'95

My dear
Darby Barbour: July

The mother church
is neither eloquent nor special in its
construction or art ~ however, it is the grand
dame in our hearts ~ its grandeur is in
its quiet simplicity; its mood is
Japanese; its Stillness is Zen, and
its "Kami" is Shinto ~

Enjoy the adventure and
good words to you

Woody

A HISTORY OF
CANTERBURY
CATHEDRAL

A HISTORY OF
CANTERBURY
CATHEDRAL

EDITED BY

PATRICK COLLINSON, NIGEL RAMSAY, AND
MARGARET SPARKS

OXFORD UNIVERSITY PRESS

1995

Oxford University Press, Walton Street, Oxford OX2 6DP

Oxford New York
Athens Auckland Bangkok Bombay
Calcutta Cape Town Dar es Salaam Delhi
Florence Hong Kong Istanbul Karachi
Kuala Lumpur Madras Madrid Melbourne
Mexico City Nairobi Paris Singapore
Taipei Tokyo Toronto
and associated companies in
Berlin Ibadan

Oxford is a trade mark of Oxford University Press

Published in the United States
by Oxford University Press Inc., New York

British Library Cataloguing in Publication Data
Data available

Library of Congress Cataloging in Publication Data
A history of Canterbury Cathedral / edited by Patrick
Collinson, Nigel Ramsay, and Margaret Sparks.
Includes bibliographical references and index.
1. Canterbury Cathedral—History. 2. Canterbury (England)—Church
history. 3. England—Church history. I. Collinson, Patrick.
II. Ramsay, Nigel. III. Sparks, Margaret.
BX5195.C3H57 1995   274.422'34—dc20   94-3723CIP
ISBN 0-19-820051-x

1 3 5 7 9 10 8 6 4 2

Typeset by Selwood Systems, Midsomer Norton
Printed in Great Britain
on acid-free paper by
Butler & Tanner Ltd.
Frome, Somerset

Preface

THERE are many histories of Canterbury Cathedral, its architecture, its stained glass, its Archbishops, Priors, and Deans, but, until the present work, there has been no history of the Cathedral as a community of people, and yet the community is the heart of what the Cathedral is. Before the Reformation, the Cathedral was the church of one of the largest monastic communities in England. After 400 years as a 'New Foundation' Cathedral, with a Dean and Chapter and a staff which now numbers over 200 full-time employees, it is still a community, with the responsibility of maintaining not just the building, but also the essential work of worship, education, and hospitality, of which the building is a symbol.

The Cathedral community is deeply indebted to the Leverhulme Trust for financing much of the work that underpins this volume, to the scholars who have written it, and, in particular, to the three editors, Professor Patrick Collinson, Dr Nigel Ramsay, and Mrs Margaret Sparks, who have given their time and expertise unstintingly to make this venture possible. The community at Canterbury, together with all who seek a fuller understanding of Christian Church life in England, and its repercussions in Europe, and, through the Anglican Communion, at a world level, are enriched by this work, and the fact that it should be published just prior to the fourteen-hundredth anniversary of the arrival of St Augustine, who laid the foundations upon which the future Canterbury community developed, is indeed a happy chance.

JOHN A. SIMPSON
Dean

Editors' Preface

THE initiators of this volume were as numerous as its contributors: Oxford University Press; Lord Coggan, when Archbishop of Canterbury; and a number of historians and other members of staff of the University of Kent at Canterbury. Andrew Butcher played an instrumental role in setting up the project; he also planned a seminar on cathedral history which met in the Precincts. Active work began in 1983. The book's realization was made possible by a grant from the Leverhulme Trust, beginning in 1984, which provided the salary of a research assistant and contributors' expenses.

The preparation of this book has met with the active encouragement of successive Deans of Canterbury and other members of Chapter. The staff of the Cathedral Archives and Cathedral Library have been patient and helpful in providing time and space for contributors and editors. In the Precincts we thank many members of the administrative staff as well as the Friends of Canterbury Cathedral for help and support of various kinds. At the University of Kent, successive Masters of Eliot College—Dan Taylor, Shirley Barlow, and Chris Cherry—have kindly provided Nigel Ramsay with an office. Among the contributors to the volume, Jeremy Gregory and Kate Eustace deserve particular thanks for their willingness to contribute at a late stage.

P. C.
N. L. R.
M. J. S.

Contents

List of Illustrations

(Between pages 192 and 193)

(*Between pages* 480 *and* 481)

Acknowledgements

The editors wish to thank the following who have kindly given permission to reproduce the plates as indicated:

Society of Antiquaries of London 5, 27, 120; B. T. Batsford Ltd. 22, 58; Bodleian Library, Oxford 18, 31, 32, 33, 39, 40, 43, 44, 45, 71, 78, 107, 125, 130, 133, 134, 137, 139, 141, 142, 144; British Library Board 2, 4, 6, 7, 88, 93, 118, 126, Col. Pl. I; Trustees of the British Museum 3; Burrell Collection, Glasgow Museums and Art Galleries 15; Dean and Chapter of Canterbury 55, 67, 119, 162, Col. Pls. II, III; Canterbury Archaeological Trust 17, 19, 20, 21, 23, 50, 51, 52, 54, 74, 75, 76, 79, 80, 81, 83, 84, 86, 106, 161, Col. Pl. V; Canterbury Museums 1, 24, 25, 41, 46, 59, 60, 61, 62; Courtauld Institute of Art Col. Pl. VI; Fisk Moore (photograph by Eric Hall) 10, 57, 64, 69; *The Guardian* 66; T. A. Heslop 29, 30; Master and Fellows of St John's College, Cambridge Col. Pl. IV; Kent Messenger Group Newspapers 61, 68, 70, 72, 82; King's School, Canterbury (photograph by Tom Jennings) 53; Master and Fellows of Magdalene College, Cambridge 85; Ben May 13, 34, 35, 36, 37, 47, 48, 49, 56, 63; Metropolitan Museum of Art, New York 12; Museum of London 28; Anne Oakley 73; Royal Commission on Historical Monuments England: National Monuments Record 14, 16; Edwin Smith 11, 132, 138; Master and Fellows of Trinity College, Cambridge 8, 9; University of Warwick 77, 131, 135, 136, 140, 143, 145–60; Dean and Chapter of Westminster 89; Whitworth Art Gallery, University of Manchester 42; Christopher Wilson 26, 87, 90, 91, 92, 94–105, 108, 109, 110, 111–17, 121–4, 128, 129.

Note on Sources

All manuscript sources are in Canterbury Cathedral Archives, and references to folios are to rectos, unless otherwise stated. The following classes or categories of material are cited: Accounts of the New Foundation; Additional Manuscripts; Almoner's Accounts; Anniversarian's Accounts; Assisa Scaccarii; Bartoner's Accounts; J. B. Bickersteth Papers; Blore Collection and Papers; Boxes in the Basement; Bunce, Schedule; Canterbury Letters; Cawston Manuscript (Lit. D. 12); Cellarer's Accounts; Chamberlain's Accounts; Chapter Act Books; Chartae Antiquae; Christ Church Letters; Deanery Papers; Dean's Books; Domestic Economy; Eastry Correspondence; Fabric; F. W. Farrar Papers; Feretrar's Accounts; File O E; Granator's Accounts; King's School Boxes; Library Archive; Literary Manuscripts; Manuscripts Catalogues; Memorabilia of Dean's Book, 1854–84; Miscellaneous Accounts; Miscellaneous Books; Music Manuscripts; Oblation Books; Petitions; Preachers' Books; Prior's Accounts; Prior's Chaplain's Accounts; Receiver's Accounts; Registers; Sacrist's Accounts; Scrap Books; Shadwell Manuscripts; Surveys and Maps; Treasurer's Accounts; Treasurers' Accounts; Treasurer's Books; X. 1. 1, etc. (Church Court Records).

Abbreviations

Arch. Cant.	*Archaeologia Cantiana*
Bede, *Hist. Eccles.*	Bede, *Historia Ecclesiastica*
BCS	W. de G. Birch, *Cartularium Saxonicum* (3 vols.; London, 1885–93)
BIHR	*Bulletin of the Institute of Historical Research*
BL	British Library
Bodl.	Bodleian Library, Oxford
Cant. Cath. Chron.	*Canterbury Cathedral Chronicle*
CClR	*Calendar of Close Rolls*
Ch. Ant.	Charta Antiqua
Christ Church Letters	*Christ Church Letters*, ed. J. B. Sheppard (Camden Soc., NS, 19; 1877)
CPL	*Calendar of Papal Registers: Papal Letters*
CPR	*Calendar of Patent Rolls*
CUL	Cambridge University Library
CYS	Canterbury and York Society
DE	Domestic Economy
DNB	*Dictionary of National Biography*
EconHR	*Economic History Review*
EHR	*English Historical Review*
Emden, *BRUC*	A. B. Emden, *Biographical Register of the University of Cambridge to 1500* (Cambridge, 1963)
Emden, *BRUO*	A. B. Emden, *Biographical Register of the University of Oxford to A. D. 1500* (3 vols.; Oxford, 1957–9)
Emden, *BRUO, 1501–1540*	A. B. Emden, *Biographical Register of the University of Oxford, A. D. 1501 to 1540* (Oxford, 1974)
Gervase, *Historical Works*	*The Historical Works of Gervase of Canterbury*, ed. W. Stubbs (2 vols.; Rolls Series, 73; 1879–80)
HMC	Historical Manuscripts Commission
James, *ALCD*	M. R. James, *The Ancient Libraries of Canterbury and Dover* (Cambridge, 1903)
JBAA	*Journal of the British Archaeological Association*

JEH	*Journal of Ecclesiastical History*
KCD	J. M. Kemble, *Codex Diplomaticus Aevi Saxonici* (6 vols.; London, 1839–48)
Knowles, *Monastic Order*	D. Knowles, *The Monastic Order in England . . . 940–1216* (2nd edn.; Cambridge, 1963)
Knowles, *Religious Orders*	D. Knowles, *The Religious Orders in England* (3 vols.; Cambridge, 1948–59)
Legg and Hope, *Inventories*	*Inventories of Christchurch, Canterbury*, ed. J. W. Legg and W. H. St J. Hope (London, 1902)
Le Neve, *Fasti*	J. Le Neve, *Fasti Ecclesiae Anglicanae*, rev. edn. (Institute of Historical Research, Univ. of London, 1962–)
Lit. Cant.	*Literae Cantuarienses: The Letter Books of the Monastery of Christ Church, Canterbury*, ed. J. B. Sheppard, (3 vols.; Rolls Series, 85; 1887–9)
LP Henry VIII	*Letters and Papers, Foreign and Domestic, of the Reign of Henry VIII*, ed. J. Brewer, J. Gairdner, and R. H. Brodie (22 vols. in 37 pts.; London, 1864–1932)
LPL	Lambeth Palace Library
Migne, *PL*	*Patrologia Latina, Cursus Completus*, ed. J. B. Migne (221 vols.; Paris, 1844–55)
Pantin, *Cant. Coll.*	W. A. Pantin, *Canterbury College, Oxford* (4 vols.; Oxford Historical Society, NS, 6–8, 30; 1947–8, 1985)
PRO	Public Record Office, London
RS	Rolls Series
S	P. H. Sawyer, *Anglo-Saxon Charters: An Annotated List and Bibliography* (London, 1968)
Searle, *Chronicle and Lists*	*Christ Church, Canterbury. I. The Chronicle of John Stone. II. List of the Deans, Priors, and Monks of Christ Church Monastery*, ed. W. G. Searle (Cambridge Antiquarian Society Publications, 8vo ser., 34; 1902)
Smith, *Cant. Cath. Priory*	R. A. L. Smith, *Canterbury Cathedral Priory: A Study in Monastic Administration* (Cambridge, 1943)
Somner, *Antiquities* (1640)	W. Somner, *The Antiquities of Canterbury* (London, 1640)
Somner, *Antiquities* (1703)	W. Somner, *The Antiquities of Canterbury*, ed. N. Battely (London, 1703), reprinted with an introduction by W. Urry (E. Ardsley, Wakefield, 1977)
TRHS	*Transactions of the Royal Historical Society*
VCH	*The Victoria History of the Counties of England*
Wharton, *Anglia Sacra*	*Anglia Sacra, sive Collectio Historiarum*, ed. H. Wharton (2 vols.; London, 1691)
Wilkins, *Concilia*	*Concilia Magnae Britanniae et Hiberniae*, ed. D. Wilkins (4 vols.; London, 1737)
Woodruff and Danks, *Memorials*	C. E. Woodruff and W. Danks, *Memorials of the Cathedral & Priory of Christ in Canterbury* (London, 1912)

Notes on Contributors

NICHOLAS BROOKS is Professor of Medieval History and Dean of the Faculty of Arts in the University of Birmingham. He is the author of *The Early History of the Church of Canterbury: Christ Church from 597 to 1066*.

MARGARET GIBSON† was lately a Senior Research Fellow of St Peter's College, Oxford. Her publications include *Lanfranc of Bec*, *The Eadwine Psalter* (edited with T. A. Heslop and R. W. Pfaff), and *Liverpool Ivories*.

BARRIE DOBSON is Professor of Medieval History at the University of Cambridge and a Fellow of Christ's College. Among his previous contributions to the history of English cathedrals are *Durham Priory, 1400–1450* and the chapter on the later Middle Ages in *A History of York Minster*, ed. G. E. Aylmer and R. Cant.

PATRICK COLLINSON is Regius Professor of Modern History at the University of Cambridge and a Fellow of Trinity College. He is the author of a number of studies of religion, politics, and society in the Elizabethan and early Stuart age, and, most recently, of a collection of *Elizabethan Essays*.

JEREMY GREGORY is a Lecturer in History at the University of Northumbria at Newcastle. He is editing Archbishop Thomas Secker's *Speculum* for the Church of England Record Society and is completing a monograph on the diocese of Canterbury, 1660–1805.

PETER B. NOCKLES is an Assistant Librarian and Methodist Church Archivist at the John Rylands University Library of Manchester. He is the author of several articles on the Oxford Movement, including a chapter for the History of the University of Oxford, as well as of *The Oxford Movement in Context: Anglican High Churchmanship, 1760–1857*.

KEITH ROBBINS is Principal of the University of Wales, Lampeter. A former President of the Historical Association and of the Ecclesiastical History Society, his many publications include *The Eclipse of a Great Power: Modern Britain, 1870–1992*, *History, Religion and Identity in Modern Britain*, and *Churchill*.

NIGEL RAMSAY is a Curator in the Department of Manuscripts in the British Library and an Honorary Research Fellow at the University of Kent, Canterbury. He has edited *English Medieval Industries: Craftsmen, Techniques, Products* (with John Blair), as well as *St Dunstan: His Life, Times and Cult*.

ROGER BOWERS is a Lecturer in Music at the University of Cambridge. He is the author of a number of articles addressing the relationship between the composition of church music during the Middle Ages and Renaissance and the resources which the Church saw fit to make available for its performance.

CHRISTOPHER WILSON is Reader in History of Art at University College, London. He is the author of *The Gothic Cathedral: The Architecture of the Great Church, 1130–1530*, and of a number of publications on English Romanesque and Gothic architecture and sculpture.

KATHARINE EUSTACE is an Assistant Keeper in the Department of Western Art in the Ashmolean Museum, Oxford; previously she was Curator at the University of Warwick. Her publications include *Michael Rysbrack, Sculptor 1694–1770*, the catalogue to the exhibition that she selected and organized at Bristol City Museum and Art Gallery in 1982.

MARGARET SPARKS has been Secretary of 'A History of Canterbury Cathedral' since 1983. She has written articles on Canterbury monastic and cathedral history, and is co-author of *The Image of St Dunstan* and author of *St Augustine's Abbey, Canterbury*. She is a member of the Council and of the Management Committee of Canterbury Archaeological Trust, and chairs its Publications Committee.

PLANS

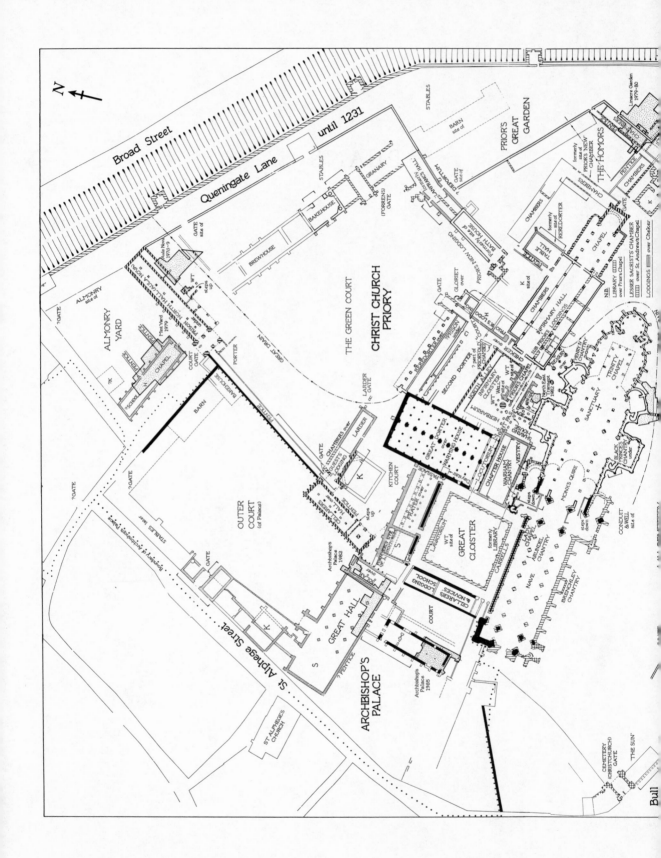

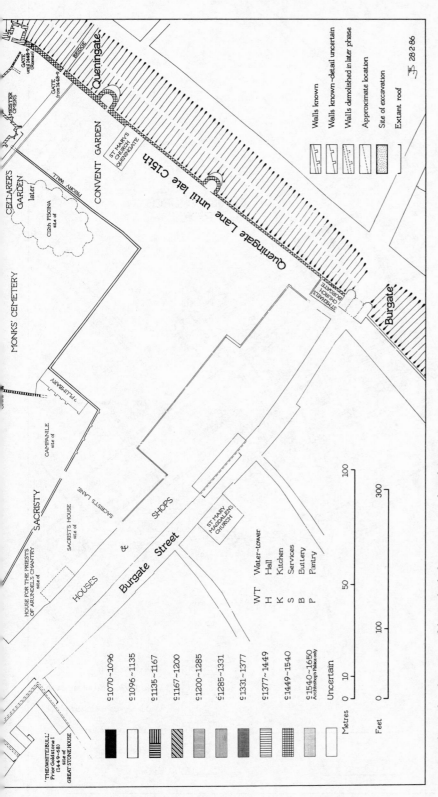

PLAN 1 The Medieval Precinct of the Cathedral Priory. Drawn by John Bowen, 1986.

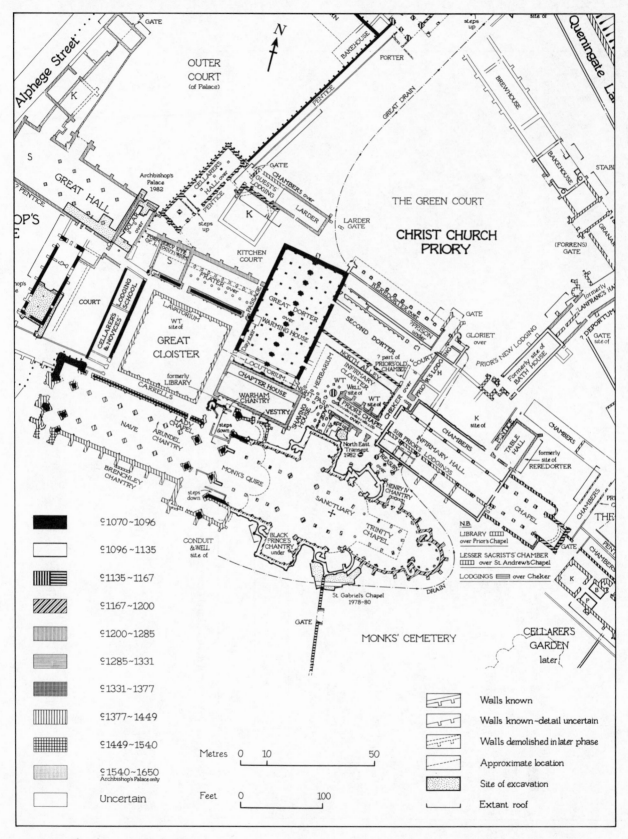

PLAN I Detail to show monastic buildings.

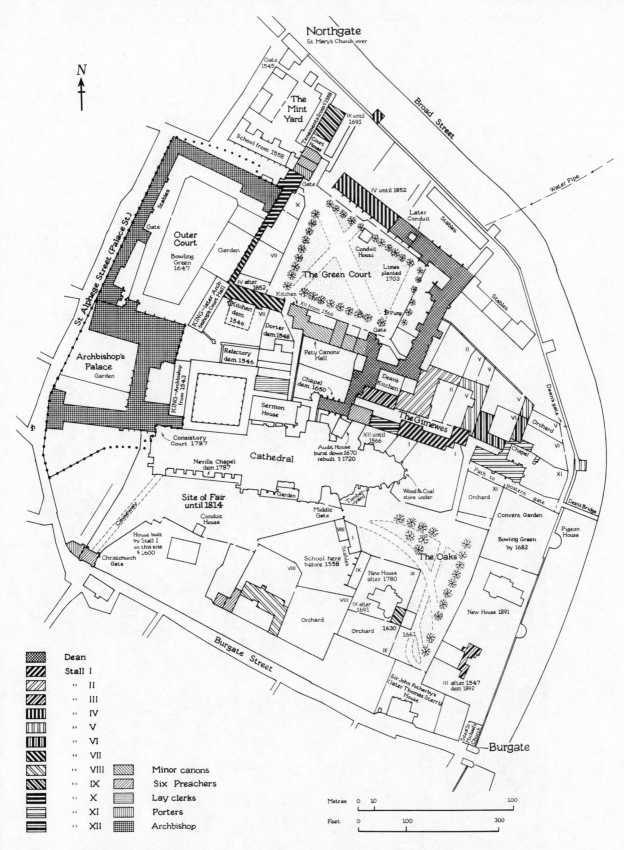

PLAN 2 The Cathedral Precinct as adapted for the Dean and Chapter after 1541. Drawn by John Bowen, 1984.

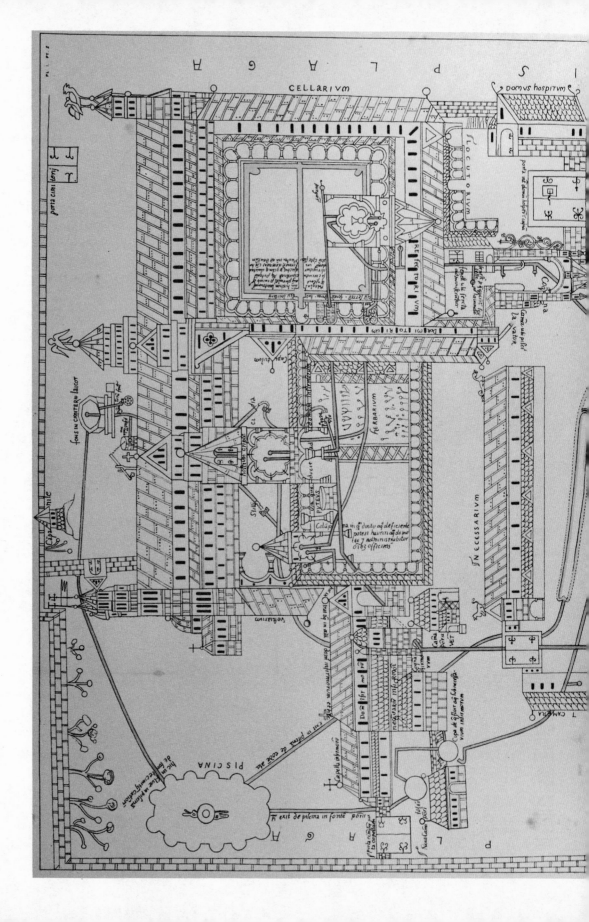

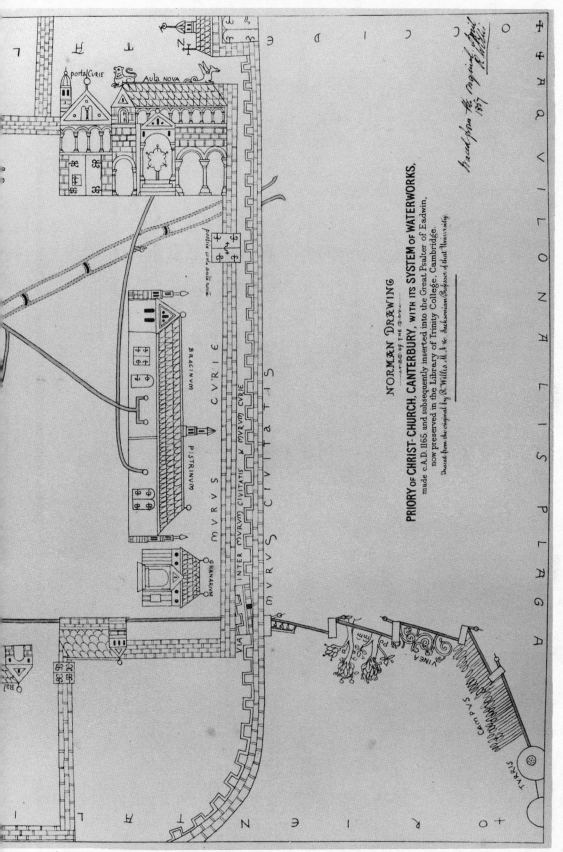

PLAN 3 The 'Waterworks Drawing' of c.1165, as redrawn by Professor Robert Willis, 1867, for *Archaeologia Cantiana*, vii (1868). The Priory buildings are shown in relation to the piped water supply installed by Prior Wibert. To the north is the city wall; the main water-pipe descends from a spring (to the north-east; lower left). The original drawing is in the Eadwine Psalter (Cambridge, Trinity College, MS R.17.1).

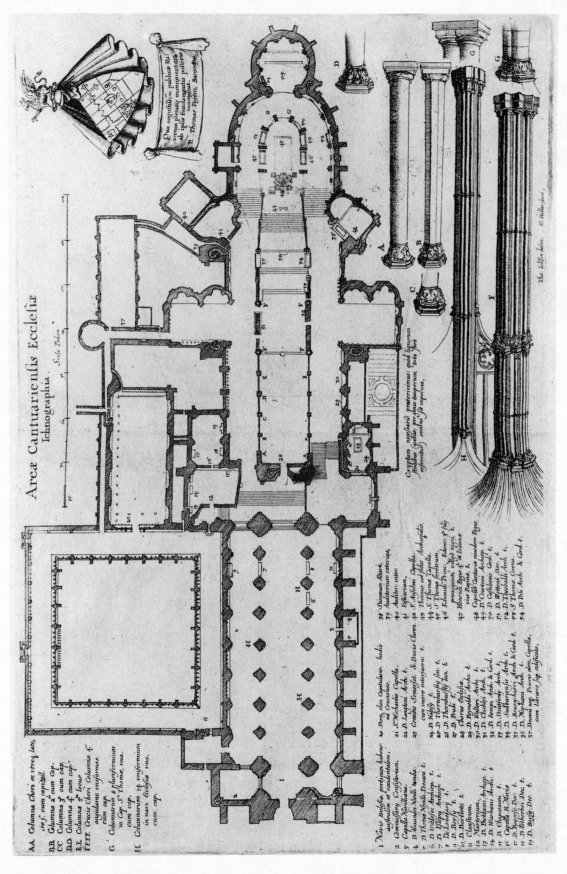

PLAN 4 The Cathedral and adjoining buildings, c.1650. Drawn by Thomas Johnson and engraved by Wenceslaus Hollar for W. Dugdale, *Monasticon Anglicanum*, i (1655).

A HISTORY OF
CANTERBURY
CATHEDRAL

I

The Anglo-Saxon Cathedral Community, 597–1070

NICHOLAS BROOKS

THE FOUNDATION

The Roman city of Canterbury (Durovernum Cantiacorum) was the capital of the tribal province or *civitas* of Kent. It is likely that during the fourth century AD there was already a Christian element in its population and an episcopal church in the city, but unfortunately we do not know even the name of any of the Romano-British bishops. A rich silver-hoard buried just outside the west wall of the town in the early fifth century is a testimony to the wealth of some of the Christian inhabitants (Pl. I); but it remains uncertain how long a British Christian population may have remained in the town once Kent came under the rule of pagan Anglo-Saxons in the mid-fifth century.[1] The archaeological evidence suggests that in the later fifth and early sixth centuries there was a real hiatus in the economic and civic life of the town and that any continuing occupation was at a minimal level and confined to inhabitants of low status. Most of the western half of the town became uninhabitable through repeated flooding and was later to be used only as water-meadows; in the east, Roman buildings and streets fell into disuse and into varying degrees of ruin. In the present state of our knowledge, the emergence of Canterbury as the first see of Anglo-Saxon England and as the metropolitan church therefore seems to have owed relatively little either to its Roman past or to any living Christian tradition maintained by inhabitants of British descent. Rather, it was the product of the particular circumstances of the closing years of the sixth century.

In 596 Pope Gregory I dispatched to Britain a group of forty monks from his own monastery of St Andrew on the Caelian Hill in Rome to convert the pagan English. The

---

[1] For possible Christian survivals, see N. P. Brooks, 'The Ecclesiastical Topography of Early Medieval Canterbury', in *European Towns: Their Archaeology and Early History*, ed. M. W. Barley (London, 1978), 487–98; for a less sanguine view, see C. Thomas, *Christianity in Roman Britain to AD 500* (London, 1981), 170–4, 183–4. For the hiatus in civic life in Dark Age Canterbury, see T. Tatton-Brown, 'The Towns of Kent', in *Anglo-Saxon Towns in Southern England*, ed J. Haslam (Chichester, 1984), 1–36, and D. A. Brooks, 'The Case for Continuity in 5th-century Canterbury', *Oxford Jnl. Archaeology*, 5 (1988), 99–114; for the Christian silver-hoard, see C. M. Johns and T. W. Potter, 'The Canterbury Late Roman Treasure', *Antiquaries Jnl.*, 65 (1985), 312–52.

missionary party was led by their prior, Augustine, who was promoted by Gregory to be abbot and was subsequently consecrated as bishop by Frankish prelates in the course of his journey to England.[2] The arrival of the group, reinforced by Frankish interpreters, in Kent in the following year was not simply dictated by the convenience of the short sea-crossing. Kent had long-established ties through settlement, trade, and diplomacy with the Frankish kingdoms and may sometimes have been subject to Frankish lordship. King Æthelberht of Kent (*c.*580–616x18) was certainly married to a Christian Frankish princess, Bertha, the daughter of Clovis's grandson, King Charibert of Paris.[3] For a decade or more, Bertha had been accompanied at the Kentish court by her Frankish chaplain, Bishop Liudhard, and had been accustomed to worship in the church of St Martin, a building

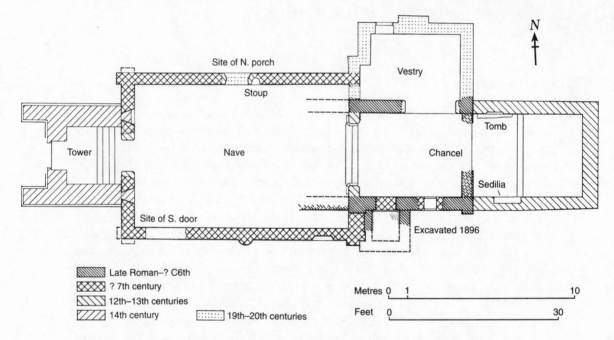

FIG. I Plan of St Martin's Church, Canterbury. Reproduced by permission of T. Tatton-Brown

believed to have been a Roman church and lying just to the east of the city (Fig. 1). Augustine and his companions were therefore assured of a hospitable welcome in Kent and may have had reason to believe that the king was ready to consider conversion. Even more advantageous was the fact that Æthelberht was at that time the most powerful

[2] The principal sources for the Gregorian mission are the letters of Gregory himself (*S. Gregorii Magni Registrum Epistularum*, ed. D. Norberg (Corpus Christianorum Series Latina 140–140A; Turnhout, in progress), vi, 51–7, 59–60; xi, 34–42, 45, 47–8, 50–1, 56) and the account in Bede, *Hist. Eccles.*, i. 23–33; ii. 1–8. For a recent critical assessment, see N. P. Brooks, *The Early History of the Church of Canterbury* (Leicester, 1984), 1–36, 63–7, 87–91.

[3] For the dates of Æthelberht's reign and of his marriage to

Bertha, see N. P. Brooks, 'The Formation and Early Structure of the Kingdom of Kent', in *The Origin of the Anglo-Saxon Kingdoms*, ed. S. R. Bassett (Leicester, 1989), 65–7. For the possibility of Frankish lordship, see I. N. Wood, 'The Merovingian North Sea', *Occasional Papers on Medieval Topics*, 1 (1983), 15–16, and J. M. Wallace-Hadrill, *Early Germanic Kingship in England and on the Continent* (Oxford, 1971), 24–32; for a minimalist interpretation see Brooks, *Church of Canterbury* (cit. in n. 2), 6–7.

English king, exercising dominion over all the Anglo-Saxon rulers south of the river Humber. His lordship proved to be of short duration, but in 597 a mission had to start in Kent if it was to have the prospect of expansion into subordinate kingdoms.

It was therefore in Kent that Augustine's mission began its work, and in Canterbury, the principal Roman town of Æthelberht's kingdom, that they were first given a former Roman church as an episcopal see. Christ Church, the cathedral church of Canterbury, has occupied the same site in the north-eastern sector of the city ever since the king's original grant to Augustine (Fig. 2). The dedication of this church to Jesus Christ, the Holy Saviour, in imitation of the papal cathedral on the Lateran, helped to create in Canterbury a little Rome. So did the relics and books which the missionary-monks had brought from Rome with them. At Christ Church the Roman monks sent by Gregory retained the leadership of the English mission as long as any of them still lived, that is until the death of Bishop Honorius, in 653.

Æthelberht's overlordship over other English kingdoms made far-reaching plans for the extension of the mission seem feasible. In 601 Gregory therefore sent to Kent a further band of Roman monks bearing instructions for the organization of the English Church. He proposed metropolitan sees at London and at York, each with twelve suffragan bishops.[4] This ambitious plan was premature with regard both to York and to London. Though new sees were established at Rochester and at London in 604, King Æthelberht is not known to have made London the focus of his authority. Augustine and his successors as metropolitan bishops of the embryonic English Church (Laurence 604x9–619, Mellitus 619–24, Justus 624–7x31, and Honorius 627x31–653) seem to have remained at Canterbury. Gregory's scheme still stood as the authoritative guidance on such matters as the number of metropolitan and suffragan sees that ought to be established. But paradoxically Canterbury's authority was reinforced when King Æthelberht died, in 616 or 618. In the pagan reaction that followed his death, both Mellitus, Bishop of London, and Justus, Bishop of Rochester, fled to Frankish Gaul. For a time, Canterbury was once more the only English see. Thereafter, its fame, as the first English see and as the sole surviving church of the disciples of St Gregory, helped to ensure its continued pre-eminence.

Bede records that Æthelberht had given Augustine and his companions 'the necessary possessions of various types'; later he tells us that the King endowed the sees of Rochester and London with many estates and possessions 'as at Canterbury'.[5] Unfortunately, we cannot determine the extent or the location of the initial endowment at Canterbury, since the surviving series of authentic early charters granting lands to Christ Church begins only in the closing years of the eighth century. Yet there is good reason to believe that the cathedral church of Canterbury, like the other major Kentish churches, acquired a landed lordship of phenomenal wealth during the period when Kent was ruled by its own dynasty, that is from 597 until 764. By comparing the estates of the archbishops and community as they existed in 1066 with those that are known to have been acquired in the ninth, tenth, and eleventh centuries, we can deduce that many of the larger manors in Kent may have formed part of the early endowment of the see. By 1066 almost a quarter of the landed

---

[4] *Greg. Epist.*, xi. 39.

[5] Bede, *Hist. Eccles.* i. 26, ii. 3. For what follows on the Christ Church endowment, see Brooks, *Church of Canterbury* (cit. in n. 2), 100–7.

To Blean

'Bertun'
c. 840

To Sturry and Fordwich

To London
and Rochester

St Dunstan

? Mill

R. Stour

'Aldberthingtun'
823

? Mill

Northgate (Roman)

'Drutintune'

Archbishop's manor
and hundred of
'Estursete'

Mill

Westgate (?Roman)

King Street

St Peter

St Ælfheah

CATHEDRAL

St Saviour   St John
(Christ Church) Baptist

'Curringtun'
786

Queningate (Roman)

To Fordwich

BINNANEA

King's Mill

Market
762

ST AUGUSTINE'S ABBEY

Meadows

lay cemetery

St Peter and St Paul

? Mill   ? Mill

'Burh Street' Burgate

St Mary

St Pancras

To Fordwich

Roman theatre

R. Stour

? Mill

To Sandwich

? St Mary

Newingate

? St Paul
845

St Martin

R. Stour

St Mildred

'Ealdan Street'

LONGPORT

To Sandwich

'Wistræt'

'Hryther caep'

Cattle-market

Worthgate (Roman)
'Weoweraget'

Ridingate
(Roman)

(Watling Street)

Wincheap

Metres 0   300

Feet 0   1000

To Wye

To Dover

Roman wall, ditch, and gate

Roman cremation cemetary

Roman inhumation cemetary

▲   Late Roman silver hoard

◆   Pagan Anglo-Saxon cremation

●   Pagan Anglo-Saxon inhumation

○   6th/7th-century hut

⌑   8th/9th-century manor

▬   Church

|||||||| Ecclesiastical precincts

FIG. 2 Anglo-Saxon Canterbury

wealth of Kent was to belong to the cathedral church, and it is likely that the bulk of this endowment had been acquired before 764. The independent kings of Kent had sacrificed their dynasty's fortune by the scale of their pious benefactions. By the eighth century, moreover, the church of Canterbury was also receiving grants of huge estates beyond Kent from the powerful overlords of the southern English. One such grant was King Æthelbald of Mercia's gift of the monastery of Cookham in Berkshire, with 100 hides of land, at some date between 740 and 756; another was the acquisition, on an unknown occasion, of 300 hides at *Iognes homme*, perhaps Eynsham in Oxfordshire. Despite the gaps in our evidence, it is clear that during the first century and a half of its existence, the cathedral church of Canterbury received a massive endowment, spread over much of south-eastern England.

It was indeed Canterbury's wealth, together with its links with Rome and with St Gregory, 'the apostle of the English', which made its ecclesiastical dominance acceptable throughout England in an age of fluctuating political fortunes. As Northumbrian, Mercian, and West Saxon rulers sought to extend their power over the southern English in the course of the seventh and eighth centuries, the metropolitan bishops of Canterbury (or '*arch*bishops', as they were styled at least from the year 679[6]) cultivated an aura of Roman authority. In England, as on the Continent, *romanitas* had an unfailing attraction for barbarian Germanic rulers. Pope Gregory I, himself adapting Roman imperial precedents, had sent to Augustine a *pallium* or 'pall', that is a long band of white wool marked with crosses, to be worn when celebrating mass. He intended it to authorize Augustine to consecrate suffragan bishops.[7] This concept of the papal *pallium* as the symbol and pre-requisite of metropolitan authority took root in England when palls were granted to Justus, Honorius, and subsequent archbishops. Thereafter, whenever an archbishop of Canterbury died, it was necessary to secure a *pallium* from Rome for his successor. The papacy was thus able to maintain contact with the nascent English Church, and at least by the early eighth century popes were accustomed to require from the archbishops-elect a written profession of faith before they would send the *pallium*.

Occasionally, in times of dispute or crisis in the English Church, as with the elevation of Wigheard in 666–8, Berhtwald in 690–2, and perhaps of Cuthbert in 740, an archbishop-elect himself travelled to Rome to receive the pall in person, and sometimes even for consecration. Personally endorsed by the Bishop of Rome in this way, an archbishop of Canterbury could be sure of his authority in England. If, as happened with Wigheard in 668, the elect died in Rome, a pope might even appoint and consecrate his successor. When Theodore, a Greek-speaking native of Tarsus, arrived in Canterbury in 669, he had been chosen directly by Pope Vitalian I for the task of reviving the English Church. Theodore's vigorous assertion of the metropolitan authority of the see of Canterbury—

---

[6] Theodore was 'bishop of the church of Canterbury' at the synod of Hertford (672), but 'archbishop' in an original charter of 679 and 'archbishop of the island of Britain and the city of Canterbury' in the synod of Hatfield (679). See Bede, *Hist. Eccles.* iv. 5, 17, and BCS 45 (S 8). For the wider significance of these terms, see E. Lesne, *La Hiérarchie épiscopale* (Lille, 1905), 31–5; F. Kempf, 'Primatiale und episcopal-synodale Struktur der Kirche vor der gregorianischen Reform', *Archivum Historiae Pontificiae*, 16 (1978), 47–66; H. Vollrath, *Die Synoden Englands bis 1066* (Konziliengeschichte, Reihe A; Paderborn, 1985), 28–30.

[7] For the pall, see Brooks, *Church of Canterbury* (cit. in n. 2), 66–7; Th. Gottlob, *Der kirchliche Amtseid der Bischöfe* (Kanonistische Studien und Texte, 9; Bonn, 1936), 26–30.

by holding regular annual synods, by appointing and even deposing bishops, and by creating new sees and dividing old ones—could not have been carried out had it not been axiomatic that an archbishop sent from Rome was entitled so to act. Even Bishop Wilfrid of York, the ablest and most determined opponent of the hierarchical policies of Archbishops Theodore and Berhtwald, could hope to resist only if he could secure from Rome explicit support upon the disputed issues.[8] But when Wilfrid returned to England with the necessary privileges from Popes Agatho, Sergius I, and John VI, he found on each occasion that the Northumbrian Church and the Northumbrian kings preferred to stick with the decisions that had been reached under the aegis of the archbishops of Canterbury. Compromises were possible only after the deaths of leading protagonists and in such a way as left the authority of the see of Canterbury intact.

By such means, the young English Church achieved in the later seventh century a far more effective and hierarchical structure than was to be found at that time in the contemporary Frankish or Lombard kingdoms. Bishops had fixed sees, and their authority was restricted to their own, clearly defined dioceses. They were consecrated by their metropolitan, the archbishop of Canterbury, who presided over synods which were intended to be annual gatherings of the whole English Church; there, matters of faith, discipline, and organization could be settled and enforced. The *pallium* served to emphasize the authority of the metropolitan and thence ultimately of Rome in such matters. In the early eighth century the Anglo-Saxon missionaries on the Continent, Willibrord and Boniface, took such concepts of ecclesiastical hierarchy, metropolitan authority, and ultimate dependence upon papal decisions into the new ecclesiastical provinces that they established east of the Rhine; from there they were to be adopted throughout the Frankish Church and to form a foundation for the medieval growth of the authority of the Holy See.[9]

THE EARLY COMMUNITY

The Christian community established in Canterbury under Augustine comprised about forty Roman monks, reinforced in 601 by a further band under Mellitus; there were also Franks, in the household of the Queen, and others recruited by Augustine on his journey to England. The traditions which Bede recorded about the way of life of these missionaries derived from Albinus, Abbot of the monastery of St Peter and St Paul, which Augustine and Æthelberht had founded just outside the walls of the city. These traditions centred upon the activities of the Roman monks and on the links with Rome. They remembered nothing, for example, of the activities of Liudhard, Bertha's Frankish chaplain. Yet Liudhard had been a bishop, not simply a household priest. This suggests that he had been intended to have a missionary role and to consecrate priests. Bede tells of the 'apostolic' life of Augustine and his companions, serving God with assiduous prayers, vigils, and fasts,

[8] Bede, *Hist. Eccles.* v. 19. 'Eddius' Stephanus, *Life of Bishop Wilfrid*, ed. B. Colgrave (Cambridge, 1927); H. Mayr-Harting, *The Coming of Christianity to Anglo-Saxon England* (London, 1972), 129–47; G. Isenberg, *Die Würdigung Wilfrieds von York* (Ph.D. thesis, Univ. of Münster, 1978); Vollrath, *Die Synoden* (cit. in n. 6), 66–123.

[9] Th. Schieffer, *Winfrid-Bonifatius und die christliche Grundlegung Europas* (2nd edn.; Darmstadt, 1972).

preaching *to whom they could* and despising everything of this world.[10] Several of the Roman monks are indeed known to have become priests. Though their disciplined and ascetic way of life and their Latin Scriptures and liturgy may have seemed a strange and potent magic to their pagan Kentish hosts, we may suspect that preaching and pastoral work would have been more effectively undertaken by Franks (whose vernacular speech was closer to Kentish) than by Romans.

Had Bede's information derived from Christ Church, we might be better informed about the Frankish role in the conversion of the English, since the Frankish clergy are likely to have been based there, leaving the monastery of St Peter and St Paul (the later St Augustine's) as a separate establishment, principally for the Roman monks. We know that Augustine was concerned about his relations with his clergy and that Gregory instructed him to follow the monastic or 'apostolic' tradition to which he was accustomed, that is to live communally and without private property. Only clerks in minor orders could take wives or have individual stipends, though they too were to be under ecclesiastical discipline.[11] In recommending that the priests and deacons of the Cathedral at Canterbury should adopt a monastic regime, Gregory was seeking to establish in the English Church the high standards that many of the early Fathers of the Western Church had sought to impose on their clergy: Augustine at Hippo, Eusebius at Vercelli, Ambrose at Milan, and Martin at Tours, to name only the best known.[12] He was not enjoining that the Canterbury clergy should all be monks, observing a full monastic liturgical regime and seeking a secluded communal life. That was, however, to be the interpretation adopted both by tenth-century monastic reformers and by later Canterbury forgers in an age when the future of the monastic chapter was in doubt.[13] Rather, the great Pope was seeking to bring the life of the Canterbury clergy closer to that of Roman monks and to his own personal practice. Indeed, the arrangement of cathedral and separate monastery which Augustine set up in Canterbury suggests that the intention was to mirror arrangements in Rome, where monks from the monasteries of the city joined the cathedral clergy for the morning and evening offices (lauds and vespers), but were alone responsible for the regular recitation of the shorter daytime offices and for the long night-vigil (nocturns).

Such liturgical co-operation helped to make the 'church of the people of Kent' famous in the seventh and eighth centuries as a source of choirmasters skilled in chanting the Office 'according to Roman custom', a tradition maintained at Canterbury first by 'the disciples of St Gregory' and then by their pupils.[14] Augustine had indeed been authorized to adopt any liturgical practices of the Frankish Church which met with his approval, but his loyalties must have remained predominantly with Rome. Certainly, when, in the eighth century, we first have detailed evidence of the practice at Canterbury, we find that Rome and Gregory remained the models. It was the Roman, not the Gallican, psalter text that

[10] Bede, *Hist. Eccles.* i. 26.

[11] Ibid. i. 27 (Resp. 1), pp. 78–80. For the authenticity of the *Responsiones*, see P. Meyvaert, 'Les *Responsiones* de S. Grégoire le Grand à S. Augustin de Cantorbéry', *Rev. d'hist. ecclésiastique*, 54 (1959), 879–94.

[12] G. Lawless, *Augustine of Hippo and His Monastic Rule*

(Oxford, 1987); M. Zacherl, 'Die *Vita Communis* als Lebensform des Klerus in der Zeit zwischen Augustinus und Karl dem Großen', *Zeitschrift für katholische Theologie*, 92 (1970), 385–424.

[13] Brooks, *Church of Canterbury* (cit. in n. 2), 90–1.

[14] Ibid. 91–3; Bede, *Hist. Eccles.* ii. 20; iv. 2; v. 20. 'Eddius' Stephanus, *Life of Wilfrid*, ed. Colgrave, ch. 14.

was used,[15] while Archbishop Cuthbert's synod of *Clofesho* of 747 prescribed the general use of a written exemplar from the Church of Rome in the office of baptism, in the mass, and in liturgical chant; it also advocated the adoption of an annual cycle of observance of saints' festivals according to the martyrology of the Roman Church, with the appropriate psalmody.[16] Rome, then, continued to be the model that the Church of Canterbury sought to imitate.

In monastic observance it is unlikely that the Gregorian missionaries were bound by one single code or rule. This was the age of the *regula mixta*, when abbots had an eclectic attitude to monastic practice. But Gregory the Great had devoted the whole of the second book of his *Dialogues* to the miracles of St Benedict, so it is likely that his disciples in Canterbury would have had a very high regard for Benedict's authority. An early interpolated text of the Rule of St Benedict is known to have been extensively studied and glossed in seventh-century Canterbury. So too were Gregory's *Dialogues*.[17] It is therefore likely that the Anglo-Saxon veneration for the Rule, so evident in the careers of men like St Wilfrid and St Boniface, owed something to the honour in which the Rule was held in the English metropolitan see.

The establishment of a school at Canterbury, to train young English clerks to read and to understand both the Latin Scriptures and the Church's liturgy, must have been among Augustine's first concerns. Already by 631 or 632 Canterbury was able to send teachers and masters to East Anglia to establish a comparable school there. But it was under Archbishop Theodore (668–90) and Abbot Hadrian of St Augustine's (670–708) that Canterbury became an outstanding centre of instruction, famous above all for their teaching of the Scriptures, but also for the training they provided in other essential ecclesiastical skills: metre (the rules for the composition of Latin poetry), the computus (the workings of the calendar), law, and astronomy.[18] Many of the outstanding English churchmen of the early eighth century acquired a foundation in Greek and deepened their Latin learning from the teaching of these two scholars. Unfortunately, none of the library books from the Canterbury of Theodore and Hadrian's day have survived; nor have any library catalogues. But we can attribute to the pen of Augustine of Canterbury two sermons preserved in a manuscript from Mainz, and to Theodore some octosyllabic verse and an extensive body of judgements on penitential discipline.[19] Moreover, collections of glosses which survive in numerous Continental manuscripts have been shown to derive from a collection first made at Canterbury in the late seventh century. They establish that a wide range of Latin authors, both patristic and monastic, were studied there. The extensive biblical glosses in these collections have preserved something of Theodore's exegesis of the Pentateuch and

---

[15] *Le Psautier romain et les autres anciens psautiers latins*, ed. Dom R. Weber (Collectanea Biblica, 10; Rome, 1953), pp. ix–xxii; *The Vespasian Psalter*, ed. D. H. Wright and A. Campbell (Early English Manuscripts in Facsimile, 14; Copenhagen, 1967).

[16] Synod of Clofesho, 747, c. 13; *Councils and Ecclesiastical Documents Relating to Britain and Ireland*, ed. A. W. Haddan and W. Stubbs (Oxford, 1869–78), iii. 367.

[17] M. Lapidge, 'The School of Theodore and Hadrian', *Anglo-Saxon England*, 15 (1986), 45–72. For the authenticity of the

Dialogues, see P. Meyvaert, 'The Enigma of Gregory the Great's *Dialogues*: A Response to Francis Clark', *JEH*, 39 (1988), 335–81.

[18] Brooks, *Church of Canterbury* (cit. in n. 2), 94–9; Lapidge, 'School of Theodore', 45–72.

[19] L. Machielson, 'Fragments patristiques non-identifiés du ms. Vat. Pal. 577', *Sacris Erudiri*, 12 (1961), 488–539; Lapidge, 'School of Theodore' (cit. in n. 17), 46–9; P. Finsterwalder, *Die Canones Theodori Cantuariensis und ihre Überlieferungsformen* (Weimar, 1929).

of the Gospels.[20] It is clear that what made Canterbury virtually unique in the Latin West was that Theodore followed the Eastern or Antiochene style of commentary; that is to say, he used the Greek Fathers in preference to the Latin, and adopted factual and literal interpretations rather than following the Western, allegorical tradition.

Under Theodore's successors the ephemeral pre-eminence of the school of Canterbury in the study of Greek slipped away, probably because texts of the Greek Fathers were lacking. But several of the archbishops of the first half of the eighth century were competent Latin scholars. Tatwine (731–4) was the author both of a grammar and of a collection of riddles; Cuthbert (740–60) has left us some skilled inscriptions in hexameters.[21] Such men are likely to have maintained a good level of Latin scholarship in their cathedral church.

KING OFFA AND THE IMPOSITION OF MERCIAN RULE (764–805)

The second half of the eighth century proved to be a decisive watershed in the history of the Church of Canterbury.[22] At that time, all the southern English kingdoms came under the increasing domination of the rulers of Mercia, with the result that the archbishop's responsibilities for the province necessarily involved difficult adjustments to changing political realities. Moreover, in Kent itself the rule of the native dynasty, which had established and endowed Christ Church so handsomely, came to an end, after a prolonged and fluctuating struggle. From the year 764, when Offa of Mercia (757–96) first intervened directly in Kent at the head of a large Mercian following, the Kentish kings, Egbert and Heahberht, came under increased pressure. They gained some respite in 776, when the men of Kent seem to have defeated the Mercians in a battle at Otford; but at least by 785 Offa was ruling Kent as 'King of the Mercians', without reference to any local king. On Offa's death, in 796, the rising of Eadberht Præn briefly re-established Kent as an independent kingdom. But from 798 King Cenwulf had imposed Mercian rule once more, though initially he set up his brother Cuthred (798–807) as a subordinate king there.

These political changes had obvious dangers for the archbishops and for the community of Christ Church. Victorious kings could annul the bequests of defeated kings to a church, as grants either of rebellious nobles or of unjust foreign invaders. To a Mercian king, the major Kentish churches would need to be purged of any residual loyalty to the dynasty which had founded and enriched them. The two Kentish bishoprics and the Kentish 'minster' churches were therefore obvious targets after the dynasty had been suppressed, particularly since both Offa and Cenwulf needed land and offices to reward the nobles on whom their victories had depended. But they also needed the support of the ecclesiastical hierarchy. Each claimed descent from the Mercian royal house, but neither Offa nor Cenwulf could number a king among their immediate or near ancestors. They were both

[20] Lapidge, 'School of Theodore' (cit. in n. 17), 53–67; B. Bischoff, 'Wendepunkte in der Geschichte der lateinischen Exegese im Frühmittelalter', *Sacris Erudiri*, 6 (1954), 187–279, at 191–5, trans. as 'Turning-points in the History of Latin Exegesis in the Early Middle Ages', in *Biblical Studies: The Medieval Irish Contribution*, ed. M. McNamara (Dublin, 1976), 73–160.

[21] M. Lapidge, 'Some Remnants of Bede's Lost *Liber Epi-*

grammaticum', *EHR*, 90 (1975), 812–14.

[22] The fundamental studies of the Mercian kingdom are F. M. Stenton, *Anglo-Saxon England* (3rd edn.; Oxford, 1971), 202–38, and the chs. of C. P. Wormald in *The Anglo-Saxons*, ed. J. Campbell (London, 1982), 70–128. See also Brooks, *Church of Canterbury* (cit. in n. 2), 111–27.

well aware of the contemporary example set by the Carolingian dynasty's successful usurpation of the Frankish throne, which had depended upon episcopal and papal support and had utilized new rituals of royal 'ordination' or consecration. Like the Carolingians, both Offa and Cenwulf sought to legalize their extended rule and to pass it on to their descendants. They therefore hoped to control the metropolitan Church of Canterbury. Otherwise they might need to transfer its metropolitan authority to a see which was more easily dominated from the Mercian heartland. The stage was set for a titanic struggle, whose outlines can be only dimly discerned in the extant sources.

The conflict began during the archiepiscopate of Jænberht (765–92). Though consecrated in Offa's presence, Jænberht had previously been Abbot of St Augustine's, and his ties were with the Kentish dynasty and nobility. Through friendship with King Egbert II and kinship with Aldhun, reeve in Canterbury, he secured for Christ Church in 780 or thereabouts three valuable manors in East Kent: Charing, Great Chart, and Bishopsbourne. Offa, however, soon annulled Egbert's grants on the grounds that 'it was unlawful for his thegn [*minister*] to give away land granted to him by his lord without his lord's testimony'.[23] It seems clear that the Mercian King regarded the Church of Canterbury as one of the centres of opposition to his rule and was determined to punish it. In 779, when he had won control of the upper Thames valley, after defeating the West Saxons in battle at Bensington, he acquired the wealthy minster of Cookham (Berkshire), which his predecessor, King Æthelbald, had once granted to Christ Church. Despite the evidence of Æthelbald's charter, and despite the best efforts of both Jænberht and his successor, Æthelheard (792–805), Offa retained Cookham in his own hands and passed it on to his widow, Queen Cynethryth, to rule as abbess.[24] Not until 798–9, when the Mercian throne had passed from Offa's kin to Cenwulf, was Æthelheard able to recover (at a price) Charing, Chart, and Bishopsbourne, and to secure some recompense in Kent for the loss of Cookham's extensive properties.

The conflict of Church and State was not limited to these property disputes and to Jænberht's support for Kentish independence. From 781 (the year in which Charlemagne had had his sons, Pippin and Louis, anointed by the Pope) Offa began to attend the annual synods of the Canterbury province, perhaps as a means of pressurizing Jænberht or of countering his influence. Moreover, the Mercian king also sought to secure the succession of his only son, Ecgfrith, to his enlarged kingdom. The papal legates, Bishops George of Ostia and Theophylact of Todi, who visited England in 786, are known to have concerned themselves with the 'ordination' of legitimate kings.[25] But it would seem that Archbishop Jænberht was determined to avoid consecrating Ecgfrith, lest that might appear to legitimize Ecgfrith's rule throughout the province of Canterbury, that is over all the kingdoms

---

[23] BCS 293 (S 155) and cf. BCS 319, 332 (S 1259, 1264). For differing interpretations of Offa's confiscations, see E. John, *Land Tenure in Early England* (Leicester, 1960), 48; H. Vollrath, *Königsgedanke und Königtum bei den Angelsachsen* (Köln, 1971), 163–8; C. P. Wormald, 'Bede, the Bretwaldas and the Origins of the *Gens Anglorum*', in *Ideal and Reality in Frankish and Anglo-Saxon Society*, ed. id. (Oxford, 1983), 115–16; Brooks, *Church of Canterbury* (cit. in n. 2), 114–15.

[24] BCS 291 (S 1258); Brooks, *Church of Canterbury* (cit. in n. 2), 116–17.

[25] *Councils*, ed. Haddan & Stubbs (cit. in n. 16), iii. 453–4. The best discussion of the report of the papal legates and of the relations of Mercian rulers with English synods is now K. Cubitt, 'Anglo-Saxon Church Councils, *c*.650–*c*.850' (Ph.D. thesis, Univ. of Cambridge, 1990), chs. 7, 9.

south of the Humber. To resolve the issue, a 'contentious synod' was held in 787 at Chelsea, where two momentous steps were taken. Not only was Ecgfrith consecrated as king during his father's lifetime, seemingly by the Mercian Bishop Hygeberht of Lichfield, but the province of Canterbury was also divided in such a way that London and all the sees south of the Thames remained subject to Jænberht, while Dunwich, Elmham, Lindsey, Leicester, Lichfield, Worcester, and Hereford were formed into a new province of Lichfield under Hygeberht, who received a *pallium* and metropolitan rank from Pope Hadrian I.[26]

The Church of Canterbury had suffered a heavy price for Jænberht's determination to resist Offa's consolidation of his power. It had failed to secure the right to consecrate the most powerful English king. Its metropolitan authority was now restricted to the Kentish and Saxon bishoprics (Canterbury, Rochester, London, Selsey, Winchester, and Sherborne). Its endowment had been severely pruned. When Archbishop Jænberht died, in 792, he was replaced by an abbot from the new province, that is by Æthelheard of Louth in the subkingdom of Lindsey. Offa was clearly not prepared to tolerate another Kentish archbishop of Canterbury, and he continued to attend the synodal assemblies of the two provinces, over which the two archbishops now presided jointly.[27] At Christ Church, Æthelheard seems to have been regarded as a foreign intruder, for on Offa's death he fled, on the community's advice, to the Mercian court. His flight may not have safeguarded his church, for either during or after the rising of Eadberht Præn (796–8) Christ Church seems to have lost all its early archives.[28] Meanwhile King Cenwulf negotiated with Rome in order to transfer metropolitan authority from Canterbury to the vacant see of London, but when Pope Leo III refused to allow any further tampering with the structure of the English Church, Cenwulf re-established Æthelheard at Canterbury by force of arms. Thereafter, the Mercian King and the Archbishop worked together to restore the confiscated Canterbury properties and, with papal support, to secure the abolition of the metropolitan see of Lichfield and the restoration of Canterbury's authority over its province (803).[29]

At Christ Church, from 798 and for most of the ninth century, a careful record was kept of the professions of faith and of obedience to the archbishop made by bishops-elect of the Canterbury province. The terms in which some pledged their loyalty were indeed deliberately reminiscent of secular oaths of fealty:

I declare that whatever thou, father, whatever thy successors as prelates of the holy church of Canterbury, affirm in truth I shall lovingly affirm; whatever they shun as unjust, that I too shall hasten to shun in every way.[30]

Thus the Church of Canterbury sought to buttress its metropolitan authority by maintaining the earliest record of such professions of obedience to survive in Europe. They serve as a reminder that the see had survived the greatest threat to its status, but at the

---

[26] *Anglo-Saxon Chronicle: A Revised Translation*, ed. and trans. D. Whitelock with D. C. Douglas and S. I. Tucker (London, 1961), s.a.787. For the division of the sees, see Brooks, *Church of Canterbury* (cit. in n. 2), 118–20.

[27] At Chelsea in 789 (BCS 255, 256, 257; S 131, 1430, 130), and in 793 (BCS 267; S 136); at *Clofesho* in 794×6 (BCS 274; S 139)

and 798 (BCS 289, 291; S 153, 1258); at Tamworth in 799 (BCS 293; S 155).

[28] Brooks, *Church of Canterbury* (cit. in n. 2), 121.

[29] BCS 310; Brooks, *Church of Canterbury* (cit. in n. 2), 123–7.

[30] *Canterbury Professions*, ed. M. Richter (CYS, 67; Torquay, 1973), no. 28.

cost of accepting a Mercian archbishop. Never again would the Church of Canterbury work for Kentish independence.

ARCHBISHOP WULFRED (805–32)

In 805 Wulfred, who had served as archdeacon during the later years of Æthelheard's archiepiscopate, was chosen to succeed him. The election of a member of the Christ Church community accorded with the advice that Alcuin had given during Æthelheard's flight, and doubtless served to satisfy local pride. But the new Archbishop was in fact a member of a noble Middle Saxon family;[31] his elevation may reflect the introduction of Mercian clergy into the community by Archbishop Æthelheard. Be that as it may, Wulfred's pontificate is surprisingly well documented, thanks to a splendid series of Canterbury charters and episcopal professions of faith, as well as the canons of his great reforming synod, held at Chelsea in 816. From such sources, we can show Archbishop Wulfred to have been a dynamic leader and reformer who made a major impact on the whole English Church.

Fundamental to his work was the reform of his cathedral community at Christ Church along lines very similar to those that had been pioneered at Metz by Bishop Chrodegang and which were to form the standard for cathedral clergy that Louis the Pious and Benedict of Aniane sought to impose throughout the Frankish realms in a series of reforming councils of the years 813–16. In a former charter of 808x13, Wulfred announced that he had 'revived the holy monastery of the church of Canterbury by renewing, restoring and rebuilding it': he insisted that the Christ Church community maintain the Office at the canonical hours, eat their meals in a communal refectory, and sleep in a communal dormitory, and that any property owned by individual members be bequeathed to the community.[32] His reforms represented a marked tightening of the regime at Christ Church, a return to some of the monastic ideals that Pope Gregory the Great had recommended to Augustine and his clergy. In referring to the priests and deacons of Christ Church as being subject 'to the rule of the life of monastic discipline', rather than calling them cathedral 'canons' subject to a 'canonical' rule, Wulfred was sticking to the terminology of an older tradition and avoiding the new language of the Carolingian reforms. The difference, however, was one of nomenclature rather than of substance.

As Archbishop, Wulfred enjoyed fluctuating relations with the secular powers. He quarrelled with King Cenwulf early in his period of office and again more dramatically from c.815 to 821; thereafter, the rapid changes in the Mercian royal succession and, from c.825, the subjection of Kent to the rule of the West Saxon Kings Egbert and his son Æthelwulf, all required nimble political footwork.[33] None the less, the evidence suggests that as far as circumstances allowed, Wulfred followed a consistent and vigorous territorial

[31] Brooks, *Church of Canterbury* (cit. in n. 2), 132 for Wulfred's family. For Alcuin's advice that the archbishop be elected from the community, see *Alcuini Epistolae*, ed. E. Dümmler, MGH Epist., 4 (Berlin, 1895), no. 128, trans. in *English Historical Documents c.500–1042*, ed. D. Whitelock (2nd edn.; London, 1979), no. 203.

[32] BCS 342 (S 1265); Brooks, *Church of Canterbury* (cit. in n. 2), 153–60; R. Schieffer, *Die Entstehung von Domkapiteln in Deutschland* (Bonner Historische Forschungen, 43; Bonn, 1976), 262–78.

[33] Brooks, *Church of Canterbury* (cit. in n. 2), 132–7.

policy in the acquisition of estates for his own use and in reorganizing and extending the properties of the community. By spending a considerable personal fortune, he purchased estates in Kent and in Middlesex and disposed of properties (or claims to properties) in the Thames valley or even further afield. By a series of exchanges and planned purchases, he accumulated adjacent properties, both for himself and (separately) for the community, which could be efficiently administered as single manors. Indeed, many of the great medieval manors of the archbishops and of Christ Church (Bishopsbourne, Eastry, Lympne, Graveney, Harrow, Otford, and Petham) seem to have taken their definitive form in his time. He also insisted that grants made to Christ Church were inalienable and permanent gifts, so long as the community maintained the reformed life that he had established for them.

By contrast, Wulfred was careful to insist that he himself had full powers of disposal over the huge lordship that he accumulated for his own use. Indeed, in one charter he expressed resentment at the idea that he should be any more restricted in the disposition of his own booklands than other men were in the disposition of theirs.[34] Wulfred's will has not survived, but while he certainly used some properties to help build up a permanent endowment for the archbishops, he is known to have passed on the bulk of his estates to his kinsman the priest Werhard, who can be shown to have risen very rapidly in the Christ Church community: a deacon in 824 and only a junior priest in 825, Werhard was presiding over the community as 'priest-abbot' by the mid-830s. Indeed, if, as seems likely, other members of the same Middle Saxon family may be recognized in the Wulfhard who had been the senior priest at Christ Church from 803–13, and in the Wernoth who was 'priest-abbot' in 811 and 813 then Wulfred's kin may be seen to have dominated the Christ Church community from the beginning of the century until after our last record of 'priest-abbot' Werhard, in 845.[35] Though Wulfred had indeed observed his own regulation that individual members of the community should not grant their lands outside it, his immediate concern would seem to have been to exalt the members of his own family.

Little is known of the life of the community during Wulfred's archiepiscopate, except from the charters and books which may, with some probability, be ascribed to the Christ Church scriptorium. During the second and third decades of the ninth century, a number of Christ Church scribes, led and probably trained by Archbishop Wulfred himself, developed a highly calligraphic and mannered variety of insular cursive minuscule. The Canterbury script represents one of the high points in the development of insular min-uscule, and they evidently regarded it as suitable for the more formal synodal charters (Pl. 2) and for important books. Astonishingly, however, at the very time when Christ Church scribes were attaining the high point of the script's calligraphic potential, their standards of Latin grammar and orthography were at a low ebb. Indeed, the two charters which may plausibly be attributed to the hand of Archbishop Wulfred himself are already replete with false agreements and with spellings affected by the scribe's vernacular pro-nunciation.[36] It is clear that under Wulfred several of the Cathedral clergy were well able to produce a finely written charter or copy a book in a handsome script; they could also

---

[34] S 1622, discussed and quoted ibid. 139.
[35] Ibid. 139–42.

[36] BCS 370 and 373 (S 186, 187); for the attribution to Wulfred's hand, see Brooks, *Church of Canterbury* (cit. in n. 2), 168.

compose, utilizing earlier models, elaborate professions of faith for bishops-elect to present to the Archbishop, and perhaps for archbishops-elect to send to the Pope.[37] Doubtless many of them could comprehend the routine services and familiar passages of the Scriptures; but few, if any, of them appear to have had sufficient command of grammar to be able to compose in Latin for new needs. With standards of learning so low in the metropolitan church, there must have been a danger that the decline would be irreversible and would seriously hamper the routine pastoral work of the Church.

Canterbury's metropolitan responsibility for pastoral standards in the English Church was also at the root of the major dispute of Wulfred's archiepiscopate. For a century and more, leading English churchmen had been concerned lest 'monasteries' or minster-churches should fall under the hereditary control of the local noble or royal families, to the detriment not only of their 'monastic' discipline, but also of effective pastoral care in their extensive territories or *parochiae*.[38] In 803 Archbishop Æthelheard and the bishops of his province had decreed that minster communities should never choose laymen as their lords and should henceforth observe monastic discipline. But it was left to Wulfred to attempt to enforce such general pronouncements against the entrenched proprietorial rights of lay lords. He presided over the synod of Chelsea (816), which prohibited the alienation of monastic estates for more than a single lifetime (can. 7), asserted the duty of bishops to choose (with the consent of the *familiae*) worthy abbots and abbesses for the minsters of their diocese (can. 4), and finally authorized them to intervene to secure the property of communities which were threatened by the rapacity of laymen (can. 8). Thus the synod overrode the traditional canonical restrictions on episcopal interference in monastic elections and property. The stage was set for a major clash of Church and State.

Wulfred was immediately embroiled in a bitter test-case with King Cenwulf of Mercia over the lordship of the Kentish 'monasteries' of Reculver and of Minster-in-Thanet. In the course of a long struggle (816–21), the King secured papal privileges confirming his acquired and inherited rights over monasteries, while the Church of Canterbury produced forged charters which purported to grant control of monastic elections and property to the archbishops.[39] The King used his influence at Rome and at the court of the Emperor, Louis the Pious, to secure the Archbishop's suspension from office, and the Archbishop may in turn have tried to depose the King. At all events, most of the moneyers of the Canterbury mint preferred in these years to produce a unique series of 'anonymous' coins (Pl. 3), bearing the royal or archiepiscopal bust but omitting the King's or Archbishop's name. Shortly before his death, in 821, Cenwulf imposed a solution whereby the Archbishop retained the lordship of Reculver and Minster, but at the price of ceding to the King 300 hides of land at *Iognes homme* (perhaps Eynsham in Oxfordshire) and of paying a

---

[37] For Wulfred's charters and the attribution of charters to the Christ Church scriptorium, see Brooks, *Church of Canterbury* (cit. in n. 2), 164–74; M. Brown, 'Paris BN lat. 10861 and the Scriptorium of Christ Church, Canterbury', *Anglo-Saxon England*, 15 (1985), 119–37; J. Crick, 'Church, Land and Local Nobility in Early Ninth-Century Kent: The Case of Earldorman Oswulf', *Hist. Research*, 61 (1988), 251–69.

[38] Brooks, *Church of Canterbury* (cit. in n. 2), 173–80. Arch-

bishop Æthelheard's decree against lay lordship is BCS 312; the canons of Wulfred's 816 synod of Chelsea are printed in *Councils*, ed. Haddan & Stubbs, iii. 579–85.

[39] The forged privileges of Wihtred and Æthelbald are BCS 91, 162 (S 22, 90); Cenwulf's papal privileges are BCS 337, 363. See also W. Levison, *England and the Continent in the Eighth Century* (Oxford, 1946), 255–7, and Brooks, *Church of Canterbury* (cit. in n. 2), 185–6.

massive fine, equivalent to the *wergild* or blood-price of a king. In Canterbury eyes, however, even this savage settlement did not stick, since from 822 to 824 the King's daughter, Abbess Cwoenthryth of Minster, did not in fact pay the rents and obedience due from her house. After the succession of King Beornwulf of Mercia (823–5), Wulfred reopened the dispute on more favourable terms at a synod at *Clofesho* in 825 and subsequently at *Oslafeshlau*. There the Abbess was compelled to compensate the Archbishop for the injuries done him by her father; she gave up control of Minster and in addition ceded an estate of 100 hides at Harrow, Wembley, and Yeadding in Middlesex, which thereafter was to form one of the greatest archiepiscopal manors.[40]

Wulfred's remarkable, though partial, victory was to be short-lived. The days of Mercian rule in Kent were numbered. In 825 Egbert of Wessex defeated Beornwulf's army at Wroughton (Wiltshire) and then sent his son, Æthelwulf, to establish West Saxon power in the south-eastern kingdoms (825x7). The new rulers of Kent did not recognize Wulfred as sole lord of the Kentish minsters and they confiscated an estate at 'Malling' (probably East Malling in Kent) which, they claimed, had been given to the Church of Canterbury by King Baldred, a Mercian subking, when in flight from the West Saxon forces. The interruption of the archbishops' minting-rights during the initial years of West Saxon rule may be another indication of their strained relations with the metropolitan church. The only acquisition of Wulfred's later years (825–32)—King Wiglaf of Mercia's grant of Botwell, near Hayes (Middlesex) in 831—suggests that the great Archbishop still preferred to operate within the Mercian political stage.[41] His Middle Saxon origins and the political loyalties of a lifetime were not easily set aside.

WEST SAXON RULE AND THE IMPACT OF THE VIKINGS (832–923)

It was left to Archbishop Ceolnoth (833–70) to adjust the stance of the Church of Canterbury in order to bring it into keeping with a political situation in which the West Saxons ruled south of the Thames and had claims over Essex as well, while the Mercians remained the dominant Midland kingdom. Nothing is known of Ceolnoth's origins, since the late story that he had previously been the 'dean' of the Christ Church community is a typically anachronistic monastic invention.[42] Early in his archiepiscopate, namely in 836, he presided over a provincial synod, which was held at Croft (Leicestershire), deep in Mercian or Middle Anglian territory. This synod was attended by King Wiglaf and his nobles,[43] and was the last known occasion when a Mercian king and his retinue attended such a gathering, as had been the norm since the 780s. Thereafter, Ceolnoth attended the West Saxon court under Egbert (802–38), Æthelwulf (830–58), and his sons, in the company of the southern English bishops; and he also attended, though less frequently, the Mercian court under Kings Berhtwulf (840–55) and Burgred (855–75). As metropolitan, he probably

---

[40] The only account of the Reculver and Minster dispute is the Canterbury record of its settlement, BCS 384 (S 1436). For the interpretation followed here, see Brooks, *Church of Canterbury* (cit. in n. 2), 173–206, at 180–3.

[41] BCS 400 (S 188). For Wulfred's relations with the West Saxon kings, see Brooks, *Church of Canterbury* (cit. in n. 2), 138.

[42] Gervase, *Historical Works*, ii. 348; for the reasons to discount this assertion, see Brooks, *Church of Canterbury* (cit. in n. 2), 145.

[43] BCS 416 (S 190); for the interpretation of the changing pattern of English synods in the mid-9th cent., see Cubitt, 'Anglo-Saxon Church Councils' (cit. in n.25), ch. 9.

also needed to attend the East Anglian court on occasions during the reigns of the successive Kings Æthelstan, Æthelweard, and Edmund (825–69), but none of their charters have survived. Henceforth, when the bishops of the entire province gathered in synod, as at *Astran* in 839 and London in 845,[44] their meeting was a purely ecclesiastical occasion. We may therefore suspect that the archbishops continued to preside over the annual synods of their province in the second half of the ninth century; but in the absence of any king, these were no longer occasions which produced royal charters, the principal evidence for English synodal activity in the period from 780 to 836. We must therefore hesitate before assuming from the silence of our sources that the archbishops of the later ninth century neglected their duty to exercise metropolitan authority through regular provincial synods.

In general the rule of the West Saxon kings seems to have greatly reduced the flow of royal benefactions to the Church of Canterbury. It is difficult to be certain whether Archbishop Ceolnoth and his successors were less wealthy and less active in the land market than Wulfred had been, or whether the West Saxon dynasty was less well disposed towards a see which they considered already more than adequately endowed. However, in 838–9 a window of opportunity opened for Ceolnoth, because of King Egbert's desire to secure for his son, Æthelwulf, who was already ruling as subking in Kent, the succession to the whole of his enlarged kingdom. It was almost 200 years since the West Saxon succession had last passed from father to son, so it is not surprising that Egbert was willing to be generous in order to secure ecclesiastical support for his efforts to establish a dynasty. In 838 the Archbishop presided over a 'venerable council' of southern bishops, meeting with Kings Egbert and Æthelwulf and their nobles at Kingston in Surrey. There the two kings restored to Christ Church the estate at Malling, which had been confiscated at the time of the West Saxon take-over. They also settled the long-running dispute over the control of minster-churches, by reaching agreement that Æthelwulf and his father had been chosen for (secular) protection and lordship, while the bishops had been constituted as spiritual lords, so that the rule of the monastic life and liberty of election in these 'free monasteries' might thenceforth be preserved.[45] This was a compromise, reflecting similar developments in Carolingian Frankia, by which the bishops and the Crown attempted to co-operate in a shared lordship in order to protect the minsters from the abuse of local aristocratic power.

Neither in this agreement, nor in grants of a series of properties on the edge of Romney Marsh and of an estate near Lyminge in the closing months of the same year,[46] is there mention of any cash payment by the Archbishop or his Church to secure these favours from Æthelwulf and his father. What is recorded, however, is a solemn undertaking by the Archbishop and the community at Christ Church on their own behalf and that of their successors that they would thenceforth offer firm and unbroken friendship, patronage, and protection to Egbert and Æthelwulf and to their heirs. It is unlikely to be an accident

[44] For the synod at *Astran*, see BCS 421 (S 1438); for that at London, BCS 448 (S 1194). ·

[45] BCS 421 (S 1438); for the interpretation of this difficult charter, of which three contemporary copies survive, see

Brooks, *Church of Canterbury* (cit. in n. 2), 145–6, 197–200, 323–5.

[46] BCS 407, 408, 419 (S 323, 1623, 286); Brooks, *Church of Canterbury* (cit. in n. 2), 145.

that this promise of friendly support was made at Kingston, the place where the river Thames ceases to be tidal and where West Saxon and English kings were normally to be consecrated as king in the tenth century.[47] It may even have been part of this agreement that Archbishop Ceolnoth should consecrate Æthelwulf as King of the Saxons at Kingston during his father's lifetime. Be that as it may, what is clear is that Ceolnoth had tied the fortunes of his church to those of Egbert's dynasty. In the ensuing century, Egbert's lineage was to go on to forge, through its conquests, a unitary English kingdom. The Archbishop's choice therefore proved prescient. This time the Church of Canterbury had avoided the dangers—implicit in the policies of Wulfred's later years—of committing itself to the losing cause. Ceolnoth was no Jænberht.

Despite his success in steering his Church into calmer political waters and recovering confiscated property, Ceolnoth's chief hope of attracting benefactions for Christ Church lay in establishing good relations with the leading nobles of south-eastern England, especially with the ealdormen of Kent and with their wives, daughters, and other kinsfolk. Ceolnoth's friendship with Ealdorman Ealhhere and Ealhhere's powerful kin—his brothers, Ealdorman Æthelmod and (probably) the reeve Abba, his sister Ealhburg, daughter Ealawyn, and grandson Eadwald—brought a steady flow of Kentish estates and of food-rents from Kentish manors into the Christ Church lordship during the 840s and 850s. In the next generation, Archbishop Æthelred's friendship with Ealdorman Ælfred of Kent and Surrey was to prove equally beneficial. Critical too were Ceolnoth's links with a number of the widows of Kentish nobles (Heregyth, widow of reeve Abba, Ealhburg the widow of Ealdred, and Cynethryth the widow of Ealdorman Æthelmod) and with others wishing to devote their lives to God's service, such as Lufu 'handmaiden of God'. Noble testators appreciated the prospect of the Archbishop's protection of their widows (who might otherwise be pressurized into unwelcome remarriages) and of their young children. A similar need was met by Ceolnoth's willingness to offer a haven at Christ Church to nobles, such as Badanoth Beotting, who wished to abandon the secular life and end their days in some form of religious observance. Above all, the community's ability to promise to commemorate in perpetuity the anniversaries of their benefactors with prayers and psalmody tied the interests of the local Kentish nobility to their Cathedral church. Such were the factors which enabled Christ Church under Ceolnoth's and Æthelred's guidance to acquire substantial estates and food-rents in Kent—at Challock, Mongeham, Bishopsbourne, Little Chart, Finglesham, Chartham, Nettlestead, and several properties in and around Canterbury itself.[48]

The benefits of these good relations with the Crown and with the lay nobility were put at risk by the growing threat of pagan Viking armies. The sources do not provide an adequate account of Viking activities in south-eastern England in the ninth century. Incidental references in charters show that Viking forces were already active in Kent at the close of the eighth century and were building fortresses there by the second decade of the

---

[47] For consecrations at Kingston, see S. D. Keynes, *The Diplomas of King Æthelred the Unready, 978–1016* (Cambridge, 1980), 270–1, and C. P. Wormald, 'Celtic and Anglo-Saxon Kingship: Some Further Thoughts', in *Sources of Anglo-Saxon Culture*, ed. P. E. Szarmach and V. D. Oggins (Studies in Medieval Culture; Kalamazoo, Mich., 1986), 151–83, at 160 and n. 42.

[48] For archiepiscopal relations with the Kentish nobility and the estates acquired at that time, see Brooks, *Church of Canterbury* (cit. in n. 2), 147–9, 151–2.

ninth century.[49] Presumably some Viking armies were by then overwintering in England and constructing camps as bases for their raiding. Moreover, not only is the record of Viking activity in Kent in the *Anglo-Saxon Chronicle* under the years 835, 841, 851, 853, 855, 865, 885, and 892–3 extremely sparse; it also shows no interest in the fortunes of individual churches.[50] None the less, the events of which we are told—the ravaging of Sheppey in 835, the storming of Canterbury itself in 851, the attempt to dislodge a 'heathen army' from Thanet in 853, the wintering of the heathens on Sheppey in 855 and on Thanet in 865, their attempt to besiege Rochester in 885, and their two-pronged attack on Kent in 892–3—were all likely to have included threats to the major Kentish churches in these places, since they were such easy targets for booty-seeking raiders. The disappearance of the communities of such minsters as Folkestone, Dover, Minster-in-Thanet, Reculver, Minster-in-Sheppey, and Hoo from all records for a century and more after *c*.850 suggests that these houses were indeed attacked and their communities dispersed and disrupted. The beautifully illuminated eighth-century Kentish gospel-book, the Stockholm Codex Aureus (Pl. 5), which Ealdorman Ælfred and his wife Werburg purchased from 'the heathen army with much clean gold' and then presented to Christ Church, is itself likely to have been pillaged from one of the Kentish minsters during these raids.[51]

The estates of the major churches, and of Canterbury in particular, must also have suffered from the Viking wasting of the Kentish countryside in order to induce the payment of tribute. Indeed, one of Christ Church's benefactors, Ealhburg, when making a bequest to St Augustine's, provided for the eventuality that her estate might be unable to pay any food-rent to the community for three years because of the devastation caused by the 'heathen army'.[52] As major landowners, the archbishops and the Christ Church community would also have had to make substantial contributions to the payments of tribute offered, as in 865, in the hope of persuading the Danish army to move elsewhere. It would therefore be unwise to underestimate the Viking impact upon the economy of the Cathedral church. Indeed, we do not even know the fate of Christ Church during the attack on the city in 851. Whilst its early charters certainly survived, none of its library books and altar-books would seem to have done so, since those that are extant all came into its possession after the 851 raid. It therefore seems unlikely that the oldest and most important church in England escaped damage.

More insidious than the immediate financial and physical difficulties, however, was the damage caused to Christian morale by the unchecked activities of armies of pagans. If neither the Kentish minsters nor even the Cathedral church itself could provide a secure environment for the pursuit of a religious vocation, it would be surprising had the quality and quantity of recruits not been affected. We have, of course, no means of knowing to what extent the progressive decline in the Latinity of charters produced by the Christ Church scriptorium in the ninth century may have been associated, directly or indirectly,

[49] For the charter references to early Viking activity in Kent, see BCS 848, 332, 335, 348, 370 (S 134, 1264, 168, 177, 186); for their interpretation, see N. P. Brooks, 'The Development of Military Obligations on 8th- and 9th-Century England', in *England before the Conquest: Studies in Primary Sources Presented to D. Whitelock*, ed. P. Clemoes and K. Hughes (Cambridge, 1971), 69–84, at 79–80.

[50] Brooks, *Church of Canterbury* (cit. in n. 2), 151, 201–2.

[51] F. E. Harmer, *Select English Historical Documents of the Ninth and Tenth Centuries* (Cambridge, 1914), no. ix.

[52] Ibid. no. vi (S 1198).

with Viking activity throughout that century. What is clear is that the two processes were coeval and that the low point of Latin learning at Canterbury between *c*.850 and *c*.880 coincided with the period when the Viking assaults were at their height. Indeed, the principal Christ Church charter-writer of the 850s and 860s adopted none of the features of the beautiful 'mannered minuscule' of earlier Canterbury scribes. His crude and uneven script eschewed all attempt at calligraphic adornment, and his Latin abounded in mis-spellings and orthographic oddities. He would seem to have joined the Cathedral com-munity soon after the town had been sacked in 851, and to represent a significant lowering of standards there.[53] By the archiepiscopate of Æthelred (870–88), the situation had become critical. By then, charters had apparently to be written either by a scribe who could no longer see what he had written, or by men who had no effective command of Latin grammar at all. To judge by the standards in the metropolitan church, the future of Christian education and worship was indeed in the balance in England in these years. The community was failing to produce men who could read and interpret the Latin Scriptures and services, let alone pass those skills on to the next generation.

The elevation of one of King Alfred's court scholars, the Mercian Plegmund, to the archiepiscopal see in 890 is likely to have been intended to reverse this precipitate decline. Plegmund was one of the scholars who instructed King Alfred in the task of translating Gregory the Great's *Cura Pastoralis* into English. Though the Archbishop must therefore have been at court often in his early years, he was clearly well equipped to introduce a new standard of education to the Cathedral clergy. Only two charters written in the Christ Church scriptorium survive in contemporary manuscripts from his long archiepiscopate (890–923), but both show that under his guidance there were scribes in the community who used a handsome rounded version of the insular minuscule script and whose command of Latin grammar was excellent.[54] Though the evidence is certainly slight, it seems clear that Canterbury participated in the Alfredian revival of learning.

It is also likely that Plegmund lent his support to the King's administrative and military reforms. Certainly we find him in 898 assembling in London with Bishop Werferth of Worcester, King Alfred, Ealdorman Æthelred, and Lady Æthelflæd of the Mercians to confer about the laying-out (*instauratio*) of the borough of London.[55] Alfred's programme of burghal foundation, renewal, and garrisoning offered to the Church the prospect of secure places where major churches could be built within protective town-walls of stone or of earthwork and timber. Though no detail is yet known of any strengthening of the defences of Canterbury itself at this time, nor of the fate of the city during the double assault on Kent in 892–3, it is likely that the Cathedral city had become a garrisoned borough and was in a position to resist attack. The laying-out of a new High Street and the construction of a new gate ('Newingate') may plausibly be attributed to the reign of

---

[53] For the level of learning at Christ Church and the work of 'scribe 7', see Brooks, *Church of Canterbury* (cit. in n. 2), 171–4; for a more sanguine interpretation of standards in the whole of England, see J. Morrish, 'King Alfred's Letter as a Source on Learning in England in the 9th Century', in *Studies in Earlier Old English Prose*, ed. P. E. Szarmach (Albany, NY, 1985), 87–107.

[54] BCS 539, 638 (S 1203, 1288); Brooks, *Church of Canterbury* (cit. in n. 2), 173–4, 214.
[55] BCS 577/8 (S 1628); T. Dyson, 'Two Saxon Land-Grants for Queenhythe', in *Collectanea Londiniensia: Studies Presented to R. B. Merrifield*, ed. J. Bird, H. Chapman and J. Clark (London and Middx. Archaeol. Soc., Special paper 2 (1978), 200–15.

Alfred or to that of Edward the Elder (899–924).[56] The Church of Canterbury will have benefited both from the new security and from the urban revival. As the greatest landlord in east Kent and in the city itself, it will also have made a major contribution to the cost of the work. In an age of Viking attacks, it was more than usually apparent that the interests of Church and State coincided.

WIDENING HORIZONS (924–1016)

The political and military success of the descendants of Egbert and of Alfred in the tenth century brought new opportunities and responsibilities. The conquests of Edward the Elder, of Athelstan (924–39), and of their successors extended their rule first to the whole province of Canterbury and then to part of that of York. What was to be Canterbury's role in the unification of the kingdom?

First, it is clear that the archbishops were brought firmly within the West Saxon patronage system. From the appointment of Athelm, Bishop of Wells, as Archbishop in 923 until that of Lyfing, also of Wells, in 1013, every new archbishop had held one of the southern English sees before his appointment to Canterbury. This was a radical break from previous practice. With the possible exception of Cuthbert, who may have been Bishop of Hereford before being transferred to Canterbury in 740, none of the archbishops had been translated from another see since the early days of the Roman mission. Such translations were indeed prohibited by canon law and therefore needed express papal permission. Cuthbert is believed to have travelled to Rome to receive the *pallium* from the Pope in person. Every tenth-century archbishop from Wulfhelm (926–41) onwards is likewise known to have commenced his office by journeying to Rome for the *pallium*, so it is possible that Athelm had already done the same in 923.[57]

The early tenth century was a time when the papacy was beset with local political difficulties, and most of the popes had themselves been translated from other Italian sees. They were scarcely in a position to assert papal authority over the English Church by requiring a translated archbishop-elect to come to Rome, instead of themselves sending a pall to England. It is much more likely that the motive for the change came from the English kings, who wanted to appoint to Canterbury men whom they trusted and whose record they knew. As the kingdom grew and royal visits to Kent were necessarily less frequent, the kings dared not risk promoting Kentish clerics trained in the Christ Church community, lest Canterbury should once again be the focus of local antagonisms. Nor could they allow there to be doubt about their metropolitan's status, so the kings' interest was to secure papal support for their archbishops. Wealthy kings may have been prepared to pay substantially to get their way. Certainly by the early eleventh century, when resources were tighter, archbishops bitterly objected to being expected to pay in order to

[56] Brooks, 'Ecclesiastical Topography' (cit. in n. 1), 487–98.
[57] Brooks, *Church of Canterbury* (cit. in n. 2), 216–17; for the evidence for *pallia* sent from Rome and obtained in Rome, see Levison, *England and the Continent* (cit. in n. 39), 241–8; for the

Continental development of papal *pallia*, see H. Jedin and J. Dolan, *History of the Church*, iii (London, 1980), 72, 166–9, 288–90.

secure the *pallium*.[58] The West Saxon bishops whom the English kings promoted to Canterbury were mostly from West Saxon aristocratic families whose interests were closely tied to those of the monarchy.[59] They were also men who, as bishops, had attended the royal court regularly and on whose advice the kings had come to rely. Such men owed their careers entirely to the king. It was a policy designed to cement the alliance of Crown and archbishops.

One role that the archbishops fulfilled in return for their promotion was to preside over the English king-making rituals. The earliest English coronation order may have been in use at royal inaugurations from the middle of the ninth century, that is, from the archiepiscopate of Ceolnoth and the consecration of Æthelwulf to succeed his father, Egbert, in 838 or 839.[60] The 'second English *ordo*' seems to have been composed either for the coronation of Edward the Elder (900) or for that of Athelstan (925). It was therefore either Archbishop Plegmund or Archbishop Athelm who introduced into English royal ritual the ring, the crown itself, and much liturgical ceremony that was perhaps of West Frankish origin.[61] Most of the tenth-century coronations took place at Kingston-upon-Thames,[62] and it is clear that they were occasions for all the bishops and leading secular nobles to witness and to join the feasting that followed. In the first half of the tenth century, when Canterbury was the only metropolitan see in the kingdom, such coronations were therefore occasions when the authority of the see of Canterbury was manifested. Again in 956 (when Wulfstan of York was close to death), Archbishop Oda seems to have presided alone. But at Edgar's 'imperial' coronation at Bath, in 973, Archbishop Dunstan officiated jointly with Oswald of York, and that was to be the normal pattern in Anglo-Saxon coronations thereafter.[63] A kingdom that now comprised, as the second English *ordo* stated, 'the sceptres of the Saxons, the Mercians, and the Northumbrians', could readily accommodate two metropolitan sees.

The unification of the English kingdom in the tenth century removed the clear geographical distinction between the assemblies (*witenagemots*), to which kings summoned their nobles and bishops, and ecclesiastical synods, where all the bishops of the province met under the authority of the metropolitan. Charters show that from the reign of

[58] The letter of protest against the simonious expenses of the *pallium*-journey is printed in *Councils and Synods Relating to the English Church*, i. 871–1204, ed. D. Whitelock, M. Brett, and C. N. L. Brooke (Oxford, 1981), pt. I. 441–7, no. 61. For its attribution to Archbishop Wulfstan of York, see D. Bethurum, 'A Letter of Protest from the English Bishops against the Expenses of the Pallium Journey', in *Philologica: The Malone Anniversary Studies*. ed. T. A. Kirby and H. B. Woolf (Baltimore, 1949), 97–104.

[59] Brooks, *Church of Canterbury* (cit. in n. 2), 214–16, 222–3, 237–40, 243–4, 278–9.

[60] J. L. Nelson, 'The Earliest Royal *Ordo*: Some Liturgical and Historical Aspects', in *Authority and Power: Studies in Medieval Law and Government Presented to Walter Ullmann*, ed. B. Tierney and P. Linehan (Cambridge, 1980), 29–48.

[61] C. E. Hohler, 'Some Service Books of the Late Saxon Church', in *Tenth-Century Studies*, ed. D. P. Parsons (Leicester, 1975), 67–9; *The Claudius Pontificals*, ed. D. H. Turner (Henry Bradshaw Soc., 97; 1971 for 1964), pp. xxxi–xxxiii; J. L. Nelson, 'The Second English *Ordo*', in her *Politics and Ritual in Early*

Medieval Europe (London, 1986), 360–74.

[62] For the coronations of Athelstan (925) and Æthelred (979), see *Anglo-Saxon Chronicle*, trans. Whitelock *et al.*, 924 B C D, 978 E, 979 C. For Eadred (946) and Eadwig (956), see *Florentii Wigorniensis Monachi Chronicon ex Chronicis*, ed. B. Thorpe, 2 vols. (Eng. Hist. Soc.; London, 1848), i. 134, 136; for Edward the Elder (900), Edmund (939), and Edward the Martyr (976), see Ralph de Diceto, *Opera Historica*, ed. W. Stubbs, 2 vols. (RS, 68; 1876), i. 140, 146, 153, whose authority for 10th-cent. events is very doubtful.

[63] 'Florence' of Worcester names the officiating archbishop(s) in 925, 946, 956, 973, 975, and 979: see *Chronicon*, ed. Thorpe, i. 134, 136, 142, 145–6. For the wider activities at coronations, see B.'s *Vita Sancti Dunstani*, in *Memorials of Saint Dunstan, Archbishop of Canterbury*, ed. W. Stubbs (RS, 63; 1874), 32–4; for the 973 coronation, see Byrhtferth's *Vita S. Oswaldi*, in *Historians of the Church of York*, ed. J. Raine, 3 vols. (RS, 71; 1879–94), ii. 436–7.

Athelstan it was normal for there to be at least one royal assembly every year, and sometimes as many as four, attended by all the bishops of Canterbury's province. From 928 until 939, from 944 to 950, and again from 954 or 955, when the Viking kingdom of York had been brought under English rule, the Archbishop of York was also usually present at the *witan* and was ranked immediately after the Archbishop of Canterbury.[64] Such regular assemblies of all the leading clergy of the kingdom made purely provincial synods superfluous. The *witan* therefore took over the functions of the synod. The law-codes of Athelstan and Edmund, issued from such assemblies, include individual laws, substantial sections, or even whole codes, devoted to ecclesiastical law. Thus Athelstan's first code concerned the payment of tithes and was enacted 'on the advice of Wulfhelm, my archbishop, and also of my other bishops'. Edmund's first code, also devoted to canon-law matters, declares that the king:

assembled a great synod [*micelne synoð*] at London in the holy Easter season, both of ecclesiastical and secular orders: there Archbishop Oda and Archbishop Wulfstan and many other bishops were taking thought for the good of their souls and of those subject to them.[65]

That was to be the pattern throughout the late Anglo-Saxon period. When King Æthelred II summoned a *sinodale concilium* to Winchester on Whitsunday 993, those present included not only the bishops and abbots of the entire kingdom, but also 'the other leading magnates of mine', that is the *æthelings*, ealdormen, and king's thegns.[66] Ecclesiastical law (like secular law) was declared at meetings of the *witan* attended by bishops and nobles from the whole kingdom; the leading role of one or both archbishops is often mentioned in the preambles to the extant codes, or is associated with particular enactments on fasting, pledges, tithes, and so forth. But the law that was determined was the king's law, and the assembly was that of the whole kingdom. There can be little doubt that these arrangements represented a deliberate attempt to foster the concept of a single nation and of a single national Church. The kings were concerned to incorporate the Northumbrian kingdom and Church firmly into the institutions of their new state. Though it is possible that when the members of the *witan* were assembled, the English bishops were sometimes able to meet without the king, it is significant that neither in the ecclesiastical codes of the tenth and eleventh centuries nor in the canonical writings of Archbishop Wulfstan of York, is there any indication that the 'synod' or 'the bishops' ever referred to a provincial assembly rather than to a meeting of bishops from the whole kingdom.

Thus the political needs of the kingdom seem to have overridden the traditions of the provincial organization of the English Church. The fact that York in the tenth and early eleventh centuries normally had only one suffragan, the Bishop of Chester-le-Street (later of Durham), made the integration of the northern province into a national structure seem appropriate. York was never at this time a rival of Canterbury. The two metropolitans were

[64] Hrothward attests BCS 663, 664 (S 400, 399) of 928; BCS 667, 669 (S 404, 403) of 930; Wulfstan's attestations begin in 931: BCS 675, 677, 680, 683 (S 413, 416, 410, 409). For the relationship of synod and *witenagemot* in the 10th and 11th cents., see *Councils and Synods* (cit. in n. 58), pt. 1, pp.vi–vii, and Vollrath, *Die Synoden Englands* (cit. in n. 6), 210–29.

[65] I Athelstan, prologue; I Edmund, prologue (F. Liebermann, *Die Gesetze der Angelsachsen*, (3 vols.; Halle, 1903–16), i. 146, 184).

[66] See S 876, a charter of 993, the best edition of which appears in *Councils and Synods*, i (cit. in n. 58), pt. 1, no. 39. For a somewhat different interpretation, see Vollrath, *Die Synoden Englands* (cit. in n. 6), 308–10.

independent and formally of equal status. When one archbishop died, the arrangement laid down by Pope Honorius I in 634—that the other should be responsible for consecrating the archbishop-elect to the vacant see—was followed faithfully.[67] None the less, the Archbishop of Canterbury almost always took precedence in English councils, despite the personal eminence or the seniority in age or appointment of particular Archbishops of York. Canterbury was the older see, its province was larger, and it had more suffragans. The establishment of the single kingdom of the English does not seem to have given rise to any rivalry between York and Canterbury before the Norman Conquest.

For the Church of Canterbury, however, participation in the making of the English kingdom was not an unmixed blessing. Early in Athelstan's reign, in his Grately code, the King had enacted that there was to be 'one coinage throughout all the king's domain'. The result of this policy seems to have been that Archbishop Athelm lost the right to issue silver pennies in his own name. From Jænberht to Plegmund every pontificate had been marked by the production of coins, normally by two moneyers concurrently, which bore the archbishop's name on the obverse (Pl. 3). No such coins were produced for Athelm or for any subsequent archbishop, though Athelstan's code indicates that the profits from the work of two moneyers of the Canterbury mint continued to go to the archbishops. Henceforth, however, the coins that the archiepiscopal moneyers produced bore the king's name, and their design was indistinguishable from other English pennies.[68] This curtailment of the visible sign of the privileged status of the see of Canterbury serves as another indication of the precocious uniformity achieved by the tenth-century English state.

The political and military successes of the dynasty also brought a new widening of the territorial interests of the Church of Canterbury. Some acquisitions continued to be made in Kent—such as the great estate of Reculver, which Archbishop Wulfred had fought to retain from Mercian royal hands but had lost to the West Saxons; King Eadred with the support of his mother, Eadgifu, granted the whole 26 sulungs of Reculver to the Cathedral Church in 949 in a charter, which was apparently written by Abbot Dunstan of Glastonbury himself.[69] Other Kentish estates were given by wealthy nobles, such as the bequest of the downland manor of Meopham by the king's thegn Byrhtric and his wife, Ælfswith.[70] But King Eadred's grant of Twickenham (Middlesex) in 948 (if we may accept a very strange charter full of Continental features),[71] King Eadwig's grant of Ely to Archbishop Oda (possibly intended to provide a foundation for his monk-nephew, Oswald),[72] the bequest to Christ Church by Ealdorman Ælfgar of Essex of the reversion to an estate at Eleigh (Suffolk),[73] the gift of Vange (Essex) to Archbishop Dunstan by the king's thegn Ingeram,[74] and the acquisition of the huge manor of Pagham (Sussex), seemingly after a successful

[67] Honorius's letter is in Bede, *Hist. Eccles.* ii. 17, which is cited in the rubrics for the consecration of an archbishop in the 'Dunstan Pontifical' (Paris, Bibl. Nat., MS lat. 943) and in later pontificals. See *Canterbury Professions* (cit. in n. 30), p. lxiii and n. 2.

[68] II Athelstan 14 (Liebermann, *Gesetze* (cit. in n. 65), i. 158); C. E. Blunt, 'The Coinage of Athelstan', *British Numismatic Jnl.*, 42 (1974), 40–1, 64–5.

[69] BCS 880 (S 546); the critical view of its authenticity in Brooks, *Church of Canterbury* (cit. in n. 2), 232–6, is withdrawn

in id., 'The Career of St Dunstan', in *St Dunstan: His Life, Times and Cult*, ed. N. L. Ramsay, M. J. Sparks, and T. Tatton-Brown (Woodbridge, 1992), 1–23, at 17–18.

[70] D. Whitelock, *Anglo-Saxon Wills* (Cambridge, 1930), no. 11 (S 1511).

[71] BCS 860 (S 537); for the traditional view of its authenticity, see Brooks, *Church of Canterbury* (cit. in n. 2), 232.

[72] BCS 999/1347 (S 646).

[73] Whitelock, *Wills* (cit. in n. 70), no. 2 (S 1483).

[74] BCS 1101 (S 717).

joint programme of forgery with the see of Chichester in the late 950s[75]—all are signs that the see and the community were profiting from the wider contacts made through the archbishop's regular participation in the meetings of the *witan*.

The renewed Viking threat in the closing decades of the tenth century restricted once again Canterbury's income from rents, drained its cash resources, and at times threatened the safety of archbishops and community directly. Viking armies are known to have been active in Kent and neighbouring shires in 991, 994, 999, 1006, 1011, 1013, 1014, and 1016. Their unchecked tactics of deliberate devastation in order to extort mounting payments of tribute disrupted the routine extraction of resources by great landlords. Thus in the autumn of 994 the 'pagan' army of Olaf Trygvason and Svein Forkbeard threatened to destroy the Cathedral church by fire unless Archbishop Sigeric paid the sum promised to them. Unable to raise the sum from his own resources, Sigeric had to borrow 90 pounds of silver and 200 mancuses of gold (in all £115) from Bishop Æscwig of Dorchester in return for ceding to him an estate of 30 hides at (Monks) Risborough (Buckinghamshire).[76] In 1009 Thorkell's army landed at Sandwich and made straight for Canterbury: 'and would quickly have captured the borough if all the citizens had not still more quickly asked them for peace. And all the people of East Kent made peace with that army and gave 3,000 pounds.'[77] In September 1011 the Cathedral and city were threatened for a third time, but on this occasion Thorkell's forces were not bought off. Admitted to the city, they captured Archbishop Ælfheah and other leading ecclesiastics and laymen, together with 'all those in holy orders'. They proceeded to sack and burn both the Cathedral and the borough, before carrying off the Archbishop as a hostage. Just how devastating a blow to English morale was the capture of the Archbishop and the ransacking of the cradle of English Christianity is indicated by the huge tribute of £48,000 that had to be paid by the following Easter to secure peace. It seems that the money was not all gathered in time. Six days later, on 19 April 1012, Archbishop Ælfheah was battered to death by the pagan army in a display of festive and drunken barbarity. Regarded immediately as a Christian martyr, the Archbishop was said to have been killed because of his refusal to allow any money to be paid as a personal ransom.[78] What is clear, however, is that this further act of terrorism was effective. Full payment of the huge sum due to Thorkell's army was soon completed.

We do not know the size of the tribute due from the Canterbury estates in the winter of 1011–12, nor its share of other huge payments, which culminated in the £72,000 paid in 1018. A general impoverishment of English magnates, secular and ecclesiastical, has been suggested because of the use of baser metals in the extant metalwork of the period and because of the quantity of English silver found in Scandinavian hoards at this time.[79] But even these unsettled conditions were by no means entirely unfortunate for a major church

[75] Brooks, *Church of Canterbury* (cit. in n. 2), 240–3.

[76] KCD 689 (S 882); Brooks, *Church of Canterbury* (cit. in n. 2), 283.

[77] *Anglo-Saxon Chronicle* (cit. in n. 26), 1009 CDE.

[78] Ibid. 1011, 1012 CDE; Thietmar of Merseburg, *Chronicon*, ed. R. Holtzmann, MGH Script. Rer. Germ., NS ix (Berlin, 1935), vii. 42, trans. in *English Historical Documents* i (cit. in n. 31), no. 27.

[79] D. Hinton, 'Late-Saxon Treasure and Bullion', in *Ethelred the Unready*, ed. D. Hill (British Archaeological Reports, 59; Oxford, 1978), 135–58; for contrasting views of the authority of the Anglo-Saxon Chronicle's figures for the payments of 'Danegeld', see J. Gillingham, 'Levels of Danegeld and Her-egeld in the Early Eleventh Century', *EHR*, 104 (1989), 373–85, and M. K. Lawson, 'Levels of Taxation in the Reigns of Æthelred II and Cnut', ibid. 385–406.

like Canterbury. Thus the death of both Ealdorman Byrhtnoth of Essex (in the battle of Maldon in 991) and subsequently of his wife, Ælfflæd, without offspring, brought to Christ Church estates at Lawling in Essex and Monks Eleigh and Hadleigh in Suffolk.[80] Another heirless noble, Æthelric of Bocking, gave his patrimonial estate to the community, and Archbishop Ælfric was able to persuade the King to allow the bequest to stand despite the suspicions of Æthelric's treachery in 991.[81] The King's eldest son, the *ætheling* Athelstan, made a deathbed bequest of his Kentish estates at Hollingbourne and Garrington (in Littlebourne) to Christ Church in 1014, and successive archbishops—Ælfric, Ælfheah, and Lyfing—all bequeathed substantial estates to the community.[82] In times of violence and insecurity, belief in the efficacy of the prayers of the community for the souls of benefactors, lay and ecclesiastical, ensured a substantial flow of endowments.

The sources tell us more about the fortunes of the endowment than they do about the life of the community in the tenth century. One charter, which records the terms on which Archbishop Oda (941–58) and the Christ Church community leased their property at Ickham to a Kentish noble, gives us the names of three mass-priests, five deacons, one priest, and twelve others who are not given any rank.[83] But without comparable lists from the tenth or eleventh century it is not possible to trace changes in the community's composition. There is, however, evidence that in the second quarter of the tenth century the community acquired a few learned Continental scholars. The first was the author of an elaborate dedicatory poem entered into the richly but simply ornamented gospel-book (BL, Cotton MS Tiberius A. ii), which King Athelstan had received from the German King Otto I and his mother, Matilda, and had then given to Christ Church, seemingly in the closing years of his reign (c.937x9). The poem, *Rex Pius Æthelstan*, celebrates in twenty lines of elegiac couplets the English king's conquest of fierce and proud kings and his gift to Christ Church of the gospel-book, which he had had adorned with golden letters and bejewelled covers.[84] This poet wrote excellent Latin, in the 'hermeneutic' style, aiming to display as many obscure and learned words as possible; he also used an elegant and practised Continental Caroline minuscule script (Pl. 4).

Another Continental scholar, Frithegod—or Freðegod, as he is called in the list of the community under Archbishop Oda—was a deacon at Christ Church and was remembered as a teacher of unique learning. His principal extant work, the *Breviloquium Vitae Beati Wilfridi*, is a rendering of 'Eddius' Stephanus' *Vita Wilfridi* into 1,400 hexameters. It was written to honour the installation of the bones of St Wilfrid in an altar at Christ Church. The relics had been seized from their shrine at Ripon (along with the text of the *Vita*) in King Eadred's punitive sack of the monastic church there in 948. The poem survives in two manuscripts of the mid-tenth century: one a copy in which five Christ Church scribes, experimenting with the Caroline script, combined to produce a working text, the other

[80] Brooks, *Church of Canterbury* (cit. in n. 2), 285–6.
[81] Whitelock, *Wills* (cit. in n. 70), no. 16 (i) and (ii) (S 1501, 939).
[82] Ibid., no. 20 (S 1503).
[83] A. J. Robertson, *Anglo-Saxon Charters* (2nd edn.; Cambridge, 1956), no. 32 (S 1506).
[84] The text of *Rex Pius Æthelstan* is printed and discussed by

M. Lapidge, 'Some Latin Poems as Evidence for the Reign of Athelstan', *Anglo-Saxon England*, 9 (1981), 61–98, at 93–7. For the history of the gospel-book see S. D. Keynes, 'King Athelstan's Books', in *Learning and Literature in Anglo-Saxon England: Studies Presented to Peter Clemoes*, ed. M. Lapidge and H. Gneuss (Cambridge, 1985), 143–201, at 147–53.

in Frithegod's own hand, incorporating his subsequent revisions of the text. Frithegod's poem is notable not only for obscuring the awkward fact that Wilfrid had been in constant conflict with Archbishops Theodore and Berhtwald, but also for the author's unequalled command of Greek vocabulary and syntax in coining new Latin words from Greek roots in forms designed to meet the needs of his verse. This was indeed a virtuoso display of scholarly one-upmanship.[85]

The Caroline minuscule script was introduced at Christ Church by scholars such as this, and perhaps by others—such as the four clerks who were remembered as bringing relics of St Audoenus ('St Ouen') from Rouen in 957x8;[86] it was adopted gradually at Christ Church in the second half of the tenth century. Dunstan himself seems to have learned the Caroline hand when in exile at Ghent, in 956–7.[87] By the last decade of the tenth century, when we first have books surviving from the Christ Church library (as opposed to gospel-books and psalters which were kept on the altars of the church), the traditional 'insular minuscule' had been abandoned for all texts in Latin (though it was retained for the vernacular). By that time, there were twenty or more scribes at Christ Church trained to write a highly calligraphic English Caroline script and to ornament important initial letters with elaborate pen-drawn interlacing patterns of fronds and animals (Pl. 6). In the first two decades of the eleventh century a substantial number of Christ Church scribes mastered this stately script, achieving what has been described as its 'possible limit of perfection'.[88]

The development of an outstanding scriptorium using the new script was one of the distinctive changes in the life of the Christ Church community in the tenth century, as it came under the growing influence of the English revival of monasticism. Archbishop Oda had himself received the monastic habit at Fleury (one of the principal offshoots from Cluny), probably when he visited the court of the Capetian Duke, Hugh the Great, in 936. Archbishop Dunstan (959–88) had been the first English reforming abbot to establish (at Glastonbury) a community of monks observing the Benedictine Rule. His successors at Canterbury—Æthelgar (988–90), Sigeric (990–4), Ælfric (995–1005), Ælfheah (1006–12), and Lyfing (1013–20)—had all been abbots of reformed houses before their elevation to the episcopate and their subsequent translation to the metropolitan see.[89] The reforms that Archbishop Wulfred had imposed upon the community in the ninth century, especially the common dormitory and refectory and the insistence on monastic discipline, would certainly have appealed to these monk-archbishops. Under Oda, the Canterbury clergy were clearly differentiated from monks by being ranked in the various clerical grades; to

---

[85] *Frithegodi Monachi Breviloquium Vitae Beati Wilfridi et Wulfstani Cantoris Narratio Metrica de Sancto Swithuni*, ed. A. Campbell (Zurich, 1950). There is now a major critical study of Frithegod and his work in M. Lapidge, 'A Frankish Scholar in Tenth-Century England: Frithegod of Canterbury/Fredegaud of Brioude', *Anglo-Saxon England*, 17 (1988), 45–65.

[86] Frithegod wrote a lost verse *Life of St Ouen* (Lapidge, 'A Frankish Scholar', 48); Eadmer's story of the four clerks arriving with the saint's relics at Edgar's court (presumably in Mercia) is in his *De Reliquiis Sancti Audoeni et Quorundam Aliorum Sanctorum quae Cantuarie in Aecclesia Domini Salvatoris Habentur*, ed. A. Wilmart, *Rev. des sciences religieuses*, 15 (1935), 364–5.

[87] Brooks, 'Career of St Dunstan' (cit. in n. 69), 1–23. Since

this chapter was written a much-needed reassessment of the introduction of Caroline scripts at Christ Church has been provided by D. N. Dumville, *English Caroline Script and Monastic History* (Woodbridge, 1993), 86–110, 141–5.

[88] T. A. M. Bishop, 'Notes on Cambridge Manuscripts, Part VII: The Early Minuscule of Christ Church, Canterbury', *Trans. Cambridge Bibliog. Soc.*, 3 (1959–63), 412–23, at 416–17. See now the masterly survey in Dumville, *English Caroline Script* (cit. in n. 87), 111–39, 146–51.

[89] For the monastic careers of these archbishops, see Brooks, *Church of Canterbury* (cit. in n. 2), 222–3, 278–80, and Brooks, 'Career of St Dunstan' (cit. in n. 69), 1–23.

judge from Continental parallels, they may also have worn better clothing and have continued to retain some private but inalienable property for their lives. But there is no evidence that they were an aristocratic body of hereditary married clergy, like that which caused Æthelwold such offence at Winchester. Stories of the expulsion of secular clerks from Christ Church by Archbishop Sigeric in 990, by Ælfric in 995 or 1006, or by Æthelnoth in 1021, all seem to be late monastic inventions from periods when the monastic chapter was under threat.[90] Rather, it is likely that successive archbishops encouraged a growing proportion of the community to follow their own example and take the monastic profession. Thus the balance in a mixed community of clerks and monks would gradually have swung to the monks.

Certainly in the extant altar-books we have evidence that the liturgical regime of the Christ Church community was increasingly Benedictine. The Bosworth Psalter is a manuscript written by a scribe associated with Archbishop Dunstan and is prefaced by a calendar which adapts a Glastonbury model for use at Christ Church; it contains all the important texts of the Benedictine Office: the Roman psalter, with the divisions of particular psalms in accordance with the Rule, the canticles for daily singing, the hymns of the New Hymnary brought to England with the monastic reform movement, and the monastic canticles which belong to the third nocturn of the Office (Pl. 7).[91] Both in this psalter and in the magnificently illustrated copy of the Utrecht Psalter that was produced at Canterbury at the turn of the century (Pls. 8, 9),[92] and in the Arundel Psalter, written by the Christ Church monk Eadui Basan about the year 1020, Christ Church practice remained loyal to the use of the Roman rather than the Gallican text of the psalms. Contemporary Continental houses, both those of the Lotharingian and of the Cluniac reforms, knew only the *Gallicanum*. Increasingly in the eleventh century that was the practice of English reformed houses too. But at Christ Church the tradition of Roman authority remained supreme in matters liturgical. The deliberate compromise which this involved is apparent in the Arundel Psalter, where a Winchester calendar is adopted (presumably replacing the Glastonbury model hitherto in use at Christ Church), but where the *Romanum* psalter text is none the less retained. That Canterbury found no difficulty in marrying Roman and Benedictine authority is vividly revealed in the superb illustration which Eadui Basan placed between the end of the psalms and the start of the monastic canticles in the Arundel Psalter (Col. Pl. 1).[93] The illustration shows the artist-monk kneeling in a position of humility and holding the psalter at the feet of St Benedict, who,

[90] For the context in which these stories were fabricated and the historical errors perpetuated, see Brooks, *Church of Canterbury* (cit. in n. 2), 257–60.

[91] BL, Add. MS 37517; P. M. Korhammer, 'The Origin of the Bosworth Psalter', *Anglo-Saxon England*, 2 (1973), 173–89; E. Temple, *Anglo-Saxon Manuscripts, 900–1066* (Survey of Manuscripts Illuminated in the British Isles, 2; London, 1976), no. 23 and pls. 81–3. For the monastic canticles, see P. M. Korhammer, *Die monastischen Cantica im Mittelalter* (Münchener Universitäts-Schriften; Munich 1976), and for the hymnary, see H. Gneuss, *Hymnar und Hymnen im englischen Mittelalter* (Tübingen, 1968) and G. R. Wieland, *The Canterbury Hymnal* (Toronto Medieval Texts, 12; Toronto, 1982). For the Roman and Gallican psalter

texts in England, see C. and K. Sisam, *The Salisbury Psalter* (Early English Text Soc., OS, 242; London, 1959), 48–51.

[92] BL, Harl. MS 603; F. Wormald, *English Drawings of the Tenth and Eleventh Centuries* (London, 1952), 44–5, 54–6; Temple, *Anglo-Saxon Manuscripts* (cit. in n. 91), no. 64.

[93] BL, MS Arundel 155, fo. 133; for the hand, see T. A. M. Bishop, *English Caroline Minuscule* (Oxford, 1971), 24. The fullest discussions of the iconography of this important drawing are J. Higgitt, 'Glastonbury, Dunstan, Monasticism and Manuscripts', *Art History*, 2 (1979), 275–90, and R. Deshman, '*Benedictus Monarcha et Monachus*: Early Medieval Ruler Theology and the Anglo-Saxon Reform', *Frühmittelalterliche Studien*, 22 (1988), 204–40, at 211–16.

authorized by the hand of God, delivers the Benedictine Rule to a group of genuflecting monks. Scholars have disagreed whether the model which Eadui was here adapting came from Æthelwold's Winchester or from Dunstan's Canterbury, but what is clear is that by 1020 the Christ Church community saw itself as avowedly Benedictine and bound by the terms of the Rule.

The surviving books from the pre-Conquest library at Christ Church tell very much the same story. Nothing remains from the Cathedral library of the days of Theodore, or even of Frithegod. But some sixty-two manuscript books, written at Christ Church seemingly during the period from *c.*990 to 1066, are extant, mostly executed in the Christ Church version of the English Caroline minuscule script.[94] It is clear that a major effort was made, particularly in the early part of that period, to produce a library with copies of the works that were considered essential for the reading and instruction of the Cathedral community. The Christ Church books are a characteristic example of what has been called 'the late Anglo-Saxon monastic curriculum'.[95] The reading of the community would seem to have concentrated upon the Gospels, the psalms, and monastic hymns, that is, on the core texts of the communal worship of the monastic Office. Prominent too were the works of Juvencus and Arator, who retold New Testament stories in Latin verse, the collections of moral maxims and exemplary stories of Prosper, Defensor, and Smaragdus, Aldhelm's prose and verse eulogies of the conventual life, collections of the lives and passions of saints and martyrs, as well as a number of individual monastic *vitae*. The intention of this library was clearly to provide the Canterbury monks with a good literary training from Christian or moralizing authors. Of Virgil and the pagan classical poets on whom Frithegod had drawn so freely, there is no trace. Remarkably, there are also very few of the fundamental theological, exegetical, and historical works of the Christian Fathers: Ambrose, Augustine, Eusebius, Isidore, Gregory, Orosius, nor even of England's own Bede. It was a library intended to produce devout and humble Benedictine monks, who would know the psalms and much of the New Testament by heart and who would appreciate the skills of Latin hexameters and hymns. It does not seem to have encouraged intellectual curiosity or, indeed, new writing. It is characteristic that neither of the two pre-Conquest Lives of St Dunstan was written at Christ Church. The first was written by 'B.', an Englishman and a former clerk of Glastonbury who had been abroad at Liège throughout Dunstan's archiepiscopate, and the second by Adelard, a monk of Ghent who also had no knowledge of the Archbishop's life at Canterbury.[96]

THE GATHERING STORM (*c.*1020–1066)

The accession of the Danish barbarian warrior Cnut to the English throne in 1016 brought an end to the long agonies of political and military disaster that had characterized the

[94] Brooks, *Church of Canterbury* (cit. in n. 2), 266–78.

[95] M. Lapidge, 'The Study of Latin Texts in Late Anglo-Saxon England: (i) The Evidence of Latin Glossses', in *Latin and the Vernacular Languages in Early Medieval Britain*, ed. N. P. Brooks (Leicester, 1982), 102.

[96] For the Lives by B. and Adelard, see Stubbs, *Memorials of Saint Dunstan* (cit. in n. 63), 1–68; M. Lapidge, 'B. and the *Vita S. Dunstani*', and A. Thacker, 'Cults at Canterbury: Relics and Reform under Dunstan and His Successors', in *St Dunstan: His Life, Times and Cult* (cit. in n. 69), 247–59 and 221–45.

reign of Æthelred the Unready. Cnut was determined to rule as a lawful Christian ruler, not as a pagan conqueror, and he therefore relied heavily on the advice of his archbishops, whom he was prepared to reward. In 1018, when Archbishop Lyfing had returned from Rome with the *pallium*, the King and his new wife, Ælfgifu / Emma, the widow of Æthelred, visited Canterbury; they first granted to the Archbishop a small property adjoining one of his manors in Sussex, and then, in a public ceremony in the Cathedral, Cnut confirmed the privileges granted to Christ Church by earlier kings by taking the charters of freedom (*freolsas*) and laying them on the high altar. The shire court of Kent was notified of this demonstration of the King's support for the lands and rights of the Church of Canterbury, and a record of this message was inserted by the monk and master-scribe Eadui Basan into one of the church's gospel-books.[97] One of the privileges which the King laid on the altar was evidently the forged charter of King Wihtred of Kent, purporting to cede to the Kentish churches freedom from all secular burdens and to the archbishops control of the Kentish minster churches. The surviving text of this ninth-century forgery is a fair copy seemingly written for this occasion by Eadui Basan himself.[98] It seems unlikely that Cnut knew what he was confirming.

Just how far the King was prepared to dance to the monks' tune was made clear when Lyfing died, on 12 June 1020. In his place, on 13 November, there was consecrated Æthelnoth, who had previously been the 'dean' of the Christ Church community, that is to say, he had presided over the monastic chapter. This was the first time for a century that the incoming archbishop had not been translated from a southern see; it was also the first time since 805 (Archbishop Wulfred) that a member of the Christ Church community had succeeded to the archbishopric. We do not know whether Æthelnoth's elevation was the product of a free election by the monks of Christ Church, in accordance with the Rule and the provisions of the English *Regularis Concordia*.[99] But the monks clearly regarded it as an important precedent, since they entered documents connected with Æthelnoth's elevation into one of their gospel-books.[100] No other archiepiscopal succession was commemorated in this way, so it would seem that the election of their dean, however it had been achieved, was regarded as a triumph, which they intended should be remembered.

Other successes followed in 1023, when Æthelnoth returned from Rome with the *pallium*. In the summer of that year, King Cnut authorized the Archbishop to remove the body of the martyred Ælfheah from St Paul's in London, where it had been taken in 1012 from Greenwich and where miraculous cures had already been reported. According to the post-Conquest monk Osbern, Archbishop Æthelnoth and a party of Christ Church monks—including Ælfweard the Tall and Godric, who was later dean of the community— broke open the tomb and removed the body as speedily as possible under the protection of a troop of Cnut's housecarls and against the wishes both of the clergy of St Paul's and

[97] BL, Stowe Charter 38 (S 950); *Anglo-Saxon Writs*, ed. F. E. Harmer (Manchester, 1953), no. 26 (S 985), which is entered into BL, Royal MS 1 D. ix, fo.44ᵛ. See Brooks, *Church of Canterbury* (cit. in n. 2), 288–90. For Cnut's benefactions to other English monasteries, see L. M. Larson, *Cnut the Great* (New York, 1912), 175–8.

[98] BCS 91 (S 22); for the hand, see Bishop, *English Caroline Minuscule* (cit. in n. 93), no. 24; for the context, see Brooks, *Church of Canterbury* (cit. in n. 2), 289–90.

[99] *Regularis Concordia*, ed. T. Symons (Nelson's Medieval Classics; London, 1953), ch. 9.

[100] *Writs*, ed. Harmer (cit. in n. 97), nos. 27, 28, which are entered into the MacDurnan Gospels (LPL, MS 771, fos. 69, 114ᵛ). See Brooks, *Church of Canterbury* (cit. in n. 2), 290–1.

of the citizens of London.[101] Removed from London on 8 June, brought to Canterbury in a cortège led by Queen Emma and her child, Harthacnut, on 11 June, the body was enshrined in the Cathedral just on the north side of the altar of Christ on 15 June, in a ceremony attended by several bishops. Thus the community acquired with maximum publicity the relics of a recent and already potent martyr. It cannot be said, however, that the pre-Conquest monks of Christ Church made the most of their acquisition. They neither produced a Life of Ælfheah while there were still contemporaries of the Archbishop in the community to remember his deeds; nor did they commission a Continental scholar to write one for them; nor did they collect details of miracles occurring at the tomb. In short, they failed to establish the cult of St Ælfheah—a failure which had to be remedied by the Anglo-Norman community in the closing years of the century.

Other important but somewhat uncertain royal gifts to the Cathedral church belong to the same year and probably to the same visit to Canterbury. Queen Emma donated a notable relic, an arm claimed to be St Bartholomew's, which she had purchased in Italy from the Archbishop of Bari;[102] King Cnut was claimed to have granted his gold crown, which he placed on the altar of Christ in the Cathedral, together with all tolls and rights in the port of Sandwich for the monks' food ('ad victum monachorum').[103] Sandwich was a major herring-port and its haven was the largest sheltered anchorage for naval fleets in eastern England. Control of Sandwich was therefore of vital strategic importance in the eleventh-century struggles for the English throne. To give it to Christ Church could be considered an act of foolish generosity; certainly Harold Harefoot was to repossess it in 1037.[104] Moreover, in the 1030s the abbey of St Augustine's acquired land on Thanet, on the northern bank of the Wantsum channel. For more than a century there were constant disputes between the two Canterbury houses over port dues and the unloading of cargoes on one bank or the other. The fact that none of the numerous extant single-sheet versions of Cnut's Sandwich diploma is in a pre-Conquest hand, and that the charter purports to give to the Christ Church monks a monopoly of revenues from the port and all landing-rights on *both* sides of the Wantsum therefore suggests that the extant diploma is a forgery. But the details of the witnesses and the formulation show that the forger had access to a genuine diploma of Cnut granted in 1023. It is probable that the King did grant the monks some rights in Sandwich in that year, but not as fully or precisely as the extant charter claims.

Cnut and Emma's astounding largesse may have been intended to ensure the Church of Canterbury's support for their rule and for the succession of their only son, Harthacnut. Certainly Æthelnoth was to prove faithful to his benefactors, even refusing to crown the illegitimate Harold Harefoot in 1036. When Harold established his authority over the whole kingdom in 1037, he confiscated the port of Sandwich, doubtless in order to close it to Harthacnut's fleet. By that time, moreover, the tide of history was no longer running in the monks' favour. Since Cnut had attended the imperial coronation of Conrad II in Rome in 1127, he had developed the royal chapel on the imperial model as the chief route

[101] *Anglo-Saxon Chronicle* (cit. in n. 26), D 1023; Osbern, *Historia de Translatione S. Elphegi*, in Wharton, *Anglia Sacra*, ii. 143–7.

[102] Brooks, *Church of Canterbury* (cit. in n. 2), 292.

[103] KCD 737 (S 959); Brooks, *Church of Canterbury* (cit. in n. 2), 292–4.

[104] *Charters*, ed. Robertson (cit. in n. 83), no. 91 (S 1467).

for ecclesiastical preferment in England. In the later years of his reign, he and Emma were grooming one of the king's priests, Eadsige, as Æthelnoth's successor. Eadsige became a monk for the purpose in 1035 and granted to Christ Church a series of properties on the edge of Romney Marsh in return for the community's 'staunch support and loyalty to him'. In the same year, Æthelnoth consecrated Eadsige as bishop, probably with a seat in St Martin's Church in Canterbury, and Eadsige took over the Archbishop's role in the shire court of Kent.[105] In 1038, when Æthelnoth died, Eadsige succeeded to the metropolitan see without interference. Whilst the formality of promoting a member of the Christ Church community had thus been maintained, in reality Cnut had arranged for the succession of one of the priests of his chapel. It was a dangerous precedent, which ran counter to the canonical prohibition both of auxiliary bishops (*chorepiscopi*) and of bishops consecrating their own successors. In 1035–8 determined kings could ignore the canonical proprieties, but the age of reform was near.

Eadsige's archiepiscopate (1038–50) was remembered as an unhappy time at Christ Church because it coincided with the rise of Earl Godwine of Wessex. After the Conquest, when denigration of the Godwine family was politic, Eadsige was considered to have permitted Godwine to steal the monks' manor of Folkestone, to have lost to him the 'third penny' of shire revenues in Kent, which Æthelnoth was said to have received, and to have 'given' to Godwine Kentish properties at Richborough, Langport, Newenden, and Saltwood.[106] The reality seems to be that Christ Church estates were leased out to leading Kentish nobles, not only to Godwine but also to local men like Æthelric Bigga and his son, Osbern, for one or more lives.[107] It could always prove difficult to recover such estates from powerful sitting lords, and after 1066 it was particularly difficult to prevent the confiscation of estates that had been in the hands of those who had fought at Hastings. Godwine, however, may not have been the scourge of Christ Church whom it was later convenient to depict. Certainly, when Eadsige fell ill in 1044, the Earl seems to have co-operated with the Archbishop in securing King Edward's consent that Abbot Siward of Abingdon should be consecrated as bishop to be his replacement, reportedly in order to prevent an unsuitable candidate from purchasing the office.[108] Though not a monk of Christ Church, Siward, as an Abbot of Abingdon who had been trained at Glastonbury, had an impeccable monastic pedigree. In the event, Siward died before Eadsige, in 1048, and Eadsige consecrated a certain Godwine (of whose connections we know nothing) as 'Bishop of St Martin's' in his place. So far as we can tell, in these arrangements the initiative lay with Eadsige, and the Earl was co-operative.

When Eadsige died, on 29 October 1050, the community sought to continue this alliance by electing a monk of Christ Church, named Ælric, who was a kinsman of Godwine. But they had miscalculated the political situation disastrously, for King Edward the Confessor chose this moment to throw off the tutelage of the Godwine family. At a *witan* held at

---

[105] For Eadsige's relations with Cnut and with the community, see ibid., no. 86 (S 1465), BL, Stowe Charter 41 (S 974), and *Writs*, ed. Harmer (cit. in n. 97), nos. 29, 30 (S 987, 988); Brooks, *Church of Canterbury* (cit. in n. 2), 295–6.

[106] Brooks, *Church of Canterbury* (cit. in n. 2), 300–2.

[107] *Charters*, ed. Robertson (cit. in n. 83), no. 101 (S 1471); BL,

Cotton MS Augustus II 36, discussed and trans. in F. R. H. Du Boulay, *The Lordship of Canterbury* (London, 1966), 38–41. For the general problem, see Brooks, *Church of Canterbury* (cit. in n. 2), 301–2.

[108] *Anglo-Saxon Chronicle* (cit. in n. 26), 1043 D, 1044 C; Brooks, *Church of Canterbury* (cit. in n. 2), 299–300.

London in March 1051, the King forced through the translation to Canterbury of his Norman friend Robert of Jumièges, the Bishop of London.[109] The recognition of Duke William of Normandy as the heir to the English throne, and the exiling of Earl Godwine and of all his sons soon followed. As Archbishop, Robert set about recovering the Christ Church lands that had been in Godwine's hands. But in September 1052 the Earl and his sons forced the King to restore their earldoms, and the Norman Archbishop to flee to his homeland. In his place the *witan* nominated Bishop Stigand of Winchester, who had been the intermediary who had negotiated the Earl's return.[110]

For Christ Church the elevation of Stigand was a disaster. Stigand, despite his tenure of the monastic see of Winchester, was not a monk and showed no willingness to become one. He was already a pluralist, holding the sees both of East Anglia (Elmham) and of Winchester. Though in 1052 he seems to have passed Elmham on to his brother, Æthelmær, he retained Winchester, which, after Canterbury, was the richest see in England. He had also been involved in simony, as in the attempted promotion of Spearhafoc to London in 1051, which Archbishop Robert had quashed. In Edward the Confessor's eyes, Stigand was the man who had usurped the office of his friend Archbishop Robert. Royal benefactions to the see of Canterbury came to an end. As a pluralist and a simoniac, Stigand had no chance of securing a *pallium* from Pope Leo IX or from any of his reforming successors. Though the Tusculan pope Benedict X, who seized control of Rome for ten brief months (1058–9), did send a pall to Stigand, his acts were soon annulled by Pope Nicholas II. Except in 1058–9, English bishops therefore went abroad or to York for consecration. Stigand, it would seem, was neither excommunicated nor deposed by the reforming popes; he continued to be given first place among the bishops at meetings of the *witan*, even when the papal legates were present,[111] but was prevented from exercising authority as metropolitan of the southern province. The popes were apparently well aware that Stigand was a key figure in the balance of power between the King and the Godwine family and in the dispute over the English succession. Perhaps wisely, they seem to have decided not to choose between the claims of a Norman duke and an English earl to the throne of the childless Edward.

Stigand therefore survived in possession of the sees of both Winchester and Canterbury. He also amassed a huge personal lordship of estates, primarily in East Anglia, where his family interests lay, but also in Gloucestershire; there were no less than thirty-nine burgesses on his properties in Norwich, and numerous East Anglian freemen had taken him as their lord by commendation. The patronage of this successful operator was evidently worth having, and several major English churches (including Ely, St Alban's, St Oswald's, Gloucester, and the Old Minster at Winchester) leased properties to him, seemingly as a retainer for his political services and maintenance.[112] He must have cut a remarkable figure as a great lord, on a par with the greatest earls. But all this manipulation seems to have brought no advantage to the see of Canterbury or to the monks of Christ Church. In

---

[109] *Anglo-Saxon Chronicle* (cit. in n. 26), 1050 C, 1051 E; *Vita Ædwardi Regis*, ed. F. Barlow (London, 1962), 18–19.

[110] For Stigand's career, which is summarized here, see F. Barlow, *English Church, 1000–1066* (London, 1963), 77–9, 217, and Brooks, *Church of Canterbury* (cit. in n. 2), 304–10.

[111] 'Florence' of Worcester, *Chronicon* (cit. in n. 62), i. 220; William of Malmesbury, *Vita Wulfstani*, ed. R. R. Darlington (Camden 3rd ser., 40; 1928), 16–18; *Anglo-Saxon Chronicle* (cit. in n. 26), 1060–1 D.

[112] Brooks, *Church of Canterbury* (cit. in n. 2), 308.

Stigand's eighteen years as archbishop (1052–70), Canterbury probably saw very little of him. Certainly the neglect of any record-keeping of the community's land transactions in these years, the virtual absence of new grants, and the declining output of books written in the Christ Church scriptorium[113] all speak of a community and a church that desperately lacked leadership, spiritual or political. It was Canterbury's misfortune that the most secular of all its archbishops should have proved so long-lived and that his notoriety in an age of ecclesiastical reform should have created the false impression at the time of the Norman Conquest that both Canterbury and the Anglo-Saxon Church as a whole were in need of a radical reform. His record should not obscure the achievement of his predecessors in securely establishing the metropolitan church with a monastic constitution and a landed endowment (Fig. 3) that were to be its twin foundations throughout the Middle Ages.

THE PRE-CONQUEST CATHEDRAL

Nothing of the structure of the Anglo-Saxon Cathedral survives above ground to this day. The church and most of the monastic buildings were gutted by a great fire on 6 December 1067, and the shell of the old buildings was soon demolished and totally replaced by Archbishop Lanfranc's new Norman Cathedral. However, in the spring of 1993 traces of the foundations of the pre-Conquest Cathedral were revealed when the need to renew the marble floor of the present nave and south transept provided an opportunity for limited archaeological investigations.[114] Combining this recent archaeological evidence with the scraps of information in pre-Conquest written sources and with the detailed account of the principal altars by the English monk Eadmer, based upon his childhood memories,[115] it is possible to establish the main features of the plan of the church (Fig. 4).

The Cathedral was remarkable in being bipolar, that is, in having apses and altars at both the east and west ends. Eadmer tells us that the principal altar, that of Christ, was in the raised sanctuary on the chord of the eastern apse, with the tombs of the archbishop-saints Ælfheah and Oda located immediately to the north and the south. A second altar, containing the relics of St Wilfrid, was at the extreme east end of this apse. Beneath this 'presbitery' (as Eadmer termed it) was the crypt, seemingly a ring-crypt, with a central passage leading to the tomb of St Dunstan, the principal Anglo-Saxon saint of the Cathedral church.

Westward from the sanctuary steps stretched the choir, where the community could maintain the daily liturgical cycle of prayer and psalmody at the canonical hours, cut off from the laity by a screen. Here was the stone column or 'pyramid' erected immediately

[113] Only 8 out of the 62 books ascribed to the Christ Church in Brooks, *Church of Canterbury* (cit. in n. 2), 266–70, were written in *saec. xi med.*, and most of them were probably from Eadsige's rather than from Stigand's archiepiscopate.

[114] Through the kind co-operation of the excavation director, Paul Bennett of the Canterbury Archaeological Trust Ltd., it is possible to offer here a provisional plan and interpretation in advance of the publication of his excavations.

[115] Eadmer, *De Reliquiis S. Audoeni*, ed. Wilmart (cit. in n. 86),

305–6. For Eadmer's age, see R. W. Southern, *St Anselm and His Biographer: A Study of Monastic Life and Thought 1059–c.1130* (Cambridge, 1963), pp. 231, 274–87. Full references to the written sources may be found in Brooks, *Church of Canterbury* (cit. in n. 2), 37–59. Important earlier interpretations are H. M. Taylor, 'The Anglo-Saxon Cathedral Church at Canterbury', *Archaeol. Jnl.*, 126 (1969), 101–29, and F. Woodman, *The Architectural History of Canterbury Cathedral* (London, 1981), 13–32.

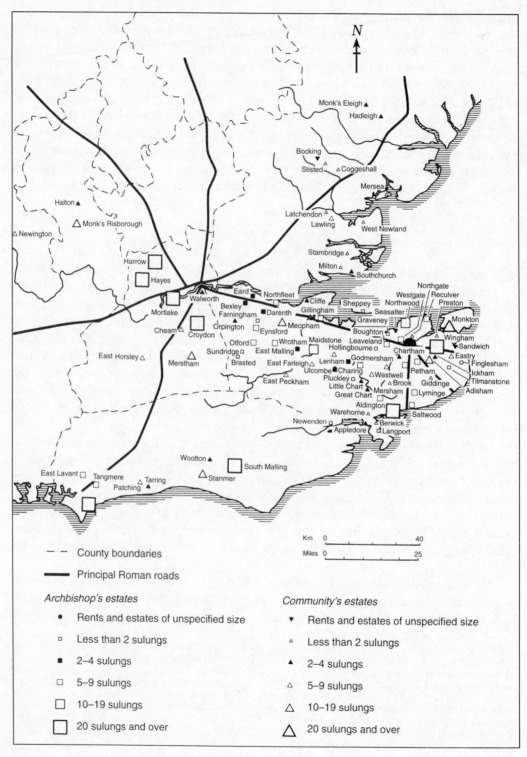

N

Monk's Eleigh ▲
Hadleigh ▲

Bocking ▼
Stisted △   △ Coggeshall

Mersea

Halton ▲
Latchendon △
Lawling
West Newland

△ Newington
△ Monk's Risborough

Stambridge △
Milton △
Southchurch

Harrow
Hayes
Eard   Northfleet
Walworth   Cliffe   Sheppey   Northwood
Bexley   Darenth   Gillingham
Mortlake   Farningham   Graveney
Orpington   Meopham   Boughton
Cheam △   Croydon   Eynsford
Otford □   Wrotham   Maidstone   Leaveland
Sundridge □   East Malling ■   Hollingbourne △   Chartham
East Horsley △   Brasted   East Farleigh △   Lenham ■   Godmersham
Merstham △   East Peckham   Ulcombe   Charing   △ Westwell
Pluckley □   Little Chart △   △ Brook
Great Chart   Mersham △   Lyminge
Aldington △
Warehorne △
Newenden □   △ Berwick
Appledore □   Langport

Northgate
Westgate / Reculver
Seasalter   Northwood   Preston
Monkton
Wingham
Sandwich
Eastry
Finglesham
Ickham
Tilmanstone
Adisham
Petham
Giddinge
Saltwood

Wootton ▲
South Malling
East Lavant □   Tangmere   △ Tarring
Patching ▲   Stanmer △

Km 0 _____ 40
Miles 0 _____ 25

--- County boundaries

━━━ Principal Roman roads

Archbishop's estates

- •   Rents and estates of unspecified size
- ▫   Less than 2 sulungs
- ■   2–4 sulungs
- ▢   5–9 sulungs
- ☐   10–19 sulungs
- ☐   20 sulungs and over

Community's estates

- ▼   Rents and estates of unspecified size
- ▵   Less than 2 sulungs
- ▲   2–4 sulungs
- △   5–9 sulungs
- △   10–19 sulungs
- △   20 sulungs and over

FIG. 3 Estates of the Church of Canterbury in 1066

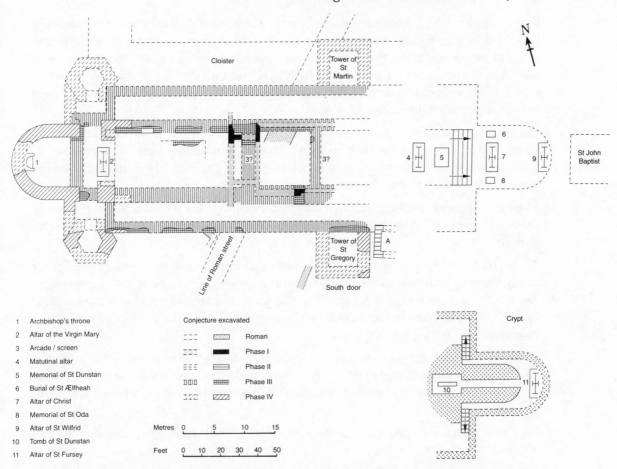

1	Archbishop's throne
2	Altar of the Virgin Mary
3	Arcade / screen
4	Matutinal altar
5	Memorial of St Dunstan
6	Burial of St Ælfheah
7	Altar of Christ
8	Memorial of St Oda
9	Altar of St Wilfrid
10	Tomb of St Dunstan
11	Altar of St Fursey

Conjecture excavated

Roman
Phase I
Phase II
Phase III
Phase IV

Metres 0   5   10   15

Feet   0   10   20   30   40   50

FIG. 4 Plan of the pre-Conquest Cathedral and Crypt. [The eastern end of the church, the position of altars, tombs, memorials, choir screen, and of the archiepiscopal seat and the layout of the crypt are at present known only from written sources. The plan of the western half is reconstructed on the basis of the excavation of those fragments which have survived destruction by the foundations of both the Norman and the present Cathedral and by the construction of tombs in subsequent centuries.]

above the tomb of St Dunstan, and further to the west the matutinal altar for morning or 'Morrow' masses, which English practice had added to the Benedictine Office. Near the mid-point of the church were two towers: that of St Gregory on the south contained the south door, which was the main entrance to the Cathedral; that of St Martin on the north gave access to the cloister. At the western extremity of the Cathedral, at clerestory or first-floor level and accessible only by means of stair-towers at the western corners of the building, was the massive apsidal 'oratory of St Mary', containing an altar of the Virgin, and behind it, against the wall of the apse, the archiepiscopal *cathedra* or throne. This altar would seem to have been the one used for pontifical masses and for all rites involving the laity.

In the Anglo-Saxon period it was believed that this Cathedral was indeed the same

Roman church which Augustine had received from King Æthelberht and had recovered for Christian use. While that is certainly not true of those parts of the early Cathedral revealed by the recent excavations, it remains possible that the most easterly portion of the Anglo-Saxon Cathedral, where the high altar and the crypt were situated, had at its core a Romano-British church.[116] The excavations have brought to light four main phases in the Cathedral's construction (Fig. 4):

Phase I The early church of the seventh and eighth century, whether or not it embodied a Romano-British core, seems likely to have been of typical Kentish form. That is, it had an apsidal chancel and a simple nave, which had gradually come to be surrounded on the west, north, and south sides by porches (*porticus*).

Phase II A separate building, perhaps a baptistery-church, lay within 2 feet of the south-eastern corner of the nave of the early Cathedral and had also been extended in subsequent periods.

Phase III A massive enlargement of the Cathedral in the ninth or (more probably) the tenth century involved widening the foundations (presumably to permit a heightening of the walls), incorporating the *porticus* into side-aisles and virtually doubling the length of both church and aisles by extending them westwards. This had the effect of providing a nave that was distinct from the choir.

Phase IV The final westward extension, and the rebuilding of the west end of the Cathedral, involved the construction of a large western apse with the oratory of St Mary at clerestory level and with access by means of hexagonal stair-towers built at the western end of the church.

A provisional interpretation of the Cathedral's structural history can therefore be essayed.

1.   The early church is likely to have had a Roman core, to have been developed by Augustine as a simple building with a nave and apsidal sanctuary, and to have had a series of *porticus* added successively by later archbishops.

2.   Archbishop Cuthbert (740–60) built a church dedicated to St John the Baptist as close as possible to the sanctuary of the Cathedral church, with the intention that it should serve as a baptistery and as a place of burial for the archbishops. The latter function made subsequent extensions necessary.

3.   Archbishop Wulfred (805–32) 'rebuilt, renewed and restored the holy monastery of the church of Canterbury' as part of his reform and reorganization of Christ Church. It seems that this programme may have concerned the monastic buildings.[117]

4.   Archbishop Oda (941–58) restored the church, removing damaged roofs and beams, and taking down parts of the walls so that the walls could be raised in height by some 20 feet.[118] We should probably equate this reconstruction of the Cathedral with Phase III of

[116] For the Roman core of the church of St Martin's, Canterbury, see T. Tatton-Brown, 'St Martin's Church in the 6th and 7th Centuries', in *The Parish of St Martin and St Paul, Canterbury: Essays in Memory of James Hobbs*, ed. M. J. Sparks (Canterbury, 1980), 12–18.

[117] Above, p. 12.

[118] Byrhtferth, *Vita S. Oswaldi*, in *Historians of the Church of York* (cit. in n. 63), i. 407.

the excavated sequence, rather than with a subsequent reinforcement of the wall of the south aisle.

5. Some reorganization of the choir and of the crypt must have been necessitated by the construction of the tomb of St Dunstan in the years immediately after his death in 988.

6. Finally, the reconstruction of the western end of the Cathedral, with the apsidal oratory of St Mary and its hexagonal stair-towers (Phase IV), seems most likely to have been the work of Archbishops Lyfing (1013–20) or Æthelnoth (1020–38) and to be associated with the widespread development of the cult of the Virgin Mary in Benedictine circles at that time.[119] The southern tower may probably be identified with the tower of St Gregory, which incorporated the south door, the main entrance to the Cathedral.

By the end of the Anglo-Saxon period, the Cathedral was a very substantial church indeed, measuring some 100 feet (31 m.) in width. The overall length is unknown (in the absence of excavations in the crypt) but, since the tower of St Gregory was near to the middle of the Cathedral, may have reached almost 300 feet (95 m.). Canterbury Cathedral is therefore likely to have been the largest church in England and would certainly have ranked among the major early medieval churches of northern Europe. Like many European churches of the ninth, tenth, and eleventh centuries, it had come to have a bipolar form, with both western and eastern apses. Here and in the arrangements of the eastern crypt it was reminiscent of, and doubtless in part modelled upon, the Constantinian basilicas of Rome and upon St Peter's in particular. Imitation of Rome, a liturgy that was becoming ever more elaborate and more explicitly Benedictine, and the burial of the growing number of venerable or saintly archbishops—these seem to have been the dominant ideas that had shaped the Cathedral's development over the five centuries that separated St Augustine from the Norman Conquest. Had any of the church's walls or decoration survived intact above ground, we might appreciate better how worthily the Anglo-Saxon Cathedral had served these purposes.

[119] M. Clayton, *The Cult of the Virgin Mary in Anglo-Saxon England* (Cambridge, 1990).

II

Normans and Angevins, 1070–1220

MARGARET GIBSON†

THE ALIEN ARCHBISHOPS

> The hills stand about Jerusalem: so even the Lord standeth round about his people.
>
> Ps. 125: 2

Lanfranc (1070–1089)

On 29 August 1070 Lanfranc rode up Harbledown Hill and saw, for the first time, the city of Canterbury lying below him, where the road drops to cross the river Stour. Eastwards he saw what remained of the Cathedral after the fire, and beyond that the white stone of the new rotunda at St Augustine's.[1] Further east lay the oldest of the Canterbury churches, St Martin's; immediately on Lanfranc's route into the city lay one of the newest, St Dunstan's. Martin stood for the origins of the monastic life in the West, and Dunstan for its most recent effective manifestation in England. Lanfranc himself had been a monk for nearly thirty years—at Bec (to the south-west of Rouen) and then in 1063 as Abbot of Duke William's new model foundation of St Stephen's at Caen. The Duke had planned Caen as his principal residence, and St Stephen's as his mausoleum—which indeed it became. Thus Lanfranc was already close to William the Conqueror. In an age of quick decisions and minimal administrative machinery he was the Duke's trusted adviser and, perhaps, his friend. In 1070 Lanfranc was about 60 years old, and he spoke no English.

He entered Canterbury as its archbishop, wearing his ceremonial ring and carrying his pastoral staff. The monks of Christ Church and of St Augustine's received him in procession, the two communities no doubt vying with each other in the splendour of their entourage. They passed under the cross at the Westgate, over the bridge at King's Mill,

---

[1] Wulfric's German rotunda was demolished to make way for Abbot Scotland's new church of 1093. See R. Gem, 'The Significance of the 11th-century Rebuilding of Christ Church and St Augustine's, Canterbury, in the Development of Roman-esque Architecture', in *Medieval Art and Architecture at Canterbury Before 1220*, ed. N. Coldstream and P. Draper (British Archaeol. Assn., Conference Trans., 5; London 1982 for 1979), 1–19, rotunda at 16, with refs.

and thence to the Cathedral, where Lanfranc was consecrated by the Bishops of Winchester and London and six others.[2] But whereas outwardly the ceremonial forms were observed, the sole ground of Lanfranc's appointment was the King's decision. William the Conqueror had already played his part by investing Lanfranc with ring and staff and receiving his homage for the Cathedral estates.[3] Four of the eight bishops who had consecrated him had been appointed by William;[4] the King had acquiesced in (if not prompted) the deposition of Stigand;[5] there had been no consultation of either the Dean of Christ Church or the monastic chapter. That William would support Lanfranc to the hilt may be seen from the royal judgement on the primacy, to which we shall turn in a moment. But the corollary also held good: that Lanfranc was in Canterbury to do the King's work.

Serving the King could mean, literally, fighting on his behalf. In 1075 a baronial revolt broke out in several areas of southern England. It was the more dangerous in that the dispossessed or threatened Anglo-Saxon nobility were making common cause with the Norman incomers. William was overseas, and his kingdom was saved by an alliance of Geoffrey of Coutances, Odo of Bayeux, and Lanfranc himself—all bishops, but acting here as territorial magnates loyal to their lord the King.[6] More normally, the King's service entailed drafting legislation and participating in ceremonial occasions. When the King appeared in state at Christmas in Gloucester, at Easter in Winchester, and at Whitsun in Windsor, most of the higher clergy, episcopal and monastic, found it expedient to be present.[7] Things were on a much grander scale than in the parvenu little court at Caen. Lanfranc was no longer a court prelate in the sense that he had been as Abbot of St Stephen's: nevertheless the King's interests were ever-present and seldom, if ever, set aside.

Lanfranc's enduring contribution to the government of England is his 'restructuring' of the English Church. In Stigand's day, each bishop had minded his own affairs, and the primacy of Canterbury was purely a primacy of honour. It is easy to regard such a lax reign as yet further proof of Stigand's personal negligence and the decay of the Anglo-Saxon Church. Several contemporary analysts took this view.[8] Yet, as we have seen in the preceding chapter, it was only in the rarest of circumstances that Anglo-Saxon archbishops (of Canterbury or of York) exercised and enforced legal control over other bishops.[9] They

[2] *Scriptum Lanfranci de Primatu*, in *Die Fälschungen Erzbischof Lanfranks von Canterbury*, ed. H. Boehmer (Leipzig, 1902), 165; cf. *Acta Lanfranci*, in *Two of the Saxon Chronicles Parallel*, ed. C. Plummer (2 vols.; Oxford, 1892), i, 287–8. See further M. T. Gibson, *Lanfranc of Bec* (Oxford, 1978), chs. 6–7 and App.

[3] Lay investiture (as distinct from 'simony'—the purchase of spiritual office) was regarded as perfectly normal until the 1070s—Gregory VII formally condemned the practice in 1075; text lost, but see his letter of May 1077 to Hugh of Die (*Gregorii VII Registrum*, iv. 22, ed. E. Caspar, 2 pts. (Berlin: Epistolae Selectae ex Monumentis Germaniae Historicis, 1920–3), 330–4). Even then the issue was perceived as a layman conferring spiritual office (investiture) as distinct from the estates pertaining to that office, for which the new bishop did 'homage'.

[4] The Bishops of Winchester, Dorchester-on-Thames, Elmham, and Chichester.

[5] The best analysis of a murky episode is F. Barlow, *The English Church, 1000–1066* (2nd edn.; London and New York,

1979), 302–10.

[6] The best account is Orderic Vitalis, *Historia Ecclesiastica*, lib. iv, ed. M. Chibnall, ii (Oxford Medieval Texts; Oxford 1969), 310–19; contemporary evidence in *The Letters of Lanfranc, Archbishop of Canterbury*, ed. H. Clover and M. T. Gibson (Oxford Medieval Texts; Oxford 1979), nos. 31–6.

[7] See the anecdote of the foolish courtier who exclaimed at the king's magnificence, 'Ecce deum video!'—'Look, it is God himself!': *Vita Lanfranci*, ch. 13 (Migne, *PL*, cl, cols. 53C–54A); cf. Gibson, *Lanfranc* (cit. in n. 2), 198.

[8] See, e.g. William of Malmesbury, *Gesta Pontificum*, i. 23, ed. N. E. S. A. Hamilton (RS, 52; 1870), 35–7; but note the judicious words of Barlow, *English Church* (cit. in n. 5), 26–9.

[9] Bede regarded Archbishop Theodore (668–90) as 'the first archbishop whom the whole English Church consented to obey': *Hist. Eccles.*, iv. 2. But even Theodore failed to establish full jurisdiction over York, and none of his successors showed much interest in the question.

might hold synods, but did they enforce attendance, and if so, by what means? They might promulgate canons, but how was such law enforced? In any case, they had little opportunity, for the western Church as a whole had no single agreed code of canon law, nor the legal independence that such a code would foster. What Lanfranc did was to lay the first foundation of the new, independent Church in England. He assumed that each bishop owed a personal loyalty to the head of his province. Thus, when a man came to Canterbury to be consecrated as, say, Bishop of Salisbury, he should make a profession of orthodoxy to the archbishop, and then offer him a written profession of loyalty as 'his humble and obedient son'. The profession itself was normally a little strip of parchment measuring some 6 × 2 inches (150 × 50 mm.), declaring (in Osmund's case) that:

'I, Osmund, bishop-elect of the church of Salisbury, and about to be consecrated by you, reverend father Lanfranc, archbishop of the metropolitan see and primate of the British Isles, humbly promise to you and your successors due and canonical subjection and obedience'.[10]

These professions were then placed in the Cathedral archive, as precedents for the future. Lanfranc had the law on his side, in the sense that the early Church councils had provided for metropolitan jurisdiction over diocesan bishops,[11] but to contemporaries it may have seemed rather that he was treating his episcopal colleagues as William the Conqueror treated his lay nobility when he exacted the oath of Salisbury. At a stroke, Lanfranc was asserting jurisdiction rather than dignity, and claiming power rather than honour. Archbishop Thomas of York protested vigorously, citing the original directive of Gregory the Great (which had not even mentioned Canterbury), and no doubt the simple truth that as head of the northern province it was not practicable for him to submit to the jurisdiction of another archbishop. The case was taken to Rome; Alexander II sent it back to England, and there William the Conqueror decided in favour of Lanfranc himself, but not (or not clearly) in favour of Canterbury in perpetuity.[12] This disastrous ruling—for so it was to prove—committed Lanfranc and all his successors to the wrangle, first for power and eventually merely for precedence, which is still expressed in York's title of 'primate of England' as against Canterbury's designation of 'primate of all England'. In Lanfranc's case it is striking evidence of how the King's word closed a case. For Lanfranc's successors the exercise of primacy drove a fatal wedge between the archbishop and his Cathedral chapter. Should the archbishop tend and govern his Cathedral close, or should he administer the English Church?

In the short term, however, Lanfranc discharged both sides of his duties with apparent ease. He sacked the Dean.[13] He called in 'new blood', notably Henry, the new prior, and

---

[10] *Canterbury Professions*, ed. M. Richter (CYS, 67; 1973), no. 40.

[11] See the councils of Nicaea (325), cans. 4–6; Antioch (341), cans. 9, 11, 14–16; and Chalcedon (451), can. 49. These canons clarify the role of the metropolitan in his province. For Lanfranc's use of such canons, see H. Fuhrmann, *Einfluß und Verbreitung der pseudoisidorischen Fälschungen*, Monumenta Germaniae Historica, Schriften xxiv (1974), II, 419–22, citing Z.

N. Brooke, *The English Church and the Papacy* (Cambridge, 1931), 57–83.

[12] *Letters of Lanfranc* (cit. in n. 6), item 11.

[13] The office of dean, held by Godric until *c.*1070, was replaced by that of prior. Lanfranc may have associated deans with colleges of canons, and priors with the more 'regular' monastic life.

Ernulf the schoolmaster; and he sent at least one young English monk to Bec.[14] French-speaking monks now held the key positions; it was they who had to restore the damage of 1067 in stone and lime, and to maintain or establish proper monastic observance. The material side of the recovery was completed within a decade. The new church, with its spacious crypt, was finished in 1077; the extensive monastic building included the great dormitory, sections of which still stand to the north of the present nave.[15] High on the central tower, Lanfranc set a gilded seraph as a weather vane, which the traveller would see glinting in the sun as he came down the hill into Canterbury.

The monastic life within the new buildings is described in the *Constitutions* that Lanfranc drew up for Prior Henry at some time in the 1070s.[16] His covering letter being undated, an internal date of 1079 + has been derived from the inclusion of 'St Alphege the martyr' among the feasts of the second rank.[17] Recognition of Alphege is said to have followed Anselm's elegant proof of the equipollency of justice and truth: to die for justice is to die for truth, therefore Alphege—whose death at the hands of the Danes was in defence of justice—is properly regarded as a martyr.[18] We should, however, allow that no manuscripts of the *Constitutions* are earlier than *c*.1100, and the feast of Alphege is easily interpolated at this point in the text. The date of 1079 or later depends entirely on this feast. On the other hand, common sense would suggest that the *Constitutions* were available to Prior Henry within months, rather than years, of his taking up office. Here the span is 1070–6: perhaps by 1072, the year of Lanfranc's long absence on his journey to Rome. For, as Anselm might have put it, a community is like a child: new patterns of behaviour may be imposed at the beginning of its life much more easily than later on.[19] Lanfranc would have been ill-advised to delay ten years before specifying the type of monasticism that he wished to see in operation at Christ Church.

Lanfranc had lived as monk and prior at Bec and as abbot of St Stephen's, Caen. Mid-century Bec was on too small a scale and possibly also too austere in its way of life to be a useful model for Canterbury. The foundation of St Stephen's, Caen, as a major ducal monastery certainly called for constitutions of some kind, drawn up by Lanfranc, or on his instructions. No relevant texts survive. Yet with seven years' experience at Caen behind him, it is unlikely that Lanfranc began from scratch in reading, excerpting, and amalgamating the available monastic customaries to make a rule-book for Canterbury. 'I have followed', he wrote to Prior Henry, 'the practice of the principal monastic houses

---

[14] Prior Henry (*c*.1074–96)—disliked by many, but very efficient—went on to be Abbot of Battle. Ernulf, who succeeded him as prior, rose to be Abbot of Peterborough (1107) and Bishop of Rochester (1114). The Englishman sent abroad was Osbern: see Anselm, Letters 39, 66–7, ed. F. S. Schmitt, *Anselmi Opera* (Siegburg, 1938—Edinburgh, 1946), iii. 150, 186–7, elucidated by R. W. Southern, *St Anselm and His Biographer: A Study of Monastic Life and Thought 1059–c.1130* (Cambridge, 1963), 248.

[15] See the classic work of R. Willis, *The Architectural History of the Conventual Buildings of the Monastery of Christ Church in Canterbury* (London, 1869), 3 *et passim*, and now H. J. A. Strik, 'Remains of the Lanfranc Building in the Great Central Tower and the North-West Choir/Transept Area', in *Medieval Art and Architecture at Canterbury* (cit. in n. 1), 20–6.

[16] Lanfranc's *Monastic Constitutions* are conveniently available ed. and trans. D. Knowles (Nelson's Medieval Classics; London, 1951), repr. with an expanded introd. in *Corpus Consuetudinum Monasticarum*, ed. K. Hallinger, iii (Siegburg, 1967).

[17] *Constitutions* (cit. in n. 16), 59. The case for 1083 as the *terminus ante quem* is well put by D. Sheerin, 'Some Observations on the Date of Lanfranc's *Decreta*', *Studia Monastica*, 17 (1975), 13–27.

[18] *Vita Anselmi*, i. 30, ed. R. W. Southern, 2nd edn. (Oxford Medieval Texts, 1972), 50–4. Anselm gave the proof during his visit to Canterbury in 1079.

[19] Cf. *Vita Anselmi*, i. 11 (cit. in n. 18), 20–1.

active today.'[20] Although he does not name Cluny, it has long been evident (and was no doubt vividly clear to contemporaries) that what Lanfranc advocates is essentially Cluniac: it should be compared specifically with Abbot Odilo's *Liber Tramitis Aevi*, written 1030x48.[21] In the 1070s Cluny was still, for all but the radical reformers, the ideal of monastic life and liturgy. Cluny had deeply influenced Norman monasticism, including (I would suggest) the new ducal foundations in Caen; the same Continental and Norman pattern was maintained in Christ Church.

Each house had its own needs.[22] For Christ Church, Lanfranc increased the ceremonial on feast-days to a degree 'appropriate to a primatial see'.[23] He saw himself as archbishop and primate within the context of a traditional monastic community: his successors were increasingly to live apart within their households. Lanfranc proposed no root-and-branch alteration in the annual liturgical round; even when he listed the five principal festivals, the twenty-two solemn feasts, and the seventeen feasts of the third rank, he added to the last category 'and any other such feasts as may be appointed for celebration in the same way'.[24] The community was thus free to celebrate the Conception of St John the Baptist or any other traditional local feast, so long as it also observed the forty-four feasts listed in the *Constitutions*. The degree to which Lanfranc had departed from pre-Conquest liturgical practice may be seen by comparing the requirements of the *Constitutions* with the calendar in the Arundel Psalter, written *c*.1020 by the great Christ Church scribe Eadui Basan.[25] Lanfranc's three grades are:

1. Christmas, Easter, Pentecost, Assumption, *festivitas loci*.
2. Stephen, John the Evangelist, Innocents, Circumcision,[26] Epiphany, Purification, Gregory, Annunciation, Octave of Easter, Alphege, Ascension, Augustine of Canterbury, Octave of Pentecost, Nativity of St John the Baptist, Peter and Paul, Translation of Benedict, Nativity of the Virgin, Michaelmas, All Saints, Andrew, Dedication of the Church.
3. Sylvester, Vincent, Conversion of Paul, Philip and James, Invention of the Cross, James the Apostle, Peter in Chains, Laurence, Octave of the Assumption, Bartholomew, Augustine of Hippo, Decollation of St John the Baptist, Exaltation of the Cross, Matthew, Simon and Jude, Martin, Thomas.

[20] *Constitutions* (cit. in n. 16), 1: 'Mittimus vobis nostri ordinis consuetudines scriptas, quas excerpsimus ex consuetudinibus eorum coenobiorum quae nostro tempore maioris auctoritatis sunt in ordine monachorum.'

[21] Ed. P. Dinter, *Corpus Consuetudinum Monasticarum*, x (Siegburg, 1980). Bernard of Cluny, to whom Knowles draws particular attention in his edition of Lanfranc's *Constitutions*, is available only in M. Herrgott's edition as sect. 9 of *Vetus Disciplina Monastica*, ed. by the monks of St. Blasien im Schwarzwald (Paris, 1726)—a rare book, of which a copy is BL 4071. e. 7. Neither the date of the text nor Bernard's own status is secure.

[22] The principle is emphasized in *Constitutions* (cit. in n. 16): 'nulla fere ecclesia imitari aliam per omnia potest.'

[23] Ibid.: 'We have added very little, but we have made some alterations, particularly in respect of certain feasts which we

think should be celebrated with more splendour in our church because it is the primate's see.'

[24] Ibid. 14–15, 55, 59, 64–5.

[25] BL, MS Arundel 155, fos. 2–7'. The calendar is edited by F. Wormald, *English Kalendars Before A.D. 1100* (Henry Bradshaw Soc., 72; 1934), 169–81 (no. 13). Eadui Basan's activity is lucidly summarized by J. J. G. Alexander and C. M. Kauffmann, *English Illuminated Manuscripts 700–1500*, exhib. cat., Bibliothèque Royale Albert I (Brussels, 1973), no. 10. The calendar in the Bosworth Psalter, if it is indeed Christ Church (which I gravely doubt), represents an older form, displaced by 1020: see P. M. Korhammer, 'The Origin of the Bosworth Psalter', *Anglo-Saxon England*, 2 (1973), 173–87, and, crucially, N. R. Ker, *Manuscripts Containing Anglo-Saxon* (Oxford, 1957), 161–2, no. 129.

[26] Grade 2 feasts are listed in the *Constitutions* (cit. in n. 16), 14–15 (Stephen—Circumcision) and 59, 64–5 (all the rest).

The Arundel Psalter omits (1) *festivitas loci*; (2) Octave of Easter, Ascension, Octave of Pentecost; (3) Octave of the Assumption and Augustine of Hippo; Sylvester and Bartholomew have been added in the twelfth century. Thus Lanfranc found in established Christ Church procedure the great majority of his principal feasts. Many further saints appear in Arundel, to be commemorated with less ceremony; so in any calendar—their absence from the *Constitutions* does not imply their absence from post-Conquest Christ Church devotion. What should be remarked are the six major feasts in Arundel, entered in capitals. These are the feasts of: Matthias, Edward king and martyr, Benedict, Dunstan, Paul, Clement. The first three fall, or can fall, in Lent. Of the others, the most controversial at Canterbury was that of Dunstan, to whom we shall return in a moment.

To what extent did Lanfranc alter Christ Church observance in the direction of Cluny? The two relevant customaries are Abbot Odilo's *Liber Tramitis Aevi* and the highly discursive account of Cluniac practice attributed to Bernard of Cluny and dated to 1067;[27] but only the former is available in a critical edition such as permits accurate comparison with Lanfranc's *Constitutions*. In the *Liber Tramitis Aevi* the forty-four Lanfrancian feasts occur as follows:

1. Odilo omits *festivitas loci*.
2. Odilo omits Alphege, Augustine of Canterbury, translation of Benedict (March).
3. Odilo omits the Octave of the Assumption.

Setting aside such peculiarly Cluniac feasts as Maiolus and the reception of St Gregory, Cluniac observance not found in the *Constitutions* is generally to be found already in the Arundel Psalter. In other words Christ Church practice was already broadly Cluniac *c*.1020. Lanfranc largely, and prudently, left the calendar alone, specifying the feasts to be observed rather than identifying those (if any) which should or might be deleted. He is, besides, at pains to point out that the *Constitutions* are not the last word. Changes and additions reflect a living community. His *Constitutions* are merely the tramming on which the community will embroider its own liturgical tapestry. It is by viewing the *Constitutions* as open rather than closed that we may understand Lanfranc's attitude to the local saints of Canterbury, above all St Dunstan.

The omission of Dunstan from the *Constitutions* has convinced generations of historians that on arriving in England Lanfranc expunged him from the liturgy.[28] So Walter of Evesham (Lanfranc's own former chaplain) cast into the fire the relics of Anglo-Saxon saints; so, notoriously, Lanfranc's own nephew, Paul of St Albans, threw the bones of King Offa of Mercia on to the dunghill.[29] It is assumed that Lanfranc 'the lawyer', being well versed in the criteria for formal canonization newly established by Leo IX,[30] considered that these Anglo-Saxon saints lacked credentials. Just as title to a disputed estate increasingly turned on written documentation, so veneration of a saint now required either universal recognition or a papal bull. Dunstan and Alphege failed to make the grade.

[27] For both, see n. 21 above.
[28] Southern, *Anselm* (cit. in n. 14), 250–1; cf. *Vita Anselmi*, i. 30 (cit. in n. 18), 50–1.
[29] Gibson, *Lanfranc* (cit. in n. 2), 171 and 166 with refs.
[30] In 1050 Leo IX canonized his own predecessor in the see of Toul, Bishop Gerard: Migne, *PL*, cxliii, cols. 644D–7D. As Lanfranc was then in Rome, he presumably witnessed the ceremony: Gibson, *Lanfranc* (cit. in n. 2), 171. For the history of canonization in the western Church, see E. W. Kemp, *Canonization and Authority in the Western Church* (Oxford, 1948).

Alphege was reinstated, as we have seen; so, no doubt, on some unrecorded occasion in the 1080s, also Dunstan. But this entire line of reasoning is at best plausible; it falls far short of proof.

Lanfranc found a community in a ruined church holding their services by the tomb of St Dunstan, huddled under the eleventh-century equivalent of a tarpaulin.[31] When the church was rebuilt, the relics of Dunstan and other Anglo-Saxon saints were removed with honour—and miracles—provisionally to the transept and ultimately to positions on either side of the altar of the Holy Cross in the centre of the church. This was in 1076–8. Osbern, who recorded it all in his *Miracles of St Dunstan*, and Eadmer, who subsequently revised Osbern's book, both stress that these were saints, that they were active and efficacious, and that they were treated with respect.[32] Dunstan twice came to the assistance of Lanfranc himself: when he was hard-pressed in litigation, and when he was sick.[33] On the latter occasion, Dunstan swept in on a white horse, with his entourage streaming before him— the Anglo-Saxon magnate that he had been in life. I quote this latter vision as showing how clearly Lanfranc and his community at Christ Church saw the real Dunstan: no plaster saint, but an effective, energetic patron. The great bell in one of the west towers of the Cathedral bore his name, the Dunstan bell—again as early as *c*.1080.[34] Dunstan had a Continental reputation—however undeserved—as the author of the *Regularis Concordia*.[35] Do we require a calendar entry to eradicate the belief that the cosmopolitan Lanfranc cleared away Dunstan with the other unintelligible, forgotten local cults? Dunstan was an essential bridge between two worlds—the pre-Conquest community and its modern successor—and Lanfranc was far too experienced and conservative a monk to think of removing him.

The Cluniac monasticism that Lanfranc introduced was workable, by those of moderate attainments and moderate commitment. The liturgy was to be performed with military precision, especially on the great feast-days. At no time should a monk be idle, chatting to his friends or in any other way taking time off. Monks should read books—according to their ability, but every man some. The children and the novices should be well cared for and vigilantly guarded from indiscipline and bad company. As we might expect, this sober, low-risk monasticism commanded approval and worked well for several generations. It is the kind of clearly defined order that recurs time and again in the annals of the Church. It is feasible; the obedient monk can fulfil every requirement without having a breakdown. What we cannot recover, even speculatively, is the characteristic piety of the last generation of Anglo-Saxon monasticism. Was anything wrong with pre-Conquest monasticism except that it was out of fashion? Even if the pre-Conquest monks had worn fine clothes and gone hunting,[36] they had also been among the earliest practitioners of liturgical drama.[37]

---

[31] Southern, *Anselm* (cit. in n. 14), 245–6, with refs.

[32] Both edited by W. Stubbs, *Memorials of Saint Dunstan, Archbishop of Canterbury* (RS, 63; 1874).

[33] Gibson, *Lanfranc* (cit. in n. 2), 218–19, with refs.

[34] Goscelin, *Vita S. Edithae*, ed. A. Wilmart, *Analecta Bollandiana*, 56 (1938), 38; cf. Osbern, *Miracula S. Dunstani* (cit. in n. 32), 138.

[35] *Anselmi Epp.* 39, ed. F. S. Schmitt, *Anselmi Opera*, iii (Edinburgh, 1946), 151.

[36] Eadmer, *Miracula S. Dunstani* (cit. in n. 32), 237–8.

[37] See the 'Easter play' in *Regularis Concordia*, ed. T. Symons (Nelson's Medieval Classics; London, 1953), 49–50; cf. K. Young, *The Drama of the Medieval Church* (2 vols.; Oxford, 1933), i. 249–50, 581–3, pl. vii. For its performance in the 1060s, see Southern, *Anselm* (cit. in n. 14), 246, with refs.

From time to time, no doubt, they thought and prayed, often in English and perhaps not always communally. If the English monks who had learnt their psalter and their monastic life before Lanfranc's arrival never fully adjusted to his government, they were simply the losers—like their dispossessed secular counterparts who went to be mercenaries in Byzantium,[38] or who married their sisters to the men who now held their land.[39]

The children and the novices adapted to the new regime, and benefited from its strength. Lanfranc recovered the lost estates of the Cathedral, and audited its very miscellaneous forms of income. Domesday Book and related records well illustrate the economic potential of Christ Church;[40] that this wealth was real and accessible was due above all to Lanfranc's persistence in verifying the community's claims to property and, where necessary, enforcing these claims by legal action in the shire court.[41] Thus the Norman community could feed its members and fund its buildings.

The new generation received a good grounding in Latin. Ernulf of Beauvais taught them Priscian's grammar, according to the method that was being developed in the Continental schools.[42] They learned Virgil and they read such classics of the Christian Fathers as the *Moralia* of Gregory the Great and the *Letters* of Jerome.[43] That is, they not only studied Scripture and Christian doctrine, they achieved linguistic fluency in Latin. Osbern (the Englishman who was sent to Bec) writes well,[44] but the prize goes to another Englishman, the monk Eadmer, who was 10 years old when Lanfranc came to Canterbury.[45] There is a better-than-even chance that when Lanfranc first came through the Westgate, in the summer of 1070, there was a choir of children in the upper storey of the gate, with Eadmer among them.[46] In Eadmer the community had a monk of the traditional sort, from a local Canterbury family. Nevertheless, he proved to be the most articulate exponent of Lanfranc's achievement and the most devoted servant of his successor. His *Historia Novorum* and *Vita Anselmi* are both full of direct observation and illuminating prejudice;[47] right or wrong, they display the easy Latin style that reflects wide reading in the library and close reading of Jerome. Both in his convictions and in how he expresses them, Eadmer is proof that the new regime was understood and embraced by those who really mattered: the monks of the next generation.

[38] S. Blöndal, *The Varangians of Byzantium*, rev. and trans. B. S. Benedikz (Cambridge, 1978), 141–7.

[39] The most vivid evidence is still Domesday Book for Kent: see now, conveniently, *Domesday Book* i: *Kent*, ed. Philip Morgan (Chichester, 1983), in *Domesday England*, ed. J. Morris.

[40] See Domesday Book for Kent (cit. in n. 39) and the *Domesday Monachorum* and related documents (n. 57 below).

[41] See J. Le Patourel, 'The Reports of the Trial on Penenden Heath', in *Studies in Medieval History Presented to F. M. Powicke*, ed. R. W. Hunt, W. A. Pantin, and R. W. Southern (Oxford, 1948), 15–26.

[42] A glossed Priscian of *c*.1100 from St Augustine's, Canterbury (now CUL, MS Ii. 2. 1; see pp. 52–3 below), gives an impression—even at one remove—of the style of exegesis then current in Christ Church. In broad terms, the material and method derive from the modern commentary known as the *Glosule*. See M. T. Gibson, 'The Early Scholastic *Glosule* to Priscian, *Institutiones grammaticae*', *Studi Medievali*, 20/pt. 1 (1980), 235–54.

[43] *Anselmi Epp.*, 64 to Ernulf's student, Maurice (Virgil) and 23 and 25 to Lanfranc (Gregory, Ambrose, Jerome) (cit. in n. 35), 180–1, 130, 132–3.

[44] *Memorials* (cit. in n. 32), 69–161.

[45] Southern, *Anselm* (cit. in n. 14), 231.

[46] *Acta Lanfranci*, i. 287–8 (cit. in n. 2). For the ceremonial entry by the same gate on Palm Sunday, see *Constitutions* (cit. in n. 16), 24–5.

[47] The *Historia Novorum* is ed. by M. Rule (RS, 81; 1884); Eadmer's 'History of Recent Events in England' is trans. by G. Bosanquet (London, 1964). For the *Vita Anselmi* see n. 18 above.

Anselm (1093–1109)

After the death of Lanfranc (28 May 1089), Canterbury was without an archbishop for nearly five years. Anselm was consecrated on 4 December 1093. He had visited the community fourteen years before,[48] and maintained some slight correspondence with a few of its members. Some of these letters are of monastic friendship, or at least practical assistance with the needs of Christ Church; but the majority either overtly concern the English property of Bec, or are letters of introduction on behalf of Bec monks who are travelling through Kent on their way to administer that property:

Commendo vestrae paternae caritati et caritativae paternitati fratres nostros et vestros, quos in Angliam mittimus; quatenus, ubi opus erit, vestro sustineantur auxilio, vestro regantur consilio.[49]

I commend to your fatherly love and loving paternal care our brothers and yours, whom we are sending to England. Where there is need, let them be sustained by your help and directed by your advice.

These men are administering the wealth of Bec overseas. There is no continuing influx of Continental monks to Christ Church itself, nor indeed to any other major foundation. The last such transfer on any scale was from Fécamp to Battle in 1076, and that was a special case.

Anselm was not a stranger to the community at Christ Church, but neither was he a friend. He was at ease with the small group of French-speaking intellectuals who had come with him from Bec: Alexander, who was to collect and edit Anselm's table-talk, Baldwin, and a few others who are only names. His intellectual stimulus came from men who were not in Canterbury: Boso, monk and future Abbot of Bec, who is cast as the interlocutor in the *Cur Deus Homo*, and Gilbert Crispin, also a Bec monk but since 1085 Abbot of Westminster, who has some part in shaping the argument. Anselm wrote to Gilbert and Boso, and they presumably wrote back—in Latin. It may be that by the 1090s Anselm was more at ease with the written than with the spoken word. Certainly he had little contact with the monks of Christ Church as a community. There is really no evidence that he assumed the burden of regular liturgical preaching. The only sermon that he is known to have given is the valedictory address to his monks as he went into exile in 1097.[50] But that was a unique occasion, or was perceived to be so at the time.

Anselm excelled in conversation—not conversation as we know it, but the godly anecdote. The monastic life, he said, was like fire:

A false coin can look absolutely genuine; but if it is cast into the fire it is at once shown to be false. In the same way a man of bad character seems to be of good character when he is in the world. But if he becomes a monk, his faults press upon him and he is at once shown not to be what he seemed. The man who seemed humble and long-suffering shows up now as impatient and proud. If he blames the monastic life, it is as though the coin were to say to the fire, 'You made me false!' The fire did not make the coin false, it showed it up for what it was. In the same way the monastic

---

[48] Eadmer, *Vita Anselmi*, i. 29 (cit. in n. 18), 48.

[49] *Anselmi Epp.* 91, p. 219; cf. nos 90, 93–4 (cit. in n. 35), 217–21. See further M. Morgan, *The English Lands of the Abbey of Bec*

(Oxford, 1946), 12–13.

[50] Southern, *Anselm* (cit. in n. 14), 362–4.

life has not caused that man's bad character; it has revealed it. Let him blame himself, not the monastic life, and change his evil character to good. For unless his character is seen to be good, the good works which he performs are of little worth.[51]

That is a characteristic report of Anselm's conversation: fully explicated and solidly edifying. Much rarer is the epigram, with its condensed meaning, which the disciple must elicit for himself. 'Sicut enim ferrum ignitum quaqua sui parte continet ignem, sic et in se boni voluptatem, mali vero sentient anxietatem.' ('Just as red-hot iron has fire within some part of itself, so good men have pleasure within themselves, but evil men have stress.')[52] The virtue of the epigram is that it can be memorized—as meditation on a journey, while working in the garden, or during a tedious chapter-meeting. It is where Anselm comes closest to the more radical piety of the new monastic orders; more radical in that it was written for the individual rather than the group. Guy I, Prior of La Grande Chartreuse, was a master of such spiritual wit: 'Ignoras te ligatum, et non resistas vinculis: sicut canis' ('You do not know that you are fettered, you do not resist your chains—like a dog!').[53] But Guy was addressing an élite, as the Carthusians always remained: men who had chosen the pure monastic life. Anselm's community at Christ Church embraced men of all sorts, who had come in for many different reasons: vocation, family tradition, disinheritance, the desire to study, the inability to fight. They recognized in Anselm a great theologian and teacher, but they were the natural constituency neither for his theology nor for exploring the frontiers of the spiritual life.

Eadmer

The voice of Christ Church in the last decade of the eleventh century, through into the 1120s, is that of the monk Eadmer, for a few years Anselm's close companion, thereafter scribe and historian within the community, and finally the improbable and unsuccessful claimant to the senior Scottish see of St Andrews. He is himself the subject of an edifying anecdote, preserved by William of Malmesbury in the *Gesta Pontificum*:

When as archbishop he [Anselm] owed obedience to no one, he asked Pope Urban to appoint him someone by whose commands he might order his life. The Pope pointed to Eadmer; whom Anselm used to obey so scrupulously that were he to direct him to lie down Anselm would not turn over without his permission, far less get up again.[54]

Eadmer was appointed not as Anselm's confessor but as the man whom he should obey in practical life, in modern parlance his 'minder'. He was an opportunity to exercise publicly a virtue that was denied to archbishops, yet enjoined on monks. Eadmer was a constant occasion of Anselm's showing obedience, in small things. He never says or implies that he directed Anselm on issues of principle; it was precisely to the indifferent action that he was appointed. He was Anselm's hair shirt. For some three years he

[51] *De Humanis Moribus*, 95, in *Memorials of St Anselm*, ed. R. W. Southern and F. S. Schmitt (Auctores Britannici Medii Aevi, 1; London, 1969), 79.
[52] Ibid. 59, in. 56.
[53] *Le Recueil des pensées du b. Guigue*, ed. A. Wilmart (Études de philosophie médiévale, 22; Paris, 1936), 74, no. 30.
[54] *Gesta Pontificum* (cit. in n. 8), 122.

shadowed Anselm: from the encounter with Urban in 1097 until not long after Urban's death. Then the relationship grew more distant, but it had given Eadmer material for his remarkable biography, the *Vita Anselmi*. He writes of the man and saint, the scholar wrestling with an argument, and the unwilling but recalcitrant archbishop. 'Many reasoned arguments were adduced against [the recognition of Pope Urban II]. Anselm countered with: 'Render unto Caesar the things which are Caesar's and unto God the things which are God's (Matt. 22: 21).'[55] In Anselm, William Rufus had chosen a man who was quite unable to sustain the common purpose that had marked Lanfranc's relations with the old king. As Abbot of Bec, Anselm had already acknowledged Urban II as pope, and that closed the matter. Not only was Anselm mentally unable to negotiate, the problem held no intellectual interest for him. His response was to go away: in 1097–1100 and again, following the impasse over homage to Henry I, in 1103–6. Eadmer records his farewell to the brethren in 1097: 'I have the choice of acting against God and my own honour, or of leaving this kingdom forthwith. Indeed I am glad to go, trusting that by God's mercy my exile will in some way promote the freedom of the Church in days to come.'[56] The Archbishop's conscience was clear, but his absence could only be to the detriment of the daily life of the community. Their revenues were more vulnerable and their secular support was diminished, in defence of an ideal which few would understand and in which few were interested. Long afterwards, Anselm might be seen as a precursor of Becket in his readiness to be exiled for a principle, but his actual years in office served only to loosen the bonds between the community and its increasingly nominal head.

THE AGE OF THE PRIORS

> I was glad when they said unto me, we will go into the house of the Lord.
>
> Ps. 122: 1

In the five years before Anselm's consecration, the six years of his exile, and the further five-year vacancy after his death, it fell to the priors to safeguard the interests of the archbishopric and the status of the community. What we can glimpse of their work commands respect. They established an archive; they presided over (and funded) the golden age of the Christ Church scriptorium; and they transformed the fabric of the Cathedral. While they could not entirely compensate for an absent or preoccupied or incapacitated archbishop, they did establish the reputation of their community in Canterbury and in the world.

Prior Henry (c.1074–1096)

The text known as the *Domesday Monachorum* records three kinds of fiscal information:[57] the traditional ecclesiastical payments, notably chrism-money, which Lanfranc had secured from various churches within the diocese of Canterbury, including St Augustine's; the

---

[55] *Vita Anselmi*, ii. 16 (cit. in n. 18), 86.
[56] Ibid. ii. 21, p. 93.
[57] Fac. with detailed analysis by D. C. Douglas, *The 'Domesday*

Monachorum' of Christ Church Canterbury (London, 1944), 3–4 et *passim*.

estates of the archbishop, the Christ Church monks, and the bishop of Rochester, essentially as in Domesday Book; and a list of sixty-six men who had to provide, or who were, *milites archiepiscopi*. The limiting dates for this information are 1089–96 for the first two categories, and 1093–6 for the third.[58] All is set out in a tricolumnar quaternion of ample dimensions: 14 × 10¼ inches (355 × 260 mm.)—about as large a page as the Kentish sheep could supply. The format is that of the luxury polyptych in which a monastery recorded its title-deeds; we may justly compare it to the *Textus Roffensis* of c.1120[59] A companion volume (now lost) was the earliest post-Conquest cartulary, inferred by Nicholas Brooks from later Christ Church records and dated by him to c.1090.[60] Next came a collection of archiepiscopal letters: the fifty letters and miscellaneous items from Lanfranc's rule at Canterbury that still survive in BL, Cotton MS Nero A. vii.[61] Although this manuscript may not itself be from Christ Church, the letter-collection can reasonably be attributed to the years immediately after Lanfranc's death; and it must originate in Christ Church. It includes a full account of Lanfranc's primatial dispute with Thomas of York and its settlement by royal writ.[62] These diverse records—ancient ecclesiastical rights, modern estate-records, and archiepiscopal business—can well be attributed to Prior Henry in the years when he was in sole charge: 1089–93. His activity in setting in order the revenues and rights of the archbishopric may be compared to Henry of Eastry's reaction to an equally dangerous situation in the 1290s, and again in 1306–8.[63]

So far, so good. Did Prior Henry go further? Had he any part in assembling the dossier of papal privileges that was presented at Rome in 1123 in support of the absolute primacy of Canterbury over York? The dossier is commonly seen as inept; the privileges failed utterly to find credence in the papal court. Inept is not the first epithet that even his enemies would apply to Prior Henry, yet it seems to me that he may well have had some part in assembling these privileges. So far as it concerns us here, the drama has four stages. In 1072 Lanfranc listed eight popes by whose privileges the primacy of Canterbury was strengthened.[64] These were: Gregory the Great (sixth century); Boniface, Honorius, Vitalian (seventh century); Sergius, twice, Gregory (eighth century); Leo (ninth century); Leo (eleventh century). As R. W. Southern argued thirty years ago, while papal letters of this type are at best standard *pallium* documents, they do lend support to Lanfranc's case.[65] The second stage, and that which concerns Prior Henry, is the letter of welcome written by the monk Osbern to Anselm as his newly elected (but not yet consecrated) archbishop. It may be dated to the summer of 1093. For Osbern, Christ Church is 'sanctorum Bonifacii, Honorii, Vitaliani, Agathonis et ceterorum orthodoxorum patrum singulari semper privilegio donata'. ('Perpetually endowed with a unique privilege by saints Boniface, Honorius, Vitalian, Agatho, and other orthodox fathers'.) It is to Christ Church that the churches

[58] The list of *milites archiepiscopi* relates to 1093–6. Douglas's assumption that the script in which it is written must be dated to the mid-12th cent. seems to me unnecessary; it is another late 11th-cent. hand.

[59] *Textus Roffensis*, ed. P. H. Sawyer, 2 vols (Early English Manuscripts in Facsimile, 7 and 11; Copenhagen, 1957 and 1962), ii. The *Textus Roffensis* is a smaller book: 9 × 6⅒ inches (225 × 155 mm.).

[60] N. P. Brooks, *The Early History of the Church of Canterbury* (Leicester, 1984), 39; reviewed by M. T. Gibson, *Jnl. Theol.*

Studies, NS, 38 (1987), 227–9, at 229.

[61] *Letters of Lanfranc* (cit. in n. 6), 15–16.

[62] Memorandum on the primacy of Canterbury: ibid. 38–49, no. 3.

[63] J. H. Denton, *Robert Winchelsey and the Crown, 1294–1313* (Cambridge, 1980), chs. 3–5.

[64] Lanfranc to Alexander II: *Letters of Lanfranc* (cit. in n. 6), no. 4, 52–3.

[65] R. W. Southern, 'The Canterbury Forgeries', *EHR*, 73 (1958), 193–226, at 210–17.

of all the regions round about habitually turn for the defence of their own freedom.[66] All these popes but Agatho are on Lanfranc's list, and for Agatho no Christ Church privilege of any kind now survives. The third stage of the drama is a major collection of primatial material that appears to have been drawn up for the consecration of Thomas II of York, in June 1109.[67] Once again there was a vacancy at Canterbury; Thomas had been nominated in the spring of 1108, but he delayed his consecration—we can only suppose deliberately—until after Anselm's death (21 April 1109). The last four documents in the collection are letters from Anselm summoning Bishop William of Exeter and Thomas himself to the consecration, the petition of the clergy of York, and Thomas's profession: 'Ego Thomas, Eboracensis aecclesiae consecrandus metropolitanus, profiteor subiectionem et canonicam oboedientiam sanctae dorobernensi aecclesiae et eiusdem aecclesiae primati canonice electo et consecrato, et successoribus suis canonice inthronizatis'.[68] ('I Thomas, who am about to be consecrated metropolitan [bishop] of the church of York, offer duty [lit. 'subject status'] and canonical obedience to the holy church of Canterbury and to the primate of that same church, canonically elected and consecrated, and to his successors canonically enthroned').

The supporting *pièces justificatives* include an impressive series of episcopal professions to Canterbury from the late eighth century onwards,[69] the *Scriptum Lanfranci de Primatu*,[70] and ten papal letters: 1. Gregory the Great to Augustine; 2. Boniface IV to King Ethelbert; 3. Boniface V to Archbishop Justus; 4. Vitalian to Archbishop Theodore; 5. Sergius to the kings of the English; 6. Sergius to the bishops of England; 7. Gregory III to the bishops of Britain; 8. Leo III to Archbishop Æthelheard; 9. Formosus to the bishops of England; 10. John XII to Archbishop Dunstan.[71] Eight of these letters (nos. 2–9) plus 11. Honorius I to Archbishop Honorius, may be found in one of the major heirlooms of Christ Church, the so-called Athelstan Gospels.[72] The letters have been added to the flyleaves by several hands of the early twelfth century: in approximate terms *c*.1100. We note the omission of Agatho and Leo IX from both collections, and the presence of Honorius in the gospel-book only. Whereas the letter of Gregory the Great to Augustine, in which he defines the complementary jurisdictions of York and London, was readily available in both Gregory's *Register* and Bede's *Ecclesiastical History*, the others survive only within this Canterbury dossier. The basic texts may well be genuine,[73] but they all contain phrases that can only reflect the aspirations of post-Conquest Christ Church. Boniface V (619–25) confirmed 'ut in Doroberniae civitate semper in posterum metropolitanus totius Britanniae locus habeatur, omnesque provinciae regni Anglorum ut praefati loci metropolitanae ecclesiae subiiciantur, immutilata perpetua stabilitate decernimus' ('that in the city of Canterbury the metropolitan see of all Britain be established for ever, and that all the provinces of the

---

[66] *Anselmi Epp.* 149, ed. F. S. Schmitt, *Anselmi Opera*, iv (Edinburgh, 1949), 8; cf. Southern, 'The Canterbury Forgeries', 207.

[67] BL, Cotton MS Cleopatra E. i, fos. 40ra–56^tb. For Thomas's profession (fos. 55vb–56ra), see now *English Episcopal Acta*, v, *York 1070–1154*, ed. J. E. Burton (Oxford, 1988), no. 12.

[68] *Canterbury Professions*, ed. Richter (cit. in n. 10), 37, no. 62.

[69] Ibid. 1–39.

[70] See n. 2 above.

[71] See, conveniently, William of Malmesbury, *Gesta Pontificum*, i. 30–9 (cit. in n. 8), 46–62 [= 2, 3, 11, 4–10]. The collection is printed by Boehmer, *Die Fälschungen* (cit. in n. 2), 145–61. There is no full critical edition.

[72] BL, Cotton MSS Faustina B. vi and Claudius A. iii; see Southern, 'Canterbury Forgeries' (cit. in n. 65), 217–18.

[73] Nos. 2–3 = Bede, *Hist. Eccles.*, ii. 8 and 18, pp. 158–61, 196–9.

kingdom of the English be subject to the metropolitan church there situated—this we decree as an unchangeable law for ever').[74]

Later popes invoke Augustine: all such jurisdiction as he had from Gregory the Great appertains to the see of Canterbury, now and for ever. 'Your primacy,' writes John XII to Dunstan, 'whereby you act on behalf of the apostolic see, as your predecessors did: this we confirm to you in full, to the full extent that St Augustine and the bishops who succeeded him are known to have enjoyed it.' There is much here that is relevant to the consecration of the Archbishop of York; and if Thomas II actually made the profession just quoted, then in 1109 the dossier served its turn. The fourth and disastrous act of the drama we shall return to below.

As to when the interpolated privileges first came into being, Lanfranc quotes none of the crucial phrases in 1072; in any case, what he needed—and what he got—was a royal writ. But by 1093 Osbern could refer to a collection of privileges; and by 1109 the dossier as we know it was in existence and adequate for its purpose. So the limiting dates are 1089x93 to 1109. Given Prior Henry's concern for archiepiscopal rights in general, it is likely enough that he ordered a fair copy to be made of all papal privileges relevant to the primacy of Canterbury. I do not say that he was incapable of doctoring the texts—though I doubt that he did so. In the *sede vacante* years 1089–93, when neither Urban nor Clement was recognized in England, *cui bono*? On the other hand, Prior Henry was a man of the cartulary, the polyptych, the systematic collection. That he manufactured an *archaic* record, such as is stowed away in the gospel-book, is scarcely credible. His place in the drama of the Canterbury forgeries may rather have been to set beside the *Domesday Monachorum*, the cartulary of *c*.1090, and Lanfranc's letters a volume of primatial material that sooner or later (and in my view by 1109) incorporated nine or ten interpolated privileges.

Prior Ernulf (1096–1107)

As a fellow student with Ivo of Chartres, and a scholar in his own right, Ernulf of Beauvais was among the half-dozen creative intellectuals of eleventh-century Bec.[75] His cast of mind was not Anselm's, he was never a close disciple; but having known the Archbishop for twenty years, he understood him better than did most people in Canterbury. So he was an excellent choice for Prior.

Ernulf's principal monument is the Norman library—not in its entirety but, we may be relatively certain, in its essential structure. Lanfranc had acquired books as he could, by purchase and commission in Normandy and latterly by the employment of Norman-trained scribes.[76] But the establishment of an in-house scriptorium capable of preparing and ruling parchment, writing at book length in an even script, and finally binding the result—all that was the work of the 1090s. The *Domesday Monachorum* is halfway there—a skilfully prepared page written in a less-than-confident hand. One of the leading scribes in the early days was Eadmer himself, whom R. W. Southern has seen as the designer of the

[74] Boehmer, *Die Fälschungen* (cit. in n. 2), 148.

[75] P. J. Cramer, 'Ernulf of Rochester and Early Anglo-Norman Canon Law', *JEH*, 40 (1989), 483–510.

[76] Gibson, *Lanfranc* (cit. in n. 2), 177–82; see further C. R. Dodwell, *The Canterbury School of Illumination, 1066–1200* (Cambridge, 1954), 17–20.

new Christ Church script, a felicitous blend of Norman and English style.[77] Certainly Eadmer helped to set up the scriptorium which produced the biblical and patristic library of the late eleventh and early twelfth centuries.

Cluniac custom provided for the distribution of books among the community at the beginning of Lent; and this practice Lanfranc had confirmed in his *Constitutions*.[78] Thus there was need for a good quantity of individual books of the Bible and volumes of main-line Christian authors: a long run of Augustine, Jerome, Ambrose, Gregory the Great; a plentiful supply of Bede; and a few Carolingian texts. For most monks, that was already a lifetime's reading. The Christ Church library had, in addition, an extensive collection of the works of Anselm: both his letters of friendship and pastoral admonition and the great philosophic treatises.[79] For about a generation, Anselm was the sole modern author. By the 1140s Hugh of St Victor was being added, and to a lesser extent, St Bernard. That completed the Norman library of Christ Church, some 300 volumes in all.[80] By the same token, the local monastic scriptorium, for the production of high-quality library volumes—which is an unusual and expensive element in the economy of any monastery—ceased to function. From the mid-twelfth century the library was augmented either by a few exceptional luxury volumes, such as the Eadwine Psalter,[81] or (more commonly) by purchase and gift. The Christ Church scriptorium spans the period from Prior Ernulf, as founder, to Prior Wibert (1152x4–67), by whose time the few luxury productions were the main concern.

The new library was a great collaborative endeavour not only within Christ Church but throughout Norman England: exemplars were borrowed; artists, and occasionally scribes, travelled from one house to another. In rare cases, the detailed links can be reconstructed between a manuscript and its immediate exemplar.[82] A major source of material and ideas was St Augustine's, Canterbury. Whatever the political tensions between the two houses, there can be no doubt that they exchanged books. St Augustine's developed a script that owed rather more to English Caroline than did that of Christ Church; the best St Augustine's manuscripts were an example and a challenge to contemporary Christ Church. One may stand for all: the St Augustine's manuscript of Lanfranc's commentary on the Pauline Epistles, in its original binding, has recently returned to Canterbury after centuries of exile;[83] the elegance of the script and page-design equals the quality of the text—and that in all likelihood was taken from the author's own manuscript. The same care was taken with secular texts, judging by a fine folio Priscian now in Cambridge, the text of which has been collated with 'liber archiepiscopi' ('the archbishop's book'), again presumably Lanfranc's book.[84] It can only have been to the advantage of Christ Church that so fine a scriptorium was operating just outside the city walls. St Augustine's had its own sources of exemplars, notably Mont-Saint-Michel, and was willing to lend: Neil Ker

[77] Southern, *Anselm* (cit. in n. 14), 371–4.
[78] *Constitutions* (edn. cit. in n. 16), 19.
[79] Details in Southern, *Anselm* (cit. in n. 14), 67–8 and 238.
[80] Surviving volumes are listed by N. R. Ker, *Medieval Libraries of Great Britain* (2nd edn.; London, 1964), 29–40; suppl. A. G. Watson (London, 1987), 10–12. The greater part of the Norman library appears in Prior Eastry's catalogue of *c.*1326: ed. in

James, *ALCD*, 13–142, nos. 1–303 (at pp. 13–51).
[81] See n. 128 below.
[82] N. R. Ker, *English Manuscripts in the Century After the Norman Conquest* (Oxford, 1960), ch. 3.
[83] MS Add. 162.
[84] See n. 42.

has identified several instances of the same exemplars being used in both the Canterbury houses. So too for the elaborate historiated initials of the time. St Augustine's was at once a source of exemplars and a bench-mark of quality.[85]

Prior Conrad (1107–1126)

Whereas Ernulf took the critical decisions in respect of the scriptorium and the library, Conrad is remembered as a builder. The reconstruction of Lanfranc's choir, which was already under way by *c*.1100, was essentially Prior Conrad's work. The new building entirely replaced Lanfranc's choir and crypt. Whereas Lanfranc's choir had extended some 68 feet (21 m.) east of the crossing, the new choir ran 190 feet (58 m.) east, with commensurate extension to the north and south. Whereas Lanfranc had built on the site of the venerable complex of churches and baptistery that had made up the old Cathedral, Conrad took in new land to the east. An upper church on so ambitious a scale required not only the extension of the crypt eastward but its total reconstruction.[86] Lanfranc's crypt already had stood partially above ground level, but now the vaulting was raised still further, to create the spacious undercroft that we know today. The entire eastern section of the church was new, starting from the solid west wall of Lanfranc's crypt, beneath the western piers of the crossing. It took the best part of forty years to build, being eventually dedicated in 1130—four years after Prior Conrad's departure. In its day it was perhaps the most lavish Romanesque choir in England, in the embellishment of which neither expense nor ingenuity was spared; yet the design was obsolescent long before the work was complete. There may be truth in the surmise that the destructive fire of 1174 was—at the least—opportune.

The undercroft still stands. The planned alternation of its columns and capitals, focusing the eye on the sanctuary, is convincingly explicated by Eric Fernie: here the original design is still valid.[87] Some of Lanfranc's stonework—columns and capitals—may have been used again, but the most dramatic carving is certainly of Conrad's generation.[88] C. R. Dodwell has observed how that carving correlates with the inhabited initials in Canterbury and Rochester manuscripts of the first quarter of the twelfth century.[89] Two capitals in the crypt have marked similarities to initials in contemporary patristic manuscripts (Pl. 10 and Col. Pl. V): the more exactly if the stonework were painted in equivalent colours. Rather than ask whether the manuscript illuminators peered round the crypt, or the sculptors visited the scriptorium, we should see both capitals and initials within the spectrum of Kentish workshop practice *c*.1120. What survives is the brilliant detail rather than the sculptural programme or the full-page miniature.[90]

Above stairs, so to speak, Conrad's 'glorious choir' has vanished, being replaced by the

[85] Dodwell, *Canterbury School* (cit. in n. 76), 122–3, *et passim*.

[86] Gem, '11th-Century Rebuilding' and Strik, 'Lanfranc Building', cit. in nn. 1 and 15.

[87] E. Fernie, 'St Anselm's Crypt', in *Medieval Art and Architecture at Canterbury* (cit. in n. 1), 27–38.

[88] G. Zarnecki, *English Romanesque Sculpture, 1066–1140* (London, 1951), pl. 11, 35, 47, 49–57. See now further Deborah Kahn, *Canterbury Cathedral and its Romanesque Sculpture* (London, 1991).

[89] Dodwell, *Canterbury School* (cit. in n. 76), 62 and 70 and pl. 35, 42.

[90] The icon of Dunstan being taught by the Holy Ghost (BL, Cotton MS Claudius A. iii, fo. 8) is the sole exception, if we follow T. A. Heslop, '"Dunstanus Archiepiscopus" and Painting in Kent Around 1120', *Burlington Mag.* 126 (1984), 195–204.

Gothic choir built by William of Sens and William the Englishman.[91] But although the fire of 1174 completely gutted the interior, the foundations remained, and indeed the greater part of the outer walls to the height of the triforium base was incorporated in the Gothic choir. Only the Trinity Chapel is new. Thus the ground-plan of Conrad's choir has exactly determined the ground-plan of the present Cathedral, except for the Trinity Chapel and the Corona at its eastern end. Conrad's choir was divided into eight bays, with alternating round and octagonal pillars, as in the Gothic choir that we see today. But the total effect was very different: the old piers were not so tall, they had undecorated capitals, and they were of plain ashlar, unrelieved by the shiny little columns of Purbeck marble—Gervase calls them *columnae* rather than *pilarii*—that were the new fashion in the 1170s.[92] Conrad's choir had eastern transepts, as today. It is this feature in particular that leads the eye to the great Third Church at Cluny: that architectural miracle which ruined Cluny's finances for a generation.[93] Although Conrad's choir was on a much smaller scale, if he had the proportions right (and all observers say that he had), then to stand in the crossing looking eastward was to stand in the Cluny of England. The final magniloquent gesture was to increase the height of the central tower and construct two ancillary towers over the present chapels of St Andrew and St Anselm. The whole undertaking well merited a new conventual seal,[94] displaying the new choir in dramatic visual shorthand.

The lower walls of Conrad's choir were decorated externally with elaborate blind arcading, a stretch of which may still be seen just to the east of the south transept.[95] Above this were large aisle windows. Within the building, the chronicler Gervase (who was professed in 1163, just over a decade before the fire[96]) records two tiers of windows above the arcade. The lower range was small and dark, the upper range was set between the triforium and 'the wonderfully painted wooden ceiling' ('*caelum ligneum egregia pictura decoratum*').[97]

Above the wall was the roof, its ceiling adorned with a wonderful fresco (*pictura*). William of Malmesbury is an earlier witness, characteristically oblique. There is nothing in England, he writes, to touch the choir of Christ Church 'for the light of its glass windows, its glistening marble pavement and its pictures in many colours'.[98]

Again the eye is drawn upwards to the windows above the triforium and on to the painted ceiling. Given that there were eight steps up from the nave to the choir itself, another three from the choir to the presbytery, three more to the high altar, and then a

[91] Gervase, *De Combustione et Reparatione Ecclesiae Christi Cantuariensis*, in Gervase, *Historical Works*, i. 27–8; cf. 12–16. See the accessible and reliable account by N. Pevsner and P. Metcalf, *The Cathedrals of England*, i. *Southern England* (Harmondsworth, 1985), 50–81.

[92] Gervase, *De Combustione* (cit. in n. 91), i. 27 and 12; also Pevsner and Metcalf, *Cathedrals of England*, 54, 56.

[93] Plan of Cluny III in C. Brooke and W. Swaan, *The Monastic World* (London, 1974), p. 61.

[94] T. A. Heslop, 'The Conventual Seals of Canterbury Cathedral 1066–1232', in *Medieval Art and Architecture at Canterbury* (cit. in n. 1), 94–100 and pl. XXVII, with refs. Although the earliest extant example of the 'second seal' is on an archiepiscopal document of 1155 × 61 (A. Saltman, *Theobald, Arch-*

bishop of Canterbury (London, 1956), no. 31), the total loss of original documents issued by the community (as distinct from the archbishop) in the first half of the 12th cent. makes it impossible to determine when, and in what circumstances, this seal was first made and used.

[95] Zarnecki, *English Romanesque Sculpture* (cit. in n. 88), pl. 34.

[96] Gervase, *Historical Works*, i. 173, 231.

[97] Ibid. 27 and 13.

[98] 'Nichil tale possit in Anglia videri in vitrearum fenestrarum luce, in marmorei pavimenti nitore, in diversicoloribus picturis': *Gesta Pontificum* (cit. in n. 8), 138. As William is concerned only with bishops (pontiffs), the Canterbury choir is included in the section on Rochester, as an early achievement of Bishop Ernulf.

further eight to the archbishop's throne, against the wall of the apse, the 'glory' of the choir on a summer morning must have been vertiginous.

Further testimony to the scale and character of Conrad's patronage is his provision for the ongoing liturgy of the Cathedral.[99] He gave furnishings and vestments, a great seven-branched bronze candlestick, of the type still to be seen in Henry the Lion's church at Brunswick,[100] and a series of five enormous bells—bell-ringing was a lively tradition at Christ Church throughout the twelfth century.[101] What is irretrievably lost is the ceremonial within which these treasures had a reasonable place: the day-to-day music, the reception of important visitors, the funerals, the five great festivals for which the entire circle was lit in the great chandelier before the high altar.[102] An easy parallel, and perhaps a useful one, is Cluny in the time of Peter the Venerable.[103] This was the definitive, fully articulated era of Benedictine life in Western Europe. Fundamentally too, it was 'the end of the Empire', but Conrad was spared that knowledge.

His last years saw the fourth (and for our purposes final) act in the drama of the primatial privileges. The collection that had apparently passed muster for the consecration of Thomas II of York in 1109 was presented in Rome in 1123 to safeguard the rights of the archbishopric on the consecration of William of Corbeil. How the documents were received is less than clear, for the sole witness is a canon of York, the historian Hugh the Chanter.[104] He says that they were laughed out of court. At any rate, no papal confirmation was secured, and the dispute rumbled on through the years, becoming a ritual element in archiepiscopal consecrations down to the Reformation and beyond. Its shadow persists even today: York is 'primate of England'; Canterbury is 'primate of *all* England'.

THE SETTLED COMMUNITY *C.*1120–1170

> Walk about Sion, and go round about her:
> and tell the towers thereof.
>
> Ps. 48: 11

In the 1120s the first heroic generation of Norman Christ Church was passing on. Eadmer, who had been a child at the time of the Conquest, died in his late sixties *c.*1130. The memory—or, if we may risk the word, the trauma—of the Conquest was fading; the

---

[99] Details in Conrad's obit: BL, MS Arundel 68, fos. 12–52ᵛ, at 16ᵛ–17; partly ed. Wharton, *Anglia Sacra*, i. 136–7, and Legg and Hope, *Inventories*, 44.

[100] K. Jordan, *Heinrich der Löwe* (Munich, 1979), pl. 9.

[101] 'Quinque signa permaxima, quorum primum .x. similiter secundum .x. tertium xi. quartum viii. quintum vero xxiv homines ad sonandum trahunt' ('There were five great bells. The first took ten men to ring it, as did the second; the third took eleven men, and the fourth eight, but the fifth needed twenty-four'), Wharton, *Anglia Sacra*, i. 137; see further n. 140 below. The fifth bell had been unsuccessfully cast by Prior Ernulf.

[102] Lanfranc, *Constitutions* (cit. in n. 16), 59–60: 'accendantur

duae partes cereorum coronae presbyterii' (for feasts of the *second* rank).

[103] *Statuta Petri Venerabilis*, ed. G. Constable, *Corpus Consuetudinum Monasticarum*, ed. K. Hallinger, vi (Siegburg, 1975).

[104] Hugh the Chanter, *The History of the Church of York 1066–1127*, 2nd edn., rev. M. Brett, C. N. L. Brooke, and M. Winterbottom (Oxford Medieval Texts; Oxford, 1990), 193–5; cf. Southern, 'Canterbury Forgeries' (cit. in n. 65), 223–4. Note that St Augustine's had presented analogous forged privileges to Pope Calixtus II only three years before, and secured a privilege in return: W. Levison, *England and the Continent in the Eighth Century* (Oxford, 1946), 179; cf. Gibson, *Lanfranc*, 235–6.

distinctions between Norman and English were being concealed; and the community was reverting to the normal monastic concerns of performing the liturgy, overseeing the revenues, and criticizing the archbishop. These conditions persisted for half a century, virtually two monastic generations. I do not mean that the community was lax, only that it went about its business without undue self-analysis, whether historical or philosophical.

The Price of Independence

In broad terms, the second quarter of the twelfth century saw the clarification of the economic and political status of the monastic community in Christ Church. Absolute independence was not in question, nor did the community really want it: they wanted at one and the same time a monastic archbishop who would understand their needs and speak on their behalf in the outside world, and complete control of their own affairs and of promotion within the community. Their outlook is well expressed by Gervase of Canterbury, who recounts Theobald's bruising exchanges with the community as the background—and more ominously the precedent—for the intolerable policies of Archbishop Baldwin.[105] While recognizing the archbishop's right to intervene, he is appalled when it is exercised.

In both Domesday Book proper and the *Domesday Monachorum*, the monastic estates are separate from those of the archbishop;[106] the division was (says Gervase) ratified by Lanfranc and confirmed by Anselm.[107] Thus, in an archiepiscopal vacancy, only the archbishop's estates fell to the king: monastic revenues were unaffected. But this arrangement fell far short of comprehensive protection of the revenues and liberties of the monastic community. It did not, for instance, cover the traditional burdens on monastic revenues to the benefit of the archbishop. That such burdens were real may be seen from Archbishop Theobald's removal of some recent and improper financial impositions, and his assumption that others were the community's due service.[108] In such ways the community was bound to the archbishop, and he in turn could not hope to balance his books without their help. As late as 1150, Theobald was wrestling with the most basic questions of organization and the extent to which he had a voice in the community's affairs.[109] In the absence of systematic obedientiaries' records at so early a date, and given the scarcity of monastic, as distinct from archiepiscopal, documents of the time of Theobald, we cannot tell how—or indeed whether—the (at least) six obedientiaries had regular and adequate funding *c*.1150.[110] We do not know how independent they really were. That Theobald successfully removed two priors from office[111] suggests that it was still the archbishop who had ultimate control of the community and its resources.

The second quarter of the twelfth century was a time of economic uncertainty for Christ Church, as for many other long-established monastic houses. They were not in

[105] Gervase, *Chronica*, s.a. 1150, in Gervase, *Historical Works*, i. 142–6; see further Saltman, *Theobald* (cit. in n. 94), 56–64.

[106] *Domesday Kent* (cit. in n. 39), ad loc.: *Domesday Monachorum* (cit. in n. 57), 88–95; see further Southern, *Anselm* (cit. in n. 14), 256–60, with refs.

[107] Gervase, *Imaginationes*, in Gervase, *Historical Works*, i. 43–4.

[108] Saltman, *Theobald* (cit. in n. 94), 183–4, esp. no. 30.

[109] Ibid. 62–3.

[110] The best and most accessible account is still Smith, *Cant. Cath. Priory*, 14–22.

[111] Saltman, *Theobald* (cit. in n. 94), 56–64.

financial crisis, but they were stagnant. No doubt the community could afford the 'glorious choir', built and paid for over many years. The issue is rather one of how soon and how well they understood the difference between static income from their estates and ancient rights (as scrupulously itemized in the *Domesday Monachorum*) and dynamic income from commerce in the city of Canterbury and such control as they could establish over regional trade. They did, after all, control the ports of Dover and Sandwich.[112] William Urry's seminal work on the city of Canterbury 'under the Angevin kings' indicates that Prior Wibert had a sound economic relationship with the city of Canterbury.[113] We know nothing of his ambitions further afield. A firm alliance with the city—not only socially but economically—was worth much.[114] Archbishops came and went, but the community had a secure base in Canterbury itself. In this respect it was exactly on a par with St Augustine's.

By contrast, the archiepiscopal household was clearly articulated and well run. It was becoming a source of employment for the new class of *magistri* who had studied in the schools of Paris, providing access for the few to the glittering prizes of a place at court, an archdeaconry, a bishopric.[115] These were unthought-of developments as late as 1120. Archbishops William of Corbeil and Theobald transformed their households, while the monastic community *c*.1125–50 continued unchanged. By *c*.1140 several men who were to be leading intellectuals in the circle of Thomas Becket were already in archiepiscopal employment at Canterbury.[116] The mere contrast of community and household, both in structure and in the kind of people attracted by one or the other, throws a good deal of light on the tensions within Christ Church between the departure of Conrad (1126)[117] and the appointment of Wibert (1153).

Finally, two sources of legal conflict emerge in the time of Theobald, theoretically of long standing, but in practice of major importance only in the 1150s. The Archdeacon of Canterbury was the archbishop's senior representative in the diocese, *and within the community*. His seat in the chapter-house was the archbishop's footstool.[118] In so far as the community retained pastoral responsibilities and pastoral income in the diocese as a whole, there was occasion here for a sharp clash of interests with the archdeacon. But the community had no say in choosing the man, nor in his formal assumption of office.[119] Having archdeacons at all was a post-Conquest novelty,[120] for which monastic customaries (such as Lanfranc's *Constitutions*) made virtually no provision.[121] Yet this cuckoo in the nest, this magpie, had the power to settle disputes, adjust finances, and sway local courts.

---

[112] Both Dover and Sandwich were 'de vestitu monachorum': see *Domesday Kent* (cit. in n. 39), fo. 3ᵃ. For Sandwich see further W. Boys, *Collections for an History of Sandwich in Kent* (Canterbury, 1792), 654–9.

[113] W. Urry, *Canterbury Under the Angevin Kings* (London, 1967), ch. 2 *et passim*.

[114] For details of 12th-cent. Canterbury, see the excellent maps published by the Canterbury Archaeological Trust: *Topographical Maps of Canterbury* (2nd edn.; Canterbury, 1982).

[115] Saltman, *Theobald* (cit. in n. 94), 165–77.

[116] Herbert of Bosham lists 20 *eruditi*, *c*.1165: *Materials for the History of Thomas Becket, Archbishop of Canterbury*, ed. J. C. Robertson and J. B. Sheppard, 7 vols. (RS, 68; 1875–85), iii. 523–32; cf. F. Barlow, *Thomas Becket* (London, 1986), 77–9.

[117] He became Abbot of St Benet, Hulme.

[118] Saltman, *Theobald* (cit. in n. 94), 258–9, no. 30.

[119] There is no evidence for 'monastic archdeacons' in Christ Church in the period, *pace* D. Knowles, Lanfranc's *Constitutions* (cit. in n. 16), 112, n. 2. See further J. Sayers, 'Monastic Archdeacons', in *Church and Government in the Middle Ages: Essays Presented to C. R. Cheney*, ed. C. N. L. Brooke, D. E. Luscombe, G. H. Martin, and Dorothy Owen (Cambridge, 1976), 177–203.

[120] C. Morris, *The Papal Monarchy: The Western Church from 1050 to 1250* (Oxford History of the Christian Church; Oxford, 1989), 222.

[121] In all 12 volumes of Hallinger there is a single reference to an archdeacon, and that relating to his role at mass: *Corpus Consuetudinum Monasticarum*, ed. K. Hallinger, vii, pt. 3, 211 apparatus.

When Thomas Becket was appointed archdeacon in 1154, it was his first serious promotion, in which he learned the basics of acquiring friends and neutralizing enemies.[122] To the community, the archdeacon was always a potential enemy: the archbishop's exercise of power through his official was less tolerable than exactly the same demand made to the prior and community face to face.

The second source of conflict was the facility with which modern monks appealed to Rome. In the great world beyond Canterbury, the papal Curia was becoming the familiar and accepted court of final resort. Whereas in 1123 the community had presented their dossier of privileges at Rome only as an exceptional measure, and in defence (be it said) of their own archbishop, now they saw Rome as the guarantor of monastic independence against him. Had they not challenged Theobald's deposition of Prior Jeremiah in Rome, and been vindicated?[123] It was heady stuff. On the whole, however, in Theobald's day, community and archbishop were at peace. If occasionally the Archbishop put his foot down, it was for the community's profit, not his own. The proof may be found in Theobald's promotion of the subprior Wibert to the prior's office in 1153. In him the community had a man of energy and certitude to steer it through the last feeble years of Theobald's archiepiscopate and the turmoil of Becket's.

Prior Wibert (1153–1167)

Within Christ Church, though not on the wider stage, Wibert was a figure comparable to Suger at Saint-Denis;[124] he deserved his own *vita* or, better, a *de administratione sua*. He restored Conrad's church. It was not a complete reconstruction, but—judging by the surviving evidence in the crypt—it was a radical repair. On the north side of the choir ambulatory he strengthened the chapels of the Holy Innocents (crypt) and St Andrew (above); and on the south side correspondingly the chapels of St Gabriel (crypt) and St Anselm (above).[125] Such expensive and inconvenient internal works at that point in a cathedral are normally in response to instability in the central tower or towers; and this was almost certainly the case in Christ Church. The towers that Conrad had set above the apsidal chapels and the transepts—which may be seen on the second conventual seal—had settled unevenly and now threatened the entire structure. Wibert built a treasury[126]— to serve the needs of the sacrist and the recently created *thesaurarii*, the last of the major monastic offices to be defined. From the end of the century (1198–9) onwards, a long series of treasurers' accounts provides the kind of solid information that in the twelfth century still survives only by chance.[127]

Wibert's most celebrated achievement is symbolized by the octagonal tower which

[122] Barlow, *Thomas Becket* (cit. in n. 116), 37–9.

[123] Saltman, *Theobald* (cit. in n. 94), 57–8, with refs.

[124] G. Panofsky-Soergel, *Abbot Suger on the Abbey Church of St-Denis and its Art Treasures* (2nd edn.; Princeton, NJ, 1979), *passim*.

[125] D. Kahn, 'The Structural Evidence for the Dating of the St Gabriel Chapel Wall-Paintings at Christ Church Cathedral, Canterbury', *Burlington Mag.* 126 (1984), 225–9, with valuable observations on the mid-12th-cent. reinforcement of the four chapels.

[126] R. Willis, *Conventual Buildings* (cit. in n. 15), 74–9 (treasury, or *vestiarium*), and 51 with fig. 7 and 158 ff. with further plans; F. Woodman, *The Architectural History of Canterbury Cathedral* (London, 1981), 76–84.

[127] Smith, *Cant. Cath. Priory*, 14–22; id., 'The Central Financial System of Christ Church, Canterbury, 1186–1512', *EHR*, 55 (1940), 353–69, with (368–9) a critical edn. of the earliest surviving treasury account-roll (1198–9).

controlled the water-supply to the whole complex of Cathedral and monastic buildings. It is a highly decorated, slightly old-fashioned little edifice, opposite the infirmary cloister; and it is easily recognizable in the more detailed of the two contemporary plans of the waterworks, which were added to the last folios of the Eadwine Psalter.[128] These plans are unique in twelfth-century Europe. What is more, they work: they are not what theoretically might be,[129] but represent the actual condition of the site *c*.1160. The spring was a thousand yards away, at Horsefold;[130] the water thus dropped 40 feet on its way to Christ Church: in principle, then, a pipe 2¼ inches in diameter would maintain an acceptable pressure at the point of use. The system was overhauled two centuries later by Prior Chillenden, and adapted to the reduced needs of the Dean and Chapter at the Dissolution.[131] So Wibert built well. Whether he was building from scratch is not so clear. Had Christ Church a uniquely efficient water-supply before the elegant Cistercian systems were laid out at Rievaulx and Fountains? Twelfth-century plumbing is a subject that would repay further study, not in cathedrals (where excavation must be limited) but ideally in royal palaces such as Wolvesey and Clarendon, where the need for a reliable water-supply was far greater even than in a monastery of a hundred monks and their servants.[132] Technically the work is not unduly difficult, and Roman prototypes were and are scattered across southern England. It is hard—and, I would argue, unnecessary—to see Wibert's waterworks as a brilliant, isolated *tour de force*.[133] What is exceptional is the quality of the cartography by which they are recorded. Decorative and apparently accurate, it constitutes most of the evidence for the disposition and architecture of the Cathedral and monastic buildings in the mid-twelfth century. It is a sober reminder of how little we know.

Wibert could employ the best artists of the day in the decoration of the Cathedral, in sculptural ornament, and in the illumination of luxury manuscripts. By the 1150s it is very unlikely that the Cathedral still had its own workshops and scriptorium: not only were these expensive to maintain; in a time of changing fashions, their limited, local repertoire ceased to please. Economy and quality were better served by calling in talent from outside. That this was Wibert's policy is vividly evident in the frescos with which he completed (and concealed) the reconstruction of the four chapels mentioned above.[134] Nothing can effect a stylistic reconciliation between the John the Baptist cycle, fragments of which remain in the chapel of St Gabriel, and the scene of Paul picking up the viper in the chapel

---

[128] Fac. *The Canterbury Psalter*, ed. M. R. James (London, 1935), fos. 284ᵛ–6ᵛ. See further n. 138 below. Although Wibert's tower was partially rebuilt *c*.1400, it is still clearly recognizable on the 12th-cent. plan.

[129] Contrast *The Plan of St Gall*, fac. edn. and commentary by W. Horn and E. Born (3 vols.; Berkeley, Calif., Los Angeles, and London, 1979).

[130] Saltman, *Theobald* (cit. in n. 94), no. 46.

[131] R. Willis, *Conventual Buildings* (cit. in n. 15), 158–73; good analysis with photographs by W. Urry, 'Canterbury, Kent, circa 1153 × 1161', in *Local Maps and Plans from Medieval England*, ed. R. A. Skelton and P. D. A. Harvey (Oxford, 1986), 43–58; report on excavation of conduit house by T. Tatton-Brown in *Arch. Cant.* 97 (1981), 292–3. For the water-supply to St Augustine's,

which was from the same escarpment and on the same scale, see the report on the excavation of 'St Augustine's Conduit House' by P. Bennett, ibid. 106 (1988), 137–41.

[132] Gervase says that Lanfranc had envisaged a full complement of 140 monks: *Actus Pontificum*, in Gervase, *Historical Works*, i. 368. 64 monks went into exile in 1207: *Annales de Wintonia*, ed. H. R. Luard (RS, 1865), 80. These figures are the basis of all other estimates and assertions. See further Urry, *Canterbury Under the Angevin Kings* (cit. in n. 113), ch. 7.

[133] The date and complexity of the St Augustine's waterworks system is not yet clear (cf. P. Bennett, 'St Augustine's Conduit House' (cit. in n. 131)).

[134] See Kahn, 'Dating of the St Gabriel Chapel Wall-Paintings' (cit. in n. 125).

of St Anselm, upstairs.[135] But we have reached an era in Romanesque taste when no reconciliation is called for: the wealthy patron could choose among diverse practitioners, develop his taste, and change his mind. In architecture and sculpture Wibert was more conservative, judging by his water-tower. As a bibliophile he broke no new ground textually, but he may have gone further—or permitted others to experiment—in the choice of illuminators. He gave the community a fine gospel-book,[136] but he is not among the several twelfth-century priors whose individual collections could still be identified in the library *c.*1326.[137] At the same time, two manuscripts of exceptional splendour were produced in Christ Church in the mid-twelfth century: the Eadwine Psalter and the Dover Bible.[138] These are essentially treasures, rather than books for normal liturgical or scholarly use; but in that they were made for the community, they were made with the Prior's approbation, and perhaps indeed with his active encouragement.

Wibert is remembered too as the open-handed donor of embroidered hangings, liturgical vestments, and yet another great bell: 'Signum quoque magnum in clocario posuit, quod triginti duo homines ad sonandum trahunt.'[139] This was a considerably grander bell than even the biggest of Prior Conrad's.[140] Visually, Dunstan and Alphege were still the principal saints, over the high altar on each side of Christ in glory.[141] These were saints in the old style, invested by the king, holding their lands of the king, and distantly courteous to the pope. They were known by their works rather than by their doctrine. Had they quite the right image for a modern primatial see? Such considerations may underlie the attempted canonization of Anselm in 1163,[142] and they do explain the presentation of Dunstan as the expositor of the Rule of St Benedict, in a fine illumination of *c.*1170.[143] Perhaps too it was at this time that a traditional rendering of Gregory the Great—book in hand, inspired by the Holy Ghost, and his papal feet embraced by a bishop and a monk— was crudely retitled *Dunstani Archiepiscopi*.[144] Such refurbishment of the traditional calendar we know with hindsight to have been superfluous.

[135] Pevsner and Metcalf, *Cathedrals of England* (cit. in n. 91), 73–4 (St Paul and the Viper); cf. L. Eleen, *The Illustration of the Pauline Epistles in French and English Bibles of the Twelfth and Thirteenth Centuries* (Oxford, 1982), 90–101.

[136] Legg and Hope, *Inventories*, 44.

[137] James, *ALCD*, 52 and 96.

[138] C. M. Kauffmann, *Romanesque Manuscripts 1066–1190* (A Survey of Manuscripts Illuminated in the British Isles, 3; London, 1975), 96–9, nos. 68–9. The Eadwine Psalter is now considered to be about a decade later than the date of '*c.*1147' (which derives from the assumed date of the comet on fo. 10). See also *The Eadwine Psalter: Text, Image, and Monastic Culture in Twelfth-Century Canterbury*, ed. M. T. Gibson, T. A. Heslop, and R. W. Pfaff (London, 1992).

[139] 'He set up a great bell in the bell-tower, which took 32 men to ring it': LPL, MS 20, fol. 225ᵛ, quoted by Legg and

Hope, *Inventories*, 44.

[140] The free-standing bell-tower, 'campanile', to the south of the choir is shown in Prior Wibert's waterworks plan: *Canterbury Psalter* (cit. in n. 128), fo. 284ᵛ.

[141] *De Combustione*, in Gervase, *Historical Works*, i. 13.

[142] See conveniently Barlow, *Thomas Becket* (cit. in n. 116), 85– 7: tactically the petition may have been a reply to the canonization of Edward the Confessor (1161).

[143] BL, Royal MS 10 A XIII, fo. 2ᵛ; good reproduction in N. L. Ramsay and M. J. Sparks, *The Image of Saint Dunstan* (Canterbury, 1988), front cover.

[144] BL, Cotton MS Claudius A. iii fo. 8; good reproduction in *Image of Saint Dunstan* (cit. in n. 143), 19. A case for identifying the drawing itself as of Dunstan, made at Canterbury *c.*1120, is put by Heslop, '"Dunstanus Archiepiscopus" and Painting' (cit. in n. 90).

THE CULT OF THOMAS BECKET 1170–1185

> We took sweet counsel together, and walked in the house of God as friends.
>
> Ps. 55: 15

The myth of Becket is nowhere better expressed than by the irreconcilable contrast between the Archbishop in his life, who neglected the community and in the view of some dishonoured it, and the martyr, by whose *life* the monks of Christ Church were edified and enriched. Gervase of Canterbury, who had been professed in 1163 and had seen Thomas's indifference to the community at first hand, could still recall him *c.*1186 as the perfect archbishop:

All his life Thomas did nothing to the disadvantage of the monks of Christ Church, but showed them every mark of affection and goodwill. It was his custom to preside at their chapters, listen to their sermons and study with them in the cloister; pray with them in church, and take counsel in private with the prior and the senior monks for the welfare of their church. He was a good shepherd and a loving father.[145]

Thomas Becket

Thomas's ecclesiastical career began in the household of Archbishop Theobald, in whose service he accumulated useful preferment, culminating (1154) in the archdeaconry of Canterbury itself.[146] He traded these skills for the highest position at the court of Henry II: in the first month of the new reign (January 1155) he became the King's chancellor. But he remained archdeacon; indeed he was still archdeacon after his own consecration as Archbishop of Canterbury. A conflict of interests was hard to avoid or to restrain. Within a few years, Theobald had to confirm that the archdeacon of Canterbury had no jurisdiction within the Cathedral precincts, and might not intervene in the community's affairs.[147] The man who stalked through the court with a tame wolf at his heels was a threat to the sheepfold of Christ Church long before he became archbishop.[148] It is not enough to say that Thomas put his old life behind him when he came to Canterbury. However sober his dress and however modest the archiepiscopal table, he could not please the community.[149] As a secular clerk, he broke the tradition of monastic archbishops,[150] and as a patron of learning and the arts he looked outside Canterbury, beyond England even, to find talented and original men. In Gerard la Pucelle he had a canonist and theologian from Paris, and in John of Salisbury an old-style humanist.[151] These and other *eruditi* are sufficiently

[145] Gervase, *Persecutio Contra Baldewinum Archiepiscopum*, in Gervase, *Historical Works*, i. 48; cf. R. W. Southern, *The Monks of Canterbury and the Murder of Archbishop Becket* (William Urry Memorial Lectures, 1; Canterbury, 1985), 18.

[146] Barlow, *Thomas Becket* (cit. in n. 116), 28–40. Thomas remained archdeacon until 1163: ibid. 82.

[147] Saltman, *Theobald* (cit. in n. 116), nos. 30 and 50; see also the charge of irregular levying of archidiaconal revenues (ibid. 168).

[148] B. Ross, 'Audi Thoma', *EHR*, 89 (1974), 333–8, at 337 n. 4,

quoting Oxford, Corpus Christi College, MS 32, fol. 96ʳ⁻ᵛ.

[149] Barlow, *Thomas Becket* (cit. in n. 116), 74–87, *et passim*.

[150] Though not a monk, William of Corbeil had at least been a canon regular.

[151] For Becket's *eruditi* as a group, see n. 116 above, and for Gerard la Pucelle, see *The Letters of John of Salisbury*, ed. W. J. Millor, H. E. Butler, and C. N. L. Brooke, 2 vols. (Oxford Medieval Texts; London, 1955; rev. Oxford, 1986 and 1979), ii. nos. 158, 184–6, 226, 277, and 297, with further refs.

commemorated in their writings; but they were only one segment in a spectrum of patronage which included scribes and illuminators, metalworkers, and vernacular poets.[152] Under Becket, the archiepiscopal household became a little princely court, like those of Henry of Blois at Winchester, Count Henry the Liberal and his wife at Troyes, and Henry the Lion at Brunswick.[153] International in context, it brought honour to Canterbury but not to the monastic community of Christ Church. Their mental horizons were those of Prior Wibert, and of Odo the subprior who succeeded him: maintenance and embellishment of the fabric, orderly distribution of revenues, and defence of established rights and custom. Thus the gulf was not only between the secular clerk and the monks, or between Becket as an individual and his monastic community, but between the old local world and the new perspective of England in Europe. At the practical level, on the other hand, it has to be allowed that Becket was in exile for the last three years of his archiepiscopate, and that even when he was resident in Canterbury, he made no attempt to alter the structure of the community or (so far as the documents survive) to appropriate its wealth.[154] The division was not between one individual and another, but between the traditional monastic world and the new world of royal clerks and international lawyers.

The New Saint

Becket was killed on 29 December 1170. Contemporary sources throw vivid and inconsistent light on the day's fatal events. In the early afternoon, Henry II's knights forced their way into the precinct and confronted Becket in his palace. He refused to go with them to the King. As darkness fell, the Archbishop slipped across to the Cathedral for vespers and there, at the foot of the steps leading up to the choir, waited for his pursuers. He fell before the altar of St Benedict, one secular clerk having stayed to defend him.[155] Even at his death the community was divided and very cautious in its response. There was an element of relief at his departure.

Within a week a cure was reported by the dead Archbishop's blood; local enthusiasm grew, and over a few crucial months the transient shock-reaction to the murder became stabilized as a permanent cult.[156]

The creation of a structured cult of Thomas Becket had (as I see it) four elements. Henry II's legal responsibility for the murder released quite substantial royal funds for the shrine. Thomas's refusal to accept secular jurisdiction over the clergy could now be

[152] For Becket's personal library, see C. F. R. de Hamel, *Glossed Books of the Bible and the Origins of the Paris Booktrade* (Woodbridge, 1984), ch. 4; and for Becket as a patron, U. Nilgen, 'Intellectuality and Splendour: Thomas Becket as a Patron of the Arts', in *Art and Patronage in the English Romanesque*, ed. S. Macready and F. H. Thompson (Soc. of Antiquaries of London, Occasional Papers, NS 8; 1986), 145–58.

[153] For the reputation of Henry of Blois, see John of Salisbury, *Historia Pontificalis*, ed. M. M. Chibnall, 2nd edn., Oxford Medieval Texts (1986), 78–80; for Henry the Liberal, see P. D. Stirnemann, 'Quelques bibliothèques princières et la production hors scriptorium au xii siècle', *Bulletin archéologique*, NS, 17–18 (1984), 7–38, with further bibliography; and for Henry

the Lion, Jordan, *Heinrich der Löwe* (cit. in n. 100). The great exemplar of the day was the court of Frederick Barbarossa: see now P. F. Ganz, in *Friedrich Barbarossa*, 2 vols. (Konstanzer Arbeitskreis für Mittelalterliche Geschichte, Vorträge und Forschungen, 1991).

[154] Of Becket's few surviving archiepiscopal *acta*, none is addressed to Christ Church: *English Episcopal Acta*, ii: *Canterbury 1162–1190*, ed. C. R. Cheney and B. E. A. Jones (London, 1986).

[155] Barlow, *Thomas Becket* (cit. in n. 116), 240–7.

[156] B. Ward, *Miracles and the Medieval Mind: Theory, Record and Event, 1000–1215* (2nd edn; Aldershot, 1987), ch. 5, and cf. shrewd observations in ch. 7.

presented as the cause of his death: he had died for justice and thereby for truth; he was not only a saint but a martyr. So Anselm had justified Alphege a century before.[157] Third, and crucially, Alexander III formally canonized Thomas within a year of Henry II's submission and penance.[158] The fourth element is truly paradoxical, in that the international perspective which had been so alien to the community in Thomas's lifetime brought him in death instant celebrity from the Baltic to Sicily. Churches were dedicated and reliquaries inscribed. Thomas stands in the iconostasis of protective saints in the Gospels of Henry the Lion.[159] Such universal recognition forced the community at Christ Church to shift its mental gear. By no act or thought of its own, Dunstan and Alphege— the saints of yesterday, in the eyes of many—had been joined by a modern saint, whose defining characteristic was his defence of the freedom of the Church against an encroaching State.

The New Cathedral 1174–85

Thus it was that when fire destroyed Conrad's 'glorious choir' in 1174, the community had not only the funds to begin rebuilding, but a clear architectural strategy: provision for the cult of Thomas Becket.

When all was done, Gervase of Canterbury told the story of the rebuilding: the work of a distinguished foreign architect completed, and well completed, by an Englishman trained in France.[160] William of Sens found Conrad's choir roofless and burnt out, but in its lower structure basically sound. (He had Wibert to thank for that.) Thus essentially what William did was to construct triforium and clerestory levels that would take the stress of a vaulted stone roof without overburdening the older masonry beneath. He was working within the proportions of the old choir. New decorative elements were introduced,[161] but structurally the building was an extremely intelligent repair. William the Englishman, who took over when his predecessor was injured, had a much freer hand in planning and building the Trinity Chapel and the Corona beyond. It was he who developed the building beyond the limitations of Romanesque into the new architecture of the thirteenth century. He had a better grasp of practical mathematics than his predecessors. We need only compare Wibert's shoring-up of the eastern towers with William's confident reliance on the accurate transmission of stress through the skeleton of his new building. So he provided the ample Trinity Chapel for the major shrine of the new saint, and the little Corona to the east, to display Becket's skull fragment for separate veneration. A generation was to pass before the whole complex was complete and in operation; but

[157] Eadmer, *Vita Anselmi*, i. 30 (cit. in n. 18), 50–4.

[158] Henry submitted 21 May 1172; the bull of canonization was issued 21 Feb. 1173: Barlow, *Thomas Becket* (cit. in n. 116), 260–2 and 268–9.

[159] Jordan, *Heinrich der Löwe* (cit. in n. 100), pl. 3. Thomas is the last martyr to the right in the register below Christ. For the cult of Becket in Europe as a whole, see T. Borenius, *St Thomas Becket in Art* (London, 1932); also P. A. Newton, 'Some New Material for the Study of the Iconography of St Thomas Becket', in *Thomas Becket. Actes du colloque international de Sédières, 19–24 août 1973*, ed. R. Foreville (Paris, 1975), 255–63. A

fine early piece of jewellery is the gold reliquary inscribed DE SANGVINE SANCTI THOME MARTYRIS that was presented to Queen Margaret of Sicily by the Bishop of Bath (Pl. 11): see Neil Stratford in *English Romanesque Art 1066–1200*, exhib. cat., ed. G. Zarnecki (London, 1984), no. 303.

[160] *De Combustione*, in Gervase, *Historical Works*, i. 6–29; lucid analysis by Pevsner and Metcalf, *Cathedrals of England* (cit. in n. 91), i. 59–65.

[161] Gervase draws attention to the elaborately-carved capitals (formerly plain) and the polished black marble colonnettes: *De Combustione*, in *Historical Works*, i. 27.

the requisite building was finished much sooner: the Trinity Chapel *c*.1180 and the Corona *c*.1200.

A pilgrimage church of the eleventh or twelfth century had, almost as a matter of course, a major sculptural programme on the west front. Alternatively, an elaborately decorated porch might be added on the north or south side for the reception of pilgrims. Madeline Caviness has observed that the experience of the pilgrim to Canterbury was that of being inside a vast enamelled reliquary:[162] the newly liberated areas of the upper walls of choir, transepts, and Trinity Chapel had been put to immediate and dazzling use. It was not the first stained glass at Canterbury, by many years; but it was of a new order in scale and splendour. In the highest, clerestory range—running right round the horseshoe of choir, north transept, Trinity Chapel, Corona, and back again—were the eighty-six Ancestors of Christ. In the triforium range below were the ancient Canterbury saints, Dunstan and Alphege, near their shrines. Dunstan appears in a sequence of six miraculous events, including King Eadwy's escape from Hell (Col. Pl. III*a*)[163] That was a fully fledged anecdote by the late eleventh century—as eloquent to William Rufus as it might be to Henry II. Although formally the image bears comparison with Christ bringing Adam (and Constantine) out of Hell, its function here is solely to honour Dunstan; there is no link with the Passion scenes in the south choir transept. These belong to the great series of typological windows, showing the life of Christ set within the framework of prefiguring events and prophetic utterances.[164] There are twelve windows in the series, to be found in the eastern transepts and north and south choir aisles, with, in addition, the great east window in the Corona. They run below the saints' lives in the triforium and the procession of Ancestors in the clerestory, having not only a greater area of glass than these, but a more complex significance. Here, the events of the Old Testament balance and foreshadow Christian truth. Take the second monastic canticle, the song of Hezekiah: 'I said in the midst of my days, I am going down to the gates of Hell.' The prophet Isaiah told the king that if he would repent, his life would be lengthened by fifteen years (Is. 38: 1–20). So Hezekiah arose from his bed of sickness . . . as Christ ascended to the Father. We may recall that the enamels on the imperial crown showed Christ ('by me kings reign') and the three exemplary kings of the Old Testament: David, Solomon, and Hezekiah.[165] It may be thought that the icon of the devout king has more force than the slightly strained parallel with the Ascension of Christ.

This lowest range of Canterbury windows is full of inscriptions.[166] Some are plain to the modern reader, others arcane in their reference or in a damaged condition. Fortunately, they survive also in manuscript; the written text in turn is related to the inscriptions on a

[162] M. H. Caviness, *The Windows of Christ Church Cathedral Canterbury* (Corpus Vitrearum Medii Aevi, Great Britain, 2 London, 1981), 159.

[163] Osbern, *Vita Sancti Dunstani*, ch. 30, and Eadmer, *Vita Sancti Dunstani*, ch. 21, in *Memorials of Saint Dunstan*, ed. Stubbs (cit. in n. 32), 104–5 and 196.

[164] Caviness, *Windows* (cit. in n. 162), 7–62 (Ancestors); 63–75 (saints); 77–156 (life of Christ). For details of lost glass and reconstructed iconography, see ibid. See also ead, *The Early Stained Glass of Canterbury Cathedral: c.1175–1220* (Princeton, NJ,

1977), 101–6 and (schemata), 168–75. Two fine Ancestors are illustrated in *English Romanesque Art* (cit. in n. 159), no. 94a–b.

[165] P. E. Schramm and F. Mütherich, *Denkmale der deutschen Könige und Kaiser*, i, 2nd edn. (Munich, 1981), no. 67.

[166] M. R. James, 'The Verses Formerly Inscribed on Twelve Windows in the Choir of Canterbury Cathedral', *Cambridge Antiquarian Soc.*, 8vo ser., 38. (1901); see also Caviness, *Windows* (cit. in n. 162), and N. Stratford, 'Three English Romanesque Enamelled Ciboria', *Burlington Magazine*, 126 (1984), 204–16.

1 (top) Part of the late-Roman hoard of Christian silver from Canterbury. (Canterbury Museums.)

2 (above) Opening part of the record of the Synod of *Clofesho* of 825. The charter records the settlement of the dispute for the control of the Kentish minsters of Reculver and Minster-in-Thanet, and was written by a contemporary Christ Church scribe in a fine example of insular cursive minuscule. (BL, Stowe Charter 15.)

3 (right) Silver pennies bearing the name of archbishops and produced by moneyers of the Canterbury mint from *c*.770 to *c*.925. 1. King Offa—Archbishop Jænberht. 2. King Offa—Archbishop Æthelheard. 3. King Cenwulf—Archbishop Æthelheard. 4. Archbishop Wulfred—*Doroverniae Civitatis*. 5. Anonymous (Wulfred) Wilnoth *moneta*—*Dorobernia Civitas*. 6. Archbishop Ceolnoth—Biornoth *monet'*. 7. Archbishop Æthelred—Ethered *mon'*. 8. Archbishop Plegmund—Æthelfreth *mon'*. (British Museum, Dept. of Coins and Medals.)

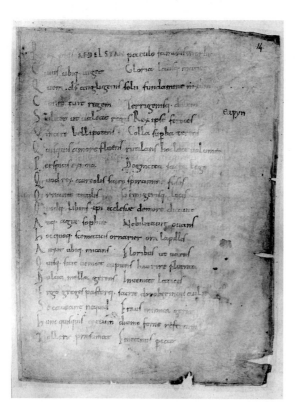

4 Verse dedication in elegiac couplets recording King Athelstan's gift of the Athelstan Gospels to Christ Church, written by a contemporary Continental scribe. (BL, Cotton MS Tiberius A. ii, fo. 15.)

5 (*below left*) Beginning of the Gospel of St Matthew, with illuminated Chi-rho initial, from the eighth-century *Codex Aureus*. The inscription recording the purchase of the gospel-book from the heathen army by Ealdorman Ælfred and his wife and their gift of it to Christ Church was added in the second half of the ninth century. The reproduction is taken from the facsimile in J. O. Westwood, *Facsimiles of the Miniatures and Ornaments of Anglo-Saxon Manuscripts* (London, 1868), pl. II, which was made before the pages were trimmed and the inscription in part lost. (Stockholm, Kungliga Bibliotek, MS A.135, fo. 11.)

6 (*below*) Decorated initial U and the opening of book II of Julian of Toledo's *Liber Prognosticorum*. Written at Christ Church in a graceful English Caroline minuscule script at the end of the tenth century. (BL, Royal MS 12.C.XXIII, fo. 23ᵛ.)

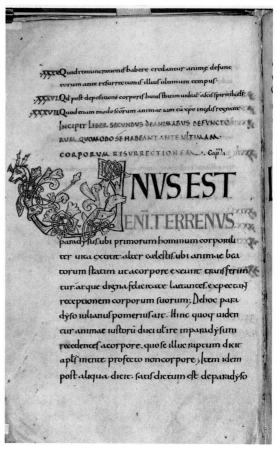

7 Illustration and text of Psalm 26 from the Harley Psalter. The drawings were based on those in the Carolingian 'Utrecht Psalter', but the text is Roman rather than Gallican. Here the psalmist's enemies are shown encamped against him, whilst (above) the psalmist approaches the Temple (centre) and seeks to hide in the Lord's pavilion (right). Script and drawings are of the early eleventh century. (BL, Harl. MS 603, fo. 16.)

8 Illustration of Psalm 21 (22), from the Eadwine Psalter, a version of the Utrecht Psalter made *c.*1160. Christ with angels (top); psalmist surrounded by oxen, dogs, and a unicorn (right); Temple with people, a feast, mothers, and armed men (left; illustrating later verses); in the centre are the Cross and instruments of Christ's Passion. (Cambridge, Trinity College, MS R.17.1, fo. 36ᵛ.)

9 Text and illustrations of Psalm 120 (121) from the Canterbury or Eadwine Psalter. Text in three columns, for the three versions of the Psalms (Hebraicum, Romanum, and Gallicanum), with notes for Gallican in the fourth column. (Note the French translation of Hebraicum and the English translation of Romanum, both interlineations.) The psalmist looks up to the hills and the protection of Christ (right); King David is in a walled city (left), with people going through a gate. (Cambridge, Trinity College, MS R.17.1, fo. 228.)

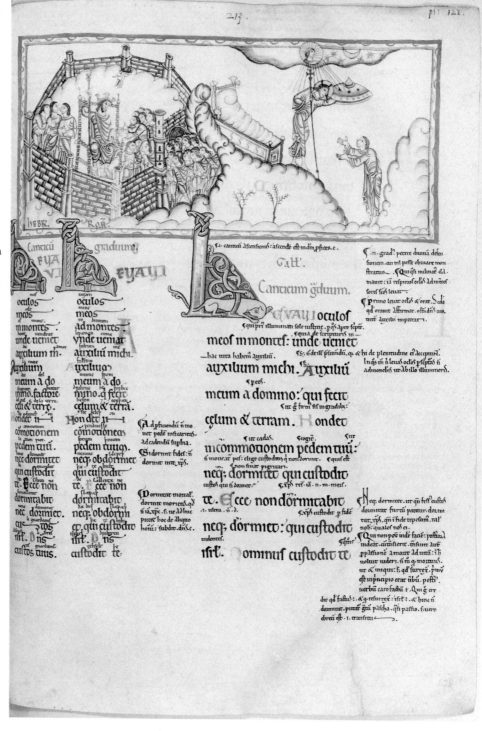

10 (*top right*) Western crypt, built by Archbishop Anselm *c.*1100; looking south-west.

11 (*right*) Fighting dragons. Capital in western crypt.

12 (*far right*) (*a,b*) Reliquary pendant given by Reginald Fitz Jocelin, Bishop of Bath, to Queen Margaret of Sicily, possibly in 1177. It contains blood-stained fragments of St Thomas Becket's clothing. (New York, Metropolitan Museum of Art, 63.160.)

(a)   (b)

13 Presbytery and Trinity Chapel, built to the designs of William of Sens and William the Englishman, 1178–84; with the high altar (as reordered to its medieval position in 1977), the archbishop's throne, marble pavement, and site of St Thomas's shrine.

14 (*left*) Eastern crypt, built when William the Englishman was master mason, 1180–4. St Thomas's tomb was between the two central marble pillars.

15 (*above*) Châsse for relics of St Thomas Becket, showing his martyrdom and his soul assisted by angels. Champlevé enamel on copper, gilt; *c*.1200x10. Once owned by John Batteley, archdeacon of Canterbury and canon of stall I, 1688–1708. (Glasgow Museums & Art Galleries, Burrell Collection, 26/6.)

16 Iron gate to the chapel of St Anselm. First half of twelfth century.

17 The prior's throne in the Chapter House which Prior Eastry rebuilt in 1304.

18 Archbishop Arundel with monks of Christ Church. From a table of contents added to a harmony of the Gospels which he gave to the Priory. (Bodl., MS Laud Misc. 165, fo. 5.)

19 Head of a monk from the vault of All Saints' Chapel; stated to be Dom John Wodnysborough (d. 1457).

20 Henry IV's chantry chapel, dedicated to St Edward the Confessor. Consecrated in 1440.

21 Dom John of Sheppey (d. 1439). East cloister walk.

22 (*left*) The Christ Church Gate, completed *c*.1520; the turrets were removed *c*.1803. Photographed before its restoration by the Friends of the Cathedral (1931–7).

23 (*below*) Meister Omers, built by Henry Beaufort, Bishop of Winchester, and completed in 1444. Later used as the best monastic guesthouse.

24 (*right*) The Water Tower and the Cheker, *c*.1775. Watercolour by Richard Bernard Godfrey. (Canterbury Museums.)

25 (*lower right*) 'Arundel Tower and Cloisters, north side, Canterbury Cathedral', watercolour by John Buckler, 1804. The tower was demolished in 1832. (Canterbury Museums.)

26 The nave, completed in 1405, with the strainer arches added for the central tower of *c*.1500.

27 Flemish panel painting of the Martyrdom of St Erasmus, showing Dom John Holingborne as donor; dated 1474. (Society of Antiquaries of London.)

(a)   *(b)*

28 Pilgrim tokens. (*a*) Ampulla. The Martyrdom of St Thomas. (Museum of London, TL74 1671.) (*b*) Badge. St Thomas returning from exile. (Museum of London, 82.8/3.)

(a)   *(b)*

29 Third seal of the prior and chapter (in use from 1232; Birch, *Catalogue*, no. 1373). (*a*) Obverse. Stylized view of Cathedral. SIGILLVM ECCLESIE XPISTI CANTUARIE PRIME SEDIS BRITANNIE. (*b*) Reverse. Martyrdom of St Thomas, between transepts of Cathedral. EST HVIC VITA MORI PRO QUA DUM VIXIT AMORI. MORS ERAT ET MEMORI PER MORTEM VIVIT HONORI.

30 Seal *ad causas*. (Birch, *Catalogue*, no. 1383.) (*a*) Obverse (in use from 1221). Martyrdom of St Thomas. SIGILLUM ECCLESIE XPISTI CANTUARIE AD CAUSAS. (*b*) Reverse (later date). The Trinity. DEUS PATER DEUS FILI(US) DEUS SP(IRITU)S.

(a)   *(b*

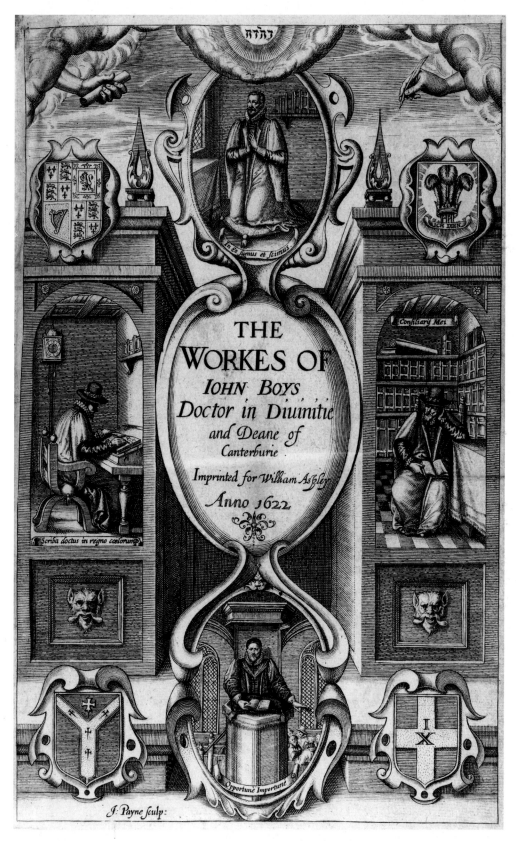

THE
WORKES OF
Iohn Boys
Doctor in Diuinitie
and Deane of
Canterburie.

Imprinted for William Aspley
Anno 1622

Scriba doctus in regno cœlorum

In eo sumus et scimus

Consistory Mei

Opportunè Importunè

J. Payne sculp:

31 John Boys, Dean 1619–25. Engraved frontispiece by J. Payne to his *Works* (1622).

The South Prospect of the Cathedral and
Metropoliton Christ Church of Canterbury

Ecclesiæ Cathedralis et Metropoliticæ
Christi Cantuariensis, facies australis,

Tho. Johnson delin: Wenceslaus Hollar fecit.

The Prospect of part of ȳ Metropolitane
Church of Canterbury: 1683:

Church yard.

32 South view by Thomas Johnson, engraved by
Wenceslaus Hollar, for W. Dugdale, *Monasticon
Anglicanum*, i (1655).

33 West front of Cathedral and Archbishop's
Palace, in 1683. South range of Palace built by
Lanfranc *c.*1080, adapted by Parker 1565, and
demolished 1844. (Bodl., MS Tanner 123, fo. 24.)

group of enamelled ciboria, the record of the lost frescos in the chapter house at Worcester and finally to an early thirteenth-century pattern-book of unknown origin that has long been in the library at Eton.[167] They are in the ancient genre of verse epigram that distils the meaning of a familiar biblical scene.[168] 'As Moses lifted up the serpent in the wilderness, so shall the Son of Man be lifted up' (John 3: 14):

> Mors est exanguis dum cernitur eneus anguis.
> Sic Deus in ligno nos salvat ab hoste maligno.[169]

Christ is the new David and the new Samson, destroying the gates of Gaza:

> Salvat ovem David sic Christum significavit
> Est Samson fortis qui rupit vincula mortis.[170]

As Jonah escaped from the belly of the whale, so Christ rose from the dead:

> Redditur ut salvus quem ceti clauserat alvus.
> Sic redit illesus a mortis carcere Ihesus.[171]

While the three related series of epigrams permit the reconstruction of missing scenes in the Canterbury windows, they are also a warning to the historian of late twelfth-century Christ Church. Indeed doubly so. Specifically, it is not possible to infer from the written evidence which came first—the Canterbury glass, the ciboria, or the frescos in Worcester. We do not know whether Christ Church is leading or following. More generally, such epigrams belong to the older literary tradition—monastic, but not exclusively so—that John of Salisbury had already perceived to be under threat in the 1160s, and would be overwhelmed by scholastic learning—the technical learning of the universities—by the early thirteenth century. Here the divergence of design between the glass of Christ Church and the glass of Saint-Denis expresses a real difference of sentiment, of cast of mind, and (be it said) of worldly prospects.

Setting the glass in context is worth attempting, if only to spell out what we do not know. Although the colours and the technique, and some stylistic details, recall the glass of the previous generation in Saint-Denis and Chartres,[172] these early Canterbury windows are not directly or primarily of Continental inspiration. Installed *c.*1180–1200, as soon as the Trinity Chapel was finished, it is likely that they repeated some of the details of the windows in the old choir, and even possible that they retained elements of its programme— for instance the lives of Dunstan and Alphege. The Ancestors of Christ are new; but here the closest parallels are in Winchester and the work of Winchester artists at Sigena in northern Catalonia.[173] The Canterbury windows would seem to be by English artists, working within a tried and familiar programme.

---

[167] Stratford, 'Enamelled Ciboria' (cit. in n. 166), with a concordance of *tituli* and good pictures.

[168] An immediate precedent has recently been detected in Augsburg a generation earlier: Caviness, *Windows* (cit. in n. 162), 81. The temptation to postulate an ultimate derivation from the work of Honorius Augustodunensis, of Canterbury and Regensburg, should perhaps be resisted.

[169] Ibid. 153.

[170] Ibid. 154.

[171] Ibid. 155.

[172] L. Grodecki, *Les Vitraux de Saint-Denis*, i (Corpus Vitrearum Medii Aevi, France, Études, 1; Paris, 1976), 25–8 *et passim*; Y. Delaporte, *Les Vitraux de la cathédrale de Chartres* (4 vols.; Chartres, 1926).

[173] W. Oakeshott, *Sigena: Romanesque Paintings in Spain and the Artists of the Winchester Bible* (London, 1972), *passim*; G. Zarnecki in *English Romanesque Art* (cit. in n. 159), no. 87.

THE MODERN WORLD 1185–1220

I had rather be a doorkeeper in the house of my God: Than to dwell in the tents of ungodliness.

Ps. 84: 11

The Archbishop's Business

Historians of Christ Church, then and now, have identified the archiepiscopate of Baldwin as a watershed in the fortunes of the community. Richard of Dover, who had spent all his adult life within Christ Church, had been archbishop through the early years of the cult of Becket and the great building programme. Richard was succeeded by a stranger and a Cistercian. On the face of it, Baldwin of Ford, Bishop of Worcester 1180–4 and postulated as archbishop in December of the same year, had excellent credentials. A learned monk, whose scholarly writings fill half a volume of Migne's *Patrologia Latina*, he also understood both the theory and the practice of running a diocese.[174] That indeed was the sticking-point. The successful conduct of archiepiscopal business had long required clerks to write letters and negotiate lawsuits. These were, increasingly, professional men: Baldwin himself had held just such a position as a young man in the service of Bishop Bartholomew of Exeter, the great canonist.[175] But these clerics who were permanently available to the archbishop were not best accommodated within his often itinerant household; they needed their own social and religious framework, and a steady income. William of Corbeil, if not his predecessors, had considered organizing them as a college of canons;[176] Theobald had simply maintained a large household; Becket's had been an alien entourage, disliked by the community but absent for long periods in exile with the Archbishop; Richard of Dover had been primarily concerned with the internal affairs of Christ Church. To an outsider like Baldwin, provision for the archbishop's clerks was a long-standing problem to be solved forthwith. He proposed the establishment of a house of canons half a mile north of the city.[177] The college of St Stephen and St Thomas Becket at Hackington would promote the efficient conduct of archiepiscopal business and remove secular disturbance from the precinct at Christ Church. On 1 October 1186 Baldwin secured three privileges for its support from Pope Urban III,[178] and set about the construction of the church and collegiate buildings.

The monks of Christ Church regarded the creation of a college at Hackington (or anywhere else) as detrimental to their practical interests and a devastating insult to their traditional role as the community of Augustine, founded by Gregory the Great, the first monastic house in England. The college was to be financed in part from a percentage of

[174] Migne, *PL* cciv, cols. 403–774.

[175] A. Morey, *Bartholomew of Exeter, Bishop and Canonist* (Cambridge, 1937), 105–12.

[176] William of Corbeil's proposal to refound St Martin's, Dover, as a house of canons had been condemned by the community at Christ Church: *Chronica*, s.a. 1136, in Gervase, *Historical Works*, i. 97–9.

[177] The dossier of this bitterly contested case survives in LPL,

MS 415 (s. xiii in.): *Epistolae Cantuarienses*, ed. W. Stubbs (RS, 1865). The monastic view is eloquently articulated by Gervase, in his *Imaginationes*: Gervase, *Historical Works*, i. 29–68. See now C. Holdsworth, 'Baldwin of Forde, Cistercian and Archbishop of Canterbury', in *Friends of Lambeth Palace Library, Annual Report, 1989* ([London], [1990]), 13–31.

[178] *Epistolae Cantuarienses*, nos. vi, dlx, and dlxi.

the offerings made at Becket's shrine: but money was not the crux of the matter. What the community feared, and justifiably, was that the archbishop would go away. Hackington would be no ordinary college of canons: one stall was allocated to the king, one to every bishop in the southern province, and one to every church in the archbishop's gift.[179] There would be sixty to seventy canons when all was complete. When the archbishop was not at court or on a journey, he would surely live at Hackington; visits to Christ Church would be few and fleeting. The unique primatial status of the community would fade away, and Christ Church be no better than other ancient houses: St Albans, Glastonbury, or St Augustine's, Canterbury.

By December 1186 there was deadlock. Prior Honorius was suspended from office, and both sides quickly marshalled far-flung and glittering support.[180] Baldwin could rely on his fellow Cistercians, the community invoked the Cluniacs. Most of the English bishops supported Baldwin, as did Henry the Lion. But Philip Augustus was for the monks. In Rome, Prior Honorius found the cardinals divided. The *deus ex machina*—for there would be no way forward without one—was Saladin, whose victory at Hattin the following summer prompted the Third Crusade. In December 1189 Richard I left for the East, and Baldwin followed him in March 1190. Settling his affairs before he departed, the Archbishop agreed to remove all the building materials that were lying at Hackington to another site, at Lambeth.[181] Thus, inauspiciously, Lambeth Palace assumed its role as the archbishop's alternative residence.

Baldwin died in the Holy Land; and his successors let the grass grow in Hackington. When the community secured a bull from Innocent III specifying that the proposed college should forever remain unbuilt (June 1201),[182] the monks might well feel satisfied. With great labour and expense they had defeated the Archbishop. But for the community it was an empty victory. What the monks wanted was not a defeated archbishop but a politically effective, modern archbishop who still lived in his community at Christ Church. They wanted the old days back again.

The Future of the Past

For the next fifteen years or so, the community may still have cherished that hope, for Hubert Walter was fully occupied in royal government throughout his archiepiscopate. As negotiator for Richard I's release from a German prison (1193), as justiciar and then chancellor for the decade following, and as *éminence grise* to King John, the Archbishop had little time for the community at Canterbury.[183] In the King's service he had clerical and legal assistance, and income, as he needed. Hubert Walter's archiepiscopal seal had the martyrdom of Becket on the reverse,[184] but he himself was always primarily the servant

---

[179] *Chronica*, s.a. 1186; in Gervase, *Historical Works*, i. 338.
[180] *Epistolae Cantuarienses*, pp. xlii–xlvi.
[181] *Chronica* s.a. 1190: Gervase, *Historical Works*, i. 483–4.
[182] *Epistolae Cantuarienses*, nos. dlii–dliii.
[183] C. R. Cheney, *Hubert Walter* (London and Edinburgh, 1967), 37–9, 90–114. Only three of Hubert's surviving *acta* concern Christ Church: *English Episcopal Acta*, iii: *Canterbury*

1193–1205, ed. C. R. Cheney and E. John (London, 1986), 56–60, nos. 387–9.

[184] The inscription runs: 'Martir quod stillat, primatis ab ore sigillat' ('By the primate's mouth the martyr puts his seal to the words that are distilled here'): W. de G. Birch, *Catalogue of Seals in the Department of Manuscripts in the British Museum* (6 vols.; London, 1887–1900), i. no. 1187.

of the King. So the community was left to its own devices. That so little is known of Prior Geoffrey (1191–1213) is proof that these were quiet years.

They were interrupted only by the crisis that followed the death of Hubert Walter (July 1205). Two men were almost established as his successor: Reginald the subprior, elected by the community, and the King's candidate, John de Gray, bishop of Norwich. Innocent III would have neither, consecrating instead Stephen Langton, theologian and cardinal, at Viterbo in June 1207. When King John refused to admit Langton to England, the Pope retaliated with an interdict on the whole country, which lasted from the spring of 1208 until the late summer of 1213.[185] The King replied by seizing the property of those who submitted to the papal ruling; the dispossessed redeemed their lands by heavy payments to the King. Thus it was King John who gained, substantially, in the first instance. Thereafter, Christ Church, like the rest of the English Church, had only to sit out the interdict: it was not catastrophic. But the considerable financial loss, both by the payment to the King in 1207 and by the inhibition of public liturgical ceremony, delayed the completion of the Trinity Chapel, and rendered unthinkable the proposed translation of the relics of Thomas Becket. The installation of glazing in the ambulatory of the Trinity Chapel ceased, and was resumed only in the autumn of 1213, under Prior Walter (1213–22).[186] Now at last the life and miracles of Becket were displayed in what the historian is not permitted to call glorious technicolour. That completed, a new and splendid shrine could be installed in the centre of the Trinity Chapel, and plans at last finalized for the translation of the relics.

The description of these great events falls to Professor Dobson; but they throw a retrospective light on the present chapter. By 1220 the only common ground between the community and its Archbishop was the cult of Becket. In all other respects the interests of the two were at best divergent and (as we have seen) at heart incompatible.

---

[185] For a clear analysis of events, with assessment of the effects of the interdict, see C. R. Cheney, *Pope Innocent III and England* (Stuttgart, 1976), 147–54 (election), 302–7 (interdict) and 308–12 (confiscation of property). King John had already evicted the monks of Christ Church for having accepted Langton (July 1207: ibid. 298).

[186] Caviness, *Windows* (cit. in n. 162), 157–64; 175–214; inception and resumption of work, 164. See also usefully, ead., 'Canterbury Cathedral Clerestory: The Glazing Programme in Relation to the Campaigns of Construction', in *Medieval Art and Architecture at Canterbury* (cit. in n. 1), 46–55.

III

The Monks of Canterbury in the Later Middle Ages, 1220–1540

BARRIE DOBSON

THE CHAPTER AND THE ARCHBISHOPS, 1220–1285

'Cantebire, chef de igleses de engleterre.'[1] When, in the middle of the thirteenth century, Matthew Paris produced his celebrated itinerary of the journey from London to Apulia, his description of the English kingdom's senior metropolitan cathedral could afford to be brief and to the point. Even for a St Albans monk, there could be no doubt of Canterbury's pre-eminence among the churches and monasteries of Britain, a pre-eminence recently and strikingly reinforced by its fame as the place where the most astonishingly popular of English thaumaturges had met his death. As they were always at pains to remember, it was to St Thomas Becket that the monks of Christ Church owed their unique position as not only the most powerful but also the most visited religious community in the land; and, for that reason above all, Tuesday, 7 July 1220, the day on which the body of the saint was translated from the crypt to the magnificent new chapel of the Holy Trinity at the east end of the Cathedral, represents the most appropriate point of departure for what was to be an illustrious monastic future. Presided over by Archbishop Stephen Langton himself, and attended by the twelve-year-old Henry III, as well as his Justiciar, Hubert de Burgh, together with seventeen bishops and numerous magnates, the translation of Becket's mortal remains in July 1220 was both 'one of the grandest state occasions' of medieval England and also the inauguration of the Jubilee of St Thomas, held regularly at Canterbury thereafter until 1470.[2] For Archbishop Langton, who had identified his cause with that of his famous predecessor during his own years of exile between 1207 and 1213, this was a ceremony which must have seemed the climax of his career:[3] but for the community of

---

[1] BL, Royal MS 14 C. VII, fo. 2.

[2] Walter of Coventry, *Memoriale*, ed. W. Stubbs, 2 vols. (RS, 58; 1872–3), ii. 245–6; Matthew Paris, *Chronica Majora*, ed. H. R. Luard, 7 vols. (RS, 57; 1872–83), iii. 59–60; R. Foreville, *Le Jubilé de Saint Thomas Becket du XIIIᵉ au XVᵉ siècle, 1220–1470* (Paris, 1958), 8–11; A. J. Duggan, 'The Cult of Saint Thomas Becket in the Thirteenth Century', in *St Thomas Cantilupe, Bishop of*

Hereford: Essays in His Honour, ed. M. Jancey (Hereford, 1982), 38–9.

[3] For Langton's enthusiastic reception at Rome when he brought relics of Becket there in 1220, see F. M. Powicke, *Stephen Langton* (Oxford, 1928), 145; cf. Duggan, 'Cult of Saint Thomas Becket', 37–8.

Christ Church too, the translation of St Thomas brought to a triumphant end the fifty most testing and tumultuous years in its history. No one present at Canterbury Cathedral in July 1220 had a greater cause for celebration than those elderly monks who could remember not only their imprisonment within their precinct at the hands of Archbishop Baldwin, in 1188–9, but also the greater and more recent calamity of a five-year exile (1209–13) at the Abbey of Saint-Bertin in the Pas-de-Calais for their loyalty to an archbishop thrust upon them by Innocent III.[4]

The resilience with which the monks of Canterbury recovered from the disasters of the reign of King John, to resume their traditional place as one of the wealthiest ecclesiastical corporations in England, is indeed the most striking feature of their financial records during the early thirteenth century. As early as 1215 the chapter had recovered almost all the property alienated during its exile, and its treasurers were thereafter soon able to repay the debts incurred before the Interdict.[5] Even more impressive were the large sums now being offered by visitors to the shrines of the Cathedral, and especially to those of St Thomas Becket, which reached a record level of over £1,142 in 1220 itself.[6] Such beneficence coincided with one of the most intensive building campaigns in the history of the Cathedral, a campaign deliberately designed to glorify the memory of the saint. By the 1220s the decoration of the Gothic choir and the new Trinity Chapel of the Cathedral was complete, and so too was the construction of Becket's own shrine, under the architectural supervision of Elias of Dereham and Walter of Colchester.[7] Within the next thirty years, and certainly by the time the exceptionally stylish Martyrdom door had been built to provide a suitably grand entrance from the Cathedral cloister into the holy place of Becket's martyrdom, the latter's canonization had long elicited many other sumptuous gifts to the fabric of Christ Church. Among these perhaps the most remarkable were the inlaid stone roundels possibly donated by the Abbey of Saint-Bertin to adorn the approach to the saint's mortal remains: these formed part of the display created by a splendid mosaic floor of *opus Alexandrinum*, quite probably donated by King Henry III himself.[8] In no way could the monks of Christ Church be unaware of their personal debt to the saint to whom

[4] According to an apparently well-informed chronicler at Winchester, 64 members of the community were forced to abandon their Cathedral during the interdict: *Annales Monastici*, ed. H. R. Luard, 5 vols. (RS, 36; 1864–9), ii. 80. For their dispersal to Saint-Bertin and other French abbeys, see Powicke, *Stephen Langton* (cit. in n. 3), 76. The names of only 29 of these Christ Church monks *in exilio* are preserved in Searle, *Chronicle and Lists*, 172.

[5] *Interdict Documents*, ed. P. M. Barnes and W. R. Powell (Pipe Roll Soc., NS, 34; 1960), 46–55; Smith, *Cant. Cath. Priory*, 16–18.

[6] Misc. Accts., 1, fo. 53; C. E. Woodruff, 'The Financial Aspect of the Cult of St Thomas of Canterbury As Revealed by a Study of the Monastic Records', *Arch. Cant.*, 44 (1932), 17–19.

[7] Matthew Paris, *Historia Anglorum*, ed. F. Madden, 3 vols. (RS, 44; 1866–9), ii. 242; cf. A. H. Thompson, 'Master Elias of Dereham and the King's Works', *Archaeol. Jnl.*, 48 (1941), 1–35. For the conception of the Trinity Chapel as a 'new kind of shrine-house' for pilgrims to the Cathedral, see M. H. Caviness, *The Windows of Christ Church Cathedral Canterbury* (Corpus Vitrearum Medii Aevi, Great Britain, 2; London, 1981), 158–64;

also *Age of Chivalry: Art in Plantagenet England, 1200–1400*, ed. J. Alexander and P. Binski, exhib. cat., Royal Academy of Arts (London, 1987), 197–8.

[8] Although the date of the (later mutilated) Martyrdom door remains controversial, this 'ripe production' seems more likely to have been built after rather than before 1250, as suggested in F. Woodman, *The Architectural History of Canterbury Cathedral* (London, 1981), 136; cf. J. Newman, *The Buildings of England: North East and East Kent* (2nd edn.; Harmondsworth, 1976), 216. The pavements surrounding Becket's shrine are well discussed in E. Eames, 'Notes on the Decorated Stone Roundels in the Corona and Trinity Chapel in Canterbury Cathedral', in *Medieval Art and Architecture at Canterbury Before 1220*, ed. N. Coldstream and P. Draper (British Archaeol. Assn. Conference Trans., 5; London, 1981 for 1979), 67–70. The 1220s and 1230s were characterized by exceptional expenditure on other *nova opera*, notably the building of a new refectory: see [R. C. Hussey], *Extracts from Ancient Documents Relating to the Cathedral and Precincts of Canterbury* (London, 1881), 7–8.

they owed such generosity and such good fortune. In 1221 they themselves decided to replace the traditional design of their common seal by a new one which included a representation of Becket's martyrdom half a century before. Thanks to their new saint's almost instantaneous celebrity, they could confidently look forward to a future in which— not least because of Honorius III's grant of an indulgence in perpetuity to all who visited Canterbury to worship at Becket's shrine—the cult of St Thomas was certain to experience 'un essor extraordinaire'.[9]

It is therefore all the more ironic that a monastic chapter which owed so much of its prestige and prosperity to a deceased archbishop should find it exceptionally difficult to establish an amicable *modus vivendi* with his successors. Yet such is in fact the major theme in the recorded history of the Christ Church community during the sixty-five years between 1220 and the appointment of Henry of Eastry as their prior, in 1285. Throughout this long and often dispiriting period, of no cathedral church in the kingdom was it more true that archbishop and chapter were dissatisfied partners, trapped in a marriage from which there was no escape. Paradoxically enough, the extraordinary posthumous popularity of St Thomas did more to exacerbate the inherent tensions between archbishop and monks than to reduce them. Whereas most other English bishops were gradually distancing themselves, both geographically and pastorally, from their cathedral communities, the awareness of the thirteenth-century archbishops of Canterbury that they were Becket's most immediate heirs normally led them to visit their Cathedral frequently; it also induced them to take a highly interventionist attitude to the conduct of worship and the monastic life within the Christ Church precincts. It was no doubt partly for these reasons that Stephen Langton completed Hubert Walter's great archiepiscopal palace-hall, to the northwest of the Cathedral, at 'prodigious' expense.[10] With the one exception of Boniface of Savoy, who spent long periods of his pontificate in France, all the thirteenth-century archbishops paid frequent and often lengthy visits to their palace at Canterbury.[11] More often than not, however, the Christ Church monks themselves, always careful to be well-informed as to their archbishop's whereabouts, awaited these visits with apprehension rather than eagerness.

For the monks of Christ Church, even more than for their counterparts in the seven other English monastic cathedrals, there was accordingly the greatest possible incentive to influence, if they could, the choice of their archbishop and titular abbot. In their own eyes, the ideal solution to this delicate relationship was naturally to elect a member of their own community to the metropolitan see; and on three occasions in the thirteenth century they hoped that they might achieve that desirable objective. As Prior John Sittingbourne observed—too hopefully—to his chapter as they prepared for the election

---

[9] Woodruff and Danks, *Memorials*, 122–3; Foreville, *Jubilé* (cit. in n. 2), 163–6; Duggan, 'Cult of Saint Thomas Becket' (cit. in n. 2), 39.

[10] For Archbishop Boniface's well-known claim that he deserved 'to be truly the builder of this Hall', because he paid the debts incurred by his predecessors, see Somner, *Antiquities* (1703), 128. Cf. 'The Great Hall of the Archbishop's Palace at Canterbury', *Arch. Cant.*, 43 (1931), 298–300; Woodman, *Architectural History* (cit. in n. 8), 133–5.

[11] See, e.g., Gervase, *Historical Works*, ii. 134–80; *Registrum Epistolarum Fratris Johannis Peckham Archiepiscopi Cantuariensis*, ed. C. Trice Martin, 3 vols. (RS, 77; 1882–5), i. 389–92; ii. 403, 538; iii. 1057, 1074, 1078; C. H. Lawrence, *St Edmund of Abingdon: A Study in Hagiography and History* (Oxford, 1960), 183–5. For a violent assault on the archbishop's palace when he was present in Canterbury in 1303, see *CPR 1301–7*, 197–8; J. H. Denton, *Robert Winchelsey and the Crown 1294–1313* (Cambridge, 1980), 182.

which followed Stephen Langton's death, in July 1228, 'if we are constant in charity we will be invincible, and if inseparable then insuperable'.[12] Such pious hopes were doomed to disappointment; and although Master Walter de Eynsham (in 1228), Prior Sittingbourne himself (in 1232), and Prior Adam Chillenden (in 1270) were all elected in turn by their fellow monks to the chair of St Augustine, these elections were all duly *cassata* at the papal Curia.[13] Like King John before them, neither Henry III nor Edward I was willing to accept the prospect of a Benedictine monk in the supreme ecclesiastical office of the realm, an objective attained only once thereafter, in the person of Archbishop Simon Langham (1366–8). More significantly still, the fact that the thirteenth-century English monarchy and the Canterbury chapter often failed to adopt a united front on the death of an archbishop enabled the papacy to control the appointment to the see of Canterbury more successfully than ever before or after. The result was that 'of the seven archbishops chosen in the thirteenth century, six were in effect designated by the pope'.[14] Even the one apparent exception to this rule, Boniface of Savoy, probably owed his *pallium* as much to the influence of his Savoyard relatives at the papal Curia as to Henry III's advocacy; and he too was capable of taking a markedly anti-monarchical stance during the political crises of the mid-thirteenth century.[15] One of Becket's legacies to his successors in the chair of St Augustine was that for well over a century after his martyrdom, the archbishops of Canterbury were not drawn—like most English bishops—from the ranks of the royal administrative establishment. Curiously enough, until the pontificate of Archbishop Stratford (1333–48), the most powerful prelate in England was often among the least typical of his colleagues on the episcopal bench.

Not that this development can in itself have been much comfort to the monks of thirteenth-century Christ Church, who found themselves subjected to the direct authority of archbishops who were more often theologians than civil servants, men of considerable academic talent who were thoroughly imbued with the 'reforming' zeal of the post-Lateran papacy but usually had no deep sympathy for the monastic ideal as such. Master Richard Grant, Chancellor of Lincoln Cathedral for the six years before Gregory IX provided him to the see of Canterbury as Langton's successor in January 1229, died in Italy less than two years later; but even within that short pontificate, he had proved a determined advocate of papal policy towards the English Church, as well as an opponent of too great an involvement by his suffragan bishops in secular affairs.[16] On neither of these two crucial issues do the sympathies of the monks of Christ Church appear to have been with the Archbishop; and it was accordingly hardly surprising that, on receiving the news of Richard Grant's death in August 1231, they proceeded to postulate as his successor the royal

[12] Gervase, *Historical Works*, ii. 115–22.

[13] Ibid. ii. 121–2, 127, 129, 252–3; Le Neve, *Fasti, 1066–1300*, ii. 6–7. In 1270 the Christ Church monks elected as archbishop one of their own brethren, Prior Adam de Chillenden, against the express wishes of Edward I. Only in Oct. 1272 did a new pope, Gregory X, break the deadlock by providing the first mendicant to the see of Canterbury, in the person of Robert Kilwardby: see Gervase, *Historical Works*, ii. 252; F. M. Powicke, *King Henry III and the Lord Edward* (Oxford, 1947), 586–7, 591–3.

[14] C. H. Lawrence, 'The Thirteenth Century', in *The English Church and the Papacy in the Middle Ages*, ed. id. (London, 1965), 119–56, at 146.

[15] M. Gibbs and J. Lang, *Bishops and Reform, 1215–1272* (Oxford, 1934), 19–23; but for a different view, see R. Stacey, *Politics, Policy and Finance Under Henry III, 1216–1245* (Oxford, 1987), 220–1. Cf. L. E. Wilshire, 'Boniface of Savoy, Carthusian and Archbishop of Canterbury, 1207–70', *Analecta Cartusiana*, 31 (1977), 4–90.

[16] Powicke, *Henry III and Lord Edward* (cit. in n. 13), 74–5; Gervase, *Historical Works*, ii. 128.

chancellor, Ralph Neville. However, Gregory IX was dissuaded by Archbishop Langton's brother Simon from translating Neville from Chichester to Canterbury, on the grounds that he was 'curialis et illiteratus'; he then quashed the elections of two other candidates (Prior Sittingbourne and John le Blund) acceptable to both Crown and chapter, before imposing Edmund of Abingdon upon the Cathedral community as its new archbishop, towards the end of 1233.[17] This was a choice that the monks of Christ Church were soon bitterly to regret. As early as 1235 the new archbishop was already taking legal action against his chapter for its failure to pay its alleged share in furthering the cause of John le Blund; and in the following year the monks were in their turn accusing Archbishop Edmund in the papal Curia of withholding not only the advowsons of several of their churches, but also the *exennia* to which they were entitled on their own manors.[18] So was inaugurated the most spectacular and least edifying dispute between an archbishop and his cathedral chapter in the later Middle Ages.

Most modern commentaries on the dramatic confrontation between Archbishop Edmund and his monks in the late 1230s have been at pains to stress the insubordination of the latter 'and how impossible it was for even the best of archbishops to manage his captious and litigious chapter'.[19] It might be more accurate to suggest that the 'multae controversiae et dissensiones' of 1238–40 bring little credit to either of the two protagonists but do reveal—like no other episode in the thirteenth century—the obsessive and not entirely unjustified nervousness with which the monks regarded their titular abbot. Appropriately enough for a religious house perhaps more notorious for its fabrication of documents advantageous to itself than any other English monastery, it seems to have been exposure of the forgery of charters within the cloister which precipitated the complete collapse of confidence between Archbishop Edmund and his monks. The former, aided and abetted by the convent's accursed Achitophel, Archdeacon Simon Langton, enlisted the support of the papal legate Otto to such effect that Prior John Chatham was abruptly forced, early in November 1238, to resign his office and enter the Carthusian order.[20] Within a few days of this initial victory, Edmund entered the Christ Church chapter house and made a serious error in announcing his dismissal of the convent's subprior, Ralph de Westgate, recently departed on a mission to the Roman Curia. After several weeks of further protest and perturbation, the monks themselves took the equally contentious step of electing Roger de la Lee as their new prior, in early January 1239: this unauthorized election was a 'nova res' which Archbishop Edmund never confirmed and which led him by a steady process of escalation into imposing a long series of sentences of excommunication on his errant flock.[21] Despite the public scandal of a conflict which allegedly brought the citizens of Canterbury to the verge of financial ruin, because of 'the withdrawal

[17] Paris, *Chronica Majora* (cit. in n. 2), iii. 206–9; Gervase, *Historical Works*, ii. 129–30; Le Neve, *Fasti, 1066–1300*, ii. 6; *CPR 1225–32*, 497; Lawrence, *St Edmund* (cit. in n. 11), 124–9.

[18] *CClR 1234–7*, 356, 524, 540; Lawrence, *St Edmund* (cit. in n. 11), 164–5.

[19] For Bishop Stubbs's comments on this 'tedious quarrel', see Gervase, *Historical Works*, i, pp. xx–xxi; cf. Knowles, *Religious Orders*, i. 261–2. The comparatively favourable interpretation of the archbishop's personality in Lawrence, *St Edmund* (cit. in

n. 11), 181–2, makes his intransigence towards the Christ Church monks even harder to understand.

[20] Gervase, *Historical Works*, ii. 131–4; Paris, *Chronica Majora* (cit. in n. 2), iii. 492.

[21] Gervase, *Historical Works*, ii. 134–80; cf. HMC, 5th *Report*, app. p. 439. A very different account of the factions among the Canterbury monks is provided by Matthew Paris's *Vita Sancti Edmundi* (Lawrence, *St Edmund* (cit. in n. 11), 254–6).

of merchants and pilgrims', the dispute was still raging as fiercely as ever when Archbishop Edmund died unexpectedly, on 16 November 1240, at Soisy, near Pontigny, on his way to Rome.[22]

So ended with unexpected abruptness what the late Dom David Knowles described as 'perhaps the most deplorable' of all controversies between medieval English cathedral chapters and their bishops.[23] Predictably enough, it had brought to the surface most of the sensitive issues at stake in the relationship between the archbishop and his monks, including the former's right to appoint the prior of Dover and his selection of obedientiaries in the Cathedral Priory, as well as the convent's insistence that suffragan bishops of the southern province ought to be consecrated at Canterbury.[24] This last claim has a good deal of bearing on what was the community's most obsessive fear of all. Ever since Archbishop Baldwin had first proposed the establishment of a handsomely endowed prebendal church immediately north of his Cathedral city, at Hackington, in 1186, the Christ Church monks had become notoriously alarmed by the danger that such a foundation might take over their role as the electors of the archbishops and as the Cathedral clergy of Canterbury.[25] Despite their success in preventing either Baldwin or Hubert Walter from implementing their proposals, there seems every probability that this was the most fundamental *casus belli* between Archbishop Edmund and his chapter over a generation later. Moreover, the monks were not unjustified in their anxieties on this source. According to a letter from Master Philip of Arden, a royal clerk at Rome in late 1228, no less a person than Pope Gregory IX had at least been prepared to discuss the possibility of suppressing the Canterbury community as the Cathedral clergy and replacing them by secular canons.[26] Among the monks themselves it was already believed that Edmund of Abingdon was contemplating the creation of a 'prebendal church' and the replacement of monks by secular canons as early as his visit to the Curia in 1238; and during the next few months plans for a great church at Maidstone, comprising no less than fifty prebends, were certainly drawn up by Elias of Dereham. In the event, the royal government intervened to halt the building operations at Maidstone; but there is a real sense in which the Canterbury monks of the late 1230s were justified in believing that their contest with Archbishop Edmund was a struggle for the continued primacy of their Cathedral church.[27]

For the monks of Canterbury, Archbishop Edmund accordingly proved a good deal more profitable dead than alive; and by the time of his canonization, in 1246, they could already afford to remember him with respect and veneration, as indeed they did at the altar within the Cathedral crypt dedicated to his memory.[28] Meanwhile, and after the painful trials of enduring the rule of a saintly archbishop, the Christ Church monks seem

[22] Gervase, *Historical Works*, ii. 173, 179–80; Lawrence, *St Edmund* (cit. in n. 11), 177.

[23] Knowles, *Religious Orders*, i. 261.

[24] Gervase, *Historical Works*, ii. 134, 153; C. R. Haines, *Dover Priory* (Cambridge, 1930), 82–3; I. J. Churchill, *Canterbury Administration* (2 vols.; London 1933), i. 273–4.

[25] Gervase, *Historical Works*, i. 335–8, 474–81; ii. 408; William of Newburgh, *Chronicles of the Reigns of Stephen, Henry II and Richard I*, ed. R. Howlett, 4 vols. (RS, 82; 1884–9), ii. 392; Knowles, *Monastic Order*, 319–20, 325–6.

[26] *Royal and Other Historical Letters Illustrative of the Reign of Henry III*, ed. W. W. Shirley, 2 vols. (RS, 27; 1862–8), i. 339; Gibbs and Lang, *Bishops and Reform* (cit. in n. 15), 78–9.

[27] *Annales Monastici* (cit. in n. 4), iii. 1501; Gervase, *Historical Works*, ii. 174; Lawrence, *St Edmund* (cit. in n. 11), 165–7.

[28] Woodruff and Danks, *Memorials*, 128. St Edmund's own ring was sufficiently highly esteemed to be placed on the altar of the Sword Point in the Martyrdom (Legg and Hope, *Inventories*, 135).

to have been generally content with the promotion of Boniface of Savoy. Throughout and ever since the pontificate of this longest-serving late medieval Archbishop of Canterbury (1245–70), Boniface has been a much-maligned prelate. He was certainly often an absentee one: he first visited his Cathedral in 1245, but was enthroned there (in the presence of Henry III and Queen Eleanor) only in 1249. So frequent and lengthy were his travels abroad that it was entirely characteristic that he should eventually have died in his native Savoy, in 1270. Perhaps more alarming to the convent than such absences were the consequences of having as their titular abbot a 'forceful, ruthlessly businesslike foreigner ... principally interested in pressing to their legal and logical conclusion his own rights'.[29] Undoubtedly the Canterbury chapter's attitude to Archbishop Boniface often manifested signs of acute suspicion. In the course of a struggle to defend their delinquent brother, Hugh de Cretinge, from punishment by Boniface, they actually denied the latter access to his own chapter house. Not too surprisingly, the Archbishop for his part held the opinion that 'simple fellows you are, but clever enough in mischief'.[30] Nevertheless, and despite these currents of animosity, Boniface of Savoy's long tenure of the see of Canterbury witnessed the crucial stages whereby the relationship between the archbishop and his chapter began to be stabilized and redefined after the disputes of the previous half-century. At Canterbury, as elsewhere in England, the reign of Henry III witnessed the emergence of a series of influential trained lawyers and administrators whose skills were soon applied to resolving the legal disputes which divided the archbishop from his monks. It was due to the services of men like Master Omer, a paid employee of the convent for over thirty years after 1249, and resident at the famous house—which still bears his name—within the Cathedral precinct, that some oil was now applied to previously troubled jurisdictional waters.[31]

Of all the many concordats and compromises relating to issues at stake between archbishop and monks which were produced in the middle of the thirteenth century, much the most significant was a definitive agreement made between Archbishop Boniface and Prior Roger of St Alphege before Hugh de Bigod, then Justiciar of England, in 1259.[32] At long last, a clear and workable division was made between the *baronia* or franchise of the archbishop on the one side, and the *libertas* of the Cathedral chapter on the other. In return for a payment to the archbishop's treasurer of 40 marks a year, secured on their manor of Godmersham, the Christ Church community was thereafter to enjoy the return of royal writs in the case of their own tenants: this was not only a privilege to be cherished because of the status it brought them, but also a responsibility whose exercise in practice was to test their administrative skills to the utmost for the rest of the Middle Ages. Of more symbolic portent for the future of the relationship between the archbishop and his chapter was Boniface of Savoy's firmly expressed commitment to defend and protect the laws and liberties of the Christ Church community by sentences of excommunication and

[29] Gibbs and Lang, *Bishops and Reform* (cit. in n. 15), 22–3; cf. Wilshire, 'Boniface of Savoy' (cit. in n. 15), 4–90; Gervase, *Historical Works*, ii. 186, 193, 202–3.

[30] Woodruff and Danks, *Memorials*, 130–2.

[31] Gervase, *Historical Works*, ii. 208–9, 221, 250–1; Smith, *Cant. Cath. Priory*, 69–70. For the origins of the Omer family, see J.

B. Sheppard, 'The Meister Homers, Canterbury', *Arch. Cant.*, 13 (1880), 116–7; cf. below, p. 95.

[32] *CPR 1429–36*, 415–24; Gervase, *Historical Works*, ii. 208–9, discussed in F. R. H. Du Boulay, *The Lordship of Canterbury* (London, 1966), 292–5.

interdict whenever called upon to do so by the prior or a member of the convent.[33] All in all, the later medieval archbishops of Canterbury usually honoured this commitment; and from 1259 onwards it was rarely indeed that the Christ Church chapter found itself needing to appeal to either king or pope against the aggression of its archbishop. From about the same time, the archbishops of Canterbury often began to see the monks themselves as their most natural allies in ecclesiastical politics. Accordingly, Prior Henry of Eastry could be relied upon to give the wisest—and most cautious—advice during the political struggles of the reign of Edward II, just as Canterbury Cathedral was the safest place of refuge to Archbishop John Stratford in 1340–1.[34]

The compromise of 1259 is therefore only the most obvious instance of the truism that the delicate relationship between the archbishop and his chapter was destined to become one of mutual reciprocity. However often they were at odds with one another, nothing henceforward united both parties more closely than any perceived threat to the liberties of the church of Canterbury from others. In particular, and again and again throughout the later Middle Ages, it was the monastic community of Christ Church which increasingly emerged as more sensitive than the metropolitan himself to metropolitan privileges. Of no issue perhaps was this more invariably the case than that of the obligation upon all suffragan bishops of the southern province to be consecrated in the Cathedral at Canterbury, unless they had received from the chapter a special licence to be consecrated elsewhere. Such an obligation seems to have been a cause of comparatively little anxiety to the Christ Church monks during the twelfth century; and it was only in the late 1230s, and at the height of their struggle with Archbishop Edmund, that the community fabricated the 'Magna Carta Beati Thome' to validate, amidst much else, their claim that suffragan bishops should be consecrated only within the church of Canterbury, 'cui tenentur ex professione et debita subiectione'.[35]

No doubt this particular cause was so vigorously promoted by the late medieval monastic chapter because of its sensitivity to the increasingly remote possibility that the metropolitan status of their Cathedral might be challenged by future archbishops of the see, as it had once been by Archbishops Baldwin, Hubert Walter, and Edmund. In the event, they were to be more or less completely successful in establishing the convention that all suffragan bishops should either be consecrated at Canterbury or be compelled to secure a capitular licence *alibi consecrari*.[36] When, for example, Archbishop Pecham provoked a *cause célèbre* in October 1284 by consecrating a new Bishop of Salisbury, Walter Scammel, at Sonning near Reading, Henry of Eastry (not yet prior of the Cathedral community) was sent to Northampton to discuss the monks' objections with the Archbishop: thanks to his intervention, as well as to the chapter's appeal to Rome, Archbishop Pecham paid his chapter £100 as compensation for this breach of their now traditional privileges.[37] From the late thirteenth century onwards, most English bishops of the

[33] Gervase, *Historical Works*, ii. 209.

[34] *Lit. Cant.*, i. 162–4, 172–4, 180–1, 194–5, 202–3, etc.; R. M. Haines, *Archbishop John Stratford* (Toronto, 1986), 283.

[35] Reg. I, fo. 85ᵛ; C. R. Cheney, 'Magna Carta Beati Thome: Another Canterbury Forgery', in id., *Medieval Texts and Studies* (Oxford, 1973), 87–9, 107.

[36] Churchill, *Canterbury Administration* (cit. in n. 24), i. 247, 273–5.

[37] LPL, MS 242, fo. 86ᵛ; BL, Cotton MS Galba E. iv, fo. 108; Decima Douie, *Archbishop Pecham* (Oxford, 1952), 184–5, 188, 286; cf. *CPR 1281–92*, 372.

southern province were in fact usually consecrated at Canterbury; and the Priory's registers leave no doubt that whenever this was not the case, the archbishop was careful to ensure that the convent's licence *alibi consecrari* was secured.[38] Until their final suppression, in 1540, the Christ Church monks continued to base this cherished privilege on the forged 'Magna Carta Beati Thome'; and the consecration of suffragan bishops at Canterbury continued to be one of the more notable liturgical events in the Cathedral.

Equally successful was the Christ Church chapter's campaign to exercise its authority in the much more significant and responsible arena of provincial and diocesan jurisdiction during vacancies of the archiepiscopal see itself. In this contentious field, the convent's major adversary was the archdeacon of Canterbury, most dangerously during the years between 1227 and 1248, when the archdeaconry was held by Archbishop Stephen Langton's brother.[39] In the weeks immediately after the death of Edmund of Abingdon, in 1240, Archdeacon Simon Langton launched a well-orchestrated assault on the prior and chapter's traditional right to exercise archiepiscopal authority during the vacancy.[40] Although this exceptionally bitter struggle was temporarily resolved by a compromise which allowed the archdeacon considerable powers of institution and collation within the diocese, the Canterbury monks never had any intention of making a permanent surrender of their jurisdictional authority during archiepiscopal vacancies. At the end of a long series of appeals by successive archdeacons of Canterbury, culminating in that made by Richard de Ferryng in the vacancy of 1292–4, the chapter seems to have made good, *de facto* if not *de iure*, its claim to exercise *sede vacante* jurisdiction within the diocese of Canterbury itself.[41] Of even greater consequence for the prior and chapter, and indeed for the English Church as a whole, was the outcome of the disputes which inevitably arose out of the convent's claim to exercise metropolitical, and not just diocesan, jurisdiction during vacancies in the archiepiscopal see. The principle that the clergy and the laity of the southern province owed obedience to the prior and chapter of Canterbury during vacancies had in fact been conceded by Pope Alexander III as long ago as 1179: but given that this issue brought the Canterbury community into direct and frequent confrontation with the bishops and with other cathedral chapters of the southern province, and that it regularly made them subject to the criticism that they were 'putting their scythes in another's harvest', it is perhaps remarkable that they were as successful as they were.[42] Of the many attempts made to resolve the multifaceted controversies which sprang up on the deaths of Archbishops of Canterbury, the most significant and long-lasting was the compromise of June 1278, whereby, after previous approval by the Bishop of London, the prior and chapter were formally conceded the right to appoint an Official of the vacant see, who would thereafter

---

[38] *Litterae licentiatoriae*, whereby the prior and chapter authorized their archbishop to allow one of his suffragan bishops-elect to be consecrated elsewhere than Canterbury, abound in the convent's late medieval registers; see Reg. S, fos. 115, 229, 251, 255, 256; Reg. T, fos. 445ᵛ–446, 448ᵛ, 450. Such a licence *consecrari alibi* was often requested of the prior by the archbishop himself (e.g. Reg. S, fo. 252) and perhaps only a minority of English bishops were eventually consecrated in Canterbury Cathedral (but see Searle, *Chronicle and Lists*, 21, 118).

[39] Gervase, *Historical Works*, ii. 131–3; Powicke, *Stephen Langton* (cit. in n. 3), 5, 7, 45, 104–5, 166–7; Le Neve, *Fasti, 1066–1300*, ii. 14.

[40] Gervase, *Historical Works*, ii. 180–2; Churchill, *Canterbury Administration* (cit. in n. 24), i. 550–1. For Simon Langton's earlier attempts to restore the archdeaconry of Canterbury to its previous dignity, see Ch. Ant. A. 43; HMC, 9th *Report*, app., p. 430.

[41] CUL, MS Ee v. 31, fos. 48ᵛ–49, 52ᵛ–53; Gervase, *Historical Works*, ii. 301; Churchill, *Canterbury Administration* (cit. in n. 24), i. 560–1; ii. 224; cf. Ch. Ant. A. 43–7, 101–6.

[42] *Papsturkunden in England*, ed. W. Holtzmann (3 vols.; Berlin, 1930–52), ii. 371–8; *CPL* 1484–92, 202–8; Churchill, *Canterbury Administration* (cit. in n. 24), i. 552–3.

exercise jurisdiction throughout the province on their authority. At the same time, the convent was officially conceded its right to confirm the election of all suffragan bishops during vacancies of the see of Canterbury, a right it regularly exercised as part of its general responsibility for the spiritual jurisdiction of vacant suffragan sees.[43]

In these and many other related spheres, the copious surviving registers of their exercise of jurisdictional powers during vacancies of the metropolitical see leave no doubt of the thoroughness and effectiveness with which the prior and convent took on administrative responsibilities which utterly transcended those of any other English monastic chapter.[44] That these responsibilities often created irritation among the secular clergy of late medieval England was all too often the case; but it was equally true that their occasional role as the supreme source of ecclesiastical authority within the kingdom afforded the monks of Canterbury unrivalled opportunities for prestige, influence, and indeed self-gratification. What other English cathedral chapter, after all, could wield the power exercised by Prior Thomas Chillenden and his brethren in January 1396, when they commissioned their archbishop-elect, Thomas Arundel, to crown a Queen of England at Westminster Abbey?[45] Well might the monks of fourteenth- and fifteenth-century Canterbury be pleased with the final outcome of their predecessors' long struggle to halt the erosion of their remarkably extensive jurisdictional rights *sede vacante*; and it was certainly with very considerable pleasure that, during the vacancy of 1292–3, the prior and chapter not only exercised metropolitical powers in vacant sees within the southern province, but also 'visited their chapters as well as the clergy and people, both in head and members, without contradiction from anyone'.[46] Although such supreme jurisdiction within the province during vacancies of the archiepiscopal see was not in fact entirely unchallenged in later centuries, the monks of Christ Church were more or less completely successful in maintaining their position intact. As late as 1487, for example, Pope Innocent VII had no hesitation in responding to a request from Prior William Sellyng with an explicit confirmation that he and his chapter enjoyed full jurisdictional and visitatorial rights in the province of Canterbury during vacancies of the see.[47] The chapter's legal victories of the thirteenth century remained victories to the end.

Quite apart from what was in many ways their single most weighty responsibility—the preservation of the spiritual overlordship of the archbishop of Canterbury when there was no archbishop—the prior and chapter of Christ Church were often a source of important advice and administrative assistance to their archbishops while the latter were very much alive. On the copious evidence of the chapter's surviving letter-books, the prior and his monks invariably showed great expedition in confirming and registering, as they were legally entitled to do, all the archbishop's most important acts, and especially his appoint-

[43] *Calendar of Institutions by the Chapter of Canterbury Sede Vacante*, ed. C. E. Woodruff and I. J. Churchill (Kent Archaeol. Soc., Records Branch, 8; 1923), 144; Smith, *Cant. Cath. Priory,* 9; Churchill, *Canterbury Administration* (cit. in n. 24), i. 553–4. For Archbishop Pecham's support of the convent's jurisdicton *sede vacante* (in a letter to the Curia) see *Reg. Epist. Peckham* (cit. in n. 11), i. 32–3.

[44] The best guide to the voluminous registers of the spiritual

jurisdiction exercised by the prior and chapter during vacancies of the see from 1292–4 onwards is D. M. Smith, *Guide to Bishops' Registers of England and Wales* (Royal Hist. Soc., 1981), 3–18.

[45] Reg. G, fo. 256; Churchill, *Canterbury Administration* (cit. in n. 24), i. 563.

[46] Gervase, *Historical Works*, ii. 301.

[47] CPL 1484–92, 193–4.

ments to the most responsible offices in the diocese.[48] At a much more personal level, the most important 'liaison officer' between the convent and its titular abbot was the Christ Church monk seconded to be a chaplain in the archbishop's household. Such an arrangement had obvious attractions, not only for the archbishop, who could, for instance, seek the expert advice of his monk chaplain before his visitations of the Cathedral Priory, but also for the prior. During the last years of his life, Henry of Eastry normally used Thomas Godwynston, the archbishop's resident monk, as his main channel of communication with his superior.[49] For obvious reasons, however, the office of monk chaplain was one of considerable ambiguity as well as influence, likely to lead either to the rapid promotion or to the personal downfall of its holder. Indeed, in the case of Thomas Ringmere, the chaplain of Archbishop Kilwardby who was appointed Prior of Christ Church in 1274, promotion was eventually followed by disgrace. Perhaps because of these dangers, the office of monk chaplain gradually went into eclipse. By 1324 Prior Eastry was already lamenting a long lapse in such appointments; and they were soon to be replaced by more occasional and *ad hoc* commissions to individual monks, who were dispatched to consult and advise the later medieval archbishops on particularly pressing business.[50]

Much more formal were the senior administrative offices in the archbishop's service which were held, albeit intermittently, by the Priors of Canterbury themselves at various times in the fourteenth and fifteenth centuries. Most responsible of all was the position of vicar-general in the diocese of Canterbury, an office so strenuous that it was naturally not compatible with the prior's duties towards his own community. When Archbishop Walter Reynolds asked Prior Eastry to serve as his vicar-general in 1319, the subprior and convent were quick to point out that such a responsibility would overtax the strength of an already overburdened superior.[51] Nevertheless, in October 1375 Archbishop Sudbury was not deterred from appointing Prior Richard Gillingham, together with two secular clerks, as his vicars-general; and in 1418, and again in 1420, Archbishop Henry Chichele commissioned Prior John Wodnesbergh as vicar-general during his own absences abroad at Henry V's side.[52] In such ways the priors of late medieval Christ Church were pleased to do what they could to serve their archbishops loyally; but there can equally be no doubt that the closest ties between the latter and the community were forged at common meetings in Canterbury itself. From the pontificate of John Stratford (1333–48) onwards, most archbishops were too heavily involved in senior administrative work for the Crown to visit their palace adjoining Christ Church as frequently as had their thirteenth-century predecessors; but they were certainly more regular visitors of their own Cathedral than most members of the English episcopal bench.[53]

[48] See, e.g., CUL, MS Ee v. 31, fos. 11ᵛ, 20, 258ᵛ; *Lit. Cant.*, ii. 251, 267; iii. 201–2 (the confirmation made by Prior Thomas Goldstone and his chapter of Archbishop Stafford's foundation of the college of Wye in 1449). Cf. W. A. Pantin, 'English Monastic Letter-Books', in *Historical Essays in Honour of James Tait*, ed. J. G. Edwards, V. H. Galbraith, and E. F. Jacob (Manchester, 1933), 202.

[49] *Lit. Cant.*, i. 36–7, 117–18, 239, 334, 390, 413–14.

[50] Gervase, *Historical Works*, ii. 278; *Lit. Cant.*, i. 509–10; ii. 10–11; iii. 138–40; Pantin, *Cant. Coll.*, iii. 43.

[51] Reg. I, fo. 364; CUL, MS Ee v. 31, fo. 31; cf. *Lit. Cant.*, i. 190,

for Eastry's complaint two years later that he was too ill to mount a horse.

[52] Churchill, *Canterbury Administration*, i. 30–1; ii. 5–6, 180–1, 223; E. F. Jacob, *Archbishop Henry Chichele* (London, 1967), 20, 22.

[53] Compare the relatively few visits to Canterbury recorded in Haines, *Archbishop John Stratford* (cit. in n. 34), 470–508 (Itinerary, 1323–48), with the many allusions to Archbishop Reynolds's journeys to his Cathedral recorded in *Lit. Cant.* i, *passim*. 15th-cent. archbishops also visited their Cathedral less often than one might expect, although they not infrequently made private visits

There were, however, some archiepiscopal visits to Canterbury which were awaited by prior and monks with particular apprehension. It was during the second half of the thirteenth century that the practice (it never evolved into a logical system) of disciplinary visitation of the Christ Church chapter by the archbishop first became properly established. At Canterbury, as elsewhere, such visitations have the double fascination of allowing the historian not only to observe a medieval religious house under close and critical scrutiny, but also to examine the relationship between a bishop or archbishop and his monastic chapter when the latter was at its most vulnerable. Admittedly, the procedure followed in English episcopal visitations provided no guarantee against *suppressio veritatis* on the part of a monastery intent on keeping its visitor at bay; and it has to be said that, compared with most English cathedral monasteries, the surviving visitation records of medieval Christ Church are neither very abundant nor very revealing.[54] However, these records, still insufficiently analysed, do at least testify to the fact that the monks of Canterbury never denied the archbishop's right to diagnose their spiritual and material failings before producing injunctions for their amendment. The chapter of a metropolitan cathedral which itself customarily used the spiritual arm of visitation against other churches during vacancies of the see could hardly resist being visited itself; and on this issue at least, the cloister at Canterbury was spared the bitter disputes which disfigured the history of a cathedral monastery like Durham.[55] Nevertheless, it seems to have been quite late in the century, and many years after the Fourth Lateran Council of 1215, that Christ Church was first subjected to a thoroughly well-documented archiepiscopal visitation. However, and although no direct evidence survives, it is hard to believe that Boniface of Savoy failed to visit his own Cathedral chapter at the time of his first recorded metropolitan visitation of the province of Canterbury, in 1250–1. Similarly, Boniface's successor, Archbishop Robert Kilwardby (1273–8) was so assiduous and vigorous a visitor of monastic houses elsewhere that it seems hardly plausible for him not to have turned his attention to his monks of Christ Church too.[56]

However, it is only in 1279, with the papal provision of the Franciscan John Pecham to the see of Canterbury, and the survival of the first extant archiepiscopal register, that the community of Christ Church can at last be seen exposed to the full rigours of a conscientious visitation. Whether or not actuated by a hostility towards the Benedictine order, Pecham clearly saw the formal visitation as both his favoured instrument for moral regeneration and also the ideal method of imposing his spiritual authority throughout the diocese and province.[57] Accordingly, it is no surprise that within a few months of his

to their palace and entertained distinguished guests there (Searle, *Chronicle and Lists*, 43–4). For the very dilapidated condition of the latter in the 1340s, see *Lit. Cant.*, ii. 284.

[54] See, e.g., J. Dahmus, *William Courtenay, Archbishop of Canterbury, 1381–1396* (University Park, Pa., 1966), 110–11; and for a partial exception, see *Kentish Visitations of Archbishop William Warham and His Deputies, 1511–1512*, ed. K. L. Wood-Legh (Kent Archaeol. Soc., Kent Records, 24; 1984), 1–5.

[55] Such disputes provide the major theme of C. M. Fraser, *A History of Antony Bek, Bishop of Durham, 1283–1311* (Oxford, 1957), and R. Brentano, *York Metropolitan Jurisdiction and Papal Judges*

Delegate (1277–96) (Berkeley, Calif., 1959).

[56] Churchill, *Canterbury Administration* (cit. in n. 24), i. 289–90; E. M. F. Sommer-Seckendorff, *Studies in the Life of Robert Kilwardby, O. P.* (Rome, 1937), 90–9. For Archbishop Hubert Walter's visitation of Christ Church as early as 1197, see C. R. Cheney, *Episcopal Visitation of Monasteries in the Thirteenth Century* (Manchester, 1931), 32–3.

[57] *Flores Historiarum*, ed. H. R. Luard, 3 vols. (RS, 95; 1890), iii. 82; Douie, *Pecham* (cit. in n. 37), 143–76; R. C. Finucane, 'The Registers of Archbishop John Pecham and His Notary, John of Beccles: Some Unnoticed Evidence', *JEH*, 38 (1987), 406–36.

promotion to the see of Canterbury, the new Archbishop informed Prior Thomas Ring-mere that he intended to visit his chapter 'in head and in members'.[58] Ironically enough, Pecham's visitation of his Cathedral Priory in 1279, like its sequel two years later, not only elicited the first full accounts we possess of the spiritual and economic welfare of the convent, but also occurred at a time when the monks themselves were undergoing a greater constitutional crisis than at any later point of their history. According to the revelations made at and between Pecham's two visitations, the chief cause of the monks' misfortunes was the financial incompetence of Thomas Ringmere himself, a prior probably thrust upon the chapter by Archbishop Kilwardby, very ill-advisedly, in 1274.[59] Although it was Pecham's own, mistaken policy to maintain Ringmere in office, a stream of letters that the Archbishop subsequently dispatched to Canterbury leave no doubt that the prior's authority had been eroded beyond repair, almost certainly as a result of the Archbishop's own two visitations of the convent. Fortunately, the creation of a series of more or less irregular monastic councils, committees, and caucuses allowed at least some of the convent's official business to be carried on in the absence of an effective prior. The early 1280s accordingly witnessed the largest number of constitutional and administrative experiments in the late medieval history of the monastery, not least because of Pecham's own iconoclastic reforming zeal. Most of these experiments proved abortive, like the Archbishop's attempt to terminate the traditional practice of prolonged absence on the convent's manors by the four monk wardens, criticized by the Archbishop on the grounds that monks who lived outside their religious house 'were not monks but demons'. However, other constitutional reforms during the last years of Ringmere's priorate, notably the council of senior monks at the convent's *scaccarium* or exchequer established in 1281, proved to have an enduring effect in accelerating the tendency for the prior of Christ Church to become 'in effect a constitutional monarch'.[60] On the other hand, it has to be admitted that the exceptionally turbulent as well as heavily indebted state of the Christ Church community between 1279 and 1285 demonstrates the dangers rather than the strengths of archiepiscopal visitation as an instrument of reform. Despite the lengthy and elaborate injunctions prepared by Pecham in the months after his 1281 visitation of the convent, Prior Ringmere was subjected to acts of extreme insubordination, including an appeal to Rome, by many of his brethren; he excommunicated no less than thirteen of them in June 1282. Despite Archbishop Pecham's attempts to act as a dispassionate arbiter among the convent's factions, the near-scandalous feuds and controversies within the community were not resolved until early 1285, with Prior Ringmere's dramatic and pre-sumably impulsive decision to take refuge at Beaulieu Abbey, where he temporarily adopted the Cistercian habit, before he finally ended his long and erratic career at Chertsey Priory, in 1311.[61]

The visitations of the Christ Church monks by John Pecham therefore reveal the difficulties facing any archbishop who wished to impose radical administrative reform

[58] *Reg. Epist. Peckham* (cit. in n. 11), i. 61; Churchill, *Canterbury Administration* (cit. in n. 24), i. 295–6.

[59] Gervase, *Historical Works*, ii. 278; Douie, *Pecham* (cit. in n. 37), 176.

[60] *Reg. Epist. Peckham* (cit. in n. 11), i. 89, 160–1, 188–9, 346–8,

389–90; ii. 397–403; DE 2, 106, *passim*; Douie, *Pecham* (cit. in n. 37), 177–86; Smith, *Cant. Cath. Priory*, 59–60.

[61] DE 73, *passim*; Gervase, *Historical Works*, ii. 292, 295; Douie, *Pecham* (cit. in n. 37), 182–8; Woodruff and Danks, *Memorials*, 158.

upon a deeply divided convent. By contrast, the visitations conducted by Pecham's successor, Archbishop Robert Winchelsey (1293–1313), took place after Henry of Eastry had replaced Ringmere as prior and restored a high degree of stability and harmony to the Canterbury cloister. In his own injunctions, quite unlike those of Pecham, Winchelsey could accordingly concentrate more or less exclusively upon comparatively minor shortcomings in the community's religious life, as well as upon a certain amount of disorderliness in and around the cloister.[62] In these familiar and hardly startling complaints, Archbishop Winchelsey's visitations were of course to be highly typical of the others conducted by his successors during the next two centuries. Later archbishops of Canterbury, if they lived long enough, were certainly at pains to undertake a visitation of their Cathedral Priory at least once; and an incomplete list of such occasions would include visitations by Archbishops Winchelsey (1298, 1301), Reynolds (1324, 1327), Stratford (1335), Islip (1350, 1355), Langham (1368), Wittelsey (1370), Sudbury (1377, 1378), Courtenay (1393), Arundel (1397), Chichele (1414), Stafford (1444), perhaps Kempe (1453), Bourchier (1484), Morton (1490), and Warham (1511).[63] Such a pattern of comparatively infrequent and episodic visitation by the ordinary is very similar to that encountered in other late medieval English cathedrals; and given the irregularity of these inquisitions by bishop or archbishop, it is hardly surprising that they never proved a fully satisfactory agency for achieving radical reform or sustained supervision of life in the cloister.[64] This generalization certainly seems to apply in the case of the Christ Church community, where it is admittedly only occasionally that the injunctions, let alone the *detecta* and *comperta*, of an archiepiscopal visitation survive.[65]

Fortunately, the first of Archbishop Winchelsey's visitations of his Cathedral church, on 6 February 1296, is comparatively well documented and gives a detailed impression of the procedure adopted at Christ Church on these occasions. After arriving in the Canterbury chapter house and preaching the usual preliminary sermon, Winchelsey was confronted with the not unfamiliar difference of opinion as to how many secular clerks he was entitled to keep by him during the subsequent proceedings. Once this had been resolved by a compromise, the prior and all the monks present were examined individually about all issues relating to the state of their convent. After returning to his palace, where it seems to have been customary for the archbishop to hold a dinner for the prior and his senior monks, it was as long as a month later before Winchelsey returned to the Christ Church chapter house to announce the preliminary results of his findings and impose penances

[62] BL, Cotton MS Galba E. iv, fos. 67–70; cf. *Registrum Roberti Winchelsey, Cantuariensis Archiepiscopi, 1293–1313*, ed. R. Graham, 2 vols. (CYS, 51–2; 1952–6), i. 68.

[63] Cheney, *Episcopal Visitation* (cit. in n. 56), 57, 60–1; T. L. Hogan, 'The Memorandum Book of Henry of Eastry, Prior of Christ Church, Canterbury' (Ph.D. thesis, Univ. of London, 2 vols., 1966), i. 212–14; *Lit. Cant.*, i. 119, 132–3, 152–3, 175, 209, 232, 240; LPL, Reg. Reynolds, fos. 80–1; Churchill, *Canterbury Administration* (cit. in n. 24), i. 139–47; ii. 38–9; Haines, *Archbishop John Stratford* (cit. in n. 34), 56, 459; *Registrum Simonis Langham*, ed. A. C. Wood (CYS, 1956), 229–31; *Lit. Cant.*, ii. 4; Reg. S, fo.

71; Searle, *Chronicle and Lists*, 34; *Registrum Thome Bourgchier, Cantuariensis Archiepiscopi, 1454–1486*, ed. F. R. H. Du Boulay (CYS, 1957), 457–60.

[64] Knowles, *Religious Orders*, i. 79–84; ii. 204–18; iii. 62–8; cf. R. B. Dobson, *Durham Priory, 1400–1450* (Cambridge, 1973), 231–8.

[65] See, e.g., *Reg. Bourgchier* (cit. in n. 63), 457–60. Visitations of the Christ Church community tend to be recorded with formal brevity only in surviving archbishop's registers; and the otherwise voluminous archives of the Cathedral Priory are similarly, and singularly, devoid of extensive visitation material.

on offending monks.[66] No less than another two years elapsed before the Archbishop produced his carefully edited *statuta in prima visitacione sua*.[67] To a much greater extent than Pecham's injunctions of fifteen years earlier, these *statuta* provide the first systematic review to survive of the conduct of the religious life within the Christ Church cloister. All in all, the results were not too discouraging; and it seems immediately obvious that eleven years after Henry of Eastry had succeeded Thomas Ringmere as prior, the monks of Canterbury were comparatively free from serious faction and personal scandal.

For Archbishop Winchelsey, quite unlike John Pecham two decades earlier, the chief cause for concern at the Cathedral Priory was less monastic indebtedness and insub-ordination than a dangerous relaxation of spiritual standards. Attendance by the monks at the *opus Dei* in the choir needed to be improved, while Winchelsey also ordered that the eating of meat ought to be confined to the convent's guest houses, the prior's *camera*, the infirmary, and the monastic *deportus* or small dining-chamber. Significantly enough in the case of a monastery which received more guests than any in the realm, the Archbishop criticized the Canterbury monks for not being hospitable enough to their visitors, especially when the latter were members of religious orders. Archbishop Winchelsey was also at particular pains to deprecate prolonged absence from the cloister by all members of the community. Only the treasurers, almoner, cellarer, and sacrist were allowed to leave the precinct without a companion; and the four monk wardens of the Priory's manors were enjoined to spend most of the year in Canterbury.[68] In many ways, these and the later injunctions produced by Archbishop Winchelsey after his 1298 visitation are the all too familiar commonplaces of episcopal visitation as practised at all late medieval English religious houses everywhere. They are none the less revealing for all that. Already by the close of the thirteenth century it apparently seemed to their Archbishop that the greatest danger facing the monks of Christ Church was neither internal faction nor economic bankruptcy, but rather the decline of their religious fervour and the trend towards what the late Dom David Knowles once called 'spiritual rusticity'.[69] If so, such a development was all the more ironical among a monastic community which in all other respects could pride itself on being more sophisticated than any other religious house in the country. However, and as the events of Thomas Ringmere's turbulent priorate may serve to remind us, a cathedral chapter may suffer even worse fates than a lack of intense religious zeal. For the future success of the Christ Church chapter in averting serious financial crisis and personal dissension, the main credit must go not to the archbishops but to the priors of Canterbury—above all to the most energetic and long-lived of them all, Henry of Eastry.

---

[66] *Reg. Winchelsey* (cit. in n. 62), i. 68–9, 91–3, 280; ii. 813–27, 1303–7; and for comments on this 'fullest account of [visitation] proceedings in the thirteenth century', see Cheney, *Episcopal Visitation* (cit. in n. 56), 59–61. In Feb. 1368 the Canterbury monks seized the opportunity of being visited by a monk archbishop, Simon Langham, to persuade him to dispense with all secular clerks during the proceedings (*Reg. Langham* (cit. in n. 63), 229–31).

[67] BL, Cotton MS Galba E. iv, fo. 67.

[68] Ibid., fos. 67–70; cf. Hogan, 'Memorandum Book of Prior Eastry' (cit. in n. 63), i. 145–63.

[69] Knowles, *Religious Orders*, iii. 460.

HENRY OF EASTRY (1285–1331) AND THE ROLE OF THE PRIOR IN THE COMMUNITY

During the four centuries since Archbishop Matthew Parker first drew attention in his *De Antiquitate* of 1572 to 'a Prior of the Church of Canterbury, Henry by name, one of great Prudence and singular skill in the Rights of the Church', the forty-six years during which the community of Christ Church was ruled by Henry of Eastry have usually been seen as the most dynamic and materially prosperous period in the history of the post-Conquest monastery. Nor is it hard to appreciate why the impressive administrative, financial, and architectural achievements of this 'explorator sedulus et sagax' should have won the admiration of scholars as diverse as William Somner and Robert Willis.[70] More recently still, Eastry's national significance as perhaps the leading English exemplar of efficient medieval monastic administration and estates management has been the subject of some of the more eloquent pages written by the late R. A. L. Smith and Dom David Knowles.[71] By any standards, the complex administrative machine so energetically directed by Prior Eastry during his long priorate is better documented than that of any English religious house of the period. Although only a small proportion of the voluminous archives of that priorate have yet to appear in print, it is in fact Eastry's own, almost obsessive, preoccupation with the written record which has earned him, not undeservedly, the high opinion in which he has long been held by historians of medieval Canterbury.

At times, the abundant original evidence for Prior Eastry's rule has admittedly tempted his admirers into giving him credit for supposed innovations in monastic policy and practice which had in reality been anticipated by his much less well-recorded thirteenth-century predecessors. However, not only does the extraordinary range and bulk of Eastry's correspondence tempt one to the thought that he may have been a more assiduous letter-writer than any other monastic prelate of medieval England: it seems equally evident that he was the first prior of Christ Church to inaugurate a methodical system of registration of documents, most fully represented perhaps by the convent's massive 'Register of charters, letters patent, and letters close' now preserved in the Cambridge University Library.[72] Among the archives of the Dean and Chapter of Canterbury themselves, there remains a large miscellaneous series of smaller registers and *libelli* which seem to owe their genesis to Eastry's determination to commit even the most insignificant financial account to preservation in register form. Similarly, it must have been at the Prior's own command or request that the correspondence he received from notables throughout the realm still survives as one of the greatest original letter-collections of medieval England.[73] No doubt the care with which these, and other more ephemeral documents produced at

---

[70] M. Parker, *De Antiquitate Britannicae Ecclesiae et Privilegiis Ecclesiae Cantuariensis cum Archiepiscopis Ejusdem* (Lambeth, 1572), 217; Somner, *Antiquities* (1703), 144–6; R. Willis, *The Architectural History of the Conventual Buildings of the Monastery of Christ Church, Canterbury* (London, 1869), 182–8.

[71] R. A. L. Smith, *Collected Papers* (London, 1947), 67–70; Smith, *Cant. Cath. Priory*, 70–85, 139–41, 162–79; Knowles, *Religious Orders*, i. 49–54.

[72] CUL, MS Ee. v. 31, fo. 1. This register, devoted to the period 1285–1327, contains 1,266 separately itemized documents.

[73] For a now somewhat outdated guide to the 'Eastry Correspondence', in the archives of the Dean and Chapter, see R. L. Poole, 'Eastry Letters', in HMC, *Reports on Various Collections*, i. (1901), 250–81. A small selection of the letters and other documents drawn from the convent's registers during the latter part of Eastry's priorate is published in *Lit. Cant.*, i. 40–360.

Canterbury in Eastry's priorate were preserved, testifies to the Prior's well-known caution and reliance on precedent in all his business dealings. It seems equally certain that the Prior deliberately amassed copious documentation, not least statistical, of his convent's affairs in order to defend his own reputation against his critics, as well as to impress his contemporaries—as he has impressed posterity—with his energy and diligence. Appropriately enough, the most handsomely produced administrative record of Eastry's priorate to survive is the aptly named *Memoriale multorum Henrici Prioris* (BL, Cotton MS Galba E. iv). The 244 folios of this volume not only document the financial success of his administration by a bewildering variety of calculations (e.g. by demonstrating the way in which the total income received by the convent's treasurers rose from only £1,927 when he became prior, in 1285, to £2,926 16s. 5d. in 1331), but also contains Eastry's most impressive piece of self-justification, his impressive list of *Nova Opera* carried out in the church and precincts as well as on the manors of Christ Church during the first thirty-seven years of his priorate.[74]

The long period of Henry of Eastry's priorate accordingly provides the historian of the church of Canterbury with the first real opportunity to observe the heavy responsibilities and ceaseless administrative routines of the prior of Christ Church as they were experienced by that prior himself. No doubt the strains and stresses of the office had always been considerable, sufficient indeed to force two of Eastry's recent predecessors into complete retirement: John Chatham as a Carthusian in 1238, and Thomas Ringmere as a Cistercian at Beaulieu (and later a hermit in Brookwood Forest) in 1285.[75] By contrast, Henry of Eastry was prior for no less than forty-six years, a term of office hard to parallel at any medieval religious house and one certainly unrivalled by any of his sixteen successors at Canterbury: of the latter, only four ruled as prior of Christ Church for more than twenty years, namely Robert Hathbrand (1338–70), Dr Thomas Chillenden (1391–1411), Dr William Sellyng (1472–94), and Master Thomas Goldstone (1495–1517).[76] So long a priorate had many obvious advantages, not least that Eastry himself enjoyed the unique experience of close collaboration with no less than four successive archbishops of Canterbury.

Indeed, perhaps the most significant conclusion that can be drawn from Prior Eastry's voluminous correspondence is the central importance of that collaboration to the harmony and welfare of the Christ Church community. Despite occasional periods of tension, the Prior was generally remarkably successful in squaring the difficult circle of presenting himself as his archbishop's loyal subject while at the same time dissuading the latter from intervening too peremptorily or too closely in the affairs of his Cathedral. Thus, although there was usually little love lost between the Benedictine monks of Canterbury and the zealous Archbishop John Pecham (1279–92), a letter of remonstrance on Eastry's part was sufficiently strongly worded to ensure that this first Franciscan to

---

[74] BL, Cotton MS Galba E. iv, fos. 101–109ᵛ; cf. Hogan, 'Memorandum Book of Prior Eastry' (cit. in n. 63), esp. i. 328–40. The remarkable multiplication of registers and cartularies compiled at Christ Church during Eastry's priorate almost certainly made its estates and other properties the most assiduously documented in early 14th-cent. England: see, e.g., Regs. J and K, and G. R. C. Davis, *Medieval Cartularies of Great Britain: A*

Short Catalogue (London, 1958), 21–2. For a slightly inaccurate English translation of only a small section of Eastry's account of his *Nova Opera*, see Knowles, *Religious Orders*, i. 322–5.

[75] BL, Cotton MS Cleopatra C. vii, fo. 15ᵛ; Gervase, *Historical Works*, ii. 133–4, 292, 295; see above, pp. 73, 81.

[76] Le Neve, *Fasti, 1300–1541*, iv. 5–6.

become primate of all England was buried not, as he had originally intended, at the new Grey Friars church in London, but within the Martyrdom of the Cathedral which he had failed to reform as thoroughly as he would have wished.[77] Robert Winchelsey's courageous defence of what he saw as the liberties of the *ecclesia Anglicana* during the twenty turbulent years (1293–1313) of his archiepiscopate inevitably exposed his monks of Canterbury to political dangers only too reminiscent of the age of Stephen Langton and King John. On 21 February 1297, for example, royal agents took possession of the priory and locked up its cellars and storehouses shortly after Archbishop Winchelsey had used the Cathedral church at Canterbury to preach a sermon aimed directly against Edward I himself. In the event, Prior Eastry displayed his usual discretion and was able to extricate his convent from the worst consequences of supporting Winchelsey in his struggles against Edward I and Edward II; he did so while retaining the favour of the Archbishop himself, who not only regarded him as a 'faithful' ally but also employed him as his vicar-general throughout the diocese of Canterbury in 1308.[78]

Prior Eastry was clearly much more whole-hearted in his support, circumspect though it was, for the campaign to canonize Robert Winchelsey in the years after the latter's death in 1313; but the acquisition of yet another saintly archbishop among the patrons of Canterbury Cathedral was a triumph which eluded him as it eluded all the other advocates of Winchelsey's canonization.[79] By contrast, the latter's successor as archbishop, Walter Reynolds (1313–27), could certainly not be regarded as a saint, and may even have been 'of all archbishops of Canterbury the least deserving of respect'.[80] Prior Eastry himself, to judge from the exceptionally large number of letters he wrote to Lambeth during the second half of Edward II's reign, showed little enough respect for Reynolds's political acumen. It seems clear enough that the Archbishop rarely resented, usually welcomed, and often acted upon the advice he received from the Prior in such profusion, especially during the national political feuds and faction of the 1320s.[81] So, to an even greater degree, did Archbishop Simon Meopham (1328–33), whose occasional attempts to take new initiatives affecting his Cathedral—for example, by permitting holy orders to be conferred in the monastic infirmary—were brought to nothing by Henry of Eastry, that masterly exponent of procrastination and self-confessed advocate of the *via media* in public affairs.[82]

Henry of Eastry's success in keeping his four archbishops at a respectable if respectful distance by varying the tone of his responses to their requests and demands seems to have been emulated by most of his successors as prior of Christ Church. From Eastry's time onwards, bitter disputes between the archbishop and his prior were very infrequent, even

[77] Wilkins, *Concilia*, ii. 184–5. In the event, Pecham's heart was buried behind the high altar of the London Franciscan priory, but his other mortal remains, together with his oak effigy, went to Canterbury (Douie, *Pecham* (cit. in n. 37), 182–91, 338).

[78] *William Thorne's Chronicle of Saint Augustine's Abbey, Canterbury,* trans. A. H. Davis (Oxford, 1934), 326–7; *Bartholomaei de Cotton Historia Anglicana,* ed. H. R. Luard (RS, 16; 1859), 332; Denton, *Winchelsey and the Crown* (cit. in n. 11), 111–12, 246; HMC, 9th *Report,* app., pp. 446–8.

[79] Ch. Ant., 169; HMC, 5th *Report,* app., p. 433; Wharton,

Anglia Sacra, i. 11–17; *Lit. Cant.,* iii. 398, 401–2; Denton, *Winchelsey and the Crown* (cit. in n. 11), 15–33; C. E. Woodruff, 'The Miracles of Archbishop Winchelsey', *Trans. St Paul's Ecclesiological Soc.,* 10, pt. 4 (1938), 111–23.

[80] *DNB,* s.v. Reynolds. For a not altogether successful attempt to rehabilitate Reynolds's reputation, see J. R. Wright, *The Church and the English Crown, 1305–1334: A Study Based on the Register of Archbishop Walter Reynolds* (Toronto, 1980).

[81] *Lit. Cant.,* i, pp. lxxxiv–xc, 172–206.

[82] Ibid. i. 244–50, *et passim;* Knowles, *Religious Orders,* i. 52.

by the standards of other monastic cathedrals. For example, not one late medieval prior of Canterbury Cathedral ever seems to have been threatened with deposition; and as there were no instances of resignation, all the priors did in fact die in office. The prospects of the archbishop being able to work harmoniously with his Cathedral prior were in any case probably enhanced by the highly unusual electoral procedure at Canterbury, which gave the former considerably more scope to intervene in the selection of the latter than was true of other English monastic cathedrals. Admittedly, the right to elect its own prior in vacancies of the metropolitan see had been conceded to the Canterbury chapter long ago, by bulls of Popes Alexander III and Urban III in 1174 and 1187 respectively.[83] However, the much more important and potentially extremely contentious issue of the role of the archbishop in the electoral process *sede plena* seems only to have been fully determined and agreed by both parties in the second half of the thirteenth century. In theory at least, the archbishop never surrendered his own traditional right to appoint the Prior of Canterbury.

According to the *Forma electionis prioris* preserved in Prior Eastry's memorandum book, it was for the archbishop himself, after he had received news of the death of the previous prior from a monastic delegation, to direct the subprior to summon all the members of the community to meet him in the chapter house at Canterbury on a predetermined day. As the appointment of a new prior rarely took place at a date later than three weeks after the death of his predecessor, it was only after a short interval that the Canterbury monks assembled in the chapter house, where their votes were duly recorded on a parchment roll, usually by the archbishop himself, but sometimes by his chaplain or another deputy. On the following day, after a night in his palace considering the qualities of the candidates, the archbishop or his representative returned to the chapter house to announce the name of the monk whom not necessarily the majority but the 'sanior pars' had nominated and whom he now appointed ('prefecit') as prior.[84] The elect, after a customary declaration of his unworthiness for so high an office, was then led in procession to the choir of the Cathedral for his installation at the hands of the archbishop, before they both returned to the chapter house, where the prior was placed in the seat he was to occupy at chapter meetings for the remainder of his life. With a very few exceptions, most surprisingly in the case of William Petham, who was apparently nominated prior in the politically turbulent year of 1471 by Nicholas Faunt, Mayor of Canterbury, this procedure was followed more or less exactly until the suppression of the monastery.[85] Most late medieval archbishops did in fact regard the appointment of a new prior of Christ Church as a sufficiently important cause to warrant the journey to Canterbury.[86] It must seem likely that their personal position as scrutators of the votes cast by the monks afforded them the opportunity to exercise real control over the choice of the successful candidate, unless a very clear majority

[83] *Papsturkunden in England* (cit. in n. 42), ii. 323, 445; Smith, *Cant. Cath. Priory,* 29.

[84] BL, Cotton MS Galba E. iv, fo. 26; and cf. Reg. O, fo. 151. Of the many surviving accounts of prior's elections recorded in the convent's registers, that of Prior Richard Oxenden on 26 Apr. 1331 (Reg. G, fo. 22ᵛ) is especially informative.

[85] Searle, *Chronicle and Lists,* 21, 39, 46, 105–6, 116. An important feature of 15th-cent. prior's elections was the long *collatio*

or address delivered by the archbishop or his representative, like that of Master Richard Andrew on behalf of Archbishop Chichele at John Salisbury's election in Mar. 1438 (HMC, 9th *Report,* app., pt. 1, p. 102).

[86] Thus Archbishop Pecham was present at Eastry's election in Apr. 1285 (Douie, *Pecham* (cit. in n. 37), 186): for some 15th-cent. examples, see Reg. S, fos. 231, 249, 251–3.

existed within the convent. At the least, the unique electoral procedure practised at Canterbury must have minimized the chances of appointing a prior who was highly antipathetic to either archbishop or chapter; and at the most it appears—unless the quite copious evidence misleads—to have reduced the dangers of the factionalism which frequently disfigured elections of abbots and priors in other late medieval English monasteries.

Immediately after their appointment by means of this selection process, the priors of Christ Church, like Henry of Eastry on 8 April 1285, were entitled to the use of the *pontificalia*, undoubtedly the most important and highly valued symbol of their prestige. Their prior's right to use the mitre and the ring in processions and on the chief festivals of the year was of especial significance in the eyes of the Canterbury monks, because the acquisition of these *pontificalia* in January 1221 seems to have been the first of its kind and had given the greatest possible publicity to the outstanding fame of their Cathedral and their recently translated saint.[87] By the late thirteenth century, however, papal grants of mitre and ring to English abbots and priors were sufficiently common to deprive them of any particularly distinctive value; indeed, in 1341 and 1355 Prior Robert Hathbrand was highly concerned that other cathedral priors, especially the prior of Worcester, enjoyed the use of various *pontificalia* (like the tunic, sandals, and pastoral staff) not yet possessed by himself. For Hathbrand, as for his predecessors and successors, such an injustice deserved urgent amendment by the pope on the grounds that 'the priors of Christ Church excel all other priors in England in dignity and honour'.[88] In the event, Urban VI did rectify this anomaly, in 1378, by adding to the prior's existing *pontificalia* of mitre, ring, dalmatic, and gloves the right of wearing the sandals and carrying the crozier of a bishop, together with the legal authority to confer a solemn benediction after mass and other notable liturgical offices. After 1434, when these highly prized privileges were confirmed by Eugenius IV, the honorific dignity of the priors of Christ Church was as secure as papal grants could make it.[89]

Valuable though such *pontificalia* were to the self-esteem of the late medieval priors of Christ Church, much more significant in practice were those jurisdictional and other privileges which they tried to extract, often with considerable difficulty, from their archbishops. Most important of all was the ability to control, if not absolutely to determine, the recruitment of novices into the cloister and the right to appoint most, if not at all, of the monastery's obedientiaries. Both issues were controversial and, in the event, both were resolved only by compromise solutions which left the archbishop with a good deal of his formal authority intact while allowing the prior considerable influence on the matters of substance. In particular, it was obviously of very considerable importance to a prior of Christ Church not to have uncongenial monks intruded into high administrative office within the convent by an unsympathetic archbishop. Accordingly, only the archbishop himself is ever likely to have been content with Urban III's bull of 1187 which entitled him to appoint the subprior, precentor, and sacrist of the monastery, as well as

[87] Bodl., MS Tanner 165, fo. 118; *Annales Monastici* (cit. in n. 4), iii. 66; Knowles, *Religious Orders*, i. 259.

[88] *Lit. Cant.*, ii. 241–3, 328–32.

[89] Bodl., MS Tanner 165, fo. 117ᵛ; Reg. A, fo. 26; Woodruff and Danks, *Memorials*, 225. Chief credit for gaining these privileges was given by the convent to Prior Thomas Chillenden (BL, Arundel MS 68, fo. 58).

the prior himself, leaving to the latter the choice of all the other obedientiaries, after consulting his senior colleagues.[90] Such an arrangement was predestined to become a source of friction between the archbishop and his chapter thereafter. Despite several attempts to do so, the prior and chapter were never successful in releasing the archbishop's titular hold over the appointment to these offices, and that of the chamberlain too; but at least they were quick to protest when any archbishop, such as John Pecham in 1281, tried to extend his control over monastic appointments even further.[91] Much more contentious was the procedure to be adopted by the prior and chapter when one of the obediences to which the archbishop had the right of appointment became vacant. After a long series of disputes on this issue, notably with Archbishop Winchelsey in the late 1290s, the monks reluctantly conceded that they were obliged to send forward at least three names to the archbishop when the offices of (at least) subprior, sacrist, precentor, or chamberlain needed to be filled.[92] However, as the priors of Christ Church can often be seen trying to influence the archbishop's choice by informing him of the monk they considered most suitable for the office in question, it seems likely that in the great majority of cases Prior Eastry and his successors did come to enjoy what they most desired—effective control of appointment to obediences within the cloister.[93]

Whether the priors of late medieval Canterbury would have found it wise to promote members of their community to office or to take other important initiatives without securing the consent of at least their senior colleagues in the monastery is another matter entirely. All the available evidence suggests that, even in the case of a superior as formidable as Henry of Eastry, the priors of Christ Church—whatever their high status and prestige in the outside world—found it advisable to consult their brethren as fully as possible. In August 1282 Archbishop Pecham had specifically enjoined that all appointments to the Cathedral's offices should be carefully discussed in the convent's *scaccarium* by the prior and at least six of his senior monks before the recommendation of suitable persons was made to a subsequent chapter-meeting. More than forty years later, Prior Eastry himself was at pains to point out to Archbishop Reynolds, when discussing the proposed return to the Canterbury cloister of a penitent fugitive monk, that 'arduous business should be dealt with by the counsel and assent of all the brethren and nothing should be determined against the will of the convent'.[94] Although Eastry sometimes had to face acts of defiance on the part of dissident members of his flock, his correspondence suggests that he was highly skilled in the important art of managing the monks of so large a community.[95] Only

[90] *Papsturkunden in England* (cit. in n. 42), ii. 447–8; Smith, *Cant. Cath. Priory*, 33.

[91] *Reg. Epist. Peckham* (cit. in n. 11), i. 245. For an attempt by Prior Richard Oxenden in the 1330s to persuade the archbishop to give up his right of appointment to these obediences, see *Lit. Cant.*, ii. 106–8.

[92] However, the chapter's claim to appoint its sacrists and chamberlains without the intervention of the archbishop seems to have been a novel and at times controversial matter; and by the late 14th-cent. it was also generally accepted that the monk warden of Canterbury College, Oxford, as well as the two monk penitentiaries of the Cathedral should be chosen by the archbishop from three names submitted to him by the prior

and chapter: see LPL, Reg. Islip, fos. 21ᵛ–22; Reg. Wittelsey, fo. 13; *Reg. Langham* (cit. in n. 63), 282–3, 287, 293, 310, 315; Pantin, *Cant. Coll.*, iv. 77.

[93] In 1344, and again nine years later, Prior Hathbrand tried to dictate the choice of obedientiary by the device of pronouncing one of the chapter's three candidates to be the most suitable monk to hold the office (*Lit. Cant.*, ii. 276–7, 318–19; cf. DE 51).

[94] *Reg. Epist. Peckham* (cit. in n. 11), ii. 403–4; *Lit. Cant.*, i. 232–3.

[95] For Eastry's advice to his subprior on the qualities needed by successful obedientiaries, see *Lit. Cant.*, i. 309. The most serious conspiracy against Prior Eastry's rule was that led by the apostate monk, Robert of Thanet, and his colleague Robert de Alyndon; see Eastry Correspondence, i, nos. 18, 29, 32, 56;

occasionally did he or his successors have to face a serious challenge to their authority; and although evidence for personal faction within the convent may well have been suppressed by the chapter, an argument *ex silentio* would at least suggest that acts of deliberate insubordination were less frequent at Canterbury than at many monastic cathedrals.

In the case of all but very serious offences, however, the responsibility for preserving discipline within the cloister was delegated by the prior to other senior monks, and in particular to his *priores claustrales*, who were both more numerous and more important at Christ Church than in other major Benedictine houses. Admittedly, the chapters of other monastic cathedrals, like the community of St Cuthbert at Durham, normally used the services of a third prior, in addition to the subprior; but at Canterbury there emerged a fourth as well as a third prior, both entrusted with such miscellaneous supervisory responsibilities as the security of Archbishop Chichele's new monastic library in the middle of the fifteenth century.[96] Of much more, and indeed critical, significance for personal harmony within the convent was its subprior, usually a senior monk who held the office for several years and sometimes later became prior himself.[97] At least by the end of the fourteenth century, the subprior of Christ Church enjoyed the use of his own *camera* (now completely destroyed), in the south aisle of the infirmary hall, and was assisted in his duties not only by a lay servant but also by a young monastic chaplain assigned to his service.[98] The duties of the subprior were naturally at their most onerous and indispensable during the vacancies, short though these were, between the death of one prior and the appointment of his successor. However, the subpriors were almost equally important in maintaining administrative continuity at the monastery during incapacitating sickness on the part of the prior: in the last decade of Henry of Eastry's rule, when the Prior was often ill, his subpriors were entrusted with matters as important and delicate as the presentations of clerks to the convent's benefices and the correct course of action in the case of an apostate monk.[99] For the great majority of the late medieval monks of Christ Church, their subprior must often have been a more effective source of authority than the prior himself, above all because of the frequent absences of the latter from Canterbury itself.

In 1298 Archbishop Winchelsey was in fact sufficiently concerned at the possibility of prolonged absenteeism on the part of Henry of Eastry that he instructed the Prior 'to reside in the cloister when he can and supervise the monks there in such a way that they will be both well behaved and well governed'.[100] Exactly how often and for how long Eastry and his successors were away from Christ Church for purposes of business or recreation proves to be a matter less well documented than one would wish in the prior's

CUL, MS Ee. v. 31, fos. 163, 185, 191–6; *Lit. Cant.*, i. 118, 147–52, 160–1.

[96] Searle, *Chronicle and Lists*, 106, 194–5; Pantin, *Cant. Coll.*, iii. 152–3; MS Lit. E. 6, fo. 41. The third and fourth priors often served simultaneously as the convent's *magistri ordinum* (Searle, *Chronicle and Lists*, 194–5).

[97] The Oxford graduates John Salisbury and William Petham served as subpriors before their appointments as prior in 1438 and 1471 respectively (Emden, *BRUO*, iii. 1470, 1631–2). For another ex-warden of Canterbury College, John Wodnesbergh, who was subprior from 1449 until his death eight years later, see ibid. 2074.

[98] BL, Arundel MS 68, fo. 66; *Lit. Cant.*, iii. 115; Bodl., MS Tanner 165, fo. 221; Searle, *Chronicle and Lists*, 69, 187; Willis, *Conventual Buildings* (cit. in n. 70), 56.

[99] *Lit. Cant.*, i. 142–3, 232–3; cf. 308–9, 320. As early as 1324 (ibid. 117) Eastry had asked his subprior to deputize for him during his periods of disability: in fact he remained 'physically deteriorating but mentally robust' until his death at 92, seven years later (Hogan, 'Memorandum Book of Prior Eastry' (cit. in n. 63), i. 345–6, 374).

[100] *Reg. Winchelsey* (cit. in n. 62), ii. 815; Smith, *Cant. Cath. Priory*, 36 n. 4.

chaplain's accounts and other records of the later Middle Ages; but the prior's well-stocked stable in the precincts of the Cathedral, staffed by a farrier, groom, and stableman, testifies in general terms to his regular commitment to a strenuous round of financial and administrative responsibilities outside Canterbury.[101] As befitted prelates of national renown who were frequently summoned to meetings of Parliament and Convocation, the priors of Christ Church certainly visited London and Westminster very frequently indeed, if usually for comparatively short periods of time. According to the detailed accounts of several such expeditions which survive from the fifteenth century, the prior and his entourage would usually ride from Canterbury via Sittingbourne and Rochester to Gravesend, where they would customarily spend the night, before taking a barge to London on the following morning. Accommodation was most conveniently available at the prior's own 'place' or inn at Southwark, almost completely rebuilt during the priorate of Thomas Chillenden, and later known as 'The Flower de Luce', sited in Tooley Street, where London Bridge railway station now stands.[102] Apart from consultations with royal exchequer and other clerks at Westminster, a regular feature of these visits to the capital must have been a meeting with the archbishop at Lambeth; but it was even more common for priors of Canterbury to visit their spiritual overlord at one of the latter's favourite Kent, Surrey, or Sussex manors, like Maidstone or Mortlake, Mayfield or Knole.[103]

Much more frequent were the prior's absences from Canterbury to stay at one of his manor houses, most of them concentrated in east Kent and the object of a remarkable amount of capital expenditure at almost all periods of the later Middle Ages. Thus, during the first thirty-seven years of his priorate, Henry of Eastry spent no less than £3,739 4s. 6d. on 'nova opera in maneriis', of which a considerable proportion was devoted to improving the residential accommodation of the manor houses by such additional buildings as the 'new hall with a solar' and 'new stone chamber with chimney, [*capella*] and garderobe' constructed at Monkton on the Isle of Thanet.[104] A century later, and although the convent had by then embarked on a systematic policy of leasing its manorial demesnes, Prior Thomas Chillenden similarly lavished a good deal of capital on repairs and renovations to the Christ Church manor houses.[105] The length of time spent by individual priors in a particular manor no doubt varied very greatly and is in any case rarely possible to determine with any precision. Not too untypical perhaps was Henry of Eastry's itinerary during the summer of 1327: in addition to a visitation of those of the convent's Kentish manors, like Meopham and Merstham, whose financial situation needed the Prior's personal attention, Eastry also stayed—at least partly for purposes of recreation—at the

[101] Bodl., MS Tanner 165, fos. 186–221; Treasurers' Accts., nos. 1–5 (1282–1374); Smith, *Cant. Cath. Priory*, 31.

[102] DE 13, 16, 17, 18, 35, 60; *Lit. Cant.*, iii. 118; and for Prior Thomas Goldstone's later repairs to his inn at Southwark, see BL, Arundel MS 68, fo. 66. Cf. M. Carlin, 'The Urban Development of Southwark, *c.* 1200 to 1550' (Ph.D. thesis, Centre for Medieval Studies, Univ. Toronto, 1983), 288–94, no. 162, a reference I owe to Mrs Margaret Sparks.

[103] See e.g. Treasurers' Accts., no. 26 (1381–3), and Prior's Accts., no. 14 (1473–4). Unless official responsibilities to the Crown dictated otherwise, the late medieval archbishops were always more likely to be found at their Kent manors rather

than at their Lambeth or Canterbury palaces: indeed, of the 22 archbishops between 1279 and 1532, only 5 died at the former, and none at all at the latter.

[104] BL, Cotton MS Galba E. iv, fos. 102–8; Knowles, *Religious Orders*, i. 324. For an 'Inventory of the stuff, sent by my Lord Prior for his use at the Almonry at Monkton', see HMC, 5th *Report*, app., p. 445.

[105] For the new rooms built by Prior Chillenden at Ickham, Chartham, Godmersham, and other manor houses, see BL, Arundel MS 68, fo. 58; C. E. Woodruff, 'A Monastic Chronicle Lately Discovered at Christ Church', *Arch. Cant.*, 29 (1911), 68–9; cf. *Lit. Cant.*, iii. 116–19.

manors of Ickham, Brooke, Chartham, Cliffe, and, above all, Godmersham.[106] Only 7 miles south-west of Canterbury, in the Stour valley, the prior's manor house at Godmersham was still unusually well equipped when it was provided with a new stable for the prior's horses during the years of Thomas Chillenden's rule: it may well have retained its position as one of the most frequented of all the prior's manor houses throughout the fifteenth as well as the fourteenth century.[107]

However, neither in their size nor in their ability to offer lodging on a lavish scale to all comers can any of the prior's manors have rivalled the accommodation to be found in his own suites of apartments at Christ Church Priory itself. Within the notoriously complex plan of the late medieval Canterbury precincts, the prior's quarters were unquestionably the most complex group of chambers, increasingly dispersed rather than concentrated in and around the area occupied by the convent's huge monastic infirmary to the north-east of the Cathedral church. So difficult are the architectural problems presented by the successive campaigns of building in this area of the monastic *curia* that no satisfactory history of the prior's apartments at Canterbury is yet in print.[108] However, it is immediately obvious from the plentiful if scattered documentary sources that few if any decades from the early thirteenth to the early sixteenth century failed to witness some major addition to, or renovation of, the rooms at the disposal of the prior and his household. Although the latter already used the facilities of a *camera vetus* and *camera nova* (both located near the infirmary cloister) by the late twelfth century, perhaps the most critical stage in the highly unsystematic development of the prior's quarters was the building of a large new chapel at the end of a long building-campaign between the 1220s and 1250s. This prior's chapel, finally completed during the priorate of Roger of St Alphege (1258–63), was built over the south alley of the infirmary cloister, and extended into the cloister garth to gain extra width. Refurnished and redecorated on several occasions in the later Middle Ages, for instance by paintings of St Thomas, Pope Alexander III, and Louis VII of France, this 'chapel of the Blessed Mary within the Gate' was not merely the prior's personal chapel: it was often made accessible to laymen who wished to worship there, and also served, for example, as a suitable setting for the conferment of holy orders towards the close of the fifteenth century. Less happily, in 1382 a bitter quarrel led to bloodshed in this chapel, by no means a haven of tranquillity. Unfortunately little now remains of what was once one of the most important buildings in the Christ Church precinct: the prior's chapel—together with the monastic library constructed over it in the 1440s—was destroyed beyond repair during the Interregnum.[109]

---

[106] Reg. L, fos. 152ᵛ–153, *Lit. Cant.*, i. 221, 232–4, 239.

[107] *Lit. Cant.*, iii. 117; cf. ibid. i. 136; ii. 56; Smith, *Cant. Cath. Priory*, 108, 126, 143, 150, 192 n; cf. *Christ Church Letters*, 89–90. For an especially instructive account of intensive late medieval building-works at a Christ Church manor house which was 'reserved as a country house for the prior and a holiday house for the monks' 3 mls. south-west of the Cathedral, see M. J. Sparks and E. W. Parkin, 'The Deanery, Chartham', *Arch. Cant.*, 89 (1974), 169–82.

[108] The following brief account of the prior's apartments at Canterbury is heavily indebted to a much more extended survey recently prepared by Mrs Margaret Sparks.

[109] Little can be known from documentary sources about the prior's quarters in the precinct before 1200 (but see Smith, *Cant. Cath. Priory*, 30, for references to an 'old' and 'new' *camera prioris* by the 1160s). The earliest stages of the new prior's chapel of the 13th cent. were apparently financed by Benedict the Jew in 1222: see [Hussey], *Extracts from Ancient Documents* (cit. in n. 8), 7; Woodruff and Danks, *Memorials*, 128–99, *passim*; Somner, *Antiquities* (1703), 96; HMC, 5th *Report*, app., p. 444; *Reg. Bourgchier* (cit. in n. 63), 418, 419.

Even more instructive is the complex building-history of the prior's hall and other apartments, including a 'camera magna prioris cum pictura' and 'nova camera plumbata', built by Prior Eastry between 1285 and 1290 to the north of the monastic infirmary. After creating a new gateway through the eastern part of the existing *necessarium*, Eastry was able to find space to build several new chambers and a counting-house or Cheker around the 'Prior's Entry'.[110] The result was a series of interconnecting or adjacent apartments, providing the priors of Christ Church thereafter with the refinement and privacy normally available only in a large private country-house. Thus the prior's hall was adorned with tapestries and regularly attended at mealtimes by the convent's guests and servants, as well as by several monks and the prior himself.[111] In what must now often seem a highly uncoordinated and even chaotic manner, successive priors after Eastry continued to supplement all this spacious accommodation with additional private chambers, studies, solars, and bedrooms in profusion. In particular, the increasing need for high-quality lodgings for guests was met in a variety of ways, most sumptuously it seems by Prior Thomas Goldstone's 'New Lodgyng', completed by 1517 and of which part still survives as the south end of the present Deanery.[112] However, there can be no doubt at all that the most important pressure upon the ceaseless if erratic development of the prior's apartments at late medieval Canterbury was the demand for privacy and personal comfort, including private garderobes, washrooms, and even bathrooms. One extant example is 'Prior Sellyng's Tower', built as a *studium* in the 1470s and now constituting the south-west corner of the present Deanery. Yet another instance of the same trend is Le Gloriet, located near the gate from the *curia* north of the Cathedral into the monastic quarters of the convent. Apparently of a convenient size for small business-meetings, Le Gloriet was much patronized by Prior Thomas Chillenden and was also the *camera* in which Prior Wodnesbergh chose to die, in 1428.[113] Despite, or because of, their lack of centralized design, the history of the prior's quarters at Canterbury illustrates to perfection the fragmentation of the unitary monastic plan, the transformation of the house of God into many minor mansions, so characteristic of late medieval English monasticism as a whole.[114]

However, the size and variety of the residential and administrative accommodation at the disposal of the prior of Christ Church was also a direct reflection of the complexity of his roles as *paterfamilias*, as affable host to visiting notables, and, above all, as the director of a complicated administrative machine. From at least the first half of the thirteenth century, the prior's own household, long since detached from the other spending departments of the convent, was large enough to be subdivided into several smaller administrative units, notably the chamber, kitchen, pantry and buttery, scullery, and stable. According to an unusually detailed account of 1377–8, twenty-five servants were then in the permanent paid employ of the prior, ranging from his marshal to his butler's boy (*garcio botellarie*) and

[110] Reg. G, fos. 214, 218; BL, Cotton MS Galba E. iv, fo. 101; Woodman, *Architectural History* (cit. in n. 8), 138; Woodruff and Danks, *Memorials*, 225.
[111] Reg. G, fos. 213, 217; Prior's Accts., no. 14 (1473–4); DE 32.
[112] BL, Arundel MS 68, fo. 66; see ibid., fo. 58, for Prior Chillenden's extensive renovations to the 'Pavid Chamber' and
other parts of the prior's quarters a century earlier (cf. Woodruff and Danks, *Memorials*, 237).
[113] Bodl., MS Tanner 165, fo. 5; BL, Arundel MS 68, fo. 66; DE 44; *Lit. Cant.*, iii. 115.
[114] R. Gilyard-Beer, *Abbeys* (HMSO, 1958), 45–9; cf. Dobson, *Durham Priory* (cit. in n. 64), 91–3, 100–3.

the woman (a certain Christine Sharp in 1475) who washed his clothes.[115] The wages and especially the liveries of clothing annually distributed to these servants are well documented in surviving records, where the recipients are usually categorized as *armigeri* or *valetti prioris* and are found in the company of others whose services to the prior did not necessarily imply permanent residence in the precinct.[116] Most important of the laymen regularly in attendance on the prior was the steward of his hall (*seneschallus aule prioratus*), who also often held the office of porter of the Priory's inner—or northern—gateway into the prior's and monks' domestic buildings. At least by the time of Henry of Eastry's priorate, this steward was the ceremonial head of his master's household and was expected to be constantly in the prior's company, either in the hall itself or when they rode out of Canterbury on business together.[117] On even closer terms with the prior were his monk chaplains, of whom there were usually more than in any other English cathedral priory— often two in the thirteenth century and regularly as many as three in the hundred years before the Dissolution.[118] The senior of these *capellani* accounted annually for at least a part of the income and expenditure of the prior's household; but as this 'high chaplen' enjoyed little independent income by virtue of his office, being reliant on the prior himself for subventions to produce a sum of £100 or so a year, his surviving account-rolls throw disappointingly little light on the disbursements of his superior. Nevertheless, it is clear enough that the post of prior's chaplain, and especially senior chaplain, in a monastery as large as Christ Church was one of very considerable influence. Not surprisingly, this was an office often held by young monks who, like John Wodnesbergh and William Molashe in the fifteenth century, themselves later became priors of Canterbury.[119]

In addition to his chaplains and the permanent members of his household, the prior of Christ Church relied on the more specialized and professional skills of a large and highly heterogeneous group of councillors. The great importance of these individuals for the welfare of the monastery was first analysed in detail by the late R. A. L. Smith in what has deservedly proved one of the most influential chapters of his study of *Canterbury Cathedral Priory*. Although Smith probably exaggerated the stability and institutional ethos of what he called the prior's 'inner council of legal experts', he was certainly right to draw a major distinction between those lay counsellors who lived in or near Canterbury and the even larger number of senior clerical administrators who were retained by the prior to work primarily at Lambeth or Westminster.[120] As Smith also appreciated, it was during the middle years of the thirteenth century that the operations of both the Church and—even more—the English common-law courts rapidly became too technical and sophisticated to be readily intelligible to most monks of Canterbury themselves. Accordingly, it was at

---

[115] Prior's Chaplain's Accts., no. 2 (1377–8); DE 53; cf. Smith, *Cant. Cath. Priory*, 31–2.

[116] See esp. the long lists of individuals entitled to liveries at late 15th-cent. Christ Church recorded in Bodl., MS Tanner 165.

[117] Reg. G, fo. 217; Reg. S, fos. 230ᵛ, 245, 249ᵛ; HMC, 5th *Report*, app., p. 429; *Lit. Cant.*, i. 87.

[118] Assisa Scaccarii, 1230–3, 1243–4, 1263–4; Treasurers' Accts., no. 1 (1282–4); Prior's Chaplain's Accts., nos. 1–17 (1347–1416); Reg. O, fo. 107; *Lit. Cant.*, i. 207–8; Searle, *Chronicle and Lists*, 192; Pantin, *Cant. Coll.*, iii. 152–3.

[119] Prior's Chaplain's Accts., nos. 3–4 (1397–9), 7 (1405–6), 8–10 (1410–24), 14–15 (1415–17). The personal expenses of the prior in hospitality, gifts, and travel expenses were normally recorded in day-books or on parchment and paper bills, kept quite separately from the prior's chaplain's annual accounts of his master's ordinary household expenses (DE 3, 16, 17, 18, 31, 35, 95, 96).

[120] Smith, *Cant. Cath. Priory*, 68–82.

this time, and in the persons of men like Master Roger Cantelupe, Master Omer, Robert of Ludlow, and Hugh Mortimer, that the prior became very heavily dependent indeed on highly trained lawyers for the conduct of his Cathedral's affairs.[121]

Perhaps the most valued of all the prior's counsellors, because of their exceptional responsibility for complex issues of ecclesiastical jurisdiction during vacancies of the see, were a small élite of prominent church-lawyers, themselves heavily involved in the mechanisms of royal government and of the archbishop's *curia*. Senior clerks with this type of experience, headed by Gilbert of St Liffard, later Official of the court of Canterbury, figure prominently among the nineteen councillors who received annual retaining pensions of £5 or so from Prior Eastry in the 1280s and 1290s.[122] All allowances made for the ever-increasing elaboration of royal and archiepiscopal administration during the fourteenth and fifteenth centuries, a not dissimilar group of prior's retained counsellors is still readily detectable in the list of *clerici* entitled to the prior's general livery of clothing at Christmas 1439. In that year, these counsellors included among their number ecclesiastical administrators as powerful as: Master John Stopyngton, royal clerk of the Rolls; Master Richard Andrew, the archbishop's *auditor causarum* as well as first Warden of All Souls College, Oxford, and future Dean of York Minster; and Master William Lyndwode, keeper of the privy seal and author of the *Provinciale*.[123] The chief duty of these counsellors and their colleagues was to uphold the interests of the church of Canterbury in the king's and Church courts; but as their names and previous experience suggest, the retaining of such distinguished canon lawyers was equally important in fostering ties of friendship and fraternity between the prior of Christ Church and the most influential bureaucrats of the late medieval English State and Church.

Exactly the same principle inevitably applied, if within a more restricted geographical area, in the case of the prior's senior lay counsellors and *iurisperiti*. Although there can have been few magnates in medieval England totally indifferent to the spiritual advantages of placing their services at the disposal of the monks who guarded the shrine of St Thomas, it was above all to members of the knightly and gentry families of east Kent that the prior turned for constant legal advice and practical support amidst bitter and often violent disputes. The most assiduously helpful of these *armigeri prioris* were entitled to benefit from the convent's annual distribution of livery; and in this and other ways, families like the Fogges, Culpepers, and Ropers profited from their close association with a Cathedral they often represented at law.[124] Most prominent of all these *generosi* was the prior's chief steward or *seneschallus libertatis*, whose time-consuming duty it was to supervise the courts of the Christ Church manors, as well as to protect and maintain the prior's servants and officials throughout England.[125] Thus, in 1330, to take a comparatively early example, when

---

[121] Thus Cantelupe and Ludlow were used as intermediaries by the Canterbury chapter in their struggle against Archbishop Edmund Rich in 1239; and Prior Ringmere conducted the funeral service for Mortimer in 1275 (Gervase, *Historical Works*, ii. 142–3, 281; cf. Smith, *Cant. Cath. Priory*, 69–70).

[122] Treasurers' Accts., nos. 1 (1282–4) and 4 (1290). For some examples of the *litterae pensionariae* whereby Prior Eastry retained the services of Ralph de Hengham, Thomas de Cobham, and other lawyers in the 1280s, see CUL, MS Ee. v.

31, fos. 16ᵛ, 19ᵛ, 22ᵛ, 25, and Smith, *Cant. Cath. Priory*, 70–2.

[123] Bodl., MS Tanner 165, fo. 221ᵛ; cf. Emden, *BRUO*, i. 34–5; Emden, *BRUC*, 379–81. On 9 Mar. 1438 Richard Andrew delivered the opening address in the Canterbury chapter house at the election of Prior John Salisbury (HMC, 9th *Report*, app., pt. 1. 102).

[124] Bodl., MS Tanner 165, fos. 186, 191, 196, 201ᵛ; cf. Reg. S, fo. 250ᵛ (letter of fraternity to Sir John Fogge and his family, 1472).

[125] *Lit. Cant.*, ii. 69; Smith, *Cant. Cath. Priory*, 85–6.

Prior Eastry was forced to replace his steward, Sir John de Ifield, he was anxious to find a local knight who had the commitment and the desire to engage himself strenuously in the management of the convent's estates.[126] As in other major English religious houses, moreover, the influence of the prior's steward at Canterbury tended to increase considerably after the convent adopted a policy of leasing its demesnes, and so became more dependent upon the negotiation of legally enforceable leases of land with its tenants. By 1475 the Kentish gentleman chosen by Prior Sellyng as his chief steward was the prominent lawyer John Fyneux, who had already served Christ Church as an attorney for several years.[127] Eleven years later, the Prior aimed higher still and secured as his chief steward an Earl of Essex, not too surprisingly perhaps, in that Lord Henry Bourchier was a great-nephew of the Archbishop.[128] As not only the chief stewards but also the other lay *iurisperiti* of the prior so often acted in the interests of the Archbishop of Canterbury, whose retainers they might also be, not the least important consequence of this 'cosinage' of local gentlemen-lawyers was to minimize the prospects of serious seigniorial conflict about property between the two greatest landlords of east Kent.[129]

In few other spheres, however, could the priors of Canterbury from Henry of Eastry to the two Thomas Goldstones (1449–68; 1495–1517) ever be free from the endless strains and stresses of perpetual litigation. To preside over the intensely jealous monastic chapter of the primate of all England was *ipso facto* to be exposed to a series of legal conflicts on a bewildering variety of different fronts. In many ways, indeed, the public history of the late medieval community of Christ Church is nothing less than the history of its lawsuits. Accordingly, no assessment of the role of the prior of late medieval Canterbury can avoid coming to the final conclusion that an ability to defend their liberties and privileges at law was the quality to which his monks were always likely to give the highest priority. It was, for instance, because of his own prowess in legal combat that Henry of Eastry himself seems to have emerged as prior, somewhat unexpectedly, in 1285. During the preceding dozen years, Eastry had often represented his convent at London and elsewhere on such contentious matters as its claims to superiority over Dover Priory and its right to enforce the consecration of the southern province's suffragan bishops at Canterbury Cathedral.[130] Perhaps the best general impression of the financial and other burdens caused by exposure to so much litigation is afforded by Eastry's own list of the twenty major law-cases still awaiting final judgement on the day of his election. These causes ranged from the 'intolerable dissension' caused by appeals to Rome against the ex-prior, Thomas Ringmere, to a minor dispute about the right to exploit a mill at Faversham.

Most striking of all, however, are the large sums of money expended on the monastery's most notorious and long-standing *causes célèbres*, notably its conflict with Dover Priory over a host of long-running grievances, and the jurisdictional explosions caused by the

[126] *Lit. Cant.*, i. 334–7; cf. i. 68–9.

[127] HMC, 9th *Report*, app., pt. 1. 117. Cf. the appointment of an even more prominent Kentish gentleman, James Fiennes, to the life stewardship of the Archbishop of Canterbury in 1443 (*Lit. Cant.*, iii. 182–3; Du Boulay, *Lordship of Canterbury* (cit. in n. 32), 395).

[128] HMC, 9th *Report*, app. pt. 1. 118; *Reg. Bourgchier* (cit. in n.

63), pp. xviii–xix. Cf. the analogous development of the prior's steward's office noted in Dobson, *Durham Priory* (cit. in n. 64), 125–31.

[129] Very few references to such conflict occur in Reg. S (1390–1500) or Reg. T(i) (1506–32).

[130] LPL, MS 242, fos. 86⁰, 242; Hogan, 'Memorandum Book of Prior Eastry' (cit. in n. 63), i. 16–30, 41–44.

prior's attempts to maintain his spiritual authority in the southern province during vacancies of the see.[131] According to a survey made at Eastry's orders in 1322, of all the prior's extraordinary expenditure incurred during the preceding thirty-seven years, the cost of lawsuits in Rome and England amounted to no less than £3,624, as much as 16 per cent of the grand total. One does indeed wonder, in Dr Hogan's words, 'how many modern corporations spend as high a proportion of their operating expenses on legal fees'.[132] Perhaps for that reason, among others, it seems clear that fifteenth-century priors of Canterbury, like their counterparts elsewhere, were generally much more reluctant than their predecessors to resort to the royal law-courts when they could use the cheaper and less formal method of arbitration instead. Thus, in the late 1420s Prior William Molashe's disputes with both Merton College, Oxford, and the citizens of Canterbury were resolved by the use of neutral arbiters.[133] Admittedly, and to judge from a series of brief biographical sketches of Christ Church priors compiled by a Canterbury monk during the priorate of John Wodnesbergh (1411–28), after the Black Death of 1348–9 successful prosecution of the convent's rights at law was beginning to seem less crucial than ensuring that the Cathedral was financially solvent and unencumbered by past debts.[134] Here again, however, Henry Eastry served as the best exemplar for later priors, because of his exceptional and much publicized capacity to liquidate the enormous debts incurred by his predecessors. Like British university vice-chancellors of the early 1990s, the superiors of the largest religious houses of the later Middle Ages were judged by those who knew them best as the Marthas rather than the Marys of the Lord's monastic vineyards.

For the heads of these major monasteries, moreover, the most fitting expression of successful financial management took a highly corporeal form—the financing of major building or rebuilding works within the precinct. It is no coincidence that among the tributes paid to recently deceased Priors of Christ Church in the fourteenth and fifteenth centuries, it is their contributions to the architecture of the Cathedral and its environs which always receive pride of place.[135] Once again, Henry of Eastry's achievements as a sponsor of building works set standards which were hard for his successors to surpass. In the first thirty-seven years of his rule, Eastry spent no less than £2,184 on *nova opera* in the Cathedral church and the monastic buildings, the most expensive items being the £230 16s. 0d. spent on the prior's own quarters and the £839 7s. 8d. which went towards the modernizing of the church choir and chapter house.[136] By the beginning of the fifteenth century, Prior John Finch (1378–91) and, above all, Prior Thomas Chillenden, that 'greatest builder of a prior that ever was in Christs Church' (1391–1411), were being remembered for their restoration of the monastic dormitory and especially for their contribution towards Henry Yevele's new Cathedral nave, the greatest building-campaign in the late medieval

[131] BL, Cotton MS Galba E. iv, fos. 108–9; Haines, *Dover Priory* (cit. in n. 24), 88–94; Churchill, *Canterbury Administration* (cit. in n. 24), i. 552–6.

[132] BL, Cotton MS Galba E. iv, fo. 109; Hogan, 'Memorandum Book of Prior Eastry' (cit. in n. 63), i. 308; ii. 1121–3.

[133] *Lit. Cant.*, iii. 150–2.

[134] Woodruff, 'Monastic Chronicle' (cit. in n. 105), 56–84.

[135] BL, Arundel MS 68, fos. 4, 5, 58, 65–6; Cotton MS Galba E. iv, fos. 102–2. The best example is the exceptionally detailed account of Prior Chillenden's building works printed in Woodruff, 'Monastic Chronicle', 61–77.

[136] BL, Cotton MS Galba E. iv, fo. 101; Knowles, *Religious Orders*, i. 323–4.

community's history.[137] Fifty years later still, Prior Thomas Goldstone was praised in his official obituary for a personal charm ('pius et benignus ... humanus, affabilis atque benevolus') which served his community well when threatened by involvement in the Wars of the Roses. However, his most lasting memorials were his 'ornamenting' of the recently completed south-western tower of the Cathedral and the creation of a highly decorated new Lady Chapel east of the Martyrdom. It was within this chapel, built by the Cathedral's master mason, Richard Beke, that Goldstone's own bones were laid to rest.[138] A generation later, the construction of the last major addition to the fabric of Canterbury Cathedral, its central tower or 'angyll stepyll', was being co-ordinated by the second Prior Thomas Goldstone (1495–1517). He too ensured that his name would always be associated with Bell Harry by the prominent display of his initials ('T G P': 'Thomas Goldstone Prior') and rebus (three gold stones) not only within its interior crossing vault but upon the strainer arches, 'most beautifully completed in carefully carved stone', below the tower.[139] Even Goldstone's successor, Thomas Goldwell, now best remembered as the superior who surrendered his monastery to Henry VIII and Thomas Cromwell, must have hoped that the appearance of his arms in the vault of the spectacular new Christ Church Gate of the early sixteenth century would ensure him too an honoured place in the long line of Canterbury priors who rightly saw themselves as amongst the greatest builders of their times.[140]

The greatest memorials to the financial competence and organizational skills of the successive priors of Christ Church still survive in the form of the much-visited remains of the most elaborate building-complex ever produced by an English monastic cathedral community. Not surprisingly, the monks of late medieval Christ Church themselves tended to visualize their convent's history in terms of their priors almost as much as of their archbishops.[141] By the end of the Middle Ages it would also have been hard for the Canterbury monks to avoid a more poignant reminder of their illustrious deceased priors in the form of the many large stone or marble memorial slabs set into the floors of the Cathedral church and its adjacent chapels. Regrettably enough, few of these gravestones, usually adorned with a brass or other effigy of the prior, survive at Canterbury today.[142] By a happier fate, however, what is almost certainly the tomb of Henry of Eastry himself

[137] *CPR 1377–81*, 460, 530; *1381–85*, 164; *Lit. Cant.*, iii. 114–16; Woodman, *Architectural History* (cit. in n. 8), 151–64; J. H. Harvey, 'Archbishop Simon of Sudbury and the Patronage of Architecture in the Middle Ages', *Cant. Cath. Chron.*, 76 (1982), 22–32; id., 'Henry Yeveley and the Nave of Canterbury Cathedral', ibid. 79 (1985), 20–32; John Leland, *Itinerary*, ed. L. Toulmin Smith (5 vols.; London, 1907–10), iv. 41.

[138] See the tribute to Thomas Goldstone ('bella civilia in quibus magna cum gravitate et prudentia ita hanc ecclesiam feliciter gubernabat') in BL, Arundel MS 68, fo. 5. For the Prior's contributions to the fabric of the Cathedral's south-west tower, see C. E. Woodruff, 'The Rebuilding of the South-West Tower of Canterbury Cathedral in the Fifteenth Century', *Arch. Cant.*, 45 (1933), 37–47. Cf. Searle, *Chronicle and Lists*, 104–5; D. I. Hill, *Canterbury Cathedral* (London 1986), 38, 85–6; J. H. Harvey, *English Mediaeval Architects* (2nd edn.; Gloucester, 1984), 17.

[139] BL, Arundel MS 68, fo. 65; Wharton, *Anglia Sacra*, i. 147;

Woodman, *Architectural History* (cit. in n. 8), 199–211. For Prior Sellyng's involvement in the design of the central tower before Goldstone succeeded him, see *Christ Church Letters*, 61–2.

[140] P. H. Blake, *Christ Church Gate, Canterbury Cathedral* (Bridge Place, Canterbury, 1965), 34 ('sable, a gold well'). The appearance of Prior Goldwell's arms on the vault of the gate makes it virtually certain that it was not completed until after 1519 (Woodman, *Architectural History* (cit. in n. 8), 215).

[141] Wharton, *Anglia Sacra*, i. 1–151; Searle, *Chronicle and Lists*, 7–118; Woodruff, 'Monastic Chronicle' (cit. in n. 105), 47–84.

[142] Prior's Accts., no. 12 (1472–3: 'pro lapide posita super sepulcrum domini Johannis Oxne nuper proris'); Searle, *Chronicle and Lists*, 105; cf. Woodruff and Danks, *Memorials*, 268–71, with the suggestion that Prior William Molashe's burial-place is still marked by a large marble slab in the floor of the south aisle of the crypt.

still remains at the west end of the south choir aisle. Here at least, the most remarkable of Christ Church's superiors can be seen, in somewhat sombre majesty, occupying the bay immediately east of the tomb of the archbishop, Walter Reynolds, whom he had served somewhat less loyally than he had served the interests of his own community. Given the recognition of Eastry's exceptional achievements by the medieval monks of Christ Church, as more recently by modern historians of Canterbury, it seems only proper that he may be the only monk of his community ever to have been accorded the unusual distinction of a standing monument.[143] No other prior in the history of the Cathedral is as self-revealing as is Henry of Eastry in much of his voluminous correspondence: it is all the more appropriate that only in the case of his own damaged and emaciated effigy do we have an opportunity to see a prior of Canterbury as he himself would have liked to be seen.

MONASTIC LEARNING AT THE UNIVERSITY AND IN THE CLOISTER

By its very nature, the history of an undying monastic corporation like medieval Christ Church underwent few absolutely decisive turning-points; but of all the years between the translation of St Thomas to his new shrine in 1220 and the surrender of the monastery to the Crown in 1540 the most significant date might seem, at least in retrospect, to be 1331. It was in that year (on 8 or 9 April) that Henry of Eastry's unprecedentedly long priorate of forty-six years came to its end, when the convent's grand old man died as mass was being celebrated in his Cathedral.[144] Much more important for the future, however, was the appearance at Oxford University towards the end of that same year of a small group of Canterbury monks. The three brethren who took up residence in a hired hall near the church of St Peter in the East in October 1331 included the first Oxford bachelor (Hugh of St Ives, in 1332) and the first doctor of theology (James of Oxney, in 1358) to be found within the ranks of the medieval community.[145] At long last the most academically talented members of Canterbury Cathedral were to be exposed to university education in systematic fashion; and it accordingly followed that from the 1330s, as never before, Oxford scholarship and Oxford academic connections came to exercise the most important new influence on the intellectual, cultural, and even religious horizons of the community at Christ Church. For this reason, and to a greater extent than even the monks of Canterbury themselves appreciated, the erratic but finally successful campaign to establish a *studium* of their own at Oxford now seems the most important issue in the history of the Cathedral monastery during the half-century after Prior Henry of Eastry's death. Only in January 1384, when Archbishop William Courtenay published his revised statutes for Canterbury College during the course of a visitation of Christ Church, can the future of the monks' academic colony at Oxford be said to have become absolutely assured.[146] Although the smallest of all academic institutions in late medieval Oxford, the college thereafter became

[143] Misc. Acct. 2 (Treasurers' Accts. 1307–37); [Hussey], *Extracts from Ancient Documents* (cit. in n. 8), 11; M. J. Sparks, 'Henry of Eastry, Prior of Christ Church, Canterbury, 1285–1331', *Cant. Cath. Chron.*, 79 (1985), 19; Woodman, *Architectural History* (cit. in n. 8), 253; cf. C. Wilson, below, pp. 490–1.
[144] BL, Cotton MS Galba E. iv, fos. 109ᵛ, 183ᵛ; Reg. G, fo. 22ᵛ;

Wharton, *Anglia Sacra*, i. 141; *Lit. Cant.*, i. 360–1.
[145] Reg. L, fos. 10, 13, 32; Emden, *BRUO*, ii. 1416; iii. 1627; Pantin, *Cant. Coll.*, iv, 4–5; *Lit. Cant.*, i. 392–3, 414–18.
[146] Pantin, *Cant. Coll.*, iii. 172–83; iv. 44–6; Dahmus, *Courtenay* (cit. in n. 54), 200–8.

one of the Canterbury prior and chapter's central concerns, not least because—somewhat surprisingly in comparison with other great Benedictine monasteries—it was the only daughter house or cell they possessed.[147]

At first sight it might seem no less surprising that the monks of Christ Church were such latecomers to the Oxford academic scene. Well over fifty years before Hugh of St Ives and James of Oxney received their higher degrees, the representatives of the English Black Monks had met in their general chapter at Reading, in September 1277, and agreed to establish a common Benedictine *studium* (the future Gloucester College) at Oxford, 'in order to make learning flourish once again within our order'.[148] So, on the whole, it had done; but during these critical early years for the introduction of the 'university monk' into Oxford, the state of higher education at Christ Church itself still left a good deal to be desired. Whether or not the pre-eminently practical Prior Eastry was prejudiced against the study of any academic subject but canon law, he seems in any case to have preferred to send his most talented young monks to study not at Oxford but at Paris: members of the Christ Church community are recorded there in 1288, 1304–6, and probably again in 1307–9.[149] Even for Canterbury monks, however, study abroad could be no proper substitute for regular recourse to the Oxford schools; and in the years around 1300 it became notorious that England's premier cathedral priory lacked monks capable of providing competent lectures in theology within the cloister. Between 1286 and 1314 Prior Eastry continued the unusual and somewhat demeaning practice of employing a series of Franciscan friars to make good this deficiency by acting as lectors in theology within the convent; and even this arrangement was regarded with acute suspicion by some of the more conservative Christ Church monks, who argued that such innovations were likely to 'bring forth discord' in the community.[150]

However, there can be no doubt that the real explanation for the delays and hesitancy with which the Christ Church community entered the academic milieu of Oxford was less an indifference to learning on the part of the chapter than an acute nervousness by the prior and monks that they might thereby compromise their self-proclaimed position as 'that church of Canterbury, blessed by the precious blood of that glorious martyr, the blessed Thomas, which excels all the other churches of England in name, honour, and dignity'.[151] So exalted, not to say arrogant, a sense of their own superiority over other religious houses had long helped to create, and then prolong, Christ Church Priory's notoriously long-running feuds with its Benedictine neighbours in Kent, most notably

[147] Throughout the three centuries after 1136, when 12 Christ Church monks allegedly refounded the religious house at Dover as a Benedictine monastery, the frequent attempts made by the Canterbury prior and chapter to reduce this priory to complete dependence upon themselves were never absolutely successful: for G. G. Coulton this was 'a struggle in the law courts which throws into insignificance even the great Jarndyce case in *Bleak House*' (LPL, Reg. Islip, fos. 24ᵛ–26ᵛ; *VCH Kent*, ii. 133–4; Haines, *Dover Priory* (cit. in n. 24), pp. xiii, 59–110).

[148] *Documents Illustrating the Activities of the General and Provincial Chapters of the English Black Monks, 1215–1540*, ed. W. A. Pantin, 3 vols. (Camden, 3rd ser., 1931–7), i. 75; R. B. Dobson,

'The Foundation of Gloucester College in 1283', *Worcester College Record* (1985), 12–24; id., *Durham Priory* (cit. in n. 64), 343–5; cf. Emden, *BRUO*, i. 272.

[149] Pantin, *Cant. Coll.*, iv. 3–4, 9–10. For a perhaps unduly favourable view of Eastry's patronage of learning, see Hogan, 'Memorandum Book of Eastry' (cit. in n. 63), i. 340–4.

[150] CUL, MS Ee. v. 31, fo. 28; Gervase, *Historical Works*, ii. 281; Pantin, *Cant. Coll.*, iv. 3.

[151] See the draft of a petition against the presidents of the English Black Monks addressed to the pope in 1360 (*Lit. Cant.*, ii. 398–9).

with Dover Priory and St Augustine's Abbey just outside the walls of Canterbury itself.[152] For similar reasons it became even more important to the prior and chapter of fourteenth-century Canterbury not to take any initiative at the University of Oxford which might lead to the subjection of some of their monks to the direction of the English Benedictine Order's national chapters. Accordingly it followed, as the late W. A. Pantin pointed out, that the creation of an effective academic college of Christ Church monk-scholars at Oxford was first inhibited and then delayed by the mother house's determination not to accept the legality of any other authority over its university monks than its own. In the long struggle to achieve this objective, the prior and chapter lost many battles but eventually gained the final victory. Canterbury College finally emerged not only as the Christ Church community's most important centre of higher education but also, and almost as important in the monks' eyes, as 'a symbol of an exemption claimed and won'.[153]

It could nevertheless be argued now, as it was argued by many of the leading Benedictine abbots and priors of the fourteenth century, that in failing to respond to their summonses to the long series of triennial general chapter meetings of the English Black Monks, which began at Oxford in 1218–19, the prior and chapter of Christ Church were in flagrant breach of a decree (*In singulis regnis*) of the 1215 Lateran Council.[154] However, it was only after the publication, in 1336, of Pope Benedict XII's great reforming constitutions for the Black Monks—constitutions so important that even the monks of Christ Church, Canterbury, could hardly ignore them—that the presidents of the English Benedictine chapter of 1340 decided to grasp the nettle directly, and sent two monks to Benedict XII himself with the information that the Prior of Christ Church was guilty of persistent contumacy in refusing to attend their chapter meetings. With the traditional Christ Church argument at such times, namely that 'it is unfitting for a mother to be in tutelage to her daughters', Prior Robert Hathbrand successfully fought off this particular challenge through the agency of his proctors at the papal Curia.[155] However, the conflict entered a new and more contentious phase when, in 1360, Abbot Thomas de la Mare of St Albans, one of the very few medieval English Benedictine prelates with the force and authority to risk a confrontation with the Prior and chapter of Christ Church, procured a papal declaration that the *Benedictina* of 1336 were intended to apply to metropolitan cathedral priories. In a highly uncomfortable position, Prior Hathbrand exploited the exceptional range of patrons available to a prior of Canterbury by making personal appeals for protection against de la Mare and the Black Monk chapter to the three most powerful laymen in England: the Black Prince, John of Gaunt, and Edward III himself.[156] In the event, and from a point of near-surrender of their claim to total exemption from the authority of the English Benedictines, the community at Christ Church was rescued by a highly unusual

[152] Neither of these two notorious and voluminously documented disputes has yet been analysed in detail; but see the understandably confused Haines, *Dover Priory* (cit. in n. 24), 59–110, and for the conflicts created by the Abbey of St Augustine's extraordinary attempts to secure exemption from archiepiscopal authority, *Lit. Cant.*, i, pp. lv, 29, 341, 467, 511, 517; ii. 7, 10, 17–19, 41–3; iii. 364–8; *Christ Church Letters*, 9.

[153] Pantin, *Cant. Coll.*, iii. 3; cf. H. Rashdall, *The Universities of Europe in the Middle Ages*, ed. F. M. Powicke and A. B. Emden (3 vols.; Oxford, 1936), iii. 210–13.

[154] *Lit. Cant.*, i. 370; ii. 224–5; *Chapters* (cit. in n. 148), iii. 158, 193; Pantin, *Cant. Coll.*, iv. 2.

[155] Reg. L. fo. 75ᵛ; *Lit. Cant.*, ii. 224–5; *Chapters* (cit. in n. 148), ii. 23.

[156] *Gesta Abbatum Monasterii Sancti Albani*, ed. H. T. Riley, 3 vols. (RS, 28; 1867–9), ii. 403–4; *Chapters* (cit. in n. 148), iii. 56–60; Knowles, *Religious Orders*, ii. 44–5.

personal intervention on the part of John of Gaunt at the 1366 Northampton chapter; and throughout the next ten years or so the convent was also able to rely upon the support of Archbishops Langham, Wittelsey, and Sudbury.[157] Even more important were the steps taken by the Prior and his monks to secure influential friends at the Curia, where they enjoyed the exceptional good fortune of having Cardinal Simon Langham, their own ex-archbishop, as their most powerful patron. However, it was only in 1379, after Langham's death, that the prior and chapter at last secured the long-awaited bull from Urban VI completely exempting them from the authority of the Black Monks' chapters.[158] So complete a triumph for Christ Church's splendid isolationism did not entirely relieve the community from anxiety that this sensitive issue might one day be reopened; and several papal confirmations of Urban VI's bull were accordingly obtained at the request of William Sellyng and other Christ Church monks during the course of the fifteenth century.[159] However, the victory of 1379 was indeed remarkable, one of the greatest of all testimonials to the Canterbury monks' unrivalled capacity to resist external pressure, win friends, and influence the great.

The most practical consequence of the monks' success in maintaining their freedom from intervention by the Benedictine chapters was that at last the way was open for the establishment of their own academic college at Oxford on a secure constitutional foundation. Even so, and even by the standards of other late medieval university institutions, the 'pre-history' of Canterbury College was exceptionally complex, and indeed erratic to a degree. The promising start made by the handful of Canterbury monks who resided in a chamber near the church of St Peter in the East was succeeded in the 1330s and 1340s by a period of profound unease because of uncertainty at Canterbury itself about both the cost of university education and the availability of suitable accommodation for the scholar monks. It was at this time that the Canterbury community went so far as to acquire a *camera* in the Black Monks' common Oxford *studium* of Gloucester College, despite the risk that such a chamber might make its monks vulnerable to the authority of the Benedictine academic superior there, the '*prior studentium*'. In fact, probably very few Canterbury monks ever used this *camera*, for in 1355 Archbishop Islip rebuked the chapter for sending no new monks at all to the Oxford schools; and it is accordingly no surprise to discover that their quarters at Gloucester College were ultimately sold off to Westminster Abbey by the Christ Church chapter in 1371.[160]

By that date a completely different and much more attractive solution to the problem had already emerged in the shape of Archbishop Simon Islip's ambitious if curiously muddled plan to found a mixed college of twelve monks and seculars on the site of what is now the Canterbury Quad of Christ Church. However, a few months before his death by a stroke, in April 1366, the Archbishop unpredictably decided to eject all the Canterbury monk-fellows from his new foundation, and then appointed Master John Wyclif as warden of what was now an entirely secular college. Fortunately for the monks of Canterbury,

[157] Ch. Ant. S. 395; *Gesta Abbatum* (cit. in n. 156), ii. 403–4; *Chapters* (cit. in n. 148), iii. 57–60, 73–5, 77–8; Churchill, *Canterbury Administration* (cit. in n. 24), i. 143.
[158] Reg. G, fo. 213; Wilkins, *Concilia*, iii. 126; cf. *Lit. Cant.*, ii.

510–11.
[159] *CPL 1484–92*, 202–8; Pantin, *Cant. Coll.*, iv. 3.
[160] Searle, *Chronicle and Lists*, 179; Pantin, *Cant. Coll.*, iii. 21–2, 38–9; iv. 4–6, 178–81, 212, 217; *Lit. Cant.*, ii. 332–3.

their next archbishop, Simon Langham, had been a Westminster Abbey university monk himself and was consequently eager to restore Islip's foundation to its original mixed collegiate status.[161] However, as there were by now many vested interests in Oxford itself opposed to the readmission of monks to Canterbury College, the Christ Church chapter soon found itself involved in one of the great ecclesiastical *causes célèbres* of late fourteenth-century England. Both parties appealed repeatedly to the Curia, where a protracted and closely contested lawsuit was finally resolved by a sentence of July 1369 to the effect that the monks of Christ Church were to enjoy exclusive use of Canterbury College thenceforward.[162] Two years later a small group of monks began to inhabit the college; but its economic survival was only assured when Thomas Chillenden, the future Prior of Christ Church, went to Rome in 1378–9 and procured papal confirmation of the appropriation of the Sussex church of Pagham to this new *studium*.[163] By the time of these tortuous negotiations about Canterbury College's future, the most serious conflict of interests had come, ironically enough, to lie between the archbishops and their monks. Only after a good deal of bargaining on practical matters did Archbishop Courtenay (in 1384) produce the lengthy statutes which were to govern the life of Canterbury College until its dissolution, in 1540. In effect these statutes offered the monks of Christ Church the substance of what they wanted, above all complete control over the selection of those brethren who were to become fellows of the college. Without the support of their mid-fourteenth-century archbishops, the Christ Church community would never have been able to found a college in Oxford at all; but that did not prevent the monks from forcing those archbishops to acknowledge that on this issue 'a chapter is immortal and has the last word'.[164]

The lengthy struggle to establish Canterbury College, Oxford, is therefore a remarkable tribute to the ability of the monks of Christ Church to outfight and outmanœuvre not only English Benedictine presidents and the University of Oxford's secular scholars but even their own archbishops. It is hard to believe that any other monastery in fourteenth-century England could have achieved so much against such odds. Admittedly, it could be argued, at least at first sight, that the academic results of the long campaign to establish the college were hardly commensurate with the strenuous efforts that had gone into that campaign. Despite the high hopes of Archbishop Langham and Prior Chillenden, for most of its history Canterbury College was the smallest academic institution in late medieval Oxford. After a short period in the 1380s and 1390s when there were as many as seven monk fellows, for much of the fifteenth century the number of monks recorded as receiving pensions in the college's annual accounts rarely exceeded two or three, in addition to the warden. As Dr W. A. Pantin once observed, there seem to have been several periods after 1400 when, despite the rare distinction of having its own Oxford college, the Christ Church

[161] Despite the increasing sophistication with which the early history of Canterbury College has been analysed (most scrupulously by W. A. Pantin in *Cant. Coll.*, iv. 9–46), the motives of several of the protagonists, and especially of Archbishop Islip, remain highly obscure.

[162] Ibid. iii. 184–206; iv. 20–9.

[163] Reg. B, fo. 376; Reg. G, fo. 217; Pantin, *Cant. Coll.*, iii. 34–6; iv. 40.

[164] Pantin, *Cant. Coll.*, iv. 44–6. For the less persuasive view that the settlement of 1384 represented 'a victory for moderation and compromise', in which it was Archbishop Courtenay who 'emerged the victor', see Dahmus, *Courtenay* (cit. in n. 54), 200–8.

chapter failed to fulfil even the minimum requirements for university education imposed upon the Black Monks by Benedict XII in 1336.[165] However, the explanation for the comparatively poor Christ Church response to the academic opportunities provided by their Oxford college was less lack of enthusiasm for university learning as such than the college's very inadequate initial endowment. It is hardly surprising that revenues from only one appropriated church, moderately wealthy though Pagham was, proved a slender base from which to sustain the operations of an entire college.[166] From this financial impasse Canterbury College was rescued only by Prior William Sellyng, whose enthusiasm for university learning led him to sustain additional monks at Oxford at no expense to the college itself. As a result, the number of Canterbury monks, including the warden, in residence at Oxford rose from only two in 1469–70 and three in 1470–71 to six in the years between 1498 and 1505.[167] Indeed, by the time Cardinal Morton made his will, in 1500, he could assume that his Cathedral community would maintain six brethren at the college, a number he then proceeded to augment by a bequest of £6 13s. 4d. to each of two additional monk-fellows for a term of twenty years. When, a generation later, an agent of Thomas Cromwell compiled an annotated list of the last fifty-six Christ Church monks, it is true that only two of the brethren were then alleged to be studying at Oxford; but there were another two 'nowe being at Parrys at stody', as well as three doctors and five bachelors of divinity among the ranks of the community.[168]

Education at Oxford was therefore undoubtedly always confined to an élite of Canterbury monks, even if an élite which became considerably larger during the fifty years before the catastrophes of the 1530s. As befitted an élite, this small group of Christ Church monks at Oxford came to be increasingly well housed and maintained, even by the comfortable living-standards of their mother house. One of Prior Chillenden's greatest contributions to the college he had done so much to establish securely was to provide 'most beautiful and suitable rooms ... which will be a source of delight and delectation to our scholars studying there'.[169] As the building and decorating of chapel, hall, and residential chambers at Canterbury College are perhaps better documented than those of any other medieval Oxford college, it is not at all hard to demonstrate that the physical environment within which the Christ Church monks lived, worshipped, and studied at Oxford was positively enviable by contemporary university standards. Not the least of their advantages was a site, immediately north of the churchyard of St Frideswide's Priory, which was more centrally located than any other Oxford monastic or mendicant convent. After the complicated process of acquiring and demolishing the many tenements previously occupying the area was complete, the serious work of transforming a heterogeneous collection of small halls and houses into a new regular quadrangle was begun by at latest the 1370s, the decade in which the hall and at least two adjacent *camere* were also being built.[170] During the early years of the priorate of Thomas Chillenden, when

[165] Pantin, *Cant. Coll.*, ii. 129, 133, 135, 137, 139, 147, 150; iv. 55–6. Cf. Wilkins, *Concilia*, ii. 588, for Benedict XII's requirement that one out of every 20 members of Black Monk communities should be sent (with an adequate pension) to study at a university.

[166] Pantin, *Cant. Coll.*, ii. 173–261; iv. 122–9.

[167] Ibid. ii. 191, 193, 226, 229, 232, 233–4, 236, 239, 241; iv. 56–7.

[168] BL, Arundel MS 68, fos. 67–8; *Sede Vacante Wills*, ed. C. E. Woodruff (Kent Archaeol. Soc., Records Branch, 3; 1914), 89; Pantin, *Cant. Coll.*, iii. 151–4, 227–45; iv. 57–8.

[169] BL, Arundel MS 68, fo. 58.

[170] *Lit. Cant.*, iii. 116; Pantin, *Cant. Coll.*, iv. 143–4.

expenditure on the *novum opus* of the college cost £340 between 1394 and 1397, the chapel, gateway, and most of the rooms were completed in their turn. By the time the north wing of the quadrangle was finished, in or about 1439, Canterbury College was spacious and attractive enough to capture the interest of those paying lodgers—monks and seculars alike—who provided the college with its most varied, and occasionally even exotic, inmates.[171]

More significant for the academic life of the monks at Canterbury College were its collections of books. Admittedly, the college's common library-building itself, the *novum opus librarie*, was apparently only under way by the 1440s and was finally completed during the early years of Prior Thomas Goldstone I. Compared with the other new, custom-built libraries constructed in this period at many of England's major churches and academic colleges (e.g. at Durham College between 1417 and 1418 and at Gloucester College in the 1420s), that at Canterbury College was adequate ('satis amplis') rather than particularly large.[172] However, there is no doubt that most of the brethren built up personal book-collections of their own, many of which ultimately passed into the libraries either of the college or of Christ Church itself. Thus five of the manuscripts, including a volume containing Wyclif's sermons, once owned by Robert Lynton, warden of the college between 1443 and 1448, found their way into the collection of college books housed in the chapel and warden's *camera* by 1459.[173] Although only four or five manuscripts from Canterbury College can now be traced, the survival of no less than seven lists or inventories of the college's books (1443; 1459; two in 1501; 1520; 1524; 1534) makes it possible to study the evolution of this late-medieval English college library in unparalleled detail. The cumulative impression is of a very great expansion in the number of books available at Canterbury College, rising from 132 in 1459 to 336 in 1501.[174] Otherwise, and somewhat predictably, the Canterbury College library catalogues reveal a highly traditional and even conservative policy of book acquisition on the part of the warden and his fellows. The inventory produced in 1501, when Thomas Chaundler ceased to be warden, reveals a library dominated by theological and biblical works (150) at the expense of books on canon law (36), civil law (13), and even philosophy (4).[175] Not only were individual monks somewhat quicker to respond to the new opportunities provided by the printed book than was the common college library, but they occasionally leave evidence of what seems to be a personal taste in recreational reading. Thus the books pledged by Thomas Anselm when fellow of Canterbury College in the second decade of the sixteenth century included a copy of the *Travels* of Sir John Mandeville and 'a bocke of the cronacles in Englysse', which had cost him 3s. 4d., as well as a Latin life 'of oure blessyd patrune sencte Thomas of Canturberi', acquired for 20d.[176] As so many of the Canterbury College fellows eventually brought their books home with them to Christ Church, not the least of the college's

[171] Pantin, *Cant. Coll.*, ii. 126–57; iv. 91–9. The residential accommodation available to the warden, monks, and sojourners of the college is carefully described ibid. iv. 139–51.

[172] BL, Arundel MS 68, fo. 3; Pantin, *Cant. Coll.*, ii. 173, 176, 179; iv. 161–6. Cf. Dobson, *Durham Priory* (cit. in n. 64), 350; J. Newman, 'Oxford Libraries Before 1800', *Archaeol. Jnl.*, 135 (1978), 248–65.

[173] Pantin, *Cant. Coll.*, iv. 159; Emden, *BRUO*, ii. 1195.

[174] James, *ALCD*; N. R. Ker, *Medieval Libraries of Great Britain: A List of Surviving Books*, 2nd edn. (Royal Hist. Soc.; 1964), 145; Pantin, *Cant. Coll.*, i. 3–6, 11–16, 18–28, 36, 39–44, 45–50, 59–62, 70–2, 73–4, 113–15; iv. 155–66.

[175] Pantin, *Cant. Coll.*, i. 91–2.

[176] Ibid. i. 18–28; cf. ii. 206.

services to its mother house was to act as the most important agency for the acquisition of new manuscripts and printed books.

It is hardly surprising that most of these volumes were directly related to the academic study of theology. Christ Church was a convent whose university monks would increasingly aspire to at least a bachelor's degree in divinity. Unlike the monks of St Cuthbert studying at Durham College, the fellows of Canterbury College were not debarred from the study of canon law; but of the thirty-nine Christ Church monks ever known to have attained a higher degree at Oxford (i.e. between 1363 and 1540) only seven graduated in canon law—most notably, Prior Thomas Chillenden—as opposed to thirty-two in theology.[177] In the case of either degree, an elaborate system of university graces and dispensations, especially from the requirement that Benedictine monks should graduate in arts at Oxford before entering a higher faculty, rarely removed the necessity for a Christ Church monk to be more or less continuously in residence for at least ten years. Robert Eastry was a fellow of Canterbury College for as long as sixteen years after 1474 before he secured his bachelor's degree in theology; and several other Canterbury monks are known to have been recalled to the mother house after ten years of study in Oxford with no degree at all.[178] Fellows who were promoted to the wardenship naturally spent an even greater part of their lives at Oxford. However, of the twenty Christ Church monks known to have been wardens of Canterbury College between 1434 and 1534, the only ones to have held that office for a period much over five years were John Wodnesbergh, a relative of the prior of that name (warden at various times between 1428 and 1449), as well as the two most controversial Canterbury monks of the early sixteenth century, Dr Edward Bocking (warden 1510–18) and Master Richard Thornden (warden 1524–34).[179] It follows that neither the wardens nor indeed the fellows of Canterbury College were allowed to entrench themselves at Oxford as perpetual students or 'professional' scholars. Nevertheless, the decision to send particular monks to Canterbury College was not one to be taken lightly by the prior of Christ Church: the long years of residence at Oxford, even if interspersed with vacations at the mother house, eventually created a small academic élite within the convent whose influence was quite out of proportion to its numbers.

The most influential members of this élite, both at Oxford and later at Christ Church, were the wardens themselves. Like several of the more important officials at the mother house itself, the superiors of Canterbury College were appointed by the archbishop after three names had been submitted to him by the prior and chapter. Although academic distinction rather than administrative ability seems to have been the main qualification for the office, the surviving correspondence of the wardens leaves no doubt of their heavy responsibilities in supervising not only their own fellow monks but secular scholars,

[177] 5 of these 39 Canterbury College fellows received their degrees from universities overseas; and one (Henry Wodehull, the first warden of the college in 1363) had already graduated before migrating from Abingdon Abbey to Christ Church (ibid. iv. 64, 227). Monks of Durham College were debarred from studying canon law by the college's statutes of 1381; and at Westminster Abbey all but 2 of the 24 monks who graduated at Oxford between 1350 and 1540 were theologians: see *Historiae Dunelmensis Scriptores Tres*, ed. J. Raine (Surtees Soc., 9; 1839),

140; B. F. Harvey, 'The Monks of Westminster and the University of Oxford', in *The Reign of Richard II*, ed. F. R. H. Du Boulay and C. M. Barron (London, 1971), 114.

[178] Emden, *BRUO*, i. 621; iii. 1429, 1666; Pantin, *Cant. Coll.*, iv. 62–3.

[179] Emden, *BRUO*, iii. 2074 (Wodnesbergh); ibid. 1501–40, 54 (Bocking), 564–5 (Thornden). Cf. Pantin, *Cant. Coll.*, ii. 147, 150, 252, 255, 259; iv. 229–30.

servants, and paying lodgers or sojourners as well.[180] John Langdon cannot have been the only warden of Canterbury College to inform his prior, which he did in the 1480s, that a group of sojourners, in this case from Peterborough Abbey, were not 'gydyd as scolerys schuld be, for they be noo studentys'.[181] Wardens of Canterbury College could also find themselves involved in heavy administrative work on behalf of the university. Thus an earlier Dr John Langdon, warden of the college between 1410 and *c.*1413, served as the university chancellor's commissary as well, becoming a member of an anti-Wycliffite committee of investigation in Oxford.[182] For the exceptionally gifted monk, the wardenship of Canterbury College might even lead to a prominence which cut short his life as a member of the Christ Church community. William Dover, warden at Oxford in the 1380s, thereafter became Prior of Dover (1393–1414); and Warden Thomas Chaundler went on to be the head of three monasteries in succession (Horsham, Wymondham, and Eynsham) between 1501 and 1519. One or two wardens of Canterbury College even found themselves on the English episcopal bench, most notably the earlier John Langdon, promoted to the see of Rochester in 1421, and who died while present at the Council of Basle in 1434.[183] Indeed, the university monks of Christ Church were still in demand outside their community even after that community had come to an end. The second last warden of Canterbury College, Master Richard Thornden, not only served as university preacher, *cancellarius natus*, and pro-Vice Chancellor at Oxford, but later became the first Bishop of Dover (1545–58). As 'Dick of Dover' he won notoriety for himself in various ways, most notably by reintroducing mass to Christ Church towards the end of a career which illustrates to perfection a personal ambition and an independence of religious attitude that were not at all uncharacteristic of Canterbury monks at Oxford towards the end of the Middle Ages.[184]

However, the great majority of Canterbury College monks did return—sometimes reluctantly—to their mother house and then resumed the life of a cloistered Canterbury monk which they had left a decade or more previously, usually in their early twenties.[185] The subsequent careers of these Oxford-educated monks at Canterbury conformed to no single pattern. Most of the ex-fellows of the college went on to hold a variety of offices in the convent, none more so than William Chart, who vacated the Oxford wardenship at the end of the fourteenth century to become successively treasurer, penancer, cellarer, almoner, coroner, granger, almoner, and subprior of Christ Church before his death in

---

[180] From 1383 each of the five *pueri collegii* was appointed by the archbishop (as vacancies occurred at the college) after he had selected one from the three names submitted to him by the prior and chapter (LPL, Reg. J. Stafford, fos. 12, 18ᵛ, 19ᵛ; Pantin, *Cant. Coll.*, iii. 100–2; iv. 85–9); for the significance of this 'secular undergraduate colony, however small, in an Oxford monastic college', see A. B. Cobban, *The Medieval English Universities: Oxford and Cambridge to c.1500* (Cambridge, 1988), 184–5. The hiring of the college's servants (especially the manciple and the cook) figures prominently in the registers of the early 16th-cent. university: see e.g. Bodl., University Archives, Reg. EEE, fo. 375; Reg. F (reversed), fos. 105–6, 180.

[181] *Christ Church Letters*, 59–60; Pantin, *Cant. Coll.*, iii. 120–1.

[182] Emden, *BRUO*, ii. 1093; Pantin, *Cant. Coll.*, iv. 224.

[183] Cawston MS (Lit. D. 12), fo. 20ᵛ; Emden, *BRUO*, i. 399–400, 589; ii. 1093; Searle, *Chronicle and Lists*, 191; Pantin, *Cant. Coll.*, iv. 224.

[184] Bodl., University Archives, Reg. Cancell. B (reversed), fos. 138, 237ᵛ–242, 270, 365ᵛ; Pantin, *Cant. Coll.*, iii. 146–7, 257–9, 265–9; iv. 64–5, 75–8, 226, 230; Emden, *BRUO, 1501–40*, 564–5.

[185] As at Durham, Westminster, and many other major Benedictine monasteries, most (but not all) Christ Church university monks were sent to study at Oxford within four to six years of their profession at the Cathedral. It followed that several of the fellows of Canterbury College were still not in priest's orders when they arrived at the university: see e.g., Emden, *BRUO, 1501–40*, 184, 256, 258, 339–40, 426; Pantin, *Cant. Coll.*, iv. 55; and cf. Dobson, *Durham Priory* (cit. in n. 64), 352–3; Harvey, 'Monks of Westminster' (cit. in n. 177), 113.

1418.[186] By contrast, John Waltham, warden of the college between 1438 and 1441, seems to have held only the offices of penancer and keeper of Becket's Corona after his return to Canterbury.[187] From 1400 onwards it became especially common for the office of subprior to be held by a monk who had once been at Oxford.[188] However, the most significant tribute to the increasing importance of an Oxford education in the eyes of chapter and archbishop must be the fact that of the thirteen priors of Christ Church (between 1376 and 1540), eight were ex-fellows of Canterbury College. Although not as dominated by university monks as was Durham Cathedral Priory in the later Middle Ages, it seems clear that from the 1470s it would have been more or less inconceivable for the Christ Church community to be ruled by a prior without a higher degree from Oxford.[189] To that extent at least, the priors and some of the senior monks of late medieval Canterbury had come to enjoy intellectual and religious horizons considerably wider than those of their predecessors in the age of Henry of Eastry.

No doubt the influence of the university monks on their brethren in the Canterbury cloister was most pronounced when it was least formally expressed and therefore most poorly recorded. However, there is no doubt at all that the ex-fellows of Canterbury College were in frequent service as preachers within and near the Cathedral. All the available evidence suggests that the demand for sermons at Christ Church increased considerably during the fifteenth and early sixteenth century; and it may even be that the Priory came to be regarded by contemporaries as the home of the most celebrated Benedictine preachers in late medieval England. Admittedly, by no means all the many sermons preached in Canterbury Cathedral were delivered by members of the Christ Church community; but a very large number of sermons, in both Latin and English, were regularly preached by the convent's university monks. Throughout much of the fifteenth century it was the prior's custom to recall two or three young fellows of Canterbury College to their mother house, like William Peckham and Richard Thornden in 1521, in order to display their preaching prowess during Lent and Holy Week.[190] To judge from the numerous allusions in the fifteenth-century chronicles and obituary lists of Canterbury, oratorical ability was one of the most highly valued skills the community hoped for from their university-educated colleagues. The latter were often asked, like William Thornden

---

[186] Cawston MS, fo. 19; Searle, *Chronicle and Lists*, 9; Emden, *BRUO*, i. 394.

[187] LPL, Reg. J. Stafford, fo. 17; Searle, *Chronicle and Lists*, 54, 56, 60, 117; Emden, *BRUO*, iii. 1974.

[188] Of many possible examples, quite representative are the careers of John Aleyn (lector, penancer, and subprior at Christ Church in the years immediately after he acquired his doctorate in theology at Oxford in 1381–2) and James Grove (sacrist, penancer, and subprior during the 1420s after his years as warden of Canterbury College): see Searle, *Chronicle and Lists*, 16, 182; Emden, *BRUO*, i. 22; ii. 833. By the 15th cent. both monk-chancellors of Christ Church were also increasingly recruited from the convent's graduates; thus in 1470 the two chancellors were Dr William Sellyng and Master Thomas Chartham, the community's most distinguished university monks of their generation (Reg. S, fos. 1, 200, 234, 245ᵛ, 248ᵛ, 249ᵛ; Reg. T(i), fos. 1, 442, 445ᵛ, 448; Cawston MS, fo. 27ᵛ; Searle, *Chronicle and Lists*,

116–17; Emden, *BRUO*, i. 394; iii. 1666).

[189] Of the last 13 priors of Christ Church (between 1376 and 1540), only 5 do not appear to have been fellows of Canterbury College (John Fynch, John Wodnesbergh, John Elham, Thomas Goldstone I, and John Oxney): see Le Neve, *Fasti, 1300–1541* (cit. in n. 76), iv. 6; Pantin, *Cant. Coll.*, iv. 74, 218–28. At Westminster only one abbot in every two studied at Oxford during the later Middle Ages, whereas at Durham all priors after 1416 were university monks (Harvey, 'Monks of Westminster' (cit. in n. 177), 122; Dobson, *Durham Priory* (cit. in n. 64), 353–8).

[190] Treasurers' Accts., 1521; Pantin, *Cant. Coll.*, iv. 66–7, 193, 206; and cf. Harvey, 'Monks of Westminster' (cit. in n. 177), 118–20. For the text of the highly sophisticated Latin sermon preached by Dr William Uttyng, Archbishop Bourchier's chaplain, on the election of John Oxney as prior in 1468, see Reg. S, fos. 232–233ᵛ; and cf. Searle, *Chronicle and Lists*, 34, 64, 76, 86, 93.

in 1460, to preach to a large lay audience in the nave of the Cathedral; but it was equally common for them to deliver a sermon exclusively to their own brethren, most notably at such important ceremonies as those which accompanied the election of an archbishop or prior.[191] Of the many Canterbury College graduates who received acclamation among their fellows as an *egregius predicator*, several even became prominent preachers on the national scene. It was Dr John Langdon, later Bishop of Rochester but then warden of Canterbury College, who delivered the main sermon when Convocation met at St Paul's Cathedral in 1411; and as late as July 1537 William Sandwich, one of the very last of Canterbury's university monks, was appointed to preach at Paul's Cross by none other than Thomas Cromwell himself.[192]

Of even greater significance for the younger members of the Christ Church community than the sermons delivered by ex-members of Canterbury College was the specialized instruction in arts and theology which they could derive from the same source. An advanced academic teacher, holding the office of claustral lector, had emerged at Christ Church as early as 1275: this position was held by three Franciscan friars in succession until 1314, after which it was the convent's own Oxford-educated monks who gradually became the natural choice as *lectores claustri*.[193] Although there is considerable uncertainty about exactly where their teaching was conducted, these lectors seem to have played a more prominent role at Christ Church than at any other English cathedral monastery. According to the visitation injunctions of Archbishop Winchelsey in 1298, the theology lectures delivered by the lector should have been attended by all, or nearly all, the brethren: if so, which admittedly seems hardly likely, Christ Church may well have become the most academically learned monastic community in the country.[194] However, after a long period when the educational life of the Cathedral was dominated by two highly influential *lectores in schola claustrali* in the persons of the Oxford graduates Dr William Gillyngham (from 1382 to *c*.1410) and Dr Richard Godmersham (from *c*.1412 to *c*.1430), the office of claustral lector seems to have gone into partial abeyance.[195] The most probable explanation is not a collapse of theological study at Christ Church as such, but rather an increased diversification of intellectual interests on the part of the last generations of Canterbury monks. In any case, some form of education in elementary theology as well as arts must have been available from the masters of the novices, at Christ Church not usually identified with the *magistri ordinis*.[196] A chamber assigned for use as the *scola noviciorum* was certainly in existence by the late 1280s; but most reading and study in the Cathedral Priory probably took place in more or less private *studia*, often carrels in the cloister like the eighteen new

[191] Reg. G, fo. 237ᵛ; Reg. S, fo. 249; Searle, *Chronicle and Lists*, 60, 78, 105, 106. When Thomas Guston preached a sermon *ad populum* in the Christ Church cemetery, his audience included Archbishop Henry Chichele (Cawston MS, fo. 22).

[192] Wilkins, *Concilia*, iii. 273; G. R. Owst, *Preaching in Medieval England* (Cambridge, 1926), 52; Cawston MS, fos. 17ᵛ, 28; Searle, *Chronicle and Lists*, 190, 193; Pantin, *Cant. Coll.*, iv; Emden, *BRUO*, ii. 1093–4; *BRUO*, 1501–40, 504.

[193] CUL, MS Ee. v. 31, fos. 24ᵛ, 28–9, 34, 63, 78ᵛ; Gervase, *Historical Works*, ii. 281; C. Cotton, *The Grey Friars of Canterbury, 1224 to 1538* (Manchester, 1924), 34–6; A. G. Little, *The Grey Friars in Oxford* (Oxford Hist. Soc., OS, 20; 1892), 4–8, 66; Hogan,

'Memorandum Book of Prior Eastry' (cit. in n. 63), i. 340–1.

[194] BL, Cotton MS Galba E. iv, fo. 67ᵛ. These lectures were also available to the chantry priests of the Cathedral (Pantin, *Cant. Coll.*, iv. 69–70).

[195] Cawston MS, fo. 24ᵛ; Searle, *Chronicle and Lists*, 29, 182, 184; Emden, *BRUO*, ii. 770, 779; Pantin, *Cant. Coll.*, iv. 221–2. The first Christ Church monk to become a lector at the Cathedral (in 1314) was Stephen de Faversham, who had studied at Paris (BL, Harl. MS 6981, fo. 37; Pantin, *Cant. Coll.*, iv. 71, 209–10, 217).

[196] Searle, *Chronicle and Lists*, 17, 71, 74, 106, 183, 187, 192–6.

ones provided by Prior Eastry at a cost of over £32 in 1318.[197] Prior Chillenden's thorough remodelling of the Christ Church cloister between *c*.1395 and 1414 involved the destruction of several of the monastic carrels there; and it was probably for that reason that a 'nova schola monachorum' appeared within the Cathedral precincts at the beginning of the fifteenth century.[198]

A more obvious symptom of the increasing sophistication of academic learning at fifteenth-century Christ Church was the construction of a new and purpose-built common library over the prior's chapel, constructed in the 1430s and 1440s under the auspices of Archbishop Henry Chichele and Prior Thomas Goldstone I.[199] This was certainly not the first library building in the history of the Cathedral: in 1320–1, for example, scribes were being paid for writing manuscripts 'pro bibliotheca' and a century later one of the charges brought against the delinquent monk Robert of Alendon was that 'he stole many books of great price from the convent's library'.[200] Mr Tim Tatton-Brown has recently suggested that this 'old library', a two-storeyed building adjacent to the north transept of the Cathedral, may have been badly damaged by the earthquake of 1382. Its replacement 'took a long time to complete'; but by 1444, at approximately the same date as at Canterbury College, Oxford, the monks of Christ Church were at last provided with a new specialized library, large enough to serve as a reading-room as well as a spacious book-store. According to Robert Willis, this new library may have measured approximately 55 by 22 feet, in which case it was somewhat larger than the first-floor library built a little earlier by the monks of Durham.[201] On the assumption that the list of 293 books compiled in 1508, by the monk bibliophile William Ingram, represents a more or less complete inventory of all the chained books then in the common library, the latter seems to have housed sixteen bookcases, each containing four shelves.[202] Of these sixteen bookcases, eight on each side of the room, no less than nine were devoted to Bibles, biblical commentaries, the Fathers, and works of scholastic theology, whereas only three cases were reserved for canon and civil law, with just one each for philosophy, medicine, history, and mathematics.[203] Not that these chained books constituted the whole, or indeed the majority, of the convent's collections of manuscripts. The Cathedral Priory already possessed some 1,850 books at the time of Prior Eastry's great catalogue of the early fourteenth century; and the evidence of later catalogues, as well as of surviving inscriptions on Christ Church manuscripts, leaves no doubt that the convent's book collections were in a constant state of development and change.[204] The new Canterbury common library of the 1440s should accordingly be seen only as the most important reference-library within a convent which abounded with other

[197] BL, Cotton MS Galba E. iv, fos. 101–2; *Lit. Cant.*, i. 46; Pantin, *Cant. Coll.*, iv. 71.

[198] BL, Arundel MS 68, fo. 5; *Lit. Cant.*, iii. 116; Woodman, *Architectural History* (cit. in n. 8), 164–6; Woodruff and Danks, *Memorials*, 176–7.

[199] BL, Arundel MS 68, fo. 5; Jacob, *Archbishop Chichele* (cit. in n. 52), 99.

[200] Assisa Scaccarii, 1230–31; Reg. L, fo. 128; *Lit. Cant.* i. 151.

[201] T. Tatton-Brown, 'The Mediaeval Library at Canterbury Cathedral', *Cant. Cath. Chron.*, no. 82 (1988), 35–42; James, *ALCD*, l–li (by no means a definitive discussion); J. W. Clark,

The Care of Books (Cambridge, 1901), 106, 190; cf. Dobson, *Durham Priory* (cit. in n. 64), 365–7.

[202] James, *ALCD*, pp. liv–lv; Ker, *Medieval Libraries* (cit. in n. 174), 29. See, however, N.L. Ramsay, below, pp. 364–6.

[203] James, *ALCD*, pp. liv–lv.

[204] See e.g. the way in which the 36 books probably acquired by Prior Thomas Chillenden at Oxford during his years as a canon-law student there in the 1370s and 1380s eventually came to supplement Christ Church's somewhat limited collection of legal texts (Lit. MS C. 16; *Lit. Cant.*, iii. 121–2; Emden, *BRUO*, i. 415; James, *ALCD*, pp. xxxv–xl, l).

book-depositories, for instance in the infirmary, the prior's *camera*, the cloister carrels, and the private rooms of many monks, above all those who had once been fellows of Canterbury College. By the end of the fifteenth century at least, the cumulative impression left by ever more abundant evidence is of considerable numbers of the Christ Church fraternity probably reading very widely indeed.

Indeed, one of the more unusual features of the surviving Christ Church book-lists and inventories is that many of them itemize not only the contents of the convent's formal 'libraries' but also the personal collections of individual monks, like those of Robert Holyngborn (in *c.*1495 and *c.*1508), Thomas Goldwell (in *c.*1496), and John Dunstone (in 1501–2).[205] In the case of many monks who had studied at Canterbury College, like Robert Holyngborn and Robert Eastry (*c.*1500), their personal libraries consisted primarily of their Oxford textbooks; but Richard Stone, not a university graduate, showed a more personal predilection for saints' lives (including a *Vita Sancti Thome Martiris*) and for works of history, ranging from Bede's *Ecclesiastical History* and Higden's *Polychronicon* to a mysterious *Cronice Anglorum*.[206] Unfortunately, it is the service books and the recreational reading of the Christ Church community which are least adequately represented by surviving manuscripts; but it seems clear enough from inscriptions in the latter that by the end of the fourteenth century it was quite unusual for a monk to write or illuminate a text for himself or his convent. A hundred years later still, Prior Thomas Goldstone II was prepared to pay no less than £60 6s. 8d. for the copying of the *Rationale Divinorum*; and when he wished to present 'a large and new' service book for the precentor's use in the Cathedral choir, he had it sent up to London for binding after 'gilding and decoration' at Christ Church by a local stationer.[207] Few of the new books acquired by the monks of Canterbury during the fourteenth and fifteenth centuries were so lavishly bound; but it remained a library of national importance for all that. A check-list of seventy-four books missing from the common library in 1338 demonstrates better than any other source quite how intensively its contents were used. Apart from twelve books lent to outsiders—including some volumes of *Vitae et Miraculae* still unreclaimed after being lent to Edward II several years earlier—the overwhelming impression provided by the books borrowed is of a Christ Church community especially eager to read accounts of the history of their own church and, above all, of their patron St Thomas.[208]

Not that many lives of St Thomas Becket seem to have been composed or copied by Christ Church monks themselves towards the end of the Middle Ages; and it is ironical that their monastic library should have reached its most elaborate stage of organization when the golden age of their scriptorium was undoubtedly over. It has indeed to be conceded that fewer of the fourteenth- and fifteenth-century brethren, and fewer ex-fellows of Canterbury College in particular, became men of letters than one might have had a reasonable right to expect. However, what M. R. James once described as 'a dearth of literary output' in the early sixteenth-century convent does not necessarily imply a

[205] Pantin, *Cant. Coll.*, i. 80–8; iv. 222, 223; James, *ALCD*, 498.

[206] Pantin, *Cant. Coll.*, i. 88–9; C. E. Woodruff, 'An Inventory of the Contents of the Bed-Chamber of Brother Richard Stone, Monk of Christ Church, Canterbury', *Arch. Cant.*, 43 (1931), 103–10.

[207] Woodruff and Danks, *Memorials*, 384–5; DE 117.

[208] Reg. L, fo. 104; *Lit. Cant.*, ii. 146–52; James, *ALCD*, pp. xliv–xlvi.

complete lack of intellectual distinction and achievement within the Canterbury cloister.[209] Precisely because they belonged to so large a monastic community, the brethren of Christ Church tended to include among their ranks several monks with highly specialized and at times unorthodox intellectual interests. In the course of the fifteenth century, for example, the convent produced two celebrated astronomers in the persons of Thomas Aldyngton (who died in 1501) and John Trendle, who had died of asthma in 1433. The latter was the author of a treatise on the seven planets and was regarded, by his brethren at least, as an outstanding *calculator*.[210] Several other late medieval Canterbury monks occupied themselves in rearranging the Priory's manuscripts and archives, thereby developing an antiquarian interest in the history of their house. John de Gloucestre compiled an inventory of the convent's records in 1370; and William Ingram's catalogue of the common library in 1508 was only the most ambitious of the large variety of memoranda he produced, usually on quasi-historical topics.[211] One of Ingram's contemporaries in the Christ Church cloister, Thomas Cawston, deserves greater praise than he has yet received for compiling ('fecit fieri, AD 1466') obituary notices of all the monks of Christ Church since 1286 with an accuracy and attention to detail which surpasses similar lists in any English medieval religious house at any time.[212] According to Cawston's own obituary, he died in 1504 at the age of 76, after residing over half a century within the community he had served as chancellor, third prior, feretrar, sacrist, treasurer, coroner, and master of the infirmary, as well as the 'collector of the names of the living and dead monks of the church of Christ Church from the eighth year of King John to the nineteenth year of Henry VII'.[213]

The desire to preserve one's brethren's names and dates of death for purposes of posthumous commemoration is a common enough feature of all religious corporations; but at fifteenth-century Christ Church the impulse to create comprehensive lists of deceased monks seems to have become almost obsessive, not least because such lists helped to satisfy a growing historical, or at least antiquarian, curiosity about the past of so famous a monastic community. Both the two Christ Church 'chronicles' of the fifteenth century, one written by William Glastonbury before his death in 1449 and the other by John Stone (Canterbury's most enjoyable 'compositor istarum cronicarum') in the period from 1467 to 1471, are primarily and sometimes solely a series of biographical tributes to deceased Christ Church priors and monks.[214] It was precisely because John Stone found himself unable to resist elaborating informally upon what was planned as a pious commemoration of his dead fellows that his 'chronicle' finally developed into the most engagingly vivid piece of historical writing to survive from any fifteenth-century monastery.

[209] James, *ALCD*, p. lii; cf. Woodruff and Danks, *Memorials*, 384; Harvey, 'Monks of Westminster' (cit. in n. 177), 122–6. In 1494 one ex-fellow of Canterbury College, John Holyngbourne, took the exceptional initiative of commissioning a Netherlandish painting (see pl. 27).

[210] Cawston MS (Lit. D. 12), fos. 23ᵛ, 33; Searle, *Chronicle and Lists*, 71, 82, 189.

[211] Lit. MS C. 11; HMC, 5th *Report*, app., p. 435; Searle, *Chronicle and Lists*, 181; Pantin, *Cant. Coll.*, iv. 217; Ker, *Medieval Libraries*, 29; G. H. Rooke, 'Dom William Ingram and His Account-Book, 1504–1533', *JEH*, 7 (1956), 30.

[212] Lit. MS D. 12, now known as Cawston's *Historia Duplex* because it also contains the longest and fullest profession-lists to survive from medieval Christ Church. For some comments on the complete composition of this manuscript see J. Hatcher, 'Mortality in the Fifteenth Century: Some New Evidence', *EconHR*, 2nd ser., 39 (1986), 23–5.

[213] Cawston MS, fo. 35.

[214] Oxford, Corpus Christi College, MS 256, only partly printed in C. E. Woodruff, 'The Chronicle of William Glastynbury, Monk of the Priory of Christ Church, Canterbury, 1419–1448', *Arch. Cant.*, 37 (1925), 121–51. Cf. Searle, *Chronicle and*

However, although Stone's chronicle offers its readers the rare opportunity to share the perspective of a Canterbury monk upon his own central preoccupations, ranging from liturgical observance and monastic attitudes to office-holding in his convent to an endless sequence of visits by kings, magnates, and prelates, it has to be conceded that the author's intellectual horizons seem limited to Canterbury itself.[215] Not surprisingly in the case of a Cathedral priory whose claims to ascendancy in the English Church were based on its antiquity, a strong sense of historical tradition continued to be very apparent in the late medieval cloister. However, that tradition had tended to become steadily more attenuated as it progressed from Eadmer and Gervase of Canterbury to the latter's anonymous, and much less accomplished, continuators. Considerable historical work was still being attempted at Christ Church in the fourteenth century, most notably an anonymous chronicle for the period from 1346 to 1367 and the *Vitae Archiepiscoporum Cantuariensium*, both once erroneously attributed to Stephen Birchington.[216] However, by the beginning of the fifteenth century the writing of narrative history at Canterbury had atrophied beyond repair; and despite the charm of William of Glastonbury's and John Stone's biographical collections, Christ Church Cathedral exemplifies only too well the familiar theme of the decline and fall of the monastic chronicle towards the end of the Middle Ages.

It is therefore neither to William Glastonbury nor to John Stone but to the ex-fellows of Canterbury College that one must again return for a final impression of the most creative intellectual activity within the late medieval Christ Church cloister. At the end of the fourteenth century, for example, it was the university-educated William Gillyngham who allegedly produced such successful summary accounts of the history of Canterbury and of the dignitaries of the Benedictine order that his work was used as the basis for illuminated paintings on the north side of the cathedral choir.[217] Much more significantly, and apparently earlier than in any other monastery in the country, some Christ Church monks were soon to show their awareness of the new Italianate emphasis—on the style as much as the substance—of what should be read and written. By the 1440s, William Chart, for example, who died in Ireland in 1458, was trying to write Latin letters on the new Italian model, even if with only partial success.[218] An even more interesting portent

Lists, 48, 107 *et passim*; Woodruff, 'Monastic Chronicle' (cit. in n. 105), 47–84; A. Gransden, *Historical Writing in England* (2 vols.; London, 1974, 1982), ii. 401, 413–17.

[215] However, it seems most likely that Stone himself regarded his 'chronicle' as a private commonplace-book, probably designed for informal circulation among a few members of the community only; cf. Gransden, *Historical Writing* (cit. in n. 214), ii. 417.

[216] Gervase, *Historical Works*, ii, *passim*; *Chronica Johannis de Reading et Anonymi Cantuariensis. 1346–67*, ed. J. Tait (Manchester, 1914); *Stephani Birchingtoni Historia de Archiepiscopis Cantuariensibus, A.D. 597–1369*, in Wharton, *Anglia Sacra*, i. 1–48, and cf. ibid. 49–176; Searle, *Chronicle and Lists*, 183. See also BL, Harl. MS 636, a version of the French Brut (to 1313) written at Canterbury in order to extol the Christ Church community above all other English religious houses: see J. Taylor, *English Historical Literature in the Fourteenth Century*

(Oxford, 1987), 118.

[217] T. Tanner, *Bibliotheca Britannico-Hibernica* (London, 1748), 357, 363; Pantin, *Cant. Coll.*, iv. 221; Emden, *BRUO*, ii. 770. For the popularity of such lists of saints and other worthies within Benedictine monasteries at the beginning of the 15th cent., see W. A. Pantin, 'Some Medieval Treatises on the Origins of Monasticism', in *Medieval Studies Presented to Rose Graham*, ed. V. Ruffer and A. J. Taylor (Oxford, 1950), 189–215.

[218] William Chart was almost certainly the compiler (at Christ Church) of the handsome collection of humanist texts, which includes two of his own letters, presented to the then Imperial University of Tokyo by Canon B. H. Streeter in 1931: see Univ. of Tokyo Library, MS A. 100. 1300, fos. 79–80 (a fac. edn. of the entire manuscript was ed. by K. Nishimoto and publ. under the title of *Codex Streeterianus* by the Univ. of Tokyo in 1987). Among the many items in this collection is a letter (fos. 75–6) of Master Richard Petworth, once secretary of Cardinal

of the future was the interest shown in classical authors by another graduate of Canterbury College and would-be Ciceronian, Henry Cranebroke, who had become an acquaintance of Sir John Tiptoft while at Oxford in the early 1440s. One of the manuscripts bought by Cranebroke a few years later still survives as BL Royal MS 10 B. IX and includes several works by Poggio and Guarino da Verona, as well as a letter of 1452 in which the Christ Church monk is complimented for his literary elegance ('stilo Tulliano') by Tiptoft himself.[219]

By that date the most illustrious of all Christ Church's university monks, William Tyll or Sellyng, had entered the community, from which he was soon sent (by 1454) to Canterbury College. There he not only supplicated for his baccalaureate of theology in 1458 but was also introduced by Stefano Surigone, Thomas Chaundler, and probably Sir John Tiptoft to the delights of contemporary Italian learning.[220] Although much discussed, the precise nature of the literary achievements and contributions to English 'humanism' of this supposed 'foremost English classical scholar of his time' are hard to assess. However, the fact that William Sellyng made no less than three lengthy visits to Italy (in 1464–*c*.1467; 1469–71; 1487–*c*.1489) can leave no doubt either of his own enthusiasm for the new methods of studying Latin and Greek available at Florence, Padua, and Bologna, or of the value set upon the services of so accomplished an English Benedictine scholar by his king and community alike.[221] It may have been at Bologna (where he became a doctor of theology in March 1466), or possibly at Padua, that Sellyng learnt the Greek which he was later to teach in his turn to some of his fellows at Christ Church. More remarkably still, Sellyng's translation into Latin (1488) of a sermon of St John Chrysostom is the earliest known translation from the Greek language made by an Englishman in the fifteenth century.[222] Otherwise, William Sellyng's literary output was comparatively slender; and it was as a teacher, preacher, and orator that he exerted much of his influence outside as well as within his monastery's walls. He was, for example, chosen to address the Convocation of the southern province during the turbulent years of Richard III's and Henry VII's reign. Of the many non-monastic pupils who perpetuated Sellyng's influence after his death perhaps the most influential was Thomas Linacre, who according to John Leland accompanied him on his last journey to Rome in 1487.[223]

Within his own community of Christ Church, William Sellyng also built up a small circle of like-minded enthusiasts for the new scholarship, a process which quite probably

Henry Beaufort and an early English admirer of Italian humanist learning, with whom Prior John Salisbury was in regular communication during the 1440s: see *Lit. Cant.*, iii. 189–90; R. Weiss, 'Some Unpublished Correspondence of Guarino da Verona', *Italian Studies*, 2 (1938–9), 110–17; id., *Humanism in England During the Fifteenth Century* (3rd edn.; Oxford, 1967), 20, 128–9.

[219] BL, Royal MS 10 B. IX, fo. 122, a manuscript which contains copies of several other letters to and from Cranebroke, as well as an erudite and cryptic satire on the then members of Canterbury College (fos. 32ᵛ–33ᵛ; printed in Pantin, *Cant. Coll.*, iii. 68–72). For Cranebroke's later career at Christ Church, see Searle, *Chronicle and Lists*, 97; Emden, *BRUO*, i. 509. John Tiptoft's close association with Canterbury Cathedral is discussed in R. J. Mitchell, *John Tiptoft, 1427–70* (London, 1938), 20–3.

[220] Weiss, *Humanism* (cit. in n. 218), 153–4; Emden, *BRUO*, iii. 1666. For a selection of Sellyng's later correspondence with Thomas Chaundler on Canterbury College business, see *Lit. Cant.*, iii. 260–2, 267–71.

[221] The primary purpose of Sellyng's second journey to Italy was to secure indulgences for the 1470 jubilee of St Thomas Becket from Pope Paul II (Pantin, *Cant. Coll.*, iii. 108–9; Emden, *BRUO*, iii. 1666)

[222] BL, Add. MS 15,673, fo. 28ᵛ; Reg. S, fos. 235, 237ᵛ; Weiss, *Humanism* (cit. in n. 218), 157–8; cf. the tribute to Sellyng's linguistic skills ('lingua greca atque latina valde eruditus') in his obituary notice of 1494 (Cawston MS, fo. 27ᵛ).

[223] Searle, *Chronicle and Lists*, 105, 108; Weiss, *Humanism* (cit. in n. 218), 156–9; Knowles, *Religious Orders*, iii. 88–90; Emden, *BRUO*, iii. 1666.

made Canterbury the most important fixed centre in England for the dissemination of Italianate learning during Sellyng's own priorate, from 1472 until his death in 1494. The most influential members of Sellyng's monastic circle appear to have been William Hadley, with whom the future prior travelled to Italy in 1464, and Reginald Goldstone, his travelling companion in Rome and Flanders during 1469–71. Throughout most of Sellyng's twenty-two year tenure of the priorate, Hadley served as his subprior (1471–98) and Reginald Goldstone acted as the Prior's confidential agent until ill health drove him to the chamber in the monastic infirmary, where he eventually died, in 1504.[224] Prior Sellyng himself had died in December 1494, to be warmly remembered by his monks for introducing Greek learning into the cloister and, more generally, for his encouragement of the study of humane letters within the convent. Not only did he adorn the common library with 'beautiful carved work', but he also glazed the south walk of the cloister and installed several comfortable new carrels there for private study by his monks: 'O quam laudabiliter se habuit!'[225] For once, the conventional eulogies of the fifteenth-century Christ Church brethren about one another seem altogether warranted. The Canterbury community had every right to be gratified at William Sellyng's highly surprising success in becoming the most notable and well regarded of all their university monks since the early fourteenth century. Alas, it was not a success which could be readily repeated. By the year of Sellyng's death, it was already apparent that the tradition of humanist scholarship which he had inaugurated at Canterbury was already in decline there. More seriously still for the future of his own Cathedral Priory, Sellyng's enthusiasm for the educational values of fifteenth-century Italy was soon to be inherited by a new generation of English humanists who saw those values as an alternative rather than a complement to the monastic ideal.[226]

THE CHRIST CHURCH MONKS AFTER THE BLACK DEATH

Although there are many reasons why the monks of late medieval England's largest religious house deserve to be remembered, perhaps their greatest claim to attention in the late twentieth century is quite simply that so very much can be known about them. Only perhaps at the cathedral priories of Durham and Norwich, as well as at Westminster Abbey, is a pre-Reformation monastic community documented in comparably profuse detail. While it would be misleading to suggest that more than the occasional Christ Church monk has left a vivid impression of his personality or his individual aspirations to posterity, as a group more can be discovered about their origins, recruitment, diet, daily routines, education, administrative responsibility, and life expectancy than in the case of almost all other Englishmen of their age. It follows that the major problem confronting the historian of the late medieval monks of Canterbury is not the scarcity but the abundance of their surviving records. Not until those muniments have been subjected to intensive scrutiny will it be possible to produce more than a provisional impression of life in the Cathedral cloister.

---

[224] Cawston MS, fos. 32ᵛ, 35; Searle, *Chronicle and Lists*, 193; Emden, *BRUO*, ii. 782, 846; Pantin, *Cant. Coll.*, iv. 222.

[225] Cawston MS, fo. 31ᵛ; BL, Arundel MS 68, fo. 2; Wharton, *Anglia Sacra*, i. 145–6.

[226] J. K. McConica, *English Humanists and Reformation Politics Under Henry VIII and Edward VI* (Oxford, 1965), 13–14, 46–9.

The following brief survey of the Christ Church community is, moreover, naturally determined by the latter's own archival practices, as well as by the unpredictable vagaries of record survival, perhaps even more unpredictable at Canterbury than at any other medieval English cathedral. Although the convent's voluminous official registers deserve to hold pride of place in any account of its administrative records, a more accurate impression of the prior and chapter's priorities and problems may often emerge from its obedientiary and other accounts, as well as from its large collections of miscellaneous correspondence. It is the fortunate survival at Canterbury of a very wide and almost unclassifiable variety of apparently ephemeral documents, of the sort often destroyed in other cathedral priories, which can sometimes allow the historian to rescue the Christ Church monks from oblivion with a sense of real immediacy.[227] An even more distinctive feature of the Cathedral chapter, especially in the fifteenth century, is the intense and perhaps almost obsessive interest displayed in the lives, deaths, and achievements of Christ Church monks within the monastery itself. Although this interest was one clearly shared by several members of the community, fascination with the biographies of the living or deceased members of the community clearly reached its climax in the celebrated *liber* of John Stone, that indefatigable 'compiler of the chronicles' of his fellow monks from 1415 to 1471.[228] In this sphere, John Stone and his colleagues have no rivals in the religious history of late medieval England: they were the first, and in many ways are still the best, of all the prosopographers of their age.   ·

The preoccupation of Thomas Cawston, John Stone, and others with the names and dates of every monk who had entered religion in their house was itself an indirect reflection of their sensitivity to the numerical size of their community. The chapter's ability to maintain its membership at an outstandingly high level, regarded as an important index of its prestige and welfare by the Christ Church monks themselves, was not, however, always achieved without effort. Although nearly always the largest religious house in England, the Canterbury community was never absolutely stable in size, its numbers being in particular a good deal more volatile in the fourteenth than the fifteenth century. In some ways, the greatest demographic disaster in the history of the convent had occurred long before the arrival of the Black Death, being caused by its involuntary involvement in Archbishop Winchelsey's dispute with Edward I. This was a conflict which at times reduced the monastery's effective complement to as low as thirty; and in July 1297 the Archbishop himself wrote to the prior and chapter from Charing reminding them that the maintenance of divine worship in the Cathedral depended on the urgent recruitment of thirty new novices to restore 'the ancient and proper number of monks' there. Winchelsey's advice was presumably taken, for after his own death, in May 1313, seventy-one Christ Church monks were able to participate in the election of his successor, Walter Reynolds.[229] On the

[227] Particularly valuable for this very reason are the highly miscellaneous 164 documents which now constitute the misleadingly titled 'Domestic Economy' accounts in the Canterbury archives: many of these were transcribed by W. P. Blore in his years as Cathedral librarian, between 1936 and 1948 (see MSS Cat. 91); cf. N. L. Ramsay, *Provisional Guide to the Principal Categories of Material in the Archives of the Dean and Chapter of* *Canterbury* (Canterbury, 1985).

[228] Searle, *Chronicle and Lists*, 107.

[229] *Reg. Winchelsey* (cit. in n. 62), i. 257–8; Denton, *Winchelsey and the Crown* (cit. in n. 11), 112; Reg. Q, fo. 81; R. M. Haines, *Ecclesia Anglicana: Studies in the English Church of the Later Middle Ages* (Toronto, 1989), 27. This demographic recovery is confirmed in general, if at times disconcertingly erratic, terms by

limited evidence available, the community thereafter usually numbered between sixty and seventy during the fifty years before the first onslaught of bubonic plague in 1348–9, a calamity which had (at least in the short term) a much more catastrophic effect on the life expectancy of the prior and chapter's tenants than on that of the monks themselves.[230] According to a well-known, but possibly misleading, entry in Thomas Cawston's obituary list, 'only [*tantum*] four of the brethren died of the pestilence' in 1349 itself; but, if so, the convent's often-mentioned immunity from plague was not to last for long. The same obituary list records the death of no less than twenty-five monks, including the subprior and the distinguished Dr James of Oxney, between June and October 1361, when the second great national outbreak of plague in England was at its height.[231] In the circumstances, it is hardly surprising that between the 1350s and the 1380s the community was at times reduced to a total strength of less than sixty; and it is even more understandable that Archbishop Sudbury should have ordered the monks to increase their recruitment urgently when he discovered that as few as forty-five monks had appeared at his visitation of the Cathedral in 1376.[232]

The size of the Christ Church community was never allowed to fall so low again during the remainder of its history. Five years later, in the crisis year of 1381, sixty-one monks took part in the election of the unfortunate Sudbury's successor, William Courtenay; and by the beginning of the next decade numerical recovery was even more complete, when eighty of his fellows elected Thomas Chillenden as their prior, in February 1391.[233] Before the beginning of the new century it therefore seems clear that whatever their causes, the community's most acute demographic difficulties had been satisfactorily surmounted. A wide variety of different sources, ranging from detailed records of elections and visitations of the convent to surviving prior's and other accounts, make it clear that in any given year between 1400 and 1520 the number of monks usually totalled between seventy-five and ninety. In the middle years of the century, the latter figure was occasionally even exceeded; and as late as 1511 there were still to be found as many as eighty-eight monks (including eight novices) subject to Archbishop William Warham's visitation of that year.[234] Admittedly, minor chronological irregularities in recruitment were not infrequent, being a natural consequence of the customary practice whereby novices were usually admitted

---

the numbers of monks recorded as receiving black cloth for their habits from the monastic chamberlain each year (Chamberlain's Accts., 1310–49).

[230] Reg. G, fo. 60ᵛ records the presence of 59 monks at the election of Archbishop Thomas Bradwardine on 4 June: there were still almost that number alive to elect Bradwardine's successor 3 months later (ibid., fos. 76–7). Cf. Haines, *Ecclesia Anglicana* (cit. in n. 229), 35; HMC, 8th *Report*, app., p. 341.

[231] Cawston MS (Lit. D. 12), fos. 16ᵛ, 17; Searle, *Chronicle and Lists*, 181; *Lit. Cant.*, ii, pp. xxi–xxv.

[232] Reg. G, fo. 173ᵛ: Churchill, *Canterbury Administration* (cit. in n. 24), i. 142. As Dr Joan Greatrex points out, this alarmingly low figure may be misleading, as in this very year the chamberlains' accounts made provision for the habits of 58 brethren in addition to the prior: on the other hand, Archbishop Sudbury's

concern seems genuine enough (Wilkins, *Concilia*, iii. 110).

[233] Reg. G, fo. 229ᵛ; Dahmus, *Courtenay* (cit. in n. 54), 200. In Aug. 1396 Thomas Arundel was elected as Courtenay's successor by 79 monks (Reg. G, fo. 237).

[234] *Kentish Visitations of Warham* (cit. in n. 54), 2–3; cf. M. H. Bateson, 'Archbishop Warham's Visitation of Monasteries, 1511', *EHR*, 6 (1891), 18–21. A century earlier, in 1414, Henry Chichele had been elected archbishop by 77 brethren (Jacob, *Henry Chichele* (cit. in n. 52), 20; cf. Reg. G, fo. 285); and in 1454 and 1455 there seem to have been over 90 members of the community (Prior's Accts.; Smith, *Cant. Cath. Priory*, 3). The evidence of obedientiary accounts and of various lists of monks compiled at about the beginning of the century (DE, 24, 27–8) confirms that there was usually a complement of considerably more than 70 monks during the decades after 1400.

into the convent in groups of six, eight, or even more, rather than singly.[235] However, despite not only that complication but also the volatility of the late medieval death-rate within the convent, throughout almost the entire course of the fifteenth century Christ Church Cathedral Priory was remarkably successful in preserving its complement of monks at a size only a little below, and often above, eighty. Not until the years immediately before the Dissolution—even in the very late 1530s there were still fifty-eight members of the community—are there any signs of a scarcity of would-be recruits to the monastic life at the Cathedral.[236]

It was perhaps because so many aspirant monks were eager to join the celebrated Christ Church community that the latter seems to have been more scrupulous than most convents in its selection of its future brethren. The formalities of entry into the fraternity were certainly more complicated at Canterbury than in many Benedictine monasteries, not least because of the anomaly that the late medieval archbishops consistently, and annoyingly, refused to make a formal surrender of their legal right to approve the admission of novices before the latter were clothed with the habit.[237] In practice, however, the choice of new members of the community was controlled by the prior, in consultation with all or part of the chapter; and to the extent that existing monks were often encouraged to recommend suitable candidates for profession to the prior, Christ Church was in many ways a self-selecting, as well as a self-perpetuating, corporation.[238] Nowhere was such selection likely to be better informed than in the case of those novices who had been scholars of the convent's own almonry school, in continuous existence within the precincts from at least the late thirteenth century to the Dissolution. Its pupils were not only taught by a professional grammar-master, but received training in the type of singing essential for the religious life. Unfortunately, it is only occasionally—as when John Stone recorded the entry of four *pueri de elemosinaria* into the community in October 1468—that evidence survives of recruitment from this school into the chapter; but that the latter was, as in other monastic cathedrals, one of the most frequented of all gateways into monastic life at Christ Church there can be no reasonable doubt.[239]

Admittedly, the national prestige of Canterbury Cathedral, even in the later Middle Ages, continued to attract some candidates for the religious life who were considerably older and from much further afield than was usually the case at the other cathedral priories such as Durham. The German ancestry ('natione teutonicus') of Brother John Browne, who died in 1412 after over thirty years in the community, was admittedly highly exceptional; and there cannot have been many inmates of Christ Church who were actually born on shipboard in the English Channel as seems to be alleged of Nicholas Winchelsea,

---

[235] Cawston MS (Lit. D. 12), fos. 2ᵛ–36; for the identical practice at Durham Cathedral Priory, see Dobson, *Durham Priory* (cit. in n. 64), 62–3.

[236] Pantin, *Cant. Coll.*, iii. 151–4; cf. Woodruff and Danks, *Memorials*, 218.

[237] The issue remained highly controversial long after Gregory IX (1227–41) granted priors of Christ Church the right to receive professions during vacancies of the see: HMC, 8th *Report*, app., p. 318; *Lit. Cant.*, ii. 160–4, 216, 244–6; Knowles,

Religious Orders, i. 256.

[238] During Henry of Eastry's absence from the convent in September 1330 he commissioned the subprior to admit two scholars to the habit (Reg. L, fo. 174ᵛ); cf. *Lit. Cant.*, i. 320–2, 402, 417–18.

[239] Searle, *Chronicle and Lists*, 106; cf. S. Evans, 'Ely Almonry Boys and Choristers in the Later Middle Ages', in *Studies Presented to Sir Hilary Jenkinson*, ed. J. Conway Davies (Oxford, 1957), 159.

professed in 1465.[240] Considerably more frequent were those Christ Church monks who appear to have entered the community late in life, after successful careers as secular clerks. Perhaps the most notable of these mature and experienced recruits were: Dr Richard Vaughan, a Welsh canon lawyer and royal orator at the Roman Curia, who joined the community in 1352; Master John Kyngton, who as prothonotary of Henry IV and chancellor of Queen Joan of Navarre was 'a great and powerful man in the secular world' he chose to abandon in favour of the monastic life six years before his death in 1416; and finally Ralph Waller, who had been marshal of the hall of Queen Catherine of Valois and then served the Prior of Canterbury in the same capacity before joining the community 'cum magna devotione' in 1447.[241]

The entry into the Christ Church fraternity of such prominent administrators, who clearly already knew the Cathedral well and wished to spend their closing years as monks there, is a not insignificant tribute to the community's esteem in the eyes of experienced civil servants; but the latter were much exceeded in number by the surprisingly numerous recruits into the Canterbury cloister from other, predominantly Benedictine, monasteries in England. During the century between 1333 and 1433, when such migrations are best documented, at least twenty-five Christ Church monks had earlier followed the religious life elsewhere. Throughout that period, it seems that the prior and chapter at Canterbury positively welcomed such recruitment, provided the monks in question were of suitable quality and had secured the assent of their previous monastic superiors to the change of allegiance.[242] Not surprisingly, most members of the community who had travelled by this indirect route into the religious life at Canterbury did so from monasteries in south-east England and the London area, most frequently from the abbeys of Faversham and Bermondsey, as well as from the priory of Dover.[243] However, Christ Church was also capable of attracting new recruits from monasteries as far away as St Albans, Chester, and Ely Cathedral: in 1388 the prior of the latter granted Brother Peter of Ely licence to transfer to Canterbury, on the grounds that he would find the air more salubrious there.[244] Not all of these entrants to the monastic life at Christ Church from other religious houses proved an unqualified success; and by 1438 Thomas Fynden, a monk admitted to the convent seven years earlier, after his original profession at Westminster Abbey, was reported to have fled the convent as an apostate.[245] While it would be a mistake to exaggerate the impact upon the convent of a small (less than 3 per cent) minority of ex-monks or canons from elsewhere, such unorthodox recruitment clearly helped to provide the Christ Church chapter with wider perspectives than those enjoyed by any other cathedral priory in the country.

Otherwise, Canterbury Cathedral Priory in the later Middle Ages, both before and after the Black Death, undoubtedly conforms to the general rule that entry to even the largest

[240] Searle, *Chronicle and Lists*, 117, 183.

[241] J. Dunbabin, 'Careers and Vocations', in *History of the University of Oxford*, i: *The Early Oxford Schools*, ed. J. I. Catto (Oxford, 1984), 579; Searle, *Chronicle and Lists*, 7–8, 185; Emden, *BRUO*, ii. 1075–6; Cawston MS, fo. 25ᵛ; cf. Hatcher, 'Mortality in the Fifteenth Century' (cit. in n. 212), 27.

[242] *Lit. Cant.*, ii. 413–14, 432, 497; Searle, *Chronicle and Lists*, 7–

118, *passim*.

[243] *Lit. Cant.*, ii. 485; Searle, *Chronicle and Lists*, 7, 11, 12, 33, 38, 181, 182, 184, 185, 187.

[244] HMC, 5th *Report*, app., p. 436 (although there seems no evidence that this monk did in the event migrate from Ely to Cambridge); cf. Searle, *Chronicle and Lists*, 27, 185–7.

[245] Searle, *Chronicle and Lists*, 187.

English religious house was overwhelmingly local. Surprisingly few direct references to the paternity or geographical origins of individual monks survive among their archives; but here, as elsewhere, the evidence of the monks' second names is cumulatively irresistible, if suspect in any one particular case. In matters of nomenclature, the Christ Church fraternity seems to have remained to the end highly conservative in its usages, more traditional, indeed, than the late Dom David Knowles once assumed. Neither first nor second names of Christ Church monks were often derived from English saints or the Fathers of the Church; and of the eighty professed members of the community visited by Archbishop Warham in 1511, all but fifteen bore the Christian names of John (27), William (15), Thomas (10), and Richard (8), almost invariably the commonest men's first names in any section of late medieval English society.[246] Of those eighty monks, approximately 75 per cent were identified by the use of a place-name as their second name or surname, a proportion almost exactly identical with that for all the 414 individuals who had been members of the community between January 1395 and May 1505. During that century, as is now well established, a toponymic surname was in general readily heritable and is by no means a reliable guide to its holder's place of birth; and much remains obscure too as regards Christ Church practice in the matter of a monk's possible adoption of a new surname when he entered the religious life.[247] Despite these qualifications, it is immediately obvious from the second names of the last 500 monks of Christ Church that the associations of those monks with villages in eastern Kent, and especially with the area south and west of Sandwich, were exceptionally close. Nor are these surnames too likely to mislead in suggesting that several of the Canterbury monks stemmed from burgess stock in towns like Ashford, Faversham, and the Cinque Ports. For obvious reasons, a monk born in Canterbury was unlikely to use that particular place-name for the purposes of identification within the convent; but names like 'John Westgate', 'Henry Northgate', and 'William Wynchepe' testify to the probability that there were always several natives of the city within the ranks of the community.[248]

The routes whereby the future brethren of Christ Church found their way from these Kent towns and villages into the convent were no doubt many and diverse. Here, as always in the history of the medieval English religious orders, considerable obscurity tends to surround the two crucial issues of the social origins and early patronage of the future monk. For many recruits to the cloister, the ability to secure maintenance at the Priory's almonry school has already been emphasized as the first and critical step towards entry into the chapter. Nor is that at all difficult to understand: many later medieval priors of Christ Church, like Henry of Eastry in 1324, would have been reluctant to admit young men to their cloister until they had acquired the 'usum et artem cantandi et legendi' and were already familiar with 'terminos grammaticales'.[249] Nor is there any doubt that the convent's bailiffs and other manorial officials were alert to the possibility of recommending for admission to the community any appropriate young candidate in their vicinity: in 1363,

[246] *Kentish Visitations of Warham* (cit. in n. 54), 3.

[247] Cawston MS (Lit. D. 12), *passim*; Hatcher, 'Mortality in the Fifteenth Century' (cit. in n. 212), 25; Dobson, *Durham Priory* (cit. in n. 64), 56–8.

[248] Cawston MS, fos. 18, 26ᵛ; *Kentish Visitations of Warham* (cit. in n. 54), 3.

[249] Reg. L, fo. 116; *Lit. Cant.*, i. 126–7.

for example, Richard de Stisted arrived at Christ Church carrying such a recommendation to his deep commitment to God, to the Cathedral, and to St Thomas.[250] It seems more probable still that many boys were recommended to the prior because of their ties of family acquaintance, or even of blood relationship, with existing monks. The frequent duplication of surname within the convent, as well as the heavy concentration of monastic toponymics within quite localized areas of Kent, lend not a little support to the hypothesis that the late medieval Canterbury community may well have been honeycombed by a number of ever-changing kindred connections. One of many possible examples is the relationship between Dr John Wodnesbergh, one of the convent's outstanding scholars at Canterbury College between 1424 and 1449, and his exact namesake and patron, John Wodnesbergh, prior from 1411 to 1428.[251] The likely prevalence of such blood-relationship must have enhanced the cohesion of the convent, even more perhaps than the elaborate rites of passage which marked the initiation of the young monk into his new religious family.

On the evidence of occasional episcopal dispensations to receive holy orders outside their native diocese at a later stage of their careers, from at least the early fourteenth century the great majority of Benedictine monks in England were between 16 and 20 years of age at the time of their profession. To this plausible, if not particularly well-documented, generalization the community of Christ Church can be no exception; and it was probably when slightly below rather than above the statutory minimum age of 18 that many of Canterbury's monks were admitted to religion there.[252] By the fifteenth century, as no doubt long before, the processes of initiation into the ranks of the community were not only deliberately elaborate, but also marked by a series of solemn ceremonies at the high altar in the presence of the community. The prior himself, sometimes but not always after consultation with the archbishop, normally received the formal oaths taken by the would-be novices in turn: each of the latter was obliged to swear that he was legitimate, of free condition, suffering from no contagious disease, and under no sentence of excommunication. Thereafter, the new group of novices received the tonsure and was provisionally admitted to the community by means of a ceremonial clothing with the monastic habit.[253] The welfare of these new recruits to the convent was then entrusted to a senior monk (only occasionally more than one) who had been specially selected to be their *magister ordinis* (master of observance). In 1524 the latter's official responsibilities were quite specifically equated with the 'rule of the novices' of that year; and his role was no doubt primarily that of personal and spiritual adviser to the latter, as distinct from the more specifically educational duties performed by the monk who held, at Christ Church

---

[250] *Lit. Cant.*, ii. 452–5.

[251] It seems, for instance, not unlikely that brothers Reginald Goldstone (d. 1504) and Thomas Goldstone (d. as prior 1517) were related in more than intellectual interests; cf. the similar case of Richard Sellyng and Prior William Sellyng, two other Canterbury College monks of the late 15th cent. who knew each other well (Emden, *BRUO*, ii. 782–3; iii. 1666–7).

[252] Admission to the convent below the prescribed *vicesimum annum* seems the most probable reason why several monks had

to wait for as long as five, six, or more years after profession before receiving priest's orders: see *Register of Henry Chichele, Archbishop of Canterbury, 1414–1443*, ed. E. F. Jacob, 4 vols. (CYS, 42, 45–7; 1937–47), iv. 317–92.

[253] By the late 15th cent. lists of Christ Church novices normally specify precisely both the date of admission or tonsure and that of profession: Searle, *Chronicle and Lists*, 183, 190–6; Woodruff and Danks, *Memorials*, 248–9.

as elsewhere, the title of 'master of the novices'.[254] It was the custom at Christ Church for the *magistri ordinis* to be senior members of the chapter, often already holding important office, who only retained responsibility for a particular group of novices before their successors were entrusted in turn to another monk. In a large monastery like that of Canterbury Cathedral, such a practice had the obvious advantage of involving the most junior members of the convent in close contact with one of the most experienced of their colleagues from the very outset.

Not that the newly clothed aspirants to the religious life at late medieval Christ Church normally had to wait long for their official entry into the ranks of the community. At Canterbury, as elsewhere, the Benedictine statutes requiring a year's probationary period were usually ignored; and in 1488 it was noted with some concern that six new monks had been tonsured (*rasi*) for more than a year but had not yet been professed. In the exceptional case of the distinguished canon lawyer Master John Kyngton, it was on the very same day (21 March 1410) that he both received the monastic habit and also made his profession before Archbishop Thomas Arundel.[255] However, the interval between receiving the monastic habit and the making of profession was rarely more than a few months, a period whose passage was itself marked by a series of lesser ceremonies. During the year (1457–8) he was serving as *magister ordinis* himself, John Stone was at pains to note that the six new brethren for whom he had personal responsibility were received into religion on 13 December, and then claimed their privileges of the *parvum servitium* on 12 February and the *communem servitium* on 26 February, before their final profession to the prior on 21 April.[256] Whether so short a probationary period was sufficient to allow the prior and chapter to discover unsuitable candidates for entry into their community may well be doubted; but at least one would-be monk of Christ Church in the fifteenth century (John Mersham in 1430) was expelled before his profession.[257] The ceremony of profession itself was invariably conducted before the high altar of the Cathedral church, unless in very exceptional circumstances, as in 1422, when Nicholas Younge was allowed to make his profession in the infirmary chapel because of the serious illness which was to cause his death shortly thereafter.[258] In the great majority of cases, professions were made before either the archbishop or the prior. Although the latter was often given authority to act on the titular abbot's behalf, there is every indication that most archbishops of Canterbury from the thirteenth to the fifteenth centuries were assiduous in attending these ceremonies and that the prior and chapter not only tolerated but welcomed their participation. The new monk's formal profession of commitment to the demands of the religious life at Christ Church was normally read aloud from a written copy; and it was at about this stage of the proceedings too that a note was made of his admission to the fraternity.[259] The ceremony was normally concluded by a celebration of mass, attended by most members of the convent: on such an occasion in August 1447, for example, John Stone thought it

[254] The name of the *magister ordinis* for a particular intake of novices was systematically recorded by the prior and chapter from at least 1356 (Searle, *Chronicle and Lists*, 181–96). For a different interpretation of this practice at Christ Church, see Knowles, *Religious Orders*, ii. 232.

[255] Cawston MS, fos. 20ᵛ–21; Searle, *Chronicle and Lists*, 192,

185.

[256] Searle, *Chronicle and Lists*, 71; cf. 81.

[257] Ibid. 187.

[258] Ibid. 12, 186, 194.

[259] LPL, Reg. Islip, fo. 22; Reg. Wittelsey, fo. 21; cf. Searle, *Chronicle and Lists*, 41–2, 187, 192.

worth noting that the community was clothed 'in froccis' as Archbishop John Stafford celebrated a high Sunday mass. So time-honoured a procedure survived to the final days of the convent. Ironically enough, it was on the feast of the deposition of St Benedict himself in 1534 that eight new recruits to the chapter made, in the predictable absence of the equally new Archbishop Thomas Cranmer, the last of all monastic professions ever to be recorded at the high altar of Canterbury Cathedral.[260]

The group of six or more monks who had made their profession together in the Cathedral church normally continued to retain its cohesion as a practical unit for education and instruction in the immediately following years. Thus, the seven novices who had read their professions at the high altar in 1416 were more or less identical with the seven young monks who were ordained as acolytes by Archbishop Chichele in April of the following year.[261] For most Christ Church monks, four or five more years would elapse before their progress through the orders was made complete with the conferment of their priestly status that qualified them to say mass at one or other of the Cathedral's many altars.[262] Throughout their novitiate, the convent's new monks probably remained under the disciplinary authority of their *magister ordinis*; but they were instructed in grammar and arts by the master of the novices, who for much of the fifteenth century seems to have held his school in an upper room in the west range of the cloister.[263] The provision of more specialized monk-lectors within the fifteenth-century cloister was designed to ensure that academic instruction continued after the end of the novitiate; but it was the acquisition of priest's orders which undoubtedly symbolized the young monk's 'emergence from tutelage' and his entry into the full life of the community. When John Ecchynham died, in January 1438, before he could be received into *sacris ordinibus*, his demise was a matter for genuine regret.[264] The ordinations of Christ Church monks themselves are abundantly but not comprehensively documented in contemporary archiepiscopal registers; and it is hardly surprising that although members of the convent occasionally travelled to Rochester or to the chapels of the archbishop's palaces at Charing, Saltwood, and elsewhere to be ordained, they usually received their first tonsure, and subsequently the orders of acolyte, subdeacon, deacon, and priest, within their own Cathedral.[265] During the fifteenth century, ordinations at Christ Church were increasingly likely to be celebrated by the suffragan bishop of Canterbury in the infirmary or prior's chapel rather than in the Cathedral church itself. As the monks' own records make very clear, the archbishop's suffragan was usually very well known indeed within the precinct: he often held the office for a considerable period, if rarely quite as long as the thirty years (1436–65) during which Richard Clerk, Bishop of Ross, regularly consecrated chrism or celebrated orders within the Priory as the suffragan of four archbishops in succession.[266] For the newly priested monk himself, the

[260] Searle, *Chronicle and Lists*, 41–2, 196.

[261] *Reg. Chichele* (cit. in n. 252), iv. 327; cf. Searle, *Chronicle and Lists*, 186.

[262] e.g. LPL, Reg. Wittelsey, fos. 165–74; Reg. John Stafford, fos. 196–207; *Reg. Chichele* (cit. in n. 252), iv. 317–52.

[263] Many of the masters of novices held the office for a long term of years; and at least one, John Newton (d. 1457), had been a scholar at Oxford (Pantin, *Cant. Coll.*, ii. 173; Emden, *BRUO*, ii. 1358).

[264] Searle, *Chronicle and Lists*, 22–3; Knowles, *Religious Orders*, ii. 232–3.

[265] e.g. *Reg. Langham* (cit. in n. 63), 383–91; LPL, Reg. Wittelsey, fos. 165–73; *Reg. Chichele* (cit. in n. 252), iv. 317–92.

[266] Although Richard Clerk had occasionally served as the suffragan of the bishop of London, his primary allegiance was to Canterbury: when he died at his rectory of Otford in 1465,

most obvious mark of his different status was naturally his celebration of his first mass, normally the occasion of a gift of 16*d.* from the monk treasurers, and his subsequent immersion into the religious routines of his Cathedral.[267]

It was precisely because those routines were so exceptionally diverse and complex that the monks of Christ Church had the opportunity for a wider variety of vocations than their counterparts in smaller and more remote monasteries. Nevertheless, at Canterbury as elsewhere, the most important distinction within the community was undoubtedly that between the choir monks and those of their colleagues promoted to important administrative office. Alert to the dangers of this development as early as the late thirteenth century, Archbishop Pecham had enjoined that no junior monk should be appointed to an obedience until he had mastered the litany; but in practice the fifteenth-century sources reveal a community in which the responsibility for communal worship rested in the hands of the *conventuales*, monks who held no important office and who numbered less than half the community.[268] To some extent, this development was the result of the increasing specialization of the liturgy itself, as well as of the tendency to multiply the range of administrative duties within the convent. At first sight, the general outlines of the performance of the *opus Dei* at Christ Church seem to have remained comparatively unchanged during the fourteenth and fifteenth centuries. Thus, in 1500 as in 1300, the monastic *horarium* at Christ Church began with Matins in the choir and was followed, after sleep in the dormitory, by the offices of Prime, Terce, and Sext, themselves followed by masses and the bell for daily chapter. However, the gradual introduction of such innovations as more masses to the Blessed Virgin Mary in the Lady Chapel, of sophisticated organ music, and of more accomplished choral singing necessitated a more professional approach to communal worship. For many members of the community the most desirable quality was that ascribed to Brother Thomas Chart, who died soon after 1500 at the age of 70 with a reputation for being 'in musica et organis bene instructus'.[269] In the absence of visitation injunctions and chapter ordinances which comment directly on the performance of the liturgical round at Christ Church, it is hardly possible to make a clear assessment of how effectively the community fulfilled this most fundamental of all its responsibilities. Much no doubt depended on the musical direction of the monastic choir provided by successive precentors and their assistants, the succentors and third chantors. For connoisseurs of cathedral liturgy and worship in fifteenth-century England, Christ Church must often have had much out of the ordinary to offer. When John Borne died of plague in 1420, after many years' service as precentor, it was to be long remembered—at least within the Canterbury cloister itself—that he had possessed the most excellent voice of any member of a religious order in England.[270]

the event was carefully recorded by John Stone (*Reg. Chichele* (cit. in n. 252), i, pp. lxviii, lxx, 285, 303; iv, 383–92; Searle, *Chronicle and Lists*, 26–89, 91).

[267] After the future Prior William Sellyng had received priest's orders in 1456, he celebrated mass at the high altar for a whole week (Searle, *Chronicle and Lists*, 66).

[268] *Reg. Epist. Peckham* (cit. in n. 11), 399. By the late 15th cent. the word *conventualis* (like *claustralis*) was generally applied to those members of the community who were neither important

office-holders nor *stationarii*, incapacitated by age or illness (Cawston MS, fos. 28–36).

[269] Cawston MS, fo. 29; Searle, *Chronicle and Lists*, 189; cf. W. P. Blore, 'A Fourteenth-Century Account for Cathedral Organs', *Laudate*, 24 (1946), 38–41. The liturgy and music of the late medieval community are described by R. Bowers, below, pp. 413–26.

[270] Searle, *Chronicle and Lists*, 11.

As the duties of the precentor were concerned primarily with matters of the voice rather than the pen, his role in the community is much less well documented than those of most other monk office-holders. Indeed, the 'obedientiary' system at Christ Church presents an extreme case of the need to distinguish between offices utterly central to the welfare of the convent and others which might be performed more casually and could indeed be transitory. However, there is no doubt that the main patterns of monastic administrative responsibility within the convent, first fully revealed by the surviving obedientiary accounts of the late thirteenth century, underwent no major transformation in the later Middle Ages. In their responses to new needs and opportunities inside the cloister, the prior and chapter sometimes gave additional authority to one official (usually the prior himself) at the expense of another; but they did so within what was essentially a traditional, and indeed at times atrophied, command structure. No attempt can be made here to do full justice to the complexities of that structure, especially because there was a tendency at Canterbury for several obedientiaries' duties to be increasingly subdivided among several monks rather than to be consolidated into fewer and fewer hands as at some other cathedrals.[271] As a result of these vicissitudes, the prestige and influence of particular obedientiaries was always liable to fluctuate from period to period. Nevertheless, a special status always pertained to the seven monastic officials who were traditionally appointed, much to the community's displeasure, by the archbishop of Canterbury from three names submitted to him by the prior and chapter. For obvious reasons, these obedientiaries— normally the subprior, sacrist, precentor, cellarer, chamberlain, and two penitentiaries— continued to be leading figures in the life of the Cathedral until its suppression.[272] There were, however, many other offices quite as important to the conduct of the chapter's affairs. According to a series of ordinances produced within the convent's exchequer in 1375, at least fourteen other obedientiaries (the subsacrist, subcellarer, almoner, prior's chaplain, treasurers, feretrar, keeper of St Thomas's Corona, keeper of Our Lady's shrine in the crypt, keeper of St Thomas's tomb, granator, bartoner, and keepers of the manors) held offices which excluded them from the ranks of the ordinary *conventuales*.[273] However, perhaps a more pragmatic and meaningful distinction within the long series of conventual obediences is that between those offices which involved the financial administration of a separate department and those whose primary responsibility was to the spiritual rather than material welfare of the brethren. Of the former, all involving strenuous financial responsibility as well as an obligation to render a detailed annual account, the offices of the almoner, anniversarian, bartoner, cellarer, chamberlain, feretrar, granator, infirmarian, keeper of the manors, prior's chaplain, sacrist, and treasurer were the most central to the Cathedral's welfare.[274] Of the latter, the subprior was obviously the most important source

---

[271] For the extreme case of the concentration of virtually all the important obediences at Rochester Cathedral under Prior William Fressel in 1511–12, see Smith, *Collected Papers* (cit. in n. 71), 52–3; cf. H. W. Saunders, *An Introduction to the Obedientiary and Manor Rolls of Norwich Cathedral Priory* (Norwich, 1930), 68–75.

[272] See above, pp. 88–9. The prior and chapter's nominations of candidates for archiepiscopal appointment to these seven obediences are regularly recorded in surviving registers: see,

e.g., LPL, Reg. Islip, fos. 21ᵛ–22; Reg. Wittelsey, fo. 13; *Reg. Chichele* (cit. in n. 252), i. pp. lxxxiii–lxxxiv; iv. 114–15, 150, 152; HMC, 5th *Report*, app., p. 427; *Lit. Cant.*, i. 117, 506–10; ii. 106–8, 276–7, 394–8; Smith, *Cant. Cath. Priory*, 35–6.

[273] DE 77; cf. *Lit. Cant.*, iii. 5.

[274] For information about the highly uneven sequences of separate obedientiary account-rolls among the Dean and Chapter's muniments, I am most indebted to Dr Joan Greatrex, Dr Nigel Ramsay, and Mrs Margaret Sparks.

of authority in a Cathedral community whose prior was so often absent or distracted by secular cares.

Although monastic discipline and welfare at Christ Church were also the responsibility of a fourth as well as a third prior, for long periods of the year it was accordingly the subpriors who directly supervised the spiritual welfare of the community. As so important a source for stability within the cloister, it is hardly surprising that they often held the office for long periods and were usually monks of some distinction in their own right. William Hadley, who had been warden of Canterbury's Oxford college before becoming subprior at the mother house in 1471, held that office for twenty-seven years, until 1498: he died a year later, to be remembered by his brethren, no doubt sincerely if conventionally enough, as 'vir laudabilis vite honeste et religiose conversationis'.[275] Although few subpriors of Christ Church were ever to become prior, a remarkably large number had been students, and often warden, of Canterbury College; as such, they clearly contributed to the distinctive academic tone of the mother house, as well as deputizing for the prior in such matters as the conduct of the monks' funeral services.[276] By the fifteenth century at least, the subprior's especial responsibilities for his elderly and sick colleagues led him to occupy apartments in the south aisle of the infirmary hall, accommodation (casually destroyed in the nineteenth century) he shared with his own junior monk-chaplain.[277] The priors of Christ Church, for their part, gradually came to depend on the services of as many as three chaplains, of whom the senior was in financial charge of his master's household and therefore a figure of considerable importance for the economy of the convent as a whole. Although the seven surviving accounts of this prior's chaplain throw disappointingly little light upon the internal operations of the prior's household, it is very notable that the office was often held for several years by a young monk whose administrative rather than academic talents might finally lead him (as with John Wodnesbergh senior and William Molashe) to appointment as prior.[278]

These chaplains also constituted an informal secretarial department within the prior's apartments; but it was the monastic chancery and its seals, always at the superior's service, which formed the all-important executive agency of both prior and chapter. The convent's two chancellors (an office which emerges clearly only in the mid-fourteenth century) were often and increasingly Canterbury College graduates, like those two 'witty' university monks John Throwley and John Ambrose, who were the very last to hold the office, in 1538–9.[279] The fact that the convent's chancery was administered by two monk *cancellarii* rather than one (as was usual elsewhere) is itself a testimony to the remarkable range of the prior's and the chapter's official correspondence. As in other large Benedictine monasteries of the later Middle Ages, copies of the latter—issued under the convent's

[275] Reg. S, fos. 359ᵛ, 362ᵛ; *Reg. Bourgchier* (cit. in n. 63), 457; Cawston MS (Lit. D. 12), fo. 32ᵛ; Searle, *Chronicle and Lists*, 116, 188; Emden, *BRUO*, ii. 846.

[276] Pantin, *Cant. Coll.*, iv. 218–28; see above, p. 108; see below, p. 135.

[277] Searle, *Chronicle and Lists*, 68–9, 187; M. Sparks, 'The Monastic Infirmary and Choir House', *Cant. Cath. Chron.*, 85 (1991), 32; Willis, *Conventual Buildings* (cit. in n. 70), 56; Woodman,

Architectural History (cit. in n. 8), 242–3; Smith, *Cant. Cath. Priory*, 36–7. Liveries to the servants of the subprior and other obedientiaries are fully recorded in Bodl., MS Tanner 165, fo. 221 ff.

[278] During the late 14th and early 15th cent. the annual income of the prior's chaplain was in the order of £100 (Prior's Chaplain's Accts., nos. 1–17). Cf. LPL, Reg. Arundel, fo. 132; Reg. S, fo. 97; Searle, *Chronicle and Lists*, 184; Emden, *BRUO*, ii. 1288.

[279] Pantin, *Cant. Coll.*, iii. 152; iv. 74.

common or lesser seals—were more or less systematically entered into one of a series of large conventual registers. Of all the voluminous archives of the Cathedral Priory to survive, these registers remain the most enduring memorial to the labours of chancellors like Thomas Bungay, previously a canon of Lesnes, who died in 1421, and of John Waltham a century later.[280] Within the long roll-call of the late medieval *cancellarii* are to be found names of monks (like Thomas Cawston) to whom the historian of medieval Canterbury is particularly indebted. As the late W. A. Pantin once pointed out, William Sellyng was elevated directly from the chancellor's office to that of prior in 1472. During the course of the previous year he had been the first Canterbury monk to introduce, shortly after his return from his second visit to Italy, an italic hand into the monastic register then under his care.[281]

Whatever the complexities of the routines of the monastic chancery at Christ Church, those of the major financial departments of the Priory were labyrinthine by comparison, involving at least a dozen members of the community in very considerable responsibility indeed. Despite the late R. A. L. Smith's remarkable pioneering attempt to impose cohesion on a highly unsystematic and often centrifugal series of accounting practices, the patterns of financial administration at Canterbury Cathedral are still in urgent need of full elucidation. Somewhat ironically, and as Smith himself observed, that process may well prove to be most difficult of all in the case of the last hundred years in the history of the Priory: after 1450, minor monastic accounts still survive in profusion, but the large central accounts of the convent's officers (particularly those of the prior himself) are regrettably notable by their absence.[282] However, the central clue to the processes of 'getting and spending' at England's largest monastery is obvious enough. By the late thirteenth century, Christ Church, like the great majority of English Benedictine houses at that date, had deliberately adopted a financial system whereby the most important obedientiaries were allowed to retain sufficient independent resources to maintain their own offices, but the greatest proportion of the convent's income was now channelled towards a central receiving office administered by monk treasurers.[283] Such a system was bound, at Christ Church as elsewhere, to create its own internal tensions; but it was no doubt the exceptional range and value of the convent's temporalities and spiritualities which tempted successive priors and *seniores scaccarii* in the fourteenth and fifteenth centuries to a series of often incompatible and usually short-lived schemes for rationalization. As the subsidiary accounts of Christ Church monks in the early sixteenth century bear witness, in many ways the Priory's financial administration became more centrifugal and less rational in the decades immediately before the Dissolution. Nevertheless, R. A. L. Smith was almost certainly correct to suggest that the most important date in the financial and administrative history of the late-medieval convent was 1391, when the new prior, Thomas Chillenden, transferred many of the common revenues of the monastery from the treasurers' to his own office,

[280] Reg. S, fos. 200, 234, 245ᵛ, 248ᵛ, 249ᵛ; Reg. T(i), fos. 1, 415, 442, 445ᵛ, 448; Searle, *Chronicle and Lists*, 11; Emden, *BRUO*, iii. 1974; Smith, *Cant. Cath. Priory*, 64–5.

[281] Reg. S, fo. 249 ('manu Willelmi Sellyng'); cf. Pantin, *Cant. Coll.*, iv. 83–4; Emden, *BRUO*, iii. 1666–7.

[282] 18 prior's accounts survive for the period from 1396 to

1475 but many of these do so only in fragmentary and badly damaged form; cf. Smith, *Cant. Cath. Priory*, 196–205.

[283] R. A. L. Smith, 'The *Regimen Scaccarii* in English Monasteries', *TRHS*, 4th ser., 24 (1942), 65–85; cf. R. H. Snape, *English Monastic Finances in the Later Middle Ages* (Cambridge, 1926), 23–70.

and so became something of a 'prior treasurer' of his convent.[284] Although perhaps not quite so much of an administrative 'revolution' as Smith supposed, the fact that this important financial change more or less coincided with the convent's fateful decision to lease most of its manors and demesnes undoubtedly gave the priors of Canterbury from 1391 to 1540 the opportunity to adopt a more directly energizing role in the financial administration of the community than ever before, even in the age of Prior Henry of Eastry. During the fifteenth and early sixteenth centuries, the prior and his councillors normally made the effective decisions about those issues—the negotiation of the terms of leases, the proper delivery of the convent's farms, the purchase and sale of land—on which the prosperity of the Cathedral chapter now fundamentally depended.[285] Similarly, it is the prior's own annual accounts, revealing a net income of almost £2,500 in the 1470s, which now become the most essential guide to the economic welfare of the community.[286]

Within such a general context, it followed that the obedientiaries who served the central financial departments of the convent enjoyed somewhat less financial authority after the 1390s than they had done at an earlier period. The most obvious casualties in this sphere were inevitably the two (occasionally three) monk treasurers, first created to centralize the collection and disbursement of the community's revenues as long ago as the 1160s, under Prior Wibert. From the 1280s to the 1380s these treasurers had usually enjoyed an income of over £2,000 per annum; but throughout the fifteenth century, when their accounts happen to survive in considerable numbers, that figure was almost always below £1,000.[287] Nevertheless, the *thesaurarii* of Christ Church continued to be responsible for the collection of a large and miscellaneous body of rents, not least from urban tenements in Canterbury itself; and their expenditure touched on the life of the monks at every level, from the grant of oblations at Christmas and Easter to the washing of their clothes.[288] Although they were usually to be found at work in the convent's Checker (quite distinct from the monastic treasury or Spendiment) on the east side of the infirmary cloister, they travelled extensively throughout Kent, as well as to London, in pursuit of low prices for the purchase of food and high prices for the sale of livestock.[289] By definition, the monk wardens of the convent's manors were even more peripatetic; but after 1350 theirs too was an office which had lost much of the importance it had held in the age of 'high farming' and the direct exploitation of manorial profits especially associated with Henry of Eastry. When Brother William Woghope ('a man of great discretion and worldly wisdom') died in 1396, it was recorded not only that he had successfully held the office of *gardianus omnium maneriorum* for a long time but also that he was the first such warden at Christ Church to rule all the convent's manors without a colleague.[290] Possibly because of the opportunities it offered for influence, and at times even corruption, among influential

[284] Smith (*Cant. Cath. Priory*, 191) exaggerates in suggesting that henceforward Prior Thomas Chillenden 'received all the money from manors and oblations'.

[285] *Christ Church Letters*, 60–1; Smith, *Cant. Cath. Priory*, 200–4; M. Mate, 'Agrarian Economy after the Black Death: The Manors of Canterbury Cathedral Priory, 1348–91', *EconHR*, 2nd ser., 37 (1984), 341–54.

[286] Prior's Accts., nos. 12–14 (1472–4).

[287] Treasurers' Accts., nos. 1–25; LPL, ED. 80–8 (Treasurers'

Accts. 1406–1509); Smith, *Cant. Cath. Priory*, 14–28, 190–1, 195.

[288] Treasurers' Accts., nos. 17, 18; LPL, ED. 80–4.

[289] Treasurers' Accts., nos. 1, 5, 7–8, 17–18; *Christ Church Letters*, 82. For the romanesque Treasury building (originally the *vestiarium*) see Woodruff and Danks, *Memorials*, 50; Woodman, *Architectural History* (cit. in n. 8), 80.

[290] Cawston MS (Lit. D. 12), fo. 17ᵛ. The 29 surviving account-rolls of the *custodes maneriorum* almost all date from the period after 1460.

Kent laymen, the office of warden of the manors continued, however, to attract the interest of able and ambitious monks until the Dissolution. In January 1534 Dr Richard Thornden, warden of Canterbury College, was able to persuade Thomas Cromwell himself 'to make me (unwordye) warden off our maners'.[291]

More mundane, but as essential at Christ Church as at other religious houses, were the duties of those obedientiaries whose business it was to provision and to clothe the community. The activities of these monastic officials are abundantly but erratically recorded in their surviving accounts, with the ironical result that the comparatively minor office of bartoner is the best-documented obedience of all within the late medieval convent. Although originally the keeper of the community's most important home farm (hence the title of his office), by the fifteenth century the bartoner's basic responsibility was to supply barley and oats to the convent's brewhouse, located to the north of the precinct and operated by a master brewer and three or four servants.[292] Similarly, the monk granger or *granator interior* had to ensure that sufficient quantities of corn reached the convent's bakehouses every day to satisfy the community's insatiable demand for different types of bread.[293] The major responsibility for conduct at the meals actually eaten by the monks pertained to the refectorer; but the latter held little financial responsibility himself and was under no obligation to render annual accounts. A much more powerful figure was the monastic cellarer, whose duties were perhaps more diverse, and more confused, than those of any other obedientiary.

Unfortunately, less than a dozen late medieval cellarer's account-rolls survive, too few to do justice to the range of this obedientiary's expenditure, or indeed of the monastic diet he provided; but there is no doubt at all of the way he complemented bartoner and granger by providing the community with large amounts of fresh meat and fish (his biggest sources of expenditure). The cellarer also provided the refectory and other dining-halls in the precincts with more occasional deliveries of poultry, spices, and wine; by the late fifteenth century, many senior monks regularly supplemented these luxuries by private purchases of even more exotic foods like tongue, sausages, turbot-pasties, and 'dysches of conger'.[294] So important, however, were the cellarer's duties as the main provisioner of the community that he travelled often and widely throughout eastern Kent in search of suitable livestock. However, he was most often to be found within his extensive offices and stores, which had expanded northwards from the cloister to the original monastic Domus Hospitum and Aula Nova. According to the chapter's exchequer ordinances of 1375, the cellarer was to receive the great majority of his annual income (£521 6s. 8d. in that year) from the wardens of the manors; and in 1397 this sum rose to a subvention of no less

[291] *LP Henry VIII*, v, no. 757; Pantin, *Cant. Coll.*, iii. 147–8, 152; Emden, *BRUO, 1501–40*, 564–5.

[292] Of all the convent's obediences, that of the bartoner (over 100 surviving accounts between 1299 and 1460) is the only one to have received full-scale scholarly attention: R. A. L. Smith, 'The Barton and Bartoner of Christ Church, Canterbury', *Arch. Cant.*, 55 (1942), 16–25.

[293] Granator's Accts., nos. 1–78 (many in a fragmentary

condition). According to an ordinance of 1304 (Smith, *Cant. Cath. Priory*, 213), neither the granator nor the bartoner might sell grain without the express consent of the president of the chapter.

[294] In 1396–7 the cellarer, Henry Cranebroke, spent £234 on fresh meat and £86 on poultry, but as much as £282 on fresh-water and salt fish (Cellarer's Accts., no. 2); Lit. MS C. 11, *passim*; Rooke, 'Dom William Ingram' (cit. in n. 211), 38.

than £657 18s. 2d., now made—as remained the case until the Dissolution—by the prior.[295]
In similar dependence upon regular liveries of cash, either from the treasurers or (after
1391) the prior, was the chamberlain of the Priory, another indispensable member of any
obedientiary system. Throughout the fifteenth century the Christ Church *camerarius*
normally had well over £100 at his disposal every year, a substantial sum but by no means
as much as the £320 recommended in the chapter's ordinances of 1375.[296] In addition to
providing the monks with their basic sartorial requirements in woollen (black and grey)
and linen cloth, the chamberlain supervised the convent's tailors' workshop, as well as its
bath- and shaving-houses.[297] Although his was an office of the utmost importance to the
conventual monks, it carried little independent authority and was almost always held by
a comparatively obscure member of the chapter.[298]

Much more influential was the sacrist, the most important of the many monk obedientiaries whose responsibility was to the Cathedral church itself, either to its fabric and
furnishings as a whole or to its most important shrines and altars. The sacrist's own duties
were sufficiently onerous to justify the assistance of a subsacrist and no less than three
petty sacrists or sextons: the sacrist's office, untypically of most major churches, was
located at some distance from the Cathedral, near the southern perimeter of the precinct,
with a separate entrance by a lane from Burgate street.[299] After 1341–2, the year of their
first surviving account-roll, the sacrists usually received a comparatively small income of
only £100 or so per annum, insufficient to support a substantial building-programme of
nova opera, for which separate accounts occasionally survive. However, the sacrist's
accounts are the best available guide to the endless succession of minor building-works
and repairs within the Cathedral during the two centuries before the Dissolution. They
document even more comprehensively the convent's expenditure on wax for candles
(1,300 lbs. at a cost of £2 15s. per cwt. in 1394–5), as well as on vestments, altar linen, and
even the cathedral clock.[300]

However, no section of the Cathedral demanded closer supervision on the part of the
community than did the famous shrine of St Thomas, before the high altar. It is therefore
hardly surprising that two feretrars were required at Christ Church; and at least one of
these, Thomas Cawston in 1471, was appointed by the subprior, after nomination by the
seniores assembled in the prior's chapel.[301] According to the solitary surviving feretrars'
account-roll of 1397–8, the two brothers who held the office then enjoyed an income of
about £250, from which they distributed oblations and pittances to their fellow monks.[302]

[295] DE 77; Blore Coll. 121, p. 48; Cellarer's Accts., no. 2 (1396–
7); Prior's Accts., nos. 12–14 (recording the dispatch of over £600
a year to the cellarer 'for the expenses of his office' in 1472–4).
[296] Chamberlain's Accts., nos. 1–71; DE 77; Lit. Cant., iii. 6. In
the 1470s the prior's contribution to the chamberlain's expenses
was usually between £70 and £80 (Prior's Accts., nos. 12–15).
[297] Chamberlain's Accts., no. 5 (1311–12); Blore Coll. 120;
Woodruff and Danks, Memorials, 241–2. The domus rasturae was
rebuilt by Prior Thomas Chillenden between 1390 and 1411 (Lit.
Cant., iii. 115).
[298] Chamberlain's Accts., passim; Smith, Cant. Cath. Priory,
44–5.
[299] Sacrist's Accts., nos. 16–36; Pantin, Cant. Coll., iii. 152–3; C.

E. Woodruff, 'The Sacrist's Rolls of Christ Church, Canterbury', Arch. Cant., 48 (1936), 38–80.
[300] Sacrist's Accts., nos. 10–25; Woodruff, 'Sacrist's Rolls' (cit.
in n. 299), 43. It is hard to know whether the 'great new clock'
installed by Prior Henry Eastry at a cost of £30 in 1292 was
replaced or renovated in the later Middle Ages; but both sacrists
and treasurers were responsible for the upkeep of the main
Cathedral clock: see BL, Cotton MS Galba E. iv, fo. 101;
Knowles, Religious Orders, i. 323; Treasurers' Accts., no. 14 (1473–
4).
[301] Reg. S, fo. 248ᵛ; Pantin, Cant. Coll., iii. 152–3.
[302] Feretrars' Accts., no. 1 (1397–8).

Fortunately, rather more can be known about the financial responsibilities of the keepers of the subsidiary shrines within the Cathedral; of these, the master of the Corona and the wardens of the Martyrdom, of St Thomas's tomb in the crypt, and of Our Lady Undercroft were all monks and all in regular receipt of offerings made by visitors to these four centres of pilgrimage.[303] Not too dissimilar in status to all these monastic *custodes* of the shrines were the *custodes anniversariorum*, one of whose accounts actually incorporates an inventory of the valuable items at Becket's shine in 1447. Whether or not the anniversarians (usually only one after 1480) were generally scrupulous in ensuring that their brethren duly commemorated the distinguished departed at altars in the Cathedral is not easy to discover; but their small income of between £20 and £30 a year at least gave the anniversarians a limited opportunity for gifts to the brethren, and especially to the infirm.[304]

It is in fact with the more formal arrangements for the care of the infirm, the sick, and the needy that this excessively cursory survey of the most elaborate series of monastic obediences in late medieval England might most appropriately conclude. The offices of almoner and infirmarian were alike both in servicing the largest units of accommodation within the precinct (but outside the cloister) and also in being dedicated—at least in theory—to the work of Christian charity rather than of material gain and subsistence. Admittedly, it is more or less impossible to form any reliable impression of the extent of the convent's almsgiving from the fifty-four almoner's account-rolls which survive from 1269–70 onwards; and the latter, which reveal an increase in annual income from less than £100 in the 1290s to over £180 in 1368–9, are almost exclusively concerned with the administrative expenses of supervising a substantial endowment of rents and tithes.[305] Nevertheless, there can be little doubt that the almoner and his junior colleague, the subalmoner, were always among the most influential members of the community: not only did they head a particularly large and self-contained department, with its own household staff, but they also enjoyed close and regular contact with visitors and pilgrims to the Cathedral. The almonry buildings over which they presided were immediately adjacent to the great gate into the precinct; and they included a very large hall (the *domus participationis*) as well as various offices, some sleeping-accommodation, the almonry school, and a chapel which was served (after 1319) by no less than six priests.[306] By an understandable process of accretion, it seems clear that at Canterbury the almoner's original function of distributing alms to the local poor had been partly replaced by that of providing hospitality to guests who were less than destitute.

By the fourteenth century, the responsibilities of the monastic infirmarian too had come to extend very considerably beyond care for his sick colleagues. At Canterbury, as in other large monasteries of the fifteenth century, it is in the infirmary that one can best observe the privatization of space created by a growing demand for private monastic

[303] Lit. MS C. 11 incorporates the accounts of William Ingram as warden of the Martyrdom between 1503 and 1510; the contents of the account-book of Thomas Anselm sen. recording his receipt of oblations as warden of Our Lady Undercroft in 1510–11 are briefly summarized in C. E. Woodruff, 'The Chapel of Our Lady in the Crypt of Canterbury Cathedral', *Arch. Cant.*, 38 (1926), 153–71.

[304] Anniversarians' Accts., nos. 8–10 (1420–51).
[305] Almoner's Accts., nos. 8–17, 36 (unfortunately no almoner's accounts survive for the period after 1391–2).
[306] See Almoner's Accts., *passim*, and Smith, *Cant. Cath. Priory*, 46–8, for an impression of what was once one of the most impressive monastic almonries in the kingdom.

chambers. For that and many other reasons, the infirmary hall was emphatically not only a haven of rest for the infirm and dying. As its spectacular ruins suggest, and as C. E. Woodruff once pointed out, this hall could have housed the entire Christ Church community.[307] The disappearance of all but two very late (1517–18; 1520–1) infirmarian's account-rolls may make it difficult to re-create in detail the life once led within the infirmary's walls, above all by its elderly monk residents, the *stationarii*. However, all the evidence available makes it absolutely clear that its rooms and chambers played not a peripheral but a central role in the life of the community, and of many of the city's secular clergy too. More central still perhaps was the large infirmary-chapel leading eastwards out of the hall: used by the monks for a great variety of purposes while they were alive, it was to this chapel that their bodies were first brought when human life was no longer their concern.[308]

At no time—appropriately enough perhaps—was a fifteenth-century conventual monk of Christ Church so likely to receive individual attention on the part of the convent as immediately after his demise. The elaborate rituals which surrounded the funeral, burial, and commemoration of every member of the Cathedral Priory naturally have their analogies elsewhere; but on the copious evidence available, it is hard to think of any other religious house so preoccupied—and perhaps even fascinated—with disease, with the transitoriness of the monastic life, with mortal illness, and with death. Such apparently exceptional sensitivity to mortality on the part of the Christ Church monks may have been enhanced by their frequent presence in the Cathedral at some of the most spectacular royal and aristocratic funerals fifteenth-century England had to offer; and the very fact that they had more regular access to the services of highly skilled medical and surgical consultants than any other cathedral chapter in the kingdom probably increased their interest in the epidemiology of their community.[309] More obviously still, so large a monastery lived with the knowledge that the lives of its own members could be very short, and unexpectedly and harshly short at that. Between 15 July and 25 September 1457, during the most serious Christ Church 'mortality crisis' of the fifteenth century, fourteen monks died of plague. A subsequent outbreak of plague in 1471 caused the sudden deaths of eleven monks; and during the national epidemic of sweating-sickness fourteen years later (1485), there were nine victims in the Canterbury cloister.[310] However, even in less disastrous years, there were usually two or three monks to be mourned within the community.

[307] Woodruff and Danks, *Memorials*, 255. For a recent survey of the very complicated architectural history of the infirmary complex, see Sparks, 'Monastic Infirmary' (cit. in n. 277), 28–35; cf. Woodman, *Architectural History* (cit. in n. 8), 78–80, 146, 229, 242–3.

[308] Almoner's Accts., nos. 1 (1391–2) and 2 (1269–70); Woodruff and Danks, *Memorials*, 255–6; Searle, *Chronicle and Lists*, 27, 30, 40, 51. In 1376 the chapter amended its regulations to add greater precision to the privileges of the *stationarii* lodged in the infirmary (DE 77; *Lit. Cant.*, iii. 4–5).

[309] For some examples of the many surviving references to medical practitioners in the service of the prior and chapter, see HMC, 5th *Report*, app., p. 441; *Lit. Cant.*, i. 120–1, 151; iii. 4; Smith, *Cant. Cath. Priory,* 46; C. H. Talbot and E. A. Hammond, *The Medical Practitioners in Medieval England: A Biographical*

Register (London, 1965), 198–9, 230. Of the various local manors (which included Chartham) used by the monks for purposes of convalescence and recreation, Caldicote is the best known because it was presented to the chapter by Archbishop Reynolds in 1326 for precisely that reason; but it was apparently common enough for individual members of the community to seek exercise by 'walking in the fields' (HMC, 5th *Report*, app., p. 434; Woodruff and Danks, *Memorials*, 142, 262).

[310] Cawston MS (Lit. D. 12), fos. 24–6; Hatcher, 'Mortality in the Fifteenth Century' (cit. in n. 212), p. 28. It was in direct response to the severe outbreak of plague in Aug. 1471 that the prior and chapter carried their shrine of St Ouen in a 'great procession' through the cemetery (Searle, *Chronicle and Lists*, 117; cf. 67).

Although John Stone, Thomas Cawston, and their colleagues were no doubt unaware of the fact, throughout the course of the fifteenth century, death was becoming more rather than less of a spectre within the cloister. Perhaps the most important result of Dr John Hatcher's meticulous analysis of Christ Church's incomparable data on this topic is that the life expectancy (at approximately the age of 20) of the monks there rose from the comparatively low level of 28 years in 1395–1405 to a slightly higher 32.2 years in 1405–30, only to fall well below 25 years in the period between 1450 and 1490.[311]

Not that all the monks of Christ Church chose to stay and die there. A little surprisingly perhaps, a small, if not insignificant, minority of the convent (approximately fifty between 1300 and 1500) departed to lead the religious life in another place. As in the case of immigrants to the community from other religious houses, the prior and chapter appear to have placed fewer obstacles in the way of these 'migrations' than their counterparts elsewhere. A very few Christ Church monks admittedly brought honour on their chapter by moving to high office in another monastery: the most notable example in the later Middle Ages was Dr Thomas Chaundler, successively Prior of Horsham St Faith (1501), Abbot of Wymondham (1511), and Abbot of Eynsham (1517), once praised by Cardinal Wolsey as 'the flower of St Benet's order'.[312] Many more expatriate monks found shelter, predictably enough, in the local monasteries of Dover, Faversham, and Folkestone; and one or two sought a more ascetic religious life in the Cistercian order, like the exceptionally mobile William Pownse, who entered the Christ Church cloister as a professed St Albans monk but subsequently moved to Boxley Abbey in Kent.[313] A very few Canterbury monks also joined one of the mendicant orders, sometimes with very different results. Brother John Borne was licensed by Archbishop Warham to join the Carmelite friary at Coventry, where he eventually died; but six years later William Taylor's similar licence to enter the London Blackfriars led to his complete withdrawal from religion.[314] Migration to another house or order was indeed a not uncommon step towards apostasy, an occasionally distressing rather than positively alarming feature of monastic life at Christ Church. On the evidence of surviving Canterbury profession lists, which appear to record cases of *apostasia* quite scrupulously, it seems unlikely that the convent lost many of its members in this way. A few monks, predictably perhaps, disappeared while they were still novices; but for their seniors, after all, there was no obvious place of comfortable exile had they wanted to find one. Perhaps it was when armed with a papal bull of capacity to hold a benefice, or when on a mission to the Curia itself, that the *stabilitas* of a Christ Church monk was at gravest risk. Much more representative of the community's cohesiveness in the later Middle Ages were Brothers William Brygge and John Ashford, monks who died in Italy indeed, but as pilgrims and agents of the chapter rather than as apostates.[315]

The great majority of the Christ Church monks therefore died, as they had lived, at

[311] Hatcher, 'Mortality in the Fifteenth Century' (cit. in n. 212), 26–38.

[312] Searle, *Chronicle and Lists*, 191; Pantin, *Cant. Coll.*, ii. 221–32, 268–70; iv. 219; Emden, *BRUO*, i. 399–400. One of Chaundler's near contemporaries, James Burton, became prior of Folkestone but later resigned that office to end his days 'religiose' in the Christ Church infirmary (Searle, *Chronicle and Lists*, 190).

[313] Reg. S, fo. 225; Cawston MS, fo. 6; Searle, *Chronicle and Lists*, 184, 186–7, 191–2; HMC, 9th *Report*, app., pt. 1, p. 111.

[314] Cawston MS, fo. 9ᵛ; Searle, *Chronicle and Lists*, 192.

[315] The exact date of Ashford's death at the Curia (25 July 1452) and the place of his burial (the Benedictine abbey of Santa Balbina in Rome) were recorded by John Stone (Searle, *Chronicle and Lists*, 53; cf. 182, 184; Cawston MS, fo. 4ᵛ).

Canterbury. To this generalization the only important exceptions were apparently those members of the community who expired, often of plague, while studying at Oxford. Although interment in the cemetery of St Frideswide's Priory, located very close to Canterbury College, was the common solution to such a problem, the corpse of John Wy was brought by cart from Oxford to Canterbury in 1418 for all due exequies ('cum nota et psalmis') and eventual burial in the monastic cemetery there.[316] At Christ Church, as at Oxford, sudden death was common enough; but deaths by violence seem to have been remarkably few by the standards of late medieval lay and even religious society. Perhaps the most horrific end to befall any late medieval Canterbury monk occurred on the anniversary of Becket's martyrdom (29 December) in 1425, when, after the end of Compline, John Grove decided to climb up to the vaults of the still-incomplete north-western tower of the Cathedral; after losing his footing, he plunged to the pavement, so sustaining multiple fractures from which he died in the infirmary during the course of the night.[317] At the beginning of the next century, Brother Percival Wysynden came to a less dramatic but equally depressing end by drowning himself in a fountain located in the convent's new garden.[318] However, no other case of suicide emerges from the community's records; and it can go without saying that bubonic plague (almost invariably termed 'pestilentia' by the monks themselves) was the most common and most dreaded cause of sudden death. Unfortunately, it is only in the second half of the fifteenth century that the Canterbury obituary lists begin to record the cause of a monk's death at all regularly; according to Dr Hatcher's recent analysis of the cases of forty-eight monks who died between 1485 and 1507, even at that late date eight monks were diagnosed as dying of plague.[319] During the same period, nine members of the community were the victims of the more novel scourge of sweating-sickness; but most other infectious diseases seem to have been much less lethal. Despite the occasional occurrence of paralytic strokes, heart disease also seems to have been an infrequent cause of death; and in general few of the medical conditions diagnosed in the convent would seem to owe their origins to dietary problems.[320] On the other hand, pulmonary illnesses were very common indeed; and in years unaffected by outbreaks of plague, it was diseases like consumption, pleurisy, asthma, emphysema, and (above all) tuberculosis which were most likely to bring a monastic career at Christ Church to a premature end.[321]

Few monks, even those struck down by the most virulent strain of bubonic plague, were unable to die in bed; and wherever possible, it was the convent's usual practice to bring their dying colleagues from the common dormitory to a chamber in the infirmary. In his last hours the dying monk was comforted by his fellow monks, who often recorded the hour (usually in the middle of the night) as well as the date of his decease.[322] For obvious reasons, and no doubt especially after death by plague, little time was lost in

[316] Searle, *Chronicle and Lists*, 9; Pantin, *Cant. Coll.*, iv. 76–7.

[317] Searle, *Chronicle and Lists*, 12.

[318] Cawston MS, fo. 8; Searle, *Chronicle and Lists*, 189.

[319] Hatcher, 'Mortality in the Fifteenth Century' (cit. in n. 212), 30; cf. Searle, *Chronicle and Lists*, 10, 16, 17, 67, 70, 92, 115, 117.

[320] In this and similar respects the Christ Church community

seems analogous to that at Westminster Abbey, discussed in detail by Miss Barbara Harvey in her *Living and Dying in England, 1100–1540: The Monastic Experience* (Oxford, 1993).

[321] Searle, *Chronicle and Lists*, 183–92; Hatcher, 'Mortality in the Fifteenth Century' (cit. in n. 212), 30.

[322] Cawston MS, fos. 32ᵛ–36; Searle, *Chronicle and Lists*, 11–118, *passim*.

preparing for the funeral. The deceased monk was carried into the infirmary chapel, where he was laid on a special stone slab, with his face uncovered, so that all his fellows could gaze upon him for the last time. Depending on what liturgical acts were currently taking place in the Cathedral, the corpse might remain on this slab for some time; but the exequies would usually begin with little delay. Even if the prior was present in the infirmary chapel for the funeral, it was generally the subprior who conducted the service. The latter normally comprised three main phases: a personal commendation of the deceased to God, the singing of as many as fifty psalms, and finally the recitation of the Placebo and Dirige, followed by a requiem mass.[323] The body was then carried, still with the face open to view, to the choir; after more prayers and perhaps a sermon, it usually rested there all night, before being taken back to the infirmary chapel. There the corpse was properly shrouded and taken out for interment either in the monastic cemetery or—increasingly commonly in the fifteenth century—within or around the infirmary chapel itself.[324] To an extent no longer possible to appreciate, pilgrims to the shrine of St Thomas must have seen the Cathedral precinct of Canterbury as one of the greatest necropolises of medieval England. More important still perhaps was the impact upon the living community of its deceased fellows lying in such close proximity to themselves as they went about their daily business.[325] Such, no doubt, has always been the case in all monastic cathedrals, and indeed all monasteries. However, few religious houses in late medieval England can have rivalled the determination of the monks of Christ Church to make the celebration of the memory of their departed brethren an inseparable part of their own communal life, to fuse the concerns of the next world with their own.

ST THOMAS OF CANTERBURY: FROM TRIUMPH TO DISASTER

'The happy church of Canterbury can therefore sing a new song to the Lord ... made beautiful by the precious blood of the martyr Thomas and visited by the multitudes of people who come there from every nation under heaven.'[326] Amidst the economic stresses and political dangers of the three centuries which followed Honorius III's jubilant letter to Archbishop Stephen Langton in 1219, the monks of Christ Church could continue to sing more confidently than most members of the English clergy. As the custodians of the physical remains of the most celebrated thaumaturge in medieval England, they enjoyed one inestimable source of strength and comfort denied to all other religious communities in the kingdom. Admittedly nothing can be more difficult than to assess the quality and extent of a saint's appeal with any real precision; and not even St Thomas was entirely immune from 'the ebb and flow of fashion' which has led one recent historian to suppose that pilgrimage to his shrine was a sporadic phenomenon, already in decline by the late thirteenth century. In fact, the abundant evidence points to a much more positive

---

[323] Compare, e.g., the funeral services provided for William Hadley, subprior, in 1499 with those for Prior Thomas Goldstone in 1468 (Cawston MS, fo. 32ᵛ; Searle, *Chronicle and Lists*, 104–5).

[324] John Stone thought it worthy of record when a heavy fall of snow prevented the brethren from being present at the burial of a late colleague (Searle, *Chronicle and Lists*, 72).

[325] Ceremonial processions through the monastic cemetery to the east of the Cathedral were a common feature of the religious life at Christ Church (ibid. 81, 101).

[326] Foreville, *Jubilé* (cit. in n. 2), 163–4.

conclusion. Of course 'Thomme of Cankerbury', as he was impolitely known to some East Anglian Lollards of the early fifteenth century, was not without his critics in later medieval England.[327] However, the most remarkable feature of the saint's unique position in the *ecclesia Anglicana* is that he continued to preserve his ascendancy and magnetic attraction so comparatively intact—until the ultimate humiliation of the dismantling of his shrine in September 1538 deprived the Christ Church community at a stroke of its most important *raison d'être*.

It is now well known that a saint's cult is rarely what at first sight it might seem. For that reason above all, it would be dangerous to assume that the complicated and ever-changing psychological and spiritual ramifications of St Thomas Becket's own cult can now be properly understood, let alone subjected to quantitative assessment. How, for example, should one interpret the apparently startling revelation of the Christ Church prior's accounts (themselves a very incomplete series) which seem to show a decline from over £500 to less than £20 a year in oblations to the shrines in Christ Church between 1396 and 1473? A similar decline in offerings to cathedral shrines is evident throughout fifteenth-century England; and it is always as well to remember that many pilgrims to Canterbury and elsewhere preferred to offer jewels and plate to such shrines, rather than cash.[328] In any case, and without denying that the income the Christ Church monks received from oblations at St Thomas's own shrine seems never to have been as high again as it was in the year of his fifth jubilee (1420), in comparative terms Becket's capacity to elicit alms from the faithful remained more or less unrivalled to the end. On the eve of the dissolution of the convent, the *Valor Ecclesiasticus* reveals that although the oblations at St Thomas's shrine were then only valued at the suspiciously low figure of £36 2s. 10d. this was a sum still unsurpassed—except by Our Lady of Walsingham—at any monastic church in England.[329] There is, however, much more powerful testimony to the continued national celebrity of St Thomas until, and even beyond, 1500. Above all, it is clear that he never altogether lost his reputation, deserved or not, as the most effective source of physical remedy and comfort to the sick and infirm in north-west Christendom.

Naturally enough, this thaumaturgical role could normally be performed only at Becket's own shrine, situated after 1220 immediately behind the choir of Canterbury Cathedral and therefore in very close proximity to the monks of Christ Church as they conducted the *opus Dei*. Those monks were also well aware that, quite apart from the shrine's own inherent attractions, it had the great additional advantage of being located on the main route from London to the most popular Channel ports of later medieval England. In Prior Eastry's words of 1318, 'we are more than any community on earth exactly on the high road at the point of entry to, and departure from, your realm'.[330] For that reason too, perhaps no interior space in late medieval England, not even the royal mausoleum at

[327] *Heresy Trials in the Diocese of Norwich, 1428–31*, ed. N. P. Tanner (Camden 4th ser., 20; 1977), 1, 14, 45, 57, 71; J. Sumption, *Pilgrimage: An Image of Mediaeval Religion* (London, 1975), 150–1; cf. R. C. Finucane, *Miracles and Pilgrims: Popular Beliefs in Medieval England* (London, 1977), 191–202.

[328] Prior's Accts., nos. 1–15 (1411–57); Woodruff, 'Financial Aspect of the Cult of St Thomas' (cit. in n. 6), 13–32; Woodruff

and Danks, *Memorials*, 81–2; Dobson, *Durham Priory* (cit. in n. 64), 29–30.

[329] A. Savine, *English Monasteries on the Eve of the Dissolution* (Oxford Studies in Social and Legal History, ed. P. Vinogradoff; Oxford, 1909), 103–4.

[330] Reg. L, fo. 189ᵛ; *Lit. Cant.*, i. 42–5.

Westminster Abbey, was visited by so many and observed so minutely as was the tomb of St Thomas and its surroundings. Most of the several visitors who have left written record of their impressions concurred with the Venetian ambassador who reported to his Doge at the end of the fifteenth century that the tomb was of a magnificence 'which surpasses all belief'; and of the many priceless treasures which surrounded the shrine itself, there was general agreement too that Louis VII's famous ruby, the *Régale*, 'left everything else far behind'.[331] For those with an antiquarian or historical turn of mind, an even more remarkable sight must have been the extraordinary variety of conspicuous votaries and statues clustered around the tomb: such curiosities ranged, to take only two examples, from the wax model of one of Edward I's ailing gyrfalcons (presented by the King in 1286 at a cost of 3s. 4d.) to the projected and probably life-size kneeling silver-gilt image of himself which Henry VII wished to be 'set as nigh to the shrine as may well be'.[332]

It has sometimes been suggested that so vast an assemblage of marvels and exotica progressively tended to transform the most celebrated of English religious shrines into a national museum, and even (as for Erasmus and Madame de Montreuil) into a spectacle of dubious moral value and questionable aesthetic taste.[333] However, Canterbury Cathedral in the later Middle Ages is no exception to the general rule that all flourishing centres of pilgrimage must by definition attract an inseparable if uneasy agglomeration of the genuinely needy, the genuinely devout, and those for whom curiosity is a stronger motive than either need or devotion. For all three categories of visitors to Christ Church, moreover, it was important not only that St Thomas had worked celebrated miracles at his shrine in the past, but that he might still be capable of working them in the present. In August 1394, Richard II wrote enthusiastically to Archbishop William Courtenay, hoping that the recent unspecified miracle reported at Becket's shrine ('en une persone estrange') would regenerate the spiritual life of his realm; and in 1445 Prior John Salisbury testified to another miracle there, this time upon a cripple from Aberdeen.[334] Like the fifteenth-century monks of St Cuthbert at Durham, those of St Thomas sometimes found it difficult to reconcile themselves to the fact that the age of notable and verifiable miracles seemed to have passed. Nothing delighted the Christ Church chapter more than the prospect, to cite a poem composed to celebrate the saint's alleged triumph over the forces of Satan during the course of a storm in the English Channel, that 'novis fulget Thomas miraculis'.[335]

However, during the last two medieval centuries, the continuing *réclame* of St Thomas

[331] *English Historical Documents*, v: *1485–1558*, ed. C. H. Williams (London, 1967), 196; Woodman, *Architectural History* (cit. in n. 8), 221–2; A. P. Stanley, *Historical Memorials of Canterbury* (10th edn.; London, 1909), 221–90.

[332] M. Prestwich, 'The Piety of Edward I', in *England in the Thirteenth Century: Proc. 1984 Harlaxton Symposium*, ed. W. M. Ormrod (Woodbridge, 1985), 121; Stanley, *Historical Memorials* (cit. in n. 331), 237. Cf. M. Prestwich, *Edward I* (London, 1988), 112, for that monarch's offering of gold florins at the shrine in 1300 in order to secure Becket's protection of 'the foetus then existing in the queen's body'.

[333] *The Colloquies of Erasmus*, ed. C. R. Thompson (Chicago, 1965), 286–7, 303–11; *LP Henry VIII*, i. 583–4. For a valuable account of the administration of the shrine, see D. H. Turner,

'The Customary of the Shrine of St Thomas Becket', *Cant. Cath. Chron.*, 70 (1976), 16–22.

[334] Reg. S, fos. 142, 163; HMC, 5th *Report*, app., p. 462; *Lit. Cant.*, iii. 26–9; J. Stuart, 'Notice of an Original Instrument Recently Discovered Among the Records of the Dean and Chapter of Canterbury, Describing the Miraculous Cure Effected on a Citizen of Aberdeen, 1445', *Proc. Soc. Antiquaries of Scotland*, 10 (1872–4), 528–35; Stanley, *Historical Memorials* (cit. in n. 331), 276–81. For a cryptic allusion to a miracle performed somewhere in the Midlands during the 1470s and probably by St Thomas, see *Christ Church Letters*, 29.

[335] Searle, *Chronicle and Lists*, 100; for St Thomas's earlier miracles, see B. Ward, *Miracles and the Medieval Mind: Theory, Record and Event, 1000–1215* (2nd edn.; Aldershot, 1987), 89–109.

Becket's cult owed much less to any new miracles on his part than to two other factors. The first of these is obvious enough. By 1300, and indeed earlier, not only the religious and spiritual life, but the physical environment and even the linguistic usages of Englishmen and Englishwomen had become so permeated with the influence of Becket that he was firmly entrenched in their thoughts as the supreme national exemplar of the miracle-working Christian saint. The monastic, collegiate, and parish churches of later medieval England (and not England alone) were literally honeycombed with chapels, chantries, and altars dedicated to St Thomas, and hence with the acts of intense and, usually, personal devotion which those dedications implied. As is well known, more English parishioners worshipped in churches (over eighty) dedicated to St Thomas of Canterbury than to any other English saint, even his much longer established rival at Durham.[336] By the fifteenth century, however, a much more sensitive guide to the cult of Becket at a local level is provided by devotional practices at altars within the village and urban parish church. In late medieval Oxford, for example, record has been found of five altars or chapels and three lights dedicated to St Thomas, more than to any other saint in the town's churches except the Blessed Virgin Mary and St Catherine. More numerous still, no doubt, although now almost completely vanished, were the many representations of the saint of Canterbury installed in private chapels, like the painting commissioned by Edward of Caernarvon for the small chapel of Chester Castle not long before his father's death—on the feast of the translation of St Thomas in 1307—at Burgh-by-Sands.[337] Even in the city of York, notoriously reluctant to accept the primacy of the southern province in religious matters, by the fifteenth century it must have been more or less impossible for even the most casual visitor to avoid observing altars, sculpture, and, above all, stained-glass windows dedicated to the inimitable patron saint of Canterbury.[338] To a limited extent, and especially in the city of London, it may be the case that some of the new and vigorous parish fraternities of fifteenth-century England were diverted from enthusiasm for St Thomas to the more novel and fashionable holy cults of the period. However, London itself provides the best of all possible examples of the deep imprint Becket could make on the collective psychology of English burgesses. As befitted a figure who had been transformed by its citizens into a Londoner's saint, the alleged grave of his parents outside St Paul's, as well as the church and hospital of St Thomas of Acon and the recently rebuilt St Thomas's Chapel on London Bridge, were among the most notable sights fifteenth-century London could offer.[339]

Even more important in preserving the continued ascendancy of St Thomas than his

[336] F. Bond, *Dedications and Patron Saints of English Churches* (Oxford, 1914), 17, 129–33; cf. Duggan, 'Cult of Saint Thomas Becket' (cit. in n. 2), 21–44.

[337] *VCH Oxford*, iv: *City of Oxford*, 71–2, 174; H. Johnstone, *Edward of Carnarvon, 1284–1307* (Manchester, 1947), 25, 45, 61, 96, 98, 126.

[338] P. Mackie, 'Chaplains in the Diocese of York, 1480–1530: The Testamentary Evidence', *Yorks. Archaeol. Jnl.*, 58 (1986), 129; Royal Commission on Historical Monuments, *City of York* (5 vols.; London, 1962–81), iii. 8; iv. 12; v. 25, 46; A. Raine, *Mediaeval York: A Topographical Survey* (London, 1955), *passim*.

[339] *The Register of John Morton, Archbishop of Canterbury, 1486–* 1500, ed. C. Harper-Bill, 2 vols. (CYS, 75 and 78; 1987 and 1991), i. 4–7; M. B. Honeybourne, 'The Pre-Norman Bridge of London', in *Studies in London History Presented to P. E. Jones*, ed. A. J. Hollaender and W. Kellaway (London, 1969), 30–2; *The British Atlas of Historic Towns*, iii: *The City of London from Prehistoric Times to c. 1520*, ed. M. D. Lobel (Oxford, 1989), 79, 92; D. W. Robertson, jun., *Chaucer's London* (New York, 1968), 30, 39, 57, 76–7, 173, 199, 217, 220; cf. C. M. Barron, 'The Parish Fraternities of Medieval London', in *The Church in Pre-Reformation Society: Essays in Honour of F. R. H. Du Boulay*, ed. id. and C. Harper-Bill (Woodbridge, 1985), 32.

omnipresence in religious ritual throughout the country was the ability of the monks of Christ Church to publicize and organize his cult. Like the deans and chapters of most late twentieth-century cathedrals when faced with the onslaughts of modern mass tourism, the Canterbury Cathedral community was no doubt often overwhelmed by the problems created by its own popularity. In 1318, for example, Prior Eastry excused himself from granting a corrody at Edward II's request because of the chapter's expenses in receiving the many visitors who 'come and stay with us several times'.[340] All the available evidence, however, suggests that the Christ Church monks normally saw it as their duty to welcome, to encourage, and often to accommodate, the hordes of pilgrims who 'from every shires ende of Engelond to Caunterbury they wende, the hooly blisful martir for to seke'.[341] It was during the first century after Becket's martyrdom that the prior and chapter first established their reputation as the most energetic publicists of their age. The rewriting of St Thomas's life, the compilation of his miracles, and the production of appropriately illuminated manuscripts naturally continued to be a constant preoccupation inside the Cathedral community, as did the sponsorship of the attributes of his martyrdom and of subsidiary relics.[342] In particular, however, 'no Continental sanctuary of the thirteenth century sent away its pilgrims with such eye-catching propaganda for its saint'.[343] The most celebrated of such pilgrimage souvenirs, the famous Canterbury ampullae, had begun to be produced in large numbers within a few years of Becket's martyrdom, in response to the remarkable demand for a few drops of the holy water tinged with his blood. By the late fourteenth and fifteenth centuries, these ampullae had been increasingly replaced in popularity by the manufacture of lead pilgrim-badges, themselves a guide to the way in which the saint's iconographical characteristics were constantly altered over the decades.[344] Until at least the late fifteenth century, the images of the saint and his murder were by no means stereotyped, itself perhaps an indirect comment on the vitality of his cult. Above all, the accidental survival of so many ampullae and pilgrim's badges, once again unsurpassed in the case of any other English saint, is the most impressive memorial we have to the countless late medieval anonymous pilgrims who 'peered fast and pored high' as they marvelled at a shrine they could not always understand.[345]

How many of these anonymous, and poorer, pilgrims actually had an opportunity to talk to a Christ Church monk in Canterbury Cathedral is a more difficult and open question. At no time between 1190 and 1538 can more than a small minority of St Thomas's pilgrims have been lodged within the monastic precincts. It is also doubtful whether, as R. A. L. Smith once suggested, the erection of the capacious 'Cheker of the Hope' inn on the south-west corner of Mercery Lane (by Prior Thomas Chillenden in the 1390s at a cost

---

[340] *Lit. Cant.*, i. 44–5.

[341] *The Works of Geoffrey Chaucer*, ed. F. N. Robinson (2nd edn.; London, 1957), 17. The best account of the most famous route to St Thomas's shrine remains F. C. Elliston Erwood, 'The "Pilgrim's Way", Its Antiquity and Its Alleged Mediaeval Use', *Arch. Cant.*, 37 (1925), 1–20.

[342] *Materials for the History of Thomas Becket, Archbishop of Canterbury*, ed. J. C. Robertson and J. B. Sheppard, 7 vols. (RS, 67; 1875–85), *passim*; Gransden, *Historical Writing* (cit. in n. 214), i. 296–306; T. Borenius, *St Thomas Becket in Art* (London, 1932);

id., 'Some Further Aspects of the Iconography of St. Thomas of Canterbury', *Archaeol. Jnl.*, 83 (1933), 171–86.

[343] *Age of Chivalry*, ed. Alexander and Binski (cit. in n. 7), 219.

[344] Ibid. 218–22; cf. P. A. Newton, 'Some New Material for the Study of the Iconography of St Thomas Becket', in *Thomas Becket: Actes du colloque international de Sédières, 19–24 août 1973*, ed. R. Foreville (Paris, 1975).

[345] *The Tale of Beryn*, ed. F. J. Furnivall and W. G. Stone (Chaucer Soc., 2nd ser., 18; 1887), ll. 8777–82.

of nearly £900) marked a new determination to avoid 'the trouble of receiving guests in person'. In the event, the famous 'Le Cheker' proved a highly successful piece of property speculation: in addition to the income from the many pilgrims who lodged there, the prior and chapter enjoyed valuable rents from shops on its ground floor. [346] Many pilgrims and other guests were regularly found accommodation within *camerae* in the precincts thereafter, notably perhaps in the almonry, the Cellarer's Hall, the Aula Nova, and Hog Hall. Most luxurious of all was the thirteenth-century Meister Omers, located immediately to the east of the infirmary chapel and ideally suited for conversion into a long-term residence or retirement home for a distinguished bishop like John Buckingham of Lincoln in 1398, or Cardinal Henry Beaufort in 1445–6. [347] Naturally enough, it is the lengthy visits to Canterbury, particularly when made by members of the royal family and by the lay and spiritual aristocracy, which are best documented in the Chapter's archives. Indeed, it cannot be emphasized enough that the great majority of medieval pilgrimages to St Thomas, even by most distinguished individuals, are completely unrecorded. It is, for example, only from a brief remark in one of his letters that we learn of John Paston III's proposal 'to go to Canterbury on foot' in 1470; and only from a casual entry in a Durham account-roll of 1437–8 that evidence survives of Prior John Wessington's visit to a shrine even more celebrated than that of St Cuthbert. [348] Indeed, it might well be surmised, although it cannot be proved, that there were few late medieval Englishmen (and even Englishwomen) who did not harbour at some time or other of their lives the desire to go on pilgrimage to Canterbury.

Not Englishmen and Englishwomen alone. Ever since Louis VII's visit to the shrine in 1179 had given the French monarchy's seal of approval to Becket's cult, Canterbury Cathedral had been the most cosmopolitan centre of pilgrimage in north-western Christendom. In this sphere too, the prior and chapter had positively welcomed successful papal initiatives in applying the concept of the jubilee to England's most internationally celebrated saint. Although the responses to St Thomas Becket's six jubilees (1220, 1270, 1320, 1370, 1420, and 1470) are very unevenly documented, there can be no doubt at all that the widespread distribution of papal indulgences had a dramatic effect on the number of pilgrims visiting Canterbury in these—and indeed other—years. On the feast of the saint's translation (7 July) in 1420, for example, the chapter recorded that there was such 'a sudden and unexpected concourse of people' within the Cathedral that it was full to capacity and most masses had to be suspended. [349] Admittedly, St Thomas's sixth jubilee, fifty years later, was much less successful, being plagued from the outset by administrative and political planning problems of the sort which later aborted the jubilee of 1520 completely. However, Prior John Oxney's decision to send William Sellyng and Reginald Goldstone to the Curia in 1469 to negotiate with pope and cardinals on the issue is one of several indications that the prior and chapter's own commitment to the jubilee and to papal indulgences remained

---

[346] Treasurers' Accts., no. 17 (1455–6); Shadwell MSS, no. 28; BL, Arundel MS 68, fo. 58; Smith, *Cant. Cath. Priory,* 200.

[347] For this 'Cardynalysplace', see G. L. Harriss, *Cardinal Beaufort: A Study of Lancastrian Ascendancy and Decline* (Oxford, 1988), 367–8; cf. J. B. Sheppard, 'The Meister Homers, Canterbury', *Arch. Cant.,* 13 (1880), 116–21.

[348] *Paston Letters and Papers of the Fifteenth Century,* ed. N. Davis, i (Oxford, 1971), 560; Dobson, *Durham Priory* (cit. in n. 64), 93.

[349] Foreville, *Jubilé* (cit. in n. 2), 177–85 *et passim*; cf. *Lit. Cant.,* iii, pp. xxxiii–xxxvi, 215, 245, 252–3.

as firm as ever.[350] Such commitment was, after all, in their own obvious best interests. As late as 1487, Innocent VIII granted an act of remission to those prepared to visit the church of Canterbury ('very famous in the realm of England') in a state of penitence during each of the three succeeding years: and in the very same year, Archbishop Morton issued an indulgence to those who came to the assistance of the hospital of St Thomas of Acon, 'the birthplace of the glorious martyr, and where his memory is venerated second only after the church of Canterbury'.[351] For the Christ Church community, papal indulgences were still to be eagerly sought rather than shunned.

During the century or so before the Dissolution, there are similarly few signs of a general decline of interest in St Thomas and his shrine outside England itself. If visitors to the shrine from mainland Europe between 1340 and 1440 included King John II of France (1360), Jean Froissart (1395), and the Emperor Sigismund (1416), then between 1440 and 1540 they included a future pope (Aeneas Sylvius, the future Pius II, in 1436), the Bohemian Leo of Rozmital (1466), Giovanni de Giglis in the 1470s, and the Emperor Charles V in 1520.[352] So frequent were such visits that many of the ceremonies and procedures which accompanied them had developed into a set and elaborate form. Thus when Campeggio arrived in Canterbury as papal legate on 24 July 1518, he processed to the high altar and then to St Thomas's shrine while the monks sang *Summae Trinitati*, almost their invariable responsory on these occasions.[353] No doubt in the eyes of the Christ Church monks themselves these were among the most imposing of all visits paid to their Cathedral. In retrospect, however, the most telling of tributes to St Thomas's fame were made by the obscure rather than the famous pilgrims from overseas, like the four Bridgettine nuns from Sweden who made a vow to visit St Thomas's shrine while sailing across the North Sea to their new home at the Abbey of Isleworth in 1417.[354] Nor was St Thomas's fame confined within the bounds of Christendom itself: in 1489 three mysterious travellers arrived in Jerusalem by the land route from India with the express objective of visiting, before their return to the East, what they considered the most celebrated holy places in Europe, namely Rome, Compostella, Finistère, Mont-Saint-Michel, and Canterbury.[355] But then the geographical extent of St Thomas's influence was as immeasurable as it could be, almost by definition, beyond reason. Did Giovanni Becchetti, that distinguished Augustinian friar and theologian of both Padua and Oxford universities at the end of the fourteenth century, actually believe his family's remarkable claim to be descended from the Italian branch of the family of St Thomas Becket?[356]

On balance, however, their unique and widespread international connections were

[350] Foreville, *Jubilé* (cit. in n. 2), 188–95; Weiss, *Humanism in England* (cit. in n. 218), p. 155.

[351] *CPL 1484–92*, 188–9; *Reg. Morton* (cit. in n. 339), i. 5.

[352] Froissart, *Œuvres*, ed. Kervyn de Lettenhove (28 vols.; Brussels, 1867–77), xv. 143; *Gesta Henrici Quinti*, ed. F. Taylor and J. S. Roskell (Oxford, 1975), 151–7; *The Commentaries of Pius II*, ed. L. C. Gabel (Smith College Studies in History, 22/1–2; 1936–7), 21–4; *The Travels of Leo of Rozmital*, ed. M. Letts (Hakluyt Soc., 2nd ser., 108; 1957), 43–4, 50–1; HMC, 5th *Report*, app., p. 446; *Christ Church Letters*, 35–6; Stanley, *Historical Memorials* (cit. in n. 331), 237–8.

[353] *British Library Harleian Manuscript 433*, ed. R. Horrox and P. W. Hammond, 4 vols. (Richard III Soc.; Gloucester, 1979–83), iii. 164–6; V. J. B. Torr, 'Campeggio's Progress Through Kent in 1518', *Arch. Cant.*, 43 (1931), 262–3; cf. Searle, *Chronicle and Lists*, 56, 93.

[354] *Reg. Chichele* (cit. in n. 252), iv. 167. For the most remarkable tribute to Becket's popularity in Scandinavia and Iceland, see *Thómas Saga Erkibyskups*, ed. E. Magnússon, 2 vols. (RS, 65; 1875–83).

[355] *CPL 1484–92*, 312.

[356] Emden, *BRUO*, i. 144–5.

always more likely to provide the Christ Church community with spiritual comfort in the next world rather than with material assistance in this. Becket might be able to perform many miracles; but he proved unable to protect from gradual erosion the prior and chapter's jealously guarded rights to the Wine of St Thomas originally conferred upon them by Louis VII of France.[357] Nor did the saint's considerable reputation in Ireland do much to liberate the Christ Church monks from yet another endless and expensive source of tribulation, the collection of rents and a pension of 13 marks a year deriving from a twelfth-century grant of a group of churches near Waterford.[358] In both these cases, and in countless others much nearer to home, the community's best interests were always to be served by turning to the servants of the English Crown, and in particular—as it did more often than any other monastery in his realm—to the person of the king himself. Fortunately for the prior and chapter, there was never a period between the reigns of Henry II and Henry VIII when an English monarch failed to appreciate the importance of as close and appreciative a relationship with St Thomas's community as his other commitments allowed. Very occasionally, a king's individual obsession with another English shrine or chantry foundation (Henry III at Westminster Abbey, Henry VI at Windsor, perhaps Richard III at York) might threaten to divert royal interest and royal patronage away from Canterbury. However, such comparative distraction never lasted for long; and in any case the king's affections were invariably supplemented by those of his immediate family, the latter in many ways even more important to the welfare of the Cathedral than his own. To take only the case of the two most important laymen ever buried in their Cathedral, after their deaths as during their lives, the monks of Christ Church owed considerably more to the Black Prince than they did to Henry IV.[359]

From the early thirteenth to the early sixteenth century, royal visits were accordingly regular rather than unusual features of cathedral life at Canterbury. Edward III, for example, normally visited Canterbury at least once a year throughout his long reign, worshipping at St Thomas's tomb and the Lady Chapel in the Cathedral before moving on to distribute alms at the shrines at St Augustine's Abbey as well.[360] Most late medieval sovereigns probably visited the Cathedral even more often, especially as the royal coronation cult of the Holy Oil of St Becket ('with which kings were accustomed to be consecrated') gathered impetus in the decades after its first appearance under the sponsorship of Edward II.[361] There were several years in the reign of Henry VI when that

---

[357] As the occasion for one of the longest and best-documented conflicts in Anglo-French relations during the Middle Ages, the complex history of the Wine of St Thomas deserves more attention than it received over a century ago in *Lit. Cant.*, i, pp. lxxvi–lxxxiii; iii, pp. xix–xxiv. The wine consumed by the Canterbury community itself was apparently more often shipped from Rouen to Sandwich or Deal than from Gascony: see the especially informative account of an expedition up the Seine to buy wine recorded in DE 150; cf. Treasurers' Accs., nos. 1–18.

[358] J. B. Sheppard's view that the chapter's possessions in Ireland were a source of 'at least as much vexation as profit' (*Christ Church Letters*, p. viii) is fully borne out by all the voluminous evidence (e.g. ibid. 6–7, 10–13; Reg. S, fo. 236ᵛ; *Lit.*

Cant., iii. 2–3, 6–7, 10–12, 48; HMC, 5th *Report*, app., p. 445; *CPR 1272–81*, 317, 386, 397).

[359] For the Black Prince's munificent legacies to Christ Church, see Legg and Hope, *Inventories*, 96. Despite Leland's view to the contrary, it seems less than certain that Henry of Bolingbroke contributed substantially to the rebuilding of the Cathedral's nave and cloister during the priorate of Thomas Chillenden (BL, MS Arundel 68, fo. 58; Woodruff and Danks, *Memorials*, 188).

[360] W. M. Ormrod, 'The Personal Religion of Edward III', *Speculum*, 64 (1989), 857–8; cf. id., *The Reign of Edward III* (New Haven, Conn., 1990), 44.

[361] For the stress placed on this implausible validation-myth by the Yorkist monarchs, see W. Ullmann, 'Thomas Becket's

unfortunate monarch made three or four expeditions to Canterbury; and it might not be altogether a coincidence that the Yorkist royal family also visited Becket's shrine particularly frequently during the early and most volatile stages of the Wars of the Roses.[362] It was, in fact, while at Canterbury on 18 July 1465 that Edward IV and Queen Elizabeth Woodville heard the welcome news of Henry VI's capture in Ribblesdale, an event they immediately celebrated by attending a sermon in the Cathedral choir, a Te Deum, and a procession to Becket's tomb.[363] At more tranquil periods, the king and his consort usually tried to make their visits to Canterbury coincide with a major feast-day, preferably that of Becket's own translation; and on these and other occasions they might occupy the archbishop's palace or the prior's quarters for several days at a time. In November 1415 Henry V spent only two days in Canterbury on his return from Agincourt to an ecstatic welcome by the Londoners; but he was there again with the Emperor Sigismund for as many as twelve days in the following August. Even longer were the visits to Canterbury of his son, the considerably more lethargic Henry VI: no king of medieval England can have worshipped at St Thomas's shrine more often—and no doubt devoutly—than did the last of the Lancastrians.[364]

The effect on the Christ Church community of such a regular bombardment of royal and aristocratic visitation will never be altogether easy to assess. At times, one even suspects that St Thomas's immense fame outside the Cathedral precincts made it more, rather than less, difficult for the Canterbury monks to identify very closely with this supernatural colossus in their midst. Among the copious records of the fifteenth-century convent, unlike in those of Durham Cathedral Priory, personal invocations to the patron saint tend to be as infrequent as rhetorical tributes to his fame are ubiquitous.[365] Nor is it likely that the visits made by kings and queens were often of much material profit to the monks themselves, not least because of their own obligation to present a visiting monarch with a suitably lavish gift of plate on these occasions: in 1343, for example, the Prior presented Edward III and Queen Philippa of Hainault with a set of silver ewers and bowls, as well as a palfrey and a pony ('parvum equum').[366] There were, however, more important ways still in which the community of Christ Church could be of service to the English Crown and nobility. By definition, Canterbury Cathedral was the most efficacious prayer-house in the kingdom; and the extensive surviving correspondence of the prior and chapter with the monarchs and magnates of the later Middle Ages rarely failed to conclude with either a request for a prayer to St Thomas or an expression of a readiness to make one.[367] For an English king of the later Middle Ages, the most urgent request for the monks'

Miraculous Oil', *Jnl. Theol. Studies*, NS, 8 (1957), 129–33; J. W. McKenna, 'The Coronation Oil of the Yorkist Kings', *EHR*, 82 (1967), 102–4.

[362] Searle, *Chronicle and Lists*, 110–17, 150; B. Wolffe, *Henry VI* (London, 1981), 81, 94, 338; *Chronicles of London*, ed. C. L. Kingsford (Oxford, 1905), 176, 222, 231.

[363] Searle, *Chronicle and Lists*, 93–4.

[364] *Gesta Henrici Quinti* (cit. in n. 252), 100–1, 150–5; Wolffe, *Henry VI* (cit. in n. 362), 361–71; R. A. Griffiths, *The Reign of Henry VI* (London, 1981), 864.

[365] It is, e.g., noticeable how rarely St Thomas's name is invoked in the personal correspondence between 15th-cent.

Canterbury College monks at Oxford and their fellows at the mother house (Pantin, *Cant. Coll.*, iii. 88–142); cf. Dobson, *Durham Priory* (cit. in n. 64), 27–32.

[366] Woodruff, 'Financial Aspect of the Cult of St Thomas', (cit. in n. 6), 28–9.

[367] Incidental pious references to St Thomas seem much more common in Eastry Correspondence and the registers of that prior than they are in the convent's letters of the 15th cent. (*Lit. Cant.*, i–iii, *passim*): in 1452, however, John Tiptoft, Earl of Worcester, obviously thought it appropriate to commend Henry Cranebroke, a monk he knew well, 'Deo sanctoque Thome' (Pantin, *Cant. Coll.*, iii. 103).

prayers tended to be when he was in military danger from either external or internal enemies. No doubt this had always been the case; but it was Edward I in the 1290s who began to systematize the practice of calling for prayers within Canterbury and other cathedrals at times of national crisis.[368] In 1394 Richard II asked the Christ Church monks to pray for the success of his Irish expedition; and to the very end of its existence the convent was the recipient of a continuous succession of requests to seek St Thomas's protection against military defeat, disease, and bad weather.[369]

Such prayers were all the more likely to be willingly performed at Canterbury because there can have been few monastic communities in the south of England more conscious of the threat that war presented to their own prosperity. Although the prior and chapter were sometimes, however reluctantly, compelled to raise troops and money for the English war effort against the Welsh and Scots during the reigns of Edward I and Edward II, they were naturally much more apprehensive of raids by the French on the Kent coast.[370] All in all, they were certainly right to be so. In the event, the Hundred Years War proved to be less catastrophic for the Christ Church monks and their tenants than might have been predicted; and it was to Kentish rebels rather than to a French *chevauchée* that both city and Cathedral of Canterbury were compelled to open their gates on 10 June 1381.[371] However, and as the violent events of the following days prove only too well, the Cathedral precinct was acutely vulnerable to armed attack. The community's life at Canterbury during the fourteenth and fifteenth centuries was never, in other words, quite as isolated from the threat of external aggression as John Stone and their other chroniclers might seem to imply. The monks accordingly had a vested interest in presenting themselves to the Crown, as to Edward III in 1340, in the guise of royal watchdogs gazing over the English Channel and 'watching to defend your realm from attacks by sea'.[372] In practice, however, one supposes that English kings and magnates found the services of the community much more effectively deployed when providing them with accommodation on the way to or from battle. For obvious reasons, Canterbury was in any case even more ideally located for the making of peace than for the preparation of war. It was there, for instance, that John, Earl of Warenne, and Aymer de Valence negotiated with the envoys of Philip the Fair of France in the spring of 1301;[373] and it was at Canterbury too that in 1416 and 1520 respectively Henry V and Henry VIII enjoyed the rare pleasure of welcoming a German emperor to English soil.[374]

For the monks of Christ Church, however, it might well be claimed that the kings and magnates of medieval England were of greater significance when dead than alive. Although important matrimonial alliances (notably Edward I's second marriage to Margaret of France in 1299) were sometimes concluded by a wedding in Canterbury Cathedral, it was

[368] D. W. Burton, 'Requests for Prayers and Royal Propaganda', in *Thirteenth Century England*, 3, ed. P. R. Coss and S. D. Lloyd (Woodbridge, 1991), 25–35.

[369] Reg. S, fo. 14ᵛ; *Lit. Cant.*, iii. 30–1; HMC, 9th *Report*, app., pt. I, p. III; cf. A. K. McHardy, 'Liturgy and Propaganda in the Diocese of Lincoln During the Hundred Years War', *Studies in Church History*, 18 (1982), 215–27.

[370] *Lit. Cant.*, i. 70–3, 126–7, 182–4, 212–22; ii. 56.

[371] W. E. Flaherty, 'The Great Rebellion in Kent', *Arch. Cant.*, 3 (1860), 73–7; *The Peasants' Revolt of 1381*, ed. R. B. Dobson (2nd edn.; London, 1983), 127, 133, 139–40, 205.

[372] *Christ Church Letters*, 2–3.

[373] *CPR 1292–1301*, 580, 582, 586.

[374] *Gesta Henrici Quinti* (cit. in n. 352), pp. xxvii–xxviii, xliv–xlvi, 150; J. J. Scarisbrick, *Henry VIII* (London, 1968), 75–6.

undoubtedly the burials there which had the deepest and most sustained impact on monastic life at Christ Church.[375] The prospects of procuring a final resting-place in close proximity to the shrine of the most celebrated of all English saints were not to be lightly disregarded; and even a French king (John II in 1364) might prefer to direct his body to the Abbey of Saint-Denis but his bowels to St Paul's and his heart to Canterbury Cathedral.[376] On the whole, the archbishop and chapter seem to have prepared to give way to these pressures; and licence for the burial of both clergy and laity within the church as well as in the lay cemetery seems to have been less restrictively applied than in the case of several other monastic cathedrals.[377] Naturally enough, however, it is the burials of the spiritual and lay aristocracy which have left the most abundant documentary evidence, as well as surviving memorials. In 1437 the funeral services of Queen Joan of Navarre, buried in the Cathedral choir by the side of a royal husband who had died twenty-four years earlier, were carefully planned by Humphrey, Duke of Gloucester, and the royal council.[378] It is similarly clear from the record of the extraordinarily elaborate final rites of passage which accompanied the corpse of Archbishop Henry Dean—in its progress by barge and funeral car from Lambeth to interment within the Cathedral Martyrdom in 1503—that these Canterbury funerals were among the most important (and now neglected) State occasions of late medieval England.[379]

More important, no doubt, to those who decided to leave their mortal remains within Canterbury Cathedral was the assurance of the prayers of the monastic community thereafter. As in many of the major churches of late medieval England, the existence of a multiplicity of different types of chantry and obit foundation can bewilder the historian, as it must once have confused the monks themselves.[380] Although a community of religious inevitably finds it more difficult to assimilate the concept and practice of the chantry within its routines than does its secular counterpart, it can be safely said that Christ Church was the scene of more, and more substantial, chantry establishments than any other English monastic cathedral. Not all of these, it has to be said, were a source of satisfaction to the prior and chapter, partly perhaps because they were usually served by secular chaplains rather than by the monks themselves. Even the most celebrated of all the Canterbury chantries, founded for two chaplains—and endowed with Vauxhall manor— by the Black Prince in 1363, was involving the convent in serious financial loss by 1472; and earlier in the century the two chantry priests were sufficiently at odds with one another

---

[375] Gervase, *Historical Works*, ii. 317; cf. Prestwich, *Edward I* (cit. in n. 332), 395–6.

[376] *Chronicon Johannis de Reading*, ed. Tait (cit. in n. 216), 216, 238; *The Anonimalle Chronicle, 1333 to 1381*, ed. V. H. Galbraith (Manchester, 1927), 50.

[377] Most such burials are unrecorded; but see Searle, *Chronicle and Lists*, 44, for the interment of Elizabeth Septvans at Canterbury Cathedral in 1448; cf. B. Golding, 'Burial and Benefactions: An Aspect of Monastic Patronage in Thirteenth-Century England', in *England in the Thirteenth Century* (cit. in n. 332), 65–72.

[378] *Proc. and Ordinances of the Privy Council*, ed. N. H. Nicolas, 7 vols. (Record Commn.: 1834–7), v. 56; *Chronicles of London* (cit. in n. 362), 143; *History of the King's Works*, i: ed. H. M. Colvin,

The Middle Ages, (London, 1963), i. 488.

[379] A. Way, 'The Will of Henry Dene, Archbishop of Canterbury', *Archaeol. Jnl.*, 18 (1861), 260–1; *Sede Vacante Wills* (cit. in n. 168), 93–5; cf. ibid. 85–6 (Archbishop Morton, 1500); L. L. Duncan, 'The Will of Cardinal Bourgchier, Archbishop of Canterbury, 1486', *Arch. Cant.*, 24 (1900), 244–52.

[380] Much the best-documented of the Christ Church chantries are the chapels of St Thomas in the almonry and of the Black Prince in the undercroft: see, e.g., HMC, 5th *Report*, app., p. 435; 9th *Report*, app., pt. 1, p. 102; *CPR 1327–30*, 448; *1381–5*, 98; *1467–77*, 388, 415; *1476–85*, 12, 123; *Lit. Cant.*, i. 88–91, 103, 129, 130–3, 166; ii. 248–9, 257–9. No satisfactory account of these or the other Cathedral chantries yet exists.

to make it necessary to produce new regulations for their better behaviour.[381] Despite such difficulties, the enthusiasm for chantry foundation at Canterbury shows few signs of abating before the Reformation, dominated as it was by the archbishops of Canterbury themselves. Indeed, William Warham's minuscule chantry chapel, to which he was brought for burial in 1532 but which had been built near the Martyrdom as long ago as 1507, was the occasion for the last significant structural modification to the fabric of the Cathedral before the Dissolution.[382] Even more lavish had been the perpetual chantry-foundations of Bishop John Buckingham and Archbishop Thomas Arundel at the end of the fourteenth century: the latter provided his two priests with a house on the south side of the Cathedral and intended his chantry chapel itself to serve as an occasional oratory for laymen and laywomen.[383] The incidental spiritual benefits for the laity of the presence of chantry priests within a cathedral should not perhaps be too rapidly discounted; but it is even more clear, as in the case of Lady (Joan) Brenchley's chantry, founded in the late 1440s within the Cathedral nave, that the prior and chapter appreciated the ways in which chantry intercession could strengthen their links with local—and not so local—magnates and gentry.[384]

There were, however, other ways in which the community at Christ Church might use, yet again, the fame of St Thomas to reward allies and win friends in high places. Perhaps the most obvious of these was the admission of favoured clerks and laymen (including women) into the fraternity of the monastery, a practice widespread enough among many of late medieval England's major churches but rarely as energetically pursued as at Canterbury.[385] Only from the late fourteenth century do copies of letters of confraternity begin to survive among the prior and chapter's records; but thereafter they proliferate, to constitute a roll-call of the nation's ruling élite. Prominent ecclesiastical figures, like Cardinal Beaufort in 1433, Cardinal John Kempe in 1447, Archbishop Thomas Rotherham in 1465, and Bishop Richard Fox in 1503, were naturally members of this élite; but so too were less exalted clerks (like the physician Master John Cokkys, and Master Thomas Chaundler, chancellor of York Minster) who had befriended Canterbury monks at Oxford.[386] Equally prominent were the names of the higher aristocracy (Thomas Holland, Duke of Exeter, in 1422; Anne, Duchess of Buckingham, in 1469; Henry, Duke of Buckingham, in 1482); and it is not without irony that Queen Elizabeth Woodville and Richard, Duke of Gloucester, were both received into the Christ Church fraternity within a few years of their fateful struggle for political ascendancy in 1483.[387] Less anticipated and more

[381] Reg. N, fos. 182[v], 239[v]; HMC, 9th *Report*, app., pt. I, pp. 102, 106; *Lit. Cant.*, iii. 210–12, 257.

[382] HMC, 5th *Report*, app., p. 435; *Wills from Doctors' Commons, 1495–1695*, ed. J. G. Nichols and J. Bruce (Camden Soc., 83; 1863), 21–7; Woodruff and Danks, *Memorials*, 214–15.

[383] HMC, 5th *Report*, app., p. 435; 9th *Report*, app., pt. I, p. 112; *Reg. Morton* (cit. in n. 339), 119, 147, 151, 153, 161; *Sede Vacante Wills* (cit. in n. 168), 100–5; Woodruff and Danks, *Memorials*, 194–5.

[384] HMC, 5th *Report*, app., p. 435; 9th *Report*, app., p. 114; *Reg. Morton* (cit. in n. 339), 155; Woodruff and Danks, *Memorials*, 203, 350; cf. C. Burgess, 'By Quick and by Dead: Wills and Pious Provision in Late Medieval Bristol', *EHR*, 102 (1987), 837–58.

[385] As in the case of most other religious houses, letters recording admission to the confraternity were usually copied into the main conventual registers: see esp. Regs. S and T(i). For a famous exception, see BL, Cotton MS Nero D. vii (the famous Liber Benefactorum of St Albans); and cf. E. Bishop, 'Some Ancient Benedictine Confraternity Books', in id., *Liturgica Historica* (Oxford, 1918), 359–60.

[386] Reg. S, fos. 115[*], 211, 220, 229; Reg. T(i), fo. 434[v]–435; HMC, 9th *Report*, app., pt. I, p. 115; cf. Pantin, *Cant. Coll.*, iii. 107, 110–14, 123–5; iv. 101, 148–50.

[387] Reg. S, fos. 86, 237; HMC, 9th *Report*, app., pt. I, pp. 112, 117–18.

distant recipients of letters of admission to the fraternity were the convent's friends or patrons at the Curia (Master Peter de Mellinis in 1469), in the Loire Valley (King Louis XI himself in 1477), and even in Iceland (Vigfus Ivarson, an alleged descendant of Thomas Becket, in 1415).[388]

More valuable still to the prior and chapter were the good offices of those lords and gentlemen who dominated the operations of the legal system either at central or local level. In 1509 John More had served as one of the chapter's attorneys-at-law in London; so it is not perhaps particularly surprising that in 1530 his son, Sir Thomas More, then Chancellor of England, was to be one of the last of all entrants to the Christ Church fraternity. However, a much more representative member of the convent's all-important if diversified group of retained common lawyers and estates-management consultants was Sir John Fogge, admitted to confraternity in 1472.[389] John Fogge and his family, together with John Culpepper, John Tattershall, Edmund Langley, Sir John Fyneux, Sir Edward Poynings, John Roper, and other gentlemen who held the office of steward of the convent's liberties and manors between the early fifteenth and early sixteenth centuries, were the crucial figures in integrating the affairs of the convent within county society in Kent.[390] They usually held the office of steward for life, and their contacts with other prominent Kent families made these gentlemen indispensable guides through the thickets of local legal and administrative practice. During the century and more which followed Thomas Chillenden's rule, only an imprudent prior would have dared to neglect their advice. As one of Sir John Fyneux's letters to William Sellyng in 1474 serves to suggest ('for wee thynke that yee have been agreable and appliable to every thynge for the weell of the matier'), it was now very often the gentleman lawyer who told his supposed master how to conduct the monastery's affairs.[391] Whatever the dangers of such a change of emphasis, for good or ill the Cathedral Priory of Canterbury had become—despite its great size—as increasingly dependent on the counsel and services of leading gentry families of the county as the other English monasteries of the age.

By contrast with the much-courted gentry members of Kent society, the burgesses of the city of Canterbury itself are generally notable by their absence from the confraternity of the Cathedral. Such an absence is all the more conspicuous when compared with the many London merchants, like Mayor William Estfield in 1429, who not only received this much cherished privilege, but were among the convent's trusted counsellors.[392] The prior and chapter's extremely close business associations with the city of London, where they had maintained 'our great stone house in Chepe' since at least the priorate of Henry of Eastry, was no doubt inevitable, but perhaps in itself provocative to the inhabitants of Canterbury.[393] However, there were many and more immediate occasions for conflict

[388] Reg. S, fos. 82ᵛ–83, 237ᵛ; HMC, 9th *Report*, app., p. 117; *Lit. Cant.* iii. 137–8.

[389] LPL, ED 88 (Treasurers' Accts., 1508–9), fo. 7; Reg. S, fo. 250ᵛ; HMC, 9th *Report*, app., pt. I. 121.

[390] Reg. T(i), fos. 59, 448ᵛ–5; Searle, *Chronicle and Lists*, 27; HMC, 9th *Report*, app., pt. I. 110, 113, 114, 117, 118, 120. R. A. L. Smith's cursory survey (*Cant. Cath. Priory*, 81–2) of the role of the prior's counsellors and attorneys after 1400 is exceptionally brief: but their importance and status emerges clearly in Du

Boulay, *Lordship of Canterbury* (London, 1966).

[391] *Christ Church Letters*, 27–8; see above, p. 96.

[392] HMC, 9th *Report*, app., pt. I, p. 113; cf. S. L. Thrupp, *The Merchant Class of Medieval London* (Ann Arbor, Mich., 1948), 338.

[393] Detailed financial accounts of several of the innumerable expeditions to London made by the prior and other monks survive as, e.g., DE 16, 17, 18, 96; cf. *Lit. Cant.*, i. 200–1, 268, 400–1; *Christ Church Letters*, 7–9.

between city and Cathedral; and between 1220 and 1538 it is hard not to believe that all of them were adopted at one time or another. Although the legal and constitutional issues at stake in the strife between citizens and Christ Church monks were rarely as fundamental as at St Albans or Bury St Edmunds, a condition of uneasy propinquity was always liable to break into outright violence. In 1327, for example, a disagreement about the convent's failure to make its due contribution to the Scottish wars escalated into a positive boycott on the part of the burgesses, who dug ditches outside the precinct gates and stopped all pilgrim traffic into the Cathedral.[394] A not entirely dissimilar riot of 1500 led to a personal assault on Brother Thomas Ickham ('yeld the, horeson monk') and to an embargo on the community's essential supplies of fresh fish. Other disputes, predictably enough, involved long-standing grievances about rights to common pasture as well as to sanctuary, as in 1428 when the civic bailiffs dragged a young goldsmith called Bernard from the iron grille around the site of Archbishop Chichele's tomb to which he was clinging.[395]

At times one might well be tempted to suppose that the monks of Christ Church met with admiration everywhere except in their own Cathedral city. Perhaps so; and there is certainly evidence that from the 1520s some of Canterbury's burgesses were not at all indifferent to Lutheran and other radical criticism of the established Church. However, a serious attempt was eventually made in 1492 'to end all discord' between city and Cathedral on the vexed issue of the disputed line of the precinct walls. Moreover, many of the citizens must always have been conscious of their own material debt to St Thomas, even if rarely as lucratively as in the jubilee year of 1420, when they were proud to claim that they had been able to lodge no less than 100,000 (!) pilgrims.[396] As late as 1530 there was still no obvious reason for a long-standing if somewhat truculent *modus vivendi* to disintegrate completely. Perhaps the most telling commentary on relations between townsmen and monks in their expiring moments is provided by an account of a Sunday spent at Canterbury by an obscure tiler, William Goldwyn, in 1533–4: despite his attendance at various services within the city's parish churches, he had time to breakfast with one of the monks and then after evensong 'went agayn to Christeschyrche and delivered Master Goodnestoun a ribbe of bef, and a surloin for young monks, and there was with M. Botley till VII of the clok, and then went streyte home to bed'.[397] In this scene, more reminiscent perhaps of Pepys and Trollope than of Henry II and Becket, one supposes that neither the tiler nor his monastic friends can have seen any particular reason why such pleasant Sundays should be about to end for ever.

For indeed, in the words of the late Dom David Knowles about English medieval monasticism as a whole, 'none could have foreseen the total destruction that was to come upon them so suddenly and so soon'.[398] On what must have seemed to many monks the critical issue of recruitment, there would appear to have been no cause for alarm, even into the early 1530s. Between 1511, the year of Archbishop Warham's visitation, and 1534

---

[394] *Lit. Cant.*, i. 212–21.

[395] E. F. Jacob, 'Chichele and Canterbury', in *Studies in Medieval History Presented to F. M. Powicke*, ed. R. W. Hunt *et al.* (Oxford, 1948), 389; Jacob, *Henry Chichele* (cit. in n. 52), 93–5; HMC, 5th *Report*, app., p. 434.

[396] *Lit. Cant.*, iii, pp. xxxvi–xxxix, 146, 150, 379–80; HMC, 5th

Report, app., pp. 433–4; Somner, *Antiquities* (1730), pt. 1, app., p. 51; Foreville, *Jubilé* (cit. in n. 2), 180–1.

[397] J. Brent, *Canterbury in the Olden Time* (2nd edn.; London, 1879), 185.

[398] Knowles, *Religious Orders*, iii, p. ix.

(the last year in which a group of novices are recorded as having made their professions at the high altar) no less than seventy-one new monks had joined the community.[399] Seventy monks, reluctantly or not, acknowledged the royal supremacy in October 1534; and there were still fifty-eight members of the convent in 1538.[400] When, in 1517, the monks had elected another university monk, Thomas Goldwell, to replace Dr Thomas Goldstone as their superior, they can certainly not have envisaged either that he was to be the last of the priors of Christ Church or that his régime was to be placed under such intolerable stress that he would finally be accused of murdering his fellow monks.[401] However, that unhappy fate still lay somewhere in the future. As late as the early 1530s, Prior Goldwell still enjoyed the royal favour, to the extent at least of being one of the monastic superiors in regular receipt of a handsome New Year's gift of £20 or so from Henry VIII. Even in October 1532 the Prior was still capable of thinking that it might ingratiate himself and his convent with the already formidable Thomas Cromwell if he expressed the hope that 'St Thomas Becket will be good to you'.[402]

Such a sentiment was self-evidently not to be reciprocated. By 1532 the time had passed when the reputation of St Thomas could be relied upon to safeguard the monks of Christ Church from external criticism; and in retrospect it was the widespread erosion of trust and faith in their patron saint which seems to be the first significant intimation of the cataclysm to come. On the highly ambiguous evidence available, that erosion was probably sudden rather than gradual. Admittedly, as long ago as 1395 one of the Twelve Conclusions of the Lollards had denied that 'seyn Thomas' died a genuine martyr's death; and for the next half-century attacks on his sanctity and the validity of the pilgrimage to Canterbury became 'a standard Lollard exercise'.[403] However, and for whatever reasons, recorded expressions of hostility to St Thomas seem to decrease rather than the reverse in the last half of the fifteenth century. At first sight, it may even seem that the saint's reputation can never have been higher than when Henry VIII entertained the new Emperor Charles V at Canterbury during Whitsuntide in 1520, an occasion when the latter first met his aunt, Queen Catherine of Aragon, 'standing at the top of the marble stairs in the archbishop's palace'.[404] From another perspective, however, this particular year may serve to symbolize a collapse of initiative or of nerve on the part of St Thomas's community. Although the citizens of Canterbury had been careful, as so often in the past, to arrange for 'the orderyng of vetell and ledgyng of pylgrymes', the long-expected and much-debated jubilee of 1520 did not in fact take place. Pope Leo X's misguided refusal to grant a plenary indulgence to pilgrims to Canterbury unless half their offerings were made over towards the cost of rebuilding St Peter's, had deprived the Christ Church monks of the most powerful available manifestation of their saint's unique spiritual prowess.[405] Cardinal Wolsey's attempt to

[399] Cawston MS (Lit. D. 12), fos. 35–6; *Kentish Visitations of Warham* (cit. in n. 54), 3; Searle, *Chronicle and Lists*, 194–6.

[400] *LP Henry VIII*, vii, no. 1594; xii, pt. 1, no. 120; xii, pt. 2, no. 437; Pantin, *Cant. Coll.*, iii. 151–4.

[401] T. Wright, *Three Chapters of Letters Relating to the Suppression of the Monasteries* (Camden Soc., 26; 1843), 90. No record of Prior Goldwell's election seems to survive: see Le Neve, *Fasti, 1300–1541*, iv. 6.

[402] *LP Henry VIII*, v. 329, 618; xvi. 179.

[403] *Selections from English Wycliffite Writings*, ed. A. Hudson (Cambridge, 1978), 27, 153–4; J. F. Davis, 'Lollards, Reformers and St. Thomas of Canterbury', *Univ. of Birmingham Hist. Jnl.*, 9 (1963), 1–15; Finucane, *Miracles and Pilgrims* (cit. in n. 327), 210–11.

[404] J. G. Russell, *The Field of the Cloth of Gold* (London, 1969), 64, 163; Scarisbrick, *Henry VIII* (cit. in n. 374), 75–6.

[405] *Lit. Cant.*, iii. 340–6; Foreville, *Jubilé* (cit. in n. 2), 83–6.

compensate for this inadequacy seven years later, when he spent three or four days in Prior Goldwell's apartments to supervise 'the great Jubilee and a fair in honour of the feast of St Thomas', proved an insufficient substitute. It does, however, raise the intriguing if hypothetical question of how different the fortunes of Christ Church—like those of the English Church—might well have been if the cardinal had ever been archbishop of Canterbury.[406]

By the time of Wolsey's death, at the end of 1530, St Thomas was in any case being engulfed by a fate far worse than that of indifference. Once the divisive religious ideologies of the 1520s had gained momentum, the ambivalences always inherent in the image of a saint martyred for his opposition to a king were bound to be cruelly exposed. So indeed they were, especially as these problems were compounded by the notorious ambiguities and delays in Henry VIII's own religious attitudes. Ironically enough, for some of the more conservative figures of the 1530s, Becket's readiness to defy an English king *à outrance* began to win him more of their respect than ever before: in his famous last letter from the Tower to his daughter, Margaret, on 5 July 1535, Thomas More expressed his desire to be executed on the following day, 'for it is Saint Thomas's Eve ... and very meet and convenient for me'.[407] By 1535, however, a very different view of Becket was already widely expressed. The banning of 'a book against Saint Thomas of Canterbury' at St Paul's Cross in late 1531 failed to prevent James Bainham from informing Master Latimer when under interrogation at Newgate the following year that he was damned if he repented the view that Becket was a traitor: 'for he was in arms against the Prince and provoked other princes to invade the realm'.[408] Perhaps more symptomatic and even more dangerous was the rhetorical question asked that same year by William Umpton, one of the king's own grooms: 'Why was Saint Thomas a saint rather than Robin Hood?'[409] By 1533, when Henry VIII visited Canterbury without entering Christ Church or St Augustine's Abbey at all, it seems clear that he had already been convinced by Cromwell, Cranmer, and others that the cult of St Thomas was worse than superstitious: it was politically dangerous too. A sustained official propaganda campaign, when combined with the hostility of religious radicals within the city, took less than five years to undo the work of almost five centuries. In September 1538, twenty-six cartloads of gold and silver left Canterbury, the spoils of the greatest collection of earthly treasure ever seen in medieval England; and a few weeks later (on 16 November) the name of Thomas Becket was finally expunged from the calendar of national saints' days.[410]

There can be little doubt that the prevailing emotions among most members of the

---

[406] According to George Cavendish, the monks' singing of the litany on this occasion made 'the Cardinal weep very tenderly': *Two Early Tudor Lives*, ed. R. S. Sylvester and D. P. Harding (New Haven, Conn., 1962), 48–9. For a recent reassessment of Wolsey's plans for monastic reform at large, see P. Gwyn, *The King's Cardinal: The Rise and Fall of Thomas Wolsey* (London, 1990), 469–80.

[407] In his recent biography (*Thomas More* (London, 1985), 512), Richard Marius is, of course, mistaken in supposing that More's last thoughts were with St Thomas the Apostle rather than with St Thomas of Canterbury; but within half a century More himself had joined the company of both saints to become one

of Thomas Stapleton's illustrious *Tres Thomae* (Antwerp, 1588).

[408] *LP Henry VIII*, v, app., no. 30; BL, Harl. MS 422, fo. 90; S. Brigden, *London and the Reformation* (Oxford, 1989), 189–94.

[409] *LP Henry VIII*, v. 551 (no. 1271).

[410] Ibid., vi. 588; xiii, pt. 2. 133, 303, 317; P. L. Hughes and J. F. Larkin, *Tudor Royal Proclamations*, i: *The Early Tudors, 1485–1533* (New Haven, Conn., and London, 1964), 270–6; D. J. Hall, *English Mediaeval Pilgrimage* (Bath, 1965), 159–62; G. R. Elton, *Reform and Reformation: England, 1509–1558* (Cambridge, 1977), 277, 279. For the dismantling of the shrine by Cromwell's agent Richard Pollard, see *The Lisle Letters*, ed. M. St Clare Byrne (6 vols.; Chicago, 1981), v, no. 1217.

Christ Church community during these final years were those of shock, of bewilderment, and, above all, of fear. In August 1532 the long-awaited death of Archbishop Warham, still invoking the name of Becket in his last-ditch stand against the King's 'great matter', had deprived the monks of their last great clerical protector. By contrast, Archbishop Cranmer was an unrelenting opponent of St Thomas and his monks, as instinctively ready to think ill of the Christ Church chapter as to argue that the saint's legendary blood was in fact red ochre.[411] After Cranmer's consecration as archbishop, in March 1533, the community was accordingly exposed to a sustained onslaught on its liberties and status for which there was no real precedent in its long history. Not surprisingly, Prior Goldwell's authority over his flock was seriously jeopardized; and the chapter could itself no longer express a consensual view and contain the factions within the fellowship.[412] More damaging and demoralizing still was the extremely close involvement of two of the most senior and learned Canterbury monks, Dr Edward Bocking and Master John Deryng, in the case of Elizabeth Barton, the greatest *cause célèbre* of perhaps the most critical year in the progress of the English Reformation, 1533.[413] That Dr Bocking and several (probably many) Christ Church monks sincerely believed in the validity of the nun of Kent's revelations, which threatened early death to the King for his plans to divorce Catherine of Aragon, seems much the most likely conclusion to be drawn from a notoriously tangled and partial collection of sources. Even the nervously apprehensive Prior Goldwell admitted to Thomas Cromwell, after the latter began to instigate legal proceedings against her in the summer of 1533, that Elizabeth Barton 'hath been with me at dinner divers seasons, as I suppose 6 or 7 times at most'.[414] A fulsome petition for mercy to Henry VIII by the entire community did something to avert the royal wrath; but the community must have counted itself fortunate that only two of its members, Bocking and Deryng, finally joined Elizabeth Barton on the gallows at Tyburn in April 1534.[415]

No doubt the violent ends of two fellow monks did more than anything else to produce Archbishop Cranmer's objective of a 'veray tractable' disposition within the Christ Church community. The monks duly signed their acknowledgement of the royal supremacy in December 1534 and patiently underwent the indignity of a visitation by Richard Layton in the following October. After an eventful start to his visit, when he was nearly burnt alive in his bed, Layton issued a series of injunctions which stressed the need for the monks to eat in common and not to wander outside their precinct. He also—in perhaps the last of all tributes to the ideal of the medieval university monk—instructed the chapter to maintain a further three or four monks at Oxford in addition to the five they habitually sent there.[416] Much more significantly, Layton's visitation reveals how completely Prior Thomas

[411] Cranmer's profound distaste for the way his Canterbury monks 'prated' rather than prayed emerges particularly clearly in *LP Henry VIII*, xii, pt. 1. 121, 210 (nos. 256, 436).

[412] See, e.g., Pantin, *Cant. Coll.*, iii. 147–8.

[413] *LP Henry VIII*, vi. 549, 587–9 (nos. 1381, 1468). Despite the fact that brothers Bocking and Deryng 'remain dim figures' (Knowles, *Religious Orders*, iii. 190), there seems to be no doubt that the former at least deliberately (and bravely) encouraged Elizabeth Barton to pronounce openly on the king's divorce and then publicized her visions as widely as possible (Elton,

Reform and Reformation (cit. in n. 410), 180–1).

[414] Wright, *Suppression of the Monasteries* (cit. in n. 401), 19–22; G. H. Cook, *Letters to Cromwell on the Suppression of the Monasteries* (London, 1965), 27; Searle, *Chronicle and Lists*, 193.

[415] *LP Henry VIII*, vi. 590 (no. 1469); Wright, *Suppression of the Monasteries* (cit. in n. 401), 22–4; Emden, *BRUO, 1501–40*, 54, 168.

[416] *LP Henry VIII*, xi, nos. 669, 707, 784, 832, 840, 879, 881; Woodruff and Danks, *Memorials*, 217.

Goldwell had managed to lose the trust not only of his monastic subjects but of Archbishop Cranmer and Thomas Cromwell too. Accused by one of the latter's agents of planning to smuggle 'owt of the same howse into the handys of his secrett fryndys thowsandys of pundes to hys conforte herafter', it is at first sight highly surprising as well as scandalous that Goldwell managed to survive as prior to the very end.[417] Unfortunately for all parties, Cromwell and Cranmer failed to agree on the choice of his successor. Whereas the former favoured Dr William Sandwich, the last warden of Canterbury College, with a reputation for 'lernyng in holly letteres and incorrupte iugement in the same', the Archbishop preferred Dr Richard Thornden, warden of the Oxford college from 1524 to 1534 and 'as redy to sett forwarde hys pryncis causes as no man more of hys coote'.[418] Within a few years both Sandwich and Thornden were to be canons of the New Foundation, not a future that awaited Prior Thomas Goldwell himself.[419] Indeed, Canterbury has the unusual distinction of being the only ex-monastic cathedral of Tudor England whose first dean was not its last prior.[420] Properly enough, deaf ears were turned to Goldwell's own final abject plea that he should be appointed dean in order to avoid being 'put from my chamber and lodging, which I have had all these 22 years'.[421]

It is indeed hard to deny that the life of the most famous of all English medieval monasteries came to an end in an atmosphere of squalid pathos as much as of high ecclesiastical tragedy. Even if they had been under the authority of a prior less incompetent and self-serving than Thomas Goldwell, the monks of Christ Church were ill-equipped to withstand the sustained pressures of governmental hostility during the late 1530s. From 1533 onwards several monks had found the invidious role of informer thrust upon them; and there are clear indications too that both Cromwell and Cranmer at times maintained spies within the precinct.[422] It was a matter of considerable if melancholy irony that what had long been the Cathedral Priory's greatest political asset—its exceptionally close ties with the royal family and the most notable magnates of English Church and state—now threatened to be its gravest weakness. Faced with a monarch of Henry VIII's disposition, it is not too surprising that the monks not only did what their monarch told them to do but also lived down to their self-styled obsequious status of 'poore simple religious men, of small learning and judgement'.[423] That there was a serious *trahison des clercs* among the last monks of Christ Church it would be impossible to deny; but theirs was not altogether unintelligible treason. Above all, perhaps, the ability of the chapter to retain its religious and psychological cohesion, of the community to act genuinely in common, had been eroded by the centrifugal pressures of the previous century and more.

The Cathedral Priory of Canterbury in its expiring decades accordingly provides a classic illustration of the strengths and weaknesses which can befall a religious community

[417] Cook, *Letters to Cromwell*, 70–1.

[418] *LP Henry VIII*, xiii, pt. 1, no. 527; Pantin, *Cant. Coll.*, iii. 148–55; iv. 48.

[419] *LP Henry VIII*, xvi. 380. For the later career of Richard Thornden ('Dick of Dover'), see Emden, *BRUO, 1501–40*, 564–5: after the accession of Queen Mary he was accused by Cranmer of becoming a 'false, flattering, lieing and dissimulating monke' again.

[420] *LP Henry VIII*, xvi. 380; cf. S. E. Lehmberg, *The Reformation of Cathedrals: Cathedrals in English Society, 1485–1603* (Princeton, NJ, 1989), *passim*.

[421] Woodruff and Danks, *Memorials*, 219–20.

[422] *LP Henry VIII*, vi, no. 1512; xii, pt. 1, no. 210; xvi, no. 146; Pantin, *Cant. Coll.*, iii. 151–4.

[423] *LP Henry VIII*, vi, no. 1469; xi, no. 550; J. Youings, *The Dissolution of the Monasteries* (London, 1971), 39.

whose members increasingly pursue their separate, individual ways to material welfare and self-satisfaction—and indeed to salvation too. Appropriately enough, such individualism made the monks of Christ Church react to the urgent religious debate of the 1530s with not one but many voices. Although most members of the community seem to have tried to preserve old routines to the very end, others certainly wished to destroy them. Yet another Christ Church university monk, William Jerome, adopted Lutheran views with such enthusiasm that he was dispensed from his monastic vows, only to find himself burnt alive at Smithfield in July 1540.[424] Four months earlier, on 20 March 1540, when Archbishop Cranmer headed a royal commission to receive the surrender of his former brethren, the long ordeal of the monks of Christ Church was at last coming to an end. During the following weeks the religious houses of Canterbury Cathedral and Canterbury College, Oxford, were both dissolved; and on 8 May Prior Goldwell and twenty-eight of his colleagues were assigned pensions and left the monastery for ever. Less than a year later (on 8 April 1541) the remaining twenty-eight monks of Christ Church would face the even greater challenge of inaugurating new religious routines in a metropolitan Cathedral so fundamentally reconstituted as to be unrecognizable to their predecessors.[425] Whatever the future of that Cathedral church, it would never again be said that '[elle] est la pluis sollempne et la pluis franche, come vous bien savez, qi soit desouth la Court de Rome'.[426]

---

[424] *LP Henry VIII*, xv, nos. 158–9, 680; Pantin, *Cant. Coll.*, iii. 48–9; Emden, *BRUO, 1501–40*, 316–17. Contrast the lack of any sense of impending disaster in a letter written from Christ Church to Lady Lisle by Brother Nicholas Clement in Apr. 1536 (*Lisle Letters* (cit. in n. 410), iii, no. 688).

[425] *LP Henry VIII*, xv, no. 488; xvi. 380, 700, 718; VCH *Kent*,

ii (1926), 119; Woodruff and Danks, *Memorials*, 218, 287–8; Legg and Hope, *Inventories*, 111.

[426] Reg. L, fo. 149; *Lit. Cant.*, i. 212–15. To the generous help and advice of Dr Nigel Ramsay and Mrs Margaret Sparks this chapter owes more than its author can adequately express. He is very grateful indeed.

IV

The Protestant Cathedral, 1541–1660

PATRICK COLLINSON

THE FUNCTIONLESS CATHEDRAL

Why worship God? Because, the pre-Reformation Church replied, he is, and because he is here. But how, the post-Reformation Church asked, should he be worshipped? Not with the work of human hand, not with art, as if mankind can offer to God anything of worth. The great churches of medieval Christendom represented the supreme achievement of hand and heart, the noblest expression of *Opus Dei*. Even Erasmus of Rotterdam, an acerbic critic of ecclesiastical magnificence, confessed to a sense of religious awe when he surmounted the hill at Harbledown and confronted what he called 'the church sacred to St Thomas', on a religious jaunt to Canterbury in company with John Colet, in about 1513.[1]

But what could a cathedral contribute to the service of God after the Protestant Reformation had undermined the value of good works, attributing salvation to faith alone? And when the transcendence and otherness of God had replaced the medieval notion that the holy could be localized, even possessed? This question was posed in the late 1530s, when the English monasteries, including the Priory of Christ Church, Canterbury, were found to be redundant and were dissolved. At the same time, the State (Henry VIII) began to discourage, and even proscribe, the cults of saints established in churches great and small, by ordering the physical destruction of their shrines. These included, at Canterbury, the politically symbolic shrine of Becket. In 1538 this holy of holies was systematically dismantled and packed into chests so heavy that they could hardly be shifted, twenty-six cart-loads. Devotion to St Thomas had declined in recent years, some of it displaced by more recent and localized cults. Among the educated, Erasmus's ironic account of Canterbury's holy treasures may have played some part in undermining the old devotion. 'Good God! what a pomp of silk vestments was there, of golden candlesticks!' he wrote in the colloquy called *A Pilgrimage for Religion's Sake*.[2] But it does not follow that

---

[1] *The Colloquies of Erasmus*, transl. Craig R. Thompson (Chicago, 1965), 303–12.

[2] Here I follow N. Bailey's translation of *Peregrinatio religionis ergo* in *The Colloquies of Erasmus* (London, 1878), ii. p. 28. On the declining fortunes of St Thomas, see C. E. Woodruff, 'The Financial Aspect of the Cult of St Thomas of Canterbury. As Revealed by a Study of the Monastic Records', *Arch. Cant.*, 44 (1932), 13–32.

the summary eviction of the saint had no impact upon religious consciousness.

What Erasmus half anticipated (and his colloquy was published in 1537) was legal iconoclasm, expropriation. But in Canterbury there was also the subversive iconoclasm of a proto-Protestant group consisting, not of the poor and dispossessed, but of some leading citizens. Walter Hook, an apothecary, was heard to say that images were 'but mammettes and puppetts'. Alderman Starkey said that St Thomas was no true martyr. A Westgate shoemaker railed on the image of the Virgin, saying that 'her arse is worme eten'.[3] And if these were mere words, which break no bones, the town clerk Christopher Levins took it upon himself to remove certain of the most ancient of Canterbury's relics, which had once protected Becket himself. He was said in 1543 to have burnt in his own house the bones of St Blaise, which had been displayed to the faithful as recently as 1537.[4]

But even while shrines were desecrated and abbeys depopulated, new cathedrals were being constituted. Someone in government circles thought it a rational plan to make every county a diocese in itself, each presumably with its own cathedral church.[5] This radical blueprint was not implemented, but some of the larger bishoprics were subdivided, and monastic churches at Bristol, Chester, Gloucester, Oxford, Peterborough, and Westminster all became cathedrals for the first time in their histories. Meanwhile, the ancient regular cathedrals, Canterbury included, were given a new lease of life as secular foundations, with new statutes and with chapters consisting of a dean and canons (or prebendaries), sustained by a resource-base comparable to that enjoyed in their monastic past.[6]

But, to press the point, what purpose did a cathedral now serve? For some, the same old purpose. A hundred years after the Reformation, 'outlandish papists' (foreign Catholics) knelt in the street before the image of Christ on the south gate of Canterbury Precincts.[7] Evidently, the old stones had not lost all their numinous power. But for Protestants, that was a motive for destruction, not preservation. It is all very well for Kathleen Edwards to speak of 'constant adaptation to meet the changing needs of the Church and society'.[8] Not everyone in the later sixteenth century would have confessed to having a need which a cathedral was capable of meeting. Bishops were distanced from their cathedrals by law and protocol, except on the rare occasion of a visitation conducted in person. If the Elizabethan Archbishop Parker held court in his palace, like his princely antecedents, his successor, Grindal, and the Jacobean Archbishop Bancroft seem not to have visited Canterbury at all.[9] The early seventeenth century saw the revival of the rite of confirmation, after a period of neglect, and witnessed, perhaps for the first time, the

---

[3] BL, MS Stowe 850, fo. 45. I owe this reference to Mr F. Lansberry. On the Canterbury 'radicals', see Peter Clark, *English Provincial Society from the Reformation to the Revolution: Religion, Politics and Society in Kent, 1500–1640* (Hassocks, 1977), 38–44.

[4] *LP Henry VIII*, xviii, pt. 2, 313; *Miscellaneous Writings and Letters of Thomas Cranmer*, ed. J. P. Cox (Parker Soc.; Cambridge, 1846), 334–5.

[5] S. E. Lehmberg, *The Reformation of Cathedrals: Cathedrals in English Society, 1485–1603* (Princeton, NJ, and London, 1988), 84–5.

[6] See esp. *Peterborough Local Administration: The Foundation of*

Peterborough Cathedral A.D. 1541, ed. W. T. Mellows (Northants. Record Soc., 13; 1941).

[7] Richard Culmer, *Cathedrall Newes from Canterbury* (London, 1644), 23.

[8] K. Edwards, *The English Secular Cathedrals in the Middle Ages* (2nd edn.; Manchester, 1967), 323.

[9] Patrick Collinson, *Godly People: Essays on English Protestantism and Puritanism* (London, 1983), 413; id., *Archbishop Grindal 1519–1583: The Struggle for a Reformed Church* (London, 1979), 224–5; Kenneth Fincham, *Prelate as Pastor: The Episcopate of James I* (Oxford, 1990), 292.

appearance in the Cathedral of small groups of youthful candidates.[10] But that was far from making it a diocesan centre in a twentieth-century sense. Perhaps an investigation of wills would reveal some popular attachment to cathedrals as mother churches, although such evidence is hard to interpret. The Kentish country carrier who left the sum of sixpence to Canterbury Cathedral may not have meant that as an insult. None of his fellow-townsmen made a similar bequest.[11] The truth is that for a hundred years, no very convincing answer to our question was forthcoming, until, in the 1640s, it was answered abruptly with the suppression of cathedrals and their endowments, a temporary extinction which must have appeared irrevocable at the time.

If that act of dissolution had occurred sixty years earlier, it might well have proved in historical hindsight as inevitable and irreversible as the dissolution of the monasteries, the logical completion of that secularizing process of which the 'Reformation' in England had so largely consisted. And it very nearly happened. From the late 1570s, the government of Elizabeth I was under strong pressure, some of it exerted from within the regime itself, to intervene in those wars in the Netherlands which seemed bound to decide not only the political but the religious destiny of Europe. In 1585 Archbishop John Whitgift wrote: 'Some of calling have openly given it out that these wars must be maintained by the dissolution of cathedral churches, which God forbid.' There is independent evidence that his fears were justified.[12] Presently, open war with Spain, the Armada War, had somehow to be paid for, and Whitgift was obliged to defend the cathedrals more strenuously.[13]

His *apologia* is instructive as much for what was not said as for what was. Not a word about the merits of cathedrals as buildings. Not until the time of Archbishop Laud do we find Canterbury Cathedral celebrated (in the revised statutes of 1636) as 'most beautiful', 'fabrica illa pulcherrima'. For Whitgift, cathedrals were justified by their support of learning and religion, in the sense that without the attraction of cathedral preferments, few would have the incentive to study divinity or enter the ministry. Not many benefices outside cathedrals could support a learned man, 'no, not to buy him books'. Among further benefits were the provision of 'hospitality' (a broad category in early modern England[14]), the support of grammar-school education, the relief of poverty, and the substantial taxes levied on cathedral incomes. Cathedrals were also an essential part of local urban economies, which their dissolution would damage irreparably. These points all had their merits. And so had Whitgift's plea that the war was but for a time, 'and for howe shorte a tyme God knoweth', whereas the cathedrals, once destroyed, would be lost for

[10] Fincham, *Prelate as Pastor* (cit. in n. 9), 124–5; Patrick Collinson, *The Religion of Protestants: The Church in English Society 1559–1625* (Oxford, 1982), 51–2.

[11] Collinson, *Godly People* (cit. in n. 9), 413.

[12] Whitgift to Lord Burghley, July 1585, BL, MS Lansdowne 45, art. 45, fos. 98–100. Whitgift had been asked to lend his weight to the campaign for more active intervention in the Netherlands. In 1581 Sir Francis Walsingham had advocated the mortgaging of bishops' temporalities to pay for the 'enterprise' of the Duke of Anjou in the Low Countries: BL, MS Harl. 1582, fos. 38–41. I owe these references to Dr S. L. Adams. Inner Temple Library, MS Petyt 538. 38, fos. 122–4, contains notes of the approximate valuations of the ecclesiastical establishments at Canterbury,

Ely, and Oxford, each bearing Walsingham's signature.

[13] Westminster Abbey Muniments, Muniment Book 15, fo. 93. The document is not dated and is headed (confusingly) 'Impropriations'. Whitgift's authorship and the approximate dating are inferred from the surrounding, related material in the same volume. The next military crisis revived these proposals, when in 1624 the divine John Preston advocated the sale of cathedral lands in order to settle the King's debts and to pay for a Palatine army: John Hacket, *Scrinia Reserata* (London, 1693), 202–6. I have been helped with these references by Dr Anthony Milton.

[14] Felicity Heal, *Hospitality in Early Modern England* (Oxford, 1990).

ever. Yet only a few words were said about what today is the principal rationale for a cathedral's existence. In these churches God was daily served. 'Musick likewise onely is in them mayntayned.'

These were weak arguments for the perpetuation of foundations whose incomes were collectively worth, on paper, £35,000 (or as many millions in modern values), representing a capital resource of £1,000,000 in Elizabethan money. Some of this funding came from the impropriated tithes of parish churches and was detrimental to religion at a more localized level. And could it be right to concentrate so much talent in ivory towers at a time when only a minority of the parochial clergy were graduates or had any capacity to preach? In the late 1580s, Whitgift estimated that of 7,433 ministers in his province, 2,949, or only some 37 per cent, were graduates, a mere 426 with degrees in divinity; while scarcely more than half were licensed preachers.[15] Since these figures were deployed for a defensive purpose, they are likely to have erred on the sanguine side. On the other hand, it has been calculated that some 90 per cent of the members of cathedral chapters were graduates, while at least 896 out of 2,849 who have been made the subject of a prosopographical survey extending over the sixteenth century, or almost one in three, held theological doctorates, compared with no more than one in fifty of the entire clergy of the province, cathedral clergy included.[16] How many of these well-qualified clerics were active preachers, and to what kinds of congregation, is a question which might well have embarrassed Whitgift. Moreover, how suitable were cathedrals for the pronouncement and reception of sermons?

With or without the benefit of comparative statistics, Puritan critics of the post-Reformation ecclesiastical establishment wrote scathingly of 'dens of loitering lubbers', maintaining 'in great idleness' 'unprofitable members', 'drones'; of 'that huge, dry flintie Rocke, called a cathedrall'.[17] Nor were such complaints confined to the radically critical fringe. Bishop Nicholas Ridley's farewell to Canterbury, as he contemplated martyrdom, was censorious: 'that thou mayest be found of God (after thy name) Christ's Church in deed and in truth'.[18] Archbishop Cranmer wrote contemptuously of the 'superfluous conditions' of cathedral prebendaries, wishing the very name abolished, for 'commonly a prebendary is neither a learner, nor teacher, but a good viander', spending his time in 'superfluous belly cheer'.[19]

That was not entirely fair. Many members of Canterbury's reformed Chapter were to prove themselves as good at reading—and even writing—books as at eating and drinking. Some were among the most learned men of their times, including scholars of the

---

[15] Westminster Abbey Muniments, Muniment Book 15, fos. 72–74ᵛ, with much accompanying material relating to specific dioceses, parts of it in Whitgift's hand. (I owe this reference to Dr Milton.) Note these statements: 'The whole number of Preachers in the Province of Canterbury, not reckoning the dioceses of Bathe and Wells and St Davids from whence certificates are not yet made 3992. Of Cathechizers 2158.' 'The preachers within the province of Canterbury are more in number then they were at the last survey, which was taken Aᵒ 1583, 1989.' Cf. the surveys prepared in 1603–4 in BL, Harl. MSS 280 and 595.

[16] Lehmberg, *Reformation of Cathedrals* (cit. in n. 5), ch. 9, 'Canons, Prebendaries, and Deans'.

[17] C. Cross, ' "Dens of Loitering Lubbers": Protestant Protest Against Cathedral Foundations, 1540–1640', in *Studies in Church History*, ix: *Schism, Heresy and Religious Protest*, ed. D. Baker (Cambridge, 1972), 231–7; Culmer, *Cathedrall Newes* (cit. in n. 7), Epistle.

[18] *Works of Nicholas Ridley*, ed. H. Christmas (Parker Soc.; Cambridge, 1843), 407–8.

[19] Archbishop Cranmer to Thomas Cromwell, 29 Nov. 1539, *Miscellaneous Writings and Letters* (cit. in n. 4), 396–9.

international stature of Pierre du Moulin, Isaac and Meric Casaubon, and Gerard John Vossius; rather as if twentieth-century Canterbury were to command the services of a Barth, a Bonhoeffer, or a Tillich. Yet Isaac Casaubon seems to have resided in Canterbury for just one week, and to have attended only one Cathedral service, which prompted the reaction: 'O utinam linguam hanc intellegerem!' ('Oh, would that I could understand this language!'); while Vossius and du Moulin were perpetually non-resident and to be found at Amsterdam and Sedan respectively.[20] Prebendaries who kept residence lived in their own private households, not in a collegiate setting, and with no structured means of imparting their learning to others. If Archbishop Parker had not shared Cranmer's doubts that Canterbury could ever compete intellectually with the universities, he would hardly have alienated so much of the Cathedral library to his own Cambridge college.

Cranmer and some of his successors had more realistic hopes that the new Canterbury would flourish as a centre of what we now call secondary education. The new foundation provided for a grammar school of fifty scholars, each on a stipend of £4, with a master and an usher. This was the largest of the cathedral schools re-endowed by Henry VIII. Its early masters were men of distinction, particularly the humanist and famous antiquary John Twyne and the Elizabethan John Gresshop, who owned a library of over 300 books. There were some notable early alumni, including the most learned of Elizabethan catholic controversialists, Thomas Stapleton, who followed in his master's steps in his fine translation of the Venerable Bede (1565). If Stapleton was a recognizable Twyne product, the fervent Puritan preachers Josias Nicholls and John Carter of Suffolk, both natives of Canterbury and its vicinity, are evidence of the distinctly Protestant impress left by Twyne's successors, Anthony Rushe and Gresshop, as perhaps, in a very different and reactive fashion, was the near-atheist, Christopher Marlowe.[21] But Canterbury failed to become one of the top schools of early modern England, and in 1635 the long-serving master John Ludd confessed that knowledge of Greek among his pupils was a rare accomplishment, while success in university entrance was not great. Most parents were not very ambitious for their sons, and those who were withdrew them and sent them to other schools of the royal foundation (perhaps Eton or Westminster), 'where hopes are of better maintenance, better future and present'.[22]

[20] *Ephemerides Isaaci Casauboni*, ed. J. Russell (2 vols.; Oxford, 1850), ii. 821; Mark Pattison, *Issac Casaubon 1559–1641* (London, 1875), 315, 389; Vossius to Dean and Chapter of Canterbury, Dec. 1640, *Doctissimi Clarissimique Gerardi Vossii ... Epistolae* (London, 1693), 381, no. 421; LPL, Reg. Laud, fos. 80ᵛ–81ʳ. Isaac Casaubon, as a layman, was installed without ceremony, du Moulin with appropriate rites but affirming his primary allegiance to the King of France: Lucien Rimbault, *Pierre du Moulin* (Paris, 1966), 78. I owe this reference to Dr Anthony Milton. Meric Casaubon, whose association with Canterbury lasted for 43 years (1628–71), was thoroughly Anglicized, and Anglicized.

[21] On Twyne, see *The History of Parliament: The House of Commons, 1509–1558*, ed. S. T. Bindoff (3 vols.; London, 1982), iii. 494–5; and A. B. Ferguson, 'John Twyne: A Tudor Humanist and the Problem of Legend', *Jnl. British Studies*, 9 (1969), 24–44. Twyne's *De Rebus Albionicis, Britannicis atque Anglicis Commentariorum Libri Duo*, publ. by his son in 1590 but apparently deriving from scholarly exchanges of the 1530s, is described by Ferguson as 'perhaps the earliest attempt at anything like a scientific enquiry into the origins of British history'. However, Twyne is mildly censured by Stuart Piggott for first introducing into the story the tin-hungry Phoenician traders: Levi Fox (ed.), *English Historical Scholarship in the Sixteenth and Seventeenth Centuries* (Oxford, 1956), 99–100. On Nicholls, see Peter Clark, 'Josias Nicholls and Religious Radicalism, 1553–1639', *JEH*, 28 (1977), 135–50, and on Carter, Samuel Clarke, *A Collection of the Lives of Ten Eminent Divines* (London, 1662). Gresshop's inventory, including a full book-list, as well as 'iij course sheetes for boyes', is printed in William Urry, *Christopher Marlowe and Canterbury* (London, 1988), 108–22. I am also indebted to Dr Robert Franklin for information on this.

[22] John Ludd to Archbishop William Laud, 25 Feb. 1634 [/5], PRO, SP 16/283/85. Ludd was on oath, responding to Laud's visitation articles.

THE NEW FOUNDATION, 1541–1547

The royal charter creating what Cranmer called the 'new establishment' of Christ Church, Canterbury, was sealed on 8 April 1541. The financial basis of the monastic foundation was substantially preserved, and permitted the erection of the elaborate superstructure defined in detail in the accompanying statutes[23] and handsomely remunerated. If the dean (styled in the earliest documents 'provost'[24]) was perpetually resident, he could achieve an income of £300. In practice, he was expected to reside for a minimum of ninety days and to draw £100, the twelve prebendaries £40. (In reality, as we shall see, their incomes were much higher than that.[25]) The foundation also included six preachers, twelve minor canons (later reduced to six and the savings used to secure two cornet players and two sackbutteers)[26], a full musical establishment of lay clerks and choristers, and a variety of lesser functionaries, down to the two porters who were to double up as barbers, and the school. In the first year, the treasurer dispensed £780 in stipends to the Dean and prebendaries, and a total sum of £2274 3s. 11d., all but £500 of this in the form of wages of one kind or another.[27]

Instead of so many expensive (and in his estimation nearly useless) prebendaries, Cranmer would have spent the money on twenty divines, modelled on Oxbridge fellows, each costing £10, together with forty students at 10 marks apiece. But both this scheme and a plan to include in the foundation professorships in the three learned languages, divinity, law, and medicine, foundered.[28] If Canterbury could not be a kind of third university, then Cranmer would make it a powerhouse of reformed preaching. That must have been the rationale for a Chapter of thirteen, standard in the new foundations (compared with fifty-two prebendaries at Lincoln and forty-five at Salisbury), since each member was obliged to preach once a quarter, or to procure a substitute, ensuring at least one sermon a week. And in addition, Cranmer (in all probability it was Cranmer) invented the unique institution of a college within a college, the 'six preachers', who, for £25 a year, were to provide sermons in the Cathedral and an itinerant preaching ministry in the parishes, especially those with a Canterbury connection, for which purpose they were supplied with horses, stabling, and fodder, as well as houses within the Precincts.[29]

But the new Cathedral was only potentially an engine of conversion and instruction. Cranmer's first choice for dean was the fashionable London preacher Dr Edward Crome, like Cranmer himself a cautious and sometimes prevaricating Protestant.[30] Instead, Canterbury got Dr Nicholas Wotton, a civil lawyer and ranking diplomat without clearly

[23] The Statutes of the Cathedral and Metropolitical Church of Christ, Canterbury. With Other Documents (Canterbury, 1925) (sc. the statutes of 1636) compared with the original statutes, Lit. MS E. 34. See also King Henry the Eighth's Scheme of Bishopricks, ed. H. Cole (London, 1838), incorporating material from PRO, E 315/24, calendared in LP Henry VIII, xiv, pt. 2. 151–2.

[24] Henry the Eighth's Scheme of Bishopricks (cit. in n. 23), 1.

[25] See a fuller discussion of prebendal incomes below.

[26] 'Papers Relating to Archbishop Laud's Visitations, Canterbury, 1634', House of Lords Suppl. Calendar, HMC, 4th Report, pt. 1, app., p. 125.

[27] Misc. Accts. 40.

[28] Cranmer, Miscellaneous Writings and Letters (cit. in n. 4), 396–9; Henry the Eighth's Scheme of Bishopricks (cit. in n. 23), 1.

[29] D. Ingram Hill, The Six Preachers of Canterbury Cathedral

1541–1982: Clerical Lives from Tudor Times to the Present Day (Ramsgate, 1982). For itinerant preaching as a distinct and relatively transient phase of the English Reformation, see Patrick Collinson, 'The Elizabethan Church and the New Religion', in The Reign of Elizabeth I, ed. C. Haigh (London, 1984), 187–9; and (forthcoming) the Cambridge Ph.D. thesis by Miss S. Wabuda, 'The Provision of Preaching During the English Reformation: With Special Reference to Itineration, c.1530 to 1547'. There is evidence of non-residence among the Six Preachers from c.1590 in Westminster Abbey Muniments, Muniment Book 14, fo. 6; and from 1618 in Chapter Act Book, 1604–28, fo. 80.

[30] Cranmer, Miscellaneous Writing and Letters (cit. in n. 4), 369; S. Wabuda, 'Equivocation and Recantation During the English Reformation: The "Subtle Shadows" of Dr Edward Crome', JEH (forthcoming).

advertised religious views, and from 1544 a decanal pluralist who combined York with Canterbury.[31] Of the first twelve prebendaries, six were former monks, of whom four have left traditional, Catholic wills, one written as late as 1565.[32] All in all, no less than twenty-six, or exactly half of the complement of the old Christ Church, including six chantry priests, held some sort of office in the new.[33]

So the predominant religious climate was at first anything but Protestant. Of the original Chapter, only Richard Champion, a formidable Oxford academic, and Nicholas Ridley, the future bishop and martyr, were moving in that direction. Champion, who was dead within two years, left to Ridley and his cousin Lancelot Ridley, 'my harty frendes', his great Complutensian Polyglot Bible and the Works of St Ambrose.[34] Dr Lancelot Ridley was a Six Preacher and one of four reformers among the original six, the others being Thomas Brook, Michael Drum (or Drome), and the former Canterbury Dominican John Scory, a man destined for episcopal office. By contrast, their two remaining colleagues, Robert Searles and Edmund Shether, were arch-conservatives, most demonstrably Searles, who in a will proved in 1570 bequeathed his soul to God, 'our blessed Lady his mother', and all the holy company of Heaven, arranging Catholic obsequies for the repose of his own soul and those of his nearest kindred, with 'all Christian sowles'. It says much for the persistence of the old faith in Canterbury that such a will should have achieved probate in the year that Pius V excommunicated Elizabeth I.[35]

The first years of the New Foundation, Henry VIII's last, were a period of pronounced religious reaction. At Dr Champion's funeral, in 1542, Ralph the bellringer snatched the censer from a choirboy and in the sight of all poured the hot coals on to the corpse, to signify that Champion had been 'a heretic worth burning'.[36] To the senses, the Cathedral was still in every way Catholic, richly adorned and burning—in candles and tapers—200 lbs. of wax in a single year.[37] For another eight years, masses would be sung at its many altars, including the high altar of silver, parcel gilt—Prior Chillenden's gift. An inventory of 'plate, ornamentes, vestmentes and other utensils' taken at the inauguration of the New Foundation contains not far short of 300 items, including hundreds of richly embroidered copes and quantities of other vestments.[38] The choir was still hung, as it would be until the 1640s, with the six large 'arras' tapestries given in 1511 by Prior Goldstone and the

[31] J. Meadows Cowper, *The Lives of the Deans of Canterbury* (Canterbury, 1900), 19–21; Barbara Ficaro, 'Nicholas Wotton: Dean and Diplomat' (Ph.D. thesis, Univ. of Kent at Canterbury, 1981).

[32] Wills of John Daniel alias Chillenden, William Gardiner alias Sandwich, John Menys, and John Mylles alias Warham. Maidstone, County Record Office, PRC 32/19, fo. 28ᵛ; 32/30, fos. 18ᵛ–19ᵛ; 32/22, fos. 77–8; 32/30, fos. 177–81ᵛ. Information on the tenure of prebends is provided by John Le Neve, *Fasti, 1541–1857*, iii: *Canterbury, Rochester and Winchester Dioceses*.

[33] The will of William Page, chantry priest, dated 30 Nov. 1539 (Maidstone, County Record Office, PRC 32/31, fo. 14) leaves a bequest to 'the fyve chantry priests of Christ Church'. The 1548 will of one of the 5, John Wright, is in PRC 17/26, fo. 255. Were the Six Preachers in effect the successors of the six chantry priests?

[34] Ibid. 32/18, fos. 77ᵛ–78.

[35] Ibid. 17/41, fos. 26–9. Many authorities (e.g. Lehmberg, *Reformation of Cathedrals* (cit. in n. 5), 97) state that only three of the original Six Preachers were Protestant reformers. But that is to take too literally Cranmer's words about a balance in the college. Michael Drum (or Drome), sometimes said to have been a conservative, was a notable Grecian and a member of the early reforming cell which Wolsey brought in to Cardinal College from Cambridge. Foxe reported that he 'afterwards fell away, and forsook the truth'. It is not clear when the alleged defection occurred, but Drum's Canterbury sermons of *c.*1541 were the utterances of an advanced radical: (*The History of the University of Oxford*, iii: *The Collegiate University*, ed. James McConica (Oxford, 1986), 55–6, 364; *The Acts and Monuments of John Foxe*, ed. S. R. Cattley (8 vols.; London, 1838–41), v. 4–5.)

[36] *LP Henry VIII*, xviii, pt. 2. 300.

[37] Misc. Accts. 40.

[38] Legg and Hope, *Inventories*, 168–94.

cellarer Richard Dering. With their thirty scenes from the life of Christ and the Virgin, these added a touch of 'Christian humanism' comparable to the contemporaneous windows of King's College Chapel in Cambridge and alien to the iconophobic Protestantism of the next hundred years.[39]

The Six Preachers, as originally constituted, effected an unequal confessional balance, the precarious balance of the 1530s which the English Church began to lose in the reactionary 1540s. Cranmer suggested that this tension was creative, a way to get at the truth. When one of the prebendaries retorted that it was rather a recipe for chaos, the Archbishop said, more convincingly, that the King would have it so. At Ashford, Searles denounced 'you fellows of the new trickery that go up and down with your Testaments in your hands', and at Sandwich declared, 'Beware of these false preachers, which preach to you new fangells.' Scory, on the contrary, taught at Faversham that 'this sumptuous adorning of churches' was itself a new 'fangell', contrary to the fashion of the primitive Church: 'They had no such copes.' And Drum, preaching in the Cathedral itself, suggested that the material church, with all its visual splendour, was a thing which gave God no pleasure but which he tolerated much as a father might indulge his child with an apple or a hobby-horse.[40]

It was not only the preachers who were divided by these issues, but the whole of east Kent, the gentry included. If the country leant for the most part towards the old religion, the Archbishop, who was not really as even-handed as some of his pronouncements suggested, inclined to the new. Many of the 'heretics', Champion included, enjoyed his patronage,[41] and the sequel to a critical interview with the prebendaries and Six Preachers on Trinity Sunday 1541 damaged the conservatives more than their enemies. Shether and Searles found themselves in real trouble, while the provocative reformers received only token punishment. Hence the so-called Prebendaries' Plot of 1541-2—a conspiracy with national as well as local ramifications, designed not only to topple Cranmer but to halt the Reformation in its tracks, a dry run for the Marian reaction of ten years later.[42] The King's genuine affection for the man he jocularly addressed as 'the greatest heretic in Kent' saved the Archbishop's bacon, and Cranmer was appointed to conduct his own inquiry into the affair.[43] But in Kent the Protestants were now obliged to pull in their horns and behave more discreetly. Presently, Cranmer faced a different kind of crisis, in the partial destruction by fire of his Canterbury palace, in which his brother-in-law, amongst others,

[39] M. R. James, 'The Tapestries at Aix-en-Provence and at La Chaise Dieu', *Cambridge Antiquarian Soc. Proc. and Communications*, 9 (1907), 506–14; W. D. Caröe, 'Canterbury Cathedral Choir During the Commonwealth and After. With Special Reference to Two Oil Paintings', *Archaeologia*, 72 (1911), 353–66.

[40] *LP Henry VIII*, xviii, pt. 2. 323, 334, 337, 348, 304–6; Cambridge, Corpus Christi College, MS 128, p. 49. For the adversarial preaching of the prebendaries and Six Preachers, see Brian M. Hogben, 'Preaching and the Reformation in Henrician Kent', *Arch. Cant.*, 101 (1984), 169–85.

[41] Champion was Cranmer's chaplain. Cranmer sent him to preach in Calais and collated him to the benefices of Eastry (Kent), and St Vedast, London. I owe this information to Miss S. Wabuda.

[42] For accounts of the Prebendaries' Plot, see Glyn Redworth, *In Defence of the Church Catholic: The Life of Stephen Gardiner* (Oxford, 1990), 176–207; Clark, *English Provincial Society* (cit. in n. 3), 63–6; Michael Zell, 'The Prebendaries' Plot of 1543: A Reconsideration', *JEH*, 24 (1981), 257–78; Jasper Ridley, *Thomas Cranmer* (Oxford, 1962), 229–45.

[43] Recorded in a register annotated in his own hand and preserved in Corpus Christi College, Cambridge as MS 128. The register is very fully calendared (but with the omission of some precious details, e.g. of Drum's preaching) as 'Cranmer and the Heretics of Kent', *LP Henry VIII*, xviii, pt. 2. On Cranmer's survival, see the testimony of his secretary, Ralph Morice, in *Narratives of the Days of the Reformation*, ed. J. G. Nichols (Camden Soc., 77; 1859), 252–3.

perished. The fire left intact a board 25 feet in length bearing this text from Proverbs: MAKE NOT THY BOOST OF TO MOROWE FOR YE KNOWEST NOT WHAT MAYE HAPPE TODAYE—not a bad motto for Archbishop Cranmer, nor for Canterbury.[44]

'HALFLY FORWARD AND MORE THAN HALFLY BACKWARD':[*] CANTERBURY 1547–1580

And now the morrow brought the death of Henry VIII and, for Cranmer and the cause of Protestant reformation, the false dawn of the reign of Edward IV. Though creating an epoch in the history of the Church of England that is only now coming to an end (the age of the Prayer Book), these events are poorly documented in Canterbury. The remaining chantries were now suppressed and their revenues confiscated or redeployed. The first and second Edwardian prayer-books made a liturgical revolution. Ecclesiastical Latin was replaced with Cranmer's plain English, not yet antique. The mass was suppressed in favour of a Protestant service 'of the Supper of the Lorde'. Altars were replaced by communion tables. This was to put the central Protestant doctrine of justification by mere grace and only faith into liturgical action, for Cranmer the first of priorities. There was progressive wastage of church goods now redundant. At Canterbury, Chillenden's silver-gilt altar and other, unspecified items were surrendered to the Crown, and some other plate, including 'five brass candlesticks of Archbishop Sudbury', sold. Meanwhile, money was laid out to purchase Bibles and copies of the Paraphrases of Erasmus for parish churches with a Christ Church connection. Twenty-six new psalters were secured for the choir, together with the new book of official sermons, the Homilies, which contained Cranmer's definitively Protestant statements on salvation, faith, and works.[45]

Yet only by a kind of legal fiction and under duress was Canterbury now a Protestant cathedral.[46] The governing body still wore a very conservative appearance and contained only four prebendaries identifiable as of the new religion: Thomas Willoughby (and we cannot be sure of him[47]); the Archdeacon of Canterbury, who was the Archbishop's brother, Edmund Cranmer; John Ponet, who on being promoted to the bishopric of Rochester was succeeded by the French-speaking Pierre Alexandre, called 'la merveille d'Arras';[48] and another foreigner, the eclectic Italian Bernardino Ochino.[49] Alexandre preached in

---

[*] In 1586 William Fuller complained to Queen Elizabeth I that 'Gods matters went so but halflie forward and more than halflie backward' (*Second Parte of a Register*, ed. A. Peel (2 vols.; Cambridge, 1915), ii. 60).

[44] I am indebted for details of destruction and preservation in the palace fire to Tim Tatton-Brown.

[45] Misc. Accts. 40, fo. 43. For the background in eucharistic doctrine, see esp. Peter N. Brooks, *Thomas Cranmer's Doctrine of the Eucharist* (London, 1965; 2nd and enl. edn. 1991).

[46] Evidence of coercion in Cranmer's visitation articles and injunctions, 1550: in *Miscellaneous Writings and Letters* (cit. in n. 4), 159–62; *Visitation Articles and Injunctions of the Period of the Reformation*, ed. W. H. Frere and W. M. Kennedy (Alcuin Club Collections, 14–16; 1910), ii. 246–53. See C. E. Woodruff, 'Extracts from Original Documents Illustrating the Progress of the Reformation in Kent', *Arch. Cant.*, 31 (1915), 111–12.

[47] Willoughby appears in Cranmer's investigation of the Prebendaries' Plot as an ambivalent figure: *LP Henry VIII*, xviii, pt. 2. 319–20. The question has been put whether this Dr Willoughby was the same man who had been physician to Queen Ann Boleyn and was threatened with deprivation in the diocese of Norwich in 1572 when 'of the age almost of an hundred yeares': *The Letter Book of John Parkhurst*, ed. R. A. Houlbrooke (Norfolk Record Soc., 42; Norwich, 1975), 146. This seems unlikely, given that the Canterbury prebendary died in 1581.

[48] Baron F. de Schickler, *Les Églises du réfuge en Angleterre* (3 vols.; Paris, 1892), iii. 173; A. Pettegree, *Foreign Protestant Communities in Sixteenth-Century London* (Oxford, 1986), 150–62; Collinson, *Godly People* (cit. in n. 9), 220–7.

[49] Philip McNair, 'Ochino's Apology: Three Gods or Three Wives?', *History*, 40 (1975), 353–73.

Latin on predestination, matrimony and Church discipline, excommunication and purgatory.[50] But this was hardly a team to convert English hearts and minds, indeed not a team at all. To be sure, the Six Preachers now included two outstanding reformers, Rowland Taylor and Thomas Becon. Taylor was huge in physical bulk and equally large in personality. But while traditionally supposed to have been absorbed pastorally with his Suffolk parish of Hadleigh, he was in fact a national figure and trouble-shooter, Archdeacon of both Bury St Edmunds and Cornwall, administrator of two dioceses and active in the reformation of the ecclesiastical laws. He was, after all, a lawyer.[51] Meanwhile, Becon used Canterbury as a base from which to exert a national apostolate as a popular religious writer, publishing books with such alluring titles as *The Castell of Comforte* (1550), *The Fortresse of the Faythfull* (1550), and *The Iewel of Ioye* (1553). Protestantism in Cranmer's Canterbury was still an affair of small cells, one of them French. For what appears to have been the earliest foreign Protestant congregation on English soil was briefly gathered somewhere in the city under the leadership of Alexandre and of Jan Utenhove, later an elder of the Dutch Church in London and a figure of some international importance.[52]

If the cause in east Kent required clerical leadership, this was provided by a handful of country clergy, including another Six Preacher, Richard Turner, and the fiery vicar of Adisham, John Bland, a northerner, sometime monk of Sedbergh, and tutor to two future archbishops, Grindal and Sandys.[53] But for the most part the new religion was still a rank-and-file movement of lay 'gospellers'. Such at least is the impression left by evidence gathered for the Commissioners who enforced the Edwardian injunctions in east Kent. One witness was a thirty-two-year-old soldier from the Sandwich garrison who complained that his parson had forbidden him to read the Bible, saying that it 'doeth passe your capacitie'. The same cleric, who expected to die in his unreconstructed, transubstantiationist faith, fumbled with his spectacles and made 'such heckyng and hemynge' when he read the new English service that no one could understand; whereas he could read the old service distinctly and plainly, without spectacles.[54] One assumes that the Commissioners took a sympathetic view of the Sandwich soldier. But many of the gospellers were far to the left of Cranmerian Prayer Book Protestantism, radical heretics who were denounced by the Edwardian authorities as 'Anabaptists' and who in the Marian persecution would scandalously divide the anti-Catholic ranks.[55]

After Edward's death and Mary Tudor's successful *coup d'état*, Canterbury Cathedral may have been one of those places where the mass returned 'of mere devotion', without

---

[50] Cambridge, Corpus Christi College, MSS 115, 126; BL, MS Add. 48040, art. 3. Pettegree (*Foreign Protestant Communities* (cit. in n. 48), 153) refers to another manuscript in the Bodl., and to further information in *Les Lettres à Jean Cauvin de la collection Sarrau*, ed. R. Peter and J. Rott (Paris, 1972), and in O. Michotte, *Un Réformateur, Pierre Alexandre* (Nessenvaux, 1913), 134–89.

[51] I have been helped with Rowland Taylor by Mr. J. S. Craig. See his article, 'The Marginalia of Dr Rowland Taylor', *Hist. Research*, 44 (1991), 411–20.

[52] F. W. Cross, *History of the Walloon and Huguenot Church at Canterbury* (London, 1893), 3–9; Pettegree, *Foreign Protestant Communities* (cit. in n. 48), 34, 52; F. Pijper, *Jan Utenhoven: Zijn leven en zijne werken* (Leiden, 1883).

[53] Collinson, *Archbishop Grindal* (cit. in n. 9), 34. Bland was placed in Adisham by Cranmer's commissary Christopher Nevinson (who had married his niece), a more uncompromising Protestant than his master. (Hogben, 'Preaching and the Reformation' (cit. in n. 40), 173.)

[54] MSS X. 10. 3 (esp. fos. 57–8) and X. 10. 4. Some of the cases are noted by Woodruff, 'Extracts from Original Documents' (cit. in n. 46), 92–105.

[55] On the Kentish radicals, see J. F. Davis, *Heresy and the Reformation in the South East of England, 1520–1559* (London, 1983); J. W. Martin, *Religious Radicals in Tudor England* (London, 1989), 41–81, 125–46; C. J. Clements, 'The English Radicals and Their Theology, 1535–65' (Ph.D. thesis, Univ. of Cambridge, 1980).

waiting for a legislated change. In October 1553, money was spent on the musical notation of four books, 'to set forthe the olde service', and thereafter the Cathedral steadily restocked with the necessary adjuncts of the traditional liturgy: service-books, vestments, altar cloths, and veils.[56] But some of these items were still being acquired two and three years later, and it was not until 1557 that the Catholic Cathedral was restored to something like its former glory, minus only its shrines and relics. The crowning touch was the replacement of the great crucifix or rood on its beam in the crossing below Bell Harry, with the figures of Mary and John, images newly carved and gilded. Even the treasurer's accounts manage to convey what a strenuous business this was: 'Item, paid to xii laborers ii dayes abowt the reringe of the crosse with all the furniture and pulling at the wienshe'.[57] The 'rearing' of the rood, together with a general clean-up campaign which took in the effigies on the royal tombs, was called for by the visit of the King and Queen, Philip and Mary, in July 1557. England was at war, and the King was on his way to the Netherlands and the battle of Saint-Quentin, never to return to England.

Often, the physical location of Canterbury, abreast the main road to the Continent, has alone redeemed it from profound provinciality. But in the reign of Mary and her Habsburg consort, some eminence was regained by the metropolis of English Christianity. The metropolitan was now Reginald Pole, not a man of decisive action but a prince of the ecumenical Catholic Church and an architect of the Catholic Reform who had articulated its programme in his opening address at the Council of Trent. He was also a Plantagenet. The mainspring of Pole's scheme for renewal, embodied in canons enacted at a national synod of both provinces held in London in the winter of 1555, was the project to establish seminaries in diocesan centres, for the formation of a new, more uniform, and impeccable race of clergy—the representative, model Christians of the centuries after Trent. And now there was renewed hope of realizing Cranmer's higher educational ambitions for Canterbury. By the end of Mary's reign, the physical setting for such an enterprise had been secured, with the recovery from the Crown of property in the Mint Yard, which Pole designated for educational purposes and conveyed to the Dean and Chapter. That was where the grammar school would regroup in 1573.[58]

But it was in its negative, repressive form that the Marian religious reaction lent Canterbury a lurid kind of metropolitan distinction. Between July 1555 and November 1558 there were seven separate *autos-da-fé* in the city, more burnings than anywhere else in England, London only excepted. Some of these were spectacular affairs, with as many as seven persons incinerated in the same fire.[59] Most of the victims were not natives of

---

[56] Misc. Accts. 39, fo. 30ᵛ. See Woodruff, 'Extracts from Original Documents' (cit. in n. 46), 111–17.

[57] Woodruff, 'Extracts from Original Documents' (cit. in n. 46), 111–17.

[58] W. Schenk, *Reginald Pole, Cardinal of England* (London, 1949). For the *Constitutiones Legatinae* of 1555, see Wilkins, *Concilia*, iv. 121–6, esp. Decretum XI, 'De pueris educandis in ecclesiis'. For some account of Pole's intentions for the school, I am indebted to Dr Robert Franklin.

[59] The Canterbury seven, three men and four women (including Alice Benden, referred to below), were burned on

19 June 1557. Another group of seven had been burned at Maidstone the day before. My statistics for the Marian persecution in Kent, which correct those of some other historians, add to the information in Foxe's 'Book of Martyrs' material from *significavit* certificates of relaxation to the secular arm, PRO, C 85/27/20, 85/144/33–6, and from Cecil's list (Lansdowne MSS) printed by John Strype, *Ecclesiastical Memorials* (3 vols.; Oxford, 1822), iii. pt. 2. 554–6. Other sources discussed by Martin, *Religious Radicals* (cit. in n. 55), 171–8. The relevant passages in Foxe are at *Acts and Monuments*, ed. Cattley, vii. 287–321, 328–41, 383–4, 604, 750–2; viii. 130–1, 300, 320–32, 376–7, 504–5.

Canterbury (indeed it is not now possible to identify a single one who was) but artisans from parishes in the Weald, 20 miles to the south-west, who were first confined in the Castle and the Westgate and then taken to the stake to play their parts in a kind of edifying religious theatre.[60] Some of the trials themselves were dramatic set-pieces, not least the appearance made in the chapter house by the outspoken John Bland, to be interrogated by the suffragan Bishop Richard Thornden, 'Dick of Dover', a principal plotter against Cranmer in 1542, and by Archdeacon Nicholas Harpsfield, the most active agent of reaction and repression throughout the diocese.[61] Bland and another minister, John Franklin, vicar of Rolvenden, were kept in Westgate for nineteen weeks, with the Chapter bearing the cost of their meat and drink: 33s. 4d.[62] These, the only clerics among sixty-one Kentish martyrs (unless we include 'the greatest heretic in Kent'), were burned on 12 July 1555, together with four lay heretics who were by no means orthodox Protestants but Bland's theological opponents, a joke which may have been lost on the authorities: two stakes in one fire.[63] Twenty years later, the Chapter would give 5s. 'to John Blande whose father was brent, to helpe him withall'.[64]

In the six months which followed Bland's burning, the tally of Canterbury victims rose to twenty-three. This was half the total martyred at Smithfield in the whole of the reign. By November 1558 it had reached forty-one, when five perished eight days before the Queen's death, one of them 'an aged woman', the last to suffer not only in Kent but in all England.[65] The scene of these obscenities in what Dr Urry called 'the sandy hollows at Wincheap's' is marked today by the late Victorian memorial which in due course will make its appearance in Professor Robbins's chapter.[66]

However, the more immediate monument to these events was literary, the book compiled in Elizabethan days by John Foxe and called *Acts and Monuments*, or, more popularly, the 'Book of Martyrs', transforming what might soon have been forgotten as a series of unusual criminal proceedings into a timeless legend. It is in the pages of Foxe that we encounter the four female victims, 'who, when the fire was flaming about their ears, did sing psalms'; the young man called Roper, 'of a fresh colour, courage and complexion', who on his way to the stake in Canterbury 'fetched a great leap'; and Alice Benden, the sister of two prominent townsmen of Maidstone, Roger and John Hall, who was confined in an underground vault in the Precincts called 'Monday's Hole', with the result that her skin 'did so wholly peel and scale off, as if she had been with some mortal venom poisoned'.[67] Two copies of the 'Book of Martyrs' were set up in the Elizabethan Cathedral, one in the choir, another in the north aisle.[68]

---

[60] Cf. David Nicholls, 'The Theatre of Martyrdom in the French Reformation', *Past & Present*, 121 (1988), 49–73.

[61] *Acts and Monuments* (cit. in n. 35), vii 287–306. The evidence for Harpsfield's energetic participation in the recatholicization of the diocese is in MS Z. 3. 32, publ. as *Archdeacon Harpsfield's Visitation, 1557*, i, ed. L. E. Whatmore (Catholic Record Soc., 45; 1950), and *Archdeacon Harpsfield's Visitation, 1557*, ii, *Together With Visitations of 1556 and 1558*, ed. L. E. Whatmore (Catholic Record Soc., 46; 1951).

[62] Accts. New Foundation 2, 1–2 Philip and Mary; Misc. Accts. 39, fo. 19.

[63] Patrick Collinson, 'Truth and Legend: The Veracity of John Foxe's Book of Martyrs', in *Clio's Mirror: Historiography in Britain and the Netherlands*, ed. A. C. Duke and C. A. Tamse (Zutphen, 1985), 31–54. On 2 of Bland's fellow victims, the 'free will men' Humphrey Middleton and Nicholas Shetterden, see Martin, *Religious Radicals* (cit. in n. 54), 41–70.

[64] Misc. Accts. 40, fo. 442.

[65] *Acts and Monuments* (cit. in n. 35), viii. 504.

[66] Urry, *Marlowe and Canterbury* (cit. in n. 21), 13; below, 300.

[67] *Acts and Monuments* (cit. in n. 35), viii. 505.

[68] Legg and Hope, *Inventories*, 241.

Professor Peter Clark has found 'little evidence of any popular backlash in Kent against the Marian persecutors'. The prevalent religious conservatism of east Kent may have inhibited such a backlash, but it could also have served to provoke it. In the first summer of Elizabeth's reign, 'the clergie that was most Catholike in Canterbury', led by Archdeacon Harpsfield, 'together with the better sort of devout people and citizens', made a 'solemn procession', perhaps to celebrate Corpus Christi, an extraordinary provocation and indicative of the religious temper of both Cathedral and city. This moved a number of Dover townsmen, led by a certain Burden, to stage a parodic counter-procession, which they called 'The Popes taking his farewell of his friends of Canterbury and his shipping over at Dover'. Burden was their 'Pope', and his supporters, identified as a preacher, the town clerk, two of the Dover jurats, a baker, and a smith, brought with them all the 'church stuff' from Dover, including a pyx 'with some filthy thing in it', and with these objects processed before the doors of those known to be affected to the Catholic religion, 'in all scornefull maner . . . most ungraciously'. This piece of street theatre acted out the picture of shipping the pope and popery overseas which Foxe would soon include in his 'Book of Martyrs'. Such parodic rituals of inversion were a standard part of the popular repertoire of the Lutheran Reformation in Germany, but there appear to be no other recorded examples of this kind of theatrical practice in England. The continuing resistance of Canterbury to the Protestant Reformation is underlined by the fact that a record of the incident, complete with details of the grisly fates suffered by the perpetrators, was said to have been found in the closet of Dr Benjamin Carrier, a long-standing Canterbury prebendary who in 1613 came out of that closet and publicly defected to Rome.[69]

By 1559 England had experienced, within the lifespan of half a dozen modern parliaments, several legislated changes of a religion which, in conventional perception, was changeless. For, 'questionless, there can nothing be more spitefully spoken against the religion of God than to accuse it of novelty, as a new-come-up matter'.[70] Consequently, Peter Clark speaks of the county as in 'a state of shock' by the end of the 1550s. The shock felt in many more obscure Kentish churches when the roods were once again toppled was especially severe when in Christ Church the expensive crucifix and rood statuary, erected only three years before, came crashing down to the floor of the Cathedral. This must have happened before September 1560, when there was confusing talk of putting it all up yet again. But in Canterbury there was no general holocaust of the popish 'trumpery' which

[69] P. Clark, *English Provincial Society*, 151; *A copy of a letter, written by M. Doctor Carier beyond seas, to some particular friends in England, Whereunto are added certaine collections found in his closet, made by him (as is thought) of the miserable ends of such as have impugned the Catholike Church* (1615) (*STC* 4621), 41–2. I am indebted to Miss Alexandra Walsham for the latter reference, and to Dr Mary Dixon for the following notes on the Dover men named in the story: The 'pope', William Burden, was controller of the customs in Dover, served as mayor in 1564–5, and died about 1566. The two jurats involved were Alexander Minge (jurat from 1560) and John Robbins, a wealthy mariner with cross-Channel links. The town clerk was Roger Wood, common clerk of Dover from 1546 to 1560. Nothing seems to be known about the preacher Storer, who carried the defiled

pyx, nor of Farrer the smith, 'a wealthy man when he was an actor in this lewde Procession', and the baker, Goustridge. There may well be elements of fiction in the report, particularly in the details of the 'providences' visited upon the demonstrators. But it is unlikely that the entire story was fictional. Alexander Minge was said to have died in his own house at the pier in Dover when a loft collapsed, crushing him to death. Dr Dixon confirms that Minge lived at the pier, and that his death was followed by a coroner's jury. But whatever accident befell him, it did so many years after the Canterbury procession.

[70] *An Apology of the Church of England by John Jewel*, ed. J. E. Booty (Folger Documents of Tudor and Stuart Civilization; Ithaca, NY, 1963), 83.

elsewhere was consigned to flames perhaps intended to replicate and parody the martyr fires.[71]

Of the dazzling riches inventoried in 1540, much had been siphoned off already. Archbishop Matthew Parker thought that only a tenth of the ornaments and plate present when Wotton became dean were still to be found when he came on the scene in 1559.[72] Yet it ought to surprise the historian how much survived to be listed in the new inventory taken at the time of Parker's metropolitical visitation in 1563: five out of the original eight chalices (two had recently been melted down and turned into a larger communion-cup), more than fifty copes, not to speak of sundry other vestments, altar cloths, processional crosses, and such redundant curiosities as 'Saint Thomas banner of my lorde cardinalls gyfte': for there was now no use for such things.[73] Parker's visitors were informed that the daily services were sung at a communion table which stood 'wheare the high aulter did stande', with the 'minister' wearing a simple surplice. Communion was ministered only twelve times in the year (and poorly attended at that, according to later evidence[74]) by three clergy wearing copes.[75] These arrangements were in line with general orders or 'Advertisements' which Parker published a year later, and they required no more than three copes, not fifty. In 1567 the Chapter resolved to sell much of this material in aid of general expenses, things 'now not [at] all to be usyd in or abowte the servyce of the same churche'. There were rumours that the new Dean, Thomas Goodwyn, had made £1,000 of private profit out of this deal. But Parker, hinting at Wotton's culpability, insisted that only £243 11s. 6d. had been realized, entirely for the benefit of the church. Two years later, 'other vestry stuff' was disposed of to meet the Chapter's obligations towards the suppression of the northern rebellion. And so vanished a great deal of the finest English needlework in existence.[76]

There was now a limited change of personnel. As with the gradual scaling-down of vestments and other ornaments, these human changes made, as it were, a glacis of partial continuity rather than a precipice of drastic alteration. The old Henrician prebendaries Arthur St Leger and John Mylles took the Elizabethan oath of supremacy, together with their Marian colleagues Prebendaries Darell, Jackson, and Turnbull (but Jackson was master of the Savoy in London and Turnbull dean of Chichester). Five other Marians, including Archdeacon Harpsfield, had their careers abruptly terminated when they refused the oath. And the great 'flu' epidemic of 1558 made its own purge, carrying off (besides Cardinal Pole himself) the 1541 prebendary Richard Parkhurst and the Marian John Warren. Two more Marians died in 1559, one of them, George Lily, leaving behind some large

---

[71] *The Diary of Henry Machyn*, ed. J. G. Nichols (Camden Soc., 42; 1847), 208.

[72] *Correspondence of Matthew Parker*, ed. J. Bruce (Parker Soc.; Cambridge, 1853), 303–4.

[73] Legg and Hope, *Inventories*, 195–233; Misc. Accts. 40, fo. 219.

[74] Thomas Jackson, in a Canterbury sermon of 1623 (*The Raging Tempest Stilled* (London, 1623), 327), deplored the fact that 'even in this renowned Mother Church', where the sacrament was administered monthly, 'how few are there that come, for all our calling?' Those communicating in the earlier Elizabethan years consumed quantities of wine varying from a pint to a gallon, which suggests a maximum of 50 communicants: Misc. Accts. 40, fos. 332ᵛ–333.

[75] John Strype, *The Life and Acts of Matthew Parker* (3 vols.; Oxford, 1821), 365.

[76] Chapter Act Book, 1561–8, fo. 73ᵛ; ibid. 1568–81, fo. 7; *Parker Correspondence* (cit. in n. 72), 304.

investments in Italian banks: the end of an epoch.[77] But of the new appointments to the Chapter, only those of the former Six Preacher Thomas Becon and of John Bale (two returned Marian exiles) promised Protestant reformation in any aggressive and decisive sense. To these names we could add that of the up-and-coming establishment figure Alexander Nowell, author of the official Catechism, except that Nowell was also preferred to the deanery of St Paul's and would be rarely, if ever, resident. The Edwardian Willoughby was restored, and also the Frenchman Alexandre, but Alexandre was fighting for control of the French Protestant Church in London and soon he would be dead.[78]

Moreover, these few swallows promised a summer which, as with so many English summers, proved a sad disappointment to ardent Protestants. Among their successors, one searches in vain for a single name which historians of the Elizabethan Church would recognize as belonging to a 'godly' preacher in the sense of an outspoken evangelist, tending to what would presently be called Puritanism. Among the thirty-eight Elizabethan prebendaries, there is scarcely one who can be so described. In the universities, and especially at Cambridge, there was an expectant sense of liberation as young men in their twenties and thirties discarded the 'popish' liturgical and academic costume imposed by authority as a litmus test of conformity; and in so doing rejected the compromised leadership of their seniors. Soon, some of the fundamentals of the Elizabethan religious settlement would be called in question, including bishops and cathedrals.[79] In the 1570s some of these 'hotter' Protestants, with their burning ambition to convert a generation whose Protestantism was still skin-deep, began to fan out into the Kentish countryside, where 'preacher of the word of God' was soon the ordinary designation of what had once been called a parish priest. By the 1580s there was a marked sense of collegiality among these 'preachers of Kent' who tended to nonconformity.[80] But in the Cathedral Precincts there was very little of this spirit, and in the Chapter hardly a tincture.

The explanation lies in part in the patronage process. Perhaps that very conservative Protestant, Queen Elizabeth I, who was unable to prevent the promotion of forward men to bishoprics,[81] reserved these minor but lucrative preferments for a different kind of client, or to satisfy rather different patronage pressures. Archbishop Parker told Secretary Cecil that if the Queen chose to regard Canterbury prebends as rewards for her own chaplains, no one could prevent her, but that this was having detrimental consequences.[82] Yet those appointed to the three prebends in the archbishop's own gift were not noticeably different in temper and quality from the Crown's nominees.[83] None of those three prebends fell

[77] PRO, PROB 11/41, fos. 116–17, 193ᵛ–4ᵛ, PROB 11/42B, fos. 280ᵛ–281. That the 'influenza' of 1558 (Professor David Palliser informs me that 'flu' in this case is no more than a term of art) had a hand in these deaths is a plausible inference, no more.

[78] Pettegree, *Foreign Protestant Communities* (cit. in n. 48), 150–62.

[79] H. C. Porter, *Reformation and Reaction in Tudor Cambridge* (Cambridge, 1958); Patrick Collinson, *The Elizabethan Puritan Movement* (London, 1967); *History of the University of Oxford*, iii (cit. in n. 35); Patrick Collinson, 'Andrew Perne and His Times', in *Andrew Perne: Quatercentenary Studies* (Cambridge Bibliog. Soc. Monograph, 11; 1991), 1–34.

[80] Patrick Collinson, 'Cranbrook and the Fletchers: Popular and Unpopular Religion in the Kentish Weald', in id., *Godly People* (cit. in n. 9), 399–428.

[81] Id., 'The Religion of Queen Elizabeth I' (forthcoming); id., *Archbishop Grindal* (cit. in n. 9), ch. 5; id., *Elizabethan Puritan Movement* (cit. in n. 79), pt. 2, ch. 1.

[82] *Parker Correspondence* (cit. in n. 72), 318–19.

[83] In 1567 Parker put into the fourth stall his nephew John Bungey, and in 1569 preferred to the first stall his commissary-general Thomas Lawse, who never resided in the Precincts but at Eastbridge Hospital, of which he was master, and where, towards the end of his life, he was to entertain Archbishop Whitgift in grand style: Chapter Act Book, 1581–1607, fo. 99ᵛ; MS X. 11. 11, fos. 18, 40ᵛ.

vacant during the primacy of that more advanced Protestant, Edmund Grindal.

Nor, and this is perhaps more surprising, have the Elizabethan Six Preachers made much impression on the historical record, even as preachers. The exception was Robert Pownall, a Marian exile and a client and ordinand of Grindal, who in his will asked to be buried 'harde by Mr Bale'. Pownall christened his sons with resounding biblical names (Abdias, Barnabas, Ezekiel) and wrote the 'godliest' of all Canterbury wills, in which he gave thanks 'for mye vocacion bye the voice of the gospell from idolatrye, superstition and that false Religion ... to the beleeving and professing of the pure Religion of God, taught and set forthe in his sacred woorde'. Of his children, he wrote: 'Oh lorde, make them I beseeche thee vessells and Instrumentes of thye honour and distill into their hartes the fructefying dewes of thy grace'.[84] Mrs Pownall and Mrs Bale were paid generous widows' pensions for life, which looks like a tribute to all that remained of the first, heroic generation of the Reformation.[85]

But all in all, the prosopography of Elizabethan Canterbury helps to explain the indignation expressed by Puritan critics of the system. 'Ah Mr Secretary,' Bishop John Hooper had exclaimed to Cecil in 1552, 'that there were good men in the cathedral churches!'[86] In Elizabethan Canterbury there were a few bad, or at least unsuitable, men. They included one of the Queens's chaplains and special clients, George Boleyn (1556–1603), who, as a putative son of Lord Rochford, claimed to be her first cousin. Boleyn confessed to being 'somewhat chollerick' and often threatened, and sometimes perpetrated, violence. In 1575 he attacked a Six Preacher with a dagger and stood suspended for four months, whereupon he appealed against the sentence to his royal cousin. Perhaps it was just as well that Boleyn was chronically non-resident, especially after he secured the deanery of Lichfield—in spite of which he made a great fuss about his house in the Precincts and tried to exchange it for a better one.[87] At Court he angled engagingly and wittily for a bishopric.[88] In his will, Boleyn spoke of the Queen and of other blood-relations of the Queen, but of no one else, except in this remarkable statement: 'And because I understande the Creede simplie, nott allegoricallie as some doe, for which I am sorie, and doe finde by the Creede that I shall have remission of my sinnes, I doe forgive all the people in the worlde, as I expect forgivenes at Gods handes.'[89]

The Marian veteran William Darell (1553–80), one of the four members of Chapter present to elect Archbishop Parker in 1559, was another prebendary who can hardly be called 'good', even if we discount the extraordinary story told in court of one of the ladies of the town carried to his chamber in a laundry basket. His reputation was tarnished in other respects, and he was eventually deprived.[90] Another bad character, according to the staunchly Protestant lawyer Sir James Hales, was the long-serving John Langworth (1577–

---

[84] Maidstone, County Record Office, PRC 32/31, fos. 286–8; *The Registers of Canterbury Cathedral*, ed. R. Hovenden (Harleian Soc.; London, 1878), 1.

[85] Accts. New Foundation 17, 14–15 Eliz.

[86] *Later Writings of Bishop Hooper*, ed. C. Nevinson (Parker Soc.; Cambridge, 1852), p. xix.

[87] Chapter Act Book, 1568–81, fos. 84ᵛ, 87, 41, 56; ibid. 1581–1607, fo. 57ᵛ.

[88] PRO, C 115/Box/M 17. I owe this reference to Dr W. Tighe.

[89] PRO, PROB 11/101, fo. 1.

[90] MS X. 10. 14, fos. 1–2; A. F. Butcher in Urry, *Marlowe and Canterbury* (cit. in n. 21), pp. xxxiv–xxxv. As an antiquary, Darell was more than respectable, an active member of Archbishop Parker's scholarly circle and author of a treatise on Kentish castles: May McKisack, *Medieval History in the Tudor Age* (Oxford, 1971), 20, 29–30, 49.

1614), who in 1584 briefly threatened to become the third Dean of Canterbury: 'a man ...
of a smooth and fayer tongue', but in truth 'a most notable ypocrite, given to many lewd
qualities', 'commended of none that be of the better sorte, not lyked by any of his owne
company'. Many years later, the Jacobean Archbishop Abbot renewed the charge of
hypocrisy and called Langworth 'a great papist', 'a man suspected all his time, but went
to churche and received the communion'. A Catholic priest was present when Langworth
died, although his services were refused.[91] It was just as well that the Elizabethan Church
opened no windows on such equivocal, ambivalent souls.

But these were exceptions in a clerical society which otherwise seems to have been
marked by humdrum worthiness. Richard Rogers, the suffragan Bishop of Dover who in
fact became Dean in 1584, had impeccable Protestant credentials and Cranmer relations.
Prebendary John Bungey (1567–95) was the beneficiary of his uncle Archbishop Parker's
nepotism, and a man of considerable substance. But his worthiness is reflected in his will,
where he calls himself 'an unprofitable minister of Jesus Christ' and confesses to 'this one
great sinne': 'I have not so diligentlie as I ought nor so often as I shoulde performed my
duetie in the administration of that office and function which I had in the Church of God,
nor taught the people committed to my charge in such duetifull manner and sorte as in
conscience I was bownde to doe, againe and againe.'[92] Robert Hill, a Six Preacher for more
than thirty years, may remain for us a thoroughly obscure figure. Yet this former fellow
of Lincoln College had a sizeable private library, which included a Hebrew psalter.[93]
Naturally, all these men had other livings. Bungey was rector of Chartham, and Hill was
a pluralist in a modest way, for the Six Preachers were now country clergy who came to
regard their Cathedral office as a useful perk, let out their Precincts houses, and lived in
their parishes.

So, to look beyond the death, in 1563, of John Bale, who cannot be accused of obscurity,[94]
is to see his three years in early Elizabethan Canterbury as a matter of ends rather than
beginnings: the end not only of the picaresque career of this former Carmelite friar and
Irish bishop, but of an era when the history of our Cathedral can be recounted as a kind
of epic ecclesiastical roller-coaster, full of ups and downs and violent changes of direction.
These years also witnessed the beginning of the end of the kind of Protestantism which
Bale himself symbolized, with the accent on protest.[95] Bale's own especial protesting forte
was the drama—anti-Catholic parodies of the old Bible plays and moralities, with the vices
and villains now dressed up as monks and bishops. Some of the last of these theatrical
productions were staged in Canterbury with a cast consisting of the boys of the grammar

[91] Hales to Sir Francis Walsingham, 23 Mar. 1584, PRO, SP
12/169/31; SP 14/76/48; Westminster Cathedral, Old Brotherhood Archives, ser. A xiii, p. 58. I owe the latter two references
to Dr Kenneth Fincham.

[92] PRO, PROB 11/87, fos. 37–42.

[93] Ibid. 11/57, fos. 189–90.

[94] W. T. Davies, 'A Bibliography of John Bale', Oxford Bibliog.
Soc. Proc. and Papers, 5 (1936), 201–81; J. W. Harris, John Bale: A
Study in the Minor Literature of the Reformation (Urbana, Ill.,
1940); Honor McCusker, John Bale, Dramatist and Antiquary
(Bryn Mawr, 1942); L. P. Fairfield, John Bale, Mythmaker for the

English Reformation (W. Lafayette, Ind., 1976); J. N. King, English
Reformation Literature: The Tudor Origins of the Protestant Tradition (Princeton, NJ, 1982). See also the picaresque autobiography The Vocacyon of John Bale, ed. Peter Happé and John
N. King (Medieval & Renaissance Texts and Studies, Renaissance English Text Soc., 7th ser., 14; 1989, and Binghamton, NJ,
1990).

[95] King, English Reformation Literature (cit. in n. 94), 275;
Patrick Collinson, The Birthpangs of Protestant England: Religious
and Cultural Change in the Sixteenth and Seventeenth Centuries
(Basingstoke and London, 1988), 102–6.

school, boys a few cohorts ahead of Christopher Marlowe, who enrolled in 1578. In 1560 a little unscripted scene occurred in John Poole's tailor's shop within Christ Church gate.[96] The son of Alderman John Okeden happened to be in the shop when he overheard some discussion of the making of a friar's habit to be used 'in derision' in a play which Bale and his company were to perform for Alderman George May at his house in the dissolved Priory of St Gregory.[97] The tailor called it 'an apes cote', 'and therat the company their present laughed'. But not Okeden, who announced that he would rather see 'a good play' at New Romney, where the traditional mystery-plays were still performed,[98] and he denounced Bale for staging plays about friars instead of preaching. But, he said, as an ex-friar, the knave Bale should know all about their knavery. Someone said that not all priests were knaves. Okeden said that he didn't mean priests, he meant ministers.

The young Okeden personified the still very conservative face of Canterbury's ruling oligarchy, a little world re-created for us by evidence given in the ecclesiastical court concerning a certain Agnes Butterwick, a woman of mixed reputation who served as midwife to the 'worshipful women' of the aldermanic class, including Mrs Okeden and the wife of Mr Thomas Mainwaring, Dean Wotton's man of business.[99] A few weeks after the incident in the tailor's shop, Okeden senior, the alderman, invaded a private party at the house of Alderman John Twyne, the schoolmaster (and another client of that 'apt woman' Mrs Butterwick), bringing news that the crucifix and rood imagery were about to be restored to Christ Church. This was an inaccurate echo of London news that the Queen was unhappy about the wholesale removal of crosses from the churches in the royal visitation of 1559. And it was a fact, not rumour, that she had reinstated the crucifix in her own royal chapel.[100] Mr Twyne's guests, who included Bale's son, hoped that the news was false, whereupon Okeden rounded on the young Bale, denouncing his father as a heretic and an Anabaptist and explaining what his son might have meant by 'knavery' among friars. The old Bale was a tall man, and yet his son was a little fellow: 'Som fryar lept yn when he was away . . . and begat the.'[101] Twyne, the host to these embarrassing proceedings, was Canterbury's most distinguished citizen, a former MP, a scholar and pedagogue of some reputation, and in his younger days a reformer in the Christian humanist and, presently, Lutheran senses, but now grown more conservative in his views.[102] As an alleged papist, he was about to be forced out of his schoolmastership in favour of his usher, Anthony Rushe, who was also present to hear Okeden's tirade and who had collaborated with the elder Bale in staging his polemical plays.[103]

Such undertones of religious strife can hardly have been dissipated overnight. Yet the

---

[96] MS X. 10. 7, fols. 36–9. There are references to the performance of plays by the scholars in both Chapter Acts (Chapter Act Book, 1561–8) and accounts (Misc. Accts. 40, fo. 219).

[97] The piece was probably *A Newe Comedy or Enterlude Concernynge Thre Lawes* (S T C 1288), printed in 1563. In my *Birthpangs of Protestant England* I mistakenly attributed the criticism of Bale in Poole's shop to Alderman Okeden rather than to his son.

[98] Harold C. Gardiner, *Mysteries' End: An Investigation of the Last Days of the Medieval Religious Stage* (New Haven, Conn., 1946), 68; Clark, *English Provincial Society* (cit. in n. 3), 153–4.

[99] Agnes Butterwick was a material witness in the matrimonial cause of *Coppyn* v. *Richard*, copiously documented in MS X. 10. 8. See also MS X. 10. 11, fo. 5.

[100] Collinson, *Archbishop Grindal* (cit. in n. 9), 97–9; W. P. Haugaard, *Elizabeth and the English Reformation* (Cambridge, 1968), 185–200.

[101] MS X. 10. 7, fos. 136ᵛ–141.

[102] Clark, *English Provincial Society* (cit. in n. 3), 29, 38, 40–3, 98, 168.

[103] 'To Mr Ruesshe for rewards geven him at settynge out of his plays yn Christmas, £3 6s. 8d.': Misc. Accts. 40, fo. 219.

Canterbury historian, as he advances into the reign of Elizabeth, has the impression of dying echoes of confessional thunder and finds that the story he has to tell becomes progressively less ideological. Indeed, a story, as such, becomes more difficult to construct, as the history of the Cathedral turns from a narrative of events into the anatomy of an institution.

ESTABLISHMENT AND PERSONNEL, 1559–1633

What was this institution, this community, as it settled down to occupy the plateau which lay beyond the Elizabethan Church settlement? For an answer, we naturally turn to the formal minutes or 'acts' of the Chapter, documents sadly spoiled by fire and missing altogether before 1560 and after 1628, but which would be less than fully informative even if they were complete and undamaged.[104] No fellow of a Cambridge college would be so naïve as to suppose that the minutes of the governing body contain an adequate account of the daily life of the society. Even as a record of the meetings themselves, such documents represent what Sir Keith Thomas has called 'a highly selective rendering of experience into a deceptively orderly mould'.[105] But perhaps the imaginative historian can make something of such entries as the decision recorded at a general Chapter in 1597 that the prebendaries were to sit in their seats (in the choir or in Chapter?) 'leaving no spare seate betweene them'.[106]

It is hard to resist the impression which the act books leave of a body primarily concerned with its own interests, collective and individual, and, in the spirit of the age, with considerations of prestige and status. In 1619 it was a question whether the archdeacon took precedence, after the vice-dean, over the senior prebendary.[107] Four items of business loom large. First comes the leasing of property and all its pecuniary incidents, including the division of entry fines, the lump sums payable upon the granting of a lease. Moreover, the readiest investments available in order to secure these profits were Canterbury properties, which the prebendaries were constantly leasing to each other. In 1615 it was noted that the customary division of certain manors and farms among members of the Chapter had diminished 'that peace and unitie which ought to be betweene them'.[108] The second, related item concerned the granting of patents to the many offices of profit in the gift of the Dean and Chapter, and the power to present to livings. In 1621 we hear of the practice of conferring benefices upon the prebendaries or on their 'especiall frendes at their suit', and of some who had 'not heretofore been pleasured by the churche' in this respect.[109] The third leading item of business was the question of residence and the responsibilities and emoluments which degrees of residence or non-residence entailed. And the fourth had to do with the prebendaries' houses. The inevitable concomitant of private housekeeping (as distinct from collegiate co-residence and commensality) was social competition. Some of the prebendal houses allocated to particular prebendal stalls were too

---

[104] Chapter Act Books, 1561–8 (fire-damaged), 1569–81 (damage affecting entries after 1578), 1581–1607, (hiatus June 1607–Dec. 1608), 1608–28; no continuous series of acts from 1628 until after the Restoration.

[105] Keith Thomas, *History and Literature* (Swansea, 1988), 9.

[106] Chapter Act Book, 1581–1607, fo. 210ᵛ.

[107] Ibid. 1608–28, fos. 92ᵛ, 97, 108.

[108] Ibid. 1561–8, fo. 2; 1608–28, fo. 61ᵛ.

[109] Ibid. 1608–28, fo. 116ᵛ.

small for growing families, or too old-fashioned, or even decrepit. Everyone wanted to live in the spaciousness of that grand house called Meister Omers, to which John Ponet had moved his family in 1546, thus setting the stage for the domestic politics of the Precincts for a century to come and more.[110]

Some of this business was inherently contentious, doubtless more of it than the formal and stylized record reveals. In 1637 the Dean would complain not only of 'canvisings or preingagements before elections' but of 'threatenings or uncivill language in our chapters'. The Archbishop, William Laud, told him: 'I think you have power enough in your hands to keep the Prebends in good order at your public meetings.'[111] Sixty years earlier a meeting of the Chapter had been stymied for an entire day with 'debate of matters towching the state of the churche', with the consequence that it was agreed that henceforth no leases should be granted or patents confirmed and sealed except at the two general Chapters, held in June and November. The intention, reinforced at Archbishop Parker's visitation a few years later, was that a rump of the Chapter, composed of those few prebendaries who happened to be in residence, should not be in a position to exploit vacant leases and offices to their own peculiar advantage.[112]

The Chapter was not a watertight institution, impervious to the pressures of the world beyond Christ Church gate. The letter-book of the Elizabethan civil lawyer and parliamentarian Francis Alford contains no less than ten letters written by Alford or his patrons in pursuit of prebends or similar sinecures in three or four cathedrals. On one occasion, Alford came down to Canterbury to remind the Dean of the promise of an office made to his cousin Lord Buckhurst on his behalf. But the Dean had in the meantime offered the same place to Sir Christopher Hatton—which was awkward, since Hatton, the up-and-coming star at court, was also Alford's patron. Alford was willing to pay the Dean £100 if that would help.[113] The patronage interests both of the gentry of the region and of the Court bore on three of our four major items of business—leases, offices and benefices, and residence—and they underlay the institution more fundamentally by tending to determine the very composition and personnel of the Chapter itself. In 1573 the Suffolk manor of Hadleigh was leased to the courtier and official Henry Seckford 'at the contemplation of the earl of Leicester'.[114] Shortly after this, the Queen was present in Canterbury on an official visit, which enabled 'divers' of the Privy Council to demand the grant of a manor in Devon to 'Mr Charles Smythe her Majesties servant'. Smythe was keeper of beds and armoury at Windsor Castle, and similar pressure applied in the north had secured him a Durham coal-mine. He had nothing otherwise to do with either Durham or Canterbury.[115] When the Chapter awarded an exhibition to a young Oxford scholar called Richard Hooker, 'towarde the furtherance of his studye', that looks like money prudently invested in the future interest of the Church of England. But the deed

[110] For a fuller discussion of the residential development of the Precincts, see below. I am grateful to Mrs Margaret Sparks for much information about prebendal houses.
[111] Dean Bargrave to Archbishop Laud, 30 May 1637, and Laud to Bargrave, 3 June 1637: PRO, SP 16/357/122; 16/361/15.
[112] Chapter Act Book, 1561–8, fo. 39ᵛ; Strype, *Life of Parker* (cit. in n. 75), i. 562.
[113] Inner Temple Library, MS Petyt 538. 10, fos. 12, 16ᵛ–17, 23, 49ᵛ, 52ᵛ, 53ᵛ, 54, 67ᵛ, 69, 76, 77ᵛ, 78ᵛ.
[114] Chapter Act Book, 1568–81, fo. 56ᵛ.
[115] Ibid., fo. 60. For Smythe, see *The History of Parliament: The House of Commons 1558–1603*, ed. P. W. Hasler (3 vols., London, 1981), iii. 403.

was done at the request of the Earl of Leicester and Sir Francis Walsingham.[116]

The influence of the Court was particularly unhelpful in respect of residence. The old secular cathedrals with forty or fifty canons apiece could afford to be complacent about residence, indeed to restrict it, but not Canterbury. Such a small Chapter assumed at least statutory residence (ninety days in the year, twenty-one of them to be continuous) if basic religious duties were to be performed and the obligation of hospitality fairly shared. 'Hospitality' meant two things: the entertainment of the upper crust and the sustenance of the poor. In 1573 and 1583 the problem was to ensure sufficient presence to receive the Queen and her courtiers with due ceremony. In 1596, in the midst of one of the most severe economic crises in English history, the concern of those few prebendaries who were 'keeping house' was how to cope with the demands made upon them by 'the multitude of the poore'.[117] In one quarter of 1569, only the Dean and two other members of Chapter resided according to statute. Others were in residence for less than a week, and three prebendaries, two of them royal chaplains, not at all.[118]

In Archbishop Whitgift's time there was much talk of revising the Canterbury statutes (as there had been under Parker) and Whitgift was in correspondence with Burghley about a general review of the statutes of all the Henrician foundations. New statutes for Canterbury had even been engrossed.[119] But the matter hung fire, largely because of the Queen's chronic lack of interest in reforms of this kind. The drafts and lists of local complaints in Whitgift's files[120] suggest that residence outweighed all other concerns. The original statutes were read as meaning that a prebendary whose annual income was no more than £10 above his prebend should not be required to keep house but should sit at the Dean's table or take his commons with the petty canons. But as one of the Archbishop's correspondents asked: 'Who is a prebendary resident and who is not?' It was one thing to keep a private table for your own family, another to maintain open house for rich and poor. Some resided for only the statutory twenty-one days and then 'brake up house'. On the answers to such questions depended who was, and who was not, entitled to a dividend of corn and other income drawn from those manors which were set aside for the funding of hospitality, or to a share of entry fines, and how large a dividend and share.

So much for the Chapter as a board of management, which is how it appears in the record of its formal meetings. As for duties, the only function specifically laid on the prebendaries by statute was that of preaching four times a year, or providing a substitute. From time to time, doubts were expressed or specific evidence disclosed of failure to fulfil even this obligation. Can we assume the regular appearance of the residentiaries in the choir? In 1590 someone said: 'Yt were good that the prebendaryes being at home in theyr howses were more strately bounde to be present at dyvyne servyce, to the good example

[116] Chapter Act Book, 1581–1607, fo. 43. Hooker is curiously named 'John Hooker'; but there can be no doubt about the identity of the scholar otherwise described as 'Reader of the Ebrewe Lector in Corpus Christi College in Oxford'.

[117] Chapter Act Book, 1568–81, fo. 56; 1581–1607, fo. 198; Heal, *Hospitality in Early Modern England* (cit. in n. 14), ch. 7, 'The Clergy After the Reformation'.

[118] Misc. Accts. 40, fos. 377–9.

[119] Archbishop Whitgift to Lord Burghley, 4 Aug. 1595,

Westminster Abbey Muniments, Muniment Book 14, fo. 2. I owe this and the reference which follows to Dr Anthony Milton.

[120] There are three drafts relating to Canterbury in Muniment Book 14 in the Westminster Abbey Muniments: fos. 3–7, endorsed 'Reformacion' and (in another hand) 'Christs Church in Canterburye'; fos. 8–9, headed 'Christs Church in Canterburye' 'The Questions are these' and endorsed 'To our good Lorde the L. of Canterburie his grace'; and fos. 10–11, 'Certeyn notes to be consydered of in the makyng of new statutes'.

of others.' And in 1630 it was thought desirable that meetings of the Chapter should not be held at the same time as the choir service.[121]

'Others' performed the work of the Cathedral. They were its 'ministers' and they related to the governing body as employees to employers. If that suggests a modern industrial relationship, it would be anachronistic to analyse the inequalities of the Cathedral community with the dubious benefit of post-industrial hindsight. To the medieval mind, such differences in status were an edifying demonstration of a divinely ordained hierarchical order. For Archbishop Parker, who had not been told that the Middle Ages had come to an end, his Cathedral provided a little model of an ordered universe, which the restoration of his Canterbury palace, completed in 1565 at a cost of £1,400, enabled him to put on visual display, in deliberate emulation of his predecessor, Archbishop Warham. The initial house-warming took the form of a dinner for the assize judges, attended by the quality of city and country, men and women placed in alternate ranks. This seating-plan was said to have been observed 'in honour of the queens highness', but may have been meant to make a point against a queen who had tried to ban women from cathedral closes. At Whitsuntide in the following year, there was feasting for two days, and on the following Sunday, Trinity Sunday, Parker himself ministered communion and then entertained the entire complement of the Cathedral, together with the local worthies: no ladies on this occasion, although 'the best of the weomen' enjoyed 'very exquisite fare' in inner parlours. In 1570 there was yet another convivium, graced by some newly consecrated bishops and Parker's colleague Edmund Grindal, who had been promoted to York. All the ministers and servants of the church were present, 'even the children', and, at the lowest tables of all, but in sight, the poor of both sexes from the hospitals.[122]

Grindal, who had qualms about the lordliness of his own episcopal state, offered this comment on Parker's grand entertainment of the Queen in 1573: 'I think it shall be hard for any of our coat to do the like for an hundred years, and how long after God knoweth.'[123] Parker's motive, as his panegyrist insists, was not self-gratification but the recovery of ecclesiastical dignity, an objective shared with Archbishop Laud in the seventeenth century but pursued by different means and with more success. 'Ye Gods,' the French ambassador was heard to say when his ears were assaulted by the Cathedral choir in full voice, 'I believe no prince in the whole of Europe, no, not even the most holy father, ever heard the like.'[124]

The minor canons who were at the top of the second 'ministerial' and servile tier viewed the world from a rather different vantage-point, their sense of solidarity perhaps

[121] Chapter Act Book, 1568–81, fo. 73ᵛ; 1581–1607, fo. 195ᵛ; Westminster Abbey Muniments, Muniment Book 14, fo. 10ᵛ; PRO, SP 16/286/55.

[122] The principal source is the 'historiola' of Parker's archiepiscopate, composed by his secretary John Joscelyn, headed 'Matthaeus' and appended to some surviving copies of the original 1572 edn. of Parker's *De Antiquitate Britannicae Ecclesiae*, of which some 50 copies were printed for private circulation. An accurate translation, albeit exploited in its margins for a polemical-satirical purpose, was printed overseas in 1574, *The Life Off the 70 Archbishoppe of Canterbury presentlye Sittinge Engl-* ished. Strype merely reproduces the 'historiola' in his *Life of Parker* (cit. in n. 75), i. 346–8. For the 1570 and 1573 'convivia', see ibid. ii. 20–1; iii. 291–3, 319; and *Remains of Archbishop Grindal*, ed. W. Nicholson (Parker Soc.; Cambridge, 1843), 347. For the significance of such entertainments, see Felicity Heal, 'The Archbishops of Canterbury and the Practice of Hospitality', *JEH*, 33 (1982), 544–63; and ead., *Hospitality in Early Modern England* (cit. in n. 14).

[123] Collinson, *Archbishop Grindal* (cit. in n. 9), 182–3, 191; *Remains of Grindal* (cit. in n. 122), 347.

[124] *Letter Book of John Parkhurst* (cit. in n. 47), 82.

enhanced by the collegiality of their common table, as long as it lasted. One commentator hoped, perhaps in vain, for decorous meals, with passages of Scripture read and only 'honest and vertws talkynge'.[125] The stipends of the minor canons were increased in 1564 to £13 6s. 8d. but remained inelastic, although if they chose to live in the Precincts, they paid no rent. It was said on one occasion that the wages of the 'poore mynisters of the churche' were usually in arrears. So they doubled up as parish clergy in the city and suburbs, or even further afield. The Chapter complained about these 'moonlighting' arrangements and fined both petty canons and lay clerks who were missing from any of the three daily services.[126]

The twelve lay clerks or 'singing-men' represented in the common perception a less respectable class of person, 'speciall favourers of religion', one Puritan pamphleteer remarked sarcastically, 'so ungodly' wrote another.[127] These critics would have savoured the sordid story told in court of Prebendary William King's servant girl Juliana Lobly, of her liaison with a fellow servant, John Ellis, her pregnancy and abortion, the stern Trollopian interview with King's wife (who was Thomas Becon's widow) and her daughter, leading to Lobly's dismissal. The beans had been spilt by King's nephew, William Yetman, some-time his servant but now a singing-man in the Cathedral. Other witnesses suggested that Yetman's respectability was no more than skin-deep. Before his marriage to another of the Kings' servants, Yetman, his fiancée, Lobly and Ellis, had all been seen together, naked in one bed.[128] But the lay clerk Richard Turpyn wrote an exceptionally godly will in 1573. And his colleague James Benskyn, who died in 1583, left over £200 in legacies, with the strictest instructions to his son not to waste his substance in riotous living.[129] So the Canterbury singing-men may not have deserved their dubious reputation, and, as Roger Bowers knows, some were very talented musicians.[130]

There was a good case to be made for the minor canons and lay clerks, across the considerable social divide which distanced them from their employers. In a prepared statement, they complained that the custom of having one service, matins, at seven, and another, Communion (or more properly ante-Communion), at ten was not only a scandalous relic of popery (the second service was still familiarly called 'the mass') but thoroughly inconvenient. The lay clerks found it hard to hold down the secular jobs needed to make ends meet, the choristers had no time for school work, and the petty canons, especially those living at a distance, tended to hang about in the alehouse between services.[131] Reforming 'admonitions' of 1601 were not entirely consistent with these realistic

[125] Westminster Abbey Muniments, Muniment Book 14, fo. 10ᵛ.

[126] Chapter Act Book, 1561–8, fo. 43; MS Y. 11. 4, fos. 52ᵛ, 195ᵛ; Westminster Abbey Muniments, Muniment Book 14, fo. 10ᵛ.

[127] *Puritan Manifestoes*, ed. W. H. Frere and C. E. Douglas (London, 1954), 32; Nicholas Bownd, *Sabbathum Veteris et Novi Testamenti, or The True Doctrine of the Sabbath* (London, 1606), 424. That it was a commonplace that 'singing men' were at least as good at drinking as they were at singing is suggested by John Earle's character of 'The Common Vicars in Cathedrall Churches': *John Earle: The Autograph Manuscript of Microcosmographie* (Leeds, 1966), 23–6.

[128] MS X. 10. 6, *passim*. A. F. Butcher writes on the Lobly case

in Urry, *Marlowe and Canterbury* (cit. in n. 21), xxxvii–xxxviii.

[129] Maidstone, County Record Office, PRC 32/32, fo. 66; 17/44, fo. 36 ff.

[130] Below, 432, 438. The Norwich lay clerks seem to have been a more disorderly lot. See *Extracts from the Two Earliest Minute Books of the Dean and Chapter of Norwich Cathedral, 1566–1649*, ed. J. F. Williams and B. Cozens-Hardy (Norfolk Record Soc., 24; 1953), *passim*.

[131] 'The Allegations of the petycanons of the Cathedrall Church of Canterburye for there service to be had wholye at one tyme in the forenoone' (n.d., but apparently c.1595), Westminster Abbey Muniments, Muniment Book 15, fo. 126. I owe this reference to Dr Anthony Milton.

reflections. Their main aim was to keep women out of the Precincts. Minor canons with city parishes were told to keep their families off limits, and lay clerks were forbidden to admit wives or other women into their flats in the old monastic dormitory. 'Item ther shall not be anye shoole kept for maiden children within the Close or precinct of the church.'[132]

A different class of cathedral employee altogether consisted of those 'men of business', surveyors, stewards, and especially the cathedral-close attorneys and auditors whom Trollope in the nineteenth century called 'almost clergy'. We may take as representative of their kind Thomas Cocks the auditor and Chapter clerk (or registrar), who enjoyed his fair share of plums in the form of profitable Chapter leases of town and country property. At one time, Cocks lived in the Archbishop's Palace, perhaps as its keeper.[133] In his declining years he kept what its editor calls a 'diary' but which is really a set of running accounts, detailing the life of this old man-about-town. Cocks, something of a dandy, with his velvet and silk lacings, elegant gloves, and fancy sword, had a deranged wife to whom he made an allowance of £22 a year, while he himself boarded out with the Archdeacon and other friends, or at the 'Sign of the Sun', by the Christ Church gate. Few days passed without expenditure on a quart of claret, and careful account was taken of money won or lost at cards or bowls. Cocks went both to the theatre and the sermon, bought tobacco-pipes, and rape-seed for his pet bird, and opportunistically purchased lobsters, fish (including a 'Fordwich trout'), prunes and gooseberries, strawberries and cream, and marmalade, as these good things became available.[134] Cocks was clearly a gentleman, and his successor as auditor, John Wilde, would be knighted.

It would be good to know half as much about the rhythm of everyday life in the Cathedral. Was it 'reasonable', asked a correspondent of Archbishop Whitgift, for the petty canons to sit with their hats on in the choir? Or for the people coming to services to be herded like cattle?[135] The nave and the cloisters were places for strolling up and down, a provincial equivalent to 'Paul's Walk' in London. On one occasion we overhear a conversation between two gentlemen at 10 o'clock on a Sunday morning, 'walking together in the body of Christ Churche'. Unless the conventions were different from those of St Paul's, the walkers would all have been towns*men*, and, we may assume, men of a certain social rank.[136] But a different social note is struck, another echo of Old St Paul's, in an injunction of Archbishop Parker that the cloister and church should 'be no highway or passage for market folks', to which the Chapter replied that such an order was not enforceable unless various points of access to the Precincts, and especially the back

---

[132] Bodl., MS Tanner 123, fo. 81. Similar concerns colour Archbishop Whitgift's 1598 injunctions and orders published by Archbishop Bancroft at his metropolitical visitation, 1608: *Elizabethan Episcopal Administration*, ed. W. P. M. Kennedy, iii: *1583–1603* (Alcuin Club Collections, 27; 1924), 295–7; LPL, Reg. Bancroft, fos. 226ᵛ–227.

[133] Details of Cocks's affairs in Chapter Act Book, 1581–1607, fos. 99, 103, 110, 121, 123ᵛ, 132, 199; MS X. 11. 12, fos. 85–8. See also J. Meadows Cowper, *The Memorial Inscriptions of the Cathedral Church of Canterbury* (priv. printed, Canterbury, 1897), 116.

[134] *The Diary of Thomas Cocks, March 25th 1607, to December 31st 1610*, ed. J. Meadows Cowper (Canterbury, 1901). The original is Lit. MS E. 31.

[135] Westminster Abbey Muniments, Muniment Book 14, fo. 3ᵛ (I owe this reference to Dr Milton). I have made the best sense I can of the following sentence: 'That the people that commyth to the church be not so rayled and yorgede where at when ther canne be no ryght occacion be fownde and not to course them as they doo.'

[136] MS X. 11. 3, fo. 75; 'Paules Walke', in *The Autograph Manuscript of Microcosmographie* (cit. in n. 127), 142–6.

windows of the various premises on its periphery, should be stopped up, which would reduce the value of their rents.[137]

By the turn of the century, Protestant Canterbury was entering upon its heyday under the presidency of Thomas Neville, Dean from 1597 to 1615, a famous and princely figure, 'non eius academiae tantum sed totius Europae celeberrimi' ('celebrated not only in his own university but throughout Europe') and, as master of Trinity College Cambridge, the creator of Great Court. However Neville left nothing to chance and was careful to set up his own memorial in the Cathedral long before his death.[138]

The delivery and hearing of sermons was now more than ever the Cathedral's *raison d'être*, as it was the principal preoccupation of the entire late Elizabethan and Jacobean Church. The preacher of the visitation sermon in 1624 spoke with the authentic voice of Jacobean Protestantism, Archbishop Abbot's churchmanship, when he told the clergy of the diocese that 'the Word must be applyed with power, for it is quicke, and powerfull, and sharper than any two-edged sword.' Like the Elizabethan Puritan Thomas Cartwright, he was emphatic that the mere reading of Scripture was not sufficient. There was some continuing tension on this point, for at another Canterbury visitation sermon seventeen years earlier, Prebendary Martin Fotherby, the future Bishop of Salisbury, had argued that in many respects reading was *more* powerful and effective than preaching, and this had obliged him to defend himself against 'certain malignant and captious hearers'.[139] To preach systematically on the Church's prescribed lectionary was to find a middle way in this dispute, which may explain why this was the especial forte of Neville's successor as Dean, after four years of Martin Fotherby's brother Charles (1615–19), the humdrum John Boys (1619–25), styled in a posthumous edition of some of his sermons 'that reverend and famous postiller' (Pl. 31). His monument was an exhaustive and exhausting exposition of all the readings in the Prayer Book calendar, and of the Proper Psalms for good measure, a hefty thousand pages of middle-brow theology. These 'postils' originated as weekly sermons preached throughout Boys's tenure of the deanship.[140]

That was to set an example which almost everyone now seems to have followed. In 1610 the statutory preaching obligations of the dean, prebendaries, and Six Preachers were reviewed. It was agreed that the dean and prebendaries should preach 'in their courses' on Sundays, the Preachers on certain holy days, and the divinity lecturer (a new institution, paid for by members of the Chapter at £20 a year and available to serve as their substitute) on Wednesdays and the remaining holy days.[141] The impression this leaves of somewhat desperate efforts to stitch together a rota may be false. Rather, it may have been the case that members of the foundation were competing for space and time in the pulpit, like Roman priests queueing for altars. In the Boys years, a visiting preacher fond of typically Jacobean 'conceipts' characterized all the members of the Chapter and the Six Preachers under Greek and Latin pseudonyms which were meant to be expressive of their various

[137] *Visitation Articles and Injunctions* (cit. in n. 46), iii. 235; Strype, *Life of Parker* (cit. in n. 75), ii. 23, 311.

[138] Cowper, *Memorial Inscriptions* (cit. in n. 133), 92–3; PRO, PROB 11/126, fos. 410–11; see below, pp. 517–18.

[139] Alexander Udny, *A Golden Bell and a Pomgranate* (London, 1625), sig. E; Martin Fotherby, visitation sermon 14 Sept. 1607,

in *Foure Sermons Lately Preached* (London, 1608).

[140] *Remaines of That Reverend and Famous Postiller, John Boys, Doctor in Divinitie, and Late Dean of Canterburie* (London, 1631); *The Workes of Iohn Boys Doctor in Divinitie and Deane of Canterburie* (London, 1622).

[141] Chapter Act Book, 1608–28, fo. 20.

and distinctive preaching styles: 'powerfulnesse in Demosthenes; gravitie in Aphrican; smoothnesse in Loelius; copiousnesse in Carbo . . . the mincing-like of Adelphius . . .'[142]

The chapter house was the scene of such exertions no later than 1547, when the bell-ringers were required to keep the doors shut so that the noise of the people outside should not disturb the preacher. At first, there may have been more outside than in. Bishop Stephen Gardiner noted that at the sermon preached on Ascension Day of that same year, the congregation drawn from beyond the Precincts was no more than a hundred strong, perhaps one in forty of Canterbury's population. Fifty years later, the preachers still regularly complained of the Sunday-morning strollers who ignored the sermon, some-times falling foul of the apparitor, much as a modern motorist might collect a parking-fine.[143] But by this time, what was now familiarly called the 'Sermon House' was well-used by those citizens who took their religion seriously. An early Elizabethan refur-bishment catered for substantial sermons in the Protestant style, preceded and followed by the congregational singing of metrical psalms. These 'Geneva psalms' were religiously and culturally a world away from the professional 'pricksong' of the choir, and in them-selves implied a devout, committed congregation. (At the Convocation of 1563, some radicals had proposed that 'organs and curious singing' be wholly replaced by psalms sung 'distinctly, by the whole congregation'.[144]) The accounts record the purchase of an hourglass and the erection of 'a table to singe the psalmes by'.[145] Forty years on and we hear of the parishioners of St Alphege's singing a psalm 'in the very same tune . . . in which the said psalme is and hath bin accustomed to be sunge in Christ Church'.[146] At the funeral in 1621 of Thomas Wilson, for thirty-six years preacher of St George's parish, the preacher reminded his auditory: 'You have on every side such as are both able and willing to instruct you; you are well neighboured also by the cathedrall Church adioyning to you, whether you doe often resort, and receive instructions from divers very learned Divines.'[147]

At the turn of the century, the theology of the Sermon House was sufficiently con-formable to the teaching of the Reformed churches—a broad-based and nearly consensual 'Calvinism'—to cause a minor explosion when it collided with something different. In 1595, Archbishop Whitgift collated to the sixth prebend Hadrian Saravia, a Dutch divine now making his career in the Church of England. According to Whitgift, news of 'con-tention about matters of religion in Canterbury' was soon common knowledge in London, where the rumour was that Saravia had 'broached new opinions'. So we may well believe, for we know that he held novel opinions on such keystones of the Calvinist edifice as the

---

[142] James Cleland, *Iacobs Wel, and Abbots Conduit* (London, 1626), 24–5.

[143] *Visitation Articles and Injunctions* (cit. in n. 46), ii. 143; *The Letters of Stephen Gardiner*, ed. J. A. Muller (Cambridge, 1933), 356; MSS X. 10. 7, fo. 339, and X. 10. 19, fos. 55–6.

[144] Haugaard, *Elizabeth and the English Reformation* (cit. in n. 100), 168–70; Collinson, *Elizabethan Puritan Movement* (cit. in n. 79), 65–6.

[145] Misc. Accts. 40, fos. 220–1. As early as 1547, Edward VI's injunctions for Canterbury Cathedral required the psalms to be sung 'with such leisure and deliberation as the pronouncing

of them may be perceived both by the singer and of the hearer': *Visitation Articles and Injunctions* (cit. in n. 46), ii. 143. Cf. Norwich practice in 1614: 'the psalmes shalbe songe both before and after the sermon', with one of the singing-men appointed to 'begin and sett the psalme both before and after the sermon': *Extracts from the Two Earliest Minute Books* (cit. in n. 130), 49, 52.

[146] MS X. 11. 11, fo. 30ʳ.

[147] William Swift, *A Sermon Preached at the Funerall of that Painful and Faithfull Servant of Iesus Christ Mr Thomas Wilson* (London, 1622), sign. D2ʳ. I owe this reference to Mr Arnold Hunt.

doctrines of assurance and the perseverance of the saints, while almost inventing a Protestant doctrine of episcopacy as of divine institution, *iure divino*. Saravia represented the idea of an anti-Calvinist High Churchmanship almost before its time had come. But Whitgift, whose personal and primatial role in these late Elizabethan theological debates was so ambivalent as to cause their modern historians some difficulty, regarded Saravia as a man of learning and gravity and refused to believe that he was a novelist: 'I think rather the falt to be in some others.' But most of all he blamed the Dean and Archdeacon, who ought not to have tolerated controversy in the pulpit, and they each got a stiff letter.[148] At the other end of the ecclesiastical spectrum was Thomas Wilson of St George's, a 'professed enemy' to idolatry and superstition. In 1609 Wilson reported that his doctrine had been 'calumniated', 'charged by some to be erronious and by others to be humerous'. These controversies were not forgotten at the time of his death, twelve years later. He had 'reaped the malice of some', and of one enemy in particular, who 'opposed him to the uttermost of his power'.[149] Some historians have been tempted to write of a Jacobean religious consensus, but a preaching Church is not necessarily a quiet Church.

A more representative and emollient figure than either Saravia or Wilson was Prebendary Thomas Jackson (1614–46), who has left behind enough evidence of his career to make him at this point the hero, or perhaps anti-hero, of our story.[150] Jackson was born into a Catholic family in Lancashire in 1571 and took his advanced Protestantism from Emmanuel College, Cambridge, where he was a contemporary of the future Bishop Joseph Hall, 'mine ancient colleague'. At Cambridge he adopted the theology and the fervent pulpit style of William Perkins, in whom so much of the spirit of theological and pastoral Puritanism was both consummated and stabilized. An early patron was Robert Honywood of Charing, son of the famous and godly matriarch Mrs Mary Honywood; and for the Honywoods he preserved and praised the memory of the archetypical Puritan, Mrs Honywood's spiritual physician, Edward Dering, 'a learned and zealous Divine, long since lamented'.[151] For twenty years Jackson laboured, obscurely enough, in a combination lecture at Ashford and Wye, until a chance word dropped in Lord Melville's ear by Lady Maidstone brought him to Canterbury, at the age of 43, 'the first stone in the foundation of my preferment'. So Jackson was saved from the fate of 'alienated intellectual' dubiously

[148] 'His Gr. letters to the deane and Archd. of Canterbury concerning newe opinions broached there in sermons', Westminster Abbey Muniments, Muniment Book 15, fo. 89 (I owe this reference to Dr Anthony Milton). For Saravia's 'new opinions', see Willem Nijenhuis, *Adrianus Saravia (c.1532–1613): Dutch Cavinist, First Reformed Defender of the English Episcopal Church Order on the Basis of the Ius Divinum* (Leiden, 1980); W. J. D. Cargill Thompson, 'Sir Francis Knollys's Campaign Against the *Jure Divino* Theory of Episcopacy', in his *Studies in the Reformation: Luther to Hooker*, ed. C. W. Dugmore (London, 1980), 94–130; Porter, *Reformation and Reaction* (cit. in n. 79), 364–75; Peter Lake, *Moderate Puritans and the Elizabethan Church* (Cambridge, 1982), 201–42.

[149] T[homas] W[ilson], *An Exposition of the Two First Verses of the Sixt Chapter to the Hebrewes* (London, 1609), Epistle; Swift, *A Sermon Preached at the Funerall of Thomas Wilson* (cit. in n. 147), sig. C4'. Richard Culmer later recorded that Thomas Rogers,

the celebrated lecturer of Dedham in Essex, said in a sermon: 'You talke of miracles: Is it not a miracle that Master Thomas Wilson of Canterbury should continue preaching so neere the Throne of the Beast there?' (Culmer, *Cathedrall Newes* (cit. in n. 7), 12.)

[150] Jackson's career retrieved from *DNB* and from autobiographical information to be found in his publications: *Davids Pastorall Poeme: Or Sheepheards Song: Seven Sermons on the 23 Psalme of David* (London, 1603); *Judah Must Into Captivitie: Six Sermons on Jerem. 7. 16* (London, 1622); *The Raging Tempest Stilled* (London, 1623); and *An Helpe to the Best Bargaine: A Sermon on Mat. 13. 46* (London, 1624).

[151] Jackson, *Davids Pastorall Poeme* (cit. in n. 150), Epistle. On Mary Honywood, see Thomas Fuller, *The History of the Worthies of England* (London, 1662), ii. 85–6, and Collinson, *Godly People* (cit. in n. 9), 284, 317, 318, 324.

prescribed for the 'radicals' of the Jacobean Church by some modern historians.

Like an older contemporary, Archbishop Tobie Matthew of York,[152] Jackson was an incessant preacher, who kept a tally of the many hundreds, if not thousands, of sermons which he preached from the day that he took up his prebend—and the post of divinity lecturer in the Cathedral—in 1614: courses of Canterbury lectures on such themes as Peter's fall and repentance, the wise and foolish virgins, Dives and Lazarus; 'sixe sermons in sixe dayes' preached at St George's in wartime, in 1624; four hours of exhortation at a fast held in 1625 for the stay of the plague and 'the prosperitie of our navie'; and umpteen sermons preached at his various country livings—Great Chart, Chilham, Ivychurch. He preached many scores of funeral sermons, one of them for Mrs Drake, the mother of Archdeacon Kingsley and noted as the youngest of thirty-three children, another for the ancient matriarch Mrs Honywood, mother of sixteen.[153] Jackson said that preaching was almost his only pleasure: 'either to be preaching or preparing for it: fishing or mending my net'.[154] The character attributed to him in 1620 was 'Fluviosus', 'such is the volubility of his speech'.[155] The Canterbury sermons which Fluviosus chose to publish were all prophetic utterances in the manner of Perkins, full of sin, national apostasy, judgement; and of the special place in the divine scheme of things of the elect, 'us': 'How ever thinges goe, it shall bee well with the just.'[156]

Jackson recorded not only his sermons but every detail of his prebendal income, 'the profit of my prebend', and these accounts suggest that things went very well for him in a rather different sense. Canterbury prebends were supposed to bring in about £40 a year, and some historians have innocently supposed that that indeed was what they were worth.[157] But that takes account only of what Jackson calls his 'wages', and not of all the other sources of profit available to him, including an additional £20 salary as divinity lecturer, plus dividends in money and corn, wood and timber, and, above all, a share of entry fines. In 1573 evidence had been supplied to Archbishop Parker that of £750 yielded in fines in a single year, only £26 10s. had been paid into the common chest, the remainder being divided among the Dean and prebendaries.[158] Such 'casualties' were an unpredictable quantity. But taking one year with another, Jackson could hope to make about £250 out of his prebend, 'laus deo', and sometimes more than £400.[159] His contemporary, Prebendary John Jeffray (1629–55), also kept a running account of entry fines. 'We sold him a greate pennyworth' was Jeffray's comment on the fine of £1,000 for only one life taken when 1,113 acres of Romney Marsh grazing were leased to a Mr Barrow in 1634. His own share (and Jackson's) of this single windfall was £71 8s. 6d.[160] Surviving letters from

[152] Collinson, *Religion of Protestants* (cit. in n. 10), 48–9; Fincham, *Prelate as Pastor* (cit. in n. 9), 89–90, 265–7.

[153] Misc. Accts. 52 is inscribed on the cover 'Dr Iacksons Book'. Pp. 245–56 contain an apparently exhaustive list of 'Places of Scripture where and when preached on since my prebend'. On Mrs Drake, see Cowper, *Memorial Inscriptions* (cit. in n. 133), 56. Her father was described as 'a fruitfull old Gentleman' by a tourist who inspected the grave in 1634: 'A Relation of a Short Survey of the Western Counties', ed. L. G. W. Legg, *Camden Miscellany*, 16 (Camden Soc., 3rd ser., 52; 1936), 15.)

[154] Jackson, *Judah Must Into Captivitie* (cit. in n. 150), sig. A.

[155] Cleland, *Iacobs Wel* (cit. in n. 142), 25.

[156] Jackson, *Judah Must Into Captivitie* (cit. in n. 150), 37. For the intellectual and rhetorical parameters of Jackson's words, see Collinson, *Birthpangs of Protestant England* (cit. in n. 95), ch. I, 'The Protestant Nation'.

[157] Lehmberg, *Reformation of Cathedrals* (cit. in n. 5), ch. 7, 'Elizabethan Cathedral Finance'.

[158] Strype, *Life of Parker* (cit. in n. 75), ii. 303–4.

[159] Misc. Accts. 52, pp. 174–5, 198–200.

[160] Misc. Accts. 48, p. 48. This was presumably Thomas Barrow, the London mercer who married the sister of Henry

Prebendary Benjamin Carrier to his friend and colleague Isaac Casaubon are all about money, to the exclusion of other topics. In 1611 Carrier thought that the latest round of entry fines would bring in £400 but discovered to his delight that the true figure was at least £800. Casaubon, with prospects of another prebend at Westminster (unfulfilled), rather optimistically thought of an income reckoned not in hundreds but in thousands: 'Quid magis sperare potui?'[161] On this evidence, it is hard to share Professor Stanford Lehmberg's concern about the ignorance of economics and estate management which he believes afflicted cathedral personnel: 'Probably they did not realize the extent of the inflation under which they were living, since their own stipends remained fixed.'[162] When these words were printed, in 1988, one might have heard echoes of hollow laughter in the Canterbury Precincts!

Taking account of his other, parochial livings and, for all that we know, what his money was able to earn in the world beyond the Precincts, Jackson must have been worth a cool five or six hundred a year. His will,[163] written in 1642, was spiritually buoyant, looking forward to the prospect of praising God with the remainder of his elect in 'everlasting Halleluyas', after a long life spent 'in these most happie dayes of peace and the Gospell', separated to the holy and high calling of the ministry and furnished with 'competent graces and giftes ministeriale', ever resistant to the 'curious tenents' of papists, Arminians, and sectaries. But Jackson's will spoke of more than spiritual prosperity. He was the father of many children, the Chapter on one occasion noting that he was 'much straightened for want of lodging of his great family'.[164] He was proud of having spent on children and grandchildren more than £4,000. 'And yet there is a considerable porcion remaininge', which he proceeded to disburse in various annuities and other bequests; and to his eldest son, 'my best beaver hat and my cane tipped with silver'. When his widow died, in 1658, she was still able to dispose of more than £600, besides some real estate, including two houses in Mercery Lane.[165]

It is hard not to share some of the indignation of the Puritan critics of cathedrals, especially when two comparisons are made. We may set Jackson's personal fortune against the sums devoted by the Chapter to charity, 'eleemosina'. In the late sixteenth century these stood at £150 a year, £10 of which was always set aside for Cipriano de Valera, an exotic Spanish refugee who lived in the Precincts for decades. But in the mid-nineties, a time of exceptional penury, when real wages reached their lowest point for a century or two on either side, this fund was cut to £100, where it still stood in the 1630s and even after the Restoration, although by then it received some augmentation.[166] It is, of course, possible that the members of the Chapter, who were all supposed to maintain 'hospitality', were individually generous to the poor in ways that have left no record. But if we compare

Oxinden and differed from him in politics and religion on the eve of the Civil War, as such a beneficiary of the Canterbury Chapter might well have done. (*The Oxinden Letters 1607–1642: Being the Correspondence of Henry Oxinden of Barham and His Circle*, ed. Dorothy Gardiner (London, 1933).)

[161] *Ephemerides Isaaci Casauboni* (cit. in n. 20), ii. 1183–9, 798–9.

[162] Lehmberg, *Reformation of Cathedrals* (cit. in n. 5), 174–5.

[163] PRO, PROB 11/201, fos. 205ᵛ–207ᵛ.

[164] Chapter Act Book, 1608–28, fo. 135. It was agreed to build Jackson an enlarged study. In 1626 he was provided with a new stable. (Ibid., fo. 150ᵛ.)

[165] PRO, PROB 11/275, fos. 342–344ᵛ.

[166] Accts. New Foundation, Treasurer 9, 10; 'Papers Relating to Archbishop Laud's Visitations' (cit. in n. 26), 126; Bodl., MS Tanner 128, fo. 57ᵛ.

Jackson's will with those made by members of the Christ Church community who had died a hundred years earlier, we find that while he left virtually everything to his extended family, remembering the poor with a pittance of £5, the last generation of Canterbury Catholics, ex-monks, celibate prebendaries, and chantry priests gave away every penny, to a variety of good and spiritual ends.[167] On this showing, an age of religiously inspired generosity had given way to an age of self-interested accumulation.

The true glory of Jacobean Canterbury (Archbishop Abbot's Canterbury) was not Prebendary Jackson but Dr Richard Clerke, who, if not destined to waste his sweetness on the desert air, was relatively mute and inglorious until a handsome collection of his Canterbury sermons was posthumously published, in 1637.[168] Clerke was ineffably learned, a Hebraist who had worked on the early books of the Bible for the Authorized Version. But he was without ambition, or was at least content for more than thirty years to combine a Six Preachership with the comfortable living of Minster-in-Thanet. With the exception of his visitation sermons, what he preached was non-polemical, even non-controversial, expressing a warmly evangelical, nicely balanced doctrine of freely available, saving grace. Jesus Christ came into the world to save sinners. All sinners. 'All, All, but take this withall … All that repent.' 'The object of salvation is the whole world.' Prayer and preaching were 'holy actions both', 'sisters in god's service'. The sacraments, 'awful mysteries', had the power to purge sins. 'Our Liturgy confesseth it.' Clerke is evidence of the persistence of what we may call a Whitgiftian (but distinctly pre-Laudian) Conformist churchmanship in a Canterbury where the centre of gravity, in the days of Deans Neville, Fotherby (both the Fotherbys), and Boys was well to the right of Thomas Jackson: Prayer Book Protestantism, we may want to call it, if we wish, for sound reasons, to avoid the anachronism of 'Anglican'. And for a time there was a presence in the Chapter still further to the right. In 1613 one of the anti-Calvinist canons, Benjamin Carrier, defected to Rome and was deprived, to the embarrassment of Isaac Casaubon, who was unfairly implicated in this disgrace. Carrier was a close friend of the crypto-papist John Langworth, whose thirty-seven-year enjoyment of the second prebend ended with his death, in 1614.[169] It seems that

---

[167] Wills of John Menys (prebendary), Thomas Payne (chantry priest), John Mylles (prebendary), Robert Searles (Six Preacher): Maidstone, County Record Office, PRC 32/22, fos. 77–8; 17/34, fo. 245ᵛ; 32/30, fos. 177–81ᵛ; 17/41, fos. 26–9; and of John Warren (prebendary), Richard Parkhurst (prebendary): PRO, PROB 11/41, fos. 116–17; 11/41, fos. 193ᵛ–194ᵛ.

[168] *Sermons Preached by that Reverend and Learned Divine Richard Clerke*, publ. Charles White (London, 1637). White dedicated the collection of 74 sermons to the Dean and Chapter. A copy in Cambridge University Library (Syn. 4. 63. 68) was the gift of Bishop John Hacket, the biographer of Archbishop John Williams and an extreme moderate. In his youth, Clerke had been leader of the anti-Puritan faction in bitter disputes dividing Christ's College, Cambridge, a militant leader who in 1590 had come to blows with George Downham, the future Bishop of Derry. Some time after his enforced withdrawal from the college, he became a hot candidate for the mastership in the politically charged election of 1609. (Stephen A. Bondos-Greene, 'The End of an Era: Cambridge Puritanism and the Christ's College Election of 1609', *Hist. Jnl.*, 25 (1982), 197–208.)

[169] Clerke's ninth Christmas sermon on 1 Tim. 1: 15 (unpag.), and *Sermons*, 91, 93, 264, 23. However, if William Prynne is to be believed, citing in great detail the sworn testimony of Clerke's editor, Charles White, given at Laud's trial, the *Sermons* were tampered with extensively, even 'castrated' by Laud's censors: the effect being to 'purge' many anti-papal passages and to misrepresent Clerke as more Arminian and less Calvinist than he really was. Where Clerke was made to say in print 'to men onely and to all', he had in fact written 'to men onely but not all', and had insisted that 'the Elect are few compared with the Reprobated'. (Prynne, *Canterburies Doome* (London, 1646), 257–348.) I am grateful to Dr Peter Lake for drawing this material to my attention, and to Dr Anthony Milton for encouraging me to have confidence in Prynne's testimony. I suspect that Clerke's moderated Calvinism resembled the 'hypothetical universalism' of Bishop Arthur Lake of Bath and Wells. (Fincham, *Prelate as Pastor* (cit. in n. 9), 261, 269–70.) For the Carrier–Langworth connection, see George Hakewill, *An Answere to a Treatise Written by Dr Carier* (London, 1616); Westminster Cathedral Archives, Old Brotherhood Archives, i, no. 39. (I owe

the 'false brother' Carrier was the source of Thomas Wilson's troubles until, we are told, his vizard was pulled off, revealing the mark of the Beast in his forehead. Calvinists saw in lifelong anti-Calvinists like Carrier and Langworth only thinly disguised popery. Their obsession was a worrying portent of what lay in store for Canterbury under Archbishop Laud.

LAUD, 1633–1640

It was not the uncharitable wealth of the Canterbury Chapter which, in the very year that he wrote his will, began to visit with disaster what Dr Jackson called 'this flourishing and renowned cathedral'. Canterbury fell victim to a religious, not a social revolution, albeit one tinged with the politics of envy. The story of its downfall begins no later, and perhaps—in spite of such disturbers of the ecclesiastical peace as, in their several ways, Wilson, Saravia, and Carrier—no earlier, than the archiepiscopate of William Laud (1633), or Laud's upward trajectory, which can be traced from about ten years before that.[170] For Laud presided over a profound reaction, not merely against the kind of Church which godly, grasping Jackson personified, but against the Protestant Reformation itself, in many of its manifestations. At Dunblane in Scotland someone said in Laud's hearing that 'this was a brave kirk before the Reformation'. 'What, fellow, Deformation, not Reformation.'[171] Whether or not Laud really said that—and the quip was too obvious to be entirely original—it was the kind of thing which he was expected to have said.

This was the latest of the successive reformations (or deformations) to buffet the Church of England in the century and a half after the breach with Rome. It no longer appears wholly satisfactory to characterize this episode as 'Arminianism' in action, since the Laudian programme was wider in scope and less coherent than the doctrine of salvation attributed to the Dutch theologian Jacobus Arminius and condemned at Dort in 1618. It was also rooted in the native anti-Calvinist, or pre-Calvinist, tradition.[172] Nevertheless, somewhere near the heart of the matter, whether explicitly spelt out or, as with Laud himself, implicit, was an Arminian or quasi-Arminian rejection of the doctrine of salvation

the first of these references to Dr Milton and the second to Dr Kenneth Fincham.) See the forthcoming article by Arnold Hunt 'Daniel Featley's *Clavis Mystica* (1636): A Case Study of Laudian Licensing Policy'. Since copies survive of *Clavis Mystica* in both states, corrected and uncorrected, it is possible to observe the care and sophistication with which alterations were made to the text in order to meet specific objectives. In this case at least, Prynne's account of the matter, while not patently false, is something of a caricature.

[170] However, Clarendon's sense of Archbishop Abbot's elevation in 1611 as the initial destabilizing factor has recently found renewed support. (Peter White, 'The Rise of Arminianism Reconsidered', *Past & Present*, 101 (1983); and the argument in its entirety of id., *Predestination, Policy and Polemic: Conflict and Consensus in the English Church from the Reformation to the Civil War* (Cambridge, 1992).) Dr Kenneth Fincham thinks that Abbot's appointment may have intensified some 'theological tensions'. But his conclusive opinion is that 'we should abandon the traditional view of 1610–1 as the crucial watershed of the

early Stuart Church . . . The real watershed of the early Stuart Church occurred in 1625.' (*Prelate as Pastor* (cit. in n. 9), 47, 303.)

[171] Hugh Trevor-Roper, *Archbishop Laud, 1575–1645* (3rd edn.; London, 1988), 141. In 1630 John Cosin and Augustine Lindsell were accused of talk about 'deformation not reformation'. (*Correspondence of John Cosin*, i (Surtees Soc., 52; 1869), 164, 178. I owe this reference to Dr Anthony Milton.)

[172] N. R. N. Tyacke, *Anti-Calvinists: The Rise of English Arminianism, c.1590–1640* (2nd edn.; Oxford, 1990). See the debate about early Stuart Arminianism and Calvinism (Peter White, Peter Lake, Nicholas Tyacke) in *Past & Present*, 101 (1983) and 114, 115 (1987); also K. Fincham and P. Lake, 'The Ecclesiastical Policy of King James I', *Jnl. British Studies*, 24 (1985), 169–207. On Dort, see, most recently, W. Brown Patterson, 'The Synod of Dort and the Early Stuart Church', in *This Sacred History: Anglican Reflections for John Booty*, ed. D. S. Armentrout (Cambridge, Mass., 1990), 199–221; and forthcoming work by Anthony Milton.

as limited to the elect, since Christ died in principle 'for all men and every man'. This served as premiss to a more general challenge to the religious apparatus of Reformed Protestantism, its exclusive Scripturalism, its Sabbatarianism, and especially its cult of the sermon as the sole vehicle of saving grace, together with the prejudicial ecclesiology of the self-defining 'godly' group which this preaching sustained and which was of the essence of 'Puritanism'.

The positive obverse to the denigration of preaching (and, under Laud, efforts to limit and redirect it) was a relatively novel (but we find much of this in Richard Hooker in the 1590s)[173] enhancement of the public prayers and sacraments; a new regard for holy places and holy things, the church and its material contents; and an insistence on the reverent gestures and postures appropriate to these things, especially kneeling and bowing. There was a particular emphasis on the Holy Table, as in some sense an *altar*, symbolic of God's very presence, to be placed altar-wise at the east end of the church, protected with rails and treated with greater reverence than the pulpit. Laud, as Dean of Gloucester, and the more senior Richard Neile, when Bishop of Durham, had pressed the new altar policy as early as 1617, but it was as late as 1637 that efforts were made to enforce it generally in Canterbury diocese, although kneeling to receive the communion, a ceremony more securely anchored in the Canons of the Church, was an issue somewhat earlier.[174] Many of these things (including the veneration of the font) were widely regarded as 'innovations', which was not a term of approval. Only an informed sense of the iconoclastic lengths to which the Reformation process had gone at the parochial level, and of the scrupulous legalism of the seventeenth-century mind, as well as the strength of its anti-Catholic sentiment, can render credible such a vigorously hostile reaction to what may look to us like relatively innocuous changes, far from the full efflorescence of Latin 'popery'.

'The beauty of holiness' (a concept expounded in 1617 by Bishop Lancelot Andrewes)[175] embodied its own aesthetic and iconic programme, an English version of the Baroque. Laudianism exalted the clergy as a *priesthood*, and the Church as the prerogative of priests, in which all lay initiative and, it almost seemed, lay interest, was treated with suspicious disdain. Bishops now claimed to owe their office to God directly, ruling *iure divino*, a doctrine compatible with Calvinism and only potentially subversive, since Charles I took no exception to a school of thought which simultaneously advanced divine-right monarchy; but political dynamite when embodied in the dubiously legal Canons of 1640. It required some finesse, as well as a measure of confidence in Laud's good intentions, to distinguish between these 'superstitious' innovations and popery in a covert and insidious form, and many failed to make the distinction, or chose not to make it. The diary kept by the Canterbury resident and MP Thomas Scott contains ample evidence of one man's progressive alienation and of the polarization of an urban community whose always turbulent politics were exacerbated by hostility to the Cathedral clergy and their court

[173] Peter Lake, *Anglicans and Puritans? Presbyterianism and English Conformist Thought from Whitgift to Hooker* (London, 1988), 225–30.

[174] Trevor-Roper, *Laud* (cit. in n. 171), 45–6; Tyacke, *Anti-Calvinists* (cit. in n. 172), 199–209; Peter Clark, 'Thomas Scott and the Growth of Urban Opposition to the Early Stuart Regime', *Hist. Jnl.*, 21 (1978), 24. For some of the Kentish reaction to the Laudian altar-policy, see *Proceedings Principally in the County of Kent, In Connection with the Parliaments Called in 1640*, ed. L. B. Larking (Camden Soc. 80; 1862), *passim*.

[175] Fincham, *Prelate as Pastor* (cit. in n. 9), 281.

connections and to ceremonial innovations.[176] In the early 1630s the kneeling posture was a particularly divisive shibboleth in Canterbury. The preacher Richard Clerke thought it 'unseemly' and 'singular' to refuse to kneel. Scott thought it spiritual tyranny to insist on kneeling.[177] The weather forecast was stormy.

Protestant suspicions were further aroused by the apparent hostility with which Laud's Church regarded other reformed Churches, in effect unchurching them and repudiating the common religious heritage which had hitherto bound together Continental and English Protestants.[178] By contrast, if the Roman Church was still formally opposed it was no longer regarded as wholly alien, anti-Christian.[179] And this at the very time when the reformed Churches of the Continent had their backs to the wall in the Thirty Years War, events to which Thomas Scott, for one, was constantly alert. As the minister of the French Church in Canterbury put it: 'There is a Combination on Foot, whole Countries Beyond-Sea are moved. Many Churches are desolated.'[180] With England signally failing to redress the balance of a rampant Catholic Counter-Reformation, these anti-ecumenical Anglican attitudes had a further potential for political damage.

And what of that kirk, somewhat 'braver' than Dunblane: Christ Church, Canterbury? Laud had a revived sense of the cathedral church as the mother church of the diocese (Ezekiel 16: 44–5, 'as is the Mother, so is her daughter'). The controversial Canons of 1640 declared it fit and convenient that 'all churches and chapels do conform themselves in this particular to the example of the Cathedral or mother churches'.[181] This 'particular' concerned the positioning of the communion table altar-wise,[182] a change either effected at Canterbury in Laud's first year, when a new table was installed, with the added dignity of graduated steps—a communion table of degrees'[183]—or already established practice, since William Somner wrote, in 1640, that at Canterbury 'this Altar was and still is called the high Altar'.[184] The same imagery of mother and daughter had been employed in Charles I's judgement relating to altars in the test-case of the London church of St Gregory's (1633), and it became a Laudian commonplace.[185]

Given the intensity of Arminian-Laudian concern for the material fabric of churches, and of cathedral churches especially, the Laudian episode at Canterbury ought to have repaired decades of neglect with a new and golden age of loving care and embellishment. Did it? There is certainly some sense of the massive Catholic inertia of the building

[176] Clark, 'Thomas Scott and the Growth of Urban Opposition' (cit. in n. 174).

[177] *Sermons Preached by Richard Clerke* (cit. in n. 168), 264; Clark, 'Thomas Scott and the Growth of Urban Opposition' (cit. in n. 174), 24.

[178] But see W. J. Tighe, 'William Laud and the Reunion of the Churches: Some Evidence from 1637 and 1638', *Hist. Jnl.*, 30 (1987), 717–27.

[179] Anthony Milton, 'The Laudians and the Church of Rome *c*.1625–1640' (Ph.D. thesis, Univ. of Cambridge, 1989).

[180] J. Delmé, *A Spiritual Warning for Times of War* (London, 1701).

[181] *The Works of Archbishop Laud*, ed. W. Scott and J. Bliss, v, pt. 2 (Library of Anglo-Catholic Theology; Oxford, 1853), 625.

[182] Tyacke, *Anti-Calvinists* (cit. in n. 172), 199–209.

[183] Prynne, *Canterburies Doome* (cit. in n. 169), 89; Culmer,

Cathedrall Newes (cit. in n. 7); Legg and Hope, *Inventories*, 251.

[184] Somner, *Antiquities* (1640), 170. As W. D. Caröe remarked ('Canterbury Cathedral Choir During the Commonwealth' (cit. in n. 39), 359), the high altar, with its 'screen of tabernacle work', is 'a difficult subject'. Prebendaries Thomas Jackson and Thomas Blechinden differed in the evidence they gave at Laud's trial about the novelty of Laudian altar-drill in the Cathedral. (*Works of Laud* (cit. in n. 181), iv. 223; Prynne, *Canterburies Doome* (cit. in n. 169), 79.) But Blechinden, who thought that it was not new, was not instituted until Nov. 1633. Peter Heylyn alleged that an altar-wise setting, with appropriate reverence shown, was the position before Laud. (*Cyprianus Anglicus* (London, 1668), 291.)

[185] LPL, MS 943, pp. 457–8; Prynne, *Canterburies Doome* (cit. in n. 169), 86–9.

reasserting itself in William Somner's book on Canterbury and its antiquities, written towards 1640, in what he calls 'such blessed days of peace as our Church (by Gods mercy) now enjoys', looking back with longing approval to the Cathedral described by Erasmus as striking 'a sensible Impression of Religion in their minds that beheld it afar off'.[186] On her visit to Canterbury, the French Queen Mother heard a speech from Prebendary Meric Casaubon about 'these fair structures', erected by kings and queens or 'holy prelates' elevated by kings and queens, and she was seen to alight from her sedan chair to bow towards, some said to kiss, the place of Becket's martyrdom.[187]

But in the special case of the 'mother church' of all England, we face a contradiction. In no other decade since the Reformation, perhaps in no period whatsoever, was Canterbury so dominated by its archbishop. The Chapter knew very well that its diocesan and Visitor was the most powerful of the King's subjects, and they framed their obsequious letters accordingly.[188] But, like other archbishops, Laud was almost never there, and, more than most, was a desperately busy man. After Bishop Williams's suspension, the administration of Lincoln diocese was added to his many other burdens. Hugh Trevor-Roper's biography consequently hardly mentions Canterbury, whereas it devotes a whole chapter to Laud's dealings (as chancellor) with the University of Oxford. Even for this Archbishop, it seems, Canterbury was peninsular and peripheral. It was St Paul's in London which provided the symbol for ecclesiastical regeneration, with thousands of pounds raised under political duress for its restoration, in Kent as in other counties.[189] So far as Canterbury was concerned, Laud was an occasional Visitor (but the visitations were conducted by his officers) and a frequent correspondent. Trevor-Roper speaks of his visitations as 'like a passing wind and no more'.[190] It has been said that he displayed 'a naïve trust in the power of pieces of paper ... worthy of Neville Chamberlain'.[191] Once a year he rendered an account of his stewardship to the King, but in these reports he could only pass on such crumbs of news as were fed to him.[192] The antiquary Somner, in his professional life Laud's registrar, was told: 'You have not now in this whole year given me any the least information of any one man.' Perhaps that meant that all was well. But Laud doubted it.[193]

So this somewhat remote new broom could be no more effective than his officers and others on the spot. His principal agent, the vicar-general, Sir Nathaniel Brent, was part of the legacy of Archbishop Abbot, by no means at one with Laud in his outlook, and at first not trusted. Isaac Bargrave, dean from 1625, was another wobbly plank, in Laud's perception. All should have been well, since Bargrave was the Duke of Buckingham's choice for the job,[194] and upholder equally of the altar and the royal prerogative and closer

---

[186] Somner, *Antiquities* (1640), 170, 164. Erasmus's words were quoted (without acknowledgement) in the English edn. of William Camden's *Britannia* (London, 1610), 337. Since the rendering is word-perfect, this must be where Somner found them.

[187] PRO, SP 16/400/125; Culmer, *Cathedrall Newes* (cit. in n. 7), 7.

[188] See the following letters from the Dean and Chapter in State Papers, Domestic: PRO, SP 16/251/39, 16/258/25, 16/259/50, 16/271/44, 16/311/69, 16/337/38, 16/382/55.

[189] Trevor-Roper, *Laud* (cit. in n. 171), 121–6, 346–7, 350–1, 428–9.

[190] Ibid. 194.

[191] Anthony Milton, in *JEH*, 41 (1990), 504.

[192] *Works of Laud* (cit. in n. 181), v, pt. 2. 309–70.

[193] Ibid. vii. 268–9.

[194] Sir John Hippisly to Buckingham, 29 Sept, 1625: 'and nowe my lord the deane of Canterbury is deade and if please you to make doctor Bargrafe in his place howe [who] hathe the kings promise for yt yt will besides give me credit in this place and make them see that I ame still and I hope ever shall be in your good fafor'. (PRO, SP 16/6/122.) This is unusually firm

to Paolo Sarpi's Venice than to Geneva.[195] But Laud, even before he was archbishop, went out of his way to do Bargrave a gratuitous injury and subsequently wrote to him from a lofty and hostile vantage-point.[196] In his turn, Bargrave maintained poor relations with his Chapter, a singularly ill-tempered crew, who at about this time wrote of the indignities inflicted upon them by the Dean of the Arches, Sir Henry Marten: 'undervaluings, affrontings, scorning, cheating tricks, daring disruptions and multiple contumelies'. Marten suggested that both parties should cease to behave like fishwives.[197] A Chapter which still contained the ambivalent and very senior figure of Dr Jackson could not be relied upon to give the Archbishop unflinching support. Jackson first went along with the new ceremony of bowing to the altar, and then opposed, saying that 'this bowing was to his grief'. At his trial Laud would say: 'I could tell your lordships how often Dr Jackson hath shifted his opinions in religion.'[198] This critically important relationship began badly, with Laud reminding the prebendaries that most of them owed their places to the King, as if they were in danger of summary dismissal: 'For I cannot take it well to be ill used, and undeservedly, especially at such a time as I was endeavouring your good.' Three years later, he lamented that all his pains had had 'so little success'. 'One peevish difference or other, for better I cannot name them, still arising to disturb all that is well meant.'[199]

Laud attached importance to the new statutes[200] of 1636, which he intended as a model for other New Foundation cathedrals. The principle of freshly minted statutes may have concerned him more than their specific content, since he professed to believe that hitherto cathedrals had drifted rudderless, almost as if they had no statutes.[201] Although two years in the making, they were less than a radical revision of the Henrician statutes, those relating to the Six Preachers, minor canons, and lay clerks containing many details which were already effectively redundant. But Statute 34, 'Of the Celebration of Divine Service', was rewritten, since the 1541 statutes still referred to the mass. And here we find the authentically Laudian insistence on altar drill and other manifestations of the beauty of holiness.

Other documentation reveals that Laud had two interconnecting objectives for cathedrals, which at Canterbury were unveiled in his primary metropolitical visitation of 1634 and subsequently pursued with indifferent success.[202] One related to the establishment, its personnel and financial base; the other to the fabric and, as it were, plant, a comprehensive plan both for the Cathedral and its internal arrangements and liturgical function, and for the surrounding Precincts as a space which Laud was determined to make not only decent but sacred.[203]

evidence of the *ego et rex meus* character of Buckingham's dealings.

[195] *DNB*, s.v. Bargrave; Isaac Bargrave, *A Sermon Preached Before . . . Parliament: February the last 1623* (London, 1624); id., *A Sermon Preached Before King Charles, March 27 1627* (London, 1627).

[196] In 1627 Laud (still bishop of London) countermanded Archbishop Abbot's collation of Bargrave to the vicarage of Lydd, proposing another appointment 'upon his Maiestyes Title by prerogative'. (PRO, SP 16/83/48.)

[197] Ibid., SP 16/258/24, 55.

[198] *Works of Laud* (cit. in n. 181), iv. 223.

[199] Ibid. vii. 55–6.

[200] Ibid. v, pt. 2. 332; Laud to Dean and Chapter, 26 Jan. 1636(/7), ibid. vi, pt. 2. 484–5.

[201] Laud said at his trial that 'they had extreme need of statutes, for all lay loose for want of confirmation, and men did what they listed'. (Ibid. iv. 192.)

[202] 'Papers Relating to Archbishop Laud's Visitations' (cit. in n. 26).

[203] We say that Laud had these objectives. They were shared with the King and it remains possible (as Dr Kevin Sharpe believes), but not, I think, probable, that they were first and

The keystone of the first policy was to proscribe the leasing of property for three lives, which was lawful practice under an Act of Parliament of 1559, limiting leases to twenty-one years or less. This was a matter on which both King and Archbishop issued repeated instructions and which was written into the new Cathedral statutes. By placing tighter constraints on the granting of 'beneficial' leases, this change was intended to displace the irregular income from entry fines into regular and predictable rack-rents. The political intention was to strengthen the ecclesiastical interest, if necessary at the expense of the gentry as tenants of Church property, who would be obliged to regard their landlords with 'a greater respect'.[204] Peter Heylyn connected this policy of confrontational estate-management with Laud's failure to maintain the conventional obligations of courteous hospitality at Canterbury and Lambeth,[205] and believed that it backfired in the parliamentary attack upon the Archbishop in 1640–1, in which the Kentish MP Sir Edward Dering playing a prominent part. Although the true facts of the relations of Dering and other gentry with the ecclesiastical presence in the county were naturally a little more complicated than that, there was truth in the allegation of Laud's indifference to hospitality.[206]

The Dean and Chapter responded to the royal and metropolitan order by assuring Laud that for the past ten years they had granted no leases for lives, 'notwithstandinge the ernest importunity of some persons of quality'.[207] Perhaps this was generally true, but in Canterbury itself, inside and outside the precincts, they were still granting the traditional forty-year leases.[208] One might have expected Laud to insist that such entry fines as were still payable should benefit the Cathedral and not individual members of the Chapter. But of this there is no evidence, unless the Archbishop was behind a Chapter decree of 1638 that out of every £20 taken in fines, £1 should be sequestered for the benefit of the fabric.[209] Instead, the Archbishop floated a more modest reform. Commenting on 'the meanness of your quire for a church so great and so well endowed', he proposed that the bulk of the 'entertainment money' paid by tenants to the Dean and receiver-general under covenant when their farms were visited and surveyed should be used to cost-index the stipends of the lay clerks. This was done, but at some inconvenience and even detriment. And in any

foremost royal rather than archiepiscopal objectives. (Kevin Sharpe, 'Archbishop Laud and the University of Oxford', in *History and Imagination*, ed. H. Lloyd-Jones, Valerie Pearl, and Blair Worden (London, 1981).)

[204] Trevor-Roper, *Laud* (cit. in n. 171), 149–50; Wilkins, *Concilia*, iv. 478, 480–1, 493–4; PRO, SP 16/270/6; Bodl., MS Tanner 128, fos. 41–3; *Statutes of Canterbury Cathedral* (cit. in n. 23), 15–19; *Works of Laud* (cit. in n. 181), iv. 192. For the wider implications of this policy, see Christopher Hill, *Economic Problems of the Church from Whitgift to the Long Parliament* (Oxford, 1956), 14–15, 311–14; and W. J. Sheils, 'Profit, Patronage, or Pastoral Care: The Rectory Estates of the Archbishopric of York, 1540–1640', and Felicity Heal, 'Archbishop Laud Revisited: Leases and Estate Management at Canterbury and Winchester Before the Civil War', in *Princes and Paupers in the English Church 1500–1800*, ed. R. O'Day and F. Heal (Totowa, NJ, 1981), 91–109, 129–51.

[205] Heylyn, *Cyprianus Anglicus* (cit. in n. 184), 46–7.

[206] S. P. Salt, 'The Origins of Sir Edward Dering's Attack on the Ecclesiastical Hierarchy, c.1625–1640', *Hist. Jnl.*, 30 (1987),

21–52; Heal 'The Archbishops of Canterbury and the Practice of Hospitality' (cit. in n. 122), 558–9; Fincham, *Prelate as Pastor* (cit. in n. 9), 79–80, 261–3. Dean Bargrave, by contrast, was a securely established member of East Kentish society, living in the country, occasionally hunting, and thick with his kindred and neighbours. (*The Oxinden Letters 1607–1642*, ed. D. Gardiner (London, 1933).) Mr. Peter Salt has helped me with this point.

[207] PRO, SP 16/271/44.

[208] See a collection of about 50 counterparts of leases, mostly of Canterbury tenements, c.1600–c.1634, in LPL, Carte Antique et Miscellanee III. The 1636 statutes permitted 30-year leases of houses and buildings 'et non ultra'. (*Statutes of Canterbury Cathedral* (cit. in n. 23), 14–15.)

[209] Misc. Accts. 48, p. 75. In 1573–4, Archbishop Parker had insisted that no division of fines should occur without his consent, but this more to avoid contention than to preserve the interest of the foundation. (*Visitation Articles and Injunctions* (cit. in n. 46), iii. 360.)

case, the Chapter was already augmenting the salaries of both lay clerks and minor canons from other sources.[210]

Laud's interest in a well-fed choir was part and parcel of the 'beauty of holiness' programme, which demanded a thorough overhaul of the physical setting of cathedral worship. Soon after the primary visitation, the Chapter was put to 'extraordinary expences' for 'ornaments of the altar etc.';[211] with the result that towards 1640 Somner could describe what had been achieved as 'very rich and becoming', while a visitor from Norwich enthused over 'the fayre Organ sweet and tunable' and the 'deep and ravishing Consort of Quristers'.[212] The altar-like communion-table was now adorned with a carpet of purple velvet edged with gold lace, silver candlesticks, a silver bowl, and a kind of embroidered reredos called a 'glory cloth', of which horrified anti-Laudians have left a detailed description, a nice example of Arminian aesthetics.[213]

On a related point Laud was insistent, but eventually impotent. It had long been a question whether sermons, and which sermons, should be preached in the Sermon House, 'the ordinary place', or in the Cathedral itself. An anonymous member of the Chapter insisted that the chapter house was not a consecrated building, and that sermons displaced the business of the Chapter, with all its attendant traffic of tenants, beadles, and poor suitors, into the Cathedral, which *was* such a building. Sermons should be preached from the pulpit in the nave, a place 'of little use now save for people to walke and talke in'. All that was needed was some moveable seats for the Dean and Chapter, mayor and aldermen, and for some gentlemen of quality.[214] But soon Laud revived and imposed the practice of preaching in the choir, in the setting of the Cathedral service. Here were some of the ingredients of what has been identified as a common pattern of town–gown conflict in cathedral cities under the Laudian regime, which also included friction over marketing, rates, and taxes.[215] The pattern always involved the rights of the mayor and other lay persons of consequence, particularly in their formal processions to sermons, and in the seating provided for them, often described as 'convenient' but in the Canterbury Chapter in 1634 called 'exorbitant', Laud being told that they had obeyed his direction in 'pulling downe the exorbitant seates within our Quire, whereby the Church is very much bewtified'.[216] But the occupants of the seats were scandalized, and more so by their exclusion from those no less exorbitant seats of honour in the Sermon House.

Soon after Christmas 1640, with the Laudian regime already staggering, the choir witnessed noisy cries of 'This is idolatry!' and 'Down with the altar!', together with an unusual form of protest: the congregation insisted on singing the *entire* 119th Psalm in

[210] Laud to Dean and Chapter, 23 June 1636, *Works of Laud* (cit. in n. 181), vi, pt. 2. 257–8; Dean and Chapter to Laud, 1 July, 15 Dec. 1636, PRO, SP 16/328/5, SP 16/337/38; Laud to Dean Bargrave, 24 Nov. 1636, MS Cat. 80; Dean and Chapter to Archbishop Juxon, 6 Dec. 1661, ibid.; LPL, Reg. Bancroft, fo. 226ᵛ. These fees, an intricate matter, had been reviewed as recently as 1627 (Chapter Act Book, 1608–28, fo. 159). PRO, SP 16/283/83 lists what each property was liable to pay. PRO, SP 16/283/84 reveals that the receiver-general visited annually, the Dean never more than once in his deanship.

[211] PRO, SP 16/371/44.

[212] Somner, *Antiquities* (1640), 94; 'A Relation of a Short Survey of the Western Counties' (cit. in n. 153), 11.

[213] Legg and Hope, *Inventories*, 243, 247–8; Prynne, *Canterburies Doome* (cit. in n. 169), 78–9; Culmer, *Cathedrall Newes* (cit. in n. 7), 6.

[214] PRO, SP 16/286/55. 'This I have spoken of both in publique and in private, but the alteration has seemed so difficult that it had no successe.'

[215] Anthony Fletcher, *The Outbreak of the English Civil War* (London, 1981), 318; Fincham, *Prelate as Pastor* (cit. in n. 9), 92–5; Collinson, *Religion of Protestants* (cit. in n. 10), 141–5.

[216] PRO, SP 16/271/44.

metre and in competition with the choral service.[217] After this the Chapter moved the preaching back into the Sermon House. Soon, on the eve of the Civil War, the Laudian altar-furnishings were sold, to the benefit of the King's war treasury.[218] All that remains of the Laudian Cathedral is the marble font given by Prebendary John Warner upon his episcopal promotion and now standing at the north-west corner of the nave, after a series of sad misadventures in the Interregnum. What a petition to the House of Commons in 1640 spoke of as a 'superstitious font' with 'tempting images' was described by Somner as 'a rare piece of Novelty', and he noted that it represented the first private benefaction to the fabric of the Cathedral since the Reformation.[219] Much more than that, with the Laudian altar, it affirmed the novel emphasis on the sacramental infusion of grace.

If the Laudian liturgical innovations proved to be as short-lived as they were skin-deep, the onslaught on what Laud regarded as the Augean stables of the Precincts cast the Archbishop as Sisyphus rather than Hercules, in another doomed enterprise.[220] In the early years of the New Foundation, much of the churchyard had been a green field, rented out for grazing and for the quarterly Canterbury fairs. But now new houses and walled gardens were encroaching on ground where burials had once taken place and clothiers had more recently shown their cloths. If some of this was, technically and canonically, consecrated ground, it was also desirable real estate, attracting the gentry and near-gentry who were moving into provincial towns and creating a new kind of urban civilization.[221] In the early 1630s, there were as many as thirty lay householders within the Precincts, including several 'persons of quality', renting the property of the Chapter and conveniently meeting its obligation to pay Ship Money.[222] Moreover, several members of the Chapter were themselves active in the business of leasing and building, abandoning their poky prebendal house and making long-term provision for their growing families.

Laud and his royal master set their faces against such 'encroachments', requiring that leases should not be renewed (but they were forty-year leases, and most very recent!) and that the new and intrusive buildings should be demolished as the leases fell in.[223] This became a general policy for cathedral closes and was written into the new statutes. Laud was also anxious to get rid of commerce, whether in the shape of the money-making fairs or of shop windows opening on to the Precincts.[224] According to a later report, there was provocation in the minor scandal of human bones being unearthed while ground was broken to build a house for Robert Turner, a lay clerk who doubled up as a vintner. For

[217] Christ Church Letters, iii, no. 76; Culmer, *Cathedrall Newes* (cit. in n. 7), 18; Woodruff and Danks, *Memorials*, 322–3.

[218] Christ Church Letters, iii, no. 73; C. E. Woodruff, 'Some Seventeenth Century Letters and Petitions from the Muniments of the Dean and Chapter of Canterbury', *Arch. Cant.*, 42 (1930), 93–139; Legg and Hope, *Inventories*, 246–7.

[219] Somner, *Antiquities* (1640), 99–100; Culmer, *Cathedrall Newes* (cit. in n. 7), 2.

[220] What follows is based on 'Papers Relating to Archbishop Laud's Visitations' (cit. in n. 26), 124–7; PRO, SP 16/284/3, 16/304/42, 16/311/69 and 69(I), 16/357/122; Woodruff, 'Some Seventeenth Century Letters' (cit. in n. 218), 110–13; *Works of Laud* (cit. in n. 181), vii. 351; on post-Restoration documentation

in Bodl., MS Tanner 123; and on Mrs Margaret Sparks's unrivalled knowledge of the Canterbury Precincts in the 17th cent.

[221] Alan Everitt, 'Country, County and Town: Patterns of Regional Evolution in England', in id., *Landscape and Community in England* (London and Ronceverte, 1985), 11–40; Peter Borsay, *The English Urban Renaissance: Culture and Society in the Provincial Town 1660–1770* (Oxford, 1989).

[222] 'Papers Relating to Archbishop Laud's Visitations' (cit. in n. 26), 126; PRO, SP 16/382/55/

[223] PRO, SP 16/311/69(I), and 16/304/42.

[224] Ibid.

three centuries this house was No. 8 The Precincts.[225] But the strength of vested and competing interests was insuperable: witness the case of the Archdeacon William Kingsley.[226] Dr Kingsley had allowed his prebendal house to fall into disrepair while he lived in a more convenient and modern house, now No. 11 The Precincts and familiar to many as the administrative offices of Canterbury Cathedral. Kingsley's forty-year lease dated from 1626 and cost him a modest 4s. 6d. in rent, whereas in 1650 the parliamentary commissioners would put its true (and improved) rental value at £12. Neither the envious malice of Dr Jackson, nor the tactful diplomacy of the Chapter, nor yet a solemn canonical 'monition' from the Archbishop himself produced any lasting results. In 1665, with the lease coming up for renewal, No. 11 was still occupied by the Widow Kingsley, and, for that matter, No. 8 by Widow Turner and the widow of Dean Bargrave, into whose family the Turners had married. The 1660s witnessed sundry 'capers' of these widows, who made Dean Turner's life a misery while they pulled strings at Court to obtain a royal dispensation requiring the Chapter to renew these leases, contrary to statute. In 1685 Kingsley's granddaughter was still ensconced, with the Chapter bound to renew her lease from time to time, and in 1704 the lease belonged to a great-grandson.[227] So much for Laud's best-laid schemes.

Last but not least in this catalogue of doomed enterprises we come to Laud's campaign against the Kentish congregations of French and Dutch-speaking 'strangers', the largest of which gathered Sunday by Sunday in the crypt of his own Cathedral. The fact that it has been possible thus far to explore the history of post-Reformation Canterbury without mentioning the Francophone Belgian (or 'Walloon') community who made up a quarter, or even a third, of its population is some tribute to its self-contained, deeply endogamous character, which Laud resented so strongly. Since the migration of the core of the community from Sandwich in the mid-1570s, many hundreds of these people, mostly settled in the poorer quarters of St Alphege and Northgate, had done much to revive the flagging urban economy and had enjoyed the privilege of free exercise of their own, reformed, religion, from about 1576, in the western crypt of the Cathedral, a few yards from the Black Prince's Chantry, where their spiritual progeny still have their *culte* to this day. From 1617 the Canterbury church enjoyed remarkable pastoral continuity under the leadership of Philippe Delmé, a native of Norwich, and Jean Bulteel, an alumnus of Leiden.[228]

The Walloons seem to have had few active enemies in Caroline Canterbury, but there was some ecclesiastical resentment, which is hardly surprising when we envisage a congregation of as many as 2,000 making its way through the Cathedral to the crypt, where it proceeded to lift the roof with psalms which were said to make 'very harsh and

[225] Evidence of the Turner lease of uncertain reliability in Bodl., MS Tanner 123, fos. 92–106.

[226] Chapter decisions in respect of Kingsley's lease, 13 Apr. 1626, 7 Apr. 1628, Chapter Act Book, 1608–28, fos. 146, 161ᵛ; counterpart of Kingsley's lease, 2 Sept. 1626, LPL, Carte Antique et Miscellanee III, no. 60; Jackson's account of the matter in a letter to Laud, 1 Mar. 1634(/5), PRO, SP 16/284/3; evidence that Jackson was doing much the same as Kingsley, Misc. Accts. 48, p. 38, Bargrave to Laud, 30 May 1637, PRO, SP 16/357/122; Laud's formal monition and Kingsley's ostensible compliance, Woodruff, 'Some Seventeenth Century Letters'

(cit. in n. 218), 110–13; subsequent repercussions in the case of the Canterbury widows, Bodl., MS Tanner 123, fos. 92–106.

[227] George Thorpe to Archbishop Sancroft, 10 Dec. 1685, Bodl., MS Tanner 123, fo. 107; information supplied by Mrs Sparks.

[228] Cross, *History of the Walloon and Huguenot Church at Canterbury* (cit. in n. 52); Anne M. Oakley, 'The Canterbury Walloon Congregation from Elizabeth I to Laud', in *Huguenots in Britain and Their French Background, 1550–1800*, ed. I. Scouloudi (Basingstoke and London, 1987), 56–71.

34 Thomas Turner, Dean 1643–72 (not installed until 1660). Artist unknown; *c*.1645. (Canterbury, Deanery.)

35 John Tillotson, Dean 1672–89, by Mary Beale; *c*.1672. (Canterbury, Deanery.)

36 George Horne, Dean 1781–90. Artist unknown; 1790. (Canterbury, Deanery.)

37 The Hon. Hugh Percy, Archdeacon 1822–5, Dean 1825–7. Artist unknown; *c*.1825. (Canterbury, Deanery.)

Cantuariensis ecclesiæ cath:
ab occidente prospectus.

Sic deficiente Christiana pietate, prius
tiua pietatis indicia simul pereant:
Christi ecclesiam Cantuariensem, cætero
ruin in Anglia matrem, sic à fronte e
liberi voluit præsenti seculo, et post
ris. Gulielmus Duci:

Tho: Johnson delin:
Daniel King sculp:

A Prospect of the Choir of the Cathedral Church of Canterbury.

To the Right Honoural & Reverend D.ᵉ Edmund Gibson Lord Bishop of London.

A Prospect of the Inside to the Choir of the Cathedral Church of CANTERBURY.

To the Most Reverend Father in God, D.ᵉ Lancelot Blackburn, Lord Arch bishop of York.
This Plate is most humbly Dedicated by your Lordship most Obedient Serv.ᵗ Sam.ˡ Cole.

38 (*left*) West front, drawn by Thomas Johnson and engraved by Daniel King, for W. Dugdale, *Monasticon*, i (1655). The spire on the north-west tower was damaged in a storm in 1703 and taken down in 1704.

39 (*above*) The choir, showing panelling by Roger Davis, 1676, and altar and screen by Peter Hartover, 1664, and Thomas Lingall, 1694. Drawn and engraved by S. Cole, *c.*1716. From John Dart, *Cathedral Church of Canterbury* (1726).

40 (*top right*) The nave, showing the former rood screen (*c.*1400) and font (1639; restored 1663). Drawn and engraved by S. Cole, *c.*1716.

41 (*right*) The choir, showing screen by James Burrough (1733). Watercolour by Frederic Nash, 1805. (Canterbury Museums.)

42 (*far left*) 'St Anselm's Chapel with Part of Thomas-a-Becket's Crown, Canterbury Cathedral'. Watercolour by J. M. W. Turner, 1793. (Manchester, Whitworth Art Gallery, D.113.1892.)

43 (*left*) William Gostling, minor canon 1727–77. Drawn by —— Raymond and engraved by R. B. Godfrey as frontispiece to Gostling's *Walk . . . in the City of Canterbury* (1777).

44 (*lower left*) Cathedral from the east, looking across the site of St Augustine's Abbey. Drawn by Thomas Hastings and engraved by William Woolnoth for his *Cathedral Church of Canterbury* (1816).

45 (*right*) 'Section of S. Transept and Part of Tower: Elevation of Transept and Part of Tower'. Drawn by Edward Cresy and G. L. Taylor, and engraved by J. le Keux for John Britton, *Metropolitical Church of Canterbury* (1821).

46 (*below*) 'East View of the City of Canterbury'. Watercolour by George Fennel Robson; not later than 1827. (Canterbury Museums.)

47 (*top far left*) The Hon. Richard Bagot, Dean 1827–45 (Bishop of Oxford 1829–45). By Francis Grant, 1846. (Canterbury, Deanery.)
48 (*top left*) Robert Payne Smith, Dean 1871–95. By Mathew Ridley Corbet, 1886. (Canterbury, Deanery.)
49 (*far left*) Frederic William Farrar, Dean 1895–1903. By H. A. Olivier, 1892. (Canterbury, Deanery.)
50 (*left*) Benjamin Harrison, archdeacon of Maidstone and canon of stall IX, 1845–87. Drawn by George Richmond, 1880.
51 (*above*) 'From the Bishop's Garden'. Watercolour by William De la Motte, July 1844. Deanery garden, showing a seat made of architectural fragments by order of Lady Harriet Bagot. (Add. MS 45, no. 16.)

52 Presbytery and high altar, showing Dean Percy's screen and siting of altar (1824–5), and later painting of screen (1898); new altar rails (1897).

53 (*right*) Demolition of the house of stall I (ordered 1864). Watercolour by L. L. Razé; undated. (Canterbury, King's School.) The house had been built in the south aisle of the infirmary chapel and part of the infirmary hall.

54 (*left*) 'Banqueting Room'. Watercolour by William De la Motte; August 1844. Demolition of Lanfranc's south range of Archbishop's Palace; 'These ruins all removed 1844' (note at bottom). (Add. MS 45, no. 17.)

55 (*lower left*) The Dean and Chapter in the Green Court, *c.*1922. From left to right: Canons A. J. Mason, A. W. Robinson, S. Bickersteth (back view with Dean Wace behind), T. G. Gardiner, L. J. White-Thomson, J. V. Macmillan.

56 (*right*) George Kennedy Allen Bell, Dean 1924–9. By Philip de Laszlo, *c.*1930. (Canterbury, Deanery.)

57 (*below*) Margaret Babington, Steward and Treasurer of the Friends, 1928–58, in her office over the Christ Church Gate; *c.*1945.

58 (*left*) Water Tower Garden and north-east transept, showing columns from the Saxon church at Reculver which stood there 1860–1932.

59 (*right*) 'Air Raid Precautions in Canterbury Cathedral', with sandbags round Henry IV's tomb. Watercolour by William Townsend, 1939. (Canterbury Museums.)

60 (*below*) 'Air Raid Precautions in Canterbury Cathedral'. Watercolour by William Townsend, 1939. (Canterbury Museums.)

61 From the bombed city, 1942.

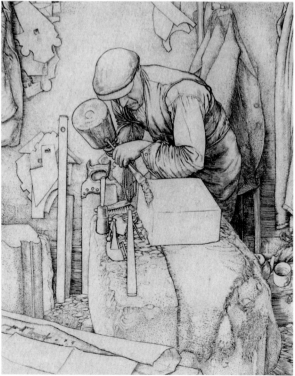

62 'The Mason's Yard'. Etching by Robert Austin, 1948. Charles Goodey, chief mason, repairing war damage.

63 Chapel of St John the Evangelist, refurnished by Stephen Dykes-Bower in 1951 as a memorial to William Temple, Archbishop of Canterbury 1942–4.

64 Hewlett Johnson, Dean 1931–63, at the Deanery.

65 The Papal Visit, 29 May 1982. The Canterbury or
'St Augustine's' Gospels are brought from St Augustine's
Chair to Pope John Paul II and Archbishop Robert Runcie.
Dean and Chapter (from left to right): Canons J. A. Simpson
and D. I. Hill, Dean V. de Waal, Canons J. H. R. de Sausmarez
and A. M. Allchin. Former Archbishops Michael Ramsey and
Donald Coggan in right background.

66 The Enthronement, 19 April 1991. Archbishop George
Carey makes his corporal oath on the Canterbury or 'St
Augustine's' Gospels to observe the customs and defend the
liberties of the Cathedral.

untuneable discords in our singinge'. Somner wrote of 'that tribe', 'a hive too little to containe such a swarme', while a visitor from Norwich was told that they numbered 10,000 communicants.[229] But no one except Laud seems to have wanted to get them out. In 1634 the three foreign churches in Kent (the others were Dutch-speaking, in Sandwich and Maidstone) were summoned to appear before the Archbishop's primary visitation. In vain their delegates pleaded that while they were in the diocese of Canterbury, they were not of it, enjoying exemption. Thus began two years of relentless pressure from Laud and, for the Churches, an endless Kafkaesque round of appearances, hearings, petitions, and political maneovres, all recorded with impeccable fidelity by the minister Jean Bulteel.[230] There were also gratuitous insults from a primate who on one occasion assured the delegates, not very convincingly, that he was not 'made of sower leaven': 'I know your doctrine, parity of Ministers, haile fellow well met.'[231]

Laud's demands were that all members of the community who were born in England as subjects of the Crown must adhere to their parish churches, and that the foreign Churches must abandon their own forms of prayer for translated versions of the English liturgy. Nominally this was royal policy, but Laud made no secret of his personal responsibility, while Charles, when petitioned directly, said: 'We must beleeve our Archbishop of Canterbury.' Later (and uncharacteristically) Laud relaxed the second of his two injunctions but continued to insist upon the first, against all persuasions to the contrary: not only from the strangers themselves but from the Dean and Chapter, the mayor and commonalty of Canterbury, the Kentish gentry, and the friend of Charles I, the grand Huguenot Duke of Soubise. The knock-down argument for the defence was that the poor among the foreigners, who had been generously sustained within their own congregations, would now become an insupportable charge on the parishes. Laud replied, preposterously, that the Churches would still have to look after their own poor, even if they ceased to be members of their congregations.

It was a typical Laudian story. There were several stays of execution, but the Archbishop never offered to give way, and never did. Eventually the order was solemnly pronounced in the Walloon congregation by Somner, the ministers and elders having declined to be their own executioners. And then very little happened. Laud's optimistic report to the King in 1636 that the Walloons 'do come orderly to their parish churches' was hardly consistent with the true facts.[232] The historian of the congregation writes of 'friendly inertia' and thinks that Laud's efforts failed for want of 'moral force' and favourable local opinion.[233]

[229] PRO, SP 16/286/55; Somner, *Antiquities* (1640), 175; 'A Relation of a Short Survey of the Western Counties' (cit. in n. 153), 17. But note a 1634 reference to 'the Walloons Church doore': Misc. Accts. 48, p. 49.

[230] J[ohn] B[ulteel], *A Relation of the Troubles of the Three Forraigne Churches in Kent* (London, 1645), agrees in all particulars, and textually, with the large body of related documents gathered in *Ecclesiae Londino-Batavae Archivum: Epistulae et Tractatus*, ed. J. H. Hessels, iii (Cambridge, 1897). See also de Schickler,

Les Eglises du réfuge (cit. in n. 48), iii. 23–63; O. P. Grell, *Dutch Calvinists in Early Stuart London* (Leiden, 1989), ch. 6, 'The Struggle for Survival: Archbishop Laud and the Foreign Congregations', 224–48.

[231] Bulteel, *A Relation* (cit. in n. 230), 38, 7.
[232] *Works of Laud* (cit. in n. 181), v, pt. 2. 337.
[233] Cross, *History of the Walloon and Huguenot Church at Canterbury* (cit. in n. 52), 115–17.

REVOLUTION, 1640–1660

Bulteel remarks that the Archbishop 'had many irons in the fire', and his narrative feeds the story of his own little local difficulty into the great events by which the metropolitan was soon overwhelmed: Scotland, the Short Parliament, the Long Parliament, root-and-branch petitions against episcopacy, the Tower. Presently, Laud's treatment of the foreign congregations would form one of the charges brought against him in a trial for high treason.[234] Meanwhile, in Canterbury, the Chapter decided that it was time to appoint a full-time librarian.[235] But such brave attempts at business-as-usual were not very convincing. The Cathedral could not hope to escape the revolutionary and counter-revolutionary turmoil which now engulfed and polarized the county of which it was a part. Nor did it expect to. In 1641 the Chapter leased the rich manor of Eastry to the Dean and his son, Robert Bargrave, but by means of a trust exercised for them by a local gentleman, Bargrave paying the fine of £300.[236] One is reminded of the parable of the unjust steward.

Soon the Cathedral was deemed by parliamentarians to be 'delinquent', collectively and *tout court*.[237] Whether its delinquency derived from such particular acts as the sale of the altar furniture in aid of the royalist cause or was held to be simply inherent matters little. At St Mary Bredin in June of 1642, the royalist incumbent, John Marston, exhorted his people to lay their hands on their hearts, consult their Bibles, and see where they could find any warrant for taking up arms against their king. Many weighty parishioners were scandalized, and it was said that there was such animosity against those who took Marston's part 'that we can hardlye looke on[e] upon another in Charitie'.[238] The Cathedral itself was split. Dr Jackson played both ends against the middle and bathed his troubled conscience from the bottles in his study. It was his colleague Meric Casaubon who spread that smear, after his withdrawal to Oxford had stripped that doughty royalist and Anglican propagandist of the prudent moderation which had marked his last Canterbury sermon, preached in January 1644.[239]

In the summer of 1642, as England drifted inexorably into civil war, Kent found itself in an unenviable situation. Such was its strategic importance that the moderate royalism or neutralism to which it was disposed were unaffordable luxuries. Anti-episcopal root-and-branchism provoked a royalist backlash, the Kentish petition of March 1642, and this in its turn played into the hands of the parliamentary leadership in London and its need to secure what was at once a back door and a lifeline. A 'great meeting' held at Dean Bargrave's country house on 16 July rallied behind the royal Commission of Array, thus serving to align the Cathedral against the Parliament.[240] In the atmosphere of phony war

[234] Prynne, *Canterburies Doome* (cit. in n. 169), 393 ff.

[235] The only Chapter Acts surviving from between 1628 and 1670 date from Nov. 1639 and Dec. 1641 and relate to this matter: PRO, SP 28/210B, sequestration papers for Kent.

[236] Misc. Accts. 48, p. 93.

[237] Culmer's preferred term was 'malignant': 'the malignant disease, called the *Canterbury evill*'—'that malignant Cathedrall': *Cathedrall Newes* (cit. in n. 7), Epistle, 19.

[238] House of Lords, Main Papers, 27 June 1642.

[239] *The Razing of the Record. Or, An Order to Forbid Any Thanks-*

Giving For the Canterbury Newes Publisht by Richard Culmer (Oxford, 1644), 2, 4; *Culmers Crown Crackt With His Own Looking-Glass* (London, 1657); Meric Casaubon, *A King and his Subjects Unhappily Fallen Out, and Happily Reconciled. Being the Substance of a Sermon, with Very Little Alteration Fitted for the Present Time. Preached in the Sermon House, Canterbury Cathedral, 15 January 1643* (London, 1660).

[240] Alan Everitt, *The Community of Kent and the Great Rebellion 1640–1660* (Leicester, 1966), ch. 4, 'The Community Divides, 1640–2', 84–124; Clark, *English Provincial Society* (cit. in n. 3), 383–

still prevailing in August, Colonel Edwyn Sandys descended on the county with a small military force, commissioned to secure strong points and to disarm prominent recusants and other presumed delinquents.[241]

It was towards the end of the month that part of the raiding party reached Canterbury and forced their way into the Deanery in the middle of the night, surprising Mrs Bargrave and her son, newly returned from his historical studies with Vossius at Amsterdam.[242] Reports were inconsistent and probably unreliable. Either no weapons were found or three cart-loads. All agree on the seizure of a quantity of gunpowder, 'fourteen barrels . . . about the bignesse of a beer-barrel'. But whether this had been laid up intentionally, indeed hidden in the roof of the Deanery, which would have been provocative and foolish, or whether, with the weaponry, it constituted part of the regular county arsenal, which our Norwich tourist, himself an artillery man, had inspected in 1634,[243] is not clear.

The next day, some of the soldiers are reported to have entered the Cathedral, where they indulged in one of the more spontaneously expressive and violent acts of iconoclasm in the long history of the English Reformation. At the centre of the storm was the Laudian altar, which was overturned, its hated altar-rails smashed. (It is surprising that the rails were still there to provoke the troopers, since it was now nearly a year since the Commons had ordered their general removal. In most churches, altar-rails had gone by the end of 1641, much like domestic iron railings by 1941.) The arrases were attacked and numerous pot-shots taken at the image of Christ on the south gate. Sandys himself was laconic in his account of these exploits.[244] The soldiers 'made havock of all their popish reliques' and did 'their pleasure', almost as if the Cathedral had been raped. But Dr Paske, as subdean in charge in Dean Bargrave's absence, promptly sent an account of these outrages to the Earl of Holland, Chancellor of Cambridge University.[245]

Paske may have regretted his sense of duty and the verbal inventiveness with which he described how the soldiers 'Giant-like began a fight with God himselfe'. Not only was he summoned to explain himself before a parliamentary committee, and otherwise 'much troubled',[246] but also his narrative achieved a more than ephemeral fame, being incorporated in the Oxford newspaper *Mercurius Rusticus*, which, as royalist and Tory propaganda, became a hardy annual, several times reprinted.[247] What was forgotten, or perhaps

8. On 20 July Henry Oxinden (a strong parliamentarian) wrote: 'Mee thinks my Condition betwixt the Commission of Array and Ordinance of Parl: [the Militia Ordinance] is like his that is between Silla and Carybdis.' But he referred caustically to 'the Araymen' and speculated about 'what a blunder and ravage' Sandys and his little cavalry-force would make upon them. *The Oxinden Letters* (cit. in n. 206), 312.

[241] Everitt, *The Community of Kent* (cit. in n. 240), 107–16; Derek Hirst, 'The Defection of Sir Edward Dering, 1640–1641', *Hist. Jnl.*, 15 (1972), 193–208; Salt, 'The Origins of Sir Edward Dering's Attack on the Ecclesiastical Hierarchy' (cit. in n. 206).

[242] PRO, SP 16/424/88.

[243] *A Perfect Diurnall of the Severall Passages in Our Late Journey into Kent* (London, 1642), 9; *A True Relation of the Late Expedition into Kent* (London, 2 Sept. 1642), 3; *The Copy of a Letter Sent to an Honourable Lord by Doctor Paske, Subdeane of Canterbury* (London, 9 Sept. 1642), 4; 'A Relation of a Short Survey of the Western

Counties' (cit. in n. 153), 20. C. E. Woodruff discovered the following note in a chapter act of 10 June 1642 which I have been unable to trace: 'For carrying our powder from Vincents to the Church and paper to divide it in and packthred': manuscript annotation to p. 323 of Woodruff and Danks, *Memorials*, in Woodruff's own copy, Canterbury Cathedral Library.

[244] *A Perfect Diurnall* (cit. in n. 243), Dr J. S. Morrill tells me that he is sceptical about some of this evidence and suggests that what purports to be Sandys's account may have been forged.

[245] Thomas Paske to the Earl of Holland, 30 Aug. 1642, House of Lords, Main Papers, printed as *The Copy of a Letter* (cit. in n. 243).

[246] S. R. Gardiner, *History of the Great Civil War 1642–1645* (London, 1901), i. 12, n. 4; A. G. Matthews, *Walker Revised: Being a Revision of John Walker's Sufferings of the Clergy* (Oxford, 1948), 202.

[247] *Mercurius Rusticus, Or, The Countries Complaint of the Sac-*

never known, was that Paske wrote a second letter to Holland, after the troopers had returned to Canterbury from Dover. Sir Michael Livesey, who was nominally in charge at the time of the acts of iconoclasm, now came to apologize, explaining that his subordinates had been told to conduct themselves 'civilie in the church' and had exceeded their orders, Livesey himself had been 'readie to feint' when he saw their handiwork.[248] But Paske, a long-serving royal chaplain, was from now on a marked man. In January 1644 he told a Canterbury congregation 'that the people were departed from the King, that they must come as Benhadad's Servants did with halters about their necks'.[249]

As for Dean Bargrave, the soldiers having arrested him in an inn in Gravesend, he spent the next three weeks in the Fleet Prison, emerging to die a few months later. The notion that shortly before his demise Bargrave received the King in Canterbury at a restored altar service in the Cathedral is inconsistent with the known royal itinerary and indeed, in the circumstances of Kent in the first winter of the Civil War, inconceivable.[250] Thomas Jackson, noting the Dean's death, allowed himself this comment: 'God have mercye on his poore church Amen.'[251] Bargrave's successor, George Aglionby, was appointed by the King in his Oxford exile but died without seeing Canterbury. Aglionby was succeeded by the Dean of Rochester, Thomas Turner, who had to wait seventeen years before seeing it. Jackson's predictable concern amidst all this confusion was that the Dean's share of any income should be distributed among the prebendaries, most of whom were now living in London, only three being still resident.[252] By the end of 1643, no one could any longer pretend that it was still a matter of business as usual. Nevertheless, in what appears to be the same spirit with which Livesey had apologized to Paske, Parliament made an order protecting the persons of the prebendaries from any violent interference, and the fabric of 'the famous and magnificent Church of Canterbury', and especially its windows, from any private and unauthorized iconoclasm on the part of soldiers or townsmen.[253]

But that was only to preserve the Cathedral for the official iconoclasm which followed. In August 1643, a parliamentary ordinance, reminiscent of the Reformation statutes and injunctions of a hundred years before, called for the utter demolition and removal from churches, including cathedrals, of all 'monuments of superstition and idolatry', specifying altars and altar-rails, together with crucifixes, crosses, and images or pictures of the persons of the Trinity, or of the Virgin Mary, or of other saints.[254] It was with a commission issued

riledges, Prophanations and Plunderings, Committed By the Rebells on the Cathedrall Churches of this Kingdome (16 Dec. 1643), reprinted in *The English Revolution*, iii. *Newsbooks*, i, *Oxford Royalist* (London, 1971), 136–43. Later eds. (1646, 1685) attributed the outrages to 'sectaries' rather than to 'rebells'. Paske is repeated word for word in Peter Heylyn, *Aerius Redivivus* (London, 1672), 443. See also *A Whisper in the Eare, Or, A Discourse Between the Kings Majesty and the High Court of Parliament* (Oxford, 1642), which is equally dependent upon Paske. See Margaret Aston, *England's Iconoclasts*, i: *Laws Against Images* (Oxford, 1988), 71–4.

[248] Paske to the Earl of Holland, 1 Sept. 1642, House of Lords, Main Papers. I owe my knowledge of the originals of Paske's two letters to the kindness of Dr John Adamson.

[249] BL, MS Add. 14827, fo. 20ᵛ. Anthony Fletcher (*The Outbreak of the English Civil War* (cit. in n. 215), 319) dates Paske's sermon to Jan. 1642. However, the manuscript volume in which

a report of the sermon occurs is inscribed 'A Book of Parliament Business 1644–1645'.

[250] Woodruff and Danks, *Memorials*; Culmer, *Cathedrall Newes* (cit. in n. 7), 20. The royal visit in question occurred in Feb. 1642 (New Style), when Charles I accompanied Queen Henrietta Maria through Kent on her way to Holland, arousing much royalist enthusiasm: Everitt, *The Community of Kent* (cit. in n. 240), 94. Henry Oxinden wrote to Elizabeth Dallison: 'Upon Tuesday last the King went up to the top of Bel Harry steeple': *Oxinden Letters* (cit. in n. 240), 290.

[251] Misc. Accts. 52, p. 233.

[252] Ibid. pp. 233–4.

[253] Woodruff and Danks, *Memorials*, 326. Woodruff and Danks give no reference and I have been unable to trace their source.

[254] *Acts and Ordinances of the Interregnum 1642–1660*, ed. C. H. Firth and R. S. Rait (3 vols.; London, 1911), i. 265–6.

under this ordinance that the preacher Richard Culmer set about the 'more orderly and thorough reformation' of the Cathedral which he later announced to the world in *Cathedrall Newes from Canterbury*.[255] Culmer was the archetypal Puritan, one of the dubious ordinands of Bishop Dove of Peterborough and a muscular rather than intellectual Christian.[256] At Harbledown he campaigned against cricket, and at Minster in Thanet, the living with which Parliament rewarded him for his services, it was said that he called upon 'you that fear God', as if some in the parish feared God and some not, so setting all 'at difference'.

Culmer's narrative is justly famous, especially for its spirited description of his own exploits at the top of a 60-foot ladder as he wielded his pike against the window above the Martyrdom, 'the superstitious glory of that cathedral'. These acts of iconoclastic destruction were the most extensive ever carried out in the Cathedral. Culmer exaggerated the harm done to the stained glass (as anyone can now see), but he told no more than the sober truth of what happened to a variety of sculpted objects, which, as 'graven images', were, as always, the main target. Large gangs of workmen toiled strenuously to topple the archangel, with his great brazen cross, over the south door, and the figure of Christ on the south gate. In the cloister, crucifixes and mitred saints, including St Dunstan, were 'battered in pieces'.

Culmer subsequently became such a controversial figure in the public prints, lambasted from Oxford as 'Blue Dick of Thanet', and defended by his own son, that most accounts inflate his personal role in this legendary story, much as such things are otherwise attributed to 'Cromwell'. What Culmer dramatized and symbolized was not merely the anti-Laudian backlash, but the triumph of religiously inspired secularity, national and local. It was the Mayor of Canterbury who supplied the musketeers who protected the iconoclasts. Lay encroachment upon the Precincts, which, as we have seen, had begun long before the Civil War, was now nearly complete. It was not that the great gates swung on their hinges. They had been burnt.

The legal position of the Cathedral foundation as civil war led to an interregnum, and as the rule of king and parliament gave place to a commonwealth and then a protectorate, takes some sorting out, as indeed does the situation on the ground. Heylyn later wrote that Parliament, having begun by practising upon the Church by little and little, at the last played 'sweep stake' and took all.[257] But it was a long game. And the revolution was subject to much amelioration. Canterbury Cathedral, after all, still stands.

The skein of events, decisions, and non-decisions ravels (rather than unravels) from the root-and-branch petitioning and debating of 1640–1, in which the Kentish MP Sir Edward Dering, spurred on by the Canterbury preacher Thomas Wilson and other radicals, played such a centrally ambivalent role.[258] ('I have seen God in you,' wrote Wilson to Dering.[259])

[255] Culmer's title deserves to be quoted in full: *Cathedrall Newes from Canterbury: Shewing, The Canterburian Cathedrall To Bee in an Abbey-Like Corrupt and Rotten Condition, Which Cals For a Speedy Reformation or Dissolution* (London, 1644).

[256] Fincham, *Prelate as Pastor* (cit. in n. 9), 180–1. Most biographical information on Culmer is culled from his son Richard Culmer's defence of his father, *A Parish Looking-Glasse for Persecutors of Ministers* (London, 1657). On both 'Cromwell' and Culmer, see Aston, *England's Iconoclasts*, i (cit. in n. 247), 63–8, 84–92.

[257] Heylyn, *Aerius Redivivus* (cit. in n. 247), 431.

[258] Hirst, 'The Defection of Sir Edward Dering' (cit. in n. 241); Salt, 'The Origins of Sir Edward Dering's Attack on the Ecclesiastical Hierarchy' (cit. in n. 206).

[259] Thomas Wilson, *Davids Zeale for Zion* (London, 1641), Epistle.

The original London petition of 11 December 1640 spoke of the eradication of episcopacy, with 'all its dependencies, roots and branches', and there can be no doubt that these were meant to include cathedrals, deans, and chapters. When the committee appointed to deal with these matters reported to the Commons on 9 March 1641, the third of three points flagged for further consideration was 'the greatness of the revenues of deans and chapters, the little use of them, and the great inconveniences which come by them'. John Crew, who presented the report, offered reasons in support of the first two items, in favour of a drastic attenuation of diocesan episcopacy, but thought no argument was called for in respect of deans and chapters, 'because the matter was plain evident'.[260]

In the subsequent debate of 12 May 1641, which brought on to the stage representatives of friendly and unfriendly opinion in the ranks of the clergy and the universities, views were split between outright abolition, preservation, and moderate reforms designed to strengthen the cathedrals and cathedral cities as power-houses of a preaching ministry, and to associate deans and chapters more closely with a reformed diocesan government. Dean Bargrave headed up the defensive lobby, pleading that any foundations which might prove to have been delinquent and 'obnoxious' should be dealt with appropriately rather than attracting a general onslaught on the whole. 'This did spinne out a long debate.' Finally the House agreed, against opposition, to hear petitions on behalf of the cathedrals from Cambridge University and Canterbury, the Canterbury petition being said to have emanated from the 'officers of the Church'. The divines with whom Bargrave stood shoulder to shoulder on this occasion (Samuel Ward, Ralph Brownrigg, and John Hacket) were all anti-Laudian moderates, as indeed in many respects was Bargrave himself. Hacket's defence made many tactful concessions to hostile opinion, granting that preaching in cathedrals had been too much neglected. As for the learned men who composed the chapters, 'they are indeed somewhat better provided than other divines in the Reformed churches, but this is the honour of England'.[261] Later in the year, Bargrave launched a further petition, favouring the retention of traditional church-government. This was said to have caused 'a great uprore' at a Canterbury hostelry, some putting their hands to the petition, others refusing.[262] Within a year, cathedrals would have to manage without Dean Bargrave's politicking.

The only real question by now was whether the 'better uses' to which cathedral endowments were to be applied meant other religious or charitable uses or the general needs of the State. When, on 15 June 1641, the Commons resolved that deans and chapters were to be 'utterly abolished', it was also decided that their lands should be employed for the advancement of learning and piety, with a 'competent maintenance' assured to all personnel currently in post, unless they were deemed to be delinquent. But Parliament,

[260] *The Journal of Sir Simonds D'Ewes from the Beginning of the Long Parliament to the Opening of the Trial of the Earl of Strafford*, ed. Wallace Notestein (New Haven, Conn., 1923), 458–9; W. A. Shaw, *A History of the English Church During the Civil Wars and Under the Commonwealth 1640–1660* (2 vols.; London, 1900), i. 47–8.

[261] John Rushworth, *Historical Collections*, 2nd edn., iv (London, 1692), 269–73; BL, Harl. MS 163, fos. 165–7, and ibid.

477, fos. 59–61; *To the Right Honorable the Lords and Commons Assembled in the Parliament the Humble Petition of Divers of the Clergie of the Church of England Whereunto Is Added Five Motions With Reasons Concerning Deanes and Chapters* (London, 1641); Shaw, *History of the English Church* (cit. in n. 260), i. 58–60. I have been helped in my understanding of Bargrave's conduct on this occasion by Mr Peter Salt.

[262] *Oxinden Letters* (cit. in n. 206), 230, 232.

too, had many irons in the fire, and beyond these resolutions nothing was done.[263]

The summer of 1641 was the last occasion when it was possible to contemplate the luxury of devoting the entirety of cathedral wealth to 'good uses' in this sense. With the outbreak of the Civil War, there were to be more pressing calls upon these resources, as idealism was overtaken by necessity. In the early months of 1643, various parliamentary ordinances empowered the seizure of rents and other assets of delinquents, including some deans and chapters, while an ordinance of 27 March 1643 ordered the sequestration of the estates of fourteen named bishops and included in a general sequestration order all deans and chapters which had contributed to the royalist war-effort.[264] The ever-changing function of cathedrals had now become one of sustaining a Great Rebellion, although the ordinances also made provision for the preservation of sundry charitable uses. In the autumn of 1647, the Civil War being concluded, the restive and now politicized Army repeatedly proposed to Parliament that its arrears of pay should be met from the dean and chapter estates.[265] But it was not until eighteen months later, on 30 April 1649, three years beyond the extinction and expropriation of the bishops, that a parliamentary ordinance finally abolished deans and chapters, a full eight years after Parliament was first minded so to do.[266]

But in the condition of post-war financial stringency, anti-prelatical ideology was now more or less irrelevant, as were so-called 'better uses'. The cause given for dissolution was 'the necessity of raising a present supply of Moneys for the present safety of this Commonwealth'. Other statements included Ireland and the Navy among the cost areas which cathedral lands were capable of refreshing. Politics (the politics of the Army and of the City as well as of Parliament) now determined the fate of the cathedrals. The preference of the Army was that their own arrears of pay should be met from the dean and chapter lands directly. But in the event, Parliament determined that these arrears should be settled, less satisfactorily, from confiscated Crown lands, while the City demanded both the dean and chapter estates and the bishops' lands as security for loans to pay off the Scots and to finance the expedition to subjugate Ireland. Consequently, the financial community enjoyed the main advantage of the sales of dean and chapter lands, promising £300,000 to pay for Ireland on the surety of property worth considerably more. This was done by the device of 'doubling' loans already secured on the 'public faith', loans which could be converted into the purchase price for church lands, both episcopal and capitular. The ingenuity of this arrangement lay in persuading the State's creditors to commit further sums, equal to those already advanced, in order to enjoy tangible security in the form of land for both old and new investments, sold at well below the market rate. But the device was more ingenious than successful, and by the early 1650s it was hard to persuade the creditors to send good money after bad, so that the sale of other forms of confiscated property (Crown lands and fee farms) hung fire. Dean and chapter lands (the second type

[263] Rushworth, *Historical Collections* (cit. in n. 261), iv. 285; Shaw, *History of the English Church* (cit. in n. 260), i. 55, 90, 93–4, 99.

[264] *Acts and Ordinances* (cit. in n. 254), i. 60, 74–6, 79–80, 106–

17, 124–7, 669–74, 840–1.

[265] John Rushworth, *Historical Collections*, 3rd edn., vii (London, 1721), 820, 835, 837–8.

[266] *Acts and Ordinances* (cit. in n. 254), ii. 81–104.

of property to be disposed of) were put up for sale under an Act of 30 April 1649, and on terms which made them, initially at least, a bargain.[267]

Sir John Habakkuk estimates that the capitular estates yielded £455,621 from 'doubling' and a further £22,951 from sales. The bishops' lands, the first to be disposed of, had a sale value of £676,387 and sold briskly, although nothing like that sum was ever raised, still less the £1,700,000 which was estimated to be the market value of all dean and chapter lands, together with the impropriated rectories belonging to both chapters and bishops.[268] These 'spiritual' revenues were to be retained by Parliament and administered by those trustees for the maintenance of a preaching ministry and the encouragement of learning whom W. A. Shaw saw, with only mild anachronism, as a body of Church Commissioners, born before their time.[269]

At Canterbury, the consequences of both sequestration and confiscation were less drastic than might have been expected. Thomas Jackson noted that 'the Church was sequestered about thannunciation [25 March] 1644 (as Monins told me)'.[270] Captain Thomas Monins of Dover was appointed treasurer-general of the sequestered Cathedral estates of Canterbury, responsible under Parliament to the sequestration committees for Kent. In effect he took over from Jackson, who had recently acted as treasurer, conducting all Chapter business, in the absence of the Dean and virtually all the other prebendaries.[271] At the Restoration, Monins claimed to have been a crypto-royalist who had exercised his function in the interests of conservation.[272] Maybe so. But, as his accounts[273] make clear, all disbursements were made by order of the responsible committee which met from time to time in the Cathedral.

Jackson himself survived more than two years of sequestration, dying in November 1646. He was not himself delinquent nor sequestrated but continued to receive his full prebendal stipend (a negligible amount, of course, compared with what he was accustomed to), plus £1 a time for the weekly lecture which he continued to provide to the very last.[274] His widow went on living comfortably in the house which her husband had leased from the Chapter, and she outlived all her children.[275] Most of the Six Preachers were also *personae gratae*, including Jackson's son-in-law John Banks, Richard Clerke's editor Charles White, and the iconoclast Richard Culmer. Their stipends were still paid in the 1650s, after the abolition of deans and chapters, with substantial augmentations allowed to Jackson's

[267] H. J. Habakkuk, 'Public Finance and the Sale of Confiscated Property During the Interregnum', *Econ HR*, 2nd ser., 15 (1962–3), 70–88; Ian Gentles, 'The Sales of Crown Lands During the English Revolution', ibid. 16 (1973), 614–35; id., 'The Sales of Bishops' Lands in the English Revolution, 1646–1660', *EHR*, 95 (1980), 573–96; id. and W. J. Sheils, *Confiscation and Restoration: The Archbishopric Estates and the Civil War* (Borthwick Papers, 59; York, 1981). I have been helped with these technicalities by Mr Paul Gladwish and by his forthcoming article, 'The Sale of Confiscated Properties During the "English Revolution"'.

[268] Habakkuk, 'Public Finance' (cit. in n. 267); I. J. Gentles, 'The Debentures Market and Military Purchases of Crown Land, 1648–1660' (Ph. D. thesis, Univ. of London, 1969), 8.

[269] W. A. Shaw, *The Financial Administration of the Revenues of the Disendowed Church Under the Commonwealth* (London, 1893).

[270] Misc. Accts. 52, p. 234.

[271] Ibid. p. 235; Reg. 27, fo. 277, cited in Le Neve, *Fasti*, 1541–1857, iii. 13 n.

[272] Edward Hasted, *History of Kent*, xi (Canterbury, 1800), 349–50.

[273] Partly in MS Add. 80; and more extensively in an 18th-cent. transcript, in Bodl., MS Gough Kent 19, fos. 148–84.

[274] Misc. Accts. 52, pp. 234–6; MS Add. 80.

[275] C. E. Woodruff, 'The Parliamentary Survey of the Precincts of Canterbury Cathedral in the Time of the Commonwealth', *Arch. Cant.*, 49 (1937), 206–7; will of Elizabeth Jackson, 12 Jan. 157[/8] (proved 14 Mar. 1657(/8), PRO, PROB 11/275, fos. 342–344ᵛ.

successors, the regular preachers of the main Cathedral and Sermon House lectures.[276] There was consequently no lack of preaching and no need of the special parliamentary ordinances which in other places set aside substantial sums for the recruitment and reward of a preaching ministry.[277] A fifth portion of their husbands' stipends was paid to the widows or wives of deceased or absent prebendaries, even to the spouse of the distinctly malignant Meric Casaubon, who was also allowed enough firewood to keep her warm. The minor canons were paid their full stipends, the school was kept going, and the statutory £100 was paid to the poor. Money was found for the most urgent repairs to the Cathedral fabric and for keeping the weather out of the archbishop's palace. But all that surplus revenue which in the past had enriched Dr Jackson and his colleagues now paid for the army in the Kentish garrisons: £850 in one quarter alone.[278]

With 1649 came confiscation and sale. Professor Gentles, the authority on the dispersal of the bishops' lands, remarks that the dean and chapter lands 'await their historian'.[279] They are not going to find him in the final pages of this chapter. Many episcopal estates were bought up by the State's creditors and other prominent political and financial figures, not by the sitting tenants, even though the tenants had first option to buy.[280] Sir John Habakkuk and Mr Paul Gladwish can demonstrate, by contrast, that a significant proportion of capitular property (perhaps as much as a third) was acquired by the sitting tenants, whom other purchasers would have had to buy out, if they hoped to enjoy the immediate benefit of their acquisitions.[281] The estates having been surveyed in 1650,[282] Canterbury sales were not very brisk; while £600 of rent from property remaining unsold was reserved for pious and charitable uses. In 1657 the trustees administering unsold church land (presumably both episcopal and capitular) still accounted for nearly £5,000 received in Kent, and in 1658 the receiver of the revenues of Canterbury deanery was still being paid for his services. As late as 1659 the parliamentary committee to remove obstacles to the sale of church lands still had work to do.[283] On the other hand, urban tenements in Canterbury worth £1,209 5s. 3d. were disposed of without apparent difficulty.[284]

In 1651 Great Yarmouth applied to buy Norwich Cathedral in order to use it as a quarry for stone to build a new harbour. So far as is known, nobody put in a bid for the fabric of Canterbury Cathedral, which, like other cathedrals, remained the property of the State until the Restoration. In this respect, the history of this episode differed from that of the dissolution of the monasteries. There was a moment of danger in 1652, when a parliamentary committee selected Canterbury Cathedral for demolition, as a contribution to

[276] MS Add. 80, fos. 5–8; Shaw, *History of the English Church* (cit. in n. 260), ii. 533–4. The sources used by Shaw identify three Six Preachers not included in Ingram Hill's *Six Preachers* (cit. in n. 29). They are Nathaniel Ward, who succeeded Charles White in Nov. 1647, John Laurey, and John Lyne: ibid. 346, 533–4.

[277] *Acts and Ordinances of the Interregnum* (cit. in n. 254), i. 669–74, 840–1.

[278] MS Add. 80; Bodl., MS Gough Kent 19, fos. 148–84; PRO, SP 28/291; Hasted, *History of Kent* (cit. in n. 272), xi. 349–50.

[279] Gentles, 'The Sales of Bishops' Lands' (cit. in n. 267), 573. They have acquired that historian in the person of Mr Paul Gladwish, so far as concerns Bristol and the counties of Gloucestershire, Herefordshire, Shropshire, and Worcester-

shire, the subject of a forthcoming Cambridge doctoral thesis.

[280] Gentles, 'The Sales of Bishops' Lands' (cit. in n. 267), 573–96; id. and Sheils, *Confiscation and Restoration* (cit. in n. 267).

[281] Habakkuk, 'Public Finance' (cit. in n. 267), 205–7, 219, 221; Gladwish, 'The Sales of Confiscated Properties' (cit. in n. 267).

[282] Survey 22, Parliamentary Survey of 1650. Parts of the survey relating to property in the Precincts are printed by Woodruff, 'Parliamentary Survey' (cit. in n. 275).

[283] Woodruff, 'Parliamentary Survey' (cit. in n. 275), 215, 217; PRO, SP 28/289; Shaw, *Financial Administration* (cit. in n. 269), 18, 21.

[284] Shaw, *History of the English Church* (cit. in n. 260), ii. 555–6.

the extraordinary expenses of the First Dutch War. But this awkward corner was turned, thanks, thought S. R. Gardiner, to 'some relics of piety and good sense'.[285] Things could have been worse. It appears that the altar furniture was only pawned, not sold. Bishop Warner's font was safely hidden, and so, thanks to a loyal lay clerk called Abraham Goldsborough, was the communion plate.[286] It was said that another lay clerk, the vintner Robert Turner, had suffered persecution for his fidelity. His namesake, the Restoration Dean, said that that was probably true, in so far as the parliamentary soldiers had drunk his wine while not always remembering to pay for it.[287]

But that is to trivialize a wounding, cathartic chapter in the history of Canterbury, reminding the historian of Lucy Hutchinson's famous remark that each local community had the Civil War more or less within itself. The parliamentary regime, in the shape of Sir Anthony Weldon's county committee and its local henchmen in the government of the city, was narrowly based and lacking local legitimacy. Political sentiment, from the upper crust of established gentry families and their many connections with 'the cathedral men', down through the middle and lower strata and strands of Canterbury's social fabric, was overwhelmingly hostile. It is only a slight exaggeration to say that the street riots in Canterbury over the celebration of Christmas in 1647 provoked, by chain reaction, the Second Civil War. Certainly they amounted to a full-scale local insurrection, with the slogan 'For God, King Charles, and Kent!' The sequel was the slighting of Canterbury's walls and the burning of its gates, as Weldon took his revenge.[288]

At this point, with the gifted Independent preacher John Durant, sometime a soap-boiler and maker of 'washing balls', sometime naval chaplain, ministering to a gathered company of saints in the Sermon House ('you whom I hope Christ hath taken out of the world'[289]), we are as far away from the intention of a cathedral as it is possible to travel. How Durant's role in a small and exclusive congregation of no more than 100 related to his larger responsibilities as a Six Preacher, to his collegial relations with the other Six Preachers, and to the ministry of a community of Cathedral ministers still in some sense catering for the needs of a national Church, is another aspect of the interregnal situation which it is difficult to reconstruct or to comprehend as if from the inside. When Durant declared that 'the most are the worst, and the best are always the fewest', that was to repeat a commonplace which had been stated again and again from the Puritan wing of the Church, for at least fifty years. It was part of Prebendary Jackson's mental furniture, built in late Elizabethan Cambridge by William Perkins. But, to change the metaphor, this was unsuitable ground on which to erect an all-inclusive, national Church, such as a cathedral, above all objects, symbolized.[290] And now the sectarian implications of the commonplace were made explicit. Durant's 100 aspired to the rule of the saints but faced a longer-term future as a conventicle.[291]

[285] S. R. Gardiner, *History of the Commonwealth, 1649–1656* (4 vols.; London, 1903), ii. 187. I owe the reference to Norwich Cathedral to Dr John Morrill.

[286] Culmer, *Cathedrall Newes* (cit. in n. 7); Legg and Hope, *Inventories*, 268–9; Bodl., MS Tanner 33, fo. 261.

[287] Bodl., MS Tanner 123, fo. 92.

[288] Everitt, *The Community of Kent* (cit. in n. 240), 231–5.

[289] John Durant, *A Discovery of Glorious Love Or the Love of Christ to Beleevers Opened* (London, 1655), Epistle.

[290] *Protestantism and the National Church* ed. P. Lake and M. Dowling (London, 1987); Collinson, *Birthpangs of Protestant England* (cit. in n. 95); id., 'The English Conventicle', in *Studies in Church History*, xxiv; *Voluntary Religion*, ed. W. J. Sheils and D. Wood (Oxford, 1986), 223–59.

[291] Madeline V. Jones, 'The Divine Durant: A Seventeenth-Century Independent ', *Arch. Cant.*, 83 (1968), 193–203.

The way back for the Cathedral is a subject for the next chapter. However 'sad, forlorne and languishing' the condition of Christ Church may have been by 1660, 'more like a ruined Monastery than a Church',[292] the restored cash-flow, mainly secured from the accumulated entry-fines on repossessed property, enabled the restored Chapter to devote nearly £29,000 to public and corporate expenditure in the first ten years of the restored foundation: £7,921 of this on the fabric and furnishings alone.[293] Preaching in the Cathedral in 1663, Samuel Hinde exulted, as well he might, in 'the Churches Resurrection after a tedious Ilyad of affliction, her glorious Triumphs after her bloody Vespers'.[294] But it was full circle in other respects too. Soon Archbishop Sheldon would be warning: 'You cannot be ignorant with what an evil Eye some men look upon the possessions of the Church'; and how, in particular, deans and chapters were charged with 'having much and doing little good'.[295]

[292] J. C. Robertson, 'The Condition of Canterbury Cathedral at the Restoration in AD 1660', ibid. 10 (1876), 93–8.

[293] Ibid.; 'Laid out by us the Deane and Chapter of Christ Church Canterbury' (19 Nov. 1670), Bodl., MS Tanner 128, fo. 57.

[294] Samuel Hinde, *Englands Prospective-Glasse: A Sermon at a Metropolitical Visitation Held at the Cathedral Church of Christ in Canterbury, on the 29th of April 1663* (London, 1663).

[295] Archbishop Sheldon to Dean and Chapter, 29 July 1670, Bodl., MS Tanner 128, fos. 58^v–59.

V

Canterbury and the Ancien Régime: The Dean and Chapter, 1660–1828

JEREMY GREGORY

INTRODUCTION

The Cathedral, State, and Society

The aim of this chapter is to explore the nature and purpose of Canterbury Cathedral as an institution and as a community in the century and a half from the Restoration in 1660 to the outbreak of parliamentary legislation in the early nineteenth century that so drastically affected the Constitution and cathedral bodies. In the course of this exploration, some opportunity will be taken to examine the relationship of the Cathedral community with the city and diocese of Canterbury, as well as with the wider world beyond Kent. Wherever possible, Canterbury will be looked at within the general context of religious life in eighteenth-century England, so as to see what light a detailed and focused examination of the ideals and practice of one such institution can shed, not only on the function of cathedrals within society, but also on the nature and extent of the Church of England's involvement in the English *ancien régime*.

In one sense, of course, the Cathedral community at Canterbury was a society within a society, with its own rules, officials, customs, traditions, lands, and revenues. In this respect it exemplified the decentralized nature of administration in the Church of England in this period. But it was always more than a closed world. It was intimately connected to the locality through its ownership of land and its use of patronage, and, through the activities and careers of those of its members who were bound up in the world beyond the Precincts, it provided an important link between provincial and national society. And so often it was the demands and concerns of that outside world which shaped the underlying assumptions and constraints within which the community operated. This is, then, an attempt to reconstruct not only the activities of the community, but also the attitudes and mental framework in which its members lived.

I would like to thank Nigel Ramsay and Margaret Sparks for their help and advice in writing this chapter.

It is no exaggeration to say that the upheaval of the mid-seventeenth century, so vividly detailed by Professor Collinson in the previous chapter, was the main determinant in shaping the ideologies of Canterbury churchmen in this period. To a large extent, the memory of what had happened when the world was turned upside down[1] formed the habits of mind and fashioned the behaviour of Church of England clergy in the late seventeenth and eighteenth centuries. In Canterbury itself, the challenge to order and stability posed by religious and political radicals had had tangible expression in the damage inflicted on the interior of the Cathedral by parliamentary troops in 1642 and by Richard Culmer and his following in 1643. The soldiers were not so boisterous at Canterbury as they were at other cathedrals such as Winchester and Worcester, where they defecated in the font, or at Hereford, where they danced during morning service, but nevertheless they were not above using pieces of Cathedral decoration for target practice.[2] In 1660 William Cooke petitioned the recently reconstituted Chapter for a reward for his help in resisting Culmer when the latter was smashing the stained glass.[3] Religious life in the city was effectively transformed during the 1640s with the stabling of horses and weapons in the Cathedral by the 'intruders', the destruction of the archbishop's palace in the Precincts, the abolition of deans and chapters by Act of Parliament in 1649, the use of the office of Six Preacher to defend the Cromwellian regime, and in the general proscription of Anglican worship in the city and diocese. It had been the Puritan attack on Christmas Day services which had led to rioting and protests against the new order in Canterbury after Edward Aldey, the rector of St Andrew's, preached a sermon in defence of Anglican services in 1647. His stand was widely believed to have been instrumental in rallying support for Charles I in Kent during the second civil war in 1648.[4] Not surprisingly, Aldey was rewarded for his attempt to maintain Anglican orthodoxy by being made a prebendary of the Cathedral in 1660 (stall XI, 1660–73). And it was not only the prebendaries and Cathedral fabric and buildings that had suffered during the 1640s and 1650s. The officials, servants, and dependants of the Cathedral must all have been dismayed at the abolition of their community.

The memories of the Civil War, when the Church had been overthrown and cathedral bodies made redundant, became extraordinarily deep and fixed within Anglican consciousness and provided an important structural coherence to the world of thought and behaviour covered by this chapter. After 1660 the anti-Puritan reflex within the English Establishment was wide-ranging, and well into the early nineteenth century, clergy were plagued and terrified by the prospect of having another civil war on their hands. As long

[1] The phrase is a contemporary one. At the 1663 visitation, Samuel Hinde, the incumbent of St Mary's, Dover (1662–70), reminded his congregation in the Cathedral that 'it was not above a few years since ... the world turned upside down'. Samuel Hinde, *Englands Prospective-Glasse: A Sermon at a Metropolitical Visitation held at the Cathedral Church of Christ in Canterbury, on the 29th of April 1663* (London, 1663), 2.

[2] A. L. Rowse, *Reflections on the Puritan Revolution* (London, 1986), 26; W. H. Hunt, *The Puritan Moment* (Cambridge, Mass., 1983), 299, 300, 308; D. Underdown, *Revel, Riot and Rebellion: Popular Politics and Culture in England, 1603–1660* (Oxford, 1985), 139, 177–8.

[3] Petition 232.

[4] *Canterbury Christmas: or, a true relation of the Insurrection in Canterbury on Christmas Day last ... written by a Citizen there, to his friend in London* (London, 1648); *The Declaration of many thousands of the City of Canterbury, or County of Kent. Concerning the late tumult ... provokt by the Mayor's violent proceedings against those who desired to continue the celebration of the feast of Christs Nativity ... Together with their resolutions for the restitution of His Majestie to his crown and dignity* (London, 1647); Alan Everitt, *The Community of Kent and the Great Rebellion, 1640–1660* (Leicester, 1966), 230–40.

as the Civil War was remembered, any activity which seemed to smack of disorder would meet the same reaction—in case it might prove to be another outburst of religious fanaticism foreshadowing a revival of those Civil War horrors which had only just been contained. The clergy in Canterbury were well aware of the fragility of the restored regime. The city had long had a reputation for harbouring radical religion and politics. Canterbury had sheltered radicals who had been forward in petitioning for the King's death in 1649, and it remained a centre for dissent and subversion throughout the 1660s and 1670s.[5] The early Restoration Nonconformist plots against the political and religious establishment were not chimerical, at least not in the eyes of the restored clergy. In 1660, for example, the Cathedral Chapter encouraged servants to keep 'arms in the Church on the arrival of the King' in case of any trouble, and complaints were made in 1663 of fanatics with cudgels who 'frightened the countryside' in and around Canterbury.[6] Prebendary John Williams (stall II, 1692–6) was concerned enough by the radical tradition to write in 1694 *A True Representation of the Absurd and Mischievous Principles of the Sect Commonly known by the name of Muggletonians*, which aimed 'to give the world an instance of the power of Enthusiasm',[7] and as late as the mid-eighteenth century, George Horne, the future Dean of Canterbury (1781–90), knew of Ranters as well as anti-monarchist Presbyterians in the area.[8] This explains why clergy were always on the look-out for attributes of disorder, and it accounts for their hostility towards those they considered potentially subversive. Indeed, members of the Canterbury Chapter were among the leading analysts of the dreaded 'enthusiasm', a peculiarly religious disease leading to social anarchy, which could be diagnosed, depending on the situation, in all groups who seemed opposed to Anglicanism. One of the first large-scale treatments on this theme was written by Prebendary Meric Casaubon, whose *Treatise Concerning Enthusiasm* (1655) argued that this disease was not the work of the devil or divine inspiration but was the result of mental or physical illness, fraud or perversion, and led to social disorder. The analogy between Nonconformists and Catholics as showing symptoms of enthusiasm became a common theme in Anglican discourse after 1660; both groups could be portrayed as inimical to the Anglican position, and both were depicted, especially in the early years of the Restoration, as king-killers. The preoccupation of the age with the quest for universal values encouraged the belief that such disorder was a recurring disease, susceptible to the same diagnosis and requiring the same treatment. As Isaac Terry, the incumbent of St Andrew's, Canterbury (1736–45), observed in a sermon preached in the Cathedral, such behaviour would 'in all ages if a timely stop be not put to [it] produce like tragical effects as having a natural tendency to subvert government, and to introduce anarchy and confusion amongst mankind'.[9] In the 1780s George Horne could argue that 'heresies seem like comets to have periodical

[5] Underdown, *Revel, Riot and Rebellion* (cit. in n. 2), 231.

[6] Petition 231; *Cal. State Papers Domestic, 1663–4*, 177, W. Kingsley to Secretary Bennet, 20 June 1663. See also R. L. Greaves, *Deliver Us From Evil: The Radical Underground in Britain, 1660–1663* (Oxford, 1986).

[7] J. Williams, *A True Representation of the Absurd and Mischievous Principles of the Sect Commonly known by the name of Muggletonians* (London, 1694), pref.

[8] C. Hill, *Collected Essays* (3 vols.; Brighton, 1985–6), ii: *Religion and Politics in Seventeenth Century England* (1986), 108.

[9] Isaac Terry, *The Religious and Loyal Subject's Duty considered, with regard to the present Government and the Revolution. A Sermon Preached in the Cathedral Church of Canterbury, on Wednesday, January 30. 1722–3* (London, 1723), 2.

returns'.[10] This frame of mind allowed novelty to be reduced to manageable proportions and provided an instant remedy in conformity to the established regime. The very strength of this attitude was its flexibility: it imposed a curious order on the variety of the Church's opponents in this period. It was not, as some historians have suggested, because the Church establishment of the eighteenth century was irreligious that it found the outbreaks of religious enthusiasm so perturbing. Rather, it was because religious preoccupations were deemed to be central to social, political, and intellectual order, that any religious experience which threatened that order needed to be anaesthetized. This attitude and understanding of events to a great extent provides the key to the function of the late seventeenth- and eighteenth-century cathedral as perceived by the ecclesiastical and secular authorities. For in this light, the prime object of the cathedral at Canterbury and elsewhere was to be an instrument of religious, and thereby social and political, stability, by preaching orthodox Anglican doctrine and by supporting the forces of order within provincial society.

It is often argued that the eighteenth century saw the dawning of the modern age, but this obscures the powerful urge for tradition and continuity with the past which dominated clerical thinking in England. A recent analysis of the role and function of cathedrals within French society in this period has condemned them for being 'citadelles du passé',[11] an irrelevance in a world dominated by the ideals and values of the Enlightenment. But such criticism would be misplaced in the English context. It was their very connection with the past, their place in the Garden of Eden, before the Fall of the Civil War, which was often seen as an indication of the necessary role played by cathedrals within English society. After all, the purpose of the Restoration in 1660 had been to re-establish the world which seemed to have been lost, and there is no doubt that the activities of the cathedrals go some way to accounting for the relative stability of eighteenth-century provincial life. We are witnessing here one of those subtle shifts in the purpose and identity of Canterbury Cathedral's position within society. From being a leader of new ideas within Kentish society under Archbishop Cranmer in the 1540s, and being used by Archbishop Laud as a centre for militant clericalism in the 1630s, its purpose after 1660 had been transposed into a perceptibly different mode: to work for stability within society.[12] It is worth asking how far such changes in the purpose of the institution shaped and altered the nature and ethos of that institution. Perhaps the purpose of creating and sustaining the sinews of stability resulted in creating an institution that was itself stable and thus, in the eyes of its critics, liable to the charge of sterility.

The achievement of seeming permanence was no easy task: it was something which had to be worked for. It is tempting to see eighteenth-century Canterbury as a precursor of that cosy world so tellingly portrayed in Trollope's nostalgic Barchester novels (*The Warden* was first published in 1855): a bastion of complacent ecclesiastical privilege and domination, a clerical citadel set within an untroubled world. But we should do so only if

[10] Magdalen College, Oxford, MS 534, no. 119.

[11] B. Plongeron, *La Vie quotidienne du clergé français au XVIIIe siècle* (Paris, 1974), 113. Cf. O. Hufton, 'The French Church', in *Church and Society in Catholic Europe of the Eighteenth Century*, ed.

W. J. Callahan and D. Higgs (Cambridge, 1979), 20–1.

[12] P. Clark, *English Provincial Society from the Reformation to the Revolution: Religion, Politics and Society in Kent, 1500–1640* (Hassocks, 1977), 73, 187, 363–7.

we remember that the stability was being constantly challenged and threatened. George Horne, the late eighteenth-century Dean of Canterbury, saw the city as a centre of vice: 'Lord enable me to avoid the snares and dissipation of the place, and both by doctrine and example to sanctify thy name, and do all the good in my power, during my continuance in it.'[13] And if stability and tranquillity existed at all, it was in no small part the creation of those bewigged clergy who look down at us from their portraits in the Deanery. They prized order, form, and proportion on all fronts, not because of any easy complacency about the eventual triumph of sanity and decorum, but because they everywhere saw the forces of chaos and dark night threatening to overwhelm them. It was this ideological context which to some extent suggests a fundamental difference between the attitudes of eighteenth-century clergy and their counterparts in France, where, at least in pre-Revolutionary Angers, clergy were 'free from the inhibitions that fear engenders'.[14] English clergy were constantly aware of possible threats to their world.

THE RESTORATION IN CANTERBURY

As befitted its status as the metropolitical cathedral, and its proximity to Dover and the coast, Canterbury Cathedral played a major part in the festivities and heady celebrations of the summer of 1660. John Reading, who had been vicar of St Mary's, Dover, from 1616 until his sequestration in 1647, and who was to be appointed to a Canterbury stall in 1660 (stall VIII, 1660–7), was chosen to present Charles II with a Bible at his landing in England on 25 May. His eloquent oration expressed hopes for the restored regime, and stressed the relationship between political and religious order.[15] Charles's progress to London was accompanied by the ringing of church bells in the Kentish towns through which he passed, and in Deal, herbs were strewn in his path. The King spent his first night in England in Canterbury, staying in the former St Augustine's monastery, and he attended a service in the Cathedral on Sunday, 27 May 1660, before continuing his journey to the capital. Clarendon, who was part of the royal entourage, noted that the Cathedral was 'much dilapidated and out of repair, yet the people seemed glad to hear the common prayer again'.[16] But such royal honours paid to the Cathedral could not obscure the very real problems which confronted Canterbury in the early years of the Restoration, and the time and effort which it would take for the Cathedral to resume its position within local society.

The Restoration Chapter

The most obvious and immediate requirement before the Cathedral could recommence its activities was the election of new prebendaries to make up the statutory number, since

---

[13] CUL, Add. MS 8134/B/8, manuscript Notebook, fo. 106, 27 Aug. 1788.

[14] J. McManners, *French Ecclesiastical Society at the End of the Ancien Régime: A Study of Angers in the Eighteenth Century* (Manchester, 1960), 40.

[15] *A Speech made before the King's most Excellent Majesty Charles II, on the shore where he landed at Dover, by John Reading B. D. who presented his Majesty with a Bible, the Gift of the Inhabitants there, May 25th 1660* (n. p.).

[16] E. Hyde, Earl of Clarendon, *The History of the Rebellion and Civil Wars in England* (3 vols.; Oxford, 1819), iii, pt. 2. 1021.

ten had been lost during the Interregnum.[17] This was perhaps even more pressing at Canterbury than elsewhere, because a Chapter meeting was required before the *congé d'élire* could be issued for the appointment of a new archbishop. But the main concern was the need for a body of men to defend the restored regime. It was this task which dominated the activities of the Chapter during the 1660s and 1670s, and which seems to a large extent to have been the reason for the promotion of certain men to Cathedral stalls. Besides the Dean, Thomas Turner (appointed in 1643), only two prebendaries had survived to continue the Cathedral tradition: Thomas Paske (stall V, 1625–62) and Meric Casaubon (stall IX, 1628–71). Paske had been the senior prebendary resident in 1642 when parliamentary troops had first descended on the Cathedral.[18] Meric Casaubon was the son of another Canterbury prebendary, the international scholar Isaac (stall VIII, 1611–14). He was himself a scholar and churchman of some repute, publishing works on a variety of topics. Nothing more dramatically reveals the effect of the Civil War on Canterbury life than this crisis of personnel; in this respect at least, it seems that the Interregnum was far more calamitous to the life of the community than the Reformation had been, when there had been a large measure of a continuity between the monks and newly created prebendaries and other members of the Cathedral staff. Other posts within the community also needed to be filled at the Restoration. Only a few of the minor canons and lay clerks had survived, and although the Six Preachers had been maintained during the Interregnum, they were all replaced in 1660 in favour of clergy who had not been so closely involved with the Cromwellian government.[19]

Since Canterbury was near to London and the Court, the vacant places were filled by August 1660. Six of the new appointees had local links and ties, having been born in the diocese or having previously been incumbents of Kentish livings, and were thus familiar with the customs and precedents of the area: Edward Aldey, William Belke, Peter Gunning, Pierre du Moulin, Peter Hardres, and John Reading. The government may well have realized the value of using local men in its attempt to restore its institutions into the interstices of provincial life. Some of the new appointees at Canterbury, together with George Hall, the new Archdeacon (1660–8), had conformed to some extent to the Cromwellian regime, which suggests not only a shortage of surviving totally unblemished clergy, but also perhaps a desire to found the restored regime on as broad a base as possible. Not that conformity to the Cromwellian government necessarily meant that these clergy had compromised their Anglican principles. Some of them at least were noted for their efforts in keeping alive Anglican traditions even in the face of adversity, and many Anglican royalists may have had no real option but to stay in England during the Interregnum. While remaining in England, the royalist du Moulin had written *Regii Sanguinis Clamor ad Caelum* (1652, reprinted 1661), a counterblast to Milton's defence of Charles I's execution,

[17] Stephen Goffe, who had been presented to stall X in 1644, was still alive in 1660. But he had converted to Catholicism in 1652 and was deprived of his prebend in May 1660. For a detailed analysis of the process of restoration at Canterbury and Winchester, see I. M. Green, *The Re-Establishment of the Church of England 1660–1663* (Oxford, 1978), esp. chs. 3 and 5.

[18] He complained to Henry, Earl of Holland, of the treatment received by the Cathedral and members of his family at the hands of Col. Sandys's regiment. In the absence of the Dean, he had been ordered by the parliamentary commander, Sir Michael Livesey, to give up the keys. *The Copy of a Letter sent to an Honourable Lord, by Dr. Paske, Subdeane of Canterbury* (London, 1642).

[19] Reg. Z, fos. 206–7.

the title-page appropriately being printed in red. Meric Casaubon had been approached by Cromwell to write a history of the Civil War, which he had declined to do. John Reading had been a Calvinist in the diocese and had opposed the introduction of Arminian theology at Canterbury during the 1630s. But he had been imprisoned in the 1640s for his support of Charles I, and in 1650 at Folkestone he had attacked the right of unordained people to preach.[20] One future Canterbury prebendary who had been able to go into exile, John Bargrave (stall V, 1662–80), the nephew of the early seventeenth-century Dean Bargrave, spent the 1640s and 1650s travelling in the Low Countries, France, Germany, and Italy, acquiring a remarkable collection of curiosities, which he kept in his house in the Precincts. In 1662, after his installation at Canterbury, he was put in charge of the mission to ransom English captives at Algiers, for which purpose £10,000 had been raised by the bishops and clergy; with this money he claimed that he bought them one by one, like horses in Smithfield. The Dean and Chapter contributed financially to this and other programmes to support the government in the 1660s.[21]

The polemical nature of the problem for the restored regime in the 1660s and 1670s is apparent: those appointed to the Cathedral were men noted and known for their orthodoxy and their willingness to defend the Restoration in print. John Reading's pamphlet of 1660, *Christmass Revived: Or, an Answer to certain Objections made against the Observation of a Day in Memory of Our Saviour Christ His Birth*, had clear resonance in the Canterbury context. In this task, old sermons could be adapted to the new situation. Meric Casaubon had printed in 1660 a sermon which he had first preached in Canterbury Cathedral in 1643 concerning the need for harmony between the nation and the monarch.[22] Indeed, a distinctive feature of the Canterbury prebendaries in the first two decades after the Restoration was their rigid orthodoxy and their support of Charles II. The most satisfactory way of explaining their readiness to uphold the position of the government is not just in terms of mindless obedience, but of obedience bred out of what was perceived to be a necessary antidote to the horrors of the previous two decades. In this vein, John Aucher (stall VI, 1660–1701), who had already written a damning treatise against the Engagement that had required citizens to declare their allegiance to the Cromwellian regime, published *The Arraignment of Rebellion; or the Irresistability of Sovereign Powers Vindicated and Maintained* (1684). This was largely a reworking of his earlier work. Thomas Pierce (stall VII, 1660–91) was known, along with Henry Hammond and Peter Heylyn, as 'the chiefest champion of the old, regular and conformable clergy'.[23] He articulated the widely held belief that the traumas of the mid-century had been a divine judgement on the sins of the nation. He observed that it was 'more than twenty years, since His Rod has been speaking to us

[20] J. Reading, *The Ranter's Ranting, with the apprehending examinations and confession of John Collins* (London, 1650); *Anabaptism Routed: or a survey of the controverted points concerning 1. Infant Baptism 2. Pretended Necessity of Dipping 3. The Dangerous Practise of Rebaptising* (London, 1655).

[21] Lit. MS E. 16, fo. 60; Bodl., MS Tanner 48, fo. 15, Turner to Barwick, 27 June 1662; ibid., fo. 28, Turner to Barwick, 18 Aug. 1662. The Dean and Chapter gave £340 in total for this

purpose. They also gave £1,000 to the King in 1661 as part of the 'royal present'.

[22] M. Casaubon, *A King and his Subjects unhappily fallen out, and happily reconciled. Being the substance of a sermon, with very little alteration fitted for the present time. Preached in the Sermon House, Canterbury Cathedral, 15 January 1643* (London, 1660).

[23] A. Wood, *Athenae Oxonienses*, ed. P. Bliss (4 vols.; London, 1813–20), iv. 299.

in several Dialects of severity'.[24] For this group of clergy the execution of Charles I in 1649 had been the culmination of the nation's sins, and obedience to monarchy was a lesson it had to learn. In the 1680s, as part of the widespread 'Tory' reaction after the Exclusion crisis, Samuel Parker (stall II, 1672–85; Archdeacon of Canterbury, 1670–88) published a series of works arguing for 'unlimited submission' to monarchy.[25] Originally a Puritan, Parker claimed that the later Stuarts should exercise a Hobbesian sovereignty to crush Nonconformity and subversion.[26] Another prebendary who shared in the defence of the later Stuarts was James Jeffreys (stall IX, 1682–9), brother of the notorious judge.[27]

What is also noteworthy about this group of Restoration prebendaries is that some of them held important positions in the universities and in other areas of the Church and political life. Peter Gunning, for example, was an influential Master of St John's College, Cambridge, before relinquishing that and his Canterbury stall on his elevation to the bishopric of Chichester in 1670. He was largely responsible for fashioning St John's into a bastion of loyalty and orthodoxy, whose reputation as a breeding-ground for religious traditionalism remained well into the eighteenth century. Thomas Pierce was President of Magdalen College, Oxford, and Dean of Salisbury. He announced that his royal dispensation for non-residence 'came down from heaven'.[28] Edmund Castell (stall VIII, 1667–86), who had collaborated with Brian Walton on his *Biblia Sacra Polyglotta* (1657) and so could be seen as having maintained the traditions of learned scholarship during the Interregnum, was excused the duties of residence as prebendary at Canterbury because he was also Professor of Arabic at Cambridge.[29] To some extent this doubling of positions also reflects the shortage of men sufficiently learned and well-qualified to fill the leading positions in the Restored Church.

Restoring the Cathedral

The most obvious task facing the newly restored Chapter at Canterbury in the years immediately following the Restoration was the repair of the damaged buildings. The scale of the destruction inflicted upon the Cathedral fabric is revealed in an account of 1662 which indicates the extent of the physical damage:

we shall here recount and represent the sad, forlorne and languishing condition of our Church at our returne; which (in short) was such as made it look more like a ruined Monastery than a

[24] Thomas Pierce, 'The Embassy of the Rod and the Audience which it Requires', in *A Collection of Sermons upon several occasions* (Oxford, 1671), 146.
[25] S. Parker, *A Discourse of Ecclesiastical Politie: wherein the Authority of the Civil Magistrate over the Consciences of Subjects in matters of external Religion is asserted* (London, 1670); id., *An Account of the Government of the Christian Church, for the first Six Hundred Years* (London, 1683); id., *Religion and Loyalty; or, a demonstration of the Power of the Christian Church within it self. The Supremacy of Sovereign Powers over it. The Duty of Passive Obedience, or non resistance to all their commands* (London, 1684).
[26] Esp. in his *Discourse of Ecclesiastical Politie* (cit. in n. 25).
[27] Other works published by members of the Chapter on this

theme include Pierre du Moulin, *A Vindication of the sincerity of the Protestant Religion in the Point of Obedience to Sovereignes, opposed to the Doctrine of Rebellion, authorised and practised by the Pope and Jesuits* (London, 1664). See also id., *The Great Loyalty of the Papists* (London, 1673); Bodl., MS Tanner 282, fo. 97, du Moulin to Sancroft, n. d. (c.1668); R. Beddard, 'Of the Duty of Subjects: A Proposed 40th article of Religion', *Bodleian Library Record*, 10 (1978–82), 29.
[28] Thomas Pierce obtained a dispensation because he was President of Magdalen and then Dean of Salisbury. Bodl., MS Tanner 123, fos. 17, 40.
[29] For Castell's dispensation see *DNB*.

Church; so little had the fury of the late Reformers left remaining of it besides the bare walles and roofe, and these, partly through neglect, and partly by the daily assaultes and batteries of the disaffected so shaken, ruinated and defaced, as it was not more unserviceable in the way of a cathedral, then justly scandalous to all who delight to serve God in the beauty of holines. The windowes (famous both for strength and beauty) so generally battered and broken down, as it lay exposed to the injury of all weathers: the whole roofe, with that of the steeples, the Chapterhouse and Cloyster, extremely impaired and ruined, both in timber work and lead: the water-tables, pipes and much other of the lead in almost all places, cut off, and with the leaden cisterne of one of our Conduites, purloyned: the Quire stripped and robbed of her faire and goodly hangings, her Organ and Organ-loft: the Communion table, of the best and chiefest of her furniture and ornaments, with the raile before it, and the skreen of Tabernacle-worke, richly overlayd with gold, behind it ... and in fine, a goodly brave Cathedral become no better (in respect of those who gott and kept possession of it) than a Den of thieves and plunderers: and to make the better way for such invaders to abuse it, the Churches guardians, her faire and strong Gates, betimes turned off the hooks and burned.[30]

This inventory is revealing not only of the damage, but also of the habit of mind which attempted to recreate the 'beauty of holiness'. The physical repair of cathedrals and their refurbishment was a necessary, if expensive, aspect of the activities of the Restoration Church. And whilst the prebendaries at Canterbury were not faced with reconstruction on the scale of Lichfield and Lincoln, there was far more to do than at, say, York, where the damage was minor. As elsewhere, they had to spend much time and effort in bringing back order and dignity to the appearance of the Cathedral. Gradually, relics of the past were restored to place. Some items were returned, like the magnificent font which had been presented in the 1630s by John Warner (stall I, 1616–38, then Bishop of Rochester) and had been lovingly hidden away by William Somner, the Canterbury antiquary and auditor to the new Chapter.[31] The font was fully repaired and set in position by 1663, attracting appreciative comments from visitors to the Cathedral. The Chapter informed Warner that they wished to preserve it 'from the rude, unhallowed and sacrilegious hands and approaches of a sordid and malignant generation in these licentious times, whose meat and drink it is to invade, abuse and violate all that ever may adorn either the house or service of God'.[32] They were clearly aware of the ideological significance of their activities, recognizing that their re-creation of decency and order would not be effected without some opposition. Somner played a crucial role in the complex and often messy business of Restoration in Canterbury, especially since many records had been lost or misplaced during the Interregnum. He had precisely the intimate local knowledge which was required

[30] Quoted by J. C. Robertson, 'The Condition of Canterbury Cathedral at the Restoration in A. D. 1660', *Arch. Cant.*, 10 (1876), 95–6. Cf. C. E. Woodruff, 'The Parliamentary Survey of the Precincts of Canterbury Cathedral in the Time of the Commonwealth', ibid. 49 (1937), 195–222; Add. MS 80, account book of Thomas Monins, sequestrator 1644–9.

[31] Treasurer's Book, 1661–2, entry for 18 July, £1 paid to Dr Castillon 'for recovering the old seale'; Bodl., MS Tanner 123, fo. 57, 13 Dec. 1662.

[32] Quoted by C. E. Woodruff, 'Some Seventeenth Century

Letters and Petitions from the Muniments of the Dean and Chapter of Canterbury', *Arch. Cant.*, 42 (1930), 123, Dean and Chapter to Bishop Warner of Rochester, 5 Oct. 1663. The first person to be baptized in the restored font was Somner's daughter, Frances, on 16 Aug. 1663. Woodruff and Danks, *Memorials*, 321. See also *The Register Booke of Christninges, Marriages, and Burialls within the Precinct of the Cathedrall and Metropoliticall Church of Christe of Canterburie*, ed. R. Hovenden (London, 1878), 12.

in order to advise the new Chapter on precedents and traditions and to restore to the church its rightful estates and revenues.

There are frequent references to repairs in the records and correspondence of the early 1660s, and the Precincts must have been a scene of almost frenetic activity as builders, glaziers, plumbers, carpenters, ironsmiths, cleaners, and workmen were employed on both physical repairs and also the refurbishment of the Choir. Money was laid out on the purchase of rich hangings for the Choir, of communion plate, a lectern, linen, candles, and candlesticks.[33] Central to this activity was the Dean, Thomas Turner, who lavished time and attention on the problem. Turner brought down prayer-books from London and also arranged for cushions for the Choir to be delivered. He presented to the Cathedral a magnificent folio Bible, covered in silver. Spurred on by Turner, the Chapter had spent £5,248 on the fabric by 1662.[34] Archbishop Juxon gave money towards the repair of the gates to the Precincts.[35] So much had been achieved by 1665 that John Evelyn noted that the Cathedral was 'exceedingly well repaired since His Majesties returne'.[36] The success of the Restoration Chapter in securing respect and admiration for cathedral worship can be seen in a painting of the interior of the Cathedral, depicting the new panelling of 1676, and the new organ of 1663, co-existing with the surviving medieval stalls.[37] Such activity and expense was used as a justification by Cathedral clergy for the large sum in fines for leases that they received in this period. In reply to lay criticism that the restored clergy had received an inordinate sum of money at the Restoration, Pierre du Moulin stressed the amounts spent on repairs, claiming that without such fines the Cathedral would have been 'a heap of ruines'. He was quick to point out the relationship between the physical manifestation of the Church as an institution within society and its spiritual role:

And it is that ruin and another following upon it of a better Church than the material, which such men as the libeller aim at, when they cry out against fines and would have them converted to other uses. God keep the Church from such stewards; and enrich us with a better patrimony of the Church, than this temporal wealth, which brings little plenty and breeds much envy.[38]

The Dean and Chapter were also anxious for it to be known that they had been very generous in taking low fines and in treating tenants favourably. Clarendon's account of the attitudes of clergy in the early years of the Restoration highlights what he felt to be the understandable bitterness expressed by cathedral dignitaries. He claimed that 'they made haste to enter upon their own' and that in the treatment of their tenants they showed

---

[33] Treasurer's Books, 1660–1, 1661–2, 1662–3, 1663–4, 1669–70. For some of Turner's gifts to the Cathedral, see P. du Moulin, *A Sermon Preached in the Metropolitical Church of Canterbury, October 17. MDCLXXII, at the Funeral of the Very Revd. Thomas Turner, D. D.* (London, 1672), 23.

[34] Bodl., MS Tanner 123, fo. 57, 13 Dec. 1662.

[35] *Mercurius Publicus*, no. 23 (5–12 June 1662), 358–60.

[36] *The Diary of John Evelyn*, ed. E. S. de Beer (6 vols.; Oxford, 1955), iii. 395, 6 Jan. 1665. For evidence of a similar restoration at Salisbury, see R. Beddard, 'Cathedral Furnishings of the Restoration Period: A Salisbury Inventory of 1685', *Wilts.*

Archaeol. and Natural History Mag., 66 (1971), 147–55.

[37] For the new wainscoting, see Fabric 50, nos. 4–6; *Canterbury Cathedral, Choir Viewed from the West, c.*1680, anon., in possession of the Dean and Chapter.

[38] Pierre du Moulin, *A Letter to a Person of Quality, Concerning the Fines Received by the Church at its Restoration, By a Prebendary of the Church of Canterbury* (London, 1668), 5; and Bodl., MS Tanner 45, fos. 159–60, du Moulin to Sheldon, 1668. It may be that over £17,000 had been received in fines by Nov. 1661. But this was clearly an anomaly. By 1663–4, fines were only £1,121: see Green, *Re-Establishment of the Church* (cit. in n. 17), 105.

'more passion than justice'.[39] However, the Canterbury Chapter was willing to take into account the 'suffering' of its tenants during the Civil War when setting fines. Some tenants sought to excuse their purchase of Church land during the Interregnum. The Earl of Winchilsea, writing on behalf of Richard Nevett, a former lessee, explained that Nevett's purchase was 'rather from necessity than choice; and yet is it the only support he hath, for himself, his wife and diverse small children'.[40] Another former tenant claimed that he had been 'forced to kiss the Rod' to preserve himself and his family.[41] Some tenants of smaller properties were let off their fines altogether. This was usually because the tenant had 'suffered' for the royalist cause. Other reasons instanced are a reminder that Church property was used as a way of supporting the friends, families, and dependants of the Church hierarchy. The abatements to Chapter tenantry during the 1660s amounted to several thousand pounds.[42]

Other forms of charity during the series of disastrous harvests in the early 1660s included giving the city corporation a 'considerable sum of money by way of stock', so that corn could be 'bought in and provided for at reasonable rates, for the supply of the necessity of the poor'.[43] The Chapter also obeyed royal policy by augmenting the salaries of vicarages in its patronage and by raising the salaries of lower members of the community. All in all, the Chapter was said to have spent or forgone £28,933 by 1670.[44]

THE PERSONNEL OF THE DEAN AND CHAPTER: 1660–1828

Social Origins

The Dean and Chapter formed an important part of the religious life of the city and diocese, providing a clerical élite which stood apart from, and yet was not divorced from, the parish clergy. The stalls were highly prized for their prestige and the financial benefit which they conferred upon their holders: in 1698 the ambitious Jonathan Swift attempted to secure a Canterbury stall. On the whole, Canterbury clergy were a distinguished body during the eighteenth century, since those making appointments drew on a national network of patronage and recruitment; it is somewhat misleading to suggest, as later critics of the eighteenth-century Church have done, that cathedral posts were the pickings for the younger sons of the aristocracy and gentry. Certainly, clerical apologists may have exaggerated the degree to which the Church remained open to all groups within society and thereby acted as an agent of social cohesion, but it is clear from the social origins of the Canterbury Chapter that high birth was not necessary for promotion. The Church could be a catalyst of social mobility, its hierarchical structures providing a ladder of preferment. If a pattern emerges, it seems that Canterbury prebendaries were increasingly

[39] *The Life of Edward, Earl of Clarendon Containing I. An Account of the Chancellor's life . . . to the Restoration in 1660 II. Continuation of the History of England, Written by himself* (Oxford, 1759), 98–9.

[40] Canterbury Letters, i, no. 87.

[41] Ibid., no. 95. Such charity was especially necessary in the early Restoration period. W. G. Hoskins shows that the harvests of 1660 and 1661 were bad: 'Harvest Fluctuations and English

Economic History, 1620–1759', *Agricultural History Rev.*, 16 (1968), 16.

[42] Bodl., MS Tanner 123, fo. 57.

[43] *Mercurius Publicus*, no. 23 (5–12 June 1662), 358–60; no. 13 (27 Mar.–3 Apr. 1662), 207–8.

[44] Bodl., MS Tanner 123, fo. 68, Turner to Sheldon, 22 Nov. 1670; MS Tanner 128, fo. 57, Sheldon to Turner, 29 July 1670.

drawn from a clerical background, indicating a growing tradition of family clerical service and the creation of clerical dynasties in the period after 1660. As at Lincoln, the sons of the clergy were more likely to achieve high office within the Church than were the sons of any other social group.[45] Even some of those members of the Chapter with aristocratic connections can be placed within this category. William Nelson (stall V, 1803–35), who was the brother of Admiral Nelson and succeeded to the title of Earl Nelson of the Nile, was the son of a Norfolk cleric.

Such a pattern of recruitment is indicative of the ways in which the Church of England clergy were a professional group in this period, set apart by their education, interests, and status. To a great extent, the Cathedral clergy at Canterbury represented a highly clericalized society. Being taught at school by clergy, attending universities where they were educated by clerical dons, mixing with clerical friends, and defending clerical interest—all these were ways in which the clergy were able to retain some form of independence in the world after 1660, helping to foster a spirit of professional loyalty which could override differences in wealth and status. With such a background of common interests, it is not surprising that the Church of England clergy shared a common outlook, marking them off from their French counterparts, whose social divisions became increasingly pronounced throughout the eighteenth century.[46] A crucial way in which this sense of professionalization could be imbued was through marriage connections. Prebendaries married into the families of diocesan clergy, as well as into each other's families, encouraging the clergy to see themselves as a cohesive group within society.

Patronage and Politics

Patronage was a crucial factor in determining the nature of the Cathedral body. The deanery and nine out of twelve prebends were in the gift of the Crown, while the remaining three prebends (stalls I, IV, and VI) and the Six Preacherships were part of the archbishop's patronage. Archbishop Laud had attempted to use his Cathedral patronage and his influence over that of the Crown to build up a clerical following within his Cathedral city in the 1630s,[47] and archbishops after the Restoration were likewise able to use their patronage to help build up a body of support within the Cathedral community. Members of the Chapter provided a crucial link between the community, the city, and the archbishop. It has often been assumed that the archbishops had very little contact or involvement with the concerns of the Cathedral and the diocese, living as they did in Lambeth. But through correspondence and contacts with the Cathedral they were able to retain a surprising amount of involvement with the religious and political concerns of the region. Certain members of the Cathedral community could supply archbishops with much-needed information and local knowledge. While the large number of local men appointed during the

---

[45] For Swift's petition, see D. Nokes, *Jonathan Swift: A Hypocrite Reversed* (Oxford, 1985), 34; J. H. Pruett, 'Career Patterns Among the Clergy of Lincoln Cathedral, 1660–1750', *Church History*, 44 (1975), 208. On the clerical profession in this period, see id., *The Parish Clergy Under the Later Stuarts: The Leicestershire Experience* (Urbana, Ill., and London, 1978); G. S. Holmes, *Augustan England: Professions, State and Society, 1680–1730* (London,

1982); D. McClatchey, *Oxfordshire Clergy, 1777–1869: A Study of the Established Church and of the Role of Its Clergy in Local Society* (Oxford, 1960); A. Warne, *Church and Society in Eighteenth-Century Devon* (Newton Abbot, 1969).

[46] *Church, State and Society Under the Bourbon Kings of France*, ed. R. M. Golden (Kansas, 1982), 1.

[47] Clark, *English Provincial Society* (cit. in n. 12), 362–4.

Restoration period was not maintained, there remained a strong connection between the Cathedral, the city, and the county. Julius Deedes (stall IX, 1738–52), for example, the son of a local physician, had been born and educated in Kent, and in 1713 Thomas Brett (unsuccessfully) stressed his Kentish connections as a reason for preferment.

Mr Netterville has encouraged me to acquaint your Lordship with the highest preferment I desire, which is a prebend of Canterbury. Though I cannot plead any desert which will entitle me to such a favour, but a fair plea for it is, that from the foundation of the Dean and Chapter to this day either the Dean or some of the prebendaries have always been natives of Kent. Dr Belk, the last prebendary that died, was also the last Kentish man of the society, and Dr Higden succeeded him; so that there is not at this day one man on that foundation who was born in this county, which never happened before since the Reformation. I acknowledge this cannot give me or any native of Kent a right to a prebend, but if it be allowed that there has been such a custom, and that you are willing to continue it, the gentlemen of the county in general must think themselves obliged by the favour.[48]

In its connections with the locality, the community retained something of its medieval ideal as a centre of advice to the archbishops. Although this was rarely demonstrated on an institutional level, certain archbishops relied on this kind of support. Archbishop Sancroft received almost weekly reports from George Thorp (stall V, 1680–1719), who was something of a patronage broker for him, acting as an intermediary between the parish clergy and Lambeth.[49] Archbishops might also use the patronage in their control to promote outstanding clergy to the Cathedral. In 1684, for example, Sancroft promoted William Beveridge (stall VI, 1684–1704), who was noted for his scholarship and devotional writings and was regarded as one of the most distinguished luminaries of the late seventeenth-century Church. Archbishops at Canterbury, as at York, might also use the patronage at their disposal to reward or promote members of their own families or dependants. A fair proportion of clergy promoted to the first, fourth, and sixth stalls were related in some way or other to an archbishop: Tenison, Wake, Potter, Secker, Moore, and Manners Sutton all promoted relations or former chaplains to Canterbury stalls. John Potter was presented to a Canterbury stall in 1745, later becoming Dean. The Archbishop did not approve of his son's marriage to a domestic servant and disinherited him, having provided for him in the Church. Archbishop Moore collated both his sons, Robert and George, to Canterbury stalls. To critics of the Church it was precisely this kind of activity which was the clearest testimony of the corrupt nature of the institution at the highest level, and early nineteenth-century pamphleteers attacked Archbishops Moore and Manners Sutton on these grounds.[50] But in the eighteenth century it was part of a patron's duties to reward his dependants. And it was a constant complaint of archbishops that they did not have enough patronage to satisfy all the legitimate claimants. Archbishop Secker explained to one such petitioner in 1758 that

no one thing hath fallen in my gift hitherto; and though probably in time several may, yet my relations, chaplains, dependents, friends and acquaintances, the number of which put together

[48] HMC, *MSS of Duke of Portland*, v (1899), 377, Brett to the Earl of Oxford, 31 Dec. 1713.

[49] Bodl., MSS Tanner 33 and 123, *passim*.

[50] J. Wade, *The Black Book; or, Corruption Unmasked!* (London, 1820), 286.

hath risen to a very large one in the many years that I have been a Bishop and no Patron, will think, and some of them with very good reason, that they have a title to more preferment from me than I may ever live to bestow.[51]

It does not seem that these prebendaries were any less assiduous in their duties than other members of the Chapter. Hugh Percy, for example, had received much preferment after marrying Archbishop Manners Sutton's daughter, becoming a prebendary in 1816 (stall II) and Dean in 1825. It was during his term of office that the Chapter embarked on a vigorous programme of repair.

Because so much of the Cathedral's patronage lay in the hands of the Crown, the community was a stronghold of Establishment ideology. One of the most likely career-patterns before becoming a prebendary was to have been a royal chaplain, thereby gaining monarchical favour. During the politically sensitive decades following the Revolution of 1688–9, the Cathedral became a centre of support for the new regime: Dean Tillotson was promoted to the archbishopric of Canterbury (stall II, 1670–2; Dean of Canterbury, 1672–89; Archbishop of Canterbury, 1691–4), and one of the Chapter, Edward Stillingfleet (stall XII, 1669–89), became Bishop of Worcester. But clearly the wider political tensions can be seen in the differing views held within the Chapter. William Beveridge (stall IV, 1684–1704) was nominated to the see of Bath and Wells but refused it because it had become vacant by the deprivation of the nonjuror Thomas Ken. In this politically charged atmosphere, the Cathedral pulpit became the scene for a number of set-piece battles where the various merits and grievances associated with the post-Revolutionary settlement were aired. One participant was William Cade, the rector of Brook and a minor canon who had married Laud's niece and whose admiration for that archbishop led him to call his son Laud. In 1689 he preached a controversial sermon attacking the legality of the new regime and defending the behaviour of the nonjurors who had declined to take the oaths of obedience to William and Mary.[52] He later complained of the rough treatment he received after this sermon. During 1690, government proclamations were issued in the Cathedral, bells were rung in honour of the new King, and a thanksgiving service was held on William's return from Ireland.[53] Some of the clergy who had been brought up to believe in obedience and loyalty were more readily able to accept the new political situation because of the stability provided by Queen Mary as a focus of Anglican loyalty. Her proven devotion to Anglican ceremonies during her time at The Hague made it possible to believe that Church of England principles were not at stake. In 1691, during William's absence, Mary promoted George Hooper, her former chaplain at The Hague, to the deanery (Dean, 1691–1704). Perhaps at Hooper's invitation, she visited the Cathedral in 1694 and presented silver and purple hangings for the altar, throne, and pulpit, and demonstrated her loyalty and commitment to Anglican worship.[54]

Again, in the potentially problematic years after 1714 the Cathedral was a bastion of

[51] LPL, MS Secker 2, fo. 10, Secker to Kennicott, 8 Nov. 1758.
[52] BL, Harl. MS 3790, fos. 169–72, 'The Case of a Sermon Preach't at Xst Ch. Cant. 9 March 1689'.
[53] Treasurer's Book, 1689–90: entries for 6 Mar., 16 Aug., 19 Oct.

[54] G. S[mith], *Chronological History of Canterbury Cathedral* (Canterbury, 1883), 330; J. Battely, *A Sermon Preach'd before the Queen in Christ's-Church, Canterbury; May vi. 1694* (London, 1694); W. M. Marshall, *George Hooper, 1640–1727: Bishop of Bath and Wells* (Milborne Port, Sherborne, 1976), 55.

support for the Hanoverian succession. George I was entertained at the Deanery in 1717 on his way to the Continent,[55] and members of the Chapter were used to keep an eye on politically suspect Tory parochial clergy. Some clergy received their prebendal preferment for their activity in government service. William Ayerst (stall III, 1724–65), for example, had been secretary and chaplain to the embassy in Holland in 1714 and in France in 1720. John Robinson (stall II, 1697–1710), who became Bishop of London in 1714, was for many years chaplain to the embassy in Sweden, securing alliance between England and Sweden in 1692 and negotiating the Treaty of Utrecht in 1713. He was also the last ecclesiastic to be promoted to high political office, being appointed Lord Privy Seal in 1711. One erstwhile nonjuror, William Higden, was promoted to Canterbury (stall III, 1713–15) because he had later conformed to the new regime and written in its support. It is not then surprising to find that members of the Chapter were quick to use the pulpit as a means of defending the Hanoverian regime, interpreting the succession as saving the nation from Popery and arbitrary government.

What is clear is that the support that members of the Chapter gave to the Whig government did not imply any lessening of their commitment to Anglican principles, and a large number of those who can be considered High Churchmen took the oaths and accommodated themselves to the new situation.[56] It was neither unusual nor inconsistent to be both a Whig and a High Churchman.[57] The Church of England was safe in Whig hands; after all, the alliance was cemented not by the arch-latitudinarian Benjamin Hoadly but by that stickler for church traditions, Edmund Gibson. In part this may explain the Tory Thomas Gooch's decision to become part of the Establishment, for which he was rewarded with a Canterbury prebend[58] (stall IX, 1730–8). Nevertheless, throughout the period, anxieties were expressed if the church seemed to be in danger, resulting in some opposition to Whig policies. In the 1754 general election, for example, there was quite a furore in Canterbury in the aftermath of the attempts of the previous year to put through Parliament a bill naturalizing Jews. This attempt was widely perceived as an attack on the essential Christian underpinning of the nation, and the Church interest in the city was able to mount a vociferous attack on the MP Matthew Robinson Morris.[59]

Sermons preached in the Cathedral during the eighteenth century, especially on fast-days, in times of national danger, or at thanksgivings for victories, stressed the ways in which political events could be interpreted and analysed as evidence of the workings of God's providence and intervention within the world. The Restoration itself had been explained in this way, and the defeat of the Jacobite rebellions was seen in similar terms. Situated near the south coast, Canterbury was always considered liable to foreign invasion, and, not surprisingly, members of the Cathedral community were alive to the dangers of

[55] Christ Church, Oxford, MS Wake 7, fo. 182, Green to Wake, 17 Jan. 1716/17; E. Sydall, *The Insupportable Yoke of Popery, and the Wickedness of bringing it again upon these Kingdoms, after so many Deliverances from it; Consider'd and Apply'd with regard to the Present Rebellion: In a Sermon Preach'd at the Cathedral-Church of Canterbury on Saturday, Nov. 5. 1715* (London, 1715).

[56] This point was recognized by Christopher Wordsworth in *Social Life at the English Universities in the Eighteenth Century* (Cambridge, 1874), 80.

[57] Despite the recent assertion that High Churchmen were opposed to the Whig regime by Linda Colley in *In Defiance of Oligarchy: The Tory Party 1714–60* (Cambridge, 1982), 107.

[58] C. N. L. Brooke, J. M. Horn, and N. L. Ramsay, 'A Canon's Residence in the Eighteenth Century: The Case of Thomas Gooch', *JEH*, 39 (1988), 546–7.

[59] T. W. Perry, *Public Opinion, Propaganda and Politics in Eighteenth-Century England: A Study of the Jew Bill of 1753* (Cambridge, Mass., 1962), 169.

their position. For them the wars of the eighteenth century could be considered as 'wars of religion'. During the tensions of the Jacobite scare of 1744–5, Samuel Lisle (stall VII and Archdeacon of Canterbury, 1728–44) saw the last 150 years of English history as evidence that God would intervene on the side of the government if the nation repented of its sins.[60] The Chapter gave £200 to help fight the rebellion 'for Defense of His Majesty's Person and Government'.[61] The perceived connection between divine providence and politics was a useful way in which clergy could explain England's success or failure and impress the importance of religious behaviour on their congregations. In 1780 James Cornwallis (Dean, 1775–81) accounted for the set-backs Britain was facing in the war in America in terms of God's providence: divine displeasure was a consequence of the neglect of public devotions.[62] The world-view displayed in such sermons preached in the Cathedral suggests that the logical implications of Newtonian science, that God will not intervene in His creation, could be tempered by religious ideology.

The Church and the World of Learning

The members of the Chapter in this period were a learned body, closely allied to the universities. During the years immediately following the Restoration, many of the prebendaries had been educated at Oxford—a choice which reflected the perception of Oxford as the centre of political loyalty and religious orthodoxy. Indeed, it became almost a policy of Restoration churchmen to turn their attention to the more politically suspect Cambridge, notorious for being a breeding-ground of Puritans, in an attempt to win it over to the restored regime.[63] The activities of clergy such as Peter Gunning at St John's, and later the appointment of the Cambridge-educated William Sancroft to the archbishopric of Canterbury in 1678, helped to remove the stigma of dissent at Cambridge, and both universities during the eighteenth century can be seen as operating as clerical seminaries, producing men trained and prepared to defend the Anglican order. Taking the period as a whole, Cambridge became marginally the more likely university for Canterbury prebendaries to have attended. In part this reflected the intimate connections which existed between Corpus Christi College, Cambridge, and the Cathedral school, through the scholarships founded by Archbishop Parker in the sixteenth century. Several members of the Canterbury Chapter, such as Leopold Finch (stall XII, 1689–1702), Julius Deedes (stall XI, 1739–52), and John Lynch (stall IV, 1728–34; Dean, 1734–60) had themselves attended the King's School. This close connection had much to do with the perceived role of the Cathedral school in this period, as defender of the Church and the Christian religion. David Jones, the headmaster in the early eighteenth century, saw his school as 'a perpetual

---

[60] S. Lisle, *A Sermon Preached before the House of Lords, in the Abbey-Church, Westminster, on Wednesday, April 14, being the Day appointed by His Majesty's Royal Proclamation for a General Fast, on the Occasion of the Present War* (London, 1744), 19–20. For the invasion scare, see *The Letters of Spencer Cowper, Dean of Durham, 1746–74*, ed. E. Hughes (Surtees Soc., 165; 1956), 39.

[61] Chapter Act Book, 1727–45, fo. 224, 26 Oct. 1745.

[62] James Cornwallis, *A Sermon Preached in the Cathedral and Metropolitical Church of Christ, Canterbury, On Friday, February 4, 1780. Being The Day appointed to be observed as a day of General Fasting and Humiliation* (Canterbury, 1780).

[63] J. Gascoigne, 'Politics, Patronage and Newtonianism: The Cambridge Example', *Hist. Jnl.*, 27 (1984), 3.

nursery to the Church'.[64] The connection between the King's School and Cambridge was strengthened when George Thorp (stall V, 1680–1719) bequeathed money for scholarships to the university, with the stipulation that preference be given to the sons of orthodox clergy of the diocese of Canterbury. In 1728 Dean Stanhope also left money for an exhibition from the school to the university. Both Thomas Green, who was Master of Corpus, and Elias Sydall, who was a Fellow of the college, were promoted to Canterbury stalls by their old college friend Archbishop Tenison. This link with Corpus matches the eighteenth-century connection of other cathedrals with particular schools and colleges.[65] In the eighteenth century, Corpus Christi College was the home of clerical antiquarian learning.[66] But this went further than mere antiquarianism. For eighteenth-century clergy, such knowledge held positive value for understanding the present realities in which they and their contemporaries lived.

Most of the Canterbury prebendaries held higher degrees, but this is not necessarily a reliable guide to their learning. A better indicator of commitment to scholarship is the number of their publications. The great majority of prebendaries published something: most commonly sermons or religious tracts, but sometimes works of a more substantial nature. George Stanhope delivered the prestigious Boyle Lectures in 1701 to an admiring London audience which included John Evelyn, and members of the Canterbury Chapter were frequently invited to preach at Court, before Parliament, and to the annual meetings of the Society for the Propagation of the Gospel in Foreign Parts. It was an important function of the Cathedral to be a focus for learning and to participate in the religious and theological controversies of the day. As Pusey noted in his defence of the cathedrals in 1833, the Chapter at Canterbury in the late seventeenth and eighteenth centuries had provided a home and a base for a number of influential writers. He picked out Parker, Castell, Stillingfleet, Beveridge, Tenison, and Mill as instances of Cathedral clergy who appeared on the national stage. This was part of the Cathedral's role in linking local and provincial culture to national concerns. At the Restoration, Meric Casaubon suggested that a series of high-powered lectures should be delivered in the Cathedral for the benefit of country clergymen.[67] Indeed, it may have been one of the most significant contributions of eighteenth-century prebendaries to the achievement of stability, that they were able to disseminate ideas and attitudes from the centre to the peripheries. In this way, the

[64] David Jones, *Some Remarks upon Modern Education. A Sermon Preach'd in the Cathedral-Church of Canterbury, on Thursday September 5, 1728. At the Anniversary Meeting of the Gentlemen Educated at the King's School* (London, 1729), 5.

[65] E. G. W. Bill, *Education at Christ Church, Oxford, 1660–1800* (Oxford, 1988), 87, 99. On the links between the Church and the universities, see G. V. Bennett, 'University, Society and Church 1688–1714', in *The History of the University of Oxford*, v: *The Eighteenth Century*, ed. L. S. Sutherland and L. G. Mitchell (Oxford, 1986), 359–400; J. Gascoigne, *Cambridge in the Age of the Enlightenment: Science, Religion and Politics from the Restoration to the French Revolution* (Cambridge, 1989), and id., 'Church and State Allied: The Failure of Parliamentary Reform of the Universities, 1688–1800', in *The First Modern Society. Essays in English History in Honour of Lawrence Stone*, ed. A. L. Beier, D. Can-

nadine, and J. M. Rosenheim (Cambridge, 1989), 401–29. On the King's School, see the praise showered on it by Eliza Berkeley in *Poems by the late George-Monck Berkeley*, ed. Eliza Berkeley (London, 1797), pp. xxviii, clxxvi.

[66] John Nichols referred to Corpus as a seminary for antiquaries: *Literary Anecdotes of the Eighteenth Century* (9 vols; London, 1812–15), iii. 525.

[67] E. B. Pusey, *Remarks on the Prospective and Past Benefits of Cathedral Institutions in the Promotion of Sound Religious Knowledge and of Clerical Education . . . Occasioned by Lord Henley's Plan for Their Abolition* (London, 1833), 79–80; Meric Casaubon, 'On Learning', app. 2 in M. R. G. Spiller, *Concerning Natural Philosophy: Meric Casaubon and the Royal Society* (The Hague, 1980), 201.

eighteenth-century Cathedral, though fiercely proud of its independence and local ties, might also act as an agent of centralization.

The breadth of learning displayed by these writers in defending the Christian faith is striking. The defence of Anglicanism required a wide range of materials and subjects: history, classics, science, and literature. It has sometimes been suggested that knowledge of such matters is in itself an indication of how far prebendaries in this period had lost sight of the central importance of the Christian faith, and it has been argued that clerical interest in topics such as classical learning and science is a testimony to the growth and dominance of secular forms of thought in the eighteenth century. Yet these areas of scholarship were seen not as independent of religious and theological considerations, but as part and parcel of a Christian culture, and were defined as legitimate branches of study precisely because they could help shed light on the Christian faith. All aspects of human knowledge could be marshalled for this cause. Indeed, it is only in the context of the changing needs of Anglican apologetics that the interest shown by clergy in other disciplines makes sense. In Canterbury the first sixty years after the Restoration saw great interest in Anglo-Saxon scholarship as part of the task of demonstrating the historic roots of the Church in England against Catholic arguments: John Battely (stall I, 1688–1708) and John Mill (stall IV, 1704–7) were both notable in this field.[68] But from the early eighteenth century greater interest was shown in classical and philosophical scholarship to meet the threats from science and deism. In such a climate the highest priority was accorded to those disciplines which would help consolidate the Established Church against its perceived enemies: at first Papists and Dissenters, and then Deists and Unitarians. Members of the Canterbury Chapter were among the most vociferous in maintaining Christian orthodoxy. John Hancock (stall V, 1719–28), for example, joined in the Whistonian controversy of the early eighteenth century by using evidence from the Church Fathers to show that Arianism was not the form of true primitive Christianity.[69]

The fundamental conception of the relationship between learning and religious faith held by Anglican clerics in this period owed much to the tenets of Renaissance Christian Humanism. The need to understand the Bible contextually drew clergy into other areas of knowledge; it was precisely their regard for the Scriptures which guided their extra-biblical intellectual pursuits. William Beveridge, for instance, in his monumental histories of the early church, stressed the importance of history and tradition in interpreting the Bible, in contrast to Jean Daillé, who, in his *Traité de l'employ des saints pères* (1632), had rejected the authority of the Fathers, arguing that Scripture alone was sufficient.[70] *The Sacred and Profane History of the World* (1728) of Samuel Shuckford (stall X, 1738–54) was an

[68] Cf. S. Taylor, 'Church and Society After the Glorious Revolution', *Hist. Jnl.*, 31 (1988), 978. J. Battely, *Antiquitates Rutupinae* (Oxford, 1711); J. Mill, pref. to T. Benson's *Vocabularium Anglo-Saxonicum* (Oxford, 1701); E. Stillingfleet, *Origines Britannicae* (London, 1685); D. Wilkins, *Leges Anglo-Saxonicae Ecclesiasticae et Civiles* (London, 1721). For Mill's support of Anglo-Saxon studies, see D. Fairer, 'Anglo-Saxon Studies', in *History of the University of Oxford*, v: *The Eighteenth Century* (cit. in n. 65), 810–11, 813, 815. Charles Elstob (stall VIII, 1666–1721) was the uncle and guardian to William and Elizabeth Elstob, two of the leading Anglo-Saxon scholars of the early 18th cent. On the subject more generally, see D. C. Douglas, *English Scholars, 1660–1730* (2nd edn.; London, 1951).

[69] John Hancock, *Arianism not the Primitive Christianity; or, the Antenicene Fathers vindicated from the Imputation of being Favourable to that Heresy, design'd as an Answer (in part) to Mr Whiston's Primitive Christianity Reviv'd* (2nd edn.; London, 1719).

[70] W. Beveridge, *Synodicon* (Oxford, 1672).

ambitious attempt to collate biblical and ancient histories. Even the highly influential *Essay on the Learning of Shakespeare* (1767) by Richard Farmer (stall IX, 1782–8) can be fitted into this context, arguing as it did for the divine inspiration which guided the bard's genius. As George Horne observed in a sermon to the King's School, such scholarship was necessary, since the 'days of inspiration have been long since at an end. God has ceased to communicate immediately the treasures of wisdom and knowledge to any man.'[71] Anglican clerics were wary of those who claimed to have direct communication with God and who thus had no need of an education. They considered them to be unreliable, showing another trait of enthusiasm.[72] For Church of England clergy in this period, their own mastery of learning distanced them from the perceived superstition of Popery and the ignorance of the Nonconformist clergy.

During the second half of the eighteenth century the Cathedral became something of a centre for the dissemination of anti-rationalist and especially anti-Socinian doctrines. Dean Horne was the leader of the 'Hutchinsonian' group, which stressed the centrality of the Trinity and the limits of human reason in religious matters. The group took their name from John Hutchinson (1674–1737), whose writings on natural philosophy and theology became the basis of their work. His appeal to such men was obvious: he had argued that a proper reading of the Bible demonstrated that both it and the natural world held sure proofs of the Trinity. Their main targets were the Unitarians and Rational Dissenters, in particular Joseph Priestley and Richard Price, who were responsible for leading an attack on the Anglican liturgy. The Hutchinsonians were largely Oxford-educated during the 1750s and rose to some prominence within the Church after 1760. George Berkeley, the son of the famous theologian and philosopher, had been collated to a Canterbury stall (VI, 1768–95) by Archbishop Secker. He supported the Hutchinsonians, and their views received more backing in the Cathedral when Horne was promoted to the deanery in 1781. Horne had been born in Kent, was educated at Maidstone School, and was well connected in the diocese. He was also President of Magdalen College and travelled regularly between Oxford and Canterbury. A constant visitor to the Deanery at this time was Horne's great ally William Jones, who shared his interest in Hutchinsonianism, occasionally preaching in the Cathedral, and who later received preferment within the diocese. In 1776 Horne published his celebrated *Commentary on the Book of Psalms*, which maintained that the Old Testament contained a full understanding of Christ's life and purpose, illustrating the crucial connection between the Old and New Testaments. In Hutchinsonian fashion, Horne also emphasized the link between the natural world and theology. The Psalms, he argued, used imagery from nature to describe Christ's power and attributes and the blessings of redemption.[73]

At Canterbury the influence of this group was very strong. Archbishops Moore and Manners Sutton were both noted for their support of these High Churchmen, and the

---

[71] G. Horne, *The Character of True Wisdom, and the Means of Attaining it. A Sermon preached in the Cathedral Church of Christ, Canterbury, before the Society of Gentlemen educated in the King's School, on Thursday Aug. 26. 1784* (Oxford, 1784), 4.

[72] I. Terry, 'The Gradual Advances of Religious Knowledge', in *Sixteen Sermons Upon Select Subjects* (Canterbury, 1746), 21.

[73] G. Horne, *Commentary on the Book of Psalms* (2 vols.; Oxford, 1776).

minor canon Henry Todd was a protégé.[74] In 1786, at the primary visitation of Archbishop Moore, Horne urged the necessity of defending the Trinity. The Hutchinsonians also had links with evangelicals of the period. In conventional historiography, the evangelicals of the eighteenth century are seen as standing apart from mainstream Anglicanism, but it is clear that there are areas of important overlap. John Wesley, for example, was much impressed by Horne's *Commentary*, while Horne sent his daughters to be educated at Hannah More's school near Bristol.[75]

Attitudes towards learning as demonstrated by these clerics indicate something of the relationship between clerical and lay society. The fusion of sacred and secular forms of knowledge mirrors a wider fusion of lay and clerical attitudes which depended on working with, rather than against, lay society. Thomas Randolph, who had been educated at the King's School and who later became the Lady Margaret Professor of Divinity at Oxford, claimed in his King's School sermon of 1733, that the school had 'brought forth more men of learning than all the private tutors in the kingdom'.[76] The division between clerical and lay spheres was perceived to be a sign of Popery. It was another indication of the unnaturalness of Popery that it set the clergy apart from the rest of the world. As Elias Sydall (stall IV, 1707–28; Dean, 1728–33) observed in 1715, for clergymen 'to affect a Dominion over the Minds and Consciences of Men, by insisting that the Laity surrender the right to think independently and give absolute obedience to them ... was to lay the very base and ground work of Popery'.[77] It is this attitude which explains the clergy's concern to strengthen and build up lay spirituality within the Church, as well as to further the laity's understanding of the tenets of Christianity, as a way of buttressing the position of the Church within society.

Restoration and eighteenth-century clergy wanted to be able to claim, against the criticisms of their opponents, that piety was a prerogative of their lay followers, and the development of a distinctly Anglican piety was seen as the best way of entrenching the Church within the hearts and minds of the nation. This stemmed from the realization, after 1660, that the Church's position could not be defended by clergy alone but would have to find support in the wider world. It also gave the individual layman a certain responsibility; clergy were well aware of the temptations and attractions offered by certain forms of dissent and wanted to channel individual initiatives into the mainstream of Anglicanism. This concern with personal piety is usually seen as the prerogative of Puritan and evangelical clergy, who stood to some degree outside the main currents of Anglican life. But such a concern is also evidenced on the part of the Canterbury Chapter. Most outstanding in this respect was Dean Stanhope (1704–28), whose main contribution to

[74] See *Memoirs of William Stevens Esquire*, ed. J. A. Park (London, 1812), 22; 'a vast number' of Horne's friends were Hutchinsonians (p. 160); *VCH Norfolk*, ii. 305, Archbishop Manners Sutton's support of High Churchmen; BL, Add. MS 39312, fo. 122, Horne to Berkeley, 9 Apr. 1791; A. B. Webster, *Joshua Watson: The Story of a Layman, 1771–1855* (London, 1954), 23–5.

[75] G. Horne, *The Duty of Contending for the Faith. A Sermon preached at the Primary Visitation of the Most Reverend John, Lord Archbishop of Canterbury, in the Cathedral and Metropolitical Church, on Saturday, July 1, 1786* (Oxford, 1786); CUL, Add. MS 8134/A/3, fo. 52.

[76] Thomas Randolph, *The Advantages of Publick Education. A Sermon preached in the Cathedral Church at Canterbury, Thursday, September 17 1733 at the Anniversary Meeting of the Gentlemen educated at the King's School* (Oxford, 1733), 18–19.

[77] E. Sydall, *The True Protestant and Church of England Clergy Vindicated from the Imputation of Preaching up themselves. Preached at Tunbridge Wells, 14 August 1714* (London, 1715), 21–2.

Anglican piety was to appropriate the traditions of the Catholic Church for Anglican ends. His *Paraphrase and Comment on the Epistles and Gospels* (1705–8) was extremely popular, often being reprinted, and it became one of the mainstays of devotional literature during the eighteenth century. What Robert Nelson had done for the festivals and fasts, Stanhope did for the Sunday Epistles and Gospels: he defended his collection from the usual Puritan charge that the readings were Popish, by saying that as they were scriptural, it mattered very little from where they came. Stanhope also translated works by St Augustine, Thomas à Kempis, and Robert Parsons into devotions suitable for an Anglican liturgy.[78] In doing this, he was consciously fitting Anglicanism into a historical Christian tradition, seeing it as one way to counter the charges of novelty which were laid at the door of the Church of England. Above all, Stanhope seems to have been concerned to develop a practical religion, where Christian dogma shaped the way in which people lived out their lives. Such writings continued the tradition of manuals of holy living which had been so important in medieval and Reformation spirituality. The eighteenth-century pre-occupation with morality can then be seen as a way of linking religious precept and practice: an impious life could endanger the individual's chances of salvation.

It is clear that Stanhope attempted to put his ideas into practice, and during his time as Dean efforts were made to tighten up on the behaviour of those living in the Precincts. For instance, in 1718 one of the lay clerks, Charles Blogg, was made to do penance for his immorality in 'laying with a whore within the Precincts'.[79] The eighteenth-century clergy's interest in moral teaching stemmed from this concern—that only when truly moral would England be living up to its role as God's Elect Nation. As John Johnson, the incumbent of Cranbrook, preached in an assize sermon in 1708:

Habitual intemperance and sensuality do by degrees harden the heart and deaden all sense of religion in the minds of men, and when this is once done, all the most sacred obligations they are under to God and their superiors are soon forgotten. Houses of debauchery and drunken clubs are the great seminaries of atheism and irreligion, and consequently one great occasion of all the mischief that can light upon the kingdom.[80]

Another phenomenon of the period is the growth of clerical JPs. Historians often interpret this as an indication of the worldliness of eighteenth-century clerics. But in a world where practical Christianity was important and the theory of the Christian Commonwealth was still a crucial way of understanding the relationship between religion and society, it is not surprising that Cathedral clergy like the Six Preachers John Duncombe (1766–86), Osmund Beauvoir (1765–89), and Richard Harvey (1793–1821) took an active part

[78] George Stanhope, *A Paraphrase and Comment upon the Epistles and Gospels, Appointed to be used in the Church of England on all Sundays and Holy Days throughout the year. Designed to excite devotion, and promote the knowledge and practice of sincere piety and virtue* (4 vols.; London, 1705), i, p. x. Also id., *Parsons: His Christian Directory* (London, 1703), and a trans. of Thomas à Kempis's *Imitatio Christi*, *The Christian Pattern* (London, 1696), which by 1814 had reached 19 editions. In a similar vein, T. Wise, a Six Preacher, translated works for an Anglican audience: T.

Wise, *The Truth of the Christian Religion, Written originally in Italian for the Benefit of the Court of Savoy, by the Marquis of Pianezza* (London, 1703). And T. Dorrington, the incumbent of Wittersham, published a collection of medieval hymns and prayers as *Reformed Devotions* (4th edn.; London, 1696).

[79] Dean's Book, 1718–42, p. 1.

[80] J. Johnson, *Reasons why Vice ought to be punished, but is not, in a Sermon Preached at Maidstone in Kent, at the Assizes held there before Mr. Justice Tracy, 17 March 1708* (London, 1708), 13–14.

on the Commission of the Peace in Kent.[81] Duncombe wanted to be an active magistrate to do justice, 'for no one in that department was more open to the poor and friendless'.[82]

What we are seeing here is not so much a secularization of religion as its laicization. One of the clearest testimonies to the link perceived between immorality and irreligion can be found in the Church's involvement in the voluntary religious organizations which emerged at the end of the seventeenth century. These organizations, headed by the Society for the Propagation of Christian Knowledge, saw the need to bring about a religious and social reformation and endeavoured to achieve this by a concentrated effort at the parish level. It has been suggested that the different types of voluntary organizations had clearly separate intentions and that they appealed to different sections of the clerical community: the SPCK and the religious societies, which were given early support by William Beveridge, were favoured by the Tory clergy, while the societies for the reformation of manners claimed the adherence of the Whig party and Low Church clergy. But it is dangerous to adopt such a schematic approach. For example, Dean Stanhope, a prominent High Churchman, warned against the religious societies, suggesting that they had separatist inclinations. He likened the societies to the religious conventicles that had played such an important part in the turmoil of the Civil War. His concern was that they might again become the agents of social and religious unrest by 'invading' the priestly office, and he reminded their supporters of the importance of steadfast obedience to the Church: 'there is no inconsistency between wishing all the Lord's people were prophets, and dreading the consequences of their thinking themselves prophets when they are not so'.[83] Stanhope was displaying a typical reaction to the dangers and consequences of religious fragmentation. He gave more praise to the work of the societies for the reformation of manners and he supported the society that had been established in Canterbury in 1698. Stanhope wished to see the nation reformed by the growth of religious principles, and when vicar of Lewisham he had told the Kent gentry and magistrates at the 1701 assize that the 'work of correcting vice and the Reformation of Manners is truly great and glorious'.[84] The intentions of the societies for the regulation of behaviour—an end to swearing, and the reassertion of Sunday as a day devoted to worship—clearly mirrored the aim to create a Christian commonwealth.

Cathedral Life

The services performed at the Cathedral were its prime function and also a way in which local spirituality and piety could be strengthened. Archbishops could enforce order on Cathedral life and activities and inquire into the performance of services through the visitation system. The questions in visitation articles reflect current events and concerns, but the answers are nearly always significant for their reserve. There is a united front caused by the possibility of external interference. Occasionally, however, tantalizing glimpses of

---

[81] B. Keith-Lucas, *Parish Affairs: The Government of Kent Under George III* (Kent County Library, 1986), 14–18.

[82] Quoted by John Nichols, *Literary Anecdotes* (cit. in n. 66), viii. 274.

[83] G. Stanhope, *The Duty of Rebuking, a Sermon . . . to which is added a Post-Script to the Religious Societies* (London, 1703).

[84] Id., *The Duty of Juries. Preached at the Lent Assizes, Maidstone, 1 April 1701* (London, 1701), 25.

evidence survive to suggest that the answers, especially of the minor canons, were not always the whole story.[85] This underlines the nature of the hierarchy within the Cathedral. The Dean and Chapter were responsible to none but God and their Visitor, and they left the day-to-day performance of worship to the subordinate members of the community. The twelve prebendaries were not required to keep constant residence: the statutes committed them to ninety days' residence a year, with at least twenty-one days' continuous residence, and usually only four or five prebendaries were in Canterbury at a time, except at the general audits or on important occasions. Nevertheless, there was constant pressure for greater attendance. George I informed the chapters of all English cathedrals that full attendance was important, to fulfil the demands of preaching and of keeping hospitality within their cities.[86] Dean Stanhope was especially concerned to ensure that residence was maintained. He was able to write to Wake in 1724, 'Our Residence is duly observed and generally a very laudable appearance at Prayers, and since my coming not one prebend's course has been preached by a stranger.'[87] But members of the Chapter could sometimes get dispensations for non-residence, if they held a university position, were royal chaplains, or were present at Convocation; non-residence was one of the disadvantages of having prebendaries who held important positions in the outside world. On the whole, it seems that there was a constant group of prebendaries who resided—for instance the du Moulin circle in the Restoration period, the Thorp circle in the late seventeenth century, the Berkeley circle in the 1770s and 1780s, and, in the early nineteenth century, the circle around Canon Welfitt, who spent nine months of the year at Canterbury—while others were more peripatetic. Another problem was that there was no concept of clerical retirement, so some of the older prebendaries who were sick or dying were unable to play their part within the life of the community. Minor canons and Six Preachers commonly preached on Sundays as substitutes for prebendaries. During the 1760s and 1770s, in particular, much of the preaching seems to have been done by the Six Preachers, especially Hearne, Duncombe, Bunce, and Beauvoir. This was partly because in these decades there was a rapid turnover of deans, who did not stay long enough to impose their authority on the community. But matters improved in the 1780s and 1790s with the longer tenure of Deans Horne and Powys, and by 1800 it was rare for a minor canon to preach on a Sunday.

Thus the minor canons were crucial in keeping the life of the community going: if the prebendaries provided a link between the Cathedral and the wider world, the minor canons connected it to the life of the city and diocese. It was they who led the daily services, read the lessons, and were responsible for the musical life of the Cathedral: the precentor and sacrist were chosen from their ranks. It is clear that in the late seventeenth century the Dean and Chapter had difficulty finding suitably qualified and talented clergy for these posts. John Langhorne was suspended in 1675 for being 'a reproach to his profession by his vitious and debaushed Manner of life and conversation, thereby greatly dishonouring this Church whereof hee is a Member'.[88] A series of regulations concerning

[85] E.g. Bodl., MS Tanner 123, fo. 54, 'Answers of minor canons and choirmen', 1682.

[86] Ibid., MS Dep. c. 233, fo. 77, George I to deans and chapters, 9 July 1724.

[87] Christ Church, Oxford, MS Wake 10, fo. 126, Stanhope to Wake, 20 Jan. 1724.

[88] Chapter Act Book, 1670–1710, fo. 31[v].

the behaviour of minor canons, lay clerks, and bedesmen during the eighteenth century brought about something of a transformation in the activities of these lower clergy and members of the community; by the end of the period, they had become much more orderly.[89] Nevertheless, they continued to bear the brunt of the Dean and Chapter's criticism if services were not adequately performed. John Moore (Dean, 1771–5) reprimanded one minor canon for not reading early morning prayers because (he said) they were not well attended.

Sir, that shall not be admitted as an excuse; if there are so few, I will pay so much a morning to half a dozen poor aged persons to attend them; for I am fully resolved that they shall never be given up while I am dean of this Church.[90]

In 1660 two minor canons and seven lay clerks returned to the restored Foundation, and they were not necessarily very suitable. Of Henry Nicholls it was said in 1663: 'a pitiful man, of parts scarce sufficient for a minister, once an apothecary, after a pettycanon at the Cathedral. The Church finding him weak gave him £10 to quit his place.'[91] A major factor in accounting for the low standards was the poor salary the minor canons received. They were originally paid out of the 'common fund', and in 1663 their salaries were increased to £18 6s. 8d. p.a. In 1704 this was raised to £20, but this was still seen as insufficient. In an attempt to solve this problem, Archbishop Wake encouraged the Dean and Chapter in 1724 to join the salaries of the substitutes to those of the minor canons.[92] By the 1790s minor canons were receiving £50 p.a., and a house and firewood. At a time when the income of the Dean and Chapter was increasing greatly, this low income caused much resentment, fuelling antagonism between the minor canons and the Dean and Chapter. William Gostling complained of 'the gentlemen who think themselves poorly off if every one at the end of the year, does not receive more money from the Church than all our Fraternity of the tattered cape and drudgery of prayer put together'.[93] Another source of ill-feeling was the allocation of livings in the Chapter's gift. The minor canons, who depended on being able to combine their office at the Cathedral with the duties of a parish incumbent, complained that they were being denied their rights to such livings. During the 1820s the Chapter Act Books reveal signs of tension between the minor canons and the 'gentlemen', with the minor canons refusing to obey new regulations imposed upon them by the Dean and Chapter. This reached something of a climax in 1828, when they complained of the newly refurbished organ, which they said, by its 'overblowings above' and 'undermoanings below' drowned out their singing. The Chapter voted to support the Dean in his dealings with the minor canons' 'subordination' and called in the minor canons to interview them. William Bennett was suspended for his rudeness.[94] There are inklings here of the outbursts of 1839, led by the irascible Bennett, in the publication of *The Case of the Minor Canons and Inferior Officers of the New Foundation. Particularly with Reference to Canterbury.*

[89] Chapter Act Book, 1670–1710, fo. 54.

[90] Quoted in G. Berkeley, *Sermons*, ed. Eliza Berkeley (London, 1799), p. xxiv.

[91] LPL, MS 1126, s. v. 'Boughton Aluph'.

[92] Chapter Act Book, 1670–1710, fo. 201; ibid. 1711–26, fo. 150ᵛ.

[93] Nichols, *Literary Anecdotes* (cit. in n. 66), ix. 345.

[94] Dean's Book, 1822–1854, p. 46. Fabric VIII, 22 Feb. 1828, Dean Bagot to Vice-Dean.

Music in the Cathedral

At the Restoration there was some difficulty in recreating the musical tradition at Canterbury which had been such a noted feature of worship before the Civil War. The Dean and Chapter were faced with the practical problem of an acute shortage of trained choristers, which was not helped by the tendency of government officials to kidnap able young singers for service in the Chapel Royal. One of the minor canons, Blaise White, was lured away from Canterbury to sing there. The visitation return of 1663 noted that the choir 'is furnished of as able singers as in this barren time (by reason of the long intermission of Cathedral service) they could procure'.[95] The Puritan tradition had attacked the Anglican musical scene, and at the Restoration the clergy had to confront the intellectual problem of defending the place and role of music within religious services. In 1663 John Reading delivered a sermon in the Cathedral in support of Church music against Puritan condemnations. He maintained that, far from being a devilish practice, music could help draw the congregation nearer to God by providing an intimation of heavenly joys, and would act as an instrument of conciliation in the years after 1660.[96] Gradually, more regular choir-practices were introduced and stricter examinations were encouraged, so as to improve the choristers' singing.[97] The kind of music performed at Canterbury is worth noting: in 1695 the Dean and Chapter agreed that Tallis's Te Deum and Creed be used every Sunday, together with Batten's Evening Service. In 1698 the organist was paid for teaching the choristers Tallis's Great Service.[98] Tallis himself had been at Canterbury in 1541–2, and the post-Restoration Chapter encouraged the publication of a new edition of his works. An inventory of 1689 reveals that the Cathedral also had in its possession the works of the early seventeenth-century composer Thomas Tompkins.[99] The Cathedral was self-consciously using the music of the era before the Civil War to emphasize its links with that tradition. This had the effect of making the Tudor and Jacobean period seem to be a musical golden age and explains why music from this time was accorded a high place in cathedral services throughout the late seventeenth and eighteenth centuries. In the early nineteenth century, the music of the composers popular before the Civil War remained part of the staple diet of the choir.[100] Canterbury was fortunate in its organists, for example Daniel Henstridge (1699–1736), William Raylton (1736–57), and Samuel Porter (1757–1803), who were noted as composers of church music in their day, and who wrote music for their own choirs. Raylton's *Service in A* remained popular until the end of the nineteenth century. The organist was responsible (with the precentors) for the provision of scores, and by the end of the period had built up a fairly large music-library, mostly in manuscript.[101] An organ was installed in 1662; this was replaced in 1683 by a new instrument, subsequently rebuilt in 1752, 1784, and 1828.

[95] Captain Cooke, master of choristers, was promised payment in June 1671 for 'going to Westchester, Litchfield, Canterbury and Rochester to look for boyes'. Quoted by C. Dearnley, *English Church Music, 1650–1750* (London, 1970), 29; 'unmarked Box'/4, 'The Answers to the articles of Enquiry, 1663', no. 4.

[96] J. Reading, *A Sermon Lately Delivered in the Cathedral Church of Canterbury, Concerning Church-Musick* (London, 1663).

[97] Chapter Act Book, 1670–1710, fo. 94; Dean's Book, 1777–92, fo. 135.

[98] Chapter Act Book, 1670–1710, fo. 152.

[99] Ibid., fo. 138ᵛ. See Legg and Hope, *Inventories*, 285.

[100] See *A Collection of Anthems as Performed in the Cathedral and Metropolitical Church at Canterbury* (3rd edn.; Canterbury, 1848).

[101] e.g. the Dean and Chapter encouraged the buying of music. Chapter Act Book, 1775–96, pp. 358, 360.

Much of the credit for the resumption of this tradition in Canterbury must go to the minor canons, who played a leading part in the musical life of the Cathedral. Auditions were held when a new minor canon was to be appointed, and the Dean and Chapter showed concern to promote clergy who showed an adequate musical ability. In 1760, for instance, Thomas Freeman, who had been a minor canon at Wells, beat an internal candidate because he 'sings a good contra tenor (a part difficult to be got) and pleased so much, that the most indifferent to Church-Musick of our Chapter agreed with the majority, and he came in without opposition'.[102] In particular, members of the Gostling family had a long association with the Cathedral and not only helped to raise the musical standard of the services but also made the Cathedral a centre for concerts in the area. John Gostling (minor canon 1674–1733) was the most distinguished bass soloist of his generation: he inspired Purcell in the 1680s and 1690s at the Chapel Royal and provided a link between the London musical scene and Canterbury. His son William (minor canon, 1727–77) not only helped to organize the Cathedral music, procuring music books and cataloguing the collection, but was also an active supporter of the Canterbury musical society.[103] It was from the Cathedral that the vogue for Handel's music spread into Kent, since his oratorios were performed in the Cathedral and his chamber music in the Deanery. Dean Friend (1760–6) was an early supporter of these concerts. This interest in Handel's music became a feature of other cathedral cities in the provinces, such as Salisbury and Bristol, in the century after 1760. For the clergy at Canterbury, Handel's music became a weapon in their battle against immorality and rationalist religion. The fear of a rising tide of disbelief led many clergy in the eighteenth century to see the musical arts as a means of spreading piety, and Handel's work seemed supremely suited to the task.[104] That great defender of Trinitarian doctrines, Dean Horne, made particular efforts to champion Handel's music. In 1784 diapasons from the organ which had been used in the great Handel centenary celebrations in Westminster Abbey were installed in the rebuilt Cathedral organ, and at the service commemorating this, Horne argued that Handel's music 'furnished the best idea we shall ever obtain on earth of what is passing in heaven'. Horne also claimed that 'in England choral service was first introduced in this Cathedral, and the practice of it long continued in the churches of Kent, from whence it became gradually diffused throughout the whole kingdom'.[105] Clerical admiration for Handel's oratorios, and especially for the *Messiah* (1741), rested on their explicit Trinitarian emphasis and their stress on a personal God, who intervened in the affairs of the world.

[102] The internal candidate was William Gostling's son: Nichols, *Literary Anecdotes* (cit. in n. 66), xi. 343.

[103] John Gostling acted as an intermediary for other minor canons, sometimes purchasing goods for them in London. See Add. MS 43, 'Private account Book of Simon D'Evereux, Minor Canon and Rector of Harbledown 1691–1733', fos. 12, 15ᵛ; J. Meadows Cowper, *The Lives of the Deans of Canterbury, 1541 to 1900* (Canterbury, 1900), 171. For a detailed study of the Gostling family, see R. F. Ford, 'Minor Canons at Canterbury Cathedral: The Gostlings and Their Colleagues' (Ph.D. thesis, Univ. of California, 1984).

[104] R. Smith, 'Intellectual Contexts of Handel's English Oratorios', in *Music in Eighteenth-Century England. Essays in Memory of Charles Cudworth*, ed. C. Hogwood and R. Luckett (Cambridge, 1983), 127; For evidence of the connection between Handel's music and cathedral bodies see *VCH Cheshire*, iii. 193.

[105] G. Horne, *The Antiquity, Use and Excellence of Church Music, A Sermon Preached at the Opening of A New Organ in the Cathedral Church of Christ, Canterbury, on Thursday, July 8. 1784* (Oxford, 1784), 276.

Celebrations of the Eucharist

Besides the daily morning and evening services, the Cathedral provided the main Sunday services and the major celebrations of the Eucharist within the city, since Canterbury lacked a large parish church. Traditional interpretations of the age have emphasized the relative infrequency of celebrations of the Eucharist by comparison with nineteenth-century standards and have concluded that the Communion played a small part in Anglican worship in the eighteenth century as a result of latitudinarian churchmanship. It is, however, becoming increasingly apparent that our perceptions of eighteenth-century piety need some modification. The Eucharist was an essential part of eighteenth-century Anglicanism, and indeed, its relative infrequency might only have served to highlight its importance.

It is clear, nevertheless, that the Restoration Church hierarchy found great difficulty in persuading its people to return to the sacrament. Whilst the restoration of Church of England morning and evening prayer was easy enough, the Eucharist proved more of a problem. Even at the Cathedral it was not until the 1680s that the sacrament was celebrated weekly. This was in response to pressure from Archbishop Sancroft, who wanted this rule to be achieved in every cathedral in the country, as part of a vigorous Anglican reaction to the perceived growth of dissent and immorality. Dean Tillotson, who was responsible for putting these demands into practice, wrote to Sancroft in 1683:

As to the Rubrick concerning Communion in Cathedral Churches every Sunday, I moved it last week to the Chapter, and we resolved to begin it next month, which was as soon as we could engage a convenient number of communicants, and I am very glad your Grace designs it throughout the province, because it is plainly required, and will I doubt not be of good example, and of great efficacy to promote piety.[106]

Tillotson is often portrayed as the archetypical latitudinarian, unimpressed by outward forms of devotion. Yet clearly his latitudinarianism could embrace a commitment to frequent communion. In 1683 he published his popular *Persuasive to Frequent Communion in the Holy Sacrament of the Lord's Supper*, in which he accounted for the present reluctance to take communion by the Reformation stress on the dangers of receiving it unworthily, which had encouraged people not to receive it at all. He concluded:

I doubt not but it hath been a thing of very bad consequence to discourage men so much from the sacrament, as the way hath been of late years: and that many men who were under some kind of check before, since they have been driven away from the sacrament, have quite let loose the Reins, and prostituted themselves to all manner of impiety and vice. We exclaim against the Church of Rome with great impatience, and with a very just indignation, for robbing the people of half this Blessed Sacrament, and taking from them the cup of Blessing, the cup of Salvation: and yet we can patiently endure for some months, nay years, to exclude ourselves wholly from it.[107]

Tillotson received some savage criticism while he was Dean of Canterbury for his policies

---

[106] Bodl., MS Tanner 34, fo. 176, Tillotson to Sancroft, 11 Oct. 1683. Similar efforts were made in other cathedrals to obtain a weekly sacrament. For Archbishop Dolben's efforts at York in 1685, see *VCH Yorkshire, The City of York*, 351.

[107] J. Tillotson, *A Persuasive to Frequent Communion in the Holy Sacrament of the Lord's Supper* (London, 1684), 69.

of moderation towards Dissenters and for his supposed betrayal of Anglican orthodoxy, characterized by his observation to William Beveridge that 'charity is better than rubrics'. In 1683 the writer of a pamphlet, *Some Select Queries humbly Offered to the Consideration of the D—n of C—t—b—y*, attacked Tillotson as a betrayer of Church of England principles and expressly blamed him for 'defacing the Altar piece of his own Cathedral, for fear of offending tender consciences'.[108] The Dean mentioned the incident in a letter to Robert Nelson. 'We only took down the sun over the screen behind the communion table which was done with so little noise that several days passed before it was taken notice of to be remov'd; and nothing done besides, not so much as the Table stirr'd out of its place'.[109]

The problem of persuading people to attend the sacrament was long-lasting. Thomas Williamson, a minor canon and incumbent of St Dunstan's, Canterbury, resigned himself to the fact that 'being a very old man ... I take all the pains I can to win souls to Christ ... I am heartily sorry that all my pains will not prevail with some to take their Saviour in the Sacrament'.[110] It is arguable that the clergy themselves were in part responsible for this situation. Their insistence on the importance of the sacrament and their stress that prospective communicants should be spiritually well prepared before receiving Communion led sections of their congregations to feel that they were unworthy to receive. It is significant that post-Restoration clergy were no longer content with a general reception at Easter: they urged their parishioners to come well prepared. George Berkeley (stall VI, 1768–95), for many years Vice-Dean at the Cathedral, warned his parochial congregation of the consequences of treating the communion lightly: 'as (in respect of our natural food) it will as infallibly destroy any one of you to abstain from all food as to eat poison, so (in this case) it will be equally fatal to you, never to receive the holy communion as to come to it unprepared'.[111] And some clergy found that some of their poorer parishioners objected to attending the sacrament since they were superstitious. Perhaps, too, such attitudes were a legacy of the separatist and Puritan opinions which had become so pervasive and entrenched in the diocese during the seventeenth century.

One of the most prominent High Churchmen in the diocese, John Johnson, vicar of Cranbrook (1707–25), occasionally preached in the Cathedral. Cranbrook was a large Wealden parish with a strong Puritan tradition and Johnson stressed the importance of Communion as a badge of Church membership. He wrote to Archbishop Wake in 1716:

I rejoice to understand that your Grace is disposed to revive Discipline; I take it for granted, that you mean true Primitive Discipline, without respect of persons, which in truth is the destruction of it. Now the first step towards this most Glorious end, I humbly conceive to be this, that the absolute necessity of communion with the Church to all that live within the pale of it, be universally pressed on the consciences of men. For if communion be not absolutely necessary to salvation, then excommunication can be no real punishment, nor can there be sufficient reason for men to undergo just penances for the regaining the communion, when they are deprived of it.[112]

[108] *Some Select Queries humbly Offered to the Consideration of the D—n of C—t—b—y* (London, 1683).

[109] BL, Add. MS 4236, fo. 223, Tillotson to Nelson, 19 Oct. 1680.

[110] Christ Church, Oxford, Wake MSS, 1716 Visitation Returns, s. v. 'St Dunstan's, Canterbury'.

[111] Berkeley, *Sermons* (cit. in n. 90), 89–90.

[112] Christ Church, Oxford, Wake MSS, 1716 Visitation Returns, s. v. 'Cranbrook'.

Johnson aroused controversy with his *Unbloody Sacrifice* (1713), a work which stressed the 'proper nature of the sacrifice' at the Eucharist. Thomas Wise (Six Preacher, 1709–19) took the opportunity, when preaching in the Cathedral, to attack Johnson's views, arguing that Johnson's ideas represented the 'boldest step to Popery since the Reformation'.[113] But although Johnson's views were regarded with some suspicion, his stress on the centrality of the Eucharist within Anglican worship was significant. Indeed, George Gilbert, an old King's School boy, writing his memoirs in the nineteenth century (1864–73), suggested that Johnson's writings were a great influence in restoring Communion in Canterbury.[114] And the weekly sacrament at the Cathedral attracted a congregation from all over the city, providing a centrepiece for lay piety. Edward Hasted noted that 'on a Sunday, when [the] altar is dressed up for the sacrament', it was 'covered with its costly and splendid service of rich plate'.[115] During the 1790s the weekly sacrament was replaced by a monthly celebration.[116]

Other Services and Sermons

Setting a standard for religious practice and providing the central focus for Anglican worship in the city and locality were seen as two of the major functions of the cathedral in this period. In the early years of the Restoration, Archbishop Sheldon argued that 'our Cathedrals are the standard and Rule to all parochial churches of the solemnity and decent manner of reading the liturgy and administering the Holy Sacrament' and that if these were not well done it would be to the 'offense of some of our friends, the advantage of sectaries, and her [the Church's] own just reproach'.[117] It is clear that the standards of cathedral worship were higher and the continuation of 'High Church' liturgical practices more thorough than the Church's later detractors claimed. At Canterbury a series of conscientious deans ensured that Cathedral services were regularly performed. Tillotson, Stanhope, Friend, Moore, Horne, and Percy were all concerned with this aspect of their office, and Canterbury also gained a reputation for its good preachers.[118] There was, at that time, something of a debate concerning the proper place for Cathedral preaching. In the early seventeenth century, sermons had usually been delivered in the chapter house, which was known in consequence as the Sermon House. This was objected to by Laud, who thought the separation of preaching a Puritan practice. At the Restoration, Meric Casaubon reiterated the potential danger of this separation of sermon and service, which encouraged the 'prattlings of enthusiasts'. 'I conceive it to be one main reason that so few are acquainted, and by consequence, not more in love, with the service.'[119] And so after the Restoration the Sermon House was abandoned. But some Low Church clergy in the diocese wanted the practice to be resurrected. John Lewis, a local incumbent who often

[113] T. Wise, *The Christian Eucharist Rightly Stated* (London, 1711), and *The Christian Eucharist No Proper Sacrifice* (London, 1714), 7, 9.

[114] *Reminiscences of the Reverend George Gilbert (1796–1874)*, ed. F. J. Shirley (priv. printed [Canterbury, 1938]), 32.

[115] E. Hasted, *The History and Topographical Survey of the County of Kent* (2nd edn.; 12 vols.; Canterbury, 1797–1801), xi. 372.

[116] Oblation Books.

[117] Bodl., MS Tanner 282, fo. 65, Sheldon to Seth Ward, 4 June 1670.

[118] *Diary of John Evelyn* (cit. in n. 36), v. 223.

[119] M. Casaubon, *The Question to whom it belonged anciently to preach* (London, 1663), 2.

preached in the Cathedral, suggested to Archbishop Wake in 1724 that preaching in the Cathedral would improve if this was done:

But the Quire is very ill contrived for any considerable auditory, and that Venerable Body have thought fit for a long time to disuse the Sermon House commonly so called tho' a most commodious place for divine worship, and where on Sundays, morning prayer and preaching might be used without prejudice to the Cathedral service.[120]

Preachers' Books indicate how far Anglican liturgical tradition was maintained at Canterbury. The Cathedral was decorated for the major Church festivals, rosemary and bay being used at Christmas, with incense in the organ loft.[121] And sermons were regularly preached on the anniversaries of the great days within the history of the Church and nation: 30 January, the anniversary of Charles I's execution, when the pulpit was decked in mourning; 29 May, the accession of Charles II; and 5 November, both the failure of the Gunpowder Plot and the arrival of William of Orange. During the Restoration period, probably while Turner was Dean, a portrait of Charles I as martyr was placed in the choir.[122] These festivals were kept up throughout the eighteenth century: they became absorbed within the tradition of Whig High Anglicanism, providing a framework for Anglican piety, and helping to give a sense of tradition and permanence to the Cathedral's activities. These anniversaries could also be used to make political points: Isaac Terry used the anniversary of Charles I's martyrdom to warn of the dangers of mixing with seditious persons.[123]

The dignity and splendour of Canterbury services were noted by various commentators, from John Evelyn in 1665 and Celia Fiennes in 1697, to Viscount Torrington in the 1790s. George Berkeley was highly impressed by the service performed at Archbishop Cornwallis's primary visitation in 1770.

An honest scriptural sermon, expressly teaching the eternal power and Godhead of Jesus, by Dr Tanner, our Senior Prebendary. The very finest anthem I ever heard; nothing like it did I ever hear even in the King's Chapel. At the entrance of the choristers into the Choir, when the Archbishop was yet at the Western door, the organ joined the voices of all choristers, singing men and minor canons, thro' these melodious lanes the Canons, Dean, Archbishop and Bishop of Peterborough passed along.[124]

Indeed, what is striking about the theological and liturgical concerns of the Canterbury Chapter in the eighteenth century is the presence of prebendaries who, far from typifying what historians have rather derogatorily labelled 'the age of latitudinarianism', actively practised High Church ideals. They are a testimony to the fact that there was an unbroken tradition of High Church devotion and spirituality stretching from the Caroline Divines of the early seventeenth century to the Oxford Movement, stressing the integrity of the

[120] Christ Church, Oxford, Wake MSS, 1716 Visitation Returns, s. v. 'Minster'.

[121] Preachers' Books, 1712–66; 1767–1822; 1822–7; Treasurer's Book, 1669–70, fo. 37. This was a traditional form of decoration at Christmas. Pepys observed these as unusual decorations at the first Christmas after 1660: *The Diary of Samuel Pepys*, ed. R. C. Latham and W. Matthews (11 vols.; London, 1974–83), ii. 321, 23 Dec. 1660.

[122] Legg and Hope, *Inventories*, 281.

[123] Terry, *Religious and Loyal Subject's Duty* (cit. in n. 9).

[124] BL, Add. MS 39311, fo. 272, G. Berkeley to Mrs Berkeley, 9 July 1770.

Church, independent of the State.[125] It may be that eighteenth-century churchmen of the period before the Oxford Movement were able to practise such ideals with less hostility than their successors. George Gilbert, for instance, remembered hearing Archbishop Manners Sutton preach in the Cathedral in 1806, at his primary visitation, on the subject of confession and its history, which by the mid-nineteenth century, he felt, would have seemed 'very Popish'.[126]

The concern to tighten up the standards of liturgical practice may, however, have had the effect of alienating some members of the public from Cathedral life and worship. Throughout this time, various injunctions were made by the Dean and Chapter to regularize the behaviour not only of the choristers and minor canons but also of the public, who, at least in the first half of the period, seem to have treated the nave as a public meeting-place. There were complaints of the unruly behaviour and noise of the 'rabble', and of women walking about in 'pattens' during services. In 1712 the Dean and Chapter instructed their officers to 'prevent all rudeness and noyse by walking and talking in the Body and Isles of the Church in time of divine Service and women bringing Children with them unless they keep them quiet, and not suffer any Burden to be carryed through the Church or make it a common throughfare'.[127] This did not mean, however, that the Cathedral services, especially on Sundays, became divorced from the life of the city, or were only attended by a select group. The Dean and Chapter tried to encourage attendance by making the times of services more convenient. In 1722, for instance, evening prayer was moved to 3 o'clock, except in the summer. In 1786 the incumbent of St Alphege's commented that 'Many persons in all parishes in this town go to the Cathedral in the morning, to the Presbyterian meeting in the afternoon, and to the Methodist meeting at night.'[128] Clearly we should be wary of imposing a strict denominational straitjacket on religious affiliations in this period, and the Cathedral played a part in overriding such distinctions. This function of the Cathedral, providing a model for services throughout the city and diocese, was urged by members of the Chapter against criticism in the 1820s and 1830s, on the grounds that without the guidance and inspiration of cathedral worship, parish worship would soon die out.[129]

In this context, it is worth recollecting that the Cathedral also provided the focus for Huguenot worship within the region. The presence of Huguenots in the city dated from the Elizabethan period and their numbers were augmented after their expulsion from France by Louis XIV, in 1685. They were allowed to hold services in the undercroft. There is some indication that the authorities in the early years of the Restoration were wary about the potentially divisive aspects of the Huguenot presence in the city: when splits developed in the congregation, the Cathedral Chapter favoured M. Jannon's party, which conformed to the Anglican liturgy.[130] The sufferings of the Huguenots who streamed into Kent in the 1680s could be portrayed by the Church authorities as those which might

[125] On this point more generally, see P. B. Nockles, 'Continuity and Change in Anglican High Churchmanship in Britain, 1792–1850' (D.Phil. thesis, Univ. of Oxford, 1982), *passim*.

[126] Gilbert, *Reminiscences* (cit. in n. 114), 10.

[127] Chapter Act Book, 1711–26, fo. 14.

[128] Ibid., fo. 116; LPL, VG 3/1/a, Archbishop Moore's Primary Visitation 1786, s. v. 'St Alphege's, Canterbury'.

[129] G. Pellew, *A Letter to the Right Honourable Sir Robert Peel. Bt. M.A. on the Means of 'Rendering Cathedral Churches Most Conducive to the Efficiency of the Established Church'* (London, 1837), 6–8, 32–7.

[130] Bodl., MS Tanner 136, fo. 152.

happen to Protestants under a Catholic monarch. The Cathedral gave money to support them. It can be argued that the presence of the refugees contributed to the unanimity with which James II was expelled in 1688.[131] The eighteenth century saw many Huguenots in the Canterbury area taking Anglican orders. David Durell, one of the prebendaries (stall XII, 1767–75) was of Huguenot stock: this was part of the gradual assimilation process whereby the 'strangers' became integrated into English cultural life.[132]

The Cathedral Fabric

The maintenance and repair of the Cathedral fabric was a continuing problem for the Dean and Chapter. The running costs for repairs were high, largely caused by the detrimental effects of weather and erosion on a medieval building. The great storm of 1703, which proved so disastrous to cathedral buildings all over England, and which killed Bishop Kidder of Bath and Wells, took its toll at Canterbury by damaging the Arundel Tower. Although some repairs were made to the tower, it remained a constant source of worry and was eventually rebuilt between 1832 and 1840.[133] Traditionally, the costs for such repairs came from the 'timber money', but this proved insufficient. Early in the eighteenth century it was agreed that the money customarily given by new prebendaries on their installation, as well as the money given by archbishops at visitations, should now be used for repairs and decoration.[134] From time to time, some of the money from fines was used for this purpose too. In 1704, for example, the architect Nicholas Hawksmoor was consulted on the best way to spend £400, part of Colonel Lee's fine, on beautifying the church, and in 1751, after a specially lush crop of fines, money was set aside for ornamenting it.[135] But a survey in 1721 showed that at least £14,000 would be needed to put the fabric in decent repair, and in 1722 the Dean and Chapter added up their expenses on the fabric since the Restoration and asked Archbishop Wake about the possibility of some kind of public provision for the Cathedral, 'which being the metropolitan and first in dignity of all England, we hope it will find a prominent place in his Majesty's and the parliament's care and regard'.[136] The attempt was unsuccessful. But clergy and members of the local laity made gifts to the Cathedral, indicating the affection in which it was held. In 1704 Archbishop Tenison gave a throne elaborately carved by the famous woodcarver Grinling Gibbons. Some prebendaries left money in their wills to be spent on the fabric: Samuel Shuckford and John Grandorge, for instance, bequeathed money for a new altar-piece, which was designed by Sir James Burrough, and for candlesticks.[137]

Despite all the problems with the fabric, a report of 1768 by the architect Robert Mylne stated that few Gothic Churches were in as good repair.[138] From 1773 the Dean and Chapter

[131] This kind of argument persuaded the Chapter to contribute to the collection for the Huguenots. Chapter Act Book, 1670–1710, fo. 64ᵛ.

[132] R. D. Gwynn, *Huguenot Heritage: The History and Contribution of the Huguenots in Britain* (London, 1985).

[133] W. Gostling, *A Walk In and About the City of Canterbury* (6th edn.; Canterbury, 1825), 148; Dean's Book, 1822–54, p. 113.

[134] E.g. Chapter Act Book, 1727–45, fo. 48ᵛ.

[135] Ibid. 1670–1710, fo. 191ᵛ; ibid. 1746–60, fo. 68.

[136] Dean's Book, 1718–42, fo. 62.

[137] For a more detailed account of Grandorge's charities, see R. Blomer, *A Discourse Concerning Conscience. With an Appendix Occasioned by the Death of the Reverend Dr. Grandorge, Late Prebendary of Canterbury, and Chaplain to the Right Honourable the late Earl of Thanet. A Sermon Preach'd in the Cathedral Church of Canterbury, Feb. 1. 1729–30* (London, 1730), 40.

[138] Fabric V, 22, Mylne's Survey and Report, 1768.

collected money to repave the nave, a scheme finally carried out in 1787. This received much criticism in the nineteenth century, especially from the Gothic Revivalists, but at the time, Hasted noted that it was 'much admired for its simplicity and neatness'.[139] Indications of concern for the fabric were the taking out of an insurance policy in 1796 and the purchase of a lightning-conductor in 1775, after a series of English churches had been damaged by lightning.[140] From 1797 the Chapter decided to place all business concerning the repairs of the Cathedral in the hands of one surveyor. The bells also received attention. They played an important role in the life of the city, signalling the approach of important events and calling people to service. In 1802 the bellringers petitioned the Dean and Chapter for more pay, claiming that they liked the new bells and that they would try to ring them well 'to please the Ear of all the City'.[141]

In the early nineteenth century, Dean Percy took great pains to improve the state of the fabric, importing Caen stone, as had been used in the medieval building. He was something of an amateur architect and he saw his work at Canterbury as part of his policy of making the building and services more orderly. In gratitude for his work, the Chapter agreed in 1827 to place his armorial bearings in the Cathedral.[142] There is no doubt that his term of office saw a great deal of activity on this front, which was not always appreciated by fellow members of the community. Canon Welfitt commented on Percy's 'rank activity and alertness on the scaffold of promotion'.[143]

By the end of the period, however, the Dean and Chapter were overwhelmed by the financial problem of maintaining a large medieval building, and a crisis began to loom as expenditure on fabric greatly exceeded the sum reserved for the purpose. In 1817 it was agreed that 10 per cent of fines should be used to augment this sum, and in 1830 matters had become so bad that the Chapter petitioned Parliament to be allowed to borrow on the security of their woods.[144] George Pellew (stall VI, 1822–8) was later to argue that instead of taking money from suppressed canonries to augment stipends of the parochial clergy, the Ecclesiastical Commission ought to encourage more expenditure on cathedral fabrics.[145]

The Library

This period also saw the development of a more regularly organized library within the Cathedral: the Chapter bought new books, appointed one of their body as librarian, and attempted to control borrowing rights. In particular, the Dean and Chapter encouraged scholarly research by subscribing to new books such as Robert Holmes's massive collation of the Septuagint (1788–1805).[146] Not surprisingly, theology, natural philosophy, and ecclesiastical and Kentish history dominated their reading, and Dean Horne seems to have been especially concerned to strengthen the library in these areas. He also encouraged the Chapter to buy Gibbon's *History of the Decline and Fall of the Roman Empire* (1776–88): 'As to Gibbon, he is in religious matters, bad enough, but a publick library cannot well do

[139] Hasted, *Kent* (cit. in n. 115), xi. 353.
[140] Dean's Book, 1793–1822, fo. 42; Chapter Act Book, 1775–96, fo. 11.
[141] Fabric VII, Petition of Cathedral Bell-Ringers, 1802.
[142] Dean's Book, 1822–54, pp. 53, 55.
[143] Add. MS 298, Canon Welfitt's Diary, fo. 33.
[144] Dean's Book, 1793–1822, p. 262; ibid. 1822–54, p. 99.
[145] Pellew, *Letter to Peel* (cit. in n. 129).
[146] Chapter Act Book, 1775–96, p. 359.

without such a history.'[147] It is worth recalling that in his memoirs Gibbon paid Horne the compliment of describing him as one of the very few assiduous dons during his time at Oxford.[148] The close relationship which existed between Lambeth and Canterbury enabled the library to receive duplicate volumes from the archbishop's library, and members of the diocesan clergy were able to borrow books. Prebendary Samuel Lisle informed Samuel Pegge, the antiquary and vicar of Godmersham (1731–51): 'I have desired Mr Norris [the auditor] to send you at any time such books of the library as you shall desire . . . and I think it very reasonable and proper that a collection of books should always be open for the assistance of any clergyman in the diocese, for the prosecution of his studies.'[149] An analysis of the reading patterns of the Dean and Chapter near the end of the period indicates that the library was well used. The years 1797–1817 saw a remarkable spate of borrowing activity, with 1,884 loans to forty-seven separate borrowers.[150] What is interesting to note is that William Paley's *Evidences of the Christian Religion* (1794), the most sustained and comprehensive argument for the existence of God from the argument from design, and a work which is often taken to be illustrative of the dominant latitudinarian tendencies of the late eighteenth-century clergy, was borrowed only four times, whereas the theological works of Horne and Jones, and the High Church *Guide to the Church* by Charles Daubeney (1798), were considerably more popular.

The Cathedral and the Public

The vogue for tourism, which has become so significant in defining the social function of Canterbury Cathedral in the present century, developed into a minor industry during the eighteenth century. The post-Reformation city lacked the throngs of pilgrims to Thomas Becket's tomb which had helped to make medieval Canterbury such an important centre, but as a diocesan capital and the seat of the Cathedral, the city continued to attract a substantial body of visitors. The city was geographically well placed to attract tourists, being an obvious stopping-off place for visitors to and from the Continent, on the main London to Dover road. Indeed, part of the route between Gravesend and Canterbury was the first to be turnpiked in the early eighteenth century.[151] Such a location brought a whole range of visitors to the city, from clergy and gentry on business to the military who descended on the area in times of war and who occasionally mustered in the Precincts, and the crowds who met at the Canterbury races on the nearby Barham Downs. The Cathedral had no rival for the attraction of tourists. It was by far the largest and most imposing edifice within the city, dwarfing all other buildings, dominating the Canterbury skyline, and making an immense visual and aural impact on the city and its visitors. As early as 1665 visitors such as John Evelyn could pay to be shown round the Cathedral,

[147] BL, Add. MS 39312, fo. 73, Horne to G. Berkeley, 2 Sept. 1788; CUL, MS 8134/B/7, fo. 16.

[148] Edward Gibbon, *Memoirs of My Life*, ed. B. Radice (Harmondsworth, 1984), 80. The Dean and Chapter bought Gibbon's *History* in 1785: Chapter Act Book, 1775–96, p. 361.

[149] Bodl., MS Eng. Lett. d. 43, fo. 138, Lisle to Pegge, 21 June 1752.

[150] 'Register of the Books Borrowed and Returned 1797–1827'; Paul Kaufman, 'Reading Vogues at English Cathedral Libraries of the Eighteenth Century', *Bull. New York Public Library,* 67 (1963), 644–55.

[151] F. W. Jessup, *A History of Kent* (2nd edn.; London, 1974), 48.

noting that 'the Cathedral is the finest sight here'.[152] In 1735 John Whaley observed that 'the Cathedral is the most magnificent one I have seen'.[153] Not all visitors, however, experienced the same 'gothic' sensation as did the young William Beckford in 1780, who recorded that

The moment after I got out of the carriage, brought me to the cathedral: an old haunt of mine. I had always venerated its lofty pillars, dim aisles, and mysterious arches. Last night they were more solemn than ever, and echoed no other sound than my steps. I strayed about the choir and chapels, till they grew so dark and dismal, that I was half inclined to be frightened; looked over my shoulder; thought of spectres that have an awkward trick of syllabling men's names in dreary places; and fancied a sepulchral voice exclaiming: 'Worship my toe at Ghent, my ribs at Florence, my skull at Bologna, Sienna and Rome. Beware how you neglect this order; for my bones, as well as my spirit, have the miraculous property of being here, there, and everywhere.' These injunctions, you may suppose, were received in a becoming manner, and noted all down in my pocket-book by inspiration (for I could not see).[154]

Nevertheless, other tourists clearly enjoyed their visit. In 1790 Viscount Torrington admired the well-performed service he attended in the Cathedral. He remarked that 'the screen and painted windows would yet do honour to the Popish Faith; and might raise a sigh over the Ruins of Religion'.[155] And during the 1790s exiled French Catholic clergy often felt homesick when they saw the Cathedral; it reminded them of their own ecclesiastical institutions which they had left behind.[156] Some of these refugees were taken up and supported by the Cathedral clergy, who seem to have had a slight penchant for the exiles. In 1799 one such *émigré*, Francis Charles D'Villars, was buried in the Precincts.[157]

The Cathedral was not slow in responding to its position as a tourist attraction. The Dean and Chapter helped to finance histories, and even guide books, which pointed out the most important sights, and they allowed authors to consult manuscript sources.[158] Such histories, forming part of the developing genre of county histories, highlighted the Cathedral's role within the life of the city, Kentish society, and the nation. These books expounded a Protestant, and specifically Church of England, historiography through which the past and the present could be understood. Most eighteenth-century writers of the Cathedral history explained its past in the form of an aggressive Anglicanism, shown in denigration of the medieval era and in the ignoring of the part played by Dissenters and Nonconformists within the life of the city and nation except as agents of social and political disorder. This Protestant attitude, which found it hard to say anything positive about the

[152] *Diary of Samuel Pepys* (cit. in n. 121), i. 172; *Diary of John Evelyn*, ed. de Beer (cit. in n. 36), iii. 395, 610; HMC, *Report on the Manuscripts of the Earl of Egmont*, ii (Dublin, 1909), 53: in 1676 Sir Philip Perceval 'paid 1s. to see the Church at Canterbury'; *The Illustrated Journeys of Celia Fiennes 1685–c.1712*, ed. C. Morris (London, 1982), 120–1; D. Defoe, *A Tour Thro' the Whole Island of Great Britain* (2 vols.; London, 1968), i. 117–18.

[153] *Horace Walpole's Miscellaneous Correspondence*, ed. W. S. Lewis and J. Riely (3 vols.; Oxford, 1980), i. 4.

[154] *The Grand Tour of William Beckford*, comp. and ed. Elizabeth Mavor (Harmondsworth, 1986), 22.

[155] *The Torrington Diaries*, ed. C. Bruyn Andrews (4 vols.;

London, 1934–8), iv. 165.

[156] McManners, *French Ecclesiastical Society* (cit. in n. 14), 293.

[157] *Register Booke*, ed. Hovenden (cit. in n. 32), 152.

[158] Somner, *Antiquities* (1703); J. Harris, *The History of Kent* (London, 1719); [J. Burnby], *An Historical Description of the Metro-political Church of Christ, Canterbury, Containing an Account of its Antiquities, and of its Accidents and Improvements, since the First Establishment* (Canterbury, 1772), intro.; J. Britton, *The History and Antiquities of the Cathedral Church of Canterbury* (London, 1821); Chapter Act Book, 1775–96, p. 27; Dean's Book, 1793–1822, p. 281.

Middle Ages, was expressed by Archbishop Herring in 1752 to Dean Lynch, concerning a request by the King of Sardinia to have the remains of Archbishop Anselm removed from the Cathedral.

You will believe I have no great Scruples on this Head, but if I had I would get rid of them all if the parting with the rotten Remains of a Rebel to his King, a slave to the Popedom and an Enemy to the married Clergy (all this Anselm was) would purchase Ease and Indulgence to one living Protestant. It is believed, that a Condescension in this Business may facilitate the way of doing it to thousands. I think it is worth the Experiment, and really for this End I should make no Conscience of palming on the Simpletons any other old Bishop with the Name of Anselm.[159]

But by the 1770s Hasted, in his *History of Kent*, was able to praise certain aspects of the medieval Cathedral, appreciating in particular medieval learning.[160] Hasted was a member of the important antiquarian and publishing circle around Canterbury: the local printers Simmons and Kirkby handled the printing of many works of obviously local interest, and of many of the sermons delivered in the Cathedral. Before the Civil War, local histories had tended to be very expensive and had been heavily dominated by London; it was only after the Restoration and in the eighteenth century that it became easier for provincial writers to participate, as local publishing centres and publication by subscription developed. In 1733 that doyen of antiquarian studies, Browne Willis, could say of Canterbury that 'there has been more wrote of this Cathedral than any other'.[161]

The most significant example of this genre was *A Walk In and About the City of Canterbury* (1774) by a minor canon, William Gostling (Pl. 43). Gostling's intimate knowledge of the Cathedral, and his acerbic commentary, made this an immediately popular and entertaining work. He himself conducted tours round the building. The Dean and Chapter helped with its publication, providing money for an illustration of the screen,[162] and Gostling's *Walk* soon almost received the status of an official guide. Gostling himself had done some original research on the medieval period of the Cathedral's history. In particular he entered into a debate with Samuel Denne concerning what he thought was the medieval baptistery (actually the Water Tower). Denne argued that since Canterbury had been a monastery, there would have been no need for a baptistery, and that the object was a lavatory.[163] Other Cathedral clergy participated in the tourist vogue: John Duncombe, better known for his satire on Gray's Elegy, extolled the history of the Cathedral and the charms of its buildings in a poem which soon found its way into the histories[164].

A nice indication of the developing interest in the history and the continuity of the cathedral tradition and community at Canterbury was the growth of the collection of portraits of past deans and other members of the community. In the mid-eighteenth century there were twenty-six portraits in the Deanery.[165] An especially interesting group was the series of late seventeenth- and early eighteenth-century portraits, Dean Tillotson

[159] HMC, *Report on MSS in Various Collections*, i (1901), 226, Herring to Lynch, 23 Dec. 1752.

[160] Hasted, *Kent* (cit. in n. 115), xi. 497.

[161] B. Willis, *Parochiale Anglicanum* (London, 1733), pref.

[162] Chapter Act Book, 1775–96, p. 27.

[163] S. Denne, 'Observations on Canterbury Cathedral', *Archaeologia*, 10 (1792), 37–49.

[164] J. Duncombe, *An Elegy Written in Canterbury Cathedral* (Canterbury, 1778).

[165] BL, Add. MS 6391, fos. 88–89ᵛ, 'Painted Portraits in the Deanery-house, Canterbury, 1796'; J. Ingamells, *The English Episcopal Portrait, 1559–1835* (Guildford, 1983), 31.

being painted by the gifted Mary Beale. Another series of portraits was painted in the late eighteenth century of Deans Brownlow North, Cornwallis, and Moore by the society portrait-painter George Romney. The Cathedral was not alone in this search for a sense of continuing tradition in visual images. At Lambeth the archbishops of the period built up an impressive collection of portraits of their predecessors, so that by 1783 the gallery at Lambeth held a portrait of every archbishop since the Reformation.[166] Of especial interest to the Cathedral visitor in search of the past were the monumental tombs and inscriptions, commemorating local and national worthies who had played some part in the life of the Cathedral. Amongst such tombs which were pointed out in the guidebooks of the period, alongside that of the Black Prince and that of Dean Neville, was that of Miss Ann Milles, 'the beauty of Kent'; she had died in 1720 aged 20, 'known for her beauty, charity and religious devotion'.

As part of the vogue for tourism and the interest in the Gothic architecture of the past which developed in the eighteenth century, views of Canterbury Cathedral could be purchased, set in a suitably pastoral and nostalgic light. Canterbury received several entries in Samuel and Nathaniel Buck's *Venerable Remains*, which was begun in 1720. During the 1790s the young J. M. W. Turner made some water-colour paintings of the Cathedral, including a splendidly dramatic view of St Anselm's Chapel (1793) (Pl. 42). This shows the contemporary appeal of the picturesque, while the choice of viewpoint, a low one, ensured that Turner could make the most of the dramatic effects of soaring masonry and steep perspective. The *Prospect of Canterbury* (*c*.1820) by G. F. Robson depicts the Cathedral as glimpsed in the distance from an Arcadian vantage-point (Pl. 46). The most notable local artist was Thomas Sidney Cooper (1803–1902). He was best known for his paintings of cows, but his earliest attempt at drawing was a picture of Bell Harry tower, and he remembered visitors coming to the city in the early nineteenth century and buying his drawings of the Cathedral.[167] Gerrard Andrewes (Dean, 1809–25) suggested that the canons and minor canons should encourage such artistic talent by subscribing to copies of Cooper's drawings. One of the minor canons, William Chafey, wanted one, but his wife remarked that they had plenty already. To which Chafey replied, 'Well, my dear . . . the old cow has given me a good deal of milk. I really must have another portrait of her.'[168]

The attraction of the Cathedral to professional and amateur artists was so great that in 1812 the Dean and Chapter forbade anyone from taking drawings of the interior without permission.[169] By the 1820s it was possible to purchase lithographed copies of Cooper's drawings and those of other artists at one of the many print-sellers within the city as a souvenir of the visit. Canterbury and its Cathedral were a place to visit or to stay at for a holiday, a historic cathedral city whose rural surroundings provided a contrast to the rapid urban growth of the early nineteenth century. But being a tourist attraction did not always bring advantages to the community. Then, as now, the stream of visitors could interfere with the Cathedral services and disturb the tranquillity of the Precincts. In 1784 the Chapter

[166] Dorothy Gardiner, *The Story of Lambeth Palace* (London, 1930), 223; S. and N. Buck, *Perspective Views of the Ruins of the most noted Abbeys and Castles of England* (3 vols.; London, 1726–36).

[167] T. S. Cooper, *My Life* (2 vols.; London, 1890), i. 43; ii. 219–21.

[168] Ibid. ii. 222.

[169] Dean's Book, 1793–1822, p. 203.

ordered that 'the custom be discontinued of admitting the rabble, during the Fair and other holiday times, to see Bell Harry'[170] and in 1819 they hung up a notice forbidding tourists to look around the Cathedral at all on Sundays and during service times on other days.[171]

The Cathedral as Landlord

The usual picture of eighteenth-century cathedrals as spiritually torpid, complacent, and self-satisfied institutions often centres on their financial activities. The position of Canterbury Cathedral in this argument is dominant: its wealth received adverse attention from as early as Blue Dick Culmer's attack in 1643 to the criticisms of the unitarian and political radical John Wade, who, in his *Black Book; or Corruption Unmasked!* (1820) singled out Canterbury as a special object for his venom.[172] Given the importance of Canterbury as the centre of anti-Unitarian ideology in the late eighteenth century, it is not surprising to find that Wade, an heir to the Church's opponents Price and Priestley, should find it so corrupt and oppressive. The reformers of the nineteenth century were to bring about a series of financial changes which ultimately took the responsibility for the administration of the Cathedral's wealth out of the prebendaries' hands and placed it firmly in those of the Ecclesiastical Commissioners, believing that involvement in financial matters had diverted prebendaries from their true role. Such a line of thought would, however, have been fundamentally wrong-headed in eighteenth-century terms. Far from being seen as a separate aspect of the prebendaries' activity, the leasing of Cathedral property in Kent and elsewhere (including Norfolk, Sussex, Essex, Surrey, and Devon) was regarded as integral to the maintenance of the community's position within local society.

The leasing of its property involved complex relationships between the Cathedral and its tenants, while a concentration of lands in Kent (87 per cent) meant that the estates would be a sensitive tool in the relationship between clerical and lay society. To attempt an adequate assessment of the administration of Church property in this period, we must view it in terms of the criteria applied by members of the community themselves. They needed to maintain their income and preserve their property. But most prebendaries had little experience in estate management, and their other commitments meant that they could not become directly involved in the day-to-day running of their estates. Yet they were the heirs of Archbishop Laud in seeing that the Church could neither take active leadership in society nor battle against what was seen as the increasing immorality of the age unless it was economically independent. The argument was neo-Harringtonian: power and influence in society went hand in hand with landed wealth. Anglican thought in Kent on the question of Church property had a highly respectable pedigree: Richard Hooker

---

[170] Ibid. 1777–92, fo. 117.

[171] Ibid. 1793–1822, p. 277.

[172] R. Culmer, *Cathedrall Newes from Canterbury*, repr. in G[eorge] S[mith], *Chronological History* (cit. in n. 54), 282–317; Wade, *Black Book* (cit. in n. 50), 286, 298. But despite the criticisms which highlighted the wealth of Canterbury, it is clear that other cathedrals were more lucrative. N. Sykes, *Church and* *State in the Eighteenth Century* (Cambridge, 1934), 149, shows that in the mid-century, prebends at Windsor, Oxford, and St Paul's were worth more than at Canterbury. A sympathetic treatment of cathedral finance is C. Clay, ' "The Greed of Whig Bishops"?: Church Landlords and Their Lessees 1660–1760', *Past & Present*, 87 (1980), 128–57.

during his time as incumbent of Bishopsbourne in the 1590s had expounded on this theme. He had justified the Anglican Church's landed wealth in terms of the close interconnection between ecclesiastical and lay society. Church lands had divine sanction, but they also had foundations in civil property-rights which must be firmly established. Thus the defence of ecclesiastical property-rights meant far more than the careful management of property: it grew out of the overriding conviction that the clergy must retain a separate status and independence in the world.

It had also long been a central thread in Anglican propaganda to stress that the wealth of the Church was beneficial to society at large. At the Restoration the Cathedral's defence of its financial position rested on its concern for the relief of the poor 'and the good and benefit of the Publick and Posterity'. And the way in which a hard-line administration of property could sour relations with local society had been seen during the 1630s. The consequences of the economic dimension of Laud's aggressive clericalism in the diocese had been disastrous. He had made little attempt at cordial relations with the local gentry and had encouraged the Dean and Chapter to follow his example. Under Laud's direction the Cathedral had curtailed its charitable expenditure and hitched up its rents.[173] Post-Restoration and eighteenth-century clergy were well aware of the criticisms of Laud. They had to work within a framework where they could defend Church rights but could not afford to alienate their supporters. They had to understand the limitations within which they moved and realize that the administration of Church lands required delicate handling. Cathedral property was one of the areas where the life of the community impinged most fully on lay consciousness. In a county like Kent, where leading members of the laity had long been sensitive to the delicate balance of lay and clerical relations, the Church would not be free to act without considering the implications for its position within local society.

An important concern for the Cathedral community in this period was to acquaint itself with the fortunes and developments of its estates in earlier periods. It was then that the rights and privileges belonging to its lands had first emerged; and at a time when clergy found it necessary to defend such privileges in the face of criticism, a knowledge of their historic basis was essential. Deans and those most concerned with the administration of the lands and property, the receiver and treasurer, took the trouble to familiarize themselves with the extent and past fortunes of the lands. This was not out of any purely antiquarian motive. An interest in the historical formation of their estates was, in a legally minded age, necessary for an understanding of the present position and responsibilities of the Church within the local community.

It is not surprising, then, that the Dean and Chapter felt compelled to preserve and order the records relating to their lands and rights. At the Restoration, Dean Turner admitted that 'our Audit Bookes ... were not soe exactly kept as they ought' and the problem was only exacerbated with the destruction of many records in a fire which burnt down the Audit House in 1670.[174] There was much correspondence between certain

---

[173] Clark, *English Provincial Society* (cit. in n. 12), 367; Felicity Heal, 'Archbishop Laud Revisited: Leases and Estate Management at Canterbury and Winchester Before the Civil War', in *Princes and Paupers in the English Church 1500–1800*, ed. R. O'Day and ead. (Leicester, 1981), 129–51; D. A. Heaton, 'A Study of the Structure of Corporate Estate management of the Lands of the Dean and Chapter, 1640–1760' (MA thesis, Univ. of Kent, 1971), 28.

[174] Bodl., MS Tanner 123, fos. 68, 21.

members of the Cathedral community and the archbishops' librarians at Lambeth in order to ascertain the rights of the Church. The two most substantial collection of documents relating to the customs, privileges, and rights of the Anglican Church produced in the period, Edmund Gibson's *Codex Juris Ecclesiae Anglicanae* (1713) and David Wilkins's *Concilia Magnae Britanniae et Hiberniae* (1737), drew extensively on medieval and post-Reformation records at Lambeth which referred to the rights of the archbishops and the Cathedral at Canterbury. In both cases the records of the see and the Cathedral were used to reveal the rights and workings of the national Church. This interest can be seen as part of the wider eighteenth-century fascination with the medieval era; the disruption to records caused by the Civil War encouraged clergy to investigate what seemed to be a more stable society. In some ways this was a continuation of the tradition established by Archbishop Matthew Parker in his *De Antiquitate Britannicae Ecclesiae et Privilegiis Ecclesiae Cantuariensis* (1572), of which a new edition was printed in 1729. This work was a demonstration of the continuity of the historical tradition at Canterbury. Clergy were not only concerned to defend the economic privileges of the Cathedral: the lands belonging to the parish clergy were in as much need of defence. In the 1760s Henry Hall, the vicar of Harbledown, helped provide information from the Cathedral registers for the Lambeth Librarian, A. C. Ducarel,[175] who produced a new edition of Gibson's *Codex* and, in 1763, a *Repertory of the Endowments of the Diocese of Canterbury,* which listed the tithe rights and privileges of each parish, in order to settle incumbents' rights against the encroachments of the laity. And clergy from within the Cathedral community and diocese helped Edward Hasted to compile his popular *History of Kent* (1778–99), a large part of which consisted of information concerning ecclesiastical rights.[176]

But however concerned the Cathedral authorities were to safeguard the rights of the Church, their freedom for manœuvre was severely constrained by custom and local demands, and in some cases by self-interest and inertia. Charles II, in the tradition of his father and Archbishop Laud, forbade the Cathedral in 1660 to convert leases for years into leases for lives, as an attempt to keep a tighter check on Church property.[177] But in 1660–1 fourteen of the Cathedral estates were newly let on leases for a period of three lives, and in the early nineteenth century six estates were still leased for lives.[178] A three-life lease was considered a better bargain for the tenants than one for twenty-one years, and most changes from lives to years happened when a lease changed hands or when the nature of the lease was altered, as at Monkton manor in 1781.[179] At times, too, the financial self-interest of the prebendaries could not be overcome. A lease for lives meant that the Dean and Chapter would receive a large fine, to the detriment of their successors. George Berkeley while vice-dean in the 1760s attempted to persuade the rest of the Chapter not to agree to leases for lives. He wrote to his wife: 'I have strenuously opposed the present

---

[175] LPL, MS 1163, fos. 108, 156; Nichols, *Literary Anecdotes* (cit. in n. 66), ix. 315–17.

[176] Hasted's account of the Deans was based on the minor canon H. J. Todd's *Some Account of the Deans of Canterbury; From the New Foundation of that Church, by Henry the Eighth, to the Present Time* (Canterbury and London, 1793); J. Boyle, *In Quest of Hasted* (Chichester, 1984), 61, 62, 67, 70, for evidence of other

clergy connected with the Cathedral who helped Hasted in his researches.

[177] Bodl., MS Tanner 128, fo. 41, Charles II to Dean and Chapter, 22 June 1662.

[178] Heaton, 'Lands of the Dean and Chapter' (cit. in n. 173), 86.

[179] Ibid.

mood of renewing life estates and I hope to good effect . . . this Chapter has afforded us an opportunity to reject a considerable fine on such a lease.'[180] His plan failed, but later that year a resolution was passed not to allow such leases.

The Cathedral's income remained fairly static for nearly a century after 1660, despite the fact that between the Restoration and the mid-eighteenth century increased costs, inflation, and rising taxes put pressures on the Cathedral to increase its revenue. In the late seventeenth century the deanery was worth about £540 per annum and canonries about £220, and similar figures prevailed in the 1740s.[181] The Restoration policy of treating tenants charitably had the result of constraining the Chapter for the next century: having leased at easy rents, it found it difficult to effect change. Thomas Bowers (stall III, 1715–24; archdeacon of Canterbury, 1721–4) recognized this:

Tis probable that the low value of money, the dearness of all things belonging to house-keeping and the more expensive way of living among all ranks and degrees of men, may awaken Churchmen to look more carefully into their estates, and to go a little out of the old track which their predecessors for a long time have gone in, without due thought or consideration, regarding only which had formerly been taken and not considering the present state of the world.[182]

But the Canterbury Chapter was bound by past precedent and found it difficult to raise its income to an economically realistic level. Tenants fared better from beneficial leasing, which was easier to administrate than the more active policy of rack-renting, which necessitated a more constant supervision but worked against any real economic exploitation of Church estates. During the 1720s, the Dean and Chapter did try to alter the basis of their fines from one and a quarter years' value for a renewal of seven years to one and a half years' value.[183] In 1720 Dean Stanhope explained to Archbishop Wake that they had attempted this with their largest lease and had informed the Dean and Chapter of Rochester 'so we do not stand alone'.[184] He argued that it was necessary to do this because of the different ways in which clerical and lay landlords dealt with their tenants. But the attempt met with a great deal of hostility, and eventually, in 1727, tenants' complaints forced the Chapter to revert to its former policy. It is clear that the Chapter had to move warily. In 1722 Sir Hewit Aucher protested against the new policy and in 1723 John Penton wrote a hectoring letter to the Chapter about an 'exorbitant fine'.[185] In the face of such attacks, the Dean and Chapter defended their action on the grounds that the fines they asked were still less than the real value of the land, that they were also less than the amounts taken by lay landlords, and that 'some men would always have the Church tied down by old fines'. They concluded that: 'it is said that the Church by Raising their Fines, Grow Harder Landlords than they were Formerly: And that it is by No Means a Proper Time for Churchmen to Do This, when They have so much Need of doing Evr'y Thing to Oblige the Laity to stand by them & Protect them from their Enemys'.[186]

[180] BL, Add. MS 39311, fo. 226, Berkeley to Mrs Berkeley, 30 June 1770.

[181] Bodl., MS Tanner 123, fo. 32. By 1759 the deanery was worth £900, the prebends £350. E. N. Williams, *The Eighteenth-Century Constitution* (Cambridge, 1970), 348.

[182] T. Bowers, *The Value of Church and College Leases Consider'd, and the Advantages of the Lessees made very Apparent* (2nd edn.; London, 1722), 12.

[183] Westminster Abbey Muniments, 25096 A/B, fo. 79.

[184] Christ Church Library, Oxford, MS Wake 8, fo. 20, Stanhope to Wake, 25 June 1720.

[185] Dean's Book, 1718–42, p. 75 and letter bound between 98 and 99.

[186] Ibid., p. 2 of 3 pages inserted between pp. 100 and 101.

The 1720s and 1730s were a time when the Church's economic position was viewed with suspicion. The Church went through a time of crisis, the object of attack being its wealth, property, and power. Norman Sykes likened the hostility to that experienced by the Church in the Reformation parliament of the 1530s,[187] and there are also close similarities to the 1830s, when radical politicians again denounced the privileges of the Church. In all these periods cathedrals were viewed as the most overt symbol of the Church's power, and not surprisingly became the centre for attack. In 1723 the Chapter advised 'any prebendaries in London to resist any attempt to bring a Bill for ascertaining fines or rents of Ecclesiastical estates',[188] and in 1736 the Dean and several prebendaries met together for a similar purpose.[189] During the previous parliamentary session a bill to let Quakers off paying their tithes had been debated and the bishops and cathedral dignitaries rallied to support the Church.[190] This is one instance of how far concern for Church interests could override feelings of compliance to the government, and how, in times of crisis, the decentralized Church could unite. In 1769 the Chapter noted with concern that 'there seems to be a dangerous Association formed among the Farmers in Essex and Suffolk to destroy the rights of collecting and gathering Tithes in the usual and legal way in defence of which we think ourselves and all persons concerned'. Along with the chapters of St Paul's, Ely, and Norwich, the Canterbury Chapter contributed to this defence.[191]

Some idea of the constraints under which the Dean and Chapter operated as landlords can be seen in the hostile reaction from tenants to any attempt to defend and strengthen church interests. The laity were quick to react when they felt that changes were afoot. In 1748 a vicious satire on Dean Lynch included criticism of his handling of Church lands as part of a general condemnation. The pamphlet is revealing not as an accurate portrayal of the Dean's behaviour, but for indicating how the laity expected clerical landlords to behave. It was alleged that the Dean had disregarded the traditional policy of 'being prudent and easy with tenants'. Instead he treated 'yeoman and farmers . . . as his dogs'.[192]

A major factor in explaining the inability of the Canterbury Chapter to secure a realistic return from its lands was its reliance for most of the period on its own members to survey and value them, and its acceptance of the values given by tenants when negotiating a fine. During the early years of the Restoration and at periodic intervals afterwards, the prebendaries would value their estates: John Bargrave's notes of his tours of the Cathedral's estates during the 1670s, when he was receiver, still survive.[193] It is clear that at the

[187] N. Sykes, *Edmund Gibson, Bishop of London, 1669–1748* (Oxford, 1926), 149.

[188] Chapter Act Book, 1711–26, fo. 135ᵛ.

[189] Ibid. 1727–45, fo. 112ᵛ.

[190] S. Taylor, 'Sir Robert Walpole, the Church of England, and the Quakers Tithe Bill of 1736', *Hist. Jnl.*, 27 (1985), 51–77.

[191] Dean's Book, 1761–76, fo. 135.

[192] *The Life of Dean L—ch by a Yeoman of Kent. No Canterbury Tale. And shall they escape for such Wickedness?* (London, 1748), 29. Pyle called Lynch a 'vast carcass', quoted in *Memoirs of a Royal Chaplain, 1729–1763. The Correspondence of Edward Pyle, D. D. Chaplain in Ordinary to George II with Samuel Kerrick, D. D., Vicar of Dersingham, Rector of Wolferton, and Rector of West Newton*, ed. A. Hartshorne (London, 1905), 288. For some

defences of Lynch from within the Cathedral community, which stress his charity, see *Poems by the late George-Monck Berkeley* (cit. in n. 65), p. ccxl; W. Jones, *Memoirs of the Life, Studies, and Writings of the Most Reverend George Horne* (London, 1795), 339.

[193] Bodl., MS Tanner 123, fo. 68; Surveys 12–21; C. E. Woodruff, 'A Seventeenth-Century Survey of the Estates of the Dean and Chapter in East Kent', *Arch. Cant.*, 38 (1926), 29–44; C. E. Woodruff, 'A Survey of the Sussex Estates of the Dean and Chapter of Canterbury', *Sussex Archaeol. Collections*, 53 (1910), 192–7. The Chapter relied heavily on their auditors. There were especial problems in finding a successor to the omniscient William Somner. Bodl., MS Rawlinson 93, fo. 47; MS Tanner 123, fo. 8, Turner to Sheldon, 28 Aug. 1672.

Restoration the Chapter recognized the importance of having accurate surveys: from 1681 the Hill family was employed from time to time to map the Cathedral's estates.[194] But this seems to have been rather a haphazard policy, and in the 1750s the Chapter was still accepting the tenants' valuations of lands and rents before renewals. It was not until 1762 that the Chapter agreed that 'for the future all such of our estates as are not mapped, shall be surveyed and mapped'.[195] In 1772 the Chapter purchased a theodolite to help such surveying.[196] Fines were supposed to be based on a notional rack-rent, but until the 1770s the Cathedral did not have an accurate record of the acreage by which such assessments could be multiplied. By and large, the Chapter had to rely on the rent which the tenant 'confessed' to be receiving from the undertenant. Tenants would not always reveal what they themselves made from their undertenants. Sometimes a measure of secrecy was required before the Cathedral could gain an impression of the exact amount made by their tenants. It was not unusual for the Chapter to ask clergy who lived near the estate in question to undertake investigations on their behalf.[197]

Gradually this rather haphazard policy changed. This process was partly the result of the increasing sophistication of estate-management techniques, especially the employment of professional land-agents to survey and value their estates. Reliance on members of the Chapter, who were not trained in such matters, had always been problematic. Some of the prebendaries were more interested than others in the Cathedral's property. Hasted noted that Lynford Caryl (stall XI, 1766–81) was 'a person to whom the body is much indebted for his indefatigable care and industry in the regulation and improvement of their estates'.[198] During Caryl's tenure of office in 1769, entries were made in books and not on parchment, which made it easier to cross-reference, and in 1772 the Chapter agreed that a week before each Chapter meeting the mason and carpenter would inspect Cathedral property in the Precincts, as a way of ensuring that improvements were kept up.[199] This, together with the general economic boom of the late eighteenth century, enabled the Cathedral to demand a higher return from its lands. Yet even as late as 1808 the Chapter was not really sure about the value of some of its outlying lands.[200] An increasing concern to use professional land-agents at the end of the eighteenth century can be found in other cathedrals, too, such as Winchester.[201]

But it was not only the fact that the Canterbury Chapter might not have the expertise or inclination to raise more money from their lands, it was also a matter of policy. The Chapter wanted to present itself as a paternalistic landlord. Prebendary Thomas Bowers maintained that 'Churchmen should be better landlords than laymen are'.[202] Being charitable to tenants and agreeing on moderate fines was part of a conscious policy of building up support within local society. The Chapter Act Books are full of references to the needs

[194] See A. Oakley, 'The Hill Family of Canterbury, St Paul, Mapmakers', in *The Parish of St Martin and St Paul, Canterbury*, ed. M. Sparks (Canterbury, 1980), 68–70.
[195] Chapter Act Book, 1761–75, fo. 28.
[196] Ibid., fo. 297.
[197] Dean's Book, 1718–42, fo. 11.
[198] Hasted, *Kent* (cit. in n. 115), xi. 528.
[199] Chapter Act Book, 1761–75, fos. 212, 284.

[200] Ibid. 1794–1824, fo. 231.
[201] F. Bussby, *Winchester Cathedral, 1079–1974* (Southampton, 1979), 173.
[202] Bowers, *Value of Church Leases Consider'd* (cit. in n. 182). It seems that French canons were also more interested in maintaining revenues than in enhancing profits. See O. Hufton, *Bayeux in the Late Eighteenth Century: A Social Study* (Oxford, 1967), 28.

of tenants being taken into consideration. The image of the Church as a charitable organization was a powerful one in Anglican propaganda, and the treatment of tenants could be seen within this framework. Through its clientèle of tenants in the area, the Cathedral could establish and maintain 'friends to the Church'. Such 'friends' were viewed as the backbone of lay Anglicanism within provincial society, providing support for the Church against Dissenters, helping in the upkeep of parish churches, and ensuring that a significant proportion of the leading members of the Kentish gentry had a vested interest in the continuation of the Church of England's position within society. The list of the Cathedral's tenants in this period reads like a roll-call of Kentish society. The families of Honeywood, Oxenden, Hales, Brook-Brydges, and Guilford appear constantly, the very continuity of names from the Restoration to the early nineteenth century being in itself one consequence of that stability which the Restored Church brought to the provinces. It was this level of Kentish society which Jane Austen came to know so well in the early nineteenth century: her relations at Godmersham were for much of this period lessees of the Church, and in her correspondence she notes the importance of audit day at the Cathedral, when civilities were exchanged between the prebendaries and local gentry.[203] The continuity in the lessees, especially on the larger estates, was in any case beneficial, encouraging tenants to spend money on improvements. And the Chapter needed to have tenants with enough local prestige to ensure that the name of the Church was not harmed, and rich enough to pay their fines.

Much of the responsibility for maintaining a satisfactory relationship between ecclesiastical landlords and their tenants rested on the estate officials. The Dean and Chapter employed a whole host of receivers, agents, and wood-reeves to help them in the administration of their estates. Such officials could be a vital bridge between the interests of the Church and the preoccupations of lay society. Their intimate knowledge of the layout of the Cathedral's property was crucial in helping prebendaries obtain information about their lands and tenants, the Church benefiting from the continuity of administration offered by such long-standing officials. The estate officials could help iron out tenants' grievances, especially during the delicate time when fines were being assessed. Officials were so important in maintaining the relationship between Church and local interests that it was essential to employ men who had the tenants' confidence. As was pointed out by the writer on estate management Edward Laurence, stewards and estate officials must be reasonable with tenants, 'not in the blustering manner of agents sent down from London'.[204] Once rapport had been gained, the Church authorities might be able to learn more about their property. There was much competition among local families for such posts. Archbishop Sancroft was informed in 1681 that 'woodreeves' places in Kent are to my knowledge coveted by the best gentlemen in Canterbury'.[205] The post of gamekeeper was also much sought after by local gentry, since it gave a tacit right to game.

[203] Among the larger estates which remained in the hands of the same gentry family throughout this period are Adisham (Oxenden family), Tenterden (Hales), East Peckham (Twysden), and Eastry (Bargrave). For this, see C. R. Bunce's *Schedule* (1805); *Jane Austen's Letters to Her Sister Cassandra and Others*, ed. R. W. Chapman (2nd edn.; London, 1952), 215, 20

June 1808. The use of estates to build up a body of support in the area had long been a feature of leasing-policy. See Clark, *English Provincial Society* (cit. in n. 12), 43.

[204] E. Laurence, *The Duty and Office of a Land Steward* (Dublin, 1731), 11.

[205] Bodl., MS Rawlinson letters 106, fo. 181.

The Cathedral and the City

The houses in the Precincts were an unusual type of urban property owned by the Cathedral. It had been part of Archbishop Laud's policy to attempt to remove lay tenants from these houses,[206] but this policy had ended abruptly in the Civil War, when parliamentary forces took over the buildings. At the Restoration some attempt seems to have been made to revive this aspect of Laudian policy. But Laud's vision of the collegiality of the clerical community, set apart from lay society, had little relevance after 1660, when the clergy's wives were such a feature of the Precincts. In the early seventeenth century, only four of the prebendaries were married, but after 1660 clerical marriage became the norm, and the clergyman's wife became a distinctive feature of the community at Canterbury. The wives of the prebendaries, minor canons, and Six Preachers helped foster a sense of Cathedral community: during the late eighteenth century, life in the Precincts seems to have been dominated by Eliza Berkeley and Susanna Duncombe, the poet and illustrator, who was notorious for breeding cats. The presence of wives and children within the Precincts is testimony to the developing family atmosphere of the Cathedral and represents an immensely important change in the nature of the community which existed under the shadow of Bell Harry. A satirical pamphlet of 1718 noted how the prebendaries' wives were famed for their beauty and how they attracted tourists.[207] The extent of the community is apparent from the names of the people buried within the Precincts—the wives and children of prebendaries and minor canons, the lay-clerks, and the cathedral servants.[208] These people living in the Precincts served to make the Church more of a self-sustaining and close-knit institution, as well as helping to integrate the Cathedral into the wider cultural world. Indeed, the literary and artistic connections of the community were strong, bringing relatives and friends to stay: the religious poet Sarah Dixon, a relation of John Bunce; the bluestocking Hester Chapone, the niece of Edward Donne's wife (stall IV, 1736–46); Joseph Highmore, the society portrait-painter and illustrator of Richardson's novels, who retired in 1760 to live with his daughter, Susanna Duncombe, in the Precincts, where he was later buried; and the author and classical scholar Elizabeth Carter, known as the most pious woman in England, who lived in Deal. And Allen Fielding (Six Preacher, 1816–23) was the son of the novelist. It may be, too, that the influence of the wives of the prebendaries can be seen in the changes in the appearance of many of the houses within the Precincts in this period. The 'modernization' which they encouraged, including the addition of bay-windows, porches, and mathematical tiles to the façades of the houses, as well as the enlargement of some of the rooms, suggest a response to the pressures of more sophisticated tastes and the need to find room for larger families.[209]

The Chapter was wary about leasing out property in the Precincts to people from the city. In 1687, when John Younger (stall II, 1685–92) leased out his house to Colonel Henry

[206] Clark, *English Provincial Society* (cit. in n. 12), 393.

[207] A great deal of information relating to life in the Precincts in the late 18th cent. can be gleaned from the gossipy preface to *Poems by the late George-Monck Berkeley* (cit. in n. 65); Dorothy Gardiner, 'The Berkeleys of Canterbury', *Arch. Cant.*, 69 (1956 for 1955), 117–24; *A Panegyrical Poem on the Fair and Celebrated Beauties in and about the City of Canterbury* (Canterbury, 1718); cf.

The Oaks; or the Beauties of Canterbury. A Comedy as performed at the Theatre in Canterbury. Written by Mrs Burgess (Canterbury, 1780).

[208] *Register Booke*, ed. Hovenden (cit. in n. 32).

[209] On some of the 'improvements' in the Precincts, see T. P. Smith, 'Deception in the Precincts', *Cant. Cath. Chron.*, 83 (1989), 18–22.

Lee, the Mayor of Canterbury, an agreement was drawn up which necessitated the mayor's leaving his mace, the symbol of his authority, outside the Precincts.[210] Some of the Precinct houses belonging to the Six Preachers were rarely used as their place of residence and were also leased out. But relations between the lay and clerical residents in the Precincts were not without their tensions. That High Churchman, George Stanhope, was anxious to safeguard his prestige as Dean of the metropolitical Cathedral and reacted strongly whenever he felt that his status was being undermined. After a particularly exuberant soirée at the house of Sir Richard Head, the Dean claimed to have been woken up and insulted by members of the party.[211] Yet by the 1780s Hasted could refer to the 'genteel families, who form a very respectable neighbourhood within these precincts, which are kept remarkably clean and neat, and being gravelled and well planted with rows of trees, make a most pleasant and desirable residence'.[212] For such families, and for other gentry within the city and locality, the Cathedral was becoming a favourite place for christenings, marriages, and burials.

Another source of potential grievance was the tendency for shopkeepers and house-owners in Canterbury to extend their own properties in ways that might be detrimental to the Cathedral's property. Orders were issued to prevent people depositing rubbish in the Precincts.[213] The Cathedral authorities sought to preserve the peace and separate character of the Precincts. They demanded the removal of cattle, horses, and geese from grazing within the cloisters and in 1722 ordered the keeper of their gaol to drive out all beggars 'and not to suffer such Nastiness about the church or Precincts as is so intolerably otherwise at present'.[214] In the early nineteenth century the Dean and Chapter were concerned about the havoc caused by the annual fair. In 1810 by their resolution 'All Puppet Shews, Gin Stalls, Roundabouts, Wild Beasts, Swings etc. were refused admittance, and no Stalls allowed but on the Broad Pavement and one under the Gateway for Gingerbread, Toys and Merchandise'.[215] In 1814 it was agreed to remove the fair from the Precincts altogether and move it to the Cattle Market in the city.[216]

The presence of lay tenants within the Precincts was symptomatic of the Church's relations with the city at large. The Dean and Chapter were a dominating force within city life: they owned many of the inns, shops, and properties within Canterbury; they provided employment for many of its inhabitants; they contributed to the upkeep of the roads; and they played a large part in shaping the economic fortunes of the city. The Church's economic presence in the city led, on the whole, to the achievement of good relations between the city and the Cathedral. This had not, of course, always been the case. In earlier periods, the city had been a centre of anti-clericalism, often in bitter dispute with the Cathedral clergy. But by the eighteenth century, matters had improved and the mayor and corporation attended services in the Cathedral. Most of the houses in the

---

[210] Treasurer's Book, 1663–4, copy of a letter from Lord Treasurer Southampton to Sir Thomas Peyton and Sir Anthony Aucher, 22 Oct. 1664; Reg. 29, fo. 291, Col. Lee's Agreement, 28 Oct. 1687; Bodl., MS Add. c. 307, fo. 174. For the wider problem of maintaining corporate independence, see R. Beddard, 'The Privileges of Christchurch, Canterbury: Archbishop Sheldon's Enquiries of 1671', *Arch. Cant.*, 87 (1973), 81–100.

[211] Chapter Act Book, 1711–26, fos. 71ᵛ, 75.
[212] Dean's Book, 1718–42, fo. 197; Hasted, *Kent* (cit. in n. 115), xi. 542.
[213] Dean's Book, 1776–93, fo. 63.
[214] Chapter Act Book, 1711–26, fo. 51.
[215] Dean's Book, 1793–1822, pp. 158, 169, 210.
[216] Hasted, *Kent* (cit. in n. 115), xi. 100.

parishes of St Andrew, St Mary Magdalen, and St Alphege, the major trading area of the city, were held under lease from the Chapter, and the number of people employed on a regular and part-time basis made the Cathedral the largest employer within the city and its environs. The range of employment is also striking—from the holders of important offices such as the auditor, to the rat-catcher (paid 6*d*. a rat) and the old people who were given small jobs such as sweeping the library and making brooms, mending carpets and washing surplices.[217] In 1676 the Chapter paid for people to go to London to be touched for the King's Evil, and in the next year it gave money to a dying man and for a woman to watch over him.[218] All this was part of the Cathedral's paternalist role within the city: providing help and giving alms to the poor, who were paid after sacrament; paying for the education of tradesmen's sons and finding choristers apprenticeships; looking after the relations of former employees and administering the charity for clergy widows; and maintaining a prison.[219] A testimony to the relationship between the Cathedral, the city, and the county was the foundation of the Kent and Canterbury Hospital in 1791. The Dean and Chapter helped contribute towards its building and paid for the maintenance of the hospital chaplain.[220]

The Chapter also contributed to the spate of improvements in the city at the end of the eighteenth century, helping to participate in Canterbury's 'urban renaissance'. These helped transform it from being Defoe's 'general ruin a little recovered'.[221] Members of the Chapter frequented the new Playhouse, which was erected in the 1790s, and the Cathedral gave generously to the programme of lighting and paving, subscribing £50 to the new corn-market and in 1827 installing gas lighting in the Precincts.[222] Hasted noted that the new paving had been in imitation of London styles 'and the improvements would have been carried still further, had not the short tenure by which most of the Houses in it were still held under Church lease (which is in every place the bane of all industry) deterred the lessees from hazarding more on such uncertain property'. Hasted claimed that without this, the city 'would in all likelihood have been second to few others in the kingdom'.[223]

The Cathedral Economy and the French Revolution

There is some indication of an alteration in the Cathedral's attitude to its tenants, and perhaps in its relationship with the city, in the late eighteenth and early nineteenth centuries. No doubt part of this change of attitude can be explained by the fear engendered by reports of the fate of the Church and monarchy in France during the Revolution. Marie-Antoinette's close friend the Princess de Lamballe, who was savagely murdered in 1792 by the Revolutionaries, had stayed in Canterbury and met members of the Chapter, and they were horrified to learn of her fate.[224] The old fears of social anarchy were renewed, and

---

[217] Treasurer's Book, 1670–1.

[218] Ibid. 1676–7.

[219] Records of Sykes's Charity; Chapter Act Book, 1761–75, fo. 105.

[220] F. M. Hall, R. S. Stevens, and J. Whyman, *The Kent and Canterbury Hospital, 1790–1987* (Ramsgate, 1987).

[221] P. Borsay, 'The English Urban Renaissance: The Development of Provincial Urban Culture, *c*.1680–*c*.1760', *Social History* 5 (1977), 581–603; Defoe, *Tour* (cit. in n. 152), i. 118.

[222] Chapter Act Book, 1775–94, fo. 323.

[223] Hasted, *Kent* (cit. in n. 115), xi. 99.

[224] See *Poems of George-Monck Berkeley* (cit. in n. 65), p. dxiii.

the Cathedral intensified its efforts to maintain its full rights and privileges. In 1801 Prebendary Welfitt divulged his innermost feelings in his diary:

this Island will be left alone to defend its existence, political and religious, with above 400 million of debt, and almost a famine sore in the land ... malgré which ... a Peace seems more to be dreaded, from the consequent pestilential infusion of French Principles and Manners, subversive of all Religion, Morality, Honour and Order.[225]

The Revolution was perceived in terms of a collapse of religious institutions and thought, and so it is not surprising that clergy saw the necessity of defending Church privileges at all costs. As part of the war effort, the Dean and Chapter gave money to the Canterbury Volunteers and in 1815 subscribed 100 guineas to the sufferers in the British army at Waterloo.[226] The Kentish coast was always vulnerable to invasion, and in 1814 the Dean and Chapter were pleased to note that their lessee at Leysdown had erected a semaphore system at Sheerness.[227] Such defence might necessitate the abandonment of the previous policy of charity towards tenants. Indeed, in 1837 Christopher Hodgson, receiver-general to the archbishop, informed Parliament that, although Church leases were far less restrictive than lay leases, there had been a distinct change in policy since the end of the eighteenth century.[228]

An indication of this new attitude is to be found in the voluminous archive left by Archbishop Manners Sutton (1805–28). His letters reveal a meticulous attention to detail and an almost daily preoccupation with the administration of Church lands. A similar policy is detectable in the Cathedral too: it is shown in the better upkeep of records, and in the more vigorous way in which Church rights were pursued. Estates were surveyed more regularly and more interest was shown in getting an economic return from them. By the late 1790s the prebends were worth about £600 p.a., and the Dean was receiving £1,200.[229] In 1804 the Dean and Chapter agreed to follow the precedent of other cathedral and collegiate institutions and demand one and a half years' income for the grant of a seven-year lease.[230] There are indications that this caused a shift in the Cathedral's relations with its lessees. From the 1790s complaints from tenants about the prebendaries begin to appear in the Act Books, and relations evidently became more strained. In 1803 the tenants refused to pay the fine for Milton Rectory.[231]

One of the consequences of the war with France was that, in response to the Act for

[225] Add. MS 298, Canon Welfitt's Diary, fo. 21, 10 Jan. 1801.

[226] Chapter Act Book, 1794–1824, p. 9; Dean's Book, 1793–1822, fo. 232.

[227] Dean's Book, fo. 220.

[228] Parliamentary Papers, 1837, IX, *Select Committee Report on Church Leases*, 23.

[229] By the 1830s the prebends were worth £1,000 and the deanery £2,111; ibid. 1835, XXII, *Report of the Commissioners Appointed by His Majesty to Inquire into the Ecclesiastical Revenues of England and Wales*, 30–111.

[230] Dean's Book, 1793–1822, fo. 232: 'Ordered & agreed that as since the incumbency of the present Dean, the principal Estates belonging to the Dean & Chapter have been survey'd and estimated by Messrs. Kent, Pierce & Kent, & other smaller estates by competent surveyors; The Dean & Chapter do adopt the principle already establish'd in almost all Ecclesiastical & Collegiate Bodies in the Kingdom of not taking a fine of less than a year and a half for a septennial renewal of Estates on 21-year leases'; *A Brief Statement as to Some Existing Calculations and the Practice of Several Lords, and the Alterations Newly Made and Making By Some of Them in the Mode of Fining* [c.1804], pasted into Balliol College Archive lease log-book, fo. 173. The pamphlet regarded one and half years as normal, and observed that the Chapter of Canterbury, as well as the chapters of Westminster, Chichester, Windsor, Gloucester, Lichfield, Bath and Wells, and Winchester College had recently increased to this level; it mentioned that changes were in progress at Lincoln and that the chapter of Durham thought its fines too low.

[231] Dean's Book, 1793–1822, fo. 104.

the Redemption of the Land Tax (1797), the Dean and Chapter agreed to sell off all their tenements in the city, except those in the Precincts, and all those estates which were held for lives out of Kent. The Act was one of Pitt's measures for raising the necessary finances for the war against France, and it enabled ecclesiastical bodies to sell their estates to lessees at terms that were advantageous to the tenants. In 1800 the Dean and Chapter sold parcels of land to Mr Austen at Godmersham. The effect of such sales was to make the church's estates even more concentrated within the diocese. Indeed, the argument that the Cathedral church at Canterbury had an intimate and inalienable right to its Kentish lands was strongly made in the 1830s, when the Dean and Chapter urged that money from lands in Kent should not be taken to support the Church in other areas of the country.[232]

Challenges to the ancien régime, 1780–1828

During the last two decades of the eighteenth century and the first three decades of the nineteenth century, Church of England clergy felt themselves to be attacked on many fronts. Not only were there dangers from abroad and from the Unitarians, but the clergy also felt their position within the State and society was threatened by efforts to gain emancipation for Catholics and by the attempts to abolish the Test and Corporation Acts, which had debarred non-Anglicans from holding office.[233] To the historically minded, such attempts were anathema, implying the destruction of the Anglican regime which, since 1660, so it was believed, had been a prime instrument in maintaining social and political stability. Canterbury's prebendaries shared in this attitude. In 1773 Richard Farmer warned of the dangers of altering this state of affairs:

Suppose the Remedy should prove worse than the Disease—it would at least make one Schism more—We shall have the Old Liturgists, and they join'd by the Methodists, would make a formidable figure. Those, who are able to find difficulties in the Old Form are able likewise to explain them: and these bear a very small proportion to the Bulk of Mankind . . . As if Religion was intended for nothing else but to be mended.[234]

In a remarkable series of sermons in the 1780s and 1790s, members of the Cathedral community stressed the urgency of the times and the necessity of maintaining tradition in worship and politics. In 1794 the Six Preacher Charles Moore preached a sermon in the Cathedral pointing out the dangers of novelty in religion, especially in evangelicalism and

[232] Parliamentary Papers, 1837, XLI, *Return of All the Remonstrances Made to the Church Commissioners Respecting the Union of the Sees of St. Asaph and Bangor and Further . . . Return . . . Memorials . . . Relating to Cathedrals*, 4.

[233] J. C. D. Clark, *English Society 1688–1832: Ideology, Social Structure and Political Practice During the Ancien Regime* (Cambridge,

1985), ch. 6.

[234] Farmer to Thomas Percy, 18 Feb. 1773, in *The Correspondence of Thomas Percy and Richard Farmer*, ed. Cleanth Brooks (Louisiana, 1946), 171. I owe this reference to Dr Grayson Ditchfield.

in the vogue for rational religion, and emphasizing the need to abide by tradition and convention.[235]

This stance is not surprising, since governmental patronage had been used to promote orthodox clergy to the Canterbury stalls. Many of the canons in the period after 1780 were intimately linked with William Pitt, Lord Liverpool, or Lord Chancellor Eldon, and with what have been called the forces of 'Tory' reaction. Folliott Cornewall (Dean, 1793–7) had been tutor to Lord Liverpool's son; Houstonne Radcliffe (stall IV, 1795–1822; Archdeacon of Canterbury, 1803–22) had been a tutor at Brasenose College, Oxford, where his pupils had included Sidmouth; and George Horne had been a friend of Liverpool's since their days at Oxford. Thomas Coombe (stall VII, 1800–22) had defended Britain's position in America in the 1780s, before being banished for his loyalism. The elevation of such men was part of the government's strategy for strengthening the profile of the Church. In 1790, Dean Horne was promoted by Pitt to the bishopric of Norwich at the same time as Samuel Hallifax and Samuel Horsley were also brought to the bench. Richard Farmer, who was known to be a 'determined enemy of Levellers', was twice offered a bishopric by Pitt because of the Tory principles which he strove to propagate in Cambridge, when he was Master of Emmanuel College. It is not surprising that the deanery of Canterbury was noted as being a stepping-stone to high office in the Church after 1780. Samuel Denne observed in 1797 that 'The Deanry of Canterbury has of late been a principal step to a Bishopric; and I question whether the ecclesiastical annals of this country will furnish, in any other Cathedral, instances of six Deans in succession being elevated from it, and that within a quarter of a century.'[236]

Eldon headed the Ultra-Tory party which emerged during the 1810s, and it was he who articulated most succinctly the idea of the Anglican establishment as understood by the Dean and Chapter. He wrote in 1825 to his fellow north-countryman and Canterbury prebendary, Matthew Surtees (stall XI, 1803–27): 'My opinion is that the Establishment is formed, not for the purpose of making the Church political, but for the purpose of making the state religious.'[237] And Eldon's brother, Sir William Scott, as Vicar-General to the Archbishop and commissary for the city and diocese of Canterbury, was well known in the locality. His defence of the Church in a speech to the House of Commons in 1802 was much appreciated by the Canterbury clergy.[238]

The defence of the Anglican constitution rested on the firm conviction that the world

[235] Charles Moore, 'Against Love of Novelty in Religious Matters. Preached in Canterbury Cathedral 26 May 1794', in his *Sermons* (3 vols.; London, 1818), iii. 340–60. Other sermons on this theme preached in the Cathedral include: George Berkeley, *The Danger of Violent Innovations in the State exemplified from the Reigns of the Two First Stuarts, in a Sermon preached at the Cathedral and Metropolitical Church of Christ, Canterbury, on Monday, Jan. 31, 1785* (Canterbury, 1785); George Horne, 'Submission to Government . . . A Sermon preached in Canterbury Cathedral on 25 October 1789', in *The Works of the Right Reverend George Horne*, ed. William Jones (4 vols.; London, 1818), iii. 384–97; and William Jones, 'Popular Commotions to Precede the End of the World. A Sermon Preached in Canterbury Cathedral on 26 September 1789', in his *Theological, Philosophical and Miscellaneous Works* (5 vols.; London, 1801), v. 274–95.

[236] J. Nichols, *Illustrations of Literary History* (8 vols.; London, 1817–58), vi. 687. The deans were Brownlow North, Moore, Cornwallis, Horne, Butler, and Cornewall. In 1824 the Earl of Liverpool presented the Chapter with a book about the Cathedral: Dean's Book, 1822–54, fo. 26.
[237] G. F. A. Best, 'The Protestant Constitution and Its Supporters, 1800–1829', *TRHS*, 5th ser., 8 (1958), 107–27; H. Twiss, *The Public and Private Life of Lord Chancellor Eldon* (3rd edn.; 2 vols.; London, 1846), ii. 124: Eldon to Surtees, Feb. 1825; Clark, *English Society, 1688–1832* (cit. in n. 233), ch. 6.
[238] See *The Substance of the Speech of the Right Honourable Sir William Scott, Delivered in the House of Commons, Wednesday April 7th, 1802, Upon a Motion for Leave to Bring in a Bill Relative to the Non-Residence of the Clergy, and Other Affairs of the Church* (London, 1802).

of stability and order would again be turned upside down unless strenuous efforts were made to keep it intact. The Dean and Chapter asked Archbishop Manners Sutton in 1812, and again in 1827, to petition Parliament against any legal changes to the status of Roman Catholics.[239] Their arguments for maintaining the status quo were based on the belief that the lessons of history had shown the necessity of such legislation and that the Anglican Establishment was essentially a tolerant one. The Chapter insisted that they were not advocating persecution in petitioning against Catholic Emancipation, but rather that they wished to save Great Britain from the nightmares of popish machinations.

Recent occurrences [show] the Romish Church is as zealous as at any former period for the political aggrandizement of Papacy and as hostile to the civil and religious Institutions by law established in this country. Your Petitioners therefore still most earnestly deprecate the dangerous experiment of engrafting the divided allegiance and encroaching spirit of Popery upon our Free Protestant Constitution.[240]

In voicing such sentiments, they and other clerical bodies like the Dean and Chapter of Windsor, who sent similar petitions, indicated that they were sharing the gut reaction of a wider stratum of society. On 24 October 1828 there was a gathering of between 40,000 and 50,000 men on Penenden Heath near Maidstone in Kent to petition Parliament against Emancipation. Such occurrences suggest a remarkable correlation between the views of the clergy and the wider world, tied together by their attachment to No-Popery.[241]

As part of this attempt to buttress the Anglican nature of the constitution, the Dean and Chapter were supporters of the foundation of King's College, London, in 1828, donating £300 to the project.[242] King's was seen as an Anglican counterblast to the recently founded University College, which admitted Dissenters and Unitarians. The foundation of King's, and the support it received from the clerical establishment, must be seen in the context of the threat to the British constitution and the need to preserve the Church and the State from what were widely perceived to be the destructive influences of liberalism. In acting on this belief, clergy in the 1820s were clearly foreshadowing John Henry Newman's attacks on non-denominational education in the 1830s.[243] In this matter, too, as in so much else, the Tractarian manifesto, far from reacting against the main currents of eighteenth- and early nineteenth-century Anglican thought, was drawing heavily upon it.

Because the Oxford Movement and parliamentary reforms happened, it is tempting to assume that they were necessary, an obvious and justifiable reaction against the appalling defects of the eighteenth-century Church. But the search for flaws is a dangerous under-taking, and their contemporary significance can be exaggerated. It would be a gross caricature to suggest that the Victorians alone were responsible for reforms within the Church, and it would be wrong to judge the Anglican cause by the yardstick of radical ideology. Even the radical critiques of the Church in this period can be seen as giving a

---

[239] Chapter Act Book, 1794–1824, p. 286: 'A Petition to be presented to both Houses of Parliament respecting the Roman Catholic Claims', 1 Dec. 1812; Dean's Book, 1793–1822, p. 199; Chapter Act Book, 1824–54, p. 52.

[240] Ibid.

[241] G. I. T. Machin, *The Catholic Question in English Politics 1820–1830* (Oxford, 1964), 148.

[242] Dean's Book, 1822–54, fo. 61.

[243] For Newman's views, see 'The Tamworth Reading Room. Letters on an Address Delivered by Sir Robert Peel, Bart. M.P. on the Establishment of a Reading Room at Tamworth (1841)', printed in his *Discussions and Arguments* (London, 1872), 254–305.

backhanded tribute to its power and relevance. If the Church was as redundant to society as the radicals claimed, there would have been little need for such attacks.

CONCLUSION

The history of the community at Canterbury within this period can be placed alongside the growing body of evidence which suggests that cathedrals played a far more central role within English religious, social, and political life than has sometimes been maintained, and that the Canterbury experience was by no means untypical.[244] In the long period between the upheavals of the mid-seventeenth century and the 1830s, the history of English cathedrals is something of a success story. At the start of our period their role was by no means clear, but within the provinces they fashioned themselves into centres of religious and political orthodoxy. In the early nineteenth century Sir Samuel Egerton Brydges, a Kentishman whose mother lived in the Precincts and who was not always well disposed towards the Church, could maintain that 'the Protestant Clergy of the Established Church are altogether, in defence of all calumnies, an excellent body'.[245] Perhaps it was their success in meshing themselves within local society which accounts for the problems that cathedrals had in changing: they were too well entrenched within the world around them for rapid alteration. Nevertheless, at Canterbury there is little evidence of that self-satisfied inertia which has been such a potent image of Church life in this period. By and large and on its own terms, the community at Canterbury fulfilled its role of creating stability. And the desire for efficiency was not just a prerogative of the Church's critics in the early nineteenth century, it was an ideal of the Church too, and we should not isolate evidence of reform and imagine that such concern was a radical monopoly. Indeed, in 1837 George Pellew, a former Canterbury prebendary, wrote to Peel on the means of *Rendering Cathedral Churches Most conducive to the Efficiency of the Established Church*.[246] And when challenge to the old regime in Canterbury did occur in the 1830s and 1840s, involving a reorganization of the Cathedral community, it was not nearly so violently anticlerical as the attacks on the Church in France in the 1790s. The changes affecting English cathedrals, as outlined in the next chapter, did not necessitate the repudiation of the cathedral community and its position within the Church and society as it had developed in the eighteenth century, but rather marked another shift in its role to fit it for the demands of a new and different age.

[244] See, e.g. Bussby, *Winchester Cathedral* (cit. in n. 201); C. J. Stranks, *This Sumptuous Church: The Story of Durham Cathedral* (London, 1973); A. Tindal Hart, 'The Age of Reason, 1660–1831', in *A History of St. Paul's Cathedral*, ed. W. R. Matthews and W. M. Atkins (London, 1957), 172–249; D. M. Owen, 'From the Restoration Until 1822', in *A History of York Minster*, ed. G. E. Aylmer and R. E. Cant (Oxford, 1977), 233–71; A. Whiteman,

'The Church of England, 1542–1837', in *VCH Wiltshire*, iii. 44–71; J. R. Guy, 'From the Reformation to 1800', in *Wells Cathedral: A History*, ed. L. S. Colchester (Wells, 1987), 148–78.
[245] Quoted in R. Furley, *A History of the Weald of Kent* (2 vols.; Ashford, 1871), ii. 674.
[246] Pellew, *Letter to Peel* (cit. in n. 129).

VI

Aspects of Cathedral Life, 1828–1898

PETER B. NOCKLES

INTRODUCTION AND HISTORICAL CONTEXT

Although a case can be made for the good order of cathedrals, in the 1830s they attracted the interest of various kinds of reformers. The Church of England as a whole was under pressure from Dissenters and from political radicals. It was eventually reformed and centralized as never before in its history. At a time of bitter pamphleteering, cathedrals increasingly stood out as visible affronts to a utilitarian age that was guided by exacting notions of efficiency and a concept of practical usefulness. The question 'What is the use of a cathedral' was raised again. In the 1830s there were many who doubted whether cathedrals in their traditional form would survive at all. They were threatened not only by radical indictments such as those in Bentham's *Church of Englandism* (1818) and John Wade's notorious *Black Book* of clerical abuses (1820); but also by the likelihood that a Whig ministry would seek to exploit anti-Church and Reforming grievances for party advantage.

Pious lay idealists such as Lord Henley subjected the cathedrals to minute and unsympathetic scrutiny: his brand of Church reform, however well motivated, seemed likely to prove fatal to the historical claims and ancient customs of cathedrals as well as to their undoubted deficiencies. Few people seemed prepared to offer them unequivocal support and protection. Even Sir Robert Peel appeared to regard cathedral chapters with an evident lack of sympathy, as 'nests of sinecurists'.[1] The fact that cathedral chapters were to survive at all, albeit in drastically pruned and reorganized form, owed much to the reforms of the late 1830s that culminated in the Ecclesiastical Duties and Revenues Bill of 1840. The most influential of these changes was the creation of the permanent Ecclesiastical Commission, in 1836, which was itself to become the agent of a far-reaching economic revolution in the Church of England.

The beliefs and arguments of a group of conservative reformers are of interest in explaining why cathedral reform was to prove the weakest and most vulnerable part of the comprehensive programme of Church reform carried out by the Commissioners. The

---

[1] G. F. A. Best, *Temporal Pillars: Queen Anne's Bounty, the Ecclesiastical Commissioners, and the Church of England* (Cambridge, 1964), 334.

I St Benedict displays his Rule to monks of Christ Church, and Eadui Basan as scribe presents his Psalter. From the Hand of God descend texts indicating the divine authority of St Benedict and the requirement of monastic obedience. (BL, Arundel MS 155, fo. 133.)

II St Paul and the Viper (Acts 28: 3–6). Wall painting of the 1160s in St Anselm's Chapel, formerly dedicated to St Peter and St Paul.

III (*a*) St Dunstan rescues King Eadwy from Hell. North choir aisle gallery, N. XI.

III (*c*) The Ascension. Corona east window, E1 panel 37.

III (*b*) Jonah cast up from the fish, as a type of the Resurrection. Corona east window, E1 panel 33.

Commissioners seemed to have little use for cathedrals except as sources of revenue to be annexed for the provision of pastoral care in poor parishes. The conservative reformers questioned not so much the need for reform as the principles and assumptions on which the Commission based its policies. In their diagnosis of the weaknesses of cathedral organization, and in their narrow definition of 'usefulness', the Commissioners were thought by these conservatives to overlook or undervalue the original uses and ideals of cathedrals. In particular, the Commission did not appreciate the cathedrals' theoretical position as centres of theological learning, their role as religious havens or retreats, and their place as 'Mother of the Diocese', with each chapter acting as the council of its bishop. The history and constitutions of cathedrals were subjected to careful study. The conservative reformers' appeal to tradition, resting on an attention to medieval cathedral statutes and involving a call for the restoration of neglected cathedral uses, thus had radical implications.

The authentic voice of this species of cathedral reform was first raised in Pusey's influential cathedral reform booklet of 1833.[2] It was propagated especially by Tractarian idealists such as Manning, in an important pamphlet in 1840, and in the writings of George Selwyn and Alexander James Beresford Hope.[3] Later, it was even to colour the documents produced by the Cathedral and Collegiate Churches Commission of 1852–5—in itself a sure sign of the growing respectability of these ideas. The propagation of this High-Church intellectual case in defence of cathedrals represented the natural complement to the Tractarian-inspired campaign to restore the ecclesiastical and 'medieval' character of the universities in the face of a similar radical assault. The essential message was that money and endowments did not matter so much as the preservation of the traditional spiritual functions of cathedrals. As a result of all this scholarly as well as popular debate and self-evaluation among the conservative reformers, the initiative was to some extent wrested from the radical, secular or Dissenting proponents of reform and turned to positive account in defence of the Church. In this way, cathedral reform almost became a High Church cause. Conscious of the need to adapt and restore, it was a High Churchman who, even in the mid-1850s, could lament that cathedrals were still the 'weak instead of the strongest part of our Church'.[4] This concern inspired a new wave of idealism about cathedral reform in the late 1860s and early 1880s, the trend being towards ever higher ideals and standards. As before, however, the emphasis was to be on the adaptation of the cathedrals' often dormant traditional uses to contemporary needs and demands. In so far as those uses were employed and the new needs met, the popular estimation of cathedrals would be transformed for the better.

[2] E. B. Pusey, *Remarks on the Prospective and Past Benefits of Cathedral Institutions, in the Promotion of Sound Religious Knowledge and of Clerical Education . . . Occasioned by Lord Henley's Plan for Their Abolition* (London, 1833).

[3] See H. E. Manning, *The Preservation of Unendowed Canonries: A Letter to William, Lord Bishop of Chichester* (London, 1840), 6–17; G. A. Selwyn, *Are Cathedral Institutions Useless? A Practical Answer to This Question, Addressed to W. E. Gladstone Esq., M.P.* (London, 1838), 1–3. In contrast, a Tory and politically High Church figure such as Bishop Phillpotts in private appeared ready to recommend a reduction in the number of canonries, if this meant that the temporal interests of cathedral bodies would otherwise be preserved. See P. J. Welch, 'Contemporary Views on the Alienation of Capitular Property in England (1831–40)', *JEH*, 5 (1954), 184–95, at 194.

[4] W. K. Hamilton, *Cathedral Reform: A Letter to the Members of His Diocese from Walter Kerr, Bishop of Salisbury* (London, 1855), 5.

THE INTERNAL STRUCTURE AND RELATIONS OF CANTERBURY CATHEDRAL

Personnel: The Structure and Organization of the Cathedral Foundation

It is easy to paint a negative and unflattering picture of the internal state of the cathedral body in the 1820s and 1830s. As the metropolitan cathedral, Canterbury tended to be singled out by contemporary radical reformers as a bastion of idleness, privilege, and uselessness. Clearly, Canterbury would be vulnerable should the axe of reform fall. As a writer in the *Christian Observer* commented, 'no man dreams, we presume, even at Canterbury, of matters continuing as they are'.[5] Yet most of the canons of Canterbury were determined that things should indeed remain as they were.

The apparent primacy of political concerns in one or two Canterbury Chapter meetings at this date might seem to give superficial credence to the popular charge that canons were animated more by a defence of vested interests and corporate rights than by spiritual or evangelistic concerns. Certainly, the Chapter's efforts to establish its electoral voting rights in 1832 seemed to occupy a disproportionate amount of its time. The city corporation, mindful of the extent to which the Cathedral represented the Tory interest, had disputed the legality of the Cathedral canons voting individually in parliamentary elections. It insisted that the canons were disbarred by being 'a corporation aggregate', since they were paid out of a common fund. The canons admitted that they were members of a corporation aggregate, but argued that they were also a corporation sole. The courts held for the canons, but hardly thereby increased the Cathedral's popularity.[6]

How justified was this apparent unpopularity? Canterbury's Chapter then consisted of twelve canons, each with an income of about £1,000 per annum, some considerably more. When judged by later standards, mutual intercourse among the canons was formal and largely social rather than spiritual. There was certainly no measuring-up to the Tractarian ideal of 'sacred fellowship' in the sanctuary, and to outsiders the Chapter must have seemed narrow and insular. One of Sydney Smith's witticisms on cathedral chapters—'the duty of the dean was to give dinners to the chapter, and the duty of the canons was to give dinners to the dean'[7]—could have been applied to Canterbury at this time. Much Cathedral patronage seemed to rest on social connections. For instance, Dean Hugh Percy had married one of the daughters of Archbishop Manners Sutton and was portioned with preferments to the value of £10,000 per annum, and Archdeacon Croft made a no less lucrative marriage with another of the Archbishop's daughters.[8] In 1836 in a Memorial to the Ecclesiastical Duties and Revenues Commissioners, the Chapter was concerned to point out that one essential object of the Cathedral was the constitution of 'a dignified body of Clergy, possessed . . . of ample estates and revenues that should never be alienated from them',[9] in addition, of course, to two objects recognized by the Commissioners: the performance of services and the reparation of the fabric.

---

[5] *Christian Observer*, 33 (1833), 45.

[6] Dean's Book, 1822–54, pp. 134–5.

[7] H. Humble, 'Cathedrals and Chapters', in *Ecclesiastical Reform: Eight Essays by Various Writers*, ed. O. Shipley (London, 1873), 190.

[8] Woodruff and Danks, *Memorials*, 354.

[9] 'Memorial from the Dean and Chapter of Canterbury', in *Memorials and Communications, Addressed to His Majesty's Commissioners of Inquiry into the State of the Established Church, from the Cathedral and Collegiate Churches of England and Wales, in 1836*

Yet it is not altogether fair to judge the Dean and Chapter of the relatively leisured 1820s by the more earnest standards of later in the century. In fact, the testimony of Archdeacon Croft to the Commissioners in 1834 revealed a surprisingly high standard of residence and sense of duty among the canons. By the Cathedral statutes, ninety days' residence were obligatory, of which twenty-one had to be continuous (extended to one month in 1803). After keeping his residence, a canon was required by the statutes to return to his benefice, or to one of them.[10] In 1832 the Dean was Bishop of Oxford and held two benefices, and all the canons except Lord Nelson held one or two benefices. It was in one of their benefices that they lived and spent most of their time. The Commissioners found that there were 'discrepancies' on 'a careful comparison of the present practice as laid down by Archdeacon Croft with the original statutes', but this in itself did not indicate undue laxity or negligence. The situation had arisen, they thought, because 'the Dean and Chapter had acted on tradition instead of occasionally referring to the statutes themselves'.[11] In 1837, stricter residential requirements were being enforced by the Chapter, each canon being made to reside, and to attend both services on Sundays during the whole of his own set period of residence and in the period immediately following.

Canterbury's case against certain aspects of the reform proposals of the late 1830s deserves some sympathy. It was inevitable and only fitting that, given Canterbury's position as the leading New Foundation cathedral, its Dean and Chapter should be at the forefront of the objections to aspects of the reform proposals.[12] Other cathedral chapters looked to Canterbury for a lead, and this was given by Dr Russell (canon, 1827–63) and Dr Spry (canon, 1828–54), who took a prominent part in defending Canterbury's interests.[13] For Canterbury was in a truly sensitive and invidious position, given the involvement of its own Archbishop in the reform proposals. As Sydney Smith pointed out, Archbishop Howley had taken an oath at his consecration in 1828 to maintain the rights and liberties of the Cathedral, but as chairman of the new Commission, he was to be responsible for seizing its patronage, taking two-thirds of its revenues, and abolishing two-thirds of its members![14]

In some respects, many of the Chapter's fears and foreboding in the later 1830s would soon come to appear exaggerated, but the Cathedral's daily life and terms of reference were profoundly changed by the passing of the controversial Ecclesiastical Duties and Revenues Bill (the 'Cathedrals' or 'Dean and Chapter' Act of 1840). By this statute, Canterbury's Chapter was to be reduced, in the course of time, from twelve to six residentiary canons, and residence was fixed at a compulsory three calendar months. In effect, the work-load of every canon was doubled, and his income, in most cases, reduced. Thus, no canon was to receive more than £1,000 per annum, and the Dean no more than £2,000 per annum. Yet Canterbury fared better than most cathedrals, which had their chapters

and 1837 (London, 1838), 9.

[10] C. E. Woodruff, 'Reminiscences of the Cathedral', *Cant. Cath. Chron.*, 39 (1943), 17.

[11] London, Church Commissioners' MSS, Canterbury, file no. 14484.

[12] The Dean, Bishop Bagot, wrote in 1838 of the Board of Ecclesiastical Commissioners as 'a power as irresponsible as it is gigantic, an *imperium in imperio*, which before long must supersede all other authority in the Church, and whose decrees are issued in such a manner as to render expostulation and remonstrance unavailing'. T. Mozley, *Reminiscences Chiefly of Oriel College and the Oxford Movement* (2 vols.; London, 1882), i. 442.

[13] Chapter Act Book, 1824–54, p. 267.

[14] Sydney Smith, *A Letter to Archdeacon Singleton on the Ecclesiastical Commission* (London, 1837), 9.

curtailed to only four canons. At Canterbury, the provision of canonries for the two archdeacons—of Maidstone (1841) and of Canterbury (1852)—eventually kept the complement up to six; a reduction to four had at first been proposed. In their Memorial, the Dean and Chapter insisted that four canons were not adequate for an 'efficient and respectable' performance of the choral service. Joint residence of at least two canons was essential in effect, to secure the constant attendance of one.[15] This vital concession was won, but not without a struggle. The Chapter was also concerned that its statutes nowhere presupposed any reduction in its size. The Chapter would have preferred a permanent annexation of some prebendal stalls to parochial uses, rather than any reduction in its numerical strength.[16] Bishop Phillpotts actually advised Sir Robert Peel that Canterbury stalls be affixed to various London livings.[17] None the less, though the Dean and Chapter were to survive the trauma of change in the 1840s and 1850s, time would bear out the fairness of their original complaint that the Commission had overlooked several other duties and uses of cathedrals in its economic reckonings.

The legislation providing for the temporary suspension of canonries, first introduced in 1835, had an immediate adverse effect on Canterbury, where a vacancy had been created by Lord Nelson's death.[18] Not surprisingly, the Chapter petitioned vigorously in 1837 against the permanent suspension of some canonries. However, relief of a kind was soon to be at hand. The Cathedrals Act of 1840 allowed a substitute to be employed by the Chapter to relieve canons from any additional duty arising from the suspension of a canonry consequent upon the death of one of Canterbury's original twelve canons. By 1845 the tenth and second canonries were vacant. In consequence, the Chapter proposed to the Archbishop that 'each of the present Canons be appointed substitutes to take a portion of the period of residences which should have been taken by the holders of the tenth and second canonries now vacant'. It was resolved that each canon should reside after his own term of residence for a similar period, so that there would always be two canons on duty.[19] Finally, in 1849, canons substitute were appointed for the performance of the duties that would have fallen to the holders of the vacant stalls. Archdeacon Harrison (who was known to be punctilious in his attendance of services) was to act as substitute for 'the performance of any duties for which in the course of the year there may be no other Canon responsible by reasons of a vacancy occurring which shall not be filled up'.[20] One striking impact of this reduction in numbers on the physical character of the Cathedral was the gradual demolition of several houses on its north side formerly occupied by canons, and the occupation of others by other Cathedral officers such as the auditor.[21]

[15] 'Memorial from the Dean and Chapter of Canterbury', in *Memorials and Communications* (cit. in n. 9), 12.

[16] Ibid. 11–13.

[17] BL, Peel Corres., Add. MS 40411, fo. 169, Bishop H. Phillpotts to R. Peel, 24 Jan. 1835.

[18] Dean's Book, 1822–54, p. 184. Lord Nelson had died on 28 Feb. 1835.

[19] Ibid. 318.

[20] Chapter Act Book, 1824–54, p. 435.

[21] Dean's Book, 1822–54, p. 312. Cf. London, Church Commissioners' MSS, Canterbury, file no. 1156, 22 July 1845. For details of houses in the Precincts and their occupants in the early 1840s, see ibid., H. Hobhouse to J. Chalk, 14 Jan. 1841. The likely architectural and social implications of this policy had been foreseen, and the proposal in the original Cathedrals Bill to allow the Commissioners to pull down the houses attached to suppressed stalls, had been opposed on the general principle that it 'would totally destroy, in many cases, the . . . appropriate character which belongs to those privileged and generally beautiful portions of our cathedral towns'. [G. Peacock], *Observations on the Plans for Cathedral Reforms Proposed in a Bill Now Before Parliament and in a Memorial Addressed to the Rt. Hon. the Lord John Russell, by a Sub-Committee of Chapters* (Cambridge, 1840), 34.

There was to be conflict well into the 1850s between the Chapter and Commissioners over the financial aspect of the measure relating to the stipends of canonical substitutes and also over the interpretation of the working of the Cathedrals Act regarding residence terms. For instance, the chapter clerk Daniel Finch was complaining in vain in 1851, that even with the system of substitutes, 'in consequence of the suspension of three stalls, each canon is now responsible for cathedral duties for a longer period of the year'.[22] However, there were also pressures to apply the legislative principles of the 1840 Act still further. In 1869 a plan was mooted at Lambeth by the Archbishops of Canterbury and York to reduce the number of cathedral canonries further and to abolish supposed 'non-residence', deemed in some quarters still to be a problem. At Canterbury, the innovative Dean Henry Alford shocked Canon Robertson and the more conservative element in the Chapter by supporting these proposals and showing a willingness to abolish canonries without regard to vested interests. Alford refused to discuss his submission with his Chapter. The influential Dean of Norwich, Edward Goulburn, took a very different view, and Canon Robertson wrote to congratulate him on his stand against the proposals. With an arch reference to his own Dean's attitude, Robertson declared that 'it is gratifying to find that there are Deans who wish to see the idea of cathedral institutions carried out instead of blotting out such institutions from the system of the church'. To disprove the Archbishop of York's case about non-residence, Robertson quoted the number of days of residence of the six Canterbury canons over the year 1868–9.[23]

The failure of the Commission adequately to allow for some of Canterbury's unique aspects became most apparent over the question of introducing Honorary Canons. The halving of the complement of residential canons under the Act of 1840 might have been offset by provision being made for the appointment of twenty-four non-residentiary or Honorary Canons. However, Canterbury already had a non-residentiary body unique to itself, the Six Preachers. The Six Preachers' traditional rights seemed threatened by the creation of new Honorary Canons. Not surprisingly, therefore, the Cathedral resisted the bare and unmodified application of this aspect of the Act. In 1841 the Chapter formally objected to the Commissioners against the appointment of Honorary Canons 'generally, and specially as interfering with the place assigned by statute to the Six Preachers in this church'.[24] The Commissioners were not impressed, and in 1842 and again in 1844 the Chapter was forced to reiterate the grounds of its opposition.[25] Daniel Finch in vain reminded the Commissioners that 'it was evidently not the intention of the legislature that Honorary Canons should be appointed where any non-residentiary dignities or preferments were founded'.[26] Direct conflict occurred between the Chapter and the Commissioners in 1844. The matter was not helped by the provision that all such Honorary Canons as held a Six Preachership should take precedence over other Honorary Canons in processions. Only in 1863 did an Order in Council finally ratify the Chapter's proposal that the Six Preachers should 'double up' as Honorary Canons and thus finally settle the

[22] London, Church Commissioners' MSS, Canterbury, file no. 1157, D. Finch to J. Chalk, 11 Mar. 1851.

[23] Norwich, Norfolk County Record Office, Goulburn Papers, MS 21644 MC 47/5, fos. 170–2, J. C. Robertson to E. M. Goulburn, 19 June 1869.

[24] Dean's Book, 1822–54, p. 271.

[25] London, Church Commissioners' MSS, Canterbury, file no. 7973, pt. 1, 'Abstract of Returns', 1842.

[26] Dean's Book, 1822–54, p. 274.

question of precedence to the advantage of the Six Preachers.[27] However, as one part was satisfied, another was upset. Those Honorary Canons who were not Six Preachers were in their turn complaining by 1871 that they were having to follow the Auditor and burgesses in processions.[28] The position of Honorary Canons within the Cathedral body remained an anomalous and almost a disturbing element. The right of appointment of Honorary Canons was vested in the archbishop, but they were entitled to no place in the Chapter, nor to any emolument. Yet in so far as they could act as substitutes and relieve the residentiary canons from their extra duties, they fulfilled a useful role.

Relations between the Dean and Chapter and the six minor canons were often difficult. In pursuit of better order at morning and evening prayer, in 1828 the Chapter instructed all the minor canons to be present daily at both services, and if necessary to find 'proper persons' to perform their duties in their churches on Sundays.[29] The minor canons had an almost hereditary understanding of themselves as the drudges of Chapter. Some were abusive when called to order.[30] Much of the strife concerned livings, both those in the city, usually served by minor canons, and those at a distance, which were staffed by curates. To this was linked the problem of adequate remuneration for their work in the Cathedral.

Before the 1840 Act, the minor canons made numerous complaints that they were not receiving the proportion of Cathedral revenue to which they felt entitled by the terms of the Cathedral statutes, and in 1835 they alleged a great 'betrayal of Founders' intentions' in this respect. They thought they had 'rights' to livings which had been gradually eroded over a long period. By the Henrician statutes, minor canons had to forfeit their position in the Cathedral if they took a living beyond a twenty-four mile radius of Canterbury. However, by custom they had always had a fair entitlement to lucrative preferment beyond that radius, so that this stipulation had been no hardship in practice. But there were complaints that such vacancies usually were given to relations and friends of the Dean and Chapter. From the 1820s the minor canons became increasingly resentful of this state of affairs.[31] In 1838 they made an unsuccessful appeal against the living of Aylsham being given to a connection of one of the canons rather than to one of their own order: Archbishop Howley formally declared against the appeal of the minor canons in this dispute.[32] It had been expected that the 1840 Act would improve things, but, as it was much later lamented, 'that blundering legislation' further eroded the minor canons' rights. The radius of 24 miles was reduced to 6 miles, but within such a distance it was no longer acceptable to employ a curate. Thus, minor canons were hard pressed, doing their full parochial work as well as Cathedral duties. Disputes over the interpretation of the Act continued to sour Chapter relations into the 1860s. Furthermore, as a result of the 1838 Pluralities Act, an incumbent could be compelled to reside in his benefice for seven months

[27] Chapter Act Book, 1854–84, p. 143. Cf. London, Church Commissioners' MSS, Canterbury, file no. 7973.

[28] LPL, Tait Papers, vol. 173, fos. 7–8, 14, Archbishop Tait to Dean Payne Smith, 12 Dec. 1871.

[29] Dean's Book, 1822–54, p. 75.

[30] At the Midsummer Chapter, 1828, on the subject of the minor canons, a note of thanks was accorded to the Dean 'for the line of conduct which he has adopted—a line in their opinion well calculated to maintain the dignity of his Office and of the Chapter, and to preserve the due subordination of the inferior Officers'. Dean's Book, 1822–54, p. 60; for further difficulties of minor canons, see ibid, pp. 80–5, 196.

[31] See *The Case of the Minor Canons and Inferior Officers of the Cathedrals of the New Foundation, Particularly With Reference to Canterbury* (Canterbury, 1839), 6.

[32] Dean's Book, 1822–54, pp. 230, 235.

each year. This created more difficulties. For instance, in 1851, the statute preventing minor canons from holding livings at a distance was enforced against William Braham. Braham contended that legal opinion upheld his right to hold Peldon in Essex, as he had been elected a minor canon prior to 1840.[33] An unfortunate anomaly was that the Act of 1840 assigned £150 a year to minor canons appointed after that date, while at least until the 1860s the older minor canons had to make do with £80 per annum. The financial plight of the minor canons was most forcefully highlighted in 1862 by one of their order, Frederick Rouch. Rouch claimed that he had been able to survive only by being granted, in 1840, a special archiepiscopal licence of non-residence on a small vicarage 20 miles from Canterbury.[34]

In 1862, the Chapter decided to augment the stipends of existing minor canons and therefore left a vacancy unfilled. Next year they secured an Order in Council which finally eased the situation by reducing the number of minor canons from six to four, thereby raising their stipends again from £150 to £227 10s. per annum. The desire was expressed that all minor canons should now be placed on the same level of remuneration.[35]

Robert Hake was an influential and learned minor canon who was precentor from 1864. Hake resented the extent to which men in holy orders like himself were treated as second-class citizens by full members of the Chapter. The Order in Council of 1863 seemed to him to create the worst of all possible worlds, for there was now a real danger that minor canons would be too few in number to perform their duties responsibly. Hake concluded that the office should be seen only as a younger man's stepping-stone to higher preferment. He went so far as to suggest that minor canons should not be beneficed at all, since the fact that they held benefices, albeit not lucrative ones, was an inducement to them to retain their minor canonries after they could no longer sing services adequately.[36] One radical solution contained in the Archbishop of York's cathedral reform proposals of 1869 was to allow an alteration in the statutes by the Visitor on a motion of members of the cathedral body, in order to put minor canons as well as Honorary Canons into the capitular body.[37] Not surprisingly, the Canterbury Chapter bitterly resisted this idea at the time. By the 1880s, however, relations between the minor canons and the rest of the Cathedral body were much improved. There was a far higher degree of conscientious attention to duty than at the start of the period. In the visitation returns for the Cathedral in 1889, the attendance of the four minor canons at the services was described as 'most exemplary',[38] and in 1893 it was stated that there were two minor canons present at almost every service.[39]

Other Cathedral officers were unhappy about their stipends. There were growing complaints from the lay clerks over the diminished value of their remuneration (£40 p.a.).

[33] Ibid., p. 443.

[34] London, Church Commissioners' MSS, Canterbury, file no. 27983, 'Memorial of Frederick Rouch', 1862.

[35] Chapter Act Book, 1854–84, pp. 133–4, 144.

[36] R. Hake, *Cathedral Reform: A Letter to . . . the Lord Archbishop of Canterbury* (London, 1872), 12. For similar advocacy of a breaking-down of distinctions between minor canons and prebendaries, see H. W. Pullen, *Medieval Mummery in 1870: A Few*

Words about Cathedral Installations (2nd edn.; Salisbury, 1870), 5–7.

[37] Norwich, Norfolk County Record Office, Goulburn Papers, MS 21644 MC 47/5, fos. 272–3, G. Selwyn to E. M. Goulburn [1872].

[38] LPL, Visitation Returns of the Diocese of Canterbury, 1889, MS VG 3/8c, fo. 372.

[39] Ibid. 1893, MS VG 3/9c, fo. 348.

From 1849, in response to a lay clerks' Memorial, there was to be an additional payment of one shilling for every day's attendance at both morning and evening services, with a pension fixed at £25 a year. The £25 a year was to be awarded to any of their body who might become incapable of performing his choral duties. A majority of the lay clerks angrily rejected the offer. Provocatively, they complained: 'our stipends are less than in any other Cathedral in the Kingdom in proportion to the duties required and that the duties leave us neither time or opportunity to obtain a livelihood by secular employment and that oftentimes we are pained to find our minds so harassed by pecuniary difficulties and worn with toil that we have neither voice nor heart to join in thanksgiving or to sing praises as we ought to do'.[40] In 1858, the salary of lay clerks was increased and fixed at £76 per annum.[41] In 1860 they petitioned for an increase, but the Dean and Chapter firmly declared that they had 'no intention of increasing their stipends nor is it likely that any fresh application to that effect will be entertained by them'.[42] In 1869, Archbishop Tait was even petitioned to urge the Commissioners to use income from suppressed canonries so as to augment the lay clerks' stipends.[43] In another emotional petition, in 1872, more respectful than that of 1849, they again stressed that the lay clerks of other cathedrals enjoyed far greater stipends, did far less work, and enjoyed lower living-costs than they did at Canterbury.[44] Such appeals fell on deaf ears; the Cathedral's financial circumstances were hardly conducive to any significant improvement in the lay clerks' position. Indeed, in 1893, the Dean and Chapter declared their intention of reducing the number of lay clerks at the next opportunity, on financial grounds.[45]

The bedesmen were equally forthright in the 1860s and 1870s in pleading for higher stipends. Their request in 1855–6 for salary increases was met with a further £10 p.a.;[46] Dean Alford was sympathetic to their cause, but his successor, Payne Smith, was not. When urged to intervene, Archbishop Tait rejected their demands on the ground of 'the altered circumstances of the cathedral body' and the sort of services which the bedesmen now performed.[47]

Yet it would be wrong to portray cathedral life at Canterbury as vitiated throughout this period by internecine conflict among its personnel. The ideal of a 'family' may hardly have been a reality in the earlier years, but there is evidence to suggest that from at least the 1880s the ideal began to approach reality. Among the most striking features of the 1889 visitation returns are the repeated signs of growth towards a greater sense of corporate unity. Obstacles to such unity had included confusion over the status of Honorary Canons, over their limited access to the Cathedral and their differentiation from the residentiary canons, and over the second-class status of minor canons. No less discussed were the absence of the archbishop from Canterbury and the lack of any 'Greater Chapter', where all the Cathedral body could meet together for discussion and feel an equal stake in

[40] Dean's Book, 1822–54, pp. 393, 399–401; a claim for higher remuneration in 1853, which won qualified support from the High Church press, was likewise unsuccessful. See the *Guardian*, 8 (12 Oct. 1853), 675.
[41] LPL, Tait Papers, vol. 206, fo. 363.
[42] Chapter Act Book, 1854–84, p. 118.
[43] LPL, Tait Papers, vol. 206, fo. 361.
[44] Ibid., fo. 366.
[45] Chapter Act Book, 1884–95, p. 197.
[46] Ibid. 1854–84, pp. 24, 33, 75.
[47] LPL, Tait Papers, vol. 188, fo. 38, W. Merritt and J. Crow to Archbishop Tait, 6 July 1872; fo. 39, Dean Payne Smith to Archbishop Tait, 16 Nov. 1872; fo. 41.

Cathedral life. But some of these obstacles were never removed, nor felt to be worth removing.

The Economy and Finances of the Cathedral

The Cathedral was dependent for its finances on rents from estates which had been granted at the setting-up of the New Foundation. At that time, these rents were sufficient to pay stipends and expenses, with a little left over. Rents were collected for the receiver and handed over by him to the treasurer. Out of them the treasurer paid the statutory stipends and expenses of the Cathedral. As well as this regular income, the Cathedral had income from additional rents and, on an irregular basis, from fines at the renewal of leases: this income was divided into fourteen parts and shared between the Dean and canons (two parts for the Dean and one for each canon). Money was also needed for the repair of the fabric, and the proceeds from sales of timber were set aside for this purpose. If this fund did not suffice, the deficit was made up from additional rents and fines, thus reducing the amount to be divided amongst the Dean and Chapter. This system is described in some detail in the Dean and Chapter's Answers to the Ecclesiastical Revenue Commissioners' Articles of Enquiry of 1832.[48] Average figures for the three years ending in November 1831 (i.e., at the St Catherine's Day audit) showed a total annual income of £21,551; of which the principal constituents were £5,977 from ordinary rents; £12,567 from additional rents, fines, etc.; and £2,360 from sales of timber.

Not surprisingly, with so much to lose, the Canterbury Dean and Chapter began a campaign in 1836 to force Parliament to abandon the financial changes contained in the proposed cathedral reform. It was asserted that the lands and tenancies that had devolved to the Dean and Chapter were an inalienable property held for themselves and their successors for ever under a title of unquestionable validity.[49] Their campaign was unsuccessful, perhaps inevitably. The Cathedrals Act of 1840, coupled with the earlier bill of 1835 allowing for the suspension of canonries, marked an administrative revolution at Canterbury. The proceeds from property belonging to the Dean and Chapter which were allotted to suspended canonries went straight to the Commissioners' Common Fund for the augmentation of poor parochial livings.[50] Even the individual incomes of the Dean and the remaining canons were not immune from the process of redistribution of capitular wealth. It was Lord John Russell's determination in 1837 that the new measure should give the Commissioners the authority to decide 'that any sums which should exceed £2,000 a year in the case of a Dean and £1,000 in the case of a Canon should be applied to the augmentation of small and populous livings in the Diocese'.[51]

The contemporary clerical outcry against what seemed to many to be a spoliation of cathedral property and revenue reflected more than mere vested interest. Certainly, there was concern over a potential loss of economic status. Yet although Canterbury's wealth and endowments might have seemed vast in the 1830s, they were put to good use then.

---

[48] Dean's Book, 1822–54, pp. 147–54; average income figures at p. 147.

[49] Ibid., p. 209.

[50] Best, *Temporal Pillars* (cit. in n. 1), p. 351.

[51] LPL, MS 1812, fo. 16, Lord John Russell to Archbishop Howley, 2 Apr. 1837.

For instance, there was concern that the old and traditional charitable role of chapters in helping towards the cost of rebuilding or repairing parish churches would be curtailed.[52] An important point of principle was at stake in the claim of the Canterbury Chapter to dispose of its own revenues in the way which it chose and considered appropriate. What the Chapter deplored most was the notion underpinning the new legislation, 'of laying on ecclesiastical bodies exclusively the whole of a burden which, when necessary, ought to be laid on the collective body of the realm'.[53] If the idea of a national, established Church was to be recognized as a reality, then there should have been an appeal to the nation for funds to augment parochial livings. The Chapter felt that the Cathedral should not have to provide for the cure of souls in parishes in which the Cathedral had no connection or stake. More than this, it was feared that the Chapter, though stripped of real economic independence and the control of its own resources, would yet be left the mere nominal possessor of extensive landed property and estates. This would amount to the worst of both worlds. It would mean having to sustain all the odium of collecting a large revenue, with none of the grace derived from its distribution towards, say, local charitable causes.[54] Certainly, it was later the lament of the conservative reformer Edward Goulburn that the Act of 1840 crippled cathedrals, rather than allowing them the freedom to develop their own resources in the way that was most fitting.[55] In 1880, looking back on this time, Robert Jenkins, an Honorary Canon of Canterbury, took a similar view. He felt that 'the Church in her panic forgot, and surrendered entirely, her grand legal position of a combination or congeries of corporations rather than a single corporation'.[56]

Nevertheless, it was to be a long time before Canterbury felt the full financial impact of the reforms of 1837–41. Great disparities in cathedral wealth remained for a long time. In a pamphlet of 1861 a radical critic, using figures of 1852, could still complain that, for example, Canterbury's revenues were more than thrice those of Manchester Cathedral.[57] By the mid-1850s, Canterbury was contributing about £5,000 per annum from six suspended canonries to the Commissioners' Common Fund.[58] However, the Dean and Chapter retained control of their own estates and paid themselves: they had not yet become stipendiaries. The Commissioners were increasingly anxious to take over the management of the estates, although this was still a controversial matter. Already the Commissioners had it in their power to scrutinize Chapter accounts with great care. Canterbury's Dean and Chapter distinguished themselves in long resisting all attempts by the Commissioners to get them to surrender their accounts and receipts. The Dean and Chapter insisted that the statutes of 1835 and 1840 made clear that the Commissioners had to show that the accounts required related to some matter within the Commissioners' cognizance.[59] On

[52] E. Burton, *A Sequel to Remarks Upon Church Reform, With Observations Upon the Plan by Lord Henley* (London, 1832), 17–18.
[53] 'Memorial from the Dean & Chapter of Canterbury', in *Memorials and Communications* (cit. in n. 9), 10.
[54] J. L. Knight-Bruce, *Ecclesiastical Duties and Revenues Bill. Speech Delivered in the House of Lords, On Behalf of the Deans and Chapters Petitioning Against the Bill, 23 July 1840* (London, 1840), 51.
[55] E. M. Goulburn, *The Functions of Our Cathedrals: A Letter in Answer to an Enquiry Addressed to the Deans of Cathedral Churches by the Lord Archbishop of Canterbury and the Lord Archbishop of York* (London, 1869), 7.
[56] R. C. Jenkins, *Diocesan Histories, Canterbury* (London, 1880), 406.
[57] Figures from a Cathedral Commissioners' report (1852), quoted and discussed in an anon. pamphlet, *Cathedral Wealth and Cathedral Work* (London, 1861), 10–16.
[58] LPL, Tait Papers, vol. 246, fo. 265, 'Cathedral Reform—Evidence of the Dean & Chapter' [1854].
[59] Dean's Book, 1822–54, pp. 273–4.

the other hand, the Commissioners entertained well-founded suspicions that the Chapter was withholding some of their legitimate revenue. In 1845 an inspection of Chapter accounts revealed that the Commissioners were being excluded from various payments on the technical ground that they were not present at Chapter meetings.[60]

Meanwhile, the Commissioners themselves had been under inspection, and one of their officers departed after an investigation of his financial activities had showed malpractice. In 1850 a new group was set up especially for the administration of property. There were to be three Church Estates Commissioners, two paid and one honorary, of whom one should be a layman. They formed an executive committee for the Ecclesiastical Commission and also influenced its decision as a body, since two of them were required always to be present at its meetings. Their appointment made the Commission's interest in property more professional. A long-term view could now be taken.[61]

As a result, the much-discussed enfranchisement of estates remaining in episcopal and capitular hands became possible after an Act in 1851. This allowed the ending of the old system of church leases, whereby the tenants paid modest rents but large fines on the renewal of their leases. The lessee could now purchase the freehold of the land, or the lessor could buy out, on the termination of the lease, the lessee's possible right to renew it. Estates could then be rented at rack-rents which were related to the current value of the land. The Chapter of Canterbury set up a formidable committee consisting of the Dean and Canons Croft, Spry, and Harrison, to treat with the lessees and decide what should be sold or purchased.[62] The Commissioners objected when, in 1852, the Chapter regranted a lease at Ickham for twenty-one years with a fine, according to the old system, although enfranchisement was not mandatory.[63] This was just one of several similar episodes involving friction between the two parties over Cathedral property. A report of the Estates Committee of the Commission in 1856 revealed just how unsatisfactory the financial relationship between the Chapter and the Commissioners had become. The secretary to the Commissioners clearly had Canterbury in mind when he stated that one cathedral chapter had deliberately run an overdraft and charged the Commissioners the 5 per cent interest they had to pay on it.[64]

The Cathedral's reputation for the management of its property was undermined by the Heseltine affair, when a London tenant, William Heseltine, brought a legal action against the Chapter.[65] After this unfortunate episode they were anxious to be seen to be most efficient, as well as fair and just to their tenants. The Commissioners felt they could manage the estates better. Yet it was not just self-interest that dictated Canterbury's resistance to them. Since the canons paid themselves fixed incomes after 1840, they had little to gain personally, in a purely financial sense, in fighting to retain the control of their estates. They fought for the old system because they felt it to be one of the last vestiges of

[60] London, Church Commissioners' MSS, Canterbury, file no. 1186. The inspection showed that the Commissioners were thereby in deficit of over £40.

[61] Best, *Temporal Pillars* (cit. in n. 1), 396.

[62] Chapter Act Book, 1854–84, p. 477.

[63] Dean's Book, 1822–54, p. 460.

[64] Best, *Temporal Pillars* (cit. in n. 1), 456.

[65] For the whole controversy, see William Heseltine, *A Tenant's Statement of the Conduct Recently Pursued Towards Him by the Dean and Chapter of Canterbury, on the Occasion of His Renewing His Lease* (2nd edn.; London, 1839).

independence and because the management of their own property was an activity reward-ing in itself and conducive to social and economic self-respect within the community. It was surely not an idle claim that they understood local needs better than did the ecclesiastical bureaucrats in London.

Other chapters felt the same; but they could not hold off the Ecclesiastical Com-missioners, who had long desired complete control over the estates of the Dean and Chapter. The Commissioners were certain that their Common Fund would be much increased if they managed the estates themselves professionally rather than receiving the fruits of amateur stewardship. In the case of Canterbury, the accounts show that the level of income was stable at an average figure of £22,000 between 1838 and 1859, and that the income was higher towards the end of the period. This suggests at least a respectable performance.[66]

In the 1850s there were proposals in Parliament for the compulsory transfer of episcopal and capitular estates to the Commissioners. A bill was introduced in 1858. Benjamin Harrison represented Canterbury at meetings in the Jerusalem Chamber called by Lord John Thynne of Westminster Abbey in defence of capitular property.[67] In the event, when the bill was passed in 1860, only episcopal property was to be compulsorily transferred, since the Home Secretary had been forced to drop the clause relating to capitular prop-erty.[68] There was hope in some quarters that Parliament had at last realized that cathedrals needed careful treatment, and should be considered as cathedrals, not just as suppliers of funds.[69]

However, the Commissioners pressed on with voluntary transfers. They had been determined for some time to get to grips with the problem at Canterbury. They first of all secured an Order in Council, in 1857, under which the treasurer was required to deliver annual accounts in a prescribed form and to pay to the Commissioners any divisible surplus in excess of the fixed salaries of £2,000 for the Dean and £1,000 for each canon. Then they proposed a scheme for the transfer of Chapter estates, for the provision of a temporary money-payment, and for the later provision of a 'convenient estate', which would bring in sufficient funds to meet regular Cathedral expenses.

The Chapter considered this possibility in 1859, before the outcome of the Episcopal and Capitular Property Bill was known.[70] Negotiations continued in 1860 and 1861, resulting in an awkward period when few financial decisions could be made. In 1862 the scheme was effected under an Order in Council. The greater part of the Chapter estate was to be surrendered, some land was allowed to be kept, and an annual payment of £5,700 was to be made to bring the income from land up to a desired figure of £17,500—the calculated total of all Cathedral expenses. In addition, a down payment of £20,000 was to be spent on agreed repairs to the fabric.[71] Other cathedrals accepted similar schemes. In 1866

[66] Figures quoted in this section are from the annual Receiver's or Treasurer's Accounts of the Dean and Chapter.

[67] Chapter Act Book, 1854–84, p. 74.

[68] O. J. Brose, *Church and Parliament: The Reshaping of the Church of England, 1826–1860* (Stanford, Calif., and London, 1959), 174–6.

[69] *Guardian*, 15 (12 Sept. 1860), 812.

[70] Chapter Act Book, 1854–84, pp. 97–8.

[71] The Order in Council is printed in *The Statutes of the Cathedral and Metropolitical Church of Christ, Canterbury*, ed. G. K. A. Bell (priv. printed, Canterbury, 1925), 114–30. Subsequent Orders in Council making changes to the estates are listed at 130–2.

Canterbury was provided with its 'convenient estate', which, with existing land, was to produce the necessary £17,500 each year. No provision was made for a review in case of falling rents or increasing expenditure. These arrangements and those of other chapters were confirmed by an Act in 1868. The effects are observable in the receiver's and treasurer's accounts, in the altered headings for sources of income, and in a slight but definite fall in the total figure: the average was £17,430 between 1862 and 1872, near enough to the 'official' figure of £17,500. This represents a loss of about 25 per cent on the income of the 1850s.

Canterbury was in some ways more fortunate than some other cathedrals. Salisbury surrendered property in 1861 in return for an annual payment of £4,200 towards stipends and expenses and a single payment of only £10,000 for the fabric. The Dean and Chapter there were not provided with their 'new estate' until 1875, and they found within five years or so that the rents did not produce sufficient income to meet their rising expenses.[72] All the 'new estates' were mainly of agricultural land, since the Commissioners made it a rule to retain buildings and improvable estates for their Common Fund. Had rents and tithes remained at the figures calculated, all might have been well. Sadly they did not, and at the same time cathedral expenses rose, especially as more was expected of deans and chapters.

The 1870s were a time of cathedral restoration. Money for this had to be sought from benefactors and from appeals to the public. At Canterbury there was the need to repair the roof of the Trinity Chapel after a fire in 1872 (only partly covered by an insurance policy with the Sun Fire Office) and there were plans to restore the choir in 1876. Income fell to an average of £16,800 between 1872 and 1882, with some bad years. In 1878 the Dean and Chapter composed a Memorial to the Ecclesiastical Commissioners, asking for additional endowment for the payment of the choir and improvements to the Choir School.[73] This was turned down; but, perhaps as a result, further exchanges were made with the Commissioners in August 1879 to improve the permanent estate, and a grant of £5,500 for new farm buildings was provided. In the same year, a Cathedral Establishments Commission was set up, which completed its work in 1885. The Canterbury Dean and Chapter gave evidence of having to make rent reductions in 1880–1 to farmers hit by the agricultural depression, while their own expenses grew—they claimed for increased salaries for minor canons.[74] Even the income at Durham, a very rich cathedral, was badly hit by reduced rents.[75]

Worse was to come in the early 1890s. In the years 1892 to 1894 income was approximately £15,000, £13,000, and £14,800. The Dean and canons halved their stipends in 1892 and only took £400 and £200 respectively in 1894—it was fortunate that their private incomes allowed for such charity.[76] The Archbishop's visitation of 1893 revealed their distress: 'both tithe and land are still falling in value and the rent of our farms every year diminishes'. So great was their fear, that the Commissioners were asked to take over the 'convenient estate' since the Dean and Chapter were 'but amateurs without technical experience and without capital, completely at the mercy of the farmers'.[77] In August 1894

[72] Kathleen Edwards, 'Salisbury Cathedral', in V. C. H. *Wiltshire*, iii (1956), 203–5.

[73] Chapter Act Book, 1854–84, pp. 398–402.

[74] *Cathedral Establishments Commission, Final Report* (1885), 5.

[75] P. Mussett with P. G. Woodward, *Estates and Money at Durham Cathedral 1660–1985* (Durham, 1988), 15.

[76] 1892: Chapter Act Book, 1884–95, p. 188; 1894: LPL, Benson Papers, vol. 127, fos. 165–6.

[77] LPL, Benson Papers, ibid., fo. 161, J. Duncan to E. W. Benson, 10 Nov. 1893.

a considerable portion of the permanent estate was accordingly handed back to the Commissioners in return for tithe rent charges, and in May 1896 a further portion. In August 1902 all the remaining land was transferred. Since that time the Dean and Chapter have owned only the houses in the Precincts and their perimeter and some other residential property and shops in Canterbury.[78]

In the visitation of 1898 the Commissioners were praised because they had 'most liberally met the threatened insolvency of the Chapter by exchanging the greater part of the Chapter lands, at the price at which they were handed on originally, for Tithe Rent Charges'. Though for some years it had not been possible for canons' incomes to be paid in full, 'with strict economy there is a fair prospect of four-fifths of their proper stipends being forthcoming'.[79] It was in the same year that Dean Farrar wrote: 'in the good old days all the canons had carriages; now, none of them has, and even the Dean cannot afford to keep a gig'.[80]

This perhaps was a state of affairs which some reformers had desired. Very gradually, over a period of about sixty years, the deans and chapters had been reduced from independent wealthy landed corporations to (in effect) boards of governors, running their cathedrals on money provided from a central establishment, and under considerable restraint from outside bodies, although nominally still independent. And during those sixty years the public expectation of all aspects of cathedral life was more demanding—in liturgy and the upkeep of the fabric, in general appearance and good order, and in an obvious service to the communities in which they were set.

Cathedral Worship and Liturgical Life

In the early 1830s, idealistic Church reformers such as Lord Henley, as well as the radical and Dissenting critics of the established Church, evinced little affection for the traditional forms of cathedral worship. Just as the enthusiastic adherents of the Oxford Movement were about to inspire the rising generation with visions of 'the beauty of holiness', the prosaic 'Benthamite' temper of the more radical cathedral reformers seemed impervious to such an appeal to the religious imagination. For cathedral reformers such as Henley, much of cathedral worship was deemed at best 'cold' and 'formalistic', and at worst 'vain' or 'useless'.[81] Such critics were often unconscious heirs to a Puritan tradition which regarded cathedral worship primarily in terms of preaching and ministering rather than in the performance of the liturgy. Not surprisingly, conservative defenders of cathedrals in the 1830s, such as G. A. Selwyn, took exception to reform proposals coloured by this negative outlook, as being potentially subversive of the traditional liturgical life of cathedrals. Cathedral reform was necessary, but traditionalists insisted that care must be taken that it represent a true reform, based on a return to the original principles and uses of cathedral institutions as envisaged by their founders and enshrined in their statutes. Nowhere perhaps did the conservative reformers differ more from the utilitarian, radical

[78] *Statutes* (cit. in n. 71), 131.
[79] LPL, Canterbury Visitation Returns, 1898, MS VG 3/10c, fo. 224.
[80] LPL, Frederick Temple Papers, vol. 10, fo. 75, Dean Farrar to Archbishop Temple, 21 May 1898.
[81] Lord Henley, *A Plan of Church Reform* (London, 1832), 35.

reformers than in their understanding of the liturgical dimension of cathedral life.

Conservative cathedral reformers tended to be High Churchmen. In some cases, they were influenced, to varying degrees, by the Oxford Movement, with its catholic ideal of cathedral worship in terms of prayer and the celebration of the eucharist rather than preaching. In complete contrast to utilitarian notions of practical usefulness dear to the heart of what Newman ironically dubbed 'the "march of mind" men', it was the mystical, sacramental, and 'medieval' aspect of cathedrals to which High Churchmen and Trac-tarians were attracted. Like George Herbert, and in equally poetic vein, such churchmen looked to cathedrals as spiritual havens and devotional sanctuaries in a turbulent, materi-alistic world. William Sewell argued in the *Quarterly Review* that cathedrals 'were intended, not like our present churches, as lecture rooms for teaching religion, or decent shelters against weather for the convenience of assembling on the Sabbath, but as great temples, where daily and almost hourly, a solemn service might be celebrated to God, even if no worshippers were present but those by whom it was performed'.[82] For Tractarians, Ecclesiologists, and many High Church cathedral reformers, the error of the radical reformers lay in confounding the uses and nature of cathedrals with those of parish churches, in terms of worship as well as of the economy of the church. Not surprisingly, to a new generation of Tractarian-inspired churchmen, contemporary practice in cathedral worship, and especially in cathedral music, did not always measure up to the standards desired. It was the very liturgical conservatism of this generation that often made it critical of practical abuses in the pre-1840 cathedral economy. For instance, the 'false principle' of heaping canonries and parishes on the same man was condemned on the specific ground that it thereby reduced attendance at the cathedral to one solitary canon and thus led to the 'absolute neglect of the weekly Communion' envisaged in cathedral statutes.[83]

At Canterbury, the Cathedral's liturgical practice in the relatively lax 1820s certainly did not measure up to the rising expectations of the High Church clergy of succeeding decades. Yet neither did it quite merit the censures of 'coldness' and 'formalism' so often levelled against it by radical critics. Certainly, standards of preaching and ceremonial, and even of mere attendance, do not appear to have been high.[84] From 1828, however, the attendance of minor canons in choir for morning and evening services was more strictly enforced,[85] and from 1837 each canon was instructed to attend both services on Sundays, during his period of residence.[86] Standards of musical performance were less readily improved. Complaints that since the late eighteenth century, musical standards at Canterbury had declined were genuine and not merely the result of Ecclesiological or Tractarian prejudice. This decline was blamed on the appointment, in violation of the Cathedral statutes, of minor canons who were incompetent to sing.[87] However, in line with the wider and well-attested trend towards higher standards of ritual and liturgical order in the Church as a whole, improvements in the Cathedral worship were becoming evident by the early 1840s. We have the testimony of several visitors to the Cathedral, some either Tractarian or

[82] [William Sewell], 'The Cathedral Establishments', *Quarterly Review,* 58 (Feb.–Apr. 1837), 232.

[83] 'The Cathedral Act', *British Critic,* 29 (1841), 144.

[84] G. S[mith], *Chronological History of Canterbury Cathedral* (Canterbury, 1883), 353.

[85] Dean's Book, 1822–54, p. 75.

[86] Ibid., p. 221.

[87] Edward Taylor, *The English Cathedral Service* (London, 1845), reprinted from *British and Foreign Review,* 33 (1844), 30.

sympathetic to the Oxford Movement, who painted glowing impressions of cathedral worship at Canterbury at this time. According to one such visitor, the Oxford Tractarian J. R. Bloxam, Canterbury Cathedral was 'infinitely superior to any foreign church ... The altar was covered with gold candlesticks, chalices, etc., and looked chaste and splendid.'[88] In similar vein, an American visitor, George Washington Doane, Bishop of New Jersey and a friend of the Tractarians, recorded eulogistic impressions of a service in Canterbury Cathedral on 28 June 1841, stating that 'the service was well conducted, the singing better than we had heard, and altogether admirable. We feel that nothing can go beyond this.'[89] Moreover, a marked improvement in the standard of choral services was noted by Archbishop Howley in his visitation of 1844.[90] The careful ceremonial surrounding the enthronement of John Bird Sumner as Archbishop of Canterbury in 1848 was a manifestation of this improved liturgical order.[91]

The first report of the Royal Commission on Cathedral and Collegiate Churches in 1854 proposed the introduction of Sunday evening services in cathedral naves. Canterbury's Chapter was distinctly unenthusiastic about the idea, arguing that the nave was too large and cold for use except as a novelty in the summer. They were against alterations to the traditional pattern of their services.[92] As long as W. R. Lyall, a High Churchman of the 'Hackney Phalanx' school,[93] remained Dean, little could be achieved in this direction. Jealousy was even generated by the fact that A. P. Stanley (a residentiary canon at Canterbury from 1851 to 1858) by his eloquent preaching did much to popularize Cathedral services and draw the crowds.[94] Stanley was on good terms personally with the rest of the Chapter, but his breadth of outlook and enthusiasm for liberal causes were not in harmony with the views of Dean Lyall and Dr Spry, nor with those of Benjamin Harrison, who deplored, in kindly fashion, Stanley's lack of understanding of the intricacies of Chapter business.[95] A new era began after Lyall's death in 1857, on the appointment of Henry Alford as Dean. It was not, however, an era of co-operation between the Chapter and its difficult new Dean.

Up to Alford's time, there had been only one sermon on Sunday, always in the morning. Alford now introduced a sermon at Sunday afternoon services, with himself as preacher, which proved very popular. He could not persuade the Chapter to preach. In his occasional absence abroad, the Headmaster of the King's School, the Warden of St Augustine's

[88] *Reminiscences of the Reverend George Gilbert (1796–1874)*, ed. F. J. Shirley (priv. printed, 1938), 10.

[89] W. C. Doane, *Life and Writings of George Washington Doane ... With a Memoir by His Son, William Croswell Doane* (4 vols.; New York, 1860), i. 274.

[90] W. Howley, *A Charge Delivered at His Ordinary Visitation, by William, Lord Archbishop of Canterbury* (London, 1844), 7–8.

[91] Woodruff and Danks, *Memorials*, 363–4.

[92] LPL, Tait Papers, vol. 246, fo. 264, 'Evidence of the Dean & Chapter' [1854]. Answers from the Dean and Chapter to the Secretary of the Cathedral and Collegiate Churches Commission in 1854, priv. printed by the Dean and Chapter as *Cathedral Commission* (Canterbury, 1872), 5.

[93] On William Rowe Lyall (1788–1857), see *DNB*; C. Dewey, *The Passing of Barchester: A Real Life Version of Trollope* (London,

1991), ch. 5; cf. LPL, Act Books of the Archbishops of Canterbury, VB 1/16, fos. 88, 281.

[94] *A Victorian Dean: A Memoir of Arthur Stanley, Dean of Westminster, With Many New Unpublished Letters*, ed. A. V. Baillie and H. Bolitho (London, 1930), 56. Cf. R. E. Prothero, *The Life and Correspondence of Arthur Penrhyn Stanley* (2 vols.; London, 1893), i. 535.

[95] For Benjamin Harrison (1808–87), see *DNB*; cf. LPL, Act Books of the Archbishop of Canterbury, VB 1/16, fo. 282; B. Hogben, 'Benjamin Harrison: Archdeacon, Benefactor, Tractarian', *Cant. Cath. Chron.*, 78 (1984), 21–5. For John Hume Spry, see LPL, Act Books of the Archbishop of Canterbury, VB 1/15, fo. 90, and VB 1/17, fo. 26. Cf. Mozley, *Reminiscences* (cit. in n. 12), i. 387–8; Prothero, *Stanley* (cit. in n. 94), i. 467–8.

College, and others were brought in.[96] Alford's innovation led to a full Cathedral on summer Sundays, advantage thus being taken of the new annual seaside-holiday invasion of the Kent coastal resorts now made accessible by the railways. As Alford himself noted in 1866 of the Sunday afternoon services, 'the great majority of the congregation consists of occasional attendants, and strangers. These latter flock in in crowds during the summer, when Ramsgate and Margate are full.'[97]

However, Alford's innovations attracted bitter and continued hostility from High Church as well as merely conservative elements in the Chapter. There were theological implications, and questions of liturgical priority were at stake. For High Churchmen the celebration of the Eucharist, with its attendant ritual, was the central act of cathedral worship. They felt that worship was somehow diminished by the preaching of popular sermons at uncanonical hours to draw in the crowds from the Kent seaside.

In general, it cannot be said that the churchmanship of members of the Chapter at this period was influenced greatly by the Oxford Movement, any more than it had been by the Evangelical Revival. Always a great stickler for rubrics, Canon Benjamin Harrison opposed Alford's Sunday afternoon services on grounds of liturgical conservatism.[98] J. C. Robertson, from a similar perspective, was another member of the Chapter who remained in implacable opposition to Alford's policy. In 1870, in a revealing letter to his friend Edward Goulburn, Dean of Norwich, Robertson stressed that there had always remained in Canterbury's Chapter an important element which maintained that 'preaching is not the sole use of cathedrals, nor even the principal use of them'.[99] Additional trouble was made by another controversial question which Alford on becoming Dean had almost immediately settled in a manner calculated to offend the conservative interest in the Cathedral.

During the seventeenth century, provision was made in the Book of Common Prayer for the annual commemoration of four notable historical anniversaries in the Church of England's calendar: King Charles I's martyrdom, on 30 January; the Restoration of the monarchy in 1660, on 29 May; and the discovery of the Gunpowder Plot in 1605 and the arrival of William of Orange in 1688, both on 5 November. These became known as the 'State services', since they owed their imposition to royal rather than strictly ecclesiastical authority. The commemoration of 30 January had always been a particular favourite with the old Tory High Church interest. By the 1850s, the 30 January service and sermon must have seemed very anachronistic, but for Dean Lyall, Dr Spry, and Archdeacon Harrison, these State services were part of a tradition which they wished to keep alive at Canterbury. However, in a wider sphere, the Tractarians inspired a growing reaction against the very notion of State services, as being uncanonical and unecclesiastical. Thus, two distinct

---

[96] Chapter Act Book, 1854–84, pp. 48, 69, 75, 155. Cf. Woodruff, 'Reminiscences of the Cathedral' (cit. in n. 10), 15. Cf. C. T. Longley, *A Primary Charge Addressed to the Clergy of His Diocese, by Charles Thomas, Lord Archbishop of Canterbury* (London, 1864), approving the Dean and, by implication, reproving the Chapter.

[97] 'Cathedral Life and Cathedral Reform', *Contemporary Review*, 2 (May–Aug. 1866), 488–513, at 506. From the late 1850s onwards, special South-Eastern Railway trains also brought visitors from the seaside to Canterbury, so as to be in time for morning service in the Cathedral on summer Sundays. See *A Guide to Canterbury Cathedral, With the Inscriptions and Epitaphs on the Various Tombs and Monuments* (Canterbury, 1860), 4.

[98] Hogben, 'Benjamin Harrison' (cit. in n. 95), 22.

[99] Norwich, Norfolk County Record Office, Goulburn Papers, MS 21644 MC 47/5, fo. 101, J. C. Robertson to E. M. Goulburn, 17 Oct. 1870.

strands of opinion within the Chapter combined, so that in 1857 a majority was 'entertaining strong objections to the language of these services, and repugnance to their use'. A demand was made for an end to their observance by the Cathedral, but a minority of canons was opposed, not only on grounds of custom and tradition, but also because of doubts as to the legal propriety of such a move.[100] Characteristically, Alford was untroubled by such considerations. It is true that Parliament in 1858 was to abandon the observance of King Charles's martyrdom, and in 1861 the Gunpowder Plot and the landing of William of Orange; but already in January 1859 Alford resolved on his own authority that at Canterbury the ordinary services should be used henceforth on the three State service days. Accordingly, on 30 January 1858, for the first time, 'the usual service was read without music', and it ceased to be a Precum Day.[101] Here was another breach of liturgical tradition to which the conservative element in the Precincts found it difficult to be reconciled.

Yet Dean Alford's reforms were not all in one direction. For as well as being a superb preacher, especially of extempore sermons, Alford was concerned with the conduct of morning and evening prayer. As an accomplished musician, he was far better equipped than many of his predecessors, and he took a very active part in Cathedral services. From as early as All Saints' Day 1857 he began the practice of intoning his part in the service on Precum Days, when it was the statutory custom for the Dean to read prayers. With the Precentor, he compiled and edited a hymn-book for use in the Cathedral, entitled *The Year of Praise*.[102] Moreover, the Dean's views on the importance of the meaning and value of cathedral worship deepened with time. By 1861, he was already complaining about a sermon that he had heard, 'really levelled at the Cathedral and all connected with it, assuming that none had any religion, cared anything for the beauty of nature or art, or for the regularity or decency of church ordinances'.[103]

A sign of the development of the liturgical life of the Cathedral in the period was an increase in the number of communicants from between about fifteen and forty in the 1830s, to thirty to sixty or more by the 1860s. Easter communicant figures in particular reveal a spectacular rate of increase, as shown by a comparison between Easter Day 1841, when there were forty-one communicants, and Easter Day 1868, when there were 120. Further, there was an increasing number of 'set-piece' special services, when vast numbers flocked to the Cathedral. For instance, on St Bartholomew's Day 1866, at the consecration of two colonial bishops, there were 400 communicants.[104] By the early 1870s a correspondence in the *Guardian* was commenting on a remarkable 'stirring' of liturgical life at Canterbury. Christmas Day in 1872, it was noted, 'was marked by an early Communion (8.15), the first, it is said, "since the Reformation" whatever date that may mean. And the right-minded resolve of the Dean and Chapter to make a trial of this for six months, on all Sundays and the great Festivals (there is always a midday celebration on Sunday), was amply rewarded by the appearance of forty-five communicants at the early service.'[105] Early fasting communions were to become a shibboleth of the Ritualist party in the

[100] Chapter Act Book, 1854–84, p. 67.
[101] Ibid., p. 75; cf. Precentor's Book, 1852–9, at 30 Jan. 1858.
[102] *Life, Journal and Letters of Henry Alford*, ed. Frances Alford (London, 1873), 391.
[103] Ibid. 335.
[104] Oblation Book, 1865–74.
[105] *Guardian*, 28 (1 Jan. 1873), 21.

Church of England from around this time, and it is not surprising to find that this particular liturgical innovation at Canterbury attracted favourable notice in advanced High Church and Anglo-Catholic quarters.

Alford's two immediate successors, Robert Payne Smith (1871–95; Pl. 48) and F. W. Farrar (1895–1903; Pl. 49), continued his policy of liturgical innovation and adaptation, with the introduction of a Sunday evening sermon and other popular services.[106] Dean Farrar was a powerful and persuasive preacher, and more of a popularizer than his two predecessors. These services were, however, not popular with the city clergy, who saw the Dean and Chapter as being in competition with them, holding services at the same time. The last three decades of the century were characterized at Canterbury by an 'increasing zeal for the fabric and the services of the church',[107] in spite of the difficulties caused by the dramatic fall in Cathedral income. For instance, at the 1893 visitation, Canon Rawlinson complained that 'the cathedral is not so "fully furnished and appointed suitably to its dignity in respect of ornaments, books and accessories" as I should like to see it'. The condition and number of service-books in the choir was also defective, for lack of funds. Canon Duncan felt that there was 'some room for improvement in the way of plain services and periodical celebrations at an early hour on week days'. He regretted that 'the present tendency would seem to be almost exclusively to great services at a later hour'.[108] Nevertheless, in spite of financial constraints, there is overwhelming evidence that in the latter part of the period all the Cathedral services were 'carefully and reverently performed'.

By the 1890s the Chapter was spending far more time discussing the finer points of ritual and liturgical practice than had been the case sixty years before. Two typical subjects of debate were the substitution of the new *Hymns Ancient and Modern* for *Church Hymns*,[109] and plans to hang banners in the nave.[110] Some of their discussions reflected wider divisions within the Church at large over the nature and extent of the ritual and ceremonial allowed in worship. At least until late in the century, however, the often damaging divisions over the points of doctrine and ritual that were so widespread in the Church as a whole had been well contained at Canterbury. There seemed to be a conscious determination to avoid liturgical disputes wherever possible. For example, the reluctance of High Churchmen in the Cathedral body to press for an end to Dean Alford's innovation of Sunday afternoon sermons was determined by a fear of disrupting what had become a fairly harmonious Chapter by the 1860s.[111]

The arrival of E. W. Benson as Archbishop in 1883 made for greater difficulties of this kind. He was a High Churchman and a cathedral man. He had been Chancellor of Lincoln and had begun the building of a cathedral in his diocese of Truro. He had also written about cathedral life and cathedral reform.[112] The two Deans during his time at Canterbury,

[106] LPL, Tait Papers, vol. 192, fo. 199, Dean Payne Smith to Archbishop Tait, 2 Dec. 1873.

[107] Woodruff and Danks, *Memorials*, 368.

[108] LPL, Canterbury Visitation Returns, 1893, MS VG 3/9c, fos. 387, 346, 349.

[109] Chapter Act Book, 1895–1910, p. 87.

[110] Ibid. 32.

[111] LPL, Benson Papers, vol. 127, fos. 143–4, F. J. Holland to Archbishop Benson, 4 June 1894.

[112] E. W. Benson, *The Cathedral: Its Necessary Place in the Life and Work of the Church* (London, 1878), an expansion of two essays, 'Cathedral Life and Cathedral Work', *Quarterly Review*, 130 (Jan.–Apr. 1871), 225–55, and 'The Relation of the Chapter to the Bishop', in *Essays on Cathedrals*, ed. J. S. Howson (London,

Payne Smith and Farrar, were determined Protestants. In the 1890s Benson appointed several of his friends as Six Preachers or Honorary Canons, to the distress of the Church Association, which listed them as 'Ritualistic Appointments'.[113] Benson made diligent visitation of his Cathedral; his friends in the Greater Chapter took the opportunity to comment on 'defects' in the Cathedral's worship and to express their desire for better things. Their depositions perhaps give an impression of a greater demand for High Church practices than was in fact the case. Even so, there were changes—the introduction of Chapter Retreats and Quiet Days; the setting-aside of a part of the Cathedral for private prayer;[114] and in 1895 the use of the 'eastward position' for the celebrant at early Communion, instead of the usual 'north end'.[115] Benson's friend A. J. Mason became a residentiary canon in that year. In 1896 Benson died and was buried with something of the splendour of a medieval archbishop in the space under the north-west tower, which was later refurbished as the Chapel of St Augustine in memory of A. J. Mason.

The life of the French Protestant Church within the Cathedral continued. In the late eighteenth century, numbers were few and the congregation moved into the south aisle of the crypt. After the death, in 1840, of a minister who had been blind for many years, the congregation was too poor to secure a resident successor.[116] They appealed to the London French Church at St Martin-le-Grand for assistance and secured a monthly visit from a pastor from there.[117] On these occasions there might be seventy present, but otherwise there would only be about seven or eight worshippers on Sundays, when there was a reading by a layman of the French liturgy. By 1870, the average congregation numbered only about twenty-one, 'not all of whom', according to a local newspaper, 'understand the French language, while not a few of them are wholly ignorant of French'. The fragile finances of the French Church were insufficient and funds were being mismanaged. In both 1859 and 1870, the Charity Commissioners drew up reports that highlighted the unsatisfactory financial state of the French Church. In 1874 the Church's very existence was, in consequence, under threat from the Charity Commissioners: they suggested a transference of Huguenot charitable funds towards the encouragement of the study of the French language at the King's School. The Cathedral Chapter resisted this scheme,[118] only to find themselves divided by the plans of a new pastor. Help was at hand for the French Church. One of the visiting French pastors from London, J. A. Martin, came to live in Canterbury in 1870 and began a sustained campaign to restore the flagging fortunes of the Church.

For the liberal and eirenic—as well as the more Protestant-minded—members of the Cathedral body, Canterbury's Huguenot connection was a positive source of pride and gratification. In particular, A. P. Stanley, when a canon in the 1850s, was most impressed

1872), 235–83.

[113] See 'List of Ritualistic Appointments by Past & Present Archbishops of Canterbury', in *An Indictment . . . of the Bishops, Showing How the Church of England is Being Corrupted and Betrayed by Them and (indirectly) by the Prime Ministers: Formulated by the Council of the Church Association* (London, 1898), 42.

[114] LPL, Benson Papers, vol. 83, fo. 82, F. J. Holland to R. H. Baynes, 21 July 1890.

[115] Chapter Act Book, 1895–1910, p. 22.

[116] Note by F. Rouch in a copy of Gostling's *Walk* (6th edn.; 1825), 233, 'I believe there remain now (1841) not one weaver and no Communicant; the Minister, Mieville, died 1839 or 1840 and none has been appointed to succeed him.' (Transcript of Rouch's notes by H. Enderby, Canterbury Public Library.)

[117] J. Martin, *Christian Firmness of the Huguenots; and a Sketch of the French Refugee Church of Canterbury* (London, 1881), 88–9.

[118] Chapter Act Book, 1854–84, p. 331.

by this aspect of the Cathedral's apparent liturgical eclecticism: he wrote that 'Arnold's much-abused theory of having different sects worship in the same church is here fulfilled even to exaggeration, inasmuch as a Presbyterian service is carried on in the crypt at the same hour as the Cathedral service above'.[119] The enthusiasm of such as Stanley inevitably made the High Church elements in the Chapter all the more prejudiced against the French Huguenot congregation in their midst. Pre-Tractarian moderate High Churchmen, not least at Canterbury, had always retained some sympathy, if patronizingly expressed, for the Continental reformed communions, carefully distinguishing these from Protestant Dissenters in Britain, whom they saw as nothing less than schismatics. However, in the wake of the Oxford Movement, many High Churchmen took a less benevolent view of their foreign 'reformed brethren', and were less willing to make allowances for their non-episcopal status. During the late 1870s prejudice built up in Chapter against the activities of the newly arrived Pastor Martin. One canon urged another to make 'the little ape' Martin use the Anglican service in French, as a condition of his—the second canon's—agreeing to preach at one of the Huguenot services in the crypt. The same canon complained that the congregation's continued existence 'except as a sentiment is wholly unnecessary ... there is not one soul in the said flock who does not know English better than French'.[120] Even a visiting French observer invited in 1877 to witness the 327th anniversary celebrations of the foundation of the Huguenot religion, was led to conclude that with so few descendants of the refugees left in Canterbury, the money set aside for the services would be better spent augmenting poor livings in the city.[121]

Pastor Martin was not easily disheartened, and proved indefatigable in rallying support for his congregation. He found a sympathetic and enthusiastic champion in Archbishop Tait, a Broad Churchman who was keen to foster continued Anglican links with foreign Protestant churches. In debates in the House of Lords, Tait defended the cause of Canterbury's French Church and he also touched on this in his 1876 Visitation Charge.[122] Tait's respect for Martin was not even diminished by the pastor's controversial abandonment of the use of French translations of the Book of Common Prayer in the crypt services, and his introduction of a new service-book of very Protestant complexion. Martin skilfully argued that it was only in this way that the French congregation could retain 'the position assigned to it by your Grace, that of being a connection between the Church of England and the continental Reformed churches'.[123] Martin subtly changed his ground, frankly admitting that the French Church 'as an institution for foreign worshippers has now ceased'. Instead, he played on the theme of historical continuity and the tradition of the congregation's worship in the Cathedral over three centuries.[124] In fact, it was necessary even for Tait to retain a certain distance in his dealings with the Huguenot congregation and to be careful not to appear to compromise Anglican integrity in any way, even if only to avoid offending some members of the Chapter. All the same, it was largely owing to

---

[119] Prothero, *Stanley* (cit. in n. 94), i. 428.

[120] LPL, Tait Papers, vol. 216, fo. 131.

[121] Ibid., vol. 228, fo. 271, H. M. Clavis to Archbishop Tait, 18 July 1877.

[122] J. Martin, *Christian Firmness* (cit. in n. 117), 89–91.

[123] LPL, Tait Papers, vol. 216, fo. 127, J. A. Martin to Archbishop Tait, 18 Jan. 1876. Cf. ibid., vol. 206, fo. 379, C. de Boinville to Archbishop Tait, 11 Aug. 1875.

[124] Ibid., vol. 216, fos. 136, 141, 154.

Tait's patronage, and not least his influence with the Charity Commissioners, that the French Church in the crypt now survived.[125]

Tait's death in 1882 was a blow to the French Church at a critical time. None the less, in the same year, after formal inspection had revealed financial and organizational improvements, the Charity Commissioners finally reprieved it.[126] Martin now planned an ambitious scheme of expansion. He hoped to secure the Church by means of an appeal. This plan came just too late, due to the arrival of the new archbishop. Dean Payne Smith was most supportive,[127] but Archbishop Benson was much less sympathetic than Tait had been to Martin's cause, and he now coolly informed Martin that 'the English interest will not be roused unless the French care enough for the work to assist it materially'.[128] Nothing further was done. On Martin's death, in 1889, the future of the French Church again seemed threatened, as the search for a suitable replacement proved difficult. Even High Church members of the Chapter now seemed prepared to see it survive, if only on their terms. Anxious negotiations were conducted.[129] Canon Fremantle was eager to find a pastor who could take pupils, as the idea of a French educational centre in Canterbury was mooted. Fremantle hoped that the new pastor 'could link up to the French Protestants in places like Dover and Folkestone'.[130] A suitable pastor was found, and the French Church lived on, and even flourished. In 1893, when the crypt was restored, the area within the Black Prince's Chantry was partitioned off for continued use of the French congregation.[131] By this time, average congregations had grown again to about forty-five, and with Dean Farrar as one of the French Church's trustees, its future seemed secure.[132]

Cathedral Fabric: Maintenance and Restoration

Later views of the early nineteenth century as a period of neglect and decay in Cathedral worship and in the maintenance of the fabric are both exaggerated and misleading. In fact, from the 1820s important steps in the repair of the fabric were made, initially under the inspiration of Dean Percy, while he was still Archdeacon of Canterbury.[133] The Dean and Chapter had borrowed £20,000 in 1831 from Queen Anne's Bounty to enable them to pull down and rebuild the north-west or Arundel Tower.[134] They were empowered to borrow a further £5,000. In his Primary Visitation Charge in 1832, Archbishop Howley could claim that over the previous ten years, no less than £29,000 had been spent in repairs to the Cathedral fabric,[135] exclusive of the sum for rebuilding the tower. By 1840, Dean Bagot could declare that as much as £60,000 had been spent on the fabric in the preceding twenty

[125] LPL, Tait Papers, vol. 280, fo. 237, Archbishop Tait to Charity Commissioners, 4 Feb. 1882. Cf. LPL, Benson Papers, vol. 12, fos. 177–9, 'Short Memorandum Concerning the French Church'.

[126] LPL, Benson Papers, vol. 55, fo. 362, H. Longley to Archbishop Benson, 23 Nov. 1897.

[127] Ibid., vol. 12, fo. 175, Dean Payne Smith to Archbishop Benson, 9 Feb. 1884.

[128] Ibid., fo. 180, Archbishop Benson to J. A. Martin, 12 Mar. 1884.

[129] Ibid., vol. 69, fo. 234, C. Pascal to Archbishop Benson, 15 Oct. 1889.

[130] Ibid., fo. 237, W. H. Fremantle to Archbishop Benson, 18 Oct. 1889.

[131] Chapter Act Book, 1884–95, pp. 216–18.

[132] LPL, Benson Papers, vol. 55, fo. 362, H. Longley to Archbishop Benson, 23 Nov. 1897.

[133] Chapter Act Book, 1822–54, p. 72.

[134] Dean's Book, 1822–54, pp. 99, 148.

[135] W. Howley, *A Charge to the Clergy of the Diocese of Canterbury at His Primary Visitation* (London, 1832) 23. Cf. Dean's Book, 1822–54, p. 149.

years, though he admitted that much was still to be done to make good earlier neglect.[136] On the other hand, there were those who deplored the rebuilding of the north-west tower as having been unnecessary and a serious lapse of architectural taste. The Chapter's consultant architect, Thomas Hopper, had merely recommended certain repairs.[137]

Contrary to the late Victorian caricature, the canons of pre-Reform Canterbury evinced profound concern about the Cathedral fabric, a concern that found eloquent expression in the various Memorials to Commissioners and to Parliament in the 1830s. A major restriction to more satisfactory maintenance of the Cathedral had always been the fact that no funds were explicitly reserved by statute for fabric repair. The canons wished to make good the want of such provision, and by 1836 there was a clamour for a special fabric fund to be set up. Until this time, the cost of Cathedral repairs had been met largely out of the proceeds of the estate woods. When these proved insufficient, the deficit was met out of income normally divisible amongst the Dean and Chapter.[138] The canons now expressed the fear that proposed cathedral reforms would make matters worse, in that alienation of cathedral property by the Ecclesiastical Commission would prevent the fabric from being adequately sustained out of cathedral resources—there would be less 'surplus' to expend on repairs. Parliamentary opponents of the Cathedrals Act of 1840 particularly resented the fact that the final decision on fabric repair would in future no longer rest with the Dean but with the Ecclesiastical Commission.[139]

The initial working of the 1840 Act for a time seemed to bear out these fears. Throughout the 1840s, the Chapter repeatedly pleaded for the creation of a proper fabric fund. For the meantime it was agreed that any monies from the sale of Cathedral land to railway or other companies should be invested and the proceeds used for the purposes of fabric repair. The annual income from this source was to be used for additional, special restoration-work on the fabric, and a 'special treasurer' was appointed to manage the fund.[140] No great sum was raised from this source, and the Dean and Chapter continued to make up the deficit.

In the 1850s application was made to the Ecclesiastical Commissioners for the right to retain the income of another stall, over and above that of the six otherwise left to Canterbury, so that the proceeds might be applied to a fabric fund. The Chapter claimed that only thus could the fabric be adequately maintained. The Commissioners were not responsive. On behalf of the Chapter, Daniel Finch repeatedly asked for financial support.[141] In 1858 he told the Secretary that the cost of restoring the nave roof alone would be £2,000.[142] By midsummer the Commissioners had reluctantly agreed to the Chapter's request to appropriate towards the repair of the fabric one third of the monies received from the sale of timber on estates sold by the Cathedral in enfranchisement under the terms of the Episcopal and Capitular Estates Management Act. The sum appropriated was £6,559 in Consols, and other sums in Chapter hands were added to form a fabric fund. The Dean was to act as 'special treasurer' of the fund.[143] In 1859 the Dean and Chapter

---

[136] London, Church Commissioners' MSS, Canterbury, file no. 1159, pt. 1, Aug. 1840.

[137] Woodruff and Danks, *Memorials*, 360–1.

[138] Cf. above, n. 48.

[139] Knight-Bruce, *Ecclesiastical Duties and Revenues Bill* (cit. in n. 54), 43.

[140] Dean's Book, 1822–54, p. 411.

[141] London, Church Commissioners' MSS, Canterbury, file no. 1159, pt. 1, 'Church Estates Commissioners', 23 Nov. 1854.

[142] Ibid., D. Finch to J. Chalk, 11 Feb. 1854.

[143] Chapter Act Book, 1854–84, p. 74.

spent £1,000, and the Commissioners gave £2,120 for the nave roof.[144]

No sooner was the fund set up than a new difficulty arose. In November that year the Dean and Chapter had agreed to consider the transfer of their lands to the Commissioners. The lengthy discussions about the future expenditure brought on to the scene the Commissioners' architect, Ewan Christian. In November 1861 the Chapter instructed its surveyor, Austin, to proceed with the restoration of the south-west tower 'as arranged by him and Mr. Christian'.[145] Christian soon had overall authority and during the 1860s made detailed reports on the fabric, and estimates of costs. It was in direct response to his gloomy reports on the decay of the fabric and the urgent need not just for repairs but for thorough 'restoration' of the Cathedral, that the Estates Committee in 1861 suggested an immediate expenditure of £30,000 on the fabric, and further expenditure over and above this for a twelve-year period. They suggested the provision of a fabric funding producing £2,000 per annum.[146] The new financial arrangements, after the Order in Council transferring Chapter estates in August 1862, made changes in the fabric fund. A new account was opened and the old one was wound up, though the Dean was still treasurer of the fund.[147] £20,000 was given by the Commissioners for immediate expenditure on approved repairs and improvements.

'Restoration' rather than mere repairs is the most appropriate description of the far-reaching work done on the cathedral fabric in the 1860s and 1870s. The years 1862 to 1866 saw especially dramatic progress. Increasingly, the Chapter looked on passively as Christian himself took major architectural, and not merely structural, decisions. For instance, though the south-west tower was not in any very urgent state of physical decay, Christian had resolved in 1861 to have it restored.[148] Once restoration rather than mere repair became the main object, it was inevitable that questions of architectural taste should come increasingly to the forefront and create divisions in the Chapter. Such disputes first surfaced in 1859, when Gilbert Scott's controversial designs for the 'completion' of the Corona at the east end of the Cathedral provoked heated discussion. These were eventually scrapped, after sharp criticisms of the plans had been aired.[149] However, the most stormy of all such controversies was the debate over the restoration of the choir in the 1870s.

The opportunity for further major restoration-work on the Cathedral in the 1870s was provided by the fire of September 1872, which destroyed the roof of the Trinity Chapel.[150] In 1876 the Dean and Chapter approved a plan drawn up by Sir Gilbert Scott for entirely refitting the choir. Archbishop Tait was made president of a committee to raise the necessary funds. Bitter architectural controversy was unleashed. In 1830 the panelling at the sides of the choir, dating from 1676, had been removed. The proposed restoration involved the removal of stalls and panelling at the west end, (mistakenly) attributed to Grinling Gibbons—who had in fact merely carved the decoration on Archbishop Tenison's throne. The removal was justified on the ground that the woodwork hid the eastern face of the screen, which the 'Gothicists' within the Chapter—assisted by Scott—claimed

[144] Treasurer's Accts., 1858–9.

[145] Chapter Act Book, 1854–84, p. 131.

[146] London, Church Commissioners' MSS, Canterbury, file no. 1159, J. Chalk to D. Finch, 21 Nov. 1861.

[147] Chapter Act Book, 1854–84, p. 139.

[148] Ibid., p. 131.

[149] Ibid., pp. 98, 115.

[150] The *Guardian*, 27 (1872), 1144. Part of the cost was met by a sum of £3,166 3s. 0d. from the Sun Fire Office: Chapter Act Book, 1854–84, p. 301.

(correctly) as the work of Henry of Eastry, dating from 1304–5. Eastry was hailed by this party as 'one of the most accomplished architects of his day', and Dean Payne Smith fervently advocated the restoration of Eastry's screen.[151] The chief opponents of the restoration scheme were William Morris and E. C. Bentinck—'a great champion of Renaissance work'. Bentinck insisted that the Eastry screens were 'merely copies or rather imitations of the originals and were executed as late as the time of Dean Percy'. Bentinck's most telling objection to the scheme patronized by Payne Smith was 'that it involves the sacrifice of original English work of a very high order without the gain of a single artistic advantage'.[152] Payne Smith, along with the majority of the Chapter, was put on the defensive. The Dean rebutted the arguments of his architectural critics by an appeal to capitular independence, asserting that 'we are perfectly well aware that as soon as our plans are published we shall become the objects of attack on the part of all sorts of people, and then, if we do our duty to the best of our abilities, as soon as the works are completed, we shall equally be the objects of laudation. But neither the fear of one, nor the desire of the other, will, or ought to have the slightest influence upon us.'[153] The stalls at the west end were not restored, though other parts of the scheme were carried out.

In retrospect, Scott's work in the 1870s could be said to have been an improvement on that carried out under the aegis of Austin and Christian in the previous decade. There had been many contemporary critics of what was condemned as the 'shoddy restoration' of the Cathedral carried out by the latter. For instance, in 1866, even that organ of ecclesiastical Gothic revivalism, the *Ecclesiologist*, was lamenting 'the entire want of judgment in the restoration of Canterbury Cathedral', especially what was being done to the exterior of the south side and the cloister, and was critical of virtually all the renovation work that had been undertaken since the late 1820s.[154] The Cathedral was condemned as having 'been so long celebrated for such carelessness about its antiquities that we are not at all surprised at what we know to be going on now'. The reviewer proceeded to state that after 'the destruction of the great north-west Tower for the sake of uniformity, no amount of mere destruction can be a matter of astonishment. As the so-called restoration progresses, so surely does the almost entire destruction of the original surface, both inside and out; with this difference, that on the exterior the face is rebuilt, entirely replaced, in the interior the facing is only scraped and cleaned, but in such a way as to erase the original tool marks.' One of the most catastrophic capitular decisions was the siting, in 1860, of a gas-works beside the west front of the Cathedral. This hastened the corrosive effects of the atmosphere on the portions of the fabric restored in Caen stone by Austin, so that by the 1880s further repair was required.[155]

The late 1870s witnessed the temporary close of the major phase of Victorian restoration of the Cathedral fabric. The visitation returns for the Cathedral in 1889 and 1893 both declared that the fabric was indeed in a sound state and in good repair, but that the appurtenances, especially the chapter house and cloisters, needed a complete restoration.

---

[151] LPL, Tait Papers, vol. 216, fos. 113–14, Dean Payne Smith to Archbishop Tait, 6 Mar. 1876.

[152] Ibid., fo. 119, E. C. Bentinck to Archbishop Tait, 4 May 1876; cf. ibid., fos. 111–12, Bentinck to Tait, 28 Feb. 1876.

[153] Ibid., fo. 114, Dean Payne Smith to Archbishop Tait, 6 Mar.

1876.

[154] 'Canterbury and Gloucester', *Ecclesiologist*, 27 (1866), 185–6.

[155] Chapter Act Book, 1854–84, p. 116.

In 1893 Edward Parry, Archdeacon of Canterbury and Bishop of Dover, declared that 'the decay of the fabric is gaining upon our means to maintain it'.[156] The generosity of individual canons alone saved the fabric fund from feeling the effects of the drastic fall in capitular income caused by the agricultural depression. Nevertheless, this fund remained too small and precarious. Only the emergence of new sources of income for fabric repair in the 1890s staved off what would otherwise have become a crisis.

Private benefaction was one possible lifeline for the Cathedral, and Canterbury was fortunate in being the recipient of a legacy of £1,000 from Dr J. G. Beaney. This was spent on the very necessary restoration of the crypt, under the direction of the architect Sir Arthur Blomfield, in 1893–6.[157]

None the less, far more than this was required if the Cathedral was to embark on the major programmes of restoration that was now needed. In the final report of the Cathedral Establishments Commission in 1885 it was stated that cathedral chapters could not afford to maintain their fabric out of their own resources.[158] In the case of Canterbury, this was only too true. Clearly, it was in the Cathedral's interest to put into practice some of the alternatives that came to be openly discussed in this period. One idea, in stark contrast to what might have been proposed in the 1830s, was that the repair of cathedral fabric, 'being essentially a local work', would be better placed in the hands of a 'Cathedrals Committee of the Town or County Councils'.[159] Nothing came of this proposal, but one of the new schemes that was adopted was that of allocating to the fabric fund the fees charged for showing visitors round the cathedral. But after the guides had been paid, this did not leave enough to make a significant supplement to the fund.[160] Still further measures were required.

The Dean and Chapter agreed to make an appeal to the nation for funds towards fabric restoration. As early as 1877, in connection with the work in the choir, the Chapter had made such an appeal and set up a special restoration fund.[161] In 1895 it was agreed to launch an appeal in the next year, to be called the Centenary Fund, as part of the advance preparations for the commemoration, in 1897, of the thirteen hundredth anniversary of the coming of St Augustine.[162] By May 1896 £9,100 had been subscribed, and allocations were made towards completing work on the crypt and to repairs to the cloister roofs and chapter-house windows.[163] Even the Ecclesiastical Commissioners made a contribution, 'having regard to the extent and value of the property of the Commissioners within the County of Kent'.[164] In spite of all this, there was not sufficient money for all the schemes of the Dean and Chapter. Dean Farrar lamented to Gladstone in 1897, 'we make no complaint of the fact that our own incomes have sunk to half their value; but it is sad that we are simply unable to do for the glorious cathedral . . . half that we so earnestly desire'.[165]

[156] LPL, Canterbury Visitation Returns, 1889, MS VG 3/8c, fo. 20; ibid. 1893, MS VG 3/9c, fos. 348, 346.

[157] Chapter Act Book, 1884–95, pp. 170–1.

[158] *Cathedral Establishments Commission, Final Report* (London, 1885), 7.

[159] H. W. Massingham, 'The Nationalisation of Cathedrals', *Contemporary Review*, 60 (July–Dec. 1891), 362–71, at 369.

[160] Woodruff and Danks, *Memorials*, 370.

[161] *Guardian*, 32 (2 May 1877), 616.

[162] London, Church Commissioners' MSS, Canterbury, file no. 1159, pt. 3, A. W. Blomfield to the Secretary, 22 Dec. 1896.

[163] Chapter Act Book, 1895–1910, p. 42.

[164] London, Church Commissioners' MSS, file no. 1159, pt. 3, 'Cathedral Arrangements' (Minutes of Ecclesiastical Commissioners' Meeting, 18 Apr. 1896).

[165] BL, Gladstone Corres., Add. MS 44525, fo. 135, Dean Farrar to W. E. Gladstone, 20 Mar. [1897].

None the less, as a result of Dean Farrar's exertions, £20,000 was raised by voluntary subscriptions. This enabled Sir Arthur Blomfield to carry out the restoration of the chapter house and the cloisters, and for new Renaissance-style altar-rails to be erected between the presbytery and sacrarium.[166] At the time of the 1902 visitation, while yet lamenting that 'our means are very limited—not sufficient for emergencies', Dean Farrar could point to the great progress that had been made. The fabric was once more in a good state of repair.[167] In a move symptomatic of the growing sense of unity between Cathedral and diocese, the Honorary Canons in 1902 were to suggest perhaps the most far-reaching new expedient of all, a proposal to collect offertories for the Cathedral fabric fund in the parish churches throughout the diocese of Canterbury.[168]

THE EXTERNAL RELATIONS OF CANTERBURY CATHEDRAL

The Cathedral in Relation to the City and the Diocese: Ideal and Reality

The aim of restoring cathedral chapters to their supposed original function as the council of the bishop was one of the central and recurrent notions of the cathedral reformers from the 1830s onwards, as exemplified in numerous pamphlets.[169] At Canterbury in 1837 Frederick Glover advocated the idea that prebendal colleges be set up to assist the diocesan.[170] It is true that some of the more 'high and dry' opponents of cathedral reform in the 1830s, such as W. L. Bowles, appeared to resent the threat of episcopal control as much as that of State interference in the rights and privileges of chapters.[171] However, the increasingly influential body of conservative reformers, always more concerned with restoring the spiritual uses of cathedrals than with the mere defence of temporalities, came to believe that it was the growing divorce of bishops from their chapters that had rendered cathedrals so vulnerable to State interference in the 1830s. For it was argued that if chapters had not grown so distant from their bishops over the previous 150 years, the bishops in the 1830s might not so readily have conceded the likely destruction of capitular rights in the setting-up of the Ecclesiastical Commission.[172]

At the time, it seemed possible that the Cathedrals Act of 1840 might bring about a new era in the external and diocesan relations of cathedrals. The creation of non-residentiary (honorary) canonries had as its avowed object the establishment of closer connections between leading parochial clergy and their cathedral. Yet, contrary to the reformers' intention, the 1840 Act seemed to widen the divorce between bishop and chapter.[173]

---

[166] LPL, Canterbury Visitation Returns, 1898, MS VG 3/10c, fos. 219, 224.

[167] Ibid. 1902, MS VG 3/11c, fo. 115. Cf. fo. 132.

[168] LPL, Frederick Temple Papers, vol. 56, fo. 342.

[169] For an early advocacy of the idea, see [Edward Berens], *Remarks of Lord Henley and Dr. Burton on Church Reform* (London, 1833), 11. Cf. C. A. Moysey, *Suggestions Arising out of the Proposed Alterations in the Cathedral Establishments . . .* (London, 1838), 4.

[170] F. A. Glover, *Reduction of Prebendaries: Being Portion of a Series of Papers Entitled, What Will "the Church" Say to the Sugges-*

tions of the Ecclesiastical Commission? . . . Which Appeared in the 'Kentish Observer' (London, 1837), 4.

[171] W. L. Bowles, *Further Observations on the Last Report of the Church Commissioners, Particularly as Respects the Patronage of Deans and Chapters, and Cathedral Music* (Devizes, [1837]), 3–7.

[172] Selwyn, *Are Cathedral Institutions Useless?* (cit. in n. 3), 13. Cf. Newton Smart, *The Ecclesiastical Commission Considered* (London, 1839), 40–1.

[173] H. Alford, 'The Church of the Future', *Contemporary Review*, 9 (Sept.–Dec. 1868), 161–78, at 175–6.

Manning actually complained that the suppression of residentiary stalls broke 'the bonds of the cathedral and the diocese'.[174] It was the recognized weaknesses of the 1840 legislation in this sphere that prompted the wave of cathedral proposals in the late 1860s and 1870s which showed a renewed emphasis on the need for cathedrals to forge closer links with their dioceses. It was suggested that cathedral statutes should, if necessary, be revised in order to facilitate this. By about 1880, it was being argued that it was only if cathedrals became more strictly diocesan that they could survive.[175] The main *raison d'être* of the cathedrals increasingly seemed to be as 'the Mother Church of the city' and 'the Parish Church of the diocese' to which they belonged, and as 'centres of spiritual energy and life'.[176] It was claimed that bishops no longer 'felt comfortable' in their cathedrals,[177] and that the deans' authority needed to be limited. Indeed, it was pointed out that for a chapter really to become a diocesan chapter, the bishop needed to become, in effect, the dean,[178] a suggestion already deplored by the Canterbury Chapter in 1854 but supported by Alford in 1868. Paradoxically, a great obstacle to the cultivation of capitular links with the diocese was the fact that most canons held benefices, where they usually resided. As was said in 1869, a canon 'cannot throw himself into the business and interests of the place; his residence is but a holiday, it is too short for business and also too sweet'.[179]

In the early nineteenth century, the Canterbury Chapter's links with the city and diocese were distinctly limited. Any sense of mutual sympathy and friendly feeling was lacking. Political antipathy was the most potent cause of antagonism in the 1820s and early 1830s. At the time of Archbishop Howley's first visitation, in 1832, the city mobs, augmented by intoxicated 'Reformers', displayed their displeasure in no uncertain terms.[180] In spite of the fact that from the mid-1830s this civic and popular Radicalism and anti-clericalism began to wane, popular feeling in the city against the Cathedral merely took on a new form. By the 1840s the Radical, anti-Tory political basis of ill-feeling had been superseded by a popular, Protestant, religious basis of antipathy. Although the Oxford Movement in its earlier phase did not make a great impact on cathedral life, none the less the Cathedral fell victim to the popular, anti-Puseyite phobia of the time. Local newspapers kept stressing that Canterbury as a city was 'essentially Protestant', 'despite the Puseyitish predilections of certain mistaken men in authority'[181]—a clear jibe at Cathedral dignitaries like Benjamin Harrison and the old High Churchmen Deans Bagot and Lyall and Dr Spry. Moreover, economic grievances also played their part in inflaming civic resentment against the Cathedral. Tension between Cathedral and city was manifested in the frequent clashes of the Dean and Chapter with the city authorities over supposed encroachments, on to

[174] Manning, *Preservation of Unendowed Canonries* (cit. in n. 3), p. 17.

[175] *Official Report of the Church Congress ... 1880*, ed. D. J. Vaughan (London, 1881), 361. Cf. Humble, 'Cathedrals and Chapters' (cit. in n. 7), 166–93.

[176] C. J. Ellicott, *Our Cathedral Institutions: Will They Stand? A Sermon Preached at the Re-opening of the Choir of Gloucester Cathedral, August 20, 1871* (Gloucester, [1871]), 12–13.

[177] Humble, 'Cathedrals and Chapters' (cit. in n. 7), 171.

[178] Edward Stuart, *Do Away with Deans: Cathedral Reform* (London, 1869), 3–4. Cf. *A Plan of Church Extension and Reform*

Submitted to the Rt. Hon. Lord John Russell. By a Deputation, in March 1848, With Remarks by J. C. Colquhoun Esq. (London, 1848), p. ix; W. R. W. Stephens, *Cathedral Chapters Considered as Episcopal Councils, in a Letter to the ... Bishop of Chichester* (London, etc., 1877) 5–15; Dean and Chapter, *Cathedral Commission* (1872) (cit. in n. 92), 23.

[179] [E. J. Smith?], 'Church Progress', *Quarterly Review*, 124 (Jan.–Apr. 1868), 251.

[180] Dean's Book, 1822–54, pp. 127–8; G. S[mith], *Chronological History* (cit. in n. 84), 345–7.

[181] *Kentish Gazette*, no. 7397 (15 Apr. 1845), 2.

property belonging to the Dean and Chapter within the City Ditch, as for instance in 1840 and 1843.[182]

In the 1850s relentless external pressure, political and social, began to break down the Cathedral's resistance to closer ties with city and neighbourhood. Dean Lyall's death, in 1857, marked a turning-point. Dean Alford's popular services soon endeared him to the people of the city, who 'responded with great congregations'. In the *Memorials* of Canterbury Cathedral, Canon William Danks concluded that around 1860 there 'began that improved relationship between cathedral and city which since those days has, we believe, become cordial'.[183] At the basic level of allowing the Cathedral to be more accessible to the city, improvements soon occurred under Alford's regime. Official guides were appointed to take people round the Cathedral. The popularity of such guided tours was soon apparent, even though complaints were sometimes made about the garrulousness or incompetence of individual guides.[184] In 1870 the Dean and Chapter felt called upon to enforce the rule that no more than thirty persons be shown round the Cathedral at any one time.[185] In 1879 free days for visiting the Cathedral were fixed for Whit Sunday, Whit Monday, and the last Thursday in every month.[186] However, it remained the custom, even in the 1890s, not to show strangers round the Cathedral on Sundays.[187]

From the 1850s numerous pamphlets and periodicals set forth the ideal of the cathedral as a social and moral rejuvenator. In their evidence of 1854 to the Cathedral and Collegiate Churches Commission, the Canterbury Dean and Chapter expressed their hearty concurrence with the Commission's conclusion that 'one of the chief objects, in any measure of improvement, should be the effective spiritual care of the Cathedral cities'.[188] To provide hospitality, especially to the city poor, had always been regarded as an important capitular duty. In mid-Victorian England this idea gained new potency and was revived and developed. Cathedrals could perform a unique role in meeting social difficulties in this sphere. As A. C. Tait wrote, 'the common hospitalities of a cathedral close, might do much to raise the tone of society in the cathedral town and neighbourhood, and to keep alive good feeling among men of different social positions'.[189] However, the reality did not always live up to the exalted ideal of Victorian cathedral reformers. Canterbury was to be no exception to this pattern.

In the early part of our period, High Church advocates of cathedral reform and radical and Dissenting critics of cathedrals alike might assert that cathedrals exerted little or no beneficial impact on the life of the city in which they were situated. Moreover, even in 1861 a radical critic of the whole cathedral system went so far as to complain that nowhere were irreligion and immorality so rampant as in cathedral towns.[190] The writer also complained that the expenditure of all English cathedrals on benevolent purposes in 1860 amounted only to £14,865 out of their total income of £312,000.[191] Certainly, the Cathedral

[182] Chapter Act Book, 1824–54, pp. 288, 341.

[183] Woodruff and Danks, *Memorials*, 366.

[184] *Guardian*, 30 (18 Aug. 1875), 1057. Cf. Chapter Act Book, 1884–95, p. 152.

[185] Chapter Act Book, 1854–84, p. 269.

[186] Ibid. 422.

[187] Ibid., 1884–95, p. 276.

[188] Dean and Chapter, *Cathedral Commission* (1872) (cit. in n. 92), 6.

[189] [A. C. Tait], 'Cathedral Reform', *Edinburgh Review*, 97 (Jan.–Apr. 1853), 161–2.

[190] Anon., *Cathedral Wealth and Cathedral Work* (cit. in n. 57), 23–4.

[191] Ibid. 20, 29–30.

could be said to have been no more successful in tackling the problems of city poverty and material want than it was in rooting out moral abuses.

The criticisms of material stagnation and moral decay were patent exaggerations. Such criticisms were more likely to have been true of Canterbury in 1828 than in 1861. Certainly from 1857, Deans Alford, Payne Smith, and Farrar had the highest ideals of the Cathedral as an active agent of both moral and spiritual rejuvenation and social harmonization in both city and diocese. The respect that Dean Alford inspired in the people of Canterbury was shown by the degree of public mourning on his death, in 1871. His successors were held in equal popular esteem. Payne Smith was particularly active in various local reform-movements, including Temperance, and thus made close contacts with local Non-conformist leaders.[192] And no one held a more exalted vision of Canterbury Cathedral as a civilizing social and moral influence on the surrounding city than did Dean Farrar in the 1890s.[193] It was also a sign of changing times that Archbishop Benson should become actively involved in the life of the city of Canterbury, whereas his predecessors had always remained remote. For instance, it was Benson who personally supported a plan for a public recreation-ground in the city, near the Cathedral.[194]

None the less, for all the real advances towards mutual understanding made in the latter part of the century, the fact remains that for most of the time the gulf between citizens of Canterbury and the Cathedral dignitaries continued to exist. Henry Alford himself confessed that in spite of all his efforts to break down the barriers, his own experience as Dean in the 1860s confirmed this. It was his perception that the people of Canterbury identified far more with the 'needy clergy' of the poor city cures than with the apparently wealthier dignitaries of the Cathedral. He expressed his regret that the 1840 Act and the general policy of the Commissioners had not better provided for the many poor parishes in cathedral cities. For instance, money from Cathedral revenues should have been assigned to Canterbury parishes, instead of augmenting unknown distant benefices.[195] Such a policy would have encouraged the people of the city to identify themselves with the Cathedral's interests, instead of seeking to undermine them. Something of the old anti-Cathedral bias of the city authorities of the early 1830s occasionally resurfaced later in the period. For instance, in 1873 a clear anti-clerical bias was displayed by the city corporation and the mayor, in their support of demands for State Board Schools as a means of diminishing the Cathedral's influence in the city.[196] Nevertheless, the factor that perhaps most inhibited fuller integration of Cathedral and city was not so much municipal or popular anti-clericalism as the jealous attitude of the city clergy towards the Dean and Chapter.[197]

The most obvious stake of the Cathedral in the religious life of the city had always been through its patronage of benefices within the city boundaries.[198] Yet despite this, the Cathedral had little hold on the city clergy. The ideal that was aimed at, during the latter decades of the century, was for the Cathedral to become the centre of religious work in

[192] *In Loving Memory of Robert Payne-Smith, S. T. P., Dean of Canterbury . . .* (n. p., n. d.), 19.

[193] Reginald Farrar, *The Life of Frederic William Farrar* (London, 1904), 316.

[194] LPL, Benson Papers, vol. 33, fo. 256.

[195] Alford, 'The Church of the Future' (cit. in n. 173), 177.

[196] *Kentish Gazette*, 186 (6 Dec. 1870), 3.

[197] LPL, Canterbury Visitation Returns, 1889, MS VG 3/8c, fos. 420–1, T. Field to Archbishop Benson, 7 Oct. 1889.

[198] For a list of the benefices in the patronage of the Dean and Chapter in 1832, see Dean's Book, 1822–54, p. 151.

the city. On the other hand, some thought that the rejuvenated life of the Cathedral after the 1850s actually hindered the work of the city parishes, and that things were better when the Chapter was inert and lethargic and left well alone. As the Honorary Canon G. J. Blore, Headmaster of the King's School, wrote to Archbishop Benson in 1890, the city clergy rarely attended services at the Cathedral, 'and so they get to ignore it, except as far as they think that its presence rather tends to interfere with the working of the parishes, and to regard the chapter as a body of clergy whose interests were different from theirs, whose higher status tends relatively to depress their own: so in the minds of some of them a sore feeling exists; and this was rather intensified at the time of the introduction of the Sunday Evening service to the Cathedral'.[199] To overcome such jealousy and division of feeling, Blore recommended that the Chapter should 'call the clergy into council with regard to the spiritual welfare of the city, thus showing that they have common interests with them'. Blore wanted the city parochial clergy to have 'more frequent opportunities of preaching in the cathedral', thus drawing them 'more closely to it', and making them 'feel the privilege of having it within reach'.

Thus the Cathedral's relationship to the city had for long been cold, if not frosty, though it gradually improved. Its relationship with the diocese differed in the later nineteenth century, as expectations changed. For centuries the Cathedral had had many links with individuals in the diocese, through estates, patronage, and family ties. For the new theorists, these informal links were not sufficient. The cathedral had to be seen as the Mother Church in each diocese, and the chapter ought to be the bishop's council. It was all very well to argue that the Canterbury Chapter should act as the archbishop's diocesan council, but, as Archdeacon Smith candidly observed in 1889, the fact was that residentiary canons when appointed were 'drawn from various dioceses, with no necessary local knowledge, in many cases retired from parochial work, often of advanced age, and so with an experience likely to be out of date'.[200] In any case, with the absence from Canterbury of the archbishop, there was little sense in which the Chapter could regard itself as his council. The archbishops normally resided at Lambeth and had for their country seat Addington Park, bought by Manners Sutton in 1808, in succession to the palace at Croydon.[201] The Honorary Canon R. C. Jenkins wrote in 1893 complaining that 'the purchase of Addington established a principle of non-residence. If the Common Council of London were located at York, the common action of it with the Lord Mayor would not be very easy.' At a time when 'diocesan consciousness' was becoming the fashionable idea among cathedral reformers, at Canterbury purely geographical factors were against the development of such an outlook, at least until the 1880s. As Jenkins remarked in 1889, in response to a visitation enquiry on the subject, 'Canterbury from the tide of the population foresaking it will soon become another Ely and the paralysis of the Diocese will be complete . . . this great evil began when the residence of the Archbishop was removed from the Diocese.'[202] Similarly, the Honorary Canon F. E. Carter in his submission at the 1898 visitation said

[199] LPL, Canterbury Visitation Returns, 1889, MS VG 3/8c, fos. 391–3, G. J. Blore to Archbishop Benson, 15 Jan. 1890.
[200] Ibid., fo. 385.
[201] *Memoirs of Archbishop Temple*, ed. E. G. Sandford (2 vols.; London, 1906), ii. 211.
[202] LPL, Canterbury Visitation Returns, 1889, MS VG 3/8c, fo. 401, R. C. Jenkins to Archbishop Benson, 28 Sept. 1889.

that for all the progress that was being made, the location of Canterbury in the extreme east of the diocese would always 'tend to diminish its due dignity as the hearth of Diocesan life'.[203] It was inevitable that canons of Canterbury would have little knowledge of parishes in the western portion of the diocese, which was 'in respect of population and industry, the most important part'.[204]

In spite of all this, the Chapter themselves had argued in 1854 that one of the canons should assist with the Diocesan Board of Education and that others should devote themselves to diocesan branches of societies, such as the Clergy Orphan Society.[205] Two canons were in any case archdeacons and were active throughout the diocese. There was knowledge of diocesan affairs within the Precincts. In 1872 a suffragan for the diocese was appointed with the title of Bishop of Dover. The first holder of the office was the then Archdeacon of Canterbury, Edward Parry. He was keen that one or two canons might be appointed by Crown or archbishop, 'for some special Diocesan work, e.g., superintendence of Religion, inspection of schools, Foreign and Home Missions, Church History lectures, or lectures in Theology. But they should have no parish or office outside the Diocese.'[206] This certainly represented a markedly different conception of what canonical duties should entail. As another canon of Canterbury had said in 1893, the old idea, so eloquently restated by Pusey in 1832, of a canonry as a 'quiet resting place where a professor . . . knows nothing of Diocesan work'[207] was being overturned by the revolutionary notion of utilizing the persons as well as the revenues of a chapter for diocesan purposes. That the new ideal became something of a reality at Canterbury towards the end of the century is clear from the Honorary Canon M. A. Nisbett's evidence at the 1893 visitation. Nisbett pointed out that of the six residentiary canons, three were actively engaged in diocesan work, and another was a member of the council of the Church Reading Society. Of the Honorary Canons, two were bishops, seven were rural deans, and seven were members of boards and councils or committees of diocesan societies. Nisbett listed the main departments of diocesan work that were appropriate to be undertaken by the Chapter at this date: the promotion of temperance, purity, and the spiritual life; church building and endowment; mission work, mainly parochial; spiritual and social agencies such as organizing hop-picking missions; and what was called 'Church Defence'. It was hoped that in future each canon would become involved in at least one of these spheres of activity.[208] Moreover, the presence of Chapter representatives at the annual meeting of archdeacons and rural deans in the 1890s helped promote diocesan links.[209] By 1898, Dean Farrar could report that the Chapter was 'in close connexion with Diocesan work'. There were 'constant meetings for every sort of good object . . . held in the Chapter House or Library. Services for various Guilds, etc., are held in St. Anselm's & the Holy Innocents' chapels. Very real progress has been made.'[210]

From the time of the appointment of the first Honorary Canons in 1863, there was a

[203] LPL, Canterbury Visitation Returns, 1898, MS VG 3/10c, fos. 253–4.

[204] Ibid. 1889, MS VG 3/8c, fo. 399.

[205] Dean and Chapter, *Cathedral Commission* (1872) (cit. in n. 92), 16.

[206] LPL, Canterbury Visitation Returns, 1889, MS VG 3/8c, fo. 375.

[207] Ibid. 1893, MS VG 3/9c, fo. 366.

[208] Ibid., fo. 384.

[209] Ibid. 1889, MS VG 3/8c, fo. 397.

[210] Ibid. 1898, MS VG 3/10c, fo. 220.

IV Josephus dictating to Samuel, shown as a monastic scribe. Initial from Josephus, *Jewish Antiquities*, written and illustrated at Christ Church, *c*.1130. (Cambridge, St John's College, MS 8, fo. 103ᵛ.)

V Initial showing animals with instruments like those on capitals in Anselm's Crypt. From a leaf of a Christ Church passional, *c*.1120, preserved by having been used as a book-wrapper. (Canterbury, Cathedral Library, Lit. MS E.42, fo. 36ᵛ.)

VI Oil on canvas. Inscribed on pavement: 'Thos. Johnson fecit. Canterbury Quire as in 1657. Ye prospecte from ye Clock House'. (Private collection.)

further problem which caused bitterness. There was no provision in the statutes of New Foundation cathedrals for a meeting of non-residentiary canons with the residentiaries, such as the meetings held from time to time in Old Foundation cathedrals. No non-residentiary canons had ever been intended in New Foundations. The Honorary Canons had no part in the capitular framework. A new gathering to include them was required. In fact, some of the Honorary Canons rarely came to Canterbury. The expense of the journey was sufficient to deter some of them from preaching when asked.[211] Various expedients began to be adopted in an endeavour to improve matters. Hostels in or near the Precincts were established to enable them to stay several consecutive days in Canterbury. A new Church House, on the model of one at Salisbury, was proposed; this was designed to be a meeting-place in the city for visiting clergy and laity.[212] Archbishop Benson even provided out of his own pocket an honorarium to cover the travelling-expenses of Honorary Canons when taking their preaching turn in the Cathedral.[213] None the less, only the creation of something like a 'Greater Chapter' would be sufficient to make all the Cathedral clergy feel that they had a stake in its future.

By the time of the 1889 visitation of the Cathedral, the idea of a 'Greater Chapter' at Canterbury was being strenuously promulgated. Both Bishop Parry and Canon Rawlinson felt that such a body could act as a useful diocesan council to the archbishop. It was proposed that this 'Greater Chapter' should meet once or twice a year, and certainly in the year prior to a Cathedral visitation. It was to assemble either by being summoned to the archbishop's residence at Lambeth or Addington, or, preferably, by meeting in the Cathedral library.[214] However, the Cathedral statutes made it difficult in practice to incorporate any of the non-residentiary clergy of the Cathedral into the capitular body. Canterbury's proposed new statutes, drawn up in 1885, both allowed for the appointment of a 'missionary canon' and also made provision for a 'Greater Chapter' that would have been truly diocesan in outlook;[215] however, these statutes were never enacted.[216] None the less, Archbishop Benson took the initiative and arranged for what was called, and indeed in effect was, a Greater Chapter to meet for the first time for devotional purposes in 1890.[217] In July 1892, the same body met to discuss specifically diocesan affairs.[218] By 1893, an annual conference of the archbishop with this 'Greater Chapter' had become an established feature of Cathedral life. Until the death of Benson, in 1896, these annual meetings continued to be held in Canterbury,[219] and his successor, Temple, was persuaded to continue the practice. Such was the progress made towards breaking down outstanding barriers between different members of the Cathedral body that in 1902 it was even proposed that Honorary Canons be assigned Cathedral stalls.[220]

Changing relations with the archbishop ushered in a new era in dealings between Cathedral and diocese. Other than at visitations, Archbishop Howley and, to a lesser

[211] Ibid. 1889, MS VG 3/8c, fo. 379.
[212] Ibid. 1898, MS VG 3/10c, fo. 237 and cf. fo. 252.
[213] A. C. Benson, *The Life of Edward White Benson, Sometime Archbishop of Canterbury* (2 vols.; London, 1899), ii. 393.
[214] LPL, Canterbury Visitation Returns, 1889, MS VG 3/8c, fo. 375, and cf. fos. 377, 385.
[215] LPL, Benson Papers, vol. 21, fos. 10–14.

[216] Ibid., vol. 83, fos. 75–8. Cf. LPL, Canterbury Visitation Returns, 1893, MS VG 3/9c, fo. 386.
[217] Ibid., fo. 347.
[218] Ibid., fo. 343.
[219] Ibid., 1898, MS VG 3/10c, fo. 233.
[220] LPL, F. Temple Papers, vol. 56, fo. 342.

extent, Archbishop Sumner, had had only severely limited contact with their Cathedral. Dividing their time between Lambeth and Addington, the Archbishops of Canterbury were rare visitors to their cathedral church. Since the early eighteenth century, archbishops had been enthroned only by proxy in the metropolitical church. Sumner's enthronement in the Cathedral in 1848 was the first personal enthronement of an archbishop at Canterbury for 133 years.[221] However, it was Tait's archiepiscopate that witnessed the most marked growth in the personal involvement of archbishops with their Cathedral. After his enthronement, in February 1869, Tait carried out a detailed personal inspection of the Precincts and expressed concern for all aspects of Cathedral life. When it came to Benson's enthronement, in 1883, the Warden of St Augustine's, G. F. Maclear, wrote to the Archbishop urging him to follow Tait's example.[222] Benson duly did.

The cardinal tenet of most cathedral reformers of the 1870s and 1880s was that the diocesan bishop must 'come home' to his cathedral close, and that no cathedral could be a true diocesan centre of religious activity so long as its bishop made a centre elsewhere. As long as the Archbishop had no residence in Canterbury, the Cathedral Chapter appeared to many like 'a body without a head', and the nexus between Chapter and archbishop a merely theoretical one.[223] Archbishop Temple's decision in 1897 to reside for part of the year in a Canterbury residence was a turning-point. Various possibilities were discussed early in 1898, including the purchase from the Dean and Chapter of Canon Rawlinson's house, Meister Omers, or the building of a house at Harbledown. In April Temple stayed at a house within the Old Palace site and decided himself that he would prefer an enlargement of the remaining wing of the medieval palace for his residence. He made suggestions to the architect on the necessary extensions to the building. Work was begun in 1899, and finished in 1901.[224] Now that the archbishop had a house of his own in Canterbury once more, Canterbury was at the heart of the diocese.

None the less, there were critics of the policy of turning cathedral chapters into what J. B. Mozley said would become 'mere representatives of Diocesan Boards and Committees'.[225] Even Dean Alford, one of the keenest advocates of that policy, complained that cathedrals had fallen between what were really two incompatible ideals—the cathedral as diocesan centre and as a place affording posts of dignified repose. The *esprit de corps* of any cathedral was, as Dean Alford admitted, inevitably 'ordinarily one of isolation from the diocese, and from common clerical work'.[226] There was a real fear in some quarters that an overemphasis on the diocesan aspect of cathedral work would undermine its more traditional, original ideal as providing a secure and quiet haven of theological learning and scholarship.

---

[221] Woodruff and Danks, *Memorials*, 363.

[222] LPL, Benson Papers, vol. 3, fo. 210, G. F. Maclear to Archbishop Benson, 19 Feb. 1883.

[223] LPL, Canterbury Visitation Returns, 1889, MS VG 3/8c, fo. 401; cf. ibid. 1893, MS VG 3/9c, fo. 378; R. C. Jenkins, *The True 'Missing Link' in the Project for Cathedral Reform: A Letter Addressed to the Rt. Hon. Alexander J. B. Beresford-Hope M.P.* (Folkestone, 1882), 3. Similarly, Dean Alford had complained in 1870 that Canterbury was 'more cut off from episcopal ministrations and presence than any other diocese in the realm'. H. Alford, *The Compacted Body: A Sermon Preached in the Chapel*

of Lambeth Palace, at the Consecration of the Ven. . . . Edward Parry, D.D., Archdeacon of Canterbury, to be Suffragan Bishop of the See of Dover, on the Festival of the Annunciation, March 25, 1870 (London, 1870), 12.

[224] *Memoirs of Archbishop Temple* (cit. in n. 201), ii. 212–13; Chapter Act Book, 1895–1910, pp. 109–24.

[225] Quoted in John Hannah, *The Pulpit, the Cathedral, and the School: An Address Delivered at His Seventh Visitation, May 5th, 7th and 8th, 1885, in the Parish Churches of Brighton; St Clement's, Hastings; and St Michael's, Lewes* (Brighton, 1885), 20.

[226] Alford, 'The Church of the Future' (cit. in n. 173), 175.

For instance, Precentor Helmore and two other minor canons of Canterbury were arguing in 1889 that the holding of professorships or lectureships at the universities, by the canons, was of 'no advantage to the cathedral or the diocese'.[227] On the other hand, Mozley felt that this new diocesan role for cathedrals by the latter part of the century was 'disconnecting them from the great stream of theological and philosophical thought in the church'.[228]

The Cathedral as a Centre of Theological Learning: Ideal and Reality

A key function and use of cathedrals argued for by numerous cathedral defenders in the 1830s was as centres of theological learning within the Church.[229] Typically, they portrayed cathedrals as 'proper centres of that knowledge which is not only to guard the Church against her enemies, but to serve as a check to the ignorance, or fondness for novelty, or self-conceit, to which active parochial clergymen are at the present day peculiarly exposed, from their very zeal in the discharge of their duties'.[230]

Cathedrals were a 'check upon innovation', and a 'safeguard of the orthodoxy of the clergy'.[231] The Tractarians, and especially Pusey, espoused a romanticized ideal of unworldly, recluse-like canons immersing themselves in sacred study in the sanctuary of a cathedral close.[232] Cathedral defenders of this type resented the way in which many reformers, such as Bishop Blomfield, assumed that the notion of cathedrals as sources of advancement of theological learning was modern and not countenanced in ancient cathedral statutes.[233]

One product of these trends was the idea that was mooted about 1832 of setting up special theological schools for the training of the clergy in some cathedral towns.[234] The universities of Oxford and Cambridge had for long had a monopoly of this role, but the liberal and secularizing campaign for university reform during the 1830s and 1840s seemed to place more of an onus than ever before on cathedrals as active centres of theological learning. Such conservative reformers as (Sir) Thomas Acland, J. R. Hope, and Gladstone argued in the parliamentary debates on the Ecclesiastical Duties and Revenues Bill of 1840 that cathedrals ought to develop facilities and resources for clerical theological training.[235] It was no longer sufficient that learning was cultivated among the men who had been preferred to canonries. A wider, more practical application of cathedral traditions of learning was needed if the Church's reputation as a learned body was to survive intact. In short, chapters were urged to provide theological teaching for ordinands, and at both Chichester (1839) and Wells (1840) theological colleges were founded in the shadow of the

[227] LPL, Canterbury Visitation Returns, 1889, MS VG 3/8c, fo. 411.
[228] Hannah, *The Pulpit* (cit. in n. 225), 20.
[229] Best, *Temporal Pillars* (cit. in n. 1), 332.
[230] [Sewell], 'Cathedral Establishments' (cit. in n. 82), 222.
[231] Newton Smart, *The Ecclesiastical Commission Considered* (London, 1839), 56.
[232] A characteristic Tractarian viewpoint was that cathedrals were 'ever designed to be, the lights of the Church, the focal points in which all pure knowledge should kindle and radiate'. 'The Cathedral Act' (cit. in n. 83), 145.
[233] *Ecclesiastical Commission: A Letter to the Bishop of Exeter, with*

Considerations on the Letter of the Bishop of Lincoln, and the Charges of the Bishops of London, and Gloucester & Bristol. By a Dignitary of the Church (London, 1839), 49.
[234] For instance, see [Berens], *Remarks on Henley and Burton* (cit. in n. 169), 13.
[235] *Speech of W. E. Gladstone Esq., M.P., in the House of Commons, July 29, 1840* (London, 1840), 24. Cf. *Ecclesiastical Duties and Revenues: Speech of T. D. Acland, Esq., M.P., in the House of Commons, Monday, June 29. 1840* (London, 1840), 16–17; J. R. Hope, *Ecclesiastical Duties & Revenues Bill: Substance of a Speech Delivered in the House of Lords, On Behalf of the Deans & Chapters Petitioning Against the Bill* (London, 1840), 64.

cathedrals. Even where this was not appropriate, it was maintained that canons could assist the Dean in the instruction of ordination candidates. Of course, cathedrals could not be expected to fulfil the role of a university. Rather, it was argued that as centres of learning, cathedrals should 'stand, as it were, between the Universities, which represent the highest thought of the country, and the parochial clergy, who represent the most complete devotion of personal service'.[236] Although this aspect of cathedral work seemed to be undervalued in the reforms of the 1830s and 1840s, it received increasing prominence from the Cathedral and Collegiate Churches Commission of 1852. That Commission suggested the assignation of one canon to every cathedral for theological study and teaching, without pastoral responsibility.[237] It seemed that the ideals espoused by Pusey in 1832 were now becoming accepted as a blueprint for reform.[238] However, for a long time the Commission's proposals were not acted upon. As late as 1869 it was a matter of complaint that the ideal of sacred study was still insufficiently recognized, and somehow considered less useful or relevant than active pastoral work. The curse of activism was already entering the Church's life.[239]

How far did Canterbury Cathedral live up to this ideal of theological learning? In the early part of the period it cannot be said that many of its canons were learned divines. But there was improvement. J. H. Spry and Dean Lyall were concerned with learning, and it might be said that Benjamin Harrison was learned. He had a national reputation as a Hebrew scholar, when at Oxford, and he was one of the Old Testament panel for the making of the Revised Version of the Bible (1885). For a time he had been identified with the activities of Newman and Pusey, contributing four of the *Tracts for the Times* and inaugurating Newman's celebrated theological correspondence with the Abbé Jager. In 1832 he had written an appendix to Pusey's influential work in defence of cathedrals, providing an impressive list of works of theological scholarship produced by cathedral clergy since the Reformation.[240]

The challenge to harness cathedral traditions of learning to new and practical ends was certainly one to which the Dean and Chapter of Canterbury tried to respond. From the late 1830s they took seriously the various proposals for the improvement of the education of clergy for the mission-field.[241] Although St Augustine's College (just east of the city wall on the Abbey site) was founded as an independent body, the success of its opening in 1848 owed much to individual members of the Chapter. No theological college was set up, though the Dean and Chapter thought Canterbury might in many ways be a suitable place for theological training. The colleges at both Chichester and Wells had attracted criticism for apparently fostering Puseyism, and for turning the cathedral close into a place of

[236] B. F. Westcott, 'On Cathedral Work', *Macmillan's Magazine*, 21 (1869–70), 311.

[237] *Cathedrals Commission, Third and Final Report* (London, 1855), p. xvi; [A. J. B. Beresford Hope], 'The Future of English Cathedrals', *Christian Remembrancer*, 30 (July–Dec. 1855), 174–218, at 190 (approving).

[238] See e.g. G. W. Pennethorne, *Theological Colleges and Cathedral Reform* (Oxford, 1869), 4–7. Cf. [E. W. Benson], 'Cathedral Life and Cathedral Work', *Quarterly Review*, 130 (Jan.–Apr. 1871), 247; Henry Boothby Barry, *Thoughts on the Renovation of Cathedral Institutions* (London, 1852), 19.

[239] E. M. Goulburn, *The Functions of Our Cathedrals* (Oxford, 1869), 15.

[240] Pusey, *Prospective and Past Benefits* (cit. in n. 2), pref. p. x. Cf. [F. A. Glover], *The Fruits of Endowments, Being a List of Works of Upwards of Two Thousand Authors, Who Have from the Time of the Reformation to the Present Time, Enjoyed Prebendal or Other Non-Cure Endowments in the Church of England* (London, 1840), pp. v–vii.

[241] Selwyn, *Are Cathedral Institutions Useless?* (cit. in n. 3), 54.

theological contention.[242] However, the membership of Canterbury's Chapter was evidently considered neutral or balanced enough to spare the Precincts from becoming a centre of doctrinal discord. As the Dean and Chapter noted in their evidence to the Cathedrals Commission in 1854, 'the larger number of Canons retained here might be considered a security against the undue influence of any one individual teacher'.[243] However, nothing came of the scheme, and the contention was not put to the test.

During the second half of the century, Canterbury came to enjoy a wider reputation for its learning. Learned men continued to be appointed from time to time. A. P. Stanley occupied himself with the history of his Cathedral, amongst other things, during his time as a canon in the 1850s. According to his biographer, Prothero, he was at home among the great monuments, pursuing the story of Becket's murder.[244] Moreover, in Alford and Payne Smith, Canterbury had two Deans distinguished as biblical scholars, while Dean Farrar was an educationalist and a skilful popularizer of learning for the middle classes. Among the minor canons, the most impressive scholarly figure was Precentor Hake, who (like Payne Smith) had been both Boden Sanskrit Scholar and Pusey and Ellerton Scholar at Oxford. A friend of Dean Alford, Hake assisted him in his commentary on the Greek Testament.[245] Yet the absolute ideal, as enunciated by Bishop Hacket in the seventeenth century and by Pusey in 1832, of the cathedral as a storehouse of theological learning and scholarship for the diocese and Church as a whole, was to elude Canterbury.

In the 1890s it was felt in some quarters that cathedral reformers had concentrated too much on fostering diocesan and parochial involvement among the canons, and that the value of theological learning for its own sake had been lost sight of. It had actually been a complaint that some of the canons of Canterbury were too involved in academic duties, and the position of Professor at the University of Oxford held by one canon, Rawlinson, had even been questioned and criticized as incompatible with a proper fulfilment of canonical duties. Yet most canons were proud of any outside academic honours and involvement, even though they tended to be careful to link these up with the life of the Cathedral. In their replies at the 1889 visitation, Canons Holland and Rawlinson stressed their academic and educational role within the Cathedral and city. Rawlinson enumerated the many theological publications undertaken by him during the tenure of his canonry, insisting that he had been appointed a canon for the pursuit of literary work and not to perform some diocesan educational role.[246] In general, the canons were anxious to defend the value of members of their body holding professional academic posts at the same time.

The Cathedral, the Nation, and the Anglican Communion

In the early part of our period, cathedral establishments were looked upon with little popular national favour. The cathedrals' defenders in the late 1830s argued that if the

[242] See W. M. Jacob, 'The Diffusion of Tractarianism: Wells Theological College, 1840–49', *Southern History*, 5 (1983), 189–209.

[243] LPL, Tait Papers, vol. 246, fos. 9–10, 'Evidence of Dean & Chapter' [1854]; Dean and Chapter, *Cathedral Commission* (1872) (cit. in n. 92), 9.

[244] Prothero, *Stanley* (cit. in n. 94), i. 430.

[245] Woodruff, 'Reminiscences of the Cathedral' (cit. in n. 10), 20.

[246] LPL, Canterbury Visitation Returns, 1889, MS VG 3/8c, fo. 376; cf. fo. 378.

Church of England's status as a national established Church meant anything at all, the cost of augmenting poor parochial livings should be met by an appeal to the nation rather than by the appropriation of cathedral resources. It was a sign of the low estimate of cathedrals in the national consciousness that such a course was deemed unthinkable by most ecclesiastical politicians of the day. The two great architects of cathedral reform, Sir Robert Peel and Bishop Blomfield, evinced a disrespect for the status of cathedral chapters in the Church. Around 1840, indeed, there was a widespread predisposition 'to sink the cathedrals if necessary'.[247] Even by about 1850, it was felt that 'the unpopularity of chapters has rather increased than diminished'.[248] Chapters were still popularly perceived as combining 'large incomes with little or no definite service'. In fact, it was later asserted that 'the cathedrals fell into disrepute so great that, in 1852, had the Commissioners advocated their abolition, few except interested voices would have been raised to arrest their extinction'.[249] From about 1860 onwards, the tide turned. In 1879, on the eve of another Cathedrals Commission, Dean Payne Smith commented to Archbishop Tait just how much higher in the national estimate cathedrals had risen since the time of the previous Commission, in the 1850s.[250] Ironically, it was what came to be viewed as the 'remoteness' of cathedrals from the bustle of national life that now lay partly behind the revived sense of their national value. As B. F. Westcott wrote in 1870, 'the conception of cathedral life as ... a life of systematic devotion and corporate fellowship is more remote from modern forms of thought than the conception of cathedral work; and yet, in other respects, it is that towards which the popular instinct is most certainly moving'.[251] By the mid-1880s, the cathedrals' hold on the affections of the nation was secure.

Canterbury's history well reflects the changing relationship between cathedral and nation in the period. In the 1830s and 1840s, Canterbury's position as the first English cathedral seemed to count for little save to attract a greater share of national opprobrium than might otherwise have been the case. In the general absence of its archbishop and at a time when the concepts of the Anglican communion and the colonial church were still only in their infancy, the Cathedral had little sense of being the primatial seat or of having any international dimension. Gradually, however, from mid-century onwards, Canterbury came to provide physical expression to the identity of an ever-wider Anglican communion. Moreover, the growing Anglican colonial identity that had Canterbury at its heart was also fostered by the inauguration of the first of the Lambeth Conferences, in 1867, for at this and subsequent conferences, the bishops came to Canterbury for a special service. Moreover, the foundation of St Augustine's College had played a part in aiding a renewed sense of Canterbury Cathedral as mother church of the colonies and Anglican communion. In this context, it was very fitting that William Grant Broughton, first Bishop of Sydney (an old King's School boy with Canterbury connections), should be buried in the Cathedral, with full honours, in 1853. It was Broughton who, from his Australian vantage-point, had looked to St Augustine's, Canterbury, to staff the growing colonial church.[252] The more

247 Best, *Temporal Pillars* (cit. in n. 1), 339–40.
248 Barry, *Thoughts on the Renovation* (cit. in n. 238), 5.
249 Humble, 'Cathedrals and Chapters' (cit. in n. 7), 191.
250 LPL, Tait Papers, vol. 246, fo. 251, Dean Payne Smith to

Archbishop Tait, 24 May 1879.
251 'On Cathedral Work' (cit. in n. 236), 248.
252 E. R. Orger, *Life of Henry Bailey* (London, 1912), 39.

Anglicanism expanded into new continents, the more Canterbury could be perceived as its spiritual home.

Finally, Canterbury's position in relation to the nation was enhanced by developments in political life and thought. In the climate of rising national self-consciousness, even self-glorification, and imperialism that characterized late-Victorian political life, it suited the national mood more readily than it could have done earlier, to appreciate Canterbury as a national ecclesiastical and historical memorial and monument, a 'true centre of Christianity' and 'cradle of English Christianity'. The thirteen hundredth anniversary celebrations of the mission of St Augustine to England, in 1897, well reflected this mood of national chauvinism. Dean Farrar was not exaggerating when he expressed the view that this anniversary 'must, I think, stir every imagination, and touch every heart', and that it presented a unique 'opportunity for conferring a boon on the cathedral for a century to come'.[253] The burial of Archbishop Benson in the Cathedral in 1896 symbolized this renewed national importance of the Cathedral as the heart of the primatial see. As the Dean and Chapter explained, it was 'fit and proper that Archbishops of the Primatial See should, if possible, be buried in their Cathedral, as was the custom in earlier times'.[254] By the 1890s, Canterbury had achieved a new-found importance as not merely the metropolitical cathedral but also as the rallying point of Anglican churchmen.

CONCLUSION

After the re-establishment of 1660, the English cathedrals, and Canterbury among them, gradually acquired stability and were agents of stability in society. By contrast, the nineteenth century was a time of almost continuous change—both change enforced from outside and also what might be called the evolution of a new kind of cathedral life, very much more in the public eye. For Old Foundation cathedrals, the changes were perhaps the greatest, since they had scarcely been disturbed at the Reformation, and the Interregnum had proved to be only an interlude. Even for New Foundations, the loss, from 1840, of half their stalls (or even more) and the income attached to them was a considerable shock. The subsequent loss of control of estates and income was tolerable only because it was gradual, and because the canons who gave up in despair in the depression of the 1890s had a different understanding of the relation between cathedral and land from that held by their fighting predecessors of the 1830s.

All the time that deans and chapters fought and laid petitions before Parliament and lobbied anyone who might use influence on their behalf, the liturgical work of each cathedral continued. Matins and evensong were sung daily, and the Eucharist was celebrated at least monthly. The musical staff of the cathedral kept things going. They felt neglected. They asked for increased salaries. Gradually they were taken more seriously. As the canons resided for longer (and increasingly there were some canons without benefices), the cathedral became more the centre of their world. More attention was paid

[253] BL, Gladstone Correspondence, MS Add. 44525, fo. 134, Dean Farrar to W. E. Gladstone, 20 Mar. 1897.
[254] Chapter Act Book, 1895–1910, p. 63. The Chapter tried to obtain permission to bury archbishops in the crypt, but without success.

to the details of worship, and to the needs of the fabric. And throughout the period, there was perpetual discussion about what cathedrals were for, and what chapters should do, in addition to the two agreed tasks—'the Performance of the services in the Churches and the continual Reparation of the Fabrics'. The cathedrals had escaped abolition, but they had to change. Continuous scrutiny is not, on the whole, good for communities, and the series of Commissions produced some confusion of purpose.

Canterbury shared in all this. The Dean and Chapter were great fighters and took on the Ecclesiastical Commission with zest and skill in the early days. In later years they showed a proper concern for the city and the diocese, and for varying good causes. In the century of church restoration they might be said to have been almost fanatical in their desire to repair and alter the appearance of the building internally and externally. Fortunately, they did not carry out all their schemes. Music improved and there was a multiplication of sermons, a matter of discord between preaching Deans and members of their Chapters. Large set-piece services for special and national occasions brought the Cathedral before the public, now curious rather than hostile. Visitors increased in number and were shown round—the beginnings of a serious twentieth-century problem. By the end of the period, the Cathedral and its staff were recognizably more like those of modern times; but the Dean and Chapter were beset with financial difficulties and increasingly worried by pressure from the general public, who had expectations of what a cathedral should be, and of what they might do within it.

VII

The Twentieth Century, 1898–1994

KEITH ROBBINS

F. W. Farrar (Dean, 1895–1903; Pl. 49) ushered in the twentieth century with a sense of sombre foreboding. He had begun to lose the use of that right hand which had penned so many books and essays over his long life. Within a matter of months, both arms hung helpless from his shoulders. Then the muscles of his neck were attacked and his head slumped permanently forward. His colleagues watched his sad decline with sympathy and alarm.

It was not difficult to discern a sense of crisis that transcended the suffering of one old man. In his prime, Farrar himself had preached five eloquent sermons in Westminster Abbey on the subject of 'Eternal Hope'. As his life ebbed away in the Deanery, he did not fear the future *sub specie aeternitatis*. As a Christian, he trusted in the love and mercy of God, yet as an Englishman and as Dean of Canterbury it was difficult to suppress anxiety about the future of State and Church. He had been born in the Fort of Bombay nearly seventy years earlier. His lifetime had coincided with the consolidation of the British Empire and, almost, with the reign of Victoria. He had witnessed the dramatic changes in politics and society. He was proud of the achievements of his contemporaries and was not disposed to rule out the possibility of progress. Lord Rosebery had felt it appropriate to offer Farrar the deanery in recognition of his distinctive place in Victorian ecclesiastical life. Farrar had felt it incumbent upon himself to accept, for the same reason. Coming to Kent in 1895 in his sixty-fifth year, he was not expected to make sweeping changes in the life of the Cathedral, but he would surely continue to write. He had an established readership, which expected him to expound. There was, indeed, to be a further volume of studies in the Life of Christ, as well as a collection of reflections on great authors— Bunyan, Shakespeare, Dante, Milton, and Thomas à Kempis. Both were instantly reprinted. Such items were perhaps predictable. The Dean's own deeper anxieties are perhaps reflected in the titles of two other books he published in the year of his removal: *Gathering Clouds: Days of St Chrysostom*, and a commentary on the Book of Daniel. Was the British Empire being weighed in the balance and found wanting?

The outbreak of war in South Africa in October 1899 was one sign that all was not well. The Dean addressed men of the East Kent Imperial Yeomanry before their departure on active service. He exhorted them to do their duty but feared that the troubles of the world extended far beyond what was thought likely to prove a little local difficulty in South Africa. He asked 'What shall be the issue of the Armageddon struggle of the nations, which apart from some special intervention of Providence, cannot be long delayed? The answer to that question, under God, depends upon ourselves.'[1] Such apocalyptic words might have seemed exaggerated to some of his listeners. The presence of a barracks in Canterbury—and places of refreshment which boasted such titles as The Military Tavern, The Gay Hussar, The British Flag and The Volunteer—served as a local reminder of military reality, but in other respects Canterbury seemed a quiet and peaceful small town, substantially untroubled by industrial expansion. It had a population of around 24,000.[2] The largest occupational group in 1901 was engaged in domestic service. In the 'khaki' general election of 1900, the borough of Canterbury comfortably returned a Conservative member to Parliament. There was general rejoicing when the war came to a successful conclusion in 1902. Had the Dean's 1899 lecture on 'Temperance Reform as Required by National Righteousness and Patriotism' played its part in securing this outcome?

It was this patriotic and conservative community which conceived itself to be *Mater Angliae*. Its place in English life derived from the past rather than the present. It owed so much to the Cathedral which loomed above it, yet the building's very bulk seemed to dwarf the town and its inhabitants. One wag described Canterbury at this time as 'all parsons and pubs'. Dean Farrar did his best to diminish the role of the latter. The relationship between town and Cathedral was not without its difficulties when viewed from the clerical perspective. The men who worshipped in the Cathedral and sustained its life experienced daily the pull of the past. Clergy and their families in the Precincts lived in the constant shadow of a building which manifested, at every turn, so many aspects of the English past. Canterbury Cathedral still had national prominence. It was appropriate, for example, that the Prince and Princess of Wales should come to the opening of the restored chapter house and be entertained to lunch by the Dean. Similarly, the Dean entertained Their Royal Highnesses Prince Albrecht and Prince Frederick William of Prussia when they came to inspect this noble English pile. Canterbury East railway station was lined with red carpeting, and an escort of lancers greeted the Duchess of Albany when she came to represent Queen Victoria on the occasion of the unveiling of the memorial to Archbishop Benson in July 1899.

It was only to be expected that the guardians of the Cathedral should be English gentlemen, who, by virtue of upbringing and education, would be embodiments of English virtues and intuitively understand their role and function. Canons of Canterbury symbolized in their persons that deep link between the English people and the English Church so emphatically asserted by the contemporary Bishop of London, the historian Mandell Creighton, whose wife had been anxious that he be addressed as 'My Lord' rather than as 'Bishop'.

It was easy in Canterbury to be persuaded that even in 1902 this link was firmly in existence. Wesleyan Methodists, Primitive Methodists, Baptists, Congregationalists, and Presbyterians all had their own congregations in the town; the Society of Friends had a

---

[1] F. W. Farrar, Diary, 1895–9, and press-cuttings.   [2] A. Bateman, *A Social History of Canterbury* (Sittingbourne, 1984), 87.

meeting-house. In the year of Balfour's Education Act, Nonconformists had no feeling that the Cathedral was theirs. Roman Catholics, who had built their church in its shadow, also knew that the Cathedral was not theirs. Inevitably, however, their new church was dedicated to St Thomas Becket. Canterbury Cathedral was the cathedral of Canterbury, but it had fixed to it the label 'Church of England'. The life and work of its clergy could not help conveying, in microcosm, a certain notion of what that Church claimed to be. All roads did not lead to Canterbury, but steps taken there could not be insignificant in the religious life of England and, possibly, elsewhere.

Canterbury was the metropolitical church, but for over 300 years the archbishops had had no residence of their own in the Precincts. They lodged with the Dean. In 1897–9, however, the remaining part of the old Archbishop's Palace was restored, and Archbishop Temple and his successors had their own home in Canterbury, to be used as occasion permitted. The work had been put in hand by the Ecclesiastical Commissioners and was not, of course, the responsibility of the Dean and Chapter. When Temple died, in 1902, he was buried in the Cloister Garth following the precedent set by the burial of Benson in 1896—the first archbishop to be buried at Canterbury since Pole in 1558. Taken together, these two developments suggested that archbishops might be feeling that they 'belonged' to Canterbury in a somewhat novel fashion. Their authority was undoubted, but its practical expression in Canterbury itself was uncertain.

A related issue was the place of Canterbury in the evolution of an 'Anglican Communion'. Visiting bishops attending the Lambeth Conferences habitually visited Canterbury. The work of St Augustine's Missionary College in Canterbury had contributed greatly to the extension of the Church throughout the British Empire. In addition, American bishops and laity had a distant fondness for the Cathedral. It was gratifying to them that the Dean of Canterbury had visited their country. In so far as the Anglican Communion world-wide could possess an identity, Canterbury provided its physical expression, even though Farrar was disappointed in the American response to his appeal for funds to assist in structural renovation.

Frederic William Farrar wrestled with these conflicting pressures and with infirmity. He had the advantages and disadvantages of literary fame, chiefly on two counts—as the author of *The Life of Christ* and of *Eric, or Little by Little*, both of which ran into many editions.[3] He was elected a Fellow of the Royal Society for his work on the origins of language. He had defended Bishop Colenso, whose views on the nature of Holy Scripture had caused offence and schism. He had been Headmaster of Marlborough College before becoming a canon of Westminster. It was an illustrious career, but it might have been more illustrious. He might have been a bishop. In 1860 he had married a woman ten years younger than himself, and she bore him ten children, five of each sex. Yet it has been suggested that he remained a man's man, and he liked boys. *Eric, or Little by Little* was deeply autobiographical, and its suggestion of homosexual love was only thinly veiled.[4] One of his sons was caught *in flagrante* with a choirboy; another was put on trial for

[3] I. Ellis, 'Dean Farrar and the Quest for the Historical Jesus', *Theology*, 89 (1986), 108–15.

[4] N. Hamilton, *Monty: The Making of a General, 1887–1942* (London, 1981), 19–25; Reginald Farrar, *The Life of Frederic William Farrar* (London, 1904).

attempting to bribe and seduce his female secretary. These personal temptations and torments are a reminder that whatever the place Canterbury occupied in Church and State, within the Precincts there was a community of men and women, boys and girls, seeking to lead a Christian life, but the gates that enclosed the community and shut it off from the city did not thereby render it immune from the pressures and temptations of the world beyond.

When Farrar died, in March 1903, the tributes naturally concentrated on the fact that he had been one of the lights of the Victorian age, which had also now come to an end. His colleagues on the Chapter noted that he had held 'a high conception of what the Metropolitical Cathedral ought to be in the life of the National Church of England' and had laboured untiringly on its behalf. The Dean whose wonderful voice had once caught the minds and hearts of thousands could at the end no longer even read a lesson in his own Cathedral. Men of rank and distinction had considered it an honour to visit him in Canterbury; he had never been too proud to visit the citizens of Canterbury. His only local shortcoming was an inability, as he put it, to see any fun in trundling a piece of leather at three bits of stick. It remained to be seen whether an incoming dean would find greater pleasure than Farrar in the exploits of Kent CCC during Canterbury Cricket Week.

The opening of the new century had given rise to a good deal of loose talk in the press about novelty. R. J. Campbell, the celebrated minister of the City Temple, was shortly to argue the need for a 'new theology'. The person of Farrar's successor, however, did not suggest that the new century required *novi homines* at Canterbury. Henry Wace (Dean, 1903–24) was 67 at the time of his appointment. He had been educated at Marlborough, Rugby, and Brasenose College, Oxford, and all his subsequent career had been spent in London. He had been chaplain at Lincoln's Inn before becoming Professor of Ecclesiastical History at King's College in 1875. He became principal of the college in 1883 and continued in that office until 1896. An honorary chaplain to Queen Victoria, he was serving in the same role to King Edward VII when he received the offer of Canterbury. As a historian, he had edited texts of the Nicene and post-Nicene Fathers, and Luther's primary works. As a controversialist, he had tangled with Huxley in his *Christianity and Agnosticism*, and with Matthew Arnold in his *Christianity and Morality*. He has been described as 'in some ways the weightiest of the Oxford evangelical authors', equipped to attempt a major work of Christian apologetics.[5] His writings in this area have been seen as 'so many preliminary studies for the one great book that he could have written on the biblical faith in God'. He had not written that book by the time he reached Canterbury. He did not write it while he was there.

Dean Wace's arrival portended no change in churchmanship. Farrar's hatred of over-weening sacerdotal claims had been well known, and he countenanced no ritual which encouraged such dogma. Conscious that one of his own ancestors, a Bishop of St Davids, had been burnt alive in Carmarthen in 1555, Farrar willingly took part in the dedication, in June 1899, of the memorial in Canterbury to the forty-one Kentish Marian martyrs. Firm Protestant principle, however, was accompanied by personal courtesy towards Roman

Catholics. Farrar personally escorted Cardinal Vaughan, the Duke of Norfolk, and other leading Roman Catholics when they visited the Cathedral in September 1897. Wace shared with his predecessor the knowledge that the Church of England was a Protestant Church for a Protestant people. A schoolboy at the time found him 'short, dour but impressive'. He did not wear a full-length cassock, but was robed in a one-button surplice over the frock-coat and apron of his gaiter suit.

Some of his colleagues soon came to the conclusion that the new Dean did not entertain any very elevated conception of what a cathedral could be. They also encountered a somewhat autocratic disposition, with the result that Chapter meetings could be misery. There was no sign of the gentle old man putting away his sword and preparing for heaven, though in this respect the Dean perhaps had a more acute assessment of his staying-power than did his colleagues. However, he did not invariably have his way. It is recorded in 1913 that the Chapter divided four to three on a matter which involved the reduction of a pension. The Dean protested at the decision and left the meeting.

The canons in 1903 were men of varied experience, commitments, and commitment. Stall I had been occupied since 1895 by William Page Roberts, born, like Wace, in 1836. A Lancashire man, he graduated from St John's College, Cambridge. Married to the niece of Earl Granville, he was to become Dean of Salisbury at the age of 71.

He was succeeded by William Danks, a banker's son from Nottingham who had obtained a pass degree at the Queen's College, Oxford. Not only was he comparatively youthful, having been born in 1845, he was unique amongst his colleagues in having pastoral experience in the province of York and in San Francisco. It is recorded that the boys of the King's School, who attended the Cathedral *ex officio* on Sunday mornings, sent a deputation to him at the close of his first series of sermons to thank for the exceptional value to them of his teaching. There is no knowledge of any other canon during this period being similarly thanked.

Page Roberts had come to Canterbury in the same year as Arthur James Mason, who occupied stall V. Born in 1851, Mason had gone from Repton to Trinity College, Cambridge. As an assistant master at Wellington, he had formed 'an almost romantic friendship' with Edward White Benson, then the headmaster of the school. When Benson was appointed Bishop of Truro, Mason followed him as chaplain and diocesan missioner. The young Mason, devoted as he was to ascetic practices, inspired great affection. Arthur Benson, the Bishop's son, remembered expeditions in the Cornish countryside with Mason, who wore a huge Corsican cloak and read poetry aloud from a little purple book. In 1882 he moved to Barking to conduct missionary work among the more educated. In the same year as he was appointed to Canterbury he became Lady Margaret Professor of Divinity at Cambridge, but in 1903 he resigned the chair, though not his canonry, on becoming Master of Pembroke College.[6] His Canterbury connection had been strengthened by his unexpected marriage to the daughter of the Headmaster of the King's School. His edition of *The Five Theological Orations of Gregory of Nazianzus* was highly regarded. He served as Vice-Chancellor of Cambridge University in 1908–10 but two years later resigned his mastership

[6] I am grateful to Dr Clive Trebilcock, Librarian of Pembroke College, for supplying certain items of information concerning Mason. See also D. Newsome, *On the Edge of Paradise: A. C. Benson, the Diarist* (London, 1980), 26.

and withdrew to Canterbury. However, his unusual knowledge of both Assyrian Christianity and the Church of Sweden was at the disposal of archbishops. His colleagues derived benefit from his expertise in stained glass and hymnology; he had a deep reverence for the Cathedral. He also felt strongly about the Balkans and the conduct there of the Turks. There was nothing parochial about Mason.

His strong Cambridge links were balanced by the new presence in 1903 of the sixty-eight-year-old Edward Moore (stall XI), also a doctor of divinity and head of a house, St Edmund Hall, Oxford. As a young man he had taken four Firsts and settled down to the first of his forty-nine years as Principal at the age of 29. Few men knew more about Dante, and in 1906 the new British Academy recognized his scholarship by electing him to its Fellowship. He had the advantage, unlike his predecessor as a canon, George Rawlinson, the Camden Professor of Ancient History in the University of Oxford, of possessing distinct speech. However, his main preoccupation was the preservation of St Edmund Hall from the predatory ambitions of the Queen's College. He continued to live for part of each term in the Hall, to ward off his neighbour. Only in 1913 did he feel that he could safely resign his Oxford post.

Francis Holland, who had occupied stall VIII since 1882, was failing and was replaced in 1907 by Edward Stuart, known to be a strong Evangelical. The Archdeacons of Canterbury and Maidstone occupied the remaining filled stalls. William Walsh (stall IV) had been Archdeacon of Canterbury since 1897, having been for a half a dozen years Bishop of Mauritius. The following year he was appointed suffragan Bishop of Dover, and thus in 1903 became the adjunct of Randall Davidson, the new archbishop. Walsh was the only canon to have been born in Kent—and the only one to sport a goatee beard. He had been an Oxford contemporary of the new Dean, though they were not at the same college. Maxwell Spooner (stall IX), the Archdeacon of Maidstone, was another Oxford man. He was the son of the brother-in-law of Archbishop Tait, and he and his brother Archibald, shortly to become Warden of New College, had had distinguished undergraduate careers. No longer able to hold his Fellowship at Magdalen after his marriage (to the daughter of the Bishop of Carlisle), he had held a series of Kent livings. Close to the Taits and, by extension, to the Davidsons, Spooner had become archdeacon in 1900. His daughter Kitty married Ralph Inge, in what David Newsome describes as 'a bustling, fashionable, ecclesiastical wedding'.[7] Newsome also notes how the signatures in the register reveal the extraordinary linking of episcopal families—Lucy Tait, Arthur Benson, William Temple, Edie Davidson.

That was the Cathedral 'team', though it was scarcely a word that a canon would have used; it lasted until changes took place during the First World War. It could not be said that this body of men lacked the maturity to cope with their responsibilities. Only two of their number possessed working experience beyond the province of Canterbury. Their close links were with the universities of Oxford and Cambridge rather than with the industrial world or, London apart, with the life of major cities. There was, however,

---

[7] Newsome, *On the Edge of Paradise*, 191.

scholarship and an appreciation of scholarship. Shared assumptions and common backgrounds should have made co-operation straightforward.

The responsibility of the Dean and Chapter was for the maintenance of the fabric and
the worthy ordering of worship. It could not be assumed that the talents of the canons
matched their obligations. Dante scholarship might, or might not, point to a ready grasp
of financial and building technicalities. At their regular meetings, the Dean and Chapter
discussed a bewildering mixture of the trivial and the profound.[8] The meetings were not
conducive to profound reflection on the function of a cathedral in the twentieth century.
It was easy to assume that it was each canon's duty simply to keep the Cathedral intact
for the next generation. Dean Wace seems not to have been a man to ask fundamental
questions. There was a routine to be observed which could, on occasion, be burdensome,
not least where fabric was concerned. It seemed that something always needed to be done.
Specialist advice could be, and was, obtained, but the ultimate responsibility rested with
the Dean and Chapter. Like directors of a company, they had to keep a careful watch over
income and expenditure, and determine what could be afforded. That even extended to
their own remuneration. In 1902 the Dean and Chapter exchanged their remaining estates
with the Ecclesiastical Commissioners in return for tithe rents. Normally, during the
Edwardian period, the Dean was able to draw a tithe dividend of £400 each half-year, and
each canon £200. It was reported at the July audit in 1911, however, that 'Tithe continues
to be paid well on the whole, but only as a result of strenuous effort and constant litigation
... the labour necessary to recover tithe increases every year, as do the expenses.' In
October 1904, when expensive repairs to the central tower were needed, there had been a
discussion in Chapter as to the desirability of applying to Parliament to suppress a canonry
on the next vacancy, with a view to providing a fabric fund for the repair of the Cathedral.
In addition, might it not be possible to transfer the Chapter's tithe rents to the Ecclesiastical
Commissioners in return for fixed payments? Indeed, the Commissioners made it clear
that they would welcome such a step, but the Chapter was not disposed to follow this
course. It was agreed in December 1910 to insure the Cathedral roof for £65,000, and the
rest of the property for £80,915. Would the colonial prime ministers, who came down to
Canterbury in July 1911, during the occasion of the Imperial Conference, have agreed that
these were sensible figures for this irreplaceable imperial symbol? The canons, aware that
they had no business expertise, coped as best they could. They felt most uncomfortable,
however, when they were confronted with examples of non-payment of rent.

There was also a certain awkwardness when matters of their own accommodation were
involved. The properties in the Precincts were substantial and desirable residences. No
less than the Cathedral itself, they required regular maintenance, but to what standard
and for whom? Canons were gentlemen and they had a certain style to maintain. William
Temple, who played ping-pong with Maxwell Spooner's daughter on his visits to Canterbury, had been accustomed a few years earlier, in Fulham Palace, to summon the

---

[8] I am grateful to the Dean and Chapter for access to the
Chapter Acts. Information in this chapter concerning the affairs
of the Cathedral derives from this source unless otherwise
indicated. For a background to the Cathedral's financial difficulties, see G. F. A. Best, *Temporal Pillars: Queen Anne's Bounty,
the Ecclesiastical Commissioners, and the Church of England*
(Cambridge, 1964), 465–79.

footman whenever more fuel was required for the library fire. Christian civilization, Ruth Spooner subsequently recalled, seemed to require one not to shake hands with the servants when paying a social visit to another house.[9] A gentleman carried a lady's parasol, but not a heavy scuttle for a woman of the working class. The 'grannies' she visited in the Canterbury workhouse seemed very remote from the world of the Precincts. The wife of the Bishop of Dover was delicate, so she had a housemaid as well as a lady's maid. Of course, she also had a cook and a kitchen maid, two further housemaids, a butler and houseboy, a coachman and gardeners. What assistance enabled the Dean and Mrs Wace to endure life in the Deanery can only be conjectured. Inevitably, the social structure did not disappear at the entrance to the Cathedral itself. The Sunday evening service continued to be largely for the female servants, dressed in plain black bonnets. Clerical ladies wearing elaborate hats bedizened with ostrich feathers and artificial flowers and fruit had attended in the morning.

Yet it was not a totally static world, and the tone and style of Cathedral life could not be dictated entirely by those to whom it appeared to belong. There was a world outside which also seemed to have a claim. Motor cars began to penetrate the Precincts, bringing passengers who were not equipped with cards to indicate that they were bent on calling upon canons. It was agreed in September 1903 that they should not be allowed into the Precincts. But this new form of transportation only raised in a more acute form the general problem posed by 'visitors'. Back in 1895 it had been remarked that no water-closet existed close to the Cathedral, and that situation could probably not continue. The fees paid by visitors were not without financial significance (1907 £1,366; 1908 £1,423; 1909 £1,432; 1910 £1,597; 1911 £1,509), but should visitors be encouraged, and should they still be charged? In 1913, when the income reached £1,760, the increase was explained by the additional facilities for touring by private and public motor-carriages, combined with fine weather. Here, in potentially acute form, was a possible conflict between the Cathedral as a national monument and as a place of worship.

Other aspects of the outside world threatened to be deliberately rather than accidentally disruptive. The Dean and Chapter agreed in August 1913 that 'in order to guard against possible outrages by women in connection with the "suffragette" movement, a police constable is now maintained on duty in the Cathedral all the time it is open'. In addition, women had to deposit their bags, parcels, and muffs with an official before entering the building. An additional watchman was employed at night. It was a little disappointing that the only female found in an unusual place by the clerk of works and the head verger turned out to be the daughter of the Archdeacon of Maidstone. She had ventured on to the roof one summer morning to read a book in peace. The police constable was dispensed with early in 1914, though in June it was agreed that it would be as well to have him back. Five days after the apparent threat to the peace posed by suffragettes had been dealt with, Archduke Franz Ferdinand was assassinated at Sarajevo. The prospect of a European conflagration had played no part in the ordinary everyday proceedings of the Dean and Chapter. The canons were not to know that the war that was about to break out would

[9] Ruth Spooner, 'Memories', unpubl. memoir.

challenge the self-contained assumptions of that quiet cathedral close in ways beyond their imagining or control.

Dean Wace, now in his seventy-eighth year, spoke on 'The Christian Sanction of War' at a service of intercession held in the Cathedral on 9 August 1914.[10] There was a personal aspect to the international catastrophe which caused him private grief. Twenty years earlier he had married as his second wife Cornelia Gertrude Schmitz, daughter of the German scholar Dr Leonard Schmitz, who had come over from Germany to teach in Edinburgh. However, in his address, he confined himself to the general issues raised by the conflict. War, he believed, was justifiable for the same reason that it was lawful to put men to death for murder and treason. Such crimes destroyed the very frame of society. War, as a last resort, had been shown for a thousand years to be the only effectual means of punishing and preventing unjust violence. If the British people could say that they had not drawn the sword from any selfish motive, they could come before God with a clear conscience. He believed they could. Britain coveted no other nation's possessions and had no desire to interfere in the internal affairs of other states. It was undoubtedly in the cause of righteousness that Britain desired to act. However, the nation had also to look within. Over the recent past there had been too much luxury, extravagance, and self-indulgence. The sacrifices to be made by soldiers and sailors would not be fruitless. They would be glorified by a sacred and divine example. It was a sermon that, like many others being delivered at this time, was inevitably being given in ignorance of the nature of the conflict that lay ahead.

It did not seem likely that the Cathedral would be affected in any immediate, dramatic fashion. It was agreed in October 1914 not to effect any special insurance of the Cathedral against war risks. It was accepted as inevitable that the fees from visitors would decline and would stay down until the war came to an end. Against this, it was reported, at the end of November 1915, that the overall income of the Cathedral had increased, no doubt largely because of the need for agricultural produce during the war, which led in turn to improved payment of tithes. Indeed, it was noted that for the first time within the memory of any of the existing members of the Chapter, it was possible for them to receive in full the amounts prescribed for them by Act of Parliament—£2,000 for the Dean and £1,000 for each of the canons. Such a fact was not generally trumpeted abroad. However, in February 1915, without specifying how, the Chapter agreed to safeguard the colours of the Buffs (East Kent Regiment) 'in case of a raid of the enemy on Canterbury'. It was generally agreed that there was an increased attendance at services. A degree of increased spiritual activity is comprehensible, but it was also the case that there were many soldiers at a loose end in Canterbury on Sundays. Ruth Spooner recalled seeing disconsolate men wandering around the Precincts on Sunday afternoons, when the Cathedral was closed except for the services. She sallied forth and gave them a guided tour. Like pantomime actors, the men reacted as if their chief interest in life was Gothic architecture. A less rewarding task came her way at her mother's suggestion, when, with a companion, she 'patrolled' the streets to keep an eye on the girls who swarmed out to catch a soldier. In May 1915 a general

---

[10] H. Wace, *The Christian Sanction of War* (London, 1914). I am grateful to Prof. Patrick Collinson for making a copy of this sermon available.

wrote to the Dean expressing the view that the renewal of pure religion was the greatest benefit of the war and that 'the aid to this revival that all ranks have received all over Kent is crowned by that afforded by the Dean and Chapter of Canterbury Cathedral'.

As the war continued, some of the early confidence that it would be 'business as usual' began to disappear. The Chapter agreed in October 1916 that its members would participate in a public procession through Canterbury in support of the National Mission of Repentance and Hope. It was recorded that the Dean received a stipend of £1,500, and each canon £750. Good workmen for the Cathedral were increasingly difficult to find. In February 1917 it was agreed to increase the insurance cover by 25 per cent against the risk of fire and aircraft action. The following month, however, as revolution in Russia threatened to tilt the balance of advantage in favour of the Central Powers, it was agreed that for the time being the Bowling Green should not be used for the cultivation of vegetables. In October the Chapter did agree to a request from the Chief Constable that if bombs were dropped from aircraft, members of the public might be allowed to make use of the Cathedral as a place of refuge during daylight. This was a development which could not have been conceived of a decade earlier. The pace of change was accelerating unpredictably. It was war, too, which indirectly made possible the participation of a Nonconformist minister for the first time in a service in the Cathedral. The occasion was the National Service of Intercession appointed by King George V. The Dean reported that he had consulted with the Archbishop on the matter. His Grace had given the opinion that such a service might properly be held in the nave and, although he was strongly opposed to interdenominational services, which frequently confused the popular mind as to the differences between Nonconformity and the Church, he was quite clear that a Nonconformist minister might be admitted on this occasion.

The Chapter emerged unscathed, but a number of changes took place in personnel, although the Dean himself, now 82, gave every appearance of being indestructible. Danks had died in 1916, at the age of 71. He was succeeded by the sixty-two-year-old Arthur Robinson. He had been connected with the city church of All Hallows, Barking-by-the-Tower—where Mason had earlier served—for thirty years. He had conducted parish missions and clergy retreats not only in England but also in Australia, New Zealand, South Africa, and Canada. Archbishop Davidson chose him to lead the National Mission of Repentance and Hope. Robinson was also a considerable scholar, possessor of a Cambridge doctorate in divinity. He was an admirer of F. D. Maurice and had written on the inter-relationship of theology, science, and philosophy. Here was a canon in touch with the wider world. It seemed that the only thing he lacked was a wife. He remedied this deficiency by inviting by letter the by no means young daughter of Dr Moore—her father too had died in 1916—to share in his life and work at Canterbury.[11] Working as a nurse in London, she at first supposed that membership of a committee was envisaged but, on learning that he had marriage in mind, gladly accepted the invitation. She had latterly been managing her father's household—two parlour-maids, two housemaids, a cook, a kitchen-maid, a gardener, and a coachman. She therefore knew what life in the Precincts

---

[11]   E. James, *A Life of Bishop John A. T. Robinson* (London, 1987), 1–6.

involved, if things continued as they had done before the war. Her father's successor was Samuel Bickersteth, son, and in turn father, of a very clerical family. Walsh, Archdeacon of Canterbury and Bishop of Dover, died in 1918. He was succeeded in the former position by Leonard White-Thomson (who in turn moved on to become Bishop of Ely in 1924) and in the latter position by Harold Bilborough, who was not made a residentiary canon. Spooner retired in 1921 and took a down train to Oxford to take up residence near his brother. He was succeeded as Archdeacon of Maidstone by John Victor Macmillan. Stuart died in 1917 and was replaced by Thory Gardiner. Gardiner had interested himself in housing and general social questions in the capital. He had been appointed a member of the Royal Commission on the Poor Law. Beatrice Webb recorded in her diary in January 1906 that Gardiner came to tea and she 'impregnated him with our views of investigation'.[12]

The overall result of these changes was to reduce slightly the average age of the canons, but not to lead to any more sweeping reassessment of priorities. Mason stayed serenely on amongst the changes, and in 1919 privately printed a sequence of Canterbury sonnets:

> Let me recount my comrades gone from hence;—
> Farrar, more admirable when he bore
> His growing palsy, than in years before,
> When London hung upon his eloquence,
> Learn'd Rawlinson, to whose munificence
> This church owes much; to Holland even more;
> Smith's quavering, silvery voice and gather'd store
> Of peaceful wisdom, pure without pretence;
>
> Walsh, Stuart, Danks, and one whose memory green
> Will never fade, so long as men desire
> To know the mysteries to Dante known;
> And two yet living, but too seldom seen,
> Page Roberts, ruling under Sarum spire,
> And you, dear Eden, on your northern throne.[13]

There was no mention in this tribute of the man who was now approaching his twentieth year as Dean.

A standard item in Chapter business over the years was the wish of certain individuals to have some kind of memorial to friend or relative established in the Cathedral. It was inevitable that the late conflict should occasion many such requests. As early as July 1917 the Chapter decided not to give leave, except in special cases, for the erection of memorials to individuals who had died in the war. It was assumed that, at the conclusion of the war, the East Kent Regiment and the public would desire to erect a substantial monument in or near the Cathedral. And indeed, in February 1919, a deputation from the Kent War Memorial Committee was received with a proposal for a memorial to be erected on the Bowling Green. The matter was referred to the Archbishop, who approved, subject to some uncertainty about the scale of the scheme and the amount of money that might be

[12] *The Diary of Beatrice Webb*, ed. N. and J. Mackenzie, iii (London, 1984), 21. Gardiner was a prominent rector of Lambeth but he is not referred to in J. Cox, *The English Churches* *in a Secular Society: Lambeth 1870–1930* (Oxford, 1982).
[13] A. J. Mason, *Canterbury Sonnets* (Canterbury, 1919).

raised. On a related matter, the Archbishop also agreed that there should be a united service of thanksgiving for peace, to be held in August 1919.

These important but formal items were predictable aspects of Chapter business. They were accompanied by other issues which pointed to the unsettling consequences of war. Within a fortnight of the Armistice, the Chapter received submissions on the question of pay. The senior vesturer pointed to the fact that 'substantial' increases of salaries and wages were being given throughout the country. He had no alternative but to request an increase.[14] The matter was thoroughly investigated, since it was becoming clear that men demobilized from the armed forces were reluctant to fall back into their old conditions of service. It was accepted in July that the days on which the choirboys would not be required to attend matins should be increased from one to three. It might be necessary to reduce staff. In his half-yearly report in November 1919, the Agent drew attention to serious financial uncertainties. There was a large increase in the number of tithe arrears, chiefly due to the breaking-up of large estates and to major land-sales. He also noted an increasing disinclination or inability to pay. More court cases might result—with consequential costs. The fees gained from visitors were beginning to recover, but the guides required to be paid increased wages. In addition, it was claimed that the Inland Revenue was holding back tax rebates which were allegedly due. In the not very distant future, there might be legislative proposals concerning the tithe which might have far-reaching financial consequences. This sense of uncertainty pervades the early post-war years, no doubt reflecting the generally unsettled social and political conditions of the country. In January 1921, however, the Dean and Chapter felt sufficiently confident of the future to recommend the purchase of a 'vacuum cleaner', subject to a satisfactory demonstration of its qualities, for which they were prepared to pay. Quite apart from the prevailing national circumstances, however, that sense of drift reflects the age of Dean Wace. In September 1919, he told his colleagues in relation to the forthcoming Lambeth Conference that he and Mrs Wace would not be able to offer as much help with accommodation as they had done twelve years previously. It was symptomatic of a general slowing-down. He was not going to be able to address himself to a new post-war world in which the Church Assembly started sending out forms of enquiry concerning the financial position of the Church and expected to receive answers. What he most relished was his continued role as a governor of various colleges and institutions beyond Canterbury. In 1924 he became the first dean of Canterbury to meet with an accidental death. He was knocked down by traffic in London. It was a sad commentary on a venerable eighty-seven-year-old's understandable inability to move with the times. His colleagues recorded the following estimate in their minutes:

His strong and vigorous character, his skill in administration, his superiority to bodily hindrances, his profound and unaffected devotion won the admiration and reverence of all who knew him. The City of Canterbury gave him the unprecedented honour of the freedom of the city to mark his eighty-fifth birthday. As a debater in ecclesiastical assemblies he made the most of his eminent

---

[14] Deanery Papers, Box 7, Senior Vesturer to Dean, 20 Nov. 1918. There are further items concerning wages in this period in the same box.

position and his learning had its full weight. His long connexion with The Times newspaper enabled him to gain the attention of the public to the needs of our Cathedral so that he obtained more than £30,000 for the reparation of it, especially of the three towers. During the Great War, his frequent sermons and addresses were an inspiration to many and a strength to thousands of our fighting men.

There was justice in this assessment, but few observers of the Canterbury scene doubted that the Cathedral at this juncture needed a man of vigour and vision.

The twentieth-century history of Canterbury Cathedral might properly be said to begin with the installation of George Kennedy Allen Bell (Pl. 56) as Dean in March 1924.[15] Unlike his immediate predecessors, he was not an eminent Victorian. Unlike them, too, he was later, in his years as Bishop of Chichester, to leave his mark on the Church of England and the world-wide Church. He had gone up to Christ Church, Oxford, from Westminster in the early years of the century, and had taken a First in Mods. and a Second in Greats. His interests were literary and he took the Newdigate prize in 1904. Ordained in 1907, he spent the next three years as a curate at Leeds Parish Church, before returning to Oxford to teach English and classics. In 1914, when he was 31, Bell moved to Lambeth, where he became resident chaplain to the sixty-six-year-old Archbishop. To the end of his life, Bell always spoke respectfully of 'Archbishop Davidson', and a relationship of such trust and intimacy developed that Davidson confessed in 1924 that it almost seemed nepotism to commend Bell's appointment to Canterbury. Bell married in 1918 and continued at Lambeth until his appointment as Dean. Looking back on his Lambeth years, he wrote that it was the task of a chaplain to be a 'nobody', but in fact he never succeeded in living in total obscurity. No one as curious and painstaking as Bell could fail to learn much from a decade spent at the hub of the Church of England. It was this experience which enabled him to move from anonymity to a high public role without apparent strain. He was an intelligent man, but he was not a scholar. Works of systematic theology or biblical criticism were not to be expected. It was already apparent that he was a man of action and theological reflection upon the issues of the day. Childless, he possessed a wide circle of friends and had no hesitation in seeking to make fresh contacts. He was a parson's son himself, and his formation was thoroughly Anglican and English, but the tragedy of war had already stimulated him to think ecumenically. In his introduction to a volume he edited on *War and the Kingdom of God*, he stated that England was morally bound to go to war in 1914 but that there was 'a greater cause than the cause of the patriot; a devotion higher than devotion to country or home'.[16] The Kingdom of God stood far beyond the idols of materialism and a false nationalism. He prayed not for the restoration of the false peace which existed before the Great War but for the establishment of that peace, within the hearts of men and between the nations of the world, which is the peace of God and 'passeth all understanding'.

What did that prayer and aspiration have to do with Canterbury Cathedral? It was

[15] R. C. D. Jasper, *George Bell, Bishop of Chichester* (Oxford, 1967), 35–55.

[16] G. K. A. Bell, *The War and the Kingdom of God* (London, 1915), 5. For a general assessment of Bell, see J. Rusama, *Unity and Compassion: Moral Issues in the Life and Thought of George K. A. Bell* (Helsinki, 1986).

apparent that Bell had been so firmly gripped by the ecumenical imperative—embracing nations as well as churches—that he would not allow himself to become completely absorbed by his local decanal responsibilities. It was equally obvious that he cared about the life and work of his new Cathedral. It would not be merely an impressive address from which to launch himself into the wider world.

In all the circumstances, the smack of firm government was congenial to his canonical colleagues, despite the fact that they were all older and might have stood upon dignity. Bell's known intimacy with the Archbishop no doubt helped, as did his modest familiarity with Canterbury when accompanying Davidson. It helped to be able to talk about hymnology with old Dr Mason. Bickersteth had been his vicar in Leeds. Macmillan had been senior chaplain at Lambeth when Bell had arrived, and Gardiner had been rector of Lambeth. He knew Robinson through the National Mission. Finally, when White-Thomson went off to become Bishop of Ely, Bell was able to start with a new Archdeacon of Canterbury, in the person of Edward Hardcastle. In most of these respects Bell was fortunate. He could make assumptions which another man without these personal and institutional links might not have been able to make. Bell was a young man in a hurry, but he carried older men with him.

Even so, there were problems, great and small, which Bell would not ignore. Things could not go on as they were. It was to be hoped that they could be changed without unpleasantness, but at all events the Dean would do his duty. Bell was disturbed to find that there was no inventory of any of the Deanery possessions; that would be remedied. He believed that a further step towards efficiency would be achieved by typing the minutes of Chapter proceedings; that was done within a matter of months. There would need to be alterations in the Deanery. They were accomplished. It was necessary to investigate the working of the Cathedral's agency and the responsibility of the Agent; after many acrimonious months, matters were resolved to the satisfaction of the Chapter, though not of the Agent, with whose services it was decided to dispense. It was agreed to make provision for a ladies' cloakroom. And so it continued. No doubt it was sometimes hard to see in these matters any particular bringing-in of the Kingdom, but no dean could expect to communicate a wider vision if he conspicuously avoided the awkward angularities of everyday life.

Bell did not lose the broader view. When his appointment was announced, the Dean of Chester, who had thought long and constructively on the role of a cathedral in twentieth-century Britain, wrote in these terms to Bell: 'it seems to me the greatest opportunity in the world a man could have'.[17] So Bell went to talk to the Dean of Chester. He came back impressed by the range of things that might be done, and the two men continued to exchange letters on how they might make their cathedrals more attractive.[18] Canterbury Cathedral would show its concern for the diocese by instituting prayers at evensong and Holy Communion on each weekday for each parish in turn. It was agreed that visitors would be helped by a colour-coded plan indicating the different phases of the Cathedral's construction. Female visitors entering with uncovered heads should not be compelled

[17] F. S. M. Bennett, *The Nature of a Cathedral* (Chester, 1925). LPL, Bell Papers, vol. 1, 1919–25, Bennett to Bell, 28 Feb. 1924.   [18] Deanery Papers, Box 7, Bennett to Bell, 27 May 1925.

henceforth to cover them—unless they intended to join in public worship. Bell's general intention was to remove the plethora of notices whose import was prohibitive. Men, women, and children should be welcome in the house of the Lord. If we treat visitors as 'trippers', the Dean told the Chapter in May 1924, that was what they would remain. In February 1925, Bell achieved his desire to follow the pattern established by some other cathedrals of removing admission charges. The Chapter agreed to a two-year experiment, and Bell successfully appealed for financial support from a few well-wishers to meet the anticipated shortfall in income. In fact, within a few years, voluntary donations exceeded the income previously received from fees, and they had the additional benefit of not being taxed. There was to be no reversion to the old practice. Finance in general, however, remained a worry, and the Dean found himself in frequent correspondence with the Ecclesiastical Commissioners. In June 1925 he and the Chapter wrote answers to the questionnaire of the Cathedrals Commission, which had been appointed the previous year. Bell had doubts about the wisdom of the Commission's report in 1927, especially the suggestion that the Greater Chapters should become the governing bodies of cathedrals. As a result of his activity, this clause was deleted from the eventual measure, passed in 1931.

The Dean also swiftly tackled the revision of Cathedral worship, particularly on Sundays. The prevailing main service consisted of matins, litany, and ante-Communion, fully choral, followed by a sermon. The remainder of the Communion service was then said. The boys of the King's School were not alone in finding its normal duration of two hours rather long. After discussion, which included schoolboys, Bell instituted a monthly sung Eucharist, with matins on the other three Sundays being sung to the end of the third collect. The Precentor was displeased and did not disguise his displeasure during worship. A few years later, the Chapter had to confront the controversial issue of the Revised Prayer Book. It happened that the Conservative MP for Canterbury, Ronald McNeill, was an Ulster Protestant. He did not like the proposed new Prayer Book and spoke against it. The Archdeacon of Maidstone thought that the Chapter should make some comment on the MP's opinions, but his brethren believed silence to be the wiser course.

It was appropriate that the editor of *Documents on Christian Unity* (1924) and the joint editor of *The Church of England and the Free Churches* (1925) should begin to take some action in this area within his own Cathedral. The occasion of the seven hundredth anniversary of the coming of the Grey Friars offered the opportunity to persuade Roman Catholics to unite in one programme of events, and they eventually did. A few months later, in November 1924, the Dean told his colleagues that the invitation to the Revd J. D. Jones, a prominent Congregational minister, to preach in the Cathedral had been accepted. Bell would go into the pulpit on the preceding Sunday to explain the invitation. In July 1927 the Dean reported that he had invited M. le Pasteur Wilfred Monod of l'Oratoire in Paris to give an address in the nave. The small French Protestant congregation which continued to worship each Sunday in the Cathedral was a remarkable historical survival, but this was the first occasion on which a pastor of the French Reformed Church had been invited specifically to address the English congregation. It was a modest fruit of the time Monod and Bell had spent in Stockholm in August 1925, taking part in the Universal Christian

Conference on Life and Work. Here was another example of the way in which Bell widened the Cathedral's horizons. The Stockholm conference—whose proceedings Bell edited with his customary efficiency—was not conceived to be a narrowly introspective ecclesiastical occasion. It was concerned with the world of work, amongst other public issues. Nine months after the Swedish discussions, there was a General Strike in Britain. The Chapter determined upon two immediate steps—a reduction of 50 per cent in fuel consumption, and the opening of the Cathedral from 5 p.m. to 7 p.m. each evening to provide some help, possibly including food, for people who were going to be without work. The role of Archbishop Davidson in the strike was perhaps not an encouragement to the view that churchmen had a prominent part to play in such confrontations. Even so, there did seem to be a gap between the ecumenical generalities of Stockholm and the strong support for the government in Canterbury itself. Should the Dean and Chapter dabble in supporting the miners in the Kent coalfields in a tangible way, whatever might be thought of their political stance?

Bell always believed that 'life and work' were never complete without art, music, and drama. He himself wrote poetry. The tercentenary of Orlando Gibbons, in June 1925, offered the prospect of a special service. Not only that, it was broadcast. In his Lambeth days, Bell had struck up an acquaintance with John Reith, general manager of the new British Broadcasting Company, and he approached him with the idea of broadcasting the Gibbons service. Chapter agreed, and Reith replied that he was delighted to be able to go ahead.[19] The success of this occasion was followed by an Armistice Day broadcast. The Archbishop preached the sermon. A carol service at Christmas was the next logical development, and it was well received. However, the canons still had things to learn about the requirements of the new medium. Bell's attention was drawn to the fact that at a crucial point, the Precentor had failed to obey his instructions to move to the Dean's stall, 'and being apparently afflicted with a severe cold, coughed and so on all through the carol singing', not to the benefit of listeners at home. It was clear, however, that broadcasting had come to stay. What was uncertain was the nature of the relationship between the BBC and the Dean and Chapter. The latter insisted that they should control the services, but they also expected the BBC to pay a fee. Some canons were not happy that divine service should even appear to be haggled over commercially, while conceding that the Cathedral was being put to extra expense because of broadcasting. In these matters, both sides were feeling their way. Bell's initiatives led deans of other cathedrals to feel that he was an expert in all the issues being thrown up by technical developments. 'I am a persistent Bore,' wrote the Dean of Winchester in June 1927, 'Now I want to ask you about the fees for organists, lay clerks and choristers, for "records".'[20]

The Dean also wished to encourage drama.[21] 'Religious drama' could be revived and be performed within the walls of cathedrals. An early attempt to stage a nativity play in the nave came to nothing, though the Chapter, with one dissentient, were agreed that under proper conditions it would be an entirely proper activity. The Dean was empowered

[19] LPL, Bell Papers, Reith to Bell, 12 Mar. 1925; Reith to Bell, 7 Jan. 1926.
[20] LPL, Bell Papers, Dean of Winchester to Bell, 6 June 1927.
[21] K. W. Pickering, *Drama in the Cathedral* (Worthing, 1985) is a general account. See also E. Martin Browne, *The Making of T. S. Eliot's Plays* (Cambridge, 1970).

to make further enquiries. It proved more difficult to find a suitable play and players than had been imagined. One particular production which he saw might have gone down well in Chelsea; it would not do in Canterbury. Bell decided that something special was required. John Masefield accepted an invitation to write a play, which turned out to be *The Coming of Christ* and which was to be performed at Whitsuntide in 1928. The fact that there were to be no charges for the seats surprised the producer, who was used to other arrangements. Masefield made no pretence to be a theologian. Was he to have a completely free hand? Could the figure of Christ actually be represented? It was a novel experience for a dean of Canterbury to be reconciling the somewhat different standpoints of archbishop, author, and producer, but he did so with great skill. In the end, all was deemed to have gone well. The Archbishop wrote to Bell that he was disappointed not to have been able to see the play but that it was a satisfaction to him that it was 'performed mainly by men and women of Canterbury. There would have been real loss had the actors, however good, been chosen from other parts of England.'[22] Gustav Holst did not feel quite the same about his music. He was so disappointed with the local talent that he insisted on bringing his own band of singers from London. Bell's verdict was that 'The whole was presented as an act of worship.' It is worth recalling that until 1913 there had been a total ban on stage plays dealing with biblical subjects, and in 1905 it had been thought shocking in some surprising quarters that Sir Henry Irving was to be buried in Westminster Abbey.

The seeds of future difficulties were already apparent, although at the time the predominant reaction—apart from that of Mr Kensit of the Protestant Truth Society who vociferously denounced such activities and detected in them the insidious hand of Rome—was that a great experiment had been bravely launched. But was this to be religious drama performed in Canterbury or by Canterbury? Holst's dissatisfaction found an echo in the comment by the Precentor in December 1928, when he reminded the Chapter that: 'we must remember that we are a county cathedral choir'. Could a festival be founded on local resources? He also drew attention to a cognate problem. Visitors in August and September swelled the congregations substantially. They expected high musical standards of the choir, but it was in those very months that the choir was weakest. Undeterred, after *The Coming of Christ*, Bell went on holiday to Salzburg—for the music festival, and to see Max Reinhardt's production of *Jedermann* (Everyman). At the end of the year he reported to his colleagues that, as a result of this experience, he had even more ambitious plans. He had been in touch with the BBC about holding a festival in the Precincts and had extracted a promise of £1,000. His colleagues approved, but thought he ought to talk to the mayor. There was a supposition that this festival would take place in August 1929. Initially it had been supposed, not least by Masefield and Holst, that the play would be put on again at Whitsun 1929, but in March the Dean announced the postponment of this idea, pleading, amongst other things, that a general election in May would rather get in the way. In the same month, however, he told his colleagues that he had accepted an invitation to become the next Bishop of Chichester. Bell had informed Sir John Reith of this and he seemed loath to continue with the provisional arrangements for the music festival. Of how many other

[22] LPL, Bell Papers, R. T. Davidson to Bell, 29 May 1928.

things initiated by Bell might a reluctance by others to continue also be true?

There were some grounds for optimism that a general interest in Canterbury Cathedral had revived. In November 1926 Bell had put a memorandum to the Chapter, floating the idea of a society which could be joined by anyone who paid a modest subscription. They might be 'Friends of Canterbury Cathedral'. Such Friends would receive an annual report informing them of work in and around the Cathedral. The income would be devoted to a special Cathedral fabric fund. At the time, no other historic cathedral had such a body, and, once again, Bell drove forward, enlisting his excellent contacts with *The Times* to contribute an article announcing the inauguration of the society. It had its own lay council, which was able to report a membership for the society of 750 at its first meeting in November 1927. Even with a subscription of only five shillings, it was able to underwrite a necessary repair to the Water Tower. Sir Anton Bertram, the initial steward, made way shortly afterwards for Miss Margaret Babington (Pls. 57, 160), daughter of a vicar of Tenterden, who was subsequently to make the life of 'the Friends' the centre of her existence. It seemed that here was a body which would, at least in part, sustain the vision of the man who was departing. There was plenty of enthusiasm, although, understandably, no one had thought through fully the consequences of establishing a lay body which controlled at least some purse-strings. The Chapter was used only to making up its own mind. It was potentially a little disturbing that others might at least have a say in policy affecting the fabric. Yet it seemed churlish to become bogged down in constitutional niceties when the magnitude of the repair work necessary became daily more evident.

In addition to the formation of the Friends, it looked as though some drama would go ahead. Voluntary collections had been taken at *The Coming of Christ*, and a sum of £800 was available for commissioning new plays. Meantime, there were to be performances in the open air or on a stage in the chapter house. Tennyson's *Becket* was an obvious choice. It was for this reason that there was slight disappointment, amidst the gratification at his acceptance, that T. S. Eliot was also going to write a play on Thomas Becket. In the event, however, *Murder in the Cathedral* was to exceed all expectations. First performed in June 1935 in the chapter house, it quickly caused a stir, even though it initially ran for only eight performances and no theatrical manager or scout was present. By the end of the year, however, it was being produced to packed houses at the small Mercury Theatre in Notting Hill Gate. Its success gave a renewed impetus both to religious drama and specifically to the Canterbury Festival.[23]

Murder in the Cathedral was performed after Bell's departure. The apotheosis of his time at Canterbury can be seen in the arrangements he masterminded for the enthronement of Cosmo Gordon Lang as Archbishop of Canterbury on 4 December 1928. Davidson's resignation was not to take effect until midnight on 12 November, being his golden wedding anniversary. Although he felt a sadness at the departure of the man whose biographer he was to become, Bell looked forward eagerly to the enthronement and relished the months he had available in which to prepare for it. He preserved among his papers a characteristically meticulous account of the entire event. He consulted widely on

[23] P. Ackroyd, *T. S. Eliot* (London, 1984), 226–8; E. Martin Browne, *Two in One* (Cambridge, 1981), 91–101.

vexed questions of procedure and precedence, not least on the delicate but historically complex issue of whether the Archdeacon or the Dean of Canterbury should actually carry out the enthronement. It seems that Bell did not conceive these matters to be trivial; but above all, in his mind, it was to be an occasion when, as it were, both the 'faith and order' and 'life and work' aspects of the burgeoning ecumenical movement should be fused. He recorded that the Chapter early decided that the congregation should be as representative as possible on all sides, both national or imperial and ecclesiastical. There were to be party leaders and vice-chancellors of universities, divinity professors of Oxford, Cambridge, and King's College, London, alongside representatives of the Trades Union Congress. 'Not the least important section', Bell wrote later, 'was the section of Artists, Musicians and Poets.' He also attached the 'greatest importance' to the representation of other Churches—the Moderators of the General Assembly of the Church of Scotland and of the United Free Church of Scotland respectively, together with the 'heads' of the Free Churches in England and, 'still more important', of the Greek Orthodox Church, the Russian Orthodox Church, the Armenian Church, the Old Catholic Church, the Church of Sweden, the German Lutherans, and the French Protestants. No invitation was extended to any representative of the Roman Catholic Church. The BBC told the Dean that it was 'their biggest effort so far'. The Southern Railway Company, at the Dean's request, arranged a special train from London. Vaughan Williams was approached to compose for the service. 'I have come to the conclusion that I can do you a "Te Deum" in time,' he replied, 'though the time is rather short'. He managed it.

A buffet luncheon for 240 was arranged at a cost of £49 including wine. The accounts of the occasion were meticulously maintained. The only doubt which the Dean appeared to entertain about any aspect of the day's complicated proceedings was whether members of the Church Lads' Brigade had joined the Scouts in lining the route within the Precincts. It was perhaps a little disappointing that the Archbishop only stayed for three-quarters of an hour at the evening reception held in his honour in the Deanery. Nevertheless, the point had undoubtedly been made. The arrangements inside the Cathedral signified that the Archbishop was the senior bishop of a world-wide Communion whose focus was Canterbury. That was to be the enduring legacy of Dean Bell.

The work of George Bell would have been hard for any man to follow. On 7 May 1929, Hugh Richard Lawrie Sheppard, CH, DD, was invited to meet Stanley Baldwin. The Prime Minister offered to put his name forward for the deanery of Canterbury—if his health was adequate. Doctors were consulted, and three days later the announcement was made. Sheppard was only 48, but he had already known much illness and suffering. He would do his best, yet 'George Bell has done practically everything; and all I must do is to try not to brick his work.' The imprint of Bell certainly confronted him on all sides. 'George has left you as a legacy', wrote Samuel Bickersteth as senior canon, 'a mass of work in which you will want all the aid we can give you ... what a success the past quinquennium has been, surely a prophecy of encouragement for you and for us.'[24]

[24] R. Ellis Roberts, *H. R. L. Sheppard: Life and Letters* (London, 1942), 194. A more convincing recent portrait is by Carolyn Scott, *Dick Sheppard: A Biography* (London, 1977).

No one who knew them both, however, could suppose that Sheppard would be a deutero-Bell: Archbishop Lang, whose lay secretary he had briefly been before his ordination, knew well the risks and possibilities which attended the appointment. Dick Sheppard's background was apparently straightforward. His father was a minor canon and subdean of the Chapel Royal. This pedigree was complemented by education at Marlborough and Trinity Hall, Cambridge. But there was nothing very conventional about his subsequent development, unless we see in his 'unconventionality' the by no means unprecedented reaction of men from such a background to the realities of life in the East End of London. He was not a scholar—the doctorate in divinity came from the University of Glasgow in recognition of his ministry—and he would not fill the Deanery with substantial tomes. The great gifts he possessed were those of a pastor and preacher. He set great store by friendship. Yet in the deepest relationship of all—marriage—there was already tension. He had eventually married in 1915, somewhat to the surprise of some of his circle of friends. He was gregarious, yet knew loneliness.

It was as vicar of St Martin-in-the-Fields from 1914 onwards that his name became increasingly well known in the Church of England and beyond. Always impulsive, he brought fresh life to a rather moribund congregation. He had a vision of a lively church serving the needs of people adrift in the capital. One visitor came to a service in June 1922 when weighed down with anxiety. It was John Reith. He came away with a renewed belief in God the Father Almighty. It is not surprising that when he came to consider religious broadcasting, he remembered H. R. L. Sheppard. The war had disclosed how remote many men in the trenches were from the assumptions of ecclesiastical Christianity. Reith wanted religion on the radio but thought he had a rather better idea of the needs of the nation than did the Church leaders he consulted. There was apprehension from all the major churches of the capital at the prospect of broadcasting ordinary services. Reith approached Sheppard—who had made his first broadcast in July 1923—and found him ready, indeed anxious, to construct a special service for broadcasting. The two men exchanged ideas, and it transpired that Reith's conception of 'BBC Christianity' accorded well with Sheppard's vision of St Martin's as the home for a diffused rather than a sectional Christianity. Eventually, on 6 January 1924, the first broadcast went out, at 8.15 p.m. There was a long queue outside the church, but it paled into insignificance beside the hundreds of thousands who would become accustomed to listening to the monthly service from St Martin's in the years that lay ahead. Sheppard wrote in the *BBC Handbook, 1929,* that 'A lack of interest in churches and church affairs may be perfectly compatible with a genuine and sincere enthusiasm for Christianity. It is here that religious broadcasting has an opportunity which probably none of us even yet recognizes.'[25] By the time these words were written, Sheppard had left St Martin's and was 'unattached'. His national stature had been recognized by his appointment as a Companion of Honour in the New Year's Honours List in 1927, but there seemed no rush to appoint the author of *The Human Parson* to another ecclesiastical position. *The Impatience of a Parson*, which he struggled against asthma to publish in 1927, displayed a dislike for the trappings of institutional religion,

[25] K. M. Wolfe, *The Churches and the British Broadcasting Corporation, 1922–1956* (London, 1984), 6, 8, and 13.

which stood in the way, Sheppard believed, of the practical living-out of the Gospel. It was not necessarily an attitude which suggested that appointment to the deanery of Canterbury was most appropriate.

After his acceptance, Sheppard himself came to wonder whether he had made a big mistake. People seemed upset that he had firmly declared his resistance to wearing gaiters. How could people be interested in what a padre wore on his legs? Canterbury itself was beautiful, but he felt that if within two years he could not do anything that seemed to him worthwhile, he would resign and go into the wilderness. As regards the services, this son of a singer thought that the services in the choir should consist of the severest plainsong, but that there should be popular services in the nave in the evening. In the event, it turned out that there was little specific planning which Dean Sheppard ever did. Illness brought on depression: depression brought on illness. Resignation presented itself as a possibility at a very early stage. He offered it in December 1929 but agreed to the suggestion that he should take a further spell of rest, in the hope that he could return to full work. 'Last week', he wrote to his colleagues, 'I crawled back to Canterbury more acutely unhappy than I have ever been before.'[26] The wishes of the Chapter gave him fresh hope. Even so, Dick knew that Canterbury needed a strong man, 'especially since George's regime'. He was not a strong man, though there remained the prospect that Continental holidays might restore him. When he took the chair at Chapter on 19 July 1930, it was for the first time in that year. He struck a blow against institutional Christianity by declaring that no meeting should last longer than two hours. As to business, he had to turn his mind to the problems posed by a Cathedral verger who introduced British Israelite beliefs while conducting tour parties. The new Dean was evidently happier meeting and talking with Cathedral workmen when they reported for duty at 6.30 a.m. It was apparent, however, that his health remained fundamentally poor, despite short periods of bright optimism and gaiety. By the end of 1930, medical opinion pronounced him totally unfit to continue. On 24 January 1931 he told his colleagues of his decision to resign as from 28 February.

It was obvious to many people, in retrospect, that even if it was right to offer him the post, Sheppard should never have accepted it. He had allowed himself to be carried away. It was, of course, true in a formal sense that he had 'failed', but one of his colleagues at Canterbury, Canon Crum, expressed the view to Sheppard's first biographer that no 'mistake' had been made. Dick Sheppard, he wrote, with perhaps a little exaggeration, was the best thing that had happened to Canterbury since the arrival of St Augustine or the Franciscans. What he was in himself stood out and refreshed the often petty world of the Precincts. Almost as if to confirm that that world could be somewhat narrow in its concerns, Chapter in May 1931 was much exercised on the subject of the address of Lady Davidson's house. It was felt objectionable that an archbishop's widow should live in accommodation merely numbered '14D'. 'Starr's House' was suggested as an alternative, but that suggested an unfortunate link with the Star Brewery. It was resolved to seek Lady Davidson's views. If Dick Sheppard had remained in Canterbury, he might well have written *The Impatience of a Dean* before many years had passed.

---

[26] Deanery Papers, Box 4, Sheppard to the Chapter, 30 Dec. 1929.

The succession was bound to be difficult. Sheppard was a national figure who became Dean. It was arguable that what the Cathedral needed above all was someone who had a record of successful administration behind him. He might, in due course, become a national figure, but it was not necessary that he should be well known at the time of his appointment. One additional factor was the existence of a Labour government. It was in these circumstances that on 30 March 1931 the Prime Minister wrote to the Dean of Manchester. 'I cannot better serve the interests of the Church', wrote Ramsay MacDonald to Hewlett Johnson, 'than by offering to you the succession to the Deanery.'[27] There are reliable suggestions that King George V had indicated his strong support, having been impressed by Johnson, who had recently preached before the royal family at Windsor. In addition, the Dean of Manchester had lost his wife a few months earlier and would benefit from a new sphere of activity.

Even before he said or did anything, Hewlett Johnson (Pl. 64) was an unusual choice. His background was both northern and industrial. Born in 1874, Hewlett Johnson was the son of a prosperous wire-worker in the Manchester region. He attended the King's School, Macclesfield, rather than one of the great southern English public schools. He read for his first degree at Owens College (later Manchester University) rather than at Oxford or Cambridge. He studied engineering rather than classical languages. That entailed a geology component, and it was the study of this subject which led him first to question the religious inheritance in which he had been brought up. By the end of the century, he had also passed his professional engineering examinations. Contemplating becoming a missionary in a posting where his engineering skills could also be useful, he was sent by the Church Missionary Society to Wycliffe Hall, Oxford, to read theology. He moved on to Wadham College and took a second-class degree. He was a little disappointed by this outcome, but it was no mean achievement to have returned to academic study in a very different area from that in which he had received his first degree. Nearly 30 and married, Hewlett returned to the area of his origins, becoming vicar of St Margaret's, Altrincham, in 1908, a few years after his ordination. The parish was busy and active but Johnson was not content with its horizons. As soon as he had left Oxford, he had decided to establish a monthly theological journal, which he called the *Interpreter*. Aware of the gaps that existed between the practical world of his early manhood and the academic world of theology, he set out to bridge them by inviting contributions from well-known scholars, and frequently contributing reviews of new books himself. The enterprise was made possible by his own private financial means—his wife also had a substantial private income—but he was increasingly being driven to the conclusion that the industrial system from which he derived that wealth was flawed. He began to move in the direction of Christian Socialism, though he did not find his congregation similarly disposed. Conrad Noel wrote in the *Interpreter* and Johnson attended the Christian Socialist conferences organized by Noel at Thaxted (where he was vicar) in the years immediately before the Great War. By the end

[27] R. Hughes, *The Red Dean* (Worthing, 1987), 55. It is argued that the initiative came from King George V. A good deal of the information in the sketch of Johnson that follows is derived from Hughes's biography and from a consultation of certain items in Johnson's papers at the University of Kent at Canterbury. See also Johnson's autobiography, *Searching for Light* (London, 1968).

of that war, he had developed a strong interest in international issues. He and his wife travelled across Germany and Austria. Even so, he continued to write, and took a doctorate in divinity at Oxford in 1924. In the same year, he became Dean of Manchester and gave up the *Interpreter*. He planned to make Manchester Cathedral a meeting-place for various groups drawn from the busy commercial life of the city. He became a favourite with the local press. His Sunday evening services were packed. There was no doubt about his socialist sympathies, though he was not active in the Labour Party as such. He kept quiet during the period of the 1926 General Strike, possibly for family as much as for political reasons. His reputation in the north of England, therefore, was substantial, but he was not a national figure. He had preached at an ordination service in Canterbury Cathedral in December 1921. It remained to be seen what more enduring impact he would make.

The Chapter made the newly widowed Dean welcome, but in private there was some apprehension. Canon Hardcastle, the Archdeacon of Canterbury, provided continuity, in company with Canon Gardiner. The new men appointed in 1928 and 1929 to succeed Robinson and Mason were Claude Jenkins and John Macleod Campbell Crum. Jenkins was Librarian at Lambeth Palace and Professor of Ecclesiastical History at King's College, London. He conformed in most significant respects to the model of an untidy and absent-minded scholar. In June 1929 the Chapter, meeting in his absence, decided that he ought to be sent a telegram reminding him of the next Chapter meeting, when it would be his turn to be vice-dean. Jenkins had a formidable range of information at his command, and it was not always confined to that which was lodged in his unlocatable books. In January 1932 he was able to inform the Chapter that the number of pigeons in the Precincts stood at fifty. It was then agreed that twenty was a more desirable figure. Expertise of this kind was to be lacking after 1934, when Jenkins became a canon of Christ Church, Oxford, on his appointment to the chair of Ecclesiastical History. Crum could be a more formidable man. An Etonian, educated at New College, Oxford, he had an original mind, not-withstanding the fact that he came to Canterbury at the age of 56, after a life spent as a parish priest. His enthusiasm for Sheppard has already been noted; whether it would also extend to Johnson was harder to say, though initially the new Dean was a frequent visitor to his home. In August 1931 the Chapter urged the Air Ministry to suggest that flyers should give the Cathedral 'a wider berth'. Crum and Gardiner, in particular, might soon feel a need to give a wide berth to some of the new Dean's flights of fancy, as they conceived them to be.

Johnson, for his part, gave clear notice that he had not come from Manchester merely to enjoy the rural charms of Kent. Formal arrangements had to be made for the fact that the new Dean would be playing himself in—in China. In his first report to his colleagues, Johnson intimated that he saw it as the task of the Cathedral to bring itself 'directly and indirectly into touch with a much wider circle even than the circle of the nation itself'. It was in this context that he defended both his attendance at a garden party given by the Soviet Embassy and his invitation to Mahatma Gandhi to come to Canterbury whilst the Indian was in London for the Round Table Conference. The latter's visit had certainly been notable. He had descended upon Canterbury in an official Rolls-Royce, which had afforded him sufficient room for his spinning-wheel. Goats were on hand to provide the requisite milk. The Dean installed his guest in a stall next to himself while evensong was sung. The canons did not find this treatment fitting, and boycotted an invitation to meet Gandhi at the Deanery subsequently.

Then there were serious floods in China, which attracted the Dean's attention. As a civil engineer, he could give some advice as well as show Christian concern. He proposed to return from China via the United States and Canada. He asked the Archbishop if he might be away from Canterbury for some four months. Lang replied that he was conscious that there was a particular need 'of giving the impression of a really resident Dean' but could not bring himself to stand in the way of the venture.

It was a novel situation for the canons. In the Dean's absence they wrestled with a particularly vexing dilemma. Two boys with catapults in a tree in Canon Gardiner's garden had broken ancient glass in a Cathedral window. It appeared that they could not be charged, because the Precincts were private property and not a street. Was there a case for a by-law? On his return from attending to the Chinese floods, Johnson had to deal with this question, and with a request from the Cyclists' Touring Club for guidance on the wearing of shorts in the Cathedral. It is perhaps not surprising that the Dean looked to a revision of the statutes which might free him from 'too sole a responsibility', as it was put. That would make it possible for the Dean to be 'better able to undertake matters of wider import connected with Church and Nation, and that becomes increasingly necessary in these days of the wide extension of the Anglican Communion'. Certainly, Johnson returned from China profoundly impressed by his experiences. He would not allow his vision of the regeneration of the world to be blotted out by narrowly ecclesiastical preoccupations.

Equally, however, he was conscious of his obligations and brought a business mind to the consideration of the Cathedral finances. It did not seem to him satisfactory that the Cathedral's income came from tithe rents, stock, and the rents from the houses round the Precincts. After the Tithe Act of 1936 the Dean and Chapter received Redemption Stock in lieu of their tithe rents. The Dean made great efforts to reinvest this in funds which would 'increase the revenue', but he was limited by the rules for 'authorized Trustee investments' and by the caution of the officers of the Ecclesiastical Commissioners, who held the stock. Socialist though he was, he preferred efficiency to what he regarded as obscurantist conservatism. There were canons who objected, for example, to the appearance of a board advertising starch on one of their city properties, though they were prepared to allow one with railway notices to remain. The revered Dr Bickersteth also objected to a planned shopping-development involving some Chapter properties, because 'it makes the Dean and Chapter enter into fierce competition in Canterbury to get some of the Motor Trade for themselves'. Yet, if they eschewed such competition, they, or their successors, were likely to face diminishing revenues.

On the other hand, there was the reality of national mass unemployment. A pilgrimage to the Cathedral to aid the unemployed was held in July 1934. It had originally been the idea of Mrs Bell, but Johnson took it up enthusiastically. The Lord Mayor of London was among the pilgrims. Lord Clydesdale arrived in his own special plane and obligingly provided Johnson with a short flight over his own Cathedral. However, the Dean commented in his report at the end of the year that 'radical reforms and much hard thinking are needed and for these a pilgrimage and the gift of half a crown are no adequate substitute'. The Dean did his own thinking, under the increasingly evident guidance of a local WEA lecturer, A. T. D'Eye, who expounded history, politics, and economics from a Marxist perspective. In his report to his colleagues in November 1935, Johnson noted that despite all the terrible drawbacks of Communism, it had apparently conquered unemployment and secured an advancing standard of life in Russia.

While the Dean reflected on Stalin's achievements, he also had to contemplate the possible unemployment of masters at the King's School. He was *ex-officio* chairman of the governors and played a leading part in the appointment of the Revd Frederick John Shirley, headmaster of Worksop College, as the new headmaster, whose task it would be to reverse the falling number of pupils and find new sources of income. Shirley had demanded a virtually free hand and set about his task with a ruthlessness that was not invariably charming.[28] Since he had also been appointed to the canonry left vacant by Claude Jenkins, Shirley's counsel was also at the disposal of the Chapter. It was apparent at an early stage that he would not be bashful in offering it. Both men were to work in close proximity for thirty years, and there were some issues on which they could agree. On the whole, however, there was a tension which was not always latent between Shirley, son of a poor Oxford carpenter, and defender of ancient institutions, and Johnson, son of a prosperous businessman, and advocate of drastic change.

It was a world of men and affairs in which the older members of the Chapter were coming to feel out of place. Canon Bickersteth resigned his stall in 1936 and died in the following year. He was not replaced, partly because of fears of 'the adverse financial position' which would result from the Tithe Act. Canon Gardiner was coming to feel unhappy with the prevailing trends. Throughout his long life he had been deeply interested in social questions and education, but the tone and temper of debate now seemed rather different from what he had experienced as a young man at Toynbee Hall in the 1880s. In July 1936 he unsuccessfully opposed the suggestion of the Archdeacons of Maidstone and Canterbury that from Christmas onwards copes with plain albs should be worn at all celebrations at the high altar. The following year, in which he was 80, he resigned his stall, to be replaced in 1938 by Frederick Brodie Macnutt, who had the misfortune to suffer a good deal of illness. On Gardiner's death, in 1941, it was observed in the Diocesan Notes that 'his robust mind avoided the snares of Utopian ideologies and impatient short cuts to the juster economic conditions for which all Christians should strive'. Archdeacon Hard-castle of Canterbury and Archdeacon Sopwith of Maidstone, on whom the weight of diocesan business fell, might have been inclined to share this disposition of their late colleague, even if they did not share his liturgical anxieties. Canon Crum's relationship with the Dean, once so close, deteriorated further.

Johnson himself appeared indifferent to snares. His public role became ever greater and his enthusiasms multiplied. Tailor-made for the Left Book Club, he longed to visit the Soviet Union but had to be content with what was described as a close friendship with Mr Maisky, the Soviet ambassador in London. It was inevitable that the civil war in Spain,

---

[28] D. L. Edwards, *F. J. Shirley: An Extraordinary Headmaster* (London, 1969), 49–55.

which had broken out in July 1936, should engage his attention. As soon as the Easter ceremonies at Canterbury were over in March 1937, Johnson went to Spain and witnessed the bombing of the Basque town of Durango. He was quite sure that the bombers were German. There was no longer any persecution of the Church in Spain. He asserted his claims fearlessly in pamphlet and pulpit on his return, earning himself a rebuke from the Archbishop of Canterbury. Unabashed, Johnson was at last able to visit the Soviet Union for three months.[29] On his return in November 1937 he reported that he was 'quite convinced that in the main they are right, and I feel also convinced that I must speak out on behalf of that right'. There was now a common front stretching from Spain to China. It was not easy to return from such illuminating experiences to debate, in the same month, the Sacrist's report. The latter wanted guidance on whether fiddle-back chasubles might be used. Such an item was commonly regarded as the badge of the Roman Catholic Church and it was also inferior to the full Gothic shape. The Cathedral Church of Canterbury, to which the whole Anglican Communion looked for guidance, could not afford to go astray in this matter. No immediate decision was reached. There appeared to be a gulf rather than a bridge between sacred and secular, between ceremony and service, opening up at Canterbury. It was perhaps a reflection of a deeper confusion on the shape and demands of holiness in British society as a whole. 'It is my impression', reported the Sacrist in November 1938, 'that the people at large shew less and less understanding of the nature of a shrine or a holy place. The Martyrdom and the Choir have been a grandiose setting for "petting parties."' Smoking and eating in the Cathedral were both becoming common.

In addition, there was now in the background the prospect of war, though it did not yet dominate everything. The Dean wondered whether the pulpit would look better if the existing heavy wooden staircase were removed and a light iron one substituted. The Chapter was divided on the matter. A few months later, however, it did agree that a new tenant, the Revd G. W. H. Lampe, then a master at the King's School, should be permitted to keep a cat in his house in the Precincts. It was in September, when the Czechoslovak crisis was at its height, that outside considerations directly obtruded on to the agenda. Canon Shirley reported that he was negotiating for a hotel in Perthshire to which the school could be evacuated in the event of war. This seemed to be a prudent step, but it was not felt necessary to set in train any protection for the Cathedral itself. In the event, of course, the crisis passed, and the Chapter could return to domestic concerns. The matter of 'special services' gave some cause for concern. Their popularity was undoubted. In 1931–2, there had been 761 such services, and that number had risen to 1,059 in 1934–5. National and civic bodies clamoured for access, despite the alleged decline in religion. The acting Precentor felt that it was imperative that the Cathedral authorities should assert their control. 'We have here,' he noted, 'surely, priceless opportunities of using our liturgical knowledge and imagination: but only so long as we are quite unfettered by the fancies of lay persons.'

In early 1939, the exercise of liturgical imagination jostled uneasily with sandbags and security. It was recognized that some 20,000 sandbags would be required in order to

[29] F. S. Northedge and A. Wells, *Britain and Soviet Communism: The Impact of a Revolution* (London, 1982), 174–5.

provide adequate protection in the crypt. In the spring, the functions of the Cathedral fire-squad were evaluated. Steps to safeguard the Precincts against IRA activity were taken, in conjunction with the Chief Constable of Canterbury. It is perhaps not surprising that, amidst general alarm, the Precentor's report on eucharistic ceremonial, requested in April, was still not available at the end of June, The Dean, meanwhile, had his own political problems. In the spring, in various publications, he had pressed strongly for co-operation with the Soviet Union, but the conclusion of the Nazi–Soviet pact in August was somewhat awkward. It was to be explained by Russia's rejection by the Western Powers. Johnson pressed on with the eulogy that was shortly to be published under the title *The Socialist Sixth of the World*. His relations with Victor Gollancz deteriorated, though publication was still guaranteed.[30]

It was in these strange circumstances in September 1939 that the Dean and Chapter again found themselves at war. In June, they had refused a request by the Fellowship of Reconciliation and the Peace Pledge Union (the latter body had been formed under the inspiration of Dick Sheppard) to rent one of their properties in Canterbury in order to mount a peace exhibition.[31] There was no doubt that the war had to be fought, but the patriotism was less strident than it had been in 1914, and no one supposed that Dean Johnson would echo the sentiments uttered by Dean Wace. Yet it was difficult to see how the small community of the Cathedral could be at peace with itself as the war unfolded in eastern Europe. Some found particularly piquant the service held on 31 December 1939, with the Dean officiating, at which the Archbishop said prayers for Finland—recently invaded by the Soviet Union. This deep tension was to some extent kept in check by the exigencies of the hour. It was likely that the King's School would be evacuated to Cornwall. There was the task of removing the priceless panes of stained glass and the 'achievements' of the Black Prince. The decision was also taken to leave the gates into the Precincts open for the duration of the war—though this decision was reversed in February 1940, after Canon Shirley complained of the number of school bicycles that were being stolen. Although the war itself still seemed far away, there was much goodwill in putting in train these arrangements. That goodwill did not extend to the issue of the protection of the Cathedral itself.

The Dean had received advice that the crypt might best be protected by a cushion of earth, 3 feet deep, laid on timbers. It would spread over the choir and the north and south ambulatories. When this work commenced, a storm of protest arose concerning the alleged 'desecration' which was being perpetrated. Strong statements were made at a special meeting of the Friends. Letters reached *The Times*. One, on 22 September, written from the Athenaeum, stated that 'To deny to worshippers the inspiration and consolation of the most important part of Canterbury Cathedral for the duration of the war in order that the crypt may be an A.R.P. shelter is deplorable.' It was a profanation of the church and a denial of its purpose. Such was the controversy that on 11 October the Dean and Chapter felt compelled to publish a statement, which was reprinted in *The Times*. Although the original plan was modified, the tone of the statement was unrepentant. Even while

---

[30] Ruth Dudley Edwards, *Victor Gollancz: A Biography* (London, 1987), 273–4, 291–2.

[31] M. Ceadel, *Pacifism in Britain, 1914–1945: The Defining of a Faith* (Oxford, 1980), 173–284.

the work was in progress, daily public worship and musical services had been fully maintained. It was right that a church should be a place of refuge. Should damage from the air be inflicted upon refugees as a result of undoing what had been done, the Dean and Chapter would never be able to forgive themselves. Nevertheless, they were all mindful of the fact that 'their Cathedral is still *first* the House of God'.[32] However, it was still to take some time for this dispute to be resolved, since it had stirred powerful emotions. It was clear that there were worthy men on all sides, who put varying stresses upon the importance of fabric and people, and of social function and liturgical continuity.

Scarcely had this issue been settled, however, when fresh controversy arose which threatened the position of the Dean himself. The notoriety brought by *The Socialist Sixth of the World* produced consternation amongst the canons. They were displeased that the Cathedral was identified in the public mind with Communism. In the past, it had still been possible to maintain social contacts—we have an account of the Dean leading off in 'Sir Roger de Coverley' at a Christmas party in the Deanery for dwellers in the Precincts—but goodwill was rapidly disappearing.[33] Johnson's marriage to Nowell Edwards in the autumn of 1938 occasioned a certain amount of gossip, since she had previously been introduced as his niece—she was, in fact, the daughter of his cousin. A first child for the Dean and his wife was expected in the early months of 1940.

The Archbishop, who had been made aware of the crisis, warned Johnson that the canons were contemplating taking their unhappiness to the press. Lang was not pleased with the 'ceaseless propaganda' on behalf of Russia, but he also expressed the view, in a letter to Johnson, that the Chapter was suffering from a strange disease which he was accustomed to call 'the Cathedral blight'. He urged Johnson to desist and he would also make sure that the canons did not go to the press. The Dean was not to be restrained and claimed to derive an authority to speak from his appointment by Ramsay MacDonald. Lang did not endorse this claim. On 12 March the Dean was informed by Canon Macnutt, the Vice-Dean, that a letter, signed by the whole Chapter, would appear in *The Times* on the following day. The canons dissociated themselves from the political utterances of the Dean, which so often gave the impression that he condoned the offences of Russia against humanity and religion. His political activities gravely impaired the spiritual influence of the Cathedral in the city and diocese of Canterbury and grievously offended many Christians throughout the world. It was a Christian duty to further social and economic reform, but not by the methods which characterized the Soviet regime. Subsequent correspondents in the press took sides in a predictable fashion. Johnson himself replied in a letter to *The Times* which the canons did not find persuasive. They were already boycotting his sermons, and Canon Crum solemnly declared that he would no longer receive Communion at the hands of the Dean. On top of this crisis came another, local, one involving the role and conduct of Mr Barker, the Chapter Agent. The case concerned the non-payment of rent by a poor tenant who lived within the ville of Christ Church. The Agent was taking her to court in the name of the Dean and Chapter. The Dean had pocketed a crucial letter in April 1940 and departed for a short holiday at his house in North Wales. Canon Shirley

---

[32] 'A Statement by the Dean and Chapter', *The Times*, 11 Oct. 1939.

[33] Archdeacon Hardcastle, *Memoirs of a Mediocrity* (Canterbury, 1941).

was inclined to see deliberate suppression of evidence in this action, but the Dean put it down to forgetfulness, for which he apologized. The canons insisted on the withdrawal of the summons. The Agent felt obliged to offer his resignation, and only the Dean voted against its acceptance. The new Agent, Reginald Tophill, was the man who had drawn the attention of the Chapter to the letter.

It took the imminent threat of invasion, after the fall of France, to achieve even a modest improvement in personal relationships. It was agreed in June 1940 that Bell Harry could be used to rally the Local Defence Volunteers in an emergency. The station commander at RAF Manston warned that it would be a matter of luck, over the next few months, whether or not the Cathedral suffered damage. In July it was felt prudent to cancel the Franco-British service of unity which had been arranged for the following month. The Chapter then turned their attention to the maintenance of worship in the new circumstances. It felt unable to accede to a request for an intercession service, or hymn-singing led by choristers, during an air raid, but the Dean suggested that good music might be played on a gramophone. However, at the next meeting he reported that he had tried his gramophone in the crypt and had been disappointed with the result. It was decided not to proceed with the suggestion. Archbishop Chichele's tomb was sandbagged. In September and October came the sad proof that the fears which had been expressed were not alarmist: Chillenden's Chambers were hit. However, it was in 1942 that the most severe damage was sustained, when Nos. 12, 13, 14, and 22 The Precincts were badly hit, along with the Deanery and various classrooms. There were at this time few visitors to the Cathedral, though it was a matter of satisfaction that a small body of day-boys was maintaining the daily services. Divided within, and assailed from the skies, the Cathedral community improvised as best it could for the rest of the war. Canon Crum, whose house was in ruins, resigned from the end of 1943, and his stall was not filled. The Dean's political position improved after the German invasion of the Soviet Union, in June 1941. It became politically expedient thereafter to be enthusiastic about Russia. It was evident that it was not only the Dean who enthused at the prospect of holding a 'Russian week' in Canterbury. The appointment of William Temple to succeed Lang in 1942 also appeared to confirm a tendency to the left. It was, of course, a homecoming for the new Archbishop, as it was also for General Bernard Montgomery, who was asked by the Chapter for his advice on the subject of a military guard of honour at the enthronement. Montgomery was the grandson of Dean Farrar. Canterbury suddenly found itself with strong links with two of the best-known men in England.

At a less exalted level, there were many local problems for the canons to worry about. The danger of fire was always apparent. Two trained men were on the roof every night. An action station of the fire brigade was established in No. 14. Was it necessary to have a tank holding 10,000 gallons of water at belfry-floor level? There was the additional responsibility which followed from the decision to accommodate the cricket records of the MCC in the crypt. In all these matters, city and Cathedral were brought together in the intimacy of emergency. In October 1942, for example, it was agreed to accede to a request from the Mayor of Canterbury that some 250 members of the Civil Defence might attend matins. The Chapter expressed the wish that popular music be played on this occasion. Other relatively novel problems required attention in these tense years. A few months earlier, Chapter had doubted whether the present was quite the time for an idea Basil Dean put to them. He had suggested that an anthology in praise of the British way of life, apparently to be not unlike the Greek tragedies in form, should be held in front of cathedrals up and down the land, beginning with Canterbury. They also declined to allow the Cathedral to be used for a commercial film, *The Canterbury Tale*, though filming was allowed in the Precincts under specified conditions. On the other hand, it was agreed that a film of *Murder in the Cathedral* might be made. The Chapter were to find, however, that film-making was not a straightforward business. After the war, a request from J. Arthur Rank that the Cathedral might be used as a photographic background for the presentation of film stars could not be entertained.

The experience of adversity brought the Christians of Canterbury a little closer to each other. In the spring of 1944 a Congregational minister wrote asking whether a ministers' fraternal might meet in the Huguenot Chapel—'as we are English we should be in place there'. Archbishop Temple approved of this interesting and attractive idea. A few months later it was agreed that the Archdeacon should attend the first meeting of a proposed Council of Christian Congregations in Canterbury. A new atmosphere was emerging, with Temple's encouragement, although he was not to live to see its further development.

In this, and other respects, prominent figures were looking to the future, since victory was in sight. The Dean received a personal copy from Field Marshal Montgomery—'You may like to have this'—of his Christmas message to the troops in Belgium in 1944.[34] Then there was the enthronement of Archbishop Fisher. His elevation appeared to suggest that sound and solid Anglican Christianity could continue, despite the upheavals of war, though Fisher specifically wrote to the Dean: 'You at Canterbury will know as we all do that there cannot be anyone to hold a candle to William Temple: all I can say for myself is that I was always his disciple, always an inadequate one—never more than now, but still his disciple.'[35] For his part, the Dean let it be known that he intended to be in the Soviet Union for two months from the end of April 1945. Which way forward for Canterbury and England? Whatever might be the answer to that question (and the constituency of Canterbury did not go with the tide and return a Labour MP in 1945), there were urgent and taxing questions of fabric and finance to attend to. Of course, Canterbury was not alone among cathedrals in suffering damage, and there was some feeling initially among English deans that a collective appeal for funds should be launched. It was inevitable that the United States would be the major target. However, it was then agreed that Coventry and Canterbury were in a unique position and should be allowed to make independent appeals. It was reported at the end of 1945 that great crowds had been visiting the Cathedral after VE day. The Cathedral clearly was still the place in which thousands of people could offer prayers of thanksgiving. It would now be necessary for thousands of people to dip into their pockets. A target of £300,000 was fixed in April 1946 and there was encouragement from the fact that the King and Queen agreed to visit the Cathedral. Early in 1947 there

---

[34] Deanery Papers, Box 8, Bernard Law Montgomery to Hewlett Johnson, 17 Dec. 1944.

[35] Deanery Papers, Box 6, Fisher to Johnson, 3 Jan. 1945. See

W. Purcell, *Fisher of Lambeth: A Portrait for Life* (London, 1969), 141–3, for a rather less friendly subsequent exchange of views.

was relief at the news that Thomas Lamont of New York was going to make a gift of £124,000. Thereafter, the appeal made only slow progress at a time of national austerity. By January 1948, for example, it had reached a total of £224,000. The emphasis in the appeal was on Canterbury as the focal point of the world-wide Anglican Communion. Renewed efforts were made in Canada. The Archdeacon of Maidstone set off for Australia. It was the Archbishop of Brisbane who made the suggestion that 'each National church' should undertake to renovate a chapel or chantry of the Cathedral. By April 1949, a further £40,000 had been received. It was enough to attend to necessary substantial repairs and renovations. There was a sense in which the Cathedral was the beneficiary of the wartime collaboration of the English-speaking world. That world came again to Canterbury on the occasion of the 1948 Lambeth Conference. The Bishop of Grahamstown, South Africa, was probably not alone in privately remarking, on his return to the Cathedral, that the magic had gone out of it.

It is not surprising that it was to take years before it could return. Alexander Sargent became Archdeacon of Canterbury in 1942. He recorded this impression of the scene at the end of the war:

the Precincts became shabbier and shabbier. There were barrage balloons in the Green Court and the Oaks; a large round static water tank stood outside the entrance to Chillenden's Chambers; the School Dining Hall was no more than a shell; the Library was in ruins; the sites of Nos. 13 and 14 a wilderness; empty houses steadily deteriorating; broken windows in abundance. We did not lose heart, but it was depressing.[36]

Sargent's robust spirit and sound common sense were to carry him through many difficult problems in the era of reconstruction, and beyond. He was to serve as archdeacon for a quarter of a century. He had been Archdeacon of Maidstone for three years and was succeeded in that position by Julian Bickersteth, who had been a headmaster, in both Australia and England. Canterbury was in his bones, too—his father was Samuel Bickersteth—and he had responded to Temple's invitation to use both his educational and Commonwealth contacts in the service of the Cathedral. Selected clergy were briefed to act as honorary chaplains during the summer months, with the intention that they should show visitors both from home and from overseas that the Cathedral was primarily the house of God, and not only a national monument of historic interest. For his part, Canon Shirley was initially preoccupied with re-establishing the school, though he was rarely reluctant to offer more general advice. In December 1948 he suggested that an appropriate topic for a lecture at the next meeting of the Greater Chapter would be 'Academic and Clerical Dress'! Canon Macnutt resigned his canonry in 1945 and it was filled two years later by Aubrey Standen. These men guided the Cathedral for more than fifteen years after the end of the war.

Continuity with the pre-war world was maintained by the Dean. He seemed as vigorous and controversial as ever. His appetite for travel remained undiminished, and he did not notice the apparent erection of an Iron Curtain at the heart of Europe. His comments on the world were constantly contentious. They did not please Archbishop Fisher, who was

---

[36] 'Reminiscences' by Canon Alexander Sargent; deposited in Canterbury Cathedral library.

at pains to distance himself from them. From time to time their impatience with each other flared into irate correspondence. As the Cold War became colder, there were inevitably suggestions that the Dean ought to restrain himself or retire. Johnson was not persuaded, and immersed himself even more heavily in the World Peace Conferences for which he was to be awarded a Stalin Prize. His colleagues were not impressed, and seemed to show their displeasure by absenting themselves from the second evensong on Sunday, which the Dean conducted. The activities of the Dean were regularly recorded in the press, without approval. To his admirers, he was a man who was courageously keeping open bridges in a bitterly divided world; to his detractors he was ludicrously simple-minded in his assessment of political situations. The year 1956 was a particularly awkward one. It was perhaps unfortunate that, apparently in ignorance of the Archbishop's presence, the Dean should have brought into the Cathedral during mid-afternoon evensong on Easter Day the Soviet Ambassador and the former Soviet Premier George Malenkov. It was an acceptance of infidelity and approval of persecution to bring such men into church at such a moment. Johnson claimed that he had not intended any discourtesy and was quite unrepentant. Non-believers should always be welcome, and what better day could there have been than Easter Day? But this episode was only a mild skirmish compared with the Suez Crisis and the Hungarian revolution later in the year. The Dean felt himself morally unable to condone either event, but politically he found he could make certain distinctions. Moscow was invited into Hungary by the Hungarian government; the Egyptian government had issued no such invitation to Britain. The British intervention was an attempt to put the clock back to colonialism. The Soviet Union's intervention was an attempt to prevent it being put back to fascism. These views were not acceptable in the Precincts, particularly as far as Hungary was concerned. In Canterbury the Dean retreated even more into the Deanery, though he kept up a voluminous correspondence which left the outside world in no doubt that he was still alive and active. Every controversial international issue received his earnest attention.

Meanwhile, the city and Cathedral community of Canterbury recovered from the experience of war. Heavy damage had been sustained from 445 high-explosive bombs and 10,000 incendiaries. Some 800 houses and other buildings were destroyed, 1,000 seriously damaged, and 5,000 slightly damaged. There had been 2,477 alerts and 115 casualties. By the early 1950s, however, the town was nearly back on its feet. The 1951 census recorded a population of 27,795, nearly two and a half thousand more than it had been in 1931 (a figure, in turn, which was slightly less than it had been in 1911). Inevitably, the redevelopment plans had occasioned controversy into which, from time to time, the Dean and Chapter were drawn. A special Chapter meeting in December 1949 decided to go ahead with building shops and flats between 16 and 23 Burgate Street. The income from these properties was likely to prove significant. Such financial considerations were important because, despite their own reduced number, the Dean and Chapter faced difficulties in dealing with everyday running-costs. It was also becoming clear that in post-war Britain, the Chapter, as employers, might not be able to employ reliable, committed, and deferential labour. In April 1948, the vergers were summoned to hear complaints about their behaviour. They were warned that 'drastic action' might follow if further complaints were received. In

March 1951, a revision of their duties was agreed. The Treasurer reported an overdraft of £27,000 in September 1950, and the Chapter accepted the need to sell appropriate investments to cover this deficiency. The lay clerks were also stressing that they needed to have sufficient time to give to other employment. A drastic reduction in the singing of matins was agreed. It was, apparently, 'almost entirely a question of economic facts', though much to be regretted. In February 1949 the Sacrist was instructed to be more economical in the use of lighting within the Cathedral, since the bills were going up alarmingly. An 'economy subcommittee' reported in January 1951 that there had to be a reduction in costs or an increase in income, or some combination of both. Some £6,000 per annum was required.

There were other problems. It had perhaps been foolhardy to restart the Canterbury Festivals soon after the end of the war, but the Friends, under the guidance of their steward, Miss Margaret Babington, had been determined. Laurie Lee's *Peasants' Priest* (1947) and Christopher Fry's *Thor, with Angels* (1948) were not failures, but somehow the genre seemed to be losing its way. It was also hard to re-establish the sense that the Festival was an important occasion. It was difficult in these circumstances to know how to proceed without upsetting feelings. In January 1949 the Dean and Chapter decided that they would assume the responsibility for the planning, conduct, and financing of the festivals. They said they would take outside advice, but in April they had to tell the Council of the Friends that they did not intend to put before them the names of those they proposed to invite. The question of responsibility rumbled on awkwardly for some time, especially since the immediately subsequent festivals were not financially successful. In 1953 the Chapter were asking themselves whether stock could be sold to meet the deficit on the Cathedral Festivals. The cost of maintaining them seemed increasingly prohibitive. The fact of the matter was that there were now bigger and better festivals elsewhere, and Canterbury seemed to have lost whatever cultural cachet it had possessed before the war. Miss Babington did not see matters in this light. She died in 1958, after a lifetime of devoted service to the Friends and to the Cathedral, and her death was indeed the passing of an era. Sadly, after an energetic start, her successor, Mrs Thoseby, was stricken with cancer, and the consequential loss of organizational skill led to a number of disasters in the early 1960s. The tradition could not continue.

To some extent, the tribulations of the Festival reflected the arrival of the television age. The Dean and Chapter were themselves hesitant about the all-intrusive camera. In March 1952, BBC Television wrote to say that they wished to bring outside-broadcast units to the Cathedral for the purpose of telling a little of its history. Chapter, in turn, wanted to know precisely what the programme was going to be. The BBC was not sure that it could say precisely. Chapter agreed in principle but wanted to able to approve all the words that were spoken. The BBC did not like this demand. In October the BBC stated that if the Dean and Chapter insisted that the Precentor should introduce the proposed programme, it would be dropped. The Dean and Chapter did so insist, and the programme was dropped. These were, of course, teething troubles. It was inconceivable that television would not one day invade the Precincts, and indeed, by the end of the 1950s, the camera had conquered. In May 1961 the BBC agreed to pay an all-in fee of £750 in order to carry the forthcoming enthronement of Arthur Michael Ramsey as Archbishop of Canterbury. For their part, the Dean and Chapter were pleased that the event would reach that ever-increasing proportion of the national population which possessed a television set.

Even so, there still lurked in the background the issue of control. Television could not be allowed to direct what went on in the Cathedral, yet it also offered the possibility that the Cathedral might make an impact on the nation in a quite novel fashion. It was a matter of balance. In other respects, too, it seemed that the Cathedral was being confronted by the need to make some kind of choice between peace and publicity. By the end of the 1950s, the 'age of austerity' had been left behind, to be replaced by an 'age of affluence'. Two small entries in the Chapter Acts for 1959 can be taken as symbolic. It was noted that car-parking in the Precincts was getting out of hand. There seemed no obvious solution. People seemed to want to take their cars with them wherever they went. It also appeared to be the case that some persons wished to take noise with them wherever they went. In October, Chapter minuted that portable wirelesses would be banned within the Precincts. On the other hand, after correspondence with the Town Clerk, it was agreed to install permanent floodlighting around the Cathedral, and permission was given for it to be switched on during August and at Christmas. Fundamentally, there was a problem of people. Canterbury was an almost inevitable port of call for visitors from the Continent. The town of Canterbury needed tourists and encouraged them to come. Figures of the precise number of visitors to the Cathedral during the 1950s are not available, but it is generally agreed that the total began to mount during the 1960s in what some regarded as an alarming manner. It was argued that the Cathedral was becoming an outpost of the English Tourist Board rather than a house of prayer and worship.

There was a feeling, indeed there had long been a feeling, that these matters might be more effectively addressed under the leadership of a new dean. It was perhaps not a good thing that there were undoubtedly some visitors who specifically came to catch a glimpse of Hewlett Johnson, now well into his eighties. His relations with his colleagues remained variable, but he seemed obdurate in his determination to stay on. Eventually, after another internal disagreement, he gave notice to Archbishop Ramsey at the end of 1962 that he would vacate his office in the following April. He was to stay in Canterbury, though not in the Precincts. He was 88. Conflict never entirely ceased, but at the moment of retirement there was a general attempt to distinguish between the man himself and his opinions. Some members of his family seem to have supposed that hostility towards him was such that there would be no invitation to hold his funeral service in the Cathedral. In fact, however, when he died, in 1966, the service was held there and he was buried in the Cloister Garth. It was a recognition that the heart of this perpetually peripatetic old man did, after all, rest in Canterbury. Amongst those present at the service were the Archbishop of Canterbury, the Mayor of Canterbury, and the First Secretary from the Soviet Embassy in London. His legacy was ambiguous to the last.

Johnson's successor was Ian Hugh White-Thomson. It was evident that he would not be likely to emulate his predecessor in seeking a major national and international role. His roots were in Canterbury itself, where his father had been archdeacon before going on to become Bishop of Ely. Educated at Harrow and Oxford, White-Thomson had considerable pastoral experience in various Kent parishes. Latterly, however, he had been serving in the Newcastle diocese as Archdeacon of Northumberland. He had been a chaplain to the Queen since 1952 and he liked golf and walking. Hewlett Johnson, aided by servants, had been supremely indifferent to aspects of household management—though he must be given credit for the installation of a new central-heating system, which served both the Cathedral and several residences in the Precincts. One of White-Thomson's first acts was to let it be known that he wanted a tumble-drier in the Deanery.

Sargent continued to bring the weight of his long experience to aid the new Dean, but his career was coming to an end. Gordon Strutt, who had been Archdeacon of Maidstone since 1959, when he succeeded Julian Bickersteth, took a major share in installing the new Dean and quickly struck up a good relationship with him, but within two years he departed north to become Bishop of Stockport. He was in turn succeeded by Michael Nott, who had substantial pastoral experience in the south of England and had also been a Senior Chaplain to the Archbishop. It was Nott who succeeded Sargent in 1967. He was in turn followed as Archdeacon of Maidstone by Thomas Estlin Prichard. Another change was made necessary by the death of Canon Standen, in 1962. He had thrown himself into many local activities throughout east Kent and, in particular, had carried most of the responsibility for maintaining a good relationship between the Chapter and the Friends. His successor was Herbert Waddams, who brought to Canterbury a wealth of international contacts and experience, having been one of the major architects of the Church of England Council on Foreign Relations, founded in 1932. He had recently been working in a parish in Ontario. He could be expected to supply, though in a different fashion, the international dimension which the former Dean had so revelled in. Also in 1962, Canon Shirley retired as headmaster of the King's School, at the age of 72. He was, however, still vigorous and now had more time to give to the affairs of the Chapter. Waddams, a much younger man, was one of those who did not altogether welcome this additional assistance, though it was still being proferred right up to the end of Shirley's life, which came in 1967. The passing of Shirley and Johnson within a year of each other inevitably provoked comment in the press that this was the end of an era at Canterbury. The two men shared a strong belief in the rightness of their opinions; it had been unfortunate that these opinions rarely coincided.

Many strange and sometimes exciting things happened in the 1960s. The son of the late Canon Arthur Robinson published *Honest to God* at the SCM Press, whose editor was the Revd David Edwards, a former pupil at the King's School. There was a general disposition to question existing conventions and institutions. Waddams did turn his mind to issues in moral theology, but the Canterbury team described above was not likely to be in the van of change. Working in Canterbury may have led to the feeling that the foundations of the Church of England were firmer than perhaps they were. Even so, change was happening in Canterbury itself. The city's population continued to grow, topping 30,000 in the 1961 census. It is in September 1959 that there is the first mention in the Chapter Acts of a possible 'University of Thanet'. The Chapter agreed that the obvious place for it was Canterbury. Looking ahead, perhaps the new vice-chancellor might like to live in the

Precincts? Canon Standen was deputed to represent the Chapter in preliminary discussions. It began to emerge, however, that although the Dean and Chapter might be able to be helpful, a new university would go its own way. The vice-chancellor would not want to live in the Precincts.

By the 1960s, the Dean and Chapter also had to come to terms with the developing ecumenical movement and decide what role Canterbury ought to play. Since the end of the war, there had been occasional visits by churchmen drawn from various denominations. In June 1945, through the good offices of the Dean, there had been a visit from a party of Russian Orthodox priests. Archbishop Damaskinos of Greece had also been received in the same year. There was, however, nothing sustained or systematic in these contacts. In the 1950s, there were occasional invitations to well-known Protestant leaders, such as Dr George McLeod when he was Moderator of the Church of Scotland, or the missionary-theologian Hendrik Kraemer, but they were gestures to prominent individuals rather than expressions of an ongoing concern for unity. The visit of the Swedish Lutheran Archbishop of Uppsala in July 1959 was, however, an indication that the link with Scandinavian Prot-estantism, which had been fostered by several canons earlier in the century, was still alive. The difficulty was to decide what to do next. A few months earlier, for example, the Chapter had refused permission to the Fellowship of St Alban and St Sergius to hold a celebration of the Orthodox liturgy in the Cathedral.

Around this time, however, a certain change of direction corresponded with the fact that in the late 1950s and early 1960s the British public was somewhat reluctantly turning its mind to the question of Europe. As early as 1954 it was reported in the Chapter Acts that attendance of youth at what was still Empire Youth Sunday had been poor. In the town, proposals had been under discussion for some time to link Canterbury with Rheims. Twinning was finally agreed, and the ceremony was to take place in Rheims in April 1959. Could the Cathedral organist give a recital there? It was agreed that he could. Perhaps the Chapter ought to do more to extend the scanty links with French Roman Catholics? As far as Roman Catholics themselves were concerned, possibilities were to be dramatically changed as a result of the Second Vatican Council, which began its work in 1962. That year also happened to be the tercentenary of the Great Ejection, and in 1960 Kent Con-gregationalists, Baptists, and Presbyterians had expressed their wish to come to the Cathedral and hold a united service there, as a token of their desire to improve relations between all Christian people.

It remained to be seen what might become of these possibilities. There were, however, certain problems within the Church of England which made it difficult to formulate a proper ecumenical stance at Canterbury. Since the end of the war, there had been an increasing disposition on the part of archbishops to travel—it was almost the only aspect of Archbishop Fisher's performance of his office which met with Dean Johnson's approval. It was Fisher who first travelled to Rome to visit the Pope, in December 1960. Air travel made such visits abroad increasingly feasible. The Archbishop of Canterbury was not a pope, but none the less was it not incumbent upon him to seek personally to strengthen the ties of the world-wide Anglican Communion? Of course, the Archbishop still had his responsibilities in the State. Archbishop Ramsey felt a need to engage himself seriously with the theological ferment he found round about him. Could any one man do all these things? It might be possible if the diocese of Canterbury was only very low among his priorities. Canterbury itself might not like that very much. As far back as 1949, the Dean had written to the Archbishop expressing the desire of the Chapter that more episcopal consecrations should take place in what was the metropolitical church. Fisher replied that he would do his best in this matter, but there were difficulties in getting down from London. It was fortunate for Canterbury that Archbishop Ramsey very evidently loved the atmosphere of the city and Cathedral. It was only to be expected that he should take Canterbury into his title when he accepted a life peerage on his retirement in 1974.

Donald Coggan, his successor, was a man of very different temperament, but Canterbury became very important for him too. The Lambeth Conference in 1978 over which he presided was, for the first time, in effect the 'Canterbury' Conference, in that it met residentially at the University of Kent at Canterbury. Coggan's international role remained extensive and he addressed a 'Call to the Nation', which did not quite have the resonance for which he had hoped. Despite the many national and international calls upon his time, it appears that Canterbury itself exercised an attraction which waxed rather than waned during his time in office. We should note that the concept of a Cathedral history was originally his—York had led the way in this respect during his time in the northern province.

The feelings towards Canterbury of Fisher, Ramsey, and Coggan were important, but the administrative problems of their office with regard to the diocese were structural rather than personal. Since 1934 the successive suffragan bishops of Dover had not held offices attached to the Cathedral. Nevertheless, there were many diocesan services and occasions which the Archbishop could not attend and at which he asked a suffragan bishop to represent him. The precedence to be accorded to such a person in these circumstances proved controversial. There was a furious exchange of letters between Dean and Archbishop on this matter in the spring of 1951. It broke out in protracted form in the following year. The Chapter implored the Archbishop to respect their convictions and not to press his wishes, with all their constitutional implications, any further. The issue in itself might appear from the outside to be farcical, but it symbolized a deeper unease about the relationship between Archbishops and the Dean and Chapter concerning the Cathedral and the diocese of Canterbury. It was not until 1980 that the new Bishop of Dover was formally recognized to have special duties over the whole diocese and to be, in effect, the archbishop's deputy. Even so, it would be rash to assume that the diocesan role of the Archbishop of Canterbury has been finally defined.

Perhaps the Dean and Chapter in the 1950s were especially sensitive in their dealings with Archbishop Fisher because there were developments in other quarters which might also have a bearing on their constitutional rights and functions. A cathedral was a cathedral, but it also had a congregation. That congregation swelled and contracted in size. At certain times of the year the great bulk of those present at services were tourists or pilgrims, but there was, in addition, a regular assembly of the local faithful. Of course, over the decades there had been various informal ways of establishing contacts between the Chapter and worshippers in the Cathedral. Some were beginning to wonder, however, whether there ought not to be some more formal representation of the laity within the organizational structure of the Cathedral. It appears that the Chapter were not impressed by such ideas. A letter was received in July 1954 advising that the Cathedral should have an electoral roll. That suggestion was not appealing. It was decided to take no action. There was also a distinct lack of enthusiasm about any further developments which might subvert the authority of the Chapter. It was bad enough, in some eyes, that as a result of the Cathedrals Measure of 1963 the Church Commissioners, as from 1 August 1963, would be paying the stipend of the Dean and the two residentiary canons engaged exclusively on Cathedral duties.[37] The Chapter agreed to make themselves responsible for the salaries of the Arch-deacon of Maidstone and the Archdeacon of Canterbury. Three years later, the Chapter felt unable to fill in a questionnaire from the Cathedrals Advisory Committee concerning the possibility of state aid for the Cathedral's fabric and fittings. They disliked anything which appeared to threaten the legal autonomy of Chapters, and they did not approve of any approach to the State for cathedrals as a special category requiring assistance.

It is against this international, national, and local background that we must look at the actual pattern of events in Canterbury. On the one hand, in May 1964 the Oecumenical Patriarch of Constantinople visited Canterbury, and on the other, it was agreed that a service should be held in the Cathedral in 1965 to mark the centenary of the foundation of the Salvation Army. A visit from the Patriarch of Rumania in the summer of 1966 maintained the flow of Eastern Orthodox contacts. It was Canon Waddams, however, who particularly wished to re-establish connections with the great French abbeys to which Canterbury had owed so much in the pre-Reformation era. In May 1966 the Chapter agreed to set aside £100 for the promotion of such contacts. A few months earlier, it had been agreed that a Canterbury Cross be carved in stone and sent to the Abbey of Bec, where it was put up in the new church. In the autumn, Waddams had a preliminary discussion with the Dean on the appropriate way to celebrate the eighth centenary of the death of Thomas Becket, which would fall in 1970. The commemoration should have a theme, and Waddams suggested 'Canterbury Cathedral—Centre of Unity'. In 1964–5 he had been struggling, not very successfully, to turn the Friends of the Cathedral into an organization which would have the official support of the Anglican executive officer and of the heads of the Anglican Churches throughout the world. It would constitute a means of strengthening a world-wide fellowship of prayer centred on the Cathedral. He also had ambitious publication plans. On the whole, however, the Friends did not take kindly to their proposed transformation. In October 1966 Waddams felt obliged to offer to resign as the body's vice-chairman, but the offer was not accepted.

It was in these circumstances that the preparation of the Becket celebration began to take priority. It was hoped that the Queen might be able to attend. It was also reported that the town authorities did not want that crepuscular entertainment, briefly popular about this time, known as *son et lumière*, but an outdoor play. The preparations steadily went forward and, as the date drew near, the inter-church aspects of the celebration became more delicate. Could a Roman Catholic mass be celebrated inside the Cathedral? In June 1969 an Anglican curate who was organizing an Anglo-French ecumenical pilgrimage to

---

[37] P. A. Welsby, *A History of the Church of England, 1945–1980* (Oxford, 1984), 162.

Canterbury wanted to celebrate at a concluding Eucharist, and asked that a French Roman Catholic priest might use a nearby altar for a simultaneous Roman mass. Permission was refused. In October it was reported that a resolution had been received from a Sussex parish regretting that apparently an archbishop of the Roman Catholic Church had been asked to celebrate mass in the Precincts. In January, a request from a local Roman Catholic priest that there should be a Roman Catholic mass in the Precincts was not approved. However, it was subsequently agreed that one could be held on 7 July. The diocesan Eucharist would be held on the Cricket Ground—because of the larger numbers expected. There was no doubt in Chapter that ardent Protestants would be hostile to the granting of permission, but it was resolved not to receive delegations wishing to discuss the decision. It was also agreed to welcome a party of monks and nuns from Bec who would join in singing evensong on 18 July. In the end, the Becket celebrations organized by Anglicans and Roman Catholics went off with great cordiality. The Archbishop of Canterbury wrote to the Dean expressing his satisfaction that the Roman Catholic mass had been successfully held. In 1975 the Dean attended mass in St Thomas's Roman Catholic Church in Canterbury, as part of the centenary celebrations of the building's erection. Meanwhile, in January 1973 the chairman of the Methodist South-East District had asked whether the members of the District Synod meeting in Canterbury might come to an Anglican communion service. It was only by majority decision that they were invited. In 1977 it was agreed that both Free Church ministers and Roman Catholic priests might be approached to see if they would assist the Honorary Chaplains in the Cathedral. In 1977, an invitation was also extended to the Cardinal Archbishop of Westminster to be present at a service to mark the dedication of Lanfranc's Cathedral in 1077—though it was in fact 1978 before he was able to attend. In the same month it was agreed that the French Protestant Pastor might robe and take part in the Cathedral procession at festivals and on special occasions—if he so desired. In February 1978 it was agreed that the Roman Catholic parish of St Thomas might hold two masses in the Cathedral each year, and that large pilgrimages might hold masses in the Eastern Crypt. However, individual Roman Catholics were not to be given permission to celebrate. The Roman Catholic Archbishop of Southwark agreed to preach during the Octave for Christian Unity in January 1979. Tentatively and hesitantly, therefore, all Christian traditions began to feel that they had a place in this House of God.

Important though these ecumenical developments were, it would be wrong to suppose that they dominated the business of the Chapter. There were always items of business, great or small, which sapped the energy of those concerned. A vision of the future was always held in check by knotty issues inherited from the past. One such was the future of the Choir School, which rumbled on, not very pleasantly, through the late 1960s and into the early 1970s. It involved some resignations and a good deal of recrimination. In January 1971 the Chapter agreed to appoint an 'educational consultant' to consider the efficiency of the school. By the end of the year, a complex arrangement was worked out for an association with St Edmund's School (in Canterbury). The plan had the unanimous support of the Dean and Chapter, but there were objectors who voiced their views cogently and forcefully. There were suggestions (which are not easy to reconcile) that the members of the Chapter were out of their depth and that they were behaving with great cunning in their disposal of this matter. Either way, there was a certain diminution of charity.

Prayer and common worship might dissipate ill feeling, but it was also regrettably the case that the form of worship in the Cathedral was itself contentious. In a cathedral, above all, there is perhaps an inescapable tension between the pursuit of excellence within an established tradition on the one hand, and a zeal for experiment and participation on the other. There was a little disagreement in April 1963, for example, concerning the words of a Latin anthem which had been sung at evensong. It was resolved that no Latin anthems should be sung without previous reference to the Dean. At the end of 1966 it was Waddams who suggested that, in the light of the alternative services of Holy Communion which had been approved in the Church of England, some general thought should be given to liturgical forms and practices in worship in the Cathedral. There seems to have been no immediate hurry to make changes. In March 1971, however, it was agreed that 'Series II' could be used at the sung Eucharist in the nave on the fourth Sunday in May, July, and August. The time at which evensong should be sung continued to present a problem. There was also anxiety about the 6.30 p.m. Sunday service which had begun at the beginning of the century, largely for the servant class. The 'servant class' was no longer identifiable, and there were those who wished in consequence to discontinue the service. There were occasions, too, when the Chapter felt overwhelmed by the volume of requests from performers—choirs, orchestras, or organists—who wished to come to the Cathedral. Such requests came from all over the world. How were they to be handled? It was essential to assert that a Cathedral was not just a concert hall, but on the other hand it was arguable that late twentieth-century man, battered by words, could respond religiously to music.

There was the further difficulty that it was obvious that there was no longer, if there ever had been, a common musical idiom which old and young could readily share. In 1969 the Chapter agreed in principle 'to the holding of a high quality concert in the "Jazz" medium', provided that it could see the programme beforehand in detail; but in February 1972 permission was not granted for a pop group called Quintessence to give a concert in the Cathedral. On the other hand, it was minuted that such performances 'be not ruled out entirely'. It was felt that the views of the organist on these matters would be helpful. In April 1976 it was minuted that the Aberavon Male Voice Choir 'should give its proposed concert in Wales rather than in Canterbury Cathedral, it being felt that the concert would have a limited appeal in Canterbury'. Were such decisions anything more than the predictable responses of middle-class, middle-aged Englishmen?

In 1976, Victor Alexander de Waal succeeded White-Thomson as Dean. His responses to the challenges confronting him were not predictable. He was middle-aged and middle-class, certainly, but his linguistic ability, his Continental family connections, and his multifarious Jewish and Christian contacts made him less 'English' in outlook than any of his predecessors. He came to Canterbury from Lincoln, where he had been chancellor. His colleagues were of varied background: Joseph Robinson, an Old Testament scholar who had succeeded Shirley in 1968; Bernard Pawley, who had become archdeacon of Canterbury in 1972 and possessed many Roman Catholic contacts stemming from his time as the representative of the Archbishops of Canterbury and York to the Vatican Secretariat for Christian Unity; Arthur Macdonald ('Donald') Allchin, who had succeeded Waddams in 1973 and had strong links with Eastern Orthodoxy; while Derek Ingram Hill supplied a wealth of local knowledge and contacts after a lifetime spent in the diocese. The new

Dean's particular interests lay in the liturgy, and he let little time elapse before indicating that he envisaged a reordering of the Sanctuary. 'An experiment' was agreed in February 1977 which entailed moving the High Altar and the archiepiscopal Marble Chair, and dismantling the brass communion-rails. In the months, indeed the years, that followed, these and other liturgical changes were a matter of controversy. Some of them were considered at special congregational meetings. It was understandable that there should be differences of view on these matters, but at least in part they also raised the issue of the nature of the Cathedral 'congregation' once more. The Dean himself, in March 1977, drew attention to the need to draw up a scheme which would enable a properly constituted group of people 'associated with the Cathedral' to elect representatives to the Diocesan Synod under the system of government which was being introduced into the Church of England. How could a cathedral Dean and Chapter work out new relationships, not only with each other, but also with the laity, in circumstances where there was now also a large floating population—a body of term-time students from the university of Kent and Christ Church College and, above all, the visitors?

It was remarked in Chapter in August 1969 that the disposal of rubbish was becoming an increasingly difficult problem. The accommodation of the makers of rubbish was also becoming more acute. Canon Derek Ingram Hill was deputed specifically to concern himself with the tourist flood. In July 1976 he drew the attention of Chapter to the complexity of the ministry to foreign visitors, especially those who spoke no English. There was a need for more guides who could converse in foreign languages. An elaborate system evolved, drawing upon the voluntary services of many committed helpers; a complex operation in itself, and one which required the skills of a specific secretary to the guides. Millions of people now passed through the Precincts and into the Cathedral each year. If the numbers kept growing inexorably, would not its ordinary life be swamped? In fact, the number of foreign visitors reached a plateau in the late 1970s—in 1979 the City of Canterbury District Plan estimated that tourism contributed some £8.5 million to the local economy and employed 10 per cent of the local labour-force—before resuming its upward path in the middle 1980s.[38] The British Tourist Authority estimated that in 1980 there were 12,393,000 visitors to Britain, 50 per cent of whom came from EEC countries, 17 per cent from North America, 13 per cent from non-EEC Western European countries, and 20 per cent 'other'. It was possible to envisage many ways in which their needs could be catered for. There was no conflict between the provision of educational assistance for schools and other parties on the one hand, and the fundamental mission of the Cathedral on the other. Indeed, properly handled, there was a unique opportunity to communicate with many millions who might have only a tenuous contact with institutional Christianity. Yet there were so many other needs, and resources were scarce.

It is as far back as March 1967 that we find the first suggestion that a business consultant be employed to advise the Dean and Chapter on a proper exploitation of their resources. In that year it was decided to take a new step with regard to the bookstall. Hitherto, this had been run by the Friends, but from that date onwards it was formed into a separate trading-company, with a paid manager who was to work initially with a staff of both paid

[38] I am indebted to Mr R. E. Steel for letting me read his 'Canterbury Cathedral and Tourism: The Organizational Response', a dissertation for an MA in management submitted to the University of Kent at Canterbury in Dec. 1986.

and voluntary people. A steady revenue might be expected from such a commercial undertaking, but there were some who were haunted by Christ's treatment of the money-changers at the Temple gates. Miss Lois Lang-Sims gave expression to this concern in a pamphlet *Canterbury Cathedral: What Are We Going to Do About It?* She discerned a situation in which the requirements of the English Tourist Board were becoming dominant. On the other hand, the scale of repairs and improvements which might be attempted was such that even 'Cathedral Gifts Ltd.' could make only a marginal contribution. Another general public appeal seemed to be necessary. It was decided in 1973 to establish a trust for this purpose, and committees were to be formed in London and Kent. Lord Astor took a prominent part and in July 1974 the Prince of Wales agreed to accept the presidency of the trust. Nearly £750,000 was raised by the end of that year; some £1,770,000 by the end of 1975; some £2,250,000 by the end of 1976; and by the time it was decided to hold the last meeting of the central co-ordinating committee, in May 1977, approximately £2,500,000 had been raised.

At one level, such a total was a magnificent achievement. It testified to the hard work undertaken by men in positions of power and influence. It was clear that the Cathedral would survive into the twenty-first century and constitute an enduring link with the past. It would survive, that is, unless some catastrophe, nuclear or otherwise, overwhelmed England. All the while, however, there were those who felt that such a financial triumph contrasted uncomfortably with the suffering of the world beyond the security of the Cathedral walls. How to reconcile the relief of famine with the establishment of a glass-workshop? How to preserve space for a 'still small voice of calm' when the air was full of the jargon of 'positive management'? At the end of 1980 the Chapter decided to ask for advice from the Industrial Society on the improvement of internal communications. Sir Peter White produced a comprehensive report, and many of his far-reaching recommendations were subsequently acted upon.

The decision of the government in 1980 to hold Budget Day on the same day as the enthronement of Archbishop Runcie in Canterbury testified to another kind of ambiguity, this time in the relationship between Church and State in late twentieth-century England. There were to be many other examples of this tension in the years that lay ahead. Unlike his two immediate predecessors, Runcie did not come to Canterbury from York, and the lack of similarity did not end there. The tensions within the world-wide Anglican Communion brought out even more strongly the multiplicity of roles that an archbishop was expected to play. Runcie struggled to balance these conflicting pressures, contriving to strike an individual note which could be both illuminating and irritating but was never irrelevant.[39] In these circumstances, Canterbury gained an increasing hold on his affections, at the same time as it had often to yield pride of place in an exhausting engagement-book.

Nevertheless, there was one early occasion when Canterbury was the centre of ecclesiastical and, to an extent, national attention: the visit of Pope John Paul II. Even so, until the glorious sunshine of the day itself, there had remained a certain amount of ambivalence about this event, scheduled for May 1982. It was an occasion which Dean Farrar, at the

---

[39] See the discussion in K. N. Medhurst and G. H. Moyser, *Church and Politics in a Secular Age* (Oxford, 1988), 282–5. Runcie himself, in his St Albans days, had edited a collection of lectures, *Cathedral and City: St Albans Ancient and Modern* (London, 1977), which reflected his own deep interest in this relationship.

beginning of the century, would scarcely have believed possible or desirable. The Dean and Canon Allchin had attended a meeting at Lambeth Palace in November 1980 at which a scheme was considered. It was first suggested that the Pope might attend evensong. Throughout the following year, however, it became clear that something more ambitious could be contemplated. Inevitably, there were delicate issues of precedence and procedure to be discussed with Rome. There were problems of security which worried the police; there were discussions with television companies; there were brochures and publications to be considered. The Chapter was asked whether it would approve the manufacture of a med-allion showing the Pope on one face and the Cathedral on the other. The members present made it very clear that they could only approve such a medallion if it bore both the Arch-bishop and the Pope together on one side, with the Cathedral on the reverse. It is not sur-prising that the actual form of the service required a number of drafts before it was accepted. In the months beforehand, very great care was taken to minimize points of controversy. The emphasis would be laid upon the welcome to the Pope as a fellow Christian. Of course, what no one had taken into account was the possibility that the United Kingdom would be at war with Argentina in the South Atlantic. For a time it looked as though the visit was in jeopardy, but in the end it was perhaps appropriate that the visit should take place in such a troubled context. The joy of an English spring day mingled with the pain of distant conflict. Two leaders of long-separated churches prayed at the Martyrdom in the Cathedral. Above and beyond was the chapel dedicated in August 1978 to the Martyrs of the Twentieth Century. There was no escaping the fact that, at the last, what Canterbury Cathedral proclaimed, despite all the difficulties that afflicted it, was a message of reconciliation and hope.

The papal visit has been followed by a decade in which Roman Catholics have become frequent and welcome visitors to the Cathedral. Relationships of affection and mutual respect have developed. New links did not replace old ones—the link with Bec was maintained. In turn, four members of the Chapter visited Rome in 1993 and were received in private audience by the Pope. It was a visit which arose in connexion with purported relics of Thomas Becket. There was also opportunity to discuss how Rome and Canterbury might mark, in 1997, the 1400th anniversary of the mission of St Augustine. Nevertheless, despite greater intimacy, hopes entertained in some quarters that the papal visit might lead to the Roman recognition of Anglican orders have not been realized.

There have been ecumenical steps in other directions—visits from the Patriarchs of Alexandria, Antioch, and Constantinople. A visit by the Metropolitan of Minsk has been one sign of increased contacts with Russian Orthodox Christians. The 1992 European Cathedrals Symposium, held in Canterbury, reflected on cathedrals as centres of liturgical excellence. Links with the Church of Sweden have been strengthened. A new pasteur of the French Protestant Church has been installed and the continuity of its history maintained. In these, and other respects, the ecumenical dimensions of the Cathedral's work have become steadily more apparent. They have gone in tandem with the enhancement of Canterbury's significance as 'mother church' for Anglicans across the world—from Japan to Uganda. One further specific example has been the development, from 1993, of a joint Canterbury Cathedral–Duke University (USA) course designed as a resource for Anglicans from all parts of the world.

Some of these special events have been occasioned by the fortuitous incidence of anniversaries—the millennium of Christianity in Russia (1988), the 500th anniversary of the birth of Thomas Cranmer (1988) and the 1300th anniversary of Theodore of Tarsus (1990) among them—while other developments have arisen out of the worldwide contacts of Archbishop Runcie. The Archbishop, in a sense, brought the world to Canterbury but he did not seek to make Canterbury his world. He showed interest and concern for its affairs, but kept an appropriate distance. The Bishop of Dover, in effect, 'ran' the diocese. Only thus could its needs be catered for in the face of the national and international role of the archbishop. The congregation which was present in Canterbury for the enthronement of George Carey in 1991 was testimony to the continuing significance of that role, even though there were also signs that the position of the Church of England as the 'Established Church' was coming under fresh scrutiny.

This national and global activity was carried forward vigorously by John Simpson who succeeded Victor de Waal as Dean in 1986. The scope of activity embraced by the Cathedral could, on occasion, sit a little uneasily alongside the life of a diocese which was essentially rural in character. The contrast made it all the more necessary to ensure that there were also special services—to celebrate the centenary of Kent County Council in 1989 for example—which provided a reminder that the Cathedral was indeed in Kent.

Tourists, however, scarcely needed a reminder. They flocked to the Cathedral in millions—around two and a half million a year in the early 1990s. In the single month of May 1994, 224,000 visitors came to the Cathedral. Such numbers have made careful planning a necessity. A Director of Visits has had this particular responsibility, with an office which organizes tours and the general control of visitors. Voluntary guides and assistants, and paid 'welcomers' meet the needs of tourists in a variety of languages. A separate Education Office and Education Officer deal particularly with school parties, providing teaching materials and other facilities. It is apparent that without such organization the life of the cathedral could become swamped. The administration has necessarily been extended and clear lines of departmental and managerial responsibilty have been established. The structures must be businesslike and efficient. Income and expenditure accounts for each financial year are now published in a lavishly illustrated and attractively presented annual *Dean's Letter*. It is evident that the substantial income from investments, property, visitors, and donations makes possible the equally substantial and constant programme of repair and maintenance, in addition to the provision of the services to the public already referred to.

It is apparent, however, that the welcome is genuine and it remains, despite all the outside pressures, a welcome to a House of God. Sign, symbol, and history have been found still to speak powerfully even to those predisposed to be sceptical or who are indifferent. There is a strong wish that the worship offered should be in harmony with its architectural setting. Music keeps its profound place. The ability to combine may indeed be thought the characteristic of the life of the Cathedral in the last years of the twentieth century: in stone, sound, and image to seek to unite past and present in a fusion which still has a message in a society very different from the Victorian England of Dean Farrar.[40]

[40] I am grateful for discussion on recent aspects of the Cathedral's history with Deans de Waal and Simpson, and with Canons A. M. Allchin, P. G. C. Brett, and D. Ingram Hill. Dom Alberic Stacpoole OSB has also discussed aspects of the papal visit with me. Support from Margaret Sparks has been invaluable.

VIII

The Cathedral Archives and Library

NIGEL RAMSAY

THE ANGLO-SAXON PERIOD

It might not seem unreasonable to suppose that St Augustine gave books to the Cathedral which he founded. It is fairly certain that he gave several to Canterbury's other great church, that of St Peter and St Paul (later dedicated also to St Augustine): until the Dissolution it preserved a group of books that were associated with Pope Gregory and the mission of Augustine. Most of these books were kept up above the high altar, and a fifteenth-century monk who chronicled his abbey's history described them as the foundation books of the whole English Church ('primitiae librorum totius ecclesiae Anglicanae').[1] The Cathedral was never to make such claims for any of its books; indeed, there is no clear evidence for its possession of a permanent library or archive until a much later date. It was not a monastic establishment until four centuries after Augustine's arrival, and it therefore lacked the continuity of personnel that is essential for the well-being of a library. Furthermore, whatever records and books it did possess in its first few centuries were almost all destroyed either in the disasters of c.796–8 and c.851, or in the fire that destroyed the Cathedral church in 1067.

This is not to belittle the achievements of the 'school of Canterbury' in the time of Archbishop Theodore (668–90).[2] Bede has related how Theodore and Hadrian of Africa, the Abbot of St Augustine's, gathered disciples to whom they taught Latin and Greek and the arts of poetry, astronomy, and ecclesiastical computation; some of these pupils were still alive when Bede was writing. Theodore and, no doubt, Hadrian must have brought books with them to England, and one or two of these may still survive—for instance a

I am very grateful for the comments and corrections of Patrick Collinson, Barrie Dobson, Margaret Gibson, Simon Keynes, Richard Sharpe, Margaret Sparks, Michael Stansfield, and Andrew Watson, who have read sections or the entirety of this chapter.

[1] Thomas Elmham, *Historia Monasterii S. Augustini Cantuariensis*, ed. C. Hardwick (RS, 8, 1858), 96–9; reprinted by James, *ALCD*, 500–2, and discussed by him, pp. lxiv–lxvii. One of these books is probably the 'Canterbury' or 'St Augustine's

Gospels', now Cambridge, Corpus Christi College, MS 286; it dates from the 7th cent.

[2] For the 'school of Canterbury' see N. P. Brooks, *The Early History of the Church of Canterbury* (Leicester, 1984), 94–9; M. Lapidge, 'The School of Theodore and Hadrian', *Anglo-Saxon England*, 15 (1986), 45–72; and G. T. Dempsey, 'Aldhelm of Malmesbury and the Paris Psalter: A Note on the Survival of Antiochene Exegesis', *Jnl. Theol. Studies*, NS, 38 (1987), 368–86.

Graeco-Latin seventh-century text of the Acts (Bodl., MS Laud Gr. 35)[3]—but there is no reason to think that this was ever claimed as the property of the Cathedral at any later date in the Middle Ages. Only from the sixteenth century were certain Canterbury books associated with Theodore, and then principally because of a misunderstanding of inscriptions written by a fifteenth-century Greek scribe of the same name. In the seventh century, books may well have been generally seen either as sacred texts, which belonged to a church or even to a particular altar in that church, or else as the property of a teacher, for him to carry away with him if he moved, or to dispose of to his pupils if he wished. Books needed for teaching purposes were too scarce to be placed in a cupboard (the normal place of storage for books) on the off-chance that the next archbishop, bishop, or abbot would be glad to make use of them.[4]

Of the splendid books that the Cathedral is likely to have had in its first three centuries, there is a poignant and solitary survivor, the Golden Gospels (or Codex Aureus), now at Stockholm (Pl. 5): this was perhaps written in Kent, in the middle of the eighth century, but it was plundered and only came back to Christ Church in the late ninth century, as a gift that had been bought back from pirates. The Cathedral's records have a continuous history that can be traced back earlier, to *c*.798.[5] There must have been still earlier charters, accompanying acquisitions of land, yet authentic texts are scarcely extant. The monk Eadmer in the early twelfth century told the tale of how Archbishop Bregowine (761–4) convened a synod in an attempt to recover the estate of the monastery of Cookham (Berkshire) which King Æthelbald of Mercia had given to Christ Church: the charters of Cookham, which Æthelbald had delivered to be placed on the altar at Christ Church, had been stolen and given to King Cynewulf, who had appropriated Cookham. Bregowine was successful in pressurizing Cynewulf into restoring the charters, but they must have perished by Eadmer's time.[6]

Starting in *c*.798, the year of Archbishop Æthelheard's restoration to the see of Canterbury, there survive both a series of episcopal professions of faith and obedience to the archbishop and a very substantial number of charters. Original documents that are written on single pieces of parchment are fragile objects, and so it is fairly remarkable that from between 798 and the death of King Alfred in 899 there survive fifty-four purported original charters from the Christ Church archives; forty-seven of these are accepted as being in contemporary or nearly contemporary hands.[7] A further sixteen charters survive as texts in Christ Church cartularies of a later date, giving a total of seventy survivors from this century—far more than for any other English church.

Documents are more portable than books. It may well be that they have survived so

---

[3] Lapidge, 'School of Theodore' (cit. in n. 2), casts doubts on the claims of Laud Gr. 35.

[4] For comments on the paucity of recorded libraries in pre-Conquest England, see M. Lapidge, 'Surviving Booklists from Anglo-Saxon England', in *Learning and Literature in Anglo-Saxon England: Studies Presented to Peter Clemoes*, ed. id. and H. Gneuss (Cambridge, 1985), 33–89, at 34–40; cf. H. Gneuss, 'Anglo-Saxon Libraries from the Conversion to the Benedictine Reform', *Settimane di studio del Centro italiano di studi sull'alto medioevo*, 32 (1984), 643–99. See also D. Dumville, 'English Libraries

Before 1066: Use and Abuse of the Manuscript Evidence', in *Insular Latin Studies. Papers on Latin Texts and Manuscripts of the British Isles*, ed. M. Herren (Toronto, 1981), 153–78.

[5] Brooks, *Church of Canterbury* (cit. in n. 2), 121, 166–7.

[6] B. W. Scholz, 'Eadmer's Life of Bregwine, Archbishop of Canterbury, 761–764', *Traditio*, 22 (1966), 127–48, at 144; Brooks, *Church of Canterbury* (cit. in n. 2), 103–4, discussing the charter of 798 from which Bregowine derived his information.

[7] Brooks, *Church of Canterbury* (cit. in n. 2), 167.

well from Christ Church simply because they could be carried off to safety when the Vikings threatened the place. With the possible exception of the Stockholm Golden Gospels, no book has survived from the Cathedral from before the Viking raid of 851.[8] And even in the following hundred years, there is only scanty evidence about either the books or the archives of the Cathedral. Christ Church may have prospered: it is hard to know how far the clerks who were resident there could share in the fortunes of the archbishop, whose authority waxed with the rise of the West Saxon regnal dynasty. Perhaps the archbishops were too involved in court politics to concern themselves with their cathedral church. However, Archbishop Oda (941–58), the most distinguished of Canterbury's churchmen in this period, did reroof the Cathedral and heighten its walls, and he gave it a new altar to contain the relics of St Wilfrid—relics which had been plundered from Ripon, probably in 948.[9]

At Oda's request, a member of the Christ Church community, Frithegod, a scholar of Frankish birth and upbringing, wrote a versified Life of Wilfrid;[10] this is more likely to have been prepared as an exercise in virtuosity, and perhaps as an adornment for St Wilfrid's altar, than as something to be read in private by other members of the community, for it is written in a particularly obscure Latin, replete with Greek-derived neologisms, and could hardly have been understood by Frithegod's colleagues.

It is to Oda's successor, Dunstan, Archbishop of Canterbury from 959 to 988, and to Dunstan's immediate successors, that credit must principally be given for establishing at Christ Church a library worth the name—a collection of books other than those intended for use in church, and understood as being the property of the community rather than of any single individual. Dunstan had lived in a monastic community, at Glastonbury, and was a highly bookish individual; his first biographer B[yrhthelm?], who knew him personally, recorded that at Glastonbury he had 'corrected faulty books, erasing the errors of the scribes', and his handwriting has been identified in five surviving manuscripts.[11] The community at Canterbury became a monastic one only in the generation after Dunstan's death, yet in Dunstan's time it must have been apparent that it was moving in that direction. Five of the next six archbishops after Dunstan probably had previously been monks of Glastonbury, and for this reason it is hard to isolate just what each contributed, for each of them, as well as Dunstan, would be likely to have looked to Glastonbury for models to follow—that is, especially, for the loan of texts to copy.[12]

Surviving books give the best indication of the achievement of Dunstan and his immediate successors. At least thirty-three extant books can be said with a fair degree of probability to have been at Christ Church by c.1000,[13] and most of these date from the later tenth century. However, it would be very difficult to say which of them date from before Dunstan's death, and in fact this is not the most important point. In the first place,

[8] Above, pp. 18, 342.

[9] Brooks, *Church of Canterbury* (cit. in n. 2), 229.

[10] Ibid. 227–9; M. Lapidge, 'A Frankish Scholar in Tenth-Century England: Frithegod of Canterbury/Fredegaud of Brioude', *Anglo-Saxon England*, 17 (1988), 45–65.

[11] See N. L. Ramsay and M. J. Sparks, *The Image of Saint Dunstan* (Canterbury, 1988), 9, with further refs.

[12] The influence of Glastonbury is argued for by J. Higgitt, 'Glastonbury, Dunstan, Monasticism and Manuscripts', *Art History*, 2 (1979), 275–90.

[13] The tally of 33 is derived from H. Gneuss, 'A Preliminary List of Manuscripts Written or Owned in England up to 1100', *Anglo-Saxon England*, 9 (1981), 1–60; there are also a few manuscripts that may be dated either side of the year 1000.

Dunstan's role was as initiator, and it was for his successors to ensure the creation of the scriptorium that was needed to produce texts in any quantity (and of a fair quality). And secondly, Dunstan's very position as initiator doubtless obliged him to buy in, or otherwise obtain, books from Glastonbury and other monastic houses, or from scribes who had worked at such places: these books and their scribes will necessarily tend not to be associable by modern scholars with Christ Church, Canterbury, and yet the presence of these books at Canterbury was an essential part of the library's creation.

Dunstan and his successors would naturally also have turned to St Augustine's Abbey for scribes and exemplars: then, as subsequently, the two establishments' libraries must, to a great extent, have developed in tandem. Archbishop Sigeric (990–4) had previously been abbot of St Augustine's (975?–90?),[14] and it may well be no coincidence that it is from the time of the start of his archiepiscopate that the creation of an organized scriptorium at Christ Church can be detected, and that the script, the form of ornament, and the choice of texts at that scriptorium all owed much to St Augustine's.[15] Of the script, for instance, T. A. M. Bishop has concluded that 'the apparently earlier minuscule of Christ Church looks coeval with second-generation St Augustine's minuscule. The appearances suggest that the scribes of both houses were equally and naturally accustomed to the Anglo-Saxon minuscule; that St Augustine's learned to write the caroline from continental models; and that Christ Church learned from St Augustine's.'[16] The decorated initial letters at both houses in the last decade or so of the tenth century are generally of a high quality, and at times so similar as to raise the possibility that certain book-artists from St Augustine's actually contributed initials to a few Christ Church books.[17] The general similarity of book titles between the two houses is also striking, although scholarship has yet to demonstrate more than a very few clear cases of textual interdependence of particular books from each of the two houses.[18] When Sigeric died (994), he made a final contribution to the library of Christ Church by bequeathing it his books.[19] His successors continued to ensure that the scriptorium maintained a high quality and level of activity for another fifteen years; at least thirty non-liturgical books survive from the scriptorium's output in the years between c.990 and c.1010.[20]

At the same time, the community took a careful interest in the preservation and study of its archives. It was most probably at Christ Church, c.1000, that a book was compiled containing a collection of letters to and from a variety of people and religious houses—to Archbishops Dunstan, Æthelgar, and Sigeric, and also to King Edgar and the Old Minister, Winchester. Some of these letters dated back as far as a generation, and the implication is

[14] Brooks, *Church of Canterbury* (cit. in n. 2), 278.

[15] T. A. M. Bishop, 'Notes on Cambridge Manuscripts, Part VII: The Early Minuscule of Christ Church, Canterbury', *Trans. Cambridge Bibliog. Soc.*, 3, pt. 5 (1963), 413–23, at 417–18.

[16] Ibid. 418. Note, however, the suggestion that the establishment of one form of the Caroline style in England ('Anglo-Caroline Style II') may have owed much to Dunstan's period of exile in Ghent: D. N. Dumville, *English Caroline Script and Monastic History: Studies in Benedictinism, A.D. 950–1030* (Woodbridge, 1992), 57, 142–3. See also ibid., chs. 3 and 4, for suggestions as to the post-Dunstan adoption of 'Anglo-Caroline Style I' at Christ Church, first for literary purposes, and then,

by the 1010s, for liturgical books as well.

[17] R. Gameson, 'Manuscript Art at Christ Church, Canterbury, in the Generation After St Dunstan', in *St Dunstan: His Life, Times and Cult*, ed. N. L. Ramsay, M. J. Sparks, and T. Tatton-Brown (Woodbridge, 1992), 187–220, at 192.

[18] See Bishop, 'Notes on Cambridge Manuscripts, Part VII' (cit. in n. 15), 417.

[19] Gervase, *Historical Works*, ii. 357.

[20] Details are given by Brooks, *Church of Canterbury* (cit. in n. 2), 267–8; cf. Gameson, 'Manuscript Art' (cit. in n. 17), 196, n. 39.

that they were all being stored at Christ Church; it is less easy to imagine their being specially borrowed for the compiler of the collection.[21] The community's wider horizons are even more clearly shown by the making of lists of English princes and bishops. The preparation of such lists had probably been begun at Canterbury in the early ninth century, but in *c.*1000 a major updating seems to have taken place.[22] It is very possible that this interest in the tenure of episcopal sees was linked with the receipt of professions of obedience by the archbishop, but it must have been a considerable enterprise to gather together the information about so many different parts of England; Glastonbury Abbey was fairly certainly one source of knowledge, but there must have been others too.

Artistically, the Cathedral community's eyes must have been opened widest by the arrival at about this time of the extensively illustrated Carolingian psalter now called the Utrecht Psalter: a variety of motifs that are clearly derived from this can be seen in several books produced in the Christ Church scriptorium in the early eleventh century, but the Utrecht Psalter's impact is best displayed in BL, MS Harley 603, a complete copy of it that was mostly made by a series of scribes and artists in the earliest years of the century and then continued a generation later. This was not intended as a mere replica: it was a new edition, so to say, with a Roman text substituted for the Utrecht Psalter's Gallican, and its pictures have a fineness of draughtsmanship that fully matches their archetype, while they surpass it by being in many cases delicately coloured. The ninth-century product of the Carolingian school of Rheims inspired the Christ Church scriptorium to undertake what is perhaps the most beautiful of all English pre-Conquest books.[23]

The flowering of the Christ Church scriptorium was abruptly terminated in 1011 by a Viking raid on Canterbury. The books and archives of the Cathedral seem largely to have escaped, but according to the chronicler Gervase, all save four of the monks perished.[24] The scriptorium resumed production within just a few years, but its role was now perhaps rather in the production of de luxe books—splendid volumes that cannot have been needed or intended for the library and which seem to have passed rapidly out of Canterbury. There were some very capable scribes and book-artists at the Cathedral—Eadui Basan was a particularly skilful scribe, who took the opportunity to record his own name for posterity—yet outside influences on the scriptorium are far more detectable than before: perhaps the Cathedral had had to draw on Winchester and Glastonbury for the membership of its brethren.[25]

The building-up of the library continued, nevertheless. Gospel-books and hymnals are

[21] Attention has been drawn to the collection (of which the sole copy is BL, Cotton MS Tiberius A. xv) by M. Lapidge, 'The Present State of Anglo-Latin Studies', in *Insular Latin Studies*, ed. Herren (cit. in n. 4), 45–82, at 58, and Lapidge, 'Æthelwold as Scholar and Teacher', in *Bishop Æthelwold: His Career and Influence*, ed. B. Yorke (Woodbridge, 1988), 89–117, at 96–7.

[22] This enterprise is now represented by BL, Cotton MS Tiberius B. v, pt. 1; fac. as *An Eleventh-Century Anglo-Saxon Illustrated Miscellany*, ed. P. McGurk, D. N. Dumville, M. R. Godden, and Ann Knock (Early English Manuscripts in Facsimile, 21; Copenhagen, 1983). The date and origin of this manuscript have been disputed, although a Christ Church origin is generally

accepted. See e.g. F. Liebermann, 'Notes on the Textus Roffensis', *Arch. Cant.*, 23 (1898), 101–12, at 106; Higgitt, 'Glastonbury, Dunstan, Monasticism and Manuscripts' (cit. in n. 12), 278; McGurk's edn., and the review of this by B. C. Barker-Benfield, *EHR*, 101 (1986), 474–5.

[23] Harley 603 is discussed by J. Backhouse, 'The Making of the Harley Psalter', *British Library Jnl.*, 9 (1983), 97–113, and by Gameson, 'Manuscript Art' (cit. in n. 17), 203–8.

[24] Gervase, *Historical Works*, ii. 360; he was probably following the chronicle of John of Worcester.

[25] T. A. Heslop, 'The Production of de luxe Manuscripts and the Patronage of King Cnut and Queen Emma', *Anglo-Saxon England*, 19 (1990), 151–95.

the commonest Christ Church products of the eleventh century to survive, and would have been needed so constantly by the monks that it is arguable that they should be considered not so much as library books as books that would be assigned on a long-term basis to particular members of the community. However, works by Ælfric and Aldhelm, the Rule of St Benedict and the *Regularis Concordia*, the writings of the Christian poets Juvencus and Sedulius, and even the occasional patristic work, such as the *Confessions* and *De Heresibus* of St Augustine, all survive, in at least one copy, from the years 1000–50.[26] It is tempting to suggest that there were other patristic works than those by Augustine, Gregory (his *Dialogues*), and Ephrem the Syrian (*De Compunctione Cordis*), and that these were subsequently disposed of as being textually inferior; but it is more realistic to judge the library by its survivors. These show it to have conformed to the Anglo-Saxon monastic norm—strongest in works that were intellectually undemanding but morally uplifting, such as collections of lives of saints and exemplary stories, rather than serious works of history or theology. It was not a library that could have impressed any scholarly visitor from beyond these shores.

FROM THE NORMAN CONQUEST TO THE LATER THIRTEENTH CENTURY

Calamitous as the defeat of the English by William of Normandy must have been felt to be, nevertheless it is certain that for the monks of Christ Church, the following year was every bit as disastrous. For in that year, 1067, a fire in the city spread to the Cathedral and destroyed both it and nearly all the monastic buildings. The monk Eadmer (in the 1120s) wrote that

the devouring flames consumed nearly all that was ... most precious, whether in ornaments of gold, of silver, or of other materials, or in sacred and profane books. ... The privileges granted by the popes of Rome, and by the kings and princes of this kingdom, all carefully sealed and collected together, by which they and theirs were bound to defend and uphold the Church for ever, were now reduced to ashes. Copies of these documents were sought for and collected from every place where such things were preserved; but their bulls and seals were irrecoverably destroyed with the church in which they had been deposited.[27]

Eadmer may have exaggerated, for at least a few of the books that would then have been deemed 'most precious' still survive; but it is true that the Cathedral has lost its original pre-Conquest charters of privileges, of the sort that still survive for Westminster Abbey (at least from the kings of England).[28] When Lanfranc came to Christ Church as its archbishop, in 1070, he would in any case have felt it necessary to build the library afresh, for he considered it a part of his mission to reform and reorder the place on the model of

---

[26] Brooks, *Church of Canterbury* (cit. in n. 2), 266–78; for England as a whole, see R. M. Thomson, 'The Norman Conquest and English Libraries', in *The Role of the Book in Medieval Culture: Proc. Oxford International Symposium ... 1982*, ed. P. Ganz, 2 vols. (Bibliologia, 3–4; Turnhout, 1986), ii. 27–40, at 28–31.

[27] Scholz, 'Eadmer's Life of Bregwine' (cit. in n. 6), 144; I

have followed the transl. by R. Willis, *Architectural History of Canterbury Cathedral* (London, 1845), 9.

[28] Of the pre-Conquest royal charters to Christ Church that are extant as purported originals, almost all are regarded as spurious or in some degree doubtful: see P. H. Sawyer, *Anglo-Saxon Charters: An Annotated List and Bibliography* (London, 1968).

Bec in Normany, where he had long been prior. He let the existing monastic community remain, but he added monks from Bec to their total, and he rebuilt the church and other buildings around it. The Priory's existing stock of books he would have regarded with distaste: to judge from what survives of it, there was hardly a volume of either the basic works of patristic theology or of recent scholastic learning, while there was much that was in English, as whole text or as gloss. Under Lanfranc, the value of the latter must have been questioned; Latin was reasserted as the language of the monks' reading.

To build up a library in the high Middle Ages required more than just a sufficiency of money: both scribes and the texts for them to copy were in short supply. Lanfranc made the creation of an adequate library one of his priorities at Canterbury, and at first, in the 1070s, he probably had to buy books that came from Bec and several other scriptoria in Normandy.[29] A number of these books survive—tall, well written, and easy to read; like those commissioned in the 1080s and 1090s, they mostly contain biblical or patristic texts. 'The pre-Conquest library with its idiosyncratic survivals and many gaps became a systematic collection of Augustine, Ambrose, Jerome, Gregory and Bede: a life-time's reading for the ordinary monk.'[30] These books were to survive the passage of the next five centuries remarkably well, and were to remain the kernel of the Priory's working collection; they were kept in use partly as a result of the high quality of their production.[31]

Like Dunstan a century earlier, Lanfranc was known to correct texts himself. For both men, books were central to the monastic existence. Lanfranc, furthermore, established a scriptorium at Christ Church with such effect that after some years it was able to supply books to other religious houses in England—to Rochester, to Durham, and not least to St Augustine's, Canterbury. The Christ Church scribes had developed a script that was distinctive to the house—we have the monastic discipline to thank for that, no doubt— but co-operation with St Augustine's still came quite as readily as rivalry to the brethren of Christ Church. This might seem so obvious as not to need to be stated, were it not that the sixteenth-century antiquary William Lambarde had stated the opposite, and that his words seem to have been influential: he wrote that the monks of the two houses 'were as farre removed from all mutuall love and societie, as the houses themselves were neare linked together.'[32]

Lanfranc was not prepared to leave it to chance that the monks of Christ Church would read what he was so patiently assembling for them. He made it a requirement that each monk should read one book a year.[33] When he had first come to Canterbury in 1070, the Priory was still following the practices that had been laid down in Dunstan's time in the *Regularis Concordia*. He ignored this, and prepared a fresh set of rules that drew in their detail on those that governed Bec. On the first Monday of Lent,

---

[29] Cf. M. T. Gibson, *Lanfranc of Bec* (Oxford, 1978), 180–1.

[30] Ibid. 180, n. 6.

[31] The relatively few books illuminated at Christ Church in Lanfranc's time are listed by C. R. Dodwell, *The Canterbury School of Illumination, 1066–1200* (Cambridge, 1954), 120; at p. 17 he lists the earliest manuscripts that entered the Norman library.

[32] W. Lambarde, *A Perambulation of Kent* (Chatham and London, 1826), 269. For one example of co-operation between

the two houses, see N. R. Ker, 'Copying an Exemplar: Two Manuscripts of Jerome on Habakkuk', in *Miscellanea Codicologica F. Masai Dicata*, ed. P. Cockshaw, M. Garand, and P. Jodogne (Ghent, 1979), 203–10; reprinted in N. R. Ker, *Books, Collectors and Libraries: Studies in the Medieval Heritage*, ed. A. G. Watson (London, 1984), 75–86.

[33] *Monastic Constitutions of Lanfranc*, ed. and trans. D. Knowles (Nelson's Medieval Classics; London, 1951), 19.

before the brethren go in to chapter, the librarian should have all the books save those that were given out for reading the previous year collected on a carpet in the chapter-house; last year's books should be carried in by those who have had them, and they are to be warned by the librarian in chapter the previous day of this. ... The librarian shall read out a list of the books which the brethren had the previous year. When each hears his name read out he shall return the book which was given to him to read, and anyone who is conscious that he has not read in full the book he received shall confess his fault, prostrate, and ask for pardon. Then the aforesaid librarian shall give to each of the brethren another book to read, and when the books have been distributed in order he shall at the same chapter write a list of the books and those who have received them.[34]

The Rule of St Benedict had laid down a general direction of a somewhat similar sort, but it was Lanfranc's ruling, in all its detail, that was to govern the monks' annual book-allocation until the Dissolution.[35] The librarian (*custos librorum*) was the precentor, as in many other monastic houses, and the library remained his responsibility throughout the Middle Ages, long after it had ceased to be particularly appropriate for one who was primarily charged with conducting the monks' services and their music.

One proof that the books in a library are being read is the making of other books that depend on them. And even more, the writing *in* books. The history of the various surviving manuscripts of the *Anglo-Saxon Chronicle* has still to be fully elucidated, despite a great many scholars' investigations; but it is apparent that in the late eleventh and early twelfth centuries the Cathedral Priory housed a number of chroniclers and annalists who were keen to record what was happening in their own lifetime, as well as to include the history of Christ Church as part of the history of England. The Parker version of the *Anglo-Saxon Chronicle* came from Winchester to the Priory at some point in the eleventh century—conceivably as part of the rebuilding of the library after the fire of 1067—and received various additions and a continuation relating to Canterbury. The scribe who made most of these additions also compiled and wrote the F version of the *Chronicle* (BL, Cotton MS Domitian A. viii), an epitome coming down to 1058 of another version, the so-called 'Northern Recension' of the *Chronicle*; but he also used a number of documents from the Christ Church archives, ranging in date from the eighth to the eleventh century.[36] What is remarkable about the F version is that it is in both English and Latin (each English annal being followed by a Latin version), while yet a further chronicle or set of annals, the I text (BL, Cotton MS Caligula A. xv), which covers the years 988–1268, is in English until 1109 (when it records the death of Archbishop Anselm). That is to say, some members of the Cathedral community were recording events in chronicles whose texts consciously went back to the pre-Conquest history of England and in a language that was alien to Lanfranc and the monks who had come with him from Normandy. And it is particularly remarkable that the English annals in Caligula A. xv were being written from *c*.1073, just three years

---

[34] Ibid.

[35] Lanfranc's *Constitutions* themselves were copied by, and were doubtless made to apply to, several other English Benedictine houses. But the Rule of St Benedict merely called for the reading of one book of the Bible each year.

[36] D. N. Dumville, 'Some Aspects of Annalistic Writing at

Canterbury in the Eleventh and Early Twelfth Centuries', *Peritia*, 2 (1983), 23–57, at 45, 49. It is also very possible that the B or Abingdon text of the *Chronicle* was at Christ Church *c*.1000: ibid. 40–1, and see also *The Anglo Saxon Chronicle: A Collaborative Edition*, iv: *MS B: A Semi-Diplomatic Edition*, ed. Simon Taylor (Cambridge, 1983), pp. xi–xii.

after Lanfranc's consecration.[37] Lanfranc's firm control over his cathedral priory was tempered by a marked tolerance in some areas.

The same scribes who copied books for the library also wrote charters for both the monastic community and the archbishop;[38] more or less the same script can be found in each of these categories of work until the 1130s.[39] There could be no hard-and-fast distinction between archive material and library books until well into the twelfth century. Differences were of quality, not of type: those documents that were deemed precious, such as papal or royal privileges, were very likely kept with some of the more precious books, in cupboards and chests. An assortment of such containers, perhaps spread over a variety of locations, might not be the most secure way of keeping such things (though it was a great deal safer than placing them on top of an altar), but it had at least the advantage that in a fire it was likely that some would escape the flames. That a charter or privilege was single-sheet or was written into a book did not necessarily bear on its value in the community's eyes: important texts might be copied into a gospel-book or some other book that was itself valued because it contained a sacred text. It has been suggested that the *Domesday Monachorum* (*c.*1100 and later) was early on bound with a gospel-book, while Eadmer relates that papal privileges were found after a diligent search through books of the Gospels.[40]

It has been a subject of debate how far Lanfranc had any part in the preparation of privilege-documents that were passed off as genuine originals.[41] What is certain, however, is that he played the leading role in initiating two major archival developments: the start of the separation of the monastic community's archives from those that pertained rather to the archbishopric, and the consequent need to make copies of a great many of these documents. Just like his contemporary Bishop Wulfstan II of Worcester (1062–95),[42] Lanfranc wished to clarify what belonged to the archbishop and to separate his estates and household from those of the monastic community: the separation of documents into two distinct archives was an inevitable counterpart to the stone wall that he built between the Cathedral church and his own palace. The earliest Cathedral cartulary to survive is a stray quire or gathering of eight leaves of approximately mid-twelfth-century date (Cambridge, Corpus Christi College, MS 189, fos. 195–202; headed in a sixteenth-century hand 'Evidentiae ecclesiae Christi', and now generally referred to by that title); its latest documents are of 1106–9, but its archetype would appear to have comprised documents coming down

[37] Dumville, 'Annalistic Writing at Canterbury' (cit. in n. 36), 39. Significantly, the annals begin with Dunstan's birth in 925.

[38] N. R. Ker, *English Manuscripts in the Century After the Norman Conquest* (Oxford, 1960), chs. 5–6, provides the best introduction to the Christ Church scriptorium in this period. That the same scribes also penned royal charters granted to the Priory in the early 12th cent. was established by T. A. M. Bishop, *Scriptores Regis* (Oxford, 1961), nos. 332, 335, 344, etc.; cf. id., 'Notes on Cambridge Manuscripts, Part I', *Trans. Cambridge Bibliog. Soc.*, 5, pt. 5 (1963), 432–41, at 433, for a mid-12th-cent. scribe who wrote both charters and a book for Christ Church.

[39] That only some of the scribes at Christ Church wrote in the house style is made clear by T. Webber, 'Script and Manuscript Production at Christ Church, Canterbury, after the Norman Conquest', in *Canterbury and the Norman Conquest: Churches,*

Saints and Scholars, 1066–1109, ed. R. G. Eales and R. Sharpe (London, etc., forthcoming, 1995), 145–58.

[40] C. R. Cheney, 'Service-Books and Records: The Case of the "Domesday Monachorum"', *BIHR*, 56 (1983), 7–15; Eadmer, *Historia Novorum*, ed. M. Rule (RS, 81; 1884), 261 (writing of 1120).

[41] See M. T. Gibson, above, pp. 49–51.

[42] Cf. *Hemingi Chartularium*, ed. T. Hearne (Oxford, 1723), pt. 1, 286; N. R. Ker, 'Hemming's Cartulary: A Description of the Two Worcester Cartularies in Cotton Tiberius A. xiii', in *Studies in Medieval History Presented to F. M. Powicke*, ed. R. W. Hunt, W. A. Pantin, and R. W. Southern (Oxford, 1948), 49–75, at 63, reprinted in Ker, *Books, Collectors and Libraries* (cit. in n. 32), 31–59, at 47.

to no later than 1037, and it is only because of references to Canterbury's primacy that the main portion of the surviving 'Evidentiae' text can be dated to no earlier than 1070.[43] Since it also contains a memorandum about the burial of archbishops of Canterbury, which is a topic that became contentious only from c.1085, it would come at the earliest from the last years of Lanfranc's archiepiscopate; more likely, however, is that it was composed in the years immediately after his death, when the Priory's estates suffered from Rufus's exactions and when the monks must have been at pains to demonstrate to royal officials which estates were archiepiscopal and which monastic. The late eleventh-century endorsements found on the earlier surviving Christ Church charters doubtless resulted either from the Lanfrancian movement towards separation of the estates, or directly from the process of preparing the cartulary.

The making of a cartulary at this date was a major enterprise for any monastic community: as with the archives themselves, responsibility would have lain directly with the monks, and it is improbable that any clerks would have been entrusted with such a task. Even in the mid-twelfth century, there are signs that such mundane documents as Priory leases were being drawn up—at least on occasion—by men of learning.[44] The episcopal and abbatial professions of obedience to Canterbury appear to have been written in the Christ Church scriptorium until about the end of the twelfth century,[45] and this may be seen as a further indication of how extensive was the role of the claustral scribes; it would be stretching the evidence to say that it also shows how slow a Priory secretariat was to develop.

Lanfranc built no library structure for his Cathedral, and his *Constitutions* contain no more than a passing reference to the presence of cupboards in the cloister;[46] by analogy with other houses, however, as well as with later Christ Church practice, it is fairly certain that the library books were kept in cupboards in the cloister. It has been suggested that the west walk of the cloister would have served best, being quiet and reasonably well lit.[47] After about 1160 a new storage-area for books became available, as the slype—a passage leading from the cloister's east walk, and between the church and the chapter house, through to the monks' cemetery—was blocked off at its further end and was thereby rendered a cul-de-sac. It is not known when the decision was taken to enclose it and turn it into a book-store: it was probably done by the 1220s, and may have been at any date from the 1160s onwards.[48]

It is possible, though no more than a guess, that the slype's enclosure came at about

---

[43] This account of CCCC 189 is entirely dependent on the analysis of it by N. P. Brooks, 'The Pre-Conquest Charters of Christ Church, Canterbury' (D.Phil. thesis, Univ. of Oxford, 1969), 103–17. The 'Evidentiae' were printed by R. Twysden, *Historiae Anglicanae Scriptores X* (London, 1652), cols. 2207–26.

[44] See H. Mayr-Harting, 'Hilary, Bishop of Chichester (1147–1169), and Henry II', *EHR*, 78 (1963), 209–24, at 218, n. 3, on a lease of 1152. Mayr-Harting links this document's authorship with the circle of archiepiscopal clerks, however.

[45] T. J. Brown, 'Handwriting of the Professions', in *Canterbury Professions*, ed. M. Richter (CYS, 67; 1973), pp. xxviii–xxxvi, at xxxiv.

[46] *Constitutions*, ed. Knowles (cit. in n. 33), 76.

[47] M. Beazeley, 'History of the Chapter Library of Canterbury Cathedral', *Trans. Bibliog. Soc.*, 8 (1904–6), 113–85, at 121–2, and cf. 132–3, 139.

[48] The continuator of Gervase, in describing the election in 1228 of a successor to Archbishop Langton, states that the compromissors retired to the 'armariolum secus hostium capituli, in quo libri precentoris includuntur' ('the cupboard near the chapter house door, where the precentor's books are kept'): Gervase, *Historical Works*, ii. 121. For this location, see also Legg and Hope, *Inventories*, 144.

the same time as the making of the earliest list of Priory books that has survived.[49] This is a puzzling as well as tantalizing document. It is a mere three leaves of parchment (with one or two columns of text on each of five sides); it clearly begins in the middle, since there is no heading, and it certainly does not include all the books that belonged to the Priory—though even so, it contains a total of 223 volumes. One of the last books in it is the *Entheticus* of John of Salisbury: John is called 'Carnotensis', and he became Bishop of Chartres only in 1176, which would of course imply that the list cannot be earlier than that year. The placing of the *Entheticus* and four other books in a separate column by themselves, entered by more than one hand, does suggest, however, that they were additions to the list; so the list can reasonably be dated to about the 1170s. For most of the list, books of the same title are grouped together, by author and title: one copy of Cicero, *De Senectute*, is followed by two entries of Cicero, *De Amicitia*; Cicero is preceded by eight entries of Sallust, and is followed by four of Arator. In the adjacent column there are no fewer than seven entries of Boethius, *De Consolatione* [*Philosophiae*]; after these has been added, in a different hand, Boethius, *Quomodo Trinitas Unus Deus*, which, like the addition of a ninth Persius after eight other Persius entries, indicates that the list remained in use for some time. But what was the function of the list? It cannot really be said to resemble any other English medieval library catalogue, for it does not refer to cupboards or shelves—and one may well wonder whether any library at this date would actually have kept its books on so rigorous an author-and-title arrangement—and it describes the books only fitfully in terms of their physical condition (whether in boards or in parchment covers) or by former owner. On the other hand, every book *is* distinguished by having some sort of mark written or drawn beside it; surviving books from this section of the library also have the same marks inscribed inside them, so that one can match them up with their entry in the list. The conclusion must be that the list functioned best as an indicator of whether a particular book that one had in one's hands was from the library: Francis Wormald was surely right in his suggestion that the list may be one that was used by the precentor when checking on book-borrowings.[50]

Two of the five books added at the end of the list are of law, and there are also about twenty miscellaneous books of theology. Otherwise, however, it is overwhelmingly a collection of Latin literature, and the multiple copies of so many of the works make plain that it was very much a working collection, for teaching purposes. The Cathedral Priory was still teaching its monks within its own premises. On the assumption that there were twice as many theological books as there were of Latin literature, and allowing for a reasonable number of chronicles and books of medicine and law, there must have been a total of six to seven hundred volumes in the entire collection.[51] It is very doubtful whether any other library in England in the twelfth century could have matched this.

The history of the archives in the twelfth century is no better ascertained than that of the library, although the materials on which such a history must be based—principally the surviving documents themselves—are far more numerous. It has yet to be shown

---

[49] The list has been printed by James, *ALCD*, 7–12, with a complete fac. on 3–6.

[50] F. Wormald, 'The Monastic Library', in *The English Library* *before 1700: Studies in its History*, ed. id. and C. E. Wright (London, 1958), 15–31, at 23.

[51] See the discussion by James, *ALCD*, pp. xxxiii–xxxiv.

satisfactorily, for instance, whether the Thidericus who acted as a scribe for Archbishop Anselm, and who on one occasion requested Anselm to send him a copy of a letter from Henry I to Paschal II, was a Christ Church monk or not. Anselm addressed letters to him rather as though he was not a monk, but it seems extraordinary that a mere scribe might have been allowed to solicit material for the Priory archive.[52]

Leaving aside the question of whether the forgeries concerning the primacy of Canterbury can be dated to the early 1120s rather than to Lanfranc's time, it is an inescapable fact that the twelfth century was a time when increasing reliance was being placed on written evidence to justify any claims of legal entitlement, and the monks of Christ Church had to do their best to provide documentary proof of what they believed to be their rights. As has already been mentioned, they conducted one search through their muniments in 1120; but there must have been many other such searches, one of which, in the mid-twelfth century, is recorded in the form of endorsements that were added to many of the charters, summarizing them and stating whether they are in Latin or English.[53] It is also undeniable that the monks continued to fabricate documents, in both the later twelfth century[54] and in the first half of the thirteenth.[55] In 1238 Archdeacon Simon Langton said to Pope Gregory IX: 'Holy Father, there is not a single sort of forgery that is not perpetrated in the church of Canterbury. For they have forged in gold, in lead, in wax, and in every kind of metal.'[56] That outburst came in the course of the investigations which followed one of the most audacious forgeries of any to be perpetrated at Christ Church, that of the charter purportedly granted to the monks by St Thomas. One upshot of the investigations carried out by the papal legate was the Pope's order to him in the same year, 1238, to examine the muniments of the Church of Canterbury and to make a permanent separation of the monks' muniments from those of the archbishop; documents of common interest were to go to the archbishop, while if there was more than one copy, the duplicates were to be given to each side. Forgeries, certain or suspected, were to be sent under seal to the Pope.[57] Documents in the past had sometimes been issued in duplicate, so that both the Priory and the archbishop would have a copy; but from 1238 it was to be the standard practice for almost all documents issued by either the archbishop or the Priory to be copied (and, very commonly, ratified) by the other. The separation of the muniments was the principal and permanent consequence of the papal decree.

The general reaction of the Priory to the legate's inquiry and its outcome can only be guessed at. There are two snippets of evidence which give a rather disagreeable impression. In the first place, a monk called Ralph of Orpington confessed to the Archbishop that he had been a party to forgery, and the Archbishop, Edmund of Abingdon, took him to the Continent with him to save him from the reprisals of the brethren. They lured him back,

---

[52] See the debate between R. W. Southern, 'Sally Vaughn's Anselm: An Examination of the Foundations', *Albion*, 20 (1988), 181–204, at 194–201, and Sally N. Vaughn, 'Anselm: Saint and Statesman', ibid. 205–20, at 212–14; for a monk named 'Theoder', see Le Neve, *Fasti, 1066–1300*, ii: *Monastic Cathedrals*, 9, n. 1.

[53] J. B. Sheppard in HMC, 5th *Report* (1876), 427, states that these endorsements are found only on charters from before the reign of Henry II.

[54] See e.g. T. A. M. Bishop and P. Chaplais, *Facsimiles of English*

Royal Writs to A. D. 1100. Presented to Vivian Hunter Galbraith (Oxford, 1957), no. 6.

[55] See e.g. C. R. Cheney, *Pope Innocent III and England* (Stuttgart, 1976), 205 (forgeries relating to St Augustine's Abbey).

[56] C. R. Cheney, 'Magna Carta Beati Thome: Another Canterbury Forgery', *BIHR*, 36 (1963), 1–26; reprinted in id., *Medieval Texts and Studies* (Oxford, 1973), 78–110, at 104.

[57] Cheney, *Medieval Texts and Studies* (cit. in n. 56), 100–1.

67 Chapter library 1868–1942.

68 Chapter library after bomb damage, 31 May 1942.

69 James Maple, bookbinder, and William Urry, archivist, at work in temporary quarters, August 1947.

70 New library, opened 18 June 1954.

71 (*far left*) Lost twelfth-century cupboard, of the sort that could have been in the Treasury. Photograph once owned by R. C. Hussey (d. 1886). (Bodl., MS Top. Gen. c. 19, fo. 41.)

72 (*left*) Fourteenth-century cupboard.

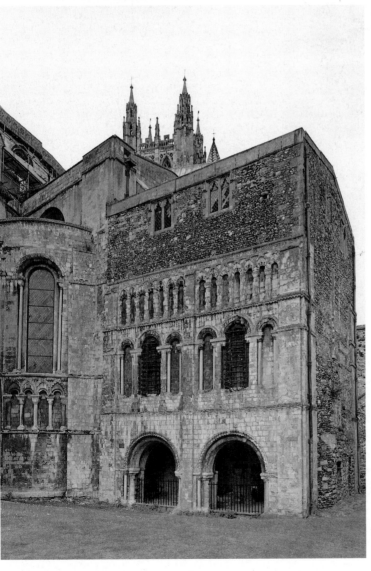

MEMENTOTE CORAM DEO
WILLELMI GEORGII
VRRY
ET HVIVS ECCLESIAE
METROPOLITICAE ET
VRBIS CANTVARIAE
CHARTOPHYLACIS
APVD OXONIENSES
PRAELECTORIS IN
PALAEOGRAPHIA
AVLAE SANCTI
EDMVNDI
SOCII
1913   1981

73 (*top left*) Priory seal press for production of large two-sided seals; thirteenth century, probably 1232.

74 (*top centre*) Seal of the official of the see of Canterbury during archiepiscopal vacancies, perhaps showing the north-west tower, site of the archbishop's court. (Birch, *Catalogue*, no. 1350.) S. OFFICIALITATIS ECCLES. XSTI CANTUARIE VACANT' SEDE.

75 (*top right*) Bundle of bills of acquittance from Priory treasurers for sums received, 1445–60, filed on string tied round a wooden tally stick. (D.E. 15c.)

76 (*left*) Treasury or vestiarium where Priory and Chapter archives were stored; built *c.*1160, with chamber above, *c.*1300. Arches below may have formed processional entry to monks' cemetery.

77 (*above*) Memorial tablet, lettered by David Kindersley, to William Urry, archivist 1948–69.

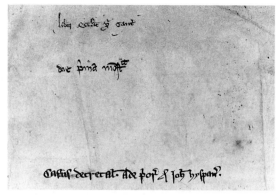

(a)

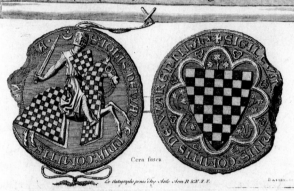

(b)

(c)

78 (*far left*) Charter of John de Warenne, Earl of Surrey and Warenne, to Archbishop and Prior and Convent of Christ Church, 1276. Engraved by James Basire in the late eighteenth century, when the original charter (which would once have been in the Priory muniments) belonged to Thomas Astle; it is now lost.

79 (*left*) Inscriptions of ownership in Priory manuscripts.
(*a*) Notes of location in the library ('de prima monstra[cione]') and of gift by Prior Adam de Chillenden (d. 1274) of John de Deo, *Casus Decretalium*. (Lit. MS D.11, f.1.)
(*b*) Note of purchase and donation to the Cathedral by Martin of Clyve, monk of Christ Church (d. 1301), at front of Hugh of St Cher's commentary on the Sentences of Peter Lombard. (Lit. MS A.12, fo. iii^v.)
(*c*) Note of ownership by John Kynton, monk of Christ Church (d. 1416), of Aegidius Romanus, *De Regimine Principum*. (Lit. MS B.11, fo. 3^v.)

80 (*lower far left*) Priory court roll book for Kentish estates, 1497–1507; parchment. Damaged in the Audit House fire, 1670. (Court Roll 65(1).)

81 (*lower left*) Dean and Chapter lease register, 1638–42; paper. Damaged in the Audit House fire, 1670. (Register Y7.)

82 (*right*) Chapel of Our Lady Martyrdom, dedicated 1455.

83, 84 *(right)* Anthem, 'O gracious God of Heaven', by George Marson, master of the choristers, 1596x7–1627, organist 1596x7–1632, minor canon, 1604–30 (MS Music 1A, fos. 142, 142ᵛ.)

85 *(below)* *Benedicamus domino à3*, by John Nesbett, master of the Lady Chapel, 1473–4 to 1487–8. (Cambridge, Magdalene College, MS Pepys 1236, fo. 126ᵛ.)

86 *(below right)* Accounts for mending organ and making service books, 1635. (Misc. Accts. 41, fo. 65.)

87 The presbytery, site of royal and archiepiscopal funeral hearses, showing (from left to right) monument to Archbishop Sudbury, remains of sedilia, monuments to Archbishops Stratford and Kempe.

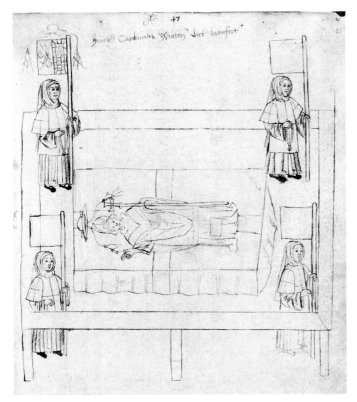

88 Funeral effigy and mourners' enclosure of Henry Beaufort, Bishop of Winchester (d. 1447). Drawing made for Sir Thomas Wriothesley, Garter King of Arms 1505–34. (BL, Add. MS 45131, fo. 21.)

89 Hearse of John Islip, Abbot of Westminster (d. 1532). Anonymous drawing in Islip's Mortuary Roll. (Westminster Abbey Library.)

90 Monument to Archbishop Hubert Walter (d. 1205).

91 Detail of lid of Hubert Walter's monument.

92 Monument to Archbishop John Pecham (d. 1292). On the right, part of Archbishop Warham's monument (cf. Pl. 107).

93 Monument to Prior Henry of Eastry (d. 1331), drawn by Edward Blore, c.1823. (BL, Add. MS 42011, fo. 45.)

94 Monument to Archbishop Simon Meopham (d. 1333), spandrel on south side of canopy.

95 Meopham monument, spandrel on south side of tomb-chest.

96 Meopham monument, spandrel on north side of canopy.

97 Meopham monument, south side.

98 Monument to Archbishop Thomas Bourchier (d. 1486), north ambulatory, detail of canopy.

99 Bourchier monument, detail of north side of tomb-chest.

100 Monument to Sir John Scott (d. 1485), at Brabourne, Kent, detail of canopy.

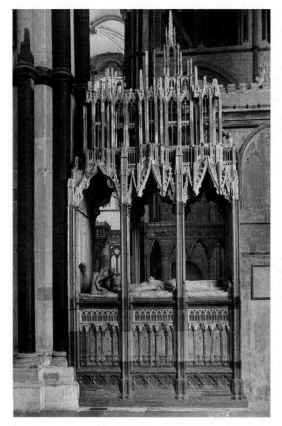

101 Monument to Archbishop John Stratford (d. 1348).

102 Monument to Archbishop Simon Sudbury (d. 1381).

103 Monument to Archbishop Henry Chichele (d. 1443), south side viewed from archbishop's throne.

Facing page

104 (*top left*) Monument to Archbishop John Kempe (d. 1454), south side.
105 (*top right*) Monument to Archbishop Bourchier, south side.
106 (*lower left*) Monument to Archbishop John Morton (d. 1500), south side. Photograph taken between 1895 and 1937.
107 (*lower right*) Monument to Archbishop William Warham (d. 1532), Martyrdom. Engraving by J. Cole from J. Dart, *Cathedral Church of Canterbury* (1726).

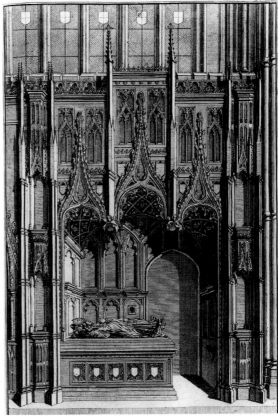

108 (*right*) Effigy of Archbishop Pecham.

109 (*far right*) Effigy of Archbishop Walter Reynolds (d. 1327).

(*below, left to right*)

110 Effigy of Prior Eastry.

111 Effigy of Archbishop Stratford.

112 Effigy of Archbishop William Courtenay (d. 1396).

113 Upper effigy of Archbishop Chichele.

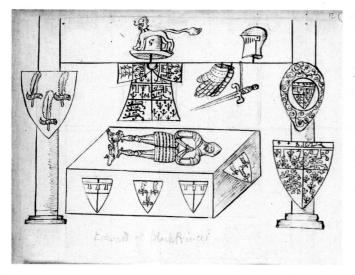

118 Monument to Edward, Prince of Wales, known as the Black Prince (d. 1376), north side. Drawing by John Philipot, 1613. (BL, Egerton MS 3310A, p. 19.)

119 The Black Prince's monument, from south-east, with railings removed.

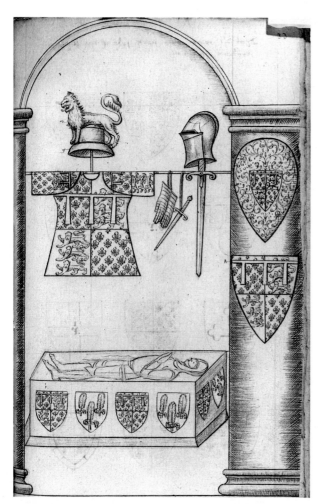

120 The Black Prince's monument. Anonymous drawing, c.1600. (Society of Antiquaries of London, MS 162, fo. 33.)

121 Head from unidentified knight's effigy of c.1340, found in 1893 in the chapel of Our Lady Undercroft.

122 Chapel of St Edward the Confessor, vault and part of east wall, showing traces of five figures formerly surmounting the altarpiece (cf. Pl. 20).

123 Effigies of King Henry IV (d. 1413) and Queen Joan of Navarre (d. 1437).

124 Upper part of effigy of Henry IV.

125 (*left*) Monument to Joan, Lady Mohun (d. 1404), south side. Engraving from J. Dart, *Cathedral Church of Canterbury* (1726), 30.

126 (*centre*) Mohun monument, from south-west. Drawing by Edward Blore, 1823. (BL, Add. MS 42030, fo. 7.)

127 (*right*) Effigy of Lady Mohun. Drawn and engraved by C. A. Stothard, *Monumental Effigies of Great Britain* (1832), pl. 88.

128 (*left*) Effigies of (from left to right) Thomas, Duke of Clarence (d. 1421), Margaret, Duchess of Clarence (née Holland; d. 1439), John Beaufort, Earl of Somerset (d. 1410).

129 (*right*) Effigy of Elizabeth, Lady Trivet (d. 1433).

however, and, it was said in a letter to Edmund, maltreated him.[58] The papal legate's inquiries disclosed another scandal, of the alteration and subsequent deliberate destruction of a privilege granted by Pope Alexander III. The Prior, John of Chatham, admitted responsibility and resigned, and, together with a monk named Simon of Hartlip, entered the Carthusian order. In a fifteenth-century list of Christ Church monks, it is recorded in red lettering beside Hartlip's name: 'Iste fregit cartam sancti Thome'—'This man broke (or destroyed) the charter of St Thomas.'[59] Did the Priory come to believe, after all, that it was innocent of wrongdoing, and that an authentic charter had been done away with?

Over the course of the thirteenth century, two factors led to a great expansion of the Priory's archive. The first was the gradual process by which the Priory regained direct possession of its lands which had been allowed to slip into private control and yield only low customary rents: the Priory now built up collections of charters as these and other lands were formally granted to it.

In the second place, the Priory sought to strengthen its hand in the event of any future challenge to its exercise of the archbishop of Canterbury's spiritual jurisdiction during the vacancy that ensued after each archbishop's death.[60] The vacancy after Edmund of Abingdon's death (1240) lasted for over four years and a certain amount of ecclesiastical court documentation was kept from this time. Far more has survived from the vacancies of 1270–3 and 1292–4. These periods came after the great series of settlements that Archbishop Boniface had overseen, and the preservation of all this material may have reflected not so much prudent necessity as the extreme carefulness of one man, Prior Henry of Eastry.

THE PRIORATE OF HENRY OF EASTRY

Just how much could be accomplished by an individual prior of sufficient energy and capability is shown by the achievements of Henry of Eastry.[61] His long priorate (1285–1331) was marked by the cataloguing of the Priory's books and—far more time-consuming—the complete overhaul of the Priory archives. It is true that by the late thirteenth century the Priory's disputes over the exercise of its *sede vacante* administrative rights (and so, too, its part in the struggles about archiepiscopal primacy) had virtually come to an end, and that the preservation of records, rather than the active prosecution of legal campaigns, was accordingly what was now needed. Eastry, however, was unquestionably a man who was ready to go to law if that was of any possible use, while he appreciated to the full that the preservation and good ordering of muniments was the Priory's fundamental safeguard. A list of Priory muniments that was drawn up in about 1307 indicates that large numbers

[58] C. H. Lawrence, 'The Alleged Exile of Archbishop Edmund', *JEH*, 7 (1956), 160–73, at 162. Edmund obtained a papal injunction to restrain the monks from victimizing informers.

[59] Cheney, *Medieval Texts and Studies* (cit. in n. 56), 101; Lit. MS D. 12, fo. 1ᵛᵇ. Beside Ralph of Orpington's name in Lit. D. 12, fo. 1ᵛᵃ, is written 'Nota de carta sancti Thome' ('Note, about the charter of St Thomas').

[60] See *Select Cases from the Ecclesiastical Courts of the Province of Canterbury, c. 1200–1301*, ed. Norma Adams and C. Donahue jun. (Selden Soc., 95; 1981), pp. 3–4, 35–7.

[61] Eastry's career is treated by T. F. Tout, in *DNB*, s.v. Henry (of Eastry); by Smith, *Cant. Cath. Priory, passim*; by T. L. Hogan, 'The Memorandum Book of Henry of Eastry, Prior of Christ Church, Canterbury' (Ph.D. thesis, Univ. of London, 1966); and by M. Mate, 'Henry of Eastry', in *DNB: Missing Persons*, ed. C. S. Nicholls (Oxford, 1993), 301–2.

of documents were kept in Eastry's *studium* in the dormitory, as well as in his *desca* in the study of the late Prior R[oger] in the dormitory, in his *desca* in the room with a leaded roof (*camera plumbata*), and in his *desca* in the room of Master Homer, one of the Priory's legal representatives.[62]

In the previous decade, the 1290s, Prior Eastry had directed a major overhaul of the Priory's main collection of charters (or title-deeds) and royal and papal letters. In common with the general English practice, the royal and papal letters were put into separate sequences, while the charters were arranged by manor or parish. Much less typical was the care with which each document had its contents very briefly summarized on its dorse (or back); the letters and those charters that recorded direct transfers of title were numbered (e.g. 'Chartham vii' or 'Langedon xxx'). Every single one of these thousands of numbered documents was then copied into a book, the cartulary in the Cathedral archives now known as Register E.[63] To clarify this process, the original documents were also endorsed 'Reg.' (meaning 'registered' or 'to be registered'), while each copy in the register was given the same number as that on the original: it should thus have been a simple matter to cross-refer between the originals and the copies in the register. Perhaps as a final safeguard, a complete transcript of Register E was also made, at almost the same time.[64]

Eastry was not the only Priory official to concern himself with the making of register-copies: it is one indication of the apparent independence of the different obediences in this period that some (at least) had their own registers compiled. A fragment of an almonry register survives from the early fourteenth century,[65] and that active administrator, the monk John de Gore (d. 1326), compiled the greater part of Register J, dealing with the Priory's rural estates, and possibly also BL, Add. MS 6160, a miscellaneous collection of extents, taxations, etc.[66]

Since some of the obediences appear to have had their own seals from the fourteenth century onwards,[67] it was only prudent that they should have their own registers. And since the different obedientiaries had their own particular archival needs, such as precedents to be followed in the fulfilment of their duties, the copying of memoranda of all sorts into registers was an obvious course of action. Perhaps the biggest of these registers was that made in the 1320s at Priory Eastry's bidding, termed by him his 'Collection of many things' (*Memoriale multorum*).[68] He put into this over 160 different texts: lists of popes, kings,

---

[62] The list's headings alone have been printed, from Reg. I, fo. 449, by J. B. Sheppard, 'The Meister Homers, Canterbury', *Arch. Cant.*, 13 (1880), 116–21, at 117–18.

[63] Cf. G. R. C. Davis, *Medieval Cartularies of Great Britain: A Short Catalogue* (London, 1958), no. 168.

[64] The transcript is in four parts, as Regs. A–D: ibid., nos. 169–72.

[65] LPL, Carte Misc. XIII, pt. i, art. 15; ibid., no. 176. See e.g. Ch. Ant. E. 186 for an endorsement mentioning registration in the almonry; C. R. Cheney, *English Bishops' Chanceries, 1100–1250* (Manchester, 1950), 159, no. 10. See also below, p. 376, for the suggestion that obedientiaries' records were particularly liable to be lost after the setting-up of the New Foundation, in 1541. Note, however, that Davis, *Medieval Cartularies* (cit. in n. 63), omits a 15th-cent. almoner's register, Bodl., MS Tanner 18, as well as fragments of a sacrist's book of the 14th and 15th cents.,

LPL, MS 1232.

[66] For Add. MS 6160 see Davis, *Medieval Cartularies* (cit. in n. 63), no. 184, and B. Mains, 'The Beneficed Clergy of the Diocese of Canterbury, 1279–1313' (D.Phil. thesis, Univ. of Oxford, 1976), 54; see also Smith, *Cant. Cath. Priory*, 104. Reg. J begins (fo. 12): 'Registrum Johannis de Gore de Redditibus et consuetudinibus ecclesie Christi Cantuariensis' ('Register of John of Gore about the rents and customs of Christ Church, Canterbury'), putting Gore's personal role in its making beyond question.

[67] Cf. W. de G. Birch, *Catalogue of Seals in the Department of Manuscripts in the British Museum* (6 vols.; London, 1887–1900), i, no. 1384, for a 14th-cent. seal of the almonry. The almoner's estates were the most substantial of any of those of the obedientiaries.

[68] Now BL, Cotton MS Galba E. iv, fos. 1–186; ed. Hogan, 'Memorandum Book of Henry of Eastry' (cit. in n. 61).

archbishops of Canterbury, and religious houses in the province of Canterbury; taxation lists; notes of bounds and weights and measures (both local and biblical); forms of profession to the see of Canterbury, and vacancy material; details of the duties of the steward of the guest-hall and of other Priory officials; royal charters and statutes; twenty signs of true friendship; details of his own works; the coming of Antichrist; and dozens more. Not least because of the sheer range of its materials, it remains one of the most fruitful of all the Priory registers; it preserves many texts that survive in no other form, thereby demonstrating the advantages of registration in terms of preservation as well as of access.

Eastry's relations with his four successive archbishops (Pecham, Winchelsey, Reynolds, and Meopham) were far from uniformly easy. He was, however, a very capable and tenacious administrator, and his knowledge of the forms and precedents that the Priory needed to follow was one good reason for the archbishops to approach him for advice. The Priory had, besides, the advantage that its own records remained in its undying care, while those of the archbishop were liable to be moved around the country, or at least to be divided between several different properties. The bulk of the archiepiscopal records were housed at St Gregory's Priory in Canterbury (where, presumably, there was no one specifically employed to look after them), but by the early fourteenth century some were housed at Lambeth, while yet more were carried about with the archbishop or were housed in different manor-houses.[69] Little wonder, then, that in 1307, after Archbishop Pecham's death, Eastry was approached with a request for information about Pecham's muniments and those of his notaries: Eastry might well have known the answer, and he certainly knew which of Pecham's notaries to approach.[70] Two decades later he wrote to Archbishop Meopham to tell him that a particular papal privilege which he wanted could be found in 'your archiepiscopal archives at Canterbury'.[71] It has fairly been said that Eastry knew a good deal more about the archbishop's records than did some archbishops themselves.[72]

Of all the documents preserved as copies in Eastry's *Memoriale multorum*, the one that has attracted the greatest amount of scholarly investigation in the last 150 years is undoubtedly the library catalogue.[73] Written almost entirely in one hand, it has an appearance of consistency and unity that is highly deceptive. By later standards it might be judged rather a poor piece of work. It is probably incomplete even in its coverage of what it purportedly contains, it does not make any mention of the shelves on which the books were located, and it does not even give much of an impression as to how the Priory's book collection was arranged. In the face of these weaknesses, it is hardly surprising to find that

[69] For the storage of the archiepiscopal archives, see I. J. Churchill, 'Table of Canterbury Archbishopric Charters', *Camden Miscellany* 15 (Camden Soc., 3rd ser., 41; 1929); F. R. H. Du Boulay, *The Lordship of Canterbury* (London, 1966), 1–15 (another version printed as 'The Archbishop as Territorial Magnate', in *Medieval Records of the Archbishop of Canterbury* (London, 1962), 50–70); J. E. Sayers, 'The Medieval Care and Custody of the Archbishop of Canterbury's Archives', *BIHR*, 39 (1966), 95–107; R. C. Finucane, 'The Registers of Archbishop John Pecham and His Notary, John of Beccles: Some Unnoticed Evidence', *JEH*, 38 (1987), 406–36, at 415–17.

[70] Finucane, 'Registers of Pecham', 416.

[71] Du Boulay, *Lordship of Canterbury* (cit. in n. 69), 7. Cf. also his letter to Archbishop Walter Reynolds, written after a search had been made in the Cathedral archives in connection with an episcopal election at Lichfield; he suggested that the desired documents were at Lambeth (Reg. L, fo. 131ᵛ).

[72] Du Boulay, *Lordship of Canterbury* (cit. in n. 69), 7.

[73] It was last ed. by James, *ALCD*, 13–142; a new edn. by L. O. Ayres and M. T. Gibson is forthcoming as part of the Corpus of British Medieval Library Catalogues.

it also fails to state the opening words of the second folio of each book, a simple and more or less foolproof method of identification of particular books that was still uncommon but was soon to become standard.

Analysis of the catalogue shows that it really comprises several collections.[74] Its first 280 or so books (as numbered in James's edition) form a theological collection, arranged in a roughly alphabetical order, but omitting the letters K to N. Most of these books date from the eleventh and twelfth centuries and were written at Christ Church. A small section of chronicles, martyrologies, and monastic rules (nos. 282–303) is followed by a group headed 'books in English' (*Libri anglici*, 304–20); these were kept together, presumably from appreciation of their antiquity, for they were in Old English, and so were hardly likely ever to be read by more than one or two of the monks, if any.[75] Next come the books that were kept in the cupboard in the cloister (321–58), a collection of such fundamental or particular works of divinity, history, science, and law as Augustine on the Psalms, Gregory's *Moralia*, the *Sentences* of Peter Lombard, Josephus, Eadmer's *Historia Novorum*, the Letters and the Miracles of Thomas Becket, and works by Pliny and Boethius. As a psalter, there was the celebrated twelfth-century Eadwine or Canterbury Psalter; basic though these works might be for the Priory, these were not run-of-the-mill copies. The catalogue continues with passionals and lectionaries (359–80), which one might have expected to find nearer to the refectory (in which they might have been read aloud); secular books follow, with grammar, rhetoric, dialectic, and philosophy (381–432), arithmetic and music (433–43), and medicine (444–*c*.507).

This arrangement by subject or location gives way, for the rest of the catalogue, to a mere list of accessions by donors' names: a series of monks, most of whom died in the 1290s or first five years of the fourteenth century (approximately nos. 508–782), then a run of books that are stated to have belonged to Becket or to members of his circle (783–900), then a few books that came from Archbishops Lanfranc and Hubert Walter (901–4), followed by a large number that were given in the course of the twelfth and thirteenth centuries by monks and others (905 onwards). A chronological order of date of accession gradually emerges, coming down to about 1326 (to no. 1638), although it ends slightly raggedly (nos. 1639–1737 are of various dates from 1307 to 1320). In two different hands are then added, first (1738–55), books from the monks Stephen of Faversham and John of Gore (d. 1295 and 1326, respectively), and, secondly (1756–1831), books from four monks and a lawyer called Brice of Sharstead (all of whom died in the years 1326–8). From all this it is clear that the copyist's text was produced in 1326, and that it was brought up to date with the accessions of the two following years.[76] It is also woefully evident that for many decades, accessions had just been allowed to accumulate, without any real effort being made to arrange them on a subject basis.

To say that the Priory's main library had become a sort of dumping-ground would, however, be unfair. There was, for instance, a tradition among Benedictine monks of

[74] James, *ALCD*, pp. xxxvii–xliv, remains the starting-point.

[75] The *Libri anglici* have been discussed by M. Förster, *Beiblatt zur Anglia*, 12 (1901), 360–2; James, *ALCD*, pp. xxv–xxviii; and R. M. Wilson, *The Lost Literature of Medieval England* (2nd edn.; London, 1970), 77–9.

[76] It is perhaps no mere coincidence that Prior Eastry's compendium of grants, compositions, etc., now in CUL, MS Ee. v. 31, was last added to in *c*. 1327.

preserving some books simply because they had belonged to well-loved or respected members of the community;[77] the books of St Thomas could be said to have come into this class. Furthermore, certain books—especially psalters and other liturgical works—may have been regarded as the property of particular monks and consequently have been inscribed with their names after those monks had died: such at least is the inference that may be drawn from the library borrowers' list of 1338, as will be seen. It made some sense, therefore, to leave at least some of the books in the grouping by donor's name in which they had come into the library (cf. Pl. 79).

Eastry was not content with having the library books listed. It was in his time, too, that they received pressmarks. And thanks to these we can reconstruct how the books were arranged. Apart from those that were kept in a cupboard in the cloister, they remained in the slype building, in the space between the chapter house and the north-west transept.[78] The catalogue divides them into two *demonstrationes*, themselves subdivided into *distinctiones*. The pressmarks as a general rule are by *distinctio* and *gradus*.[79] The *demonstrationes* have been understood since M. R. James's time to be the two sides of the library room, while the *distinctiones* were explained by him as being 'the narrow vertical divisions' of these;[80] the *gradus* were the shelves, of which there were up to fourteen in a *distinctio*. If the shelfmarks are compared with the numbers assigned by James to the books in Eastry's catalogue, it will be seen that there were on average slightly more than forty books in each *distinctio*. Yet there is not by any means a perfect correlation between shelfmarks and Eastry catalogue numbers. The Eastry catalogue reaches a total of 1,831 books, but none of the survivors from the last 650 or so books in it has a shelfmark. The highest surviving shelfmark is D.xiiii.G.xi, i.e. on a book from the eleventh shelf of the fourteenth *distinctio*; this is on a book numbered 1166 in James's edition of the catalogue, and that number does not accord with what one would expect on the basis of slightly more than forty books per *distinctio*. The next-highest surviving shelfmark is D.viii.G.ix.M°.i (M°.i. standing for the first *monstratio* or *demonstratio*); this is on a book that is no. 421 in the catalogue. All the other forty-five surviving shelfmarks are on books from the first seven *distinctiones*, which is puzzling. The majority of these shelfmarks are on books from the first 300 Eastry catalogue numbers, and can be perfectly correlated (*distinctio* i has numbers that range from 19 to 34, ii has from 47 to 79, iii has from 90 to 145(?), iv from 156 to 176, v from 206 to 244, and so forth); a few shelfmarks have numbers

[77] For the preservation of psalters at Durham Cathedral Priory and Rievaulx Abbey, see F. M. Powicke's introduction to his edition of Walter Daniel, *Life of Ailred of Rievaulx* (London, 1950), p. lxvi.

[78] This location is confirmed by references to the library as being adjacent to the chapter house, in Reg. G, fos. 77ᵛ (1349), 82ᵛ (1348; I owe this reference to Dr J. Greatrex), and 110ᵛ–111 (1349). It has been suggested that Eastry added an extra floor to the building, c. 1304–5 (T. W. T. Tatton-Brown, 'The Medieval Library of Canterbury Cathedral', *Cant. Cath. Chron.*, 82 (1988), 35–42), but the suggestion depends on the possibility that Prior Eastry's list of his own building achievements would have hidden such a work in the statement that he repaired the chapter house in 1304–5. Such modesty on Eastry's part may be

doubted. Yet an extra storey certainly was added at some point in the 14th cent., although it also must have been too dark to serve as more than a place for storage.

[79] Surviving pressmarks are printed by Ker, *Medieval Libraries of Great Britain* (2nd edn.; London, 1964), 29–39, and suppl., ed. A. G. Watson (London, 1987), 10–12.

[80] James, *ALCD*, pp. xliii–xliv. Note, however, that in the north wall of the slype there were two substantial recesses, such as could have accommodated book-presses, side by side, with a further, larger recess a little further east; these recesses were filled in, in 1896 (see Legg and Hope, *Inventories*, 144 n.), but their outlines can still be seen. The north wall would have been the better lit of the slype's two main walls.

that are slightly out of sequence (e.g. D.iii.G.xi. on no. 173); but then there is a batch of high numbers (ranging from 853 to 888 and 1182 to 1184) that also have shelfmarks from the first seven *distinctiones*. One explanation is that there were gaps on the shelves, and that some of the high-number books were transferred to fill them; in support of this hypothesis is the fact that the transferred books were mostly twelfth-century manuscripts (like so many of the first 280 or so books), but against it is the more significant fact that their subject-matter did not match that of their new neighbours. Four of these out-of-sequence books (853 and 855–7) had belonged to St Thomas Becket and his friend Herbert of Bosham, no less; it seems strange that the two great men's collections were split up. Is the answer, then, that the batch of high-numbered out-of-sequence books were shelved in a second series of *distinctiones* that ranged (on the surviving evidence) from ii to vii? There are only ten such surviving pressmarked books, which is too small a number for certainty; and yet there is a distinct lack of correlation between their pressmark and catalogue sequences even on this basis. The puzzle is worth further investigation, not least because the first 300 books in the Eastry catalogue so largely represent the library's *continuum*: they will be found to re-appear a good deal in a list in 1508, and to have survived particularly well down to the present day. Numerically speaking, that is to say, the medieval Christ Church library is over-represented today by its late eleventh- and twelfth-century books and (in subject terms) by its theological collection.

As the Eastry catalogue makes clear by its naming of donors or sources, almost all the books that entered the Priory library after the twelfth century were gifts or bequests and not purchases.[81] About 160 people figure in the catalogue, and if all the books that are written after their names actually came from them, they brought the library about 1,335 books (i.e., counting nos. 381–8 and 503–1831). Just over half of the names are identifiable as those of monks, while Archbishops Lanfranc, Becket, Hubert Walter, Langton, and Winchelsey also figure, as might be expected. Some of the remaining seventy names are probably those of monks, but others are those of men outside the Priory community who yet had some link with it: they illustrate the Priory's links with other communities in East Kent. There are members of other religious houses, like John, Abbot of Davington (thus the catalogue, nos. 1238–9; but there was only a nunnery at Davington), and W., Prior of Dover (nos. 1315–19), and there are local ecclesiastics (such as Master Robert de Gressenhale, no. 152—if he is taken as the cataloguer's error for Reginald de Gressenhale, rector of Great Mongeham and a former chancellor of Cambridge University, who died at the right date for names in this part of the catalogue, 1292 or 1293[82]). There was also at least one medical practitioner, Master Robert of Cornwall (nos. 1706–14), and most numerous of all, there was a crop of *magistri* who were probably mostly canon lawyers. These last had perhaps all once been in receipt of annual retaining fees from the Priory, but they were certainly capable of showing generosity in return. Master Michael of Barham, Doctor of Civil Law (d. by 1320)[83] gave twenty-two books, of which nine were of civil law and eight of canon law (nos. 1684–1705); Brice of Sharstead, Doctor of Civil or Canon Law (d.

---

81 This is also borne out by the absence of expenditure on book-buying in the sacrist's and prior's account-rolls.

82 See Emden, *BRUC*, 271.

83 Id., *BRUO*, iii. 2151. Barham was also rector of the Christ Church living of Eastry.

1327), gave just three volumes (nos. 1823–5), but these included two very useful texts, the constitutions of the Court of Arches and a glossed copy of William of Mandagout's *Summa de Electionibus*, together with five other canon-law items.[84]

That the monks of Christ Church should dominate the catalogue was, however, inevitable. They could not give books to people outside the Priory, and they could not make wills bequeathing books to particular monks. Since many of the monks would each wish to have the same texts in his keeping, it was bound to be the case that certain texts would frequently recur in the catalogue. For instance, the basic texts of canon and civil law occur again and again, for they were often needed by the monks; they might have been acquired at university in England, or even in Paris, Orleans, or Bologna, to all of which universities monks from Christ Church are known to have gone.[85] The system whereby monastic offices were held on a rotating basis had as one side-effect the need for a large number of the community to know the rudiments of canon law. Knowledge of the common law was either recognized as being less easily acquired from books or simply regarded as less needful; as in other monastic library catalogues, there are very few books of common law (one is no. 1792, *Liber de legibus Anglie*, which is perhaps the treatise now known as Bracton's), and it may be that they were kept not in the library but in the offices of certain of the obedientiaries. Common-law books rarely feature in English monastic catalogues, although a considerable number of surviving books of statutes and registers of writs undoubtedly belonged to religious houses. In the list of Prior Eastry's own books, inventoried at his death in 1331, there is both a Bracton and a book of statutes.[86] One may wonder if the latter would have been included in the main library catalogue if Eastry's books had already been given to the library and were being catalogued as part of it. The list of Eastry's books also includes his *Memoriale multorum* (BL, Cotton MS Galba E. iv) and three registers, which surely would not all have been regarded as library books. And yet among the books that came from John de Gore—a fairly humdrum seven volumes, including the *Lumen laicorum* in French (i.e. Peter of Peckham's *Lumière as Lais*) and a *Collectarium de multis* in Latin and French—the catalogue does include the register of his own making, Register J.

Like a post-mortem inventory, the library catalogue reflects the interests of previous generations—above all, of men who had died in the later thirteenth and very early fourteenth centuries. The late thirteenth and fourteenth centuries were a major period of growth for all the English monastic cathedrals, so Christ Church, Canterbury, was merely following the national pattern in this.[87] Yet it would hardly be stretching the truth to apply to the post-twelfth-century Christ Church library as a whole what M. R. James said of Prior Eastry's book-list, that 'the collection is a very unliterary one, that of a man of affairs rather than of a student'.[88] The catalogue rather gives the impression of a Priory that was

---

[84] For Sharstead, see ibid. 1681. His executors both gave books specifically bequeathed by him, and returned a *Speculum Judiciale* and *Summa Azonis* which he had had out on loan from the Priory: see CUL, MS Ee. v. 31, leaf inserted between fos. 263 and 264.

[85] See R. B. Dobson, above, p. 100.

[86] James, *ALCD*, 143–5, at nos. 59–60. A 14th-cent. book of statutes, now Cambridge, Trinity College, MS O. 9. 26 (no. 1438), which evidently belonged to Christ Church, has no press-mark and occurs in none of the lists of Priory books.

[87] Ker, 'Cathedral Libraries', in id., *Books, Collectors and Libraries* (cit. in n. 32), 294.

[88] James, *ALCD*, p. xlv.

full of men of affairs, while even such a highly literate individual as the late twelfth-century monk Nigel Witeker is represented by such well-known books as Peter the Chanter's *Historia scolastica*, Peter Lombard's *Sentences*, and the Chronicle of Ralph of Diss.[89] There are virtually no signs in the catalogue of any interest in Greek or Hebrew learning.[90] That is perhaps unsurprising, for the Priory was not celebrated in this period for its learning. Only in one of the last entries in the catalogue, the books that had belonged to Stephen of Faversham (nos. 1738–48), is there any clear sign of the Priory as a place of teaching— and that sign, admittedly, is detectable partly because we know that Stephen of Faversham (d. 1324 or later) was the first monk who lectured on theology to his brethren.[91] He owned such useful-sounding though imprecisely described works as *Diverse questiones theologie* and *Questiones extracte de diversis scripturis*, as well as one volume of Aquinas. The Priory's major collection of works by Aquinas had come just ten years or so previously, as part of Archbishop Winchelsey's bequest (nos. 1639–83, at 1664–75). Winchelsey possibly had attended Aquinas's lectures in Paris, between 1269 and 1272.

The historian might like to find more evidence of private devotional reading, of the sort that W. de Cherringe (d. 1296) had possessed—such as 'Psalterium de latino et gallico beate Marie' and 'Psalterium parvum beate Marie' (nos. 1552–3)—but it may be that such books escaped being put into the library. On the other hand, the catalogue is capable of shedding a great deal of light on some of the older books in the library. The books in Old English are one such category. Another is a trio of martyrologies (nos. 291–2 and 294), which were the subject of a most ingenious investigation by J. Armitage Robinson.[92] Realizing that the first two of these three volumes were both, in effect, redundant sets of constitutions for the monks, rendered out of date by Archbishop Pecham's injunctions and Archbishop Winchelsey's constitutions, he argued that the treatises that each volume contained, called in the catalogue 'Consuetudines Ecclesie Beccensis', were none other than the *Constitutions* that Lanfranc had written (or rather, adapted) for the monks of Christ Church. They were called 'Bec Customs' because that was their origin, but they were in fact the constitutions that governed the monks of Christ Church for over two centuries. And Robinson was able to show that the first volume, described as *Martilogium Vetus* in the catalogue, still survives, although now divided into two parts;[93] the first part still has its pressmark, D.vii.G.xiii. It was only thanks to the information in the fourteenth-century catalogue that the twelfth-century manuscript could be reconstructed, and it was even in part thanks to this that the Lanfrancian *Constitutions* could be shown to have been intended initially for the Cathedral Priory rather than for the English Benedictine order as a whole, while the influence of the customs of Bec upon the *Constitutions* was graphically revealed.

It is fortunate, but far from exceptional, to have a library catalogue surviving from the

[89] Ibid. 101, nos. 1084–91.

[90] cf. James's comments, ibid., p. xlii.

[91] 'Primus fuit de congregatione monachorum qui theologiam in claustro . . . legebat' ('He was the first of the monastic community who lectured on theology in the cloister'): chronicle of a continuator of Gervase, in John Leland, *De Rebus Britannicis Collectanea*, ed. T. Hearne, 6 vols. (2nd edn.; London,

1774), i. 274–5 (from Cambridge, Trinity College, MS R. 5. 41). He was appointed lector in 1324, having made his monastic profession in 1295.

[92] 'Lanfranc's Monastic Constitutions', *Jnl. Theol. Studies*, 10 (1908–9), 375–88.

[93] BL, Royal MS 7 E. VI, fos. 1–103, and Cotton MS Claudius C. vi, fos. 170–203.

Middle Ages; it is another matter altogether to be able to say anything about the use that was made of a medieval library. Although it is likely that it was the common practice of English Benedictine abbeys to allow books to be borrowed by outsiders, it is only rarely that this can be demonstrated.[94] In the early thirteenth century, however, Christ Church, Canterbury, is known to have lent a volume containing the Brut chronicle and a work by St John Chrysostom to Master Laurence de S. Nicholas (d. *c.* 1237): this is known because he failed to return it, and Prior Nicholas had to write a letter to Anglesey Abbey, seeking its restitution.[95] Even more remarkably, however, there is also still extant from Christ Church a list that records precisely who had out on loan books from the library, and what these books were. From an incidental mention in a Priory register—a note that an allowance of a loaf of 'monk's bread' and half a gallon of small beer should be given to the sacrist's servant whenever he carried books from the library to the chapter house for the annual inspection[96]—it is clear that the Lanfrancian (and general Benedictine) requirement of an annual Lenten stock-taking was still being adhered to. The list that survives from St Gregory's day (12 March) 1338 specifies the books that were missing, from the 'large tables' and the 'small tables.'[97] These 'tables' were doubtless boards covered with wax, like those used by the precentor to name the monks who were to conduct the different services each week, and in this instance recorded the names of book-borrowers. The large tables record the books missing from the two *demonstrationes*: these total about fifty-four. Remarkably, the Priory brethren were not the only borrowers from these shelves: the lion's share had indeed been assigned to monks, but sixteen books had been lent out to seculars. These were headed by Edward II, dead for over eleven years, who had borrowed both a collection of the Miracles of St Thomas Becket and a book with the Lives of Becket and Anselm. An unnamed person had been lent one of St John Chrysostom's works, at the prior's direction; all but one of the other books were of civil law, and it may be that their borrowers were all civil or canon lawyers. As in the case of the donors whose names are mentioned in the library catalogue, the interplay between the monastic community and the community of East Kent can again be seen. The *Digest* bequeathed by Michael of Barham had been lent to Master Robert of 'Bereham', who was surely his relative; and a *Codex* (i.e., of Justinian) was out to Master Henry Shorne, DCL, who had been in receipt of a retaining pension from the Priory every since 1300.[98] An *Inforciatum* (second part of the *Digest*) had gone to Master Richard de Haute, who died within a few months of the stock-taking and left the Priory a whole collection of books of civil and canon law.[99]

The books that the large tables record as assigned to monks are a much more varied assortment. Another three lives of Thomas Becket, a couple of medical books, Everard of Béthune's *Grecismus* (i.e. no. 687 or 688 in the library catalogue), three works by Aquinas

[94] Rose Graham, *English Ecclesiastical Studies* (London, 1929), 173; *Catalogi Veteres Librorum Ecclesiae Cathedralis Dunelm.*, ed. B. Botfield (Surtees Soc., 7; 1838), 37.

[95] J. Burtt, 'Notes Upon Ancient Libraries', *Notes and Queries*, 1st ser., I (1849–50), 21–3; cf. E. Hailstone, *History . . . of Bottisham* (Cambridge Antiquarian Soc., 8vo Pubn. 14; 1873), 196–201, 210–12, 340.

[96] Reg. J, p. 514 ('qui portant & reportant libros de libraria ad monstrandum in capitulo').

[97] The list is printed in *Lit. Cant.*, ii. 146–52; only part of it is given by James, *ALCD*, 146–9; for what he gives, James is more accurate than Sheppard although less clear. The date in the manuscript, 1337, is presumably by the reckoning whereby the year began on Lady Day (25 March).

[98] Emden, *BRUO*, iii. 1696; he was a donor to the library.

[99] HMC, 9th *Report* (1883), pt. I, app., p. 90a.

and two by Peter Lombard, a Brut chronicle in French, and a psalter of the Virgin Mary are among the reading of about twenty-four of the monks; there is just one law-book. The little tables go even further in countering any impression of a community composed of legally minded administrators, for they record ordinals, diurnals, processionals, psalters, antiphoners, and a missal, assigned to a total of twenty-eight monks; they are a reminder of the fact that the religious life was the monks' primary concern, and they illustrate this as the library catalogue does not, for they record books that were perhaps kept by the sacrist and not by the precentor.[100] Certainly, these are books that cannot be identified with any that are itemized in the library catalogue, and none had been entrusted to a secular person.

One point raised by the table lists is the question of where these books were believed to be. The books borrowed by both monks and secular persons are stated to be in their hands ('in manibus'), and yet a considerable proportion of the monk-borrowers had been dead for some years. If they had kept them in their offices, or in the cloister, or even in the dormitory, then the books surely would have been recovered at their deaths. Had they, then, been taken outside the Priory precincts? The implication presumably is that the table lists record not just books that had been borrowed, but books that had failed to be returned—in other words, books that were recorded as still missing after the annual stocktaking. The total annual book-borrowings would thus have been far greater. The high proportion of books out to dead monks reflects not just slack administration of the library but also punctiliousness in recording all book loans. And the only puzzle is that the late Prior Henry of Eastry was among the offenders.

THE LATER MIDDLE AGES, C.1340–1540

Not for another 500 years were both the library and the archives of the Cathedral to be again as thoroughly catalogued as they had been in the early fourteenth century. Their history in the last 200 years of the Priory is confused and uncertain: there are many scraps of evidence, but there is a lack of all-embracing lists, especially for the library. One might guess that, like other cathedrals (whether secular or monastic), Canterbury saw a distinct slowing-down in the growth of its library in the second half of the fourteenth century: this was a period when books were more likely to be given instead to the colleges of Oxford and Cambridge. The monastic cathedrals had already recognized the shift in intellectual life to the universities, by sending young monks to study at Oxford or Cambridge, or even at Continental universities; the setting-up of Canterbury College at Oxford in the 1360s was the Cathedral Priory's ultimate, long-term response to this pattern of study.[101] It is likely that the college was initially supplied with several dozen, or perhaps even as many as a hundred, books from the Christ Church library.[102]

[100] They may be compared with the 22 gospel-books with precious bindings which the sacrist had in 1316: Legg and Hope, *Inventories*, 78–9; discussed by Cheney, 'Service-Books and Records' (cit. in n. 40), 13.

[101] For Canterbury College, see R. B. Dobson, above, pp. 102–6; for its library, see esp. Pantin, *Cant. Coll.*, iv. 155–66, and N.

R. Ker, 'Books in the Colleges Maintained in Oxford by the Benedictines', in *The History of the University of Oxford*, iii: *The Collegiate University*, ed. J. McConica (Oxford, 1986), 463–5.

[102] Pantin, *Cant. Coll.*, iv. 157–9, identified books from Christ Church that were at Canterbury College in the mid-15th cent. and later.

Like the books that were given to the quasi daughter-house, Dover Priory, books that were dispatched to Oxford were in effect being permanently alienated. The college statutes (December 1365?) made clear that the books were to stay there for ever, not being lent out of the house unless to a scholar of Merton College.[103] They were to be kept together in one room, all borrowings were to be recorded in a borrowers' book, and at the front of each volume was to be inscribed, in large letters, 'Hic liber est scolarium aule Cant' ('This book belongs to the scholars of Canterbury hall'). No doubt a few books did trickle back to Canterbury, being brought back by monks who had not finished with them when their stay in Oxford was at an end; in *c*.1487 the monk Thomas Goldstone wrote from Oxford to tell the Prior that he could not find him a copy of Grosseteste's *Dicta* for sale, and he was therefore sending him the college's copy, although this was in breach of the statutes.[104] The warden and other members of the college were allowed to spend money on book purchases, but it is likely that they too resorted to taking from another library what they were unable to buy. The presence in college inventories of 1501 and later, and yet not in the two earlier inventories of 1443 and 1459, of two civil law books (two parts of the *Digest*) that had been Thomas Becket's, suggests that no book at Canterbury was beyond the college's reach.[105]

Perhaps it should not be seen as surprising that fewer books were coming into the Cathedral library. It may have been hard to formulate any policy as to what sort of books were really desirable, while it cannot have been easy to find books for sale outside Oxford, London, and Cambridge. For the fifteenth century, there is some evidence that the Priory tended to acquire such books as it specifically wanted by engaging a scribe to work locally, rather than by attempting to find them in some stationer's (or bookseller's) shop. Since the texts were likely to duplicate works already in the library, the scribe could be furnished with his exemplar. A list of the books stated to have been 'written and acquired' in the time of Prior Chillenden (1391–1411) presumably indicates that scribes had been employed to write some of these.[106] There are thirty-six in all: approximately two-thirds were works of canon law, while the rest were of civil law or were service books. If any monk wrote or acquired a chronicle or anything by way of devotional reading, it does not figure here; all the books in the list are of a legal or practical nature, rather like the books that Prior Henry of Eastry had acquired for himself.

The Priory may not particularly have welcomed all the books that it was bequeathed— tokens of favour or esteem from Archbishops Courtenay and Arundel, Bishops Courtenay of Norwich and Fitzhugh of London, and Henry V, for instance[107]—but such accessions,

[103] Ibid. iii. 167–8; cf. also 181, for Archbishop Courtenay's statutes, Jan. 1384.

[104] Ibid. 117–18, no. 144. The *Dicta* were on the twelve stones of the Apocalypse.

[105] Cf. Ker, 'Books in the Colleges Maintained by the Benedictines' (cit. in n. 101), 464.

[106] The list is printed in *Lit. Cant.*, iii. 121–2, and (with two omissions) by James, *ALCD*, 150–1. James noted that the first book in the list, a glossed Decretals, is probably identifiable with one later at Canterbury College.

[107] Courtenay's and Arundel's bequests were noted in the accounts of these archbishops in the Christ Church Mar-

tyrology and Obituary, BL, Arundel MS 68, printed from the copy in LPL, MS 20, by Wharton, *Anglia Sacra*, i. 62; Courtenay's bequest is recorded in Reg. S, fo. 73, printed by Beazeley, 'History of the Chapter Library' (cit. in n. 47), 135; Fitzhugh's will, dated 1434, is printed in *Register of Henry Chichele, Archbishop of Canterbury, 1414–1443*, ed. E. F. Jacob, ii (CYS, 42; 1937), 540–1; Henry V's bequest was in his testament dated 10 June 1421, printed by P. and F. Strong, 'The Last Will and Codicils of Henry V', *EHR*, 96 (1981), 79–102. The Priory had difficulty in obtaining Arundel's bequest: T. Rymer, *Foedera*, original edn. (20 vols.; London, 1726–35), x. 317–18.

combined with those made by commission or purchase, must in numerical terms have more than offset the removal of books to Oxford. The bookshelves in the slype (between the chapter house and the north-west transept), even with the benefit of a second storey, must have been filled to the limit—and the slype was in any case a most unattractive place to use as a book-store. Even after the rebuilding of the cloister in the 1390s and 1400s, it would also have been a practical impossibility to contemplate storing more books there; it must have been difficult enough merely to locate them there. Seasonal dampness would have affected both the slype and the carrels in the cloister, where most monks did their reading: it did not help that the slype and cloister were directly north of the Cathedral church. The obvious answer was to have a new library building.

Archbishop Chichele was the benefactor who enabled Canterbury to join the growing number of cathedrals, both secular and monastic, that were erecting new libraries at about this time. It was built as an extra storey above the prior's chapel; that is, approximately above where the Howley-Harrison Library now is.[108] It was a much larger building than the slype area, as well as being, no doubt, far better lit. It was an oblong room, 66 feet long on its north side and 63 feet 6 inches on its south, and 21 feet wide. The work on its construction must have been well under way by 1432, ten years before Chichele's death, for an agreement between the Priory and Archbishop drawn up in that year refers to both his construction of the building and his gift for it of valuable books on various subjects.[109] It was not completed until about 1442–3, however, for an account of that year mentions the purchase of glass from Chichele's executors.[110]

In 1508 a list was drawn up of the 'repairs done to the books which are in the library above the prior's chapel, that is, for their new binding and boarding with covers and giving them clasps and chains'.[111] The names are given of 293 books, bookcase by bookcase and shelf by shelf, and for each book the opening words of its second leaf are also stated, in the approved manner of any professional cataloguer. There is no reason to think that the library furniture would have been changed since the 1440s, so it is safe to assume that the library was set up with precisely what this list shows it to have had in 1508 (and, equally certainly, until the Dissolution): there was a set of sixteen book-presses, eight on each side of the room, and each book-press had an upper and lower shelf on each side.[112] That is to say, the library was furnished according to the standard later medieval model, with double-sided desks at which the monks could read and write; there would have been a seat between each bookcase, and it is almost certain that there would have been a window above each seat, as in other libraries of this date.

It is very probable, too, that the books in the new library were chained. All the evidence

[108] W. H. St J. Hope drew a parallel with earlier monastic libraries, such as at the abbeys of Castle Acre and Fountains, where there are still 'traces of an upper storey over the gallery connecting the infirmary buildings with the church, with a wide and ample stair leading up to it from the gallery itself' (Jnl. Royal Institute of British Architects, 3rd ser., 5 (1898 for 1897–8), 384). Canterbury's library and its staircase are more fully discussed by Robert Willis, The Architectural History of the Conventual Buildings of the Monastery of Christ Church in Canterbury (London, 1869), 65–7.

[109] Reg. S, fo. 111, printed by Sheppard, Lit. Cant., iii. 159.
[110] Prior's Accts., no. 6 [1442–3], s.v. Novum Opus, has payments for carpentry and glass for the new library (ex inf. Mrs M. J. Sparks).
[111] MS Lit. C. 11; printed by James, ALCD, 152–64.
[112] Cf. the conjectures of J. W. Clark, 'On Ancient Libraries: (1) Christ Church, Canterbury . . .', Proc. Cambridge Antiquarian Soc., 8 (1891–4), 359–68, and the modifications to Clark's views suggested by B. H. Streeter, The Chained Library (London, 1931), 47–9.

points to this: the books had no new pressmarks written in them, and the new arrangement of two-shelf presses was based on the presumption that the books would be read *in situ*, and on the practical difficulty of having more than two tiers of shelving with chains hanging down. Unlike the book-store in the slype, the new library would have been sufficiently brightly lit by its windows on the north and south sides for it to be a perfectly practicable proposition to require books to be read there, rather than to allow them to be carried into the cloister.

What cannot be stated with any certainty, however, is exactly which were the books that the new library housed so securely and so spaciously. It is apparent from the 1508 listing that the 293 books that were then repaired were shelved in an entirely rational way. The first case on the north side had Bibles and biblical concordances and some scholastic theology; the second had more scholastic theology and biblical commentaries and glosses; the third to seventh cases had more biblical commentaries and other works by the early Fathers, with major collections of Chrysostom, Augustine, Jerome, Bede, Gregory, and Ambrose; and the eighth case had some history books (Josephus, Bede, Vincent of Beauvais) as well as grammars and dictionaries. The cases on the south side had some more miscellaneous scholastic theology (last two cases), books of canon and civil law (the next four cases), lives of saints, and works of philosophy and medicine (second case from the west), and then a more heterogeneous assortment that included a Brut chronicle in French, a Greek book, several books of sermons, a musical book (*liber de tropis loquendi*), and the letters of Ivo of Chartres.[113]

This arrangement is clear enough. What is uncertain is how many more books there were—if any—than those that are enumerated in the list. J. W. Clark and M. R. James thought that the new library-room contained almost the whole of the Priory's book collection, since the 512 feet of shelving (as calculated by Clark) would have held about 2,100 volumes; James thought that it would have received at least 1,700 volumes when first erected, and he guessed that it might have run out of space for new accessions only in the late fifteenth century.[114] These views have, however, been questioned by N. R. Ker, who suggested that the 1508 list is in fact 'an almost complete list' of the contents of the Priory's chained library—which he saw as being a small, choice, selection of the more precious books.[115] Ker drew attention to the fact that so many of the books in the 1508 list have been identified as still extant (over two-thirds of those numbered between 31 and 155, for instance), and that the list includes 'practically all the extant Christ Church copies of works of the Fathers and of glossed books of the Bible'. On the other hand, neither the 1508 list nor any other document before the 1530s mentions any other library collection than the 'new library' and the books still kept in the cloister; the new library in all probability *could* have housed 2,100 volumes; and if the books were not all chained in it, it is strange that they were not given new, post-Eastry pressmarks. The presence in the list of so much of the Priory's patristic collection is perhaps explicable by the fact that so much of it was made up of late eleventh- and twelfth-century manuscripts: the Priory's patristic collection

[113] James, *ALCD*, pp. liv–lv.
[114] Ibid., p. liii.
[115] N. R. Ker, 'The Migration of Manuscripts from the English

Medieval Libraries', *The Library,* 4th ser., 23 (1942–3), 1–11, at 10–11; reprinted in id., *Books, Collectors and Libraries* (cit. in n. 32), 459–69, at 468–9.

forms a remarkable *continuum* in the history of its library, from the twelfth century right down to the Dissolution. The patristic books were (and are) handsome volumes, but in the later sixteenth century their appeal was naturally limited to a few book-collectors, and it was perhaps for this reason that they were to form such a large proportion of the gifts of the ecclesiastics Archbishop Whitgift and Dean Neville to Trinity College, Cambridge, so that they have been kept together down to the present day. Ker's observation of this and other aspects of the books listed in 1508 cannot be faulted, but his inferences are hard to sustain. Further research may provide other reasons for doubting his hypothesis: almost all the books in the 1508 list that are still extant come from its first half—that is to say, the presses on the north side of the library: these were the books of biblical concordances and scholastic theology, as well as of patristic writings, and all were liable to suffer benign neglect in the later part of the century. But why do only eight books survive from the presses on the southern side of the library? And why would the Priory have kept such a small number of books, ranging from two to eight, on each shelf? And finally, most seriously of all, it is difficult to say that the books in the list formed a truly 'select' collection: too many fundamental texts are absent from it.

For the years immediately following the death of Prior Eastry, there is very little to say about the Priory muniments. The recording of documents must have owed much to his personal interest in the matter, and now that he was dead, such practices seem to have ground to a halt. Eastry had had transcribed or listed all sorts of records, both financial and of a more general nature; for his priorate, the Priory registers come closer to being chapter act books and memoranda books than they had ever done previously. Perhaps the general structure or pattern of Priory life was not really conducive to the recording of events that concerned it. Members of the community relied on their memory for what they had all agreed on. From time to time a monk might show himself interested in chronicling the life that was going on around him, and there still survive several fourteenth- and fifteenth-century chronicles written by such brethren; but by no stretch of the imagination can Christ Church be compared with, say, St Albans Abbey or Durham Cathedral Priory as a centre of historical documentation. The only continuous record kept at Christ Church, Canterbury, was a listing of the names of the monks and their dates of profession, and even this record is far from complete.[116]

The Priory may or may not have suffered financially from the absence of Eastry's careful recording of its financial dealings; the historian is unquestionably hampered by the general lack of any record of chapter decisions that concerned the liturgy or organization of the house. Eastry's *Memoriale multorum* (BL, Cotton MS Galba E. iv) includes copies of a few chapter decisions, about the Priory's temporal income and the observance of the feast of Corpus Christi, for instance;[117] but such knowledge is rarely available from before or after his priorate.

It would be wrong positively to blame Eastry's successors for not leaving records

[116] Thomas Cawston, who had held the office of chancellor (amongst others), and who in 1486 compiled a list of the monks (Lit. MS D. 12), evidently had access to records of the dates of profession and of death from 1286 and of monks' names from 1210 onwards.

[117] Fos. 73 and 75^v; it is perhaps more than merely coincidental that the latter decision is also mentioned in the Christ Church chronicle which is now at Trinity College, Cambridge (MS R. 5. 41, fo. 126).

which do not still survive. A day-book of financial accounts kept by Priors Oxenden and Hathbrand[118] was discovered by J. B. Sheppard, and other records of that sort were doubtless kept by all of his successors; it may be that they filled up paper books, like the day-book, and such books were inherently less likely to be preserved than Eastry's costly parchment compilations. Still, the silence after Eastry is suggestive. The Priory was resourceful enough, however, to develop fresh, alternative strategies for dealing with its records. One method was to engage outsiders to handle some of its business affairs. In a sense, this was hardly a novelty; Master Homer in the mid-thirteenth century had clearly been a trusted agent of the Priory. But with Alexander Hauekyn (or Hawkin) in the mid-fourteenth century, the Priory went a stage further: Hauekyn is described as 'secretarius' as early as 1331, and according to Hasted he was 'secretary to several priors'.[119] Hauekyn was clearly an exceptional man, however—not least in his generosity towards the Priory[120]—and the Priory's long-term solution to the problem of record-keeping was to set up a permanent chancery.

At Durham Cathedral Priory, the chancery was a major department, and the chancellor (*cancellarius*) was responsible for both the library and the registers; the chancery even had its own permanent collection of books.[121] At most other major houses, such as Westminster Abbey and St Augustine's Abbey, Canterbury, it was instead the precentor who had charge of the registers, as well as of the library. The setting-up of a chancery at Christ Church, Canterbury, could easily be presented as a forward-looking piece of policy-making, for it can reasonably be seen as a recognition of the literary standards that were coming to be expected of the Priory's letter-writers. The chancellors—and the usual practice at the Priory was for there to be two at a time (rather like its treasurers)—were sometimes men with a university education, skilled in Latin composition. Like the prior's chaplaincy, the chancellorship was an office that might point to higher office in the future; like John Wessington at Durham, William Sellyng was promoted direct from chancellor to prior.[122] The chancellors at Christ Church are not known to have had a library of ordinary books, but they did gain a permanent office, perhaps in the Treasury (behind St Andrew's Chapel), and here they had charge of the bulk of the Priory muniments. It is only at the end of the fourteenth century that mention is first found of records being kept 'in our chancery',[123] but it is clear that their removal from the prior's quarters had taken place long before this, possibly in the aftermath of Henry of Eastry's death.

In 1370 John of Gloucester and John of Eastry, the two chancellors, attempted to put the archives to right. Gone now, if not previously, was the mass of bags, pouches, boxes, and

[118] DE 3.

[119] Ibid., fo. 31 ('secretar' domini R. Prioris'); E. Hasted, *History ... of Kent* (1st edn., 4 vols.; Canterbury, 1778–99), iv. 515, n. z. Hauekyn was still alive in 1358, when he granted (conveyed?) property to the Priory: A. Hussey, *Kent Chantries*, Kent Records, 12 (Kent Archaeol. Soc., 1936), 31.

[120] Hasted states that he gave £150 towards the south steeple and a new bell, as well as towards the reroofing of the Martyrdom area: *History of Kent*, iv. 515 n. z, 517 n. l.

[121] See W. A. Pantin, 'English Monastic Letter-Books', in *Historical Essays in Honour of James Tait*, ed. J. G. Edwards, V. H.

Galbraith, and E. F. Jacob (Manchester, 1933), 201–22, at 207–8, 211; R. B. Dobson, *Durham Priory, 1400–1450* (Cambridge, 1973), 362–3.

[122] But, as Barrie Dobson pointed out to me, the chancellorship at Canterbury was less of a stepping-stone to high office than it was at Durham; several Canterbury chancellors are not known to have held any other office.

[123] 'Sicut in quodam scripto obligatorio et indentura inde facta, que in Cancellaria nostra habentur' ('As in a bond and indenture thereof, which are kept in our chancery'): BL, Arundel MS 68, fo. 36ᵛ.

chests of Prior Eastry's day: everything was placed in one or other half of a large cupboard (*armariolum*), subdivided into fifteen or sixteen compartments (or *vasa*), some of which were further subdivided into what must have been small pigeonholes, marked with letters of the alphabet. Within these, the documents were placed in a clear order, which represented a valiant effort by the two chancellors to arrange according to subject-matter. For instance, lesser documents obtained at the papal Curia were put in the fourth *vas* in the north part of the cupboard, the fifth *vas* had the more important papal privileges, and the eighth *vas* (divided into six parts) had the lesser papal privileges; the twelfth *vas* (in two parts) had archiepiscopal charters that had been copied into one of the registers, and (presumably in a pigeonhole all of its own) a copy of the (Great) charter of St Thomas. 'Codicilli latine et anglice' in the tenth *vas* of the same cupboard were very conceivably the pre-Conquest charters; these were perhaps seen to some extent as relics, on a par with the grantors' knives (once, if not still, attached to charters in token of livery) that filled the thirteenth *vas* in the southern cupboard.

All these details are known because the two chancellors also wrote a guide to their new arrangements, prefaced by a short (though flowery) account of their achievement.[124] They had acted in order to enable their successors to locate documents more readily than before, but it is evident that they had, too, a sense of respect for the historic importance of the archives—what their preface calls '*virtus memorativa*'. By the same token, however, the chancellors' work is open to criticism as being an arrangement and selective listing that reflects their own sense of historical curiosity about an archive that was gradually falling out of regular use: the documents that they had arranged did indeed form the bulk of the Priory's muniments, but it seems probable that the documents that were likeliest to be needed for the administration of the Priory's jurisdiction and estates were located elsewhere, in the offices of the treasurers and other obedientiaries, or even in the custody of their lawyers or officials. The rise of the practice of leasing out the conventual land had as its concomitant a reduction in the need to resort to title-deeds: rentals, surveys, and counterparts of leases were what was now required by those in charge of the estates, and the older archives were thus losing their practical value. And at the same time, the Priory's jurisdictional rights, as, for instance, during archiepiscopal vacancies, were becoming still less likely to be questioned: the sort of dispute that had so exercised Henry of Eastry and his predecessors seems rarely to have arisen in the later fourteenth century or subsequently.

The history of the archives in the fifteenth century is far from being clear. Some quite irrelevant papers came into the muniments: for instance, the personal archive of John Kington (d. 1416), a monk who in earlier days had participated in diplomatic negotiations with Hanse towns and the Teutonic Knights, and who had kept the associated documentation.[125] And at about the same time, when seeking an indulgence for the jubilee of

---

[124] There survives only Somner's transcript of the inventory, Ch. Ant. C. 232.

[125] Ch. Ant. M. 301 and X. 9. Cf. *Lit. Cant.*, iii. 78–86; *Hansisches Urkundenbuch*, v: 1392–1414, ed. K. Kunze (Leipzig, 1899), nos. 687, 697, 804, etc.; Emden, *BRUO*, iii. 1075–6. Kington achieved a measure of fame this century, as the 'eld monk, whech had ben tresowrer wyth the Qwen whyl he was in seculer clothyng, a riche man, and gretly dred of mech pepyl', who told Margery Kempe that she should be put away 'in an hows of ston, that ther schuld no man speke wyth' her. *The Book of Margery Kempe*, ed. S. B. Meech and H. E. Allen (Early English Text Soc., os, 212; 1940 for 1939), 27.

St Thomas of 1420, the chapter wrote that it had lost a requisite papal bull.[126] A few years later, in 1434, a whole series of royal charters (going back to Edward the Confessor) was confirmed and consequently copied into a royal Chancery patent roll:[127] this shows that the archives could still yield the required documents, although it is also a reminder of the later medieval tendency to use the Crown's record-keeping apparatus as a supplement, or even an alternative, to an institution's or family's own archive.

In the later fifteenth century there are a few signs that some of the brethren at Christ Church took an interest in the archive that was under the chancellors' care. In 1474 the subprior, William Hadleigh, compiled a cartulary of St James's Hospital, Thanington (of which he was warden): he must surely also have cast an occasional eye on the Priory's own muniments.[128] And in the later years of the century a fresh listing of some of the older Priory documents was made:[129] this survives in an imperfect condition, and therefore cannot easily be assessed, but it appears to be a relisting of some of the groups of documents that had already been described in 1370. The receptacle containing each group is termed a *cista* (chest) rather than a *vas*, and although some of the *ciste* have numbers and contents that correspond to the numbers and contents of *vasa*,[130] other *ciste* have both a letter (e.g., .C.) or mark and contents that cannot be correlated with the older listing. It is uncertain whether a relocation of all these documents had taken place, or whether the late fifteenth-century list was simply recording the physical arrangement as it had long been (without giving what may have been an artificial impression of regularity[131]), as well as including some additional material. How far, it may even be asked, had the rearranging of the earlier muniments actually advanced since Prior Eastry's time?

What the Cathedral Priory all too clearly lacked was the equivalent of Thomas Gunwyn, an early sixteenth-century clerk who worked for Glastonbury Abbey, where he was described as 'deeply knowledgeable about the muniments of this monastery'.[132] It is perhaps indicative of loose administration at Christ Church that only some leases were copied into registers, although it must be said that very few religious houses kept such a register at all.[133] It certainly is strange to find that the Priory in the late fifteenth century

[126] See Pantin, *Cant. Coll.*, iv. 224; R. Foreville, *Le Jubilé de Saint Thomas Becket du XIIIe au XIVe siècle, 1220–1470* (Paris, 1959), 41–2, 121.

[127] *CPR 1429–36*, 415–24. Mention ought also to be made, at about this point, of an alphabetically arranged index, in roll form, to four of the Priory registers, designated 'c', 'ca', 'g', and 'k': Ch. Ant. M. 349. It has been badly damaged and lacks almost all of its heading. 'K' is Reg. K.

[128] The cartulary is now BL, Add. MS 32098. The prior of Christ Church was responsible for keeping inventories of the goods of Eastbridge Hospital, Canterbury: R. M. Haines, *Archbishop John Stratford* (Toronto, 1986), 383.

[129] PRO, E 36/138; Davis, *Medieval Cartularies* (cit. in n. 63), no. 175. A few items in this have been identified tentatively with extant or otherwise recorded documents by C. R. and M. G. Cheney in their edition of *Letters of Pope Innocent III (1198–1216) Concerning England and Wales* (Oxford, 1967), e.g. 12, no. 61; and in their 'Letters of Innocent III: Additions and Corrections', *BIHR*, 44 (1971), 98–115, at 106, no. 160; they refer to the inventory as being of the early 16th cent.

[130] e.g. *cista sexta* seems to represent south side, *vas* 6.

[131] Note the discrepancy in the 1370 account between the statement in its preface that the documents were kept in 30 *vasa* (15 in each part of the cupboard), and the actual numbers of *vasa* in the north and south divisions—15 and 16—as set out in the text.

[132] John of Glastonbury, *Chronica*, ed. T. Hearne (2 vols.; Oxford, 1726), ii. 289: 'munimentorum istius monasterii profundissime expertum'. Gunwyn assisted Abbot Beere in the making of a survey of the abbey's estates.

[133] The see of Canterbury may have had such a register, however; the Priory made copies of archbishopric leases, in Reg. T (for which see F. R. H. Du Boulay, 'Calendar of the Demesne Leases made by Archbishop Warham (1503–32)', in *Documents Illustrative of Medieval Kentish Society*, ed. id., Kent Records, 18 (Kent Archaeol. Soc., 1964), 266–97). So, too, did St Augustine's Abbey, Canterbury: see Lit. MS E. 23 (Davis, *Medieval Cartularies* (cit. in n. 63), no. 206, and cf. no. 205). See also J. N. Hare, 'The Monks as Landlords: The Leasing of the Monastic Demesnes in Southern England', in *The Church in Pre-*

made its rent collectors or bailiffs responsible for keeping and creating records of its properties and tenants: the contract for the appointment of the rent-collector of the manor of Westwell in 1494 specifies that he was to keep ledgers (or 'gaderers'), and after five years and again after seven years was to start a 'newe Rentall in parchemyn', containing a complete list of tenants, extents, boundaries, rent charges, and the like.[134] Every time he handed over a completed rental, he received a bonus of 30s. to 40s.; but it was against his own rentals that his success in rent-collecting was judged. This was 'contracting-out' in the extreme—the passing of responsibility to men with no real interest in maintaining the Priory's rights.

The last phase of English monasticism was characterized by a revival of historical interest—a concern for both the history of individual religious houses and the order to which they belonged, and also for the history of the Church and, in consequence, for the writings of the Church Fathers. Almost every English house had some early chronicle or history of itself to which it could turn, while national chronicles such as the Brut were copied on a commercial scale. Christ Church, Canterbury, of course, had absolutely no problem in finding materials bearing on its own history, as well as that of England as a whole: the revival can merely have encouraged a sense of awareness of the past that was already strongly felt. The Priory's collection of relics of saints was by itself enough to induce an almost overwhelming respect for its early history, given the part which several of these saints played in the liturgy, prayers, and art of the place; it is, nevertheless, of interest to note the renewal that took place in the cults of early saints, such as Blaise and especially Dunstan, in the course of the fifteenth century.[135]

The library was so well stocked with late eleventh- and twelfth-century copies of many of the texts that were now brought back into fashion, that there was little need to buy or commission fresh copies. Their handsome script was perfectly easy to read, and there is even reason to think that it was appreciated for its own aesthetic qualities: as at certain other religious houses, scribes were engaged in producing facsimile scripts that replicated those of the twelfth century. For instance, the Arundel Psalter (BL, MS Arundel 155) has a couple of leaves that—admittedly very feebly—imitate the earlier script of the rest of the book,[136] while the Cathedral's Lit. MS E. 42 has five leaves that look back more skilfully to twelfth-century models.[137] Textual replication was more common, however. For instance, in the early sixteenth century, two whole volumes of biblical commentaries by Bede were copied from manuscripts in the Priory library for Archbishop Warham.[138] Perhaps to avoid wear and tear, the thirteenth-century Christ Church martyrology and obituary (now

Reformation Society: Essays in Honour of F. R. H. Du Boulay, ed. C. M. Barron and C. Harper-Bill (Woodbridge, 1985), 82–94, at 87–8. Christ Church's leases are in Regs. S, T, and T2; there also survive *c.* 140 bonds entered into by Priory lessees as security for the performance of covenants in their leases, from the 1390s onwards.

[134] D. Gardiner, 'Some Notes on Petitions Concerning Canterbury Monastic Houses in the Court of Chancery', *Arch. Cant.*, 43 (1931), 199–214, at 205, from Reg. S, fos. 391ᵛ–392ᵛ. There are similar requirements in other bailiffs' or bedells' contracts of about this date in Reg. S.

[135] See N. L. Ramsay and M. J. Sparks, 'The Cult of St Dunstan at Christ Church, Canterbury', in *St Dunstan* (cit. in n. 17), 311–

23, at 321–2.

[136] For Arundel 155 (whose added leaves are fos. 145–6), see E. Temple, *Anglo-Saxon Manuscripts, 900–1066* (A Survey of Manuscripts Illuminated in the British Isles, 2; London, 1976), 84–5, no. 66. The added leaves are only roughly imitative.

[137] Fos. 69–74; see N. R. Ker, *Medieval Manuscripts in British Libraries*, ii (Oxford, 1977), 296–7.

[138] See *The Benedictines and the Book: An Exhibition to Commemorate the Fifteenth Centenary of the Birth of St Benedict. A.D. 480–1980* (Oxford: Bodleian Library, 1980), no. 55, discussing Oxford, New College, MSS 42 and 57, both of which are suggested as having been copied by the same scribe for Warham. They are in a humanistic script.

BL, MS Arundel 68) was also copied at about this time (the copy being LPL, MS 20). It is conceivable that the copy (now Bodl., MS Tanner 223) made at this time from the cartulary of the archbishopric of Canterbury, LPL, MS 1212, was also prepared for the Cathedral Priory, although it is more likely to have been made for the archbishop.[139]

Wear and tear of the twelfth-century books in the Chichele library would explain why so many of them figure among the books in it that were listed in 1508 as needing repair.[140] It would be misleading, however, to suppose that the monks' intellectual energies were all being devoted to reading library books, in either the new library or in the cloister. Increasingly, it seems, the brethren were forming private libraries, by a combination of gift, purchase, and their own writing. William Ingram, in whose account and memorandum book the 1508 list is copied, recorded the purchase of *Liber Gestorum Romanorum* (doubtless the popular collection of tales known generally as *Gesta Romanorum*), two books of the Life of St Thomas, 'Coklorels Bote', and a little Bible (described as 'scripta', as opposed to being in print).[141] He himself partly wrote BL, MS Harl. 1587, a grammatical miscellany that goes back to the late fourteenth century.[142] At a monk's death, his possessions would have been distributed as appropriate, the books perhaps first being listed: at least two such book-lists survive.[143] At St Augustine's Abbey the customary specifically stated that in such circumstances it was the precentor's duty to take such books and to write the dead monk's name in them before bearing them off to the library.[144]

William Ingram's books were a rather middle-brow assortment. Yet the humanistic revival of learning was far from passing the Priory by; and it is in one or two of the private book-lists and manuscript compilations that the renaissance can most clearly be seen to have come to Canterbury. A list of books handed over by Prior Goldstone to Thomas Goldwell, perhaps *c.* 1496, includes a few works indicative of this: four by Cicero (including *De Amicitia* and *De Rhetoricorum Inventione*), volumes of Lucan and Priscian, and commentaries on works by Virgil, as well as the more conventional *Meditations* of St Anselm and the somewhat recherché *Questiones* of John (of St German) of Cornwall.[145] Half a century earlier, the Ciceronian model aspired to by such monks as Henry Cranebroke and William Chart is shown in letters by or about them in books compiled as letter formularies.[146] It was, however, with William Sellyng, prior from 1472 to 1494, that the Italian

[139] For Arundel 68 and Lambeth 20, see e.g. [Richard Whytford], *The Martiloge in Englysshe after the Use of the chirche of Salisbury,* ed. F. Procter and E. S. Dewick (Henry Bradshaw Soc., 3; 1893 for 1891), 287. The latter manuscript cannot have been copied before 1500, since it includes the obit of Archbishop Morton (fo. 218ᵛ) in its original hand. For Tanner 223 and Lambeth 1212, see A. J. Collins, 'The Documents of the Great Charter of 1215', *Proc. British Academy,* 34 (1948), 233–79, at 240.

[140] Cf. above, pp. 364–6. The list is followed by a much shorter list of books 'that Richard hath', Richard presumably being the binder; it includes one or more books 'from the cloister library' (James, *ALCD,* 164, nos. 303, 306), reminding us that there was still a cupboard of books in the cloister. Dr M. T. Gibson has observed that the 1508 list is not actually in the hand of William Ingram, even though it occurs in a notebook of his (MS Lit. C. 11).

[141] See G. H. Rooke, 'Dom William Ingram and His Account-Book [MS Lit. C. 11], 1504–1533', *JEH,* 7 (1956), 30–44, at 42–3.

For 'Coklorel's Bote', see A. W. Pollard and G. R. Redgrave, *Short-Title Catalogue of Books Printed in England, Scotland, & Ireland, and of English Books Printed Abroad, 1475–1640,* 2nd edn., rev. W. A. Jackson, F. S. Ferguson, and K. F. Pantzer, 3 vols. (Bibliog. Soc., 1986–91), nos. 5456, 5456. 3.

[142] F. A. Gasquet, 'The Canterbury Claustral School in the 15th Century', *Downside Review,* 10 (1891), 31–45.

[143] Discussed by R. B. Dobson, above, p. 111.

[144] *Customary of the Benedictine Monasteries of Saint Augustine, Canterbury, and Saint Peter, Westminster,* ed. E. M. Thompson, 2 vols. (Henry Bradshaw Soc., 23, 28; 1902–4), i. 362.

[145] The list has been printed thrice, most recently by Pantin (*Cant. Coll.,* i. 81), who suggested that it represents books handed over to Goldwell when he became a fellow of Canterbury College; Pantin accordingly dated it *c.*1496.

[146] See R. B. Dobson, above, pp. 113–14; and cf. R. Weiss, 'Some Unpublished Correspondence of Guarino da Verona', *Italian Studies,* 2 (1938–9), 110–17.

humanistic renaissance was most strongly felt at Christ Church. Sellying had been to Italy, and as prior he was in a position to promote what he admired. He enhanced the fabric of the Cathedral library that lay above his chapel, by adorning it with 'very beautiful carved work'; and he glazed the south alley of the cloister 'for the use of studious brethren', and made there 'the new [wooden] framed constructions which are now called carrels'.[147] The monks were being encouraged to read, and perhaps write, in the cloister in greater comfort.

The pity, the tragedy, is that it probably will never be known quite what books Sellyng had acquired or commissioned in Italy or England, since most, if not all, of his collection was destroyed when a fire broke out in the prior's lodgings, where his books were kept. This was in 1535, and there are two accounts of it, one, a prosaic report to Thomas Cromwell by his agent Dr Richard Layton, making no mention of the books, and the other an exaggerated account by the Canterbury schoolmaster and bibliophile John Twyne. Putting an account of the disaster into the words of Abbot Vokes (or Foche) of St Augustine's Abbey, Twyne says that 'besides other buildings, it destroyed the library ... In that fire among many thousands of books, alas! one copy—Theodore's—of that precious book of Cicero, *De republica* perished in the flames.'[148] Layton reported that 'only three chambers were burnt, called the new or the king's lodging. The gable ends of the house, made of strong brick, kept the fire from the houses adjoining'; he made no mention of books.[149] It is regrettable that the seventeenth-century scholar William Somner is silent about the fire; it seems fairly certain, however, that it was only the Prior's books that were lost. The sixteenth-century antiquary John Leland, who came to Canterbury within just a few years of the disaster, refers to it in the course of his biographical account of Sellyng, and names a few books that were saved from it.[150]

Leaving aside Prior Sellyng's books, which in any case were not incorporated within the main library collection, it would be fair to say that the library of Christ Church in the early sixteenth century corresponded in its form and character to that of most other English monastic houses. What Knowles wrote of the medieval monastic book-collection in general can certainly be applied to the history of Christ Church Cathedral Priory's library: 'It was from the beginning, and remained in part till the end, the sacred and profane legacy of the ancient world, multiplied and broadcast under the peculiarly favourable conditions of the eleventh and twelfth centuries, and with the original comments and additions made during that [latter] century. All that came after that was in a sense accidental, the infiltration of other disciplines, theological and legal, that were not monastic.

[147] 'Australem partem Claustri ad usum studiosorum confratrum vitreari fecit, ac ibidem novos Textus, quos Carolos ex novo vocamus, perdecentes fecit.' Sellyng's obituary, in the Christ Church Martyrology and Obituary, BL, Arundel MS 68, fo. 4[r-v], printed from the copy in LPL, MS 20, by Wharton, *Anglia Sacra*, i. 145–6, at 145. The other three alleys of the cloister were glazed subsequently: see Beazeley, 'History of the Chapter Library' (cit. in n. 47), 139.

[148] John Twyne, *De Rebus Albionicis, Britannicis atque Anglicis Commentariorum Libri Duo* (London, 1590), adapted from the transl. by F. A. Gasquet, *Monastic Life in the Middle Ages* (London, 1922), 136. Cicero's *Republic* had a quasi-mythic status in the

Middle Ages and Renaissance: no complete copy of it was ever found, and Twyne must have been mistaken in his claim. Archbishop Parker believed that certain of his Greek manuscripts had been Theodore's: see M. R. James, *Sources of Archbishop Parker's Collection of MSS* (Cambridge Antiq. Soc. 8[vo] Pubn. 32; 1899), 9.

[149] *LP Henry VIII*, ix. 226, no. 669.

[150] J. Leland, *Commentarii de Scriptoribus Britannicis*, ed. A. Hall (Oxford, 1709), 483. Sellyng's books are discussed briefly by R. Weiss, *Humanism in England* (3rd edn.; Oxford, 1967), 158–9.

Of creative monastic writing between 1250 and 1540 there was relatively very little, and no monastic library ever seriously attempted to collect all the Latin Continental books of the later Middle Ages, still less the vernacular literatures of the new Europe.'[151] The only qualification to this statement would be the gloss that, as has already been seen at Canterbury, as also to some extent at other houses, the late fifteenth and early sixteenth centuries saw an increasing tendency on the part of individual monks to form personal libraries. William Ingram and Prior Sellyng were not the only members of Christ Church to collect books on their own account, and while the copying of patristic texts may be seen as a sign of institutional activity, a chance few inventories survive to show that in their own cubicles certain monks were possessed of a wide range of contemporary literature, in print as well as manuscript. The inventory of Richard Stone (1509) comprises twenty-five manuscripts and sixteen printed books, and includes works of history and hagiography (such as a Life of Becket).[152] John Holyngborne (professed in 1510) owned a Solinus, *De Mirabilibus Mundi*, which he had purchased in 1503 (now BL, Cotton MS Vespasian B. xxv), a medical collection (Oxford, Corpus Christi College, MS 189), and a psalter (LPL, MS 588); his name also occurs in the Arundel Psalter (BL, MS Arundel 155). Neither in the listing made in 1508 of books at the Cathedral Priory that needed repair, nor in the inventories of Canterbury College, do printed books make more than the briefest appearance: it was, however, the institutional libraries rather than the individual monks that lacked them.[153]

Yet although the 1508 listing does not give a full picture of the Priory library, it provides the clearest of indications that the library was being well maintained. If anything, it was being too carefully guarded: at Archbishop Warham's visitation of the Priory in 1511, it was found that the precentor needed to be reminded of his duty to see that all monks, including the novices, benefited from the distribution of books that he oversaw.[154] Yet there is also a presumption that the Priory archives were not wholly inaccessible to outsiders; in the late 1530s John Leland was permitted to make notes from Register O, and he read the library catalogue in Prior Eastry's register, while he also looked at the books in the library. It is hard to think that to him was allowed what might have been forbidden to a monk, however junior. On the other hand, by the late 1530s the entire house would have seen that drastic changes were coming, likely to overturn the monastic way of life. The loss of their library may have seemed the least of these *bouleversements*. And John Leland may have been one of the more sympathetic of their visitors.

THE NEW FOUNDATION, FROM 1541 TO THE EARLY NINETEENTH CENTURY

The high degree of continuity of personnel between the Cathedral Priory and the New Foundation might have been expected to result in the intact survival of the Priory's library

[151] Knowles, *Religious Orders*, ii. 350.
[152] Pantin, *Cant. Coll.*, i. 88–90.
[153] See R. B. Dobson, above, pp. 105–6; see also N. R. Ker, 'Books in the Colleges Maintained in Oxford by the Bene-

dictines' (cit. in n. 101), 464–5.
[154] *Kentish Visitations of Archbishop William Warham and His Deputies, 1511–1512*, ed. K. L. Wood-Legh (Kent Archaeol. Soc., Records ser., 24; 1984), 294, 297.

and muniments. It is indeed true that quite a number of the Priory's charters are still in the Cathedral's possession, together with about six hundred of the thousands of obedientiaries' accounts that it probably still had in 1541, as well as a great many of its manorial accounts and other records. In this, Christ Church compares very favourably with St Augustine's Abbey, whose account rolls and original charters are almost all irretrievably lost. But its archives still make a relatively poor showing when set beside those of, say, Durham Cathedral or Westminster Abbey, while its medieval library is notorious for having so largely ended up in other institutions' ownership. How did all this come to be?

It appears that the members of Chapter simply ignored the presence in their midst of what must have been still one of the largest collection of books in England. This is remarkable, but it is certainly suggested by the Chapter's response to Archbishop Cranmer's visitation inquiry of 1550. The Edwardian injunctions of 1547 had required every cathedral to have a library of patristic theology, with the works of Saints Augustine, Basil, Gregory Nazianzen, Jerome, Ambrose, John Chrysostom, Cyprian, and Theophylact, as well as of Erasmus.[155] In 1550 Cranmer asked the Chapter of Canterbury if it had a library of such works, and its answer can be guessed at from the fact that in the same year its treasurer's accounts record the expenditure of £12 'for the boks off the library'.[156] An indenture of 1551 records the handing-over of some twenty works by one prebendary, William Devenish, to another, John Joseph, and since seven of the nine prescribed authors figure in this list, it is a fair bet that it is a complete catalogue of the new library.[157] All the items on it could have been, and doubtless were, printed books. It may perhaps also be inferred that the collection was the responsibility of a prebendary and not of a minor canon, and that it was not kept in the same room as any of the Priory books. Injunctions of about the same date for St George's, Windsor (1547) and York Minister (1552) forbade borrowing, and, at Windsor, required the books to be chained.[158]

The inauguration of this 'approved' library shows the corporate obedience of the Chapter, but the fate of the medieval library reflects the interests of a whole series of successive individual deans and prebendaries, several of whom were well aware of the importance of many of the manuscript books in the Priory collection. Compliance with the Reformation must be the cause of no missals having survived from the Priory, but there is no reason to think that any other books were destroyed; nor does it seem to be the case that more than a very few books were abstracted by disgruntled ex-monks. The customary of Becket's shrine (BL, Add. MS 59616), which passed to the Hawkins family of Nash Court, near Canterbury, may, however, have been preserved by this sort of channel.[159] What seems generally to have happened, rather, was that particular deans and prebendaries removed those books that interested them, over a period of time that lasted

---

[155] *Visitation Articles and Injunctions of the Period of the Reformation*, ed. W. H. Frere and W. M. Kennedy, 3 vols. (Alcuin Club Collections, 14–16; 1910), i. 135, and ii. 136.

[156] Ibid. ii. 249; Misc. Accts. 40, fos. 43ᵛ, 44 (payments in Nov. 1550).

[157] Christ Church Letters, ii, no. 212; noted by R. L. Poole, HMC, *Various Collections*, i. 232. That the list is not of a personal collection is shown by its form, its present location, and its inclusion of two Bibles in English, as well as one printed by Robert Estienne.

[158] *Visitation Articles and Injunctions*, ed. Frere and Kennedy (cit. in n. 155), ii. 164, 318–19.

[159] See D. H. Turner, 'The Customary of the Shrine of St Thomas Becket', *Cant. Cath. Chron.*, 70 (1976), 16–22. The book also contains two biographies of Becket; for other possible former contents of it, see Brown, in *Canterbury Professions*, ed. Richter (cit. in n. 45), p. xxxvi n.

from the 1540s until early in the following century. The list of such men is headed by Nicholas Wotton (Dean, 1541–67), who removed such obvious treasures as the 'A', or Parker, manuscript of the *Anglo-Saxon Chronicle* and who made historical or antiquarian notes from such books as the monk John Stone's chronicle.[160]

The only member of the Cathedral community whose collecting activities have been thoroughly investigated is John Twyne (*c*.1507–81), Headmaster of the King's School, who owned at least ten manuscripts from the Cathedral Priory, including the 'B' manuscript of the *Anglo-Saxon Chornicle*, as well as a similar number of manuscripts from St Augustine's Abbey.[161] But comparable tales could undoubtedly be told of several other deans and prebendaries, such as William Darell (1553–80) and, most notably, John Bale (1560–3) and Dean Thomas Neville (1597–1615). Even men who were not of the collecting mentality joined in: for instance, Thomas Becon (prebendary, 1559–67), who presented to Archbishop Parker an English exposition of the Gospels of Mark and Luke and the Pauline Epistles. Becon sent this from Canterbury as being an old monument worthy to be preserved and embraced for its antiquity's sake;[162] he would undoubtedly have felt differently about Prior Henry of Eastry's *Memoriale multorum*, from which he quoted with abhorrence in his *Monstruous Marchandise of the Romish Bishops* a list of relics at Christ Church in 1315.[163] Archbishop Parker had been given special powers of obtaining loans of ancient manuscripts, but his correspondence shows that he had no need to exert himself in Canterbury, since the prebendaries offered them to him freely. To take another instance of this, Bale wrote to him in 1560, 'Fyve great legendes have I borrowed of maistre Mylles for your graces occupyenge, the sixt I have taken out of our lybrarye': this conceivably refers to the twelfth-century passionals, of which fragments remain at Canterbury (see Col. Pl. V) and in the Cotton collection in the British Library, and it certainly reveals a former monk, John Mylles (prebendary, 1541–65), as preserving such books, while it incidentally implies that the medieval library was still a very recognizable collection.[164]

The fate of the Priory archives after 1540 was bound to be very different from that of the library. The muniments were needed as the title-deeds for the New Foundation's estates, and there was no question of their being able to gather dust until removed by some rapacious or historically minded prebendary. On the other hand, some of the

[160] For Wotton, see May McKisack, *Medieval History in the Tudor Age* (Oxford, 1971), 28–9, 66. An excerpt by him from Stone's chronicle (now Cambridge, Corpus Christi College, MS 417) is in a volume of his collections, BL, Add. MS 38692, fo. 58 ('Ex libro scripto a monacho Cantuariensis'; 'From a book written by a monk of Canterbury'); cf. also Barbara Ficaro, 'Nicholas Wotton: Dean and Diplomat' (Ph. D. thesis, Univ. of Kent at Canterbury, 1981), 273.

[161] A. G. Watson, 'John Twyne of Canterbury (d. 1581) as a Collector of Medieval Manuscripts: A Preliminary Investigation', *The Library*, 6th ser., 8 (1986), 133–51.

[162] For Becon's letter, and the identification of the manuscript as Cambridge, Corpus Christi College, MS 32, see M. R. James, *A Descriptive Catalogue of the Manuscripts in the Library of Corpus Christi College, Cambridge* (2 vols.; Cambridge, 1912), i, pp. xxi, 269.

[163] The *Memoriale multorum* passed into the hands of John Twyne, and subsequently into Sir Robert Cotton's library,

where it is now MS Galba E. iv, fos. 1–186. Becon's quotation, which is in translation, is in his *Works* (3 vols.; London, 1560–4), iii, fos. clxxxxii[v]–clxxxxvii[v]; cf. H. B. Thomas, 'Thomas Becon, Canon of Canterbury', *Arch. Cant.*, 69 (1955), 159–70, at 165.

[164] H. R. Luard, 'A Letter from Bishop Bale to Archbishop Parker', *Proc. Cambridge Antiquarian Soc.*, 3 (1865), 157–73, at 163; the Priory library in Henry of Eastry's time had a six-volume set of *lectionalia* (James, *ALCD*, 52, nos. 371–6) and a six-volume (?) set of passionals (ibid., nos. 359 ff.; cf. N. R. Ker, 'Membra Disiecta', 2nd ser., *British Museum Quarterly*, 14 (1939–40), 79–86, at 83–5). Excerpts gathered by Parker from the *passionale sancti Ignatii* (i.e., BL, Cotton MS Otho D. viii, fos. 8–173, and Cambridge, Trinity College, MS O. 2. 51, flyleaves) are in Cambridge, Corpus Christi College, MS 298, sect. IV, fo. 54[v]. I am grateful to Mr T. Graham for providing information about the latter manuscript. It is impossible to say whether Bale was referring to the *lectionalia* or the passionals.

muniments were in a sense incriminating evidence, or would soon come to seem so, since they showed the pious uses to which many medieval benefactors had specifically assigned their gifts to the Priory. Matters were also complicated by the complete restructuring of the Cathedral's personnel: the replacement of a departmentalized structure by a basically two-tier system (of dean and prebendaries) had drastic implications for the archives, since these for the last few centuries had evolved in relation to the different monastic obediences. The prebendaries were not, and perhaps never could be, so familiar with the Cathedral estates as the monks had been: the estates were henceforth seen as sources of revenue rather than as communities of the brethren's families.

The archival victims of the transition were almost inevitable: first the records that concerned particular obediences, and then those that related to what had become unacceptable in political or religious terms. The Cathedral has lost most of the registers or cartularies that were doubtless kept by each of the obedientiaries, a dozen leaves of the almoner's register alone surviving at Canterbury;[165] gone, too, are the original charters that endowed the altars,[166] and almost all of the Priory's original *papalia*.[167] These were the immediate losses, and they were in part deliberate. A longer-term threat came from the new structure of the Cathedral's estate management, which put a growing share of the management responsibilities upon the professionals employed by Chapter: lawyers and other outsiders now took possession of chunks of the Cathedral muniments as they established and fought for the Cathedral's rights. And, to take one instance of danger, if such men died, who was going to ask their widows or executors to return whatever documents they might have been entrusted with? In July 1570 Archbishop Parker warned the Chapter that all who had 'any writings or evidences' belonging to the Cathedral must bring them in, to be kept 'in the accustomed place appointed for that purpose' (by which he presumably meant the Treasury), by Michaelmas next.[168] Such things were easier said than done.

William Lovelace was a successful common lawyer who rose to be a serjeant at law (1567); he was being employed by the Cathedral as its counsel by 1559, when someone noted that evidences delivered to him included a whole series of London rentals stretching back over 140 years.[169] In November 1570, in belated response to Parker's monition, Chapter called for the return of 'eny wrytynges, bookes or evydences belongying to thy[s] churche', and specifically warned Lovelace to bring in 'such evidence as he hath in his custodye'.[170] Six years later, however, the antiquary William Lambarde was making notes from what he called a 'vetustus liber' of Christ Church that Lovelace had in his possession, and

---

[165] Davis, *Medieval Cartularies* (cit. in n. 63), notes (no. 176) only a fragment of an almoner's cartulary. Davis's account of Christ Church cartularies and registers is far from complete, however; cf. n. 65 above.

[166] 164 charters enclosing altars had, however, been copied into Regs. A and E; these have been calendared by C. E. Woodruff, 'Endowment Charters of the Altars' (typescript, 1925).

[167] Cf. C. R. Cheney, 'Some Features of Surviving Original Papal Letters in England', reprinted in his *The Papacy and*

England, 12–14th Centuries (London, 1982), ch. 2, pp. 1–25, at 4. For the destruction of *papalia* at Canterbury and elsewhere, see e.g. *Papsturkunden in England*, ed. W. Holtzmann (3 vols.; Berlin, 1930–52), i. 11, and ii. 12–13.

[168] *Visitation Articles and Injunctions*, ed. Frere and Kennedy (cit. in n. 155), iii. 235.

[169] *Christ Church Letters*, iii, inserted loose with no. 92.

[170] Chapter Act Book, 1568–81, fo. 20 (*olim* 27).

Lambarde's excerpts are sufficiently detailed to enable the book in question to be identified as one that is now at Trinity College, Cambridge.[171]

Parker himself may not be above suspicion where the Cathedral's archives are concerned, although his motive for obtaining sight of some of its records was no doubt the perfectly reasonable one of obtaining material to assist him in his own lawsuits. There was a longstanding uncertainty as to which legal instruments of the archbishop or his Cathedral needed to be confirmed by the one or the other and there was now the added complication that some Cathedral Priory properties had passed to the archbishop. And who could blame the archbishop's legal advisors for wanting to read through records of the Cathedral Priory, in search of information for particular lawsuits? There are 'Parkerian' red chalk or crayon markings in records that are still at Canterbury,[172] and there are other markings, apparently also of the later sixteenth century, on account rolls and suchlike documents from the Priory that are now at Lambeth Palace Library:[173] all are signs of the careful perusal of the Cathedral's records. Superfluity of records, rather than abstraction of documents, must have seemed to the prebendaries to be the principal problem, and it is perhaps remarkable that so much of the inessential was retained. It is likely that at some point in the mid- to late sixteenth century a separation out of the more important materials took place; the Chapter Acts in 1612 include an incidental reference to 'our chest' in which were kept 'our dotacion [foundation charter of 1541] and other muniments of our Church'.[174]

In the early seventeenth century, scholarly collectors' depredations were to show just how voluminous and, by implication, how well arranged the Cathedral muniments were. The library's history was far unhappier, from a much earlier date. The generations of deans and prebendaries who followed Bale and his contemporaries took a narrower line as to what was of interest. It may be regarded as bad enough that such men as Wotton and Bale removed so many dozens of manuscripts, to give to patrons or to libraries at Cambridge or Oxford; but at least those books have been preserved. In the 1570s the splendid set of twelfth-century passionals was in large measure destroyed, being cut up and used in the bindings of ecclesiastical court books.[175] Strongly Protestant though he was, Bale would have been shocked by such vandalism: he did not take such a narrow view of historical significance as did this generation.

Yet if the 1570s mark the nadir of the library's fortunes, the tide was very slow to turn. A glimmer of light may be detected in the actions of Nicholas Simpson (prebendary, 1580–1610), who certainly seems to have taken a particular interest in gathering together books that related to the history of the Cathedral community. An inventory of 1584 mentions ten

[171] Lambarde's notes are in BL, Cotton MS Vespasian A. v, fos. 81ᵛ–89ᵛ; the book, which is only of the 14th cent., is Trinity College, MS O. 9. 26 (no. 1438). Lovelace appears also to have acquired a register of St Laurence's Hospital, Canterbury: cf. Soc. of Antiquaries, MS 168, fo. 22.

[172] e.g. Reg. L, fo. 141.

[173] A number of Cathedral Priory documents at Lambeth can be linked with particular lawsuits, thanks to the presence of trefoil markings in the margin (e.g. beside references to Longbeech Wood).

[174] Chapter Act Book, 1608–12, fo. 39ᵛ (*olim* p. 106).

[175] For the passional leaves in Lit. MS E. 42, made up this century from ecclesiastical court books' bindings, see Ker, *Medieval Manuscripts in British Libraries* (cit. in n. 137), ii. 289–97; for other manuscripts used for bindings see ibid. 312–30; cf. also M. B. Parkes, 'Fragments of Medieval Bindings', app. 1 (pp. 227–30) to Felix Hull, *Guide to the Kent County Archives Office* (Maidstone, 1958); rev. as 'Fragments of Medieval Manuscripts', in M. B. Parkes, *Scribes, Scripts and Readers. Studies in the Communication, Presentation and Dissemination of Medieval Texts* (London and Rio Grande, Oh., 1991), 313–17.

'old bookes' that came from his custody,[176] and in Thomas Cawston's list of the monks, which is still at the Cathedral, there is an inscription 'Si iste liber perdatur Nicholao Sympson restituatur' ('If this book is lost, it is to be restored to Nicholas Simpson').[177] But even with Simpson there is uncertainty as to his motivation and aims: it cannot be shown that he was definitely seeking to preserve these relics of the Cathedral's past for its own future use.[178] He may have been no different from his contemporary, Richard Colfe (prebendary, 1581–1613), who collected manuscripts from the Cathedral Priory and other sources, but whose sons gave them to the Bodleian Library, Oxford,[179] or, most notoriously, Thomas Neville (Dean, 1597–1615), who bequeathed about thirty books from the Priory library to his Cambridge college, Trinity.

The prebendaries of Canterbury might be men of great learning—never more so than in the early years of the seventeenth century, when most of them were doctors or at least bachelors of divinity—but they did not necessarily see the Cathedral as a centre of learning *per se*. In this, they were just like the canons of every other cathedral in England. The actions of Colfe's sons and of Dean Neville were matched in a corporate way by the Dean and Chapter of Exeter, who in 1602 presented 81 manuscripts to the newly founded Bodleian Library, while in 1612 the Dean and Chapter of St George's, Windsor, gave 159 of their medieval manuscripts to the same library.[180]

When were cathedral libraries themselves to be seen as forming part of what Thomas Bodley styled the republic of letters—as being (in the contemporary sense of the word) 'public' libraries? The early 1620s appear to have been the turning-point. In July 1622 James I instructed his librarian Patrick Young to make search in every English cathedral for all old manuscripts and ancient records, and to make inventories of these.[181] Where Archbishop Parker had sought loans (or gifts), Young was simply to produce catalogues. But Young stuck to his remit, and several of his catalogues survive; they may even have been made available to interested scholars in London.[182] No catalogue by Young of Canterbury's manuscripts has yet been located by modern researchers, and it is quite possible that he did not get to Canterbury. No matter, however; for the tide had now turned. Cathedral libraries were clearly regarded as institutions that ought to stay, and their deans and chapters responded by starting to put them into good order, both as repositories of what had survived and as working libraries stocked with useful reading-matter.

At Canterbury it was resolved in Chapter on 23 June 1628 'that every man should do his endeavour to refurnishe the ancient library of the . . . Church, And that a booke of velume should be provided wherein the names of the Benefactors should be registred and that the

---

[176] Legg and Hope, *Inventories*, 241.

[177] Lit. MS D. 12, fo. 1.

[178] Cf. Somner's assertion that many of Simpson's books had passed into the hands of Dr William Wats: N. L. Ramsay, 'William Somner's Pursuit of a Missing Cathedral Register', *Cant. Cath. Chron.*, 82 (1988), 43–5, at 43.

[179] See F. Madan, H. H. E. Craster, N. Denholm-Young, P. D. Record, and R. W. Hunt, *Summary Catalogue of Western Manuscripts in the Bodleian Library at Oxford* (7 vols.; Oxford, 1895–1953), vii. 542 (index, s.v. Colfe).

[180] Ibid. 547, 579 (index, s.v. Exeter and Windsor); see also W. D. Macray, *Annals of the Bodleian Library* (2nd edn.; Oxford, 1890), 28, 43–4.

[181] Young's Worcester Cathedral catalogue has been printed as *Catalogus Librorum Manuscriptorum Bibliothecae Wigorniensis, Made in 1622–1623 by Patrick Young*, ed. Ivor Atkins and N. R. Ker (Cambridge, 1944); for Young's Salisbury and Lichfield catalogues, see Ker, *Books, Collectors and Libraries* (cit. in n. 32), chs. 16 and 19.

[182] The catalogues passed into the collection of John Selden.

two uppermost deskes should be instantly fitted for the receipt of such books as shall be first given to the encoragement of so good a worke'.[183]

From 1625, Canterbury had as its dean a man with a strong sense of respect for the Cathedral's history, Isaac Bargrave (d. 1643). Like John Cosin at Durham (prebendary, 1624–60; bishop, 1660–72), he found no difficulty in accepting the value of his cathedral's medieval inheritance at the same time as commemorating his predecessors who had been deans of the New Foundation.[184] Bargrave was almost certainly responsible for commissioning the portraits of Deans Wotton, Neville, Fotherby, and Boys which still hang in the Deanery.[185] It is likely, too, that he played a major part in the Chapter's new-found enthusiasm for its library. The benefactors' book that was ordered to be provided in 1628 is still extant, and it includes gifts by him of such works as the medieval schoolman Alexander of Hales's *Opera Omnia*, as well as that desideratum for any seventeenth-century library, the catalogue of the printed books in the Bodleian Library (1620)—a book which every person admitted to read in Bodley was required to purchase.[186] Bargrave was supported by Archbishop Abbot, who in 1633 bequeathed to Canterbury twenty-five of the books in his study, though he left the bulk of his books to the library at Lambeth Palace which his immediate predecessor, Richard Bancroft (1604–10), had founded.[187]

In 1634 a catalogue was drawn up of the Cathedral's books, both printed and manuscript.[188] There are thirty-one printed works, in about eighty volumes, many of which can be identified as still in the Cathedral library: they are mostly patristic texts or biblical commentaries, but although a few of them date from before 1551, none appears to be a survivor from the collection set up in 1550. Of the twenty-seven manuscript volumes inventoried, one is recorded in the benefactors' book as the gift of Sir John Wilde, the Cathedral's Steward, while most of the rest are survivors from the Cathedral Priory's library.[189] Almost all can also be positively identified as still at the Cathedral today. They are, however, a fairly humdrum assortment of biblical and canon law texts and commentaries and suchlike works that, not surprisingly, had been spurned by the library's pillagers over the previous hundred years: their dullness and their chains had been their salvation.

Just at the time that the library was being re-established, however, the archives were suffering their most serious depredations since the early Middle Ages. Sir Edward Dering (1598–1644), of Surrenden Dering, near Ashford (Kent), was as assiduous in tracing or fabricating his pedigree as he was active in the politics which would bring his public career to a dramatic and scandalous conclusion on the eve of the Civil War. He somehow

---

[183] Chapter Act Book, 1608–28, fo. 162ᵛ (*olim* 304ᵛ).

[184] Cosin's cultural activities at Durham have most recently been investigated by A. I. Doyle, 'John Cosin (1595–1672) as a Library Maker', *The Book Collector*, 40 (1991), 335–57. He drew up a benefactors' book for Durham's chapter library in 1628.

[185] R. Strong, 'Portraits of the Deans of Canterbury in the Deanery', *Cant. Cath. Chron.*, 65 (1970), 102–11, at 103–4.

[186] The benefactors' book is Lit. MS E. 40; the 1628 book appears to have been incorporated within the book that was ordered to be provided in 1677. Bargrave's gifts are listed at fo. 109, and gifts by his daughter Mrs Anne Palmer at fo. 102.

[187] For Abbot's legacy, see ibid., fo. 112ᵛ; cf. [W. Oldys], *The Life of Dr George Abbot, Lord Archbishop of Canterbury, Reprinted with some Additions and Corrections from the Biographia Britannica* . . . (Guildford, 1777), 60, 62, 65.

[188] Legg and Hope, *Inventories*, 263–5. Lists of 1630, 1634, and 1638 are LA1/1, 2, and 4.

[189] Wilde had given the first book in the list, identifiable as MS Lit. B. 6—one of just two books in the list that had been at St Augustine's Abbey. The benefactors' book records him as having also given a folio manuscript of the *Sentences* of Peter Lombard.

discovered that the Cathedral's muniments were full of material that might relate to his ancestry and at the very least were of immense historical interest. What was more, Dean Bargrave was both a friend and a cousin of his, and it seems a not unreasonable assumption that it was thanks to Bargrave that he obtained access to the muniments, which he then set about ransacking for the benefit of his own and other antiquaries' collections.[190] A notebook of Dering's, with entries dated 1637–9, includes memoranda that read rather like shopping-lists: at Dover, a jar of capers, old deeds from cousin Swan, and 'patterns of stuffe for cosen Bargrave', and at Canterbury, 'all willes of Pluckley persons' (in the ecclesiastical court records), 'verses for Dr Geffrey' (John Jeffray, prebendary 1629–55), and the sinister note 'carry saxon deedes. borow some to peruse.'[191] Dering must have removed hundreds of original charters from the Cathedral; the British Library alone has many dozens, in the Cotton and Stowe collections. They are easily identifiable as having passed through his hands, since he shamelessly marked them with a simplified version of his coat of arms.[192] He had a particular liking for Anglo-Saxon and other early charters, as well as ones with fine seal-impressions, but he was more or less omnivorous. The presence in his collection of two leaves abstracted from the Cathedral's Register E is explained by his endorsement 'Deedes for Collateralls'; these leaves contain copies of a few of the altar-endowment charters, of which the originals no longer existed.[193] One of these charter copies has had a further name added to it in the seventeenth century—almost certainly by Dering, who was addicted to forging. An original charter from the Christ Church muniments, later in his collection and now in the Kent Archives Office, has had its grantor's name altered—to give just a single further instance of his (not very skilful) handiwork.[194]

Although Dering never suffered any retribution or opprobrium for his actions, it is likely that he was not undetected. Ranged against him would have been both Archbishop Laud (1633–45) and William Somner junior. Laud's visitation articles in 1634 included the standard question of whether the Cathedral archives were safely kept, 'and in such manner as is required by the statutes'. The Dean and Chapter's rather equivocal response was that their muniments 'are some of them kept in such manner as is required by our statutes, and the rest according to custome, as we are informed, though the prebendes thinke it fit to be altred'.[195] Three years later, following his next visitation of the Cathedral, Laud returned to this problem: in a letter to the Dean and Chapter, he specifically called for the dean's private door to the Treasury (where the archives were kept) to have two different locks, so that neither the dean nor the prebendaries could have access to the room without the

[190] For Dering's friendship with Bargrave, see S. P. Salt, 'The Origins of Sir Edward Dering's Attack on the Ecclesiastical Hierarchy, c.1625–1640', *Hist. Jnl.*, 30 (1987), 21–52, at 25, 26, 43; for Dering's collecting activities, C. E. Wright, 'Sir Edward Dering: A Seventeenth-Century Antiquary and his "Saxon" Charters', in *The Early Cultures of North-West Europe* . . ., ed. C. Fox and B. Dickins (Cambridge, 1950), 369–93. He obtained at least one pre-Conquest charter from the Cathedral by 1623 (BL, Cotton MS Augustus II. 98, which he gave to Sir Robert Cotton; see Wright, pp. 380, 383–4), but several more by 1630.

[191] Bl, Add. MS 47787, fos. 17ᵛ, 16.

[192] Cf. L. B. L[arking], 'On the Surrenden Charters', *Arch. Cant.*, 1 (1858), 50–65, at 57, 59.

[193] BL, Add. MS 25109; sold by Puttick & Simpson in the Dering sale of 4 Feb. 1863, lot 1103.

[194] Kent Archives Office, U2770 (uncatalogued collection of Kent charters once in Sir Thomas Phillipps's collection). For his making of 'medieval' seals and monuments to his ancestors, see R. H. D'Elboux, 'The Dering Brasses', *Antiquaries Jnl.*, 27 (1947), 11–23.

[195] HMC, 4th *Report* (1874), pt. 1, app., pp. 124, 125.

other's knowledge.[196] That was a barb aimed at Dean Bargrave. As a more general request, he called for the muniments to be inventoried and brought down from the upper into the inner room of the Treasury.[197] 'And it were very fitting, upon this removal, you would employ some skilful and trusty person to digest them all into some apt and good order, that you may, upon any occasion, with very little trouble, make use of them as often as you shall need.'

As the 'skilful and trusty person', Laud can only have had in mind William Somner junior, son of the Cathedral's registrar and himself soon to be (if he was not already) the Archbishop's deputy registrar. The younger Somner (1606–69) must be rated as one of the most attractive as well as most learned persons in the entire history of the Cathedral community. He never did produce an inventory of even part of the archives, but he made himself into a scholar of national renown by his work on Canterbury documents—his *Antiquities of Canterbury* (1640), dedicated to Laud, was the first scholarly history of any English town—while his Old English studies brought him into the mainstream of European scholarship. To Dugdale's *Monasticon Anglicanum* (1655–73) he contributed material on Canterbury Cathedral and St Augustine's Abbey as well as all the translations of passages in Old English.[198]

Somner was an ecclesiastical lawyer, and by his capability and devotion won the trust of the Cathedral Chapter so that he ultimately became their auditor and registrar (1660). A correspondence that he conducted in 1637–8 with Dr William Wats about a missing 'liegier book' (or register) shows his zeal on the Cathedral's behalf long before he held any Chapter office; this particular trail, which perhaps began in the prebendal study of Nicholas Simpson, went cold however, for Wats yielded nothing more than tantalizing statements, such as the mention that there were Cathedral manuscripts in Sir Robert Cotton's library, 'one of which [I] myself some 20 yeares ago got for him in Cambridge'.[199]

As Wats perhaps knew, Somner's position *vis-à-vis* the Chapter at this time was an informal one. By the statutes, it was the Dean, Vice-Dean, and Treasurer who were key-keepers of the Treasury; and if any outsider's assistance in searching the archives was

---

[196] *Works of the Most Reverend Father in God, William Laud*, vii: *Letters* [ed. James Bliss] (Library of Anglo-Catholic Theology; Oxford, 1860), 345–6 (9 May 1637); cal. in *Cal. S. P. Dom., 1637*, 86–7. Bargrave replied (30 May 1637), accusing Humphrey Peake (prebendary, 1633–?) of being 'my common threatener in the chapter', who had promoted the fuss about the muniments: *Cal. S. P. Dom., 1637*, 162; Laud then reiterated his point about the Dean's private door (3 June 1637): *Letters* [ed. Bliss], 349–51; cal. in *Cal. S. P. Dom. 1637*, 188–9. The door is shown in Willis, *Conventual Buildings* (cit. in n. 108), fig. 6.

[197] Somner, *Antiquities* (1640), 173, states that the Cathedral records were kept partly in the treasury and 'partly in the loft over this Vestry' (meaning the chamber over St Andrew's Chapel). The latter was presumably what Laud referred to as the upper room.

[198] Cf. his letter to Dugdale, 1654, printed in *The Life, Diary, and Correspondence of Sir William Dugdale . . .*, ed. W. Hamper (London, 1827), 282. That Somner has received less than his

due in modern historiographical studies is perhaps because his life and achievements were written up at considerable length at an early date: a biography by White Kennett was prefixed to Somner's *Treatise of the Roman Forts and Ports in Kent* (Oxford, 1693), revised and enlarged as the first section of the second edition of Somner's *Treatise of Gavelkind* (London, 1726). There are also accounts of his work by N. Battely, in the pref. to his edn. of Somner, *Antiquities* (1703); by 'C.' [i.e. P. Morant] in the *Biographia Britannica*, vi, pt. 1 (London, 1763), 3757–62; and by Thompson Cooper in *DNB*; and his life was carefully investigated by W. G. Urry in the introd. to a fac. reprint of the 1703 edn. of the *Antiquities of Canterbury* (E. Ardsley, Wakefield, 1977), pp. v–xxiv.

[199] Somner's two surviving letters are printed by Ramsay, 'Somner's Pursuit of a Missing Cathedral Register' (cit. in n. 178); Wats's letter is printed in Woodruff and Danks, *Memorials*, 393, from LA 1/3.

sought, it was to the auditor that the Chapter would turn.[200] This was to be the position until the nineteenth century, and it was not conducive to disinterested scholarly researches. Horton Drayton (d. 1649) was deputy auditor, registrar, and chapter clerk from 1613, and held the full offices from 1623 to at least 1642.[201] When the antiquary Brian Twyne (d. 1644) wanted transcripts of some of the Chapter's medieval muniments relating to Canterbury College, Oxford, it was to Horton Drayton that he would have had to apply.[202] Like several of his successors in office, including Somner, Drayton was a notary public and could thus authenticate the accuracy of transcripts that he supplied; but there was no doubt a fee to pay for this, and in any case antiquaries did not need the benefit of notarial authentication of their materials. There was, of course, no question of allowing scholars direct access to the muniments, nor was there any list of the muniments until the following century.

The Civil War was to cause massive disruption and then total dislocation to the Cathedral archives and library; it is impossible to tell if it resulted in the permanent loss or destruction of documents or books. Sequestration papers from the Commonwealth show that in 1641 a minor canon, John Bayly, was acting as library keeper, with a fee of £7 p.a.; it was his duty to 'take care that no bookes be lent out of the library'.[203] Bayly was apparently still claiming this fee in 1646, but in the absence of Chapter Act Books or accounts for the years 1642–60 it cannot be said what happened to the library and archives during most of the 1640s. But in 1649 the Act for Abolishing of Deans caused all cathedral muniments, along with cathedral lands, to be vested in a set of trustees, and Canterbury Cathedral's archives must then have gone to London, joining those of other cathedrals at Gurney House in the Old Jewry.[204] Canterbury's printed books may have joined them in the following year, when they were ordered to be catalogued and sent there;[205] other orders, however, in 1651, directed them to be sent to Mr (George) Griffith, minister of the Charterhouse in London.[206] Somner claimed that the books were sold away. They were certainly removed from their place in the library over the Dean's private chapel, since that was demolished.[207]

After the Restoration all the cathedrals gradually set about the recovery of their muniments. The documents may have been disturbed by antiquaries' perusal of them at Gurney House, while they had undoubtedly become greatly disordered by the time they had

---

[200] *The Statutes of the Cathedral and Metropolitical Church of Christ, Canterbury. With other Documents* [ed. G. K. A. Bell] (priv. printed, Canterbury, 1925), 77–81. Neither the receiver nor the auditor held a Treasury key. In practice, however, it is clear that one canon by himself was able to gain access to the Treasury.

[201] Appointment as deputy auditor, registrar, and chapter clerk, 13 Apr. 1613: Chapter Act Book, 1608–28, fo. 42; grant, jointly with two other people, of patent of the full three offices in May 1623: ibid., fo. 125ᵛ.

[202] See the transcripts, Bodl., MS Twyne 2, fos. 298, 302ᵛ, 308ᵛ, etc., with notes of Drayton's attestation. For instances of Drayton's dealing with the muniments, see also Chapter Act Book, 1608–28, fo. 152ᵛ, and the prebendary John Jeffray's memorandum book, Rental 15, fos. 17 and 18.

[203] PRO, SP 28/210B, folded sheet with copies made in 1646 of Chapter decrees of 1639 and 1641.

[204] The Act is printed in *Acts and Ordinances of the Interregnum,*

1642–1660, ed. C. H. Firth and R. S. Rait (3 vols.; London, 1911), ii. 81–104; see 82, 103. For English cathedral archives at this period, see D. M. Owen, 'Bringing Home the Records: The Recovery of the Ely Chapter Muniments at the Restoration', *Archives*, 8 (1967–8), 123–9; B. A. English and C. B. L. Barr, 'The Records Formerly in St. Mary's Tower, York', pt. 1, *Yorks. Archaeol. Jnl.*, 42 (1967–70), 198–235; and G. Yeo, 'Record-Keeping at St Pauls' Cathedral', *Jnl. Soc. Archivists*, 8 (1986–7), 30–44, at 32–3.

[205] Woodruff and Danks, *Memorials*, 388, where 'Surrey(?)' is a misreading of 'Gerny'; the original document is LA 1/5. The order is dated 6 Mar. '1650'.

[206] PRO, SP 23/88, p. 525, and SP 23/14, p. 88; cal. in *Cal. Proc. Committee for Compounding . . . 1643–1660*, ed. M. A. E. Green, i. 429, 434.

[207] J. C. Robertson, 'The Condition of Canterbury Cathedral at the Restoration in A.D. 1660', *Arch. Cant.*, 10 (1876), 93–8, at 95, quoting Somner.

undergone further removals, to Excise House in 1654 and then to Lambeth Palace in 1662. They were sorted by more than one person; in 1664 the celebrated antiquary William Dugdale recorded the receipt of £12 'towards my recompence for sorting the old Evidences of the Bishops, which were brought up to London in the times of the late troubles, and confounded together, by mixing with one another'.[208] Dugdale did not do his job with particular care, however, for most cathedrals ended up with some documents belonging to other cathedrals. Canterbury was more of a gainer than a loser overall, since it seems to have lost relatively little to other cathedrals and to have received much that undoubtedly belonged to others, as well as a certain amount whose true ownership is still difficult or impossible to determine. Furthermore, if the library did actually go to London, it too was returned virtually unharmed, since most the books that are known to have been in it before the Civil War are still at Canterbury today.

Two matters of greater long-term importance for the library and archives were events of the post-Restoration years. The first of these was the decision to rebuild the library. The Chapter was in an extremely well-funded position in the 1660s as it received arrears of rents and granted large numbers of fresh leases, but in the event it hardly needed to spend a penny of its own money, since Archbishop Juxon came forward with a gift of £500 'for the building, repairing or fitting up of the place formerly called the Dean's Chapel'.[209] A brick building was accordingly put up, being finished in 1664, on the site of the first-floor chapel, directly below the library's previous location. John Warner, Bishop of Rochester (prebendary of Canterbury, 1616–c.1638), who before the Civil War had given the Cathedral its font, by his will (dated 1666, proved early in the following year) left a further £500 'to be bestowed in bookes for yᵉ late erected Library'.[210] Books were duly bought, and from 1668–9 a library keeper was once more employed, a minor canon named Elias Robinson being paid £7 p.a., while in 1669 there was the inevitable concomitant of a new set of library regulations.[211] Somner died in March 1669 and his printed books and manuscript collections were bought from his widow for £100.[212] The Chapter could fairly feel pleased with the state of their library. In April 1670 they even paid for it to be wainscoted.[213]

But at almost the same date, disaster struck the archives. On 23 June 1670 workmen mending the leads on the roof of the chamber above the Audit House (a long narrow structure, on the north-west side of the Treasury[214]) set the roof on fire. A Miss Savin saw it and gave warning, the town bell was rung, and forty or fifty men laboured to quench

[208] *Life, Diary, and Correspondence of Dugdale*, ed. Hamper (cit. in n. 198), 117. When, one wonders, did the royalist divine Barnabas Oley (d. 1686) write (mistakenly) on the first page of Reg. J that 'This seems to belong to the ArchBp. of Canterbury; vide fol. 58 et fol. 100'? Oley expressed concern in 1666 about losses of manuscripts from Worcester Cathedral: see Young, *Catalogus Librorum Manuscriptorum Wigorniensis*, ed. Atkins and Ker (cit. in n. 181), 15–16.

[209] Lit. MS E. 40, fo. 115.

[210] E. Lee-Warner, *The Life of John Warner, Bishop of Rochester 1637–1666* (London, 1901), 62; cf. PRO, PROB 11/323, fo. 104 (Carr 14).

[211] Receipts from booksellers are LA 1/7 (John Crooke, £91

17s.) and 1/8 (Cornelius Bee, £151 6s. 8d.). The salary of the *bibliothecarius* or library keeper is entered in the Treasurer's Accounts, s.v. Feoda et Regarda. The regulations of Oct. 1669 do not survive but are referred to in Chapter Act Book, 1670–1710, fo. 1ᵛ.

[212] The receipt of Somner's widow, Barbara, 11 June 1669, for £100 8s. is LA 1/11. In 1675 she produced an account as executrix showing that though his estate was worth £1,409 4s. 2d., his debts and legacies totalled £1,485 19s. 5d.: Kent Archives Office, PRC 18/34/86. I owe this reference to Mr D. W. Harrington.

[213] Treasurer's Accts. 1669–70, fo. 34, 6 Apr. 1670.

[214] See Beazeley, 'History of the Chapter Library of Canterbury Cathedral' (cit. in n. 47), 155.

the blaze; they were successful, but not before irreparable damage had been done.[215] Chapter Act Books of the sixteenth century were among the worst victims, while a quantity of miscellaneous papers, including some of those so recently acquired from Somner, was totally destroyed.[216] Twenty years later the Cathedral's historian Nicholas Battely, writing to John Strype, reported on a visit to the archives: 'in the place where the Records [of] about the time of King Ed[ward] and Queen Elizabeth lay, were found heaps of burnt papers'.[217] And a century later, Edward Hasted wrote that 'Many of the manuscripts which suffered by the above fire, remain in the same mutilated state as at their first removal, (though many of them might with care be recovered), in a heap on the floor, in one of the rooms over the vestry.'[218]

Remarkable though it may now seem, however, despite such shocked exclamations on the part of a few researchers, the destruction of part of the Cathedral's archive seems to have caused little concern outside the Precincts. The explanation is perfectly simple: only a very few people wished to investigate the history of the Cathedral or its estates in a detailed manner, and the sheer bulk of the remaining records, combined with the lack of guides or indexes, would have been quite enough to deter any such people from even attempting to gain access to them. Besides, without resort to the records kept in the Treasury, it was still possible to read a great deal of material relating to the Cathedral's history in the Chapter library, while the dispersals of the sixteenth and early seventeenth centuries meant that there were many relevant manuscripts in the libraries of London, Cambridge, and Oxford. John Dart contented himself with using the manuscripts in the Cotton Library in London for his *History and Antiquities of the Cathedral Church of Canterbury, And the Once-Adjoining Monastery . . .* (1726), though admittedly this was not a particularly well thought of work.[219] The much more learned John le Neve, when indicating sources for his compilation of priors, deans, and canons of Canterbury, listed sixty manuscripts, of which less than half were actually at Canterbury; of these, some were registers, kept in the Treasury, but several were (and still are) treated as manuscripts to be kept in the library.[220] The medieval registers were consulted by just a very few well-connected historians—such as William Wake, whose history of Convocation of the Clergy contains a number of extracts from the Canterbury registers. It is thanks to Wake's work and that of his opponent Atterbury that we know that the registers had been given new reference-marks, doubtless as a result of their being rebound after the Audit-house fire. Instead of Somner's knobbed book and White Book, and so forth, we now find citations from the more prosaically named Registers H, I, and K.[221]

[215] Ibid. 153–5; Miss Savin was given 'twelve payre of gloves, white kidd &c.'

[216] The destruction of Somner papers is mentioned by Kennett, in his edition of Somner, *Treatise of Gavelkind* (cit. in n. 198), 121.

[217] CUL, Add. MS 3, fo. 65, in letter of 2 and 3 Mar. '1690'.

[218] E. Hasted, *History . . . of Kent*, 1st edn. (cit. in n. 119), iv. 579 n. f.

[219] Hearne called his book 'pompous' and noted that 'he took Orders & became Parson of Yeatley, & that the Parish proceeded against him for very shocking Crimes': *Remarks and Collections of Thomas Hearne*, xi, ed. H. E. Salter (Oxford Hist.

Soc., os, 72; 1921), 459.

[220] John Le Neve, *Fasti Ecclesiae Anglicanae* (London, 1716), pp. vi–vii; reprinted in T. D. Hardy's edn. of the *Fasti* (3 vols.; Oxford, 1854), i, pp. xxviii–xxxii.

[221] W. Wake, *The State of the Church and Clergy of England . . .* (London, 1703), e.g. 44 (Reg. K) and app. pp. 20–2 (Reg. H). Wake states on p. xv that the manuscripts of Canterbury Cathedral were 'carefully examined for me', by Archbishop Tenison's favour. Cf. also Francis Atterbury, *The Rights, Powers and Privileges of an English Convocation, Stated and Vindicated* (2nd edn.; London, 1701), 578, citing Reg. G (as Reg. I). Somner's White Book A is now Reg. H, and the knobbed book is Reg. K.

In the later seventeenth and early eighteenth centuries, there was no one in the Cathedral community with a particular interest in its archives; it may even have been in this period, rather than in the fire of 1670, that some of the early charters and other records that Somner had printed or referred to, were allowed to decay and perish. There were presumably enough post-medieval records of quitrents and the like for the auditor not to need to consult the medieval Priory materials, and in any case it was terriers and lease-books that were of practical value.[222] In 1684, when Archbishop Sancroft asked his friend, the prebendary George Thorp, about the Cathedral's claims in connection with episcopal consecration licences, he was told in reply that 'We know not where safely to found the original of our claym, except in the Charter [of 1541] which confirms to us all the privileges which the Priory enjoyed ... We have no memorial among any of our present members of any such book here as the Registrum album.'[223]

The library meantime went from strength to strength. Rules that were to govern it for a century or more were agreed on in 1672, to be 'ingrossed faire in parchment and put into a frame', and hung up in the library.[224] Two members of the Cathedral staff (who were thus already under oath) were to be appointed library keeper and assistant; they were to compile two alphabetical catalogues, one to lie open in the library and the other to be kept in the Treasury; a paper book was to be kept of the names of the dean and prebendaries borrowing books and of the volumes that they were signing for; the period of borrowing was to be a fortnight, after which the library keeper was to demand their return; the library was to be heated with coal in the winter and was to be swept clean once a week, and the books were to be wiped once a quarter; it was to be open on Tuesdays and Thursdays from 8 to 10 a.m. and from 1 p.m. to Evensong; the dean and prebendaries alone were to have keys and to be allowed to borrow books, although the Six Preachers, minor canons, and 'any other Gentleman or any Minister' introduced by a member of Chapter or by the library keeper, were to be allowed 'to study there (beside the fore mentioned publique houres) at any time when the Library Keeper or his assistant will bee willing to abide there, or any of the Chapter that brought them in'; the library keeper was also allowed 'to shew the Library to any Stranger or forraigner of quality, hee being careful that no Iniury bee done to the Bookes'. The library keeper, a Six Preacher named Dr Arthur Keyes (or Kaye), was to be paid £5 p.a., and his assistant, a minor canon named John Sargenson, received £2 p.a.[225]

As Norman Sykes wrote, 'it would be stretching piety to the extremes of credulity to suppose that the post-Restoration and Hanoverian prebendaries thronged to avail themselves of these privileges of study in the library'.[226] Yet at least the library must have

---

[222] The payment on 7 Oct. 1670 of £2 'to Goodman Wilks for mending and binding two Volumes of the Register leases, that were burned' is the only archival repair payment that was made that year. Treasurer's Accts. 1669–70, fo. 36ᵛ.

[223] Letter of Thorp to Sancroft, 11 Dec. 1684: Bodl., MS Tanner 123, fo. 21 (*olim* 24). The Registrum Album is in fact Reg. H, at least in part. The three crucial charters of the New Foundation were those of Foundation (8 Apr. 1541), Dotation (23 May 1542, granting manors etc.) and Permutation (9 Mar. 1546, effecting various exchanges of property).

[224] Chapter Act Book, 1670–1710, fo. 14; they were printed by Beazeley, 'History of the Chapter Library' (cit. in n. 47), 159–61, where it is plausibly suggested that they are the same as the rules of 1669, with the addition of a twelfth rule.

[225] The Treasurer's Accounts of the 1670s also show that the woman who swept the library was paid for 'rubbing the books'.

[226] N. Sykes, *Canterbury Cathedral Library: Lecture Delivered on the Opening Day, July 18, 1954* (Canterbury Papers, 9; Canterbury, 1954), 16.

been felt to be run in a secure manner, since the books had their chains removed (1677) and a larger borrowers' book was acquired (1680), while gifts of books suggest that use was being made of the collection: the benefactors' book records a number of gifts, from prebendaries, former prebendaries (such as Peter Gunning, Bishop of Ely, d. 1684), and a few of the local gentry and clergy.[227] In 1685 three chests full of books were given by Prebendary Thorp, and a quantity was received after the death of James Jeffreys (prebendary, 1682–9).[228] The library was also made more attractive by the bequest to it by John Bargrave (prebendary, 1662–80) of his 'Cabanett of medalls with the Antiquities that stand upon it in my Study, as likewise all my other Greater Medalons that hang upon the Shelves with the other things on the shelves', together with 'the great octangular round marble table that standeth in my dining-room' and 'All my large and lesser Mapps of Italy, ould Rome and new in Sheets at large very faire together with all the Cutts in my trunks of all the Antient Ruines, the pallaces, Statutes [*sic*], fountaines, the Cardinalls, souldiers, phillosophers &c. of Italy, France, high Germany'. Visitors to the library could perhaps also already see at this date the 'large draught of the Cathedral (pen wash) by F. [or rather, Thomas?] Johnson, 1651', that George Vertue was shown on the library staircase in 1738.[229] The decision in 1709 to commission a book-plate provides an indication of how large the library had become, for plates were pasted into 2,400 books. The design is an engraving of the Cathedral's coat of arms, and the original copperplate is still in use today.[230]

The local community, which the library primarily served and from which it benefited, was matched by another class of readers, the scholarly community. Somner's manuscripts were of national significance and fame, and they doubtless attracted readers almost as soon as they were acquired. The manuscripts of Canterbury Cathedral, as of most other English cathedral libraries, were listed in E. Bernard's *Catalogi Librorum Manuscriptorum Angliae et Hiberniae* (Oxford, 1697).[231] There is ample anecdotal evidence of scholars in this period coming to read in the library—historians, like Henry Wharton and Robert Plot, and philologists, such as William Wotton.[232] John Lewis, vicar of Margate, a scholar of national repute, made an expression of personal gratitude to a prebendary: 'To my Faithful Friend Dr Elias Sydal, Canon of Christ Church Canterbury, I owe the having had the Liberty of making Use of whatever is in the Library of that Church, for my Purpose.'[233] In 1712, when there were a couple of prebendal vacancies at Canterbury, William Elstob thought that his chances of getting one of them would be strengthened by the presence

[227] Treasurer's Accts. 1676–7, p. 77, 15 Jan. 1676/7; 1680–1, fo. 28ᵛ, 19 Nov. 1680; and 1685–6, fo. 43, 13 Feb. 1685/6; MS Lit. E. 40 (for which see n. 186, above).

[228] Treasurer's Accts. 1684–5, fo. 56ᵛ, 19 June 1685; and 1689–90, p. 72, 3 Dec. 1689.

[229] Bargrave's will is Kent Archives Office, PRC 32/54, fos. 481–2; partly printed in John Bargrave, *Pope Alexander the Seventh and the College of Cardinals*, ed. J. C. Robertson (Camden Soc., 92, 1867), p. xix. John Bargrave was the nephew of Dean Isaac Bargrave. For Vertue's visit, see *Vertue Note Books*, vi (Walpole Soc., 30; 1955, for 1951–2), 86.

[230] Mr Jackson was paid £1 1s. 6d. for the copperplate, £4 10s. for 3,000 'prints', at 3d. per 100, and 12s. 3½d. for pasting the prints on 2,400 books, at 6d. per 100, and for the paste: Tre-

asurer's Accts. 1708–9, s.v. Expensae Necess. Incertae, 7 Sept. 1709.

[231] ii, pt. 1. 223–5, 389. Curiously enough, the Cathedral's copy of *CMA* was acquired only in 1718: Treasurer's Accts. 1717–18, p. 57, 31 Oct. Some of Somner's manuscripts and annotated printed books were described by H. Wanley, *Catalogus Librorum Septentrionalium*, in G. Hickes, *Linguarum Vett. Septentrionalium Thesaurus* (2 vols.; Oxford, 1703–5), ii. 270–2.

[232] Wharton referred to Causton's obituary (Lit. MS D. 12) in *Anglia Sacra*, i, p. xix; for Plot, cf. Bodl., MS Ashmole 1135, fo. 67.

[233] John Lewis, *History of the Life and Sufferings of the Reverend and Learned John Wicliffe* (London, 1720), pp. xvi–xvii.

of Somner's books there, given his own design to edit the pre-Conquest English laws. He wrote to Humfrey Wanley:

Perhaps if my Lord Treasurer [Robert Harley, Earl of Oxford] were put in mind of me, and were made acquainted, that Mr Somner's Collection of Books are deposited in the Library there, which you know is pretty large, and consisting of a good choice of such books in the Canon, Civil and Common Law as he judged proper in the Work I have engaged in, and most of them adorned with Annotations and Improvements in his own hand, his Lordship would out of his great generosity, and his known favour to learning of this kind, be pleased to give me his patronage, and recommendation to the Queen, for the supplying one of these vacancies.[234]

Elstob was not successful; such pleas generally cut no more ice then than now.

Over the course of the eighteenth century, the Cathedral community included a number of men—canons, minor canons, office holders and others—whose interest in their church's history was manifested in publications or manuscript compilations. It is consequently easy to form the impression that it was a community that was conducive to scholarly activities— one which would have welcomed outsiders who shared its members' interests and who wished to carry out their own historical researches. The reverse was true, however: between the late seventeenth and late eighteenth centuries, the library became less accessible to outsiders, while the archives remained as hard of access as before, if not even a little harder. Already in 1696 the Cathedral accounts record a payment for three locks and ten keys for the library, just three years after the minor canon John Gostling had been given ten guineas 'for writing the Statutes and the Catalogue of the Bookes in the Library'.[235] Each of these payments can be seen as ominous; one explanation for the canons' wish to limit access to the library was that in a chainless age, the books were proving harder to keep on the shelves, and the catalogue further encouraged their being borrowed. That is to say, the better stocked and the more workable the library, the greater was the need to control its use. A further, related development in the eighteenth century was the tendency for the book acquisitions to veer towards the historical, the literary, and the practical, away from the patristic and the theological.

These developments should not be exaggerated. It is true that in 1718 the Chapter ordered three fresh locks and fourteen keys for the library (two for the Dean and one for each prebendary), and directed that the locksmith be strictly charged to make no keys for anyone else, but it is hard not to suspect that he would soon resume doing what he had evidently done in the past.[236] The locks had to be changed again in 1735.[237] If Stephen Hunt, a Canterbury physician, had not enjoyed relatively easy access to the library, why else would he have bequeathed to it his own library, in 1714? The Benefactors' Book states that his collection included a great many curiosities purposely purchased by him shortly before his death, 'most of them philologicall and criticall and variety of Bibliotheque French and

---

[234] BL, Harl. MS 3780, art. 134; printed in 'William and Elizabeth Elstob, the Learned Saxonists', in *Reprints of Rare Tracts*, i (Newcastle, printed by M. A. Richardson, 1847), 26–9, at 27. In 1711 Elstob had transcribed notes made by Somner in his copy of Spelman's *Concilia* (1639); Elstob's copy of the *Concilia* is now Bodl., L. 2. 12. Art.

[235] Treasurer's Accts. 1695–6, fo. 45ᵛ, 20 Aug. 1696; and 1692–3, p. 77, 16 Aug. 1693. The statutes were doubtless those of 1636.
[236] Chapter Act Book, 1711–26, fo. 73; the Treasurer's Accts. 1717–18, p. 58, 2 Dec. 1718, refer to 13 keys.
[237] Treasurer's Accts. 1734–5, fo. 31ᵛ, 29 July 1735.

severall philosophicall and medicall with variety of Classicall Authors, generally in small volumes'; that is to say, for light rather than serious reading.[238] These and other accessions caused a new bookcase to be required (1735), followed by a new catalogue, printed in 1744; the latter gives neither shelfmarks nor dates of publication, but enables us to see that the library had grown to about 5,000 titles.[239]

Hard of access though they might be, the archives were not neglected either. The German-born historian David Wilkins was a prebendary (1720–45) and had been the archbishop's librarian at Lambeth: he made some use of the Cathedral registers for his monumental edition of the medieval and later *Concilia Magnae Britanniae et Hiberniae* (1737–8). At just about the same time, the Chapter's auditor, Samuel Norris, completed a catalogue of the Cathedral's medieval charters. He was unquestionably a bookish individual—he had been allowed a key to the Chapter library in 1727, while he also had a considerable collection of books of his own—even though he was not a scholar. His catalogue assigned a letter of the alphabet and a number to each of the charters (A.1, etc.), which he arranged on a topographical basis, manor by manor. It was an indispensable piece of work, the *sine qua non* for any serious research on the charters (many of which had never been copied into the medieval registers).[240]

Knowledge of the existence of Norris's catalogue was bound to filter out beyond the Precincts. If men of an antiquarian disposition were entrusted with the task of sorting the muniments, as, for instance, the Revd Henry Hall was in the 1750s, then they were likely to communicate their discoveries to each other.[241] The first scholar who is known to have made substantial use of the medieval charters (or 'Chartae Antiquae', as they were now called) was Dr A. C. Ducarel. As the archbishop's commissary, with friends in Canterbury, he was in a very favourable position; but as an anecdote recorded by Hasted makes clear, even if (as is likely to have been the case) he got Archbishop Secker himself to request the loan of a manuscript from the library on his behalf, it was far from certain that the Chapter would agree. In this case, they refused to lend the volume (Lit. MS A. 11) to the Archbishop. He complained, and they then thought better and agreed to let Dean Friend take it up to Lambeth. Secker was still highly annoyed and 'with much coldness refused to receive it, on which [the] Dean with many apologies requested only to leave it with His Grace, who remained silent, upon which the Dean on taking his leave laid it down on a chair and departed'.[242]

Ducarel had succeeded in getting direct access to the Chartae Antiquae by 1763, when

---

[238] Lit. MS E. 40, fo. 115[v]; the books were received and catalogued in Apr. 1714 (Treasurer's Accts. 1713–14, p. 120). At least 270 are identifiable in the library today.

[239] *Catalogus Librorum Bibliothecae Ecclesiae Christi Cantuariensis* (Canterbury, 1743). James Abree was paid for printing 100 copies, 20 Nov. 1744 (Treasurer's Accts. 1743–4, fo. 68[v]). According to a note in A. C. Ducarel's copy (location now unknown), it was drawn up by the Revd Dr Eyre (not a prebendary) and Samuel Norris. For the new bookcase, see Treasurer's Accts. 1734–5, fo. 32 (£2 5s. 9d. paid to Thomas Davis 'for making a new Class in the Library').

[240] There is a sketch of Norris's life by V. A. Moyce, Add. MS 311. At the Midsummer Chapter, 1737, he was voted 50 gns. in

gratitude for his Index Chartarum: Dean's Book, 1718–42, fo. 305[v]. Norris should also be credited with having the series of Miscellaneous Accounts bound up (or rebound); see Treasurer's Accts. 1734–5, fo. 32, for a payment of £1 11s. 8d. to Edward Burges 'for binding old Register Books &c.'

[241] For the work of Hall, Ducarel's predecessor as Lambeth librarian, see J. Nichols, *Literary Anecdotes of the Eighteenth Century,* ix (London, 1815), 314–15.

[242] J. Boyle, *In Quest of Hasted* (Chichester, 1984), 108; the incident is datable to 1760 × 6. Secker lent the manuscript to Ducarel, who lent it to Hasted; the latter observed that 'there is not a single article in it that could anyways prejudice them or anyone else in the slightest degree whatsoever'.

he published *A Repertory of the Endowments of Vicarages in the Dioceses of Canterbury and Rochester*, for it is replete with references to such materials. For most enquiries, however, it was easier to turn for help to a local figure such as Dr Osmund Beauvoir, Six Preacher and headmaster of the King's School (d. 1789). In 1776 he compiled a very careful catalogue of over 400 medieval seals attached to documents in the Treasury: it is an intelligently arranged piece of work, and bears comparison with W. de G. Birch's British Museum seals catalogue of a century later.[243] Beauvoir was a familiar and trusted figure about the Precincts, and able to fulfil the sort of role of assisting visitors and scholars that the prebendaries had taken in the early years of the century; he was joined in his examination of the seals by Edward Hasted, who was then also resident in the Precincts. Hasted clearly did not get on with the Dean and prebendaries, and his *History of Kent* has relatively few references to their muniments; for his account of the Cathedral, he drew far more on the Cotton and Harleian collections in the British Museum.[244]

Hasted's *History* includes a rather jaundiced mention of the Cathedral's library, as having 'a tolerable good collection of books, the improvement of which has been much neglected for some years past'.[245] It is true that the eighteenth-century history of the library seems to be one of a constant succession of Chapter decrees and changed locks, and that even the concession of library keys in 1768 to Six Preachers and minor canons, as well as the Master and Undermaster of the King's School, was reversed in 1797.[246] Yet that reversal itself seems to have formed part of a final upturn in the library's outlook, for it must have resulted from the decision earlier in the year to request H. J. Todd, a favoured minor canon, 'to arrange the Books in the Library, to take an account of what are missing, and use his endeavours to recover them'.[247] Todd was an energetic and scholarly man who had already printed a catalogue of the Literary (or Library) Manuscripts, and before the year was out he had rearranged the books and commenced making a fresh catalogue of them.[248] A borrowers' book—not the first to be called for, indeed; but the earliest that survives— was begun, new keys were cut (this time being numbered with prebendal stall numbers), and a couple of years later the key privilege was re-extended to the minor canons and schoolmasters; more significantly, perhaps, Todd was given authority to spend up to £10 p.a. on book purchases, at his own discretion.[249] Todd was at this time called 'Librarian',

[243] For Beauvoir, see Nichols, *Literary Anecdotes* (cit in n. 241), ix. 351–9; *A Kentish Parson: Selections from the Private Papers of the Revd Joseph Price*, ed. G. M. Ditchfield and B. Keith-Lucas (Kent County Council, 1991), esp. 89–91. Beauvoir's seal catalogue is Bodl., MS Gough Kent 9 (*S.C.* 17955). The seals were in large boxes, arranged by letter of the alphabet; quite a few were safeguarded by being (still) in individual boxes.

[244] He later wrote that the dean and prebendaries 'are accounted the superior Gentry of the Place, and may be Said to Carry Themselves by far too hauty and Proud to every one else. The Gentry who hire the Houses of those Who are nonresident there take the next lead and generally follow their Example . . .': 'Anecdotes of the Hasted Family', *Arch. Cant.*, 26 (1904), 267–94, at 291 n. Samuel Denne in *Archaeologia*, 10 (1792), 273, described how, on his behalf, Hasted was accompanied to the audit room by John Lynch (prebendary, and later dean, 1781–1803) in search of a 'leiger book'; Hasted also looked at one of the manuscripts 'under lock in the library',

MS Lit. D. 10.

[245] *History of Kent*, 1st edn., iv (Canterbury, 1799), 579. However John Burnby, in his *Historical Description of the Metropolitical Church of Christ, Canterbury* (Canterbury, 1772), 79, described it as 'now well replenished'.

[246] Chapter Act Book, 1761–75, p. 186; ibid., 1794–1824, p. 52.

[247] Dean's Book, 1793–1822, fo. 52. For Todd (d. 1845), see *DNB*; he was subsequently Lambeth librarian and a canon of York Minster.

[248] The manuscripts were catalogued as the second part of Todd's *Some Account of the Deans of Canterbury; From the New Foundation of that Church, by Henry the Eighth, to the Present Time* (Canterbury and London, 1793). It is stated at the end of this that 'Eighteen Volumes of Old Registers . . . are kept in the Chapter Room' (298). For Todd's rearrangement and cataloguing, see Dean's Book, 1793–1822, fo. 56.

[249] Chapter orders for the library: Dean's Book, 1793–1822, fo. 63ᵛ; minor canons' borrowing: ibid., fo. 79.

but from 1801 a prebendary (initially Dr Houstonne Radcliffe) was termed 'Librarian' and the working librarian was called 'Sub-Librarian'.[250] This was a distinct downgrading of the working librarian's status, and came after Todd had resigned his minor canonry; the salary, £5 p.a., was also less than it had been. The library itself benefited considerably, however, since from now on it had a permanent advocate or representative in Chapter. The first indications of the library's new position were the decisions to create a library fund (£170, in 4% consols)[251] and, in the following year, 1802, to print the *Catalogue of the Books, both Manuscript and Printed, which are Preserved in the Library of Christ Church, Canterbury*: this was based on Todd's work, reprinting his catalogue of the Literary Manuscripts, with a dozen additions, and adding his alphabetically arranged listing of printed books (about 3,650 works in all). One hundred and sixty copies were printed; it was not intended for sale.[252]

The borrowers' books survive in an unbroken set from 1797 onwards. Since it is likely that all books that were consulted were signed for as loans, the borrowers' registers provide a very clear picture of how the library was serving the community.[253] Initially, in the late 1790s and opening years of the nineteenth century, it was the prebendaries who used the library most: it took some time for the minor canons to become familiar with the habit of regular use. The occasional manuscript was taken out—principally those of Somner—but otherwise it is works of literature and history, especially ecclesiastical and local history, that predominate, with a smattering of works by classical authors. All books had to be returned for the audits held at the time of the Winter and Summer Chapters. Somewhat more than a hundred books a year were borrowed, although the number of titles was less, since the same book might be borrowed by several readers over the course of a year. In 1814, for instance, the minor canon T. A. Mutlow borrowed Peck's *Desiderata Curiosa*, MacKnight on the Epistles, Campbell on the Four Gospels, and, in January to March, the seven volumes that had so far been published of Nichols's *Literary Anecdotes*. Canon Welfitt borrowed the second and third volumes of Nichols, from July to August, while the minor canon W. Bennett borrowed the first volume, from late July to late August. Bennett was a voracious reader, and took out many other books in the course of the year; Canon Marlowe (who perhaps only resided in the Precincts in the summer) borrowed little more than one unspecified volume of Nichols. The eighth volume of the *Literary Anecdotes* was published in the course of 1814, and was borrowed by Mutlow in

---

[250] Ibid., fo. 90.

[251] Library fund: ibid. Previously, the library had depended on the Gift Money account for its general book-buying income, and it was just one of a variety of competing demands on that account. Gift Money came from such sources as presents from deans and prebendaries at their installation and from archbishops at their visitations; see e.g. Fabric IV for a Gift Money account of the 1770s.

[252] Details about the catalogue were noted by Todd at the front of a copy addressed to the Dean and Chapter and in his own copy (formerly in the library of St Augustine's College, Canterbury; present location unknown). He pointed out that part of the listing of printed books on which his own work was based, the catalogue of presses A to X, had been chiefly

compiled by David Wilkins; that catalogue, in Wilkins's own hand, supplemented by Todd, survives in the library's own archive. It is striking that only two or three books are recorded as having been lost between Wilkins's time and Todd's. Todd's catalogue of manuscripts was made better known by being extensively excerpted by William Clarke, *Repertorium Bibliographicum* (2 vols.; London, 1819), i. 122–9.

[253] Borrowers' registers of eight English cathedrals are discussed by P. Kaufman, 'Reading Vogues at English Cathedral Libraries of the Eighteenth Century', *Bull. New York Public Library*, 67 (1963), 643–72; 68 (1964), 48–64, 110–32, 191–202; and separately printed; reprinted without the tabulations in his *Libraries and Their Users: Collected Papers in Library History* (London, 1969), 76–89.

December; it and the fifth volume were borrowed by the prebendary Dr Thomas Coombe in 1815, when Bennett and Welfitt also continued their reading of the series. The shared reading of such a popular work, as well as shared use of the library as a whole, must in a modest way have helped to bring together the canons and minor canons. From about the 1820s, the canons ceased to sign the borrowers' book with the prefix 'Dr' to which most of them were entitled.

At more or less the same time that Todd took the Cathedral's printed books in hand, the Chapter was faced with questions about its archives by a Select Committee of the House of Commons that was investigating the public records (as it termed them) of a whole range of institutions. The Auditor, Edward Benson, gave a singularly inadequate answer, in May 1800: he stated that in order to be able to give a satisfactory account of the earlier deeds and registers, 'it is necessary to be particularly conversant with such Materials; Mr Benson is but very little so; and after having been several Days examining them, finds himself not competent to the Execution of a Task of so much Difficulty'.[254] It surely cannot be merely coincidence that four years later the Chapter accepted the offer of C. R. Bunce 'to arrange all our Papers & Documents under the inspection of our Brother Radcliffe.'[255]

Cyprian Rondeau Bunce (d. 1807) was a middle-aged solicitor and undoubtedly a local worthy; he had been at the King's School in the early 1760s, and by this date he was an alderman of Canterbury.[256] His portrait, which hangs in the Cathedral library, is of a solid rather than an imaginative or scholarly looking man; and yet a hard-working and careful arranger and lister was just what the archives needed, and his work was, in its way, an exemplary achievement. He arranged the muniments with care, and reclassified the Chartae Antiquae into a somewhat more sensible order than that given by Samuel Norris. Almost every document was endorsed by him with a brief note of its contents, and in many cases a shelfmark or reference number, while he also neatly entered them with a slightly more detailed description into a 'Schedule', arranged in several hefty folio volumes. The antiquary David Powell has left an account of how he encountered Bunce in December 1805, working in the Audit-house: Bunce introduced himself, invited Powell to warm himself by his fire whenever he was cold in the Cathedral, and showed him into the Treasury, 'most neatly fitted up with wooden casses [i.e. cases], and in particular one large one filling up a spacious Norman wall arch, containing numerous Records which he had or was so diligently arranging'.[257] Bunce's work was finished by late in 1806; it even included an index. It has its faults: he was a lawyer, and ultimately more concerned with title-deeds than with documents that related to the history of the domestic concerns of the Cathedral, and he made no attempt to date documents that were undated. But it was none the less a very careful and accurate piece of work, and he could never have expected

[254] *Reports from the Select Committee Appointed to Inquire into the State of the Public Records of the Kingdom* ... (Ordered by the House of Commons to be printed, 1800), 332, app. N1.

[255] Dean's Book, 1793–1822, fo. 112.

[256] Bunce was born 1752; he died 1807 (see *Kentish Gazette*, 21 July 1807, 4.). See also W. J. Mercer, 'Excerpts from Sundry Works, Relative to the Family of Bunce', manuscript notebook in Canterbury City Library, pU 802.42 BUN. In November 1806

Bunce wrote a report for Chapter on the state of the archives and with suggestions for the future management of records; this is now LA1/22.

[257] BL, Add. MS 17733, fo. 69. The charters and other muniments in the Treasury are described by E. W. Brayley, *The Beauties of England and Wales*, viii (London, 1808), 843, as being 'in large wooden lockers, made in the shape of copes'; it is certainly possible that some had once served as cope-chests.

that it would still be in daily use today as the sole listing of the Chartae Antiquae and several other categories of material.

THE OPENING OF THE LIBRARY AND ARCHIVES TO A WIDER READERSHIP

In the 1820s and 1830s there was a trend nationally to attach renewed importance to the provision of libraries for the use of the clergy, while there was also a revival of the notion of government funding for the publication of historical documents. Making available sound theological, historical, and classical books for the clergy became a part of the aims of the cathedral reformers as also of their defenders: a clerical library need not be more accessible than any other subscription library, but both radical and conservative reformers and defenders deployed arguments that created diocesan clerical libraries out of chapter libraries. The provision of cathedral prebends as quasi-sinecures for men of learning was—arguably—an abuse that needed correction; but certainly it was felt that clerical learning throughout the diocese needed to be encouraged and aided, and that building up and making accessible cathedral libraries were suitable means of achieving this. The work of the Record Commission, 1800–37, helped draw attention to the riches that remained unexplored in cathedral and other archives; the Commission's publications (of which a complete set was given to every cathedral library) did not require access to cathedral archives for any more than its own employees and editors, but they undoubtedly had the effect of encouraging historians to seek after primary sources other than chronicles.

It is easy and dangerous to attribute too much in such areas of activity to the influence of particular activists. At Canterbury, however, if it is fair to give credit for improvements to any particular members of the Chapter, it would undoubtedly be owed to two men: Dr John Russell, FRS, FSA (canon, 1827–63) and Dr J. H. Spry (canon, 1828–54). And for Canterbury the year 1828 would have to be counted one of the most critical. In the Midsummer Chapter that year, Canons Pellew, Russell, and Spry were asked to report on the state of the library and especially on its duplicates; their report, in November, was far-reaching and must have required a great deal of work. Of the 4,257 volumes in the library, they had selected 324 as being fit for disposal as either duplicates or useless (such as 'antiquated treatises on medicine'). They recommended that the proceeds of such sale be applied to the purchase of better editions of the classics and the early Fathers (several 'bad or useless editions' of such works in the library being sold); that the many dirty or mutilated books in the library be cleaned, repaired, and lettered by some journeyman bookbinder, and that all unbound books be bound, and that then all the books 'be reclassed in a manner more convenient for reference'; that the library fund (then standing at £872 in 3% Consols.) and floating balance (then £178; mixed with the Chapter's general funds) in future be kept distinct and placed in the Librarian's hands; that there be an annual vote of money at the November Audit (as in fact had happened the previous year); and that the audit room be fitted up with a carpet and a table 'with drawers for each member of the Chapter', so as to make it a suitable reading-room. Faced with these suggestions, the Chapter agreed to every one of them, including an allowance of £400 (to be taken from library funds, however) and the allocation of the sale proceeds for the costs of new books, furniture and binding; and it was resolved that Dr Spry be appointed Librarian.[258]

Russell's particular concern was with the muniments. The St Catherine's (or November) Chapter of 1828 also approved the report of the Finance Committee, which included the recommendations that all Chapter documents be forthwith returned into the Treasury ('and never taken out of it except to the Audit Room for the purpose of reference') and that 'the state of the Books and Papers now in the Treasury be carefully examined, as there is reason to fear that many of them are in a state of deterioration'. A committee comprising Dr Russell and four others was then appointed to inspect the books and papers. The result was a major updating of Bunce's Schedule, in the form of a supplementary volume listing more recent documents.[259]

It must be borne in mind that the primary concern of Bunce—as also of Russell, no doubt—was for documents of continuing legal or practical value to be filed in a rational way and to be readily locatable. A notebook that has (or should have) records of all items removed from the Treasury, 1773–1869, is largely taken up with references to accounts, terriers, and maps of relatively recent date, and it is exceptional to find mention of, say, a charter of King Cnut being borrowed in 1787 by the prebendary Richard Farmer, or of the inspection of medieval registers by the historian Henry Petrie in 1824 and 1827.[260] When outsiders came to pursue historical researches, they were looked after by the Librarian. Thus it was Spry who in 1839 took out over eighty pre-Conquest and other charters which the distinguished Anglo-Saxonist J. M. Kemble had selected and which the British Museum was to clean and repair.[261]

The library borrowers' register in the 1830s shows a small number of outsiders being permitted to take out books, and in 1832 library keys were ordered by Chapter to be allowed to four of the Six Preachers who lived near the Cathedral.[262] Finally, in 1840, it was resolved that the library should be opened every Tuesday and Saturday, from 11 to 3 o'clock, and that 'the Clergy of the Diocese and other Persons at the discretion of the Dean, Vicedean or resident Members of the Chapter be admitted . . . to read in the Library'. Six small tables and twelve oak stools were to be provided for the library's visitors, while borrowing was to be restricted to the canons, minor canons, schoolmasters, Auditor, and Surveyor; authorized keyholders were entitled to read in the library at any time.[263] These Chapter decisions marked a major shift in the library's role, away from a private community library and towards a public reading-room. Spry, who remained Librarian until his death in 1854, was a conservative and a leading campaigner against the setting up of the Ecclesiastical Commission, but there is no reason to doubt that he was behind the Chapter decisions; he had already, in 1829, requested that no dictionary, lexicon, or work on

[258] Dean's Book, 1822–54, pp. 62 (request of midsummer 1828) and 72–3 (report). A copy of Todd's catalogue, interleaved and with additions in Spry's hand, is in the library's own archive; the additions perhaps date from this time. There is a brief account of Spry in the *Gentleman's Mag.*, NS, 43 (Jan.–June 1855), 124.

[259] Dean's Book, 1822–54, pp. 71, 74. Memoranda by Russell for a report on the archives in the Treasury, 1828, are LA1/23. The supplementary volume is lettered on the spine 'CCC Schedule, vol. 3, 1806–27' (i.e., supplementing Bunce's vol. iii); it received further additions, down to 1840.

[260] MB 4/3, 26 June 1787, 19 Oct. 1824, and 10 Sept. 1827. The notebook is certainly not the complete record of removals of documents that it was intended to be (cf. Dean's Book, 1770–6, fo. 149).

[261] MB 4/3, 19 July 1839.

[262] Dean's Book, 1822–54, p. 141.

[263] Ibid., p. 250.

grammar be borrowed, on the ground that these were works of reference and should always be accessible in the library.[264] Perhaps in about 1830, he had had all the books rearranged, so that they were shelved according to their subjects and not their size. The bibliographer Beriah Botfield in 1849 mentioned this rearrangement (and its unfortunate effect of rendering Todd's catalogue semi-useless) and praised the general appearance of the library: many of the books 'have been recently rebound by Mr Gough of London ... some of the older volumes having been repaired and gilt. The whole collection has a freshened aspect.'[265]

What might be seen as a form of celebration of the library's public opening came in September 1844, when the British Archaeological Association held in Canterbury its first annual meeting. It was in the course of this conference that Robert Willis first lectured about the architectural history of the Cathedral, while J. O. Halliwell, already a well-known literary scholar although only 24 years old, spoke about some of the medieval and Tudor manuscripts in the library—a cartulary of St Augustine's Abbey (Lit. MS E. 19, which Richard Farmer, canon 1782–8, had bought at a London bookstall in 1784), and a late sixteenth-century collection of English satires (Lit. MS D. 10, art. 3), which he believed to be among the earliest of its type.[266] The archaeologists were liberally treated by the Dean and Chapter, being allowed free admission to the Cathedral for a whole week, unaccompanied by any verger, while several canons and minor canons as well as the surveyor, George Austin, joined their Association: Spry read a paper, presented ten guineas to the Association, and was made one of its vice-presidents.[267]

Even J. O. Halliwell did not get into the Treasury. Anglo-Saxonists, however, were gradually getting to learn the size of the Cathedral's richness in this field, thanks to such men as Kemble; ultimately, in 1878, the Ordnance Survey was to publish a substantial group of the early charters in its series of *Facsimiles of Anglo-Saxon Manuscripts*.[268] The Norman and later muniments remained very little known, by contrast. A greedy jackdaw perhaps played as significant a part as anyone in bringing these to scholars' attention. The tale is told in a letter from the antiquary Albert Way to Sir Frederic Madden, Keeper of Manuscripts at the British Museum, in January 1852:

One of the Minor Canons was sunning himself in his garden, when one of the Cathedral Jackdaws flew over his head, and dropped at his feet a parchment scroll! He picked up the windfall, which proved to be no miraculous legend, foretelling of mitres or deaneries or other good things about to befall him, but simply a deed of the XIIth century! It concerned some matters between the Monks of Rochester and the See of Canterbury, or the like. This excited my curiosity, and on further enquiry, I succeeded in penetrating into a Norman chamber, the receptacle of the *rejectamenta* of the Muniment Room. The jackdaws had free access, on all sides, heaps and chests of parchments were there—the first fragment I took up was a tattered leaf of an Anglo-Saxon MS. in a large bold hand. Then came a bundle of royal Mandates *vacante sede*—and so forth. It seems that a lawyer

[264] Note at front of Borrowers' Register, 1829–59. In the 1850s local clergy and residents start to appear in the register as borrowers 'by permission'.
[265] B. Botfield, *Notes on the Cathedral Libraries of England* (London, 1849), 5–6.
[266] *Archaeol. Jnl.*, 1 (1845), 278.

[267] *Report of Proc. British Archaeol. Assn. ... Canterbury*, ed. A. J. Dunkin (London, 1845), 9, 255, 358, 359–60; *JBAA*, 1 (1845–6), List of Members, 6–7.
[268] *Facsimiles of Anglo-Saxon Manuscripts. Photozincographed by Command of the Majesty Queen Victoria...*, with transl. by W. B. Sanders, pt. 1 (Southampton: Ordnance Survey Office, 1878).

was employed some years ago to arrange and select the Chapter muniments; it is said that he threw out all that were of no *legal* value, and the jackdaws made their nests of the refuse. Ought not their spoil to be rescued? I am going to address the Treasurer on the subject. The Documents in the 'Treasury' proper seem to be in good care, and well arranged and docketed.[269]

Way was staying in Canterbury with his cousin A. P. Stanley (canon, 1851–8; Librarian, 1854–8), who was then keeping his first residence as a canon, and Way was in a position to achieve something. A fortnight later a further letter from him to Madden related that the Dean had ordered the parchments into the Treasury.[270] Stanley found in the history of the Cathedral ideal scope for his skills as a popularizing scholar, and Way found in the medieval registers and Chartae Antiquae some useful material that was printed as an appendix to Stanley's bestselling *Historical Memorials of Canterbury* (1854). And under Stanley's aegis and in Way's company, Way's friend Robert Willis was able to search the muniments and discover such gems as the roll that lists all the works and gifts of Prior Chillenden.[271]

Canon James Craigie Robertson succeeded Stanley as Librarian in 1859 (after short terms of office by Benjamin Harrison and Dean Alford), and continued until his death in 1882. He was never celebrated like his friend, the high-flier Stanley, and his only overtly popular work, a biography of Becket, never enjoyed the success of Stanley's *Memorials*, with their vivid account of Becket's murder. He was, however, a very fine scholar, editing six volumes of *Materials for the History of Thomas Becket, Archbishop of Canterbury* for the Rolls Series.[272] He was also a capable and effective Librarian. The Library contained over 5,000 books and was too small to house them properly, and a new library was built, on the site of the present main library building, being completed in 1868.[273] By June the following year Robertson had produced a fresh catalogue of its contents.[274] So rapidly did books continue to come in that in 1877 the Old Library (which had never been demolished and had stood empty since 1868) was assigned to take the overflow of books from the new building.[275]

Nevertheless, it is for his dealings with the Cathedral archives rather than with the printed books that Robertson must be rated most highly. It was his tenure of the Librarianship that saw the archives brought for the first time under this office. This was a far from foregone conclusion, too. The self-confident days of Spry and Russell and even of Stanley had been followed in the late 1850s and 1860s by a period when the Chapter felt particularly under pressure from the Ecclesiastical Commissioners. At the St Catherine's audit in 1868, the Chapter passed the thoroughly formalistic and awkward resolution 'that the keys of the Treasury should again be kept by the three Clavigeri [i.e. the Dean, Vice-Dean, and Treasurer], and that in answer to a question of the Surveyor [H. G. Austin] he should be

[269] BL, Egerton MS 2845, fos. 152–3. The minor canon was William Bennett, the sacrist; the jackdaw's parchment is Ch. Ant. R. 70a.

[270] BL, Egerton MS 2845, fos. 161–162ʳ.

[271] R. Willis, 'The Architectural History of the Conventual Buildings of the Monastery of Christ Church in Canterbury', *Arch. Cant.*, 7 (1868), 1–206, at 187–8; cf. MB 4/3, at 12 June 1852.

[272] Robertson edited the first six volumes, 1875–82; the seventh was edited by J. B. Sheppard, 1885. There is an account

of Robertson by W. H. Fremantle in the *DNB*.

[273] Beazeley, 'History of the Chapter Library' (cit. in n. 47), 179; cf. *Arch. Cant.*, 8 (1872), pp. xl, xlii: the Kent Archaeological Society held its AGM in the library in July 1868.

[274] G S[mith], *Chronological History of Canterbury Cathedral* (Canterbury, 1883), 363; cf. Chapter Act Book, 1854–84, pp. 201, 231, 234, 254.

[275] Memorabilia of Dean's Book, 1854–84, s. a. 1877.

informed that it is not to the Auditor [T. Godfrey-Faussett] but to the Clavigeri that he must apply for leave to take out deeds etc. from the Treasury'.[276] And in the following year an offer from the newly established Historical Manuscripts Commission to catalogue the ancient documents in the muniments was firmly turned down by Chapter; 'the Auditor was requested to reply that our documents were already well and sufficiently cat-alogued'.[277] Robertson and Godfrey-Faussett will both have known that this was not entirely true; only a couple of years previously, a group of charters and other documents had been found under the floor of a room above St Andrew's Chapel where muniments had long been kept.[278]

It was to be several years before Robertson had his way—and then it was very much as a result of the labours of his protégé J. B. Sheppard. Joseph Brigstocke Sheppard (1828–95) was a chemist and medical practitioner who had moved to Canterbury in 1857 and who had become interested in old documents as a result of being given a thirteenth-century bailiff's account by a grateful patient.[279] Robertson encountered him not long afterwards, in the early or mid-1860s, and procured for him the occasional use of keys to the church and Treasury. In about 1869 he began to work systematically at the archives in the Treasury, and in 1873 he was persuaded by Robertson (at the suggestion of Mrs Sheppard) to give up his medical practice, and in the same year Chapter authorized Robertson to make some appropriate present to him in their name, since he 'has taken great pains with some of our old documents'.[280] Next year Chapter allowed Charles Trice Martin to come to report on their manuscripts for the Historical Manuscripts Commission, but Martin, to his credit, recognized that Sheppard was better able to do this, and it was accordingly Sheppard who wrote the Commission's first report on the muniments, summarizing many of the Chartae Antiquae.[281] Finally, in 1877, Chapter agreed formally to entrust its muniments to Sheppard, 'to arrange'.[282] It was a momentous move, for, more than any other event or decision, it marked the effective surrender of the old, tight system of control over the Treasury's contents. The historical documents (as some were now termed) were removed from the Treasury and, it appears, were kept in the Old (or 'Deanery') Library. Sheppard had the enthusiasm of an autodidact and energetically set about gathering in strays from the muniments. Unofficially, he had already begun in the 1860s, when by persuasion and bribery he had gathered over a hundred more or less ragged and decayed documents from the workshops, stable, and stonecutters' shed; these tattered items had been consigned to near-oblivion by Bunce.[283] After 1877, he was able to gather in far more, from the auditor's office (1878) and the Treasury cupboards (1880), for instance.[284] His greatest discovery came much later however, in 1894, when he found other documents,

[276] Chapter Act Book, 1854–84, p. 253.
[277] Ibid. 260.
[278] Godfrey-Faussett wrote a note on this discovery in *Arch. Cant.*, 7 (1868), 341.
[279] This and other information about Sheppard is taken from his obituary by A. Jessopp in *Canterbury Diocesan Gazette*, 3 (1894–5), 168–71.
[280] Chapter Act Book, 1854–84, p. 314.
[281] HMC, 5th *Report* (1876), 426–62. Martin's report to the Dean and Chapter is LA1/24. Sheppard also wrote a report for

Chapter on his rearrangement of the seals and some other parts of the archives in 1874: LA 1/25.
[282] Memorabilia of Dean's Book, 1854–84, s. a. 1877.
[283] [J. B. Sheppard], 'Historical Records Recently Discovered in Canterbury Cathedral', *Canterbury Diocesan Gazette*, 2 (1893–4), 190–2, at 190.
[284] See his catalogue of these papers, mostly of the 19th cent., MSS Cat. 85 (kept in the library's own archive, as an obsolete catalogue).

sound and legible but also rejected by Bunce, wrapped in old leases in bundles behind heavy metal deed-boxes on the tops of Treasury cupboards. Here were many hundreds of *sede vacante* pleadings and institutions and other records and large numbers of original letters addressed to Prior Henry of Eastry.[285] It was mainly from these and his earlier discoveries that Sheppard made up the bulky scrapbooks of Canterbury Letters, Christ Church Letters, and Sede Vacante Scrapbooks and Scrapbooks A, B, and C which medievalists of the past half-century have found so useful.[286]

Sheppard was himself a prolific publisher, following up his first report for the Historical Manuscripts Commission with two more, on the medieval registers and the Literary Manuscripts;[287] his discovery in 1894, so near the end of his life, must have been bittersweet, since he had edited for the Rolls Series three volumes of Latin and Norman-French letters, mostly from the registers and Chartae Antiquae, as well as a volume of letters in English for the Camden Society.[288] The Eastry letters would have formed a far more coherent set than these, and are just as important; they remain unprinted.

Sheppard was also a wholehearted exponent of the scientific method. Mary Sibylla Holland (wife of Canon Francis Holland and niece of Dean Lyall) in 1889 wrote of him even as having 'the religion of the scientific man', although she admitted that he was 'full of the very dew of kindness, under his rough old body and face'.[289] Some of his notes show him to have been interested in the development of medieval letter-forms,[290] and it seems likely that he saw in the fledgling discipline of palaeography another form of the scientific approach. Certainly, he was among the founder members of the Palaeographical Society (1873), as were also Robert Payne Smith and the Cathedral library—the only dean and the only cathedral library in the country to be so. Nor was Sheppard the sole capable scholar to labour (at first in an entirely honorary capacity) in the library. In the 1880s and 1900s Joseph Meadows Cowper worked there on the records both of the Dean and Chapter and of the city, editing a couple of the Literary Manuscripts (one for the Early English Texts Society).[291] A detailed survey of English and Welsh cathedral libraries that was carried out in 1878 allows some informed comparative comments to be made about Canterbury.[292] It was one of the more heavily used libraries, with about ninety readers annually (exceeded only by Durham, Exeter, and Chester); its twice-weekly opening was about average (six libraries were open daily, and six others on one or two days a week);[293] and with an

[285] Sheppard, 'Historical Records Recently Discovered' (cit. in n. 283); the discovery was also reported in the *Reliquary*, NS, 8 (1894), 181, and *Proc. Soc. Antiquaries*, 2nd ser., 15 (1893–5), 177. Sheppard believed that it was Canon Russell who had rejected these documents, but it seems far likelier that it was Bunce, as Woodruff stated in a manuscript note to Sheppard's obituary in the Cathedral library copy of the *Canterbury Diocesan Gazette*.

[286] e.g. *Select Cases from the Ecclesiastical Courts*, ed. Adams and Donahue (cit. in n. 60), is almost entirely based on material discovered by Sheppard.

[287] HMC, 5th *Report* (1876), 426–62; 8th *Report* (1881), 315–55; 9th *Report* (1883), 72–129 (Sheppard also reported on the Canterbury corporation records, 9th *Report*, 129–77).

[288] *Literae Cantuarienses*, 3 vols. (RS, 85; 1887–9); *Christ Church Letters* (Camden Soc., NS, 19; 1877).

[289] *Letters of Mary Sibylla Holland*, ed. Bernard Holland (2nd edn.; London, 1898), 200.

[290] See e.g. Add. MS 208.

[291] Cf. A. M. Oakley, 'Joseph Meadows Cowper', *Cant. Cath. Chron.*, 85 (1991), 36–8. The Canterbury corporation records were first housed in the Cathedral library from 1884 to 1904; Memorabilia of Dean's Book, 1854–84, s. a. 1884, and cf. the book-plate in FA 2 and other volumes of the records; *Kentish Gazette & Canterbury Press*, 15 Jan. 1921.

[292] Herbert E. Reynolds, 'Our Cathedral Libraries: Their History, Contents, and Uses', *Trans. and Proc. First Annual Meeting of the Library Assn. ... 1878*, ed. H. R. Tedder and E. C. Thomas (London, 1879), 32–43 and app. 1; also separately printed.

[293] Since 1872 it had been open on Tuesday and Friday (and in 1878 the hours were stated to be from 11.15 to 1.15): Memorabilia of Dean's Book, 1854–84, s. a. 1872.

estimated 8,000 books (exceeded only by Durham, with 21,000, and York, with 11,000, while being matched by Exeter) it had one of the largest collections. Canterbury, Durham, and York could perhaps also claim to be most *au courant* with the scholarly world beyond the close or precinct.

Within ten years of this survey, Canterbury's collection of books was more than doubled in size. In 1887 Mrs Isabella Harrison carried out the wishes of her late husband, Benjamin Harrison (Archdeacon of Maidstone and canon, 1845–87), and presented his library to the Dean and Chapter.[294] It was a very considerable gift, comprising some 16,000 books and pamphlets, in about 11,600 volumes. The Old Library had already been refitted to house the books, and the name by which this room has ever since been generally known, the Howley-Harrison Library, is a reminder that what it houses is really more than just one man's collection. In fact, it is the major part of four libraries—the scholarly books of Archbishop Howley (whose domestic chaplain Harrison had been, 1838–45), and a substantial portion of the library of Sir Robert Harry Inglis (whose ward, Isabella Thornton, Harrison had married),[295] as well as the books of Harrison's father (Benjamin Harrison, treasurer of Guy's Hospital and, like the Thornton family, a member of the 'Clapham Sect'[296]) and, most of all, the library of Harrison himself. Inglis and Harrison were similar in character and outlook, being arch-conservatives and active in politics—the one in the Commons, the other in Convocation—and the collection includes many tracts and pamphlets sent to one or other. But they were also scholarly men—Harrison had made his name as a Tractarian, a Puseyite who had written in defence of the role of the cathedral as a centre of learning—and Inglis was a *littérateur* and a member of the Roxburghe Club. Harrison was also deeply interested in the history of the Church of England, its liturgy and its archaeology. Howley's books fit in less well than those of Inglis and Harrison, but all three men were bibliophiles who liked their books to be adequately bound, who cared for early editions, were familiar with the salerooms, and bought the occasional book just because it was rare or beautiful. Many of Harrison's books have annotations (often corrections) by him, carefully written in pencil; one of his obituarists commented that 'The one thing he could never allow to pass was an inaccurate statement.'

The Howley-Harrison Library is an ecclesiological resource *sans pareil*. It is, however, difficult to assess its importance within the history of the Cathedral library as a working collection. It was catalogued by Sheppard before the year was out, and the catalogue was made available to readers; borrowing was even permitted, albeit only in the name of a canon.[297] On the other hand, the Howley-Harrison Library room was not open to the

---

[294] For accounts of Harrison, see W. H. Fremantle in *DNB*; Beazeley, 'History of the Chapter Library' (cit. in n. 47), 180; B. Hogben, 'Benjamin Harrison: Archdeacon, Benefactor, Tractarian', *Cant. Cath. Chron.*, 78 (1984), 21–5.

[295] Harrison himself wrote of Howley that 'by his kind desire, expressed in his last illness . . . all his learned books were given to [Harrison]': *Patient Waiting: Sermons Preached in Canterbury Cathedral . . .* (London, 1889), 206. For Inglis, see G. F. Russell Barker in *DNB*.; E. M. Forster, *Marianne Thornton, 1797–1887: A Domestic Biography* (London, 1956); Clive Bigham, *The Roxburghe Club: Its History and Its Members, 1812–1927* (Roxburghe Club, [no.

188], 1928), 51; *Catalogue of the Remaining Portion of the Library of the Late Sir Robert Harry Inglis, Bart . . .*, Sotheby, 12 Nov. 1889, lots 1–468.

[296] For Benjamin Harrison sen. (1771–1856), see G. T. Bettany in *DNB*; a less attractive picture is given by Michael Rose, *Curator of the Dead: Thomas Hodgkin (1798–1866)* (London, 1981), esp. ch. 5.

[297] The Howley-Harrison Library borrowers' register, 1888–1910, shows it to have been little used save by the Librarian and the library staff.

public, and since it was a collection that was not added to, it gradually came to assume the air of a little-visited museum. Until 1986, the books remained in undisturbed order on the very presses in which they had been received. Being a collection formed by a few private individuals, it is essentially an assemblage of monographs, with very few periodicals. In a sense it tells one most about its creators' tastes: it is only by knowing their interests that one can guess what may be worth looking up in the catalogue.

THE TWENTIETH CENTURY

In 1890 G. R. Eden (Bishop of Dover and canon, 1890–7) was appointed Librarian. Perhaps because he was translated just seven years later to the see of Wakefield, he remains a shadowy figure in Canterbury's history. However, the steps that he took for the library set a pattern that lasted until recent years. Principally, he established the printed books collection as a general loan library, with most books (other than those in the Howley-Harrison Library) being freely borrowable for up to four weeks. The elderly Sheppard remained an Assistant Librarian (being sometimes called Librarian of the Howley-Harrison Library; from 1889 he had also held the ancient, honorific office of Seneschal of the Cathedral[298]), but Eden at some point arranged for the appointment of two Honorary Librarians. A lay clerk, Robert Rhodes, was paid as Library Keeper or general factotum; the role of the Honorary Librarians was 'to exercise a general supervision of the Library, and also to assist students in their researches', as one of them expressed it.[299] Eden also framed new rules for the Library, and in 1896 he had the books rearranged by John Macfarlane of the British Museum.[300]

Honorary Librarians ran the library until the death, in 1948, of W. P. Blore (who was actually Librarian, and acted without remuneration). They relieved the Canon-Librarian of much of his work, and they had time to lavish on readers of whom they approved. They had the run of the library and the archives, and became familiar with their contents. It is arguable, too, that they weakened the library's claims upon Chapter resources, since they took the library away from the Chapter's mainstream concerns. The library was set on the path to quasi-autonomy and the Canon-Librarian had both to make an effort to discover what was happening and what needed to be done in it, and then to argue its case in Chapter. There was thus a risk that it would be left alone by an uninformed and uninterested Chapter, while its Honorary Librarians would do only what work they wished. The library (which is to say, its readership) was fortunate that by and large the Honorary Librarians were helpful and conscientious, and that their personalities did not loom as large as they might have; it was as well, too, that most of the Canon-Librarians were capable men, as well as being scholars. The Honorary Librarians gave their time because they were attracted by the history of the Cathedral and the documentary riches

---

[298] He described himself as 'Keeper of the Cathedral Records' at the front of his catalogue of the Howley-Harrison library; at the Chapter's suggestion, he had been given a Lambeth LlD.

[299] Beazeley, 'History of the Chapter Library' (cit. in n. 47), 180.

[300] Ibid. 180–1. Eden's rules were more or less repeated by subsequent Librarians (1898, 1903, 1925, 1931), although extended in number.

of its muniments, and they therefore built up the collection of printed books into one that was clearly focused on the history of Canterbury in particular and on the Middle Ages in general. The clergy of the diocese retained a special position, as automatically having borrowing rights, but it cannot be said that the library particularly sought to serve their interests. The diocesan Clerical Book Association had been housed and then (in 1863) absorbed by the Cathedral library;[301] in the twentieth century, those who wished to read contemporary theological works had to resort to the library of St Augustine's College (which remained open until 1987, long after the college itself had been closed down[302]). But at least for the first half of the twentieth century, the Canon-Librarians probably helped ensure that the Cathedral library acquired some publications bearing on the contemporary Church of England, as well as ecclesiastical biographies and the like.

A glance at the book borrowers' registers is sufficient to show some of these changes. The immediate impression is one of remarkable activity, with several hundred books being borrowed every year. In 1891, the first full year of borrowing under the new dispensation, no fewer than 700 books were signed for. Admittedly, this figure was never again achieved; yet during the 1890s the tally never fell below about 550. Book borrowings declined gently, until around 1910, but they then stayed at a plateau of somewhere between 250 and 300 a year until the 1920s, rising back above 300 throughout the 1930s. On the other hand, it is remarkable what a small band of people was signing for these books: apart from a few spinsters and clergy, they were all members of the Cathedral community—the Dean, a few of the canons (principally Mason, Moore and Danks) and, above all, the Honorary Librarians and the Sub-Librarian. From the point of view of printed books, it was as though the library was reverting to being a private library of the Cathedral community.

On the other hand, it is noticeable that the sort of books being borrowed were very different from those being taken out 50 or 100 years earlier: periodicals loom large, *Archaeologia Cantiana* being the most popular, with Camden Society volumes and the *Church Quarterly Review* typical of the alternatives. The monographs that were borrowed were primarily works of local and national history, or ecclesiastical history. They were mostly, one feels, for serious rather than light reading, and one may suspect that in many cases they were being borrowed in order to enable the library's documents to be better understood.

The shift in the library's primary role, from housing a collection of printed books to being a place for the consultation of historical documents, had the wholly beneficial effect of drawing attention to the documents' need for conservation. That need has formed a *leitmotiv* of the library's history ever since 1896, when F. W. Cross, as Honorary Librarian, offered 'to deal with the burnt minute Books of the Chapter': he arranged in order the first two Chapter Act Books (still suffering the effects of the audit-house fire of 1670), which were then sent to the British Museum for repair and rebinding, at his expense.[303]

---

[301] Chapter Act Book, 1854–84, pp. 141 (1862), 154. It was agreed that the Librarian might weed the libraries of the Chapter and of the Clerical Book Association, and spend the proceeds of sale of such books on putting the latter collection into good condition.

[302] In Oct. 1989 the St Augustine's Foundation sent most of the books to the library of Pusey House, Oxford, although some were sold by auction at Phillips in London, sale of Printed Books, Atlases, and Maps, 22 Feb. 1990, lots 1–36.

[303] Chapter Act Book, 1895–1910, pp. 50, 69; see also F. W. Cross, 'The Early Minute-Books of the Dean and Chapter of Canterbury', *Archaeol. Jnl.*, 54 (1896), 235–48.

The eminent Dante scholar Edward Moore was appointed Librarian shortly after becoming a canon in 1903, and took more drastic steps to deal with the problems posed by the archives. These had by now all been gathered in to safe keeping (the last significant discovery being of a group of eighty-two documents, mostly fragmentary, found in the Treasury in 1896, apparently by the Honorary Librarian M. Beazeley[304]), although their actual place of storage remained haphazard, being either the Treasury or the Chapter library or the Howley-Harrison Library. Moore sought advice from the Bodleian Library and from J. P. Gilson of the British Museum.[305] Gilson was one of the finest and most energetic manuscript-cataloguers of this century, and his report is extremely thorough and practical, its only fault being an excessive optimism as to the time needed for his recommendations to be carried out. He had totted up the number of days and months that his proposals would take, and arrived at a total of approximately two and a half years of 'urgent' work. Even today, however, after dozens of man-years of work on the archives, several of the suggestions remain no closer to being achieved.

The short answer as to why Gilson's report was not immediately acted upon (save in such minor matters as abandoning a catalogue by Sheppard and reverting to Bunce's Schedule, for the Chartae Antiquae; the Schedule was interleaved to allow for additions) is that the Dean and Chapter did not feel that it was really their responsibility to employ the requisite cataloguer. It was part of the legacy of their dealings with the Ecclesiastical Commissioners that they would have felt that the Commissioners had, or ought to have, some responsibility for records of lands that the Chapter had had to surrender to the Commissioners. And, in the financing methods that were operative at this period, it was the Commissioners who paid the Sub-Librarian's modest salary of £20 (just as they also paid the canons' stipends too). Late in 1905, and again in 1906, some carefully selected duplicates were sold by auction for over £500; the proceeds were invested in stock, but this yielded no more than £14 10s. annually.[306] That would go only the shortest of distances in salary terms.[307]

The appointment of Charles Eveleigh Woodruff (1855–1948) as Honorary Librarian, in 1907, was in a sense the long-term response to the Gilson report. Moore may have hoped that Woodruff would be another Sheppard; it is difficult to assert that he would have been disappointed. Woodruff was not an outstanding scholar, but he was certainly industrious, and although he was not as prolific a cataloguer as Sheppard, he was certainly just as active at putting material into print.[308] As Honorary Librarian (1907–9), Deputy Librarian (1909–18), and later Honorary Librarian once more, he combined holding a series of country livings (save for the years 1906–11) with putting in a great deal of time in the library—and for him the library primarily meant its documents. He contributed the greater part of the

[304] J. P. Gilson, *Manuscripts of the Dean and Chapter of Canterbury* (priv. printed [1905]), 5.

[305] E. Armstrong, 'Edward Moore, 1835–1916', *Proc. British Academy*, 7 (1915–16), 575–84, at 584. Gilson, *Manuscripts of the Dean and Chapter* (cit. in n. 304), There is a copy of Gilson's report in the Bodleian Library.

[306] The sales at auction, on or before 27 Dec. 1905 and 25 Apr. 1906, yielded £15 1s.; in 1906 a total of £553 17s. 9d. was spent on L.B. & S.C.R. stock, giving £14 10s. 8d. interest annually.

[307] The Sub-Librarian, who from Aug. 1904 was the lay clerk W. Halward, was certainly at a later date being allowed to supplement his income by charging 1s. an hour for invigilating readers of items from the archives.

[308] Appreciative obituaries of Woodruff were written by W. P. Blore, *Kentish Gazette*, 20 Feb. 1948; H. J. Cape, *Cantuarian*, 22 (1946–8), 313–14; and W. G. Urry, *Arch. Cant.*, 61, (1949 for 1948), 192–3. See also Woodruff's entry in *King's School, Canterbury: Register, 1859 to 1931* (OKS Assn., 1932), 31.

Memorials of the Cathedral & Priory of Christ in Canterbury (1912, written in collaboration with Canon Danks) and he published over thirty articles in *Archaeologia Cantiana*, while he listed over 1,200 additional Chartae Antiquae and many hundreds of other documents in the Cathedral's archives. If he was sometimes careless and inaccurate, he nevertheless had a considerable ability for getting the most significant facts out of the materials before him. It may be that Moore was skilful at directing him; in 1910–11 Moore arranged for the publication of a catalogue by him of the Chapter's Literary Manuscripts,[309] while in 1909 he had written for Moore a short account of the volumes in the archives that needed repair and for which it was proposed to ask the Ecclesiastical Commissioners for a grant.[310] Within their different compasses, these can be reckoned two of Woodruff's best pieces of work.

Moore's next successor but one as Canon-Librarian, Samuel Bickersteth (canon, 1916–36; Librarian, 1924–36), certainly had a fairly low personal opinion of Woodruff. When he found once that Woodruff had already been paid for making a transcript of a document of which another transcript was subsequently requested, he observed that 'It was characteristic of C. E. W. to suppress the fact that he had got 5 guineas for earlier work, unless indeed his memory did genuinely fail him as it often does.'[311] This was in 1932, when Woodruff was 76 years old; he lived to be 92. Readers in the library in the 1920s and 1930s had in effect to choose which of the two Honorary Librarians they would like to help them. Those who did not wish for the assistance of the gaunt Woodruff could turn to Charles Cotton (Deputy Librarian, 1918–39). He was a cheerful and hardworking antiquary, devoted to the history of the Franciscans and the Order of St John of Jerusalem, as well as that of the Cathedral, and was a hospital doctor in Ramsgate.[312] He marked Bickersteth's retirement by presenting to the library a Franciscan breviary of 1557 and a fourteenth-century copy of Pseudo-Chrysostom's commentary on St Matthew's Gospel (Add. MSS 65 and 66), saying in a letter to Bickersteth that 'During your time happiness and harmony have reigned amongst the staff, thanks to your unfailing courtesy and consideration.'[313]

The 1920s and 1930s certainly seem to have been halcyon years for the library. For readers or borrowers of printed books, it was open on Tuesday, Wednesday, and Thursday mornings, from 11 a.m. to 1 p.m., while for those who wanted to do 'research work among the Archives' it was open on the same days from 10 a.m. to 1 p.m. and from 2 p.m. to 4 p.m.[314] The library was run rather on a shoe-string; in the year ending 30 September 1935, for instance, it cost the Chapter precisely £195 1s. 10d. (plus heating and any fabric repairs). Its other expenses were met from the interest on invested library funds (£14 10s. p.a.), supplemented by the customary gifts of £20 from every new canon at his installation, and

[309] C. E. Woodruff, *A Catalogue of the Manuscript Books (which are preserved in Study X.Y.Z. and in the Howley-Harrison Collection) in the Library of Christ Church, Canterbury* (Canterbury, 1911); cf. Chapter Act Book, 1910–19, pp. 22, 36.

[310] A copy of this letter, which was printed, is pasted into the front of Bunce's Schedule, i. pt. 1.

[311] J. B. Bickersteth Papers, Box 1, typescript memorandum, signed 'S.B.'

[312] Cf. his obituary by R. U. P[otts], *Arch. Cant.*, 51 (1940 for 1939), 232–4.

[313] A copy of this letter, dated 12 May 1936, is among the Blore Papers (Miscellaneous); it was printed in *Canterbury Diocesan Gazette*, 44 (1936), 90–1.

[314] Printed sheet of Chapter Library Regulations, over the names of Dean Bell and Canon Bickersteth; dated Jan. 1925. A copy is in J. B. Bickersteth Papers, Box 1, on cover of account of the Accord of Winchester. This is the first mention of extra hours for historical researchers: was Dean Bell responsible?

£40 from an incoming dean.[315] Chapter or library funds were used to purchase some books, but at least as many books were presented. In 1930, for example, the library purchased the revised edition of the first volume of the *Letters and Papers of Henry VIII*, seven volumes of the *Calendar of Papal Registers*, several volumes of Alcuin Club publications, and six parts of Cabrol and Leclercq's *Dictionnaire d'archéologie chrétienne et de liturgie* (earlier parts having been given by Dr Nichols of Worcester, Mass., USA). The library's set of Migne's *Patrologia Graeca* was completed with £200 that Archdeacon Maxwell Spooner had left to the library, and the books and pamphlets on the Scandinavian Church bequeathed by Canon A. J. Mason were catalogued and made available to readers. A fourteenth-century Bible (Add. MS 38) presented by Mrs E. L. Holland was restored at the British Museum, at a cost of £75 15*s*.; Dean Sheppard had persuaded the American millionaire J. P. Morgan to defray this cost. The British Museum figured significantly in the library's affairs in this period, since its photographers took the few photographs of manuscript materials that were requested, while the Friends of Canterbury Cathedral paid for the conservation and rebinding of a Cathedral register each year, usually at the British Museum.[316] Local expertise in bookbinding and repair was also deployed, and by 1932 a binder, P. J. (Jack) Maple, was working at the library on three mornings a week, dealing with both manuscripts and early printed books.[317] The sequel to these efforts was a grant of £400 from the Pilgrim Trust in 1934, for the repair of eight more registers—recognition from outside Canterbury of how well the library was being run.[318] In 1934, too, Dr Cotton enjoyed a rare distinction: a letter of his to *The Times* was accompanied by an appreciative leading article. He had suggested that an illustrated mention of a 'hairy star' ('feaxeda steorra') in a note to Psalm 5 in the Eadwine Psalter was an allusion to Halley's Comet. The Astronomer Royal confirmed that the comet had appeared in 1145, enabling the psalter to be given that year as the *terminus post quem* of its production.[319]

The library's atmosphere was clearly one of congenial learning. Under Bickersteth's successor as Librarian, its highest peak of scholarship was reached. The new Librarian, William Parry Blore (1875–1948) was not a canon, but his father, Dr G. J. Blore, Headmaster of the King's School, had been both an honorary canon and, for some years, Acting or Deputy Librarian, while his own sister, (Mary) Margaret, was the wife of Canon A. J. Mason.[320] He had been a preparatory school teacher, and had spent his holidays reading in the Cathedral library. Woodruff would have liked the post himself, but, as Bickersteth disclosed to Blore in response to his letter of acceptance, 'even C. E. W. wrote to me ... "There could be no better choice."' Blore acted without remuneration; he had taken early retirement, and enjoyed reasonable private means. In 1948 he wrote to Dr Rose Graham, whom he was assisting in her edition of the Register of Archbishop Winchelsey,

[315] Letter from T. G. Gardiner, Treasurer, to C. E. Woodruff, 19 May 1936, in Blore Papers (Miscellaneous).

[316] S. Bickersteth, 'Cathedral Library', *Canterbury Diocesan Gazette*, 39 (1931), 77–9.

[317] *Friends of Canterbury Cathedral, 6th Annual Report* (1933), 29.

[318] S. Bickersteth, 'Canterbury Cathedral Library', *Canterbury Diocesan Gazette*, 43 (1935), 16–17.

[319] *The Times*, 6 June 1934, 15. Cotton's triumph has since been qualified by the awareness that in the middle years of the 12th

cent. there was a number of comets, any one of which could have been the subject of comment in the psalter: see S. D. Keynes, 'The Comet in the Eadwine Psalter', in *The Eadwine Psalter: Text, Image, and Monastic Culture in Twelfth-Century Canterbury*, ed. M. T. Gibson, T. A. Heslop, and R. W. Pfaff (London, 1992), 157–64.

[320] Much of the material in this paragraph is taken from the appreciation by N. L. Ramsay, 'William Parry Blore', *Cant. Cath. Chron.*, 83 (1989), 38–41.

that transcribing 'is my principal form of amusement; and has been so for the last 50 years: with the result that I can supply most investigators with transcripts of documents that they wish to work on'. He was a fine Latinist and interpreter of the documents in the Cathedral's archives, interested not so much in wringing the principal facts from his materials (in the manner of Woodruff) as in patiently seeking to understand them. Painstaking in the extreme, he was the sort of person who always seeks to answer letters by return of post; for scholarly enquirers of whom he approved, he was happy to give endlessly of his time, copying, suggesting, and corresponding. To understand the Ecclesiastical Suit Rolls, he mastered the procedure of medieval ecclesiastical courts; he was too modest to wish to edit the rolls himself, although Professor Powicke was enthusiastic about his work, but his transcripts formed the starting-point for the Selden Society's *Select Cases from the Ecclesiastical Courts of the Province of Canterbury, c. 1200–1301*.[321] In all, about 300 notebooks or packets of his transcripts of medieval and sixteenth-century records survive—and they are often more like editions, complete with notes, than mere copies.

Blore's idyll was destroyed by the Second World War and its aftermath. The bulk of the archives had been put in the crypt for safety in the First World War, and in 1939 they were taken down to a room adjacent to the crypt: it was characteristic of Blore that he carried them all himself, assisted only by his friend, the Revd C. S. Phillips.[322] Disaster struck the library on the night of Trinity Sunday, 31 May, 1942: a high-explosive bomb with delayed action of about six seconds fell directly on to the north-east corner of the building and went through the floor and into the ground to a depth of 5 or 6 feet below the basement floor before exploding.[323] A large mass of earth and brick was shot up out of the crater, causing the collapse of the roof beams and consequently of much of the library furniture. There was, however, no fire, and therefore no water, and damage to the books was generally limited to their bindings. Fewer than a hundred books were actually destroyed or rendered entirely useless. Belatedly, the other books were removed to the chapter house and then to the crypt.

There then followed a period of nine years during which the library's future remained unsettled. The Howley-Harrison Library room remained in use, and in January 1946 many of the documents in the archives were brought up there. Blore had, too, the assistance of William Urry, who in August 1946 was appointed Assistant Librarian. However, the whole future of the archives was uncertain: there were suspicions that the Chapter planned to deposit them in Oxford, and a scheme for a major new building met with none of the American financial support that had been been anticipated. Eventually, in 1950, the Chapter were to settle for a building that would stand on the site of the old one, paid for out of a grant of £10,000 from the Pilgrim Trust and with compensation from the War Damage Commission (assessed at £33,154).[324] Blore's relations with the Chapter deteriorated. He did not get on with Shirley, the Canon-Treasurer, or with Standen (canon from 1947), and lamented to the medievalist W. A. Pantin that 'with the departure of [Canon] Crum (who

[321] (Cit. in n. 60.)

[322] J. M. C. Crum, reviewing Phillips's *Canterbury Cathedral in the Middle Ages*, *Theology*, 53 (1950), 113. The store-room was a chamber below the southern Corona turret.

[323] Details of the bombing and its aftermath are taken from

Blore's report, as excerpted in *Friends of Canterbury Cathedral, 16th Annual Report* (1943), 17–18, and from J. L. Denman's account in Sykes, *Canterbury Cathedral Library* (cit. in n. 226), 29–32.

[324] Cf. Chapter Act Book, 1947–53, pp. 613, 779.

did really care for the Library *and* make use of it), and ... of [Canon] Macnutt, there is now no one who really takes any interest in the Library or even uses it'.[325] In February 1948 Blore was interviewed by the Dean and was then replaced as Librarian by Standen; he remained the working librarian. His firm dealings with one or two members of the public were among the matters held against him, and it is a sign of how far the Dean and Chapter had changed in their attitude towards the public accessibility of their library that at one stage in this sad débâcle Blore was instructed 'that visitors to the Library be encouraged'.[326] He died before the year was out.[327]

Blore's successor, appointed as 'Keeper of the Manuscripts of the Cathedral Library', was William George Urry (1913–81).[328] Urry's term in charge of the Cathedral archives and library (to which were added the city and diocesan archives) has always been seen as a great success. The new library building was completed in 1954, and is on three floors (one more than its predecessor); it has a spacious and agreeable atmosphere. It echoes its predecessor and other buildings in a style that has been described as 'neo-Norman-cum-Tudoresque'.[329] It does not house many books, but this defect was remedied by the reconstruction of the Cheker Building in 1964–6.[330] Urry, like Blore, approached Canterbury's history as a native of the city; he investigated its medieval history deeply, gaining a doctorate for his thesis on 'Early Rentals and Charters Relating to the Borough of Canterbury' (completed in 1955). He was a scholar-librarian, who regarded other scholars as having priority among his readers; but he also had a scholar's curiosity about his surroundings, which led him to gather in documents, objects, and information of all kinds for his collections, and he delighted to talk to the public about the past that he could show that they still lived in. With Maple's assistance, he raised the standard of conservation of the damaged documents and books to heights that can hardly have been matched anywhere else outside London; Maple was adept at constructing apparatus to help him deal with repairs (Pl. 69). The library had been built with a dark-room for photography, and Urry acquired ultraviolet-ray reading-equipment. He had his difficulties in his relations with the Chapter—he felt underfinanced, and he would have liked assistance in the daily routine of retrieving and returning the documents—but the library was able to attract volunteers, and in the 1950s and 1960s there continued to be no more readers than in the 1930s, which is to say, slightly fewer than 1,000 a year. The rise to popularity of family history had yet to take place, and there were also still very few enquirers wishing to investigate the earlier printed books in the library; the foundation of the University of Kent made no impact in Urry's time.

Urry's tragedy was that from about 1960 he was intermittently dogged by illness, and consequently was unable to complete any further books—on Becket, the later medieval

[325] Draft letter to Pantin, Blore Papers (Miscellaneous).
[326] Chapter Act Book, 1947–53, p. 252.
[327] Blore's obituary in *The Times*, 11 Nov. 1948, records in classic style that 'A manner which was sometimes formidable at first encounter hid a heart of singular tenderness and generosity.' He bequeathed £500 to the library.
[328] Obituary of Urry: ibid. 27 Feb. 1981; see also H. Mayr-Harting, 'William George Urry: Address Given at His Memorial Service in the Church of St. Mary the Virgin, Oxford.

1 May 1981' (typescript).
[329] John Newman, *The Buildings of England: North East and East Kent* (3rd edn.; Harmondsworth, 1983), 218. It is described by its architect, J. L. Denman, in Sykes, *Canterbury Cathedral Library* (cit. in n. 226), 31–2, and more fully in the *Builder*, 188 (Jan.–June 1955), 66–70.
[330] For the Cheker or Wolfson Building, see F. J. Shirley, 'Rebuilding the "Cheker" at the Cathedral Library', *Friends of Canterbury Cathedral, 38th Annual Report* (1965), 6–7.

city of Canterbury, or Christopher Marlowe.[331] In July 1969, when he was preparing to leave Canterbury to take up the Readership in Palaeography at Oxford, he wrote in a letter: 'Life here consists mainly in rushing up and down stairs to get MSS. for readers, answering letters to dotty enquirers convinced they are descended from St Hereward the Wake, doing all the office-boy's work, petty cash, licking stamps and so forth. If I were able to do little but my real job, i.e. cataloguing MSS, I would not mind making a sacrifice in terms of pay, but life is slipping by and the setup here, doing routine jobs all day long that any teenager could do, means that there is little to show for it.'[332]

Dotty or otherwise, the genealogical enquirers became far more numerous in the time of Urry's successor, Miss Anne Oakley (appointed in 1970, after an interregnum of about a year). They came in person, and soon began to outnumber the historical researchers; initially they were attracted by the transcripts of parish registers preserved in the archidiaconal and diocesan archives, but then original registers came to be brought in to the archives. The pedigree-mongers then became even more numerous, and time-consuming because of the quantities of documents that they wanted to skim through.

Pressure was first taken off the archivist by the removal of printed books from her responsibilities. In 1977 cataloguing was begun of works in the library printed before 1801, as a project that has been funded by the British Library and directed by Dr David Shaw of the University of Kent. A second project was later added, that of cataloguing the nineteenth-century books and pamphlets; both enterprises are now virtually complete.[333] In 1978–9 the Dean and Chapter entered into an arrangement with the University of Kent comparable to agreements that had already been reached between the cathedrals and universities of Exeter and York, whereby a Keeper of Printed Books was employed by the university to work at the Cathedral.[334] Only one such keeper was appointed, Mrs Naomi Pearman (later Linnell); after she had taken early retirement (on grounds of ill health), the Chapter made a new agreement with the University of Kent, in 1989, and Mrs Sheila Hingley became Cathedral Librarian.[335]

The problem of the archives was resolved in the same year by another agreement with an outside body—in this case, the Archives Office of Kent County Council.[336] Here again, staff were brought in from outside, supplementing those already working for the Cathedral; within a complex financial structure, it has thus proved possible for moneys from the county council, the Cathedral, and the city of Canterbury to pay for a greatly enhanced level of staffing in the archives. Thanks to this and to successful appeals to charitable trusts, the last few years have seen the resumption of the cataloguing work that Urry so rightly regarded as of primary importance.

[331] The latter was sufficiently close to completion for it to be edited by A. F. Butcher and published as *Christopher Marlowe and Canterbury* (London, 1988).

[332] Copy of letter to C. R. Dodwell, 29 July 1969, in file OE.

[333] Canterbury's pre-1701 books are included in Margaret S. G. McLeod *et al.*, *The Cathedral Libraries Catalogue: Books Printed Before 1701 in the Libraries of the Anglican Cathedrals of England and Wales*, i: *Books Printed in the British Isles . . .*, ed. Karen I. James and D. J. Shaw (London, 1984).

[334] For Exeter and York, see Ker, 'Cathedral Libraries', in Ker, *Books, Collectors and Libraries* (cit. in n. 32), 299; for Canterbury, *University of Kent Library: Annual Report of the Librarian, 1978–9*, [5].

[335] She was appointed as Keeper of Printed Books, Aug. 1989, but soon afterwards her title was changed to that of Cathedral Librarian.

[336] The Canterbury city archives were the subject of a separate agreement between Kent County Council and Canterbury City Council.

Modernization of such an institution as Canterbury's library and archives is not easy. The sale of several hundred nineteenth-century printed books in 1984 was perhaps an unsurprising mishap.[337] But in general the Cathedral's manuscript and printed collections have made the transition into the age of computerized cataloguing with remarkable smoothness. The Cathedral's statutes of 1942 imply a priority of concern on the part of the library (and archives) for the study of the Cathedral Church's history, fabric, and records.[338] That remains true; on the other hand, as Blore's unhappy tale serves to demonstrate, the public too, whether scholarly, genealogically minded, or simply dotty, are seen as a priority. There is an enormous amount of manuscript material that still awaits cataloguing or calendaring—there are, for instance, the medieval Cathedral Priory registers, before whose uncalendared 'voluminous pages' even Bishop Stubbs quailed[339]—but progress is now being made as never before towards achieving what so many scholars over the last few generations have hoped for.

[337] Some of the books so disposed of are detailed in Winterdown Books, cat. 12 (Acrise, Kent, 1984).

[338] *The Constitution & Statutes of the Cathedral Church of Christ,* *Canterbury* (HMSO, [1942]), stat. xxxiii, § 6.

[339] Gervase, *Historical Works*, ii, p. xliii.

IX

The Liturgy of the Cathedral and its Music, c.1075–1642

ROGER BOWERS

THE NORMANNO-ENGLISH LITURGY AND ITS OBSERVANCE, c.1075–c.1350

The Constitutions of Archbishop Lanfranc

The monastery church which Lanfranc began to build in 1070, and of which the easternmost sections were ready for consecration and use by October 1077, was the heart and focus of a community of men, youths, and boys whose oblation and reception into the Benedictine monastic order had committed them to a life of unceasing liturgical observance. This was composed of a perpetual round of worship and prayer, of contemplation and penance, and of intercession for mankind and re-enactment of the sacrifice of the Mass. This was not an end in itself, or even simply an offering to God. The monks believed that it would be for the benefit of their fellow men, and for themselves a passport to a special reward at the Last Judgement. For 470 years before Lanfranc, the worship of God through liturgical observance in choir had been the primary reason for the existence of the Cathedral church, and so it has remained for 900 years since.

The content of the religious services, and the manner in which they were performed, were prescribed for the monks by the traditional liturgy of the Church. Over many centuries, and through many vicissitudes, Western Christendom had devised for its use an immense body of liturgical material composed of three constituent elements, namely text, music, and ceremony; as observed at the greatest of the Benedictine monasteries, this comprehended an almost infinite complexity and elaboration, which nevertheless was informed by a ground-plan that was common to all Western Christendom. The texts were written in the ecclesiastical Latin of the Vulgate and of the Fathers; the music consisted of the huge repertory of unadorned, unharmonized plainsong chant contained in such service-books as the antiphoner, gradual, and processioner.

It is fortunate that there survives from so early a period as the late eleventh century a document that yields much information on the content and manner of the Benedictine liturgical observance undertaken at Christ Church, Canterbury, in the wake of the main thrust of Lanfranc's reforms. This has become known as the *Constitutions of Archbishop Lanfranc*,[1] and can be shown to have been drawn up around the years 1075–80.[2] Principally, this heterogeneous document appears to comprehend successively: 1. a liturgical directory; 2. a summary of the responsibilities of the major officers of the Priory, with a disciplinary code; and 3. rules for the training and admission of recruits to the Priory at the beginning of their careers, and for the dispatch of deceased monks at their end.

In compiling the liturgical directory which is principally of interest here, Lanfranc drew upon a number of monastic customaries of Continental provenance; all took their fundamental inspiration from the original Rule of St Benedict, but the principal immediate influence upon Lanfranc appears to have been the liturgical practice of the monastery of Cluny, as set out in the code attributed to the monk Bernard of Cluny and written in 1067. Conspicuously absent are any direct borrowings from the English *Regularis Concordia* of about a century earlier;[3] Lanfranc's *Constitutions* appear to enunciate a fresh start in the detail of liturgical practice at Christ Church, with the reformed observances of continental Europe at its heart.

Lanfranc's directory is by no means a complete and comprehensive guide to the liturgy of his day. It naturally shares the characteristics of his exemplars, and so the light which it sheds on the daily liturgical round is apt to be somewhat fitful, confused, and oblique. Its format is that of a prototype ordinal, of pragmatic rather than comprehensive compilation. The detail of its content excludes most that was routine; it concentrates instead upon those constituent episodes in the liturgy that were least susceptible to reliance upon memory—on seasonal items of only brief currency, for instance, and on the enormous complexities of the liturgy of Holy Week. Further, the objects of its regulation tend to be the items performed by everyone present in choir, rather than those committed to individuals. Thus, like its prototypes, it bears the character primarily of a rough-hewn and imperfect attempt at the rationalization of pre-existing and piecemeal written collections of pronouncements, concerned mainly with just those liturgical points that experience showed to be most in need of an authorized source of reference. It presupposes the existence of some supplementary books (to which, indeed, there are a few passing references), and, much more, of a substantial body of liturgical custom which long and frequent usage had rendered habitual and ingrained in the memories of its enactors, and which therefore did not need to be written down. Nevertheless, the document is still of substantial length, and analysis of it can yield valuable insight into the liturgical practices of Christ Church at this critical period.

The *Constitutions* originated at a time when the sheer quantity of liturgical observance at the major religious communities of the Christian West stood at perhaps the greatest level that was ever achieved. At its core stood the daily performance of the cycle of Canonical Hours—Matins (called at this early period *Nocturnae*), Lauds (called *Matutinae*),

[1] *Decreta Lanfranci Monachis Cantuariensibus Transmissa*, ed. D. M. Knowles (Corpus Consuetudinum Monasticarum, 3; Siegburg, 1967); an earlier version of this edition, with an English translation, had appeared as *The Monastic Constitutions of Lanfranc*, ed. M. D. Knowles (Nelson's Medieval Classics; London, 1951).

[2] *Consuetudines Beccenses*, ed. M. P. Dickson (Corpus Consuetudinum Monasticarum, 4; Siegburg, 1967), p. xxxiii; but cf. *Decreta Lanfranci* (cit. in n. 1), p. xvi.

[3] *Decreta Lanfranci* (cit. in n. 1), pp. xvii–xix.

Prime, Terce, Sext, None, Vespers, and Compline; to these were added two community masses, namely the early Morrow Mass and the High Mass of the Day. Appended or prefaced to these was an inchoate and piecemeal accumulation of extra recitations of psalms, prayers, processions, and minor offices, primarily of an intercessory character,[4] adding up in all to a routine of worship and praise that was strenuous and exhausting to all committed to participation in its totality.

To a large degree, the content of the services on any particular day depended on its categorization as feast or feria. The *Constitutions* recognized five main classes of feast, and defined the shades of distinction between the ceremony of each. There were five principal feasts (the Nativity, the Resurrection, Pentecost, the Assumption of the Virgin Mary, and the patronal festival), seventeen lesser feasts, sixteen minor feasts, and others yet more minor which still qualified for the principal mark of distinction—the recitation of twelve lessons at Matins. On feasts of the least standing, and on ferias, there were only three lessons at Matins.[5] All days not designated as feasts were ferias (or non-feast days).

The sequence in which the several services were observed was fully prescribed, with slight differences between the winter (1 October–Easter) and summer timetables, and between feast-days and ferial days, but no timetable exact by clock-time can be given, since much revolved round the ever-shifting times of sunrise and sunset.[6] Matins was the night office, sung during the hours of darkness, beginning probably a short time after midnight. In the summer season, Lauds followed immediately, and then all returned to bed. During winter the community retired to sleep straight after Matins, and then, towards the night's end, all rose for a period of study or prayer followed by the singing of Lauds, which was so performed as to conclude as daylight broke. Following daybreak, throughout the year, Prime was sung, and, following an interval for further study in the cloister, Terce and then the Morrow Mass. There followed the daily chapter meeting, and more time in cloister before Sext and then the procession preceding High Mass of the day. Mass was followed by None (at about midday), and then there followed the midday meal. Vespers was the afternoon office, and Compline was recited at the end of the liturgical day;[7] all then retired to the dormitory to sleep, before rising again after midnight to sing Matins of the next day's cycle.

It may be salutary to recall that at no time before the Reformation were these religious services in any sense at all congregational. The monastery church was the monks' private chapel; lay people had no need of access to its services, and indeed they were expressly excluded from them. They could enter only as pilgrims seeking access to the shrines of the saints. The inhabitants of the city attended to their religious devotions in their own parish churches; only the very greatest of visiting dignitaries, whose presence did honour to the monastery, were welcome to attend upon the monks' devotions in the Cathedral.

Lanfranc's *Constitutions* duly, if often obliquely, disclose the monastery's condign adherence to all those elements of liturgical observance that by the late eleventh century were

---

[4] For further detail, see ibid., pp. xxi–xxii.

[5] *Constitutions* (cit. in n. 1), 55–70.

[6] For a more detailed analysis of the daily *horarium* see *Decreta Lanfranci* (cit. in n. 1), pp. xxiii–xxv.

[7] *Constitutions* (cit. in n. 1), 3–6, 7–8, 54–5; Compline was soon to develop into a fully sung community office, but at this period was still very much a private devotion, recited quietly in pairs or threes: ibid. 38.

common to all Western communities of religious. The community at worship *was* the choir, and the *Constitutions* duly allow for participation of specific kinds and characteristics for each of the community's component sections. In Lanfranc's church, the fourth bay of the nave was filled by the rood-screen and pulpitum, and the monk's choir-stalls occupied the next three bays eastward to the central crossing. Here the participants were disposed in the (liturgical) choir of the church along its two sides, in stalls facing each other across the central aisle; judging by the term *forma* employed to describe them, the choir-stalls of the early Norman Cathedral probably were not yet of any great elaboration. On the north side the principal stall was that of the prior, on the south side that of the precentor.[8]

The community of Christ Church was large; it may have had some fifty members immediately before the Conquest, was exceeding sixty by *c*.1080, was reported to have reached 100 by 1090, and by *c*.1125 may have been approaching close to Lanfranc's optimum figure of 150.[9] It appears that for much of the twelfth century the Priory may well have proved able to maintain such dimensions, as a monastery of 140 monks; after the hiatus of 1207–15, however, such a scale was not achieved again. Nevertheless, except for occasional and temporary crises, it seems likely that right down to the very eve of the Dissolution it was rare for the complement of monks to fall below a total of seventy to eighty.[10] This was the largest community of religious in England, equipped at all stages of its history, at least in terms of personnel, to undertake the observance of the *Opus Dei* in the fullest and most expansive manner considered desirable.

According to their seniority in the community, the fully professed monks were divided into two ranks, of *priores* and *iuniores*. In procession, the *iuniores* preceded the *priores*, and in choir it was probably already the custom that the junior half of the community occupied a rank of stalls in front of, and lower than, the rear stalls against the choir wall that were occupied by the older monks.[11] To these two groups of fully trained monks was committed the execution of all the principal constituent phases of each service in choir. The youngest of the *iuniores* constituted the *iuvenes*, who on the whole were not given a distinct rank of liturgical functions to execute.[12] The *conversi* (monks not in holy orders) did fulfil a characteristic role, as servers; they undertook the humbler duties as carriers of the holy water, crosses, candles, and thuribles, both in procession and at service.[13]

Finally, there were the *pueri* or *infantes*. These were oblates, boys offered (*oblati*) by their parents to be educated and brought up at the monastery, for profession as monks when they reached *adulta aetas*—perhaps around the mid-teens. Such boys, given probably at the age of around 8, 9, or 10, constituted the principal source of recruits to the Priory,[14] and their number was probably never negligible. As prospective members of the monastic community they formed an integral part of the choir at service and had their own distinctive contribution to make to it; in particular, their presence lent to the singing the characteristic timbre of production in octaves, as the boys reproduced in their unbroken

---

[8] Ibid. 68, 75, 81, 108, 125, 129–30. In procession likewise, the participants walked two by two, the two files being sometimes referred to as *dui chori* (ibid. 71).

[9] Knowles, *Monastic Order*, 714.

[10] Smith, *Cant. Cath. Priory*, 3–4.

[11] *Constitutions* (cit. in n. 1), 23, 50, 57, 58, 129; on 70–1, 'maiores'

probably denotes the same as 'priores'.

[12] Ibid. 3, 10, 28, 117–18, 129.

[13] Ibid. 12, 13, 23, 30, 36–8, 41, 44, 50, 56, 58, 64, 68, 69, 104–10, 120–1; also 23, 50 (as 'laici monachi').

[14] Ibid. 110–11, 115–17.

voices the chant being sung an octave lower by the adults.[15] The boys attended all the daytime services, and also the night Hours on certain of the days of greatest solemnity.[16] To the voices of one boy or a small group was deputed the singing of certain small-scale items in the liturgy—for instance, the incipit of a hymn, the invocations of the Litany of the Saints in the preamble to High Mass and at procession, and certain versicles and ritual antiphons on greater feasts.[17] In addition to these, there were also some large set-piece items, whose texts or liturgical symbolism suggested that they were particularly suitable for performance by the voices of boys: for instance, the alternate stanzas of the hymn 'Gloria, laus et honor' and the antiphons 'Hosanna filio David' and 'Cum angelis et pueris' in the great Palm Sunday procession, where the boys represented the 'children of the Hebrews'; the prose 'Inventor rutili' at the blessing of the New Fire on Holy Saturday; and the gradual at mass on the feast of All Saints.[18]

Diligent and competent performance of the complexities of the liturgy was sought by the commission of responsibility for its oversight to the senior monk appointed to be precentor. This was an awesome mandate, since he was in a very real sense the director of the chant and ceremony at all the services. He made out the weekly *tabula*, assigning to individuals the liturgical duties, singing and reading, that they were to perform over the ensuing seven days.[19] He was to ensure competence by hearing—if in his discretion it was necessary—all those to whom he had given individual duties rehearse their parts before the service. If, despite this precaution, any chant was begun or sung incorrectly, the precentor was to be alert personally to make good the deficiency. He signalled the start of each chant, and indicated whether its performance should be hastened or relaxed.[20] On the greater feasts, he selected those who were to be associated with him as, in effect, the *rectores chori*.[21] The precentor himself sang the incipit of several of the most significant chants on the greatest feast-days,[22] and was always to be ready to act as stand-in for the archbishop or prior when either defaulted on an expected attendance in choir.[23] He was visibly in charge of the sung processions mounted to greet distinguished visitors, and he had some supervisory role over the teaching of reading and chant to the boys.[24] In all these duties, he enjoyed the assistance of a deputy, the succentor,[25] and, by weekly turns, of some experienced monk chosen by himself to serve as *cantor hebdomadarius*. On greater occasions the latter acted as the associate of the precentor, and on lesser occasions he might deputize for him.[26]

---

[15] For provisions made for the boys' training, see ibid. 3, 4, 21, 49, 73–4, 115, 132.

[16] Ibid. 7, 13, 28, 46.

[17] Ibid. 29–30, 5, 18, 20, 34, 49, 50.

[18] Ibid. 24–5, 44, 64.

[19] By the early 14th cent. the precentor had deputed this duty to the succentor in respect of all days other than principal feasts: BL, MS Arundel 68, fo. 56.

[20] *Constitutions* (cit. in n. 1), 80; also 14, 55, 58, 60, 61, 129.

[21] Ibid. 58 (where the term 'ad regendum chorum' is employed, clearly cognate with the term *rector chori*, which does not occur at this period), 61, 81. An inventory of 1316 makes reference to the staves used by the *rectores chori* as both a tool and a symbol of their office: Legg and Hope, *Inventories*, 61, 74.

[22] *Constitutions* (cit. in n. 1), 12, 16, 20, 23–5, 45, 50, 53, 67, 68, 82.

[23] Ibid. 23, 24, 32, 58, 80; for Lanfranc's use of the term 'abbas' to denote the archbishop, see ibid. 2–3.

[24] Ibid. 71, 116.

[25] Ibid. 82; this is the sole reference to the succentor in the whole text, but in view of the weight of the precentor's responsibilities, the importance of his deputy should not, perhaps, be underestimated.

[26] Ibid. 12, 30, 46, 55, 81, 82. For a general overview of the contemporary context into which this analysis of the duties of the Canterbury precentor belongs, see M. Fassler, 'The Office of Cantor in Early Western Monastic Rules and Customaries: a Preliminary Investigation', *Early Music History*, 5 (1985), 29–51.

The picture of liturgical practice provided by the *Constitutions* is at times oblique and sketchy, and at times full and vivid. Particularly graphic are the provisions implying the enormous length of festal Matins, with its twelve lessons, twelve responsories, and abundant psalms. Equally evocative are the descriptions of the conventual processions, including the Rogation Day processions to a neighbouring parish church and back[27] and the Palm Sunday procession re-enacting in symbolic fashion the entry of Jesus into Jerusalem.[28] Noteworthy likewise were the elaborate solemnities of Christmas and Ash Wednesday, the washing of feet on Maundy Thursday, and the ceremonies of Good Friday and Holy Saturday, including the blessing of the New Fire.[29]

Indeed, in overall effect, the *Constitutions* appear to reflect a copious, not to say a bloated, liturgy, of complex structure and in need of minute management and direction. Of the degree of fervour and efficiency with which the late eleventh-century monastic community effected it, little can now be learnt. It would be naïve, of course, to imagine a consistent observance of smooth and clockwork orderliness. Rather, the text of the *Constitutions* itself reveals some hints of the types of infelicities that it was expected might arise and would have to be dealt with. For instance, the necessity to order that without the precentor's permission none of those deputed to be *rectores chori* on feast-days might take their leave from choir before the end of the service of Mass, is strongly suggestive of a widespread practice of premature departure upon the onset of ennui, which might even be commonly condoned if the offender were only a member of the rank and file and had no specific part to play in the direction of the service. In similar vein is the regulation forbidding anyone to hurry forward the pace of the singing, unless the precentor had himself specifically begun it that way.[30] In all likelihood, the sheer volume of liturgical observance at the Priory was to some extent self-defeating; the more demanding and ambitious the attempt to re-create on earth the unceasing worship of God in the courts of Heaven, the more likely was human frailty to compromise it in practice.

The Opus Dei *and Its Adjuncts, c.1075–c.1350: Plainsong, Polyphony, and the Organ*

For 470 years following the enthronement of Archbishop Lanfranc, the conduct of the Latin rite in the choir of the Cathedral church remained the central activity of the monastic community. Regrettably, no detailed history of this liturgy and its music can be written, since very little relevant documentation has survived. No consuetudinary or ordinal is known to exist; and of the books of text, only the damaged 'Burnt Breviary' of *c.*1375,[31] and, among the books of chant, only a gradual of the late eleventh century[32] and some

[27] *Constitutions* (cit. in n. 1), 49–52.
[28] Ibid. 22–6, 151–2.
[29] Ibid. 10–14, 17–18, 27–38, 38–46.
[30] Ibid. 80, 81.
[31] Add. MS 6; see C. S. Phillips, *Canterbury Cathedral in the Middle Ages* (London, 1949), 18–26. There was a close similarity between the texts of the Office as observed at Canterbury and those known to have been followed at the cathedral priory of Durham; as Phillips suggests, this congruence of textual practice indicates that Durham may have drawn widely on Canterbury materials when the former's monastic liturgy was first

set up in the late 11th cent., so that surviving books of Durham provenance may give the best recoverable idea of the character of Christ Church Use.
[32] Durham, Cathedral Library, MS Cosin V. V. 6 (K. D. Hartzell, 'An Unknown English Benedictine Gradual of the Eleventh Century', *Anglo-Saxon England*, 4 (1975), 131–44); see also BL, Cotton MS Caligula A. xiv. On the loss of the Canterbury books, see N. Sandon, *The Octave of the Nativity: Essays and Notes on Ten Liturgical Reconstructions for Christmas* (London, 1984), 58.

fragments of one of the fifteenth[33] have yet been identified. Nor can these losses be relieved by study of any comprehensive inventory of the service-books of the Priory's choir, for none is known to survive from any period of the Middle Ages.[34]

All these losses are the more regrettable since Christ Church, Canterbury, was far too prominent a church ever to become a backwater, in the liturgy and its music any more than in any other of the ecclesiastical arts. Lanfranc himself had already observed that on certain feasts at Christ Church, the service was celebrated with particular and exceptional solemnity as a reflection of the importance of the church as a primatial cathedral, and this phenomenon can only have been enhanced and extended by the increased importance of the church as a custodian of the shrines of saints, especially following the canonization of Archbishop Becket in 1174.[35]

Certainly by *c.*1200 much of Lanfranc's liturgical directory had become obsolete. Outgrowths of the tenth and eleventh centuries were pruned away in the course of the twelfth;[36] and after the practice of child oblation died out around 1150,[37] the sound of the chant was transformed by the disappearance of unbroken voices doubling at the upper octave. Meanwhile, probably at some time during the twelfth century, there was inaugurated in the Lady Chapel, then situated in the two easternmost bays of the nave north aisle, a daily celebration of Lady Mass (the votive mass of the Virgin Mary). By the end of the thirteenth century it had long been the custom that the celebration of this mass should be attended daily by the precentor and seven monks,[38] and from February 1305 these were augmented by the four clerks of the four principal side-altars in the church.[39] At this period, among the communities of religious at least, devotion to the Virgin Mary seems to have been at a peak; how long so full an attendance was maintained is not known, but certainly the daily celebration of Lady Mass continued down to the Dissolution, and, indeed, beyond.[40]

Archbishop Winchelsey's injunctions to the Priory of 1298 create the impression that if little was wrong with the due and general observance of the content of the Cathedral liturgy, yet there existed among the community a tiresome element blessed with only an imperfect understanding of the spirit of reverence in which it might best be conducted. There was, apparently, no need to re-enact Archbishop Pecham's order of 1282 defining the penalties for unlicensed absenteeism from choir; however, some old problems noted

[33] Add. MS 128/34; the saints especially honoured include Augustine of Canterbury, Audoen, and Dunstan, a constellation that makes a Christ Church provenance highly likely.

[34] An abbreviated inventory survives from 1315, listing (without detail) 15 missals, 1 gradual, 3 breviaries (of Salisbury Use), 4 gospellers, and a lectionary (Legg and Hope, *Inventories*, 75), and 22 further gospellers (ibid. 78–9).

[35] *Constitutions* (cit. in n. 1), 1. The rhymed Offices of St Thomas (Martyrdom and Translation) were written, and pre-existing chants applied to them, not at Christ Church, but by Benedict, abbot of Peterborough: A. Hughes, 'Chants in the Rhymed Office of St Thomas of Canterbury', *Early Music*, 16 (1988), 185–201.

[36] *Constitutions* (cit. in n. 1), pp. xviii, xxiv, xxv.

[37] Knowles, *Monastic Order*, 421–2.

[38] *Registrum Roberti Winchelsey, Cantuariensis Archiepiscopi,*

1293–1313, ed. R. Graham, 2 vols. (CYS, 51–2; 1952–6), ii. 820. These same eight also celebrated a votive mass of St Thomas on Tuesday of their week.

[39] BL Cotton MS Galba E. iv, fos. 72ᵛ, 75. The four clerks were those of the altars of the Blessed Virgin Mary in the nave and in the crypt, of the Martyrdom, and of the shrine of St Thomas—of whom it had previously been ordered that they be sufficiently educated to act as servers to the monks celebrating mass at their respective altars: ibid., fo. 67; see also BL, MS Arundel 68, fo. 56.

[40] By the early 16th cent., the four altar-clerks do appear to have ceased to attend; in a list of the duties which on appointment they swore to observe—of which the only surviving copy dates from 1503—there is no mention of any such obligation to attend Lady Mass: Lit. MS C. 11, fo. 37.

by Lanfranc, of premature departure before the end of service and of hurrying the psalmody, were still in evidence, and may indeed have been in practice ineradicable. Winchelsey sought to insist on enforcement of the rule that all monks, especially the *iuniores* and novices, undertake the immense task of committing to memory the totality of the liturgy; he even named fourteen monks who were to be withdrawn from all other pursuits until they had done so. Only thus could errors and omissions committed by the young and inexperienced in the execution of the liturgy be eradicated, and with them the suppressed but nevertheless unseemly levity which they might provoke. Otherwise, it seems clear that no scandal or debilitating insufficiency about the conduct of the services in the Cathedral church had been brought to the Visitor's notice: by whatever were the standards of the time, the work appears to have been competent.[41]

By the second quarter of the thirteenth century, the standard repertory of ritual plain-song at many of the larger Benedictine churches was coming to be supplemented by occasional items of music set in polyphony, as an alternative manner of rendering music in and about the liturgy. It would be wholly in keeping with its general pre-eminence to conceive of Canterbury Cathedral as having been among the earliest nurseries of poly-phonic composition and performance in England. There do indeed survive in the Cathedral archives several fragmentary manuscripts of medieval polyphony; of none is the exact provenance known, but it seems likely that a reasonable, and probably a large, proportion is of Christ Church origin, having been sung at services there, and possibly even composed by members of the community.

The adoption at service of polyphonic settings of sacred texts, both liturgical and para-liturgical, was undertaken with the same intention as the deployment of the most elaborate of the ornaments, vestments, and ceremony—to help to distinguish feast-days from ferial, and the more important services from the less. At this early period they were written for ensembles of up to four unaccompanied men's voices, one voice per part.[42] A high pro-portion of English polyphonic settings surviving from the thirteenth and fourteenth centuries are of texts from the liturgy of the daily Lady Mass (considered always to be a festal mass, no matter what the rank of day otherwise). Much of the remaining corpus of polyphony consisted of motets—settings, that is, of non-liturgical texts commonly appropriate to a particular saint or feast, and most probably sung in the principal choir to help to distinguish the major Hours or mass on the appropriate feast-day.

Among the fragments of this putatively Canterbury polyphony are two settings (dating from *c*.1250x75) of the solo portions of Alleluias for Lady Mass: these are an almost complete (and readily restorable) Alleluia *V̄ Salve virgo*, and an incomplete Alleluia *V̄ Ave rosa generosa*. Both settings are *à3*, in which two relatively high voices proceed in lively six-eight rhythms over the third voice which sustains, in longer notes, the plainsong proper to the text. The high proportion of full triads in close position lends a sense of sonority to the

[41] *Registrum Epistolarum Fratris Johannis Peckham Archiepiscopi Cantuariensis*, ed. C. T. Martin, 3 vols. (RS, 77; 1882–5), 344, 399; *Reg. Winchelsey*, ed. Graham, i. 91–3; ii. 813–21, 1324.

[42] R. Bowers, 'The Performing Ensemble for English Four-teenth-Century Church Polyphony', in *Studies in the Per-formance of Late Mediaeval Music*, ed. S. Boorman (Cambridge, 1983), 161–92.

jaunty rhythmic style that is not uncommon in English polyphony of this period.[43] A second manuscript fragment, of *c.* 1300 or a little earlier, preserves the greater part of a bitextual motet in a relatively simple style for three voices, which is fortunately almost completely restorable. Its texts, ... [lost] ... / *Virgo que fructifero in ventre* / *Virgo*, reveal it to be in honour of the Virgin Mary.[44]

There are also fragmentary survivals of numerous motets from the early fourteenth century. A third manuscript contains incomplete remains of two motets for four voices. One, *O pater excellentissime* / ... [lost] ... / Tenor / ... [lost] ..., is composed on a particularly large scale. Its text commemorates St Bartholomew, and because of the composer's rigorous exploitation of the *Stimmtausch* principle of voice-exchange and reuse of musical material, it has proved possible to reconstitute the four voices of this piece in almost their entirety. The same source contains a further fragmentary motet on the text *O crux vale, speciale mundi gaudium*, in honour of the Holy Cross: the leaf concerned survives as a flyleaf in a volume that originally belonged to Christ Church, Canterbury, and still bears the arms of the Priory on its opening page.[45]

A fourth manuscript, now very fragmentary, dates from *c.*1310x20 and contains bits of four bitextual motets. Not a great deal can now be determined of their character, but each is likely to have been for four voices. The text of one, *Quid rimari cogitas* / ... [lost] ... / Tenor primus / ... [lost] ..., honours the Virgin Mary. In both its formal structure and its melodic idiom, this motet bears an uncanny resemblance to *O pater excellentissime* discussed above, and is likewise largely restorable. The texts of the other three motets, all very fragmentary, reveal them to be in honour of St Bernard of Clairvaux and the Assumption of the Blessed Virgin; the feast of St Bernard (20 August) falls within the octave of the Assumption (15–23 August).[46] Possibly also of Christ Church provenance are two further fragments. One contains sections of up to five further motets of the early fourteenth century which have been recovered from the binding of a manuscript of the works of St Anselm that is known to have belonged to the Cathedral library in the time of Prior Henry of Eastry (1285–1331). The other, from about the second quarter of the fourteenth century, consists of two fragmentary motets preserved in the binding of a printed volume of the letters of Pope Pius II that belonged in the early sixteenth century to William Gyllyngham, a monk of Christ Church.[47]

Further manuscript music existed at the Priory at around the turn of the fourteenth century; a library inventory made late in the priorate of Henry of Eastry included a copy

[43] Formerly in Add. MS 128/8; N. Sandon, 'Fragments of Medieval Polyphony at Canterbury Cathedral', *Musica Disciplina*, 30 (1976), 37–41, with full transcription (59 bars) of Alleluia *V̄ Salve Virgo*, 48–50.

[44] Add. MS 128/62; no detailed description of this recently discovered item has yet been published.

[45] Bodl., MS New College 57, fo. 1: a copy of Bede's Commentary on the Acts of the Apostles, given to New College by Archbishop Warham. P. Lefferts and M. Bent, 'New Sources of English Thirteenth- and Fourteenth-Century Polyphony', *Early Music History*, 2 (1982), 352–3; P. Lefferts, 'The Motet in England in the Fourteenth Century' (Ph.D. thesis, Columbia University, New York, 1983), 829–43 (with transcriptions of the music); id.,

The Motet in England in the Fourteenth Century (Ann Arbor, Mich., 1986), 286–7.

[46] Add. MS 128/5; polyphonic fragment missing at the time of writing. Sandon, 'Fragments of Medieval Polyphony', 37–41; Lefferts, 'The Motet in England', 529–4 (with transcript of the music); id., *The Motet in England*, 246–8, 286.

[47] Respectively, Bodl., MS Bodley 271 (*s.c.* 1938) and Wisbech (Cambs.), Borough Library, MS C. 3. 8. I am most grateful to Dr Andrew Wathey for drawing my attention to the existence of these two fragments and to their Canterbury associations. For further details, see A. Wathey, *Manuscripts of Polyphonic Music: Supplement 1 to RISM B IV¹⁻², The British Isles, 1100–1400* (Munich, 1993), 66–8, 92–3.

of the Rule of St Benedict given by the monk Thomas of Leicester (d. 1290), which also incorporated a mass of miscellaneous items including a polyphonic setting of a text *Lex sancte trinitatis* and a setting of the text *Samson dux*[48]—of which latter, indeed, a monophonic setting of *c*.1250 does survive elsewhere.[49]

Not every one of these fragmentary musical sources was necessarily originally of Christ Church provenance. Nevertheless, there still seem to be very good grounds for considering that by not later than the third quarter of the thirteenth century a thriving cultivation of polyphonic performance—and, very possibly, of composition also—had begun to arise there. It has been said that at least until the mid-fourteenth century the principal English centres of composition and performance of polyphony appear to have been the greater Benedictine monasteries;[50] and it is entirely credible that Christ Church, Canterbury, was one of the seed-beds of sacred polyphony in England, where performances both of Lady Mass and festal High Mass, and of the Offices, were distinguished by the enhancement of the plainsong rite with performances of polyphonic elaborations such as these, executed by suitably enthused and interested members of the monastic community.

Another appurtenance of worship to make an early appearance at Canterbury Cathedral was the organ. This device was not uncommon by the late twelfth century in the greater Benedictine houses. At this period, it was apparently a machine of no great size, being a single-manual positive operated by one person and simultaneously blown by another. It seems likely that it was not yet considered to be an instrument of music, but rather a producer of cheerful though fairly random noise, a machine to help generate an atmosphere of celebration on feast-days in the same manner and spirit as peals and clashes of bells. In his description of the transepts and nave of Lanfranc's Cathedral at the time of the fire in 1174, the monk Gervase recorded that the southernmost bay of the south[-west] transept contained a tribune vault or gallery, whose upper level (at a height of some 28 feet above floor level) was the normal location of the Cathedral's organ.[51] An elevated position in fairly close proximity (but not immediately adjacent) to the ritual choir appears to have been the normal site of the church organ at this period; since this part of the building was undamaged by the fire, and indeed apparently remained unaltered until it was almost completely rebuilt in the fifteenth century, it is likely that this machine and its successors remained in this position for some considerable time after 1174, though no mention of them in thirteenth-century records has yet been found.

During 1332–3 whatever instrument was then in use was substantially refurbished and apparently sited in a new, if still elevated, location; the cost of this operation was unusually fully recorded. The total apparent cost was £17 8*s*. 11*d*., and the organ-builder was one Janyn, a name as likely to be Netherlandish as English in origin. The builder's fees

[48] BL, Cotton MS Galba E. iv, fo. 136. See A. Wathey, 'Lost Books of Polyphony in England: A List to 1500', *Royal Musical Assn. Research Chron.*, 21 (1988), 4; James, *ALCD*, 536.

[49] BL, Harl. MS 978, fos. 2–4.

[50] F. Ll. Harrison, *Music in Medieval Britain* (2nd edn.; London 1963), 113.

[51] Gervase, *Historical Works*, i. 10; F. Woodman, *The Architectural History of Canterbury Cathedral* (London, 1981), 29, 31, 33–4, 170. The clumsy and inaccurate translation of Gervase printed by J. Dart, *The History and Antiquities of the Cathedral Church of Canterbury* (London, 1726), 7, has sometimes given rise to the erroneous belief that there was a second organ in the corresponding location in the north transept; see, e.g., S. W. Harvey, 'The Organs of Canterbury Cathedral', *The Organ*, 3 (1923), 2.

amounted only to a fairly modest 18s. and the relatively small sum of 40s. 9d. expended on materials indicates considerable reuse of existing materials, including the pipe-work. The greatest part of the expense was upon timber and carpenters' wages about 'the auxiliary carpentry of the organ'. Clearly this extensive work was not upon the instrument itself, but appears to refer to the construction of an elevated gallery on which it might stand, possibly at a location closer to the choir than its former site in the south-west transept.[52] The actual function of the organ at this period is obscure; it may be that it had barely graduated from its role as a mere purveyor of joyful but random noise. Certainly its predecessor in 1322 had been sounded on feasts of St Dunstan, and to such good effect that apparently four men had been required to blow it—most probably in shifts.[53]

THE CULTIVATION OF AUXILIARY REPERTORIES, c.1350–1540

The Music of the Monastic Choir, c.1350–1438

In the principal choir of the Cathedral church, the monks' unceasing ritual of daily High Mass and the Office continued to be observed in the Latin plainsong liturgy of the Benedictine Use until the end of the Priory in 1540. Meanwhile, there continued to evolve, both in the choir and, presently, elsewhere within the church and precinct, patterns of worship parallel and complementary to the liturgy of the monastic choir. Hereby, the scope of the music cultivated within the Priory was broadened and enriched by the adoption and deployment of innovations from the forefront of contemporary musical enterprise.

While in general the monasteries were, from the second half of the fourteenth century, losing to secular churches their former leading role in the composition and performance of polyphony,[54] skill in music and singing remained highly valued at Canterbury. A motet text compiled apparently in about 1370x3 includes, among the names of fourteen notable contemporary English singers, that of John Exeter, 'by whose art Canterbury has shone for many years'; this may well refer to a Christ Church monk of that name who appears from the 1350s to the 1370s.[55] John Borne, precentor, who died in 1420, was remembered for the excellence of his voice, even though he had not been a singer of polyphony. John Stanys, who briefly succeeded him as precentor before his own death in 1421, was likewise commended as an outstanding singer who had directed all the renderings of polyphony

---

[52] DE 3, fos. 17–19 (pencil foliation) *passim*; printed with numerous significant but unacknowledged omissions (and one intrusion) by W. P. Blore, 'A Fourteenth-Century Account for Cathedral Organs' (with D. Gardiner and J. H. Harvey, 'A Note on Personalities'), *Laudate*, 24 (1946), 38–41. See also [R. C. Hussey], *Extracts from Ancient Documents Relating to the Cathedral and Precinct of Canterbury* (London, 1881), 11; not all the documents quoted by Hussey, for which he gives no references, have been traced.

[53] BL, Cotton MS Galba E. iv, fo. 99: a complete day's rations

to each of four *servientes trahentes organa*—the draught concerned being, of course, of air, not of traction.

[54] Harrison, *Music in Medieval Britain* (cit. in n. 50), 113, 156–7.

[55] Reg. G, fos. 60ᵛ, 76, 173ᵛ; R. Bowers, 'Fixed Points in the Chronology of English Fourteenth-Century Polyphony', *Music & Letters*, 71 (1990), 326, 328–9. This identification is not totally certain; two other musicians of this name are known from this period, though neither is known to have had Canterbury connections.

in choir in his time, with colleagues such as John Moundfield, John Cranbroke, and William Bonyngton.[56]

Canterbury's reputation for music stood sufficiently high at this time to tempt gifted but artistically frustrated monks of other monasteries to abjure their existing oaths and migrate. John Stanys had moved from Bermondsey Priory in 1399, and in 1408 Geoffrey Bond joined Christ Church, Canterbury, from St Albans, likewise rising eventually to the office of precentor. He in turn, in 1421, lured a second St Albans monk, William Pounsy, to join him.[57] Something of the character of the repertory of these singers may be judged from the fortunate survival in the Cathedral library of a leaf from a choirbook of *c*.1415x30 containing parts of two elaborate and demanding motets: an anonymous *Ave miles triumphalis* / . . . [lost] . . . / *Christi morte nato mundo*, and John Dunstable's *Preco preheminencie* / *Precursor premittitur* / Contratenor / *Inter natos muliere*, possibly composed in 1416.[58] Further slivers and scraps of manuscripts of polyphony in the library, datable to the second and third quarters of the fifteenth century, reveal, through the use of red ink for certain passages of the verbal text, that the enthusiasts among the monks undertaking responsibility for the performance of polyphony were able to contrast passages for solo ensemble with passages for a small chorus, and therefore must have been six to eight in number.[59] Meanwhile, William Bonyngton (monk 1381–1412) was remembered both as a player of polyphonic music and as a singer; this can refer only to playing the organ, by this time evidently recognized as a musical instrument. Indeed, from at least 1361 an annual fee of 10*s*. was paid to the Priory servants detailed to blow the organ, later transformed into a fee for the monk who played it; in 1450 this was John Pirie. By 1384 the instrument was of a size sufficient to earn it the title 'the great organ'; apparently, however, it still stood on the timber gallery built in 1332–3.[60]

The Lady Chapel Choir and the lay Cantors, 1438–1540

Of the various chantry and votive masses celebrated out of choir, the most important was the Lady Mass, observed daily in the Lady Chapel by a team consisting (historically) of eight of the monks. As the fourteenth and fifteenth centuries progressed, the deepening devotion to the Virgin Mary that so characterized late medieval Christian worship prompted the enhancement of the Lady Mass in a number of ways, including its performance with special and distinctive music. One common resort at monastic churches was the creation of a Lady Chapel choir formed to attend and sing at the mass, consisting principally

[56] Lit. MS D. 12, fos. 19, 19ᵛ, 21ᵛ; Cambridge, Corpus Christi College, MS 417, fos. 11ᵛ, 12; Searle, *Chronicle and Lists*, 11, 12, 183, 185. It may be noted that throughout this latter source, the term 'organista' means not 'organist' but 'singer of polyphonic music'.

[57] Lit. MS D. 12, fos. 5ᵛ, 25; Cambridge, Corpus Christi College, MS 417, fos. 6, 12; Searle, *Chronicle and Lists*, 12, 40, 185, 186–7; *Gesta Abbatum Monasterii Sancti Albani*, ed. H. T. Riley, 3 vols. (RS, 28; 1867–9), iii. 480, 486; *Annales Monasterii Sancti Albani a Johanne Amundesham, Monacho*, ed. H. T. Riley, 2 vols. (RS, 28; 1870–1), i. 89–91.

[58] Add. MS 128/6, recovered from the binding of Lit. MS C.

11; Sandon, 'Fragments of Medieval Polyphony' (cit. in n. 43), 41–4; *John Dunstable: Complete Works*, ed. M. Bukofzer, 2nd edn., rev. I. Bent, M. Bent, and B. Trowell, *Musica Britannica*, 8 (1970), 78; M. Bent, *Dunstaple* (Oxford, 1981), 8 and n. 17.

[59] Add. MS 128/66; for red text, see R. Bowers and A. Wathey, 'New Sources of English Fourteenth- and Fifteenth-Century Polyphony', *Early Music History*, 3 (1983), 165–8 and n. 47.

[60] Lit. MS D. 12, fo. 19ᵛ; Searle, *Chronicle and Lists*, 183; Treasurers' Accts. 26, fo. 8. Payments 'pro organis trahendis': Sacrist's Accts. 1–75; Misc. Accts. 7, 9, 10, 11, 14, 15, 16, 30; Scrapbook C, no. 22; LPL, Estate Documents, Rolls 75–9. Pirie: Sacrist's Accts. 37.

of a group of boys drawn from the almonry school and trained by a special master; he was always a secular recruited from outside the community, and was commonly given the title of cantor. Some half-dozen such choirs are known to have been created between 1384 and 1420, and the establishment of others continued to the very eve of the Dissolutions.[61]

Christ Church, Canterbury, had maintained an almonry grammar-school since at least the late thirteenth century, and it appears that at some point in 1438 Prior John Salisbury and the convent decreed that eight of the boys should form a choir for the Lady Chapel, and appointed as their master one of the most eminent and prolific composers of the period, Lionel Power.[62] For Power, by now about 60 years old, this was probably an appointment for semi-retirement, and after only a short tenure he died and was buried in the precinct on 6 June 1445.[63] After a brief interval, however, the recently elected Prior John Elham secured the appointment of a new cantor, Thomas Ware, at Michaelmas 1446, and Elham soon initiated the building of a new Lady Chapel by the Martyrdom for the choir to sing in. It was ready for use by December 1455; it was set out appropriately as a miniature sanctuary and choir, with stalls for the singers and a small organ installed in 1456.[64]

The duties of this choir were not strenuous; its regular functions probably did not extend beyond attending daily at Lady Mass and singing its plainsong, and performing each evening a plainsong Marian votive antiphon. Doubtless the boys undertook the singing of improvised descant to the plainsong; a copy of Lionel Power's vernacular manual explaining how the necessary training was undertaken is still extant.[65] However, the nature of the surviving evidence is such that it is the choir's non-routine undertakings that are best recorded. For instance, in 1446, and again in 1454, Queen Margaret visited the Cathedral as a pilgrim, and attended (Lady) Mass in the crypt, sung by the boys; in 1449 the boys sang mass at the time of the death of their benefactor, Prior Elham, for whom they had sung on numerous occasions before—sometimes, perhaps, in his personal chapel, where he had an organ installed 1447.[66]

Thanks to the availability from 1438 of the expertise of the lay cantor, it is likely that the performance of polyphony in the monastic choir by enthusiasts among the monks could now be accorded a yet higher profile. Performances took place, for instance, at the formal reception of distinguished guests to the Cathedral church, such as a visit by Queen Margaret in 1447. Polyphony was also used to mark the first High Mass which Thomas Goldstone I celebrated as prior, in 1449, and to distinguish the High Mass performed in 1470 on the occasion of the 250th anniversary of the translation of St Thomas.[67] Probably dating roughly from the period 1460–70 are some settings for four men's voices, surviving in fragmentary form in the Cathedral library, of the antiphons sung at the beginning of

[61] R. Bowers, 'Choral Institutions within the English Church: their Constitutions and Development, 1340–1500' (Ph.D. thesis, Univ. of East Anglia, 1975), 4068–100, 5032–45.

[62] R. Bowers, 'Some Observations upon the Life and Career of Lionel Power', *Proc. Royal Musical Assn.*, 102 (1975–6), 111–22.

[63] Bodl., MS Tanner 165, fos. 156–163ᵛ, *passim*; Searle, *Chronicle and Lists*, 37; BL, Cotton MS Tiberius B. iii, fo. 4ᵛ; BL, MS Arundel 68, fo. 29ᵛ; LPL, MS 20, fo. 192.

[64] Legg and Hope, *Inventories*, 147, 160–7; Prior's Accts. 15,

'Expense forinsece'.

[65] BL, MS Lansdowne 763, fos. 104ᵛ–112; S. B. Meech, 'Three Musical Treatises in English in a Fifteenth-Century Manuscript', *Speculum*, 10 (1935), 242–58.

[66] Searle, *Chronicle and Lists*, 39, 61; Misc. Accts. 4, fos. 41ᵛ, 95, 142, 144ᵛ, 145, 187ᵛ, 226ᵛ.

[67] Oxford, Corpus Christi College, MS 256, fo. 63ᵛ; Searle, *Chronicle and Lists*, 42, 46, 112.

the procession preceding High Mass on Sundays. The manuscript is in the form of a parchment roll, one of a set of four; it includes four settings of *Asperges me, domine* and one of the corresponding antiphon for the Easter season, *Vidi aquam egredientem*. Although only the tenor voice is preserved here, two of the remaining voices of one setting survive elsewhere, and create an evocative impression of the sonorous and quite extended polyphony with which the principal Sunday celebration in the monks' choir could be distinguished.[68]

Meanwhile, the ablest of the monks might well, on occasions, be entabled to attend the evening votive antiphon. Lionel Power's last compositions were all Marian antiphons for three men's voices, including his settings of *Mater ora filium*, *Ibo michi ad montem*, and *Quam pulcra es*, and very possibly these were written for the polyphonists among the monks to sing at this devotion.[69] During the 1450s and 1460s, moreover, composers first began to write formal polyphony that involved the voices of boys as well as of men, and at Canterbury by 1469 the boys, their master, and three of the monks could be thought of as a group which could perform and be called 'the singers of this church'.[70] The routine occasions on which such a group could be convened were the services in the Lady Chapel, suggesting that on days on which composed polyphony was appropriate, the choir was by now in a position to tackle even the larger compositions of the period in the five-part scoring that was becoming standard, deploying boy trebles and four adult voices (ATTB) singing one to a part.

Thomas Ware was succeeded as Master of the Lady Chapel choir in 1470 or 1471 by William Corbrand. He was followed during 1473–4 by John Nesbett, who occupied the office until 1487–8 and was then succeeded by Nicholas Bremmer. In about 1530 Bremmer gave way to Thomas Wood, who survived the Dissolution in 1540 to become one of the first lay clerks of the choir of the New Foundation Cathedral.[71] Two settings have survived of the incipit and verse of the responsory *In manus tuas* for Compline during Lent, composed by Corbrand for two equal men's voices; probably these slight but felicitous pieces give little idea of Corbrand's true capacities, since over 100 years later he was cited by Thomas Morley as one of the illustrious composers whose works he had consulted during the preparation of his *A Plaine and Easie Introduction to Practicall Musick* of 1597. John Nesbett's skilful three-voice Eastertide dismissal versicle *Benedicamus domino; Alleluia* (Pl. 85) survives in the same manuscript as the two works by Corbrand, which is likely to have originated at the Cathedral Priory.[72]

Representative, probably, of a more monumental repertory within the Cathedral's polyphony of this period is Nesbett's setting for full five-voice choir (TrATTB) of the Magnificat, surviving now only in two sources elsewhere. Perhaps this was sung as the

[68] Add. MS 128/65; Sandon, 'Fragments of Medieval Polyphony' (cit. in n. 43), 44–8.

[69] *Lionel Power: Complete Works*, ed. C. Hamm, 2 vols. (Corpus Mensurabilis Musicae, 50; Rome, 1969), i. pp. xi–xiii, xvii–xix, nos. 23–6.

[70] Searle, *Chronicle and Lists*, 109–10.

[71] Sacrist's Accts. 51–75 and LPL, Estate Documents, Rolls 78–9. Prior's Accts. 12, 14; Misc. Accts. 7, 9, 16, 36, 59; Scrapbook B, no. 49; Lit. MS C. 11, fos. 37ᵛ, 47–52 *passim*, 111–139 *passim*; DE 31, fo. 2ᵛ; Inventory 29; DE 164. For the will of Nicholas Bremmer, see Maidstone, Kent Archives Office, PRC 32/15, fo. 18.

[72] *The Music of the Pepys Manuscript 1236*, ed. S. R. Charles (Corpus Mensurabilis Musicae, 40; Rome, 1967), nos. 5, 106, 109. T. Morley, *A Plaine and Easie Introduction to Practicall Musicke*, ed. R. A. Harman (2nd edn.; London, 1962), 321.

evening votive antiphon in the Lady Chapel, where boys and monks could sing together, since a further setting of the Magnificat from this period is known from a fragmentary choirbook leaf originally found in the Cathedral library, and similarly scored apparently for full five-voice choir. Its use of red ink for sections of verbal text confirms that the choir possessed the resources necessary to differentiate between full chorus and solo ensembles; very considerately, the treble and alto parts are both written at the bottom of the page, where most readily visible to the boys, so perhaps a distribution of four boys to each of the upper parts and two men on each of the remaining (TTB) voices would constitute a plausible vocal scoring for this piece. Both settings are large-scale and call for singing of considerable virtuosity; Nesbett's consists of seven or eight minutes of bravura counter-point, including solo duets and trios involving all the parts.[73] Also, a setting for four men's voices of the Marian antiphon text *Gaude virgo salutata*, attributed to one Holyngborne, may very well have been the work of a Canterbury monk of this period, Robert Holyng-borne (d. 1508).[74]

The manner in which the Lady Chapel choir of eight boys, their master, and some suitably skilled monks was equal in the late fifteenth century to the task of singing any of the elaborate mainstream polyphony of the period is equally evident in the contents of an inventory of the choir's repertory made some fifty years later, at some point in the 1530s. The core of the repertory was evidently music in four and five parts, to which it was not impractical to add some compositions in up to six parts. The books of polyphony included quires containing settings of the sequences for Lady Mass, as well as a choirbook containing a 'Mass of two tenors' as its distinguishing feature. There were three further choirbooks, one of which contained music in four parts, supplemented by loose quires containing the mean and bass parts of six-part music; an additional set of quires contained three-part music, and there was a further set of five part-books supplemented by a *sextus* book.[75] The inventory does not mention the Lady Chapel organ; one was repaired in 1520–1, and two instruments were listed in the Dissolution inventory of 1540, available, when appropriate, to alternate with the singers.[76] The lack of detailed description in the inventory is unfor-tunate, but certainly does not compromise the evident indications that right up to the Dissolution, the Lady Chapel choir, despite the smallness of its resources, was thriving under its appointed master, and was maintaining a vigorous and challenging repertory in up to six parts, extending probably to the ordinary and some propers of Lady Mass, Magnificats, and votive antiphons.

In the monks' choir, meanwhile, the singing of plainsong was not neglected. The generosity of Thomas Goldstone II (prior 1495–1517) in providing books for use in the choir service was particularly remarked in his obituary notice, and in *c.*1505 the monk John Crosse, writing to a lay associate whose son apparently was being prepared to join the Priory as a novice, reckoned it advisable that as a preliminary training, the boy first be 'put to hys playnesong' until 'he ys sure thereoff'. In 1508 several of the books of chant

[73] *The Eton Choirbook*, ed. F. Ll. Harrison, 2nd edn., 3 vols. (Musica Britannica, 10–12; 1967–73), iii. 63. Formerly Add. MS 128, no. 46(e), at time of writing stolen from the Cathedral, though a photocopy remains (Add. MS 128/7); Sandon, 'Frag-ments of Medieval Polyphony' (cit. in n. 43), 48, 51–3.

[74] *Eton Choirbook*, ed. Harrison, iii. 154–60; see below, p. 425.
[75] Legg and Hope, *Inventories*, 164, though this transcription is not wholly accurate.
[76] Ibid. 165; Misc. Accts. 14, fo. 137ᵛ.

from the monks' choir were sent off for rebinding, with one volume that was certainly of polyphony and three others which may have been.[77]

The monastery's own record of the shortcomings revealed to Archbishop Warham's visitation of 1511 discloses the persistence of that apparently ineradicable stratum among the monastic community whose minds and hearts were less than totally committed to the execution of the liturgy: there was some absenteeism, particularly among the higher administrative officers, and silence was not well kept during service. For lack of an instructor in Latin grammar, there were even some monks who were unable to execute the texts of their parts in the liturgy without error.[78] This latter omission could, of course, readily be corrected, but the former was as much a matter of the monastery's capacity to apply an admissions policy that excluded the unsuitable as of a disciplinary exercise upon those professed.

Meanwhile, in some fashion still largely obscure, the organ in choir remained in full use. Two of the monks by whom it was played are known by name: Thomas Chart, recorded 1486–93 and lamented at his death as 'very learned in music and upon the organ, and most devout', and John Wodnesbergh, recorded 1516–33.[79] By 1508 the principal organ is found to have been installed in the location commonest for this period, in the loft over the choir screen; by 1540 the choir contained both this instrument and a second organ, probably a smaller instrument standing on the choir floor.[80]

The Liturgy and Music of the Chapel of the Almonry

The prior had his own chapel, and there was a large chapel in the infirmary; but the almonry chapel was distinguished by its own musical foundation. From at least the 1290s a small residential grammar school maintained for boys nominated by individual monks had been conducted there, taught by a professional schoolmaster. One primary purpose of this school was the provision of boys sufficiently well educated to serve the daily masses that were celebrated privately at the side-altars in the Cathedral church by each monk in priest's orders. In 1319–20 a small college of six secular chantry priests was established in the newly enlarged chapel of the almonry. These priests were committed to the daily observance of masses and of the complete liturgical cycle of Canonical Hours, all according to the secular Use of Salisbury. The regulations of the school were thereupon modified to ensure the attendance of the boys at services on Saturdays, Sundays, and holy days. From 1398, the almonry's resident population was increased by the admission of two older scholars, youths up to the age of 24, nominated by the chaplain and clerks of the small collegiate chantry of Bredgar.[81] From 1398 until the Dissolution therefore, services in the almonry chapel were attended at weekends and on holy days by groups of priests, clerks, and boys who were able between them to fulfil the liturgical roles assigned to clerks of all

[77] BL, MS Arundel 68, fo. 65ᵛ; Christ Church Letters, iii, no. 18; Lit. MS C. 11, fo. 102ᵛ.

[78] *Kentish Visitations of Archbishop Warham and His Deputies, 1511–1512*, ed. K. L. Wood-Legh (Kent Archaeol. Soc., Kent Records, 24; 1984), 294–7.

[79] Sacrist's Accts. 58 with 68, 70, 75; Misc. Accts. 7, 9, 14, 15,

16, 30; Searle, *Chronicle and Lists*, 189, 192.

[80] Lit. MS C. 11, fo. 103; Legg and Hope, *Inventories*, 192.

[81] Almoner's Accts. 10ff.; Reg. A, fos. 316ᵛ–319, and BL, Cotton MS Galba E. iv, fos. 87–90; Ch. Ant. B. 384 (see *Lit. Cant.* iii, 68–70).

three forms, and thus to give a full rendering of the plainsong and liturgy of the designated Salisbury Use.

From 1438, moreover, following the appointment of a professional lay cantor in the Priory and the progressive addition of the skills of singing-boys to the accomplishments of eight of the almonry scholars, it must have become possible to envisage the cultivation of music that was more elaborate and adventurous than simple plainsong. Indeed, it appears probable that one of the very few surviving English manuscripts of fifteenth-century polyphony originated within the orbit of the Cathedral almonry and its chapel personnel. The manuscript—Pepys 1236 at Magdalene College, Cambridge—was compiled over some years around 1465–75 and contains 122 compositions, mostly fairly brief and all for the secular Salisbury Use. Certain of its non-musical contents associate it with the county of Kent, and with the exercise of responsibility for the upbringing of boys; of the eight composers named, two—William Corbrand and John Nesbett—were masters of the Lady Chapel choir at Canterbury, while most of the others enjoyed known associations with the Cathedral. These facts create a set of criteria for establishing the provenance of the manuscript which only the almonry chapel of Canterbury Cathedral appears to satisfy. Its very small page-size and the absence of signs of use suggest, however, that it was not a working manuscript actually used in the chapel, but a private anthology kept by one of the almonry priests, into which he copied music principally for his own interest and reference, although no doubt collected with an eye to possible selection for recopying for chapel use.

The manuscript contains examples of virtually every type of item from the Office and from the propers of High Mass and Lady Mass that composers set in polyphony at this time. Represented most fully are the Alleluias for High Mass and Lady Mass, hymns for the Office and festal processions, Office responsories and their verses, and dismissal versicles. Most of the music is in three parts, with further pieces in two and four parts, as well as a few items in measured monophony. Particularly suitable for use in the context of the almonry community were the numerous settings of texts associated with St Nicholas, the patron saint of schoolboys, and with the annual boy-bishop ceremonies. The anonymous four-voice setting of the refrain of the processional hymn *Salve festa dies . . . qua caro* employs an overall compass reaching almost three octaves, demonstrating—like John Nesbett's Magnificat—early exploitation of the resources of boys' voices in polyphonic composition and performance.[82] It is indeed disappointing that nothing further can be learnt of the cultivation of music in the almonry chapel between this date and the Dissolution in 1540.

The Observance of the Liturgy at Canterbury College, Oxford

The monastic cell maintained by the Priory in Oxford from the third quarter of the fourteenth century was occupied principally by between four and seven professed monks

[82] *Music of the Manuscript Pepys 1236* (cit. in n. 76); S. R. Charles, 'The Provenance and Date of the Pepys MS 1236', *Musica Disciplina*, 16 (1962), 57–71; F. Ll. Harrison, 'Music for the Sarum Rite', *Annales Musicologiques*, 6 (1958–63), 99–144; R. Bowers, 'Magdalene College: MS Pepys 1236', in *Cambridge Music Manuscripts, 900–1600*, ed. I. A. Fenlon (Cambridge, 1982), 111–14.

sent there to study in the schools of the university and to proceed to degrees. Also to be maintained out of the revenues of the college were five 'poor scholars'—boys and youths engaged to combine the function of servants with education as schoolboys.[83] The college was equipped with a chapel, where the monks discharged their commitment to observe the *Opus Dei* just as if they were still in Canterbury. Although the constraints of study restricted this to certain principal observances, attendance at these was obligatory upon all the monks and boys. These occasions extended to Vespers and High Mass on every principal and greater feast, and also to Matins on the nine greatest days, all to be observed with the plainsong chant. In addition, Lady Mass and the Marian votive antiphon were observed weekly on Saturdays. The only daily observance was a votive mass, merely spoken.[84]

Surviving inventories reveal the chapel to have been adequately stocked with service-books of the plainsong liturgy, especially antiphoners and graduals; and by 1443 a small organ had been installed.[85] After a period of some contraction around the middle and third quarter of the fifteenth century, the fortunes of the college were revived from about 1475: full numbers of monks and boys were presently restored, most particularly during the wardenship of Robert Holyngborne, who was sent to Oxford in 1492 and succeeded as warden in 1501. The books that he owned show him to have been a man of broad interests and of considerable learning, and indicate that liturgical observance held a high place in his priorities and concerns. In particular, his listing of the chapel service-books on his inauguration inventory was deft and highly professional, and he apparently replaced the existing organ, which he condemned as 'utterly feeble' ('valde debilis'). Also in his time, the performance of polyphony was introduced in the chapel. By 1510 (and until 1524) there appears on the inventories a 'book of pricksong', which probably was to serve at the weekly Marian votive antiphon.[86]

However, this community of monk-scholars and boys was in no sense a professional choir, and it appears that whatever was being achieved at Canterbury College must simply have been the product of amateur zeal generated by the energies of one committed enthusiast. The volume of polyphony was neither supplemented nor replaced as time progressed, and after 1524 ceased to appear on the inventories at all. Apparently, the college's short-lived excursion into an adventurous musical repertory did not long survive Holyngborne's untimely death in 1508.

Throughout the lifetime of the Cathedral Priory, the maintenance of the unceasing observance of the liturgy was the fundamental reason for its very existence, to which all other functions were merely ancillary, subordinate, and subservient. The nature of the surviving documentary sources is such that no more than a sporadic and fitful picture of the nature of its content and the manner and quality of its conduct has yet emerged. Nevertheless, the impression that does arise is one that is not at all unattractive. Indeed, it should be noted that virtually all of the intermittent perceptions of liturgical observance which can

[83] Pantin, *Cant. Coll.* iii. 179–82; iv. 55–7, 86, 141, 225.

[84] Ibid. ii. 222; iii. 179–82.

[85] Ibid. i. 4, 12, 30, 36, 52–3, 58, 67–8, 73–4.

[86] Ibid. i. 36, 52, 58, 85–7, 107–9, 53, 58, 67. Emden, *BRUO*, ii. 955.

be gained originated not as consequences of sloth, inactivity, indifference, or decadence on the part of the community, but as the results of enterprise, vision, vigour, and initiative—and all this no less in the second quarter of the sixteenth century than in the last quarter of the eleventh or the thirteenth.

Nevertheless, the picture is not consistent: a certain dichotomy is apparent. Of the degree of fervour and commitment for the observance of the plainsong liturgy evinced by the common body of monks, very little is so far known; and since that little arises almost exclusively from records of visitation, it is in the nature of the record that the impression given tends to a mild negativity. Shortcomings, inattentiveness, and perhaps also incompetence, there may indeed have been. However, it seems clear that at least at most times between *c.*1270 and 1540—and very possibly continuously—there existed among the body of monks a more than adequate number of musically able, trained, and literate enthusiasts by whom the practice (and possibly also the composition) of polyphonic music, of the most advanced character, was accorded a regular role in the conduct of worship. Furthermore, it is likely that the actual number of surviving, if fragmentary, manuscripts of pre-1540 polyphony that can putatively be given a Christ Church, Canterbury, provenance is greater than that for any other single institution in England, monastic or secular. By the participation in services of monks such as those responsible for the accumulation of this collection, it would seem that a sense of competence and commitment could hardly fail to be infused into all the aspects and occasions of liturgical observance to which they contributed. Meanwhile, throughout the last hundred years of the Priory, the availability of the expertise of the appointed master of the Lady Chapel choir seems to have ensured that that small-scale choir in its diminutive chapel possessed the skill and expertise to tackle music in the most demanding and virtuosic idioms of its day. In respect of its observance of the liturgy and its plainsong, therefore, it would be churlish to fail to acknowledge that as the primatial cathedral church of medieval England, Christ Church, Canterbury, may well have fallen only little short in its fulfilment of the high expectations that could with justice be imposed upon it; and in the cultivation and deployment of polyphonic music by its professionals and enthusiasts, in choir and Lady Chapel alike, it may well have done enough to earn itself an honourable repute in a very competitive field.

THE REFORMATION AND THE VERNACULAR LITURGY, 1540–1597

The Choir of the New Foundation Cathedral

The intention of the government of King Henry VIII at the Dissolution of the monasteries was that the successor capitular bodies of the New Foundation cathedrals should embody as much continuity as possible with the former monastic personnel. Not only was a place in the new establishment to be offered to every monk who desired and was best qualified to occupy it; express order was also made that the services of such lay singing-men and boys as each monastery had formerly maintained should also be retained for the successor choir.[87]

As befitted the cathedral church of the primate, the newly founded choir at Canterbury was provided with an ample personnel, equal in number to any in the country. The Use of Salisbury, the standard secular liturgy of lowland England, now replaced the Benedictine Use, and for its execution three distinct ranks of clergy were required. As the clerks of the top form (with such of the dean and canons as were resident) there were to be twelve minor canons, all in priest's orders. With them were associated a gospeller (deacon) and epistoler (subdeacon), to read, respectively, the Gospel and Epistle at High Mass each day. All fourteen inaugural appointments were of former monks; probably only a certain proportion was able to sing in the polyphonic chorus, but their eventual successors would be skilled singers. To be the clerks of the second form, twelve lay clerks were provided; these were all professional singers, and the first appointments included Thomas Wood, last Master of the Lady Chapel choir, Thomas Tallis the composer, and Thomas Bull, from the choir of Magdalen College, Oxford. Also to be a clerk of the second form was the Master of the Choristers and Organist, and provision was made for ten choristers to be the clerks of the third form. Of the antecedents of the first Master of the Choristers, William Selby, nothing is known; in all probability, the inaugural corps of choristers was composed principally of the former Lady Chapel singing-boys.[88]

The liturgy to be observed by this choir extended to the daily High Mass and the full cycle of the eight Hours of the Office, amplified by a complex web of minor observances such as the Hours of the Virgin. Lady Mass and the votive antiphon continued to be celebrated daily in the Lady Chapel. To qualify for his receipt of quotidians, each canon residentiary was required to make in church little more than token attendance, at one service—Matins, High Mass, or Vespers—per day; the main burden of executing the services fell on the choir. The consuetudinary of Salisbury Use, as amplified by the long-established practices of the old secular churches, was designed to ensure a largely full attendance of all classes of singers at the principal services of Prime, High Mass, and Vespers, and of the adults at Matins. At the remaining services, a reduced attendance was contemplated, probably organized (if organized at all) on a rota system. In addition, authorized leave was presently defined as sixty days in each year.[89] For those former monks who had now become minor canons, the liturgical life of the Cathedral simply carried on much as before the Dissolution. However, the (putative) conversion of the Lady Chapel singing-boys into the chorister-boys of a secular choir involved a total transformation of their role, and a major amplification of their work as both singers and officiants in the ceremonial. The Master of the Choristers and his ten charges now constituted a song school, separate from the grammar (King's) school. The song school's premises are known

[87] PRO, E 36/116, pp. 19–20, 86–7; calendared in *LP, Henry VIII*, xiv, pt. 1, no. 1189, at p. 530.

[88] BL, Cotton MS Tiberius E. iv, fo. 359; H. Cole, *King Henry VIII's Scheme of Bishopricks* (London, 1838), 1–3, 48–9. Draft statutes of 1544: stat. [1], Cambridge, Corpus Christi College, MS 120, p. 16; PRO E 315/245, fos. 78–9; DE 164, fo. 1; Misc. Accts. 40, fo. 1ᵛ. C. E. Woodruff, 'Canterbury Cathedral: A

Contemporary List of the Members of King Henry VIII's New Foundation', *Cant. Cath. Chron.*, 37 (1941), 9.

[89] Stat. [15]: Cambridge, Corpus Christi College, MS 120, p. 25; *Visitation Articles and Injunctions of the Period of the Reformation*, ed. W. H. Frere and W. M. Kennedy, 3 vols. (Alcuin Club Collections, 14–16; 1910), ii. 142.

by the early seventeenth century to have abutted on the residence of the seventh prebend on the site of the former monastic dormitory.[90] The boys themselves resided in the precinct with their Master and his wife. Accommodation for the minor canons and unmarried lay clerks was fashioned out of former monastic buildings now redundant, and a common hall was established and staffed for the provision of meals.[91] Salaries were appointed for the several ranks of singers: £10 a year for the Master of the Choristers and each minor canon, gospeller, and epistoler, £8 for each lay clerk, and £3 16s. 8d. for each chorister.[92]

For the conduct of the services, the interim Guardians of 1540–1 were instructed to acquire the appropriate service-books of Salisbury Use,[93] and from the former monastery the new secular choir inherited two organs in the choir—presumably the great organ on the screen and a smaller instrument on the choir floor—and in the Lady Chapel a further two organs.[94] The principal and most urgent requirement, however, must have been a ready-made repertory of polyphonic music for full chorus of boys and men, setting texts (such as the ordinary of High Mass, and the hymns and responsories of the festal office) which the former Lady Chapel choir had never been called upon to tackle. Details of provision made in 1543 at the neighbouring cathedral of Rochester disclose that there, on all days other than the plainest feria, its choir (barely half the size of that of Canterbury) sang polyphony for the evening votive antiphon and on most days at Lady Mass also, the latter being amplified with subordinate organ polyphony. Only on the principal, major double and Marian feasts was Lady Mass merely said, doubtless because on such days an elaborate polyphonic setting was used for High Mass at the high altar. The organ contributed polyphony to Matins, High Mass, and Vespers on all feasts of nine lessons and above.[95] At Canterbury, the manner of the deployment of full choral polyphony, and of the organ, would doubtless have been of similar character, but of far wider scope and greater intensity, commensurate with its greater resources. In departments in which the repertory inherited from the Lady Chapel choir was deficient, the Canterbury musicians of 1540 clearly needed to acquire a ready-made repertory of standard five-part polyphony for rapid learning and deployment at service.

It seems possible that a surviving collection of four part-books, from a set consisting originally of five, was compiled in 1540 for use at Canterbury for this very purpose. This 'Henrician' set of part-books, now preserved at Peterhouse, Cambridge, contains a huge collection of seventy-one items, all but a very few composed on the grandest scale. There are nineteen masses, seven Magnificats, forty-three votive antiphons, and two ritual items by some thirty composers, among whom Fayrfax, Ludford, Aston, and Taverner are the most copiously represented. There are good grounds for believing that the repertory which they contain is actually that of the choir of Magdalen College, Oxford, but copied

[90] Stat. [20]: Cambridge, Corpus Christi College, MS 120, p. 33. *The Use of Sarum*, ed. W. H. Frere (2 vols.; Cambridge, 1898–1901), i. 40, 93–4, 98–9 (cf. the regulations applied in the early 16th cent. at Wells Cathedral: Wells Cathedral Library, 'Dean Cosyn's MS', fo. 19ᵛ); Misc. Accts. 40, fo. 1ᵛ; ibid. 41, fo. 286.

[91] Stats. [20], [30]: Cambridge, Corpus Christi College, MS 120, pp. 33, 36; M. J. Sparks, 'The Great Dormitory: A Documentary Study' (unpubl. paper), 2–4.

[92] Cole, *Henry VIII's Scheme of Bishopricks* (cit. in n. 88), 48. Misc. Accts. 40, fo. 1ᵛ. Stats. [30], [31], [32]: Cambridge, Corpus Christi College, MS 120, pp. 36–9; Treasurer's Accts. 1 (1547–8), fo. 4.

[93] PRO, E 36/116, p. 19.

[94] Legg and Hope, *Inventories*, 183, 192, 193.

[95] *Use of Sarum* (cit. in n. 90), ii. 235.

in haste for some other choir to use: the inclusion of a unique antiphon votive to St Augustine of Canterbury (*Exsultet in hac die*, attributed to the otherwise unknown Hugh Sturmy) suggests Canterbury Cathedral as by far the most likely intended destination for the books.[96] One of the inaugural lay clerks, Thomas Bull, had come to Canterbury from the choir of Magdalen College, and he emerges as an obvious conduit for the transmission of this collection to Canterbury.[97]

The music of these part-books makes great demands on both the skill and the stamina of the singers, and certainly its quality and content would seem to testify favourably to the skill and virtuosity of the men and boys of any choir by which it was performed. Masses such as *Spes nostra* by Robert Jones and *Veni, Sancte Spiritus* by Richard Pygott are among the longest and most taxing to have survived from this period, as likewise are Tallis's *Salve, intemerata Dei mater* and Taverner's *Gaude plurimum* among the votive antiphons. Probably the Catholic reaction of the early 1540s marked the utter apogee of the professional choral tradition of the English Church. Canterbury Cathedral had been equipped with choral forces capable of rising to a leading place in the fulfilment of such expectations, and these part-books would have supplied a wealth of suitable material for their realization.

The Reform of the Liturgy, 1547–c.1564

THE EDWARDIAN REFORMS, 1547–1553

The opening phase of the history of the music of the New Foundation Cathedral had not even ten years to run before its accomplishments were overtaken by the progress of the English Reformation. As far as concerned the Cathedral choir, the upheavals of the Reformation period were accomplished, in constitutional terms, with surprisingly little formal change; the number, character, and disposition of the singers intended for the reformed liturgy in, say, 1564, was virtually identical to that deemed suitable for the Latin rite in 1540. In liturgical and professional terms, however, the changes were momentous. The ten services of each day were reduced to three; the Latin liturgy was abolished, and with it virtually all of the immense tradition of musical elaboration associated with it; and the Cathedral musicians were perforce transformed from a body of highly skilled professional participants enacting the Catholic liturgy to a body of merely static part-time performers witnessing and commenting upon its Protestant successor.

Until the first Book of Common Prayer was ready for promulgation in 1549, the government of Edward VI was concerned principally, *faute de mieux*, with maintaining the existing Latin rite, while purging it of features which seemed to be tainted with superstition or misunderstanding irreconcilable with scriptural authority. The injunctions delivered to Canterbury in 1547 did little more than demote the Lady Mass, by (in effect) ordering its removal from the Lady Chapel to the choir on ferias, and by its suppression altogether on

[96] CUL, Peterhouse MSS 471–4; N. Sandon, 'The Henrician Partbooks at Peterhouse, Cambridge', *Proc. Royal Musical Assn.*, 103 (1976–7), 106–40; R. Bowers, 'Peterhouse, MSS 471–4', in *Cambridge Music Manuscripts, 900–1600* (cit. in n. 82), 132–5.

[97] Oxford, Magdalen College, Liber Computi 1510–30: acct. for 1526–7, unfol.; Liber Computi 1530–42, fo. 129; DE 164.

holy days so that time might be made for a vernacular sermon or a reading from the Homilies. With the same objective, Prime and the morning Hours on Sundays, Christmas Day, and Easter Day were to be omitted. All Sunday and festal masses were to be abbreviated by omission of the sequence; processions were discontinued, and the observance of Matins was to be moved from midnight to 6 a.m. There were provisions for a curfew, and requirements for less inattentive conduct among the singing-men in choir.[98] While these initial modifications to the liturgy were little more than cosmetic, the removal or defacement of windows and images was certainly under way by 1547–8,[99] indicating that the processes of reform visited upon the building anticipated the reform of the liturgy.

However, with the issue of the first Book of Common Prayer in January 1549, and even more so when this was superseded by the second Book in 1552, a Protestant liturgy existed to be imposed upon the Cathedral with rigour. The luxuriant superabundance of observance contained in the old service was now no more. It was replaced by a liturgy which instead made a virtue of repetitious simplicity, and which, moreover, contained not one note of music. The rituals of Morning Prayer, Evening Prayer, and Holy Communion were designed for parish-church use. In cathedral and collegiate churches it was left to the discretion of the chapter to decide how its professional choir could contribute—if at all. To Morning and Evening Prayer all that any choir could possibly offer were sung renderings of the responses plus the Creed and Lord's Prayer, with the psalms and canticles—and only simple unison plainsong tones, appropriately modified, were available to which to sing them. For the service of holy communion, the first Prayer Book gave scope for sung renderings of the ordinary, an introit psalm, and the sentences—but even this licence was removed from the 1552 Book. Some polyphony was composed for the new services, and would have been available for adoption at Canterbury, although that of the period 1549–53 is mostly in only four parts, bleakly simple and syllabic in style and banal in expression, placing a debilitating premium on the audibility of the words.[100] Certainly the Canterbury choir's former repertory of polyphony to Latin texts must now have been totally discarded, and probably there was little to take its place: the accounts that survive for two of the six years of Edward VI's reign record no payments at all for the copying of any new vernacular repertory of polyphony. Finally, in February 1550 the government ordered that all service-books of the Latin liturgy be delivered up for destruction.[101]

The singers on the foundation of Archbishop Cranmer's own Cathedral thus found their historic role at the centre of the church's worship suddenly belittled by the new liturgy, and pushed to an insignificant margin of the Cathedral's functions. The Protestant reform left them professionally demeaned, debilitatingly underemployed, and artistically superfluous; but at least there appears to have been no contemplation at Canterbury of the complete disbandment that overtook some professional liturgical choirs at this time.

[98] *Visitation Articles and Injunctions* (cit. in n. 89), ii. 135–46.

[99] LPL, Estate Documents, Roll 92, fo. 2; Treasurer's Accts. 1, fo. 8.

[100] For a succinct account of the impact of liturgical reform on the musical service of the Church at large at this period, see P. G. le Huray, *Music and the Reformation in England, 1549–1660* (2nd edn.; Cambridge, 1978), 1–34. For the contents of the few surviving sources of Edwardian polyphony, see ibid. 172–209.

[101] *Statutes of Lincoln Cathedral*, ed. H. Bradshaw and C. Wordsworth (2 vols. in 3; Cambridge, 1892–7), ii. 856.

THE RE-ESTABLISHMENT OF THE LATIN RITE, 1553–1558

The accession of Mary I in July 1553 threw into abrupt reverse almost all the changes of the previous six years. By the autumn, statute law was in place requiring the resumption, by not later than 20 December 1553, of all forms of the Latin service in use during the last year of Henry VIII. At Canterbury, the resident Chapter appears to have hastened to revive the Latin Mass at the earliest opportunity—even without first consulting the Archbishop.[102] Certainly, the rood was promptly re-erected, with its crucifix, Mary, and John. The need (as disclosed by the accounts, which are complete for the reign of Queen Mary) to re-equip the Cathedral with such apparatus as processional crosses, thuribles and sperges, ornaments and vessels of the altar, vestments for mass and the Office, and so on, proved to be only modest, suggesting either the receipt of substantial gifts or the surreptitious preservation of much of the former material. Very much larger was the task of re-equipping the choir with plainsong service-books. Many of the necessary volumes were hunted down by the choirmen themselves and purchased with their own money, subsequently reimbursed. Thirteen antiphoners, ten graduals, nine hymnals, thirty-one processioners, and sixteen volumes incorporating both hymnal and processioner (all, by definition, surreptitiously preserved by unreformed believers in defiance of the order of 1550) were speedily obtained, and supplemented by numerous unnotated volumes of text.[103]

There was need, too, for restoration of a repertory of polyphony. By as early as October 1553 Robert Colman, a lay clerk, had completed the copying of a set of four part-books 'to set forthe the olde service'; probably the four parts were of men's voices, since the boys must have been wholly preoccupied with learning the plainsong and ceremony of what to most of them would have been a completely new liturgy. During 1554–5 much new copying was undertaken: the large sum of 78s. was paid for producing polyphonic settings for the Marian feasts, evidently a major operation, and for the feasts of St Thomas of Canterbury and of the Transfiguration. By the following year, the choir had obtained a volume of polyphony—apparently a choirbook—called the 'Red Book', into which the lay clerk John Marden copied movements of the ordinary of the mass. In the next year, Thomas Bull completed the copying of further 'divers songs'. Evidently, this was a large undertaking, since his recompense was 53s. 4d. in a year in which one shilling sufficed to recompense the lay clerk Robert Tanner for copying one item for the evening votive antiphon, 'an Antem of our lady of five partes'. The 13s. 4d. paid in the same year for the copying of the polyphony of 'St Thomas storrye' probably related to settings of the major matins and vespers responsories for the offices on the feasts of St Thomas of Canterbury.[104] Evidently, considerable effort was being made to effect resumption of the performance of the Latin polyphony during the Marian period, and the Chapter was duly appreciative of the choir's efforts; at Michaelmas 1557 pay increases were implemented, of £3 6s. 8d. to each minor canon, £2 to the master of the choristers and each lay clerk, and 3s. 4d. to each

[102] *Writings and Disputations of Thomas Cranmer . . . relative to the Sacrament of the Lord's Supper*, ed. J. E. Cox (Parker Soc.; Cambridge, 1844), 429.

[103] Misc. Accts. 39, fos. 17–19ᵛ, 30ᵛ–31; ibid. 40, fos. 54ᵛ, 55, 57ᵛ, 58, 71–72ᵛ, 73ᵛ, 93; Treasurer's Accts. 2, fo. 10; ibid. 3, fos. 9ᵛ–10ᵛ;

LPL, Estate Documents, Roll 93, fo. 6ᵛ.

[104] Misc. Accts. 39, fos. 18, 30ᵛ; ibid. 40, fos. 54ᵛ, 71, 72ᵛ. Treasurer's Accts. 2, fo. 10; ibid. 3, fo. 9ᵛ; LPL, Estate Documents, Roll 93, fo. 6ᵛ.

chorister.[105] Meanwhile, and for reasons not disclosed, for the first half of Mary's reign, William Selby transferred to Thomas Bull the duties of Master of the Choristers. At Michaelmas 1556 he resumed the teaching of the boys, though it was in Bull's home that they continued to be brought up, until they returned to Selby in 1564.[106]

The use of the Cathedral organs was also resumed, in both the choir and the Lady Chapel. Repair to the great organ, particularly to the bellows, was in hand during 1553–4 and again in 1556–7, but the instrument was old and perhaps near the end of its working life; indeed, during the latter year its condition provoked some crisis, which was resolved by the Chapter only by resort to the expedient of temporarily borrowing the organ from St George's parish church in the city. During 1555–6 a small instrument was obtained for the Lady Chapel.[107] Probably it was for these instruments that William Selby composed his two surviving works for organ. His setting in keyboard polyphony of *Felix namque*, the offertory chant for the Lady Mass *Salve, sancta parens*, is of considerable length and in four parts. The second item, *Miserere mei, domine*, sets more briefly the chant of a psalm-antiphon for the service of Compline in the principal choir; its constraint within an overall compass of only two octaves and a fifth appears to corroborate the impression that, for the 1550s, the instrument in the choir was old-fashioned and probably elderly.[108]

An abiding problem encountered by the Chapter in this period was that of retaining the services of its ablest singers, in the face of peremptory requisition made by the two royal choirs. During 1553–4 a chorister, Richard Selby, was taken for the choir of St George's Chapel, Windsor, and apparently nothing came of the expedition made to London by Thomas Bull to see what could be done 'to save our queresters'.[109] There was a steady haemorrhage of lay clerks to the Chapel Royal: Thomas Tallis was lost in 1542, and Richard Lewcan, James Cancellor, and Roger Senton (or Centon) in the reign of Edward VI.[110] Even harder to replace were the minor canons, since men who possessed both priest's orders and the skills of a professional singer were rare. As Hugh Sully, Henry Aldred, and George Buck were successively taken for the Chapel Royal in the reign of Mary,[111] unfilled vacancies were left at Canterbury, and presently the Chapter took an obvious course of action to occupy them. In the autumn of 1556 it filled two vacancies, and then a third occurring early in 1557, with young lay singers, paid £8 per year and appointed to 'substitute' for the occupants of the minor canonries vacant and now suspended. The procedure was a success; by 1560 it was established that at any one time three of the minor canonries should be occupied not by priests but by these lay 'substitutes', so modifying the constitution of the choir to stand at nine minor canons and fifteen lay singers.[112]

[105] Misc. Accts. 40, fos. 87ᵛ–88ᵛ; Cambridge, Corpus Christi College, MS 120, p. 73.

[106] Misc. Accts. 39, fos. 21–23; ibid. 40, fo. 24ʳ⁻ᵛ; 'stipendia' sections of Treasurer's Accts. 2–5 and Misc. Accts. 39, 40; *Registrum Matthei Parker*, ed. W. H. Frere, 3 vols. (CYS, 35, 36, 39; 1928–33), ii. 632, 635; Cambridge, Corpus Christi College, MS 120, p. 83; *Register Booke of the Parish of St George the Martyr Within the Citie of Canterbury*, ed. J. M. Cowper (Canterbury, 1891), 170, 171. For identical arrangements for the teaching and boarding of the choristers at this time at Rochester Cathedral, see S. Lehmberg, *The Reformation of Cathedrals* (Princeton, NJ, 1988), 201.

[107] Misc. Accts. 39, fos. 17ᵛ, 20; ibid. 40, fos. 58, 60, 71, 72; Treasurer's Accts. 2, fo. 10; ibid. 3, fo. 9ᵛ.

[108] *The Mulliner Book*, ed. D. Stevens (Musica Britannica, 1; 1951), 27, 35.

[109] Misc. Accts. 39, fos. 17ᵛ, 18; Treasurer's Accts. 2, fo. 10ᵛ.

[110] DE 164; Misc. Accts. 40, fos. 1ᵛ, 21ʳ⁻ᵛ; Oxford, Corpus Christi College, MS 256, fo. 195ᵛ; PRO, E 179/69/61; E 101/427/6, fo. 28; BL, MS Stowe 571, fo. 36ᵛ.

[111] Misc. Accts. 39, fos. 3, 23ᵛ, 13; PRO, LC 2/4(2), fo. 31ʳ⁻ᵛ.

[112] Misc. Accts. 39, fo. 13; ibid. 40, fos. 65, 87ᵛ–88, 112–113ᵛ, etc.; Treasurer's Accts. 2, fo. 4ᵛ; ibid. 3, fo. 4; *Reg. Parker* (cit. in n. 106), ii. 631–2.

The restoration of the Latin rite was terminated by the accession of a Protestant successor to Mary I in November 1558. The vernacular Prayer Book enforced from 1559 by the government of Elizabeth I predicated once again the extinction of the choir's hard-won repertory of Latin polyphony and its mastery of the complex Latin liturgy. Essentially, the new Prayer Book was a reissue of that of 1552. However, a set of royal injunctions issued later in 1559 made up for one important matter conspicuously left unclarified, by including a provision that defined and articulated a role in the liturgy for the professional choirs maintained by the cathedral and collegiate churches. It was noted that through these churches' maintenance of livings for singing-men and boys, the 'laudable science of music' had in the past been much cultivated and brought into high esteem; and since it was the Queen's personal wish that such promotion of music be preserved, instruction was now given that those livings be retained, and that 'modest and distinct song' which did not obscure the sense of the words might be adopted for any appropriate part of the Common Prayers. Meanwhile, 'for the comforting of such that delight in music', there might be sung at the beginning and end of Morning and Evening Prayer 'an hymn or suchlike song, to the praise of Almighty God, in the best sort of melody and music that may be conveniently devised'.[113]

With this direct expression of the royal will, the English cathedral choir was preserved from reformist extinction, but probably it ought not to be imagined that the early Elizabethan cathedral service was adorned with polyphony sung by the choir on a daily basis. Even in the period immediately preceding the Reformation, plainsong had been the standard musical ingredient of the services, and it cannot be imagined that a Protestant reformation of the liturgy could result in an *increase* in the amount or proportion of polyphony sung each day. The royal injunction, however, gave scope for the daily performance of plainsong responses, psalms, and canticles at the Office, and of the Kyrie and Creed of ante-Communion; there was opportunity also for the use of homophonic settings in part-music for the canticles of the Office and for the ordinary of Communion on a few suitable days, such as the twenty-seven feast-days acknowledged by the Prayer Book. The singing of a simple anthem (even the word is the successor of 'antiphon') following the third collect of Morning and Evening Prayer was clearly envisaged by the injunction, and might even have been permitted more frequently than just on feast-days where the Chapter was sympathetic.

Canterbury duly adopted the standard pattern of execution of the Prayer Book liturgy. In 1564–5 it was reported that Morning Prayer and litany with ante-Communion were observed daily, and Evening Prayer between 3.00 p.m. and 4.00 p.m. in winter and an hour later in summer; the full Communion service was celebrated just on the first Sunday of each month, and on the major festivals.[114] The Dean, Nicholas Wotton, was largely absent, and the then residentiary canons did not attend service.[115]

For the choir, the outlook from the 1560s may have seemed fairly secure, but by

---

[113] *Visitation Articles and Injunctions* (cit. in n. 89), iii. 22–3.   [115] *Reg. Parker* (cit. in n. 106), ii. 636, 638.
[114] Ibid. iii. 78–80, 194–5; Legg and Hope, *Inventories*, 209–10.

comparison with the years before 1547 it was a security compromised by artistic impoverishment, declining status, and plain irrelevance to the theological and institutional character of an English Church now committed by its formularies and the sympathies of its leading personnel to the Reformed (rather than Lutheran) version of Protestantism. For the choristers, the content of their musical education was reduced now to slight dimensions, but at least such a contraction in one side of their training allowed them more time to attend the grammar school and gain the standard education of the day. The jobs of the singing-men likewise still required a certain natural talent, but beyond that, the acquisition of only minimal experience and but a meagre training. Their duties amounted to little more than a diversion, offering less than half-time employment, uncertain but lowly status, and a remuneration which in real terms was now in progressive decline. Indeed, for nearly forty years after 1559, whatever the choir sang, it sang not as an integral ingredient in an exercise of religious value, spiritual uplift and reward, or even devotional necessity, but merely on sufferance, as an obligatory concession (perhaps to many of the canons, such as Thomas Becon, a grudging concession) to a pernicious eccentricity of the royal will.

The Vernacular Reformed Service, c.1564–1597

It was fortunate for the choir that in its first dean and its first archbishop under the new, Elizabethan dispensation, the Cathedral was in the hands of men to whom the maintenance of at least competent standards of performance for such music as was undertaken would have appeared a desirable goal. Archbishop Parker (1559–75) concurred in expressions of the positive value of music in the church services; he even maintained musicians in the chapel of his household, and commissioned Thomas Tallis to compose music to which his metrical translation of the psalter could be sung.[116] The amateur but well-informed musical interests of Nicholas Wotton, Dean 1541–67, may well also have contributed something to the generation of esteem and value for the music of the Cathedral—in so far as his prevailing absence permitted. Music is mentioned in a number of his surviving letters, and he certainly was sufficiently well informed to be able to interview a newly appointed minor canon (Thomas Knell) in 1565, decide that he was inadequate to occupy that office, and arrange instead for the appointment of a qualified professional, the composer Clement Woodcock.[117]

It was in this spirit that as early as 1564 the Dean and Chapter made plain their rejection of the extremes of clerical austerity then current, by deciding to replace rather than remove the decayed organ in the choir. Funds were raised through the issue to the farmers of their estates, among others, of an invitation 'upon request . . . of theyre gentleness and good will . . . to contrybute towards the makyng', and before Christmas 1565 the builder, Henry Langford, had completed the new instrument, placed in a new location on a gallery above

[116] *Correspondence of Matthew Parker*, ed. J. Bruce and T. T. Perowne (Parker Soc.; Cambridge, 1853), 215; *Autobiography of Thomas Whythorne*, ed. J. M. Osborn (Oxford, 1961), 254–5; *Thomas Tallis: English Sacred Music*, ii: *Service Music*, ed. L. Ellinwood, rev. P. Doe (Early English Church Music, 13; 1974), pp. x–xi, 160–77.

[117] R. Ford, 'Clement Woodcock's Appointment at Canterbury Cathedral', *Chelys*, 16 (1987), 37–40; letter in 'Box in Basement A'; Chapter Act Book, 1561–8, fo. 34ᵛ; Misc. Accts. 40, fos. 297, 307ᵛ–309, 326, 332; Treasurer's Accts. 4, fos. 2ᵛ, 4ʳ⁻ᵛ, 15ᵛ.

and behind the stalls on the north side of the choir; for this, he was paid £56 4s. 9d.[118] The instrument proved to be less than satisfactory; substantial repair, by the Queen's organ-builder William Treasure, was required in 1573, and during 1576–7 the Chapter laid out £46 13s. 4d. for another builder, Jaspar Blankarde, to mend and even remake parts of the organ 'so that it be thoroughly and utterly perfected'.[119] After this, Blankarde took up a service contract to maintain the organ at an annual retainer of 40s.[120] Throughout this period, there was also 'the little organs in the quire'; this was periodically repaired, and both instruments were listed on an inventory of 1584.[121] Perhaps the purpose of the latter organ was to accompany anthems and services composed in embryonic 'verse' style, for which purpose the great organ would have been over-powerful.

Nevertheless, for most of the reign of Elizabeth the music of the Cathedral seems to have been managed at what, by comparison with the accomplishments of the Marian and late Henrician periods, was probably an unadventurous and uninspiringly low ebb. Two adult positions in the choir were lost in 1575, when the offices of gospeller and epistoler, redundant under the new liturgy, were suppressed.[122] In the same year, the Chapter embarked on a recruitment policy designed to reduce the number of minor canons to six, but to compensate by raising that of the substitutes also to six; this was accomplished by 1580.[123] Throughout all this time, a substantial measure of stability in the rendering of the music of the liturgical services, such as it was, must have arisen from the longevity of William Selby as Organist and Master of the Choristers; one of the original appointees of 1540–1, he accepted semi-'retirement' only in December 1583, shortly before his death in June 1584.[124]

Of the composed music actually promoted and performed in the choir between 1559 and 1583 (and indeed, until 1597), very little direct information survives. Of Selby's own composition to English words, nothing remains except a single voice-part of a full anthem for probably four voices, *Blessed are thou that fearest God*, a setting of Psalm 128 in the metrical version by Sternhold and Hopkins.[125] At Canterbury itself, there are no surviving musical manuscripts of this period, and the accounts, which up to 1581 survive reasonably fully, record dispiritingly few payments for the copying of polyphony; the repertory must be presumed to have been repetitious and of relatively meagre content. Throughout all this time, the choir was steadily acquiring a stock of printed psalters; for the most part, probably, these were unnoted prayer-book psalters for use in the liturgy. However, in 1566–7 a stock of eleven volumes of metrical psalms was obtained; these were usable not in the choir services, but at the sermon preached each Sunday in the Sermon House.[126]

[118] Chapter Act Book, 1561–8, fo. 53; Treasurer's Accts. 4, fos. 13ᵛ, 15ᵛ; ibid. 5, fos. 2, 14; Misc. Accts. 40, fos. 332, 335, 336ᵛ, 337ᵛ, 338ᵛ.

[119] Chapter Act Book, 1568–81, fos. 64ᵛ, 115ᵛ; Treasurer's Accts. 7, fo. 7; ibid. 8, fo. 9.

[120] Chapter Act Book, 1568–81, fo. 115ᵛ; Treasurer's Accts. 9, fos. 6ᵛ, 8; Misc. Accts. 40, fos. 105ᵛ, 109, 111, 112, 115.

[121] Chapter Act Book, 1568–81, fo. 64ᵛ; Misc. Accts. 40, fo. 385ᵛ; Legg and Hope, *Inventories*, 242.

[122] Misc. Accts. 40, fos. 380ᵛ, 397ᵛ, 402ᵛ, 406, 429; Treasurer's Acct. 7, fo. 2.

[123] 'Stipendia' sections of Treasurer's accounts 1575–80 in Misc. Accts. 40, 41, and Treasurer's Accts. 3–9.

[124] Chapter Act Book, 1581–1607, fo. 57ᵛ; *Names of them that were Crystyned Marryed and Buryed in the Paryshe of Saynt Mary Magdalene in Canterbury 1559–1800*, ed. J. M. Cowper (Canterbury, 1890), 98.

[125] Shrewsbury, Shropshire Record Office, MS SRO 356, Mus. MS 3, fo. 3.

[126] Misc. Accts. 40, fos. 220, 333, 340; Treasurer's Accts. 4, fo. 15; ibid. 5, fo. 12; ibid. 6, fo. 12ᵛ; ibid. 10, fo. 8.

Flurries of musical enterprise were rare, but striking when they happened. In the spring of 1567 the arrival of a new and resident dean, Thomas Goodwyn, was accompanied by, and apparently provoked, a sudden if short-lived burst of music-copying; within eighteen months the substantial sum of £8 16s. 4d. had been paid in recompense, mostly to William Selby, Richard Coste, and Clement Woodcock. The payments were for both 'makyng and pryckyng', which suggests that the music concerned was largely of their own composition.[127] No vocal polyphony by Woodcock is known to be extant; however, of Coste's compositions, a four-part anthem *He that hath my commandments* survives complete, and his four-part Short Service for Morning and Evening Prayer could probably be reconstructed from the remaining parts.[128] During Goodwyn's deanship, the formal reception of Archbishop Parker to conduct his visitation of 1570 was marked by the singing of an 'Antheme', as also was the reception of Elizabeth I upon her royal visit of 1573, at which the Chapel Royal joined the Cathedral choir.[129] After 1568, copying is next recorded in 1574–5, when 10s. was paid to George Juxon, then a lay clerk, for 'makyng and pryckyng certen songs for the quere', indicating that he too was already active as a composer.[130] However, in 1576 the succession as archbishop of Edmund Grindal, an advanced reformer, probably served as a dampener upon whatever degree of initiative Goodwyn might have been seeking intermittently to stimulate; little by way of approval or encouragement could be expected of a diocesan who (in 1567) had stated plainly enough 'We do not assert that the chanting in churches, together with the organ, is to be retained; we disapprove of it, as we ought to.'[131] It was perhaps no coincidence that no further manifestations of musical enterprise at the Cathedral occurred thereafter until late in 1583, shortly after the accession of a successor to Grindal as archbishop.

The concurrence of the new archbishop, John Whitgift, in a positive appreciation of music as a component of worship was on record,[132] and shortly after his succession new initiatives in the music of his cathedral church became apparent. In the winter of 1583, when the elderly William Selby was offered semi-'retirement', the members of the choir were allowed the initiative in seeing themselves 'furnyshed with songe bookes', with an assurance of due recompense for those who executed the work.[133] Unfortunately, in the prevailing loss of documentation for the 1580s, the result of this initiative is not known; however, it is possibly from this period that George Juxon's single surviving work originates, a broad and expansive setting in full style for six voices of a text proper to Morning Prayer on Easter Sunday, *Christ rising again from the dead*.[134]

Selby's retirement, meanwhile, had ushered in a period of instability in the management

[127] Chapter Act Book, 1561–8, fos. 66, 81ᵛ; Treasurer's Acct. 5, fo. 13; ibid. 6, fo. 15ᵛ; Misc. Accts. 40, fo. 389ᵛ.

[128] New York Public Library, MSS Drexel 4180–3 (one voice-part also in BL, Add. MS 29289); Durham, Cathedral Library, Music MSS C 8, C 13, E 11a.

[129] *Reg. Parker* (cit. in n. 106), ii. 536, 538; Misc. Accts. 40, fo. 450; Cambridge, Corpus Christi College, MS 120, fo. 55*; J. Nichols, *Progresses and Public Processions of Queen Elizabeth* (2 vols.; London, 1788), i, year 1573, pp. 36, 39, 52.

[130] Misc. Accts. 40, fo. 450.

[131] *Zurich Letters*, ed. J. Brandon, 2 vols. (Parker Soc.; Cam-

bridge, 1842–3), i. 178.

[132] *Works of John Whitgift*, ed. J. Ayre, 3 vols. (Parker Soc.; Cambridge, 1851–3), iii. 106–8, 384–8, 392.

[133] Chapter Act Book, 1581–1608, fo. 57, 57ᵛ.

[134] London, Royal College of Music, MSS 1045–51. A five-part setting of the responses attributed to a George Juxon (which in one source bears a conflicting ascription to Adrian Batten) seems more likely to be the work of George Juxon's son, also called George (born 1590, chorister of Canterbury Cathedral 1602–5).

of the Cathedral's music, marked by a rapid succession of short-lived occupants of the office of Master of the Choristers. Selby's immediate successor, Matthew Goodwyn, was a particularly risky choice, since at the time of his full appointment in June 1584 he was not yet 15 years old. It is likely that he owed his appointment to a close kinship with the then dean, Thomas Goodwyn; and once the latter had been elevated to the bishopric of Wells, late in 1584, it was not long before young Matthew was dispatched from Canterbury to the provinces to learn his trade. But after only eight months as Master of the Choristers and Organist at Exeter Cathedral, the unfortunate youth died, on 12 January 1587, having lived an eventful seventeen years and five months.[135]

Goodwyn's successor was Arthur Cock, already a lay clerk, and a former chorister of the Cathedral. The fact that his salary was increased from £12 to £15 a year in 1588 suggests that he was regarded as satisfactory; nevertheless, under circumstances now wholly obscure, Cock presently accepted the same demotion as Matthew Goodwyn before him, and departed to take up the corresponding post at Exeter in April 1589.[136] His successor at Canterbury was George Juxon; his likewise was an internal appointment, he having already been a lay clerk for nearly twenty years. Juxon was well-connected and resided in some state in the premises of the former Dominican friary; however, in December 1592, after a very brief tenure, he died.[137] During at least part of the time that Juxon was in office, the functions of Master of the Choristers and Organist became separated. Richard Coste was rewarded for playing the organ during part of 1588–9, and Thomas Stores, one of the lay clerks, during 1589–90.[138] The reasons for this change do not appear; perhaps Juxon was not in good health. Most unfortunately, the name of his successor is, for loss of documentation, unknown.

The visitations of Archbishops Parker and Whitgift disclosed no serious delinquencies in the way the Cathedral music was conducted, though some degree of absenteeism among the choirmen remained a source of perennial, if not debilitating, concern. Most likely the problem was no greater than in any modern manufacturing or service concern, and was indeed inevitable, so long as the lay clerks had to take on supplementary jobs in order to make ends meet, and the minor canons had to take on parish livings in the city for the same purpose.[139] Eventually, in about 1585, the Chapter adopted the practice of rewarding noteworthy examples of diligence and praiseworthy devotion to duty among the lay clerks with cash gratuities: Esdras Johnson, Robert Barker, and Thomas Bailey became frequent recipients.[140] The lay clerks' salaries had become badly eroded by inflation, having last been fixed in 1557.

[135] Chapter Act Book, 1581–1607, fos. 57ᵛ, 59, 61; I. C. Payne, 'Two Early Organists of Exeter Cathedral: Matthew Godwin and Arthur Cock', *Devon and Cornwall Notes and Queries*, 35 (1983), 133–42.

[136] Misc. Accts. 40, fo. 350; ibid. 41, fos. 15ᵛ–16ᵛ, 55, 88–91ᵛ; Treasurer's Accts. 9, fo. 2; Chapter Act Book, 1581–1607, fo. 111; Payne, 'Two Early Organists of Exeter Cathedral' (cit. in n. 135), 135–6.

[137] Treasurer's Accts. 7, fo. 2; Misc. Accts. 40, fo. 430ᵛ; LPL, Reg. Archbishop Whitgift, i, fo. 255ᵛ; Treasurer's Accts. 10, fo. 2ᵛ; Chapter Act Book, 1581–1607, fos. 53, 57, 89, 93, 103. *Regyster*

Booke of the Chrystenynges, Maryages and Buryalls of the Parish of St Alphaege In the Cyttye of Canterbury, ed. J. M. Cowper (Canterbury, 1889), 9, 10, 204.

[138] Treasurer's Accts. 10, fo. 7.

[139] Stat. [23]: Cambridge, Corpus Christi College, MS 120, p. 31; *Reg. Parker* (cit. in n. 106), ii. 549; iii. 931; Chapter Act Book, 1561–8, fo. 43 and index, fo. 86; ibid. 1581–1607, fos. 42, 52ᵛ, 67ᵛ, 71, 82; Reg. V 2, p. 80; Reg. V3, fos. 68ᵛ, 143ᵛ.

[140] Chapter Act Book, 1581–1607, fos. 71, 74, 77, 87ᵛ; Treasurer's Accts. 10, fo. 7; LPL, Estate Documents, Roll 94, fo. 5ᵛ.

Probably it would not have taken much singing rehearsal each day to keep the choristers adequately trained at this period, and the Chapter presently took the opportunity to expand their experience in a way that would equip them more broadly for an eventual musical career. From 1565 until his appointment in 1570 as Master of the Choristers at Chichester Cathedral, Clement Woodcock was a lay clerk of Canterbury, and is known as the composer of five surviving works for viol consort; it may therefore have been in recognition of a growth in the practice of domestic consort music in the Precincts that in December 1574 the Chapter decreed that 'For the better exercise of the Maister and of the queresters' a 'set' of viols and a 'set' of lutes be acquired.[141] Such an initiative in instrumental training seems to have been remarkably fruitful, and a number of the boys turned in adult life to professional music and to composition. Arthur Cock (chorister, 1568–75) composed for viols; Thomas Ford (admitted 1589) served as a lutenist in royal service between 1611 and 1642, and became a versatile and pioneer composer of instrumental ensemble music and of viol fantasias, anthems, and part-songs. William Corkine (left 1599) published two books of ayres, and Thomas Hunt (admitted 1587) and William West (left 1589) both composed church music. Edward Pearce (1568–75) eventually became Master of the Choristers of St Paul's Cathedral, where, as master of 'The Children of Paul's' his career is written large in the history of English drama.[142] Meanwhile, John Newstreet exemplifies those choristers who took up the musical profession at less exalted levels; he was a chorister in the 1590s, when he 'was put to Learne Musicke And hath ever since followed the same' in and about the city, a living on which he contrived to maintain himself and his wife and bring up sixteen children.[143] Meanwhile, however, in late 1581 or 1582 the Chapter decided to terminate its responsibility for the provision of residential accommodation and care in the Precincts for the choristers, and in 1593 the maintenance of a common hall for the provision of meals also ended.[144] From this time on, the choristers must be presumed to have lived at home, or with guardians or friends in the Precincts or the city; nevertheless, it does seem that the Cathedral's provision of free musical training remained in good order.

THE REHABILITATION OF SERVICE MUSIC, 1597–1642

The Prayer Book Liturgy in Jacobean Observance

During the 1590s and the first years of the new century, the practice of music in the greater churches that were equipped with professional choirs was lifted from the relatively depressed state in which it had been labouring thitherto to a new and higher plateau of endeavour, in terms of objective, accomplishment, and—in many quarters—esteem.

---

[141] Ford, 'Clement Woodcock's Appointment' (cit. in n. 117), 37–40; *Elizabethan Consort Music*, ed. P. Doe (Musica Britannica, 44; 1979), nos. 38, 41, 64–6; Chapter Act Book, 1568–81, fo. 84.

[142] See, e.g., the entries on these composers in *New Grove Dictionary of Music and Musicians*, ed. S. Sadie (20 vols.; London, 1980); for Cock, see also Payne, 'Two Early Organists of Exeter Cathedral' (cit. in n. 135), 138–42; for Pearce, see R. Gair, *The Children of Paul's: The Story of a Theatre Company*

(Cambridge, 1982).

[143] Petitions 17, 250.

[144] Chapter Act Book, 1581–1607, fo. 30ᵛ. In 1581, the choristers' stipends were still being paid on their behalf to Selby as their master, but by the time of the next surviving account, 1587–8, they were being paid into the boys' own hands: Misc. Accts. 41, fos. 55–56ᵛ, 92–93ᵛ.

Indeed, it is not impossible that it was at this time that the performance of polyphonic music was first raised to a daily occurrence, at least for the canticles and anthem at Morning and Evening Prayer and for the Kyrie and Creed at ante-Communion.

The ascendancy of Calvinism in the leadership of the Church of England was still to come in 1600—it was to be dominant through much of the reign of James I—but the high Calvinist doctrine that Christ died only for the elect was already challenged by a significant minority of senior churchmen, who described a sacramental economy of salvation which was open, in principle, to all, and which consequently valued liturgy and sacrament somewhat above the sermon. Evidently, such a doctrine possessed great potential for elevating the role in the Christian life of the liturgical service, as a means both to a revelation of godly and holy living and to exposure to prayer and the Scriptures. A well-ordered liturgy, enhanced by the beauty of holiness, concentrating on a decent and impressive offering of the sacrament of Communion and an elegant and heightened performance of the Common Prayer, now became a worthy and desirable object at which to aim. It was in this spirit that, for instance, between 1603 and 1610 the Canterbury Chapter was busy about the installation of pews in the choir to accommodate the novelty of congregational attendance at the services there.[145] That music would be included among the many possible facets of the 'beauty of holiness' was made certain through the fortuitous emergence of a new generation of composers born around the middle of Elizabeth's reign, including Tomkins, Weelkes, Orlando Gibbons, and a substantial number of lesser lights, who proved to have the capacity of creating music of the highest quality for the enhancement of the reformed liturgy. The craft of composition itself expanded to match the needs of the new approach to, and evaluation of, the practice of liturgy. Composition took on newly expanded objectives of ambition, design, and scale; polyphony became more flexible and capable of sustaining works of durations scarcely encountered since the time of the Marian restoration of the Latin rite. Longer and more diverse texts were selected for setting as anthems, and much use was made of the verse idiom to exploit voices of solo capacity and to create elegant patterns of variety of texture over long compositions.

Such views were to come to the fullness of their fruition only after 1625, but the application of an enhanced role for music at Canterbury began with the appointment as dean of Thomas Neville in 1597. He was already Master of Trinity College, Cambridge, where one of his most immediate concerns and accomplishments had been the upgrading of the content and standard of musical performance in the college chapel,[146] and it would appear that he was equally prompt to initiate the same at Canterbury. Taking advantage, it would seem, of a fortunate vacancy, he brought the twenty-five-year-old George Marson from Trinity College to act as Master of the Choristers and Organist, and he had entered office by Michaelmas 1597. Presently, in 1604, Marson was formally appointed to these offices, at a salary of £17 a year; in the same year, having taken orders, he was admitted in plurality to a minor canonry, and in 1607 was collated in addition to the rectory of St Mary Magdalen in Canterbury. Evidently he was a valued man.[147]

[145] Misc. Accts. 41, fo. 217ᵛ; Treasurer's Accts. 13, fo. 8; ibid. 16, fo. 8ᵛ; ibid. 18, fo. 5ᵛ.
[146] I. C. Payne, 'Instrumental Music at Trinity College, Cambridge, c.1594–c.1615', *Music & Letters*, 68 (1987), 128–40.
[147] A. Ashbee, 'Marson, George', in *New Grove Dictionary* (cit. in n. 142), xi. 710; Reg. Y, fos. 92ᵛ, 296ᵛ; Chapter Act Book, 1581–

The appointment of Neville and the arrival of Marson were marked by an unprecedented and sustained spate of music acquisition and copying that appears to be indicative of an immediate and major overhaul and expansion of the repertory. During 1597–8 a set of at least eight, and more probably ten, new books was purchased for use in the choir, and in the year following, to keep the newly acquired stock in order, there was obtained a new 'chest to sett in the Quire for to lay the singing books [in]'.[148] Immediately, the books began to receive new music, and until 1605–6 copying activity is recorded for every year except one—a startling departure from the prevailing inactivity of the thirty-nine years preceding 1597. Simultaneously, the existing books were repaired. The accounts unfortunately record no details identifying the music being acquired at this time. However, the sums paid to the copyists amounted between 1598 and 1606 to some £21 16s., and at the standard rate of 4d. per folio,[149] this would have procured 1,308 folios or 2,616 pages of music—enough to fill a new set of ten part-books each containing 130 folios. Considering that the actual quantity of vernacular service music of good quality at this time was far from great, and bearing in mind the sheer size of the labour involved in copying even a single whole service, this exercise in the collection and building of a repertory was no small achievement—for the Cathedral in general, and in particular for the principal scribe, the lay clerk (and later minor canon) John Ward. However, after 1606 the intensive copying of music ceased for a time, perhaps while the choir digested its new material; thereafter, up to Neville's death in 1615, only the copying by John Ward of some services in 1611–12 and 1612–13 is recorded.[150]

Another of Neville's initiatives concerned the introduction of instrumentalists to make some contribution to the choir service on the great festivals of the church. By Michaelmas 1597 the places of two of the substitutes had been suppressed, and in their stead the Cathedral was recruiting a group of wind-players. By then, three had already been appointed, and a fourth, completing the group, joined at Christmas. In 1603 the ensemble was reduced to three players (and one of the substituteships was revived), but it was restored to a membership of four in 1610, at which figure it remained until the Civil War. The trio of 1602–10 was of players all on cornett, but it would seem that the quartet retained from 1610 consisted of two players on cornett and two on sackbut.[151] The band's function was 'to make music in the quire' of the Cathedral, on feast-days and their vigils.[152] Precisely what music was played is not divulged, but at least it is clear that at this time the band can have had no contribution to make to the accompaniment of the choir's sung

1607, fo. 307ᵛ; Treasurer's Accts. 13, fo. 3; LPL, Estate Documents, Roll 94, fo. 2.

[148] Misc. Accts. 41, fos. 157ᵛ, 158ᵛ; LPL, Estate Documents, Roll 94, fo. 6ᵛ.

[149] This rate was paid at Canterbury in 1624–5 (Treasurer's Accts. 33, fo. 3), and is known to have applied also at institutions such at Eton College in 1613–14 and Durham Cathedral in the early 1630s: J. Morehen, 'The Sources of English Cathedral Music, *c.*1617–1644' (Ph.D. thesis, Univ. of Cambridge, 1969), 29–30.

[150] Misc. Accts. 41, fos. 158ᵛ, 176, 185, 213ᵛ; Treasurer's Accts. 11, fo. 5; ibid. 12, fo. 9, 9ᵛ; ibid. 13, fo. 8; ibid. 14, fo. 7; ibid. 20, fo. 8; ibid. 21, fo. 5ᵛ.

[151] LPL, Estate Documents, Roll 94, fo. 2; Misc. Accts. 41, fos. 131ᵛ–132, 168ᵛ–169, 181ᵛ, 212; Treasurer's Accts. 12, fos. 7ᵛ, 9ᵛ; ibid. 19, fo. 5. It cannot be stressed too strongly that there is no trace whatever in the Cathedral archives of the regular employment, or even occasional use, of wind-players in the course of the Cathedral service at any time prior to 1597. In particular, there is not a shred of evidence to support the assertion that 'In the list of officers appointed for the Cathedral Church of Canterbury in 1532 [*sic*] there were two Cornetters and two Sackbutters', as first claimed by F. W. Galpin, *Old English Instruments of Music* (London, 1910), 191, and without verification repeated countless times by subsequent authors.

[152] Treasurer's Accts. 12, fo. 7ᵛ; ibid. 17, fo. 5.

polyphony. Until the early 1620s, almost all the players were not merely uneducated, but barely literate, unable even to sign their names in receipt of their pay.[153] Probably they were members of the corps of city waits, in attendance merely to sound suitable pieces from their unwritten repertory at appropriate moments of the festal services—flourishes, perhaps, at the entry and departure of the clergy.

With the appointment of Charles Fotherby as dean in 1615, the music of the Cathedral was abruptly subjected to a campaign of reinvigoration and animation of unprecedented energy—for which it may well have been ready, after the momentum of Neville's original stimulus had established a new plateau of endeavour and then run down and worn off. Unlike Neville, Fotherby was undistracted by plural appointments, and his initiatives may well have been designed to lift the Cathedral's music to the forefront of what was rapidly becoming once again, as in pre-Reformation days, a very competitive field. Three years of intensive music acquisition and copying were inaugurated; John Ward earned nearly £20 for his pains as scribe. Although there is again no identification of the music copied,[154] the sum paid would have produced some 1,185 folios of material, adding up probably to some ninety anthems or the equivalent in anthems and services.

The considerable expenditure upon the Cathedral organ that began in Fotherby's time suggests a great scheme of modernization. George Pendleton, who had held the maintenance contract since 1597, was succeeded in 1615 by John Burward, by whom it was held until 1636.[155] After fifty years' use, the Langford-Blankarde organ of 1564 was probably ripe for serious attention; during 1618–19 some £83 17s. 10d. was paid to Burward for work upon it, and in view of the additional expenditure of over £5 on clearing up the dust, grime, and filth created, the work may very well have been nothing less than a complete dismantlement and rebuilding. At the same time, the case was beautified with statues (probably of angels) and pedestals for them to stand upon.[156] It is perhaps no accident that no reference to the little organ on the choir floor can be found later than 1616–17.[157] It seems likely that Burward's work included the modernization of the great organ by the physical incorporation into it of the smaller instrument as a separate *rückpositif* chair organ, all played from a single console now of two manuals—as was being accomplished at much the same time at Lichfield Cathedral.

Fotherby also sought to reverse the slight attenuation in numbers experienced by the choir in Neville's time. The second substituteship suppressed since 1597 was reinstated in 1617, restoring numbers to six. Further, one lay clerkship which since the 1590s had been occupied in absentee and sinecure plurality by Gentlemen of the Chapel Royal was surrendered by its holder (William West) in 1618, and reoccupied thenceforth by a resident choirman.[158] Only the minor canons now remained depleted, through the holding of one minor canonry in plurality by George Marson. Otherwise, the membership of this, almost the largest choir in England, was restored to full occupation.

Also subject to an enlargement of its role at this time was domestic music-making in

---

[153] See e.g. Misc. Accts. 41, fos. 131ᵛ–132, 195ᶠ⁻ᵛ, 242ᵛ, 269.

[154] Treasurer's Accts. 23, fo. 8; ibid. 24, fo. 5; ibid. 25, fo. 4ᵛ.

[155] 'Expensae necessariae' or 'Feoda et regarda extra-ordinaria' sections of Treasurer's accounts, years quoted.

[156] Treasurer's Accts. 26, fos. 2ᵛ, 3; ibid. 27, fos. 2ᵛ, 3.

[157] Ibid. 25, fo. 4ᵛ.

[158] Ibid. 24, fo. 3; ibid. 26, fo. 1ᵛ; ibid. 27, fo. 1ᵛ.

the Precincts. Already in 1600 a 'sett' of recorders had been obtained for the use of the chorister-boys;[159] with their existing full consorts of viols and lutes, the boys were now well equipped to play, as part of their recreation and training, any of the music being published at the time for either plain or broken consort. Their viols seem to have come in for intensive use, and from 1609–10 until the 1630s every single surviving account records expenditure on new strings. The teaching was shared between Marson and William Williams, lay clerk and himself a former chorister; among other occasions, the boys played their viols to entertain Archbishop Abbot in 1615.[160] Moreover, in 1615 the Cathedral acquired (for £7) a second chest of viols, and while the first was distinguished as 'the viols for the choristers' school', the maintenance of the second was committed to certain of the lay clerks.[161] The provision of this latter chest at the Chapter's expense may well suggest that it was for use by the singing-men not only for their own recreation but also, perhaps, for such purposes as the entertainment of Deanery guests; there is for this period no evidence to suggest that the lay clerks' viols were yet being adopted for the performance in choir of the newly popular large sacred consorts with viol accompaniment, of the kind then being written by composers such as Gibbons, Weelkes, Amner, and Ward.

The initiatives and innovations of Fotherby's short-lived deanship may well have elevated the Cathedral's practice of music to a view of new horizons of ambition and accomplishment, which were only likely to be maintained, or even enhanced, under his successor. John Boys (instituted 1619) sprang from a prominent Kentish land-owning family, but otherwise his sole qualification for the appointment was the ardour with which he championed the vernacular liturgy. Between 1609 and 1616 he had published four lengthy volumes of 'Expositions', of the lessons, the Epistles and Gospels, and the proper psalms, all 'as used in our English liturgie'. His writings contain numerous explicit appreciations of the contribution of music to the due observance of the Common Prayer; his posthumous eulogist 'R. P.' described him as 'a loving and carefull Deane', much remarked for 'his devotion to frequenting publique prayers', and whose deathbed conversation was all 'of musicke'.[162] A comprehensive campaign of repair, apparently of no fewer than five sets of part-books, was in hand during 1620–1, and in the same year the repertory was augmented with a substantial collection of twenty-seven anthems, copied into some existing set of books. The £6 10s. expended would have provided thirty-nine new folios for each of ten books; at two and a half to three pages per anthem, these compositions were of substantial dimensions. Further copying activity followed in every year save one (1622–3) up to Boys's death in 1625.[163]

The vigour of the Canterbury choir at this time is well attested by what would appear to be the encouragement given to the composers within its ranks, and it is fortunate that one of them, John Barnard (lay clerk, 1617–22), became a zealous collector, copier, and eventually publisher of the church music of his day, including some by his erstwhile

[159] Chapter Act Book, 1581–1607, fo. 246; Misc. Accts. 41, fo. 185; Treasurer's Accts. 11, fo. 5.

[160] 'Expensae necessariae' section of Treasurer's Accounts, years quoted; Treasurer's Accts. 23, fo. 5ᵛ.

[161] Treasurer's Accts. 23, fo. 5ᵛ; ibid. 28, fo. 2ᵛ; ibid. 30, fo. 4; ibid. 31, fo. 4ᵛ; ibid. 32, fo. 4ᵛ; etc.

[162] Eventually all reprinted in *The Works of Iohn Boys* (London, 1622); see 6–16, 28–45, 179–81. R. P., biog. introd. to *Remaines of that Reverend and Famous Postiller, John Boys* (London, 1631), sigs. a4ᵛ, b1ᵛ.

[163] Treasurer's Accts. 29, fo. 4, 4ᵛ; ibid. 30, fo. 4; ibid. 32, fo. 4ᵛ; ibid. 33, fo. 3.

Canterbury colleagues.[164] Most of George Marson's surviving composition is for full choir. This comprises one whole service, one setting of just the morning and evening canticles, a Cantate Domino, a Creed, a set of festal responses with Psalm 16, and three anthems for five and six voices; there are also two five-part verse anthems. It is, perhaps, not among the very best music of its period, and Barnard selected none of it for publication; nevertheless, the variety of forces and occasions for which Marson's music was written indicate the extent to which a sense of genuine choral purpose and endeavour was being established and reinforced in his time. Other composers who for a time were members of the Canterbury choir include John Mace (substitute, 1617–18), composer of a five-part full anthem 'Let thy merciful ears, O Lord'; John Barnard himself, who has left two sets of responses; and William West (chorister, left 1590; lay clerk by 1597, departed for Chapel Royal 1604), composer of a whole service and two anthems, one in verse style, the other full. For all three composers' music, the sole surviving source is John Barnard's manuscripts.

Very much more would be known about Canterbury Cathedral music of this period if it were possible to verify the identification made by many scholars of the composer John Ward with the Canterbury choirman of that name. This vigorous, prolific, and gifted composer created music in an extraordinarily wide variety of styles, extending to numerous services and anthems for the Church's liturgy and a number of domestic devotional consorts for voices and viols; a volume of twenty-five madrigals, plus a number of unpublished secular vocal works; and for viols some forty-two fantasias and eight In Nomines in four, five, and six parts, with a few other instrumental pieces.[165] The Canterbury archives disclose that three individuals of this name served in the choir around the period concerned: a lay clerk 1560–93 (died); a chorister admitted 1580, who is probably to be identified with the substitute (1587–90), lay clerk (1590–1607) and minor canon (1607–17) of that name, who died in 1617; and a chorister, 1598–1604.[166] The first Ward is certainly too early for the identification, but he may well have been the father of the second; the third appears to have been unrelated to either of the others. This is not the place to endeavour to unravel and resolve the mass of contradictory information by now accumulated.[167] If the second Ward were the composer, then Canterbury could claim to have nourished and sustained from boyhood to grave one of the principal composers of the Jacobean era, whose stature only the genius of contemporaries such as Byrd, Tomkins, Weelkes, Gibbons, and Wilbye can relegate to the second rank, and whose music would thus have been written largely for the Cathedral choir and community of which he was a life-long member. There are

[164] Barnard's manuscript collection is now London, Royal College of Music, MSS 1045–51. J. Barnard, *The First Book of Selected Church Musick* (London, 1641; fac. edn., ed. J. Morehen (London, 1973). For further details of composers and sources mentioned here, see *New Grove Dictionary* (cit. in n. 142); and P. G. le Huray and R. T. Daniel, *The Sources of English Church Music, 1547–1660* (2 vols.; London, 1972). Marson also contributed a madrigal to Thomas Morley's anthology *The Triumphs of Oriana* (1601).

[165] For a condensed list of works, see M. Foster, 'Ward, John', in *New Grove Dictionary* (cit. in n. 142), xx. 210–11, though the unpublished madrigals appear to have been overlooked.

[166] These dates distilled from 'Stipendia' sections of Treasurer's Accounts, years quoted.

[167] There is a substantial literature, to most of which reference is made in I. C. Payne, 'The Handwriting of John Ward', *Music & Letters*, 65 (1984), 176–88. A more recent article, R. Ford, 'John Ward of Canterbury', *Chelys*, 23 (1986), 51–63, is valuable for being the first to distinguish the second from the third of the Canterbury John Wards, but otherwise only confuses the issue further by suggesting that they were father and son, and that both between them composed the music surviving under the single name.

reasons, however, for believing that not the second but the third John Ward was in fact the composer; consequently, Canterbury can claim no more than to have offered him the chorister's experience and training that launched him on so fruitful and prolific a musical career elsewhere.

One striking feature of the choir of which Marson was director was an extraordinary degree of stability among the choral personnel. In the twenty-eight years 1597–1625, there were among the twelve lay clerks only twenty-five changes of personnel, and all but six of the new lay clerks had already entered the choir as substitutes. In the same period, among the six minor canons there were only eight departures, and most appointees remained to serve for terms exceeding twenty-five years. At Michaelmas 1625, for example, of the six minor canons and twelve lay clerks, one had served over thirty years, seven for twenty or more, four for ten or more, and only six for nine years or fewer; furthermore, seven of the lay clerks and four of the six substitutes had formerly been choristers. Of the actual quality of the singing and of the performances generated by the choir at this time, of course, no estimate can be made. Pay may have remained poor, but from the 1590s this was readily supplementable in cases of need from the Chapter's alms budget, and absenteeism was only patchily a problem.[168]

Such is the nature of the surviving documentation that only rarely does record survive of disciplinary troubles, though the minor canon William Struddles neglected to take his oath of obedience and eventually, in 1604, had to be redeemed from a debtors' prison, while in 1603 the lay clerk Thomas Bailey had to be discouraged from conducting an ale-house at his home, which was in the Mint Yard and thus temptingly adjacent to the grammar school.[169] Presently, however, the Chapter completed its retreat from its statutory perception of the chorister-boys as honoured, resident, and equal co-practitioners in a common liturgical obligation; to Jacobean clergy, to be allowed to sing in a cathedral choir was a privilege and a training which had to be paid for, a concept given effect in 1619 with the erection of a provision that each chorister thenceforth pay to Marson (as if an apprentice to a master) a fee for his teaching—of 5s. per term.[170]

The Music of the Laudian Cathedral, 1625–1642

Isaac Bargrave's appointment as dean in 1625 coincided with the accession of Charles I, and thus with the rise to influence of William Laud, as Bishop of London and then, from 1633, as Archbishop of Canterbury. Bargrave himself took an ardent delight in music, and contributed his own, apparently somewhat taurine, bass voice to the singing in choir;[171] in all likelihood he was no unwilling conduit for Laud's ambition to make of his Cathedral a cynosure and show-case of Arminian principles of worship in practice.

George Marson was nearing the end of his career, and until 1630 there was little copying of new music; nevertheless, expensive campaigns of repair for the music-books suggest that

[168] At least, only modest fines were levied in the two years for which evidence survives: Misc. Accts. 41, fos. 256 (1604–5), 265–268ᵛ (1622–3).

[169] Chapter Act Book, 1581–1607, fos. 265, 268, 281ᵛ; Misc. Accts. 41, fos. 184, 242ᵛ, 256ᵛ.

[170] The scheme was introduced progressively between 1619 and 1627: 'Feoda et regarda' sections of Treasurer's Accts. 28–35.

[171] R. Culmer, *Dean and Chapter Newes from Canterbury 1644* (2nd edn.; London, 1649), sigs. C1ᵛ–C2.

the performance of the existing repertory remained at least industrious and vigorous.[172] It appears that Bargrave sought at first to make a mark on the Cathedral's music through initiatives that were prompted very probably by practices that he had encountered on his missions to Italy, and especially to Venice: he aimed principally at the enhancement of the actual tonal splendour of the impact made by the music of the services, through expanded participation of the available instrumental resources. The lay clerks' chest of viols was kept, with a chamber organ made for Bargrave, in the Deanery, where it was probably intended primarily for the provision of elevated diversion and entertainment for distinguished guests. However, it appears that at this time it may also have begun to be put to some use for the accompaniment of verse anthems in choir; during 1626–7 the quite considerable sum of 40s. was spent on the creation or provision of a book of *cantiones*— the accountant's usual term for polyphonic compositions for the church services—'for the viols'. Indeed, one of the two surviving sacred compositions by William Pysing, the verse anthem 'The Lord hear thee in the time of trouble', was written expressly for the combination of voices and viols.[173]

A second initiative of this period concerned the character of the role of the wind-band in services on festivals and their eves; for while it remained usual for functional or even total illiterates to be appointed to play cornett, the signatures of the sackbut-players show that from about the mid-1620s their appointments were being conferred on literate men of good education. It is more than probable that the Chapter's policy in respect of the sackbutteers was now to appoint performers able to play from written notation; indeed, in 1625 repairs were put in hand on what was now described as the 'Sackbut book', and in 1634–5 payment was made 'for prickinge one service in both Sackbut bookes'.[174] From the mid-1620s, therefore, it is possible to conceive of at least one, and commonly both, of the sackbutteers (though not the players on cornett) contributing to the performance of accompanied choral music on festivals and their eves—probably to double the organ bass where appropriate, and so compensate for the absence of pedal tone on the contemporary English organ. This new distinction between the cornetteers and sackbutteers found reflection in their respective patterns of attendance; the record of one sackbutteer was exemplary and that of the other only somewhat less so, while that of the cornetteers was apparently negligent and haphazard.[175]

Early in Bargrave's deanship, the Chapter took advantage of Marson's advancing years to introduce at Canterbury a salutary development that since about 1610 had already been initiated at a number of cathedral and collegiate churches, namely the separation of the offices of Organist and of Master of the Choristers, so allowing two men each to exercise a professional specialism in these two entirely distinct fields. The formula adopted at Canterbury was that which was standard; the office of greater prestige was that of the Organist, appointed and salaried in his own right, while that of Master of the Choristers

[172] Treasurer's Accts. 33, fo. 3; ibid. 36, fo. 3ᵛ; ibid. 38, fo. 2.

[173] 'Expensae Necessariae' sections of Treasurer's Accts. 33–47; Treasurer's Accts. 35, fo. 4; Misc. Accts. 41, fo. 427; Legg and Hope, *Inventories*, 261; F. W. Galpin, 'An Old English Positive Organ', *Musical Antiquary*, 4 (1912–13), 20–30; C. Monson, *Voices and Viols in England, 1600–50* (Ann Arbor, Mich., 1982), 31, 54.

[174] Marks and signatures: Misc. Accts. 41, fos. 269, 347ʳ⁻ᵛ, 408, 474, 535; Treasurer's Accts. 33, fo. 3; Misc. Accts. 41, fo. 427.

[175] Misc. Accts. 41, fos. 474, 535.

was exercised by one whose primary employment and remuneration was as a singing-man of the choir. At Christmas 1627 Marson surrendered the latter office, his place being taken by William Pysing, who himself had been a chorister between 1615 and 1617; Pysing retained the appointment until the civil wars, and filled it again from 1660 until his death in 1684, occupying a lay clerkship also from 1630.[176]

Marson continued to serve as Organist until his death in February 1632. For a few months, the lay clerk Francis Plummer (chorister, 1612–19; substitute, 1621–4; lay clerk, 1624–Civil War) served as acting Organist, but early in November 1632 the Chapter made the appointment of its first full-time specialist Organist, Valentine Rother. He retained the appointment until some time between 1637 and 1639; he was succeeded by Thomas Tunstall, who was still in office at Michaelmas 1642. Of neither man is anything at all known beyond the dates of their Canterbury appointments.[177]

Such a departure, costing between £20 and £30 per year in salary alone, clearly reflected a substantial change and expansion in the prevailing perception of the role of the organ and organist in the music of the services. Hitherto, the function of the organ may well have been modest, extending little beyond the performance of brief 'voluntaries' before each canticle (with little objective beyond giving the singers the pitch), and the sounding of the keyboard accompaniments to services and anthems in verse style. Now, in the Laudian 1630s, the organ was being given a new role, that of adding brilliance and splendour to the ritual by accompanying also the large corpus of anthems and services that had originally been composed in full, properly unaccompanied, style. In Rother's first two years, several books of (blank) paper were procured for the organist, and 151 pages of the music of service settings ('of the Magnificats'), as well as 114 pages of unspecified music, were copied in. The scribe was Francis Plummer, who in the following year completed the task, with the copying of accompaniments to full anthems (seventy pages) and to festal psalms (fifty-three pages). This was music which its composers had never expected or intended to be accompanied, and it must be stressed that the role of the organ was not the support of feeble singing, but simply the addition of a whole new layer of extroversion and brilliance to the performance of music which had always been completely self-sufficient, if less demonstrative, without this gratuitous organ-doubling of the vocal lines. The inventory of music so created was maintained and added to thereafter, and the chest purchased for the use of the organist in 1639–40 was probably to help him keep in good order his growing stock of books.[178] As might be expected, this increased use of the organ from the early 1630s resulted in ever-growing annual bills for maintenance and repair, over and above the terms of Burward's maintenance contract.[179]

Archbishop Laud's concern for the projection of seemliness and magnificence in the services of his Cathedral church was made evident from the start. The Chapter assured his 1634 visitation that 'we do most willingly maintain for the decorum of our quire' the band of wind-players, who since Laud's accession had been appearing in choir clad in

[176] Treasurer's Accts. 36, fo. 3; ibid. 38, fo. 4.[v]
[177] *Register Booke of Christninges, Marriages, and Burialls within the Precinct of the Cathedrall and Metropoliticall Church of Christe of Canterburie*, ed. R. Hovenden (London, 1878), 9; Misc. Accts. 41, fos. 358[r–v], 419[r–v]; Treasurer's Accts. 40, fo. 2; ibid. 41, fo. 3;
ibid. 44, fo. 2[v]; ibid. 45, fo. 2[v]; ibid. 46, fo. 2[v]; ibid. 47, fo. 2[v].
[178] Treasurer's Accts. 41, fos. 3[v], 4; ibid. 42, fo. 3[v]; ibid. 44, fo. 3[v]; ibid. 45, fo. 3[v]; Misc. Accts. 41, fos. 368, 427.
[179] 'Expensae necessariae' sections of Treasurer's Accts. 39–43, 45.

surplices, newly made; Laud's revision of the statutes, completed in 1637, created for the band a formal place in the constitution of the Cathedral, as it also sanctioned the division of the offices of Master of the Choristers and Organist.[180] No less importantly, Laud also was evidently the initiating force behind the Chapter's provisions of 1636 substantially to increase the annual stipends of the minor canons (to £15 6s. 8d.), lay clerks (to £15), and substitutes (to £13), expanding the Chapter's own small-scale initiative of 1627.[181]

Further, while the progressive replacement of George Marson by younger men was probably the cause of a marked resumption in music-copying and repertory-building in 1630, it may well have been the Laudian influence (via the Chapter) that ensured that this campaign, unlike all others before it, did not burn out but continued unabated through the 1630s, possibly even gathering intensity as the decade ended. Few details are vouchsafed by the trite formalities of the accounts, but four blank paper books were bought in 1630–1, and two more in the year following; and up to 1636, £8 13s. 0d. (692 pages at the new rate of 3d. per page) had been spent on copying new music, while the old books were kept in due repair. An inventory taken in November 1634 appears to record, in very untechnical language, the current existence of no fewer than ten sets of part-books of services and anthems; this repertory was probably very similar in both volume and content to that of Durham Cathedral, where to this day there remain no fewer than twenty-seven books of choir music copied between c.1620 and 1641, surviving from at least five sets of part-books.[182] Momentum increased in 1636–7, with purchases of fresh paper and the expenditure of £7 12s. 6d. (610 pages) on copying in that single year alone; it is particularly unfortunate that the accounts for the next two years are lost, since in 1639–40 there was still substantial activity, extending to expenditure on copying of £4 14s. 3d. (377 pages). The scale of all this work may be gauged from the detail that 2s. 6d. sufficed to recompense a copyist for entering one anthem into eight books in 1634–5.[183] One driving force behind this activity may well have been the Master of the Choristers, William Pysing. Two verse anthems of his composition have survived, so the setting of the litany and the substantial 'new setting' which he himself copied into his books in 1634 and 1639–40 may well have been of his own composition.[184]

Particularly revelatory of the importance of decorum and seemliness in the public recitation of the divine office in the Laudian Cathedral was the need felt by even the Chapter to be seen to be not merely presiding observers but (as far as possible) actively participating members of the body of clerks offering the daily office. To this end, between 1631 and 1636, books of choir-parts were written out severally for the Dean and residentiary

[180] Misc. Accts. 41, fos. 367, 369; Treasurer's Accts. 42, fo. 3ᵛ; 'Papers Relating to Archbishop Laud's Visitations: Canterbury, 1634', HMC, 4th *Report* (1874), app., p. 125; *Statutes of the Cathedral and Metropolitical Church of Christ, Canterbury*, ed. G. K. A. Bell (priv. printed, Canterbury, 1925), 4, 54–6.

[181] Chapter Act Book, 1608–28, fo. 296; Treasurer's Accts. 40, fo. 4; ibid. 41, fo. 4; MS Cat. 80: letters (on leaves unfol.), grp. I, items 1, 4, and grp. II, item 5 (transcript, not wholly accurate, of first and third letters in C. E. Woodruff, 'Some Seventeenth-Century Letters and Petitions from the Muniments of the Dean and Chapter of Canterbury', *Arch. Cant.*, 42 (1930), III, 121);

Treasurer's Accts. 44, fo. 4; ibid. 45, fo. 4, etc. See also P. Collinson, above, pp. 188–90.

[182] Treasurer's Accts. 39, fo. 4; ibid. 40, fo. 3ᵛ; ibid. 41, fo. 3ᵛ; ibid. 42, fo. 3ᵛ; ibid. 43 fo. 4; Misc. Accts. 41, fos. 367ʳ⁻ᵛ, 368ᵛ; Legg and Hope, *Inventories*, 256; B. Crosby, *A Catalogue of Durham Cathedral Music Manuscripts* (Oxford, 1986), pp. xiii–xv.

[183] Treasurer's Accts. 44, fo. 3; ibid. 45, fo. 3; Misc. Accts. 41, fo. 427.

[184] A. Ashbee, 'Pysing, William', in *New Grove Dictionary* (cit. in n. 142), xv. 484; Misc. Accts. 41, fo. 368ᵛ; Treasurer's Accts. 42, fo. 3ᵛ; ibid. 45, fo. 3.

canons, eight in all; it is possible that these were merely books of the words of anthems, but the terminology used suggests that they included music also.[185] To how much, and to how good, use they were put, it may perhaps be preferable not to speculate.

It is particularly fortunate that it should be from exactly this period that a few leaves from one of the Cathedral's choirbooks should actually have survived. The Cathedral possesses one volume (First Contratenor, Cantoris) out of what must once have been a complete ten-volume set of John Barnard's printed collection *The First Book of Selected Church Musick*, which bears a publication date of 1641. This contains a comprehensive collection of compositions in all the forms used in the church music of its day: responses and festal psalms, services (elaborate whole services for feast-days, expansive evening services for their eves, and short services for ordinary daily use), and anthems, all in both full and verse style in up to seven parts. It would undoubtedly have been a most valuable resource for the Canterbury choir to have possessed; however, its current binding (marked 'Christ Church Canterbury') appears to be of Restoration rather than pre-Civil War date, and there can be no certainty that the original set of books was at Canterbury before 1660. Bound in with it, however, are fourteen folios of manuscript music that are in a hand of about the second quarter of the seventeenth century, and these do seem certain to constitute an actual remnant of a pre-Civil War volume of Canterbury provenance. As well as works of local origin, the music ranges from the finest productions of the leading composers of the day to nothing less than the good metropolitan works of the London-based professionals. In the second category are the demanding verse anthem 'Glorious and powerful God' by Orlando Gibbons, and 'Lord, let me know mine end' and 'Thou art my king, O God' by Thomas Tomkins; in the third, items such as John Ward's Second Service, Thomas Holmes's 'O Lord, I bow the knees of my heart', Albert Bryne's 'I heard a voice', and also 'Hear my prayer, O Lord' by Thomas Wilkinson, of Trinity College, Cambridge. George Marson's Second Service and five-part full anthem 'O gracious God of Heaven' (Pls. 83, 84) represent the local interest, while William Cranford's ubiquitous 'O Lord, make thy servant Charles our king' was a very appropriate item for a soundly royalist and Laudian institution. A visitor of 1635, one Lieutenant Hammond, who rather fancied himself a connoisseur of church music, was pleased to record in his journal how in the Cathedral he 'saw and heard a fayre Organ sweet and tunable, and a deep and ravishing consort of Quirsters'; and indeed, the slight and fortuitous cross-section of the content of the Cathedral's accumulation of pieces in use in the 1630s that is revealed by these manuscript leaves shows that its choir was not concerned with music on merely a small or provincial scale, but comprehended both full and verse examples of the major and most demanding mainstream sacred repertory.[186]

[185] Treasurer's Accts. 40, fo. 3ᵛ; ibid. 41, fo. 3ᵛ; ibid. 42, fo. 3ᵛ; ibid. 43, fo. 4; Misc. Accts. 41, fos. 367, 368, 368ᵛ, 392ᵛ.

[186] Music MS 1A; the manuscript music is fos. 135–42 and 173–68 (reversed). Other manuscript additions occupy fos. 143–68 and 189–74; these are in five different hands, all of post-Restoration date (c.1660–1700). The identifications here have been assisted by the typescript catalogue of the Canterbury music manuscripts prepared by Dr Robert Ford. 'A Relation of a Short Survey of the Western Counties made by a Lieutenant of the Military Company of Norwich in 1635', ed. L. G. W. Legg, in *Camden Miscellany*, 16 (Camden Soc., 3rd ser., 52; 1936), pp. vii, 11.

The National Crisis of 1639–42 and the Extinction of the Sung Cathedral Service

The deepening national crisis from 1639 onwards cannot have left the Precincts of Canterbury Cathedral unscathed, yet the remaining evidence seems to suggest that, even after the first shocks of January 1641, the community's concern was, with an obstinacy born of conviction, firmly to maintain 'business as usual'. But by the late 1630s the projection of Laud's metropolitan church as a showcase of Arminianism in action had begun to generate in the city a counter-sentiment, according to which the manner of service as conducted there was perceived as crypto-papist and subversive of the Protestant reformation of ninety years before. Rather than inspire awe and deference, the Laudian service and the apparatus by which it was sustained was generating offence, abhorrence, and complaint. Thus, by 1640, the manner in which 'The Pettie Canons and Singingmen there sing their Cathedrall Service in Prick-Song after the Romish fashion' had become a source of grievance; the practice of appointing minor canons to livings in the city, though they were insufficiently learned in theology to instruct and preach, was a further source of anger and distress.[187]

It was the elevated nature of the Cathedral music, rather than the mere facts of singing and organ-playing, that were arousing godly indignation; it was, indeed, with approval that the iconoclast Richard Culmer recorded the congregational singing of metrical psalms with organ support at the weekly public sermons that were delivered on Sunday afternoons in the Sermon House. An organ had first been installed there at Christmas 1625; George Marson and Francis Plummer had been appointed to play at sermon time, Plummer continuing alone after Marson's death.[188] It was the Chapter's decision, some time in 1640, to move the location of the weekly sermon to the choir of the Cathedral, where it was 'hemd in with their Quire service [so] that all that will partake of the Sermon, should of necessity partake of their Cathedrall-Ceremonious-Altar-Service' also, that provoked the first open outburst of popular disaffection. On the feast of the Epiphany (6 January) 1641, the sermon congregation, thus constrained to remain also for Evensong, perceived an insupportable degree of provocation in the clergy's practice of bowing the knee in reverence of the high altar: the service was seriously disrupted with cries of 'This is idolatry . . . leave your idolatry'. On the Sunday following, mere barracking became mass defiance. The preacher completed his sermon, and a metrical psalm was begun; the organist chose the first section of Psalm 119, and the three officiants processed to the altar, 'ducking, ducking, ducking like wild-geese, head to tail', to commence the liturgy of Evensong. The people would have none of this popery; Psalm 119 has not one section but twenty-two, and spontaneously the congregation took it into its collective head to frustrate the start of the Office by launching precipitately into section two, and thus defiantly to keep on singing. From among the throng was heard the threatening cry 'Downe with the Altar, downe with the Altar'. In alarm, clergy and choir forsook the sanctuary, and left their evening prayer abandoned and unsung; their object achieved, the people 'did depart home quietly'. Badly intimidated, the residentiaries prevailed upon the Dean (absent at Westminster for the Convocation) to agree to restore the preaching of the sermon to

---

[187] Culmer, *Dean and Chapter Newes* (cit. in n. 171), sigs. B1ʳ⁻ᵛ, D1ᵛ.

[188] Ibid., sig. D1; Chapter Act Book, 1608–28, p. 232, fos. 264, 271ᵛ, 275ᵛ; Treasurer's Accts. 34, fo. 3, 3ᵛ; ibid. 41, fo. 3.

the Sermon House, to distance the malcontents from the choir service they evidently abominated.[189]

Open malcontentment was for a time assuaged, and some small re-expression of the Cathedral community's royalism may be discerned in the payment to William Pysing of 5*s.* for copying 'a new Anthem upon the King's day' on 7 April 1641.[190] Nevertheless, the fact that this was the only payment for music-copying made during the whole of 1640–1, while there were no payments at all during 1641–2, suggests that there had now been generated among the Cathedral management at least a degree of hesitation and apprehension about the possible eventual visitation of retribution upon overt practitioners of Laudian High Churchmanship. On 2 February 1642 iconoclasts gained entry to the Cathedral at night and vandalized the recently installed baptismal font; the Chapter, refusing to be intimidated this time, responded with defiance. The canons effected the conversion of the communion table to a high altar restored to its canonical position at the east end of the choir, and preached a series of incendiary sermons, including one on Trinity Sunday 1642 by Dean Bargrave vehemently defending 'Church musick and Organs'.[191]

Such provocation presently reaped condign reward. On 26 August 1642, barely days after open hostilities had been declared, the parliamentary soldiery of Colonel Sandys and the future regicide Michael Livesey gained entrance to the Cathedral, and took the opportunity to visit a godly orgy of retributive plunder upon the ornaments, furnishings, and fittings of the choir. The high altar was overturned and the altar rails destroyed; images and tapestries were violated and defaced. Bibles and Prayer Books suffered without distinction; the great lectern of bronze was tumbled down. The organ was despoiled; the music books were rent in pieces and scattered about the floor, or looted for use in a burlesque horse-back parody of the Cathedral service as presently the soldiery rode away towards Dover.[192]

The Cathedral community was left to survey the damage. Some, including that to the organ, was superficial and could be repaired; but the effective extinction of the manuscript repertory of polyphonic music must have seemed irreparable. Moreover, hostilities having now broken out, the Chapter clearly believed that it had neither the right nor the duty to expose the men and boys of the choir to the danger of violence and retribution which any attempt to restore the Laudian Cathedral service must have seemed certain to provoke. The sung service was discontinued; the choir was abandoned as a place of worship, and left disused for eighteen years.[193] By the havoc of 26 August 1642 the sung liturgy of Canterbury Cathedral was silenced, and not heard again until the restoration of the king and the Anglican Church in 1660.

---

[189] Culmer, *Dean and Chapter Newes* (cit. in n. 171), sigs. B1ᵛ, D1ʳ⁻ᵛ; Christ Church Letters, iii. 76; Canterbury Letters to 1661, no. 84.

[190] Misc. Accts. 41, fo. 491.

[191] Culmer, *Dean and Chapter Newes* (cit. in n. 171), sig. C1ᵛ.

[192] Ibid., sig. D1ᵛ–2; see also P. Collinson, above, p. 195.

[193] Treasurer's Accts. 47, fo. 3; Misc. Accts. 41, fo. 555ʳ⁻ᵛ; Culmer, *Dean and Chapter Newes* (cit. in n. 171), sig. D2.

X

The Medieval Monuments

CHRISTOPHER WILSON

On 10 January 1302 the Archbishop of Canterbury, Robert Winchelsey, issued a letter intended to round off a comprehensively damning diocesan visitation which he had conducted during the previous year. The letter was addressed to the Prior of Worcester Cathedral Priory and ordered nothing less than the immediate removal of the monument which the aged and infirm Bishop Giffard had recently prepared for himself on the south side of the sanctuary. Giffard's monument was objectionable on several counts: it kept daylight from the high altar; it took up space where there ought to have been seats for the officiating clergy; it incorporated a canopy which rose higher than the nearby shrine of St Oswald; and it usurped the place previously occupied by the tomb of a bishop popularly regarded as a saint. The Archbishop conceded that the new tomb might be re-erected in a less elevated position, where it would become more accessible to passers-by. He concluded by observing that though the honour of a church could be enhanced by a prelate's much-visited and beautiful monument the ministers of that church must never be the cause of lowering its standing.[1]

Clerical protests against the invasion of church interiors by tombs were nothing new— they had been voiced for almost a thousand years[2]—but in his parting shot at the Prior of Worcester, Winchelsey seems to have come closer than any other English medieval bishop to defining the positive attributes of church monuments. His failure to make explicit reference to their primary function as stimulants to the living to pray for the early release from Purgatory of the souls of those commemorated is unlikely to have occasioned surprise, given the universal currency which this concept had attained by the thirteenth century.[3] His determination to condemn the Giffard monument on account of its intrusiveness would probably also have seemed unremarkable to most observers, for in 1302 the

---

[1] R. Graham, 'The Metropolitical Visitation of the Diocese of Worcester by Archbishop Winchelsey in 1301', *TRHS*, 4th ser., 2 (1919), 72, 91–2; J. M. Wilson, 'The Liber Albus of the Priory of Worcester', *Worcester Hist. Soc. Publ.*, 38 (London, 1919), pp. xxi, 5, 8; *Registrum Roberti Winchelsey Cantuariensis Archiepiscopi, 1294–1313*, ed. R. Graham, 2 vols. (CYS 51–2; 1952–6), 761–2.

[2] See n. 8 below.

[3] There can be little doubt that the extraordinary proliferation of both soul masses and monuments which the 12th and 13th centuries witnessed was linked to the formalization of the doctrine of Purgatory during the same period. Although this rise in the demand for monuments was not accompanied by a proportionate increase in theoretical writing about them, the subject received authoritative treatment from St Thomas Aquinas in quest. 71, art. 11 of his *Summa Theologiae*, anon. edn.

grandiose canopied tombs developed in England during the previous two decades must have become recognizable as a potentially serious threat to the liturgical, symbolic, and aesthetic integrity of the host churches. Clearly the Archbishop was ready to accept that even the new type of monument might add to the prestige and amenity of a cathedral, but it is safe to assume that he would have regarded any monument as unimportant beside the altars and shrines which were the true goal of the passers-by mentioned in his remonstrance to the Prior of Worcester. The monks of Christ Church, Canterbury, who may or may not have been aware of their titular abbot's stand over the Giffard tomb, were evidently of the same mind, for very large monuments such as they had just begun to admit into their church were never to be allowed to jostle the great array of altars and relics which was its peculiar glory.[4]

In 1302 the fittings of the eastern arm of Canterbury Cathedral were in process of renewal, but the liturgical layout which they defined remained that established after the reconstruction of the early twelfth-century choir in 1175–84. In the course of that rebuilding, all tombs had been moved out of the two main areas appropriated to the cult of St Thomas Becket, namely the enlarged Trinity Chapel, destined to house the principal shrine, and the crypt below this chapel, where the saint's original burial-place was situated.[5] Such 'tomb-free zones' were an extreme and comparatively rare way of indicating the great distance separating ordinary mortals from the sainted dead, 'the princes of the heavenly kingdom',[6] but at Christ Church, as elsewhere, the clearances

(5 vols.; Ottawa, 1941–5), v. 325–7). Aquinas's account owes much to St Augustine's writings, notably the *De Cura pro Mortuis Gerenda ad Paulinum*, cap. 2 (Migne, *PL*, xl, col. 596) and the *De Civitate Dei*, lib. 1, capp. 12–13 (ed. D. Dombart and A. Kalb, *Corpus Christianorum, Series Latina*, 47 (Turnhout, 1960), 13–15). In the latter, Augustine, who was hostile to sumptuous burial practices of all kinds, states that the decent burial of the bodies of the righteous builds up faith in the Resurrection among the living, while stressing that the hope of Resurrection is not at all dependent on such burial. Aquinas was more positive about tombs, whose relation to the Purgatory concept he spelled out. Direct appeals for prayers were inscribed on many medieval tombs, though not normally on the monuments of the nobility and higher clergy, those best placed to enhance their prospects in the next life by engaging in good works and paying for soul masses. An exception to this general rule among the Canterbury tombs is the inscription on the Black Prince's monument.

[4] In 1302 Westminster Abbey was the English church whose sanctuary was most encumbered by canopy tombs, and it is very likely that this example was in Winchelsey's mind—and indeed in Giffard's when he commissioned his monument. The surviving elements of the latter are of metropolitan workmanship. The positions of the shrines in Canterbury Cathedral at the time of the 1174 fire (which, except for that of St Anselm, were the same as when the choir was dedicated in 1130) are given in Gervase's account of the burning and rebuilding in his *Chronica*, in Gervase, *Historical Works*, i. 10–11, 14–16. A translation of these passages and a list of shrines and tombs are in R. Willis, *The Architectural History of Canterbury Cathedral* (London, 1845), 37–40, 44–7, 133–5.

[5] For the liturgical layout of the sanctuary, see A. Reader-

Moore, 'The Liturgical Chancel of Canterbury Cathedral', *Cant. Cath. Chron.* 73 (1979), 25–44. For the post-1174 moving of tombs, see Gervase, *Historical Works*, i. 22–6. The ban on tombs did not, of course, extend to saints' shrines, and those of Sts Wilfrid and Oda were installed in the Corona, the 'chancel' of the Trinity Chapel, much as they had been in the old Trinity Chapel: Legg and Hope, *Inventories*, 34–5; anonymous early 16th-cent. monk of Christ Church, Canterbury, list of archbishops' and priors' burial-places, Cambridge, Corpus Christi College, MS 298, p. 103. As Gervase makes clear, all the archbishops' tombs in the chapel of St John the Baptist and St Augustine of Canterbury, below the Romanesque Trinity Chapel, were moved out after the 1174 fire, but what is not clear is whether the numerous coffin-lids to be seen in the crypt under the Gothic Trinity Chapel in the late 18th cent. (E. Hasted, *The History of the ... City of Canterbury ...* (2 vols.; London, 1801) i. 417) were late medieval or whether they were the residue of burials moved out after 1174. Given that the floor of the Trinity Chapel crypt was tiled at the charge of a monk who died in 1414 (ibid. i. 363), the former dating seems the more likely. The present concrete floor of *c.*1893 contains only one grave-slab in the central vessel, and markings indicating the positions of two coffins in the north aisle. A burial recorded because St Thomas's tomb stood immediately to the east of it is that of William of Andeville, Abbot of Evesham (d. 1159), a former monk of Christ Church (*Chronicon Abbatiae de Evesham*, ed. W. D. Macray (RS 29; 1863), 99–100), and the only uncanonized prelate other than an Archbishop of Canterbury known to have received burial in the eastern part of the Cathedral.

[6] This phrase occurs in Goscelin of Saint-Bertin, *Historia Translationis S. Augustini Episcopi*, lib. 1, cap. 2 (Migne, *PL*, clv, col. 15).

did not endure, and the fourteenth and fifteenth centuries saw a resurgence of the primordial desire to lie *ad sanctos*.[7] Even so, the Christ Church monks succeeded in restricting burial in the eastern parts of their church to prelates and royalty, the two groups whose right to burial in church was almost universally accepted during the Middle Ages.[8] By insisting on an orderly and considered disposition of tombs within the parts of the church which were pre-eminently theirs, and by securing the symbolic and visual subordination of tombs to shrines, the monks were able to contrive an exceptionally compelling demonstration of the solidarity which existed between them, their earthly leaders, and their sanctified patrons (Fig. 2). Even in the nave, where burial of non-royal laity was permitted, the operation of the hierarchical principle inherent in all medieval concepts of order ensured that the choicest positions were reserved to archbishops and priors (Fig. 1).[9]

THE ARCHBISHOPS' MONUMENTS

The most important 'victims' of the post-1174 clearance of tombs were Archbishops Lanfranc (d. 1089) and Theobald (d. 1161). In 1180 both bodies were removed out of the small Trinity Chapel at the east of the Romanesque choir and were not readmitted to its

[7] In the 13th-cent. cathedral at Chartres no tombs have ever been introduced, despite the fact that the preceding church contained them, and at Durham Cathedral the first burial in the church took place only in 1311. For burial *ad sanctos*, see, most recently, Y. Duval, 'Sanctorum sepulchris sociari', in *Les Fonctions des saints dans le monde occidental (IIIᵉ–XIIIᵉ siècles). Actes du colloque organisé par l'École française de Rome avec le concours de l'Université de Rome 'La Sapienza', Rome, 27–9 octobre 1988*, Collection de l'École française de Rome, 149 (Rome, 1991), 333–51. While warning against vainglorious motives, Aquinas admitted the value of burial *ad sanctos*: *Summa Theologiae* (cit. in n. 3).

[8] Lay persons' graves in churches were forbidden at the Councils of Vaison (442), Braga (563), and Nantes (658), but the Council of Mainz (813) allowed the tombs of bishops and abbots, and 'fideles laici', meaning effectively kings, princes, and patrons and founders of churches: P. Hofmeister, 'Das Gotteshaus als Begräbnisstätte', *Archiv für katholisches Kirchenrecht*, 111 (1931), 450–87; A. Grabar, *Martyrium* (2 vols.; Paris, 1946), i. 550; H. s'Jacob, *Idealism and Realism: A Study of Sepulchral Symbolism* (Leiden, 1954), 278; A. Geitner, 'Grab, III: Im Christentum', in *Lexikon für Theologie und Kirche* (11 vols.; Freiburg i. B., 1957–67), iv, cols. 1154–6; P. Grierson, 'The Tombs and Obits of the Byzantine Emperors (337–1042)', *Dumbarton Oaks Papers*, 16 (1962), 6 (n. 26), 25 (n. 76); R. Krautheimer, 'Zu Konstantins Apostelkirche in Konstantinopel', *Mullus: Festschrift Theodor Klauser*, ed. A. Stuiber and H. Hermann (Münster, 1964), 224–9; K. H. Krüger, *Königskirchen der Franken, Angelsachsen und Langobarden bis zur Mitte des 8. Jahrhunderts* (Münstersche Mittelalter-Schriften, 4; Munich, 1971). At Christ Church, Canterbury, the strength of the allegiance to the Holy See must account in large part for the fact that the traditional pre-Christian Roman ban on intramural burials remained in

force until 740, when Archbishop Cuthbert obtained papal permission for a cemetery and a detached baptistery-cum-mausoleum dedicated to St John the Baptist, which was intended to house the tombs of himself and his successors: Gervase, *Historical Works*, ii. 345. Suggestively, the first burials of non-sainted popes inside the nave of the (extramural) church of St Peter in the Vatican date from immediately before the grant to Cuthbert (I. Herklotz, 'Sepulcra' e 'monumenta' nel medioevo: *Studi sull'arte sepolcrale in Italia* (Rome, 1985), 85), but the main aim in building St John's was no doubt to enhance the resemblance of Christ Church to Rome's cathedral, whose baptistery was already of such importance that the church itself, though originally dedicated to Christ, was coming to be thought of as dedicated to the Baptist. St John's, Canterbury, like the other late-Antique and early-medieval baptisteries which contained tombs, was ultimately inspired by Rom. 6: 3–4, where St Paul links baptism and burial as means to gaining eternal life through Christ. The first Archbishop of Canterbury buried in Christ Church appears to have been its rebuilder Oda (d. 958). For what may well have been the last attempt by an English bishop to limit lay burial in church, made in 1292, see *Councils and Synods Relating to the English Church*, ii. *AD 1205–1313*, ed. F. M. Powicke and C. R. Cheney (2 pts.; Oxford, 1964), pt. 2. 1117.

[9] For a 14th-cent. German treatise purporting to establish the correct placing of tombs in churches, relative to the rank of the deceased, see Geitner, 'Grab' (cit. in n. 8), col. 1154. The monuments in the nave and choir at Canterbury conformed to the usages defined in this text in so far as sites under the main arcade arches were reserved to archbishops. A recent discussion of the hierarchy of place in relation to burial is V. Harding, 'Burial Choice and Burial Location in Later Medieval London', in *Death in Towns: Urban Responses to the Dying and the Dead 100–1600*, ed. S. Bassett (Leicester, 1992), 119–35.

KEY TO MONUMENTS

1 Archbishop Richard of Dover (d. 1184)
2 Archbishop Simon Islip (d. 1366), site of
   monument from early 17th century
3 Archbishop Islip, approximate original site of
   monument
4 Archbishop William Wittersley (d. 1374)
5 Archbishop Thomas Arundel (d. 1414)
6 John Buckingham, Bishop of Lincoln (d. 1399)
7 Prior Thomas Chillenden (d. 1411)
8 Prior John Wodnesbergh (d. 1428)
9 Prior John Salisbury (d. 1446)
10 Prior John Elham (d. 1449)
11 Sir William Brenchley (d. 1406) and Lady Joan
   Brenchley (d. 1453)
12 ? Sir Robert Clifford (d. 1423)

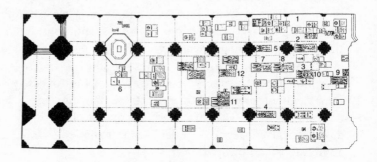

FIG. 1 Nave floor, showing brass indents etc. removed in 1787. Drawn by Jesse White, 1786. (Surveys & Maps 104.
Key numbers added.)

much more spacious replacement, completed in 1184.[10] The first, and for almost 200 years
the only, burial here was very much a special case. Archbishop **Hubert Walter** (d. 1205)
was never a candidate for canonization, but he had earned the undying gratitude of the
monks by abandoning the scheme initiated by his predecessor Baldwin to create a new
archiepiscopal foundation of Lambeth.[11] The siting of the tomb (Pl. 90) in a window
embrasure can be explained in terms of the need to avoid obstructing the future pilgrim-
route to St Thomas's principal shrine.[12] In its location on the south side, rather than on
the more honorific north side, which was symbolic of a place at God's right hand and
normally reserved to such exalted persons as founders, Hubert's tomb anticipates the

[10] At the same time as Lanfranc's and Theobald's bodies were moved, those of Archbishops Æthelred (d. 888) and Eadsige (d. 1050) were transferred from the south and north sides of the chapel in the crypt below the Romanesque Trinity Chapel, to positions under the main crypt altar, that of St Mary, directly under the high altar: Gervase, *Historical Works*, i. 26. Their bodies remained there for the rest of the Middle Ages: early 16th-cent. list of archbishops' and priors' burial places (cit. in n. 5), 101, 104. Lanfranc's tomb in the Trinity Chapel had been close to the south wall and Theobald's close to the north wall: Gervase, *Historical Works*, i. 16. Lanfranc's original burial-place, in the nave before the rood (*The Ecclesiastical History of Orderic Vitalis*, ed. M. Chibnall (6 vols.; Oxford, 1969–80), iv. 170), was even more honorific; cf. the burial of Remigius, Bishop of Lincoln in 1092 'in prospectu altaris sanctae crucis': *Vita S. Remigii*, in *Giraldi Cambrensis Opera*, ed. J. F. Dimock, 8 vols. (RS 21; 1861–91), vii. 22. See also F. Oswald, ' "In medio ecclesiae": Die Deutung der literarischen Zeugnisse im Lichte archäologischer Funde', *Frühmittelalterliche Studien*, 3 (1969), 313–26. In 1180 Lanfranc was reburied in the north-east transept (see n. 13 below), and Theobald was transferred to the Lady

Chapel in the eastern bays of the north nave aisle, a move which Gervase justified by claiming that Theobald had himself desired to lie there: *Historical Works*, i. 26. Perhaps to mitigate any slight done to Theobald's memory, Archbishop Richard of Dover (d. 1184) was entombed in the same chapel: ibid. 400. For the finding of Theobald's leaden coffin in 1787, at a spot not precisely indicated, see H. Boys, 'Observations on the ... Tomb of Theobald ...', *Archaeologia*, 15 (1806), 291–9. Richard of Dover's empty coffin was revealed in the 1993 nave excavations.

[11] Hubert Walter's monument was correctly identified for the first time since the 16th cent. in W. A. Scott Robertson, 'Christ Church Canterbury: Chronological Conspectus of the Existing Architecture ...', *Arch. Cant.*, 14 (1882), 284. For a discussion of the earlier historiography of the tomb, a report of its opening and partial dismantling on 8 Mar. 1890, see id., 'Burial Places of the Archbishops of Canterbury', ibid. 20 (1893), 280–8. On Baldwin's and Hubert Walter's proposed foundation see above, pp. 66–7, 74.

[12] The window embrasure chosen, that on the south side of the Trinity Chapel, is the best for its purpose as it is the longest and the only one which is correctly orientated.

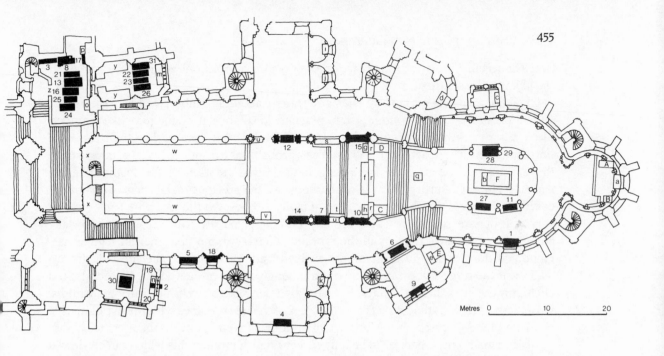

FIG. 2 Eastern parts of the church as in 1538, showing monuments in relation to other features. Drawn by Christopher Wilson.

MAJOR SHRINES

A St Wilfrid
B St Oda
C St Dunstan
D St Alphege
E St Anselm
F St Thomas

ALTARS

a Holy Trinity
b St Thomas
c St Edward
d St Andrew
e St Peter and St Paul
f Christ (high altar)
g St Alphege
h St Dunstan
i St Martin
j St Stephen
k St John Evangelist
l St Gregory
m Assumption of Blessed Virgin Mary and St Benedict
n St Michael and St Anne
o Martyrdom of St Thomas (Altar of the Sword's Point)
p The Saviour, All Saints, Blessed Virgin Mary, and St Margaret

MAJOR FITTINGS

q Chair of St Augustine
r High altar screen
s Relic cupboard
t Sedilia
u Choir enclosure
v Archbishop's throne
w Choir-stalls
x Choir screen
y Lady Chapel stalls
z Red Door

MONUMENTS

1 Archbishop Hubert Walter (d. 1205)
2 Archbishop Stephen Langton (d. 1228)
3 Archbishop John Pecham (d. 1292)
4 Archbishop Robert Winchelsey (d. 1313)
5 Archbishop Walter Reynolds (d. 1327)
6 Archbishop Simon Meopham (d. 1333)
7 Archbishop John Stratford (d. 1348)
8 Archbishop John Offord (d. 1349), approximate site
9 Archbishop Thomas Bradwardine (d. 1349)
10 Archbishop Simon Sudbury (d. 1381)
11 Archbishop William Courtenay (d. 1396)
12 Archbishop Henry Chichele (d. 1443)
13 Archbishop John Stafford (d. 1452)
14 Archbishop John Kempe (d. 1454)
15 Archbishop Thomas Bourchier (d. 1486)
16 Archbishop Henry Dean (d. 1503)
17 Archbishop William Warham (d. 1532)
18 Prior Henry of Eastry (d. 1331)
19 Prior Richard Oxenden (d. 1338), approximate site
20 Prior Robert Hathbrand (d. 1370), approximate site
21 Prior John Finch (d. 1391)
22 ? Prior Thomas Goldstone I (d. 1468)
23 ? Prior John Oxney (d. 1471)
24 Prior William Sellyng (d. 1494)
25 Prior Thomas Goldstone II (d. 1517)
26 Archdeacon John Bourchier (d. 1495) (see n. 186)
27 Edward, Prince of Wales (d. 1376)
28 King Henry IV (d. 1413) and Queen Joan (d. 1437)
29 John Beaufort, Earl of Somerset (d. 1410) and Thomas, Duke of Clarence (d. 1421), approximate site of original burials
30 Lady Margaret Holland (d. 1439), John Beaufort, Earl of Somerset (d. 1410) and Thomas, Duke of Clarence (d. 1421)
31 Sir Henry Grey, Lord of Powis (d. 1450)

later Canterbury usage of modestly forgoing northern positions while space remained available on the south.[13]

Of all the medieval monuments in Canterbury Cathedral, Hubert Walter's is the most difficult to situate within contemporary practice, for there is nothing quite like it among the few other English episcopal and abbatial tombs which are earlier than the mid-thirteenth century. In fact, the tomb itself was probably as exceptional as its placing within the Cathedral. Scholars have for a long time drawn attention to the formal likeness between Hubert's Purbeck marble monument and the precious metal *feretra* or reliquary coffins which were the chief component of major shrines. On the face of it, *feretra* were a very appropriate source of ideas for any designer charged with creating a specially ambitious tomb, since they, of all the types of funerary monument then in regular use, embodied the richest and most highly evolved traditions. Indeed, the most distinctive feature of the tomb's decoration, the interlocking pattern of quatrefoils, diamonds, and circles on the lid, is hardly explicable except by reference to twelfth-century goldsmiths' work.[14] Nevertheless, the hipped roof-like form of the lid combines with the use of marble to make Hubert's tomb as a whole recall antique sarcophagi more than *feretra*, whose 'roofs' normally end in gables.[15] The only earlier English monuments which can be viewed as direct imitations of antique sarcophagi were a pair of mid-twelfth-century marble tombs in Old St Paul's Cathedral. These commemorated Sebbi, king of the East Saxons, and Æthelred, king of England,[16] and were even more obviously evocative of Antiquity than Hubert's monument, for their lids incorporated fluting, a motif seemingly unparalleled in English Romanesque art.

[13] An example of the application of 'right' in this sense to the tomb of a founder occurs in connection with the reburial, in 1241, of Robert Fitzhamon, founder of Tewkesbury Abbey, 'in dextera parte presbiterii', that is, on the north side of the sanctuary: W. Dugdale, *Monasticon Anglicanum*, ed. J. Caley, H. Ellis, and B. Bandinel (6 vols. in 8; London, 1817–30), ii. 60. Canterbury examples of founders and major benefactors buried in northerly positions are St Augustine, in the north *porticus* of St Gregory in the church of St Peter and St Paul built by him in the early 7th cent., and the reburial at Christ Church in 1180 of Archbishop Lanfranc and Queen Eadgifu respectively *ad* (meaning 'in front of'?) and north of St Martin's altar, in the northern apse of the north-east transept.

[14] Hubert's tomb is compared to shrines in R. Gough, *Sepulchral Monuments of Great Britain* (2 vols. in 5; London, 1786–96), i, pt. 1. 25; J. Morris, *The Tombs of the Archbishops of Canterbury Cathedral* (Canterbury, 1890), 5; N. Stratford, P. Tudor-Craig, and A. M. Muthesius, 'Archbishop Hubert Walter's Tomb and Its Furnishings', in *Medieval Art and Architecture at Canterbury before 1220*, ed. N. Coldstream and P. Draper (British Archaeol. Assn. Conference Trans., 5; London, 1982 for 1979), 73–4, where a dating between Hubert's death in 1205 and the exile of the monks in 1207 is proposed. The architect of the Trinity Chapel, William the Englishman, probably alive until *c*.1214 (J. H. Harvey, *English Mediaeval Architects: A Biographical Dictionary Down to 1550* (2nd. edn.; Gloucester, 1984), 101), has a strong claim to the authorship of the tomb, whether it was made *c*.1205–7 or on the return of the monks in 1213. It is suggestive that the rare combination of lobed arcading and foliate span-

drels is anticipated on the tombs of some of the 12th-cent. Latin kings of Jerusalem in the Church of the Holy Sepulchre. This church is of significance in Hubert's career in that he visited it immediately after its reopening in 1192 and secured from Saladin the concession that the Latin rite be regularly celebrated there. For the late 12th-cent. dating of the only tomb attributable to a particular king, see Z. Jacoby, 'The Tomb of Baldwin V, King of Jerusalem (1185–1186), and the Workshop of the Temple Area', *Gesta*, 18, pt. 2 (1979), 8.

[15] This generalization holds good for virtually all of the extensive visual evidence available from Western Europe other than Italy, including the representations of the (probably not then existing) main shrine of St Thomas in windows N. III and S. VII of the Trinity Chapel aisles (M. H. Caviness, *The Windows of Christ Church Cathedral, Canterbury* (Corpus Vitrearum Medii Aevi, Great Britain, 2; London, 1981), 163, 187, 210, figs. 272–3, 366), the making of which may have overlapped with that of Hubert's tomb. The tomb has lost the stone or stones incorporating the ridge of the lid. The monument to Hubert's uncle and close friend Gilbert Glanvill, Bishop of Rochester (d. 1214), whose decorative similarity to the Archbishop's has long been recognized, had vertical gables and a single pitched roof.

[16] The Sebbi and Æthelred tombs are recorded in W. Dugdale, *The Book of Monuments* (BL, Add. MS 71474, fo. 177, 177ᵛ), and their setting is indicated in Wenceslaus Hollar's engraving in id., *History of St Paul's Cathedral* (London, 1658), 93. They may be contemporary with the 1148 translation of St Erkenwald's relics. Far less closely related to antique prototypes than to the hogback memorials of Viking northern England is the

'Ensarcophagusment',[17] as distinct from burial in coffins set below the pavement, was still very rare in early thirteenth-century England; and perhaps because the practice recalled the *elevatio* of saints' bodies from their original below-ground burial-places, it retained its capacity to signify exceptional prestige until the late thirteenth century, when tomb-chests, which might or might not contain the body, gained widespread acceptance.[18] At Canterbury, one of the most distinguished of the twelfth-century archbishops, Theobald, lay in a marble sarcophagus that may well have influenced Hubert's monument,[19] but the latter includes at least one element indicating that whoever took responsibility for the commission was aware of the prestigious sarcophagi to be seen in Rome itself. This is the series of six large sculptured heads on the lid (Pl. 91), which seems to have no antecedents in earlier funerary art other than the heads on such ancient sarcophagi as that of Constantine the Great's daughter Constantina and that reused for the tomb of the English pope Hadrian IV in Old St Peter's.[20] The Canterbury heads are more numerous and, inevitably, different in style from those on Roman sarcophagi, yet the differences are not sufficient to outweigh the resemblances, namely their disembodied form, their largeness, their very bold relief, and their location on the lid. The heads on Hubert's tomb are not identified by inscriptions, so their meaning, even the intention to impart specific meanings, is not demonstrable beyond doubt. However, there must be a very good chance that they commemorate what was to contemporaries the most remarkable thing about Hubert Walter, his position as ruler simultaneously of the Church and kingdom of England. On this hypothesis, the heads become representatives of the different communities which he had governed: mitred bishops for the English episcopate, a tonsured monk for Christ Church, long-haired and apparently minimally tonsured men for the

impressive but enigmatic early 12th-cent. monument recorded in the Precincts of Canterbury Cathedral in the 18th cent. (and now at Fordwich, 2 miles to the north-east of the city): S. Rigold, 'The Fordwich Stone and the Church Porch', in *Fordwich: The Lost Port*, ed. K. M. McIntosh (Ramsgate, 1975), 131–2. Monuments and grave-covers in the form of a hipped roof and without, or almost without, vertical faces representing walls are pre-Christian in origin and of extremely wide distribution, and the type was doubtless represented in the pre-Conquest Cathedral by the 'memoriam . . . in modum pyramidis' of Archbishop Oda (d. 958), which was located south of the altar of Christ; Osbern, *Vita Sancti Dunstani*, in *Memorials of Saint Dunstan, Archbishop of Canterbury*, ed. W. Stubbs (RS 63; 1874), 109.

[17] The coinage of Evelyn Waugh in *The Loved One: An Anglo-American Tragedy.*

[18] Above-ground dummy sarcophagi made of brick, tile, and cement enclosed the below-ground coffins of the founder saints and immediate successors of St Augustine in the early 7th-cent. lateral *porticus* of the church of St Peter and St Paul, Canterbury: W. H. St J. Hope, 'Recent Discoveries in the Abbey Church of St Austen at Canterbury', *Archaeologia*, 66 (1914–15), 387–99; R. U. Potts, 'Tombs of Kings and Archbishops in St Austin's Abbey', *Arch. Cant.*, 38 (1926), 97–100. The term 'sarcophagus' was generally used in medieval England to denote a stone coffin, by implication below ground, as in the case of St Thomas, who, immediately after his death, was placed in 'marmoreo sarcophago novo', the lid of which was level with

the floor: *Materials for the History of Thomas Becket, Archbishop of Canterbury*, ed. J. C. Robertson and J. B. Sheppard, 7 vols. (RS 67; 1875–85), ii. 81; iii. 149. *Tumba* was the usual word for an above-ground coffin or tomb-chest, the equivalent of 'sarcophagus' in its modern but classically influenced sense. Apart from the monuments of Kings Æthelred and Sebbi at St Paul's (see n. 16 above) and King Alfred's porphyry 'mausoleum' at the New Minster in Winchester (*Asser's Life of King Alfred Together With the Annals of St Neots* . . ., ed. W. H. Stevenson (Oxford, 1904), 143), the latter presumably a reused antique sarcophagus appropriate to Alfred's papally bestowed consular rank, there is no firm evidence that tomb-chests were part of English royal monuments before the reign of Henry III.

[19] Indications in Gervase's account that Theobald's tomb was a sarcophagus are the term 'tumba' applied to it and the reference to its composition of several sheets of marble enclosing an inner coffin: *Historical Works*, i. 26.

[20] For Constantina's sarcophagus, see R. Delbrück, *Antike Porphyrwerke* (Berlin and Leipzig, 1932), 219. For Hadrian IV's grey-pink granite sarcophagus, see R. U. Montini, *Le Tombe dei Papi* (Rome, 1957), 199–200, and Herklotz, 'Sepulchra' e 'monumenta' (cit. in n. 8), 100, where its likeness to porphyry in terms of colour is rightly stressed. One or more of the now lost antique sculptured sarcophagi set up in St John Lateran for the tombs of Paschal II (d. 1119), Innocent II (d. 1143), Clement III (d. 1191) and Celestine III (d. 1198) may well have incorporated large heads like those on the sarcophagi of Constantina and Hadrian IV.

clerks of the archiepiscopal household, and a man in a round cap, perhaps representative of the proto-professional judiciary created by Hubert during his justiciarship (1194–8).[21] So exceptional a concentration of spiritual and secular power would probably have seemed not totally unworthy of comparison with that aspired to by the papal occupants of the imperial or empire-evoking sarcophagi in the main churches associated with the Roman see.[22]

After Hubert's tomb, that of Cardinal **Stephen Langton** (d. 1228). appears strikingly modest in both location and design. Langton's greatest monument at Canterbury was, of course, not his own tomb but the shrine of St Thomas, whose making and installation in 1220 he had masterminded. One might suppose that the archbishop who worked harder than any other to ensure the success of St Thomas's cult would have been able to name his own burial-spot, and if Langton did indeed choose to lie in the chapel of St Michael in the south-west transept, this would have been in effect a humble admission of his need of the good offices of the angel regarded as the pre-eminent guide of men's souls.[23] Langton's Purbeck marble coffin lid, plain except for an edge moulding and a kind of cross pattée carved in reserve, is undeniably austere, but in 1228 it would not have seemed unduly so.[24] The general move towards more pretentious episcopal monuments got under way in England only during the 1240s and 1250s, when Purbeck effigies in very high relief began to enjoy a considerable vogue, and limited numbers of monuments incorporated canopies modelled on the open arcaded structures traditionally used to support the *feretra* of shrines.[25] There was no possibility that the formative phases of either of these developments

[21] A community is represented by large disembodied heads in high relief on an object undoubtedly well known to Hubert, namely the second seal of St Augustine's Abbey, made in 1198–9 (reprod. in T. A. Heslop, 'The Conventual Seals of Canterbury Cathedral 1066–1232', in *Medieval Art and Architecture at Canterbury* (cit. in n. 14), pl. XXIXc). The heads on this seal also resemble those on Hubert's monument in being enclosed within quatrefoils. There seems to be no early 13th-cent. evidence that royal justices wore hats like that on the head on Hubert's tomb, but an illumination in a manuscript of *c*.1290 of Bracton's *De Legibus et Consuetudinibus Angliae* (BL, Add. MS 11353, fo. 9) shows the king seated beside six justices, three of whom wear round red hats surmounted by a pompon or knob. Presumably both types of hat were versions of the *pilleus* worn by many ranks and conditions of men in the 13th cent.

[22] For the series of papal burials in reused antique marble sarcophagi, starting with that of Leo IX (d. 1054) in St Peter's, and also their significance as *imitatio imperii*, see Herklotz, 'Sepulcra' e 'Monumenta' (cit. in n. 8), 91, 92, 95–100.

[23] St Michael's Chapel seems to have occupied a privileged position in the devotional and liturgical life of the Cathedral. Its altar was one of the few whose offerings were listed separately in the treasurers' accounts for 1237 (*Lit. Cant.* ii, p. liii), and in 1296 there is mention of four solemn feasts of pilgrimage: St Thomas, Easter, Pentecost, and St Michael (BL, Cotton MS Galba E. iv, fo. 68). Langton's tomb was originally before St Michael's altar, and the rough sides of the freestone coffin confirm the testimony of the *Polistorie* written at Christ Church, Canterbury in the early 14th cent. (BL, Harl. MS 636, fo. 240ᵛ) that the body 'fust mÿs en tere'. When the chapel was rebuilt in

the 1430s, the coffin and its marble lid were raised and shunted eastwards to make room for the monument of Lady Holland and her husbands, with the bizarre result that its foot protrudes through the east wall: J. Morris, *Tombs of the Archbishops* (cit. in n. 14), 22–3; Legg and Hope, *Inventories*, 153–4. It can hardly be a coincidence that some time in the 1220s Archbishop Walter de Gray of York began to rebuild the south transept of York Minster, whose central eastern chapel, dedicated to St Michael, served as his own burial chapel.

[24] In 1228 only bishops of Exeter and Salisbury had been commemorated by effigies. The early 13th-cent. bishops of Winchester had very modest tombs, to judge from the plain coffin-lid of Bishop Lucy (d. 1204), still in place before the Lady Chapel entrance, and the report that Peter des Roches (d. 1238) chose a 'humilem sepulturam' in his lifetime: Matthew Paris, *Chronica Majora*, ed. H. R. Luard, 7 vols. (RS 57; 1872–83), iii. 489–90. Until 1274 the bishops of Durham were buried in the chapter house under coffin-lids bearing only a cross and their names (*The Rites of Durham*, ed. J. T. Fowler (Surtees Soc., 107; 1902), 55–6), and at Chichester all the slabs attributable to early 13th-cent. bishops are quite plain: H. Tummers, 'The Medieval Effigial Tombs in Chichester Cathedral', *Church Monuments*, 3 (1988), 4, n. 3.

[25] Apparently the earliest English bishop's tomb combining a canopy and a Purbeck effigy was that of John Bingham (d. 1246), north of the high altar at Salisbury: Gough, *Sepulchral Monuments* (cit. in n. 14), i, pt. 1, pl. xii opp. p. 41, p. 43, where it is misattributed to Bishop Poore (d. 1237). The most shrine-like 13th-cent. tomb anywhere in Europe is the posthumous monument in York Minster to Archbishop Walter de Gray (d.

would be represented at Canterbury, since Langton's four immediate successors were all buried abroad.[26]

Langton's fifth successor, the Franciscan **John Pecham** (d. 1292), also intended to be buried away from Canterbury, in the church of the London Greyfriars. But on hearing of this, Prior Henry of Eastry wrote to the Archbishop to warn him of the offence it would give to the holy fathers his predecessors in the see. Pecham yielded, though with a very bad grace and, in what was clearly intended as a pointed gesture, left his heart to be buried with his London brothers.[27] It is tempting to surmise that he had been induced to comply with the Prior's wishes by an off-the-record promise of a tomb in the north-west transept, the Martyrdom of St Thomas, where no burial had been allowed before. The placing of Pecham's monument hard up against the stair projecting into the north-west corner of the Martyrdom indicates that space was being left on the east for a successor's tomb (Pl. 92). This kind of arrangement was apparently then unknown in England except at St Augustine's Abbey in Canterbury, where a two-hundred-year-old series of four tombs of Anglo-Saxon royals extended across the end wall of the south transept.

The tombs at St Augustine's were among the few eleventh- or twelfth-century English tombs which conformed to the same basic scheme as Pecham's monument, that is, a tomb chest set in a shallow arched recess.[28] It is very likely that they were conceived as replacements for the pre-Conquest monuments of the same type which had covered the bodies of saints and founders at St Augustine's until their partial dismantling in the early eleventh century. The source which contains the reference to the Anglo-Saxon monuments does not indicate their date but notes the 'Roman elegance' of their columns and arches, and thus implies that they were early seventh-century and of a self-consciously antique

---

1255). The tombs of Bishops Robert Grosseteste (d. 1253) at Lincoln (as reconstructed by N. J. Rogers, 'English Episcopal Monuments, 1270–1350', in *The Earliest English Brasses: Patronage Style and Workshops, 1270–1350*, ed. J. Coales (London, 1987), 20) and Giles of Bridport (d. 1262) at Salisbury, incorporate important shrine-derived elements but are not wholesale imitations of shrines.

[26] The only one of Pecham's four immediate predecessors whose tomb is recorded visually is Boniface of Savoy (d. 1270, beatified 1839), who was buried at the Cistercian abbey of Hautecombe. His destroyed effigy has been dated c.1440 and attributed to the patronage of Amadeus VIII, Duke of Savoy, on the strength of its similarity to the bronze monument (also destroyed) at St Catherine's, Aiguebelle, of Boniface's fellow Savoyard Peter of Aigueblanche, bishop of Hereford (d. 1268), which was inscribed with the name of its maker, Henry of Cologne: A. Dufour and F. Rabut, 'Les Orfèvres et les produits de l'orfèvrerie en Savoie', *Mémoires de la Société savoisienne d'histoire et d'archéologie*, 24 (1886), 387. However, the Henry of Cologne patronized by Duke Amadeus is documented only as a goldsmith, and the visual records of the two effigies (S. Guichenon, *Histoire généalogique de la Royale Maison de Savoye* (2 vols.; Lyons, 1660), i. 282; Rogers, 'English Episcopal Monuments' (cit. in n. 25), fig. 11) indicate that both were late 13th-cent. work. It seems likely that Boniface's executors commissioned the effigy in emulation of his suffragan's. Both showed the deceased with closed eyes, a motif virtually never found in English medieval effigies.

[27] D. Douie, *Archbishop Pecham* (Oxford, 1952), 189. Pecham's burial-place is given as 'de coste le lyu ou seint thomas fust martirize' in *Polistorie* (cit. in n. 23), fo. 220, and 'ad martirium sancti Thome in pariete' in the early 16th-cent. list of archbishops' and priors' burial-places (cit. in n. 5), 107. Pecham's heart monument, which must have been resited, if not remade, after the reconstruction of the London Greyfriars from c.1306, is located in a late medieval burial-list 'retro magnum altare in archu partis australis in sacrario' (C. L. Kingsford, *The Greyfriars of London* (Aberdeen, 1915), 71), a description comprehensible only if one assumes that the high altar stood against a sacristy occupying the easternmost bay of the central vessel of the choir.

[28] Of the very few Romanesque tomb-recesses to have survived at other major English churches, the only ones incorporating tomb-chests are the six in the south cloister wall at Chester Cathedral, which were apparently constructed at different dates in the early and mid-12th cent. A date not much later than c.1100 for the St Augustine's Abbey tombs is indicated by the profile of their bases, but it is clear that they were not planned when the transept was built in the late 11th cent. For the identity of their occupants and their excavation in the 1920s, see Potts, 'Tombs of Kings and Archbishops' (cit. in n. 18), 108–11.

appearance appropriate to their setting in the little Rome established by Augustine in east Kent.[29] The arched-canopy motif, whose exact form naturally varied in accordance with current architectural fashion and the exigencies of space, was an ancient and universally recognized symbol of heaven and immortality, but when it occurred set above a sculptured effigy showing the occupant of the tomb recumbent and at the moment of Resurrection,[30] as in Archbishop Pecham's tomb, it became specifically an intimation of the heavenly mansions prepared by Christ Himself for each of His followers (John 14: 2).[31] Canopies also had imperial and royal connotations which were hardly less venerable than their celestial ones, and this fact must go far towards explaining why most of the few known examples of high arched tomb-recesses from Late Antiquity and the early Middle Ages belong to the monuments of popes, emperors, and kings.[32] In thirteenth-century England tomb-recesses were almost always low and plain, so it would seem that their honorific role had become less important than their capacity to minimize the obstruction of floor space caused by grave-slabs and effigies.[33] In France, by contrast, considerable numbers of tombs incorporating high and richly decorated recesses were being made from the late twelfth century onwards; and given that Pecham's tomb and the other earliest extant English examples of this type betray strong French influences in their detailing, it is difficult not to conclude that the type had virtually died out in England and had had to be reimported.[34]

[29] Goscelin, *Historia Translationis S. Augustini* (cit. in n. 6), cols. 29–30. Goscelin may have been aware of the Roman format or style of the architectural elements of these canopies, or he may merely have been guessing that they represented Roman practice, on the strength of the association of their occupants with the papal mission of 597.

[30] This is surely the most obvious interpretation of the youthful physique and open eyes shown in the great majority of 13th-cent. Western medieval effigies, but the existence of numbers of effigies which deviate from this norm suggests that a lack of precision prevailed about the nature and purpose of figural monuments, and also a toleration of incompatible readings. Dante referred to effigies as simulacra ('sembianze') of the deceased as they had been when living: Dante Alighieri, *Purgatorio*, canto xii, lines 16–24, ed. C. Singleton (Princeton, NJ, 1973), 120–3, a reference kindly given me by Alexandrina Buchanan. The general dearth of medieval writing about what effigies were supposed to represent is matched by the paucity of modern scholarly treatments of the subject, but see H. s'Jacob, *Idealism and Realism* (cit. in n. 8), 9–44; E. Panofsky, *Tomb Sculpture: Its Changing Aspects from Ancient Egypt to Bernini* (London, 1964), 49–66; P. Ariès, 'Une Conception ancienne de l'au-delà', in *Death in the Middle Ages*, Medievalia Lovaniensia, ser. 1/studia 9, ed. H. Braet and W. Verbeke (Louvain, 1983), 86–7.

[31] In a few French tomb canopies, the heavenly meaning was reinforced by blue paint and gold stars on the vault, or by representations of the Agnus Dei. For examples of the latter, see A. Erlande-Brandenburg, *Le Roi est mort: Étude sur les funérailles, les sépultures et les tombeaux des rois de France jusqu'à la fin du XIIIᵉ siècle* (Paris and Geneva, 1975), fig. 115; J. Adhémar and G. Dordor, 'Les Tombeaux de la collection Gaignières: Dessins d'archéologie du XVIIᵉ siècle', *Gazette des Beaux-Arts*, 6th ser., 84 (July–Sept. 1974), 164 (no. 913).

[32] For valuable brief discussions of the early-medieval and Romanesque derivatives of the Early Christian *arcosolium* recess-tombs, see J. Deér, *The Dynastic Porphyry Tombs of the Norman Period in Sicily* (Cambridge, Mass., 1959), 24–41; Herklotz, 'Sepulchra' e 'Monumenta' (cit. in n. 8), 56–7, 143–56. However, Deér, in emphasizing the innovatory character of the ciboria of the 12th-cent. Sicilian tombs, neglects the mortuary functions of the ciboria associated with the high altars of some of the most important Italian and French churches (see n. 34 below). One of these, the ciborium of c.1000 in S. Ambrogio, Milan, was probably not unique in being surmounted on each side by gables which anticipate those of Romanesque and Gothic recess-tombs. Because the oldest medieval gabled tombs in Italy and France date from the early 12th cent., there is no obvious way of ascertaining whether they owe their gables to the influence of ciboria, Romanesque church portals, or antique pedimented façades and aedicules honouring the Emperor.

[33] The problem of obstruction and injury caused to passers-by was mentioned by St Hugh of Lincoln when making arrangements for his own tomb; *Magna Vita Sancti Hugonis*, ed. D. Douie and D. H. Farmer, repr. with corrections (2 vols.; Oxford, 1985), ii. 192.

[34] The only English Gothic recess-tombs which certainly predate Pecham's and which have the gables and something of the upright proportioning of the French examples are the Bradfield monument at Rochester (discussed below) and the simply detailed mid- or early 13th-cent. monument at Tewkesbury Abbey to Abbot Alan, the biographer of St Thomas (d. 1202): L. L. Gee, '"Ciborium" Tombs in England 1290–1330', *JBAA*, 132 (1979), 31. The early success in France of the 'ciborium tomb', in which the compressed 'ciborium' is borne mostly or wholly on a pair of slim, free-standing supports, can perhaps

Like most of the late medieval tombs in Canterbury Cathedral, Pecham's monument was the work of London-based artists. Its architectural design can be ascribed with some confidence to Michael of Canterbury, master mason to Christ Church from the late 1270s and designer of the Cheapside Cross in London, the second most important of the twelve crosses built, from 1291, in memory of Queen Eleanor. His principal work was St Stephen's Chapel in Westminster Palace, begun in the following year. Among several Kentish works attributable to Michael in his pre-royal days is the monument of John Bradfield, Bishop of Rochester (d. 1283), the earliest English Gothic tomb-recess whose architecture is of high ambition. Its most remarkable feature, its pierced pendant cusping, shows an awareness of the decorative detailing of the cathedral portals which by the thirteenth century had become the main influence on French tomb architecture.[35] Pecham's tomb deploys a far richer vocabulary of forms than Bradfield's, a variation no doubt due partly to Michael's exposure at the start of the 1290s to the wider range of French portal-derived motifs used on the Eleanor Crosses and in the contemporary and stylistically very closely related tomb of Aveline, Countess of Lancaster, in Westminster Abbey.[36] As has long been acknowledged, the general scheme of the Pecham tomb, in particular its large gable and its arcaded and gableted tomb-chest, follows Aveline's tomb, but the rather unimaginative application in the latter of the rapidly hardening conventions of French tomb design is enlivened here by a fuller and freer use of elements drawn from the parent tradition of portal architecture.[37] The main features in this category are the large foliage 'rosette' in the canopy gable and the elegantly undulating serrated leaves which line both the gable and the main arch.[38] Pecham's tomb exerted a powerful influence on English tomb architecture of the early fourteenth century,[39] and even more importantly, it foreshadows Michael of

be attributed in part to the fact that since at least the early 7th cent. the ciboria associated with main altars in French churches had often stood over major relics enshrined above ground, rather than over the high altars near to the west ends of those shrines. The picture presented in ibid. 29–41 of direct Italian influence on 13th-cent. French ciborium tombs underestimates the strength of French artistic traditions at this period.

[35] For Michael of Canterbury's documented career, see Harvey, *English Mediaeval Architects* (cit. in n. 14), 45–6. For his *œuvre*, including Bradfield's tomb, see C. Wilson, 'The Origins of the Perpendicular Style and its Development to *circa* 1360' (Ph.D. thesis, Univ. of London, 1980), 27–111.

[36] It is very likely that when the Eleanor Crosses were commissioned, the king's works organization acquired drawings of the crosses built to commemorate St Louis some 20 years earlier, and of other Parisian and northern French works of comparable type. Thus it would have been possible to study the French sources of the Eleanor Crosses without leaving England. The main elements of the Pecham tomb which derive from the crosses are the ogee arches and the minature traceried parapet, battlements, and flower-decorated cornice on the still-visible left-hand pinnacle. The latter has been much truncated; cf. the tombs of Bishop Louth at Ely (d. 1298) and Edmund 'Crouchback', Earl of Lancaster (d. 1296) at Westminster, both almost certainly designed by Michael of Canterbury.

[37] The recess-tomb of Archbishop Eudes Rigaud (d. 1275), formerly in Rouen Cathedral, has been dated to the time of

the Archbishop's death and identified as the kind of French design which lies behind the tombs of Pecham and Aveline; Gee, '"Ciborum Tombs"' (cit. in n. 34), 33. However, the tall overall proportioning, the use of black stone (touch?), the location in the Lady Chapel begun after 1302, and the similarity in format to the tomb in the same chapel of an archbishop who died in 1306, all argue for an early 14th-cent. dating; Adhémar and Dordor, 'Tombeaux de la collection Gaignières' (cit. in n. 31), 68 (no. 344), 101 (no. 542).

[38] Very similar foliage rosettes occur in the gables on the flanks of the west portals of Rheims Cathedral (c.1260). Apparently the only English examples of this motif earlier than 1292 are on the exceptionally ambitious, and doubtless London-made, canopy over the tomb of Bishop Walter de Merton (d. 1277) at Rochester. The foliage lining the gable and arch of the canopy to Pecham's tomb may derive directly from the virtually identical but more closely spaced leaves which frame the tympanum of the south transept portal of Notre-Dame, Paris, begun in 1258.

[39] Strictly speaking, the Pecham tomb influenced later tomb design not directly but through the exceptionally splendid tomb of Edmund 'Crouchback', Earl of Lancaster, in Westminster Abbey. The Pecham tomb and the tombs of Queen Eleanor, Crouchback, Aveline, and Bishop Louth are considered in the context of the career of Michael of Canterbury in C. Wilson, 'Origins of Perpendicular' (cit. in n. 35), 33–4, 80–7. The similarities of the Pecham and Crouchback tombs were noted as

Canterbury's main contribution to European Late Gothic art, the concept of making full-scale architecture out of the decorative motifs which originated on French cathedral portals.

The tomb of Archbishop Pecham typifies major late medieval English monuments in that the imaginative richness of its architecture is not matched by iconographic inventiveness.[40] The effigy (Pl. 108) conforms to the blessing and staff-holding type almost always used for thirteenth-century English bishops' effigies,[41] and the idea of representing the chief mourners at the funeral on the tomb-chest, though comparatively newly introduced into England, was nearly a century old in France.[42] Nevertheless, the aesthetic merits of the sculpture make it fully worthy of its setting. The oak effigy, sadly battered though it is, remains recognizable as the finest medieval wooden effigy in England.[43] The idealized and youthful head (Pl. 115) with its broad brow, long eyes, prominent cheekbones, and sensitive mouth,[44] the slender physique and the bold yet fluid draperies are all closely comparable to the effigy of Aveline of Lancaster, a work convincingly attributed to the sculptor Alexander of Abingdon, who carved the figures on the Eleanor Cross at Waltham. The architecture of Aveline's tomb can be ascribed to Richard of Crundale, architect of the Eleanor Cross at Charing and of the Queen's main tomb at Westminster.[45]

long ago as 1786 (Gough, *Sepulchral Monuments* (cit. in n. 14), i, pt. 1. 67), and the interrelatedness of all the tombs mentioned in this note was recognized in P. Biver, 'Tombs of the School of London at the Beginning of the 14th Century', *Archaeol. Jnl.*, 67 (1910), 51–65.

[40] This lack of iconographic inventiveness is reflected in, for instance, the small amount of attention paid to English monuments in Panofsky, *Tomb Sculpture* (cit. in n. 30). The heavy involvement of late-medieval English architects in tomb design by comparison with their Continental colleagues raises questions about the relative prestige of architecture and image-making which have never been explored and which cannot be entered into here, but it is fair to say that art historians have generally failed to grasp this distinction, mainly because, for reasons arising from the traditions of specialization within the discipline, English Gothic monuments have persistently been pigeonholed as sculpture, notwithstanding the predominantly architectural character of many major examples (cf. n. 201 below).

[41] Apart from some of the retrospective effigies at Wells, there are no 13th-cent. English episcopal effigies which conform to any of the alternative schemes then in use in France. The tradition of showing archbishops with their primatial cross was stronger in England than elsewhere and was departed from only in Archbishop de Gray's tomb at York (an error no doubt of the southern sculptor of the Purbeck effigy) and in the foreign-made effigy of Boniface of Savoy (see n. 26 above). Pecham's primatial cross, held in his left hand, has disappeared, leaving a large mortice. The only seemingly innovatory element in the iconography of Pecham's effigy is the pair of dragon-like creatures at his feet, but these are no doubt unusually prominently winged versions of serpents, an allusion to Ps. 91: 13 which occurs in earlier French and English bishops' effigies.

[42] The earliest known instance is the series of six images of relatives on the silver-sheathed tomb-chest of Thibaut III,

Count of Champagne (d. 1201), formerly in Saint-Etienne, Troyes: s'Jacob, *Idealism and Realism* (cit. in n. 8), 86. For the earliest extant English approximation to this iconography, see n. 49 below.

[43] The aesthetic merit of the extant English wooden effigies, like the social standing of the persons commemorated, is not generally high. The only late 13th-cent. wooden effigy at all comparable in quality to Pecham's, that in Abergavenny Priory attributed to George de Cantelupe, tenth Lord of Abergavenny (d. 1273), may also have come from the workshop of Alexander of Abingdon, as it has much in common with the freestone effigy of Edmund of Lancaster in Westminster Abbey. Pecham's effigy is compared to Aveline's, the Abergavenny knight is compared to Edmund of Lancaster, and Pecham and Abergavenny are both attributed to London workshops in A. C. Fryer, *Wooden Monumental Effigies in England and Wales* (2nd edn.; London, 1924), 29, 38, 88, 90–1. No less odd than the fact that Pecham's effigy is of wood is its placing on top of a very smoothly worked Purbeck slab. Might the original intention have been to install a monumental brass? If the architecture is made of Reigate stone, as it appears to be, there must be a possibility that the entire monument was made in London and shipped to Canterbury in parts, in which case the use of wood for the effigy may have been intended to reduce carriage costs.

[44] No doubt sufficient authority for showing the deceased much younger than at death was Augustine, who said that the spiritual bodies of the blessed in heaven would be like the resurrected body of Christ, youthful and of perfect beauty: *Retractationes*, lib. 1, cap. 17 (Migne, *PL*, xxxii, col. 613); *De Civitate Dei*, lib. 22, capp. 19, 20 (*PL*, xli, cols. 781–3).

[45] For the attribution to Alexander of Abingdon of the effigy of Aveline of Lancaster, see W. R. Lethaby, *Westminster Abbey Re-examined* (London, 1925), 198; E.-A. Wendebourg, *Westminster Abbey als königliche Grablege zwischen 1250 und 1400* (Worms, 1986), 100–1; entry on the Eleanor Cross at Waltham by P. Lindley in *Age of Chivalry: Art in Plantagenet England, 1200–1400*,

The deep, gable-topped head-canopy of the latter may well have been the model for that which has been torn away from the base slab of Pecham's effigy.[46]

A spirit of triumphalism probably lies behind the determination to find room on the tomb-chest and flanking buttresses for figures of all seventeen of the Archbishop's suffragans, since the military conquest of Wales during Pecham's archiepiscopate had brought the principality's four dioceses more firmly than ever under the authority of Canterbury. The bishops are portrayed as tall, elegantly draped figures and are clearly of the same workmanship as the line-up of royal relatives on the chest of the slightly later tomb at Westminster of Aveline's husband, Edmund 'Crouchback', another monument attributed to Alexander of Abingdon and Michael of Canterbury.[47] Like the heraldically identified 'weepers' on both the Lancasters' tombs, Pecham's suffragans show no emotion, being primarily a testimony to the rank of the deceased. In their impassiveness they conform to a type almost certainly in existence in France by *c*.1200, although it is likely that more recent cross-Channel influences were also at work, for at least one late thirteenth-century French archbishop is known to have been commemorated by a monument whose arcaded tomb-chest displayed a contingent of suffragans in a state of perfect composure.[48] That the alternative tradition of presenting the mourners as grieving witnesses to the funeral rites never found much favour in England was probably due at least partly to the authoritative status accorded to Michael of Canterbury's tomb designs.[49] The original effect of the weepers and all the other sculpture on Pecham's tomb has been distorted by the loss of most of the polychromy, but enough colour remains on the canopy to indicate a bolder and simpler treatment than the elaborately naturalistic painting of the Westminster tombs.[50] The flat back and sides of the recess present ideal fields for wall-

ed. J. Alexander and P. Binski, exhib. cat., Royal Academy of Arts (London, 1987), 363, no. 374. For the attribution of Aveline's tomb-chest to Richard of Crundale, see Wilson, 'Origins of Perpendicular' (cit. in n. 35), 80–2.

[46] The evidence for the head-canopy is the three mortices which attached it to the base slab, and the protruberances on the front edge of the slab, which formed continuations of the abacus, base, and corbel of a shaft supporting the canopy. There was no balancing shaft on the virtually invisible far side.

[47] Three of the bishops were obscured when the tomb of Archbishop Warham was built in front of the east flanking buttress. Only the need to include 17 figures explains the unconventional procedure of extending weepers from the tomb-chest on to the buttresses, where they have to be stacked three deep. Pecham's weepers are shallower in relief and occupy shallower niches than those on Crouchback's tomb, a variation indicative of a lower level of expenditure.

[48] For the earliest recorded tomb-chest with figures of mourners, see n. 42 above. Early tomb-chests where the mourners show no emotion are that attributed to Queen Gertrude of Meran (d. 1213), formerly at Pilis, Hungary, made *c*.1233, and that of Adelaide of Champagne (d. 1187), made *c*.1260 and now at Joigny (Yonne): H. R. Hahnloser, *Villard de Honnecourt* (2nd edn.; Graz, 1972), 395–6; W. Sauerländer, *Gothic Sculpture in France, 1140–1270* (London, 1970), 506, pl. 295. The earliest recorded archbishop's monument with suffragans on the tomb-chest was that of Pierre de Montbrun (d. 1286), the first arch-

bishop of Narbonne buried in the new cathedral begun in 1272: M. Pradelier-Schlumberger, 'Le Tombeau du Cardinal Pierre de la Jugie à Narbonne', *Narbonne archéologie et histoire*, ii: *Narbonne au moyen-âge* (Montpellier, 1973), 273; Adhémar and Dordor, 'Tombeaux de la collection Gaignières' (cit. in n. 31), 78, no. 403. Given the stylistic orientation of the architecture of Narbonne Cathedral towards northern France, common dependence on some lost archbishop's tomb in that region seems a likelier explanation than direct influence for the iconographic similarity of the Montbrun and Pecham tombs. The lack of weepers on the surviving tombs of Pecham's successors may reflect the fact that funerals of Archbishops of Canterbury were hardly ever attended by their suffragans!

[49] The earliest example of the representation of a funeral service which includes laity as well as clergy is on the monument of Louis de France (d. 1260), son of St Louis, formerly at Royaumont and now at Saint-Denis: Erlande-Brandenburg, *Le Roi est mort* (cit. in n. 31), figs. 121–30. The earliest English monument influenced by this tradition, that of Thomas Cantilupe at Hereford (*c*.1282–7), is unique in its iconography: seated knights whose posture is expressive of sorrow.

[50] Short accounts of the medieval paint surviving on the stonework and the effigy (the latter not now visible to the naked eye) are in C. E. Keyser, *A List of Buildings in Great Britain and Ireland Having Mural and Other Painted Decoration* (3rd edn.; London, 1883), 53–5; E. W. Tristram, *Friends of Canterbury Cathedral, 9th Annual Report* (1936), 49–50; id., *Friends of Can-*

paintings. The subject most often used in this position was the deceased kneeling before the Virgin or some other intercessor.[51]

Wall-painting was allotted an unusually prominent role in the monument of Archbishop **Robert Winchelsey** (d. 1313), which stood near the centre of the south wall of the south-east transept. The 'right go[o]dly tumbe of marble; at the very but ende yn the waulle side' noted by John Leland in the early 1540s was destroyed soon afterwards on account of the cult with which it was still residually associated, but the position of a high gabled recess similar to Pecham's is defined by the traces—now little more than stains on the masonry—of a large figural composition set within a rectangular 'frame' formed of bands of Gothic tracery.[52] On the facing wall of the north-east transept, equally faint vestiges remain of a huge figure of St Thomas blessing and standing watch over the monks as they passed between the choir and their dormitory—a symmetry which highlights Winchelsey's status as a champion of the Church in its struggles with the Crown, and which more than hints at the saintly and patronal status he seemed likely to attain during the decades following his death.[53] The south-east transept was a natural choice for the site of a promising cult, since it provided ample unencumbered floor-space, as well as proximity to the relics of four sainted archbishops.[54] All that remains of Winchelsey's tomb is a very damaged mitred and cushioned head with the over-large ears typical of early fourteenth-century English episcopal effigies. Wholly untypical of this date is the use of Purbeck marble, a departure suggestive of an unusually high level of expenditure.[55]

terbury Cathedral, 10th Annual Report (1937), 47; id., *English Medieval Wall Painting: The Thirteenth Century* (2 vols.; Oxford, 1950), i. 519. The polychromy of the effigy is likely to have been much more detailed and naturalistic than that of the architecture (see the settings for imitation gems on the amice etc.). Around 1800 enough painting and gilding survived to show that the chasuble 'has been of gold richly ornamented' and the gesso base for the polychromy still concealed most of the wooden fabric of the effigy: D. T. Powell's topographical collections of c.1795–1835 (BL, Add. MS 17733), fos 5, 7. The incompleteness of the upper part of the mitre and its incorporation of a tenon suggests that this section of the effigy was originally of metal.

[51] As in the tomb-recess of Precentor John Swinfield (d. 1311) at Hereford Cathedral (Gough, *Sepulchral Monuments* (cit. in n. 14), ii, pt. 2, pl. lxxvi) and that of c.1300 attributed to Bishop Leofric (d. 1072), formerly in St James's Chapel, Exeter Cathedral.

[52] *The Itinerary of John Leland*, ed. L. Toulmin Smith (5 vols; London, 1907–10), iv. 39; J. H. Denton, *Robert Winchelsey and the Crown, 1294–1313* (Cambridge, 1980), 15. Within the painted area around Winchelsey's monument, the outline of a gable is defined by the junction between 12th-cent masonry and Victorian patching of the scar left by the removal of the monument. The fact that some of the wall arcade capitals and bases here are still 12th-cent. indicates that though the recess was of a kind frequently let into a wall (cf. Pecham's monument), it was actually mostly built out from the main wall-plane and projected well into the transept. This is confirmed by the description of the burial site as being before St Gregory's altar in *Polistorie* (cit. in n. 23), fo. 234, and in the early 16th-cent. list of archbishops' and priors' burial-places (cit. in n. 5), 108.

[53] A painting of an archbishop in this context can only have represented St Thomas. A date c.1300 is suggested by the form of the canopy over the figure. Neither this painting nor that associated with Winchelsey's tomb has previously been noticed in print.

[54] For his cult and Archbishop Reynolds's unsuccessful application for his canonization in 1327, see Legg and Hope, *Inventories*, 43; L. F. Salzman in *Sussex Notes and Queries*, 1 (1926–7), 218; C. E. Woodruff, 'The Miracles of Archbishop Winchelsey', *Trans. St Paul's Ecclesiological Soc.*, 10 pt. iv (1938), 111–23; Denton, *Winchelsey and the Crown* (cit. in n. 52), 15–33. For the shrines of the four pre-Conquest archbishops in the south-east transept, see Gervase, *Historical Works*, i. 15, 24.

[55] This is currently (1994) in store. There can be little doubt that it is the head of an effigy reported in 1888 as having been found in the crypt of the Trinity Chapel (by implication recently) along with the 'base' of the same effigy and the canopy which was over the effigy (meaning the head-canopy?): 'The Crypt of Canterbury Cathedral: First Report of a Committee Appointed "to Make an Antiquarian Investigation of the Cathedral"', *Arch. Cant.*, 18 (1889), 255. The present whereabouts of the 'base' and canopy are not known. The funerary expenses paid by Winchelsey's executors amounted to £459 8s. 7¾d. (Ch. Ant. A. 34). No details of this expenditure are recorded, but its large size can be gauged by comparison with the total of £142 16s. 5½d. spent by the executors of Bishop Thomas Bitton of Exeter (d. 1307), which included the metal components of a large brass costing £16 13s. 4d. and a marble slab for the indent costing £3: Rogers, 'English Episcopal Monuments' (cit. in n. 25), 52–3; *Account of the Executors of Richard Bishop of London 1303, and of the Executors of Thomas Bishop of Exeter, 1310*, ed. W. H. Hale and H. T. Ellacombe (Camden Soc., new ser., 10; 1874), pp. xv, 22–3.

The concern to keep the area round Winchelsey's tomb functioning as a cult area was perhaps the main reason why his successor's request for burial there was not met.[56] **Walter Reynolds** (d. 1327) was buried instead under the window in the central bay of the south choir aisle, a position surely intended to invite comparison with the monument in a southern window embrasure of the Trinity Chapel which commemorated the last archbishop of Canterbury to fill the office of royal chancellor and bear the name Walter.[57] The Reynolds tomb has lost the main components of its superstructure, a quasi-canopy formed of a shallow, free-standing arch set well in advance of the window glass. The tomb-chest and the shafts which formerly carried the 'canopy' are in the rather heavy version of Michael of Canterbury's manner current in Canterbury and north-east Kent during the 1320s.[58] Reynolds's poorly preserved effigy (Pl. 109) may never have been an outstanding work of sculpture, but its polychromy must once have made it resplendent. The precious silk used for the chasuble and the apparel of the alb was rendered as vigorously painted gold griffons on a blue ground.[59] A painted element now completely destroyed was the epitaph.[60] The position of the forearms of the effigy suggests that the primatial cross was held in the right hand and a book in the other, a scheme apparently used for only one other English bishop's effigy, that of Reynolds's contemporary Walter Stapledon at Exeter.[61]

More interesting from almost every point of view is the effigy-less monument to

[56] It would not be surprising if another factor was the low esteem in which Reynolds was held generally: Denton, *Winchelsey and the Crown* (cit. in n. 52), 20. See also n. 172 below. Reynolds's will had asked modestly that he be buried 'in plana terra' (*Sede Vacante Wills*, ed. C. E. Woodruff (Kent Archaeol. Soc., Records Branch, 3; 1914), 67; J. R. Wright, 'The Testament or Last Will of Archbishop Walter Reynolds of Canterbury, 1327', *Mediaeval Studies*, 47 (1985), 449). It seems reasonable to interpret Reynolds's planned below-floor burial as the earliest evidence that any archbishop of Canterbury contemplated being commemorated by a brass: Rogers, 'English Episcopal Monuments' (cit. in n. 25), 38. Although the commonest form of early 14th-cent. English episcopal monument, brasses were not introduced into the eastern arm at Canterbury before the 19th cent.

[57] The similarities in their names, their careers, and the placing of their tombs were sufficient to cause confusion as to the identity of the tombs' occupants once Reynolds's painted epitaph had become illegible (see n. 60 below). For the history of this confusion and that over the identity of the occupant of the adjacent tomb, now known to be that of Prior Eastry, see F. Woodman, 'Two Tombs in the South Quire Aisle', *Cant. Cath. Chron.*, 69 (1975), 14–22. Woodman repeats Scott Robertson's incorrect statement ('Burial Places of the Archbishops' (cit. in n. 11), 289) that Reynolds's effigy lacks the *pallium*, and makes the strange suggestion that it was originally on the tomb of Prior Oxenden.

[58] That the 'canopy' arch was of obtuse pitch is clear from the fragment remaining above the jamb shafts. Stylistically, the closest work in the locality is the north-west tower at Herne: Wilson, 'Origins of Perpendicular' (cit. in n. 35), 100–2. Thomas

Johnson's view of the choir in 1657 (Col. Pl. VI) shows the canopy reduced to its present state.

[59] John Philipot's Kentish church notes of *c.*1613–15, BL, Egerton MS 3310A, p. 29; Richard Scarlett's heraldic collections of 1599, BL, Harl. MS 1366, fo. 12ᵛ. Very extensive fragments of polychromy remain on the chasuble, dalmatic, and other portions of Reynolds's effigy. On the jamb-shafts of the 'canopy', traces remain of the 'barber's pole' pattern shown in Somner, *Antiquities* (1703), pt. 2, pl. between 32 and 33.

[60] The epitaph (R. Holinshed, *Chronicles* (2nd edn.; London, 1587), 1463; Scarlett heraldic collections (cit. in n. 59), fo. 12) is said by two early 17th-cent. sources to have decayed greatly in their time: F. Godwin, *A Catalogue of the Bishops of England* (London, 1601), 86; J. Weever, *Ancient Funerall Monuments* (London, 1631), 222. It was doubtless of medieval date (*pace* Woodman, 'Two Tombs' (cit. in n. 57), 16, 18), and its likely position is the edge of the base slab under the effigy, as on the monuments of Edmund 'Crouchback' at Westminster and Bishop John of Sheppey (d. 1360) at Rochester.

[61] However, at least one English prelate (possibly a bishop of Norwich) was shown in this way on an early 14th-cent. brass: Rogers, 'English Episcopal Monuments' (cit. in n. 25), 18, 44. Considerable numbers of 13th-cent. French episcopal effigies held books and croziers (Adhémar and Dordor, *Tombeaux de la collection Gaignières* (cit. in n. 31), 25 (nos. 26–7), 63 (no. 312), 66 (no. 330), 74 (no. 380), 82 (no. 429), but this scheme appears to have fallen from favour in France by the early 14th cent. The pair of dogs at the feet is among the earliest English examples of this motif, which recurs in the two later 14th-cent. archbishops' effigies still extant (Pls. 111, 112). It was current in France from the early 13th cent.: ibid. 28 (no. 108).

Cardinal **Simon Meopham** (d. 1333).[62] Its central element, a simple coped grave-slab, and its positioning at the entrance to the chapel of Saints Peter and Paul were doubtless intended to convey humility (Pl. 97).[63] Such a reading is not necessarily at odds with its unusually fine materials and craftsmanship, nor with the fact that the only recent precedent for the integration of a tomb into an openwork screen was the monument of *c*.1325 in St Paul's Cathedral to Roger Niger, an early thirteenth-century bishop reputed a saint.[64] St Paul's was also the setting for Meopham's one enduring achievement as archbishop, the establishment of the feast of the Conception of the Virgin by a council of the Canterbury province held at his demand in 1328.[65] Meopham had been elected to the see of Canterbury on this feast and, in ordering its observance, he quoted the authority of St Anselm,[66] so it is surely no coincidence that his tomb should stand at the entrance to the chapel which housed that saint's shrine.

In its small-scale architectural detailing, the Meopham tomb shows some striking similarities to a major monument attributable to Thomas of Canterbury, the documented successor to Michael of Canterbury at St Stephen's, Westminster, and almost certainly his son. The monument in question, that of Edward II at Gloucester, is admittedly wholly different in format from Meopham's, but the link is reinforced by the fact that it is the only extant English monument which anticipates the Canterbury tomb in its use of stones of highly contrasted colour and texture.[67] Unfortunately, the part of Meopham's tomb where this aspect was most apparent, the series of recesses over the grave-slab, is the least well preserved. Enough survives, however, to enable one to visualize the original effect of creamy matt Caen stone showing through openwork cusps of shiny black Belgian 'touch', with mottled brown Purbeck shafts supporting miniature vaults of Caen and set against jambs of touch. The ultimate source of this taste for 'structural polychromy' was probably

[62] Measured drawings of 1879 by Arthur Keen (*Building News*, 4 Mar. 1881, 238–9) show damage to the pierced cresting, since repaired, but omit the dowel holes below the hollow cornice on the south side, which presumably held a brass inscription fillet. This must have gone by *c*.1600, when the tomb was identified by a table hanging on it as that of Archbishop Oda (d. 958); Godwin, *Catalogue* (cit. in n. 60), 20; Weever, *Funerall Monuments* (cit. in n. 60), 214. In 1635 it was identified as Archbishop Sudbury's monument, and the latter was thought to be Oda's: 'A Relation of a Short Survey of the Western Counties made by a Lieutenant of the Military Company of Norwich in 1635', ed. L. G. W. Legg, *Camden Miscellany*, 16 (Camden Soc., 3rd ser., 52; 1936), 13–14.

[63] Among English bishops buried in places walked on by those entering church were St Swithun, Bishop of Winchester (d. 862), Michael of Northburgh, Bishop of London (d. 1361), and Philip Repingdon (d. 1424), Bishop of Lincoln until 1419. Dr Jane Geddes kindly informs me that the iron gates incorporated into Meopham's tomb are 13th-cent. work reused (Pl. 16).

[64] Niger's tomb and the associated screen were doubtless made shortly before the translation of this bishop's body in February 1326. For their appearance, see the engraving in Dugdale, *History of St Paul's* (cit. in n. 16), 87. The tomb was of grey marble: H. Holland, *Monumenta Sepulchraria Sancti Pauli*

(London, 1614), unpaginated (pp. 9–10). Meopham's and Niger's monuments both incorporated low, coped tomb-covers set under quasi-tomb-chests with the sides cut away by niches like the prayer niches of shrine bases and, at the back of these niches, slabs pierced by small apertures. The screen above Niger's tomb was much higher than that over Meopham's, and similar in its overall design to the Canterbury choir enclosure completed in 1304. It is possible that Meopham's tomb was also influenced by the screen-cum-canopy of the mid-13th-cent. monument to John Bingham, Bishop of Salisbury, for which see n. 25 above.

[65] Emden, *BRUO*, ii. 1261. Christ Church had formally decided to celebrate the feasts of the Oblation and Conception of the Virgin in 1321: Reg. A, fo. 390.

[66] R. W. Southern, *St Anselm and His Biographer: A Study of Monastic Life and Thought 1059–c.1130* (Cambridge, 1963), 295. For Meopham's election, see *Short Chronicle of S. Paul's Cathedral from 1140 to 1341*, in *Documents Illustrating the History of S. Paul's Cathedral*, ed. W. S. Simpson (Camden Soc., NS, 36; 1880), 53.

[67] The stylistic affinities of the architectural detailing of Meopham's tomb are discussed in R. K. Morris, 'The Development of Late Gothic Mouldings in England, *c*.1250–1400, Part II', *Architectural History*, 22 (1979), 29; Wilson, 'Origins of Perpendicular' (cit. in n. 35), 127.

the late thirteenth- and early fourteenth-century French royal tombs which combined white marble and touch.[68]

Meopham's monument is typical of major English tombs and church furniture of the early fourteenth century to the extent that its sculpture is of excellent quality despite being conceived essentially as filling to the interstices between architectural members. The Evangelists in the spandrels to the tomb-chest (Pl. 95) are even bisected visually by the shafts of the screen-cum-canopy,[69] a trait already found on a London-made work of the preceding generation, the base made *c.*1302–8 for the shrine of St Alban at St Albans Abbey. That the tomb-chest spandrels owe their summary handling and shallow relief to the hardness of the touch from which they are cut is evident by comparison with the same sculptor's work in eight of the main, upper spandrels, where the material is fine-grained Caen.[70] The figures in the four larger upper spandrels have tense facial expressions and contorted poses appropriate to the subject-matter: pairs of academics engaged in vigorous scholarly disputation (Pls. 94, 96).[71] Presumably Meopham's executors wished him to be remembered as a university doctor. Further sculpture from the same hand can be seen on the portal which leads to the chapter room at Rochester Cathedral,[72] but the only known parallel for the pairs of debating scholars is the series of 'weepers' on the tomb-chest of the monument in Lincoln Cathedral to Bishop Henry Burghersh (d. 1340), which was sited even closer to a major shrine than was the Meopham tomb.[73] Burghersh had been Meopham's main competitor for the see of Canterbury, and it would appear that the rivalry between these two prelates was being carried on beyond their lifetimes.

The Meopham monument exemplifies the continuing growth in the size of major English monuments during the fourteenth century, a development which, together with the Christ Church community's reluctance to allow burials near St Thomas's shrine, made virtually inevitable the eventual breaching of the splendid stone screens which had enclosed

---

[68] The earliest known example of this combination is the tomb of Isabel of Aragon (d. 1271); Erlande-Brandenburg, *Le Roi est mort* (cit. in n. 31), 168–9, figs. 152–5.

[69] Unlike the top slab of the 'tomb-chest', these spandrels relate correctly to the supports of the canopy-cum-screen.

[70] A close parallel in a French Gothic tomb for the upper spandrel sculptures of Meopham's monument was the series of similarly trefoil-framed, small-scale scenes in the spandrels of the late 13th-cent. or early 14th-cent. monument to Jean de Montmirel at Longpont: Adhémar and Dordor, *Tombeaux de la collection Gaignières* (cit. in n. 31), 21 (no. 64).

[71] The anxious-looking disembodied head below the lectern used by one pair of academics (Pl.96) apparently represents the Jew or Saracen oppressed by the weight of wisdom contained in the holy texts. A similar expression and asymmetrically knotted headdress are worn by a head on the slightly later canopy of the Percy Tomb at Beverley: N. Dawton, 'The Percy Tomb Workshop', in *Medieval Art and Architecture in the East Riding of Yorkshire*, ed. C. Wilson (British Archaeol. Assn. Conference Trans., 9; Leeds, 1989 for 1983), pl. xxiiib. That this headgear identified pagans and infidels is evident from, e.g., the depic-

tions of Roman soldiers and Jewish bystanders in the scenes of Christ's audience with Pontius Pilate and Christ leaving the Praetorium in the *Très Riches Heures* of the Duc de Berry (Chantilly, Musée Condé, MS 62, fos. 143, 146ᵛ).

[72] The close similarities between the freestone sculpture on Meopham's tomb and the Rochester door are noted in E. S. Prior and A. Gardner, *An Account of Medieval Figure-Sculpture in England* (Cambridge, 1912), 378–9. A more detailed analysis of the relationship is in R. E. Hirschhorn, 'The Chapter-Room Doorway at Rochester Cathedral' (M A report, Courtauld Institute of Art, Univ. of London, 1977), 65–7.

[73] Gough, *Sepulchral Monuments* (cit. in n. 14) i, pt. 2, pl. xxxv. That Burghersh's tomb is later than Meopham's is suggested by the more conventionally weeper-like arrangement of its sculptured scholars and is proved beyond reasonable doubt by the fact that the tomb-chest of his father, Robert, which is structurally integral with his own, has on its north side male weepers wearing the tight, low-belted *pourpoint* in fashion from the early 1340s. Uniquely, the Burghersh tomb is structurally continuous with the base of a shrine, that of St Hugh's head.

the choir and sanctuary since 1304.[74] Yet the decision to insert the tomb of Archbishop **John Stratford** (d. 1348) into the southern screen, immediately west of the *sedilia*, cannot have been taken lightly, and one should probably see the acceptance of this visually disruptive change at the liturgical heart of the Cathedral as a measure of the exceptional amity which had developed between Stratford and the monks during his 'exile' at Canterbury in 1340–1 (Pl. 87).[75] It clearly mattered a great deal that damage to the choir enclosure be minimized, for the cornice and tracery of the latter have somehow been kept in place above the vault of the tomb canopy, despite being rendered nearly invisible from the ground by the two parallel rows of spire-like tabernacles which their retention necessitated (Pl. 101).[76]

The spire-crowned canopy of Stratford's tomb places it among the most ambitious fourteenth-century monuments anywhere in Europe. Only two earlier tombs of this type are known: Edward II's at Gloucester and Pope John XXII's in Avignon Cathedral, the latter a full-blown example of the Kentish version of Decorated Gothic and, by virtue of its occupant's office, a very effective testimony to the pre-eminence which the English achieved in the field of tomb architecture during the early fourteenth century.[77] Although far more complex architecturally than recess-tombs such as Archbishop Pecham's, Stratford's spired and canopied monument functions in exactly the same way, as a symbol of the heavenly tabernacle of the soul. The extraordinarily elevated character of its architectural language is evidenced by the derivation of its linked, open-sided spires from a type of high altar screen which had been in existence for barely a generation.[78]

Stratford's tomb shows every sign of having been designed by William Ramsey, the earliest practitioner of the Perpendicular Gothic style in south-east England, 'king's principal master mason south of the Trent' from 1336 until his death in 1349, and the documented designer of some important tombs.[79] A letter which Prior Hathbrand wrote soon

---

[74] In 1304, when the enclosure was completed, the few monuments in the main vessels of the choirs and sanctuaries of other English cathedrals were almost all those of founders, builders, exceptionally important benefactors, or bishops revered as saints.

[75] The insertion of the tomb did not entail curtailing the *sedilia*, as suggested in Reader-Moore, 'Liturgical Chancel' (cit. in n. 5), 31. That Stratford's warm relations with Prior Hathebrand predated his quarrels with Edward III is evident from a letter of Aug. 1339: *Lit. Cant.*, ii. 215.

[76] A brass plaque in the south aisle floor announces to passing Latinists that the tomb was repaired on the orders of Archbishop Randall Davidson: G. K. A. Bell, *Randall Davidson, Archbishop of Canterbury* (2 vols.; 3rd edn.; London, 1952), i. 495. The repairs were carried out c.1906, and, as photographs taken before then show, they were confined to reinstating alabaster components missing from the south side of the tomb-chest and the setting of the effigy. Unfortunately, the original details were not accurately reproduced and the wrong kind of stone was employed. Of an entirely different order of skill was the earlier restoration of the southern row of spires on the canopy, which entailed piecing in a great number of original fragments. Presumably this work was done under one or other of the Austins, surveyors to the Cathedral c.1820–92. After being particularly heavily damaged in the mid-17th cent., these spires had been

replaced without the level corresponding to the vertical parts of the two-light 'windows': drawing of 1823 by E. Blore, BL, Add. MS 42030, fo. 7; albumen print 10 in 'Canterbury Cathedral VII. Ecclesiastical Tombs', one of a series of albums of drawings, prints, and photographs of English cathedrals compiled by Gerald Cobb and now in the National Monuments Record. There are indications of the intention to construct a central row of spires, but it would be a remarkable coincidence if their omission had happened to leave the right amount of space to accommodate the choir enclosure screen.

[77] The English character of John XXII's tomb was first established in F. Bond, *Congrès archéologique de France: Avignon*, 76 (1909), 390–2, but the Kentish Decorated analogies for the design have never been thoroughly analysed.

[78] C. Wilson, 'The Neville Screen', in *Medieval Art and Architecture at Durham Cathedral*, ed. N. Coldstream and P. Draper (British Archaeol. Assn. Conference Trans., 3; London, 1980 for 1977), 94, 97–8.

[79] For Ramsey, see Wilson, 'Origins of Perpendicular' (cit. in n. 35), 172–258, esp. 245–54 on his tomb designs; Harvey, *English Mediaeval Architects* (cit. in n. 14), 242–5. Harvey has tentatively attributed the tomb to the important royal architect John Box, on the strength of the latter's being documented in the employ of the Prior in 1350 (ibid., 31).

after the Archbishop's death in August 1348 to his brother Robert Stratford, the Bishop of Chichester, reveals very clearly the monastery's concern to ensure that the major monuments in the Cathedral should be of high quality. Hathbrand states that he has no one in his employ equal to the task of making the tomb, admits fearing to begin the work lest criticism of it injure the honour of Christ Church, and requests that the Bishop recommend an expert craftsman.[80] Perhaps the enquiry was passed on to the Archbishop's nephew, the Bishop of London, at whose cathedral Ramsey had built his masterpiece, the cloister and chapter house begun in 1332. It is notable that the canopy to Stratford's tomb makes use of materials of contrasting colour in a way paralleled exactly at the cloister of St Paul's, that is, Purbeck up to capital level and unpainted Caen for everything above. The cells of the canopy vault are whitewashed, with bright colour reserved for the ribs and bosses.[81] The niches of the lost weepers are of alabaster, their canopies backed by tracery pierced to show off the Purbeck behind.

Stratford's alabaster effigy resembles the handful of important earlier English effigies in this material in being of excellent quality (Pl. 111).[82] The head, cruelly damaged though it is, remains recognizable as a superbly idealized portrayal of the self-confident yet spiritually alert late medieval church leader (Pl. 117). This is apparently the earliest of the many English episcopal effigies with hands joined in prayer, a type long known in France.[83] The French influences which pervade the earliest full-scale works of architecture in the Perpendicular style are exemplified here in what remains of the exquisite head-canopy, the nearest thing yet seen in England to the half-polygonal flat-topped canopies first used on French royal tombs.[84] An afterthought was the introduction of slabs forming end walls to

[80] R. M. Haines, *Archbishop John Stratford* (Toronto, 1986), 360. Unfortunately, the damage suffered by the only known copy of the Archbishop's will affects the passage mentioning his burial site: 'in ecclesia Cant' in parte occiden' ['tal' ' and two or three words torn away] in d' [part of word torn away—originally 'dextera'?] parte hostii occidental' iuxta ipsum hostium supradictum' ('in the church of Canterbury, on the west side ... on the [right-hand?] side of the west door, beside the above-mentioned door'). The identification of the door as that on the south side of the choir in *Sede Vacante Wills* (cit. in n. 56), pp. viii–ix, is clearly incorrect, but which door was being referred to is not clear. The statement in the Prior's letter to the Bishop of Chichester that the Archbishop had been allotted an eminent burial-place may well be a reference to the decision to depart from his wishes in this matter.

[81] The ribs are coloured blue, pink, red, and black (the last doubtless the result of chemical change) and the bosses are gold. There are no traces of paint on the outside of the canopy, even in the inconspicuous parts of the spire-work hard up against the cornice of the presbytery enclosure screen, whose north side, by contrast, does retain large areas of original paint.

[82] The other effigies in question are those of Edward II (d. 1327) at Gloucester; John of Eltham, son of Edward II (d. 1336) at Westminster (on a tomb whose architecture is probably by William Ramsey); William of Hatfield, son of Edward III (d. soon after 1336), in York Minster; and John Hotham, Bishop of Ely (d. 1337), formerly in Ely Cathedral and on a tomb-chest probably also designed by William Ramsey. Stratford's effigy

retains hardly any colour visible to the naked eye, except some green or blue on the cushions and a few specks of gold on the fringes of the dalmatic, stole, etc. The restricted use of colour to offset the natural alabaster compares with the earliest French white marble effigies; Erlande-Brandenburg, *Le Roi est mort* (cit. in n. 31), 169, 172 n. 13. For English medieval artefacts in alabaster, see, most recently, N. L. Ramsay, 'Alabaster', in *English Medieval Industries*, ed. J. Blair and N. L. Ramsay (London, 1991), 29–40.

[83] However, the effigies of English clergy of less then episcopal rank had shown the deceased in prayer since the late 13th cent. The sample of French bishops' tombs drawn for Gaignières (Adhémar and Dordor, *Tombeaux de la collection Gaignières* (cit. in n. 31)) indicates a sudden shift in the late 13th cent., away from the variety of types current during most of the century and towards effigies with praying hands and pastoral staffs held under the forearm, as Stratford's cross staff is. It is possible that the emergence of this type, which effectively conveys both personal humility and the dignity appropriate to the holder of high office, was due in some measure to influence from the praying effigies made for members of the French royal family from the 1260s onwards.

[84] The superbly and minutely carved angel with outstretched wings which survives at the less damaged of the two upper angles of the head-canopy appears to have no exact parallel in contemporary tomb design, and the few English part-polygonal head-canopies earlier than Stratford's (e.g. Prior Eastry's at Canterbury) are far simpler. The part-polygonal canopy originally on the tomb of Isabel of Aragon at Saint-Denis (c.1275)

the canopy. That at the foot bore a high relief of the coronation of the Virgin, that at the head, angels bearing the Archbishop's soul heavenwards.[85]

There is no evidence that the Archbishop designate, John Offord, who perished at the height of the Black Death, in May 1349, ever received a monument over his grave in the Martyrdom.[86] **Thomas Bradwardine** died only three months later and was buried in a tomb facing Meopham's across the chapel of Saints Peter and Paul. For some unknown reason the canopy of this monument has been removed, but the parts which remain in place below the south window show that the normal urge to be up to date had yielded to a concern to make a visual counterweight to Meopham's tomb.[87] The monuments of the next two archbishops who died in office, **Simon Islip** (d. 1366)[88] and his nephew **William Wittelsey** (d. 1374),[89] were the first to be set up in the nave since Richard of Dover's tomb

may have been the earliest head-canopy not of the simpler arch-and-gable type. Yet another innovation of this tomb was the pair of vertical 'strips' of enriched images flanking the canopy and its shafts. This motif was known to London brass-makers by the first decade of the 14th cent. (Rogers, 'English Episcopal Monuments' (cit. in n. 25), 52), but the image-less version on Stratford's monument seems to be the first English example on a sculptured tomb.

[85] Figure sculpture in this position is much rarer in English than in French monuments. That the slabs bearing these sculptures are afterthoughts is evident from their relation to the originally open arches at the ends of the canopy, which they block and whose iron ties they make redundant, and from the improvised-looking pair of low arches cut through them in order to accommodate the head-canopy and feet. The purpose of the slabs was presumably to mask the sides of the aperture cut through the sanctuary enclosure screen.

[86] The original hand of the early 16th-cent. list of archbishops' and priors' burial-places (cit. in n. 5), 108, gives the spot simply as 'ad martirium sancti Thome' ('at the Martyrdom of St Thomas'). On the misidentification of Pecham's monument as Offord's, current from the later 16th cent., see Morris, *Tombs of the Archbishops* (cit. in n. 14), 23–5; 'Short Survey' (cit. in n. 62), 16.

[87] The original entry in the early 16th-cent. list of archbishops' and priors' burial-places (Cambridge, Corpus Christi College, MS 298, p. 108) places the tomb in 'capella apostolorum petri et pauli sub fenestra' ('the chapel of the Apostles Peter and Paul, below the window'). The hacking-away of the canopy is unlikely to be post-Reformation, as there is no evidence that the tomb was of cultic importance. Also, the careful patching at the points where the canopy arches sprang is in marked contrast to the gaping hole left by the removal of Archbishop Winchelsey's monument in the later 1540s (cf. n. 52 above). The lack of any mention of Bradwardine's tomb in Leland's *Itinerary* (cit. in n. 52), was probably due to the insconspicuousness of the plain tomb-chest and the lack of any indication that the wall-arcade behind it was part of the monument. The tomb-chest was opened and the Archbishop's skeleton seen in 1888: *Builder*, 54 (Jan.–June 1888), 71. An epitaph from an unspecified Cotton MS (now BL?) is given in Weever, *Funerall Monuments* (cit. in n. 60), 223. Rogers, 'English Episcopal Monuments' (cit. in n. 25), 39, 63 (n. 9), suggests that this was on the monument

itself, and that because it ran to eight lines, it must have been on a brass plate, as is its modern replacement.

[88] Islip was buried 'ante magnam Crucem in navi' ('before the great rood in the nave') (Stephen Birchington, *Historia de Archiepiscopis Cantuariensibus . . .*, in Wharton, *Anglia Sacra*, i. 46), 'in the middle of the body at the upper-end, inclining to the north side' (Somner, *Antiquities* (1640), 264). Islip's tomb-chest, one of the 'high tumbes' noted by Leland (*Itinerary*, iv. 40)—the others were those of Archbishops Wittelsey and Arundel—was 'raysed one yeard from the ground' (Scarlett, heraldic collections (cit. in n. 59), fo. 13ʳ). The brass is mentioned as still existing and the eight-line verse epitaph recorded in Holinshed, *Chronicles* (cit. in n. 60), 1465. The fact that Islip's was the only raised tomb in the central vessel of the nave enables one to be fairly sure that this was the tomb which Erasmus' Ogygius meant when he said that there was nothing to see in the nave other than chained books and 'sepulchrum nescio cujus' ('a tomb, I know not whose'): *Opera Omnia Desiderii Erasmi Roterodami, Ordinis Primi, Tomus Tertius, Colloquia*, ed. L.-E. Halkin, F. Bierlaire, and R. Hoven (Amsterdam, 1972), 487. At some date between the writing of Weever's account and Aug. 1635, the tomb and its brass were moved to a new position, under the second arch of the north nave arcade from the east; 'Short Survey' (cit. in n. 62), 16; Somner, *Antiquities* (1640), 264. The new site is shown in Surveys and Maps 104, ground-plan of the nave made in 1786 for the Chapter by 'White' to record the positions of tombs (Fig. 1): Dean's book, 1777–93, p. 141. During the repaving of the nave in 1787 the coffin was found a short distance (the exact position is not given) from the re-erected tomb: *Gentleman's Mag.*, 57 (1787), pt. 1. 222–3. A view of the tomb is in J. Dart, *The History and Antiquities of the Cathedral Church of Canterbury* (London, 1726), 37, but like all the representations of monuments there, it is more a reconstruction than a true record of what still survived. One of the defaced indents in the north cloister walk (no. XI in A. G. Sadler, *The Indents of Lost Monumental Brasses in Kent* (priv. print. 1975–90), pt. 1. 26 and app. 3, 14–16; no. 2 in Gough, *Sepulchral Monuments* (cit. in n. 14), ii, pt. 2. 88) is almost certainly Islip's, for its head-canopy agrees well with the rendering in Dart, and its length of 368 cm. is extremely close to the 4 yds. given in 'Short Survey' (cit. in n. 16), 16. A sketch of the upper part of the effigy on this indent was made in 1805, when it was in the chapter house, along with other indents ejected from the nave:

had been installed in the Lady Chapel in 1184.[90] They consisted of marble tomb-chests, plain except for brasses, and were cleared away when the nave was repaved in 1787. Since these tomb-chests, and that erected later by Archbishop Arundel, were the only monuments in the nave more ambitious than floor-level brasses, it is clear that Christ Church had set its face against the general late medieval English trend towards 'democratizing' the tomb-chest. The rest of Europe continued to restrict tomb-chests to prestigious burials, although Continental influence offers a far less likely explanation for the conservatism of Christ Church than the hierarchical habit of thought which governed all forms of commemoration within the pre-Reformation Cathedral.

The Stratford monument remained the only interruption of the choir enclosure until 1381, when the headless corpse of the murdered **Simon Sudbury** was entombed in an even more honourable position south of the high altar (Pl. 102). Sudbury, like Stratford, was an archbishop with whom the monks developed a special rapport, and there is a possibility that they took charge of commemorating this personally poor primate.[91] Sudbury's monument owes much to Stratford's as regards its general architectural form and its relation to the choir enclosure,[92] but its bolder, barer character typifies late fourteenth-century Perpendicular in the South-East, particularly the works of the likely architect of the nave of Canterbury Cathedral, Henry Yevele, who is documented as a major designer of tombs.[93]

Powell, collections (cit. in n. 50), fo. 118. The identification as Archbishop Arundel's brass made there is certainly wrong, as the latter was much shorter than Islip's brass (Fig. 1). Islip's will (*Sede Vacante Wills* (cit. in n. 56), 77–9) does not stipulate any particular burial-spot within the Cathedral. The chantry was kept at the altar of St Cross, close to the original site of the monument: A. Hussey, *Kent Chantries* (Kent Archaeol. Soc., Kent Records, 12; 1936), 48–9.

[89] Wittelsey left his body to be buried wherever his executors and friends chose: *Sede Vacante Wills*, 80. His burial near Archbishop Islip, under the third arch of the south arcade from the east (plan by Thomas Johnson engraved in 1654 by Wenceslaus Hollar, in W. Dugdale, *Monasticon Anglicanum* (3 vols.; London, 1655–73), i, between 18 and 19; 1786 plan of nave floor (cit. in n. 88)), was apt, for he was Islip's nephew. Bishop Godwin reported that the monument had been 'lately defaced by tearing out the brasse' and remembered reading the epitaph some 16 years earlier: *Catalogue* (cit. in n. 60), 100. What little remained of the epitaph *c.*1630 is given in Weever, *Funerall Monuments* (cit. in n. 60), 224. A view, with a reconstruction of the brass, is in Dart, *History and Antiquities* (cit. in n. 88), 25. The grave was seen in 1787: *Gentleman's Mag.*, 57 (1787), pt. 1. 223.

[90] It is probable that Islip's and Wittelsey's tombs were made immediately after their deaths and were dismantled and re-erected after the rebuilding of the Romanesque nave. Theobald's original monument is likely to have been destroyed at this time. The tomb of Islip's successor, Simon Langham (resigned 1368), is in Westminster Abbey; see n. 101 and p. 475 below. In the reproduction of the 1786 plan of the nave floor in Woodruff and Danks, *Memorials*, pl. opp. 195, the numbers added to identify Islip's and Wittelsey's tombs have been transposed.

[91] The request in the brief nuncupative will for burial in the Cathedral mentions neither a site nor a tomb: *Sede Vacante Wills* (cit. in n. 56), 81. By the 1630s Sudbury's tomb was identified (doubtless by means of a 'table') as that of Archbishop Oda, for which see n. 16 above; 'Short Survey' (cit. in n. 62), 13. The correct identification is given in Somner, *Antiquities* (1640), 265. Around 1833 the tomb was opened and a leaden ball found in place of the severed head: Scott Robertson, 'Burial Places of the Archbishop' (cit. in n. 11), 290. The Archbishop's head is generally believed to be that kept in St Gregory's Church, Sudbury, but a late-medieval continuator of Gervase of Canterbury's *Chronicle* states that after the burial of the body at Canterbury, the head remained for a time in St Michael's Church, London, before being brought to the Cathedral and buried honourably with the body: Trinity College, Cambridge, MS R. 5. 41, fo. 152.

[92] The concern to safeguard the integrity of Prior Eastry's choir enclosure is as evident here as in Stratford's tomb, although the solution adopted is different. The cornice and cresting of the screen are kept visible from the sanctuary by making the north side of the canopy very low (Pl. 87). In contrast to the procedure adopted for the insertion of Stratford's tomb, the cornice was dismantled and re-erected (see the insertion in darker stone), and the early 14th-cent. tracery was replaced by new blind tracery following the same pattern. From the south aisle the screen is completely invisible.

[93] Features common to Sudbury's tomb and tombs documented as Yevele's work include the trios of pendant ogee arches (cf. John of Gaunt's tomb in Old St Paul's Cathedral: Dugdale, *History of St Paul's* (cit. in n. 16), pl. at 163) and the niches in the tomb-chest (cf. the fragment from the tomb of Sir Walter Manny (d. 1372), formerly in the chapel of the London Charterhouse: J. H. Harvey, *Henry Yevele* (London, 1944), 33). Of the works attributed to Yevele by Harvey the closest stylistically to the Sudbury tomb are the pulpit in Arundel Church and the tomb of Rahere in St Bartholomew-the-Great, Smithfield,

Sudbury's vigorous patronage of the rebuilding of the nave, coupled with the martyr status which his long-lost epitaph accorded him,[94] must explain why he seems to have been the only fourteenth-century English bishop commemorated by a cast-metal effigy. With the destruction of the effigy, probably in the reign of Edward VI, all remembrance of it seems to have faded.[95] Yet the evidence for its former existence is clear: John Leland's description of the monument as 'a high tumbe of coper and gilte'; and the rough finish, incomplete mouldings and irregular form of the slab on the central section of the tomb-chest, features inexplicable unless concealed by an effigy and base-plate of metal.[96] At the time of Sudbury's murder, the Black Prince's magnificent gilt-copper effigy had probably just been installed in the Trinity Chapel, and it is very likely that this monument inspired the convent to commemorate their own 'hero' in similar style. Yet there can be little doubt that the placing of Sudbury's and all the other fourteenth-century archbishops' monuments on the south side of the sanctuary and Trinity Chapel was due to the desire to avoid the more honorific northern positions which, in the sanctuary at least, were occupied by objects of higher importance than tombs.[97] There may also have been a wish to parade the illustrious dead along the approach to the cultic and aesthetic climax at Christ Church, the shrine of St Thomas. A preoccupation with the view from the south aisle is palpable in Stratford's and Sudbury's monuments, for their relatively ill-lit north sides are simpler than their south sides, markedly so in the case of Sudbury (Pls. 87, 101, 102).[98]

The most easterly of the medieval archbishops' tombs, that of **William Courtenay** (d. 1396), almost certainly owes both its existence and its placing beside St Thomas's shrine to the intervention of Richard II, who happened to be in Canterbury waiting to cross to France when the Archbishop died.[99] Courtenay himself had prepared a large floor-level

London. The whitewashing of the vault of the canopy of Sudbury's monument, and the total absence of applied colour, suggest a concern to emphasize the visual pre-eminence of the gilt-bronze effigy (for which see below).

[94] Sudbury contributed 3,000 marks to the rebuilding of the nave and was responsible for the demolition of the old nave, for laying foundations, and for building much of the outer walls. After his death his executors gave a further 130 marks: Sede Vacante Register for June–Dec. 1381, Bodl., MS Ashmole 794, fo. 264ᵛ. For the fullest statement of the circumstantial evidence relating to the identity of the designer of the nave, see J. H. Harvey, 'Henry Yeveley and the Nave of Canterbury Cathedral', *Cant. Cath. Chron.*, 79 (1985), 20–30. A fragment of the epitaph, where Sudbury was described as 'martirizatus', is in Weever, *Funerall Monuments* (cit. in n. 60), 244. He is compared to St Thomas in John Gower, *Vox Clamantis*, lib. 1, cap. 14 (*Complete Works of John Gower*, ed. G. C. Macaulay (4 vols.; Oxford, 1899–1902), iv. 50–4).

[95] The defacing of Sudbury's tomb was probably due, as the destruction of Winchelsey's monument certainly was, to its having been the site of a cult. For the posthumous miracles, see Thomas Walsingham, *Historia Anglicana*, ed. H. T. Riley, 2 vols. (RS 28/1; 1863–4), i. 461–2. Somner surmised that the epitaph was removed because the mayor and aldermen of Canterbury had prayed for his soul on his anniversary, in gratitude for his part in building the city wall: *Antiquities* (1640), 265. For the destruction of metal tomb-effigies in Wells *temp.* Edward

VI, see P. Tudor-Craig, 'Wells Sculpture', in *Wells Cathedral: A History*, ed. L. S. Colchester (Shepton Mallet, 1982), 123, 130–1 (n. 70). The only references in print to an effigy on Sudbury's tomb—those in J. Storer, *The History and Antiquities of the Cathedral Churches of Great Britain* (4 vols.; London, 1814–19), i. 12, and J. Britton, *The History and Antiquities of the Metropolitical Church of Canterbury* (London, 1821), 67—are unlikely to have been the outcome of direct observation, as they are each accompanied by the patently untrue statement that the niches of the tomb-chest contained images.

[96] Leland, *Itinerary* (cit. in n. 52), iv. 39. The central section of the top slab is made of two pieces of marble whose edges join very roughly near the central longitudinal axis. The large, approximately rectangular depression at the west end looks like the seating for the cushion under the effigy's head.

[97] Namely, the great relic-cupboard in the bay next to the eastern crossing, and the cupboard for the gear belonging to St Alphege's altar. For the former, see Legg and Hope, *Inventories*, 80–92; for the latter see n. 144 below.

[98] The tomb-chest of the Sudbury monument is lower on the north side and quite plain, and the canopy is simpler and lower (see n. 92 above). The simplification of the north side of Stratford's monument affects only the spires of the canopy.

[99] For the very plausible suggestion that Richard II ordered Courtenay's burial in Canterbury Cathedral at the suggestion

brass at the centre of the choir of his collegiate foundation next to Maidstone Palace, but the eastern arm of the Cathedral has never contained any examples of this widely used kind of memorial.[100] Probably it was considered that the excavation of graves in the masonry infill between the floor and vaulting of the crypt would be hazardous, but a more important factor is likely to have been the feeling that the members of the Christ Church community deemed worthy of burial in the eastern arm, as well as the community as a whole, would be best honoured by the use of tomb-chests rather than floor-level slabs. Courtenay's monument at Canterbury is thus an alabaster tomb-chest, surmounted by an effigy in the same material. Presumably begun shortly after the Archbishop's burial in the presence of the King on 4 August 1396, it is, to all appearances, a 'bespoke' London-made piece rather than one of the semi-standardized products of the hugely prolific alabasterers' workshops at Chellaston in Derbyshire. As has long been recognized, the effigy (Pl. 112) is similar enough to that of William of Wykeham at Winchester to be attributed to the same workshop. Courtenay's tomb is probably a fraction later than Wykeham's,[101] for though both effigies present a similar blandly imposing image unlikely to incorporate elements of portraiture, the drapery carving at Canterbury looks like a simplified and schematized version of that at Winchester. Even more definite evidence that Courtenay's tomb is a derivative of Wykeham's is the series of 'stalks' impaling the shields on its tomb-chest, an architecturally anomalous feature hardly explicable except as a residue of the elongated

of the monks, and the implication that the lost inscription spelled out that he was buried there rather than at Maidstone or Exeter Cathedral, see Somner, *Antiquities* (1640), 266. That Richard was motivated by embarrassment at needing to hurry through the election of Courtenay's successor and by remorse at having often treated a faithful friend ungenerously, as is suggested in M. Beazeley, 'The Burial Place of Archbishop Courtenay', *Arch. Cant.*, 23 (1898), 31–54, is perhaps supported by the proximity of Courtenay's grave to that of Richard's father, for there is no obvious reason why the monks should have thought this Archbishop merited burial so close to St Thomas's shrine. Richard II's interference with burial arrangements is documented in the cases of John Waltham, bishop of Salisbury (d. 1395), buried in the Confessor's Chapel at Westminster amid general murmuring about the inappropriateness of non-royal burials there (Walsingham, *Historia Anglicana* (cit. in n. 95), ii. 218), and Thomas of Woodstock, Duke of Gloucester (d. 1397), denied burial in the same chapel.

[100] Except in the crypt; see p. 492 and n. 251 below. For the refusal to grant Archbishop Reynolds burial in the floor of the south-eastern transept see above. It was clearly thought safe to dig graves above the massive ashlar-built arches of the crypt which carry the piers of the choir and Trinity Chapel (e.g. the graves of Henry IV and Archbishop Chichele), but this was not done above the vaults carrying the floors of the main vessels and aisles, which in the main crypt are rubble-built. See also n. 232 below. It may be a coincidence that brasses are absent from the tomb-chests in the eastern arm at Canterbury, as well as from the floor there, but the presence of brasses in both types of setting in the nave makes it more likely that a policy of exclusion was being operated. Such a policy is unlikely to have been based on snobbishness about relative costs; cf. the prices of brasses and alabaster effigies mentioned on p. 492 and

in nn. 186, 217 below. Accounts of the indents of the Cathedral's brasses are: Sadler, *Indents of Lost Brasses* (cit. in n. 88); T. Hay, 'The Ledger Slabs of Canterbury Cathedral, 1991', *Arch. Cant.*, 109 (1991), 5–28; id., cat. of ledger slabs, deposited in the Cathedral Archives.

[101] Wykeham's tomb was probably ordered around 4 Nov. 1394, the starting-date of the remodelling of the Winchester nave, of which the chantry chapel is an integral part. It was certainly in existence when the Bishop made his will on 24 July 1403, as the chantry chapel is there called 'newly built': R. Lowth, *The Life of William of Wykeham, Bishop of Winchester* (London, 1759), 217, app., p. xxxv. Wykeham's effigy and tomb-chest resemble Courtenay's less than they did originally, because of their repair after Civil War damage. The two effigies and that of Cardinal Langham at Westminster are attributed to the same workshop in W. H. St J. Hope, 'On the Early Working of Alabaster in England', *Archaeol. Jnl.*, 61 (1904), 232. It is nevertheless clear that all three were carved by different sculptors. Apart from the loss of the hands, the tip of the nose, the head of the primatial cross, and the front finial of the mitre, Courtenay's effigy is notably well preserved, thanks, no doubt, to the high, and possibly contemporary, iron railing, for which see J. Geddes, 'Some Tomb Railings in Canterbury Cathedral', in *Collectanea Historica: Essays in Memory of Stuart Rigold*, ed. A. Detsicas (Maidstone, 1981), 66, 68. The main uprights of these and the similar railings round the Black Prince's and Henry IV's monuments have holes to receive some kind of terminal feature, presumably spikes for wax torches lit, e.g., on anniversaries. The present restrained colouring of the alabaster of Courtenay's tomb in gold, red, and green is apparently a reinstatement of what remained of the original scheme: E. W. Tristram, 'A Note on the Tomb of Archbishop Courtenay', *Friends of Canterbury Cathedral, 11th Annual Report* (1938), 39–40.

arch-headed panels in the equivalent position on the Winchester tomb-chest, which lacks shields because its occupant was not of noble birth.[102] Wykeham's monument was probably designed, like the chantry chapel and nave in which it stands, by the major architect William Wynford, but the garbling of its architecture by whoever was responsible for the design of Courtenay's monument effectively proves that he was not an architect[103]. The workshop which made the Wykeham and Courtenay tombs also produced the alabaster effigy on the monument erected *c.*1394 in Westminster Abbey to one of Courtenay's predecessors at Canterbury, Simon Langham. There the tomb-chest is of Purbeck marble and was supplied by Henry Yevele and Stephen Lote, London's leading designers of tomb architecture as well as of full-scale buildings.[104] Whereas the Wykeham tomb-chest seems to have been imitated only once, Yevele's and Lote's designs gave rise to numerous near-copies by marblers and alabasterers. Canterbury Cathedral contains three such imitations.[105]

Comparison of Courtenay's effigy with Stratford's illustrates the steep decline in quality which affected many of the figural arts in late fourteenth-century England.[106] The face is a strangely bloated mask, the rendering of the eyes and their sockets being particularly schematic, and the body seems to consist of a flattened and slightly flaring cylinder. In one respect, Courtenay's effigy is more naturalistic than Stratford's, for the vestments are no longer shown entirely as though their wearer were standing upright. However, the draperies are not those of a recumbent figure so much as of an upright one which has been carefully lowered into an horizontal position—a curious conceit most fully enacted in the buckled tubular folds of the alb. During the rest of the Middle Ages, naturalistically gravity-flattened and form-revealing draperies were to make little headway in English tomb-sculpture against the traditional quasi-upright convention, presumably because the latter was thought more decorous.[107] Comparison of the actual vestments portrayed in Courtenay's and Stratford's effigies shows some changes in ecclesiastical fashion. The apparel of the amice has become shallower, the sides of the mitre have become lower and the points more acute, and the vertical part of the *pallium* has acquired a rounded end and

---

[102] Islip's and Wittelsey's lost brasses (see nn. 88, 89 above) had each incorporated two shields, one of which may have been their personal arms, but it was appropriate that the tomb-chest of the emphatically armigerous Courtenay should have made far more generous provision. The arms must have become indecipherable by the 16th cent., for they are not recorded in Scarlett's heraldic collections or Philipot's church notes (n. 59 above). Not being within a chantry chapel, Courtenay's tomb-chest could be considerably larger than Wykeham's.

[103] A comparable instance of a specialist craftman's degrading a scheme taken from earlier architect-designed monuments is the Purbeck tomb-chest of the monument to Richard Beauchamp, Earl of Warwick, at Warwick, contracted for in 1456 by John Bourde, marbler of Corfe, and perhaps designed by the London marbler John Essex. In place of the three-tier blind tracery which occurs between the niches on the tombs of Edward III and Richard II, there are small niches illogically divorced from their pedestals by a residual tier of blind tracery.

[104] H. F. Westlake, *Westminster Abbey: The Church, Convent,*

Cathedral and College of St. Peter, Westminster (2 vols.; London, 1923), i. 118; Harvey, *English Mediaeval Architects* (cit. in n. 14), 364.

[105] The tomb-chests of Henry IV and Joan of Navarre, Lady Margaret Holland and her two husbands, and Archbishop Kempe, all discussed below. Archbishop Bourchier's tomb-chest, which resembles the preceding in deriving from the tombs of Edward III and Richard II at Westminster, but is a reworking by an architect of high ability, is discussed below.

[106] It exemplifies also the tendency to rely on well-established formulas, for the dogs at the feet of these two effigies are a motif apparently first used in England on the tomb of Aveline of Lancaster in Westminster Abbey, made in the 1290s. The angels at the head of the latter also established a pattern still adhered to in Courtenay's effigy.

[107] The maniples of some of the early 13th-cent. effigies of pre-Conquest bishops at Wells acknowledge the effects of gravity, and the concept is more fully applied in the effigies of Bishops Ralph of Shrewsbury at Wells (d. 1363) and John of Sheppey at Rochester (d. 1360).

has begun to contract. The stubbly jowls in vogue during the second quarter of the fourteenth century have given way to the clean-shaven look henceforth *de rigueur* for late medieval English clerics.

Archbishop **Thomas Arundel** (d. 1414) was doing no more than taking due credit for his work of completing the rebuilding of the nave when he decided to build himself a monument under the third most easterly arch of the north arcade. This position would have recalled the burials of founders and major benefactors on the north sides of sanctuaries, and, given the function of the nave as the part of the Cathedral regularly accessible to the faithful at large, the nearness of Arundel's tomb to the east end would probably have conveyed some sense of the pastor at the head of his flock.[108] Apart from the slightly later chapel of John Buckingham, Bishop of Lincoln (d. 1399), which also stood under the north arcade but much further west,[109] Arundel's monument was the Cathedral's only free-standing chantry chapel.[110] The demolition of both structures in 1540, some seven years before the general attack on chantries, is hard to understand except as an act of retribution by Archbishop Cranmer for Arundel's and Buckingham's zealous suppression of Lollardy.[111] By 1408 Arundel had built at least the chapel, and the monument it contained—a tomb-chest bearing a brass—existed by 1411, if not before.[112] Arundel's is thus

[108] Arundel's chapel would probably have stood further east had it not been necessary to avoid darkening the Lady Chapel (or at least its altar), then in the eastern bays of the north nave aisle. The exact position of Arundel's monument is not stated in any secondary work pre-dating the repaving of the nave floor in 1787. The early 16th-cent. list of archbishops' and priors' burial places (cit. in n. 5), 110, gives 'in navi ecclesie in capella ab eo fundata' ('in the nave of the church, in a chapel founded by him'). John Leland, writing soon after the destruction of the chapel, includes 'Arundel under a piller on the north side' among the 'high tumbes of bisshops ... in the body of the chirche': *Itinerary* (cit. in n. 52), iv. 40. Scarlett, heraldic collections (cit. in n. 59), fo. 13ᵛ, notes only that Arundel 'lyeth on the northe syde of the boddye of the Churche', and by recording no heraldry indicates that there was none to be seen in 1599. Somner, *Antiquities* (1640), 268, specifies that the monument had been inside the chapel and that the only part of it remaining was 'a bare Gravestone levelled with the floor, with the brass all shamefully torn away'. It is omitted from Johnson's 1654 plan (cit. in n. 89). The 1786 plan of the nave floor (cit. in n. 88) shows an indent under the third arch from the east in the north arcade, which must be Arundel's because of its shortness (due to the need to leave room for an altar within the chantry chapel) and because the only other indent shown under a north arcade arch, that in the next bay east, is definitely Archbishop Islip's.

[109] John Buckingham retired to Christ Church after resigning the see of Lincoln in 1398. His will asks for burial in the low (i.e. westerly) place where the archbishop was wont to make his station in general processions. His floor-level brass was seen in 1599 by Scarlett, who thought it very curiously made and mistook it for a prior's, doubtless because it showed a figure with mitre and pastoral staff: heraldic collections (cit. in n. 59), fo. 29ᵛ. At the corners were the arms of the Bishop and the three other individuals commemorated in the chantry: Edward III, Thomas, Earl of Warwick, and Henry Ferrers, Lord of Groby: *Sede Vacante Wills* (cit. in n. 56), 103. Somner pronounced

it 'very fair', noted that the name was missing from the inscription, and worked out the identity of the occupant: *Antiquities* (1640), 180–1. At an unknown date (in the 1660s?) the indent was succeeded by the simple ledger shown in the middle of the seventh bay from the east on the 1786 plan of the nave floor (cit. in n. 88). Somner claimed that no chantry chapel was ever built, despite the provision for one in the ordinances (Ch. Ant. C. 146, 146a, 147, and 150; Reg. D, fos. 311ᵛ–313). However, a chapel is referred to in the will of one of the chantry chaplains who died in 1468: A. C. Hussey, 'Further Notes from Kentish Wills', *Arch. Cant.*, 31 (1915), 37.

[110] The lack of a stone vault (cf. the similarly sited chantry of Bishop Edington (d. 1366) at Winchester) and the approximate height are both revealed by the post-demolition patching of the adjacent piers (kindly pointed out to me by Tim Tatton-Brown). That the north and south walls ran between the northern and southern shafts of the latter piers was proved by an exploratory excavation of the western part of the chantry site carried out in 1992 by the Canterbury Archaeological Trust.

[111] In 1546 there was no chaplain serving Buckingham's chantry who could say what had become of the chapel, but it is virtually certain that it had been demolished in 1540, as the endowments are said to have been surrendered to the king: *The Canterbury Chantries and Hospitals in 1546*, ed. C. Cotton (Kent Archaeol. Soc., Records Branch, 12, suppl.; 1934), 27. For Cranmer's appropriation of the Arundel chantry endowments, the destruction of the chapel, the selling of its materials, and the removal of its gear by the king's commissioners at the suppression of Christ Church in Mar. 1540, see ibid. 65–6.

[112] The papal permit obtained by Arundel in 1408 for his chantry foundation speaks of the 'oratory' as built: *Kent Chantries* (cit. in n. 88), 33. Permission to construct tombs was needed from the monks only when the site was in the choir or beyond, so might Arundel's papal permit have been a precaution taken in case the monks raised objections to the intrusion of a large and new-fangled kind of monument? The will made on 12 Feb.

the earliest Canterbury monument known to have been erected in the lifetime of its occupant. To the Pope, the Archbishop had represented his chapel as an oratory which would enable the laity to hear mass whenever the east parts of the church were closed off.[113]

An unexpected and intriguing postscript occurs in the form of an entry in the fabric accounts of York Minster for 1418–19: 'Paid to Marcell, carrier, for sending to the executors of the Archbishop of Canterbury in London one wooden image made as an exemplar, 3s. 4d.' It may be suggested that the reference is to a full-size wooden pattern such as is known to have been used to guide the executors and craftsmen concerned in making three later English tomb-effigies in bronze.[114] On his hypothesis it becomes possible to offer the following reconstruction of events. While Archbishop of York, Arundel embarked on commissioning a bronze effigy but let the scheme lapse on his translation to Canterbury in 1396. Some four years after his death, his executors, perhaps finding his estate in surplus, considered reviving the project, with the aim of equalling the monument of the predecessor who began the nave which Arundel brought to a triumphant conclusion.[115] It seems likely that Arundel himself had forborne to proceed with an effigy so much more splendid than the brasses on the nearby tombs of Islip and Wittelsey.

By far the best known of all the archbishops' monuments at Canterbury is that of **Henry Chichele** (d. 1443) on the north side of the choir (Pl. 103). Completed by 1426,[116] it is the earliest fully developed example to have survived of one of the most arresting inventions of late medieval art, a 'double-decker' tomb, in which an effigy of the usual lifelike kind is placed above another of equal size representing a naked, decaying cadaver.[117] There is a good chance that Chichele's monument was based on some lost French prototype dating from the late fourteenth or early fifteenth century, for although the exact combination of

1414 (*Sede Vacante Wills* (cit. in n. 56), 82) refers to the chantry (meaning the chapel) as incomplete, but presumably the only work then outstanding concerned the fittings and decoration.

[113] See n. 112 above and n. 260 below.

[114] *Fabric Rolls of York Minster*, ed. J. Raine (Surtees Soc., 35; 1859), 39. S. Whittingham, 'The Chronology of the Portraits of Richard II', *Burlington Mag.*, 113 (1971), 12 (n. 4), interprets the exemplar, correctly in my view, as a preliminary stage in the making of an effigy at York before 1396, intended to be reused for the same purpose at Canterbury. M. Aston, *Thomas Arundel* (Oxford, 1967), 282, assumes that the exemplar was made to permit the copying of an existing effigy in York Minster. However, a drawing would have sufficed for this purpose, whereas all the other known instances of full-scale mock-ups in wood (assuming that the Arundel exemplar was life-size, something not revealed in the entry) relate to a more advanced stage in the planning process than the gathering of information about suitable prototypes on which to base a design. They were, in fact, part of very careful preparations made immediately in advance of the actual execution of work using particularly costly materials, the aim being, no doubt, to give patrons the opportunity to intervene and so obtain a result which was to their liking. The documented instances of wooden exemplars for effigies are: John Massingham's for the Earl of Warwick's bronze effigy at Warwick, 1449; James Hales's for the Earl of Derby's bronze effigy at Burscough Priory,

Lancashire, *c*.1504–6; and Lawrence Emler's and Thomas Drawsword's for the white marble effigies projected for Henry VII's monument in 1506.

[115] York Minster too already contained one cast-metal effigy, that of Dean William de Langton (d. 1279): S. Badham, 'A Lost Bronze Effigy of 1279 from York Minster', *Antiquaries Jnl.*, 60 (1980), 59–65.

[116] A *terminus ante quem* for the monument is provided by a letter from the Prior of Christ Church to Chichele dated 5 Feb. 1426. This reports a commotion caused at the time of high mass on the previous day, when an escaped prisoner tried to resist arrest by holding on to the iron railings round the Archbishop's new 'monumentum': *Lit. Cant.* iii. 146–8. For the Priory's agreement to bury the Archbishop's body in the already prepared tomb and to celebrate his obit at the adjoining altar of St Stephen, see *The Register of Henry Chichele, Archbishop of Canterbury 1414–1443*, ed. E. F. Jacob, 4 vols. (CYS 42, 45–7; 1937–47), ii. 123–4.

[117] One of the inscriptions on Chichele's tomb invites the passer-by to contemplate the horrible residue of the corpse's decomposition (see below, n. 121), yet the lower effigy does not show what was actually inside the grave, namely a cadaver arrayed in full pontificals. The portrayal of insignia in decay, or associated directly with decay, would doubtless have been thought an affront to the dignity and enduring character of the archiepiscopal office.

elements used cannot be found in any one earlier tomb, the elements themselves nearly all occur in France at a considerably earlier date.[118] Cadaver effigies resemble the majority of the morbid images so favoured during the fifteenth century, in that they exploit the enhanced naturalistic capacity of late medieval art for the purpose of shocking the individual into recognition of his true, mortal nature and thereby inducing a prayerful, penitent state of mind.[119]

The effectiveness of the Chichele monument as a *momento mori* was enormously enhanced by its location at the one point in the church where it was able—almost literally—to speak to three different audiences.[120] On the north side of the slab under the cadaver effigy an inscription sharply admonitory, almost minatory, in tone addresses in the second person singular anyone passing along the aisle,[121] while the last third of the southern inscription, which faced the monks as they left the choir by the adjoining door, equates the grave and its contents with a mirror able to reveal his mortality and sinfulness to the spiritually self-aware onlooker.[122] The most obvious interpretation of the first two-thirds of the southern inscription is as a reinforcement of the message conveyed visually by juxtaposing the cadaver with the resurrected body of the prelate arrayed in the gorgeous apparel proper to his position near the summit of the earthly ecclesiastical hierarchy: 'I was born a poor man: and was afterwards raised to be Primate here. Now I am cast down:

[118] The immense tomb of Cardinal Jean de la Grange (d. 1402), formerly in Saint-Martial, Avignon, an iconographically far more complex monument than Chichele's, had in its lowest register a high-relief cadaver similar in 'pose' to that of Chichele's and also laid on a shroud. In the next lowest register was an effigy of the normal kind but backed by small statues of Christ and the Apostles similar in their iconographic function to the figures formerly on the pier east of Chichele's tomb-chest. For the Avignon tomb, see A. M. Morganstern, 'The La Grange Tomb and Choir: A Monument of the Great Schism of the West', *Speculum*, 48 (1973), 52–69, and for possible Avignon visits by Chichele, see *Reg. Chichele* (cit. in n. 116), i, pp. xxvi, xxx. The monument of Guillaume de Harcigny, physician to Charles VI (d. 1393), formerly in the cemetery of the Franciscans in Laon, consists of a single effigy, a cadaver comparable to that of Chichele's tomb in being fully three-dimensional. The late 13th- or early 14th-cent. tomb of Jean de Montmirel (d. 1219), formerly in the abbey of Longpont near Soissons, was a double-decker, with the lower effigy showing the deceased as a knight, the upper as a Cistercian monk: Adhémar and Dordor, *Tombeaux de la collection Gaignières* (cit. in n. 31), 21 (no. 64). The use of the Chichele scheme in the tomb of Johann von Sierck, Archbishop of Trier (d. 1456), formerly in the Church of Our Lady at Trier, may be due to direct English influence, but given the general dearth of evidence for such influences on Continental art at this period, it seems more likely that the Trier and Canterbury tombs share a common French or Low Countries ancestry. These monuments, and Chichele's, are discussed in K. Cohen, *Metamorphosis of a Death Symbol: The Transi Tomb in the Late Middle Ages and the Renaissance* (Berkeley, Calif., 1973). It is unlikely that the earliest English cadaver-effigy is that in the north transept of York Minster traditionally identified as Treasurer Thomas Haxey (d. 1425), as the knotting of the shroud

above its head is typologically later than the treatment of the shroud on Chichele's lower effigy.

[119] For an exposition of the thesis that 'the cadaver tomb phenomenon was orthodox, even reactionary, novel in only the manner of its plastic expression', see P. M. King, 'The Cadaver Tomb in England: Novel Manifestation of an Old Idea', *Church Monuments*, 5 (1990), 26–38. Other discussion of the intellectual context of the 15th-cent. cadaver tomb are: Cohen, *Death Symbol* (cit. in n. 118), 11–119; s'Jacob, *Realism and Idealism* (cit. in n. 8), 48, 53–4; Panofsky, *Tomb Sculpture* (cit. in n. 30), 64–5; P. M. King, 'Contexts of the Cadaver Tomb in Fifteenth-Century England' (D.Phil. thesis, Univ. of York, 1987).

[120] The most accurate printing of the inscriptions is that in J. M. Cowper, *The Memorial Inscriptions of the Cathedral Church of Canterbury* (priv. printed, Canterbury, 1897), 137. The inscription fillets are attributed by Robin Emmerson to the London workshop which made the 'Series B' brasses: R. Emmerson, 'Monumental Brasses: London Design c.1420–85', *JBAA*, 131 (1978), 73. The inscription on the upper slab outlines Chichele's career in conventional terms.

[121] Expanded, this reads, 'Quisquis eris qui transieris. rogo michi memoreris / Tu qui eris michi consimilis. qui post morieris / Omnibus horribilis. Pulvis, vermis et caro vilis' ('Whosoever you are who will pass by [here], I ask for remembrance from you, you who will be like me, you who will afterwards die, horrible in everything—dust, worms, vile flesh'). For the origins of the motif of the dead addressing the living from the tomb, of the 'as I am now so will you be' formula (also used at Canterbury on the Black Prince's tomb), and of the 'food for worms' image, see Cohen, *Death Symbol* (cit. in n. 118), 24–6.

[122] 'Ecce meum tumulum: cerne tuum speculum.' ('Behold my grave, and see in it a mirror to your [true] self.')

and turned into food for worms.'[123] The lesson that archbishops are raised up to greatness, only to sink lower in the world than they were before, was surely aimed at the current holder of the office, seated on his throne across the presbytery from the tomb. At Rochester Cathedral, a church with uniquely strong ties to Canterbury, an early thirteenth-century wall-painting of the Wheel of Fortune conveys a similar warning and occupies the exactly analogous position in the choir, so there must be a good chance that this very painting was the germ of the concept of confronting the archbishops with a humility-inducing image as they sat enthroned in quasi-regal splendour.[124] Of course, the Chichele tomb and its inscriptions were far better attuned to the increasingly individualistic, literate, and naturalism-orientated late medieval audience than was so impersonal and diagrammatic an image as the Wheel of Fortune.

The statues of Christ and intercessor saints in the piers at the head and foot of Chichele's tomb amplified and clarified the ultimately hopeful meaning of the effigies. Despite the decay of the physical body, the Archbishop was affirming the hope of resurrection of the flesh expressed in the Office of the Dead: 'I believe that my Redeemer lives and that on the last day I shall rise from the earth. And in my flesh I shall see my Saviour.'[125] Christ, whose image was no doubt placed centrally on the eastern pier, is invoked directly in the ejaculatory prayer 'Emanuel, Emanuel' inscribed at the head and feet of the cadaver.[126] The heavenly meaning of the piers as a whole is reinforced by the extraordinary, indeed unique, form of the tester which links them. This consists of two widely separated layers, the upper one solid, the lower a lattice studded with gilt stars and glazed with blue glass shedding a suitably unearthly glow.

Chichele's effigies were mutilated during the Commonwealth, inexpertly repaired in 1663–4, and enveloped in a heavy polychrome *maquillage* during the restoration of 1897–9,[127] yet despite these misfortunes they remain recognizable as distinguished works of

[123] 'Pauper eram natus: post primas hic relevatus. Iam sum prostratus: et vermibus esca paratus.'

[124] Tristram, *Wall Painting: The Thirteenth Century* (cit. in n. 50), i. 593; ii. suppl. pl 38a. Some of the imagery in Henry III's palaces was comparable in its moralizing intent and in its prominent placing relative to the enthroned king. The builders of Chichele's tomb were so determined to install it as nearly opposite the throne as they could that they allowed its western edge to overlap the outer face of the north choir door.

[125] These words are based on Job 19: 25–7. For related inscriptions on English and French 14th- and 15th-cent. tombs, see Cohen, *Death Symbol* (cit. in n. 118), 112; Rogers, 'English Episcopal Monuments' (cit. in n. 25), 28, 36 (n. 97), 62, 65, (n. 137). For Job as witness to the Resurrection in the Office of the Dead, see L. Besserman, *The Legend of Job in the Middle Ages* (Cambridge, Mass., 1979), 58, 64, 165 (nn. 28, 31).

[126] At the head of the upper effigy is the inscription which, expanded, reads 'Cetus sanctorum concorditer iste precetus / Ut deus ipsorum meritis sibi propicietur.' ('This company is prayed to in concert, that, for their own merit's sake, God may have mercy on this man.') On the use of short ejaculatory prayers on brasses, a practice far commoner there than on effigial tombs, see J. Bertram, '*Orate pro anima*: Some Aspects of Medieval Devotion Illustrated on Brasses', *Trans. Monumental*

Brass Soc., 13 (1983), 328. The prayer 'Emanuel, Emanuel' also occurs in the antechapel windows of All Souls College Chapel, Oxford, probably made in 1441: F. E. Hutchinson and G. McN. Rushforth, *Medieval Glass at All Souls College* (London, 1949), 20–1.

[127] The foundation deed of All Souls College (1438) laid responsibility for the upkeep and repair of Chichele's tomb on the Fellows, who have since then ordered at least four and probably five major restorations. John Philipot's church notes of c.1613–15 (cit. in n. 59), fo. 28ᵛ, mention that the tomb has been 'lately newly refreshed and revived at the charges of the College of All soules', and it is likely that this was a different restoration from that mentioned in Somner, *Antiquities* (1640), 269, since a date shortly before 1613 seems too early for the making of the statues of Christ and the Apostles reported to have been removed in 1642 from the north door of the choir (clearly meaning the tomb adjacent to the door); Hasted, *Canterbury* (cit. in n. 5), i. 365, n. e. For the restorations of 1663–4, c. 1836, and 1897–9, see *Gentleman's Mag.*, NS 13 (Jan.–June 1840), 82; C. G. Robertson, *All Souls College* (London, 1899), 224–5; R. H. D'Elboux, 'Shields from the Tomb of Archbishop Chicheley', *Antiquaries Jnl.*, 27 (1947), 172–6; ibid. 19 (1949), 91; E. F. Jacob, *Archbishop Henry Chichele* (London, 1967), 96 (n. 1). The 1663–4 works are documented in Bodl, MS D. D. All Souls c.

sculpture. It is possible that they are by John Massingham, the leading English sculptor of his day, who is known to have been resident in Canterbury in 1429–31, years when the main sculpture in hand at the Cathedral is likely to have been the imagery on the south-west porch patronized by Chichele. Massingham certainly worked at Chichele's foundation of All Souls College, Oxford, in 1438–42, and the face of the bronze effigy of Richard Beauchamp, Earl of Warwick, in St Mary's, Warwick, which was based on a life-size wooden pattern carved by him in 1449, is comparable in its general design to the somewhat stern physiognomy of the upper effigy on the tomb (Pl. 113).[128] The angels which support the cushions under the Archbishop's head are very refined interpretations of what had been for more than a hundred years one of the stock elements of major English tombs, but the equally small clerks flanking the feet and holding service-books are an innovation. The sense of these ancillary figures, much more explicit in the twelfth- and thirteenth-century French tombs which are their ultimate source, is that the angels are witnesses to, almost participants in, the earthly funeral rites.[129]

Chichele's funeral was of a splendour befitting his office, notwithstanding the penitential import of the cadaver on the tomb. Borne from Lambeth in a horse-drawn 'chariot',

271, item 311, a–k, misc. bills, receipts, a list of payments (a), and an article of agreement with the London 'carver' Thomas Stanton, dated 24 Aug. 1663 (k). This last specifies the restoration of the effigies and tabernacle work and the supply of seven brass escutcheons (of the arms of English dioceses), two small pieces of brass over the preceding (i.e. the 'labels' on the tomb-chest cornice), and a total of 20 alabaster figures, 12 being of the Apostles and two each of Time, Labour, Rest, and Death. The statues, like the painting and gilding by Thomas Parkinson (i) and the repair of the iron 'grate' by John Barrett (c), were thought of as reinstatements of what had existed before. At least some of the sculptural work was carried out by Alexander Crooker, a member of Stanton's workshop. The glazier John Railton's repairs to the lower tester involved renewing 40 of its blue-glass quarries and 58 of its lead stars (h). Losses from the upper effigy in the 1640s include the nose, the hands, the upper parts of the mitre and primatial cross, the heads of the angels flanking the Archbishop's head, and the heads, hands, and books of the clerks by the feet; from the lower effigy, the toes of the left foot, the right foot below the ankle, and the fingers of the left hand. Changes of 1663–4 are the replacement of the upper effigy's hands without gloves and almost perpendicular to the body, the insertion of sloping, star-decorated 'fascia' boards between the two layers of the tester (visible in several 18th-cent. engravings, the earliest being in Somner, *Antiquities* (1703), pt. 2, pl. between 32 and 33), replaced in 1897–9 by C. E. Kempe with shield-holding angels such as are just visible in Thomas Johnson's view of the choir in 1657 (Col. Pl. VI). In the 1897–9 restoration, the clerks at the feet acquired long, flowing hair; cf. Gough, *Sepulchral Monuments* (cit. in n. 14), ii, pt. 2, pl. xliv. A clear view of the south side of the monument taken before Kempe's restoration is albumen print 15 in Cobb, 'Ecclesiastical Tombs' (cit. in n. 76).

[128] For Massingham, see Harvey, *English Mediaeval Architects* (cit. in n. 14), 199–200; L. Stone, *Sculpture in Britain: The Middle Ages* (Harmondsworth, 1955), 206–9.

[129] For the funerary significance of angels, and their presence at the celebration of the divine office, the latter idea already adumbrated in the writings of Origen of Alexandria, see K. Escher, 'Die Engel am französischen Grabmal des Mittelalters und ihre Beziehung zur Liturgie', *Repertorium für Kunstwissenschaft*, 35 (1912), 100–2; J. Duhr, 'Anges', in *Dictionnaire de spiritualité médiévale*, ed. M. Viller, i (Paris, 1937), col. 602; J. Daniélou, *Les Anges et leur mission d'après les Pères de l'Église* (Paris, 1953), 84–7; C. McDannell and B. Lang, *Heaven. A History* (New Haven, Conn., and London, 1988), 37–44. For reproductions of major late 12th- and 13th-cent. northern French tombs showing earthly participants in funeral rites, as well as heavenly witnesses, see Sauerländer, *Gothic Sculpture* (cit. in n. 48), pls. 56–7, figs. 16, 33, 38; Erlande-Brandenburg, *Le Roi est mort* (cit. in n. 31), figs. 58, 109–20. A valuable, if somewhat too positive, assessment of the influence exerted on tomb imagery by burial customs is R. Kroos, 'Grabbräuche—Grabbilder', in *Memoria: Der geschichtliche Zeugniswert des liturgischen Gedenkens im Mittelalater*, ed. K. Schmid and J. Wollasch (Münstersche Mittelalter-Schriften, 48; Munich, 1984), 285–353. The tomb of Philippe de France (d. 1235), now at Saint-Denis, has two kneeling angels with arms outstretched towards the effigy's head, the earliest examples known. In conjunction with the lion at the prince's feet, they illustrate Ps. 91: 11–13. The Chichele monument's combination of such angels with book-reading clerks flanking the feet probably originated on some lost late 13th-cent. French tomb, but the oldest extant example seems to be on the strongly French-influenced tomb of Otto von Hessen and his half-brother Johann (d. 1328 and 1311) at Marburg: K. Bauch, *Das mittelalterliche Grabbild* (Berlin, 1976), fig. 216. The earliest English examples of the Chichele tomb's type of angel are on the monument of Aveline of Lancaster in Westminster Abbey, and the motif of book-reading clerks is likely to have reached England before c.1320, the approximate date of the knightly effigy at Norton (Co. Durham), to the left of whose feet sits a single book-reading figure, in this case a lady. The effigy in Winchester Cathedral of William of Wykeham (d. 1404) appears to be the oldest English effigy accompanied by angels and clerks, though the latter are three in number, are placed below the feet, face away from the effigy, and lack books.

accompanied by 200 horsemen, in addition to the gentlemen and other servants of the household, and surrounded by 100 continuously burning torches, the body lay sealed in its leaden coffin and surmounted by a realistic funeral-effigy dressed in full pontificals.[130] This is the earliest documented use of such an effigy at a bishop's funeral, predating by four years that of Cardinal Henry Beaufort, bishop of Winchester (Pl. 88), and there can be little doubt that the practice derived from English royal funerals, where effigies had been used from 1327, if not earlier. Effigies are known to have been made for use during the exequies of at least two later archbishops of Canterbury and one archbishop of York, but they never became a regular part of English episcopal funerals.[131] It seems clear that in all cases they were thought of primarily as substitutes for the actual corpse, which could not have survived display during preparations for burial at a site distant from the place of death.[132] The practice of exposing the corpses of high-ranking clerics during a 'lying in state' continued to be observed during the fourteenth and fifteenth centuries, but whether any medieval archbishop of Canterbury was treated in this way is not known.[133]

The architecture of the Chichele tomb was in all probability designed by Thomas Mapilton, who succeeded Yevele and Lote as chief master mason to the king and master mason to Christ Church.[134] The detailing is extremely close to that of the south-west porch of the Cathedral, which Lote or Mapilton built and Chichele funded,[135] but the curious concept of octagonal stone towers covered with imagery and bearing a tester has no exact analogy elsewhere. The towers are paralleled only in the image-clad stair towers on the western angles of Henry V's chantry at Westminster Abbey. This even stranger monument was built from 1439, but if, as is almost certain, detailed designs had been drawn up shortly after Henry V's death in 1422, Mapilton would automatically have been their author, and

---

[130] Thomas Cawston's obituary, MS Lit. D. 12, fo. 24[v].

[131] The sole record of Beaufort's funeral effigy seems to be the unpublished bird's-eye view in the funeral collections of Sir Thomas Wriothesley, Garter King of Arms 1505–34 (Pl. 88). Apparently the only other documented instances of late-medieval episcopal funeral effigies are those of Henry Dean, archbishop of Canterbury (d. 1503) and his successor, William Warham (d. 1532) (n. 162 below). The carved head from the tomb of Thomas Rotherham, archbishop of York (d. 1500) may have been part of a funeral effigy: F. Drake, *Eboracum* (London, 1736), 447, 480. The statement, in *A Note of the Manner of the Burieng of a Bysshop in old Tyme used*, contained in an Elizabethan funeral collection but seemingly composed *temp.* Mary I (BL, Egerton MS 2642, fo. 195), that the hearses of bishops generally bore an effigy, is definitely not correct. For the English royal effigies, which were almost certainly the source of the episcopal effigies, see W. H. St J. Hope, 'On the Funeral Effigies of the Kings and Queens of England', *Archaeologia*, 60 (1897), 517–70.

[132] It has been asserted that 14th- and 15th-cent. English funeral effigies symbolized the enduring office, in contrast to the mortality of the incumbent, represented by his coffined corpse, and that funerals where the latter was accompanied by a fictive corpse in the form of an effigy were both the source and the key to the meaning of the Chichele type of double-decker tomb: E. H. Kantorowicz, *The King's Two Bodies: A Study in Medieval Political Theology* (Princeton, NJ, 1957), 435–6. This interpretation is disputed, and the practical nature of funeral effigies as substitutes for the corpse stressed, in the discussion

of the English material in R. Giesey, *The Royal Funeral Ceremony in Renaissance France* (Geneva, 1960), 80–1, 85; and the lack of any correlation between the late-medieval Englishmen known to have had funeral effigies and those commemorated by cadaver tombs is emphasized in Cohen, *Death Symbol* (cit. in n. 118), 41. See also review of the latter by R. Giesey, *Speculum*, 52 (1977), 638–9. Further evidence which weighs against Kantorowicz's interpretation of English funeral effigies is adduced in S. Anglo, *Images of Tudor Kingship* (London, 1992), 105–6. For an English instance of the use of an effigy specifically to substitute for the corpse, see n. 163 below.

[133] Documented instances of high-ranking English prelates whose corpses were exposed between death and burial include William, abbot of St Albans (d. 1235) (*Gesta Abbatum Monasterii Sancti Albani*, ed. H. T. Riley, 3 vols. (RS 28/4, 1865–9), i. 303); Michael of Northburgh, Bishop of London (d. 1361), whose will asked that the funeral take place soon, so that the corpse could be put on view before becoming corrupt (Dugdale, *History of St Paul's* (cit. in n. 16), 34); and John Wodnesbergh, Prior of Christ Church (see n. 183 below).

[134] For Mapilton's career, including his patronage by Chichele's relations, see Harvey, *English Mediaeval Architects* (cit. in n. 14), 194–6.

[135] Particularly close are the base mouldings (already used in Yevele's and Lote's cloister at Christ Church) and the detailing of the niche canopies, heavily restored in the 1860s but validated by original pieces such as that presently in the Deanery garden.

132 (*facing page*) Detail of monument to the Hales family, erected 1592, nave north aisle, showing burial at sea of James Hales (d. 1589) and his widow Dame Alice (d. 1592). Perhaps by Epiphanius Evesham.

133 (*above*) Monument to Richard Neville (d. 1599), formerly in Brenchley Chapel, south side of nave. Engraving from J. Dart, *Cathedral Church of Canterbury* (1726). Sculptor unknown.

134 (*above right*) Monument to Dean Thomas Neville (d. 1615) and his brother Alexander Neville (d. 1614), formerly in the Brenchley Chapel. Figures now in south choir aisle. Engraving from J. Dart, *Cathedral Church of Canterbury* (1726). Sculptor unknown.

135 (*right*) Monument to Dame Dorothy Thornhurst (d. 1620), St Michael's Chapel. Sculptor unknown.

136 (*left*) Monument to Orlando Gibbons (d. 1625), nave north aisle. By Nicholas Stone.

137 (*below*) Monument to Dean Charles Fotherby (d. 1619), Our Lady Martyrdom Chapel. Engraving from J. Dart, *Cathedral Church of Canterbury* (1726). Sculptor unknown.

138 (*right*) Detail of monument to Dean John Boys (d. 1625), Our Lady Martyrdom Chapel. Perhaps by Nicholas Stone.

139 (*far right*) Monument to Alexander Chapman, canon of stall XI (d. 1629), formerly in the Martyrdom, now north choir aisle. Engraving from J. Dart, *Cathedral Church of Canterbury* (1726). Perhaps by Nicholas Stone.

140 (*below right*) Monument of Lt. Col. William Prude (d. 1632), St Michael's Chapel. Sculptor unknown.

141 (*below far right*) Monument to Dean John Bargrave (d. 1643), Our Lady Martyrdom Chapel (not erected until 1679), engraving from J. Dart, *Cathedral Church of Canterbury* (1726). Perhaps carved by Edward Pierce. Painting perhaps by Cornelius Johnson.

142 Monuments to the Revd John Clerke (d. 1700) and Mrs Priscilla Kingsley (d. 1683), now separately in Martyrdom. Engraving from J. Dart, *Cathedral Church of Canterbury* (1726). Sculptor unknown.

143 Monument to Admiral George Rooke (d. 1708), St Michael's Chapel. Sculptor unknown.

144 (*above*) Monument to Miss Ann Milles (d. 1714), south choir aisle, engraving from J. Dart, *Cathedral Church of Canterbury* (1726). Sculptor unknown.

145 (*above right*) Monument to John Sympson (d. 1748), nave south aisle. By Michael Rysbrack.

146 Monument to Lt. Col. John Stuart (d. 1808), nave south aisle. By Peter Turnerelli.

147 Memorial to members of Prince Albert's Light Infantry, 1842, nave south aisle. By Thomas Denman.

WHILST SERVING IN AFFGHANISTAN,
BETWEEN THE YEARS 1838 AND 1842,
EITHER FROM THE FATIGUES OF SERVICE
OR IN ACTION WITH THE ENEMY,
THERE PERISHED
OF THE 13TH PRINCE ALBERT'S LIGHT INFANTRY,
LIEUT. COLONEL WM H. DENNIE, C.B.
BREVET-MAJOR JAMES KERSHAW,
CAPTAINS GEO. FOTHERGILL AND WM SUTHERLAND,
LIEUTENANTS EDWARD KING, RICHARD EDWARD FRERE,
JOHN BYRON HOBHOUSE, & J.F.P.C. SCOTT,
SERJEANT-MAJOR WILLIAM AIREY,
12 SERJEANTS, 8 CORPORALS, 3 BUGLERS
AND 264 PRIVATES;

ALSO
SHORTLY AFTER THEIR RETURN FROM THAT COUNTRY,
MAJOR J.G.D. TAYLOR,
CAPTAIN WILLIAM A. SINCLAIR,
AND ASSISTANT-SURGEON G.W. BARNES.

TO THE MEMORY OF THE ABOVE,
THEIR SURVIVING BROTHERS IN ARMS
OF THE SAME REGIMENT,
HAVE CAUSED THIS TABLET TO BE ERECTED.

148 (below) Three military memorials, 1834–48, nave north aisle. By Thomas Longley and Edward Richardson.

149 (right) Memorial to members of 16th Queen's Lancers, 1848, nave south aisle. By Edward Richardson.

ALIWAL

TO THE MEMORY OF
THE OFFICERS, NON-COMMISSIONED OFFICERS AND PRIVATES ABOVE INSCRIBED,
OF THE SIXTEENTH QUEEN'S LANCERS,
WHO FELL IN THE DISCHARGE OF THEIR DUTY,
DURING THE CAMPAIGN ON THE SUTLEJ,
IN THE YEARS 1845, 1846.

THIS MONUMENT
IS ERECTED BY THEIR SURVIVING COMRADES.

150 (*left*) Monument to Lt. Col. Frederick Mackeson (d. 1853), nave south aisle. By John Graham Lough.

151 (*above*) Monument to Sir George Gipps (d. 1847), nave south aisle. By Henry Weekes.

152 Monument to Archbishop William Howley (d. 1848), north ambulatory. By Richard Westmacott the younger.

153 Monument to William Grant Broughton, Bishop of Australia (d. 1853), nave south aisle. By John Graham Lough.

154 Monument to Dean William Rowe Lyall
(d. 1857), nave north aisle. By H. G. Austin; effigy
perhaps by John Birnie Philip.

155 Monument to Archbishop Archibald Campbell
Tait (d. 1883), north-east transept. Tomb-chest by
William Brindley; effigy by Joseph Edgar Boehm.

156 Monument to Archbishop Edward White Benson (d. 1897), St Augustine's Chapel, north-west tower. Monument by Thomas Graham Jackson; effigy by Thomas Brock.

157 Model for monument to Archbishop Randall Thomas Davidson (d. 1930), by Cecil Thomas. The monument is in the Trinity Chapel north ambulatory.

SACRED TO THE MEMORY OF
THE HONᴮᴸᴱ JAMES GEORGE BEANEY M.D.
MEMBER OF THE LEGISLATIVE COUNCIL OF AUSTRALIA
BORN IN THIS CITY JANUARY 15ᵀᴴ 1828
DIED AT MELBOURNE JUNE 30ᵀᴴ 1891.
THE MUNIFICENT FOUNDER OF THE BEANEY INSTITUTE
AND FREE LIBRARY IN THIS CITY
AND A GENEROUS BENEFACTOR TO ITS CHARITIES.

THIS MONUMENT
IS ERECTED
BY THE OFFICERS
NON-COMM^D OFFICERS
& MEN
OF THE 2ND BATTALION
THE BUFFS
IN MEMORY OF
THEIR COLONEL
EDGAR EVELYN
RAVENHILL
D · S · O
WHO DIED AT WYNBERG
CAPE COLONY
ON FEB · 6 1907 ÆT · 47

159 (*above*) Monument to Col. Edgar
Evelyn Ravenhill (d. 1907), nave north
aisle. By Eric Gill.

160 (*right*) Monument to Miss Margaret
Babington, Steward of the Friends
(d. 1958), nave south aisle. By Mary and
Denis Gillick.

MARGARET BABINGTON
MDCCCLXXVIII · MCMLVIII
A DEVOTED FRIEND
OF CANTERBURY
CATHEDRAL

161 'Green Court Gate, Canterbury Precincts'. Watercolour by Job Bulman, c.1776. Almonry buildings in use as King's School on left; Archbishop's Palace Barn, later Grange House, on right. (Add. MS 45, no. 32.)

162 'New School House and the Norman Staircase'. Lithograph after a drawing by W. A. Boone, 1865. From left to right: New School Room of 1853; Norman staircase; fragment of the Aula Nova; Mitchinson's house for headmaster and boarders.

Chichele, as one of the King's executors, would have seen them in advance of ordering his own tomb.[136] The echoing of the designs for Henry V's chantry in the turriform piers of Chichele's monument might be viewed as nothing more than an architectural borrowing, but this would be to lose sight of the exceptional nature of the bond between the two Henrys, who stood shoulder to shoulder both in the war against the Lollards and in the war to recover the king's French inheritance. That both monuments presented similar images of the heavenly kingdom is a very apt memorial to an alliance which had held out the prospect, unparalleled in the post-Conquest period, of king and archbishop working together to revitalize the religious life of England.[137]

Archbishop **John Stafford** (d. 1452) was laid in a grave in the Martyrdom, next to that of Prior Finch. The juxtaposition was a meaningful one, for Finch had reroofed the Martyrdom in the late fourteenth century, and in 1448 Stafford had laid the first stone of its remodelling, which was financed from the £1,000 bequeathed to the Priory by Cardinal Beaufort, the Archbishop's erstwhile mentor.[138] For some unknown reason, Stafford's executors failed to have his grave covered by a brass directly after his death, and it fell to his registrar Robert Grout to leave 40 marks for this purpose in his will of October 1460. Since this is the only archbishop's tomb whose cost is known, it is doubly unfortunate that no more than the stripped indent still remains in place.[139]

Stafford may well have considered that space for tombs in the sanctuary was exhausted, but no such thinking deterred the executors of Cardinal **John Kempe** (d. 1454) from making room by demolishing the south choir entrance and building a replacement further west (Pl. 104). The new door was evidently designed by Mapilton's successor as architect to Christ Church, Richard Beke, but despite the latter's brilliance in the field of decorative

---

[136] Although the piers of Chichele's monument are less explicitly turriform than the staircases on Henry V's chantry, their celestial imagery enables them to function as evocations of Sion's towers (Ps. 48: 12). For the documentary evidence relating to Henry V's tomb and chantry, see W. H. St J. Hope, 'The Funeral, Monument and Chantry Chapel of Henry V', *Archaeologia*, 65 (1913–14), 129–86; *History of the King's Works*, i, *The Middle Ages*, ed. H. M. Colvin (London, 1963), 488–9. The gatehouse-like form of the chantry, surely intended to evoke the *porta coeli* of Jacob's dream (Gen. 28: 12), originated no later than 1415, for the King's will drawn up in that year mentions the two-storey structure and two sets of stairs: T. Rymer, *Foedera*, orig. edn. (20 vols.; London, 1726–35), ix. 289. Mapilton died in 1438 and the architect responsible for the building of the chantry was John Thirsk.

[137] The correspondences between these two monuments extend to the design of the tomb-chests, with three wide arches on each long side, and reinforce the implication of the inscription 'Ecce meum tumulum' ('Behold, my tomb'), below Chichele's cadaver effigy, that the structure enclosing it is a kind of cut-away tomb-chest. For relations between Henry V and Chichele see, most recently, J. Catto, 'Religious Change Under Henry V', in *Henry V: The Practice of Kingship*, ed. G. L. Harriss (Oxford, 1985), 104–8; C. Allmand, *Henry V* (London, 1992), 257–9.

[138] A final payment (£9 3s. 2d.) for the Martyrdom roof is in the treasurers' accounts for either Mich. 1383–Mich. 1384 or Mich. 1384–Mich. 1385 (Misc. Accts. vol. 2, fo. 335ᵛ). The inception of the mid-15th-cent. remodelling of the Martyrdom is recorded in Searle, *Chronicle and Lists*, 44.

[139] Stafford's will is not known to exist. Grout's will (PRO, PROB. 11/4, fos. 164ᵛ–165ᵛ) required his executors to have a marble stone placed on Stafford's grave, in accordance with the Archbishop's last wish, a request which raises the possibility that the testamentary arrangements of the latter were incomplete or non-existent. The stone was to bear a 'sculptura' and was to be made 'juxta advisamentum magistri Willelmi Clyff vel alteri viri in dicto opere satis experti' ('following the advice of Master William Clyff or someone else of sufficient skill in such work'). In Harvey, *English Mediaeval Architects* (cit. in n. 14), 62, this passage is misconstrued as referring to a carved gravestone over Grout's own tomb. For Grout's activities as registrar, see E. F. Jacob, 'Archbishop John Stafford', *TRHS*, 5th ser., 12 (1962), 16, 18. For the indent of the Stafford brass, see W. H. H. Rogers, 'Stafford of Suthwyke in North Bradley, Wilts, and of Hoke, Dorset', *Wiltshire Notes and Queries*, 3 (1902), drawing opp. 193; Sadler, *Indents of Lost Brasses* (cit. in n. 88), 16–17, app. 3, p. 9. For the verses on the marginal fillet (already partly missing by the early 1580s), see Holinshed, *Chronicles* (cit. in n. 60), 1470–1. By 1599 most of the inscriptions were lost, but the effigy and the two flanking shields of arms remained; Scarlett, heraldic collections (cit. in n. 59), fo. 14.

architecture he was not entrusted with the tomb itself.[140] The effigy-less tomb-chest is routine London marbler's work, a piquant contrast with the splendour of the polychromed wooden canopy above. There seems little doubt as to what meaning was intended here and in the considerable number of later English episcopal monuments which exhibit a similar contrast: the earthly body and its receptacle are of little importance by comparison with the resurrected body and its heavenly dwelling-place evoked by the canopy.[141] The treatment of the latter as three tall spires is obviously a nod in the direction of Kempe's neighbour Stratford, but the exact equality in size of the spires and their placing above a single, unsubdivided opening recall the much larger, stone-built monument of Henry Bowet, Kempe's immediate predecessor as Archbishop of York.[142] Perhaps there was also the intention to echo the wooden tabernacles over the silver statuary on Prior Chillenden's high altar screen. Certainly, the vaulted ceilure above the spires, a feature unique in a medieval English tomb, can best be understood as a borrowing from the architecture of timber screens, but even if the high altar screen was not a source for the Kempe monument, it will have been an important influence, in the sense that the visual dominance it achieved in the sanctuary by virtue of its great height and precious materials enabled fifteenth-century archbishops and their executors in all good conscience to commission lofty and elaborate monuments.[143]

Anxiety about possible encroachments on the pre-eminence of the high altar is unequivocally expressed in the formal permission which the convent granted in 1480 for the erection of the tomb of Cardinal **Thomas Bourchier** (d. 1486). This stands to the north

[140] The moving of the entrance to make way for Kempe's monument, first suggested in Woodruff and Danks, *Memorials*, 138, has recently been confirmed by the discovery of a payment for it, probably made in 1454: M. J. Sparks, 'Archbishop Kempe's Gate in the Quire Screen', *Cant. Cath. Chron.*, 82 (1988), 28–30. If the tracery of the 14th-cent. choir enclosure is *in situ* above the present entrance, as it appears to be, Kempe must have been buried at the threshold of the old gate, a gesture of self-abasement presumably disapproved of by his executors (cf. n. 63 above). For Beke's documented career, see Harvey, *English Mediaeval Architects* (cit. in n. 14), 17; for the attribution to him of the choir screen, see F. Woodman, *The Architectural History of Canterbury Cathedral* (London, 1981), 188–96.

[141] To some extent this concept was anticipated in the tomb of Archbishop Meopham, but its general diffusion belongs to the late 15th and early 16th centuries. An earlier example of an episcopal monument consisting of an effigy-less tomb-chest placed within a sumptuous architectural setting was that of Bishop Thomas Langley (d. 1437), formerly enclosed inside a chantry chapel in the Galilee at Durham. The plainness of Kempe's tomb-chest was originally offset a little by the use of more elaborate than usual brass inlays in the sides, and a certain ambition is evident in the derivation of its pattern of upright panels alternating with quatrefoils from the north and south sides of the platform under Henry V's tomb-chest, built in 1422. For the text of the marginal inscription, see Cowper, *Memorial Inscriptions* (cit. in n. 120), 135. The inscription fillets were made by the London workshop responsible for the 'Series D' brasses: Emmerson, 'Monumental Brasses' (cit. in n. 120), 76. Strictly speaking, the canopy has six spires arranged in two parallel rows, as on Archbishop Stratford's tomb. The northern spires are plainer than the southern but differ from the latter in having formerly incorporated images. The longitudinal stability of the structure is assured by two planks nailed to the insides of the three northern spires! For the restoration of the canopy in 1947–8, see *Friends of Canterbury Cathedral, 21st Annual Report* (1948), 26–7. The eagle crockets on the arches of the canopy allude to the Archbishop's Evangelist name-saint; cf. a canopy in the section of the Norwich Cathedral choir-stalls made during the episcopate of John Wakering (1416–25).

[142] Bowet died in 1423 but his tomb was complete by 1415. It is illustrated in Gough, *Sepulchral Monuments* (cit. in n. 14), ii, pt. 2, pl. xxvii.

[143] For Chillenden's high altar screen, see Woodruff and Danks, *Memorials*, 173–5. Traces left on the adjoining piers show that it rose slightly above Archbishop Bourchier's monument, enough to redress any damage caused to the pre-eminence of the high altar by the building of the Stratford tomb *c*.1350. The removal of the screen accounts for two apparent anomalies in the design of Bourchier's monument: the gap between it and the arcade pier to the east; the non-regular form of the south-east corner, evidently intended to echo the division of the screen into a solid 'dado' pierced by doors and a main upper stage containing imagery (cf., e.g., the Neville Screen at Durham). Kempe's monument was the first to make no gesture towards preserving the visual integrity of the choir enclosure, for even in Chichele's monument, whose insertion destroyed a large section of the north screen, the cornice of the tester is aligned with that on the screen.

of the high altar and the flanking altars of Saints Alphege and Dunstan, and its open, arched structure represents a scrupulous response to the monks' requirement that the lighting from the north aisle windows be safeguarded (Pl. 105). Archbishop Winchelsey would have approved their concern, which had indeed shown itself a hundred years earlier in the similarly open form adopted for the tomb of Archbishop Sudbury directly opposite (Pl. 87).[144] The position occupied by the Bourchier monument relative to the high altar makes it virtually certain that it fulfilled a function not mentioned in the 1480 agreement, namely the provision of a setting for the temporarily installed representation of Christ's sepulchre, which was one of the principal sites of the Easter liturgy during the late Middle Ages.[145] The open form of the monument would have permitted veneration of the Easter Sepulchre by lay people positioned in the north aisle, since, besides facilitating the conduct of the official liturgy, structures of this kind served as a focus for the distinctively late-medieval affective piety centred on the sufferings undergone by the body of Christ in the course of making His salvific sacrifice. Although very different from Chichele's tomb, Bourchier's resembles the latter in having 'earned' its extraordinarily prestigious site by significantly enhancing the devotional resources of the Cathedral; and it is even possible that both monuments were conceived to some extent as critiques of chantry chapels like Archbishop Arundel's and Bishop Buckingham's, with their assertive hiving-off of what had been communally accessible space. In the late fifteenth and early sixteenth centuries, south-eastern England witnessed a striking growth in the popularity of effigy-less monuments intended to double as receptacles for Easter Sepulchres, and it is likely that this movement derived some of its impetus from the building of Bourchier's beautiful and prominently placed tomb.[146] Such influence is very apparent in the case of the monument on the north side of the chancel at Brabourne, some 12 miles south of Canterbury, which commemorates Bourchier's retainer Sir John Scott (d. 1485) (Pls. 98, 100). There can be

[144] For the grant of 1480, see *Lit. Cant.*, iii. 301–2. The need to meet the Priory's other condition, that a new cupboard be provided for the gear pertaining to St Alphege's altar, explains the small gap between the tomb proper and the pier to the west, the high placing of the image niche at the south-west corner relative to those at the other corners, and the renewal of all the masonry below this niche. A reference to this cupboard, implying that it still existed, is in W. Gostling, *A Walk In and About the City of Canterbury* (Canterbury, 1774), 174. Bourchier's indebtedness to St Alphege in being buried close to his altar and shrine is evident in his will, where he commends his soul to the Virgin, St Thomas, and St Alphege, and presents a gold image of the Trinity to the Cathedral in honour of the Trinity, St Thomas, and St Alphege: L. L. Duncan, 'The Will of Cardinal Bourgchier, Archbishop of Canterbury, 1486', *Arch. Cant.*, 24 (1900), 244–52.

[145] Surviving documentation for the Easter Sepulchre at Christ Church seems to be confined to a payment for the lights in 1398–9: C. E. Woodruff, 'The Sacrist's Rolls of Christ Church, Canterbury', *Arch. Cant.*, 48 (1936), 48. The best account of the liturgical and devotional functions of Easter Sepulchres is in E. Duffy, *The Stripping of the Altars: Traditional Religion in England, 1400–1580* (New Haven, Conn., and London, 1992), 29–37.

[146] Important earlier effigy-less tombs which in my view are rightly regarded as having doubled as Easter Sepulchres include those of Bishop Remigius in Lincoln Cathedral, made *c*.1300, of Sir Geoffrey Luttrell at Irnham, Lincs., *c*.1340, and the Percy Tomb at Beverley Minster, of the early 1340s. For Easter Sepulchre tombs in the south-east which are contemporary with, or later than, Bourchier's monument, see B. Cherry, 'Some New Types of Late Medieval Tombs in the London Area', in *Medieval Art, Architecture and Archaeology in London*, ed. L. Grant (British Archaeol. Assn. Conference Trans., 10; Leeds, 1990 for 1984), 140–54; A. Heales, 'Easter Sepulchres: Their Object, Nature and History', *Archaeologia*, 42 (1869), 263–308. That the renewed popularity of the Easter Sepulchre tomb in the south-east predated the making of Bourchier's tomb is clear from wills of the mid- and late 1470s cited by Heales, including one of 1478 which specified that the tomb should stand between a chancel and a northern Lady Chapel, an arrangement implying an open arched structure like Bourchier's tomb, rather than the usual wall-recess. If, as seems certain, Edward IV's monument was to have been an Easter Sepulchre monument (see n. 149 below), it is likely to have played an important part in the diffusion of the type.

little doubt that Scott's tomb was designed by a mason closely connected with the Cathedral works.[147]

The stylistic affinities of the Bourchier monument are all with works in the vicinity of London. Its overall scheme—a high vaulted canopy borne on single four-centred arches and surmounted by a horizontal band of enriched images—is anticipated only in the capital's finest surviving fifteenth-century canopy-tomb, that of John Holland, Duke of Exeter (d. 1447).[148] Its distinctive combination of bold outline and delicate detailing is strongly reminiscent of St George's Chapel at Windsor, the most ambitious new church under construction near London during the late fifteenth century. The feature which contributes most to the boldness of outline, the continuation of the canopy-arch jambs down to floor level, seems to have no antecedents in fifteenth-century tomb design other than the specially treated easternmost bay of the north choir arcade of St George's, which from 1475 was intended to shelter the monument of the rebuilder of the chapel and Bourchier's kinsman, Edward IV.[149] The detailing also incorporates elements clearly derived from earlier royal monuments—so many, indeed, that it becomes tempting to view them not merely as the fruits of the architect's study of obvious sources but as the Archbishop's own tribute to his royal lineage. The most important of these quotations are: the obtusely four-centred canopy-arch with 'four-petal' tracery spandrels, from the lateral elevations of Henry V's chantry; the partly pierced, partly niched, and wholly unfunctional upper stage, from the monument in St Albans Abbey to Humphrey, Duke of Gloucester (d. 1447); and the alternately traceried and niched treatment of the Purbeck tomb-chest (Pl. 105), from the almost identical tomb-chests of the monuments to Edward III and to Richard II and Anne of Bohemia at Westminster. Since Bourchier's tomb-chest is a reworking of its model to bring it into conformity with the ultra-refined aesthetic of the canopy, there can be no question of its design having been left in the hands of the executant craftsmen, as was evidently the case with Courtenay's and Kempe's tomb-chests.[150] The only other near-copy in Purbeck of the Westminster tomb-chests, that of

[147] For Scott's tomb, see J. R. Scott, 'The Scott Monuments in Brabourne Church', *Arch. Cant.*, 10 (1876), 259–69, fig. 5 (between 8 and 9). Its elevation and vault clearly derive from Bourchier's monument. Debts to the architecture of the cathedral include the dummy shaft-rings and the spandrel tracery (cf. the arch opening into the Lady Chapel from the Martyrdom).

[148] Holland's tomb (for which see Gough, *Sepulchral Monuments* (cit. in n. 14), ii, pt. 2, pl. liv; Cherry, 'New Types of Late Medieval Tombs' (cit. in n. 146), 141–2) was originally in the chapel of the hospital of St Katherine-by-the-Tower. The inscription fillets of the Bourchier monument are from the London workshop which produced the 'Series D' brasses: Emmerson, 'Monumental Brasses' (cit. in n. 120), 76.

[149] For reasons not given, the Bourchier monument was attributed by A. Oswald to Henry Janyns, original architect of St George's, Windsor: Harvey, *English Mediaeval Architects* (cit. in n. 14), 159. Although never completed, Edward IV's monument may have influenced Bourchier's in more ways than the lack of contact between the tomb and the jambs of the enclosing arch, for, like Bourchier's, the King's tomb stood directly north of a

high altar, and hence was almost certainly intended to function as an Easter Sepulchre. The cadaver-effigy mentioned in the King's will was presumably to have lain within some kind of flat-topped and open-sided tomb-chest; cf., e.g., the monument traditionally attributed to Treasurer Thomas Haxey (d. 1425) in the north transept of York Minster. For the documentation of Edward IV's monument, see Colvin, *History of the King's Works* (cit. in n. 136), 887; for a view taken before the 18th-cent. alterations, see F. Sandford, *A Genealogical History of the Kings of England...* (London, 1677), pl. between 390 and 391.

[150] The existence of influence from Henry V's chantry is confirmed by the diminutive standing figures on the angles of the canopies to the large niches at the northern corners of the tomb canopy: cf. the canopies on the western parapet and turrets of the Westminster monument. The marble work of Bourchier's tomb-chest will have been extremely costly: cf. the £250 charged for Richard II's and Anne of Bohemia's in 1395. The badges (Pl. 99) are among the most minute carvings ever carried out in Purbeck. Some of them, together with the small standing figures mentioned above, are illustrated in Gough, *Sepulchral Monuments*, ii, pt. 3, pls. cvii, cviii. The 'toome' was

Richard, Earl of Warwick, in St Mary's, Warwick, begun in 1447, follows the royal proto-types in having gilded copper weepers, so there must be a very good chance that the figures on Bourchier's tomb-chest were of metal also.[151] The monument to Archbishop Sudbury on the opposite side of the sanctuary certainly incorporated copper-gilt sculpture, but even if the Bourchier monument did not, it is obvious that the intention was to strike a visual balance between the use made of Purbeck and Caen in the two tombs and between the open structure of their canopies. It had not been possible to contrive any such balance between the monuments in the more westerly bays of the sanctuary, and there can be little doubt that Bourchier and his architect were using near-symmetry to bring greater formality and coherence to the immediate setting of the high altar.[152]

An obituary written at Christ Church soon after the death of Cardinal **John Morton** in 1500 yields unique contemporary evidence of the thinking behind an archbishop's choice of burial spot and monument: 'Although he had been urged very often by several persons to construct for himself a tomb which was sufficiently large and commensurate with his dignity and honour, he chose instead to be buried in a place out of the public gaze and away from tumult, a secluded spot below ground known as the crypt, under nothing more than a marble stone and in front of the image of the most Blessed Virgin Mary, whom he cherished in his heart. There his favoured body rests now'.[153] Morton's wish for a comparatively modest and remotely sited monument was not respected for long, and within a few years an imposing cenotaph arose on the nearest accessible spot to his grave (Pl. 106).[154] No doubt there was a feeling abroad that the memory of so notable a statesman and improver of the Cathedral fabric deserved to be kept alive by a tomb such as he had been encouraged to build in his lifetime.

Morton's cenotaph stands within one of the Romanesque arches separating the outer aisles and ambulatory of the crypt from the chapel of Our Lady Undercroft, and in order to accommodate it, a section of the massive iron *clausura* protecting the fabulous treasures

said in 1586 to be of marble and alabaster (Holinshed, *Chronicles* (cit. in n. 60), p. 1471), but on what evidence is unclear, for no detachable sculptures are likely to have survived at Canterbury by that date. If the monument did function as an Easter Sep-ulchre, the 12 tomb-chest niches are less likely to have held weepers than saints, as on the tomb of Richard II and Anne of Bohemia.

[151] The resemblance to the Westminster monuments extends to the quatrefoiled plinth below the aisle side of the tomb-chest.

[152] Instances at other English cathedrals of approximate sym-metry between monuments on opposite sides of the sanctuary are the tombs of Bishops Simon of Ghent (d. 1315) and Roger de Mortival (d. 1330) at Salisbury, and the tombs of Bishops James Berkeley (d. 1327) and Edmund Lacy (d. 1455) at Exeter; but neither of these pairs is immediately adjacent to the high altar. More or less symmetrical pairs of chantry chapels occur at Ely, Exeter, Gloucester, Lincoln, Wells, and Winchester Cathedrals, and at Tewkesbury Abbey.

[153] *Dies Obituales Archiepiscoporum Cantuariensium, ex Mar-tyrologio & Obituario Ecclesiae Christi Cantuariensis*, in Wharton, *Anglia Sacra*, i. 63–4. For the brass indent, see Sadler, *Indents of Lost Brasses* (cit. in n. 88), pt. I. 22–3, app. I, p. 14. Although

'only' a brass, the monument was not modest in its siting, for the chapel of Our Lady Undercroft, one of the Cathedral's most prestigious cult-centres, was where the Black Prince had chosen to be buried (see below). Moreover, apart from St Thomas's original tomb, the adjacent but pre-existing tomb of William of Andeville (see n. 5 above), and Lanfranc's original grave before the nave rood (see n. 10 above), Morton's brass was the only monument on the central longitudinal axis of the church. The various desecrations and probings to which the grave has been subjected are detailed in A. J. Mason, C. E. Woodruff, and C. Cotton, *Memorandum for the Chapter on the Lady Chapel Floor in the Crypt*, dated 9 Feb. 1923. The indent was moved 'very slightly' westwards in 1893: Hay, 'Ledger Slabs' (cit. in n. 100), 14. Matthew Parker appears to be responsible for the long-accepted misinterpretation of the screenwork of Our Lady Undercroft as Morton's chantry chapel: *De Anti-quitate Britannicae Ecclesiae et Privilegiis Ecclesiae Cantuariensis cum Archiepiscopis Ejusdem* (Lambeth, 1572), 344.

[154] A south elevation, bird's-eye view of the effigy, and details of other parts are in Gough, *Sepulchral Monuments* (cit. in n. 14), ii, pt. 3, pls. cxx, cxxi. The only firm evidence for dating the tomb is its architectural dependence on Henry VII's Chapel (see n. 156 below).

of the chapel had to be transferred from the outer to the inner face of the arch. The presence of the grille hard up against the north side of the tomb accounts for the lack of detail there.[155] The canopy takes its overall form from the semicircular arch into which it is fitted, and its most prominent feature, the portal-like arrangement of six enniched images, derives from the entrance in the Cathedral's fifty-year-old choir screen. The two other major components of the architecture—the tracery 'panelling' masking the underside and jambs of the twelfth-century enclosing arch, and the badge-encrusted moulding set at the inner edge of the niches—are unmistakably quotations from the Lady Chapel of Westminster Abbey, which Henry VII rebuilt from 1503.[156] Half of the badges are Tudor roses and Beaufort portcullises such as are liberally sprinkled over the surfaces of the Westminster chapel and other buildings of Henry VII's, but here, by virtue of their alternation with Morton's rebus and cardinal's hat,[157] they become a memorial to a political association which had begun in 1483, when Morton, then bishop of Ely, assumed the role of mastermind behind the plots to put Henry Tudor on the throne. The decoration of a bishop's tomb with royal badges was virtually unprecedented and could not have failed to strike contemporaries as remarkable. What cannot be known is whether the innovation prompted comparisons with the celestial imagery of Archbishop Chichele's tomb and the very different kind of Church-State alliance which it commemorated. The religious statuary in the niches on Morton's monument, almost all showing saints named as intercessors in his will, is stylistically very close to many of the numerous figures in Henry VII's chapel, and the splendidly voluminous vestments of the effigy exhibit the rectangular 'box folds' found on the more English-looking of the Westminster statues (Pl. 114).[158] The identity of the six small figures which kneel beside the effigy and face eastwards has never been probed, but if they are academics, as their carefully differentiated clerical dress suggests, it becomes extremely likely that they commemorate the establishment under the cardinal's will of a fund to support thirty or more poor university scholars.[159]

[155] For the *clausura*, see C. E. Woodruff, 'The Chapel of Our Lady in the Crypt of Canterbury Cathedral', *Arch. Cant.*, 38 (1926), 154–5. On the north side of Morton's monument, the stone stylobate for the ironwork remains (Pl. 106), the tomb-chest is plain, there is no recasing of the Romanesque enclosing arch, and the backs of the small kneeling figures are not fully finished.

[156] The panelled arches and badge-decorated mouldings at Westminster are the transverse arches of the aisle vaults and the double ogee mouldings flanking the entrances to the eastern chapels. The monument is attributed to John Wastell, architect of the upper parts of the Bell Harry tower, in Harvey, *English Mediaeval Architects* (cit. in n. 14), 325; cf. n. 165 below.

[157] The use on the Morton monument of badges specific to an individual king is not really anticipated by the two *roses-en-soleil* on the upper cornice of Archbishop Bourchier's tomb canopy or by the hundreds of carvings of the same badge on Bishop Alcock's chantry at Ely, begun in 1488, for *roses-en-soleil* were used by both Edward IV and Henry VII, and they occur on Bourchier's and Alcock's monuments alongside motifs which are either purely decorative or without heraldic significance. On the Morton tomb, the Archbishop's own badges have been defaced, unlike those of Henry VII. The eagles on

tuns are not, as has often been asserted, part of a rebus for Morton, but the symbol of Morton's Evangelist name-saint; cf. n. 141 above. The letters 'Mor' were painted on the tuns in E. W. Tristram's restoration of the polychromy in 1937–8 (*Friends of Canterbury Cathedral, 12th Annual Report* (1939), 24–6); cf. the rebus-cum-monogram in the stained glass of *c.*1500 in the adjoining window of the crypt (Caviness, *Windows* (cit. in n. 15), fig. 585). The two courses of masonry at the base of Morton's monument were added in 1893–5, when the floor was lowered to its 12th-cent. level.

[158] Morton's will (*Sede Vacante Wills* (cit. in n. 56), 85–93), mentions the Virgin (patron of Our Lady Undercroft), Sts Peter, Paul, Thomas (of Canterbury), Christopher, Æthelred (archbishop of Canterbury; relics under the altar in Our Lady Undercroft), Catherine and Mary Magdalen (patrons of altars in the parts of the crypt under the east transepts). The saints on the canopy include Catherine, Mary Magdalen, Christopher, and Dunstan, the last being patron of the altar directly above the cenotaph. The Virgin was represented in a sculptured Annunciation group on the east jamb, which has disappeared except for the lily-pot because the figures, unlike those on the front of the canopy, were not integral with their niches.

[159] For Morton's scholars, see Pantin, *Cant. Coll.*, iii. 227.

Like Morton, **Henry Dean** (d. 1503) was content with a monumental brass. His grave was made in a still more privileged spot, namely the floor of the Martyrdom over which the blood of St Thomas had flowed more than 300 years earlier. No doubt it was as a thank-offering for this and for twenty years of soul masses celebrated at the Martyrdom altar that Dean bequeathed to St Thomas's tomb in the crypt an image of St John the Evangelist containing 151 oz. of silver gilt. A record of the heraldry on the brass made at the end of the sixteenth century shows that this originally non-armigerous archbishop had even paid St Thomas the unique compliment of recasting his own arms so as to incorporate the martyr's three choughs or beckets.[160] His will reveals that he had given great thought to the conduct of his magnificent funeral, and there is evidence that these plans were faithfully executed.[161]

In the case of his successor, **William Warham** (d. 1532), more is known about the parts of the exequies which took place in and near the Cathedral, for there exists a description of the proceedings which was written by an eyewitness, a herald with a professional interest in ceremonial forms. Much of the sanctuary was taken up with a 'barrier' or enclosure (cf. Pl. 88), within which sat the chief mourner, the Archbishop's brother, together with six further mourners. The centre-piece of the enclosure was the coffin, surmounted by the 'hearse', a gilded and painted wooden canopy formed of four 'standards'—in effect giant candelabras. Warham's standards carried a total of exactly 1,000 lights, besides numerous small pennons painted with the Archbishop's arms. On the east side of the hearse was borne the primatial cross, and at the corners stood four gentlemen bearing banners of the Trinity, the Virgin, St Thomas, and St Margaret. Between the main uprights of the standards was fixed a tester, painted with a 'maiestie', from whose edges hung a deep and richly decorated valance. On the coffin itself, a realistic effigy of the kind known to have been used at Chichele's and Dean's funerals looked up towards the image of Christ on the tester.[162] Some impression of these splendours can be gained from one of the drawings on the mortuary roll of John Islip, abbot of Westminster, who died three months before Warham (Pl. 89). The fact that this drawing shows Islip's hearse with some 200 to 300 lights fewer than on Warham's is significant, for in the early sixteenth century the scale of hearses and other funeral pomps was regulated so as to match the rank of the deceased. Thus the hearses of kings, for example, incorporated not four standards but thirteen.[163] Already by the late fourteenth century, Christ Church was operating a code of

[160] For the arms, see Scarlett, heraldic collections (cit. in n. 59), fos. 5ᵛ, 14.

[161] The burial of Dean under a brass in the Martyrdom was specified in his will: J. B. Deane, 'The Will of Henry Dene, Archbishop of Canterbury', *Archaeol. Jnl.*, 18 (1861), 261–6; *Sede Vacante Wills* (cit. in n. 56), 93–100. For the remains of the brass, see Sadler, *Indents of Lost Brasses* (cit. in n. 88), pt. 1. 16–17 and app. 3, p. 8. For the epitaph, see Weever, *Funerall Monuments* (cit. in n. 60), 232. The use of a funeral effigy and the siting of the tomb next to Archbishop Stafford's are noted in Cawston's obituary (cit. in n. 130), fos. 29, 33ᵛ.

[162] The source which mentions Chichele's and Dean's effigies is cited at nn. 130, 161 above. Warham's funeral is described in College of Arms, MS I. 15, fos. 168–170ᵛ. The account of the hearse there can be fully understood only in conjunction with the account of procedure for the burial of princes in the royal blood, ibid, fos. 96–7, and the drawing in the Islip Roll (Pl. 89). For hearses in general, see D. Rock, *The Church of Our Fathers*, (new edn.; 4 vols.; London, 1903–4), ii. 399–404, 416 and iii. 75–6; C. Beaune, 'Mourir noblement à la fin du moyen âge', in *La Mort au moyen âge. Colloque de l'Association des historiens médiévistes français* (Strasbourg, 1977), 136.

[163] W. H. St J. Hope, 'The Obituary Roll of John Islip . . .', *Vetusta Monumenta*, 7/4 (1906). Among the other elements of Islip's exequies (besides the hearse) which were less elaborate than Warham's was the use of an effigy only after the real body had been buried at the end of the first day of the funeral: College of Arms, MS I. 15, fo. 172; *Vetusta Monumenta*, 4 (1815),

practice whereby the coffins of persons other than archbishops and royalty were set up west of the sanctuary, in positions graded strictly in accordance with their place in the secular or ecclesiastical hierarchy.[164]

Warham's tomb in the Martyrdom (Pl. 107) is the largest of the Cathedral's medieval monuments. Made at least twenty-five years before 1532, it owes its two tiers of flanking niches and its three tracery-backed ogee gables to the grandest recent episcopal tomb, that of Richard Redman, bishop of Ely (d. 1505).[165] The relationship is no accident, for though personally modest, Warham was a firm believer in the value of magnificence as a means of asserting the greatness of his office.[166] The resemblance to the Redman tomb originally extended to the placing of the effigy in the west part of the recess, although here this was done in order to allow access to a tiny chantry chapel contrived in the cramped space between the transept and the chapter house. The concern to maintain overall symmetry explains the bipartite division of the blind tracery on the back wall of the recess, but since 1796–7, when the effigy was moved to a central position and the chantry entrance abolished, this has appeared an arbitrary feature, ill-judged in relation to the tripartite canopy in front. The changes of 1796–7 were part of a general refurbishing of the monument which also entailed the demolition of the chantry and the addition of parts missing from the sculpture.[167] The effigy (Pl. 116) is almost exactly contemporary with Morton's and may possibly be indebted to the latter for its general design, but its proportions are more conventional, its forms more compact, and its surface treatment metallically precise, where that of Morton's effigy conveys a sense of softness and mobility. The stripping of whitewash in the 1790s revealed that the arms on the canopy alternated between St Thomas's and Warham's. Whether or not this gesture was intended as emulation of Henry Dean's becket-incorporating arms or as a counter to the inclusion of royal badges on John Morton's cenotaph, it complements the evidence of the chantry foundation

pls. xvi–xx, pp. 2–3. The effigies of archbishops of Canterbury, like those of royalty, were used throughout the 'lying in state', procession, and funeral. Descriptions of late-medieval funerals have yet to be studied with a view to establishing what were the norms of funerary display for each of the upper echelons of English society. For Henry VII's hearse, see J. Leland, *De Rebus Britannicis Collectanea*, ed. T. Hearne (6 vols.; London, 1770), iv. 306.

[164] For the progressively eastward placing of the corpse of a monk, a person of importance (*solempnis*), and a person of great importance (*solempnior*), see C. S. Phillips, *Canterbury Cathedral in the Middle Ages* (London, 1949), 36–7; id., 'The Archbishop's Three Seats in Canterbury Cathedral', *Antiquaries Jnl.*, 29 (1949), 34, both citing the late 14th-cent. 'Burnt Breviary' (Canterbury Cathedral Library, Add. MS 6). For the placing of priors' bodies in the choir, see n. 183 below. For the placing of archbishops and royalty before the high altar, see *Polistorie* (cit. in n. 23), fo. 204ᵛ (referring to Archbishop Langton); Cawston's obituary (cit. in n. 130), fo. 25; A. P. Stanley, *Historical Memorials of Canterbury* (11th edn.; London, 1912), 167.

[165] The comparison with Redman's tomb is made in Woodman, *Architectural History* (cit. in n. 140), p. 256, where a tentative attribution is made to John Wastell. A fuller discussion is in id., 'John Wastell of Bury, Master Mason' (Ph.D. thesis,

Univ. of London, 1978), 215–23. The documentary and archaeological evidence for Warham's chapel is marshalled in Legg and Hope, *Inventories*, 138–46. The will is printed in *Wills from Doctors' Commons*, ed. J. G. Nichols and J. Bruce (Camden Soc., 83; 1863), 21–7.

[166] K. E. Hardy, 'William Warham as Statesman, Scholar and Patron' (B. Litt. thesis, Univ. of Oxford, 1943), 494–5.

[167] The monument was defaced in the mid-17th cent. (A. Wood, *Athenae Oxonienses* (London, 1691–2), i. 572). The 1796–7 restoration cost £160 (Hasted, *Canterbury* (cit. in n. 5), i. 401 and ii. 441, n. f.) and entailed mending the nose of the effigy, the primatial cross, and the angels flanking the head (cf. pencil sketch of 1785 by John Carter: BL, Add. MS 29926, fo. 241). The general authenticity of the face is vouched for by its close similarity to those of the unrestored angels on the canopy. The concern to retain original elements is evidenced by the resiting of the traceried hagioscope in the rear wall of the tomb-recess (cf. Pls. 107, 116). Despite being almost exactly contemporary, Warham's and Morton's effigies have little in common stylistically save the 'box folds' of their chasubles (Pls. 106, 107). A missal from Warham's chapel (Bodl., MS Rawlinson C. 168) is the only equipment from one of the Cathedral's chantries known to survive.

deed that devotion to the martyr of Canterbury had led the last pre-Reformation archbishop to choose burial here.[168]

THE PRIORS' MONUMENTS

The earliest recorded prior's tomb was not in the church but in the chapter house, the most honorific site aspired to by priors until the fourteenth century. Perhaps the burial here of **Elmer** (d. 1137) was by way of recognition of his work in furthering the completion of the choir dedicated in 1130.[169] **Wibert** (d. 1167) must have earned the same honour on the strength of the great improvements he made to the priory's finances, buildings, and plumbing. Firm evidence is lacking of the burial places of the few late twelfth- and early thirteenth-century priors who were not promoted to abbacies. The oldest prior's tomb still *in situ*, that of **Henry of Eastry** (d. 1331), commemorates a head of wholly exceptional calibre and was itself unmatched by any of his successors' monuments.

Before discussing Eastry's monument, mention must be made of what appear to be fragments from two prioral monuments made under Eastry's patronage. One of these fragments is a small piece of a Purbeck marble slab which has been inlaid with brass Lombardic capitals of a kind used widely for the marginal inscriptions of large monumental brasses made in London in the period *c.*1290–1330. There can be little doubt that the surviving letter-indents—NDAMPR—come from an inscription beginning HIC IACET [name] QUONDAM PRIOR HUIUS ECCLESIE (Here lies [name] formerly prior of this church). The other fragment consists of most of the head of a monk's effigy in Purbeck dating from *c.*1300. The carving, though of the severity usual in this material, is of high quality. The hood partly conceals the tonsure and is arranged in a lozenge shape strikingly reminiscent of the diagonally set square cushions under the heads of many late thirteenth- and early fourteenth-century effigies. One can be fairly confident that this monument also commemorated a prior, as there is no evidence that any Christ Church monk of lesser rank was ever accorded an effigial tomb. The lack of a mitre must mean that it covered the grave of a prior who ruled before 1220, when the Pope granted the priors of Christ Church the right to wear the mitre in processions and on major feasts. The early priors most likely to have attracted new memorials around 1300 are Elmer and Wibert, for the

---

[168] In 1599 Warham's tomb bore five different coats of arms, including St Thomas's, and one blank shield (by implication all on the tomb-chest); Scarlett, heraldic collections (cit. in n. 59), fo. 14. If the brass plates reported missing in 1640 (Somner, *Antiquities* (1640), 272) were the shields on the tomb-chest, the arms of St Thomas found in 1796–7 (Hasted, *Canterbury* (cit. in n. 5), ii. 441) must have been on the canopy. The canopy has six shields, arranged as three widely separated pairs, and at different levels—a very likely setting for the alternation of Becket's and Warham's arms which the 18th-cent. restorers employed not only there but also on the tomb-chest, extended by them so that its south face has six compartments. The small carved ornaments of the three ogee arches and the jambs of the tomb-recess include the Arma Christi and the scallop shells and goats' heads which occur in Warham's arms.

[169] For the inscription on a lead plaque identifying Elmer's grave, found 4 ins. below the pavement in 1789 (the exact spot not stated), see Boys, 'Tomb of Theobald' (cit. in n. 10), 299, pl. xi. Wibert's burial in the chapter house, the lifting of his incorrupt body from its coffin in 1404, and its subsequent reburial on the same site are reported in the early 16th-cent. list of archbishops' and priors' burial-places (cit. in n. 5), 116. For notices of the (presumably) post-1404 brass, see Somner, *Antiquities* (1640), 278; Dart, *History and Antiquities* (cit. in n. 88), 180. Wibert's tomb may have been the 'monumentum' near the entrance mentioned in the late 13th-cent. *Instructio Noviciorum Secundum Consuetudinem Ecclesie Cantuariensis*, Cambridge, Corpus Christi College, MS 441, fo. 380ᵛ, printed in *The Monastic Constitutions of Lanfranc*, ed. and trans. D. Knowles (Nelson's Medieval Classics; London, 1951), 144.

chapter house where they lay was rebuilt by Eastry, who completed that work in 1304. If the sculptured effigy was discarded in the course of the further remodelling of the chapter house from 1404, this would explain why the head was available for reuse behind the early fifteenth-century shield-decorated panelling over the west door of the Cathedral, whence it emerged during restoration work in the late 1970s.[170]

Prior Eastry's own monument was made immediately after his death and set up in the second most easterly bay of the south choir aisle.[171] By burying him at the feet of Archbishop Reynolds, the convent was commemorating a long-standing association between a ruler and a valued subordinate, a kind of gesture not too uncommon in the Middle Ages and one reinforced in this case by the lesser height of Eastry's tomb-chest relative to the Archbishop's. In terms of quality, however, Eastry's monument is so much higher than his superior's as to give rise to the suspicion that a point was being made about the respective worth of the two men.[172] Apart from its aesthetic merit, the most notable aspect of the Prior's effigy is its departure from the convention, almost universally followed in medieval England, of showing the deceased with youthful and idealized facial features (Pl. 110). Here we are confronted instead by an unflinchingly naturalistic rendering of a haggard visage such as the ninety-two-year-old Eastry must actually have possessed at the time of his death.[173] Indications of ageing had appeared in papal effigies from the late thirteenth century onwards, and the possibility of influence from that quarter is raised by the use of two motifs common in Italy but rare in England: the outward tilting of the effigy to improve its visibility to the viewer, and the folding of the hands over the stomach.[174] A

---

[170] The letters on the fragmentary brass indent are of the type classified by John Blair as 'Main Group size 1': J. Blair, 'English Monumental Brasses Before 1350: Types, Patterns and Workshops', in Coales, *Earliest English Brasses* (cit. in n. 25), 135–46, fig. 148a. The lack of a stop between the M and the P of the Canterbury fragment is slightly surprising but not unparalleled in inscriptions of this kind. In the early 17th cent., Wibert's tomb still bore an inscription in the form reconstructed above: Somner, *Antiquities* (1640), 278. The inscription fragment and the head from the monk's effigy may both have been damaged, along with the chapter house itself, in the 1382 earthquake. Information regarding the finding of the head was kindly supplied by Peter Long, Clerk of Works. Traces of an arched head-canopy are visible on the viewer's right. Head and inscription fragment are currently (1994) in store.

[171] A payment of £21 3*s.* 4*d.* 'pro tumba domini H. Prioris' in the year Mich. 1330–Mich. 1331 occurs in Misc. Accts 2 (Treasurers' Accts. for 1307–84), fo. 203', and 12*d.* (probably a gratuity) paid to the unnamed mason making the tomb in the years 26 Ap. 1331–26 Ap. 1332 is recorded in DE3 (Day book of Priors Oxenden and Hathbrand), fol. 33'. For the history of the misattributions of Eastry's tomb see Woodman, 'Two Tombs' (cit. in n. 57).

[172] Cf., e.g., Bishop Hotham and Prior Crauden at Ely; Henry IV and John Beaufort and Thomas, Duke of Clarence at Canterbury; and Charles V and Bertrand du Guesclin and Jean Bureau de la Rivière at Saint-Denis; and see n. 241 below. The burial of Prior Wodnesbergh at the feet of his teacher Prior Chillenden is the nearest sequel at Canterbury (see n. 182 below). For an official Christ Church assessment of Reynolds,

whose praise sounds suspiciously faint, see *Dies Obituales* (cit. in n. 153), 59.

[173] Two of the very few other English medieval effigies besides Eastry's which portray the effects of old age, those of Bishops Ralph of Shrewsbury (d. 1363) and Thomas Beckyngton (d. 1452) at Wells, also commemorate men known to have been aged and infirm at the time of their deaths. Earlier Northern European examples are the late 13th-cent. effigies of St Stephen at Obazine and of Rudolph I of Habsburg (d. 1291) at Speyer (Bauch, *Grabbild* (cit. in n. 129), figs 146–7), the latter famous because its maker is said to have added wrinkles to the effigy when these appeared on the face of the ageing king: *Ottokars Österreichische Reimchronik*, ed. J. Seemüller, MGH, Deutsche Chroniken, v, pt. 1 (Hanover, 1890), 508–9. Of course, we have no means of knowing whether Eastry's effigy was an attempt to portray the Prior's physiognomy or whether it resembles the vast majority of medieval effigies in showing a type.

[174] It must be admitted that there is nothing obviously Italianate about the other 14th-cent. English examples of tilted effigies, among which is that of Archbishop Reynolds. Cf. Panofsky, *Tomb Sculpture* (cit. in n. 30), 61. The motif of hands folded on the stomach, common in 13th-cent. French ecclesiastics' effigies, seems to occur earlier in England only in the early 13th-cent. effigies of the pre-Conquest Bishops Sigar and 'Leverius' at Wells. The suggestion made in Woodman, *Architectural History* (cit. in n. 140), 253, that Eastry's effigy was intended to lie on the ground and was only later installed as at present, is unacceptable. That it was made for the existing setting is clear from the omission of a canopy-shaft from the normally invisible north edge of the base slab, from the simplified detailing of

further detail suggestive of more or less direct contact with Italy is the painting in grisaille of *trompe l'œil* tracery on the uncarved sides of the head-canopy.[175] Despite these exotic traits, the effigy typifies early fourteenth-century Northern European sculpture in its mellifluously linear draperies and its elaborately naturalistic painted detail, the latter now reduced to inconspicuous fragments.[176]

The architecture of the tomb (Pl. 93) is a characteristic example of Decorated Gothic, not only in its constituent parts but also in the concern it evinces to be novel and surprising. The side sections containing gableted statue niches and delicate, deeply undercut reticulated tracery are not, as one would expect, set flush with the front of the tomb-chest but angled, rather like the wings of an altar-piece.[177] The other novel and surprising feature of the tomb has unfortunately been destroyed, but enough remains to show that the effigy was originally set behind a low, openwork screen incorporating ogee arches and diagonally set uprights continuing those on the tomb-chest.[178] This unique arrangement was probably conceived as a more radical solution than the quasi-canopy of Reynolds's monument to the problem of how to avoid obstructing the view of the stained glass in the window above the effigy.

All the later priors whose burial-place is known lay in the church. Whatever monuments may have been raised over the graves of Priors **Richard Oxenden** (d. 1338) and **Robert Hathbrand** (d. 1370) in St Michael's Chapel, they were replaced by small wall-mounted brasses when the chapel was rebuilt in the 1430s. Descriptions of these long-lost brasses reveal that the priors were shown with the pastoral staff not actually granted until 1378, an anachronism due no doubt to oversight rather than to a desire to insinuate that the privilege had been bestowed earlier.[179] Of the nine indents of later priors' brasses that have

the head-canopy on the same side, and from the exact match between the details of the sinister canopy-shaft and the shafts remaining from the arcaded 'screen' formerly in front of the effigy. The making of effigy and head-canopy from four pieces of stone was doubtless intended to ease the difficulties of installation due to their great combined length relative to the window embrasure into which they are fitted.

[175] The only comparable and contemporary English example of grisaille on stonework seems to be the quatrefoils on the image brackets in the prior's chapel at Ely: P. Binski and D. Park, 'A Ducciesque Episode at Ely: The Mural Decorations of Prior Crauden's Chapel', in *England in the Fourteenth Century: Proc. 1985 Harlaxton Symposium*, ed. W. M. Ormrod (Woodbridge, 1986), 32–4.

[176] Traces of colour are still visible on the chasuble, its lining, the apparel of the alb, the upper cushion, the head-canopy, and the flanking niches. The mitre retains traces of stamped gesso or putty simulating metalwork attachments. In 1599 it was noted that the chasuble was 'all red powdered with lions passant gold'; Scarlett, heraldic collections (cit. in n. 59), fo. 12ᵛ.

[177] The roughly contemporary monuments of the Alard family in the south aisle of St Thomas's, Winchelsea, which resemble Eastry's monument in being in the Kentish Decorated style, are the only other English tombs of tripartite format with angled side-sections, though there the angles between side and centre sections are re-entrant. The niches in the side sections

of Eastry's tomb must have contained the statues of Sts Osyth and Apollonia, between which Eastry is said to lie in the early 16th-cent. list of archbishops' and prior's burial-places (cit. in n. 5), 118.

[178] The evidence that the uprights of the arcade were continuous with those on the tomb-chest is the dowel holes and the series of gougings to provide a key for mortar. There are slight remains of the arches of the arcade above the shafts on the inner edges of the angled side-sections.

[179] In the early 16th-cent. list of archbishops' and priors' burial-places (cit. in n. 5), 119, Hathbrand is said to have been buried towards the south side of St Michael's Chapel and Oxenden towards the north side. Hathbrand's brass is located on the south side of the altar and Oxenden's on the north side in Philipot, Kentish church notes (cit. in n. 59), fo. 26, where the latter is briefly described and its inscription given. A similar but less accurate record of the same inscription and a reference to its location on the east wall is in 'The Visitation of . . . Kent . . . 1619, pt. III', ed. J. J. Howard, *Arch. Cant.*, 6 (1866), 283. Somner cites Oxenden's and Hathbrand's epitaphs, says that the former was on the east wall, and notes that Hathbrand's 'memoriall' was similar to Oxenden's: *Antiquities* (1640), 290. Both brasses are spoken of as if still existing in Hasted, *Canterbury* (cit. in n. 5), i. 400, but it is likely that this is one of several instances of Hasted's unacknowledged paraphrasing of antiquarian sources, in this case probably Philipot.

been recorded, at least six survive.[180] The main interest of these burials now consists in their placing relative to the great rebuilding which the west parts of the Cathedral underwent in the later Middle Ages. As was mentioned earlier, **John Finch** (d. 1391) lies in the Martyrdom, which had been reroofed during his priorate.[181] **Thomas Chillenden** (d. 1411) is near the east end of the nave, alongside Archbishop Arundel, his collaborator in the completion of this arm of the church.[182] At Chillenden's feet lies his pupil and immediate successor, **John Wodnesbergh** (d. 1428).[183] The next prior but one, **John Salisbury** (d. 1446), is buried at the extreme east end of the nave, on the central axis. His successor, **John Elham** (d. 1449), lies east of Wodnesbergh and on the south side of Archbishop Islip. His grave was formerly marked by a brass bought from the London marbler John Rowge for £10 6s. 8d.[184] In a unique and, for a monk, highly inappropriate display of affection for his 'carnal' family, Prior **William Molashe** (d. 1437) chose burial between his father and mother. The site selected was the crypt, close to the entrance from the south-west transept, whose remodelling had been the main architectural achievement of Molashe's priorate.[185] The desire for

[180] The six surviving priors' indents are those of John Finch, William Molashe, Thomas Goldstone I, William Sellyng, Thomas Goldstone II, and one in the north cloister walk, probably that of John Wodnesbergh. Those of Thomas Chillenden, John Salisbury, and John Elham are recorded. For further details see nn. 181–7 below.

[181] For the reroofing of the Martyrdom in Finch's time, see n. 138 above. His gentle birth, his beginning of the nave, and his burial before the door of the Lady Chapel (really the chapel of St Benedict in 1391) are noted in the early 16th-cent. list of archbishops' and priors' burial-places (cit. in n. 5), 119. The only indent in the Martyrdom which shows traces of a pastoral staff is the northernmost: Legg and Hope, *Inventories*, plan at 147; Sadler, *Indents of Lost Brasses* (cit. in n. 88) pt. 1. 20. For the epitaphs of Finch, Chillenden, Wodnesbergh, Salisbury, Elham, Sellyng, and Goldstone II, see Somner, *Antiquities* (1640), 291–6.

[182] The identification of Chillenden's burial-spot is secured by the account in Somner, *Antiquities* (1640), 291, by the note in the *ordo* for the funeral of his successor (see n. 183 below) that the latter was buried at the feet of his teacher Chillenden, and by the fact that the only ecclesiastic's brass indent shown at the head of another in the 1786 plan of the nave floor (n. 88 above) is that a little way to the south of Archbishop Arundel's. The will of Sir William Roos dated 22 Feb. 1413 makes clear that he had first refusal of the spot immediately adjacent to Arundel's chantry should he die in or near London: *Reg. Chichele* (cit. in n. 116), ii. 22–3. Roos, who was a close friend of Arundel's and a relation by marriage, as well as Henry IV's chief supporter in the northern Midlands, died in 1414 and was buried at Belvoir Priory. After the Dissolution his body and Chellaston-made alabaster tomb were moved to Bottesford (Leics.).

[183] The *ordo* for Wodnesbergh's funeral incorporated in the register of his successor Molashe as an exemplar for future prioral funerals, which perhaps represented established usage, mentions the high, cloth-of-gold-covered hearse set up where the epistle was wont to be read in the choir, on which the body lay with the face exposed to the gaze of the people: Bodl., MS Tanner 165, fo. 13, printed in F. Peck, *Desiderata Curiosa* (2 vols.; London, 1732–5), ii. 6–7. For the burial-spot, see n. 182 above. A

prioral brass indent transferred to the cloister when the nave was repaved in 1787 (no. 3 in Gough, *Sepulchral Monuments* (cit. in n. 14), ii, pt. 2. 88) and now in the north walk (Sadler, *Indents of Lost Brasses* (cit. in n. 88), 26 (no. X), app. 3, pp. 14–15) agrees quite well with the rendering of Wodnesbergh's indent in the 1786 plan of the nave floor (n. 88 above). Sadler's sketch (ibid., app. 3, p. 15) is inaccurate in several respects, notably in the shape of the mitre and in omitting shields from the ends of the canopy-pinnacles. In 1805 two prioral indents were among several in the chapter house (Powell, collections (cit. in n. 50), fo. 118), but only one of the indents now in the cloister can be identified as a prior's.

[184] For London marblers as makers of brasses, see, most recently, R. Emmerson, 'Design for Mass Production: Monumental Brasses Made in London *ca.* 1420–1485', in *Artistes, artisans et production artistique au moyen âge*, ed. X. Barral i Altet (3 vols.; Paris, 1986–90), iii. 133–71; J. Blair, 'Purbeck Marble', in *English Medieval Industries* (cit. in n. 82), 50–4; M. Norris, 'Later Medieval Monumental Brasses: An Urban Funerary Industry and Its Representation of Death', in *Death in Towns*, ed. Bassett (cit. in n. 9), 184–209. The positions of Salisbury's and Elham's graves are recorded in Somner, *Antiquities* (1640), 294. In 1787 Salisbury's indent was found to have no grave or coffin beneath it or, by implication, near it: letter of 1788 from Dr Berkeley, vice-dean, printed in Gough, *Sepulchral Monuments* (cit. in n. 14), ii, pt. 2. 89, where the indent is misattributed to Archbishop Arundel. Perhaps the grave itself was buried by the westward extension of the choir-screen steps in the 1450s. The payments for Elham's grave slab, which were probably sufficient to include the brass (cf. n. 186 below), and its carriage, are in Misc. Accts. vol. 4, fos. 187ᵛ, 188ᵛ; Harvey, *English Mediaeval Architects* (cit. in n. 14), 259.

[185] 'Willelmus Molassch ... fecit capellam Sancti Michaelis. et illa partem atrij ecclesie perfecit. Sepultus est in criptis cum patre et matre eius' ('William Molashe made the chapel of St Michael and completed the transept on that side. He was buried in the crypt with his father and mother'): early 16th-cent. list of archbishops' and priors' burial-places (cit. in n. 5), 120. For Molashe's brass indent, see Sadler, *Indents of Lost Brasses* (cit. in n. 88), pt. 1. 20–1 (no. V); app. 1, p. 13; app. 3, p. 11. For the indent

physical proximity to a favoured building project also explains the prominent burial of **Thomas Goldstone I** (d. 1468) in the Lady Chapel off the Martyrdom, and it is likely that the broken indent which lay to the south of Goldstone's until its ejection in the mid-1970s covered the grave of his successor and completer of the Martyrdom rebuilding, **John Oxney** (d. 1471). Perhaps a personal devotion to St Mary Magdalen accounts for the burial of **William Petham** (d. 1472) before her altar in the northern chapel of the crypt, under the north-east transept. Petham's coffin and the slabs for the brasses commemorating his two predecessors were supplied by the marbler William Bonevile of Corfe (Dorset).[186] The extraordinary honour of a grave directly before the Martyrdom altar must have been granted to **William Sellyng** (d. 1494) in recognition of the signal manifestation of divine favour recorded on his now lost brass, namely his death on the feast of the Passion of St Thomas. The space between the graves of Sellyng and Archbishop Stafford, the inaugurator of the Martyrdom rebuilding, was soon taken by those of Archbishop Dean and the penultimate prior, **Thomas Goldstone II** (d. 1517). Goldstone's grave completed the sequence of burials which, apart from Sellyng's exceptionally honorific grave, had been slowly edging southwards across the Martyrdom floor for more than a century and a half.[187] The existence of this sequence documents concerns which have already been identified as influences on the monuments near the high altar: the desire to delay the moment when it became necessary to place tombs in a specially hallowed part of the church, and the determination to ensure that tombs which impinged in this way justified their presence by possessing some special significance relative to their setting.

north of Molashe's, see ibid., app. 1, p. 16 (no XVI), and for that to the south, ibid., app. 1, pp. 14–15 (no. XIV) and app. 3, p. 11. Sadler's no. XVI includes indents for mid-15th-cent. and early 16th-cent. priests' brasses, so presumably Molashe *père* took holy orders after the death of his wife, and the original brass was lost and replaced within about 50 years. The statement in Woodruff and Danks, *Memorials*, 270, that 'the place of [Molashe's] burial is not recorded but it is not unlikely that the large marble slab bearing the matrix for a brass effigy of an ecclesiastic in the floor of the southern aisle of the crypt marks his tomb' would appear to be merely a lucky guess.

[186] The marble stone which Bonevile supplied for the tomb of Goldstone I in 1468 cost £4 10s. 0d., and in 1472–3 he was paid 20s. and £3 7s. 8d. respectively for Petham's 'sarcophagus' (presumably a coffin rather than a tomb-chest) and for placing a stone on Oxney's grave: R. H. D'Elboux, 'Testamentary Brasses', *Antiquaries Jnl.*, 29 (1949), 190. That both indent and brass could be subsumed under the term 'stone' is evident from, e.g., Cardinal Morton's obituary, cited above, but the sums paid to Bonevile were certainly too small to have covered brasses as well as stones (cf. p. 492 and n. 184 above). For a late-13th-cent. instance of the purchasing separately of a brass and its stone, see n. 55 above. The chapels where the three above-mentioned priors were buried are noted in the early 16th-cent. list of archbishops' and priors' burial-places (cit. in n. 5). The only indent now surviving in the Lady Chapel, that before the altar and slightly to the north, was attributed to Goldstone I, and

that further north—apparently removed in the mid-1970s—to Sir Henry Grey, Count of Tancarville and Lord of Powis (d. 1450) in Legg and Hope, *Inventories*, plan at 147. Hope's plan shows an unoccupied space immediately south of Goldstone I, which was of the right size to have been occupied by a tombstone, and Oxney may well have been buried there rather than under the slab further south which disappeared in the mid-1970s. From north to south, the three indents shown in Hope's plan correspond to nos. XXVI, XXVII, and XXVIII in Sadler, *Indents of Lost Brasses* (cit. in n. 88), app. 3. No. XXVIII is there tentatively attributed to John Bourchier, Archdeacon of Canterbury (d. 1495), whose brass remained in the Lady Chapel in 1599; Scarlett, heraldic collections (cit. in n. 59), fo. 16ᵛ; Woodruff, 'Sacrist's Rolls' (cit. in n. 145), 65.

[187] The slab for Sellyng's brass was supplied for £4 13s. 4d. by an unnamed marbler established at St Paul's Churchyard, London: Christ Church Letters, ii, no. 105. St John Hope attributed the southernmost grave to Goldstone II, and that immediately to the north to Sellyng: Legg and Hope, *Inventories*, 126, 147. That Sellyng's grave is the southernmost is evident from its location before the Martyrdom altar in the early 16th-cent. list of archbishops' and priors' burial-places (cit. in n. 5), 122, where Goldstone II is said to lie beside his predecessor. The northernmost and southernmost indents are respectively no. I in Sadler, *Indents of Lost Brasses* (cit. in n. 88), pt. 1. 15–16, and no. XV in ibid., app. 1, p. 16 and app. 3, p. 9.

THE ROYAL MONUMENTS

Apart from **Queen Eadgifu** (d. *c*.967),[188] the first royal personage buried in Christ Church was Edward of Woodstock, commonly known as the **Black Prince** (d. 1376). Some fifteen years before his death, in October 1361, he and his wife, Joan, the 'Fair Maid of Kent', had undertaken to found two chantries in expiation of their contracting a marriage within the second and third degrees of affinity. The chantries were established in the pair of chapels on the east side of the crypt of the south-east transept, and in order to make these chapels worthy of their new function, the Romanesque architecture of all the crypt within the transept was transformed into the soberly elegant example of the Perpendicular style which we see today. The work was probably complete by October 1363, when the first chaplains were appointed. The architect's name is not recorded, but by far the strongest candidate is Henry Yevele, master mason to the Black Prince *c*.1357–62.[189] The northern chapel was dedicated to the Virgin, the southern to the Trinity, whom, as was stressed in the ordinances for the chantries, the prince had 'always held in peculiar devotion'. Edward's love for the Trinity, a devotion associated particularly with Christ Church, and his feelings towards the house 'which we have cherished from the cradle', were doubtless strong influences on his choice of Canterbury as his burial-place. That this choice was made around the time of the founding of the chantries is suggested by two pieces of circumstantial evidence. The site for the monument specified in Edward's will—the crypt chapel of Our Lady Undercroft, 10 feet west of the altar—is bounded to north and south by stone screens which were almost certainly installed specifically to enclose the monument and which appear to be contemporary with the nearby chantry chapels.[190] The other indication that the burial-place was fixed during the early 1360s is the fact that by the middle of the decade all spaces had been spoken for in the main royal mausoleum, St Edward's Chapel at Westminster.[191] It is not known exactly when and by whose authority

[188] Wife of King Edward the Elder, mother of Kings Edmund and Eadred, and great-great-grandmother of Queen Matilda, first wife of Henry I. Since Henry was present at the dedication of the second Romanesque choir in 1130, it is highly probable that he was involved in the commissioning of Eadgifu's tomb, which stood near the centre of the south-east transept and was described by Gervase as a gilded *feretrum*: *Historical Works*, i. 23. Except for the tomb of William the Conqueror, made directly after his death in 1087 (Orderic Vitalis, *Ecclesiastical History* (cit. in n. 10), iv. 110–11), this is the only shrine-like English royal monument documented during the Romanesque period. After 1180 Eadgifu's tomb was north of the northern altar, St Martin's, in the north-east transept, where a 15th-cent. painting of the Queen was placed in 1921: Gervase, *Historical Works* i. 23; C. E. Woodruff, 'The Picture of Queen Ediva in Canterbury Cathedral', *Arch. Cant.*, 36 (1923), 1–14.

[189] For the Prince's and his wife's promises to found the chantries, see K. P. Wentersdorf, 'The Clandestine Marriages of the Fair Maid of Kent', *Jnl. Medieval History*, 5 (1979), 218, 227. For the dating of the remodelling of the chapels, see J. H. Harvey, *The Black Prince and His Age* (London, 1976), 102–3. For the attribution to Yevele, see id., *Yevele* (cit. in n. 93), 64; id., *English Mediaeval Architects* (cit. in n. 14), 359. The influence of William

Ramsey's works is discussed in C. Wilson, 'Origins of Perpendicular' (cit. in n. 35), 190–7, 240–5.

[190] The ordinances and will are printed in Stanley, *Historical Memorials* (cit. in n. 164), 159–71. The screenwork in the west bay of the Chapel of Our Lady Undercroft is different in its detailing and later than the screens on the east and north sides of the east bay, and predates the south screen in the east bay, a replacement of *c*.1370–80 which is structurally continuous with the monument of Joan, Lady Mohun, for which see below. The most telling indication that the chantry chapels and the western screenwork of Our Lady Undercroft are contemporary and of common authorship is the presence in both works of the same base type, a pattern rare in Perpendicular architecture after *c*.1370. Preparations for the burial of the Prince evidently got as far as digging the grave: Mason, Woodruff, and Cotton, *Memorandum* (cit. in n. 153). The crypt of the south-east transept was separated from the rest of the crypt by an iron grille and gates: Somner, *Antiquities* (1640), 177.

[191] From 1343 to 1395 the space under the western of the three arches on the south side of the Confessor's Chapel at Westminster was probably occupied by the tomb of John of Eltham, Earl of Cornwall (d. 1336): *Chronica Johannis de Reading et Anonymi Cantuariensis 1346–1367*, ed. J. Tait (Manchester, 1914),

the decision was taken to bury the Prince in the Trinity Chapel. Presumably, his well-known devotion was felt to justify burial in the part of the church pre-eminently associated with the Trinity by virtue of its dedication and its function as a container for the relics of a saint whose life had been even richer than the prince's own in Trinitarian portents.[192] One may suspect too, that at a time when the convent was in serious financial difficulties, the monks would have viewed the accessibly sited monument to the prematurely fallen flower of English chivalry as a valuable 'side attraction' for pilgrims to St Thomas's shrine.[193]

Despite gaining a more prestigious site than the Prince had requested, his tomb conforms almost exactly to the detailed specification contained in his will (Pl. 119).[194] The incorporation of a flat painted tester is the one major departure from the specification and was obviously made possible only by the change to the more spacious setting of the Trinity Chapel. The use of gilded copper rather than naturalistically painted stone and the selection of a tester in preference to an elaborate architectural canopy brings the tomb closer to the Westminster monuments of reigning monarchs than to earlier royal princes' tombs, so it would seem reasonable to interpret these features as commemorating Edward's crown-prince status.[195] His portrayal as a fully armed knight follows the con-

81–2; F. Devon, *Issues of the Exchequer* (London, 1837), 262. As early as 24 Aug. 1339 Edward III had ordered the convent to have the Earl's body moved to 'autre plus convenable place entre les Roials. Faisant toutesfoits reserver et garder les places plus honorables illoeques pour le gisir et la sepulture de nous et de noz heirs': Westminster Abbey Muniment 6300*; A. P. Stanley, *Historical Memorials of Westminster Abbey* (London, 1868), 505–6. However, by c.1365 the east arch must have been earmarked for Queen Philippa's tomb, which was partly paid for in 1367 (Devon, *Exchequer Issues*, 189). Despite Edward's reported promise to his dying queen that he would lie beside her in the same grave (*Chroniques de J. Froissart*, ed. S. Luce (15 vols.; Paris, 1869–1975), vii. 182), it seems clear that he continued to regard the central arch, the site of the existing tomb, as his burial plot, for nothing was ever done to convert the queen's tomb into a double monument.

[192] St Thomas was consecrated on the first Sunday after Pentecost, which in 1162 fell on 3 June, and ordered that the feast of the Trinity be kept as a principal feast throughout England on that day. His first mass was celebrated in the Trinity Chapel, which subsequently became the part of the Cathedral most used by him for mass and for his personal prayers. For the belief that the third day of the week was a providential day in St Thomas's life, see A. J. Duggan, 'The Cult of St Thomas Becket in the Thirteenth Century', in *St Thomas Cantilupe, Bishop of Hereford: Essays in His Honour*, ed. M. Jancey (Hereford, 1982), 40 (n. 105). The Black Prince was born within the quindene of Trinity Sunday and died on the feast itself, at three in the afternoon, having been Prince of Wales for 33 years. His wife was aged 33 when he married her. His devotion to the Trinity is amply attested by contemporary chroniclers and by the art works associated with him. No doubt he chose his burial site in the crypt at least partly because it was directly below the high altar which he, in common with many others in the Middle Ages, regarded as being dedicated to the Trinity and to which he bequeathed a precious Trinity image.

[193] For the steep rise in pilgrims' offerings at St Thomas's shrine in the year of the prince's death, and evidence of financial difficulty at this period, see C. E. Woodruff, 'The Financial Aspect of the Cult of St Thomas of Canterbury, As Revealed by a Study of the Monastic Records', *Arch. Cant.*, 44 (1932), 21. English royal tombs as a sightseeing attraction are documented in a journal of the French embassy to London in July 1445, which notes that the ambassadors spent a free Sunday afternoon at the Greyfriars and Westminster Abbey 'veoir les sepultures et ornaments, qui y sont moult riches'; *Letters and Papers Illustrative of the Wars of the English in France During the Reign of Henry the Sixth . . .*, ed. J. Stevenson, 2 vols. in 3 (RS 22; 1861–4), i. 125.

[194] The inclusion of scrolls with the motto 'ich diene' above the ostrich-feather shields may not actually be a departure from the specification: Stanley, *Historical Memorials* (cit. in n. 164), 165 n. 1. The specification gives the epitaph, which varies in only minor details from that on the tomb. On its literary source, see, most recently, D. B. Tyson, 'The Epitaph of Edward the Black Prince', *Medium Ævum*, 46 (1977), 87–104.

[195] Equally, the testers of the Westminster tombs of Queen Eleanor and Queen Philippa (the former renewed in the 15th cent.) and of the Black Prince's tomb may have been adopted in order to avoid overtopping the nearby saints' shrines in the manner criticized by Archbishop Winchelsey in 1302. The use of gilt bronze for the effigies of reigning monarchs, and by extension Crown princes, was surely intended to symbolize their quasi-divine power and authority, as embodied in the universally current formula *rex imago Dei*. It seems likely that the comparison which contemporaries would have made most readily would have been with the large-scale precious-metal statues of titular saints which by this time were often placed over the high altars of major English churches. That the use of precious metals incapable of rendering lifelike colour and texture did not significantly reduce the capacity of effigies to function as simulacra is suggested by the reference to Henry V's 'rial ymage like to him-self, of silver & gilt': *The Brut*, ed. F.

vention adopted for the effigies of earlier adult princes,[196] and, as in most English knightly effigies of the 1360s, the rigidity of the body armour virtually dictates a rigid pose. Given that the sculptor's task was primarily the careful rendering of this all-enveloping carapace, it seems beside the point to criticize the effigy's impersonal quality, as some commentators have done.[197] The effigy's visible facial features are not sufficiently individualized to allow one to decide whether they were intended as a portrait. Their similarity to those of his father's effigy at Westminster is probably due to common authorship, for the two images show many resemblances in the details of their modelling.[198]

The Black Prince's marble tomb-chest is an example of the London version of the Perpendicular style and can fairly be attributed to Henry Yevele, the leading exponent of that tradition in the late fourteenth century.[199] Its detail indicates that the tomb was put in hand soon after the Prince's death, for the octofoiled squares enclosing the shields are a motif supplanted in the repertory of London tomb-makers by the richly cusped quatrefoils apparently first used on the plinth of Edward III's monument, made shortly after 1386.[200] The marble, metal, and wooden components of the Black Prince's tomb are all of superb quality, but they are also characterized by a concern to subordinate detail to overall effect. That this coolly restrained aesthetic is also the hallmark of the work of late fourteenth-century London architects—a category which the nave at Canterbury cannot escape, despite the lack of unambiguous evidence for Henry Yevele's authorship—is not so surprising, given that one of the characteristic features of English, as distinct from Continental, late medieval tomb production is the heavy involvement of architects.[201]

W. D. Brie, 2 vols. (Early English Text Soc., orig. ser., 131, 136 1906–8), ii. 493. See also n. 30 above.

[196] Notably Edmund of Lancaster and John of Eltham in Westminster Abbey, and John of Gaunt at Old St Paul's Cathedral.

[197] e.g. D. Lüdke in *Die Parler und der Schöne Stil 1350–1400*, ed. A. Legner, exhib. cat. Kunsthalle, Cologne, 1978 (5 vols.; Cologne, 1978–80), iii. 110, and Stone, *Sculpture in Britain* (cit. in n. 128), 192. In showing the deceased wearing a bascinet rather than bareheaded, the Black Prince's effigy conforms to an English tradition rarely departed from before the 15th cent. For the Somerset origin of the even more distinctively English usage of placing the tilting helm under the head, see ibid., 262 n. 26. The earliest monument of more than local importance incorporating this feature is that of Lawrence de Hastings, Earl of Pembroke (d. 1348), at Abergavenny Priory.

[198] The attribution of these two effigies to the London latoner John Orchard, first made in W. R. Lethaby, *Westminster Abbey and the King's Craftsmen* (London, 1906), 289, has been generally accepted. Except for the missing crown, sceptres, and beast at the feet, Edward III's effigy is a single casting, whereas the quite different three-dimensional form of the Black Prince's effigy necessitated that the head, arms, torso, legs, sword, and dagger be made separately. The last is the only significant loss from the effigy.

[199] The attribution is made in J. H. Harvey, 'Henry Yevele, Architect, and His Works in Kent', *Arch. Cant.*, 56 (1943), 51, where the tomb-chest is incorrectly described as a restoration (cf. n. 200 below).

[200] The earliest stone tomb-chest decorated with shields

enclosed in octofoiled squares appears to be that of William de Valence (d. 1296) in Westminster Abbey. The unworked marble for the tomb of Edward III was mentioned in 1386: Colvin, *History of the King's Works* (cit. in n. 136), p. 487. In 1845 Sir Richard Westmacott estimated for 'reworking' the Black Prince's tomb-chest (J. Physick, 'Royal Monuments in the Nineteenth Century', *Church Monuments*, 2 (1987), 44), but the original remains in place.

[201] Cf. n. 40 above. The capacity of architects to influence the character of the sculptural adjuncts to the structures which they designed is documentarily attested by the contract of 1395 which specifies that the sculpture-encrusted cornice of Westminster Hall is to be made 'selonc le purport dune forme et molde [template (?)] faitz par conseil de Mestre Henri Yeueley': L. F. Salzman, *Building in England Down to 1540: A Documentary History* (Oxford, 1967), 472. Except in the case of the foreign-made tomb of Queen Philippa (d. 1369) at Westminster, sculptors appear to have been responsible for the architectural parts of English tombs only when these were comparatively unimportant, as in Archbishop Courtenay's monument (see above). It seems to have been rare for English architects in a large way of business to be practising sculptors, and many of the documented instances of their supplying figure sculpture probably conceal subcontracting to specialist carvers. Yevele was one of a handful of major 14th-cent. English architects who, as a sideline, ran workshops making monumental brasses (Harvey, *English Mediaeval Architects* (cit. in n. 14), 365); and though no attempt has ever been made to identify brasses from Yevele's shop, there must be at least a possibility that the influence of this exceptionally important architect and con-

It is possible that to the Black Prince's executors, part of the appeal of a tester was its capacity to display painted imagery. Earlier English examples of painting and sculpture set above tomb-effigies show Christ in Majesty, and the use here of Evangelist symbols taken from this standard image, in combination with a 'Throne of Mercy' Trinity, indicates that the Prince was expected to be faced on the Day of Judgement by all three persons of the Trinity.[202] The tester illustrates the general decline in the quality of English painting during the later fourteenth century, as well as the combination of rich surface patterning and rather formless bodies which can be seen in some of the few other surviving metropolitan paintings of *c*.1380.[203] Even so, the only undamaged face, that of the angel of St Matthew, displays an impressively bold and painterly modelling, which one of the most recent students of the tester has categorized as thoroughly Anglicized Italianate.[204]

The funeral achievements suspended above and beside the tomb are the only part of any of the Cathedral's medieval monuments to have been studied intensively, although the best source for their original arrangement, the sketch of 1613 in the Kentish church notes of the herald John Philipot, remains virtually unknown (Pl. 118).[205] Its chief value is in showing that the shield of the Prince's 'arms of war', which hung until the early nineteenth century on the pier at the head of the tomb, was balanced at the foot by the other shield borne at the funeral, the 'arms of peace', the famous ostrich feathers. When this shield and the curious *pavis* or target hung above the 'arms of war' were removed is not known, but Philipot's drawing shows that the sword, which still appears in an anonymous drawing of *c*.1600 (Pl. 120), had been stolen several decades before the traditional culprit, Oliver Cromwell, was in any position to lay hands on it.[206] The origin of the practice of hanging arms and armour near knightly graves has attracted little scholarly interest, but

tractor lies behind the severely elegant figure-style and accurately Perpendicular settings characteristic of late 14th-cent. London-made brasses.

[202] Earlier 14th-cent. examples of large images of Christ in Majesty are over the tombs of Bishops Stapledon (painting) and Grandisson at Exeter (low-relief sculpture) and the Harrington tomb at Cartmel Priory, Cumbria (painting). It is unknown how early the custom began to be observed of incorporating downward-facing images of Christ in judgement into the ceilings of the hearses of high-ranking lay persons and ecclesiastics (see p. 487 and nn. 162–3 above), but that there was a relationship of some kind between these images and the painted testers of tombs can hardly be doubted. The earliest hearse known to have been ceiled with an image of Christ in judgement was that of Henry V: Hope, 'Funeral Monument of Henry V' (cit. in n. 136), 133–5.

[203] Notably the Crucifixion page of the Lytlington Missal of 1383–4 (Westminster Abbey Library, MS 37, fo. 157ᵛ).

[204] A. Simpson, *The Connections Between English and Bohemian Painting During the Second Half of the Fourteenth Century* (New York and London, 1984), 168. P. Tudor-Craig, however, emphasizes its 'new mastery, not subservient to Cologne, Italy, or even Paris': *Age of Chivalry* (cit. in n. 45), 134. The most recent conservation undergone by the tester was the fixing of loose paint in Mar. 1974: Canterbury Cathedral Library, typescript report by Pauline Plummer dated Mar. 1975. For earlier 20th-cent. restorations, see *Cant. Cath. Chron.*, 27 (1937), 6–8. A slight

pencil-sketch made by John Carter in 1785 is in BL, Add. MS 29926, fo. 246.

[205] The most recent scholarly account of the achievements is by C. Blair in *Age of Chivalry* (cit. in n. 45), 479–81. The only references in print to Philipot's drawing (Kentish church notes (cit. in n. 59), 19) are a letter from the then owner of the manuscript, F. W. Cock, *Times Literary Supplement*, 31 July 1919, 413, and C. R. Councer, 'A Book of Church Notes by John Philipot, Somerset Herald', in *A Seventeenth-Century Miscellany* (Kent Archaeol. Soc., Kent Records, 17; 1961 for 1960), 82, but neither account includes a reproduction of the drawing or mentions the absence of the sword. Indeed, Cock mistakes the dagger in the drawing for the sword. Reference should also be made to J. Arnold, 'The Jupon or Coat-Armour of the Black Prince in Canterbury Cathedral', *Church Monuments*, 8 (1993), 12–24 (published since this chapter was written).

[206] The best rendering of the *pavis* is that in E. Bolton, *The Elements of Armories* (London, 1610), 67, reprod. in W. H. St J. Hope, 'The Atchievements of Edward, Prince of Wales (the "Black Prince") in the Cathedral Church of Canterbury', *Vetusta Monumenta*, 7/2 (1895), 20. Hope's account of the changes in the arrangement of the achievements is very full, but his suggestion that the Society of Antiquaries drawing shows 'arms of peace' which did not actually exist (ibid. 10) is negated by their appearance in the independent drawing by Philipot (cf. Pl. 118).

it was certainly current in Germany by 1240, when a leather-covered shield not too unlike the Black Prince's was suspended beside the tomb of Conrad of Thuringia, Landgrave of Hesse, at Marburg.[207] The earliest known English instance appears to have been the tomb in Tewkesbury Abbey of Richard de Clare, Earl of Gloucester (d. 1262), which his widow adorned with the sword and spurs that he had used in his lifetime.[208]

After the erection of Richard II's tomb at Westminster in the late 1390s, there was no obvious way of fitting more monuments into the Confessor's Chapel, and it is likely that in choosing burial on the north side of St Thomas's shrine chapel **Henry IV** (d. 1413) had decided to inaugurate a new royal mausoleum.[209] Henry's will of 1409 seems to leave the choice of site to the discretion of Archbishop Arundel, the chief supporter of his seizure of the throne, but there can be little doubt that this was only a polite fiction concealing a decision already taken, because in 1410 John Beaufort, Henry's half-brother and staunch ally, was buried immediately to the east of the future site of the King's tomb.[210]

For Henry IV, burial next to St Thomas possessed a significance which most later generations have overlooked. He was the first king anointed at his coronation with an oil which a legend in existence since the early fourteenth century claimed had been given by the Virgin to St Thomas during his French exile. The Virgin's intention was that the oil remain unused until the coronation of a just king who would peacefully recover the French lands ruled by his ancestors.[211] The strongly pro-Lancastrian chronicler Thomas Walsingham gives a version of the recent history of the oil which had almost certainly been concocted for circulation at the time of Henry IV's coronation. According to this, Henry IV's maternal grandfather, Henry of Grosmont, first Duke of Lancaster, recovered the oil in France and handed it over to the Black Prince, whom he naturally anticipated would be the next king. Before Richard II's coronation, the oil was searched for in vain, and when Richard came across it in the Tower of London some twenty years later, Archbishop Arundel refused to carry out a second anointing.[212] From both the Canterbury

---

[207] *700 Jahre Elisabethkirche in Marburg 1283–1983*, exhib. cat. (7 vols.; Marburg, 1983), iv. 122, fig. 26.

[208] The de Clare achievements, which appear to have escaped scholarly attention, may well have been influential, as Earl Richard was the head of the richest and most powerful baronial family in England and his tomb was exceptionally splendid, the only non-royal English tomb of the 13th cent. known to have been made of precious materials: Dugdale, *Monasticon* (cit. in n. 13), ii. 61. For the burial of his entrails in Canterbury Cathedral, see n. 249 below. A wooden shield with arms of one of the Black Prince's companions in arms, Sir Richard Fogge (d. 1407), hung until the early 17th cent. on a pier close by his grave in the nave of the cathedral: 'Family Chronicle of Richard Fogge, of Danes Court, in Tilmanstone', *Arch. Cant.*, 5 (1863), 119–20. The piers adjacent to the tomb in Hereford Cathedral of Sir Richard Pembridge (d. 1375), another comrade of the Prince, were hung with a helm and tilting shield: Gough, *Sepulchral Monuments* (cit. in n. 14), i, pt. 2, pl. liv. I am grateful to Claude Blair for confirming that no substantial work exists on the origin of the custom of suspending arms over tombs.

[209] Suggested in Woodruff and Danks, *Memorials*, 188.

[210] The will says simply that he is to be buried in the Cathedral 'aftyr the discrecion' of the archbishop: *A Collection of Wills of*

the Kings and Queens of England, ed. J. Nichols (London, 1780), 203. A later will has not survived: J. L. Kirby, *Henry IV of England* (London, 1970), 222. Until 1399 Henry was probably anticipating that he would be buried in St Mary in the Newark, Leicester, which contained the tombs of his first wife, Mary Bohun, and that of the founder of St Mary's, Henry of Grosmont, first Duke of Lancaster. John Beaufort's burial north of St Thomas's shrine is noted in Searle, *Chronicle and Lists*, 26.

[211] For the legend of the oil, see works referred to in C. Wilson, 'The Tomb of Henry IV and the Holy Oil of St Thomas of Canterbury', in *Medieval Architecture in Its Intellectual Context: Essays in Honour of Peter Kidson*, ed. E. Fernie and P. Crossley (London, 1990), 181–90; J. R. S. Phillips, 'Edward II and the Prophets', in *England in the Fourteenth Century* (cit. in n. 175), 189–201. For Arundel's role in the succession and coronation of Henry IV, see P. Heath, *Church and Realm, 1272–1461* (London, 1988), 224–32.

[212] Walsingham's dating of this incident to early 1399 (*Historia Anglicana* (cit. in n. 95), ii. 239–40) must be a slip, as the archbishop then was not Arundel but Roger Walden, and elsewhere (*Ypodigma Neustriae*, ed. T. H. Riley (RS 28; 1876), 388) he places it in Richard II's 21st regnal year (22 June 1397–21 June 1398).

and the Lancastrian viewpoints, this account was highly satisfactory, as it put Henry IV's accession under the patronage of St Thomas.[213] The references to Henry of Grosmont and the Black Prince were all too obviously designed to draw the sting from the potentially embarrassing proximity of Henry IV's tomb to that of the father of the king whom he had usurped (Pl. 19 and Fig. 2).

A detail of the monument that has been little noticed is fairly certainly an allusion to the legend of St Thomas's oil. This is the series of collars of SS painted on the tester, which differ from all other known examples of the Lancastrian livery collar in having flying golden eagles within the tirets at the centre of the wearer's breast. The eagle was an important Lancastrian badge before 1399, but it became even more significant for Henry IV once it was realized that his anointing as king could be carried out with the oil, for the outer, visible container of the holy fluid was in the form of an eagle made of gold. In the collars depicted on the tomb, the positioning of the eagles is surely a reference to the legend's account of how, when the Virgin gave St Thomas the oil, she placed the immediate container, the ampulla, inside a small gold eagle on her breast and foretold that the first king anointed with the oil would have victory over his enemies so long as he wore the eagle and its contents on his own breast. Thomas Walsingham says that despite failing to achieve unction with the oil, Richard II had worn the eagle round his neck from the time of his discovery of it in the Tower until its confiscation by Arundel in August 1399.[214] The exceptional nature of Henry IV's bond with St Thomas accounts not only for his burial at Canterbury and the siting of his tomb in the Trinity Chapel, but also for the holding of his funeral on Trinity Sunday, *roi des dimanches*. For two months and more, the coffin had lain in a candle- and pennon-decked hearse which probably rose most of the way to the vault.[215]

The identity of the patron of Henry IV's monument is not known, but the strongest candidate is his second wife, **Joan of Navarre** (d. 1437), whose effigy lies alongside that of the king. Henry's executors can probably be ruled out, since it was only in 1426 that they received the final instalment of a special grant from the executors of Henry V which enabled them to pay off the enormous debts specified in the 1409 will as a first charge on

[213] Evidence of Henry IV's devotion to St Thomas is his general practice of making a pilgrimage each May (C. Given-Wilson, *The Royal Household and the King's Affinity* (New Haven, Conn., and London, 1986), 70) and his subventions to the nave fabric. It is likely that his age at his accession, 33, was thought auspicious in itself and also in relation to the extraordinary wealth of Trinitarian symbolism in the life and death of St Thomas (see n. 192 above).

[214] The eagle symbolized not only kingship, but Christ, the Resurrection, and baptism, and there can be little doubt that its introduction into the story of the Holy Oil was an attempt to trump the legend that the French coronation-oil was originally brought direct from heaven by the Holy Spirit for the baptism of King Clovis in 496. A clear allusion to the eagle as symbol of Christ is the original placing of St Thomas's golden eagle at the Virgin's breast. For the eagle as a Lancastrian badge, see C. E. J. Smith, 'The Livery Collar', *Coat of Arms*, NS, 8 (1990), 245, where the collars on the Canterbury tester are related to one carved on the tomb of Oliver Groos (probably d. 1442) at Sloley, Norfolk. Groos was said by his son-in-law, the judge William

Yelverton, to have been in great favour with Henry IV and Henry V (microfilm of North papers in Norfolk Record Office, MF 21483/5, a reference kindly supplied by Dr Roger Virgoe), and this tends to support the suggestion made in relation to Henry IV in Wilson, 'Tomb of Henry IV' (cit. in n. 211), 187, that eagle-decorated collars of SS were marks of the king's special esteem. The eagle on the Groos tomb has half-open wings (cf. the eagles between the king's mottoes on the tester) and is typologically later than the eagles on the tester collars, being a pendant hanging from the tiret.

[215] For documentary references to the funeral expenses, see J. H. Wylie, *The Reign of Henry the Fifth* (3 vols.; Cambridge, 1914–29), i. 47–8, 209–11; *CPR 1413–16*, 64. Henry IV's and Queen Joan's hearses were both sold off shortly after their funerals (Prior's Acct. 11, c.1413; Woodruff, 'Sacrist's Rolls' (cit. in n. 145), 58). The requirement that kings' and queens' hearses rise almost to the vault is noted in an account of the workings of the Chapel Royal written c.1445–9: *Liber Regie Capelle*, ed. W. Ullmann (Henry Bradshaw Soc., 92; 1961), 112.

the estate. It is difficult to believe that Henry V, who directly after his accession ordered a copper effigy for his mother's tomb in Leicester, would have chosen to commemorate his father by a monument made of the far less expensive and prestigious material of alabaster.[216] The use of alabaster weighs slightly in favour of Queen Joan's patronage, for in 1408 she had had a monument made in this material for erection over the tomb in Nantes Cathedral of her first husband Jean IV, Duke of Brittany.[217] But the best evidence that she paid for the Canterbury monument is the punctiliously exact balance which the painted decoration of the tester strikes between her own heraldry and the King's: one shield of his arms, one of hers, one of the two impaled, all three on a background of diagonal bands formed alternately of his motto, 'soverayne', punctuated by crowned golden eagles, and what must be her motto, 'a temperance', punctuated by weasel-like ermines of Brittany.[218]

[216] For Henry's posthumous debts, see works referred to in Wilson, 'Tomb of Henry IV' (cit. in n. 211), 181–2, n. 4; P. and F. Strong, 'The Last Will and Codicils of Henry V', *EHR*, 96 (1981), 86 (a reference kindly given me by Dr Jenny Stratford). The sum of £43 for Mary Bohun's monument was paid in advance to the London coppersmith John Godeyer, only three months after Henry V's accession: Devon, *Exchequer Issues* (cit. in n. 191), 321.

[217] A parallel, possibly nearly contemporary, instance of a queen dowager's direct involvement in commissioning her husband's monument is Katherine of Valois's paying for the silver effigy of Henry V: *The Brut* (cit. in n. 195), ii. 493. The documentation for the Nantes tomb (Rymer, *Foedera* (n. 136 above), viii. 510–11) reveals the names of the carvers but not the location of the workshop. A connection with the neighbourhood of Chellaston is suggested by the most unusual of the carvers' names, viz. Poppehowe; cf. *CPR 1405–8*, 321. The appearance of the tomb is preserved in G. A. Lobineau, *Histoire de Bretagne*, (2 vols.; Paris, 1707), ii, pl. opp. 499; Adhémar and Dordor, *Tombeaux de la collection Gaignières* (cit. in n. 31), 173 (no. 970). The comparative cheapness of the Canterbury tomb might suggest that it was not commissioned while Queen Joan enjoyed her enormous, if intermittently paid, dower, that is, before her imprisonment for witchcraft in 1419–23. The estates allowed her after her rehabilitation are said to have been 'modest' (R. A. Griffiths, *The Reign of Henry VI* (London, 1981), 62), but the accounts for her household expenditure in 1427–8 (Soc. Antiquaries, MS 216) indicate that she enjoyed an income which would have enabled her easily to afford the existing monument. The monument in alabaster to Sir Ralph Greene and his wife at Lowick (Northants.), which Thomas Prentys and Robert Sutton supplied in 1419, and which incorporated an elaborate canopy, now destroyed, cost just £40 (Hope, 'Early Working of Alabaster' (cit. in n. 101), 232); and in 1421 the London sculptor Robert Broun could make a tomb incorporating two alabaster effigies on a marble slab over an alabaster tomb-chest with at least 12 weepers, for only £22 13s. 4d. (G. M. Bark, 'A London Alabasterer in 1421', *Antiquaries Jnl.*, 29 (1949), 89–91). So Henry's and Joan's tomb is likely to have cost no more than a small fraction of the £933 6s. 8d. paid for Richard II's and Anne of Bohemia's Purbeck marble and copper-gilt tomb at Westminster.

[218] The present tester-painting supersedes an earlier scheme incorporating roundels, which was apparently never finished. The roundels have been described as simple circles containing seven different types of animal (Gough, *Sepulchral Monuments* (cit. in n. 14), ii, pt. 2. 32) and as garters containing eagles and greyhounds (T. Willement, *Heraldic Notices of Canterbury Cathedral* (London, 1827), 51), but neither interpretation can be verified, as almost no details are now visible to the naked eye. For the overall design of the executed scheme, and indications of its predecessor, see Gough, *Sepulchral Monuments*, ii, pt. 2, pl. xv, for which the original drawing by J. Schnebbelie is Bodl., Gough Maps 227, leaf 6. For the motto 'soveraigne', see, most recently, C. Blair and I. Delamer, 'The Dublin Civic Swords', *Proc. R. Irish Acad.*, 88, sect. C (1988), 115–17. The Queen's motto, 'a temperance', is not otherwise attested. The ermines (now black but presumably silver originally) correspond closely to those on the collar of the Order of Ermine founded by Joan's first husband, a fact which points to her more or less direct involvement in the work. Her son demanded the return of collars of deceased members in Nov. 1437 (D. A. D'A. Boulton, *The Knights of the Crown: The Monarchical Orders of Knighthood in Later Medieval Europe 1325–1521* (Woodbridge, 1987), 275), and it might have been Joan's death which prompted this action, for one can assume that she was a *chevaleresse* of the order. It has been suggested that the trails of flowers on the tester are forget-me-nots (Blair and Delamer, 'Dublin Civic Swords', 120–1), although they have five petals instead of the normal four. The tester was restored most recently by Pauline Plummer: Canterbury Cathedral Library, typescript report dated Mar. 1975. For an earlier restoration, which embraced the whole tomb and entailed replacing missing parts of the tester with unpainted wood, see E. W. Tristram, 'A Royal Tomb at Canterbury', *Cant. Cath. Chron.*, 36 (1937), 6–8. For the shields of European royalty and English nobility on the cresting of the tester, see Gough, *Sepulchral Monuments*, ii, pt. 2. 32–3; Willement, *Heraldic Notices*, 51–3; C. R. Humphery-Smith, 'The Tomb of King Henry IV', *Cant. Cath. Chron.*, 70 (1976), 35–41. It is likely that the arms of European royalty and English nobility in the cresting were designed to perpetuate the 90 armorial banners on the King's anniversary hearse (for which, see n. 232 below). Gough noted that the eastern corners of the tester retained their carved wooden angels, and presumably these are the ones now at the south-west and south-east corners (the others being plaster casts). Under the south-eastern angel is a boss carved with the ermine of Brittany collared and with a ducal coronet hovering over its back, and it seems likely that the bosses bore alternately ermines and eagles, like those painted on the soffit of the tester.

In the large panels at the head and foot of the tomb showing the martyrdom of St Thomas and the coronation of the Virgin by the Trinity, the royal mottoes make patterned backgrounds which reinforce the playing-card flatness of the surprisingly naïvely painted figures.[219] By comparison with these panels and the tester, the colouring of the effigies and tomb-chest is restrained, with most of the natural alabaster exposed and only the decorative details picked out in gold and colour. Like the complex head-canopies, this 'parcel gilt' scheme recalls the French royal tombs in marble or alabaster, and it is probably significant that Joan's brother Charles III of Navarre and his queen lie in Pamplona Cathedral under a splendid alabaster monument of 1416–20 whose overall conception, no less than its colouring, invites comparison with those of Joan's and Charles's French royal relatives.[220]

The royal pair at Canterbury are shown in the ceremonial robes which they wore after their coronations and on other state occasions (Pl. 123). In his left hand the King held a long sceptre. His right hand rested on his chest and apparently held the ends of the cords belonging to the fastening of his mantle. The Queen's upper left arm has gone, but it no doubt held the equivalent cord. The position of her sceptre can be deduced from the remains of its supports on her shoulder and caul. That the small size of her effigy relative to her husband's corresponds to reality is clear from the reported smallness of her coffin.[221]

As long ago as 1904, W. H. St John Hope proposed that the tomb of Henry IV and Queen Joan was made in the workshops of Thomas Prentys and Robert Sutton at Chellaston in Derbyshire.[222] The basis of this attribution was the resemblance of the royal tomb to that of Sir Ralph Greene and his wife at Lowick in Northamptonshire, which Prentys and Sutton supplied in 1419. Hope's suggestion was surely correct, for the Canterbury and Lowick monuments belong to a very large and widely distributed group of late fourteenth- and early fifteenth-century alabaster tombs which are so closely interrelated as to leave no real doubt that all are products of a single, highly organized and very prolific workshop.

[219] Both panels were painted out at an unknown date after the Reformation, and by the late 17th cent., that of the Coronation of the Virgin was concealed by a painting of an angel holding a shield of the arms of England quartering Navarre: Sandford, *Genealogical History* (cit. in n. 149), pl. at 267. Sandford's text makes no mention of the Martyrdom panel, but it is shown, doubtless far less damaged than in actuality, in Dart, *History and Antiquities* (cit. in n. 88), pl. 5. The evidence of Dart's view for the visibility of the painting in the 18th cent. is difficult to reconcile with the statements by J. Milner in the description of the far more detailed rendering dated 1786 in J. Carter, *Specimens of the Ancient Sculpture and Painting now remaining in this Kingdom* (London, 1780–94), 57–8. What appears to be Carter's original on-the-spot drawing is BL, Add. MS 22926, fo. 244. The almost obliterated crowned and kneeling suppliants at the base of the Coronation panel are presumably Henry and Joan, although two kings are shown in the reconstruction by E. W. Tristram presently hanging on the north aisle wall of the Trinity Chapel. The panels are close in style to the representation of Humphrey, Duke of Gloucester, presented to the Man of Sorrows by St Alban in the Duke's book of selected Psalms, *c*.1420–30 (BL, Royal MS 2 B. I, fo. 8).

[220] The 'parcel gilt' description comes from F. Sandford, *Genealogical History* (cit. in n. 149), 268, and is confirmed by visual examination of the surface of the alabaster, large areas of which were left without paint or gilding. This is in line with the practice of the makers of alabaster altar-pieces, as noted in F. Cheetham, *English Medieval Alabasters* (Oxford, 1984), 26–7. Such details as the light scratching of the mantle linings to indicate fur would have become invisible if painted over. For the existing polychromy, see Tristram, 'Royal Tomb' (cit. in n. 218).

[221] J. H. Spry, 'A Brief Account of the Tomb of Henry IV in the Cathedral of Canterbury, August 21, 1832', *Archaeologia*, 26 (1836), 443. It is difficult to give much weight to the often-repeated notion that the smallness of the Queen's effigy is evidence for its being a later addition to the tomb; cf. the Chellaston-made monument at Arundel to John d'Arundel (d. 1421) and Beatriz of Portugal. Whereas the Queen's coffin lies on the pavement, the King's lies under it, with only its eastern part covered by the tomb-chest, an anomaly due apparently to the need for access from the north aisle to the altar of St Thomas's shrine. The lack of any gate is part of the evidence for a post-Reformation remodelling of the railings (cf. n. 224 below).

[222] Hope, 'Early Working of Alabaster' (cit. in n. 101), 232. Lawrence Stone, for whom 'it is unthinkable that a royal tomb should have been commissioned in the provinces', plumps for an attribution to the London sculptor Robert Broun, none of whose work is known to survive: *Sculpture in Britain* (cit. in n. 128), 197–8.

Henry IV's and Joan's monument is much the most elaborately finished piece of work ever produced by the Chellaston alabasterers, yet the majority of its elements were stock. The hang of the Queen's robe, the cords and fasteners of the mantle straps, the embroidered leaf borders, the arms-bearing angels on the shorter sides of the tomb-chest, even the King's puckered forehead, recur in other Chellaston-made tombs.[223] The most remarkable aspect of the tomb's manufacture has gone unnoticed, doubtless because the tester and railings make it difficult to get good views of the effigies from above.[224] The left and right sides of both effigies were worked by different sculptors, a division of labour whose effects are more obvious in the case of the King's effigy (Pl. 124). There are small yet distinct variations of detail between the right and left sides of the upper cushion, the angels, the points of the crown, the eyes, the ears, the hair, the mantle strap, etc., etc.[225] The carving on the more visible north side is consistently more competent, so Prentys evidently knew who were his better carvers. One can only speculate on whether this extraordinary and apparently unique procedure was adopted in order to achieve speed. The King's pudgy, ill-looking face and his out-of-date hairstyle are almost certainly elements of naturalistic portraiture.[226]

The stylistic evidence afforded by comparisons with other Chellaston tombs, and also the florid detailing of the robes of estate, point to a date fairly soon after Henry IV's death, and certainly well before that of Queen Joan in 1437.[227] Some time around the latter date, work must have begun on the diminutive chapel of St Edward the Confessor which opens out of the north aisle of the Trinity Chapel (Pls. 20, 122). Its consecration took place on 1 March 1441. The choice of dedication was appropriate, as Henry had been crowned on 13

[223] By 1443 the workshop was headed by Prentys's partner in the Lowick contract, Robert Sutton: P. Lindley, ' "Una grande opera al mio re": Gilt-Bronze Effigies in England from the Middle Ages to the Renaissance', *JBAA* 143 (1990), 126 (n. 21). My view that a majority of the extant early 15th-cent. alabaster tomb-effigies derived from the same workshop as the Greene monument at Lowick was reached after studying the numerous photographs of this material in the Conway Library of the Courtauld Institute of Art, Univ. of London. The ease with which the products of the Prentys–Sutton workshop can be recognized is asserted, somewhat too confidently, in Hope, 'Early Working of Alabaster' (cit. in n. 101), 232. To date, the only systematic definition of formal and technical relationships between Chellaston tomb-carvings is C. Ryde, 'An Alabaster Standing Angel with Shield at Lowick: A Chellaston Shop Pattern', *Derbys. Archaeol. Jnl.*, 97 (1977), 36–49. Similar views as to the national predominance of the Chellaston workshop and its involvement in the making of the royal tomb at Canterbury are expressed in id., 'Alabaster Tomb Manufacture 1400 to 1430', *Derbys. Miscellany*, 12 (1991), 164–77, seen only after the completion of this chapter.

[224] The evidence in the ironwork that the area enclosed by the railings has been reduced is noted in Geddes, 'Tomb Railings' (cit. in n. 101), 67–8, 73. For evidence of the same process visible in the stonework, see W. Urry, 'Some Notes on the Two Resting Places of St Thomas Becket at Canterbury', in *Thomas Becket: Actes du colloque international de Sédières, 19–24 août 1973*, ed. R. Foreville (Paris, 1975), 207.

[225] Even more obvious are the discrepancies between the

foliage on the left and right halves of the head-canopies. Badly damaged in the late 18th cent. (Gostling, *Walk* (cit. in n. 144), 164; Gough, *Sepulchral Monuments* (cit. in n. 14), ii, pt. 2, pls. xiii, xiv), these canopies were among the parts of the architecture skilfully reinstated during the conservative restoration carried out by Sir Richard Westmacott in 1847–8: Dean's Book, 1822–54, p. 348; Physick, 'Royal Monuments in the 19th Century' (cit. in n. 200), 44–7.

[226] The evidence of alabaster tomb-effigies suggests that early 15th-cent. Englishmen were generally slow to adopt the clean-shaven look sported by all the aristocratic males depicted in those of the calendar pages of the Duc de Berry's *Très Riches Heures* which were painted by 1416. However, the 'basin cut' hair of the latter, a fashion which went back to c.1400, does appear on Henry IV's effigy. If, as seems probable, the face of the statue of Henry IV on the choir-screen of York Minster (made c.1450–60?) is derived from that on the tomb, this would complement the evidence of the early painted 'portraits' that no authentic visual record of the king's physiognomy was available after his death; cf. A. J. Kempe in C. A. Stothard, *Monumental Effigies of Great Britain* (London, 1832), 81; F. Hepburn, *Portraits of the Later Plantagenets* (Woodbridge, 1986), 27.

[227] Contrast the proportions of Henry IV's ermine tippet with that on the remains of his son's effigy at Westminster, made before 1431, which is of the type shown in mid-15th-cent. representations such as those in manuscripts illuminated by William Abell. The crown on the effigy does not correspond with the known details of the 'Henry' or 'Lancaster' crown, *pace* Wylie, *Henry the Fifth* (cit. in n. 215), i. 471–1.

October, the feast of the Translation of St Edward, and at an unknown later date he had placed on the Confessor's altar, then elsewhere in the Cathedral, the miracle-working coffin-lid brought from Westminster by St Thomas at the time of the first translation in 1163. The existing chapel of St Edward was presumably intended to be the site of a perpetual chantry for the King and Queen, but no such foundation was actually established.[228] Whoever commissioned the chapel was aware of the chantry chapel of Henry's parents in St Paul's Cathedral, for both were built directly across the aisle from their associated tombs and both had to fit between aisle and crypt windows. At Canterbury the very restricted height available dictated the exceptionally flat pitch of the fan vault which is the outstanding feature of the chapel.[229]

The start of work on St Edward's Chapel must have coincided almost exactly with the completion of the much larger chapel of St Michael east of the south-west transept. Glazed by 1438 and dedicated on 18 December 1439, this is often referred to as the Holland Chapel, on account of the great tomb it was built to house.[230] Both chapels are the work of the architect to the Priory from 1432 to 1458, the Londoner Richard Beke, who here and in his other contributions to the Cathedral fabric shows himself a stylistic chameleon, capable of exploiting the capital's hundred-year-old traditions of Perpendicular architecture to yield astonishing varied effects. Thus the Holland Chapel is covered not by a fan vault but by a comparatively conventional lierne vault, whose main merit in the eyes of the patron is likely to have been its capacity to incorporate decorative, especially heraldic, bosses.[231]

[228] The 1409 will leaves the siting of the chantry to Archbishop Arundel: *Wills of the Kings and Queens* (cit. in n. 210), 203. The failure of Henry's plan for a perpetual chantry at Canterbury was probably not thought too worrying by his successors and executors, since several chantries had already been established on his behalf elsewhere. For Henry's renewal of the altar of St Edward, see Gervase, *Historical Works*, ii. 285; E. Mason, 'St Wulfstan's Staff: A Legend and Its Uses', *Medium Ævum*, 53 (1984), 166–7. The earlier existence of an altar with this dedication is attested by, e.g., Sacrist's Acct. 6 (Mich. 48 Edward III–Mich. 49 Edward III), but its location is not known. It is extremely likely that St Edward's grave-cover was also the altar *mensa* in the present chapel. The juxtaposition of St Edward's and St Thomas's chapels occurs in other English cathedrals and may have been influenced by the fact that the Confessor's main feast fell on the octave of St Thomas's. The dedication date of the Confessor's chapel is recorded only in Searle, *Chronicle and Lists*, 26. The glass contained inscriptions naming Prior Goldstone, presumably the prior from 1449 to 1468: Somner, *Antiquities* (1640), 185.

[229] John of Gaunt's and Blanche of Lancaster's chapel, called 'newly built' in the licence to found the chantry (*CPR 1401–5*, p. 214), projected from the sixth bay from the east: Dugdale, *History of St Paul's* (cit. in n. 16), pl. at 163.

[230] The starting-date of St Michael's Chapel is unknown, but fell within the priorate of William Molashe, i.e. 1428–37; see n. 185 above. A *terminus a quo* is provided by the record of an inscription in the south window (Scarlett, heraldic collections (cit. in n. 59), fo. 4) which gave Edmund Beaufort's title as Count of Mortain rather than Earl of Dorset, which he was styled from 1438. The dedication of the chapel by the suffragan Bishop of Ross is recorded in Searle, *Chronicle and Lists*, 26. It

has naturally been assumed by most writers that it was the military aspect of St Michael which prompted the selection of his chapel as the resting-place for Margaret Holland's two soldier husbands. However, the dedication is given as St Anne in a will of 1453 which attributes the foundation to the Duchess of Clarence (*Sede Vacante Wills* (cit. in n. 56), 46) and in Leland, *Itinerary* (cit. in n. 52), iv. 39, and this, along with the placing of a full-page picture of St Anne first among the miniatures of her Book of Hours (Sotheby's Sale Catalogue, 19 June 1989, p. 71), suggests a particular devotion to the Virgin's mother and perhaps even prescience of the symmetry soon to be created by the removal of the Lady Chapel into the corresponding chapel in the north-west transept. How much supervision the Duchess exercised over the building and decoration of her chapel is not known. I am grateful to Dr M. K. Jones for informing me that an unsourced statement that the Duchess was in retirement from 1428 (G. E. C[okayne], *Complete Peerage* (13 vols.; 1910–59), iii. 259) does not square with the evidence of her being active in raising the ransom for her son Thomas in the years 1429–31.

[231] The attribution of St Edward's Chapel to Beke, first made in Woodman, *Architectural History* (cit. in n. 140), 180, seems indisputable, since all the works carried out at Christ Church during his time as master mason are very closely interrelated. The interpretation advanced by Woodman that the treatment of the vault springings in the chapel indicates that the vault differs from that intended by Beke fails to take account either of the existence elsewhere of similarly mannered vault-springings or of the striking similarity of the tracery in the radial panels of the vault to that in the spandrels of Beke's choir-screen entrance. For Beke's documented career, see Harvey, *English Mediaeval Architects* (cit. in n. 14), 17.

The heraldry of the Holland Chapel was in fact remarkably systematic even by late medieval standards.

At the centre of the chapel, spiritually as well as physically, is the effigy of the builder, **Lady Margaret Holland** (d. 1439). She was the wife successively to **John Beaufort**, Earl of Somerset (d. 1410), and **Thomas, Duke of Clarence**, second son of Henry IV (d. 1421).[232] Beaufort's effigy lies to the left of Lady Margaret's, that of her second and higher-ranking husband occupying the more honorific dexter position (Pl. 128). Margaret's own arms were originally painted, with appropriate symbolism, on her inner garment, her robe, whereas her mantle bore France quartered with England.[233] Although it might seem unlikely that any fifteenth-century noblewoman would have appeared in real life arrayed as a genealogical diagram, there is incontrovertible evidence that costumes of this kind existed.[234] The heraldic surcoats of Lady Margaret's husbands were, of course, a regular part of aristocratic military dress. The lost heraldic glass in the five lights of the east window echoed the hierarchical placing of the effigies, with Clarence impaling Holland in the northernmost or dexter light, Clarence in the second light, Holland in the central light, Beaufort in the fourth light, and Beaufort impaling Holland in the southernmost light. The necessary asymmetry of the chapel in having lateral windows only on the south side was ingeniously exploited to reflect the asymmetry in Lady Margaret's progeny, all of which stemmed from her first marriage. Thus the arms of the Beaufort sons were placed in the south windows, in an east-to-west order which reflected their relative ages and also brought the arms of the eldest son Henry next to those commemorating his parents' marriage in the southernmost light of the east window.[235] The transverse rib at the

[232] Contrary to the belief of the testator mentioned in n. 230 above, there was no perpetual chantry for the soul of Lady Margaret. The hearse made for Clarence's first anniversary cost £85; cf. the £66 16s. 7¼d. received by the convent when Henry IV's funeral hearse was sold (Prior's Acct. II, c.1413) and the £236 15s. 4d. charged for the king's first-anniversary hearse: Devon, *Exchequer Issues* (cit. in n. 191), 325–6. In conventionalized form, Clarence's funeral hearse is represented on fo. 75 of Lady Margaret's Book of Hours: Sotheby's Catalogue (cit. in n. 230), 72. Expenditure made in connection with the return of Clarence's body from France, his funeral, and first-anniversary hearse, which totalled £135 13s. 6d., is detailed in the Duke's wardrobe accounts for 1418–22: Westminster Abbey Muniment 12163, printed in *Household Accounts from Medieval England*, ed. C. M. Woolgar, Records of Social and Economic History, NS, 17–18; Oxford, 1992–3), ii. 604–87. An unnamed person was paid for riding from London to Canterbury and back via Southwick (Hants) 'pro ordinacione sepulture domini': ibid. 627. Clarence Herald rode from Sandwich to London to warn the Duke's council of the landing of the Duke's body and twice sought out the Archbishop for discussions about the position of the grave: ibid. 680. The delicacy of the operation of excavating the grave out of the fill above the vault of the Trinity Chapel crypt seems to be reflected in the entrusting of the direction of this work to the London mason John Warlowe: ibid. 679. Presumably Warlowe had worked earlier for the royal family and was a relation of the brothers Edmund and William Warlowe, both of whom were employed by the Crown in the early 15th cent.: Harvey, *English*

Mediaeval Architects (cit. in n. 14), 315.

[233] The arms painted on Margaret's robe and Clarence's surcoat are recorded in Philipot, Kentish church notes (cit. in n. 59), fo. 25, and those on her robe and mantle and on both men's surcoats are given in Scarlett, heraldic collections (cit. in n. 59), fos. 1ᵛ–2, where it is noted that the arms on the surcoats were so worn that only 'England quartered' remained recognizable. Beaufort's surcoat will have shown his *bordure gobony argent and azure* and Clarence's his *label of three points*. Scarlett's description of Margaret's effigy is mistakenly applied to the glazing of the east window in Caviness, *Windows* (cit. in n. 15), 286.

[234] Comparable images of women in heraldic attire appear on the 14th- and 15th-cent. brasses, in the famous arming miniature in the Luttrell Psalter of c.1330 (BL, Add. MS 42130, fo. 202ᵛ), in the Salisbury Roll, of c.1463 (Coll. Duke of Buccleuch and Queensberry) and, most likely of all to be a faithful portrayal of actual practice, a miniature in a manuscript of before 1462 of John Lydgate's *Troy Book* (BL, Royal MS 18 D. II, fo. 6). Two documented instances of women's ceremonial robes decorated with their arms, both kindly brought to my notice by Dr Veronica Sekules, are that made in 1251 for Henry III's Queen, Eleanor of Provence (*CClR 1251–3*, 14) and that worn in 1381 by Yolande de Bar (P. J. E. de Smyttere, *Essai historique sur Iolande de Flandre, Comtesse de Bar* (Lille, 1877), 81).

[235] The main source for the heraldry of the Holland Chapel glass is Scarlett, heraldic collections (cit. in n. 59), fos. 1ᵛ–2ᵛ (shields in east window numbered 1–5 and therefore no doubt in left-to-right order; no. 5 said to be broken away), fo. 4 (shields

boundary between the two compartments of the vault carries a boss with Clarence impaling Holland, and the higher rank of the second husband is also indicated by the placing of his arms on the central boss of the east compartment, nearer the altar than the Beaufort arms at the centre of the west compartment. On bosses in both compartments are the Holland white hart and the white greyhound, the latter appearing also at the feet of Clarence's effigy. Beaufort's feet rest on an eagle such as occurs on his seal and which probably alludes to his name-saint as much as to Lancastrian family tradition.[236] The use of the white greyhound alongside the Holland white hart as a supporter to all the arms in the east window was a tactful and elegant way of indicating Beaufort's and Clarence's common descent from Edward III and John of Gaunt, both of whom used the white greyhound badge.[237] This double meaning allowed continuity with the south windows, where the arms of the junior Beauforts were flanked by greyhounds and harts *couchant*.[238]

That the glazing of the south windows commemorated Lady Margaret's sons has not been recognized hitherto, because the identities of some of the men have been muddled, despite the presence of would-be clarificatory inscriptions.[239] The third son, Thomas, Count of Perche, had been buried in 1431 in the monks' cemetery, a singular choice doubtless designed to bring him close to the tomb of his name-saint in the crypt, but at some unrecorded date his body was moved into the family chapel.[240] It is possible that this translation was carried out in 1440, that is, at the same time as Lady Margaret was interred in her chapel and her husbands were transferred from their original graves at the feet of Henry IV. The prospects for a Lancastrian mausoleum around St Thomas's shrine had already faded by 1415, when Henry V had decided to be buried at Westminster, and Henry

in south windows of Beaufort sons in order of seniority and accompanied by transcripts of remaining identifying inscriptions but without any indications of how each of the two pairs of shields was arranged in the windows). More detailed, and almost exactly contemporary, drawings of some of the arms in the glazing by an anonymous herald are in Soc. Antiquaries, MS 162, fo. 35[v].

[236] For the previous Lancastrian use of the eagle device, see works referred to in n. 214. John Beaufort's seal shows his arms hung from the neck of an eagle (W. de G. Birch, *Catalogue of the Seals in the Department of Manuscripts in the British Museum* (6 vols.; London, 1887–1900), ii. 482 (n. 7282), whereas the eagle at the feet of his tomb-effigy is gorged with a coronet to which is attached a chain ending in a ring. The eagle was the dexter supporter of the arms of John, Duke of Bedford: ibid. iii. 387–8 (no. 12698). Other examples in Canterbury Cathedral of eagles commemorating men named John are on Archbishop Kempe's and Cardinal Morton's tombs (see nn. 141, 157 above) and on a boss of the north transept vault for Prior Oxney.

[237] H. S. London, *Royal Beasts* (East Knoyle, 1956), 39–40; id., 'The Greyhound as a Royal Beast', *Archaeologia*, 97 (1959), 139–63 (but cf. n. 243 below).

[238] For the supporters in the east window, see notes in Scarlett, heraldic collections (cit. in n. 59), fos. 1[v]–2[v]. The drawings of the supporters in the south windows in ibid., fo. 4, show the greyhound with a long line attached to its collar and the hind with a chain ending in a ring attached to the coronet round its

neck. The eastern of the south windows contains numerous roundels and quarries showing greyhounds with lines more complicated than in Scarlett's sketch: Caviness, *Windows* (cit. in n. 15), pl. 207.

[239] The inscriptions were recorded by Scarlett (see prev. note). Willement attributed the first shield, that inscribed 'Th'erle of Somersett', to Lady Holland's first husband instead of to the eldest son, Henry, Earl of Somerset (d. 1416): *Heraldic Notices* (cit. in n. 218), 152. For the history of the misidentification of the third son, Thomas, see next note. The account of the heraldry in Caviness, *Windows* (cit. in n. 15), 285–7, is very confused.

[240] The Christ Church monk John Stone, our only source for Thomas's burial, was evidently unfamiliar with the latter's French title and left a space for it which was never filled: Searle, *Chronicle and Lists*, 20. In the 1540s John Leland misread the inscription in the glass as 'Percy': *Itinerary* (cit. in n. 52), iv. 40. Recently, Thomas has been confused with the previous grantee of the Comté of Perche, Thomas Montagu, Earl of Salisbury (d. 1428): F. Woodman, 'The Holland Family and Canterbury Cathedral', *Cant. Cath. Chron.*, 70 (1976), 25. For Thomas's military career in France, see M. K. Jones, 'The Beaufort Family and the War in France, 1421–50' (Ph.D. thesis, Univ. of Bristol, 1982), 26, 36–9, 77–84. Probably the last Beaufort buried in St Michael's Chapel was Edmund's daughter Isabella (d. 1453) (Searle, *Chronicle and Lists*, 58), but neither she nor Thomas seems ever to have had a monument.

VI's granting of permission for the removal of Clarence's and Beaufort's bodies indicates that he had no thought of reviving the idea.[241]

The effigies in the Holland Chapel are among the most accomplished English alabaster effigies of the fifteenth century.[242] An interest in naturalistic detail, exemplified by the downward sag of the men's surcoats and the pinning of Lady Margaret's veil within her coronet, is balanced by a boldness of conception all too rare in fifteenth-century English sculpture. There is no reason to suppose that any of the faces are attempts at portraiture, but it is notable that Beaufort's face is shown more heavily lined, to distinguish it from that of the youthful Clarence. The latter is also given slightly longer legs, a distinction which must reflect the Duke's physique rather than his higher rank, for his head and upper body are at the same level as Beaufort's. The two sets of anachronistically modern plate-armour are subtly varied, and even the most important variation, that between Clarence's coronet and Beaufort's jewelled circlet, is discreet enough to have escaped the notice of many of the heralds and antiquaries who have written about the tomb.[243] The brilliant colour of the effigies' heraldic attire would have been offset by the grey-brown Purbeck tomb-chest, which, wisely perhaps, was left free of heraldry.[244] The lost and unrecorded inscription was on a brass fillet inlaid into the raised 'rail' enclosing the effigies.[245]

THE MONUMENTS OF NON-ROYAL LAITY

Virtually all the known burials within the church of laity other than royalty were in the crypt or the nave. The crypt probably carried greater cachet, for the tombs there could be elaborate structures, in contrast to the nave, where non-archiepiscopal monuments had to be brasses in slabs laid level with the floor.[246] Unfortunately, the earliest lay monuments

[241] Henry VI's letter permitting the moving of Beaufort's and Clarence's bodies, dated 27 Jan. 1440, is printed in Legg and Hope, *Inventories*, 152. Earlier examples of royals buried at the feet of a parent or grandparent are Henry II's eldest son, William (d. 1156), buried next to Henry I in the choir of Reading Abbey; Richard I, buried next to Henry II at Fontevraud; and the eldest daughter of Philip II and Isabel of Hainault, buried next to her mother in the choir of Notre-Dame in Paris.

[242] Rivals for this accolade are remarkably few, and the only other effigies attributable to the same carver are those on the double-decker tomb of John, Earl of Arundel (d. 1435) at Arundel: Hope, 'Early Working of Alabaster' (cit. in n. 101), 232. The low quality of the alabaster effigies generally available in mid-15th-cent. England is illustrated by the crude, apparently Chellaston-made, figures on the tomb in Wimborne Minster, Dorset, of Lady Margaret's son John, Duke of Somerset (d. 1444), who ranked immediately after the king's uncles Gloucester and York. Restorations to the Holland Chapel effigies are fairly minor, although the remains of dated graffiti show that the surface has been sanded down comparatively recently. Most reinstatements of parts broken away (cf. Gough, *Sepulchral Monuments* (cit. in n. 14), ii, pt. 2, pl. xlii) seem to date from the 1940s, as do the renewal of large parts of the Purbeck

tomb-chest and the removal of dark coatings visible in photographs in the National Monuments Record; cf. *Cant. Cath. Chron.*, 42 (1947), 3.

[243] The identities of the two husbands are confused in Scarlett, heraldic collections (cit. in n. 59), fo. 1ᵛ; Willement, *Heraldic Notices* (cit. in n. 218), 40; London, 'The Greyhound' (cit. in n. 237), 146. The men are identified correctly in Philipot, Kentish church notes (cit. in n. 59), fo. 25; Weever, *Funerall Monuments* (cit. in n. 60), 211; Sandford, *Genealogical History* (cit. in n. 149), 235, but the last errs in stating that all three effigies have coronets.

[244] The extent of the polychromy is not known, in particular whether the faces and hands were painted. The statement in Gough, *Sepulchral Monuments* (cit. in n. 14), ii, pt. 2. 127, that the tomb-chest bore shields is based on a misunderstanding of the account in Weever, *Funerall Monuments* (cit. in n. 60), 211.

[245] The epitaph given in Weever, *Funerall Monuments* (cit. in n. 60), 211, begins 'Hic jacet in tumulo', but is too facetious to have been inscribed on the tomb, and, as Weever makes clear, the inscription was missing by the time he wrote.

[246] The only lay person known to have been buried in the crypt who was not of gentle birth was Prior Molashe's mother: see n. 185 above.

of which fragments remain cannot be firmly linked to any documented burials.[247] There is at least a possibility that the late thirteenth-century freestone knight's head preserved in the Cathedral until *c*.1987[248] came from an effigy commemorating the burial in 1262 of the entrails of the most powerful English baron of his time, Richard de Clare, Earl of Gloucester.[249] However, not even a tentative identification can be ventured for the admirably carved head from an early fourteenth-century knightly effigy (Pl. 121). Its facial features are unusually well preserved, on account of its having been built into a wall in the crypt from an early date.[250]

Apart from an unattributed thirteenth-century coffin-lid similar in form to Archbishop Langton's,[251] the oldest tomb still existing in the crypt is that of **Joan, Lady Mohun** (d. 1404). The costume of Lady Mohun's effigy indicates that she ordered her monument *c*.1370–80, at least twenty years in advance of the agreement which she entered into with the convent about her tomb and bequests, in 1395. There can be little doubt that permission to build a large monument beside the important altar of Our Lady Undercroft was given in return for the lavish benefactions which Lady Mohun, as a grandly connected widow of means, was well able to bestow.[252] The construction of the lierne-vaulted and gabled canopy entailed destroying and replacing in near-replica the very recently installed stone

[247] The only record of an early non-royal layman's monument is Henry III's payment in 1243 for 'unum pulchrum lapidem ... in quo fieri faciant scutum ipsius Geraldi cum armis suis' ('a fair stone ... on which is to be fashioned the sword of the same Gerald with his arms') over the grave of the son of the Justiciar of Ireland: Colvin, *History of the King's Works* (cit. in n. 136), i. 478, n. 6; R. T. D. Fitzgerald, 'Discovery of the Burial Place of Gerald Son of Maurice FitzGerald, Justiciar of Ireland, 1232–1245', *Irish Genealogist*, 5/2 (1975), 166–8. This appears to be the earliest known instance of the use of heraldry on an English monument. Presumably the gravestone was a Purbeck marble coffin-lid carved in low relief.

[248] No information is available as to the provenance of this head, which, until its theft some time in the late 1980s, was stored in the chamber over St Andrew's Chapel. I am most grateful to Philip Lankester for his detailed explanations of the reasons why it is impossible to give a more precise dating for the armour than the '2nd half C13' advanced in H. A. Tummers, *Early Secular Effigies in England: The Thirteenth Century* (Leiden, 1980), 136.

[249] Richard de Clare had a special link with Canterbury in that he entered into an agreement with Archbishop Boniface of Savoy whereby his successors in the earldom were to perform the offices of high steward and butler at enthronement feasts, by way of service for Tonbridge and other manors held of the archbishop: Somner, *Antiquities* (1703), app. to suppl., p. 20, where the document is dated 1264, two years after Richard's death. Richard died at Waltham, south of Canterbury: *Complete Peerage* (cit. in n. 230), v. 701. The entrails were buried in the Cathedral, before the altar St Edward (whose site at this date is not known), the heart was buried at Tonbridge Priory, and the body at Tewkesbury Abbey: *Polistorie* (cit. in n. 23), fo. 211ᵛ. The tomb at Tewkesbury (see n. 208 above) was of a sumptuousness so exceptional as almost to eliminate as an objection to the hypothesis advanced here the lack of parallels at this date for an entrail burial marked by a full-size effigy.

[250] The head, currently (1994) in store, was found in 1887 in the wall behind the reredos of Our Lady Undercroft: W. A. Scott Robertson, 'Sculptured Head of a Knight', *Arch. Cant.*, 17 (1887), 37. Curiously, no traces remain of the hole which its extraction must have caused. Also puzzling is the nearness in date of the head and the wall. Philip Lankester generously provided me with details of parallels of *c*.1340–50 for the fluted form of the bascinet and also pointed out to me that this and other, later effigies show a jewelled band where there ought to be (and as there actually are on the Black Prince's effigy) laces and staples (vervelles) attaching the aventail to the bascinet. The mail of the aventail, described as 'delicately sculptured', in ibid., fig. opp. 37, was presumably rendered in gesso, as it has now disappeared.

[251] This is in Purbeck marble and is situated before the altar of St Mary Magdalen in the crypt of the north-east transept. Its fine state of preservation is due presumably to its being covered when the floor was raised some time before *c*.1360. An unprovenanced fragment of a 13th-cent. coffin-lid with a stepped-cross base is currently (1994) in store. Apart from the indents of the brasses of Prior Molashe and his parents (see above), there survives only a defaced indent in the north ambulatory. In 1635 the crypt still contained 'diuerse' ecclesiastics' monuments 'all much defac'd and obscur'd by time'; 'Short Survey' (cit. in n. 62), 17. For evidence of burials in the eastern crypt, see n. 5 above.

[252] During the early 1370s she gave substantial amounts of money to the custodian of the chapel and had masses celebrated there for her good estate: Woodruff, 'Chapel of Our Lady in the Crypt' (cit. in n. 155), 157. The 1395 agreement is trans. ibid., 169–71. For Lady Mohun's life, see H. C. Maxwell Lyte, *A History of Dunster and the Families of Mohun and Luttrell* (2 vols.; London, 1909), i. 51–8. A trans. of her will is in *Somerset Medieval Wills*, 2nd ser.: *1501–1530*, ed. F. W. Weaver (Somerset Record Soc., 19; 1903), 302–4.

screen-work on the south side of the chapel. At some time during the eighteenth century, when the crypt was used as a lumber store, the canopy was severely damaged, but views taken before it had reached its present state of dilapidation show that the south side was more complicated than the north side, in that it incorporated an inner and an outer set of arches (Pl. 126). The inner arches, which survive, are part of the same blocks of stone as the canopy vault, whereas the outer arches have fallen away because they were attached to the canopy by nothing more substantial than a vertical bed of mortar. Both sets of arches had their own supports (Pl. 125), and it is the imbalance between this double row of piers and the single row on the north side which explains the asymmetrical placing of the effigy on the tomb-chest.[253] Badly mauled though it is, the 'bespoke' alabaster effigy (Pl. 127) remains a memorable portrayal of the rather bizarre notions of chic current in the 1370s: the ⊓-shaped headdress made up of innumerable layers of crimped veils held together by jewelled netting and with shoulder extensions of the same construction,[254] the 'daring' *décolletage*, the tight, form-revealing robe erupting at hip level into a dense mass of hanging folds, the open-sided *cote* soon to fossilize into an element of court dress (cf. Pl. 123), and most striking of all, the beast-decorated metal buttons of a size worthy of Mickey Mouse.[255] The brocade pattern painted on the *cote* survived into the early nineteenth century but has now perished.

At an opposite pole from this once-dazzling fashion-plate is the only other effigy in the crypt, the sombrely painted freestone image of **Elizabeth, Lady Trivet** (d. 1433) (Pl. 129).[256] Her widow's weeds are black upon black, emphasized more than relieved by the white of her triple veil and *barbe*, the ermine cuffs of her sleeves, and the red and blue cushions under her head; even the dog at her feet and the robes of the angels at her head are black. Lady Trivet's costume is, in fact, a kind of uniform worn by women who chose formally to enter widowhood, a state which entailed a vow of chastity and commitments to prayer and charitable works, but which also brought freedom from pressure to remarry, and the right to sole possession of property.[257]

[253] For the damage caused in the 18th-cent., see Gostling, *Walk* (cit. in n. 144), 130; Hasted, *Canterbury* (cit. in n. 5), i. 416. Repairs made to the canopy in 1992 entailed removing parts of the metal supports added in 1922 (for which, see J. M. Freeman, *W. D. Caröe RSTO FSA: His Architectural Achievement* (Manchester, 1990) 176), renewing the easternmost surviving inner support on the south side and reinstating the inner support and part of the vault missing from the south-east corner. Cleaning and conservation of the effigy undertaken at the same time revealed well-preserved polychromy on the southern inscription on the base slab. There is now no trace of the arms of Mohun and Burghersh (Lady Mohun's maiden name) reported to have been painted in alternate compartments of the canopy vault in Powell, collections (cit. in n. 50), fo. 17.

[254] For headdresses of this kind, see S. M. Newton, *Fashion in the Age of the Black Prince: A Study of the Years 1340–1365* (Woodbridge, 1980), 94–9.

[255] In 1372 and 1373 sets of such buttons (*botoners*) in gold were being given as presents by John of Gaunt: *John of Gaunt's Register, 1371–75*, ed. S. Armitage-Smith, 2 vols. (Camden Soc., 3rd ser.,

20–1; 1911), ii, nos. 133, 1342–3.

[256] The attribution to Lady Trivet was first established in W. H. St J. Hope, 'Note on the So-called Tomb of the Countess of Athol', *Arch. Cant.*, 27 (1905), 209–12. Her will is printed in *Reg. Chichele* (cit. in n. 116), ii. 495–7. Hope's deductions that the tomb-chest was faced in alabaster and that two of the three shields on its northern side were tinctured as for Sir Thomas Swynborne, Lady Trivet's second husband, are confirmed by Scarlett, heraldic collections (cit. in n. 59), fo. 17. The facing of the tomb-chest, shown complete in Dart, *History and Antiquities* (cit. in n. 88), pl. 31, dropped off some time in the later 18th cent. and was discarded: Gostling, *Walk* (cit. in n. 144), 130–1. The rough tomb-chest shown in Hope's illustrations, which evidently incorporated fragments of the original facing, has been succeeded by one in freestone ashlar, designed by Harold Anderson in 1951.

[257] The one element of relief in Lady Trivet's dress, the cinquefoils on her belt, is commemorative as much as decorative, since they derive from her second husband's arms: see n. 256 above. Hope's statement that the effigy came from the same workshop as that in Westminster Abbey which com-

Most of whatever non-archiepiscopal monuments stood in the Romanesque nave must have been destroyed in the course of its reconstruction from 1376, for the eleven lay people known to have had tombs in the existing nave all died after its completion c.1405.[258] The graves of members of several families at 'the apex of gentry society'[259] in east Kent occupied distinct areas, and some of the brassless indents removed to the cloister after the repaving of the nave in 1787 will have come from these informally defined mausolea.[260] Freemen of Canterbury probably accounted for the majority of burials outside in the cemetery of the laity, where, just as in any parochial churchyard, there was a yew tree.[261] The most ambitious of the now totally vanished monuments here would have incorporated a slab of some kind, and a will of 1534 indicates that some graves were marked by stone crosses at each corner.[262] Only one nobleman is known to have been buried outside, the 'war hero' Thomas Beaufort (d. 1431), who lay in the conventual cemetery at the east end of the church.[263] The subsequent removal of his remains into his mother's chapel would probably

memorates one of Lady Mohun's daughters, Philippa, Duchess of York (d. 1431), is unwarranted; the resemblance is primarily one of costume, for the Duchess, like Lady Trivet, wears the 'uniform' of the formally declared widow.

[258] Almost all the medieval lay burials in the nave which are mentioned in Somner, *Antiquities* (1640), 182–3, are included in a short list made in 1530–1: *The Visitations of Kent ... 1530–1 ... 1574 ... and 1592*, ed. W. B. Bannerman, 2 vols. (Harleian Soc. Pubns., 74–5; 1923–4), i. 3. The only nave monuments to lay people known to be recorded visually are: the brass of Sir Robert Clifford (d. 1423), Sheriff of Kent, a shire knight for the county and brother of Richard Clifford, bishop of London and a former archdeacon of Canterbury (a very free sketch of c.1645–8 in Bodl., MS Dodsworth 71, fo. 51); and the indents of the brasses of Edmund Haute, Esq. (d. 1408), a benefactor in his will to the fabric of the church, buried on the south side of the nave, near the Brenchley monument (Powell, collections (cit. in n. 50), fo. 118), Sir William Septvans and his wife, Elizabeth (both d. Mar. 1449) (ibid.), and the monument of Sir William Brenchley and his wife (see n. 260 below). Several other brasses, including one similar to the famous brass of Sir William Septvans at Chartham, were fixed at an unknown date and in unknown circumstances to the north exterior face of the Trinity Chapel, underneath St Edward's Chapel. They were later stolen, again at an unknown date, and all that remains is a series of dark areas left where they were attached to the masonry. See F. A. Greenhill, 'On the Ghosts of Some Brasses Formerly in Canterbury Cathedral', *Arch. Cant.*, 65 (1952), 137.

[259] P. W. Fleming, 'The Hautes and their "Circle": Culture and the English Gentry', in *England in the Fifteenth Century: Proc. 1986 Harlaxton Symposium*, ed. D. Williams (Woodbridge, 1987), 89, 100.

[260] The main gentry groupings were those of the Fogges and the Septvans: Searle, *Chronicle and Lists*, 43; Scarlett, heraldic collections (cit. in n. 59), fos. 28ᵛ–29; Weever, *Funerall Monuments* (cit. in n. 60), 234–6; Somner, *Antiquities* (1640), 182–3; 1786 plan of nave floor (cit. in n. 88); 'Chronicle of Richard Fogge' (cit. in n. 208), 119–20; Hussey, 'Further Notes from Kentish Wills' (cit. in n. 109), 39–40. That similar groupings of graves existed for chantry priests is revealed by the will of a chaplain of the Buckingham chantry who died in 1488: ibid. 42. The only

lay persons' chantry chapel in the nave was the Brenchley Chapel, built out from the fourth most easterly bay of the south nave aisle and intended to serve, like Archbishop Arundel's chantry (cf. nn. 112, 113 above), as an oratory for the laity when the eastern parts of the church were inaccessible: Hussey, *Kent Chantries* (cit. in n. 88), 43. Presumably this was a piece of 'forward planning', anticipating the transferral of the nave Lady Chapel into the Martyrdom and, like Archbishops Chichele's and Bourchier's monuments, an example of a specially ambitious commemoration allowed in return for an enhancement of the devotional resources of the Cathedral. Dedicated in 1448 (Searle, *Chronicle and Lists*, 45), it was positioned so as to be opposite the graves of Sir William Brenchley (d. 1406), the donor of £100 to the nave rebuilding, and his widow, Joan, which were covered by a double brass: Weever, *Funerall Monuments*, 235; Woodruff and Danks, *Memorials*, pl. opp. 195. The chapel was demolished in 1787.

[261] Hussey, 'Further Notes from Kentish Wills' (cit. in n. 109), 36, 42.

[262] The executors of Richard Burchard of Canterbury were to have two pairs of stone crosses made on the pattern of those at the grave of William Bremour: Hasted, *Canterbury* (cit. in n. 5), i. 424. Another early 16th-cent. Kentish will referring to a grave marked by four crosses is that of William Cleygate of Birling, 1503: L. L. Duncan, *Testamenta Cantiana: West Kent* (Kent Archaeol. Soc., extra vol., 1906), p. xii. For extant examples, see B. Stocker, 'Medieval Grave Markers in Kent', *Church Monuments*, 1, pt. 2 (1986), 106–14.

[263] Searle, *Chronicle and Lists*, 20. The only other known example of a lay burial within the monks' cemetery is of a Canterbury barber who died in 1347 (*Sede Vacante Wills* (cit. in n. 56), 35). No doubt the privilege was granted in recognition of work done shaving and bleeding the monks. For two secular clerks' requests to be buried here (in 1307 and 1420) see ibid., 18; *Reg. Chichele* (cit. in n. 116), ii. 198. Of memorials to the monks themselves, all that survive are some fragmentary late 12th- or early 13th-cent. inscriptions cut into the walls of the church: Gough, *Sepulchral Monuments* (cit. in n. 14), ii. pt. 1, pl. xv; anon. ('C'), 'The Cathedral Churchyard', *Canterbury Diocesan Notes*, 3 (Mar. 1929), 2.

have seemed to the monks a laudable restitution of that social decorum[264] which it was essential to maintain if the community of the universal Church incorporated as the Body of Christ were to be worthily represented by the tombs ranged around the Saviour's altar in His church at Canterbury.[265]

[264] At first sight it appears that two non-royal lay burials were intruded into areas of the church regarded as clerical preserves. However, the earlier of these burials, that of Sir Henry Grey, Count of Tancarville, buried in 1450 in the still-unfinished Lady Chapel (see n. 186 above), was in a rather attenuated sense a royal burial, since Grey was married to Antigone, natural daughter of Humphrey, Duke of Gloucester. The other apparently intruded lay burial was that of Sir John Fyneux (d. 1525) and his wife, Elizabeth, in the Martyrdom: Somner, *Antiquities* (1640), 184. As Chief Justice of the King's Bench, an executor of Cardinal Morton's will, and seneschal of the manors of the prior and chapter of Christ Church, Fyneux was clearly a very notable friend of the convent. Although the exact site of the burial is not recorded, the lack of space left by the known archiepiscopal and prioral burials to the east of the wall containing the Red Door (Fig. 2), suggests that the Fyneux were buried in the west part of the transept, outside the Martyrdom in its strictest definition. It is impossible to imagine any late-medieval citizen of Canterbury thinking in the same terms as the York merchant Thomas Doncaster, whose will of 1456 asked for burial in the 'high choir' of York Minster: *Sede Vacante Wills* (cit. in n. 56), 16.

[265] The dedication of Canterbury Cathedral to Christ (or the Saviour) was at once a sign of allegiance to Rome, whose cathedral originally had the same patron, and an assertion of hierarchic status relative to other English sees; and probably on account of the latter the primary dedication was never augmented to include the Cathedral's major house-saints. From 1130 Christ Church began to adopt the principle of making the high altar dedication govern the placing of the Cathedral's most illustrious dead; hence Sts Alphege and Dunstan were each allotted a shrine and altar flanking the high altar (Fig. 2), Alphege, as a martyr, being accorded the more honorific northern site symbolic of Christ's right (cf. n. 13 above). The issue of hierarchic ordering within the social Body of Christ has generally been addressed in relation to late medieval England in the context of discussions of Corpus Christi processions and plays (e.g. M. James, 'Ritual, Drama and Social Body in the Late Medieval English Town', *Past & Present*, 98 (Feb. 1983), 3–29 (esp. 6–12); M. Rubin, *Corpus Christi: The Eucharist in Late Medieval Culture* (Cambridge, 1991), 243–71), but see Duffy, *Stripping of the Altars* (cit. in n. 145), 26, 91–5. The consecrated host at Canterbury was in a pyx suspended above the high altar (the normal later medieval English usage), and therefore it seems legitimate to suppose that the exceptionally coherent hierarchic arrangement of the tombs in the Cathedral would have been widely viewed in much the same way as the social stratifications consciously displayed by living communities when processing with the enshrined host. Such an interpretation also accords with the contemporary sense of community which determined that the dead in Purgatory were at least as deserving of prayers as the living.

XI

The Post-Reformation Monuments

KATHARINE EUSTACE

INTRODUCTION

In 1932 J. G. Mann commented on the 'indifference with which English Post-Reformation monuments have been ... and still are regarded'.[1] There are no references to post-Reformation monuments in either Edward Blore's *Sepulchral Antiquities of Great Britain* (1826), or C. A. Stothard's *Monumental Effigies of Great Britain* (1876). The state of knowledge about English funerary sculpture, despite the pioneering work of Mrs Esdaile, Rupert Gunnis, and Margaret Whinney,[2] remains in its infancy. This neglect by historians is particularly marked at Canterbury: its historians Somner, Gostling, Hasted, Britton, and Woodruff and Danks all chose to ignore to a large extent the Cathedral's later monuments.[3]

John Dart was an exception in bringing his survey right up to date.[4] His work, with engravings by James Cole, is indispensable to the study of the years 1558 to 1726 at Canterbury, providing as it does an account of each monument, with detailed engravings of many of them. In some cases, Dart is our only source for the appearance of a monument. The other exception was Joseph Meadows Cowper, whose *Memorial Inscriptions* provides invaluable biographical detail.[5]

The primary sources in the Cathedral archives are, until the mid-nineteenth century, largely silent on the subject of monuments.[6] The problem of poor documentation exacerbates the inevitable difficulties and dangers of attribution and date based on style alone. The often recidivist nature of style, and the numbers of monuments which long post-date the deaths of those commemorated, confuse the matter further.

The register of burials is the most important source of *post* and *ante quem* dates.[7] It

---

[1] J. G. Mann, 'English Church Monuments 1536–1625', *Walpole Soc.* 21 (1932–3), 1–22.

[2] K. A. Esdaile, *English Church Monuments, 1510–1840* (London, 1946); R. Gunnis, *Dictionary of British Sculptors 1660–1851* (revised edn.; London, n. d. [1964]); M. Whinney, *Sculpture in Britain 1530–1830* (Harmondsworth, 1964).

[3] Somner, *Antiquities* (1703); W. Gostling, *A Walk In and About the City of Canterbury* (3rd edn.; Canterbury, 1779); E. Hasted, *The History and Topographical Survey of the County of Kent* (2nd edn.; 12 vols.; Canterbury, 1797–1801), xii; J. Britton, *The History and Antiquities of the Metropolitical Church of Canterbury* (London,

1836); Woodruff and Danks, *Memorials*.

[4] J. Dart, *The History and Antiquities of the Cathedral Church of Canterbury* (London, 1726).

[5] J. Meadows Cowper, *The Memorial Inscriptions of Canterbury Cathedral* (priv. printed, Canterbury, 1897).

[6] Chapter Acts for 1551–68 were badly burnt in the fire of 1670, while those for 1628–70 were destroyed.

[7] *The Register Booke of Christninges, Marriages, and Burialls within the Precinct of the Cathedrall and Metropoliticall Church of Christe of Canterburie*, ed. R. Hovenden (London, 1878).

begins in June 1571 and continues for almost 300 years, until 'burials ceased for all but privileged persons', in 1855.[8] The numbers were never great, however, and consisted largely of the members of the Cathedral Chapter and their dependants, both familial and administrative: wives, widows, daughters, infants, and domestic servants; official servants such as vesturers, vergers, bedesmen, bell-ringers, organists, stonecutters, porters, and upholsterers; masters and ushers of the King's School, choirmen and singing men, occasional townsmen, mayors and aldermen, and the odd custodian and inmate of the Cathedral gaol, as well as those inhabitants of the Precincts for whom the Cathedral was a parish church,[9] principally ministers and members of the French congregation. There were, besides, what one might describe as those who were granted the Hospitality of Death, whereby strangers were accorded burial and frequently a monument, perhaps as a result of the 1612 regulation which laid down that a stranger's grave be marked by 'a fayre tombe stone'.[10]

THE SIXTEENTH CENTURY

The Southwark Workshops

Save in one case, archbishops of Canterbury would not be buried or commemorated in the Cathedral until the mid-nineteenth century, as they were largely absentee.[11] The exception was Reginald Pole, who received the papal *pallium* in 1556, and returned from Rome as Pope Julius II's legate. He died in 1558, and was interred in the Corona, in a lead coffin under a plain plastered brick tomb-chest, inscribed simply 'Depositum Cardinalis Polis'.[12]

Cole's engraving of 1726[13] shows a wall-painting above the tomb-chest, which half obliterates a late fifteenth-century St Christopher (Pl. 130). The painting appears to be a sophisticated Italianate architectural composition in two parts, symbolic of the Resurrection. The oddity of Pole's monument is perhaps the result of expediency and historical circumstance, coinciding as it did with a change of regime and religion. The two-storeyed compartmentalization, the coffered ceiling, and the allegorical figures, here supporting Pole's coat of arms and those of the see of Canterbury, were all to become standard, three-dimensional motifs on monuments some fifty years later.

[8] Ibid.

[9] Connections with the Cathedral were crucial, and it was not enough to be a local magnate or town dignitary. In 1593 Henry Porredge was refused permission despite the detailed provisions of his will, and was buried in his parish of Bekesbourne. R. Griffin, 'Kentish Items', *Trans. Monumental Brass Soc.* 6 (1910–14), 158–77. In 1799, on the other hand, a 'Mr Edward Carlos Gregory, from Lemon Street, Goodman's Fields, London', was buried in the north cloister. The Register states that he was the son of Minor Canon Francis Gregory.

[10] Chapter Act Book, 1608–28, fo. 39'. Chapter exercised a careful control of burial regulations and fees. These were first established for breaking the ground, digging the grave, for the bells and sermon, the bell-ringers, preacher, and sexton, in the General Chapter of 5 Nov. 1592; ibid. 1581–1607, fo. 128.

[11] 'Their Burials there have been ever since discontinued; a thing the whilst to some seeming very strange, that of all the Archbishops since the Reformation, not one hath chosen to be buried there, but all, as it were with one consent declined their own Cathedral, (the ancient and accustomed place of Archiepiscopal Sepulture) affecting rather an obscure Burial in some one private Parish-Church or other.' Somner, *Antiquities* (1703), 138.

[12] Dart, *History and Antiquities* (cit. in n. 4), 169–171.

[13] Ibid. 170.

As it later suffered from over-zealous antiquarianism,[14] it is difficult to assess it fully, and Cole's engraving is our only evidence. The tomb-chest was restored from 1897 to 1900 at the expense of Cardinal Vaughan, the first official papal legate since Pole. The restoration is recorded in Latin on an adjacent brass plate, permission for which was granted 'subject to the title of Cardinal Vaughan as "Archbishop of Westminster" being removed'.[15] Above hangs an achievement of Pole's coat of arms painted by Edward Frampton RA, signed and dated 1900.

If Pole was the last archbishop for 400 years to be commemorated by a monument in the Cathedral, the first dean was to establish a tradition and to set a standard which was to be emulated by subsequent deans. As resident executive heads, they wielded great power, and many left a visible expression of it in their monuments. A highly political appointment was made by Henry VIII, when, in 1541, Nicholas Wotton became the first Dean of Canterbury on the Dissolution of the Cathedral Priory. A man of remarkable political adroitness, Wotton continued for the next quarter of a century in the service of four Tudor sovereigns.[16]

As the inscription on his monument informs us, Wotton was 'Thrice sent Embassador to the Emperor Charles V. Once to Philip, King of Spain, once to Francis I, King of France, thrice to Henry II, his son, once to Mary, Queen of Hungary, and Governor of the Netherlands, and thrice to William Duke of Cleve.'[17] He was a plenipotentiary at the peace treaties of 1546, at the Castle of Camerans in 1559, and, in 1560, in Edinburgh. When in England, however, he found time to attend General Chapters at Canterbury, and gave his attention to matters of judicial importance.[18] He died in London on 26 January 1567, 'leaving for his heir Thomas Wotton his Nephew, who has erected this monument to him'.[19] As an indication of Wotton's importance, his monument is sited in the apse between the Trinity Chapel and the ambulatory, a space traditionally reserved for royalty, archbishops, and priors (Pl. 131).

The monument, one of the finest in the Cathedral, poses several questions as to date and attribution. No one has previously questioned the date as being anything other than coincidental with Wotton's death, in 1567,[20] but if it dates from any time in the twenty years before Thomas Wotton died, it remains stylistically one of the most precocious tombs of the period. There is a cryptic entry, partly obliterated by fire, in the Chapter Acts for 25 November 1572, recording agreement to the written request by William Cecil, Lord Burghley, for such 'Cane [Caen] Stone' as may be necessary 'for a vault in the little Chappell in the north side of the upper end of this church Callyd Doctor Wotton's Chapell'.[21]

---

[14] Notebooks of M. Bardwell and E. W. Tristram: Victoria and Albert Museum, National Art Library, Box II 213. G. By 1779 William Gostling records the wall-painting as 'sadly gone to decay, and little remains to be seen': Gostling, *Walk* (cit. in n. 3), 243.

[15] Chapter Act Book, 1895–1910, fo. 167.

[16] B. Ficaro, 'Nicholas Wotton: Dean and Diplomat' (Ph.D. thesis, Univ. of Kent at Canterbury, 1981), *passim*.

[17] Trans. Dart, *History and Antiquities* (cit. in n. 4), 86.

[18] Many records of Chapter meetings are signed in a neat precise hand: N. Wotton. Chapter Act Book, 1561–8, *passim*;

Ficaro, 'Nicholas Wotton' (cit. in n. 16), app. II.

[19] Trans. Dart, *History and Antiquities* (cit. in n. 4), 86.

[20] 'The total effect is already of late Elizabethan showiness.' J. Newman, *The Buildings of England: North East and East Kent* (3rd edn.; Harmondsworth, 1983), 200.

[21] Chapter Act Book, 1568–81, fo. 54. The request comes from the 'honorable, Lord Treasurer', i.e. William Cecil, Lord Burghley. Burghley's wife, Mildred, was one of four sisters, another being Elizabeth, Lady Hoby. The chapel thus described is Henry IV's chantry chapel.

Wotton's monument has suffered from that characteristic English lack of confidence, which, when confronted with artistic innovation or quality, suggests the hand of a foreigner, probably an Italian. As early as 1736 Patrick Guthrie, writing to the architect James Gibbs, referred to 'Dean Wotton's statue in fine marble done by an Italian'.[22] William Gostling recorded that the Wotton monument, 'one of singular beauty', was 'said to be in part, if not the whole, designed and executed at Rome',[23] while Hasted declared: 'The whole is much admired for its excellent sculpture, the head especially which is said to have been executed by an eminent artist in Italy, during the Dean's residence there.'[24] In 1926 Mrs Esdaile reiterated the attribution to 'a nameless Italian sculptor'. Twenty years later she revised her opinion, giving it a firm if undocumented attribution to Gerard Johnson.[25]

All this begs the questions: who was responsible for this important monument, and when? Wotton's will seems not to survive,[26] but the inscription implies he had considered his own epitaph before his death: 'he prophetically sung his Swan-like song, and left those Things in his Study in Writing under his own Hands.'[27] This biographical epitaph was in itself an innovation.[28] Stylistically, too, there is a complete break with tradition: there is no canopy, housing, or frame, while the effigy kneels in prayer, as in life, and the monument is divested of all but secular ornament.

The innovatory kneeling figure has its source in the French royal sepulchral effigies at Saint-Denis, Paris,[29] and the cenotaph to the Emperor Maximilian in the Hofkirche at Innsbruck (c.1561).[30] The fruits which enrich the verge of the sarcophagus and the heraldic achievement are Flemish refinements of the stucco work of the Italianate School of Fontainebleau, taken up, exploited, and made available through the printed pattern-books of Vredeman de Vries and others. Many of the details find their source in Serlio's *Libri di architectura*, published between 1537 and 1547. The obelisk, symbol of eternity, and the bull's-eye ornament, reminiscent of Italian, and particularly Venetian, architectural detail of the sixteenth century, were to become ubiquitous. Obelisks, usually in two-dimensional form, were used in the late sixteenth and early seventeenth centuries as decorative finials in the upper storeys of Southwark-type wall monuments, such as the Thornhurst and Hales monument at Canterbury.

None of these details would have been foreign to the cosmopolitan Wotton, whose mind, as the epitaph informs us, 'was wholly devoted to Books and Learning, intent on the Studies of Arts, Physick, Laws, and Divinity; and beautifully stor'd with Knowledge of the Roman, Italian, French and Dutch Languages'.[31] He belonged to an important Kent family from Boughton Malherbe, one which was closely associated with court circles and was in the forefront of the intellectual renaissance that began in the late sixteenth century.[32]

[22] HMC, *MSS of Duke of Portland*, vi (1901), 62.

[23] Gostling, *Walk* (cit. in n. 3), 244.

[24] Hasted, *Kent* (cit. in n. 3), xii. 1, illustrated with a half-plate engraving by R. Pollard.

[25] K. A. Esdaile, *London Mercury*, 14 (May–Oct. 1926), 175; ead., *English Church Monuments* (cit. in n. 2), 105.

[26] Ficaro, 'Nicholas Wotton' (cit. in n. 16), 280.

[27] Trans. Dart, *History and Antiquities* (cit. in n. 4), 86.

[28] Considered an innovation of the Southwark-based Anglo-Netherlandish tomb-makers by J. G. Mann, *Walpole Soc.* 21

(1932–3), 1–23.

[29] Louis XII (d. 1515) and Anne of Brittany (d. 1514), Francis I (d. 1547), Henry II (d. 1559), and Catherine de Médicis (d. 1589).

[30] J. Stevens Curl, *A Celebration of Death* (London, 1980), 111–13, pls. 13, 14.

[31] Trans. Dart, *History and Antiquities* (cit. in n. 4), p. 86.

[32] His brother Sir Edward Wotton was one of Henry VII's executors: J. J. N. McGurk, 'Letter Book relating to the Lieutenancy of Kent, 1604–28', *Arch. Cant.*, 82 (1967), 124–42, at 124. His nephew and heir Thomas Wotton (1521–87) was the father of

Within Wotton's own circle were some of the most enlightened and cosmopolitan men of the age, many of whom were to erect monuments to themselves or members of their family. William, Lord Cobham, was chief mourner at Wotton's funeral.[33] The brothers Sir Philip and Sir Thomas Hoby were fellow diplomats.[34]

The Wotton monument has not been considered in relation to the numerous and hitherto unattributed monuments of the years 1570–1610. Certainly, it speaks of French, Italian, and classical influences, and it exhibits great command of composition, control of decorative detail, and sophistication of execution, but there is no reason to suppose that it is not the work of an English workshop. This group expresses a common formal language drawn from a repertory of motifs: kneeling figures, free-standing obelisks, three-dimensional bunches of quinces, gourds, and cucumbers,[35] masks, tasselled cushions, classical (usually Corinthian) columns, bombe-fronted sarcophagi, bull's-eye motifs, and, most significantly, good portraiture.[36] There were a number of workshops of Netherlandish origin in London in the late sixteenth century—notably those of the Cures, the Johnsons, and of Richard Stevens—which created an Anglo-Netherlandish style of vitality and orig-inality, fully capable of claiming the Wotton monument as their own.[37]

The first of those people who had no connections with the Cathedral but were never-theless commemorated in it, because they died in Canterbury, was the Protestant-inclined Odet de Coligny, Cardinal de Chatillon, Bishop of Beauvais. He died at Canterbury *en route* for France in 1571, possibly having been poisoned, and was buried in a plain plastered brick tomb in the apse between the ambulatory and Trinity Chapel, opposite Dean Wotton. The tomb's stark simplicity was recorded by Dart.[38] Application was made in the 1880s to the Dean and Chapter by the directors of the French Protestant Hospital, Victoria Park, London, to have it restored, at their expense.[39] No further embellishment was permitted at the time, but in 1952 a memorial tablet, designed and lettered by Cecil Thomas, was set up on the column behind the tomb.[40]

The memorial to the Hales family, sited on the south side of St Michael's Chapel, and

Edward, 1st Baron Wotton (who married first Hester, daughter to Sir William Pickering (d. 1574); monument in St Helen's Bishopsgate, attrib. to William Cure I) and his brother, Sir Henry Wotton: Whinney, *Sculpture in Britain* (cit. in n. 2) 16. See below, n. 98.

[33] Ficaro, 'Nicholas Wotton' (cit. in n. 16), 289. The monu-ment that Cobham dedicated to his father, George Brooke, Lord Cobham, in 1561 in Cobham Church (Kent) shows an advanced classicism and Italianate decorative detail.

[34] Philip had died in 1558, and Thomas in 1566, in Paris. Thomas Hoby had translated Castiglione's *Il Cortegiano*. His widow, Elizabeth (later Lady Russell), erected a monument to them at Bisham (Berks.). For a possible French source for this, see A. Blunt, 'L'Influence française sur l'architecture et la sculp-ture décorative en Angleterre pendant la première moitié du XVIᵉ siècle', *Rev. de l'Art*, 4 (1969), 17–29.

[35] For the popularity of these vegetable motifs, see J. Le Moyne, *La Clef des champs* (1586); and for their application to other media, esp. silverwork, cf. the Cosway Cup, hallmarked 1585–6, in the British Museum.

[36] Other examples of good likenesses are to be found on the monuments to Sir Richard (d. 1592) and Sir Michael Blount (d.

1564), St Peter ad Vincula, Tower of London; on the effigies of Peter Cappone (d. 1582), St Olave, Hart St., London, and Sir Nicholas Bacon (d. 1579) from Old St Paul's, of which only a fragment survives. The likenesses are often idealized types. Sir John Farnham (Quorn, Leics.), who was 'twice fortie and odd' years old when he died in 1587, is presented as a man of about 40. His effigy may, indeed, be based on a portrait dated 1563 attributed to Stephen van der Meulen (priv. coll.). The monu-ment to Sir Richard Alington (d. 1561) and his wife at the Public Record Office, London, exhibits the same decorative detail of swagged fruit and masks as is found on the Wotton monument.

[37] For discussion of the output of the Cure, Johnson, and Stevens workshops, see Whinney, *Sculpture in Britain* (cit. in n. 2), 16–17. The monument was restored under Prof. Tristram in the late 1940s: *Friends of Canterbury Cathedral, 20th Annual Report* (1947), 27, 34–36.

[38] Chapter Act Book, 1568–81, fos. 30–1; Dart, *History and Antiquities* (cit. in n. 4), 85, pl. 84.

[39] E. G. Atkinson, 'The Cardinal of Chatillon in England, 1568–1571', *Proc. Huguenot Soc. of London*, 3 (1888–91), 172–285.

[40] *Cant. Cath. Chron.*, 47 (1952), 12–13.

recorded, but not commented on, by Dart, was erected after 1592.[41] It has excited comment and some confusion by reason of the curious nature of its subject-matter.[42] The epitaph is, however, quite explicit, referring as it does to four people: Sir James Hales, treasurer to the Portuguese expedition of 1589, who died of fever and was buried at sea; his widow, Dame Alice, who died in 1592;[43] Cheyney Hales, their only son, who died, not having reached maturity, in 1596; and Richard Lee, Alice's widower, who erected the monument (Pl. 132).

The monument is not typical of the period. The composition is unwieldy, combining as it does high and low relief on a top-heavy two-tiered staging, with Southwark ornament. The possibility of its being associated with the work of Epiphanius Evesham (1570-post 1633) is strong. Evesham trained under Richard Stevens and was in his workshop in Southwark when Stevens died, in 1592.[44] While the Hales monument may be the work of a number of hands—which might account for its awkwardness—certain characteristics are common to other works attributed to Evesham. The low-relief panel with its strong pictorial and narrative element describing the burial at sea of Sir James Hales is comparable to a relief panel attributed by Mrs Esdaile to Evesham at Quorn in Leicestershire.[45] This depicts Sir John Farnham (d. 1587) commanding his troops in the field. The small figure of Sir John stands out from the relief in a manner not dissimilar to that of Sir James. Further, the treatment of the sea in the Hales relief bears comparison with that of the clouds on the tomb-chest of the monument to Christopher Roper, second Lord Teynham (d. 1622), at Lynsted (Kent),[46] which is signed by Evesham.

If the Hales monument could be firmly attributed to Evesham, it would undoubtedly mark an evolutionary stage in his work. There are two small tablets (about 2 feet high) in St Leonard's Church, Hythe, to Giles Collyns (d. 1586) and John Collyns (d. 1597), the latter being signed 'E. Evesham Fecit'. The painted element on the Hales monument is indeed a rather rare survival. It may not, however, be inconsistent with Evesham, who is recorded as being both a master sculptor and a master painter.[47]

The painted landscape behind the kneeling figure of Dame Alice has generally been accepted as representing the site of the drowning of her father-in-law, Sir James Hales senior, in the River Stour in 1555. The symbolic nature of this was not so much to record a tragedy as to celebrate the reinstatement of an inheritance. Sir James had handled business for the Cathedral under Henry VIII, and had been made a Judge of the Court of Common Pleas. He was knighted at Edward VI's coronation, but refused to subscribe to the King's will, in which Mary and Elizabeth were disinherited. He fell out with Bishop

---

[41] Dart, *History and Antiquities* (cit. in n. 4), 79, 178.

[42] Esdaile, *English Church Monuments* (cit. in n. 2), 108, and pl. 62; Brian Kemp, *English Church Monuments* (London, 1980), 71; J. Keates and A. Hornak, *Canterbury Cathedral* (London, 1980), 68.

[43] Her burial is recorded on 24 April 1592: 'The Ladie Hales, late Wyfe of Richard Lee, Esquire': *Register Booke*, ed. Hovenden (cit. in n. 7).

[44] Whinney, *Sculpture in Britain* (cit. in n. 2), 17 and n. 30.

[45] Esdaile, *English Church Monuments* (cit. in n. 2), pl. 66.

[46] Ill. in Whinney, *Sculpture in Britain* (cit. in n. 2), pl. 9; Esdaile, *English Church Monuments* (cit. in n. 2), pls. 81 and 82. Signed on

the base E: EVESHAM: ME FECIT.

[47] Whinney, *Sculpture in Britain* (cit. in n. 2), 18. There is painted ornament on the Giles Collyns (d. 1586) wall-tablet at Hythe (Kent) and on the monument to Christopher Roper, Lord Teynham (d. 1622) at Lynsted (Kent). Jon Bayliss, 'Giles de Witt, "marbeller"', *Bull. Monumental Brass Soc.*, 55 (Oct. 1990), 465–6, has suggested that the Hales monument should be compared stylistically to the Schietere-Damhoudre monument (1576–7) in St Salvator's Cathedral, Bruges, by Giles de Wit. De Wit worked at Cobham Hall (Kent) in the 1590s: J. Summerson, *Architecture in Britain, 1530–1830* (Harmondsworth, 1953), 44–5.

Gardiner of Winchester, and was imprisoned in the Tower, where he attempted suicide. On his release, he retired to Thanington, where he went mad and drowned himself, in 1554, aged 85.[48] His property was accordingly declared forfeit, but a court case which ensued about some of it made legal history. In a splendid example of enlightened casuistry, the jurist Dyer asked: 'Who drowned him?—Sir James Hales; And when did he drown him? In his lifetime.' Dyer concluded 'that Sir James Hales being alive caused Sir James Hales to die, and the act of a living man was the death of a dead man. And then after this offence it is reasonable to punish the living man who committed the offence and not the dead man.' As a result, his property was released to his heirs.[49] The painting shows St Mildred's Church, the River Stour, and the reinstated property. In that intensely legalistic and dynastic age, monuments were symbols, and this one re-established in society's eyes the inheritance and standing of the Hales family, by the most ostentatious and public statement of absolution for suicide, then considered both a felony and a sin.

The Hales monument was first set up in St Michael's Chapel. Here it set a precedent for the commemoration of heroes who died in the service of their country, and was to lead eventually to its designation as the Warriors' Chapel. Ironically, on account of this later development, the Hales monument was moved to its present position in the north aisle, to make way for regimental memorials.[50] There is a further dimension to the dynastic significance of the Hales monument. The year after Cheyney Hales's death, Thomas Neville became Dean and was himself immediately involved in the setting up of two monuments to his own family. The epitaph on the monument to his father, Richard, refers to Dame Margaret, Thomas Neville's maternal grandmother, who was also the widow of Sir James Hales senior.[51]

The monument to Thomas Neville, Dean from 1597 to his death, in 1615,[52] is a very good example of the dynastic motivation behind so many late sixteenth- and early seventeenth-century monuments. Neville had been chaplain to Queen Elizabeth and Dean of Peterborough before becoming Master of Trinity College, Cambridge. As his epitaph informs us, he made arrangements in his lifetime for family memorials in the chapel 'which (while he lived) he embellish'd for himself and his Family'.[53] This chapel was the former Brenchley Chantry on the south side of the nave, which had fallen into disuse. In November 1598, Chapter Acts record: 'It is agreed that the little Chapple on the side of the South Yld in the nave of the Church shall be well and sufficiently repaired, at the charge of the Church, to be ymploied and used in such manner and sort, as to Mr Deane shall be thought moste convenient.'[54] The first monument he set up was to his father, Richard Neville, his mother, and a brother, Thomas.[55] The epitaph, almost certainly written by Neville himself, gives us a precise date of erection, 3 August 1599. It informs us of the Neville antecedents, and

[48] Cowper, *Memorial Inscriptions* (cit. in n. 5), 283; *DNB*.

[49] Quoted in Esdaile, *English Church Monuments* (cit. in n. 2), 108; she has misunderstood her source.

[50] It was moved before the publication of Cowper's *Memorial Inscriptions* (cit. in n. 5) in 1897.

[51] Dart, *History and Antiquities* (cit. in n. 4), 43–5.

[52] His signature first appears in the minutes of the General Chapter in Nov. 1597. Chapter Act Book, 1581–1607, fo. 180ᵛ.

[53] Trans. Dart, *History and Antiquities* (cit. in n. 4), 42.

[54] Chapter Act Book, 1581–1607, fo. 193.

[55] Who, as his namesake, we may presume had died in infancy. Gostling wrongly records this Thomas as the Dean's uncle: Gostling, *Walk* (cit. in n. 3), 190.

that Richard spent his youth at court, adding that he passed 'the Decline of Life' at Canterbury.

The monument to Thomas Neville himself and his brother Alexander shows every sign of a premeditated scheme. The inscription quoted in Dart has gaps for the date of Thomas's death[56] and, in the case of Alexander, who died on 4 October 1614,[57] a year before Thomas, there is the unusual use of the present tense.[58] Our only source for the original appearance of the two Neville monuments is a pair of engravings in Dart (Pls. 133, 134). These present two handsome architectural wall-monuments of the standard Anglo-Netherlandish Southwark type.[59] Both have ribbon work and fruit ornament typical of the decorative detail of the period. The two kneeling effigies are in demi-relief, in a pair of niches divided by Corinthian columns. The Dean 'in his Habit'[60] closely parallels the effigy on the Wotton monument, while his elder brother, by contrast, wears armour. An entablature and broken pediment, inset with a heraldic achievement or mantled coat of arms, completes the whole.

Neville ensured that the necessary administrative procedures were in hand,[61] and left £5 for the repair and maintenance of the chapel and monuments,[62] but these were almost entirely destroyed on being moved when the Cathedral nave was repaired and the chapel pulled down in 1787. A group of fragments from both monuments was put into the Chapel of the Virgin Mary, known colloquially as the Dean's Chapel. They were set up in the south choir aisle in 1925.[63]

If the Hales monument was erected in the Cathedral through professional ties and family influence, how much more so the monument to Sir John Boys of St Gregory's, who died in 1612.[64] John Boys was MP for Canterbury in 1600–1, knighted in 1603, a counsellor at law, judge of the Chancery Court of the Cinque Ports, and recorder of Canterbury.[65] More importantly, he was steward to five archbishops.[66] He was twice married[67] but, as his epitaph informs us, died childless.[68] The monument, a handsome Southwark-type structure in three stages, relies largely on classical architectural form. Anglo-Netherlandish ornament is used sparingly, appearing only in the relief panels framing the coat of arms in the uppermost storey. The semi-recumbent effigy has a more lifelike appearance than is often associated with figure-work of this period, particularly in the treatment of legs and

[56] The interment was recorded in the Register on 7 May 1615: *Register Booke*, ed. Hovenden (cit. in n. 7).

[57] He was interred on 9 Oct. 1614: ibid.

[58] 'I dye in the [blank] year of my Age, in the year of Christs Incarnation 1614, the 4th of October. 'Tis sufficient (Good Spectator) what I inform you, know Thyself. Farewel': Dart, *History and Antiquities* (cit. in n. 4), 43.

[59] Ibid. 41, 44.

[60] Ibid. 40.

[61] In the General Chapter of 1616, the Dean and Chapter agreed to a bond being paid to the 'Executors of the last will and testament of Dr. Nevile late deane of Canterbury . . . for the performance of such conditions as are required by the said last will to be performed by the said Deane and chapter': Chapter Act Book, 1608–28, fo. 161

[62] Treasurer's Accts., 1626–7. On 30 November 1770, the Dean was instructed to give directions for 'repairing and embellishing

of Nevile's Chapel', paid for with £40 from the Archbishop and £40 from the Dean and Chapter: Chapter Act Book, 1761–75, fo. 250.

[63] Hasted, *Kent* (cit. in n. 3), xii. 11–12; Chapter Act Book, 1924–31, fos. 74, 81, 98. Substantial portions of both monuments are at present (1994) in store.

[64] 'Syr John Boyce Knight' was interred in the Cathedral on 24 Sept. 1612: *Register Booke*, ed. Hovenden (cit. in n. 7).

[65] Cowper, *Memorial Inscriptions* (cit. in n. 5), 274.

[66] Parker, Grindal, Whitgift, Bancroft, and Abbot.

[67] His second wife, Jane, daughter and co-heir of Thomas Walker, was later, in 1639, to have a monument erected to her at Great Missenden Church (Bucks.), designed by Nicholas Stone: W. L. Spiers, 'The Notebook and Account Book of Nicholas Stone', *Walpole Soc.* 7 (1918–19), 119, 125.

[68] 'Sed nulla prole relicta': Dart, *History and Antiquities* (cit. in n. 4), 48.

feet.[69] The kneeling figures of his two wives, Jane Walker and Dorothy Pawley, appear in low relief on the tomb-chest. The small effigy of a baby in swaddling bands, symbol of an heir that died in infancy, was probably destroyed at the outbreak of the Civil War.[70] The monument was, so Dart informs us, later restored by Grotius Boys.

In the same year, 1612, Adrian or Hadrian Saravia died at the age of 82. A small plain wall-tablet was set up to his memory in the north aisle by his wife Margaret Witts.[71] As the epitaph implies, he was one of the many continental immigrants who found a sympathetic domicile under Elizabeth. He became a canon of the Cathedral in 1595 and was a member of the committee appointed to translate the Bible. The tablet appears to be from the standard stock of some Southwark workshop. The panels of ornament, ribboned fruit, spades, and bones, rich in the symbolism of death and the Resurrection, are eloquent examples of the late sixteenth- and early seventeenth-century passion for morbid conceits.[72]

Another example of this stock-in-trade production of Southwark workshops is the wall-tablet to Richard Colfe, who died in 1613.[73] The formula exactly parallels that dedicated to Saravia: the shields remain blank of heraldic ornament, and the ornament itself is from the same source, the *memento mori* varying only in point of detail. The decoration may be compared to that on the relief panels supporting the coat of arms in the upper storeys of the Thornhurst and Boys monuments. Colfe was of *émigré* descent, educated at Christ's Hospital and Christ Church, Oxford. He held a number of livings in the diocese before becoming a canon in 1585, eventually being made archdeacon.

Three monuments in St Michael's Chapel to various members of the Thornhurst family exemplify the development of early seventeenth-century monumental style.[74] The most full-blown example of the stock Southwark type is that to Mary, Lady Thornhurst, who died in 1609. It combines a semi-recumbent effigy,[75] kneeling mourners in contemporary dress, Corinthian columns, obelisks, strapwork, and ribbonwork. The inscription, uncharacteristically, is uninformative. We learn only that Lady Thornhurst was married to Sir Richard Baker of Sissinghurst, had two daughters by him, Grisogone Lenerd and Cicely Blunt, and that she died aged 65. Her two daughters kneel below, in high relief on the tomb-chest, the traditional place for mourners.[76] The register of burials records the interment of 'The Lady Thornehurst wyfe unto Syrr Steene Thornhurst, Knight' in 1609.[77]

---

[69] Contrast this with the monument to Sir George Newman (d. 1627) in St Margaret's, Canterbury. Here the same formula is used, but the figure is stiff and unconvincing and the Southwark-work ornament lends a fussy air. It may be remarked in passing that polychromy is an essential ingredient of Southwark monuments, for without it the Newman monument is largely illegible. It has been boxed in as part of the 70-year lease of the church to Heritage Projects Ltd. I am grateful to Robin Westbrook for assistance and for supplying me with a photograph of the monument.

[70] This now appears only in the engraving in Dart, who goes out of his way to state that the infant 'in the plate is exactly Copied from a Model of it taken when in perfection': Dart, *History and Antiquities* (cit. in n. 4), 48.

[71] He was buried in the Cathedral on 12 January 1612: *Register Booke*, ed. Hovenden (cit. in n. 7); Dart, *History and Antiquities* (cit. in n. 4), 50–1.

[72] There are references here to Adam and Eve in the Garden of Eden amid the fruits of the Earth, to the Risen Christ taken for a gardener by Mary Magdalene, and to the Gravedigger.

[73] 'Doctor Colfe, one of the Worshipfull Prebendaries, and then vicedeane' was buried in the Cathedral 10 Oct. 1613: *Register Booke*, ed. Hovenden (cit. in n. 7). Curiously, Dart records the date in both Roman and Arabic numerals as 1643, thereby giving rise no doubt to Gostling's accusations of inaccuracy.

[74] The reason for the presence of the Thornhurst monuments is not explained, and Dart makes no comment: Dart, *History and Antiquities* (cit. in n. 4), 69–74 and pls. 71–3.

[75] The effigy is very similar to that on the monument to Sir George Newman, see n. 69.

[76] Though Dart records them intact, they have been mutilated at some time: Dart, *History and Antiquities* (cit. in n. 4), 74.

[77] *Register Booke*, ed. Hovenden (cit. in n. 7).

Sir Stephen, her third husband, kneels above her as chief mourner. He died in 1616.[78].

Sir Stephen's third wife, Dorothy, dying five years later, in 1620,[79] left a request in her will for a monument. It asks that she, a widow of Fulham, Middlesex, be buried with her husband in Christ Church, Canterbury: 'And my will and desire ys that my executor hereunder named doe within one yeare next after my decease cause and procure to be made the picture of my said Bodie of Alabaster stone, and neere or uppon the Tombe of my said late husband ... in Christchurch aforesaid to sett upp and place the same kneelinge behinde or before the picture of my said late husband ... for £40, if I myselfe in my lifetyme doe not performe the same accordinglie.'[80] The epitaph to the monument to Dorothy Thornhurst, a good example of a Jacobean hanging monument,[81] informs us that it was erected by her niece Martha Norton. (Pl. 135).

The third monument in St Michael's Chapel is to Sir Thomas Thornhurst, who was killed at the storming of the Île de Rhé, on the ill-starred expedition to La Rochelle, on 17 July 1627. The monument was erected by his widow, Barbara. His three children, Barbara, Anthony, and Cecilia, kneel in low relief in the base of the tomb-chest, carrying skulls, which suggest that they died in infancy. The monument is a fine example of a late, more subdued Southwark work, and exhibits a number of features in the new taste: the draped curtains and fringe that frame the inscription panel in its Mannerist cut-leather or strap-work frame, the two supporting figures in armour, and the greater ease and naturalism of the poses of the two effigies. These are features which suggest the influence of, if not a direct link with, the workshops of Nicholas Stone. Stone had used standing military figures as supporters as early as 1615 on the monument to Thomas Sutton at Charterhouse. The female effigy, her hand resting lightly on her breast, her head on a pair of cushions, is reminiscent of a number of female recumbent effigies by Stone, such as those of Lady Carey (1617–18)[82] and Lady Winchelsea (1623–8).[83] The male effigy reclines on one elbow, with one leg raised, a pose adopted by a number of male effigies on monuments ascribed to Stone, such as that of Sir Charles Morison (1630).[84] If it were, however, from the Stone workshop, it is unlikely that it would, at this date, have been polychromed.[85]

THE SEVENTEENTH CENTURY

Court Taste at Canterbury

Charles Fotherby (d. 1619), who was buried in the Lady Chapel, had been archdeacon for twenty-four years before succeeding Thomas Neville as Dean in 1615. His monument, a

[78] Ibid.

[79] The Lady Thornhurst was interred on 22 June 1620: ibid.

[80] PRO, PROB 11/135, fo. 470, quoted by J. H. Lea, *Abstracts of Wills in the Prerogative Court of Canterbury ... Reg. Soame, 1620* (New-England Historic and Geneal. Soc.; Boston, Mass., 1904), 229–30, no. 692.

[81] It recalls the much more elaborate monument to another widow, Elizabeth Vane (d. 1618), in St Nicholas's Chapel, Westminster Abbey, also set cater-corner, and also kneeling, but which includes the effigy of her husband: Kemp, *English*

Church Monuments (cit. in n. 42), dust-jacket.

[82] Whinney, *Sculpture in Britain* (cit. in n. 2), pls. 18A, 16.

[83] Formerly at Eastwell Church (Kent), now Victoria and Albert Museum. J. Physick, *Five Monuments from Eastwell* (London, 1973), *passim*.

[84] Watford (Herts.): Whinney, *Sculpture in Britain* (cit. in n. 2), pl. 198.

[85] Like the other monuments in St Michael's Chapel, its polychromy was restored in 1947.

bone-encrusted tomb-chest (Pl. 137), is a fine example of that obsessive early seventeenth-century morbidity which repelled later, more squeamish observers. John Britton described it in 1836 as a 'tasteless' monument and, while ignoring all other post-medieval monuments, declared: 'I cannot omit to notice and reprobate the design and effect of an altar tomb, the sides and ends of which are covered by a mass of sculptural representations of human bones.'[86] The detail is not by any means unique, indeed the treatment of the bones and skulls is very similar to that on the tomb-chest of the monument to Sir Henry Griffith (d. 1645) at Burton Agnes in Yorkshire.[87] Gostling suggests that much of the ornament on the Fotherby monument may have been cut away, and supposes that once there was more to the monument than now appears.[88] Dart records an inscription which no longer exists, so it is likely that there was a super-edifice or backplate on which John Fotherby commemorated his mother, who died in 1634.[89]

The architectural and sculptural renaissance of the early seventeenth century, which defined avant-garde court taste, was largely the work of Inigo Jones and the sculptor-stonemason Nicholas Stone. Canterbury was particularly closely linked to Court circles at this time, and three monuments that exemplify the radical changes in taste of the period are all to men with strong Court connections. The first, a rare example of a monument whose attribution is without doubt, is to Orlando Gibbons (Pl. 136). His commemoration in the Cathedral was an accident of death, but is indicative of the esteem in which he was held. Born in 1583, Gibbons was educated at Oxford, and at the age of 19 became organist of the Chapel Royal and subsequently of Westminster Abbey. He was commanded by Charles I to compose music for the King's marriage to Henrietta Maria at Canterbury on 13 June 1625. He died, however, on 6 June, perhaps of smallpox or apoplexy,[90] and was buried in the Cathedral.[91] The monument was erected by his widow, Elizabeth, née Patten, daughter of a yeoman of the vestry of the Chapel Royal. An entry in Nicholas Stone's account book for 1626 records: 'I sett up a monument at Canterbury for Erlando Gebons the Kings organest for which his wyf payed £32.'[92]

The break of the new with the old, as exemplified by the Gibbons monument, is stressed in Dart by the engraving which places the monuments to Saravia and Gibbons side by side.[93] The former is of Northern, Netherlandish inspiration, while the latter is entirely innovatory in its Italianate architecture and ornament. Three features deserve particular comment. The simplicity of its black and white marble is in stark contrast to the high polychromy of the Cathedral's Southwark-type monuments. This was very much an aesthetic issue of the time. Only two years previously, Sir Henry Wotton, in his *Elements of Architecture*, had declared against 'the Fashion of Colouring, even Regall Statues, which

---

[86] Britton, *History and Antiquities* (cit. in n. 3), 53–4, 70.

[87] Kemp, *English Church Monuments* (cit. in n. 42), pl. 144. The Fotherby monument is, however, on stylistic grounds unlikely to be by John and Matthias Christmas, whose signed monument to Archbishop Abbot (d. 1633) in Holy Trinity, Guildford, exhibits a very different treatment of the charnel-house effect.

[88] Gostling, *Walk* (cit. in n. 3), 196. It is worth pointing out that a small 17th-cent. standing figure of Father Time, now placed in a niche at the corner of the choir screen and the staircase to the south choir aisle, is precisely the kind of ornament that completed the upper stages of monuments of this period.

[89] Dart, *History and Antiquities* (cit. in n. 4), 51, 55. In Dart's suitably atmospheric mezzotint of 1726, only the tomb-chest itself is depicted.

[90] Cowper, *Memorial Inscriptions* (cit. in n. 5), 281.

[91] *Register Booke*, ed. Hovenden (cit. in n. 7).

[92] Spiers, 'Notebook of Nicholas Stone' (cit. in n. 67), 63.

[93] Dart, *History and Antiquities* (cit. in n. 4), 51.

I must take leave to call an English Barbarism'.[94] The portrait bust of Gibbons also marks a new departure. The blank-eyed head and shoulders on a pedestal are of continental origin, and, despite the contemporary ruff, are evidence of the classicizing influence of the antique.[95] The epitaph clearly expresses grief in the vein of humanist sentiment fashionable at court, in contrast to the dynastic bombast of late-Elizabethan and early-Jacobean epitaphs.[96]

An epitaph which has the same highly personal tone is that placed on Dean Boys' monument (Pl. 138) by his widow, Angela.[97] Angela Boys was the sister of Isaac Bargrave, who became Dean on Boys's death in 1625. Bargrave had accompanied Sir Henry Wotton on diplomatic missions on the Continent, and was perhaps with him in Venice.[98] The potential significance of this cannot be underestimated. Dean Boys's monument is one of the finest in the Cathedral, and an outstanding example of the discovery of the surface quality of marble. This was a taste acquired in the 1620s, when patrons and sculptors began to take more interest in antique sculpture, as a result of Continental travels.[99] The iconography, too, reflects Continental influences, and echoes, appropriately, Renaissance images of St Jerome in his study and of the Evangelists as learned men seated in their carrels.[100] The monument has been only tentatively attributed. Esdaile described it as 'of the Stone-Marshall School apparently', while Physick has suggested that it is 'in all probability connected with Stone's workshop'.[101] It exhibits a new and remarkable control of composition, each part contributing to an overall sense of scale and proportion. Details in the composition occur elsewhere in Stone's work. The use of the seated figure is said to have been introduced by him,[102] while the use of books as pilasters occurs on at least three documented monuments from his workshop.[103]

A third monument which has stylistic connections with court taste is that to Canon Dr Alexander Chapman, who died in 1629.[104] It was originally sited in the north-west transept,

[94] H. Wotton, *Elements of Architecture* (London, 1624), 89–90.

[95] Cf. the bust of Michael Drayton (d. 1631) in Westminster Abbey, attributed to Edward Marshall, or the treatment of the Apollo in Child's Bank, Strand, also attributed to Edward Marshall. See K. Eustace, 'The Influence of Collections of Antique Sculpture on Contemporary Sculpture in England, circa 1610–1650' (2 vols., MA thesis, Univ. of London, 1985), 32; and cat. entries by K. Eustace in N. Penny, *Thomas Howard Earl of Arundel*, exhib. cat., Ashmolean Museum (Oxford, 1985).

[96] In Oct. 1866 consent was given to H. H. Armistead 'to sketch or mould from the bust of Orlando Gibbons . . . for reproduction on a memorial now erecting to the late Prince Consort in Hyde Park', Chapter Act Book, 1854–84, fo. 222. The bust has been restored since the Second World War.

[97] Dean Boys was interred in the Lady Chapel on 30 September 1625: *Register Booke*, ed. Hovenden (cit. in n. 7).

[98] L. Pearsall-Smith, *The Life and Letters of Sir Henry Wotton* (2 vols.; Oxford, 1907), i, 145 n. Henry Wotton was ambassador to Venice and advisor to Henry, Prince of Wales, Lord Salisbury, and the Earl of Arundel on the purchase of works of art.

[99] Eustace, 'Influence of Antique Sculpture' (cit. in n. 95), *passim*.

[100] As in the Donatello roundels in the sacristy in San Lorenzo, Florence, or those in the ceiling of the antechamber of the Guild of the Caritá, now the Accademia, Venice.

[101] Esdaile, *English Church Monuments* (cit. in n. 2), 105; M. Whinney, *Sculpture in Britain* 2nd edn., by J. Physick (London, 1988), 435 n. 12. There are two other known links at this period between Canterbury and the Stone workshop: one is the monument to Isaac Bargrave's aunt by marriage (see n. 67), the other is the monument in Westminster Abbey by Stone to Isaac Casaubon (d. 1634), a layman who, from 1611, held a prebendal stall at Canterbury: Spiers, 'Notebook of Nicholas Stone' (cit. in n. 67), 55, pl. XVC. His son Meric was a canon at Canterbury from 1628, and throughout the 1630s Isaac's infant grandsons were being buried in the Cathedral: *Register Booke*, ed. Hovenden (cit. in n. 7).

[102] The earliest is the effigy of Elizabeth Russell (d. 1601), Westminster Abbey, followed by Nicholas Stone's monument to Francis Holles (d. 1622): J. Physick and J. Whitlock-Blundell, *Westminster Abbey: The Monuments* (London, 1989), nos. 47 and 48. The seated figure of Dean Boys is comparable to the unattributed figures of Sir Francis Bacon (d. 1626), St Michael's Church, St Albans (Herts.), and of Maria Wentworth (d. 1632), Toddington (Beds.).

[103] Thomas Bodley (d. 1613), Merton College, Oxford; Sir Henry Yelverton (d. 1629), Easton Mauduit (Northants); and Sir Thomas Lucy (d. 1640), Charlecote (Warks.).

[104] *Register Booke*, ed. Hovenden (cit. in n. 7).

or Martyrdom, and was erected by Chapman's brother Henry, as the epitaph tells us. Chapman was an erudite man of letters, and a member of the circle of Thomas Howard, Earl of Arundel.[105] As chaplain to Princess Elizabeth, the daughter of James I, he accompanied her, under Lord Arundel's escort, to be married in 1613 to Frederick, Elector Palatine. His monument bears all the hallmarks of a metropolitan workshop in tune with the radical classicism of Inigo Jones, such as a segmented pediment, and acanthus, egg-and-dart, and laurel-leaf ornament (Pl. 139). There are numerous parallels to its demi-effigy, old-fashioned when compared to that of Orlando Gibbons; it is almost identical with a work firmly attributed to Nicholas Stone's workshop, that to Sir Heneage Finch (d. 1613), formerly at Eastwell (Kent), and now in the Victoria and Albert Museum.[106]

Exemplifying a transitional stage between the old and the new taste is the monument to Lieut.-Col. William Prude, who was killed at the siege of Maastricht on 12 July 1632 (Pl. 140), and was interred in 'Somerset Chappelle' (St Michael's Chapel) on 20 September.[107] The reasons for his being commemorated are twofold. One reflects a developing sense of patriotism: like the monuments to the Haleses and Sir Thomas Thornhurst, that to Prude acknowledges service *pro patria*. The other reason is one of kinship: the monument was erected by William's son, Searles Prude, and his widow, Mary, daughter of Sir Adam Sprackling. Searles Prude was married to Ann Denne, of the distinguished Canterbury legal family.[108] The kneeling military effigy is in the Flemish tradition first seen in the Cathedral in the Neville monument. Two military herms support the arcading, above which a pair of virtues support a heraldic escutcheon. On the left is Minerva, goddess of war, and on the right, distinctly classical in appearance, is Victory, holding a laurel wreath. The fine, low-relief trophies of war around the inscriptions replace the fruit decoration seen on earlier Southwark monuments. They are an early example of such trophies entering the sculptor's repertoire, where they would remain for as long as monuments were erected to military heroes.[109]

The Civil War and the Interregnum

Although burials continued in the Cathedral throughout the Civil War, the Interregnum, and the Commonwealth, monuments were not erected until after the Restoration. The sheer number of monuments erected in England in the years leading up to 1640 may well have contributed to the outburst of iconoclasm. The taste for classical and pagan imagery, itself a reaction to an earlier iconoclasm, was indeed a subject for Puritan indignation.[110] In 1631, Weever had inveighed against 'pictures of naked men and women . . . the memories of the heathen gods and goddesses with all their whirligigs'.[111]

---

[105] Arundel presented a chalice to the Cathedral in 1636: Cowper, *Memorial Inscriptions* (cit. in n. 5), 254.

[106] Spiers, 'Notebook of Nicholas Stone' (cit. in n. 67), 88; Physick, *Monuments from Eastwell* (cit. in n. 83), *passim*.

[107] *Register Booke*, ed. Hovenden (cit. in n. 7).

[108] William Denne became recorder of Canterbury: Somner, *Antiquities* (1703), p. vii.

[109] E. W. Tristram described the monument as in a 'ruinous condition' as a result of bomb blast in the Second World War.

'The process of cleaning revealed so much of the original painted decoration that it was found possible to restore the monument with certainty as to its accuracy': F. W. Tomlinson, *The Warriors' Chapel and the Buffs* (Canterbury Papers, 2, rev. edn.; Canterbury, 1960), 17.

[110] At Paston (Norfolk) and Toddington (Beds.), monuments were severely mutilated.

[111] J. Weever, *Ancient Funerall Monuments* (London, 1631), 11.

Canterbury provides one of the few well-documented instances of localized puritanical iconoclasm. An account 'shewing the Canterburian Cathedrall to Bee in an Abbey-Like Corrupt and Rotten Condition',[112] was written by the iconoclast Richard Culmer, justifying his actions because 'the Citizens cried out "No pictures, No images, No papists, No Archbishops secretary, we have too many images and pictures in the Cathedral already"'. Ironically, it was Somner's *Antiquities of Canterbury* (1640) which was, in Culmer's words, 'a card and compasse to sail by, in that *Cathedrall Ocean of Images*'.[113] However, the monuments of the past hundred years largely survived unscathed at Canterbury, perhaps because Somner had ignored them, and perhaps also because they were simply not accessible. The Lady Chapel and St Michael's Chapel were probably locked with iron gates, as they are today. The area at the foot of the choir and the Martyrdom, on the other hand, then as now a passage open to all, was where Culmer by his own admission did the most damage in 1643. Figures were damaged on the monument to Sir John Boys in the nave, and those to Robert Berkeley (d. 1614) and William Lovelace (d. 1577) and his wife Anne nearby, were almost totally destroyed.[114] The remains of these monuments were removed at the end of the eighteenth century, when the nave and aisles were repaved and reordered.[115]

Late Seventeenth-Century Cartouche Design

The Restoration saw the reappearance of memorials, generally in the form of the less flamboyant inscribed cartouche. The first, in the Lady Chapel, to Dean Isaac Bargrave, was not set up until 1679 (Pl. 141). Bargrave had become a canon in 1622 and, as we have seen, Dean after the death of his brother-in-law John Boys in 1626. A staunch churchman and supporter of the Crown, he was committed to the Fleet Prison by the Parliamentarians. He returned to Canterbury to die, and was interred on 25 January 1643.[116] The inference to be drawn from the epitaph is that the monument was set up as a martyr's memorial by the Dean's nephew, John, himself collated to a canonry by Archbishop Juxon in 1662.

The painted portrait of Bargrave, which is inset into the cartouche, is unlikely to be posthumous. It has been attributed to Cornelius Janssen or Johnson (1593–1661), who returned to his native Holland the year after Bargrave's death. Johnson had been appointed 'His Majesty's Servant in ye quality of Picture Drawer' in 1632.[117] However, in the 1630s, Johnson lived and worked at Bridge in Kent, from where the Bargrave family came, and he made a living painting many of the local families.[118] The shallow shield-pattern surrounding Bargrave's portrait, with its clasped drapes and leafy, scrolled auricular frame, is reminiscent of the Mannerist work of the 1620s produced by the Flemish family of Van

[112] R. Culmer, *Dean and Chapter Newes from Canterbury 1644* (2nd edn.; London, 1649), *passim*.

[113] Ibid.

[114] Dart, *History and Antiquities* (cit. in n. 4), 90–1. Dart does not even bother to record Berkeley's epitaph, and lists Lovelace as among those 'whose monuments are defac'd'.

[115] Chapter Act Book, 1761–75, fo. 365; Dean's Book, 1777–93, p. 136. For the suggestion that the Lovelace monument consisted of two effigies, see C. E. Woodruff, 'Note on a Hitherto Unidentified Tomb in the Nave of the Cathedral', *Cant. Cath. Chron.*, 40 (1944), 21–2, ill.; A. J. Pearman, *Arch. Cant.*, 10 (1876), 200.

[116] *Register Booke*, ed. Hovenden (cit. in n. 7).

[117] M. Whinney and O. Millar, *English Art, 1625–1714* (Oxford, 1957), 64–7.

[118] His signed portrait of Susanna Temple, wife of the Kentishman Sir Gifford Thornhurst (grandson of the Sir Stephen in St Michael's Chapel), is now in the Tate Gallery.

Vianen.[119] The gadrooned and flaming urn, however, which surmounted the monument as a symbol of death and eternity,[120] was a motif which first appeared in the 1680s, and which was to continue in use throughout the eighteenth century.

Within its own limits it is both technically sophisticated and harmoniously designed. The sharp precision of the detail suggests a facility for ornament, while its spare, almost two-dimensional quality precludes the possibility of the monument's being from the workshops of Grinling Gibbons or the Stantons, whose output is more robust and florid. There are, however, close, though hitherto unremarked, affinities with designs which, until recently, were ascribed to William Talman and are now reattributed to Edward Pierce (c.1635–95).[121] Described by George Vertue as 'a curious Architect and Carver, a great assistant to Sir Christopher Wren',[122] Pierce, a mason-sculptor, was one of the chief contractors for St Paul's between 1679 and 1690, and he also built five of the City churches.[123] In 1678 he was employing five assistants engaged on decorative carving in wood and stone.[124] There is a substantive link between Canterbury and the work of Edward Pierce, for he was responsible for the interior ornament of St Lawrence Jewry[125] at the time when John Tillotson was archbishop. Tillotson had been lecturer at St Lawrence Jewry while he was Dean of Canterbury (1673–89), and he was buried there on his death in 1694.[126] If it is by Pierce, the recidivist nature of the design may have an explanation in the volume *Frieze-work* first published in 1640 by Edward Pierce senior, and reissued by the son in 1680. It would, after all, be fitting to decorate the monument to Bargrave, who had died in the 1640s, with ornament from the same period.[127]

Bargrave's monument is closely associated stylistically with a small group of wall-tablets in the Cathedral, one of which is to Priscilla Kingsley (d. 1683) (Pl. 142). She was exceptionally well-connected in Canterbury terms. Her grandfather, Martin Fotherby, had been a canon of Canterbury before becoming Bishop of Salisbury, while her grandmother, Margaret, was the daughter of Canon Winter. Priscilla's great-uncle Charles Fotherby was Archdeacon and then Dean of Canterbury, and her husband, Canon William Kingsley, was Archdeacon Kingsley's grandson, and a great-nephew of Archbishop Abbot.[128]

The cartouche memorial erected by his widow, Rebecca, to John Clerke in 1700[129] appears to be an example of the hospitality of death, there being no other obvious *raison d'être* for its erection in the Cathedral. The memorial to John Battely informs us that he was domestic chaplain to Archbishop Sancroft and was first a canon and then Archdeacon of Canterbury until his death, in 1708.[130] His brother Nicholas, who edited Somner's *Antiquities of Canterbury* in 1703, is buried with other members of the Battely family in St

[119] P. Ward-Jackson, 'Some Mainstreams and Tributaries in European Ornament from 1500 to 1750', *Victoria and Albert Museum Bull.* 3/2–4 (1969), passim.

[120] The flames are now missing; Dart, *History and Antiquities* (cit. in n. 4), pl. 17, p. 36.

[121] See designs in the Dept. of Prints and Drawings, Victoria and Albert Museum, nos. 3436–432, 433, 441.

[122] *Vertue Notebooks*, i, Walpole Society, 18 (1930), 69.

[123] Whinney, *Sculpture in Britain* (cit. in n. 2), 45, n. 26.

[124] J. F. Physick, *Designs for English Sculpture 1680–1860* (London, 1969), 24, n. 6.

[125] The church was destroyed in 1940: Gunnis, *Dictionary* (cit. in n. 2).

[126] Dart, *History and Antiquities* (cit. in n. 4), 176.

[127] R. Lane Poole, 'Edward Pierce, the Sculptor', *Walpole Society*, 11 (1922–3), 33–45. The engraved designs for friezes bound into a volume in the Department of Prints and Drawings, British Museum, give his name as Edward Pearce: 1937–9–15443 (73–86).

[128] Cowper, *Memorial Inscriptions* (cit. in n. 5), 286.

[129] Dart, *History and Antiquities* (cit. in n. 4), 63.

[130] The memorial used to be in the angle between St Michael's Chapel and the south-west transept door: Gostling, *Walk* (cit. in n. 3), 216.

Peter's, Bekesbourne, and the memorials there are of a similar cartouche type. The Latin inscription to John is both informative and, a new departure, upholds the deceased as an example of virtue and a worthy member of the Established Church: 'Ecclesiam Anglicanam Insigniter Ornavit.'

The small wall-plaque to Jane Hardres (d. 1675) underlines the important role that family connections played in obtaining permission for memorials to be erected in the Cathedral. The elder daughter of Thomas Hardres, King's Serjeant-at-Law, she was in fact interred in St George's parish church.[131] The Hardres family were 'of ancient Continuance in this Country, ever since the Conquest',[132] and were longstanding tenants of the Dean and Chapter.[133] Jane's sister Elizabeth was married to Canon Dr William Belke (d. 1676), whose son Thomas (d. 1712) became a canon and married into the local squirearchy.[134] Jane's monument marks a transitional stage in the evolution of the design of monuments. In its use of laurel wreaths and broken pediment it harks back to the classicism introduced by Stone in the 1620s, while the beaded callot ornament and flaming urn look forward to eighteenth-century classical-baroque. This evolutionary state is also apparent in the monument to Dean Thomas Turner, who had been a pupil of William Juxon and chaplain to Laud when the latter was Bishop of London. He became Dean of Canterbury in 1643, but was not installed until 1660. He was buried in the Cathedral on 14 October 1673.[135] The epitaph, like that of Bargrave, makes reference to the 'glorious and holy martyrs' Charles I and Archbishop Laud, and speaks of the 'Rebels Tyranny',[136] since Turner had been chaplain and confessor to both his king and archbishop, attending the King at Hampton Court and the Isle of Wight. While the book-supports on his monument recall those on Nicholas Stone's to Isaac Casaubon in Westminster Abbey, the scale, architectural solidity, and decorative detail of the piece were all to become part of the repertory of eighteenth-century monuments. Turner was the last dean for a hundred years to have a monument at Canterbury. Thereafter, deans of Canterbury by and large proceeded to bishoprics elsewhere.[137]

THE EIGHTEENTH CENTURY

The eighteenth century is extraordinarily ill-represented at Canterbury by monuments of any type. By 1720, only three had been set up, all in St Michael's Chapel. The first commemorates Admiral George Rooke (d. 1709), who was a national hero in the War of the Spanish Succession and who captured Gibraltar in 1704 (Pl. 143, detail). It is, in fact, a cenotaph, as Rooke was buried in St Paul's Church, Canterbury. His family had had links with the Cathedral for many years,[138] and his father had been Mayor of Canterbury in 1684 and High Sheriff of Kent. Mrs Esdaile described 'the excellent bust' of Rooke as being by

[131] *Register Booke*, ed. Hovenden (cit. in n. 7).

[132] Dart, *History and Antiquities* (cit. in n. 4), 65.

[133] Chapter Act Books, *passim*, esp. 1727–46, fo. 4ᵛ.

[134] He married Anne, daughter of Sir Henry Oxenden: Dart, *History and Antiquities* (cit. in n. 4), 68.

[135] Chapter Act Book, 1670–1710, fo. 120ᵛ.

[136] Trans. Dart, *History and Antiquities* (cit. in n. 4), 60.

[137] Of 18 deans from 1672 to 1845, only 6 failed to be translated to a bishopric. John Sharp (d. 1714), Dean from 1689, became Archbishop of York, where his monument is sited: G. E. Aylmer and R. Cant (eds.); *A History of York Minster* (Oxford, 1977), 448.

[138] In 1599 Elizabeth, the daughter of Thomas Rooke, was buried in the Cathedral: *Register Booke*, ed. Hovenden (cit. in n. 7).

some London master,[139] and more recently it has been given an unsubstantiated attribution to Edward Stanton.[140] The Italianate altar-form, pedestal bust under draped curtains, and swagged fruit and flowers in the upper storey, are commonplaces of the period.[141] The piece is competent and only marred by the anachronistic and erroneous use of polychromy, presumably added when the other polychrome monuments in St Michael's Chapel were restored in 1947.

One of the two men responsible for erecting the monument to Admiral Rooke was Samuel Milles (d. 1727), of Herne. Six years after Rooke's death, Milles set up a monument to his own daughter Ann (d. 1714) in St Michael's Chapel (Pl. 144). In 1726, Milles succeeded Herbert Randolph as Steward of the Cathedral Court of Record.[142] The monument was moved at the end of the last century from its original site to the staircase leading up to the south choir aisle.[143] The epitaph extols her beauty, her piety, and her chastity, and also informs us that she had been baptized in the Cathedral, daily worshipped there, and died at the age of 20. Ann Milles belonged to that social group which in death received more respect than in life—widows, spinsters, or, as the epitaph so unambiguously proclaims, virgins. Her monument belongs to the same tradition as those to Alice Hales, Dorothy and Lady Thornhurst, Priscilla Kingsley, and Jane Hardres. It is the most full-blown Baroque monument in the Cathedral. Its architecture, heavily gadrooned shelf, and tented baldacchino, with acanthus-scrolled consoles, winged cherubs' heads, and weeping putti, are all part of the repertory of Baroque funerary sculpture. The demi-effigy of the deceased *en négligée*, resting her prayer-book on a cushion, ultimately derives from Bernini's bust of Costanza Buonarelli.[144] But although the formula is just such as was employed by the Stanton workshop,[145] the quality of the carving is inferior.

The monument to Francis Godfrey erected by his parents in St Michael's Chapel depicts a fine trophy of arms supporting an escutcheon. Godfrey died of fever aged 32 in 1712, and was buried in the chapel.[146] This is a restrained Baroque monument with the kind of decorative detail typical of the late seventeenth century. Its pair of low-relief panels of *memento mori* are of a type employed by Edward Pierce,[147] the Stantons, and John Nost.[148] Like the Rooke monument, it too has been mistakenly polychromed. The last of this group is a handsome wall-tablet on the stairs leading to the south choir aisle, not recorded

[139] Esdaile, *English Church Monuments* (cit. in n. 2), 98.

[140] Keates and Hornak, *Canterbury Cathedral* (cit. in n. 42), 82.

[141] Cf. the monument of 1707 to Sir William Gore by the Fleming John Nost at Tring (Herts.), esp. in the treatment of the face, full-bottomed wig, and garlands of fruit and flowers: Esdaile, *English Church Monuments* (cit. in n. 2), pl. 115. A similar comparison can be made with the work of Francis Bird, as in Sir Orlando Gee (d. 1705), Isleworth (Middx.), Whinney, *Sculpture in Britain* (cit. in n. 2), pl. 51b.

[142] Chapter Act Book, 1711–25, fo. 181ᵛ.

[143] It was moved before the publication of Cowper's *Memorial Inscriptions* (cit. in n. 5) in 1897.

[144] Museo Nazionale, Florence. One of the earliest female busts *en négligée* is John Bushnell's monument to Mrs Pepys (d. 1669) at St Olave's, Hart Street, London. The formula was much used by the Italian sculptor Gianbattista Guelfi, who came to England in about 1715—as in his monument to Anne,

Duchess of Richmond (d. 1734), at Deene (Northants.).

[145] As in the monument to Dr Edward Tyson (d. 1708), All Hallows, Twickenham; Whinney, *Sculpture in Britain* (cit. in n. 2), pl. 51a.

[146] Hovenden records the burial of the Hon. Francis Godfrey and notes that in the Register of Affidavits is added 'buried in linnen and five pound paid to the poor, according to the Act of Parliament'.

[147] Physick, *Designs for English Sculpture* (cit. in n. 124), 46–7, figs. 21 and 22.

[148] Low-relief panels of palms and olive branches appear in the side panels of the altar chest on the monument to Sir Richard Alibon (d. 1688) at Dagenham (Essex); Sir Joseph Child (d. 1699) at Wanstead (Essex); and in the signed monument to John Digby, Earl of Bristol (d. 1698) in Sherborne Abbey. See Courtauld Institute of Art, Conway Library coll., where all are attributed to Nost.

by Dart, to Frances, wife of the Revd Samuel Holcombe, who died in 1725 of a long and painful disease, as the Latin epitaph tells us.

The great stylistic development in monumental sculpture in the eighteenth century is not represented at Canterbury, save in one monument. There are no works by Schee-makers, Roubiliac, Wilton, Cheere, or Nollekens. The only monument of the period is that to John Sympson (d. 1748) by the Flemish-born Michael Rysbrack (Pl. 145), the foremost sculptor of the previous 30 years. Sympson's father had been a merchant of Canterbury, and his uncle was mayor in 1667. Before that, the Sympsons had lived in the Precincts. John Sympson's great-grandfather Nicholas had become a canon in 1581, as had his grand-father John in 1614. The monument epitomizes the links between Chapter and town, and the inherent stability of these communities over a period of 160 years and four generations. The monument is at once a witness to an innate respect for family longevity, as well as being symbolic of the end of a line. John Sympson died heirless, his two daughters, Catherine and Mary, who were also buried in the Cathedral, having died in infancy.[149]

Leave was given to Mrs Sympson in the St Catharine's Chapter of 1750 'to erect a monument for her late Husband John Sympson Esq[r] against the South Side of the Body of our Church upon her paying Ten pounds Ten shillings tolls for such leave, and Making good all Damage thereby done. nor breaking into the wall of our said Church. Such monument to be according the plan thereof exhibited to us. the Inscription to be first approved by the Dean.'[150] This is one of the most specific entries relating to a monument in the Chapter Acts. It is very precise, indicating the extremely high cost of permission, and the extent of the control exercised by the Dean and Chapter over the care of the fabric of the church, the appearance of the monument, and the wording of its inscription.

Sympson's is the first signed monument in the Cathedral, and is dated 1752.[151] It is characteristic of Rysbrack's work of the early 1750s, in which the artist presents the cherubs or putti not merely as supporters, but as the main subject. The seated putto made its appearance in Rysbrack's work as early as 1730, on the monument to Sir Godfrey Kneller,[152] and later on the monument to the fourth Duke of Beaufort at Badminton, of 1754–6.[153] The standing putto holding an encircled serpent, emblem of eternity, appears first as one of a pair on the monument to Harriet Bouverie at Coleshill (Berks.), about 1751,[154] and again in 1753 on the monument to the Revd Thomas Busby (d. 1725) and his wife Ann, at Addington (Bucks.).[155] The broken column, which appears at Canterbury and on the Busby monument, has both a biblical and a classical significance, but more particularly signifies the extinction of an ancient line. It was first used by Rysbrack on the monu-ment to Sir Chaloner Ogle, of about 1751, at Twickenham parish church, and indeed

[149] The former in 1732 and the latter in 1734, when John Sympson is described as of St Stephen's: *Register Booke*, ed. Hovenden (cit. in n. 7).

[150] Chapter Act Book, 1746–60, fo. 61[v].

[151] It has never been illustrated before and is recorded by Webb as merely a 'Monument, wall tablet': M. Webb, *Michael Rysbrack, Sculptor* (London, 1954), 225.

[152] Ibid., fig. 8, pp. 43, 218

[153] K. Eustace, *Michael Rysbrack, Sculptor 1694–1770*, exhib. cat.

(Bristol, 1982), no. 71, fig. 47.

[154] The design is dated on the reverse '1750': Victoria and Albert Museum, Dept. of Prints and Drawings, E. 448–1946/3. Physick, *Designs for English Sculpture* (cit. in n. 124), 33, fig. 14; Webb, *Rysbrack* (cit. in n. 151), 176.

[155] A design for this monument, signed and dated 1753, sur-vives in the Victoria and Albert Museum, Dept. of Prints and Drawings, no. 4235; Physick, *Designs for English Sculpture* (cit. in n. 124), 86–7, fig. 55; Eustace, *Rysbrack* (cit. in n. 153), cat. no. 35.

Rysbrack has been credited with its reintroduction to the repertory of the symbols of mortality.[156]

The Sympson monument has a typically Rysbrackian box-plinth or base with characteristic egg-and-dart moulding under the upper ledge, and acanthus-leaf pattern along the skirting. The two putti were executed separately and put together at the time of setting up the monument. The unifying pyramidal backdrop has been considered a hallmark of Rysbrack's work, whose ubiquity drew censure from Horace Walpole.[157] It did, however, have the beneficial effect of providing a necessary foil to the often distracting surroundings of these monuments.

Ironically, the finest eighteenth-century monument which can be associated with Canterbury is not in the Cathedral but at Sowerby in Yorkshire. It is by Joseph Wilton and commemorates Archbishop Tillotson (d. 1694), and was erected by George Stansfield at Tillotson's place of birth to mark his centenary, in 1796.[158] The dearth of eighteenth-century monuments may be a reflection of Canterbury's relative obscurity during this period. Thus, one finds the Dean and Chapter devoting time to housekeeping, restoring the fabric, tidying up, and giving permission for the setting-up of some unimportant wall-tablets. One, to the Huguenot Maria le Geyt, signed by John Coles the Younger of London, was erected in 1795. Another, to the Revd William Gregory (d. 1803), a plain inscription-tablet signed by John Hacker, is the first definite example of the work of a local funerary mason at Canterbury.[159]

THE NINETEENTH CENTURY

The Advent of Neo-Classicism

The wall-tablet to Thomas Lawrence (1711–83), erected in 1806 in the north aisle, marks a turning-point and heralds the dramatic increase in the number of memorials which went up in the Cathedral aisles in the first half of the nineteenth century. The tablet, which was designed by John Flaxman RA (1755–1826), was in the vanguard of taste, and its formula, of inscription tablet and low-relief profile portrait, was to remain in use for the next 150 years.

Dr Lawrence was President of the College of Physicians, and was both friend of, and physician to, Dr Johnson. He appears to have had no other connection with Canterbury than that of retiring there to die, and was buried in St Margaret's parish church. This in itself created a precedent for the erection of cenotaphs in the Cathedral.

Like that to the other distinguished metropolitan visitor Orlando Gibbons, Lawrence's monument is well documented.[160] An entry in Flaxman's account-book for 26 July 1805 records payment of £20 by Mr Justice Lawrence of Bedford Square on account for the

[156] Kemp, *English Church Monuments* (cit. in n. 42), 180.
[157] H. Walpole, *Anecdotes of Painting in England*, ed. R. N. Wornum (3 vols.; London, 1849), iii. 754.
[158] Physick, *Designs for English Sculpture* (cit. in n. 124), 138–9, figs. 102 and 103.
[159] His work can be found in parish churches in Kent and elsewhere, and he later described himself as 'of Canterbury and London': Gunnis, *Dictionary* (cit. in n. 2).
[160] It is signed on the upper right edge: FLAXMAN R.A. Sculptor.

monument which was to cost 80 guineas. The entry is instructive because it informs us that the price is exclusive of setting-up the monument, and an entry the following year (19 May 1806) lists carriage, cartage, cramps, and two cases, adding a further £11 6s. 8d. to the bill.[161] A design exists for the work, which is the purest expression of neo-classicism in the Cathedral.[162] The medallion portrait of a head in profile is flanked by the emblem of Aesculapius and a sprig of myrtle in low relief, which in its simplicity of presentation, directness, and lack of rhetoric conforms with Flaxman's view of the Antique.[163]

The seventeenth and eighteenth centuries present a picture of a rather static society of local connections and local occupations. With the nineteenth century, however, came a marked change and a proliferation of types of commemorative monument. One of the main factors was undoubtedly the establishment of Canterbury as a garrison town. For the next half-century the names of serving officers join the list of infants, widows, and residents of the Precincts in the burial register.

Military monuments were to predominate for the next hundred years and soon begin to fill the hitherto almost empty nave aisles.[164] The earliest of these is the high-relief monument in the south aisle to Lieut.-Col. John Stuart of the 9th Regiment of Infantry, who was killed at the battle of Rolera on 17 August 1808. This monument, signed by Peter Turnerelli (1774–1839), is one of the earliest modern military monuments (Pl. 146). It is modern in two senses:[165] it is both an early example of a regimental, as opposed to a family, commemoration; and it is modern in the sense of presenting the deceased in contemporary military dress, rather than in some approximation of classical armour.

The issue of contemporary military dress had been raised as early as 1771, when Benjamin West painted *The Death of Wolfe* as the contemporary event it was. Sculptors, however, were slower to tackle the problem.[166] As late as 1807, Robert Southey commented: 'The artists know not what to do with their villainous costume, and, to avoid uniforms in marble, make their unhappy statues half naked.'[167] Turnerelli, acting on Benjamin West's advice, produced an accepted mixture of allegory, realism, and sentiment, and created a form of patriotic secularism. The classical goddess of war, Athene or Minerva, becomes Britannia, the 'Genius of Britain',[168] with the Union Flag on her shield and the lion crest on her helmet. The intention is exemplary, as is made plain by the inscription, which, significantly, is in English.

Turnerelli, who was born in Dublin and became Sculptor-in-Ordinary to the royal family, had a considerable contemporary reputation, but one which has suffered subsequently. Mrs Esdaile, in writing of the monuments of the military heroes of the Peninsula

[161] BL, Add. MS 39784 B.B., pub. in E. Croft-Murray, 'An Account-Book of John Flaxman RA', *Walpole Society,* 28 (1939–40), 51–95.

[162] Victoria and Albert Museum, Dept. of Prints and Drawings, Ionides Collection, C. A. I. 1086.

[163] It appears to relate to his design for the prize medal of the Lyceum Medicum, London, of 1785. D. Bindman, *John Flaxman RA,* exhib. cat., Royal Academy of Arts (London, 1979), 28–32, 136, and cat. no. 168.

[164] In 1800 there were only four 17th-cent. monuments (Saravia, Colfe, Boys, and Gibbons) in the north aisle, and one

(Berkeley) in the south aisle.

[165] The monument is signed on the lower right soffit: Turnerelli / Fecit / London.

[166] Joseph Wilton had presented Wolfe as a Roman general in the 1760s, while on the monument erected in Westminster Abbey in 1772, the effigy of Wolfe wears no clothes to speak of, his uniform appearing in the background.

[167] R. Southey, *Letters from England of Don Alvarez Espriella* (London, 1807), quoted in D. Irwin, *John Flaxman 1755–1826, Sculptor, Illustrator, Designer* (London, 1979), 161.

[168] Britton, *History and Antiquities* (cit. in n. 3), 71.

war, speaks 'of the lamentable failures of Flaxman, Rossi, Hopper, Chantrey and the rest',[169] while Newman has dismissed this very monument as 'Minerva attending a soldier with a headache'.[170] However, the formula espoused by Turnerelli and evolved elsewhere by Flaxman, proved popular at Canterbury for another forty years.

The monument in the south aisle to the 13th Prince Albert's Light Infantry (Pl. 147), erected c.1843, is signed by Flaxman's brother-in-law Thomas Denman (1787–1848).[171] Denman worked in Flaxman's studio, and completed the commissions that were left after Flaxman's death in 1826. Denman produced a great number of wall-tablets, many of them based, as is this one, on a Flaxman design: like caryatids, a pair of mourning figures in high relief flank the inscription tablet, with a trophy of regimental colours and medals above the architrave.[172] It is the first in the Cathedral to commemorate the collective members of a regiment, the commissioned officers being individually named with '12 Serjeants, 11 Corporals, 3 Buglers and 264 Privates' who perished in or as a result of the Afghan campaign of 1838–42 in engagements at 'Cabul, Ghuznee and Jellalabad'.

One particular campaign against the Sikhs, that of the Sutlej of 1845–6, produced three monuments. The wall-plaque in the north aisle was erected to the officers and men of the 31st Regiment of Infantry who fell at Moodkee and at Ferozeshah in December 1845 (Pl. 148), as well as to 'Ensigns Tritton and Jones killed while carrying the Colours at Sobroan' on 10 February 1846. The simple inscription-tablet, with low-relief military trophies, also informs us that 203 non-commissioned officers and men fell in battles, of which the last, Aliwal, 'concluded the conquest of the British over the Sikhs in the campaign of the Sutlej'. It is signed and dated 'E. Richardson, Sculptor, London 1848'. Richardson was also responsible for the monument in the south aisle to the 16th Queen's Lancers.[173] This was erected by 'their surviving comrades', and all ranks were listed on a pair of broken columns, while in high relief a soldier offers a wounded comrade a water-bottle, a gesture no doubt intended to evoke Sir Philip Sidney. A palm tree suggests foreign parts, while a Saracen helmet on the ground indicates a vanquished foe (Pl. 149). The whole design is still very much in the neo-classical idiom, with an added narrative element similar to that on military trophies and regimental silver of the period.

Despite a Royal Academy Schools training and the recommendation of Sir Francis Chantrey, Edward Richardson (1812–69) was held in some contempt by his contemporaries. Augustus Hare accused him of being a charlatan, while in 1844 the art critic of the *Literary Gazette* described his statue of John Gower in Westminster Hall as 'an abortion'.[174] *The Builder*, when commenting on Richardson's two monuments for Canterbury, felt 'bound to say the designs ought to have been very different in character for the proposed situation'.[175] Almost twenty years later, however, regiments still favoured Richardson as a designer, as the 101st Royal Bengal Fusiliers proposed him in 1866 for a monument which, in the event, did not receive the approval of the Dean and Chapter.

[169] Esdaile, *English Church Monuments* (cit. in n. 2), 103.
[170] Newman, *North East and East Kent* (cit. in n. 20), 214.
[171] On the right soffit: Denman / Sculp / Regent St / London.
[172] See the design for the monument to Admiral Sir Charles Thompson, reprod. in Irwin, *John Flaxman* (cit. in n. 167), Fig. 227.
[173] Signed and dated on right-hand lower edge: Edwd Richardson / Sculptor / London 1848.
[174] Quoted in Gunnis, *Dictionary* (cit. in n. 2).
[175] Ibid.

The third monument to the Sutlej campaign was erected in 1848, in the north aisle, by the officers of the 50th Regiment, the Queen's Own. It is signed by George Nelson (1810–88), and an inscription informs us that it is 'from a sketch by the late M. L. Watson'. This stated link between design and execution is so rare as to be almost unique.[176] Musgrave Lewthwaite Watson (1804–47) had died the previous year, leaving a number of clay models in his studio, to be executed in marble by his assistant.[177] Nelson exhibited a model for this monument at the Great Exhibition in 1851.[178] The design, with its robust figure of Peace or Fame, is more akin to the new classicism associated with the French Second Empire, a style that was not to find general favour for English church monuments.

During the same period, numerous small-scale inscription-tablets to individuals were set up in the nave aisles and elsewhere in the Cathedral. Most of these were the output of commercially organized funerary masons, and not all of them can be recorded here. That to George Fraser (d. 1813) is a typical example of the very large number of funerary monuments by John Bacon the Younger (1777–1859), whom Gunnis blamed for 'the mass-produced memorials' which by the middle of the nineteenth century 'had become so lamentable and frequent a blot on the wall of aisle and chancel'.[179] The wall-tablet in the north aisle to Major Robert-Macpherson Cairnes of the Royal Horse Artillery, who fell at Waterloo, is signed by Thomas Longley (*fl.* 1802–45) and Robert and Mary Rushbrooke. The two latter may have designed it,[180] for certainly it is not to a standard formula. An oval shield on a grey marble plaque rests on a heap of cannon-balls, while the soffits are the mouths of a pair of marble cannons. Longley, who had succeeded Thomas White as Master Mason to the Cathedral in 1802, is credited by Gunnis with being 'the best of the nineteenth-century Canterbury statuaries'.[181]

Longley signed other wall-plaques in the Cathedral, three of them also in the north aisle: that to Robert Chisholm (d. 1838), physician in the Kent and Canterbury Hospital,[182] and the wall-tablet to Lieut. Henry Boswell Bennett of the 45th Regiment (Pl. 148). Bennett was killed in Blean Wood during the 'Courtenay Riots', or 'The Last Peasants' Revolt', on 31 May 1838.[183]

A simpler tablet, to the memory of Lieut.-Gen. Sir William Inglis KCB, of the 57th Regiment (Pl. 148), who died in 1835, is also signed by Longley, and set in so carefully symmetrical an arrangement on the wall in relation to the monuments to Bennett and the 31st Regiment that one suspects Longley as Master Mason of being responsible for supervision of the installation of the memorials. In the south aisle the plain inscription-tablet to Lieut.-Gen. Charles Cyril Taylor (d. 1845) is a late work by John Ely Hinchliff (1777–1867), for he retired in 1847. Hinchliff had entered Flaxman's studio in 1806, and for the last twenty years of Flaxman's life was his 'most faithful, devoted and confidential assistant'.[184]

[176] The word 'sketch' does not distinguish here between drawing and clay model.

[177] It is recorded that as he lay dying, Watson had all the models brought into his sick-room, and nearly all of them were smashed on his instructions: B. Read, *Victorian Sculpture* (Over Wallop, Hants, 1982), 32.

[178] Gunnis, *Dictionary* (cit. in n. 2).

[179] Ibid.

[180] Ibid.

[181] Ibid.

[182] Signed: Longley Fecit New Road / Cant.[y]

[183] J. P. Entract, 'Henry Boswell Bennett: A Victim of the Last Peasants' Revolt, 1838', *Jnl. Soc. for Army Hist. Research*, 44 (1966), 14–18.

[184] Gunnis, *Dictionary* (cit. in n. 2).

The Mid-Nineteenth Century

Those forty years represent the full extent of Flaxman's influence. A sea change in taste had occurred, and although its roots can be found in Flaxman, it gathered momentum to become the full-blown Gothic Revival of the mid-nineteenth century, which was seen as a return from pagan classicism to 'the true style'.[185] The public debate had begun with A. W. N. Pugin's *The True Principles of Pointed or Christian Architecture* of 1841, followed two years later by his *Apology for the Revival of Christian Architecture in England.* It coincided with the emergence of a powerful reformist movement within the Anglican Church, whose impetus had its origins in Oxford and Cambridge. At Cambridge, in particular, the movement was identified with the Gothic Revival, while the Oxford Movement, as Mrs Esdaile pointed out, was quite simply hostile to monuments.[186] In 1839 the Camden Society was founded expressly to 'promote the study of Ecclesiastical Architecture and the restoration of mutilated architectural remains'.[187] Ten years later the foundation of the Ecclesiological Society provided a platform for A. J. B. Beresford Hope, whose numerous pamphlets and writings in the journal *The Ecclesiologist* were to dominate the aesthetic debate for the next half-century.

At Canterbury the appointment as successive deans of two Cambridge men, both of Trinity College, cannot be ignored. William Rowe Lyall became Dean in 1845, and in 1846 William Butterfield, who was to be the Ecclesiologists' preferred architect,[188] was engaged to design the choir pulpit. Lyall was succeeded in 1857 by Henry Alford, whose period of office was marked by a vigorous programme of restoration of the Cathedral fabric and of reforms of the liturgical service.

Two monuments which exemplify a transitional stage between the neo-classical and the Gothic are to be found in the south aisle. The classical three-quarter-length portrait-bust of Sir George Gipps (1791–1847) rests on a cusped ogee-ornamented socle, and the inscription tablet is flanked by a pair of panels of similar Gothic ornament (Pl. 151). Is it a coincidence or a conscious attempt to empathize with the architectural setting? Its sculptor, the Canterbury-born Henry Weekes RA (1807–77), would have been more familiar than most London-based sculptors with the Cathedral's architecture. While not strictly speaking a military monument, it is clearly one to a son of Kent who gained honour in the public service of his country.

Gipps was born at Ringwould, near Dover, where his father was rector, and was educated at the King's School. He fought in Wellington's campaigns against Napoleon, and, having been commissioner in Canada, went out to govern New South Wales in 1836, whence he returned in ill health in 1846. He retired to Canterbury, where he died the following year and was buried in the cloister on 8 March 1847, even though, as the burial register records, he was of St Martin's parish. In 1874 his widow, Elizabeth, herself of the Kentish family of Ramsay, was buried with him in the cloister by special dispensation.

The monument is signed by Henry Weekes RA and dated 1849. Born in Canterbury, Henry Weekes was himself educated at the King's School. In 1822 he was apprenticed to

---

[185] T. S. R. Boase, *English Art, 1800–1870* (Oxford, 1959), 226.

[186] Esdaile, *English Church Monuments* (cit. in n. 2), 79.

[187] Boase, *English Art* (cit. n. 185), 237.

[188] Ibid. 242–5.

the sculptor William Behnes in London and attended the Royal Academy Schools, where he won a silver medal in 1826. He became one of Sir Francis Chantrey's assistants, and on his master's death took over the studio and completed work such as the equestrian statue to the Duke of Wellington at the Royal Exchange. Like his master, Weekes is chiefly remembered as a portrait sculptor, and in 1837 he received the royal command to execute the first portrait-bust of Queen Victoria. The most outstanding example of his portraiture, however, is the bust of the Poet Laureate Robert Southey, in Poets' Corner in Westminster Abbey.

Weekes became Professor of Sculpture at the Royal Academy Schools in 1869, retiring to Ramsgate in 1876. His *Lectures on Art* were published in 1880 and are 'the most consistent and intelligent exposition of sculptural thinking in the Victorian era and, as far as published material goes, exceptional if not unique'.[189] He had numerous Kentish patrons, among them Lords Harris, Darnley, and Winchelsea.[190] The portrait bust of Gipps exemplifies Weekes's belief that legitimate exaggerations to compensate for the lack of colour included thickening the eyelids, sharpening the brow, deep setting of the eyes, an emphasis on the lips, and hair cut deep in relation to its natural colour.[191] Other Canterbury portraits include those to Canon William Welfitt, signed and dated 1854, now placed on a window-ledge in the north aisle, and the bust of William Masters signed and dated 1833, and presented by Masters's widow to the Beaney Institute, of which he was one of the founders.

The other monument that might be said to fall on the cusp of taste, for it demonstrates a marked stylistic ambivalence, is that to Lieut.-Col. Frederick Mackeson (1807–53) of the Bengal Army and commissioner at Peshawar (Pl. 150). He died in 1853 'of a wound inflicted by a Mahometan fanatic', as the inscription informs us. This memorial is, strictly, a cenotaph, Dean Lyall and the Chapter requesting a copy of the inscription and a model of the proposed monument before giving their consent.[192] The fact that the inscription tells us that Mackeson was born in Hythe 'in this county', educated at 'the King's School of this Cathedral', and died in the service of his country, suggests that these were the factors which told in his favour.

Cowper, in his *Memorial Inscriptions*, gives Mackeson one of the longest biographical entries, recording in great detail his distinguished career in the 14th Bengal Native Infantry. He also records a monument at Peshawar, providing the words of the high-flown epitaph composed by the Governor-General, and a brass at Hythe Church. The monument was designed by John Graham Lough (1798–1876),[193] who was also responsible at Canterbury for Bishop Broughton's effigy, and combines all the residual elements of a neo-classical relief-panel: the banner-draped urn, palm tree, mourning woman, and cross-legged male figures, one of whom probably represents Ata Mahomed, chief official at Peshawar, who was wounded attempting to save Mackeson. The panel is set in an ogeed and crocketed Gothic frame.

[189] Read, *Victorian Sculpture* (cit. in n. 177), 16–17.
[190] R. Gunnis, 'Some Monuments in the Nave', *Friends of Canterbury Cathedral, 27th Annual Report* (1954), 16–18.
[191] H. Weekes, *Lectures on Art delivered at the Royal Academy*

(London, 1880), 222.
[192] Chapter Act Book, 1854–84, fo. 6.
[193] The monument is signed on the right-hand return of the frame.

The Reaction Against Monuments

The Gipps and Mackeson monuments were set up at a time when there was not only a dramatic change in taste, but also a marked reaction to the seemingly uncontrolled proliferation of monuments. Beresford Hope, writing in the *Christian Remembrancer* for 1855, in an article on 'The Future of English Cathedrals', declared that 'even at Canterbury ... several mural tablets of a wholly incongruous character have within the last few years been allowed to blister the walls of the nave'. He went on: 'Canterbury being a military station, there seems to have grown up an unfortunate idea that military monuments, subscribed for and erected by regiments to their fallen comrades ... were exempted from the scope of capitular criticism.' This public rebuke had an immediate effect, and, as is demonstrated by a series of letters which survive in the Cathedral archives, it became increasingly difficult to obtain permission to erect memorials. In 1861, Finch, the Chapter Clerk, received a letter from Charlotte M. North of Waldershare Park, Dover, hoping for the Dean and Chapter's permission for a memorial to those of her late husband's regiment, 'the Carabinieres', who had died in the Indian Mutiny. 'Can you help us in any way,' she wondered, and ended with the warmest of open invitations to visit Waldershare Park. Perhaps Finch was impervious to such blandishments; in any event, the outside of the letter is inscribed in another hand '5. Nov. 61 / No hope / D & C discourage such appls.'[194]

In 1866 Captain Longueville Clarke of the Commandery Depot, Walmer, of 101st Royal Bengal Fusiliers, wrote requesting a memorial to those killed in the Mubeylla Pass in 1863 and 1864. He had already made a personal approach by calling on the Dean and Canon Robinson, and had been asked to 'put it in writing'. His letter devotes time to making clear that while the regiment is not a Kentish one, there are grounds for overlooking this, and continues: 'I shall be delighted to show you a design of the Memorial and I have this day written to Edward Richardson (who is going to erect it for us) for it, and if you will kindly let me know how much the site will cost, I shall esteem it a favour. I am rather particular about this, as being only limited to a certain sum I must first know what the cost of a site will be, before I can conclude the price of the memorial.'[195] Chapter Acts record the refusal of this application on 23 May 1866.[196]

There were probably two tactical errors in this approach, one being the use of a sculptor whose work was now regarded by the avant-garde as being no better than a blister, and the other being the suggestion that funds were limited, never very convincing in this sort of appeal. In the Chapter meeting of 17 September the following year, an application from Lieut.-Col. Crawley of the Inniskilling Dragoons for permission to place a monument to his late wife without payment of the usual fees was not entertained.[197]

The influence of Beresford Hope, combined with Alford's restoration programme, had, however, a very positive effect. In 1861 Beresford Hope published *The English Cathedral of the Nineteenth Century*, in which he wrote: 'For some years there has been a strong movement in favour of memorial windows in preference to mason's tablets ... it has done incalculable

[194] Fabric, X, 6–12.
[195] Ibid.
[196] Chapter Act Book, 1854–84, fo. 211.
[197] Ibid., fo. 237.

good in what it has checked . . . and in what it has produced, namely the general restoration of painted glass throughout our churches.'[198]

In Canterbury the Dean and Chapter led the way, and Dean Alford himself set an example in 1858, when two windows in the south-east transept were filled with panelled glass designed by George Austin, in memory of two of the Dean's children.[199] In the same year, Archdeacon Croft's daughter Mrs H. C. Kingsford was given permission to place a painted window in memory of her late husband in the Cathedral,[200] while in the following year Chapter agreed to a memorial window in the north-east transept 'in memory of our late brother Mr. Chesshyre'.[201] This was designed and made by Hardman of Birmingham, but has not survived.

A definite policy emerged of favouring stained-glass memorials as opposed to wall-monuments, and Chapter Acts record an increasing volume of requests for memorial windows. A letter dated 21 May 1860 to the Chapter Clerk from Leonard Sidebottom of Chatham points out that the 3rd Regiment is 'peculiarly belonging to the locality in which your Cathedral stands—the 3d are the *East Kent* Regiment and are always accustomed on that account to feel themselves allied in a particular manner to that County, and to look upon Canterbury Cathedral as the receptacle for their memorials'.[202] On 22 October he wrote a reminder, though oddly enough the matter had been presented at the Midsummer Chapter of 1860, and agreed 'upon the usual condition that it is first submitted to and approved by the Dean and Canons in Residence'.[203] Finally, on 29 November 1860 Sidebottom writes thanking the Dean and Chapter on behalf of the officers of the 3rd Regiment, and adds 'the design contemplated shall be forwarded as desired, for approval'.[204] Nowhere in this correspondence is the type of memorial described, but in fact it refers to the stained glass in the east window of St Michael's Chapel set up in 1862 by O'Connor of Birmingham.[205] This memorial to those officers and men of the East Kent Regiment who fell in the Crimean War is the first of those which came to give the chapel its soubriquet of 'The Buffs' Chapel'.[206] The window was destroyed in air raids in 1942, and was replaced in 1952 by the present heraldic window designed by William Wilson of Edinburgh.[207]

In 1865 the Chapter again deflected regimental aspirations and funds towards installing new stained-glass windows. A letter dated 17 April from Henry Castle, Major of the East Kent Militia,[208] requested permission to erect a tablet 'probably in the shape of a Monumental Brass in the Nave of the Cathedral, in memory of their late Colonel George

[198] A. J. B. Beresford Hope, *The English Cathedral of the Nineteenth Century* (London, 1861), 254.

[199] Chapter Act Book, 1854–84, fo. 77.

[200] Ibid., fo. 75.

[201] Ibid., fo. 93; Woodruff and Danks, *Memorials*, 435–8.

[202] Fabric, X, 6–12.

[203] Chapter Act Book, 1854–84, fo. 110.

[204] Fabric, X, 6–12.

[205] Woodruff and Danks, *Memorials*, 436.

[206] The 3rd Regiment, or The Buffs, appears in the first official list in 1751, and was affiliated to East Kent on 31 Aug. 1782. The title 'The Buffs (Royal East Kent Regiment)' was conferred by King George V in 1935. In 1961 they were amalgamated with The Queen's Own Royal West Kent Regiment, to become The Queen's Own Buffs, The Royal Kent Regiment: *Guide to the Museum of the Buffs* (Canterbury, n.d.); see also Tomlinson, *The Warriors' Chapel and the Buffs* (cit. in n. 109).

[207] It displays the coats of arms of the colonels of the regiment, and of the cities of London and Canterbury. It was unveiled on 10 May 1952 by the Col.-in-C. of The Buffs, King Frederick IX of Denmark. M. Babington, *The Romance of Canterbury Cathedral* (10th edn.; 1952), 76; Tomlinson, *The Warriors' Chapel and the Buffs* (cit. in n. 109).

[208] The East Kent Militia was absorbed into the East Kent Regiment, the Buffs, on 1 July 1881.

Brockman ... The Memorial would be of the value of £130, and we should be happy to lay the design before you, for approval before making any final selection ourselves.'[209] Major Castle's application was referred to the Dean and Canons in Residence.[210] In the event, the memorial was not to be a monumental brass but a window by Messrs Clayton and Bell for the south-east window of St Michael's Chapel.[211]

When Dean Alford died, Chapter agreed at a meeting in 1871 to a memorial window proposed by the memorial committee, under the chairmanship of the Bishop of Dover, and later ratified the choice of Clayton and Bell as the manufacturers. The wording of the minutes suggests that a design had been presented, which was eventually put up in the south windows of the south-east transept.[212] The policy of encouraging stained-glass memorials continued, though after Alford's death the numerous memorial windows were more often than not to members of Chapter and their families, Dean Stanley, Dean Farrar, and Canon Ellison, among others.[213]

There is some evidence of backsliding in favour of traditional memorials. In 1875 Chapter agreed 'to offer' the 16th Lancers 'an empty space on the wall', and remitted the fees.[214] When an application was received from the Buffs in 1881, however, Chapter declared that 'no sculptural designs could be put up unless our approval was previously obtained ... but that a tablet with names would be approved'.[215] At the Midsummer Chapter, consent was given to a memorial, though Chapter 'would prefer the omission of the figures on the design submitted'. The objection would not be pressed, it was promised, if the 'regiment strongly wished the figures to remain'.[216]

This may explain the unusual feelings expressed in unprecedented comments in Chapter Minutes on two subsequent occasions. In August 1882, Chapter agreed to a memorial window on the west side of the south transept, provided that Messrs Clayton and Bell were responsible for the work. The following March 'the hearty thanks' of the Dean and Chapter to L. L. Pemberton and the officers and men of the East Kent Rifles were placed on record for 'the very beautiful window' in memory of their colonel, the Marquis of Conyngham.[217] In July 1889 the 'proposed monument to Mr. Dyson' was agreed, with the proviso that this work also was executed by Messrs Clayton and Bell. Lieut. R. G. Dyson of the 3rd Dragoon Guards, and late of Denne Hill, had died in India on 12 January 1888. Two years later Chapter placed on record their sense 'of the great beauty of the window which both in colour and in grouping bears comparison with the very ancient and famous windows in its neighbourhood'.[218] This window and its inscription survives in the Trinity Chapel north ambulatory, above the screen of Henry IV's chantry chapel, but many of these memorial windows were destroyed in the Second World War. Some of the dedication inscriptions survive either under plain replaced windows, as that to Henry Kingsford (d. 1857) in the north aisle, or incongruously under modern glass, as in the south-east transept, where Dean Alford's widow is remembered in a dedication of 1878 under windows designed by Erwin Bossanyi in the 1950s.

[209] Fabric, X, 6–12.
[210] Chapter Act Book, 1854–84, fo. 186.
[211] Woodruff and Danks, *Memorials*, 436.
[212] Chapter Act Book, 1854–84, fo. 275, 287.
[213] Woodruff & Danks, *Memorials*, 435–8.
[214] Chapter Act Book, 1854–84, fo. 338.
[215] Ibid., fo. 443.
[216] Ibid., fo. 445.
[217] Ibid., fos. 439, 464, 466, 474.
[218] Ibid., 1884–95, fos. 80, 86, 140.

The Revival of the Recumbent Effigy

The views of Beresford Hope and the Ecclesiologists were to find a third sphere of influence relating to funerary memorials in the encouragement of a return to 'the Gothic tomb'. As Beresford Hope expressed it, 'what monument is so beautiful in form and so satisfactory in sentiment?' He considered the recumbent effigy most suitable for cathedrals, and declared that it would 'always continue lord of the ascendant'. At Canterbury, he singled out for praise those 'high tombs with recumbent effigies of Archbishop Howley, Bishop Broughton, and Dean Lyall'.[219]

Archbishop Howley (1766–1848) was educated at Winchester and New College, Oxford, becoming a canon of Christ Church in 1804 and Regius Professor of Divinity at Oxford in 1809. Consecrated Bishop of London in 1813, he was translated to Canterbury in 1828. It was he who announced to Queen Victoria her accession to the throne, who crowned her, and married her to Prince Albert. He was a leading figure in the work of Church reform which culminated in the setting up of the Ecclesiastical Commission. When he died, in 1848, he was buried, as so many archbishops before him, at Addington (where the archbishops owned a country house), and it has been suggested that the monument now at Canterbury was originally designed for Addington.[220] There is, however, internal evidence in the design and location of the monument which suggests that the siting at Canterbury was a conscious decision from the outset. Certainly, having the monument set up at Canterbury broke with the old tradition and created a new one, for it was the first to an archbishop to be placed in the Cathedral since the Reformation.

The effigy (Pl. 152) was the work of the sculptor Richard Westmacott the Younger RA (1799–1872), himself a member of a dynasty of sculptors, who succeeded his father as Professor of Sculpture at the Royal Academy Schools in 1857. It is perhaps significant that of sixteen monuments recorded as his work by Gunnis, after 1842 half are of recumbent effigies.[221] However, Gunnis thought Westmacott was probably given little scope in the commission 'and was merely ordered to produce a monument based on the tombs of mediaeval bishops, which it was thought would harmonize with the Cathedral'.[222] The effigy and tomb-chest were set into the Eastry screen to the north choir aisle, between Archbishops Chichele and Bourchier, in direct emulation of pre-Reformation archbishops. A preliminary design exists in the Austin Sketch-book,[223] perhaps by George Austin senior, who died in 1848, or by his son H. G. Austin, who succeeded him as Architect and Surveyor of the Cathedral. For the greater part of the nineteenth century, three generations of Austins were responsible for the restoration work and designs for furnishings, including the stained glass of the Cathedral.[224] The employment of architects in the design and siting

---

[219] Beresford Hope, *The English Cathedral* (cit. in n. 198), 254–5.

[220] R. J. King, *Handbook to the Cathedrals of England, Southern Division* (2nd edn.; London, 1876), 413.

[221] Sketch-books show Westmacott observing Gothic detail and a number of recumbent effigies here and in Italy: Courtauld Institute of Art, Conway Library photographs.

[222] Gunnis, 'Some Monuments in the Nave' (cit. in n. 190). The effigy wears a cope but, despite the suggestion of one in

Austin's sketch, no mitre. It lies on a rolled rush mat, in the manner of 17th-cent. effigies.

[223] Add. MS 210. Newman describes the open canopy as 'Dec., not Perp.': *North East and East Kent* (cit. in n. 20), 206. The leaf-ornament imitated that in the reveals of the west window in the south-west transept.

[224] A design for a brass inscription-plate for George Austin is among those in the sketch-book. H. G. Austin retired in 1889: Chapter Act Book, 1884–95, fo. 81.

of monuments came about as a result of the growing awareness of the importance of the fabric.[225] Sculptors would be commissioned for the effigy of the deceased, but architects would design the setting. The canopy of the Howley monument is less ornate than the surviving design. The leaf-ornament and, in particular, the four pendant bosses demonstrate a virtuoso skill in the articulation of oak leaves, to create a hollow sphere reminiscent of the leaf-ornament in the chapter house at Southwell Minister. This comparison is supported by other designs in the Austin Sketch-book, particularly that for Canon Lockwood, who died in 1851, where the rich ivy-leaf fringe embraces the trefoil-headed blind arcading in one sketch, and in another extends above, in a manner reminiscent once again of the sedilia in the chapter house at Southwell.

Howley's recumbent effigy was joined, in 1855, by that of William Grant Broughton, Bishop of Sydney (1788–1853) (Pl. 153). Broughton was not from Kent, but had three connections with Canterbury. He was educated at the King's School; his wife, Sarah, was the daughter of the Revd John Francis, Second Master at the school; and he was a friend and neighbour in London of the widow of his school contemporary Sir George Gipps.[226] He owed his preferment to the Duke of Wellington, who sent him to be Archdeacon of New South Wales and Van Diemen's Land. He became Bishop of Australia in 1836 and was nominated Metropolitan of Australia in 1847. His wife died in Sydney in 1849. He was one of the last people to be buried in the Cathedral. The effigy was the work of John Graham Lough (1806–76), and is signed and dated at the head.[227] The alabaster figure of the deceased rests on a cushion and mattress, eyes open, one hand resting on his chest, the other on a book. He wears a rochet or surplice, and his feet are draped in a manner akin to that of early seventeenth-century effigies. The Latin inscription around the tomb-chest is in late-Gothic script, while the six angelic figures which bear the arms of the six Australian sees were probably designed by H. G. Austin. The leaf-ornament beneath the windows above the monument is similar to that on Archbishop Howley's monument.

Lough trained in his native Northumberland as a stonemason. In 1826 he entered the Royal Academy Schools, and, like Henry Weekes, he worked in William Behnes's studio. He was in Italy from 1835 to 1839. His work was the subject of extremes of opinion during his lifetime, the *Literary Gazette* being excessive in its praise, while the *Art Journal* was outspokenly offensive.[228] Other recumbent effigies by him include those to the poet Robert Southey at Crosthwaite, Cumberland, of 1846, and Dr Gilly at Norham in Northumberland, of 1857.

On the other side of the nave in the north aisle is the third recumbent effigy singled out for praise by Beresford Hope, that to Dean Lyall (Pl. 154). William Rowe Lyall (1788–1857) had been appointed the first Archdeacon of Maidstone and a canon of Canterbury in 1841. He became Dean in 1845. As we have seen, he was the first of the reforming deans whose aesthetic judgements dominated the decisions of Chapter. His monument cost between £400 and £500, and the tomb-chest and canopy were designed by H. G. Austin, and

[225] There is a parallel at York Minster: *A History of York Minster*, ed. G. E. Aylmer and R. Cant (Oxford, 1977), 470, 485, and pl. 166.

[226] *Register Booke*, ed. Hovenden (cit. in n. 7).
[227] J. G. Lough Fec' / 1855.
[228] Gunnis, *Dictionary* (cit. in n. 2).

executed in Caen stone. The effigy, its hands clasped in prayer, is said to be after a model by John Birnie Philip (1824–75),[229] one of the most successful sculptors of the day. Philip had a large practice of individual commissions,[230] and worked extensively for Sir George Gilbert Scott, most notably on the Albert Memorial in Kensington Gardens, and at Salisbury and Lichfield. Chapter Acts record permission to erect the monument in 1857, and orders were given for raising the canopy two years later.[231]

When Archbishop Sumner died, in 1862, his monument continued the now well-established pattern of tomb-chest and recumbent effigy. John Bird Sumner had gained a scholarship to King's College, Cambridge, in 1798, and later became a Fellow. In 1828 he became bishop of Chester, and succeeded Howley as archbishop in 1848. Since he was buried, like Howley before him, at Addington, the memorial is a cenotaph. The effigy, by Weekes, is stylistically a very close parallel to that by Westmacott on the Howley monument; both effigies wear a cope and there is the minimum emphasis on drapery folds. Gunnis felt that like Westmacott, Weekes may have been 'fettered by those who ordered the monument'.[232]

Archbishop Longley (d. 1868) was commemorated only by a simple wall-tablet in the north aisle. The next great monument, therefore, was to Archbishop Tait (1811–82) (Pl. 155). This was the subject of a controversy in which Beresford Hope intervened personally. Born in Edinburgh, Tait was an undergraduate and then Fellow and Tutor of Balliol College, Oxford, until in 1842 he succeeded Dr Arnold as Headmaster of Rugby School. He became archbishop on Sumner's death, in 1862. Tait died in 1882, and was buried at Addington, where he is commemorated with five other archbishops by a standing cross in the churchyard.[233]

There was considerable delay in the decision over the type of commemorative memorial to be set up to Tait. At a Chapter meeting in April 1883, the Dean reported the strong desire of the mayor and citizens and of the Dean and Chapter that the memorial 'should take the form of a reredos in the Cathedral instead of that of a recumbent figure'.[234] In June, the Dean of Westminster and Beresford Hope visited Canterbury with the architect John Oldrid Scott. Their preferred site was behind the Archbishop's Throne. Chapter referred the matter to the Tait Memorial's London Committee, when opinion fell into two camps as to the siting of the monument and its design. Disagreement over the latter centred on whether or not it should have a canopy. Finally, in April 1884, having disposed of the canopy, Chapter gave approval to Scott's already much-amended design 'excepting the steps', which would occupy too great a space, and recommended 'that in place of the inlaid pattern, slabs of coloured marble be used'.[235]

[229] H. Pigot, *Proc. Suffolk Inst. of Archaeology,* 3 (1863), 226.

[230] Gunnis, *Dictionary* (cit. in n. 2); Read, *Victorian Sculpture* (cit. in n. 177), 266.

[231] Chapter Act Book, 1854–84, fos. 70, 98.

[232] Gunnis, 'Monuments in the Nave' (cit. in n. 190).

[233] There is a memorial inscription to Tait in Butterfield's School Chapel at Rugby, and he is commemorated in Westminster Abbey by a portrait bust by H. H. Armistead RA in the south transept at the entrance to St Benedict's Chapel. It cost

£474 1s.: *Canterbury Diocesan Gazette,* 5 (1896–7), 247. As late as 1931 two lamps were dedicated to Tait's memory in Holy Innocents at Canterbury, at the wish of his late chaplain, Henry Maxwell Spooner: Oblation Books (U3/100), 5/16, 28 Dec. 1931.

[234] Chapter Act Book, 1854–84, fo. 477. This was reported in *The Builder,* 44 (Jan.–June 1883), 740.

[235] Chapter Act Book, 1854–84, fos. 479, 480, 485, 490, 492, 494.

Unveiled in 1885 in the north-east transept,[236] it cost £2,388 10s.[237] The tomb chest executed by William Brindley of the London firm of Farmer and Brindley, the leading architectural sculptural specialists of the day, cost £825.[238] The epitaph was written by Dr Vaughan, Dean of Llandaff,[239] and executed in gilt letters on a ground of deep-red Rosso marble. The side panels are of dark-green porphyry, the other marbles being Pavonazzo and Breccia.[240] The effigy, in Seravezza marble, was the work of Sir Joseph Edgar Boehm RA (1831–90).[241] A Viennese of Hungarian descent, Boehm had trained in Paris and Italy before coming to England in 1848. He took British nationality in 1865, became Sculptor-in-Ordinary to Queen Victoria, of whom he created the portrait head for the coinage of 1887, and was knighted in 1889. He was the most successful society sculptor of the day, but was damned with faint praise by the critics F. T. Palgrave and Edmund Gosse. Gosse declared that Boehm was by 1880 'the most successful and popular sculptor in the country', his skill resting on his abilities as a modeller, but he accused him of being 'radically prosaic without distinction or style', and spoke of his 'fashionable and extensive factory of iconic monuments'.[242]

When Boehm received the commission for the Tait effigy, he was already working on effigies of Dean Stanley for Westminster Abbey and Rugby School. Tait's is very like the Stanley effigy. Both are presented in sleep, in bands and surplice or rochet, both have the deep undercutting of drapery so characteristic of Boehm, and most particularly the manner of draping the bier is almost identical.[243] It is likely that Boehm worked from a death-mask.[244]

The controversy surrounding the commemoration of Archbishop Tait contained seeds which would come to fruition in the changes of taste and custom in the twentieth century. Meanwhile, Gothic tombs with recumbent and kneeling effigies continued to be set up to bishops and archbishops. In 1890 Edward Parry, Bishop of Dover and Archdeacon and canon of Canterbury, died. He had been born in Sydney in 1830, the eldest surviving son of Rear-Admiral Sir William Parry, the Arctic explorer. Educated at Rugby School and Balliol, he became archdeacon in 1869 and suffragan Bishop of Dover in 1870. His monument in the north aisle was unveiled by the Archbishop of Canterbury in 1891.[245] It is the work of the London-based James Forsyth (1826–1910), who specialized in ecclesiastical sculpture such as fonts and pulpits, and in recumbent memorial effigies on Gothic tomb-chests of members of the Anglican hierarchy.[246] The effigy is similar in pose to that of

[236] *The Builder*, 49 (Jul.–Dec. 1885), 563; Chapter Act Book, 1884–95, fo. 13.

[237] *Canterbury Diocesan Gazette*, 5 (1896–7), 247.

[238] It was reproduced in *The Builder* in an engraving by J. D. Cooper, from photographs assisted by the architect's drawings: 50 (Jan.–June 1886), 605–7.

[239] Chapter Act Book, 1884–95, fo. 10.

[240] *The Builder*, 50 (Jan.–June 1886), 605–7.

[241] It is signed at the foot: J. E. Boehm Fecit.

[242] *Art Journal* (1894), 200, 282.

[243] Boehm's most recent biographer has compared the drapery folds of the Stanley monument to those on Cristoforo Solari's monument to Beatrice d'Este and Ludovico il Moro of 1498 at the Certosa, Pavia: M. Stocker, 'The Church Monu-

ments of Joseph Edgar Boehm', *Church Monuments*, 3 (1988), 61–75; id., *Royalist and Realist: The Life and Work of Sir Joseph Edgar Boehm* (New York, 1988), 185–6, pls. 192–6, cat. no. 244.

[244] Boehm had executed a posthumous portrait-bust of Tait in 1883, commissioned by the Queen and now at Windsor. A death-mask was presented to the National Portrait Gallery by Archbishop Lord Davidson in 1929 (NPG 2352). The National Portrait Gallery also holds the plaster cast of the three-quarter-length bust (NPG 859). A plaster bust of Tait, inscribed 'Morton Edwards Sc. London 1867', is in the Cathedral library.

[245] *Cantuarian*, 3 (1890–4), 161.

[246] Bishop Fraser (d. 1885), Manchester Cathedral; Dean Elliot (d. 1891), Bristol Cathedral: Read, *Victorian Sculpture* (cit. in n. 177), 79, 359. Others include the signed and dated monuments to

Lough's Broughton, on the opposite side of the nave, while the treatment of the marble is akin to that of Boehm's Tait. The tomb-chest of coloured marble and alabaster has high-relief end panels, which show the Bishop in scenes of ministry confirming and teaching his flock. The frontal panel shows Christ in Majesty surrounded by the symbols of the Evangelists, flanked on either side by figures of the English saints Martin, Augustine, Alphege, and Anselm. The angels at the corners carry the arms of Dover and of the Parry family.

Archbishop Benson died in 1896. Born in 1829 in Birmingham, Edward White Benson was a graduate of Trinity College, Cambridge, and was Assistant Master of Rugby School from 1853 to 1859, when he became the first Master of the newly opened Wellington College. In 1872 he became Chancellor and canon of Lincoln, and was consecrated first Bishop of Truro in 1877. In 1882 he was translated to Canterbury. Benson was the first archbishop to be buried in the Cathedral since Cardinal Pole. Permission had been sought by the Chapter to bury him in the vault in the north-west tower which had belonged to the Austin family since before the Burial Act of 1853, which prohibited the burying of corpses within the fabric of ecclesiastical buildings. It was noted that it would not be injurious to public health, as there would be a four-inch layer of porous charcoal, and the top of the vault would be made good with a layer of concrete and a layer of Portland cement.[247] Subsequently, the family and the Dean and Chapter requested a change of Order in Council to allow Benson and all future archbishops to be buried in the Cathedral proper. It was referred to the Home Office, with a request that the custom of burying archbishops in their see be restored, as it was a rare occurrence: there had only been ninety-two archbishops in thirteen centuries, and only six since 1805.[248] On 25 February 1897 the Secretary of State, Sir Matthew Ridley, approved the transfer of Archbishop Benson's remains to a brick grave in the crypt,[249] but this was not carried out.

Benson's monument (Pl. 156), which had been set up under the north-west tower, was unveiled by HRH the Duchess of Albany at a memorial service in 1899, at which addresses were given by the Lord Chancellor and Lord Mount Edgecombe. The monument was designed by the architect Thomas Graham Jackson RA, whose first design had been amended in December 1897.[250] It consists of an altar-tomb ornamented with the enamelled coats of arms of Canterbury and Benson, surmounted by a slab of Irish black marble. The canopy, in the 'decorated style', bears a close resemblance to that of Archbishop Pecham's in the north-west transept, or Martyrdom, though the representation of the Resurrection in the pediment is an innovation. The stencilled background is ornamented with Latin inscriptions, one of which is the Benson family motto, found, with other details of the design, in a memorandum among the Archbishop's papers at his death.[251]

The effigy is by Thomas Brock RA (1847–1922).[252] Brock had trained in John Henry

James Atlay, Bishop of Hereford, 1895, and Thomas Claughton, Bishop of St Albans, of the same year, and Bishop Pelham at Norwich, in the following year.

[247] Chapter Act Book, 1895–1910, fo. 59.
[248] Ibid., fos. 63–5.
[249] Ibid., fo. 81.
[250] Ibid., fo. 108.
[251] *Canterbury Diocesan Gazette*, 7 (1898–9), 277–81.
[252] Signed and dated at the foot: T. Brock, R.A. Sculptor. 1896.

Foley's studio, and later attended the Royal Academy Schools, becoming a gold-medallist in 1869. While working on the Benson monument, he was also completing his equestrian statue of the Black Prince for City Square in the centre of Leeds. The work which crowned his career and brought him a knighthood was the Queen Victoria Memorial (1901–11), part of Aston Webb's new approach to Buckingham Palace. Critics have not been unanimous in their opinion of Brock. Accused by one of being the great plagiarist of the New Sculpture,[253] he has more kindly been credited along with Lord Leighton and Henry Foley with giving a new impetus to sculpture which was to carry it into the twentieth century.[254]

Executed in white Carrara marble, Brock's effigy of Benson was described by *The Guardian* as 'a triumph of the sculptor's art'.[255] *The Guardian* went on to describe the features of the effigy with words of the strongest approbation. The portrait likeness is almost certainly based on a death-mask, of which a plaster cast is in the Cathedral library.[256] The effigy lies awake, the head and hands well modelled, the flat figure robed in cassock, rochet, and cope, the latter being the Westminster Cope worn by Benson at the service of thanksgiving for Queen Victoria's Jubilee.

Frederick Temple (1821–1902), archbishop for ten years before his death, was buried in the cloister garth.[257] He was educated at Blundell's School and went up to Balliol on a scholarship, in 1839. His tutors included Archibald Campbell Tait, Benjamin Jowett, and Matthew Arnold. He succeeded Tait as Headmaster of Rugby School in 1857. His appointment to the see of Exeter, in 1869, was greeted with a storm of opposition on account of his association with particular theological issues. At Exeter he was able to put into practice his reformist social and educational views, and when, in 1885, he was translated to London, the clergy of the diocese, who had been so opposed to him in 1869, unanimously signed a petition of regret at his departure. His tenure of the diocese of London was also marked by reforms both clerical and social. He became archbishop in 1897. He was actively engaged in the educational controversies of the day, and his name became synonymous with the Temperance Movement. He died having been taken ill while speaking in the House of Lords in favour of Balfour's reforming Education Bill in December 1902.

The proposed monument to commemorate him was the subject of a long report from the Cathedral Architect W. D. Caröe.[258] Writing in March 1903 to Lord Stanhope, Caröe informed him that he had made a tour of the Cathedral with Mr Pomeroy. F. W. Pomeroy RA (1856–1924) was a leading figure in the New Sculpture Movement. In bringing him in at the initial stages of the scheme, Caröe showed himself to be conversant with ideas current at the time.[259]

[253] S. Beattie, *The New Sculpture* (London, 1983), 230.

[254] Read, *Victorian Sculpture* (cit. in n. 177), 386.

[255] Quoted in *Canterbury Diocesan Gazette* (cit. in n. 251).

[256] It was agreed that this 'bust' should 'be put on a stand under a glass case on the Central Desk in the Library under the West window'. Chapter Act Book, 1895–1910, fo. 353. There are also two plaster busts in the library. One is signed and dated by Albert Bruce Joy, 1896, and has suffered war damage. It is a reduced version of the lifesize plaster and bronze versions in the National Portrait Gallery (2958 & 2958a). The other is signed and dated by Richard Pinker, 1883.

[257] *DNB*; his wife, Beatrice, was buried with him in 1915.

[258] LA2.

[259] Pomeroy had expressed his own views in a paper on wood- and stone-carving, given to the Architectural Association in 1891, in which he stated that the 'sculptors' work is bound up with that of the architect . . . who should endeavour to carefully select his sculptor and given him a fairly free hand in carrying out his work'. Quoted in Beattie, *New Sculpture* (cit. in n. 253), 61.

The Cathedral tour with Pomeroy was made with two considerations in mind: the type of monument and choice of site, for 'those monuments have been most successful ... which have been designed to form an integral architectural part of the Cathedral'. Caröe goes on to consider the four possible types of figure: recumbent, throned, standing, and kneeling, and here Caröe makes a positive comparison with the tomb of Dean Wotton, 'though the figure of the Dean is itself too small'. He then considers seven sites, his own preference being clearly for a kneeling figure in the south side of the corona, where 'the lighting is all that could be desired'. He concludes: 'I have no doubt that the position at the east end of the Cathedral is the more honourable.'[260]

Caröe designed the tomb-chest and setting in gilded Cornish marble, and the fretted oak canopy.[261] He pierced the tomb-chest to make the point that the Archbishop was not buried there. Pomeroy's effigy is in bronze, so that the monument reflects the fashionable interest in mixed media and the introduction of 'colour'. which is a reflection also of the Arts and Crafts Movement. The Archbishop is presented kneeling at prayer, as in life, wearing the Coronation Cope and the Collar of the Victorian Order presented to him by Edward VII after his coronation.

Mrs Esdaile saw the Temple monument as a sign 'of a revolt against the medieval convention in our conservative ecclesiastical tombs'.[262] In a letter to Canon Macnutt in 1945, the Provost of Southwell, W. J. Conybeare, asked: 'Do you know the story of the wording of the [Temple] monument? Armitage Robinson suggested pithily "Born under the Fourth George he lived to crown the Seventh Edward." Wace objected. "You have left out Victoria." "Yes," retorted A. R., "and bad art!" However, the fuller and more clumsy inscription won the day, and there it is.'[263] This inscription, and the inscription on Temple's tombstone in the cloisters, are cut in the Lombardic script devised by the young Eric Gill (1882–1940) when he was employed in Caröe's offices.[264] As McCarthy has written: 'Caröe's Lombardic letters were of Gill's origination, and he was the person who was always chosen to draw out the inscriptions which came into the office.'[265] A recent architectural historian of the Cathedral wrote of the effigy that Pomeroy 'should be better known', but was unnecessarily censorious of 'the frenetic architectural setting'.[266]

The monument to Archbishop Temple is, in effect, the last at Canterbury on a grand scale to an individual. There was, however, to be one more recumbent monument to an Archbishop of Canterbury, which, despite the great differences of time, belongs to the series of recumbent effigies which began with Archbishop Howley's in 1848. Three minor coincidences cross the apparent historical gulf, and link it with three previous archbishops' monuments. Randall Thomas Davidson (1848–1930), then Bishop of Winchester, had

---

[260] LA2.

[261] The architect's grandson, Martin Caroe, suggested in conversation with the author that the discolouration of the wood was probably the long-term result of a particular treatment of soaking the oak in ammonia, which was employed by W. D. Caröe at the time.

[262] K. Esdaile, *English Monumental Sculpture Since the Renaissance* (London, 1927), 69. Such was the success of the Temple monument that Pomeroy and Caröe collaborated again on that

to George Ridding, first Bishop of Southwell, who died in 1904. Also of a kneeling figure, the composition, unconstrained by a Gothic setting, gives full rein to 17th-cent. Mannerist influences.

[263] LA 2.

[264] Alban Caroe, in conversation with the author, Sept. 1990.

[265] Fiona McCarthy, *Eric Gill* (London, 1989), 54.

[266] F. Woodman, *The Architectural History of Canterbury Cathedral* (London, 1981), app. II.

preached in the Cathedral on the day after the unveiling of Archbishop Benson's monu-ment in 1899;[267] his wife, Edith, was the daughter of Archbishop Tait; and Provost Cony-beare of Southwell Minster had carried the primatial cross both in Temple's funerary procession and, a few weeks later, at the enthronement of Randall Davidson as archbishop, in 1903.[268]

Davidson was the first archbishop to retire from office, taking the title Baron Davidson of Lambeth in 1928. He was buried in the cloister garth on 30 May 1930,[269] and his wife was buried with him in 1936. The monument, in the north ambulatory of the Trinity Chapel, was dedicated at evensong on 20 April 1934,[270] and was designed and executed by the sculptor Cecil Thomas.[271] It is without architectural setting or embellishment, but the source for the bronze effigy and bier appears to be fifteenth-century Italian Renaissance tombs, in particular that to Cardinal Fortiguerra by Mino da Fiesole in Santa Cecilia in Trastevere, Rome.[272] It rests on a footed sarcophagus of Derbyshire Hoptonwood stone into which the inscription has been cut in relief. It is ornamented with the arms of Harrow School, the badge of the registrar of the Order of the Garter, borne by the Archbishop when Dean of Windsor, and, along the frontal panel, the arms of the sees of Rochester, Canterbury, and Winchester. The effigy is robed in the cope worn at the Coronation of King George V.[273] A model survives showing the monument as executed (Pl. 157), save for a rearrangement of the wording, simplification of the lettering, and abandonment of calligraphic ornament.[274]

Dean and Chapter Policy

Dean Alford had been extremely successful in his campaign to convert into a positive benefit to the Cathedral the human desire of the bereaved to immortalize their dead. His successor, Dean Payne Smith, was not so vigilant. The most exaggerated example was undoubtedly the monument to the Hon. James George Beaney MD (1828–91) (Pl. 158), which was unveiled in the south aisle in 1893.[275] Dr Beaney, of Melbourne, Australia, was a native of Canterbury, who, as the local newspaper reported, commenced life as an errand-boy, and 'gradually, by great energy and perseverance,' worked himself up to be 'a medical author and practitioner, whose name was second to none in Australia'.[276] A philanthropist who was generous during his lifetime to the Kent and Canterbury Hospital and Dispensary, he bequeathed £10,000 to establish a Working Men's Institute and Library,[277] and £1,000 to the Dean and Chapter, which was largely spent on restoration

[267] 9 July. The sermon was an address on the life of E. W. Benson.

[268] Letter from W. J. Conybeare to Canon Macnutt, 1945, LA 2.

[269] Oblation Books (U3/100), 5/17, for 1926–31.

[270] Ibid., 5/18; *Archbishop Lord Davidson's Memorial in Can-terbury Cathedral*, suppl. to *Canterbury Diocesan Gazette*, June 1934.

[271] Cecil Thomas was President of the Royal Society of British Sculptors and died in 1976. A plaster cast of the monument was exhibited at the Royal Academy in 1933.

[272] Curl, *Celebration of Death* (cit. in n. 30), 107, pl. 4

[273] *Cant. Cath. Chron.*, 17 (1934) 10, ill. opp. 14.

[274] The model was given to the Cathedral in 1976. The monu-ment closely resembles that to Admiral Philip Nelson-Ward (d. 1937), Boxgrove Priory (Sussex), signed and dated by Thomas, 1947. B. Kemp, *Church Monuments* (Aylesbury, 1985), 29.

[275] Add. MS 227.

[276] Ibid.

[277] *Illustrated London News*, 4 Mar. 1893, illus.

work in the crypt. At the unveiling ceremony, Dean Payne Smith expressed the wish that the memorial would prove an example to other young men.

The hanging wall-tablet in flamboyant fifteenth-century Gothic style was designed and executed by James Forsyth, who had completed Bishop Parry's recumbent effigy in the year that Beaney died. Stylistically, it is a logical development from J. G. Lough's Mackeson monument of 1853, the Good Samaritan subject of the main relief-panel extending the implied narrative symbolism of the Mackeson memorial, while the alabaster frame with the flanking figures of Saints Cosmas and Damian, and Faith and Hope, develop the Gothic eclecticism first seen in the Mackeson. The relief portrait pendant to the composition, in its own ogee-arched frame, is an addition. Critical comment at the time suggested that 'the entire work reflects the highest credit upon the artist'.[278] There is, however, evidence that, on the contrary, the exaggerated scale of the monument raised fears of its setting a precedent for a new wave of 'blisters' in the Cathedral. At a Chapter meeting on 25 February 1893, a few days before the official unveiling of the Beaney monument, the Bishop of Dover gave notice in connection with memorial tablets that at the next meeting of the Chapter he would move resolutions as to the best mode of dealing with future applications to ensure that the Dean and Chapter's control was exercised. Among the detailed and vigorous resolutions agreed on by Chapter were the rulings that the plans accepted were to be signed by the Dean for the Chapter at a Chapter meeting; that no changes would be allowed without consent; that a full-scale model be fixed *in situ* to give some indication of its appearance; and that professional advice be sought in the case of disagreement.[279]

Another sign of the tightening-up emerged later in the year when, after due deliberation over letters from the Archbishop and the Headmaster of the King's School about King's School memorial brasses, the Dean and the Chapter decided that they were 'not prepared to sanction any further memorials except in cases of eminent public distinction'. From 1886 the school had used the south-east transept for its services, and later it was fitted up as a school chapel. A dozen brass and enamel plaques, approximately 6 inches by 8, had been set up to old boys, Old King's Scholars, and masters, with inscriptions in Latin and English. The firm of S. T. Pratt and Sons of Tavistock Street, London, appears to have had a monopoly of the manufacture. This was now clearly felt to be getting out of hand, and this type of commemoration ceased. The placing of a memorial to William Somerset Maugham OKS (1874–1965) on a King's School building may be seen as a long-term or indirect result of this ruling.[280] Other forms of commemoration, however, were soon devised. An oak pulpit was dedicated on 20 December 1904 in the south-east transept in memory of Herbert Waddington OKS,[281] and this type of memorial was to become one of the features of the twentieth century.

Ironically, when Dean Payne Smith died, in 1895, his Memorial Fund Committee was told, on the advice of the architect Sir Reginald Blomfield, that in preference to a proposed new pulpit in the choir, a memorial in the form of a painted-glass window in the nave

[278] Add. MS 277.
[279] Chapter Act Book, 1884–95, fos. 201–2.
[280] Maugham's ashes were buried in the wall of the Maugham Library in the King's School, 22 Dec. 1965: *The Times*, 23 Dec.

1965; R. T. Stott, *A Bibliography of the Works of W. Somerset Maugham* (2nd edn.; London, 1973), 246–7.
[281] Oblation Books, 5/14, for 1904–12.

would be favoured.[282] In the event, however, a compromise was reached and a pulpit was erected in the nave in 1898.[283]

THE TWENTIETH CENTURY

New Memorial Policies and the Influence of Eric Gill

Two strands which were to affect policy on the erection of memorials in the Cathedral throughout the twentieth century developed from seeds sown in the 1890s. The first emerged during the debate which ensued after the Beaney monument was set up. Constructive help, such as Beaney's bequest of £1,000, was to be acknowledged in future by commemorative plaques. In 1955, on the completion of the New Library, an inscription was set up in the east cloister walk recording the generosity of Thomas William Lamont of New York, who had given $500,000 in 1947 towards the restoration of the war-damaged Cathedral.[284] Similarly, it was recorded in stone that two panels of the thirteenth-century Jesse window in the corona were restored in memory of Philip Nelson in 1953, by his widow.

The other strand of policy had been highlighted by the mayor and citizens, who, on Archbishop Benson's death, petitioned for a commemorative reredos in place of the conventional cenotaph. They were not, in the event, successful, but the movement had begun away from expensive memorials as objects and ends in themselves, towards more practical means of commemoration. When Minor Canon F. J. Helmore died, in 1938, after forty-three years as precentor, he was commemorated by a door to the belfry from the south-west transept.[285]

Not all traditional commemoration ceased, but, as in the late seventeenth century, it became largely confined to members of Chapter, and to people who had rendered particular service to the Cathedral, and was usually at the instigation of the Dean and Chapter. The moneys raised for memorials had now to be put to more practical use than merely the creation of ornate wall-tablets. In 1901 a tablet was set up to Benjamin Frederick Smith (1819–1900), Archdeacon of Maidstone and canon of the Cathedral, who had been a Diocesan Inspector of Schools from 1851 to 1875. The fund set up in his memory had the intention of installing 'a simple tablet' and also investing sums for the 'advancement of one or more pupils leaving the St Edmund's Clergy Orphan School'.[286] Other members of Chapter who were commemorated by plaques included the Revd Francis Walford MA, Canon William Danks in 1918, William Walsh, Bishop of Dover, and Canon Edward Stuart in 1921.[287] When Lieut.-Col. E. S. Newton Dickenson, late of the 19th and 20th Regiments and High Seneschal of the Cathedral, died in 1910, the marble plaque in the north-east transept was erected by the Dean and Chapter, as the inscription informs us, 'in gratitude

[282] Chapter Act Book, 1884–95, fo. 280.

[283] *A Guide to Canterbury Cathedral* (27th impression; n.d.).

[284] Verses by John Masefield, Poet Laureate, and a family friend of the Lamonts, were framed and hung below the memorial: *Cant. Cath. Chron.*, 50 (1955), 10.

[285] It was not dedicated until 1949, because of the Second World War. Oblation Books, 5/19 and 5/21, for 1938 and 1949.

[286] *Canterbury Diocesan Gazette*, 9–10 (1900–2), 23, 126.

[287] Oblation Books, 5/15, for 1912–19.

for his devoted and able services to the Cathedral'. This public acknowledgement of services rendered was to be another feature of twentieth-century commemoration.

Dean Farrar (1831–1903) was, like Dean Alford, officially commemorated by stained glass in the chapter house.[288] A simple medallion with relief portrait and inscription was set up in the south aisle, and was dedicated three years later on the anniversary of Farrar's death.[289] As the inscription informs us, the plaque was 'Placed by his grateful son, Eric', after whom the hero of Farrar's best-known edifying tale *Eric, or Little by Little: A Tale of Roslyn School* (1858) had been named. The medallion portrait was the work of the sculptor Albert Bruce Joy (1842–1924).[290] The lettering has been attributed to the young Eric Gill,[291] but it has none of the monumental quality which became Gill's hallmark. It is more likely that Gill cut the letters on Farrar's tombstone in the cloister garth, a design for which had been submitted by the Cathedral Architect, W. D. Caröe, in 1903.[292] This was a nicety of historical coincidence, for his evangelical father, the Revd Arthur Gill, had christened him Eric after Farrar's eponymous hero.

In 1908 a simple alabaster inscription-tablet by Eric Gill was set up across the nave in the north aisle to Col. Edgar Ravenhill of the 2nd Battalion of the Buffs (Pl. 159), who died at Wynberg in South Africa in 1907. The tablet was probably commissioned through Caröe. Gill, as the son of a poor clergyman, had been accepted at a reduced premium in Caröe's offices.[293] He also enrolled in the Practical Masonry classes at Westminster Technical Institute, and in Writing and Illuminating classes at the Central School of Arts and Crafts in Upper Regent Street, under the great calligrapher Edward Johnston, whose dictum 'Readableness, Beauty, Character', became symbolic of Gill's own work. He rapidly became the in-house lettercutter, and when he left in 1903 to set up on his own, Caröe continued to employ him.[294] In 1904 Gill collaborated with Caröe on the war memorial in Dane John Gardens, Canterbury, to men of the 2nd Battalion, The Buffs, East Kent Regiment, and Imperial Yeomanry of East Kent, who had died in South Africa in the Boer War.[295]

In the Ravenhill memorial, the lettering, if somewhat tentative in point of execution and of layout (the ruled guidelines are clearly visible), has nevertheless the breadth and quality, sense of space, and direct yet elegant simplicity which was to revolutionize twentieth-century epigraphy. As though aware of the significance of this simple work and its siting in the nave at Canterbury, the as yet unknown epigrapher ingeniously signed and dated it 'A. E. R. Gill 1908', by cutting a microscopic 'A' for Arthur before the letters ERG of the inscribed word 'WYNBERG', and a further microscopic 'ill 1908' in the final G.

Gill was to become the greatest typographer and lettercutter of the century, and the importance of the Ravenhill memorial-tablet cannot be underestimated in terms of the stylistic development of funerary memorials at Canterbury and elsewhere. His technique was to strip away all inessentials, and to allow the letter-forms to speak for themselves. This simplicity of approach went hand in hand with a new emphasis on

[288] Chapter Act Book, 1895–1910, fos. 275, 276, 297.
[289] Oblation Books, 5/14, for 1904–12.
[290] Chapter Act Book, 1895–1910, fos. 307, 308, 340.
[291] McCarthy, *Eric Gill* (cit. in n. 265), 61.
[292] Chapter Act Book, 1895–1910, fo. 254. No archival material

for the period up to 1927 survives from the Caröe practice.
[293] Gill described Caröe as 'the big gun' among Church architects. McCarthy, *Eric Gill* (cit. in n. 265), 38–9.
[294] Ibid. 42, 53–5.
[295] Newman, *North East and East Kent* (cit. in n. 20), 246.

material. Many other memorials in the Cathedral are evidence of Gill's pervasive and lasting influence.

During the Boer Wars and in the aftermath of the Great War, there were, inevitably, innumerable requests from individuals to commemorate their dead in the Cathedral. A series of simple engraved plates was permitted in the blind arcading of the south wall of the Warriors' Chapel, as a memorial to the fallen. A small group of wall-monuments was set up in the south-west transept to the 9th Queen's Lancers, to Sir John French (d. 1925), and to 2nd Lieut. Young, who fell at the Somme aged 19. He was the only son of Maj.–Gen. Young, Commander of the 67th Division stationed at Canterbury.

The finest of these small monuments, to the Carabinieres, was unveiled by Viscount Allenby and dedicated by the Archbishop in October 1925. It was designed by Darcy Braddell, and executed by Esmond Brunton. The figures were the work of Gilbert Bayes, and Jessie Bayes illuminated the Book of Remembrance.[296]

The sheer numbers, however, called for a united response. The official adoption of St Michael's, or the Warriors' Chapel, by the Buffs was marked by the establishment of an endowment fund. This was eventually entrusted to the Friends of Canterbury Cathedral 'for reparation to the Chapel'.[297] The Buffs Memorial 1914–19 was a reredos designed in the offices of W. D. Caröe, which included the figures of St Michael, St George, and St. Paul.[298] After the Second World War, the memorial was altered by the addition of a new altar, erected in 1952. The supports are of Bethersden marble and depict the badge of the Buffs, the green dragon, in low relief.

A pattern emerged in parallel whereby chapels were restored and refurbished to the memory of the individuals commemorated. The first of these was the chapel dedicated to St Martin of Tours, restored as a shrine sacred to the Christian spirit of service and to the memory of Alfred, Viscount Milner (1854–1925). After a funeral service in the Cathedral, he had been buried at Salehurst (Sussex).[299] His widow gave his house, Sturry Court outside Canterbury, to the King's School.[300]

Milner's commemoration in the Cathedral is a continuation of that tradition which honoured those who contributed *pro patria*. The apsidal chapel in the north choir transept was fitted out with an altar and inscription under the supervision of the architect Herbert (later Sir Herbert) Baker.[301] The lettering was cut by Lawrence Turner, while the cross and candlesticks were designed by Paul Cooper.[302] It was completed in 1928.

In the same year the Dean and Chapter proposed a memorial to Canon Dr A. J. Mason, who had recently died. This was to take the form of 'an Oratory or place of prayer at the north west corner of nave',[303] where the monument to Mason's greatest friend, Archbishop Benson, already stood. The chapel was dedicated in 1930 to St Augustine of Canterbury, in memory of Canon Mason, who had written on St Augustine, and among the new furnishings were the altar, iron screen, gates, cross and candlesticks, altar hangings, and service-book.[304]

[296] Chapter Act Book, 1924–31, fo. 136.
[297] *Friends of Canterbury Cathedral, 21st Annual Report* (1948), 24.
[298] The design exists. No accession number.
[299] Oblation Books, 5/16, 16 May 1925.
[300] D. L. Edwards, *A History of the King's School, Canterbury*

(London, 1957), 70.
[301] Chapter Act Book, 1924–31, fos. 164, 175.
[302] Oblation Books, 5/17, 3 Nov. 1928.
[303] *Canterbury Diocesan Gazette*, 36 (1928), 239.
[304] Oblation Books, 5/17, 11 June 1930.

Cosmo Gordon Lang had followed the precedent set by his predecessor, Archbishop Davidson, and had retired in 1942, becoming Lord Lang of Lambeth. The tradition of funerary effigies was not, however, continued. He died in 1945, and his ashes were committed in the chapel of St Stephen in the north-east transept, and a plain tablet with his name and dates was set under the altar.[305] In 1950 the chapel was hallowed in his memory.[306] The apsidal walls of the chapel were boldly incised with the dedicatory inscription, which was picked out in red paint, a characteristic of Gill-inspired work.[307]

William Temple (1881–1944) died in office. He was buried in the cloister garth under a simple tombstone with Gill-inspired lettering. The chapel of St John in the south-east transept was dedicated in Temple's memory in 1951. The oval altar and communion rails in black marble were designed by Stephen Dykes Bower.[308] The simple inscription 'Remember in Christ William Temple Archbishop' was cut in black marble set in the floor.

The last archbishop to be commemorated in this way was Geoffrey Francis Fisher (1887–1972), who was translated from London and enthroned in 1945. He retired in 1961 and became Lord Fisher of Lambeth. The chapel of St Gregory in the south-east transept was dedicated in his memory, and an inscription plaque was set up which stated that Fisher was Founder President of the World Council of Churches and 'by his visit in 1960 to Pope John XXIII he renewed friendship between Rome and Canterbury after 400 years'. The incised lettering is picked out in red and blue in the manner controversially established by Gill in his Stations of the Cross for Westminster Cathedral in 1913.[309]

Others who served the Cathedral well were likewise accorded memorial plaques. A plaque to Margaret Babington (1878–1958) was unveiled in the south aisle of the nave at the twenty-sixth Annual Festival of the Friends of Canterbury Cathedral, on 2 July 1960.[310] It was designed and executed by Mary Gillick, with lettering by Denis Gillick (Pl. 160). Margaret Babington, whose ashes were buried in the cloister garth, had been honorary Steward and Treasurer of the Friends of Canterbury Cathedral from 1928. To raise money for the Friends she wrote *The Romance of Canterbury Cathedral* (1932), which went into numerous editions. A redoubtable woman, her main concern was for the care and preservation of the fabric of the Cathedral. In opposition to Moberly, the Cathedral Surveyor, and Sir Charles Peers, the Cathedral Seneschal, who favoured cleaning the Cathedral heraldry and monuments by the quick, cheap, and drastic method of applying caustic soda, Margaret Babington undertook to raise the money for the restoration of Christ Church Gateway and the cloister on condition that Professor Tristram, 'the greatest expert in this class of work now living', should undertake the work.[311]

Dr William George Urry (1913–81), Archivist and Librarian, is commemorated in the east walk of the cloister, hard by the library entrance. The Cathedral and St Edmund Hall (of which Urry was a Fellow) jointly provided the memorial plaque and established a fund

[305] Oblation Books, 5/20, 10 Dec. 1945.
[306] Ibid. 5/21, 30 Sept. 1950.
[307] A bronze bust of Lang by Sir William Reynolds-Stephens, one of the last of the New Sculptors, was exhibited at the Royal Academy in 1938. The plaster cast was offered to the Friends of Canterbury Cathedral. Viscount Bennett contributed £52 10s. for the casting of the bust in bronze, now in the Library: *Friends*

of Canterbury Cathedral, 17th and 18th Annual Reports (1944, 1945), 13 and 9 respectively.
[308] D. Ingram Hill, *Canterbury Cathedral* (London, 1986), 154.
[309] McCarthy, *Eric Gill* (cit. in n. 265), 125–6.
[310] *Cant. Cath. Chron.*, 55 (1960), 1, illus.
[311] Victoria and Albert Museum, National Art Library, 86. X. 91; *Canterbury Diocesan Notes*, 70 (Oct. 1934).

for William Urry Memorial Lectures. The Latin inscription was composed by the Principal of St Edmund Hall and incised by the epigrapher David Kindersley on Delabole slate. It was dedicated by the Dean in November 1982.[312]

The Kentishman Alfred Deller (1912–79) was, as the inscription on his memorial plaque informs us, 'sometime lay clerk of this Cathedral', and the man who 'translated the male alto from the relative confines of the choir stall to the forefront of the world's stage'. The oval plaque was set up in the south choir aisle under the organ, and was dedicated at evensong on 31 May 1987.[313] The incised inscription in Delabole slate is also the work of David Kindersley's studio in Cambridge.

Kindersley trained under Gill in the 1930s, living with the Gill family at Piggotts in Buckinghamshire. During the 1940s he established a workshop at Cambridge, which was to train most of the lettercutters of the post-war generation. Kindersley came to have almost a monopoly of funerary inscription work at Canterbury and elsewhere.

Another of Gill's pupils, Ralph Beyer, was commissioned to design the lettering for a roll of honour on the wall of the west cloister walk, to remember 'those whose Ashes are Buried in this Cloister Garth'.[314] This was a means to prevent further proliferation of individual plaques. Beyer once again used the formula he had so successfully deployed in the great inscriptions that marked Sir Basil Spence's Hallowing Places in the nave at Coventry Cathedral, consecrated in 1962,[315] and which was itself based on the incised lettering and symbols of the Catacombs.[316]

CONCLUSION

At Canterbury there has been little institutionalized vandalism, and the resiting of monuments, notably the Hales, Chapman, and Milles monuments, has been carried out with consideration. The removal of the Neville monument from the chantry chapel on the south aisle was clearly an unfortunate rationalization, in the process of which irreparable but unintentional damage was done.[317] A similar view might be taken of the zealous restoration and use of polychromy in St Michael's Chapel, well-intentioned though it was.

The monuments themselves are characterized by a marked sobriety of style. There is little of the extremes of any particular style, and very little emphasis on an excess of ornament: the Baroque and Rococo are notably absent, the Gothic is very muted, and only the Mannerist evinces anything of the bizarre. Perhaps for this reason, in published compendia of British sculpture, Canterbury is never cited as possessing the outstanding example of any type. Almost all the monuments, until the advent of commercial monumental masons in the nineteenth century, appear to have been metropolitan work, occasioned by Canterbury's proximity to London and its location on the main route to the Continent. It follows that there was no significant local school of stonemasons or

[312] *Kentish Gazette*, 12 Nov. 1982.
[313] *Canterbury Cathedral News*, 16 (Summer 1987), 9, 16.
[314] H. Frazer, *Memorials by Artists* (Saxmundham, 1990), 27, illus.
[315] K. Eustace, 'Sculpture', in *To Build a Cathedral*, ed. Louise Campbell, exhib. cat., Mead Gallery, Univ. of Warwick (1987),

64–6.
[316] Oscar Beyer, *Die Katacombenwelt: Grundriß, Ursprung und Idee der Kunst in der römischen Christengemeinde* (Berlin, 1927).
[317] Less than 10 years before, William Gostling had referred to these two 'handsome monuments': Gostling, *Walk* (cit. in n. 3), 190.

stone-carvers, as there was at remote Hereford. Canterbury's own sculptor, Henry Weekes, trained in London, and must be regarded as a Metropolitan figure.

None the less, Canterbury Cathedral provides a good survey of the characteristics of monumental sculpture and lettering from 1540 to the present day, with, in each case, a modest, typical, or—on occasion—outstanding example reflecting the swings in the pendulum of national taste.

XII

The Cathedral School: The Dean and Chapter and the King's School, 1829–1896

MARGARET SPARKS

A study of the Chapter Acts of Canterbury reveals the Dean and Chapter at work considering various topics already discussed in the present volume. More pages than might be expected are concerned with the King's School, and deal with such topics as scholarships, examinations, private houses licensed for boarders, dates of vacations, buildings, the appointment of masters, even the raising of funds. From time to time, the Dean and Chapter answered questions about the school for various commissions, both ecclesiastical and educational. In the mid-1870s they were much occupied in preparing a scheme for the government of the school under the provisions of the Endowed Schools Act of 1869.

The background to their activity was a crisis in the affairs of grammar schools, and the consequent attention of the zealous proposers of questionnaires and commissions, who hoped to shed light into the darkest corners of what were regarded by some as moribund institutions. Many grammar schools had been founded by the piety of benefactors, especially in the sixteenth century, for the teaching of classics. The study of Latin and Greek was of value only for those who hoped to go to the universities, normally with the intention of becoming teachers or clergy. Although set up by their founders for 'poor scholars' (always difficult to define), by the early nineteenth century the schools were of no general use to families in trade or to the rising 'middle classes'. By the 1780s, numbers had fallen, especially in market-town grammar schools. Some schools collapsed. Being part of larger corporate bodies, the cathedral schools persisted. Traditionally, they educated the sons of local clergy and those of the legal profession, as well as the sons of local gentry. In addition, there were always some boys whose fathers were prosperous city tradesmen. The schools did send boys on to the universities and helped to pay for them by exhibitions. Most of their pupils were day-boys, though there were always some boarders.

For those who cared about cathedral schools, finance was a particular problem. The stipends for masters and the scholarships for boys were still regulated by ancient statutes: any increase had to be carefully negotiated, even if a chapter was willing to help. This topic was made painful by the pamphleteering of the Master of the cathedral school at Rochester, Robert Whiston. Further, in a small town and without boarders, it was hard to create a better school, gather a workable number of boys, pay more staff, and reserve extra money for new activities. But having boarders necessitated a decent headmaster's house or, preferably, a purpose-built boarding-house. 'Great Schools' (former grammar schools), like Harrow, Rugby, and Shrewsbury, drew boarders from all over the country. New schools specially for boarders were being founded, such as Marlborough in 1843. The smaller but active grammar-schools tried in a more modest way to do the same thing. Those with money and space—such as Tonbridge, with the Skinners' Company behind it—did best. The cathedral schools with keen and active deans and chapters did quite well. Much depended on the entrepreneurial abilities of the headmasters they appointed.

In 1827 Dr John Russell, Headmaster of Charterhouse, became a canon of Canterbury. Naturally, he took an interest in the King's School, especially after his resignation from Charterhouse in 1832. It was customary for the school to be examined by two canons appointed at the Chapter meeting held for the November Audit. On 15 December 1829 the thirty-two scholars and eight other members of the school were examined by Russell and Spry, the vice-dean. Dr Spry left an account of the examination. 'The result was not satisfactory', especially in the lower forms. The canons 'expressed strongly to Mr Jones [the Lower Master] our opinion of the disgraceful state of this part of the school'.[1] As a result, Mr Jones lost his job, and an old pupil of Russell's, George Wallace, was encouraged to apply for the post, which he obtained. Dr John Birt, the headmaster, bestirred himself, and the number of scholars rose to the statutory fifty. When, in 1832, Birt was presented to the vicarage of Faversham by the Chapter, Russell proposed Wallace as headmaster. His appointment contravened the statutes in that he was a layman and not yet of sufficient standing to take his MA. However, he was ordained to the title of the headmastership and given a Lambeth MA until, after four years, he was able to take his MA at Cambridge.

Wallace's reputation has suffered from the unfair comments of his outspoken successor, Mitchinson, who gave the impression that little was done to raise numbers or improve conditions.[2] On the vexed question of numbers, it is said that there were sixty-two boys when Wallace took over, seventy-two by 1834, and fairly soon afterwards about a hundred. It was not easy to accommodate many more, even for teaching and it was not until the 1890s that numbers rose above 150. The school buildings consisted of the thirteenth-century Almonry Hall and Chapel range in the Mint Yard, where the medieval almonry school had been held. The headmaster had a house at the west end, with space for a few boarders; the schoolroom was at the east end, near the Green Court Gate. The Lower or Second Master's house was at the north-west corner of the Mint Yard. When the school was popular, extra houses in the Mint Yard were rented for boarders. The picturesque but crumbling condition of the Almonry Schoolhouse is shown in Bulman's drawing of the 1770s (Pl. 161). It was a large stone structure with timber-framed additions.

Wallace (and no doubt Russell) looked round for some escape from the cramped

[1] C. E. Woodruff and H. J. Cape, *History of the King's School, Canterbury* (London, 1905), 185.

[2] Passages from Mitchinson's autobiography in E. D. Rendall,

'The Autobiography of John Mitchinson', *Cantuarian*, 22 (1946–7), 28.

conditions of the Mint Yard. Just outside the city wall to the east were the Findon Gate and the guest-hall of St Augustine's Abbey, at that time in use as a public house, with the confusing name of the Old Palace. Beyond were fields and gardens, covering the foundations of the abbey. The guest-hall could be used for a schoolroom; there was space for masters' houses and perhaps even for playing-fields. In 1834 the Dean and Chapter took advice about the feasibility of purchase; but they were warned (rightly) of legal difficulties, and though they attempted the purchase, in the end they did not proceed.[3] The site was later used for St Augustine's Missionary College, though only after the passage of three Acts of Parliament to secure the freehold. Had the school obtained space to build, and had the Chapter been generous, the school's history might have been very different.

No further recorded action was taken on buildings until 1848, when Wallace asked the Dean and Chapter formally if he might raise money for the building of a new schoolroom. They agreed, promising second-hand timber and other materials from their store. They also allowed him the use, at a nominal rent, of two Mint Yard houses. The next year they offered a subscription of £300. No more of this project is seen in the Chapter Acts until June 1852, when it was agreed that the new schoolroom should be built over the undercroft arches of the old Aula Nova, north of the Green Court Gate.[4] H. G. Austin (the Cathedral surveyor) prepared a plan and drawings, and by 1853 the new schoolroom was finished. The Dean and Chapter paid for the work—the cost, according to an article in *The Builder*, was about £1,000.[5] The schoolroom is in Norman style and sits neatly on the twelfth-century arches beside the Norman Staircase.

Two events perhaps expedited the completion of this building. One was the arrival, in 1851, of Canon A. P. Stanley, already the biographer of Thomas Arnold, who showed a keen interest in the Cathedral school. The other was the struggle between the Dean and Chapter of Rochester and their headmaster, Robert Whiston, in the years from 1848 to 1852. The contest was to some extent inconclusive; but Whiston's pamphleteering had not spared the Canterbury Chapter, who, along with others, were abused for dividing their surplus revenue amongst themselves rather than sharing it with the officers of their church.[6] After the Rochester affair, there was an increase in stipends. In 1854 these were raised to £200 for the headmaster and £100 for the lower master.[7]

Wallace widened the curriculum: mathematics, French, divinity, and history were taught, as well as classics—at a time when some of the Great Schools taught only classics and mathematics. In 1856 he asked the Chapter if he could appoint another master to teach useful studies 'to those scholars who do not intend to proceed to university'. The Chapter were helpful and provided a salary of £100 and the use of a house in the Mint Yard.[8] This was the beginning of what was later known as the 'Special Department'. Wallace also acquired a teacher of technical drawing, L. L. Razé, whose considerable skill in preparing drawings for engraving was employed to advertise the school. Lithographs were sold as souvenirs to visitors to Canterbury, especially in the shops in Mercery Lane.

---

[3] Legal opinion in 'The Resurrection of St Augustine's', *Cantuarian*, 23 (1948–50), 436–40; in spite of this legal opinion, the Chapter agreed to make the purchase but were presumably unable to carry it out, cf. Dean's Book, 1822–54, p. 172.

[4] Dean's Book, 1822–54, pp. 372, 404, 464.

[5] *The Builder*, 12 (27 May 1854), 278.

[6] R. Arnold, *The Whiston Matter* (London, 1961); R. Whiston, *Cathedral Trusts and Their Fulfilment* (London, 1849), 82.

[7] Dean's Book, 1822–54, p. 498.

[8] Chapter Act Book, 1854–84, p. 32.

Razé's pictures of the headmaster and scholars by the Norman Staircase (1851) and of the New Schoolroom (1855), and his often reproduced *Speeches in the Chapter House* (1845), helped to keep the school before the public. (Mitchinson remarked that Wallace also 'endeavoured to advertise the school by elaborate prize-givings'.[9])

The questionnaires of the Cathedral and Collegiate Churches Commissioners in 1854 were seen by Wallace as an opportunity. He wrote a 'very full statement . . . with suggestions for a comprehensive scheme of education for all classes', clearly regarded as too long and general to print. In 1857 he put to the Chapter a 'scheme for the extension of the school' which he had submitted to the commissioners, and also proposals for the alteration of his house.[10] But nothing more was heard of this, and early in 1859 Wallace resigned, having accepted the living of Burghclere in Hampshire. It might be said that he had put in twenty-seven years of useful, and in some ways pioneering, work, aided by members of the Chapter.

At a Special Chapter meeting in February 1859, the Dean and Chapter discussed various candidates for the headmastership.[11] The favourite was John Mitchinson, backed by a commendation from A. P. Stanley, who had departed to Oxford almost a year before. It is said that Mitchinson owed his appointment to the new Dean, Alford, but such things cannot be verified. In fact, it seems that they had little personal sympathy with each other, so far as Mitchinson's recollections go.[12] Mitchinson was duly appointed, and, until his sudden departure to be Bishop of Barbados, in 1873, he barraged the Dean and Chapter with requests and observations, often of a tactless kind. He was 25 when appointed: he had his way to make as a professional schoolmaster. He had been at the cathedral school at Durham, so he knew about deans and chapters, at least by repute.

Mitchinson immediately set about tackling the two problems of scholarships and of buildings for boarders. At the next Chapter meeting for the November Audit, he produced a 'scheme for readjusting the King's Scholarships'.[13] This had to be submitted to the archbishop as Visitor, since it required alterations to figures in the statutes. By the following Midsummer Audit, the scheme had the approval of the Visitor. After some slight changes in the autumn, it was agreed that the fifty scholarships be divided into ten senior scholarships at £30 p.a., fifteen junior at £15 15s., and twenty-five probationer at £10 16s. 8d.

Success did not come so quickly on the building front. Mitchinson thought when he went to see the school that 'anything more inconceivably squalid can hardly be imagined', which was perhaps an exaggeration. Presumably, at the time of his appointment he had expressed his views to Alford, who may have held out hope of improvement. By November 1862, more than two years after his arrival, nothing had been done. The Headmaster wrote the Dean and Chapter a letter, which was preserved in their files.[14] He reminded them of the 'ruinous condition' of the schoolhouse and of the great need to attract boarders. Parents were put off 'simply and solely from the miserable appearance of the schoolhouse buildings . . . and the general look of squalour and discomfort that the Mint Yard usually

[9] Rendall, 'Autobiography of Mitchinson' (cit. in n. 2), 28.
[10] *Appendix to the First Report of the Cathedral Commissioners* (London, 1854), 733; Chapter Act Book, 1854–84, p. 69.
[11] Chapter Act Book, 1854–84, p. 87.
[12] Rendall, 'Autobiography of Mitchinson' (cit. in n. 2), 30.
[13] Chapter Act Book, 1854–84, p. 103.
[14] Cathedral Archives, King's School Box I.

wears'. He suggested that there might be 'a sanitary outcry . . . against the school buildings', in which case he would be 'virtually ruined'. Although he had chosen schoolmastering, an academic career was still open to him (he had been a Fellow of Pembroke College, Oxford). In effect he threatened to leave if the Chapter could not give satisfactory answers to his questions. When would the school premises be rebuilt? If not this year, would anything be done in the way of repairs? Would an adequate sum be spent 'to produce such school premises as may fairly bear comparison . . . with all other schools that have been rebuilt in recent years?' Mitchinson had been to Uppingham to consult with that pioneer headmaster Thring about buildings.

The Dean and Chapter considered the matter.[15] They had been in the midst of negotiations with the Ecclesiastical Commissioners, and the previous August they had transferred to them their estates. Estimates had been made of expenditure in all departments, including the school. They had to confer with the Commissioners about a special advance of money for buildings. For once, the response was fairly speedy. By February 1863 it was agreed that the work should be put in hand.[16] The resulting headmaster's house, with accommodation for forty-four boarders and ranged round two sides of the Mint Yard, bears comparison with other Victorian school-buildings, at least in external appearance. Then it was necessary to make a boarding-house for the Lower Master. The surveyor conveniently condemned the old schoolhouse, and, after considerable negotiation, the Chapter obtained the freehold of the house opposite it, now the Grange, as accommodation for the Lower Master and twenty boarders. In these years, especially 1863–4, Dean Alford 'gave much attention to the building and alteration of the school'.[17] Between 1862 and 1867 the Chapter spent about £9,000 on building work for the school.[18] To celebrate the opening of the new headmaster's house, the new drawing-master, W. A. Boone, sketched it, and a suitably impressive lithograph was made (Pl. 162).

As a result of all this, there were 122 boys in the school in 1868. Where did they come from and who were they? From the school registers, a comparison can be made between figures for 1833–65 and those for Dr Beauvoir's headmastership, 1750–82. These suggest that while in both periods the largest number of boys came from Kent (outside Canterbury), by 1865 the number from elsewhere in Britain had increased threefold, and the number from Canterbury itself had halved. A later feature of school life was also beginning to emerge, namely the increasing number of boys from overseas. As before, pupils were sons of clergy, lawyers, farmers, and city tradesmen; but there were some notable additions—the spread of the medical profession resulted in the arrival of sons of physicians and surgeons, and the strength of the army at Canterbury Barracks produced a good number of officers' sons.[19]

Who would teach the boys? In 1861 Wallace's 'Special Department' master had been sacked,[20] and the Lower Master who had served throughout Wallace's time had left after 'seeing Mitchinson in'. He was replaced by a friend of the Headmaster's from Durham, J.

---

[15] Chapter Act Book, 1854–84, pp. 140–1.

[16] Ibid. 142.

[17] *Life, Journal and Letters of Henry Alford*, ed. F. Alford (London, 1873), 360.

[18] *Ecclesiastical Commissioners for England. Returns Relating to*

Cathedral Establishments. 1867 (n.p. [1867]), 26.

[19] These figures have been analysed by Thomas Hinde, *Imps of Promise: A History of the King's School, Canterbury* (London, 1991), 52–4.

[20] Chapter Act Book, 1854–84, p. 129.

S. Lipscomb. Masters came and went, but eventually some stayed and became part of the school framework: R. G. Hodgson was recruited for mathematics in 1868 and taught games as well;[21] R. G. Gordon came in 1867, and L. G. H. Mason in 1872, at the end of the Mitchinson reign. Science was added to the curriculum—Mitchinson had taken a First in Natural Science at Oxford, as well as his First in Greats. He taught science himself and took the boys on country walks, hunting geological and botanical specimens. At the end of his time, he had seven assistant masters. He complained vigorously that they were inadequately paid. The canons still examined the boys after the November Audit; but examiners from Oxford and Cambridge were appointed to examine at Midsummer, to select candidates for the senior and junior scholarships. The first examiner, in 1861, was Edward Moore, Fellow of Queen's College, Oxford, later to become Principal of St Edmund Hall and, later still, a member of the Chapter.[22] His report was bad, though by 1866 there had been some improvements.

Clearly, from the reminiscences of boys in the school, life under Mitchinson was hard. He was reputed to rule by fear. Boys were beaten regularly for mistakes in work as well as conduct (as was usual at this time). For Mitchinson this was just part of his ceaseless activity, and he generally bore no malice. His monitors had some difficulty in controlling the school. Eventually, in 1873, there was a strike or revolt, which did perhaps worry him.[23] He decided to accept the offer of the bishopric of Barbados, although he had already turned down two other colonial bishoprics. His approach to the Chapter seems to have been tactless in the extreme. He continually asked for improvements to the school, and in many cases he succeeded in obtaining them. But he combined these requests with refusing for over a year to pay £43 12s. 5d., a sum agreed by him to be owing for decorations at the new headmaster's house. At the same time, he complained about his position in processions in relation to the precentor, who by statute was senior to him. His suggestion that he might occasionally act as a 'substitute' for the minor canons was, not surprisingly, turned down.[24] His last campaign concerned a laboratory. In June 1870 he and Hodgson wrote a letter asking for a room for teaching science, and money for equipment. In November the Dean and Chapter repeated that they had no spare room for science, but they gave £4 for an air-pump.[25] They had arranged for some repairs to Wallace's schoolroom, said to be too hot in summer and too cold in winter.[26] For the moment they felt they had done enough. Mitchinson himself recorded that Canon J. C. Robertson once said to him (presumably in the early 1870s), 'You know, Headmaster, we do not wish the Cathedral to exist as an appanage of the King's School!'[27]

This feeling that the school was becoming something important in its own right, instead of merely a branch of the Dean and Chapter's community, was perhaps prompted by another of Mitchinson's activities: his share in the founding of the Headmasters' Conference.[28] This began in a small way as a response to the findings of the Taunton Commission (1846) and to the Endowed Schools Bill, which was before Parliament in 1869.

21 Woodruff and Cape, *King's School* (cit. in n. 1), 288–9.
22 Chapter Act Book, 1854–84, pp. 121–4.
23 Rendall, 'Autobiography of Mitchinson' (cit. in n. 2), 35–6.
24 Chapter Act Book, 1854–84, pp. 199, 209, 227 (decorations); 176, 191 (precentor); 224 (minor canons).
25 Ibid. 269, 272; supporting letter, King's School Box I.
26 Chapter Act Book, 1854–84, pp. 269, 270.
27 Rendall, 'Autobiography of Mitchinson' (cit. in n. 2), 28.
28 A. C. Percival, *Very Superior Men* (London, 1973), 199–202.

Some headmasters were worried about the bill and its implications. Mitchinson called a meeting in London in March, assisted by Harper of Sherborne, who persuaded Thring to attend. Thring then had the idea of a regular gathering and held the first conference at Uppingham. Mitchinson and his school were moving into the society of successful headmasters of larger schools, mostly endowed grammar-schools like Sherborne, Repton, and Tonbridge, but also some new schools such as Lancing and Liverpool College.

When, in 1873, a successor to Mitchinson had to be found, the Dean and Chapter looked to a very different man, who was, in fact, one of the headmasters at the first conference: G. J. Blore from Bromsgrove.[29] The son of the architect Edward Blore, he was then 34. He had been at Charterhouse and Christ Church, Oxford. At Bromsgrove (another endowed grammar-school) he had not been 'showy' but had consolidated his predecessor's work. He was tactful, kind, civilized, and married to a wife who liked schools and schoolboys. The boys at Canterbury heard of his good qualities from Bromsgrove and they were not disappointed.[30] Food improved. Studies became less spartan. Punishments were less frequent. Better pitches were found for games.

At the November Audit, the Dean and Chapter were met with the usual headmaster's report and requests. It was suggested that some boys might give up Greek and do more mathematics or science or a modern language instead. Other requests were comparatively trivial—for an extra light in the Mint Yard, for gravel in the undercroft under the school-room, for improvements in the schoolhouse latrines.[31] Next June came the request for the laboratory. The Chapter again refused. But they evidently gave it further consideration, for when the request was repeated in November, they suggested that the balance of the [Dean] Alford Memorial Fund could be used for the building of a laboratory, and they promised to add £100. In January 1875 plans were prepared for a laboratory on the west side of the Mint Yard. By September it was finished, with the inscription 'Alford Laboratory, 1875' over the door. Not all of the Chapter's £100 had been required, so the remainder was given to the Headmaster for fittings.[32] It has been said that this laboratory was secured by Mitchinson; but the success must be attributed to Blore, and perhaps to the Dean and Chapter's response to his less emphatic style.[33]

A year later, in October 1876, the Dean and Chapter 'drew up suggestions for a new scheme of management of the King's School, to be submitted to the Endowed Schools Commissioners', a task laid upon governors of grammar schools all over the country. One of their suggestions was the opening of 'a Preparatory School for Junior Boys'.[34] This idea had probably been under consideration for some time. The site of the school in the Mint Yard was too small. Already in 1865 the Dean and Chapter had acquired the freehold of the buildings on the northern side of the Archbishop's Palace Yard (the Grange) as the Lower Master's house. The former site of the palace comprised two other sizeable houses, a large garden, and shops and workshops. In June 1875 the Chapter had acquired the freehold of the remainder of the site, and it was in one of these houses (later Walpole House) facing Palace Street that they founded the Junior School. This was not a new

[29] Ibid. 232–3.
[30] Woodruff and Cape, *King's School* (cit. in n. 1), 232–7.
[31] Chapter Act Book, 1854–84, pp. 319–20.
[32] Ibid. 328, 333, 338, 340.
[33] e.g. Percival, *Superior Men* (cit. in n. 28), 205.
[34] Chapter Act Book, 1854–84, pp. 355, 357.

entity, for there had always been small boys at the school, but the opening of the Junior School took them out of the Mint Yard, making more space there. The Ecclesiastical Commissioners were again helpful. In 1877 they promised £3,000 for repairs and alterations to the house, on condition that the Dean and Chapter raise a further £1,000 'for the general improvement of the buildings of the King's School'. A public meeting was held to raise subscriptions for this fund.[35]

After much discussion between the Dean and Chapter and the Schools Commissioners, the scheme was passed, the date of agreement being 8 September 1878. Under the scheme the Dean and Chapter came together in gatherings distinct from Chapter meetings, in their capacity as school governors, with the services of a clerk to the governors, who combined the offices of secretary and treasurer. Proper accounts had to be published annually. The provisions of the scheme were based on those for Rochester and greatly resembled those of King's School, Ely: there was probably a general pattern for cathedral schools.[36] The endowments of the school were to be its new buildings and a yearly income of £1,000 from the Chapter—it had never had any separate endowment at its foundation. In June 1879 Blore came to Chapter to declare his willingness to be headmaster under the new scheme. Once it was in operation, there is little sign of the King's School in the Chapter Acts, except when special grants were made, as in November 1881, for further building.[37]

Blore reigned under the new scheme until 1886. Throughout his time he showed kindness to day-boys, an often neglected species. In 1882 he built a hall for them, with two classrooms, the original core of the building later being expanded to become first the Parry Library and later the Parry Hall. His period of office was a happy time for schoolboys, and perhaps for masters: there were parties at his house, there was cricket on the Green Court, and amateur theatricals, produced by L. G. H. Mason and admired by an audience of Precinct families.[38] However, Blore's health began to fail; he resigned and was succeeded by a highly successful Old Boy from the Mitchinson years, Thomas Field. Field had been at Oxford, where he had taken a triple First and had held a Fellowship at Magdalen, after which he had taught as an assistant master at Harrow for eight years.

There were fears among the conservatives of the Precincts, since Field's father had been 'in trade'. He had a 'stern exterior'.[39] He wrote appreciatively of Mitchinson, admiring his powers of discipline and organization and his ability to sharpen everyone's wits. He did not prove so terrifying as Mitchinson, even if he was much tougher than Blore. Like Mitchinson, he relied greatly on the monitors; but he also strengthened the position of the masters by dividing the school into Tutor Sets, in which groups of boys of all ages were assigned to the special care of one master. Field did not enlarge the school, nor was he a great builder, though he made a new home for the library, as a memorial to Bishop Parry (canon, Archdeacon of Canterbury, and Bishop of Dover). Parry had died in 1890

35 Ibid. pp. 363, 368.
36 Schemes for Canterbury and Rochester, Cathedral Archives, King's School Box II; for Ely, *The King's School, Ely*, ed. D. M. Owen and D. Thurley (Cambridge Antiquarian Records Soc., 1982), 145–59.

37 Chapter Act Book, 1854–84, pp. 414, 450.
38 Woodruff and Cape, *King's School* (cit. in n. 1), 245.
39 L. H. Evans, quoted in D. L. Edwards, *A History of the King's School, Canterbury* (London, 1957), 149–50.

and had taken a kindly interest in the school for many years.[40] Field was also concerned to have a school chapel. Needless to say, for all the headmasters mentioned, religion was of great importance. They thought it part of their work to influence the boys, and they all wished to have a school chapel, as other schools had, in which they could preach to them. The King's boys had to go morning and afternoon to the Cathedral's Sunday services, where they listened in the mornings to what seemed to them to be the tedious sermons of the Dean and Chapter. Field, who had suffered this himself, obtained some relief for the boys by getting them excused the afternoon service. He arranged for a 5 p.m. 'school only' service in the south-east transept, which was later fitted up as a school chapel. It was not a school chapel in the proper sense, but it was an improvement. Thring had completed a chapel at Uppingham in 1865; ten years later, Blore had aired the matter with the Dean and Chapter, with no great success.[41] Field achieved a compromise. In 1896 he left to become Warden of Radley. His successor, Galpin, increased the numbers in the school and extended it beyond the Precincts, in the search for extra boarding-houses.

Thus, under the care of the Dean and Chapter, the school grew from the little group of forty boys and two masters in the Almonry schoolhouse in 1829 to 143 boys and eight masters in reasonable school-buildings in 1896. In terms of other enlarged grammar-schools, it was still quite small, yet it shared the characteristics of successful boarding-schools of the 1890s, with its new buildings, its wider curriculum, and its various successes in, for example, games and securing Oxbridge scholarships, as well as sending the Army Class to Woolwich. In 1872 Canterbury and Durham were regarded as particularly successful cathedral schools, where 'the Deans and Chapters have for many years treated their schools with exceptional liberality; and the result ... shows what might have been done, but was not done, in many other places'.[42]

[40] P. G. Henderson, 'The School Library', *Cantuarian*, 54 (1990–1), 72.

[41] Woodruff and Cape, *King's School* (cit. in n. 1), 251; Chapter Act Book, 1854–84, p. 343.

[42] *Essays on Cathedrals*, ed. J. S. Howson (London, 1872), 295.

APPENDIX 1

Office Holders at Canterbury

ANGLO-SAXON ARCHBISHOPS OF CANTERBURY

Augustine	597–604x9	Æthelred	870–888
Laurence	604x9–619	Plegmund	890–923
Mellitus	619–624	Athelm	923x5–926
Justus	624–627x31	Wulfhelm	926–941
Honorius	627x31–653	Oda	941–958
Deusdedit	655–664	[Ælfsige abp. elect	958–959]
[Wigheard abp. elect	666 or 7–668]	Byrhthelm	959
Theodore	668–690	Dunstan	959–988
Berhtwald	692–731	Æthelgar	988–990
Tatwine	731–734	Sigeric	990–994
Nothhelm	735–739	Ælfric	995–1005
Cuthbert	740–760	Ælfheah	1006–1012
Bregowine	761–764	Lyfing	1013–1020
Jænberht	765–792	Æthelnoth	1020–1038
Æthelheard	792–805	Eadsige	1038–1050
Wulfred	805–832	Robert	1051–1052
?Feologild	832	Stigand	1052–1070
Ceolnoth	833–870		

ARCHBISHOPS OF CANTERBURY 1070–1532

Lanfranc	1070–1089	Stephen Langton	1207–1228
Anselm	1093–1109	Richard Grant (Wethershed)	1229–1231
Ralph d'Escures	1114–1122	Edmund of Abingdon	1234–1240
William of Corbeil	1123–1136	Boniface of Savoy	1245–1270
Theobald	1139–1161	Robert Kilwardby	1273–1278
Thomas Becket	1162–1170	John Pecham	1279–1292
Richard of Dover	1174–1184	Robert Winchelsey	1294–1313
Baldwin	1185–1190	Walter Reynolds	1313–1327
Hubert Walter	1193–1205	Simon Meopham	1328–1333

John Stratford	1333–1348	Roger Walden	1397–1399
John Offord	1348–1349	Thomas Arundel	1399–1414
Thomas Bradwardine	1349	Henry Chichele	1414–1443
Simon Islip	1349–1366	John Stafford	1443–1452
Simon Langham	1366–1368	John Kempe	1452–1454
William Wittelsey	1368–1374	Thomas Bourchier	1454–1486
Simon Sudbury	1375–1381	John Morton	1487–1500
William Courtenay	1381–1396	Henry Dean	1501–1503
Thomas Arundel	1396–1397	William Warham	1503–1532

Note: the initial date is in most cases that of the year of consecration or enthronement. This and the ensuing lists of Archbishops, Priors, and Deans depend on Le Neve's *Fasti*, as revised by D. E. Greenway, B. Jones, and J. M. Horn.

ARCHBISHOPS OF CANTERBURY 1533–

Thomas Cranmer	1533–1553	Frederick Cornwallis	1768–1783
Reginald Pole	1556–1558	John Moore	1783–1805
Matthew Parker	1559–1575	Charles Manners Sutton	1805–1828
Edmund Grindal	1576–1583	William Howley	1828–1848
John Whitgift	1583–1604	John Bird Sumner	1848–1862
Richard Bancroft	1604–1610	Charles Thomas Longley	1862–1868
George Abbot	1611–1633	Archibald Campbell Tait	1868–1882
William Laud	1633–1645	Edward White Benson	1883–1896
William Juxon	1660–1663	Frederick Temple	1896–1902
Gilbert Sheldon	1663–1677	Randall Thomas Davidson	1903–1928
William Sancroft	1678–1690	Cosmo Gordon Lang	1928–1942
John Tillotson	1691–1694	William Temple	1942–1944
Thomas Tenison	1695–1715	Geoffrey Fisher	1945–1961
William Wake	1716–1737	Michael Ramsey	1961–1974
John Potter	1737–1747	Donald Coggan	1974–1980
Thomas Herring	1747–1757	Robert Runcie	1980–1991
Matthew Hutton	1757–1758	George Carey	1991–
Thomas Secker	1758–1768		

PRIORS

Henry	*c.*1074–1096	Nicholas Sandwich	1244–1258
Ernulf	1096–1107	Roger of St Alphege	1258–1263
Conrad	1108x9–1126	Adam Chillenden	1263–1274
Geoffrey	*c.*1126–1128	Thomas Ringmere	1274–1285
Elmer	*c.*1130–1137	Henry of Eastry	1285–1331
Jeremiah	1137–*c.*1143	Richard Oxenden	1331–1338
Walter Durdent	*c.*1143–1149	Robert Hathbrand	1338–1370
Walter de Meri	1149–1152	Richard Gillingham	1370–1376
Wibert	1152x4–1167	Stephen Mongeham	1376–1377
Odo	1168–1175	John Finch	1377–1391
Benedict	1175–1177	Thomas Chillenden	1391–1411
Herlewin	1177–1179	John Wodnesbergh	1411–1428
Alan	1179–1186	William Molashe	1428–1438
Honorius	1186–1188	John Salisbury	1438–1446
Roger Norreis	1189	John Elham	1446–1449
Osbern of Bristol	1191	Thomas Goldstone I	1449–1468
Geoffrey I I	1191–1213	John Oxney	1468–1471
Walter	1213–1222	William Petham	1471–1472
John Sittingbourne	1222–1236x7	William Sellyng	1472–1494
John Chatham	1236x7–1238	Thomas Goldstone I I	1495–1517
Roger de la Lee	1239–1244	Thomas Goldwell	1517–1540

DEANS

Nicholas Wotton	1541–1567	James Cornwallis	1775–1781
Thomas Goodwyn	1567–1584	George Horne	1781–1790
Richard Rogers	1584–1597	William Buller	1790–1792
Thomas Neville	1597–1615	Folliott Cornewall	1793–1797
Charles Fotherby	1615–1619	Thomas Powys	1797–1809
John Boys	1619–1625	Gerrard Andrewes	1809–1825
Isaac Bargrave	1625–1643	Hugh Percy	1825–1827
George Aglionby	1643	Richard Bagot	1827–1845
Thomas Turner	1643–1672	William Lyall	1845–1857
John Tillotson	1672–1689	Henry Alford	1857–1871
John Sharp	1689–1691	Robert Payne Smith	1871–1895
George Hooper	1691–1704	Frederic Farrar	1895–1903
George Stanhope	1704–1728	Henry Wace	1903–1924
Elias Sydall	1728–1733	George Bell	1924–1929
John Lynch	1734–1760	Richard Sheppard	1929–1931
William Friend	1760–1766	Hewlett Johnson	1931–1963
John Potter	1766–1770	Ian White-Thomson	1963–1976
Brownlow North	1770–1771	Victor de Waal	1976–1986
John Moore	1771–1775	John Simpson	1986–

APPENDIX 2

Estates

THE Canterbury Cathedral community received the bulk of its estates before the Norman Conquest. For purposes of listing, manors were grouped together in different ways at different times, so that the count may vary; of those listed here, fifty were given before 1066. In the Priory archives, certain dates of donation were assigned to them by tradition, which may be verified when Nicholas Brooks's forthcoming edition of the Anglo-Saxon Charters of Christ Church is published. In the list printed here they are simply designated pre-Conquest. In addition, five manors were acquired in the twelfth century, two in the thirteenth, two in the fourteenth, and three in the fifteenth. Most manors were assigned to a Custody, for convenient administration. The priory also owned nineteen rectories, from which the churches were mostly appropriated for various purposes at dates ranging from 1178 to 1397. Estates were held for six chantry chapels.

In 1541 the Dean and Chapter inherited forty-three manors from the Priory, including two chantry manors. Fifteen manors had been lost in 1540 or a little earlier, and a further seven were returned to the Crown in 1546 in exchange for Godmersham, which was regarded as an essential part of the East Kent estate. The final figure was thirty-seven manors. The Dean and Chapter ownership of Priory manors is indicated under each relevant manor in the list of Priory estates, with their date of sale or transfer to the Ecclesiastical Commissioners. They also owned rectories: sixteen from the Priory and twenty-one which came to them in 1541, having formerly been the property of other dissolved religious communities. Both the Priory and the Dean and Chapter owned woodland, small parcels of land, and town properties; these are not listed here. With the exception of some East Kent manors, the estates of the Dean and Chapter were transferred to the Ecclesiastical Commissioners in 1862. Some were returned in 1866, but proved uneconomic. After further transfers, all estates were given up in 1902, apart from houses in Canterbury.

Margaret Sparks

PRIORY ESTATES: KENT

Manors

Adisham, Custody *East Kent*. Pre-Conquest to 1540. D & C 1541–1862. Adisham Court Lodge Farm 1879–94.

Agney (in Old Romney), Custody *Weald*. Pre-Conquest to 1540. D & C 1541–1862, 1866–1902.

Appledore, Custody *Weald.* Pre-Conquest to 1540. D & C 1541–1862. Appledore Mean Lands 1866–1902.

Barksore (in Lower Halstow), Custody *Weald.* c.1185–1540. D & C 1541–1862.

Barton (Farm) and *Colton,* Canterbury. Bartoner's manor. Pre-Conquest to ?1537. D & C Colton tenants included in Caldecote.

Bekesbourne, Custody *East Kent.* 1443–1538.

Berry Court (in Westcliffe), Custody *Essex.* Pre-Conquest to 1540.

Blean—Amerycourt. Almoner's manor. ?1180–1540.

Boyton (in East Sutton), Custody *Weald.* c.1473–1540. D & C 1541–1862.

Brambling (in Ickham), Custody *East Kent.* Pre-Conquest to 1540. D & C 1541–1862, 1866–94.

Brokesend (in Birchington), Custody *East Kent.* Pre-Conquest to 1540. D & C 1541–1894.

Brook, Custody *East Kent.* Pre-Conquest to 1540. D & C 1541–1862.

Caldecote, Canterbury. 1326–?1537. D & C tenants 1541–1862.

Chart (Great), Custody *Weald.* Pre-Conquest to 1540. D & C 1541–1862.

Chart (Little), Custody *Weald.* Pre-Conquest to 1540. D & C 1541–1862.

Chartham, Custody *East Kent.* Pre-Conquest to 1540. D & C 1541–1894.

Cliffe at Hoo or *Westcliffe,* Kent, Custody *Essex.* Pre-Conquest to 1540.

Copton (in Preston by Faversham), Custody *Weald.* Pre-Conquest to 1540. D & C 1541–1862.

Eastry, Custody *East Kent.* Pre-Conquest to 1540. D & C 1541–1894.

Ebony (in Stone in Oxney), Custody *Weald.* Pre-Conquest to 1540. D & C owned Kitepan Marsh in Ebony 1541–1902.

Elverton (in Stone by Faversham), Custody *Weald.* Pre-Conquest to 1540. D & C 1541–1862.

Fairfield, Custody *Weald.* Pre-Conquest to 1540. D & C 1541–1902.

Farleigh (East), Custody *Weald.* Pre-Conquest to 1539.

Farleigh (West), Custody *Weald.* 1290–1539.

Godmersham, Custody *East Kent.* Pre-Conquest to 1540. D & C 1546–1862.

Ham (in Preston by Faversham), Custody *Weald.* Pre-Conquest to 1540. D & C 1541–1862. Ham Marshes 1866–1902.

Hollingbourne, Custody *Weald.* Pre-Conquest to 1540. D & C 1541–1862.

Ickham, Custody *East Kent.* Pre-Conquest to 1540. D & C 1541–1862. 4 farms kept to 1896.

Leysdown, Custody *Weald.* c.1185 to 1540. D & C 1541–1862.

Loose, Custody *Weald.* Pre-Conquest to 1540. D & C 1541–1862.

Lydden or *Lydcourt* (near Sandwich), Custody *East Kent.* Pre-Conquest to 1540. D & C 1541–6.

Meopham, Custody *Surrey.* Pre-Conquest to 1540. D & C 1541–1852.

Mersham, Custody *Weald.* Pre-Conquest to 1540. D & C 1541–1862.

Monkton, Custody *East Kent.* Pre-Conquest to 1540. D & C 1541–1896.

Orgarswick (in Burmarsh), Custody *Weald.* Pre-Conquest to 1540. D & C 1541–1862.

Orpington, Custody *Surrey.* Pre-Conquest to 1540.

Peckham (East), Custody *Weald.* Pre-Conquest to 1539.

Ruckinge, Custody *Weald.* Pre-Conquest to 1540. D & C 1541–1862.

Seasalter (land let). Pre-Conquest to 1540. D & C 1541–1862. Seasalter Marsh to 1894.

Teston, Custody *Weald.* 1290–1539.

Westwell or *Welles,* Custody *Weald.* Pre-Conquest to 1540.

PRIORY ESTATES: EAST ANGLIA AND ESSEX

Manors

Bocking (Essex), Custody *Essex*. Pre-Conquest to 1540. D & C 1541–6 (includes land on Mersey Island).

Borley (Essex), Custody *Essex*. 1301–1540. D & C 1541–6.

Deopham (Norfolk), Custody *Essex*. 1146–1540. D & C 1541–1862.

Hadleigh (Suffolk), Custody *Essex*. Pre-Conquest to 1540. D & C 1541–1862.

Lawling (Essex), Custody *Essex*. Pre-Conquest to 1540. D & C 1541–6.

Milton or *Middleton* (Essex), Custody *Essex*. Pre-Conquest to 1540. D & C 1541–6.

Monks Eleigh (Suffolk), Custody *Essex*. Pre-Conquest to 1540. D & C 1541–1862.

Panfield (Essex), Custody *Essex*. 1472–1539.

Southchurch (Essex), Custody *Essex*. Pre-Conquest to 1540. D & C 1541–6.

Stisted (Essex), Custody *Essex*. Pre-Conquest to 1540. D & C 1541–6.

PRIORY ESTATES: OTHER COUNTIES

Manors

Charlwood (Surrey), Custody *Surrey*. Pre-Conquest to 1539.

Cheam (Surrey), Custody *Surrey*. Pre-Conquest to 1540.

Doccombe (Devon) (land let). 1174–1540. D & C 1541–1862.

Halton (Buckinghamshire), Custody *Surrey*. Pre-Conquest to 1540. D & C 1541–6.

Horsley, East (Surrey), Custody *Surrey*. Pre-Conquest to 1540.

Merstham (Surrey), Custody *Surrey*. Pre-Conquest to 1539.

Monks Risborough (Buckinghamshire), Custody *Surrey*. Pre-Conquest to 1540.

Newington (Oxfordshire), Custody *Surrey*. Pre-Conquest to 1540 (with Britwell).

Patching (Sussex), Custody *Surrey*. Pre-Conquest to 1540. D & C 1541–1862.

Walworth (Surrey), Custody *Surrey*. Pre-Conquest to 1540. D & C 1541–1862.

Wotton or *Woodtown* (Sussex), Custody *Surrey*. Pre-Conquest to 1540. D & C 1541–1862.

The Priory also owned: urban properties in Canterbury, Sandwich, London, and Southwark; Canterbury College, Oxford; port rights in Sandwich ?1023–1290; woodland and small parcels of land; estates in Ireland.

PRIORY ESTATES: KENT

Rectories

Birchington. Chapelry of Monkton. D & C 1541–1894.

Challock. Chapelry of Godmersham.

Eastry. Church appropriated for almonry 1178–86. Reappropriated 1366. D & C 1541–1862.

Edenbridge. Chapelry of Westerham.

Eynsford. Church appropriated for almonry 1178–86.

Fairfield. Church appropriated for almonry 1237. D & C 1541–1862.

Farningham. Church appropriated for almonry 1225. D & C 1541–1862.

Godmersham. Church appropriated for fabric of Priory 1397. D & C 1541–1862.

Lower Halstow. Church appropriated for the repair of books by 1205. D & C 1541–1862.

Meopham. Church appropriated for almonry 1178–86. Reappropriated for almonry and infirmary 1386. D & C 1541–1862.

Monkton. Church appropriated for almonry 1178–86. Reappropriated 1366. D & C 1541–1896.

East Peckham. Church not appropriated. 1539–40. D & C 1541–1862.

Seasalter. Church appropriated for Priory 1237. D & C 1541–1862.

Westcliff by Dover. Church appropriated for almonry 1327. D & C 1541–1862.

Westerham. Church appropriated for Priory hospitality 1328.

PRIORY ESTATES: OTHER COUNTIES

Rectories

Birstead (Sussex). Chapelry of Pagham. D & C 1541–1862.

Deopham (Norfolk). Church appropriated for Priory 1227. D & C 1541–1862.

Mundham (Sussex). Church not appropriated. D & C 1541–1800.

Pagham (Sussex). Church appropriated for Canterbury College, Oxford, 1363. D & C 1541–1801.

Warnham (Surrey). Church not appropriated. 1539–40. D & C 1541–1862.

CHANTRY ESTATES

Perpetual Chantries with chaplains

Almonry Chapel	Appropriated church of *Ash Bocking* (Suffolk) and small parcels of land in East Kent, 1321.
Arundel Chantry	Appropriated church of *Northfleet* (Kent) to provide for chantries at Maidstone and Canterbury, 1406.
Black Prince's Chantry	Manor of *Vauxhall* or *Fauxhall* (Surrey), and land in Lambeth, 4 quays on the Thames, 1362.
Brenchley Chantry	Rents in *Bilsington* (Kent), 1447.
Buckingham Chantry	Appropriated church of *Westwell* (Kent), 1399.
Henry I V's Chantry	Chapel built but no endowment made, 1437.

Perpetual Chantries with monks

Islip's Chantry	Endowment of plate and stock only, 1366.
Lady Mohun's Chantry	Manor of *Selgrave* in Preston by Faversham (Kent), 1396.

DEAN AND CHAPTER ESTATES

Manors

The Dean and Chapter's ownership of manors that had belonged to the Cathedral Priory is indicated above, in the lists of Priory manors. The Dean and Chapter also acquired certain estates that had belonged to Cathedral chantries:

Selgrave in Preston by Faversham (Kent)	1541–1862
Vauxhall (Surrey) and land in Lambeth	1541–1862

DEAN AND CHAPTER ESTATES: KENT

Rectories

Boughton under Blean (from Faversham Abbey)	1541–1862
Brookland (from St Augustine's Abbey)	1541–1862
Cranbrook (from King; formerly Archbishop)	1541–1862
Faversham (from St Augustine's Abbey)	1541–1862
Littlebourne (from St Augustine's Abbey)	1541–1862
Milton by Sittingbourne (from St Augustine's Abbey)	1541–1862
Preston by Faversham (from Faversham Abbey)	1541–1862
Preston by Wingham (from St Augustine's Abbey)	1541–1862
St Paul's, Canterbury (from St Augustine's Abbey)	1541–1862
Sheldwich (from St Augustine's Abbey)	1541–1862
Stone in Oxney (from St Augustine's Abbey)	1541–1862
Tenterden (from St Augustine's Abbey)	1541–1862
Willesborough (from St Augustine's Abbey)	1541–1862
(also listed with Rectories: Ozingel, Callis, and Alland Granges in Thanet (from St Augustine's Abbey)	1541–1862

DEAN AND CHAPTER ESTATES: OTHER COUNTIES

Rectories

Ashburnham (Sussex) (from Faversham Abbey)	1541–1800
Aylsham (Norfolk) (from Battle Abbey)	1541–1862
Bramford (Suffolk) (from Battle Abbey)	1541–1862
Exning (Suffolk) (from Battle Abbey)	1541–1800
Hempsted (Essex) (from Battle Abbey)	1541–1862
Icklesham (Sussex) (from Battle Abbey)	1541–1862
Sampford (Essex) (from Battle Abbey)	1541–1862
Ticehurst (Sussex) (from Faversham Abbey)	1541–1862

Index

Page numbers in **bold** refer to main reference to the subject. County names are those prior to the 1974 boundary changes.

minor canons (*cont.*)
for 428, parish livings in city 176,
437, stipends 176, 428, 431; 17th cent.
188, 209, 226, 227, 441, 444, 449,
stipends 190, 201, 447; 18th cent.
227, 234, income 227; 19th cent. 227,
240, 262–4, 271, 291, income 269
minster churches 14, 18, 16, 29
Minster-in-Sheppey (Kent), minster 18
Minster-in-Thanet (Kent) 14–15, 18, 183,
197; abbess of, *see* Cwoenthryth
mint, pre-Conquest 14, 15, 23, Pl. 3
missal (Bodl., MS Rawl. C. 168), from
Warham's chantry chapel
488 n. 167
Mitchinson, John, headmaster, later
bishop of Barbados 554, 556–7, 558–
9, 560
Moberly, –, Cathedral Surveyor 550
Mohun, Joan, Lady (d. 1404): chantry at
Selgrave in Preston by Faversham
569; monument 494 n. 190, 507–8,
Pls 125–7
Molashe, William, prior (1428–38) 94,
97; burial 98 n. 142, 492; funeral
492 n. 183; mother buried in crypt
506 n. 246
monastic orders, *see* Benedictines;
Carthusians; Cistercians;
Cluniacs
Mongeham, Stephen, prior (1376–7)
565
Mongeham (Kent) 17
Mongeham, Great (Kent), rector of
358
monk chaplain, *see* chaplain
monk wardens, *see* wardens
monks, *see* Canterbury Cathedral,
Priory of Christ Church, monastic
community
Monks Eleigh (Suffolk), manor 25, 568
monk's effigy, *c.*1300 489–90
Monks Risborough (Bucks.), manor
568
Monkton (Kent): lease altered 243;
manor 567; prior's manor house
91; rectory 568
Monod, Wilfred, French pastor 311
Montbrun, Pierre de, archbishop of
Narbonne (d. 1286), monument in
Narbonne Cathedral 463 n. 48
Mont-Saint-Michel (France) 141;
exemplars 52
Montgomery, Bernard, General, later
Field Marshal 325, 326
Montmirel, Jean de (d. 1219),
monument in Longpont abbey
467 n. 70, 477 n. 118
Moore, Charles, Six Preacher 252–3
Moore, Edward, canon-librarian 302,
400, 401, 402; as school examiner
558

Moore, George, prebendary 216
Moore, John, dean (1771–5) 253 n. 236,
227, 232, 240; archbishop (1783–
1805) 216, 222, 223
Moore, Robert, prebendary 216
More, John, attorney-at-law 147
More, Sir Thomas 147, 150
Morgan, John Pierpont 403
Morley, Thomas, writer on music 421
Morris, William 281
Morris, Matthew Robinson, MP 218
Mortimer, Hugh, archdeacon 95
Morton, John, archbishop (1487–1500)
82, 104, 141, 371 n. 139; monument
485–6, 488, 505 n. 236, Pls 106, 114
Moundfield, John, monk and singer
419
Mundham (Sussex), rectory 569
music 226, 228–9, 271–2, 295, 296, 408;
20th cent. 325–6, performers in the
Cathedral 336
musical instruments: cornett 440, 445;
lutes 438, 442; recorders 442;
sackbut 440, 445; viols 438, 442, 443,
445; wind 440
musicians: cornetteers (cornet players)
159, 445; sackbutteers 159, 445;
wind-band 440–1, 445, 446–7
Mutlow, Thomas Anthony, minor
canon 390
Mylles, John, monk, later prebendary
167, 183 n. 167, 375
Mylne, Robert, architect 235

Nantes (France), Cathedral, tomb of
Jean IV, Duke of Brittany 500
Narbonne (France), Cathedral,
monument of Abp Pierre de
Montbrun 463 n. 48
Neile, Richard, bishop of Durham 185
Nelson, George, sculptor 532
Nelson, Dr Philip, memorial inscription
(1953) 547
Nelson, Robert 224, 231
Nelson, William, Earl Nelson,
prebendary 215, 260
Nesbett, John, master of the Lady
Chapel choir and composer 421–
2, 424, Pl. 85
Nettlestead (Kent) 17
Nevett, Richard, lessee 214
Neville, Alexander (d. 1614), monument
518, Pl. 134
Neville, Ralph, bishop of Chichester,
royal chancellor 73
Neville, Richard (father of Dean
Neville; d. 1599), monument 517–
18, Pl. 133
Neville, Thomas, dean (1597–1615) 366,
375, 378, 439, 440, 441; monument
178, 240, 517–18, 551, Pl. 134
Newenden (Kent) 31

New Fire, blessing of 412, 413
New Foundation cathedrals 188, 288–9,
295
Newington (Oxon.), manor 568
Newman, Sir George (d. 1627),
monument in St Margaret's,
Canterbury 519 n. 69
Newman, John Henry, cardinal 254
Newstreet, John, chorister 438
Newton, John, master of novices
123 n. 263
Nicholas, St 424
Nicholas II, pope 32
Nicholls, Henry, minor canon 227
Nicholls, Josias, preacher 158
Niger, Roger (d. 1241), bishop of
London, monument in Old St
Paul's Cathedral, London 466
Nisbett, Matthew Alexander, Honorary
Canon 288
Nonconformists 168, 206, 211, 222, 238,
286, 299, 306
Norfolk 241; manors in 568; rectories in
569, 570
Norham (Northumb.), effigy of Dr
Gilly 539
Norreis, Roger, prior (1189) 565
Norris, Samuel, auditor 388, 391
North, Brownlow, dean (1770–1) 240,
253 n. 236
Northfleet (Kent), church appropriated
569
Northumbria 6, 22
Norton, Martha 520
Norton (Co. Durham), knightly effigy
479 n. 129
Norwich (Norfolk) 245; bishopric 253;
bishops of 363, 465 n. 61;
Cathedral, choir-stalls canopy
482 n. 141; Cathedral Priory 115;
dean of, *see* Goulburn, Edward;
Stigand's properties in 32
Nost, John, sculptor 527 & n.141
Nothhelm, archbishop (735–9) 563
Nott, Michael John, canon, archdeacon
of Maidstone 331
novices, *see* Canterbury Cathedral,
Priory of Christ Church, monastic
community
Nowell, Alexander, prebendary 168

Oakley, Anne Mary, archivist 406
Obazine (France), effigy of St Stephen
490 n. 173
obedientiaries, *see* Canterbury
Cathedral, Priory of Christ
Church, monastic community
obituary lists (notices) 112, 117, 134
Ochino, Bernardino, prebendary 162
O'Connor, stained-glass maker of
Birmingham 536
Oda, St, archbishop (941–58) 21, 22,